John M. ☑ **W9-CNO-714**

826-5278

PROBLEMS, CASES, AND MATERIALS ON EVIDENCE

ERIC D. GREEN
Boston University School of Law

CHARLES R. NESSON
Harvard Law School

LITTLE, BROWN AND COMPANY
Boston and Toronto

Library of Congress Catalog Card No. 81-86688

ISBN-0-316-32646-1

Tenth Printing

MV NY

Published simultaneously in Canada by Little, Brown & Company (Canada) Limited

Printed in the United States of America

Unusual, perhaps, but I want to use my half of this dedication page to express my appreciation to (and for) my co-author. Referred to in our preface as "the junior author," Eric was in truth the senior partner on this project. There is hardly a page of this book that does not show his energy, creativity, and will to finish. Friendship, too. Thanks Eric.

C.R.N.

To my mother and father, Phyllis Roth Green and Samuel J. Green.

E.D.G.

Summary of Contents

Contents

CHAPTER III   Competency of Witnesses, Direct and Cross-Examination, Making and Meeting Objections, Functions of Judge and Jury — The Rules of the Road   203

CHAPTER VII   Opinions, Scientific Proof, and Expert Testimony

633

Preface

This book is an attempt to provide a concise set of stimulating, current materials for a basic three- or four-hour course on the Federal Rules of Evidence. Our goal is two-fold: first, to provide materials from which students can draw a practical understanding of how the Federal Rules work in court. Students are entitled to expect this from any basic evidence course. This objective has caused us to keep in mind the perspective of the trial lawyer working with the rules in court. On the other hand, we have not attempted to compile a book on trial skills and tactics, a task better left to the trial practice teachers and scholars.

Our second objective is to expose the underlying principles, policy choices, epistemological assumptions, and jurisprudential values on which the Federal Rules are based. The system of evidence in any society is itself evidence about the nature of that society and its concept of justice. Examining the philosophy of proof of the Federal Rules would be a worthwhile task in and of itself, but we also believe that it is impossible to achieve a working understanding of the rules without an appreciation of the spirit, reason, and policy that underlie them. These considerations have caused us to keep in mind the perspective of the draftsman, scholarly critic, and reformer, to point out the psychological and ethical dimensions of the rules, and to draw as often as we can on the positive tension between the practical and philosophical aspects of the rules.

We have not attempted to compile a comprehensive treatise on evidence or even a textbook that covers every subject that an evidence instructor might want to teach. Rather than follow the traditional approach of including full coverage of every possible evidence topic — an approach that requires each instructor to pick and choose from a mass of material — we have chosen instead to include only what we feel is most important and teachable in a basic three- or four-hour course. This book, then, is the course we teach. We recognize that our selective approach runs the risk of excluding treatment of issues and problems held dear by others. We take comfort, however, in the expectation that such instances will be few and in the knowledge that these materials have been better received by students than any of the alternatives presently available that we have tried.

This book mixes the case and problem approaches. We regard evidence as a difficult subject to teach and think it wise to use the most effective pedagogic materials to put the subject across. Cases alone are inadequate. In many parts of the course it is impossible to find concise, well-analyzed, well-written cases. All too often lawyers relegate evidence issues to the back of their briefs, and judges decide evidence questions barely concealing their result-orientation. Attempts to build principled analytical discussions on such material necessarily suffer.

The problem approach presents a good alternative. Problems can capture evidence issues concisely and can be organized to facilitate a point-to-point developmental discussion. They can challenge and motivate students to formulate their own solutions rather than rely on the analysis of a judicial opinion. After all, a problem is only a case without a judicial answer attached to it. But problems, too, have their pitfalls. They place a heavy burden on students to think about the issues before class and to try to work out answers, sometimes to the unanswerable. This, in moderation, is stimulating. But confronting students with too many problems can dampen motivation and give students a sense of being lost in a maze of questions, thereby risking that most feared of all pedagogic questions — "Who cares?" We try to capture the best of the case and problem methods emphasizing one or the other approach where the subject matter dictates a choice and using textual material whenever we feel it will provide a clearer or deeper understanding of an important issue. In the chapters on confrontation and privilege we rely mostly on cases. In these areas doctrinal analysis is profitable — important aspects of the law have been developed in U.S. Supreme Court opinions in which theory remains unclear and unsettled. The chapters on relevance and hearsay rely heavily on problems because the concepts are best taught by working through a large number of factual situations.

The book is organized around the Federal Rules of Evidence for two reasons. First, focus on a single system of rules is a great aid in teaching and far more coherent for students than is shuttling among common law rules and various state model and uniform codes. Interrelationships among provisions can be understood, the varying philosophical objectives of the original draftsmen and of those who revised the rules can be explored, and the reasons stated in support of the rules can be examined. Second, the Federal Rules are relevant to all students, no matter where they choose to practice. States in growing numbers (22 as of the date this book went to press) have revised their own rules to conform to the Federal Rules, thus making the Federal Rules truly a model code. Although we reproduce in this book the text of particular rules in connection with the cases or problems to which they relate, we have not reproduced the Advisory Committee notes and other supporting legislative history. Students should, therefore, have a complete set of the rules and legislative history as a separate reference book, but they should not need to supplement the book with any additional texts.

A set of films has been produced to be used in connection with this book. The films were made under the directions of Eric Saltzman by the Harvard Evidence Film Project with the support of the National Endowment for the Humanities and, at inception, the Committee on Legal and Professional Responsibility. This project was conceived by the senior author and Eric Saltzman for the express purpose of creating films to be used in teaching evidence. The films are available in film and video cassette from the publisher. Each film functions as the visual statement of a case. They are not didactic; indeed, often they depict lawyers and judges doing things wrong (though always in ways that are provocative and interesting theoretically). Their function is to raise provocative questions, to bring a sense of the courtroom into class, to portray lawyers and judges operating in a courtroom context, and to reveal the varieties of tactics and styles that often go unseen in courses using only traditional teaching materials. There are no voice overlays speaking words of wisdom. We have had great success in using the films in our classes and recommend their use. We recognize, however, that some teachers may not want to take the time to show films and therefore have designed the book so that it can be used independently of them.

From our many years of teaching, we have a deep appreciation of the seamless nature of the law of evidence and a sympathetic understanding of teachers' doubts about the most effective sequence of topics. Our organization of topics, however, is one with which we feel comfortable. We begin with relevance because it is the cornerstone of the entire system — more so than ever under the Federal Rules. Chapter I explores the basic concept of relevance in the context of trial proof and the related doctrines of conditional relevancy, prejudice, and probability evidence. We have included textual material from philosophy and the social sciences here because the most advanced analyses of how people think and draw conclusions from data about uncertain events — i.e., what goes on at a trial — come from these disciplines.

Chapter II, Character and Credibility, is a logical extension of Chapter I because the basic principles involved are those of relevance and prejudice. We have departed from the approach of most course books, however, by combining the material on credibility — i.e., character for truthfulness (Rules 608 and 609) and character in general (Rules 404 and 405). It has been our experience that dealing at one time with proof of character for any and all reasons is the most effective and efficient way to get this material across. As some of the cases demonstrate, even experienced judges sometimes have trouble understanding the difference between proof of a particular character trait relevant to the litigated event and proof of credibility.

Proof of credibility leads naturally to the rules governing the examination of witnesses. Chapter III covers a number of the more technical aspects of this process including competency of witnesses; the form, scope, and limits of direct and cross-examination; the use of real proof, views, and pictures; the process of making and meeting objections; and the functions of judge and jury. An informal survey of evidence teachers reveals conflicting opinions as to when to teach this material and how much time to devote to it. Some teachers may choose to teach this material at a different point in the course, probably earlier rather than later. Some teachers may devote relatively little time to this chapter (as does one of the authors), contenting themselves with assuring technical competency in these areas; others may find it worthwhile to pause longer to explore the significance of the policy choices made by these rules (as does the other of the authors). We have tried to present this material in a way that will satisfy adherents of either approach. Thus, Chapter III represents a compromise and should be treated like any compromise — an attempt at an imperfect but broadly acceptable solution.

Chapters IV and V treat the related problems of hearsay, confrontation, and compulsory process, from *Raleigh*'s case through the latest attempts to demonstrate that the rule against hearsay should be abolished. These chapters lead naturally to the problem of privileges, the subject of Chapter VI. In that chapter, however, we are mostly concerned with uncovering the rationale for the present system of privileges. A major part of this chapter deals with how lawyers handle "hot stuff," such as a smoking gun, compromising tax records, or proof of illegal corporate payments, and thus affords an opportunity to consider the relationship between evidence and a lawyer's professional responsibility.

Chapters VII and VIII deal with the relatively self-contained topics of opinion, expert testimony, and scientific proof (Chapter VII) and writings — authenticity and proof of contents (Chapter VIII). Either or both of these chapters could be discussed out of turn without losing the coherence of doing the course as it is organized in the book. We have placed these topics near the end of the book because we feel it is preferable to teach them on a secure base of understanding of relevance, hearsay, and confrontation. Also, should the teacher or student find at the end of the term that time pressures require that some choices be made, it seems more important to us that the topics of the earlier chapters be given thorough treatment.

Strictly speaking, Chapter IX does not deal with evidence at all but with the rules relating to what effect evidence is given. This material on allocation of burdens of proof, presumptions, and inferences could be considered at any point in the course. Logically, it should probably be the first chapter on the theory that relevance and all the other rules of proof depend on who has the burden of proof, what the standard of proof is, and how devices such as presumptions, inferences, and judicial comment affect the burden and standard of proof. Our experience indicates, however, that effective pedagogy does not follow logic on this point, chiefly because of the complexity of the subject matter. This material is difficult enough for most students at the end of the course; to attempt it at the beginning of the course would be counterproductive.

The last chapter — Chapter X, Judicial Notice — has been included as a separate chapter out of deference to the traditional organization of the course, but it could be combined in one unit with the material in the preceding chapter on presumptions. Both topics deal with the problem of establishing facts without the presentation of proof. Without trying to resolve the familiar debate over whether presumptions, judicial comment, and judicial notice are "evidence," we are satisfied that the topics, at least, should be included in a coursebook on evidence.

The impetus for this book was a general dissatisfaction with the materials available for teaching evidence and a belief that our own problem-oriented, Federal Rules based approach would be an improvement. Translating that belief into this book required more time and effort than we imagined. Without the help of many other people, the translation never would have been accomplished.

First among those without whose ideas, inspiration, and support this book would not have been possible is James H. Chadbourn, the junior author's teacher and the senior author's colleague at the Harvard Law School. In addition to having been during the formative period of our scholarly lives "the dean of living evidence scholars" — a term Professor Chadbourn once used to describe his mentor, Professor Maguire — Professor Chadbourn is the source for many of the problems and cases in this book. His rationalization of the law of evidence and pedagogical approach to the subject matter so thoroughly inform this work that it is impossible to acknowledge his imprint in each specific instance. With all students of the law of evidence, we were deeply saddened by his death late last year, and feel impoverished by the loss of scholarly criticism and insight to which Chad would have subjected this effort.

Next, we must acknowledge our debt to the scholars and treatise and textbook writers who have preceded us. Although we cannot claim direct lineage through Chadbourn, Maguire, Morgan, and Wigmore back to James Bradley Thayer, any incremental advance by this book on what has come before is largely attributable to the advantage we have had in being exposed to the efforts, ideas, and experiments of our predecessors, ancient and modern. We would like to mention especially Margaret Berger, Edward Cleary, John Kaplan, Richard Lempert, John Mansfield, Mark Pettit, Stephen Saltzburg, Laurence Tribe, John Waltz, and Jack Weinstein as colleagues who have inspired us with their work in evidence.

A special debt of gratitude is also owed to Eric Saltzman, the producer and director of the films designed to be used with the book.

We also would like to thank the following student research assistants for their help in researching, editing, and criticizing drafts of the book as it developed: Joel Africk, Frances Bermanzohn, Gerri Bridgman, Emily Joselson, Tina Klein-Baker, Mary Perry, Vanessa Place, Carmin Reiss, Lisa Schwartz, and Harvey Shapiro. Thanks also go to Sharon Atkins and Ken Westhassel for their extraordinary efforts in preparing, revising, and repreparing the manuscript and to several classes of Boston University School of Law and Harvard Law School students who without loud complaint allowed us to experiment upon them with photocopied drafts of these materials.

Finally, the authors would like to thank their families for their faith and forbearance and their respective deans, Richard Speidel and William Schwartz of Boston University School of Law and Albert Sacks and Jim Vorenberg of Harvard Law School, for their moral and material support.

Eric D. Green
Charles R. Nesson

September 1982

Acknowledgments

We are grateful to the following sources for permission to reprint excerpts of their work:

American Bar Association, Model Code of Professional Responsibility, Ethical Consideration EC4-1. Excerpted from the Model Code of Professional Responsibility, copyright © 1981 by the American Bar Association, National Center for Professional Responsibility. Reprinted by permission.

American Bar Association Standards Relating to the Administration of Criminal Justice: The Defense Function — Lawyer-Client Relationship 109-112 (1974). Copyright © 1976 by the American Bar Association. Reprinted by permission.

Allen, Structuring Jury Decisionmaking in Criminal Cases: A Unified Constitutional Approach to Evidentiary Devices, 94 Harv. L. Rev. 321 (1980). Copyright © 1980 by the Harvard Law Review Association. Reprinted by permission.

Armstrong, The Count Joannes: A Vindication of a Much-Maligned Man, 36 A.B.A.J. 829 (1956). Copyright © 1956 by the American Bar Association Journal. Reprinted by permission.

Ayer, The Legacy of Hume, in Probability and Evidence 3-6 (1972). Copyright © 1972 by the Columbia University Press. Reprinted by permission of Columbia University Press and Macmillan Accounts and Administration Ltd., London and Basingstoke.

Cleary, Presuming and Pleading: An Essay on Juristic Immaturity, 12 Stan. L. Rev. 5 (1959). Copyright © 1959 by the Board of Trustees of the Leland Stanford Junior University. Reprinted by permission.

Cohen, The Probable and the Provable §30 (1977). Copyright © 1977 by Oxford University Press. Reprinted by permission.

Copi, Introduction to Logic 23-26 (4th ed. 1972). Copyright © 1972 by Irving M. Copi. Reprinted by permission of Macmillan Publishing Co., Inc.

Dr. Who. Use of the character Dr. Who by permission of the British Broadcasting Corporation.

Falknor, The "Hear-Say" Rule as a "See-Do" Rule: Evidence of Conduct,

Tague, Perils of the Rulemaking Process: The Development, Application, and Unconstitutionality of Rule 804(b)(3)'s Penal Interest Exception, 69 Geo. L.J. 851 (1981). Copyright © 1981 by the Georgetown University Law Journal. Reprinted by permission.

Tanford and Bocchino, Rape Victim Shield Laws and the Sixth Amendment, 128 U. Pa. L. Rev. 544 (1981). Copyright © 1981 by the University of Pennsylvania Law Review. Reprinted by permission.

Tribe, Trial by Mathematics: Precision and Ritual in the Trial Process, 84 Harv. L. Rev. 1329 (1971). Copyright © 1971 by the Harvard Law Review Association. Reprinted by permission.

Tribe, Triangulating Hearsay, 87 Harv. L. Rev. (1974). Copyright © 1974 by the Harvard Law Review Association. Reprinted by permission.

Westin, Privacy and Freedom 31-39 (1967). Copyright © 1967 by the Association of the Bar of the City of New York. Reprinted by permission.

Wigmore, A Student's Textbook on the Law of Evidence 10-12 (1935). Copyright © 1935 by the Foundation Press. Reprinted by permission.

Special Notice

Many of the problems in this book are based on real cases. In some instances, names and facts have been changed for educational purposes. In such event, there is no intent to represent the facts of the problem as real. Citations to cases on which problems are based are omitted in most cases in order to stimulate original thinking.

Problems, Cases, and Materials
on Evidence

CHAPTER I

Relevance

Scholars would no doubt differ sharply if asked to state the function of the law of evidence. Perhaps the simplest description is the most accurate and would be most likely to obtain the concurrence of judges, lawyers, and scholars: The function of the law of evidence is to specify (1) what types of information may be considered by the triers of fact in our law courts so that they may ascertain facts of importance to the determination of the dispute before the court, (2) in what forms this information may be communicated to the triers of fact, and (3) to some extent, what the judge, advocates, and triers of fact can do with this information.

Admittedly, this description of the function of the law of evidence says nothing about what *values* are important in determining the form and content of information to be considered by the triers of fact. Scholars, judges, philosophers, lawyers, and students debate how the goals of truth, justice, order, or certainty affect the rules of evidence. Rationality is a logical starting point for the study of the subject of evidence and relevance — rationality's operational construct — has long been treated as a fundamental foundational concept. As James Bradley Thayer stated in his Preliminary Treatise on Evidence 264-265 (1898):

> There is a principle — not so much a rule of evidence as a presupposition *axiom* involved in the very conception of a rational system of evidence . . . which forbids receiving anything irrelevant, not logically probative. . . .
>
> There is another precept which should be laid down as preliminary, in stating the law of evidence; namely, that unless excluded by some rule or principle of law, all that is logically probative is admissible. This general admissibility, however, of what is logically probative is not, like the former principle, a necessary presupposition in a rational system of evidence; there are many exceptions to it. Yet, in order to a clear conception of the law, it is important to notice this also as being a fundamental proposition.

But rationality may itself be a concept with roots in politics and culture. What does relevance mean in the law courts? Thayer despaired of

1

finding a test of relevancy in the law, referring simply to "logic and general experience, assuming that the principles of reasoning are known to its judges and ministers. . . ." Id. at 265.

Logic, the lessons of experience (i.e., precedent), and principles of reasoning are all components of relevance as that term is employed in law. As Wigmore pointed out, "the Anglo-American system of jury-trial rules of evidence . . . is *not* a pure *science* of logical proof." A Student's Textbook on the Law of Evidence 5 (1935). Some special considerations distinguishing the rules of proof in law courts from scientific or logical proof are identified by Wigmore (id. at 10-12, emphasis added):

(a) In the first place, . . . the *materials* for inference are peculiar. In the scientist's laboratory, the phenomena of chemistry, biology, botany, physics, and the like, are the chief material. But in a law court the chief material consists of human conduct in its infinite varieties, and of everyday phenomena of streets, buildings, trucks, barrels, pistols, and the like, which have no interest usually for the scientist. . . .

(b) In the second place, the scientist is not much hampered, as a court is, by limitations of *time* and *place*. A scientist can wait till he finds the data he wants; and he can use past, present, and future data; and he can go anywhere to get them. . . .

But a judicial trial must be held at a fixed time and place, and the decision must be then made, once for all. Most of the data are distant, and in the past. Many can never be re-found or revived. These limitations seriously hamper the inquiry. The only compensating advantage is that a tribunal can compel the production of data, if available, from any citizen within the jurisdiction, while the scientist cannot do this.

(c) In the third place, the tribunal deals with data presented by *parties in dispute*. Thus, human nature being what it is, there is a constant risk of fraud and bias. This makes it specially difficult for the tribunal to obtain and to valuate the evidence. . . .

(d) In the fourth place, the judicial trial takes place under dramatic conditions of *emotional disturbance*. The disputant and defiant parties are present; their witnesses and other friends sense the antagonism. The spectators make it a public drama. Everyone is keyed up. Surprise, sympathy, contempt, ridicule, anger — all these emotions are latent. Even the most honest and disinterested witness feels the mental strain. . . .

(e) And finally, the tribunal, whether judge alone or with a jury, consists of *laymen*. In a laboratory, the scientist, whatever his field, is trained in valuing the data of his special branch. But in a court room even the judge himself is not a specialist in the science of proof. The substantive law, and the law of procedure, form the main part of his equipment. And, under our system of frequent judicial change, the judge rarely has an opportunity to become a specialist in the valuing of evidence. Hence he needs the guidance of a certain set of conventional rules, based on the prior recorded experience of other judges.

In this country the history of the law of evidence over the past century has been largely one of a movement *away* from a detailed set of legal

ing a lathe his shirtsleeve caught in the machinery and his hand was
severely mangled. In defense, the employer's insurance carrier offers
the testimony of a co-worker, White, that at the time of the accident
Smith was eating a pizza and had looked away from his work momentarily to reach for a napkin. Smith's counsel objects to White's testimony.
How should the judge rule? Why?

Problem I-3
The Defective Unopened Drum of Paint

Action to recover from the manufacturer, D, the price of a drum of
waterproof roof paint. As proof of breach of D's 10-year warranty, P
offers evidence that she used *another* drum of the same brand of paint six
months earlier and that shortly after she purchased the drum in issue
but before she opened it the paint from the earlier drum allowed leaks
and also ruined the roof shingles to which it had been applied. Should
P's offer of proof be accepted?

NOTE: MATERIALITY, PROOF, AND THE
SUBSTANTIVE LAW

Morgan observed that "whether a matter of fact is provable in an
action depends, first, upon whether it falls within the area of dispute
between the litigants. In the earlier law this was determined almost exclusively by the pleadings. At present in most jurisdictions the pleadings
alone will not suffice. . . ." Morgan, Basic Problems of Evidence 160
(1954).

Other constraints on what is "provable in an action" include the pretrial order, which under F.R. Civ. P. Rule 16 supersedes the pleadings,
the issues as defined at trial, and, of course, the substantive law. Morgan
gives two examples of how the latter controls the proof at trial:

> [I]f a former judgment would as a matter of substance bar plaintiff's action
> against defendant, it will avail defendant nothing unless he has pleaded it as a
> defense. Again, assume that in a jurisdiction where the objective theory of
> contract law prevails the defendant makes an offer in language which an
> ordinary person in the position of the plaintiff offeree would understand to
> be an offer to do X, and the plaintiff accepts. The defendant when sued for
> breach of contract tenders incontestable evidence that his real intention was
> to offer to do Y. The evidence will be rejected as entirely irrelevant under the
> applicable rule of substantive law.

The point is that relevance is a relational concept; in law, relevance has
no abstract meaning.

Usually the substantive law and pleadings adequately delineate the issues, so that the purpose for which specific evidence is offered is clear. But sometimes the theory of justification at the core of a plaintiff's claim or of a defendant's defense is unclear or undergoing change. In such cases, the substantive law may not be clearly understood, stated, or perceived. Evidentiary rulings in such contexts often seem strained and hard to defend, because the evidence in question does not seem as probative on the issue for which it is ostensibly offered as it does on other, unarticulated issues. One should always ask whether such discontinuities between proof and the apparent issues in dispute reveal a problem in the handling of evidence or in the articulation of the substantive law.

Problem I-4
Dr. Who Visits Old Salem

Dr. Who sets the controls of his time machine for Salem, Massachusetts, 1686. He arrives in a strange, primitive society prone to beliefs and superstitions about witches, goblins, God, and the Devil.

Shortly before Dr. Who's arrival, three of the women in the settlement are accused by leading elders of practicing witchcraft. According to local practice, they are placed in the stockade until they can be tried in the Salem manner. In Salem at that time, an accused witch was given two options. One option was to submit to a trial, which consisted of tying the accused woman to a board and dunking her in a "pure" pond while the deacon recited the Lord's Prayer three times. If the accused survived the dunking, the purity of her soul was vindicated and she was set free; if she did not survive, guilt and sentence were simultaneously announced. No one recalled any acquittals as a result of this process. Alternatively, the accused could accept banishment from the colony, which meant exile to the western wilderness. Once banished, no one had ever been seen again.

Impressed by Dr. Who's mechanized mode of transportation, the Salem elders ask him to preside over the trial of the three witches. Dr. Who agrees on the condition that trial be conducted by what we now think of as modern trial procedures. The elders agree but insist that the jurors be selected from among their ranks. At trial, the deacon serving as prosecutor seeks to present evidence that prior to Dr. Who's arrival the three accused witches refused to submit to trial by dunking.

Should this proof be admitted? Is it logically relevant? Why should anything be kept from the trier of fact? What advantages, if any, does the common law have over the trial by ordeal? We believe, from our present vantage point, that the current adversary process more accurately determines truth. But how culture-bound is this belief? Reconsider the judgment of Solomon in light of these questions.

If you feel the Salem witch dunking is far-fetched, consider State v. Wisdom, 119 Mo. 539, 24 S.W. 1047 (1894) — the ordeal of the bier:

In the course of the examination of the witness Hill, he was asked to tell what happened down at the morgue by the dead body of Mr. Drexler, when the witness, Willard and defendant were there, prior to the inquest. This was objected to as immaterial. The objection was overruled. The witness answered that "they told us to put our hands on Mr. Drexler"; and that he and Willard did so, but defendant would not do it. Officer McGrath corroborated this statement. Defendant objected to McGrath's statement, but assigned no reason. The action of the court in this regard is now assigned as error. Who it was that told them to put their hands on Mr. Drexler's dead body does not appear. The request to touch the body was evidently prompted by the old superstition of the ordeal of the bier in Europe in the middle ages, which taught that the body of a murdered man would bleed freshly when touched by his murderer, and hence it was resorted to as means of ascertaining the guilt or innocence of a person suspected of a murder. This superstition has not been confined to one nation or people. It obtained among the Germans prior to the twelfth century, and is recorded in the Nibelungenlied, a great epic poem of that century, in the incident in which the murdered Siegfried is laid on his bier, and Hagen is called on to prove his innocence by going to the corpse, but at his approach the dead chief's wounds bleed fresh. That it dominated the English mind is attested by the passage of Matthew Paris that when Henry II died at Chinon, in 1189, his son and successor came to view his body, and, as he drew near, immediately the blood flowed from the nostrils of the dead king, as if his spirit was so indignant at the approach of the one who caused his death that his blood thus protested to God. And Shakespeare voiced the same superstition in Richard III (act I, sc. 2) thus: "Oh, gentlemen, see, see! dead Henry's wounds Open their congealed mouths, and bleed afresh."

And so does Dr. Warren, in Diary of a Late Physician (volume 3, p. 327). That it was a prevalent belief in Africa and Australia, in another form, see 17 Enc. Brit. pp. 818, 819. This superstition has come to this country with the emigration from other lands, and, although a creature of the imagination, it does to a considerable degree affect the opinions of a large class of our people. It is true, it was not shown that defendant believed that touching this body would cause any evidence of guilt to appear, or that he entertained any fear of possible consequences; but it was simply a test proposed by some bystander, and it was offered as showing the manner in which the three suspects conducted themselves when it was proposed. Clark v. State, 78 Ala. 474; Chamberlayne's Best on Ev., p. 488. While defendant had a perfect right to decline, either because of his instinctive repugnance to the unpleasant task, or because no one had a right to subject him to the test, and his refusal might not prejudice him in the minds of a rational jury, on the other hand, a consciousness of guilt might have influenced him to refuse to undergo the proposed test, however unreasonable it was, and it is one of the circumstances of the case that the jury could weigh. The jury could consider that, while it was a superstitious test, still defendant might have been more or less affected by it, as many intelligent people are by equally baseless notions, as shown by their conduct and movements. It often happens that a case must be established by a number of facts, any one of which, by itself, would be of little weight, but all of which, taken together, would prove the issue. . . .

Do you agree with the court's conclusion that the admission of this evidence was not prejudicial error? What differences, if any, are there between the *Wisdom* and *Salem* cases?

If you still feel *Salem* and *Wisdom* are far-fetched, consider State v. Mottram, 158 Me. 325, 184 A.2d 225 (1962). In *Mottram* the court had to decide whether evidence that a prosecution witness refused to take a lie detector test, the results of which were inadmissible, should have been excluded. How should the court have ruled? What differences, if any, are there between *Mottram* on the one hand and *Salem* and *Wisdom* on the other?

B.   Conditional Relevance

FRE 104
Preliminary Questions

(b) *Relevancy conditioned on fact* — When the relevancy of evidence depends upon the fulfillment of a condition of fact, the court shall admit it upon, or subject to, the introduction of evidence sufficient to support a finding of the fulfillment of the condition.

Problem I-5
The Rim

A 1969 Ford and a 1973 Chevy collide at an intersection in the country. The owner of the Ford (*F*) claims that the owner of the Chevy (*C*) was speeding and did not slow down for the intersection. *F*'s investigator found a rim from a headlight in a field 200 feet from the point of impact. *F* has an expert witness prepared to testify that in order for the headlight rim to have been thrown 200 feet the Chevy had to be going at least 75 MPH. *F* puts the investigator on the stand; she testifies to finding the rim, specifies the precise spot where she found it, and identifies the rim she found. *F* then offers the rim in evidence. What ruling? How will the judge go about deciding?

Suppose *F* tells the judge about his intention to call the expert and outlines the testimony expected from the expert?

Does *F* need a witness first who can identify the rim as having come from a 1973 Chevy? From *C*'s 1973 Chevy? Suppose *C* contests this proof with a witness who claims that the rim is from a 1974 Caddy? What ruling? By what procedure and by what standard does the judge go about deciding?

ROMANO v. ANN & HOPE FACTORY OUTLET, INC.
417 A.2d 1375 (R.I. 1980)   104(b) rejected

KELLEHER, J. This is a products-liability case in which Pio Romano, father of the minor plaintiff, Rayna Romano, instituted an action in *C* Superior Court to recover for her personal injuries. The 1973 suit alleged that Rayna received permanent injuries when she fell from a bicycle purchased from the defendant, Ann & Hope Factory Outlet, Inc. (Ann & Hope), on August 8, 1970. The Romanos contend that the bicycle's defectively designed coaster brake precipitated Rayna's injuries. . . .

The allegedly defective bicycle, a twenty-inch boy's model "Oxford" bicycle with a banana seat and high-rise handlebars, was purchased preassembled by Rayna's grandparents for her younger brother, John. The braking mechanism bore the inscription "Sturmey-Archer '69." At the time of their purchase, Rayna's grandparents received no maintenance instructions. Although Rayna and her older brother, Pio, already owned bicycles, each youngster customarily rode whichever bicycle was closest at hand. Testimony revealed that the "Oxford" bicycle functioned satisfactorily for just over a year.

On September 9, 1971, Rayna, then seven years old, mounted the "Oxford" bicycle and started down the steep hill on which the Romano home was located. The Romanos lived in Cranston on Bellevue Drive. As Rayna rode down the street, she applied the brakes "half-way" in order to keep the bicycle speed under control, but as she approached a bend in the road, the brakes failed, causing the bike to strike a curb at the foot of the hill. As a result of the impact, Rayna flew over the handlebars and hit a tree. She was hospitalized for extensive periods of time for a variety of injuries, including a fractured skull. . . .

Throughout this litigation the Romanos have claimed that the defect [in the braking mechanism] was a plastic fixture consisting of an oil cap which is attached to the top of a narrow tube. The entire fixture measures approximately one-quarter of an inch in length. The fixture is fitted into a hole found on the hub of the rear wheel. The brake chamber is lubricated by lifting the cap and letting the oil flow down the tube into the chamber. Hereafter we shall refer to the plastic fixture as the "plastic cap."

For the most part, maintenance of the "Oxford" was the responsibility of Rayna's older brother, Pio. He told the jury that prior to Rayna's unfortunate descent the plastic cap was missing from the "Oxford." Pio could not be specific as to the time when he first noticed the cap's absence. The Romanos have argued with great vigor that the trial justice committed reversible error when he prohibited their expert, Leonard Mandell (Mandell), from telling the jury that a plastic cap should never have been used because the cap could not be securely threaded into the hub's oil hole because the cap's plastic threads were destroyed once they were turned against the metal threads of the oil hole. If permitted, Mandell was prepared to tell the jury that the lack of this cap allowed debris to enter the brake chamber and oil to escape from the chamber — two conditions which, in Mandell's opinion, caused the brake failure.

In April of 1973, Mandell, a consulting engineer with a master of science degree in mechanical engineering, conferred with the Romanos at their home. As a result of their meeting, he took the bicycle to his laboratory where it was photographed and tested. Unfortunately, by the time the case was reached for trial in September 1977, the bicycle, together with Mandell's detailed notes regarding his investigation of the internal braking mechanism, had disappeared. According to Mandell, the bicycle was either taken when his office and laboratory were repeatedly burglarized sometime after September 1974, or it was "released somehow." Notwithstanding the unavailability at trial of the bicycle and the notes, Mandell was prepared to testify concerning the condition of the internal braking mechanism when he dismantled it in April of 1973.

 The attorney for Ann & Hope objected to the admission of Mandell's testimony on the ground that a proper foundation had not been laid. He asserted that the 1973 findings would be irrelevant to the condition of the bicycle at the time of the 1971 descent unless accompanied by proof that the bicycle remained unchanged during the intervening twenty months. The Romanos thereupon attempted to establish "no substantial change" in the condition of the bicycle through the testimony of Bart Costerus (Costerus), a mechanical engineer who had examined the Romano bicycle in September 1971. The bicycle was in his possession for approximately three to four weeks. He tested the braking power using a braking force of fifty pounds, Rayna's approximate weight at the time of the accident. Costerus noted that the plastic lubrication cap was missing from the hole in the rear brake hub assembly when he received the bicycle. He testified further that he neither disassembled nor lubricated the braking mechanism.

Costerus first tested the brakes on a hill in Attleboro whose contour was similar to the Bellevue Drive slope. Costerus had attached to the right pedal blocks of steel which approximated Rayna's weight at the time she was injured. The engineer, who weighed 175 pounds, would sit on the banana seat of the "Oxford" and let the bicycle roll down the hill. As the bicycle began to pick up speed, Costerus would keep his feet up in the air, and the fifty-pound weight would cause the right pedal to turn downward and thereby activate the brake. Costerus employed this technique, making some forty descents, thirty-five in Attleboro and five in Cranston on Bellevue Drive. At no time, he reported, was there a "total loss of braking power."

Other testimony also revealed that after Rayna was injured, the bicycle was stored in a basement workroom of the Romano home untouched until Rayna's father delivered it to Costerus for inspection and testing in September 1971. A few weeks later, Rayna's father picked up the bicycle from Costerus and returned it to the basement of the Romano home. Again, it remained there unused until April 1973 when Mandell acquired it for further testing.

Arguing that the tests conducted by Costerus in and of themselves could have deformed the brake's mechanism, the defense attorneys continued to object to Mandell's proffered testimony regarding his observations of the brake's inner workings. The trial justice sustained the objections. The Romanos made several offers of proof intending to establish that the test runs made by Costerus did not deplete the amount of lubricant in the braking system and that evaporation of the oil in the interim between the accident and Mandell's testing was insignificant. The trial justice rejected a final offer of proof by the Romanos relative to the presence within the braking system of dirt and debris which allegedly was sufficient to cause a brake failure. Thereafter, unconvinced that the Romanos had established the necessary similarity of braking conditions, the trial justice directed a verdict. . . .

On appeal, the Romanos argue that in excluding the testimony of their expert, Mandell, the trial justice effectively precluded testimony on the issues of defective design and proximate cause, thus making a directed verdict inevitable. They argue further that the trial justice applied an erroneous standard of admissibility in excluding the testimony of their expert. According to the Romanos, the issue of whether the condition of the brake chamber remained unchanged between the date of the accident and its subsequent examination by Mandell was a question for the jury and not for the trial justice. To support their positions, the Romanos urge us to adopt the standard of "conditional relevancy." Under this theory, all the evidence would have been submitted to the jury who would then decide, under proper instruction, whether the condition of the brake had changed substantially from September 1971 to April 1973. As authority for this proposition they rely primarily upon Fed. R. Evid. 104(b). . . . The standard of admissibility "has been variously referred to as 'some evidence' or 'prima facie' evidence. The important point is that the preliminary fact can be decided by the judge against the proponent only where the jury could not reasonably find the preliminary fact to exist." 21 Wright & Graham, Federal Practice and Procedure §5054 at 269 (1977). The Romanos argue that inasmuch as a prima facie showing of no substantial change was made through uncontradicted testimony, the issue should have been submitted to the jury.

Stated differently, the Romanos contend that because the relevancy of Mandell's examination of the brake's innards depended upon proof of another conditionally relevant preliminary fact — "no substantial change" — both should have been for the jury to decide.

At the outset, we note that the acceptance of Rule 104(b) has been considerably less than universal. Our investigation revealed a lone case in which it was applied but with virtually no explanation. A new trial was ordered because "the Court below may not have followed" the requisite procedure set forth in the rule. United States v. 478.34 Acres of Land, 578 F.2d 156, 160 (6th Cir. 1978). One leading treatise considers proof of preliminary questions of fact as "one of the most complex, as well as most common, of evidentiary concepts." It suggests that " 'laying a foundation' for the admissibility of evidence . . . is easier to do if you do not think too much about what you are doing. Thus, Rule 104 may be a provision that is best ignored." 21 Wright & Graham, Federal Practice and Procedure §5052 at 248 (1977). Another legal pundit, after a lengthy discussion highly critical of the conditional relevancy doctrine, concludes that Rule 104(b) is "an obstacle course for judge and jury alike." He declares that it is "based on incorrect analysis; it confuses the issues, invites errors, and should be repealed." Ball, The Myth of Conditional Relevancy, 1977 Ariz. St. L.J. 295, 325. Professor Ball argues that there is "no need to create a special rule to serve as a rescue apparatus to save the law of evidence from . . . mythical dangers." Id. at 310. The greater danger, he asserts, is that "once codifiers embark on this false trail, they will find a problem of 'conditional relevancy' behind every tree and will employ their rescue apparatus in a way which will confuse the jury and muddle the administration of the evidence rules far more than letting matters alone would have done." Id. at 310-11.

We are not prepared to embrace the doctrine of conditional relevancy as it is set forth in the rule. Indeed, we question how clearly the demarcation between the respective roles of judge and jury would be delineated under the rule. Professors Wright and Graham summarize commentary regarding the viability of Rule 104(b): "In short, about the only good thing that commentators have found in jury determination of preliminary questions is that it is likely to amount to a de facto repeal of the rules of evidence." 21 Wright & Graham, Federal Practice and Procedure §5052 at 249 (1977).

We have not as yet adopted the Federal Rules in this jurisdiction. Instead, we prefer to rely upon our vintage rule that the trial justice must exercise discretion regarding the admissibility of evidence when

there has been an objection of irrelevancy. A ruling made under these *SoR*
circumstances would not be reversible error unless the trial justice
abused his discretion to the prejudice of the objecting party. On review
of the record, we do not find that he abused his discretion. . . .

Turning to our own case law, we have long recognized the doctrine *R*
that conditions existing at the time of a mishap must be similar to those
subsequently proved and that these evidentiary rulings are within the
discretion of the trial justice. In Laporte v. Cook, 22 R.I. 554, 555, 48 A.
798, 799 (1901), we said that the trial justice could properly refuse to
admit testimony concerning the weight of sand that had allegedly fallen
on the plaintiff until proof fixed the exact time that the sand was removed. The sand taken from the trench "some time after the accident"
did not suffice. Id. at 555, 48 A. at 799. We have also found error when
"photographs taken of the remnants of the wrecked wagon nearly three
years after the accident" were admitted into evidence. We predicated
our ruling on the premise that the remnants were not "in the same
condition as they were immediately after the collision." Souza v. United
Electric Railways Co., 51 R.I. 124, 127, 152 A. 419, 420-21 (1930).

Accordingly, we hold that the trial justice did not commit reversible *H/*
error in excluding the testimony on the issues of defective design and
causation because, as a matter of discretion, he concluded that the condition of the brake when examined by the Romanos' expert in 1973 was
not substantially the same as it had been on September 9, 1971, the day
Rayna was injured. Here, Mandell was prepared to testify that the 1971
malfunction was due to a lack of oil and the presence of dust in the
brake's chamber. However, having in mind that there was no evidence in
regard to the temperature in the area where the bicycle was stored
during the twenty-month hiatus between Costerus's forty descents and
Mandell's inspection, the trial justice was obviously dubious about how
much of the dirt found by Mandell came about as a result of Costerus's
experiments, and he was also unsure that the oil level in the brake
chamber was the same in 1973 as it had been on the evening when the
bicycle plunged down Bellevue Drive.

On this record and in light of the views expressed herein, we cannot
fault the trial justice's refusal to allow Mandell to testify concerning the
findings he made as a result of his 1973 examination of the coaster-brake
portion of the "Oxford."

Accordingly, the plaintiffs' appeal is denied and dismissed, the judgment appealed from is affirmed, and the case is remanded to the
Superior Court.

Do you agree with the court's analysis of Rule 104(b)? Is there an
approach under the Federal Rules, other than the one rejected by the

court, that would reach the same result as the Rhode Island court reached? Under either approach, what principle is to guide the trial judge in her exercise of discretion?

The subject of judge-jury responsibility for deciding preliminary issues is considered more fully in Section E of Chapter III and, with regard to evidence offered under the co-conspirators' exclusion from the hearsay rule (Rule 801(d)(2)(E)), in Section B of Chapter IV.

C.   Logical Relevance

H. HART AND J. McNAUGHTON, EVIDENCE AND INFERENCE IN THE LAW
in Evidence and Inference 48, 50-51 (Lerner ed. 1959)

The central difficulty in a discussion of evidence and inference in the law is that the law has no single technique for connecting its conclusions with supporting data. The problems are highly varied, and techniques of decision vary correspondingly. A unified account of "evidence and inference in the law" is thus impossible. . . .

I.   THE AFTER-THE-EVENT DETERMINATION OF ADJUDICATIVE FACTS

The first type of problem we have chosen is the simplest. It is the problem presented when a tribunal is called upon to apply a legal direction of undisputed content to a disputed state of fact. Ordinarily, such a direction will be a legal "rule" in the technical sense. Such a rule can be defined as an authoritative general direction which requires for its application only a determination of the happening or non-happening of physical or mental events. In logical terms, the rule is a special kind — a "prescriptive" kind — of major premise; the conclusion follows if the propositions comprising the minor premise are proved. While such a minor premise may include a proposition that something is likely to happen in the future, generally the problem is one of determining historical facts.

ILLUSTRATIVE CASES

Here are typical examples of simple undisputed-law, disputed-fact cases:

(1) A man is charged with murder. The rule made relevant by the

facts of the case may be that any sane person who with malice aforethought kills another person shall be put to death. The facts are such that there are no difficult questions of definition, say, of "sane" or of "malice aforethought." The only question is whether it was the defendant who fired the fatal shot. (2) A man is sued for breach of warranty. The rule made applicable by the facts of the situation may be that any person who sells goods to another which are not up to the seller's representations shall, provided the buyer gives prompt notice of the defect, pay the buyer a sum of money equal to the difference between the value of the goods promised and of those delivered. The facts raise no doubts as to the exact meaning of the rule. The only issue is whether the goods delivered were as represented by the seller. (3) A large estate is to be distributed. The relevant rule may be that two-thirds of the estate of any person dying without a will shall be divided equally among his children. There are no close questions requiring the law of descent to be clarified. The only question is whether the claimant is or is not one of the children of the deceased.

In such simple situations the resemblances of the law's problems to the problems of other disciplines in dealing with evidence are perhaps at their maximum. And yet the problems are quite different.

Problem I-6
The Burned Butt

Auto accident tort action. *D*, by cross-examination, unsuccessfully sought to force from *P* the admissions that he was driving under the influence of liquor and at the time of the accident was attempting to light a cigarette. *D* also sought to testify that two days after the accident and after *P*'s demolished vehicle had been removed 10 miles from the scene of the accident, she found a slightly burned cigarette on the floor-board of *P*'s vehicle. Should *D*'s testimony be admitted? Why? *prob no*

Problem I-7
Beer Cans in the Car

Charge: driving while intoxicated. At trial, the arresting officer testifies that he stopped *D* for speeding. While writing out a speeding citation he observed a beer can on the seat next to *D*. The prosecution offers the beer can as evidence.

Should the beer can be admitted? Does it make any difference whether (1) the beer can is half empty, (2) the beer can is open and completely empty, or (3) the beer can is full and unopened?

alone in car?

NOTE: ON PRINCIPLES OF REASONING

As Wigmore and Thayer point out, the study of evidence begins with the study of logic, a branch of epistemology. The following excerpts should provide a brief but basic understanding of the most important terms and processes.

1. The uses and limits of inductive proof. A. J. Ayer confronts us with the logical problem of induction.

A. J. AYER, HUME'S FORMULATION OF THE PROBLEM OF INDUCTION, FROM THE LEGACY OF HUME, IN PROBABILITY AND EVIDENCE 3-6 (1972): A rational man is one who makes a proper use of reason: and this implies, among other things, that he correctly estimates the strength of evidence. In many instances, the result will be that he is able to vindicate his assertions by adducing other propositions which support them. But what is it for one proposition to support another? In the most favourable case, the premises of an argument entail its conclusion, so that if they are true the conclusion also must be true. It would seem, however, that not all our reasoning takes the form of deductive inference. In many cases, and most conspicuously when we base an unrestricted generalisation on a limited set of data, we appear to run beyond our evidence: that is, we appear not to have a logical guarantee that even if our premises are true, they convey their truth to the conclusion. But then what sort of inference are we making, and how can it be justified? These questions have not proved easy to answer, and their difficulty creates what philosophers call the problem of induction.

The attention which has been paid to this problem is primarily due to the work of David Hume; and it is worth taking some trouble to restate Hume's argument since, for all its essential simplicity, it has often been misunderstood. Hume starts from the assumption that we can have reason to believe in the truth of any proposition concerning an empirical matter of fact only in so far as we are able to connect the state of affairs which it describes with something that we now perceive or remember. Let us assign the neutral term "data" to what one perceives at a given moment or what one then remembers having previously perceived, leaving aside the question what these data are. On any theory of perception, their range will be very limited. Then Hume maintains that one will have reason to believe in the existence of anything which is not a datum, at the time in question, only if one has reason to believe that it is connected with one's data in a lawlike fashion. He puts this rather misleadingly by saying that "all reasonings concerning matters of fact seem to be founded on the relation of cause and effect." He then raises the question whether our belief in the existence of these lawlike connections can ever be rationally justified, and he offers a proof that it cannot.

This proof may be set out in nine stages, as follows:

(i) An inference from one matter of fact to another is never demonstrative. This is not to say that when the inference is fully set out the conclusion does not follow validly from the premisses — there is no question but that "q" does follow from "p" and "if p then q" — but rather that what one may call the guiding principle of the inference, the proposition "if p then q," when based on a supposed factual connection between the events referred to by "p" and "q," is always an empirical proposition, and as such can be denied without contradiction. Hume's way of putting this, or one of his many ways of putting this, is to say that "knowledge of the relation of cause and effect is not, in any instance, attained by reasonings a priori, but arises entirely from experience."

(ii) There is no such thing as a synthetic necessary connection between events. These are not, of course, the terms in which Hume puts it, but this is what it comes to. No matter what events A and B are, if A is presented to us in some spatio-temporal relation to B, there is nothing in this situation from which we could validly infer, without the help of other premisses, that events of the same type as A and B are connected in the same way on any other occasion. There is no such thing as seeing that A *must* be attended by B, and this not just because we lack the requisite power of vision but because there is nothing of this sort to be seen. No sense can be given to a "must" of this type.

(iii) So the only ground that we can have for believing, in a case where A is observed by us and B not yet observed, that B does exist in such and such a spatio-temporal relation to A is our past experience of the constant conjunction of As and Bs.

(iv) But clearly the inference from the premiss "Events of the type A and B have invariably been found in conjunction," or to put it more shortly, "All hitherto observed As bear the relation R to Bs," to the conclusion "All As bear the relation R to Bs," or even to the conclusion "This A will have the relation R to some B," is not formally valid. There is what we may call an inductive jump.

(v) To make it valid an extra premiss is needed assuring us that what has held good in the past will hold good in the future. Hume's formulation of this principle in the Treatise of Human Nature is "that instances of which we have had no experience, must resemble those of which we have had experience, and that the course of nature continues always uniformly the same."

(vi) But if all our reasonings about matters of fact are founded on this principle, we have no justification for them unless the principle itself is justifiable. But what justification could it have? There can be no demonstrative argument for it. It is clearly not a logical truth. In Hume's own words "we can at least conceive a change in the course of nature; which sufficiently proves that such a change is not absolutely impossible."

(vii) Even if the principle cannot be demonstrated, perhaps we can at least show it to be probable. But a judgement of probability must have some foundation. And this foundation can lie only in our past experience. The only ground we can have for saying that it is even probable that the course of nature continues uniformly the same is that we have hitherto found this to be the case. But then we are arguing in a circle. To quote Hume again, "probability is founded on the presumption of a resemblance betwixt those objects of which we have had experience, and those of which we have had none; and therefore it is impossible that this presumption can arise from probability."

(viii) The same objection would apply to any attempt to by-pass the general principle of the uniformity of nature and argue that inferences from one matter of fact to another, though admittedly not demonstrative, can nevertheless be shown to be probable. Again, this judgement of probability must have some foundation. But this foundation can lie only in our past experience. And so we have to assume the very principle that we are trying to by-pass, and the same objections arise.

(ix) We must, therefore, admit that since the inferences on which we base our beliefs about matters of fact are not formally valid, and since the conclusions to which they lead cannot be shown without circularity even to be probable, there is no justification for them at all. We just have the habit of making such inferences, and that is all there is to it. Logically, we ought to be complete sceptics, but in practice we shall continue to be guided by our natural beliefs. Hume is not, indeed, so inconsistent as to regard this generalisation about human behaviour as being more warranted than any other. He just expresses his natural belief in it, and leaves the matter there.

————————

Bertrand Russell presents two vivid examples of the force and limits of inductive reasoning.

B. RUSSELL, ON INDUCTION, IN THE PROBLEMS OF PHILOSOPHY 60-69 (1912): Let us take as an illustration a matter about which none of us, in fact, feel the slightest doubt. We are all convinced that the sun will rise to-morrow. Why? Is this belief a mere blind outcome of past experience, or can it be justified as a reasonable belief? It is not easy to find a test by which to judge whether a belief of this kind is reasonable or not, but we can at least ascertain what sort of general beliefs would suffice, if true, to justify the judgement that the sun will rise to-morrow, and the many other similar judgements upon which our actions are based.

It is obvious that if we are asked why we believe that the sun will rise to-morrow, we shall naturally answer, "Because it always has risen every day." We have a firm belief that it will rise in the future, because it has risen in the past. If we are challenged as to why we believe that it will continue to rise as heretofore, we may appeal to the laws of motion: the earth, we shall say, is a freely rotating body, and such bodies do not cease to rotate unless something interferes from outside, and there is nothing outside to interfere with the earth between now and to-morrow. Of course it might be doubted whether we are quite certain that there is nothing outside to interfere, but this is not the interesting doubt. The interesting doubt is as to whether the laws of motion will remain in operation until to-morrow. If this doubt is raised, we find ourselves in the same position as when the doubt about the sunrise was first raised.

The *only* reason for believing that the laws of motion will remain in operation is that they have operated hitherto, so far as our knowledge of the past enables us to judge. It is true that we have a greater body of evidence from the past in favour of the laws of motion than we have in favour of the sunrise, because the sunrise is merely a particular case of fulfillment of the laws of motion, and there are countless other particular cases. But the real question is: Do *any* number of cases of a law being fulfilled in the past afford evidence that it will be fulfilled in the future? If not, it becomes plain that we have no ground whatever for expecting the sun to rise to-morrow, or for expecting the bread we shall eat at our next meal not to poison us, or for any of the other scarcely conscious expectations that control our daily lives. It is to be observed that all such expectations are only *probable;* thus we have not to seek for a proof that they *must* be fulfilled, but only for some reason in favour of the view that they are *likely* to be fulfilled.

Now in dealing with this question we must, to begin with, make an important distinction, without which we should soon become involved in hopeless confusions. Experience has shown us that, hitherto, the frequent repetition of some uniform succession or coexistence has been a *cause* of our expecting the same succession or coexistence on the next occasion. Food that has a certain appearance generally has a certain taste, and it is a severe shock to our expectations when the familiar appearance is found to be associated with an unusual taste. Things which we see become associated, by habit, with certain tactile sensations which we expect if we touch them; one of the horrors of a ghost (in many ghost-stories) is that it fails to give us any sensations of touch. Uneducated people who go abroad for the first time are so surprised as to be incredulous when they find their native language not understood.

And this kind of association is not confined to men; in animals also it is very strong. A horse which has been often driven along a certain road resists the attempt to drive him in a different direction. Domestic animals expect food when they see the person who usually feeds them. We know that all these rather crude expectations of uniformity are liable to be misleading. The man who has fed the chicken every day throughout its life at last wrings its neck instead, showing that more refined views as to the uniformity of nature would have been useful to the chicken.

But in spite of the misleadingness of such expectations, they nevertheless exist. The mere fact that something has happened a certain number of times causes animals and men to expect that it will happen again. Thus our instincts certainly cause us to believe that the sun will rise tomorrow, but we may be in no better a position than the chicken which unexpectedly has its neck wrung. We have therefore to distinguish the fact that past uniformities *cause* expectations as to the future, from the question whether there is any reasonable ground for giving weight to such expectations after the question of their validity has been raised.

What implications do Ayer's and Russell's observations have for the law of evidence? Do they add anything to your understanding of the differences between what is typically called "circumstantial" evidence and what is often called "direct" or "eyewitness" evidence? If, as Russell writes, the business of science is "to find uniformities . . . to which, so far as our experience extends, there are no exceptions," what is "the business of the law of evidence"?

2. *Deductive reasoning.* Judicial proof also employs deductive reasoning. Irving M. Copi, in Introduction to Logic 23-26 (4th ed. 1972), explains what deductive argumentation is:

> Arguments are traditionally divided into two different types, *deductive* and *inductive*. Although every argument involves the claim that its premisses provide some grounds for the truth of its conclusion, only a *deductive* argument involves the claim that its premisses provide *conclusive* grounds. In the case of deductive arguments the technical terms "valid" and "invalid" are used in place of "correct" and "incorrect." A deductive argument is *valid* when its premisses, if true, do provide conclusive grounds for its conclusion, that is, when premisses and conclusion are so related that it is absolutely impossible for the premisses to be true unless the conclusion is true also. Every deductive argument is either valid or invalid; the task of deductive logic is to clarify the nature of the relation between premisses and conclusion in valid arguments, and thus to allow us to discriminate valid from invalid arguments. . . .
>
> If a deductive argument is valid, then its conclusion follows with equal necessity from its premisses no matter what else may be the case. From the two premisses *All men are mortal* and *Socrates is a man* the conclusion *Socrates is mortal* follows necessarily, no matter what else may be true. The argument remains valid no matter what additional premisses may be added to the original pair. . . .
>
> Accordingly, we characterize a deductive argument as one whose conclusion is claimed to follow from its premisses with absolute necessity, this necessity not being a matter of degree and not depending in any way upon whatever else may be the case. And in sharp contrast we characterize an inductive argument as one whose conclusion is claimed to follow from its

premisses only with probability, this probability being a matter of degree and dependent upon what else may be the case.

If this is not clear, perhaps the following exercise (adapted from Copi at 30) will demonstrate what deductive reasoning is. How good are your deductive faculties?

> In a faraway land there were two tribes. The Lynx were inveterate liars, while the Cougars were unfailingly veracious. Once upon a time a stranger visited the land, and on meeting a party of three inhabitants inquired as to what tribe they belonged.
>
> The first murmured something that the stranger did not catch. The second remarked, "He said he was a Lynx." The third said to the second, "You are a liar."

What is the tribe of the third person?   *truth Cougar*

3.   *Proof in the law courts.* Which kind of argument, inductive or deductive, is more persuasive? Do trials lend themselves to one kind of proof more than the other? With which part of the deductive process is the law of evidence primarily concerned?   *induct*

JAMES, RELEVANCY, PROBABILITY AND THE LAW, 29 CALIF. L. REV. 689 (1941): Dean Wigmore, recognizing this priority of logic, discusses the form of argument involved in the use of circumstantial evidence. His views deserve extended quotation and criticism. After stating that proof reduces to two great forms, inductive and deductive, and quoting Professor Sidgwick's description of the two, Wigmore states:

> A brief examination will show that in the offering of evidence in Court the form of argument is always *inductive.* Suppose, to prove a charge of murder, evidence is offered of the defendant's fixed design to kill the deceased. The form of the argument is: "*A* planned to kill *B*; therefore, *A* probably did kill *B*." It is clear that we have here no semblance of a syllogism. The form of argument is exactly the same when we argue: "Yesterday, Dec. 31, *A* slipped on the sidewalk and fell; therefore, the sidewalk was probably coated with ice"; or, "Today *A*, who was bitten by a dog yesterday, died in convulsions; therefore, the dog probably had hydrophobia." So with all other legal evidentiary facts. We may argue: "Last week the witness *A* had a quarrel with the defendant *B*; therefore, *A* is probably biassed against *B*"; "*A* was found with a bloody knife in *B*'s house; therefore, *A* is probably the murderer of *B*"; "After *B*'s injury at *A*'s machinery, *A* repaired the machinery; therefore, *A* probably acknowledged that the machinery was negligently defective"; "*A*, an adult of sound mind and senses, and apparently impartial, was present at an affray between *B* and *C*, and testifies that *B* struck first; therefore, it is probably true that *B* did strike first." In all these cases, we take a single or isolated

fact, and upon it base immediately an inference as to the proposition in question.

It may be replied, however, that in all the above instances, the argument is implicitly based upon an understood law or generalization, and is thus capable of being expressed in the *deductive* or syllogistic form. Thus, in the first instance above, is not the true form: "Men's fixed designs are probably carried out; *A* had a fixed design to kill *B*; therefore, *A* probably carried out his design and did kill *B*"?

There are two answers to this. (1) It has just been seen that every inductive argument is at least capable of being transmuted into and stated in the deductive form, by forcing into prominence the implied law or generalization on which it rests more or less obscurely. Thus it is nothing peculiar to litigious argument that this possibility of turning it into deductive form exists here also. It is not a question of what the form might be — for all inductive may be turned into deductive forms — but of what it is, as actually employed; and it *is* actually put forward in inductive form. (2) Even supposing this transmutation to be a possibility, it would still be undesirable to make the transmutation for the purpose of testing probative value; because it would be useless. We should ultimately come to the same situation as before. Thus, in one of the instances above: "*A* repaired machinery after the accident; therefore, *A* was conscious of a negligent defect in it"; suppose we turn this into deductive form: "People who make such repairs show a consciousness of negligence; *A* made such repairs; therefore, *A* was conscious of negligence." We now have an argument perfectly sound deductively, i.e. if the premises be conceded. But it remains for the Court to declare whether it accepts the major premise, and so the Court must now take it up for examination, and the proponent of the evidence appears as its champion and his argument becomes: "The fact that people make such repairs indicates (shows, proves, probably shows, etc.) that they are conscious of negligence." But here we come again, after all, to an inductive form of argument. The consciousness of negligence is to be inferred from the fact of repairs, — just as the presence of electricity in the clouds was inferred by Franklin from the shock through the kite-string, i.e. by a purely inductive form of reasoning. So with all other evidence when resolved into the deductive form; the transmutation is useless, because the Court's attention is merely transferred from the syllogism as a whole to the validity of the inference contained in the major premise; which presents itself again in inductive form.

For practical purposes, then, it is sufficient to treat the use of litigious evidentiary facts as *inductive* in form.

Note, Wigmore does not deny that in every instance proof must be based upon a generalization connecting the evidentiary proposition with the proposition to be proved.[15] Conceding this, he argues that the

15. The argument thus far may be summarized as follows: Relevancy is formal relation between two propositions. To determine the relevancy of an offered item of evidence one must first discover to what proposition it is supposed to be relevant. This requires analysis of the express or tacit argument of counsel. Then, since evidence is admissible only if relevant to a *material* proposition, analysis of the pleadings and applicable substantive law is

generalization may as well be tacitly understood as expressed, that "the transmutation [from the inductive to the deductive form] is useless, because the Court's attention is merely transferred from the syllogism as a whole to the validity of the inference contained in the major premise." Yet it is precisely in this transfer of attention that the value of the transmutation lies. The author's own examples illustrate the point. In the case of the repaired machinery we are told: " 'People who make such repairs [after an accident] show a consciousness of negligence; A made such repairs; therefore, A was conscious of negligence.' " Before this deductive proof can be evaluated, ambiguity must be eliminated from the major premise. By "people" shall we understand "some people" or "all people"? If the argument is intended to read, "Some people who make such repairs show consciousness of negligence; A made such repairs; therefore, A was conscious of negligence," it contains an obvious logical fallacy. If intended to read, "All people who make such repairs show consciousness of negligence; A made such repairs; therefore, A was conscious of negligence," it is logically valid. However, few could be found to accept the premise that *all* persons who repair machinery after an accident show consciousness of guilt; that is, that no single case could be found of one who, confident of his care in the past, nevertheless made repairs to guard against repetition of an unforeseeable casualty or to preserve future fools against the consequence of their future folly. Here the result of transmuting a proposed direct inference into deductive form is discovery that it is invalid — at least in the terms suggested.

The other proposed argument is equally interesting: " 'Men's fixed designs are probably carried out; A had a fixed design to kill B; therefore, A probably did kill B.' " Once one attempts to deal, in a quasi-syllogistic form, not with certainties but with probabilities, additional opportunities for fallacy are presented. Suppose that it is argued: "Most As are X, B is an A, therefore B is probably X"; or "Nine-tenths of all As are X, B is an A, therefore the chances are nine to one that B is X." Neither of these arguments is logically valid except upon the assumption that As may be treated as a uniform class with respect to the probability of their being X. This can be because there really is no way of subdividing the class, finding more Xs in one sub-class than in another, or because no subdivision can be made in terms of available data. Suppose that nine-tenths of all people in the world have dark eyes. If absolutely all one knew about B was that he was a person, it would be an apparent

---

required to determine whether the proposition ultimately sought to be proved is material. Having isolated the material proposition sought to be proved, we still must determine whether the evidentiary proposition is relevant to it — does tend to prove it. This tendency to prove can be demonstrated only in terms of some general proposition, based most often on the practical experience of the judge and jurors as men, sometimes upon generalizations of science introduced into the trial to act as connecting links. If the evidentiary proposition itself is material, there is no problem of relevancy.

nine-to-one chance that *B* had dark eyes. But if one knew *B* to be a Swede, the percentage of dark eyes in the total population of the world would no longer be important. One would want to know about the proportion of dark-eyed Swedes, which might differ from the ratio among humans generally.[19] Similarly in Wigmore's example. We know that we are interested in the probability of execution of a fixed design of a particular kind: to commit murder. There may be variation in the probability of execution of fixed designs on various subjects. As an initial criticism, therefore, the primary generalization should be "Men's fixed designs to kill are probably carried out." In this form we have a valid, quasi-syllogistic argument based upon the limited data available.[20] Still, is the premise sound?

"Men's fixed designs to kill are probably carried out," as a major premise in this argument, must mean that they are carried out more often than not. While the word "probable" can be used in other senses, its meaning here is clear. Hence one would conclude from the single datum that *A* had a fixed design to kill *B*, no other evidence being offered, that more likely than not *A* actually did kill *B*. But when this argument was presented to a group of law students and teachers, only one was willing to accept the indicated conclusion. Several would accept it if supported by adequate evidence that *B* had been intentionally killed by some one. Others refused to accept it without still further evidence connecting *A* with *B*'s death, or at the very least evidence that *B* had no other enemies. Moreover, there was less hesitancy in accepting the argument in its "inductive" form. Once the generalization was made explicit, and particularly after discussion of the meaning of "probably" as there used, doubts as to the propriety of the inference arose or sharpened. The demonstration, however "valid," is no better than its major premise, and the more one considers this premise the less reliable it looks. Certainly a permitted inference should rest upon some more easily acceptable law.

Of course, it does not follow that a proposed inference is improper because it can be shown not to follow on the basis of one possible generalization, or because another — which by the rules of logic would validate the inference — is unacceptable. There may be a third law, as yet unexpressed, which would justify the inference and at the same time be commonly accepted as true. And it may be very important to find the valid and accurate link, since the form of the link will control the form of the conclusion.

19. The form of the invalid argument would be as follows: Nine-tenths of men have dark eyes. *B* is a Swede. All Swedes are men. Therefore nine chances to one *B* has dark eyes.

20. Probability is not an actual state. Nothing really *is* probable. It is true or false. Probability is a matter of appearance. Apparently probability is always relative to the data available at the time judgment is exercised. If all possible data were available we should be dealing not with probability in an ordinary sense but with the approximation of certainty.

Persons who are unwilling to agree that men's fixed designs (at least in case of murder) are "probably" carried out — or, even conceding the fact of murder, that proof of A's fixed design to kill B establishes A, more likely than not, as B's killer — still agree that somehow this bit of evidence does have some tendency to indicate A's guilt. What form of general statement can reconcile these views? Perhaps something like this: "Men having such a fixed design are more likely to kill than are men not having such a fixed design." Those who contend that even fixed designs to kill are more often abandoned or thwarted than carried out can and doubtless will still concede that enough such designs are carried to execution so that the percentage of murderers is higher among persons entertaining such a fixed design than among the general public. Obviously this proposed generalization does not lead us from A's fixed design to kill B to the conclusion that A probably did kill B. There is nothing disturbing in this. This conclusion simply does not follow from the evidence of design. The error was in the original "direct induction." In fact, no useful conclusion about A's guilt can be drawn from design or intent alone. On the basis of an acceptable generalization we are able only to place A in a class of persons in which the incidence of murder is greater than among the general public. We cannot now say that A is probably guilty, but we can say that *the apparent probability of his guilt is now greater than before the evidence of design was received.*[21] This is logical relevancy — the only logical relevancy we can expect in dealing with practical affairs where strict demonstration is never possible.[22] The advantage of the transmutation into deductive (though not strictly syllogistic) form is that we know to what degree of proof we have attained, and do not overstate our results.[23]

Before leaving the subject of induction and deduction, consider one more example. Wigmore asserts: "There is just as much probative value in the argument 'A is quarrelsome, therefore he probably committed this assault,' as in the argument, 'B is peaceable, therefore he probably did not commit the assault. . . .'" So it may appear when the two arguments are stated as direct inductions. But transmutation of the two argu-

21. Or, the apparent probability of his innocence is now less. The two statements mean the same.

22. It should be unnecessary to point out the fundamental distinction between relevancy of evidence and the degree of probability necessary to establish a prima facie case. . . . If the sum total of evidence received falls short of satisfying the burden of persuasion, the jury is there for the express purpose of finding against the party who must bear that burden. If the sum total of evidence received is so slight that the jury as reasonable men could not be persuaded, the trial judge may enter a non-suit or direct a verdict. There is no reason for worrying about such issues while passing upon an offer of evidence. The one exception might be an item of evidence which, although logically relevant in a very remote sense, is so slight that in the opinion of the trial judge it could not sway an even balance.

23. In some cases we may be able to discover no acceptable generalization to connect the offered evidence to any material proposition. Such cases will be very rare, unless they involve errors of pleading or substantive law.

ments shows a different result. In the second case we say: "Peaceable men are not likely to commit assaults. B is a peaceable man. Therefore he was not likely to commit (this or any) assault." In the first case the most we can say is: "Quarrelsome men are more likely than others to commit assaults. A is quarrelsome. Therefore he is more likely than others to commit assaults." This may be equally good if there is no doubt of an affray between A and B, one of them surely being the aggressor. But suppose that we know someone assaulted C and are attempting to decide whether A or B or some third person was the culprit. We know that B, the peaceable man, was unlikely to commit any assault, hence unlikely to have committed the one in issue. All we know of A, the quarrelsome fellow, is that he has a general predilection for trouble. While it is some help, it does not show an affirmative probability of his guilt in any particular case. There is a definite difference in the probative value of the two offers of proof.

Nevertheless, both offers of proof are logically relevant; the apparent probability of guilt in each case would be changed, though not in the same degree, by the evidence of character. Why then is the evidence rejected in the weaker case? A possible answer would be simply because it is weaker — too weak. Although logically relevant, it falls short of the minimum requirement of legal relevancy. Such an answer merely raises a further query. Why should there be a standard of "legal relevancy" more strict than, or in any respect different from, the standards of logic? Why exclude any data which if admitted would change the apparent probabilities and hence serve, even to a slight degree, to aid the search for truth? Justice Holmes suggested one answer, it is "a concession to the shortness of life" — and perhaps to the shortness of purse of harassed litigants. If any and all evidence may be admissible which — in terms of some commonly accepted generalization about human conduct or natural events — would operate to any extent to alter the apparent probability of some material proposition, the field of judicial inquiry in most cases would be almost unlimited. Trials could come to an end only by the exhaustion of lawyers' ingenuity or clients' money, and the trial judge or jury might be overwhelmed and bewildered by the multiplicity of collateral issues. Such a rule would result in the apparent justice and the practical injustice characteristic of English Chancery practice a century and a half ago. Hence the requirement, in many cases, of something more than bare logical relevancy.

In addition to the simple factors of time, confusion and expense, other practical considerations may justify the exclusion of relevant evidence of but slight probative weight. As noted above, evidence is irrelevant in the clearest sense if its tendency is to prove some proposition not properly provable in the action. Sometimes the same evidence may be remotely relevant to a material proposition and directly relevant to an immaterial one; in such a case its exclusion could be justified lest the jury be misled into deciding the case on the immaterial issue. Or evidence might be excluded because under the issues as framed in the pleadings such evidence would unreasonably surprise the opponent.

Probably the greatest part of judicial rulings excluding evidence as irrelevant go primarily on the first principle — that the evidence is relevant, but its probative value is so slight as not to justify the time and expense involved in receiving it and the confusion of issues which might result in the mind of the trier of fact. Does this sound practical policy justify creation of the concept of "legal relevancy" — higher and more strict than logical relevancy, to which offers of proof must be referred? On the contrary, the concept can only be a nuisance. In the first place, it defies definition. No statement of a standard of probative value higher than logical relevancy can be made precise enough for use without excluding much evidence which is used daily, without argument and to good effect. And there is a definite reason for this. When a judge must decide whether a particular item of evidence, logically relevant, is of sufficient force to justify the time and expense necessary to establish it, he should not confine his attention to the effect of the offered evidence alone. He should consider how difficult it will be to establish the evidentiary fact — whether there is any real contest about it and whether confusing side issues must be explored. He should consider how the offered evidence may fit in with other evidence. It may form a small but useful part of a pattern of proof. It may stand alone, lending its negligible aid to unconnected lines of proof. It may be merely cumulative, so that the trouble of establishing it will result in little of practical value. He may even want to consider the importance to the parties of the issues being tried, in the light of mounting trial expense. Such considerations cannot usefully be reduced to a simple formula for relevancy of particular items of evidence. . . .

The remedy lies in Thayer's advice in holding to logic and general experience, assuming that the principles of reasoning are known to the judges and ministers of the law. In this analysis evidence is relevant if it can be demonstrated, in terms of some generalization acceptable to the court, to alter the apparent probability of any material proposition in the case. The generalization may rest either upon the general experience of the court or upon expert testimony, but it should be susceptible of expression. . . .

D. Prejudice and Probativeness

J. THAYER, A PRELIMINARY TREATISE ON EVIDENCE 266 (1898): [W]e must not fall into the error of supposing that relevancy, logical connection, real or supposed, is the only test of admissibility; for so we should drop out of sight the chief part of the law of evidence. When we have said (1) that, without any exception, nothing which is not, or is not supposed to be, logically relevant is admissible; and (2) that, subject to many exceptions and qualifications, whatever is logically relevant is admissible; it is obvious that, in reality, there are tests of admissibility other than logical relevancy. Some things are rejected as being of too slight a significance, or as having too conjectural and remote a connection; others, as being dangerous, in their effect on the jury, and likely to be misused or overestimated by that body; others, as being impolitic, or unsafe on public grounds; others, on the bare ground of precedent. It is this sort of thing, as I said before, — the rejection on one or another practical ground, of what is really probative, — which is the characteristic thing in the law of evidence; stamping it as the child of the jury system.

Problem I-8
A Picture Is Worth a Thousand Words

Defendant, Jack Lopinson, is charged with having secured the murder of his wife, Judith, and his partner and accountant, Joseph Malito, whose bullet-ridden bodies were found early one morning in the basement office of defendant's Philadelphia restaurant, Dante's Inferno. Defendant's explanation was that the restaurant had been held up by an unknown man, who had fatally shot Judith and Joseph and wounded Lopinson.

At trial, the state calls Dr. Marvin Aronson, the County Medical Examiner, to testify to what he observed at Dante's the morning of the crime. As part of Dr. Aronson's testimony the state offers eight color slides of the crime scene. The defense objects. As part of the state's offer of proof Dr. Aronson testifies that the slides will aid him in describing to the jury the scene and the cause of death. Specifically, the state contends that the slides are offered for the following purposes:

(1) To show the scene of the murders — that is, where the murders were committed;

(2) To show the location of the dead bodies;

(3) To show the position and condition of the bodies and the posture of the bodies in relationship to other things in the room;

(4) To show the location, nature, character, and extent of the wounds inflicted and where each wound was in relationship to the other;

(5) To show the location of the points of entry of the bullets into the bodies; to show distinctly the existence of powder burns and the residue of gun powder around the wounds; to show that the injuries were to the vital parts of the bodies;

(6) To show the cause of death of the two victims — that is, to show the severity and the violence of the assault; and

(7) To aid the doctor in giving his testimony to the jury.

The defense contends that the prejudicial effect of the slides outweighs their probative worth and offers to stipulate to the cause of death. The state refuses the offered stipulation.

How should the court rule? How should the court go about deciding how to rule?

UNITED STATES v. GRASSI
602 F.2d 1192 (5th Cir. 1979), vacated and remanded on other grounds,
448 U.S. 902 (1980)

CLARK, J. An eleven-count indictment charged Michael John Grassi, Jr., and three other persons with violating various statutes forbidding the interstate transportation of obscene materials. . . .

The indictment against Grassi was based on the distribution of five obscene films. During the course of Grassi's trial, the government asked the court for permission to show these five films to the jury. Objecting to the admission of the films on grounds that their obscene contents would prejudice the jury against Grassi, the defense attorney offered to stipulate that the films were obscene. After the prosecutor had refused to accept the proposed stipulation, the district court partially overruled the defendant's objection and allowed the jury to view three of the films. These films, which require between ten and eleven minutes to show, portray homosexual acts of the most bizarre and repulsive nature. They are also largely repetitious.

Grassi urges that, under Rule 403 of the Federal Rules of Evidence, the films should have been excluded since their probative value, in light of the proffered stipulation, was substantially outweighed by the prejudice arising from them. He argues, in the alternative, that the judge should have permitted the jury to view only a portion of one of the films. The government asserts that it had a right to refuse the stipulation and to show the films since they were necessary to prove the obscenity element of the crime with which Grassi was charged and to show that Grassi was aware of the contents of the films. Asserting that a decision concerning the obscenity of the films could not be made by viewing excerpts from them, the government also contends that the district court did not err in allowing the prosecution to present the three films in their entirety.

The process of evaluating the probity and prejudice inherent in a particular piece of evidence can be a complex one calling for a sifting of many disparate factors. Among the central considerations in determining probative value are, first, "how strong a tendency" the proffered evidence has to prove an issue of consequence in the litigation, 22 C. Wright & K. Graham, Federal Practice and Procedure, §5214 at 271 (1978); see United States v. Beechum, 582 F.2d 898, 914-915 (5th Cir.

1978) (en banc), and, second, the proponent's need for the evidence, United States v. Spletzer, 535 F.2d 950, 956 (5th Cir. 1976); Wright, supra, at 268-270. Since the films are admittedly the strongest available proof on the obscenity element of the crime, only the second probity consideration is at issue here.

But for the defendant's offer to stipulate, our task in reviewing the district judge's determination under Rule 403 would be an easy one. The government was required to prove that all the films which were the subject of the indictment were obscene. A work is obscene if "the average person, applying contemporary community standards would find that the work as a whole appeals to the prurient interest," if "the work depicts or describes, in a patently offensive way, sexual conduct specifically defined by the applicable state law," and if "the work, taken as a whole, lacks serious literary, artistic, political or scientific value." Miller v. California, 413 U.S. 15, 24 (1973). Under the *Miller* standard, a jury is required to view a film in its entirety in order to determine whether the film is obscene. United States v. Levine, 546 F.2d 658, 668 (5th Cir. 1977). Thus, in the absence of the stipulation, the probative value of the films here is as high as it could possibly be; any conclusion that the films were inadmissible because of prejudice would mean that the obscenity element could not be proven and that the defendant could not be tried. Whatever prejudice would arise from admission of the films in this situation could not substantially outweigh the probative value of the films. See Wright, supra, §5213 at 266.[3]

However, the defendant offered to stipulate that all of the films were obscene. Thus, the central issue in this case is how that offer to stipulate affects the probative value of the films. We examined the effect of an offer to stipulate on the Rule 403 balancing process in United States v. Spletzer, 535 F.2d 950, 956 (5th Cir. 1976). At his trial, Spletzer, who was charged with escaping from a federal prison, offered to admit the fact that at the time of his escape he had been confined in a federal prison pursuant to a judgment of conviction. Despite this tender, the district court permitted the government to introduce a certified copy of Spletzer's prior bank robbery conviction. This court held that the proposed stipulation eliminated the prosecutorial need for the copy of the judgment and that the district court abused its discretion in admitting the copy. The court also noted that the prejudice resulting from the

---

3. The government also urges that even if the three films should not have all been admitted on the obscenity issue, they were admissible to show Grassi's knowledge of the obscenity of the films and to show the extent of Grassi's participation in the scheme to distribute them. In order to prove a person has knowingly transported obscene materials, it need not be shown that the defendant was aware that the materials are legally obscene; the knowledge element is satisfied by proof that the defendant knew "of the materials' sexual orientation." United States v. Thevis, 490 F.2d 76, 77 (5th Cir. 1974). Here, the government proved that the films were distributed in boxes, the outside covers of which contained a graphic description of the contents of the films, and that Grassi had viewed the boxes. In light of this evidence, the additional probative value, if any, of showing three of the films to prove knowledge and participation was slight.

introduction of the prior conviction could have been substantially reduced by deleting the language revealing the nature of the prior offense.

Although *Spletzer* holds that an offer to stipulate should be among the factors considered in making a decision to admit or exclude the evidence under Rule 403, it does not indicate what result should be reached with regard to the films at issue here. The *Spletzer* court noted that the prosecution could, by introducing the expurgated conviction, still have proven the elements of the crime even if it chose not to accept any part of the defendant's stipulation. Here, the prosecution must show all five films to the jury in order to meet its burden of proof on the obscenity issue. Thus, if the Rule 403 balancing process, taking into account the stipulation, requires the exclusion of any of the five films, then the prosecution must either accept a stipulation regarding the obscenity of the excluded films or face dismissal of that portion of the charges.

In Parr v. United States, 255 F.2d 86, 88, cert. denied, 358 U.S. 824 (1958), we held that, as a general rule, a party may not preclude his adversary's proof by an admission or offer to stipulate. At Parr's trial for the distribution of obscene films, some of the films were shown to the jury over Parr's objection and offer to stipulate that the films were obscene. Upon Parr's appeal, this court affirmed on the ground that it was permissible for the government to present proof on the obscenity issue notwithstanding the stipulation since obscenity was an essential element of the crime with which Parr was charged.

The government contends that *Parr* holds that the probative value of a piece of evidence necessary to prove an element of the crime can never be substantially outweighed by the unfair prejudice arising from it even if the defendant offers to stipulate to the matter. Acceptance of this argument would mean that Rule 403 could never be used to require the government to accept a defendant's stipulation regarding an element of the crime. We decline to adopt this reading of *Parr,* which was decided before Rule 403 was adopted. The government's contentions are inconsistent with the holding in *Spletzer* that an offer to stipulate should be given weight in the Rule 403 balancing process. In addition, both *Spletzer,* 535 F.2d at 955, and *Parr,* 255 F.2d at 98, recognized that the rule against requiring a party to accept an opponent's stipulation is a general rule and proceeded to examine whether the rule should have been applied in particular fact situations. This implies that the *Parr* rule is not a blanket prohibition against compelling the government to accept a defendant's stipulations.

Moreover, acceptance of the government's arguments could cause ludicrous results in specific cases. In this case, for example, the shipment that was the subject of the indictment contained 871 separate reels of film. If the government had chosen to indict Grassi on a separate count for each individual film, then the government would have been required to show each of the 871 films at the trial in order to establish their obscenity. Adopting the government's reading of *Parr* would allow the prosecution to exhibit this massive amount of highly inflammatory material even if the defendant offered to stipulate to its obscenity. This result would directly contravene the policies underlying Rule 403. Thus, we hold that *Parr* does not entirely preclude the requirement that an offer to stipulate must form a part of the Rule 403 weighing of probity and prejudice.

It could also be argued that the offer of a stipulation, as a matter of law, totally eviscerates the probative value of a piece of evidence relevant to the matter stipulated and thus mandates exclusion of that evidence under Rule 403. The effect of adopting this opposite extreme in construing the Rule would be to require a party to accept any stipulation offered by his opponent and thus would allow a party to control the proof presented by his opponent at trial. We also reject this construction of Rule 403. A piece of evidence can have probative value even in the event of an offer to stipulate to the issue on which the evidence is offered. A cold stipulation can deprive a party "of the legitimate moral force of his evidence," 9 Wigmore on Evidence §2591 at 589 (3rd ed. 1940), and can never fully substitute for tangible, physical evidence or the testimony of witnesses. In most cases, a party has the right "to present to the jury a picture of the events relied upon." *Parr,* supra, 255 F.2d at 88.

Rule 403 also requires a trial court to determine the amount of unfair prejudice resulting from the introduction of a piece of evidence. The phrase "unfair prejudice" does not refer alone to the fact that a particular piece of evidence will have adverse effects on a party's case. Most evidence offered by an opponent should have this effect. Rather, " 'unfair prejudice' within this context means an undue tendency to suggest [a] decision on an improper basis, commonly, though not necessarily, an emotional one." Notes of the Advisory Committee on Proposed Federal Rules of Evidence, 28 U.S.C.A. Rule 403 at 102; see Wright, supra §5215. Thus, it is not enough for a party who asserts that Rule 403 requires an opponent to accept a stipulation merely to show that the evidence that is the subject of the stipulation is detrimental to his case.

In formulating a rule for the application of Rule 403 in instances in which a stipulation is offered, we reject any per se approach. Rather, as is the case with other applications of Rule 403, determining the weight to be given an offer to stipulate in the balancing process is committed to the sound discretion of the trial court, tempered by the particular facts presented. This discretion should be exercised to so balance probity against prejudice that the trial is fundamentally fair. In achieving this balance, the court has the power to require the government to accept a tendered stipulation in whole or in part as well as to permit it to reject the offer to stipulate in its entirety.

In this case the district court allowed the prosecution to show three of the films to the jury despite the defendant's offer to stipulate to the obscenity of all of the films. The less prejudicial alternative was to show fewer films and require the stipulation to be accepted as to the rest. However, in the context of this case, we cannot fault the trial judge for not requiring it. With the initial showing, the shock value was largely, if not entirely, spent. The films were repetitious to the point of boredom rather than revulsion. Given the probative value of these films which, even in light of the offer to stipulate, was substantial, we cannot hold that showing three films mandates a finding that the district court abused its discretion in allowing three films to be shown instead of two or one.

STATE v. POE
21 Utah 2d 113, 441 P.2d 512 (1968)

CALLISTER, J. Defendant, Roy Lee Poe, was convicted of the first degree murder of Kenneth Hall. The murder occurred in St. George, Utah (population about 5,130), and the trial was held there. The deceased had been a life-long resident of the community, whereas the defendant was a comparative newcomer. The jury, in returning its verdict of guilty, did not recommend life imprisonment. Whereupon, the court pronounced the death penalty. . . .

Defendant contends the trial court abused its discretion in admitting some colored slides into evidence and permitting them to be displayed to the jury by means of a slide projector and screen. With this contention, we are in agreement.

To begin with, the identity of the deceased, his death and its cause had already been established. Black and white photographs had been introduced showing the victim lying in his bed, in a sleeping position, with two bullet holes in his head. The colored slides were made during the course of an autopsy. To describe them as being gruesome would be a gross understatement. One of them, for example, depicted the deceased's head, showing the base of the skull after the skull cap and brain had been removed by the pathologist. The skin is peeled over the edge of the skull showing the empty brain cavity. Another is a top view of the empty cavity. They would have been gruesome in black and white but the color accentuates the gruesomeness.

Initially, it is within the sound discretion of the trial court to determine whether the inflammatory nature of such slides is outweighed by their probative value with respect to a fact in issue. If the latter they may be admitted even though gruesome. In the instant case they had no probative value. All the material facts which could conceivably have been adduced from a viewing of the slides had been established by uncontradicted lay and medical testimony. The only purpose served was to inflame and arouse the jury.

It must be remembered that the jury in this case not only determined the question of guilt but also fixed the punishment itself. The only use of the slides from the prosecution's standpoint was to arouse the emotions of the jury so that they would not recommend life imprisonment. It could very well be that the jury would have returned the same verdict absent its views of the slides. However, with the defendant's life at stake, this court should not hazard a guess. The slides could very well have tipped the scales in favor of the death penalty. . . .

Because the trial court abused its discretion in permitting the slides into evidence and because of the other doubtful aspects of the trial, this case is reversed and remanded for a new trial.

ELLETT, J., dissenting. I dissent from that part of the main opinion holding that the trial court abused its discretion in admitting colored slides into evidence. In the first place, colored pictures should be dealt with exactly the same as black and white pictures. All pictures are admissible in evidence if they tend to prove a matter which would be relevant for a witness to testify to orally. 23 C.J.S. Criminal Law §852(1)a. When pictures are thus competent there cannot be any proper objection made to them on the ground that they may prejudice the jury. All evidence given tends to prejudice the jury, and pictures are no exception. Just why anyone should ever have supposed a colored picture should be rejected because it shows a true likeness of any given scene escapes me. One would think that of two pictures, the one more accurately portraying the scene would be the proper one to place in evidence.

The fact that a picture may be gruesome is no reason for excluding it from evidence if it is otherwise competent and relevant. It is a matter of discretion with the trial judge to determine whether the probative value of the picture outweighs the possible adverse effect which might be produced upon being shown to the jury. 23 C.J.S. Criminal Law §852(1)c. This discretion on the part of a trial judge to admit or reject evidence should not be interfered with by an appellate court unless manifest error is shown.

In this case the defendant on appeal complains because some colored pictures were admitted into evidence and claims that the jury was prejudiced against him by reason of the gruesome appearance of those pictures.

It is true that the pictures taken of the deceased before he had been removed from his bed showed a considerable amount of blood on his face and on the bedding. He was lying with his arms folded across his chest exactly as if he were asleep. He had two holes in his face, and one could not tell by looking at the holes what had caused them. . . .

Since most cases involving gruesome pictures are concerned with conditions created by the defendant, the jury is much more apt to be affected against the defendant than it would be when the condition is caused by a surgeon in the quest for truth. The pictures so vividly described in the prevailing opinion were no more gruesome than was the open heart surgery portrayed on television a few nights ago.

The evidence given to the jury in this case would warrant a finding that the defendant was a guest in the home of the deceased; that while the deceased slept, the defendant shot him twice with a .22 caliber rifle; that defendant immediately sold the murder weapon and deceased's high-powered rifle; and that defendant stole the deceased's station wagon and was intending to get to Old Mexico down the back roads from Las Vegas, Nevada, where he was arrested. The verdict of murder in the first degree without recommendation was warranted by the evidence. The defendant had a fair trial before an unbiased jury, and I think this conviction should be affirmed.

Problem I-9
The Coppertone Corpse

EVANSVILLE SCHOOL CORP. v. PRICE, 208 N.E.2d 689 (Ind. 1965): This action was commenced by Alfred Price, father of Alfred Lee Price (deceased), against the Evansville School Corporation, to recover damages for wrongful death allegedly sustained as the result of the decedent, Alfred Lee Price, being injured while a spectator attending a baseball game at Bosse Field in the City of Evansville, Indiana. The boy, age 11, was struck on the head with a baseball on May 27, 1960, and died as a result of said injuries on May 29, 1960. . . .

At the trial the appellee offered in evidence a color photograph designated Plaintiff's Exhibit No. 5. It depicted the deceased youth lying in his casket, after preparation by a mortician, and prior to internment. The photograph shows the white satin interior of the casket and that portion of the body exposed to public view. The decedent's face bears a deep tan, and he is clothed in a white sport coat and a blue shirt open at the neck. The photograph is not gruesome, nor does it depict any physical markings, wounds, defects or other bodily abnormalities. The appellant objected to the admission of Exhibit No. 5 for a number of reasons.

How would you argue the relevancy and admissibility, or the irrelevancy and inadmissibility, of the photograph? How should the court rule? 401 - tends to show what? that he's dead?

E.   Evidence About the Person

Problem I-10
Stella's Silk Stockings

PEOPLE v. ADAMSON, 27 Cal. 2d 478, 165 P.2d 3 (1946), aff'd., 332 U.S. 46 (1947): [Defendant was charged with murder and burglary. He pleaded not guilty and was tried and convicted of murder and one count of burglary. The defendant did not testify at trial and produced no witnesses.]

The body of Stella Blauvelt, a widow 64 years of age, was found on the floor of her Los Angeles apartment on July 25, 1944. The evidence indicated that she died on the afternoon of the preceding day. The body was found with the face upward covered with two bloodstained pillows. A lamp cord was wrapped tightly around her neck three times and tied in a knot. The medical testimony was that death was caused by strangulation. Bruises on the face and hands indicated that the deceased had been severely beaten before her death. . . .

[The defendant admitted that Stella Blauvelt was murdered but contended that the evidence was not sufficient to identify him as the perpetrator.]

The tops of three women's stockings identified as having been taken from defendant's room were admitted in evidence. . . . The stocking parts were not all of the same color. At the end of each part, away from what was formerly the top of the stocking, a knot or knots were tied. When the body of the deceased was found, it did not have on any shoes or stockings. There was evidence that on the day of the murder deceased had been wearing stockings. The lower part of a silk stocking with the top part torn off was found lying on the floor under the body. No part of the other stocking was found. There were other stockings in the apartment, some hanging in the kitchen and some in drawers in a dressing alcove, but no other parts of stockings were found. None of the stocking tops from defendant's room matched with the bottom part of the stocking found under the body. . . .

How should you go about analyzing the relevance of the stocking evidence in this case? What methodology should you employ in deciding relevance in general?

Suppose that the prosecution rests its case after proving the discovery and condition of the body and introducing the stocking evidence, over the defendant's objection. Defendant then moves for a directed verdict. If the court grants defendant's motion, are the rulings on the admissibility of the stocking evidence and the motion for a directed verdict compatible? Consider the court's opinion:

To be admissible, evidence must tend to prove a material issue in the light of human experience. The stocking tops found in defendant's room were relevant to identify defendant because their presence on his dresser and in a drawer thereof among other articles of wearing apparel with a knot or knots tied in the end away from what was formerly the top of the stocking indicates that defendant had some use for women's stocking tops. This interest in women's stocking tops is a circumstance that tends to identify defendant as the person who removed the stockings from the victim and took away the top of one and the whole of the other. Although the presence of the stocking tops in defendant's room was not by itself sufficient to identify defendant as the criminal, it constituted a logical link in the chain of evidence. Evidence that tends to throw light on a fact in dispute may be admitted. The weight to be given such evidence will be determined by the jury.

It is contended that the admission of the stocking tops deprived defendant of a fair trial and therefore denied him due process of law. Defendant states that their admission could serve no purpose except to create prejudice against him as a Negro by the implication of a fetish or sexual degeneracy. No implication of either was made by the prosecutor in his brief treatment of the evidence in oral argument. Moreover, except in rare cases of abuse, demonstrative evidence that tends to prove a material issue or clarify the circumstances of the crime is admissible despite its prejudicial tendency. . . .

The judgments and the order denying a new trial are affirmed.

Problem I-11
Prophylactics in the Pocket

STATE v. STONE, 240 N.C. 606 (1954): [Defendant was convicted of incest with his daughter.] As disclosed in the record, the principal State's witness told a story involving her father in sex crimes with her, beginning when she was nine years old and continuing until 15 August, 1952. On 15 August, 1952, the defendant and his wife were taking the witness to task for keeping company with a married man, whereupon a fight took place in which she testified the defendant pulled her hair and she kicked him. She immediately left home, not to return. At that time she was 15 years old. Immediately after she left home, on 15 August, 1952 she told a married sister and her sister's husband of her father's conduct toward her. In corroboration, they testified for the State as to what she had told them. The defendant testified in his own behalf, entering a complete denial. The wife and other members of the family testified in his behalf, corroborating him. . . . [The daughter] testified on some occasions her father used rubbers, others he did not.

[Defendant was arrested seven months after his daughter left home. At the time of his arrest, two condoms were found in his wallet. These were admitted as evidence over his objection.]

Did the trial court err? Consider the Stone *court's opinion:*

The rule of relevance is stated by Greenleaf (1 Greenleaf, Evidence, sec. 51a), "It is not necessary that the evidence should bear directly on the issue. It is admissible if it tends to prove the issue or constitutes a link in the chain of proof, although alone it might not justify a verdict in accordance with it." . . .

"Where the particular fact sought to be proved is equally consistent with the existence or nonexistence of the fact sought to be inferred from it, the evidence can raise no presumption either way, and should be excluded." S. v. Brantley, 84 N.C. 766.

In S. v. Brantley, supra, after discussing the necessity for the use of circumstantial evidence and the dangers incident to such use, the Court said: "Among other hazards and inconveniences it was found that to allow evidence to be given touching every collateral matter that could be supposed, however remotely, to throw any light upon the main fact sought to be established, had the effect to render trials too complicated and to confuse and mislead the juries, and at the same time to surprise the party on trial who could not come prepared to disprove every possible circumstance, but only such as he might suppose to be germane and material. And therefore the main rule was adopted of restricting the inquiry to such facts as, though collateral to the matter at issue, had a *visible, reasonable* connection with it — not such a connection as would go to show that the two facts, the collateral one and the main one, sometimes, or indeed often, go together, but such as will show that they *most usually* do so."

When tested by the foregoing rule, the possession of prophylactics on 16 March, 1953, does not tend to prove the defendant committed rape on the — day of June, 1949, and it does not tend to prove he committed incest or that he had sexual intercourse with an innocent and virtuous female over 12 and under 16 years of age on 15 August, 1952.

The admissibility of this evidence over defendant's objection was prejudicial error.

Is the approach of the Stone *court consistent with the approach of the* Adamson *court? Are the results in these two cases compatible? Do the courts use different standards? What standard does the* Stone *court employ in ruling on the relevancy of the prophylactic evidence? Are there unarticulated reasons for excluding this evidence?*

Problem I-12
The Case of the Malodorous T-Shirts

D was charged with having committed a sexual assault in Langley Park, a Baltimore suburb, on June 11, 1966. He was arrested in November 1966 and brought to trial in May 1967. At trial, the victim testified that she had been sexually assaulted at her home in Langley Park by a man wearing a tight black ski mask who emitted a strong, nauseating body odor. The arresting officer testified that at the time of arrest, *D* was wearing seven T-shirts, each dirtier and smellier than the one before. The prosecution offered the seven T-shirts into evidence.

Should *D*'s objection to this evidence be sustained? Are the T-shirts admissible? What is their relevance? If there were no additional evidence beyond that set forth above, should the judge direct a verdict in favor of the defendant?

Problem I-13
Look Ma, No Prints

Charge: armed robbery of a post office. At trial, the prosecution introduces evidence that *D* was apprehended shortly after the robbery, about two blocks from the abandoned getaway car, with a pair of gloves in his possession. The gloves are offered by the prosecution as Exhibit *A* in order to explain the absence of fingerprints at the scene of the crime and on the getaway car. None of the eyewitnesses recalled whether or not the robbers wore gloves. *D* objects on grounds of irrelevancy.

What ruling and why? Does your answer depend on whether the prosecution has offered other evidence of *D*'s guilt? Is evidence that proves guilt by negative implication relevant? Even if relevant, is the inference to be drawn so weak as to be outweighed by its prejudice to the defendant?

Problem I-14
Bombs, Bats, and Hammers

Consider these three cases together. Is the offered evidence relevant in any of them? Should it be admitted? Should its admission depend on anything else?

(1) Charge: assault with intent to commit murder. The state introduces evidence that the victim began to open an inner screen door of his trailer and an explosion took place. The state also introduces evidence that *D* had borrowed a clothespin from his girl friend the day before the explosion. The prosecution calls an expert on bombs and offers to have the expert testify using a model bomb to illustrate how a triggering device could detonate a charge of dynamite. The triggering device used in the model is a clothespin. The expert will testify that a clothespin was only one of a number of devices that might have been used to trigger the bomb and that he did not know what device was actually used. He will testify that he used a clothespin for the model only because it was easily available to him. *D* objects to the expert's use of the model and of the clothespin trigger and explains that he used the borrowed clothespin to attach a map to his car's dashboard. (When arrested in his car a map was attached to the dashboard in this manner.)

(2) Charge: murder in the first degree. M.O.: battering the victim

with a blunt instrument. The state's evidence establishes that the victim had over 20 fresh wounds on his body, some of which were consistent with injury inflicted by a blunt instrument such as a baseball bat, others that could have been made by the claws of a hammer, and some by the rounded head of a hammer. The murder occurred in the home shared by *D* and the victim. *W,* a friend of the defendant, testifies that, on the day the beating occurred, she found a baseball bat and a hammer under the bed in the room in which the body was found. *W* also testifies that she saw another person bring a second bat from the rear of the house to the bedroom. Both bats and the hammer had been removed from the house and disposed of by other persons. The prosecution produces a bat and a hammer. *W* testifies that they closely resemble the ones she found under the bed. The prosecutor offers the bat and hammer in evidence. *D* objects that the items are irrelevant and unduly prejudicial.

(3) Charge: murder in the first degree. M.O.: blows to the head during an alleged attempted rape. A pathologist testifies that death was caused by chop wounds to the skull and brain from some sharp and heavy instrument, such as a hatchet or a meat cleaver. *D* was employed as a construction worker on a cleanup crew. The construction job involved dry-wall construction, in which a dry-wall hammer is generally used. Such a hammer has one round flat surface and one very sharp hatchet-like edge. No murder weapon was found but a framing hammer was found in *D*'s car. The prosecution offers evidence that the victim's wounds could have been caused by blows from a dry-wall hammer. No such hammer was ever found, and it was never shown that *D* ever had one. The prosecutor borrows such a hammer from a workman in the courthouse. This hammer is identified, shown to the jury, and offered as evidence on the theory that it is illustrative of the testimony of various witnesses. *D* objects on grounds of irrelevancy and prejudice.

PEOPLE v. COLLINS
68 Cal. 2d 319, 438 P.2d 33, 66 Cal. Rptr. 497 (1968)

SULLIVAN, J. We deal here with the novel question whether evidence of mathematical probability has been properly introduced and used by the prosecution in a criminal case. While we discern no inherent incompatibility between the disciplines of law and mathematics and intend no general disapproval or disparagement of the latter as an auxiliary in the fact-finding processes of the former, we cannot uphold the technique employed in the instant case. As we explain in detail, infra, the testimony as to mathematical probability infected the case with fatal error and distorted the jury's traditional role of determining guilt or innocence according to long-settled rules. Mathematics, a veritable sorcerer in our computerized society, while assisting the trier of fact in the search for truth, must not cast a spell over him. We conclude that on the record before us defendant should not have had his guilt determined by the odds and that he is entitled to a new trial. We reverse the judgment.

A jury found defendant Malcolm Ricardo Collins and his wife defendant Janet Louise Collins guilty of second degree robbery. Malcolm appeals from the judgment of conviction. Janet has not appealed.

On June 18, 1964, about 11:30 A.M. Mrs. Juanita Brooks, who had been shopping, was walking home along an alley in the San Pedro area of the City of Los Angeles. She was pulling behind her a wicker basket carryall containing groceries and had her purse on top of the packages. She was using a cane. As she stooped down to pick up an empty carton, she was suddenly pushed to the ground by a person whom she neither saw nor heard approach. She was stunned by the fall and felt some pain. She managed to look up and saw a young woman running from the scene. According to Mrs. Brooks the latter appeared to weigh about 145 pounds, was wearing "something dark," and had hair "between a dark blond and a light blond," but lighter than the color of defendant Janet Collins' hair as it appeared at trial. Immediately after the incident, Mrs. Brooks discovered that her purse, containing between $35 and $40 was missing.

About the same time as the robbery, John Bass, who lived on the street at the end of the alley, was in front of his house watering his lawn. His attention was attracted by "a lot of crying and screaming" coming from the alley. As he looked in that direction, he saw a woman run out of the alley and enter a yellow automobile parked across the street from him. He was unable to give the make of the car. The car started off immediately and pulled wide around another parked vehicle so that in the narrow street it passed within 6 feet of Bass. The latter then saw that it was being driven by a male Negro, wearing a mustache and beard. At the trial Bass identified defendant as the driver of the yellow automobile. However, an attempt was made to impeach his identification by his admission that at the preliminary hearing he testified to an uncertain identification at the police lineup shortly after the attack on Mrs. Brooks, when defendant was beardless.

In his testimony Bass described the woman who ran from the alley as a Caucasian, slightly over 5 feet tall, of ordinary build, with her hair in a dark blonde ponytail, and wearing dark clothing. He further testified that her ponytail was "just like" one which Janet had in a police photograph taken on June 22, 1964.

On the day of the robbery, Janet was employed as a housemaid in San Pedro. Her employer testified that she had arrived for work at 8:50 A.M. and that defendant had picked her up in a light yellow car[2] about 11:30

2. Other witnesses variously described the car as yellow, as yellow with an off-white top, and yellow with an egg-shell white top. The car was also described as being medium to

A.M. On that day, according to the witness, Janet was wearing her hair in a blonde ponytail but lighter in color than it appeared at trial.[3]

There was evidence from which it could be inferred that defendants had ample time to drive from Janet's place of employment and participate in the robbery. Defendants testified, however, that they went directly from her employer's house to the home of friends, where they remained for several hours. . . .

At the seven-day trial the prosecution experienced some difficulty in establishing the identities of the perpetrators of the crime. The victim could not identify Janet and had never seen defendant. The identification by the witness Bass, who observed the girl run out of the alley and get into the automobile, was incomplete as to Janet and may have been weakened as to defendant. There was also evidence, introduced by the defense, that Janet had worn light-colored clothing on the day in question, but both the victim and Bass testified that the girl they observed had worn dark clothing.

In an apparent attempt to bolster the identifications, the prosecutor called an instructor of mathematics at a state college. Through this witness he sought to establish that, assuming the robbery was committed by a Caucasian woman with a blonde ponytail who left the scene accompanied by a Negro with a beard and mustache, there was an overwhelming probability that the crime was committed by any couple answering such distinctive characteristics. The witness testified, in substance, to the "product rule," which states that the probability of the joint occurrence of a number of *mutually independent* events is equal to the product of the individual probabilities that each of the events will occur.[8] *Without presenting any statistical evidence whatsoever in support of the probabilities for the factors selected,* the prosecutor then proceeded to have the witness *assume*[9] probability factors for the various characteristics which he deemed to be shared by the guilty couple and all other couples answering to such distinctive characteristics.[10]

---

large in size. Defendant drove a car at or near the times in question which was a Lincoln with a yellow body and a white top.

3. There are inferences which may be drawn from the evidence that Janet attempted to alter the appearance of her hair after June 18. Janet denies that she cut, colored or bleached her hair at any time after June 18, and a number of witnesses supported her testimony.

8. In the example employed for illustrative purposes at the trial, the probability of rolling one die and coming up with a "2" is $\frac{1}{6}$, that is, any one of the six faces of a die has one chance in six of landing face up on any particular roll. The probability of rolling two "2's" in succession is $\frac{1}{6} \times \frac{1}{6}$, or $\frac{1}{36}$, that is, on only one occasion out of 36 double rolls (or the roll of two dice), will the selected number land face up on each roll or die.

9. His argument to the jury was based on the same gratuitous assumptions or on similar assumptions which he invited the jury to make.

10. Although the prosecutor insisted that the factors he used were only for illustrative purposes — to demonstrate how the probability of the occurrence of mutually independent factors affected the probability that they would occur together — he nevertheless

Applying the product rule to his own factors the prosecutor arrived at a probability that there was but one chance in 12 million that any couple possessed the distinctive characteristics of the defendants. Accordingly, under this theory, it was to be inferred that there could be but one chance in 12 million that defendants were innocent and that another equally distinctive couple actually committed the robbery. Expanding on what he had thus purported to suggest as a hypothesis, the prosecutor offered the completely unfounded and improper testimonial assertion that, in his opinion, the factors he had assigned were "conservative estimates" and that, in reality, "the chances of anyone else besides these defendants being there, . . . having every similarity, . . . is somewhat like one in a billion."

Objections were timely made to the mathematician's testimony on the grounds that it was immaterial, that it invaded the province of the jury, and that it was based on unfounded assumptions. The objections were "temporarily overruled" and the evidence admitted subject to a motion to strike. When that motion was made at the conclusion of the direct examination, the court denied it, stating that the testimony had been received only for the "purpose of illustrating the mathematical probabilities of various matters, the possibilities for them occurring or reoccurring."

Both defendants took the stand in their own behalf. They denied any knowledge of or participation in the crime and stated that after Malcolm called for Janet at her employer's house they went directly to a friend's house in Los Angeles where they remained for some time. According to this testimony defendants were not near the scene of the robbery when it occurred. Defendants' friend testified to a visit by them "in the middle of June" although she could not recall the precise date. Janet further

---

attempted to use factors which he personally related to the distinctive characteristics of defendants. In his argument to the jury he invited the jurors to apply their own factors, and asked defense counsel to suggest what the latter would deem as reasonable. The prosecutor himself proposed the individual probabilities set out in the table below. Although the transcript of the examination of the mathematics instructor and the information volunteered by the prosecutor at that time create some uncertainty as to precisely which of the characteristics the prosecutor assigned to the individual probabilities, he restated in his argument to the jury that they should be as follows:

	Characteristic	Individual Probability
A.	Partly yellow automobile	1/10
B.	Man with mustache	1/4
C.	Girl with ponytail	1/10
D.	Girl with blond hair	1/3
E.	Negro man with beard	1/10
F.	Interracial couple in car	1/1000

In his brief on appeal defendant agrees that the foregoing appeared on a table presented in the trial court.

testified that certain inducements were held out to her during the July 9 interrogation on condition that she confess her participation. . . .

As we shall explain, the prosecution's introduction and use of mathematical probability statistics injected two fundamental prejudicial errors into the case: (1) The testimony itself lacked an adequate foundation both in evidence and in statistical theory; and (2) the testimony and the manner in which the prosecution used it distracted the jury from its proper and requisite function of weighing the evidence on the issue of guilt, encouraged the jurors to rely upon an engaging but logically irrelevant expert demonstration, foreclosed the possibility of an effective defense by an attorney apparently unschooled in mathematical refinements, and placed the jurors and defense counsel at a disadvantage in sifting relevant fact from inapplicable theory.

We initially consider the defects in the testimony itself. As we have indicated, the specific technique presented through the mathematician's testimony and advanced by the prosecutor to measure the probabilities in question suffered from two basic and pervasive defects — an inadequate evidentiary foundation and an inadequate proof of statistical independence. First, as to the foundational requirement, we find the record devoid of any evidence relating to any of the six individual probability factors used by the prosecutor and ascribed by him to the six characteristics as we have set them out in footnote 10, ante. To put it another way, the prosecution produced no evidence whatsoever showing, or from which it could be in any way inferred, that only one out of every ten cars which might have been at the scene of the robbery was partly yellow, that only one out of every four men who might have been there wore a mustache, that only one out of every ten girls who might have been there wore a ponytail, or that any of the other individual probability factors listed were even roughly accurate.[12]

The bare, inescapable fact is that the prosecution made no attempt to offer any such evidence. Instead, through leading questions having perfunctorily elicited from the witness the response that the latter could not assign a probability factor for the characteristics involved,[13] the prosecu-

12. We seriously doubt that such evidence could ever be compiled since no statistician could possibly determine after the fact which cars, or which individuals, "might" have been present at the scene of the robbery; certainly there is no reason to suppose that the human and automotive populations of San Pedro, California, include all potential culprits — or, conversely, that all members of these populations are proper candidates for inclusion. Thus the sample from which the relevant probabilities would have to be derived is itself undeterminable. (See generally, Yaman, Statistics, An Introductory Analysis (1964), ch. I.)

13. The prosecutor asked the mathematics instructor: "Now, let me see if you can be of some help to us with some independent factors, and you have some paper you may use. Your specialty does not equip you, I suppose, to give us some probability of such things as a yellow car as contrasted with any other kind of car, does it? . . . I appreciate the fact that you can't assign a probability for a car being yellow as contrasted to some other car, can you?" A. "No, I couldn't."

tor himself suggested what the various probabilities should be and these became the basis of the witness' testimony (see fn. 10, ante). It is a curious circumstance of this adventure in proof that the prosecutor not only made his own assertions of these factors in the hope that they were "conservative" but also in later argument to the jury invited the jurors to substitute their "estimates" should they wish to do so. We can hardly conceive of a more fatal gap in the prosecution's scheme of proof. A foundation for the admissibility of the witness' testimony was never even attempted to be laid, let alone established. His testimony was neither made to rest on his own testimonial knowledge nor presented by proper hypothetical questions based upon valid data in the record. (See generally: 2 Wigmore on Evidence (3d ed. 1940) §§478, 650-652, 657, 659, 672-684; McCormick on Evidence, pp. 19-20; State v. Sneed (1966) 76 N.M. 349, 414 P.2d 858.) In the *Sneed* case, the court reversed a conviction based on probabilistic evidence, stating: "We hold that mathematical odds are not admissible as evidence to identify a defendant in a criminal proceeding *so long as the odds are based on estimates, the validity of which have [sic] not been demonstrated.*" (Italics added.) (414 P.2d at p. 862.)

But, as we have indicated, there was another glaring defect in the prosecution's technique, namely an inadequate proof of the statistical independence of the six factors. No proof was presented that the characteristics selected were mutually independent, even though the witness himself acknowledged that such condition was essential to the proper application of the "product rule" or "multiplication rule." To the extent that the traits or characteristics were not mutually independent (e.g., Negroes with beards and men with mustaches obviously represent overlapping categories[15]), the "product rule" would inevitably yield a wholly erroneous and exaggerated result even if all of the individual components had been determined with precision. (Siegel, Nonparametric Statistics for the Behavioral Sciences (1956) 19; see generally Harmon, Modern Factor Analysis (1960).)

In the instant case, therefore, because of the aforementioned two defects — the inadequate evidentiary foundation and the inadequate proof of statistical independence — the technique employed by the prosecutor could only lead to wild conjecture without demonstrated relevancy to the issues presented. It acquired no redeeming quality from

15. Assuming arguendo that factors B and E (see fn. 10, ante), were correctly estimated, nevertheless it is still arguable that most Negro men with beards *also* have mustaches (exhibit 3 herein, for instance, shows defendant with both a mustache and a beard, indeed in a hirsute continuum); if so, there is no basis for multiplying 1/4 by 1/10 to estimate the proportion of Negroes who wear beards *and* mustaches. Again, the prosecution's technique could *never* be meaningfully applied, since its accurate use would call for information as to the degree of interdependence among the six individual factors. Such information cannot be compiled, however, since the relevant sample necessarily remains unknown.

the prosecutor's statement that it was being used only "for illustrative purposes" since, as we shall point out, the prosecutor's subsequent utilization of the mathematical testimony was not confined within such limits.

We now turn to the second fundamental error caused by the probability testimony. Quite apart from our foregoing objections to the specific technique employed by the prosecution to estimate the probability in question, we think that the entire enterprise upon which the prosecution embarked, and which was directed to the objective of measuring the likelihood of a random couple possessing the characteristics allegedly distinguishing the robbers, was gravely misguided. At best, it might yield an estimate as to how infrequently bearded Negroes drive yellow cars in the company of blonde females with ponytails.

The prosecution's approach, however, could furnish the jury with absolutely no guidance on the crucial issue: *Of the admittedly few such couples, which one, if any, was guilty of committing this robbery?* Probability theory necessarily remains silent on that question, since no mathematical equation can prove beyond a reasonable doubt (1) that the guilty couple *in fact* possessed the characteristics described by the People's witnesses, or even (2) that only *one* couple possessing those distinctive characteristics could be found in the entire Los Angeles area.

As to the first inherent failing we observe that the prosecution's theory of probability rested on the assumption that the witnesses called by the People had conclusively established that the guilty couple possessed the precise characteristics relied upon by the prosecution. But no mathematical formula could ever establish beyond a reasonable doubt that the prosecution's witnesses correctly observed and accurately described the distinctive features which were employed to link defendants to the crime. (See 2 Wigmore on Evidence (3d ed. 1940) §478.) Conceivably, for example, the guilty couple might have included a light-skinned Negress with bleached hair rather than a Caucasian blonde; or the driver of the car might have been wearing a false beard as a disguise; or the prosecution's witnesses might simply have been unreliable.[16]

The foregoing risks of error permeate the prosecution's circumstantial case. Traditionally, the jury weighs such risks in evaluating the credibility and probative value of trial testimony, but the likelihood of human error or of falsification obviously cannot be quantified; that likelihood must therefore be excluded from any effort to assign a *number* to the

---

16. In the instant case, for instance, the victim could not state whether the girl had a ponytail, although the victim observed the girl as she ran away. The witness Bass, on the other hand, was sure that the girl whom he saw had a ponytail. The demonstration engaged in by the prosecutor also leaves no room for the possibility, although perhaps a small one, that the girl whom the victim and the witness observed was, in fact, not the same girl.

probability of guilt or innocence. Confronted with an equation which purports to yield a numerical index of probable guilt, few juries could resist the temptation to accord disproportionate weight to that index; only an exceptional juror, and indeed only a defense attorney schooled in mathematics, could successfully keep in mind the fact that the probability computed by the prosecution can represent, *at best,* the likelihood that a random couple would share the characteristics testified to by the People's witnesses — *not necessarily the characteristics of the actually guilty couple.*

As to the second inherent failing in the prosecution's approach, even assuming that the first failing could be discounted, the most a mathematical computation could *ever* yield would be a measure of the probability that a random couple would possess the distinctive features in question. In the present case, for example, the prosecution attempted to compute the probability that a random couple would include a bearded Negro, a blonde girl with a ponytail, and a partly yellow car; the prosecution urged that this probability was no more than one in 12 million. Even accepting this conclusion as arithmetically accurate, however, one still could not conclude that the Collinses were probably *the* guilty couple. On the contrary, as we explain in the Appendix, the prosecution's figures actually imply a likelihood of over 40 percent that the Collinses could be "duplicated" by at least *one other couple who might equally have committed the San Pedro robbery.* Urging that the Collinses be convicted on the basis of evidence which logically establishes no more than this seems as indefensible as arguing for the conviction of X on the ground that a witness saw either X or X's twin commit the crime.

Again, few defense attorneys, and certainly few jurors, could be expected to comprehend this basic flaw in the prosecution's analysis. Conceivably even the prosecutor erroneously believed that his equation established a high probability that *no* other bearded Negro in the Los Angeles area drove a yellow car accompanied by a ponytailed blonde. In any event, although his technique could demonstrate no such thing, he solemnly told the jury that he had supplied mathematical proof of guilt.

Sensing the novelty of that notion, the prosecutor told the jurors that the traditional idea of proof beyond a reasonable doubt represented "the most hackneyed, stereotyped, trite, misunderstood concept in criminal law." He sought to reconcile the jury to the risk that, under his "new math" approach to criminal jurisprudence, "on some rare occasion . . . an innocent person may be convicted." "Without taking that risk," the prosecution continued, "life would be intolerable . . . because . . . there would be immunity for the Collinses, for people who chose not to be employed to go down and push old ladies down and take their money and be immune because how could we ever be sure they are the ones who did it?"

In essence this argument of the prosecutor was calculated to persuade the jury to convict defendants whether or not they were convinced of their guilt to a moral certainty and beyond a reasonable doubt. Undoubtedly the jurors were unduly impressed by the mystique of the mathematical demonstration but were unable to assess its relevancy or value. Although we make no appraisal of the proper applications of mathematical techniques in the proof of facts, we have strong feelings that such applications, particularly in a criminal case, must be critically examined in view of the substantial unfairness to a defendant which may result from ill conceived techniques with which the trier of fact is not technically equipped to cope. We feel that the technique employed in the case before us falls into the latter category. . . .

[W]e think that under the circumstances the "trial by mathematics" so distorted the role of the jury and so disadvantaged counsel for the defense, as to constitute in itself a miscarriage of justice. . . . The judgment against defendant must therefore be reversed. . . .

APPENDIX

If "Pr" represents the probability that a certain distinctive combination of characteristics, hereinafter designated "C," will occur jointly in a random couple, then the probability that C will *not* occur in a random couple is $(1 - \text{Pr})$. Applying the product rule (see fn. 8, ante), the probability that C will occur in *none* of N couples chosen at random is $(1 - \text{Pr})^N$, so that the probability of C occurring in *at least one* of N random couples is $[1 - (1 - \text{Pr})^N]$.

Given a particular couple selected from a random set of N, the probability of C occurring in that couple (i.e., Pr), multiplied by the probability of C occurring in none of the remaining $N - 1$ couples (i.e., $(1 - \text{Pr})^{N-1}$), yields the probability that C will occur in the selected couple and in no other. Thus the probability of C occurring in any particular couple, and in that couple alone, is $[(\text{Pr}) \times (1 - \text{Pr})^{N-1}]$. Since this is true for each of the N couples, the probability that C will occur in precisely *one* of the N couples, without regard to which one, is $[(\text{Pr}) \times (1 - \text{Pr})^{N-1}]$ added N times, because the probability of the occurrence of one of several *mutually exclusive* events is equal to the *sum* of the individual probabilities. Thus the probability of C occurring in *exactly one* of N random couples (*any* one, but *only* one) is $[(N) \times (\text{Pr}) \times (1 - \text{Pr})^{N-1}]$.

By subtracting the probability that C will occur in *exactly one* couple from the probability that C will occur in *at least one* couple, one obtains the probability that C will occur in *more than one* couple: $[1 - (1 - \text{Pr})^N] - [(N) \times (\text{Pr}) \times (1 - \text{Pr})^{N-1}]$. Dividing this difference by the probability that C will occur in at least one couple (i.e., dividing the difference by $[1 - (1 - Pr)^N]$) then yields *the probability that C will occur more than once in a group of N couples in which C occurs at least once*.

Turning to the case in which C represents the characteristics which distinguish a bearded Negro accompanied by a ponytailed blonde in a yellow car, the prosecution sought to establish that the probability of C occurring in a random couple was 1/12,000,000 — i.e., that Pr = 1/12,000,000. Treating this conclusion as accurate, it follows that, in a population of N random couples, the probability of C occurring *exactly once* is $[(N) \times (1/12,000,000) \times (1 - 1/12,000,000)^{N-1}]$. Subtracting this product from $[1 - (1 - 1/12,000,000)^N]$, the probability of C occurring in *at least one* couple, and dividing the resulting difference by $[1 - (1 - 1/12,000,000)^N]$, the probability that C will occur in at least one couple, yields the probability that C will occur more than once in a group of N random couples of which at least one couple (namely, the one seen by the witnesses) possesses characteristics C. In other words, the probability of *another* such couple in a population of N is the quotient A/B, where A designates the numerator $[1 - (1 - 1/12,000,000)^N] - [(N) \times (1/12,000,000) \times (1 - 1/12,000,000)^{N-1}]$, and B designates the denominator $[1 - (1 - 1/12,000,000)^N]$.

N, which represents the total number of all couples who might conceivably have been at the scene of the San Pedro robbery, is not determinable, a fact which suggests yet another basic difficulty with the use of probability theory in establishing identity. One of the imponderables in determining N may well be the number of N-type couples in which a single person may participate. Such considerations make it evident that N, in the area adjoining the robbery, is in excess of several million; as N assumes values of such magnitude, the quotient A/B computed as above, representing the probability of a second couple as distinctive as the one described by the prosecution's witnesses, soon exceeds 4/10. Indeed, as N approaches 12 million, this probability quotient rises to approximately 41 percent. We note parenthetically that if 1/N = Pr, then as N increases indefinitely, the quotient in question approaches a limit of $(e - 2)/(e - 1)$, where "e" represents the transcendental number (approximately 2.71828) familiar in mathematics and physics.

Hence, even if we should accept the prosecution's figures without question, we would derive a probability of over 40 percent that the couple observed by the witnesses could be "duplicated" by at least one other equally distinctive interracial couple in the area, including a Negro with a beard and mustache, driving a partly yellow car in the company of a blonde with a ponytail. Thus the prosecution's computations, far from establishing beyond a reasonable doubt that the Collinses were the couple described by the prosecution's witnesses, imply a very substantial likelihood that the area contained *more than one* such couple, and that a couple *other* than the Collinses was the one observed at the scene of the robbery. (See generally: Hoel, Introduction to Mathematical Statistics (3d ed. 1962); Hodges & Leymann, Basic Concepts of Probability and Statistics (1964); Lindgren & McElrath, Introduction to Probability and Statistics (1959).)

Do you agree with the result in *Collins*? With *all* the reasons the court gives for reversing the conviction? Would the same circumstantial evidence as was introduced in *Collins*, but without the probability testimony and argumentation, be sufficient to sustain defendant's conviction? Should probability evidence of the sort introduced in *Collins* and *Sneed* be admitted if the foundational problems — the size of the sample, the establishment of realistic individual probabilities, and the certainty of mutual independence — can be overcome? Can these problems ever be overcome? Could the court take judicial notice of individual probabilities?

For more on the use of probability theory in trials — and in the *Sneed* and *Collins* cases in particular — see Finkelstein and Fairley, A Bayesian Approach to Identification Evidence, 83 Harv. L. Rev. 489 (1970); Tribe, Trial by Mathematics: Precision and Ritual in the Legal Process, 84 Harv. L. Rev. 1329 (1971); Finkelstein and Fairley, The Continuing Debate Over Mathematics in the Law of Evidence: A Comment on "Trial by Mathematics," 84 Harv. L. Rev. 1801 (1971); Tribe, A Further Critique of Mathematical Proof, 84 Harv. L. Rev. 1810 (1971); Note, Evidence, etc., 1967 Duke L.J. 665. See also Kaplan, Decision Theory and the Factfinding Process, 20 Stan. L. Rev. 1065 (1968).

Problem I-15
License Plate Roulette

Personal injury action by *P* against Lawton's Supermarket. *P* was run down at an intersection in Lincoln, Massachusetts, by a truck with a Massachusetts license plate with five characters, the first three characters being "LAW"; *P* did not see the last two characters on the license plate. At trial, evidence is presented that Lawton's owns four trucks whose license plates read "LAW01" to "LAW04" and that Lawton's trucks were on the road making deliveries at the time of the accident. Lawton's introduces evidence that there are two other trucks with Massachusetts license plates which read "LAW — — ," one garaged in the neighboring town of Lexington and one in Springfield, 100 miles away.

What is the probability that the truck that hit *P* belongs to Lawton's? Should the statistical evidence be admitted? Is the evidence sufficient to support a verdict for *P*?

Problem I-16
Blue Bus

P is negligently run off the road into a parked car by a blue bus. *P* is prepared to prove that *D* operates four-fifths of all the blue buses that use the route. What effect, if any, should such proof be given?[1]

NOTE: THE USE OF MATHEMATICAL AND PROBABILISTIC PROOF IN THE TRIAL PROCESS

The *Collins* case and the two problems that follow it raise the issue of what effect, if any, mathematical or probabilistic proof should be given. This issue is hinted at in a general way in the material previously quoted from Ayer, Russell, and James. In application, it must be broken down into two main questions. The first question is whether mathematical proof should be admitted at all. If so, there are subsidiary questions: What should the fact-finder be told about it? In what form? One might ask this same question from a quite different perspective: Is it possible to utilize *any* proof that is *not* probabilistic? The second main question is: To what extent may probabilistic and mathematical models be used as standards on which to base a criminal conviction or civil judgment? This question deals with the *sufficiency* of proof to sustain a verdict.

In this chapter we are concerned with the first question — the admissibility or other trial use of a mathematical model or proof without regard for its sufficiency to sustain a verdict. We deal with the second question in Chapter IX, Section B, Inference and Speculation: What Is the Difference Between "Reasoning" and "Guessing"? The two questions are obviously related (Blue Bus is considered again in Chapter IX), and you may want to look ahead to those materials.

In a powerful article, Trial by Mathematics: Precision and Ritual in the Legal Process, 84 Harv. L. Rev. 1329 (1971), Professor Laurence Tribe argues that the usefulness of mathematical methods in the trial process is greatly exaggerated. In some cases, Tribe writes, such methods clash with other important values of the legal process.

Tribe divides mathematical proof situations into three categories: "(1) those in which such proof is directed to the *occurrence* or nonoccurrence of the event, act, or type of conduct on which the litigation is premised; (2) those in which such proof is directed to the *identity* of the individual responsible for a certain act or set of acts; and (3) those in which such proof is directed to *intention* or to some other mental element of responsibility, such as knowledge or provocation." Id. at 1339. Tribe argues

1. This problem is based on Tribe, Trial by Mathematics: Precision and Ritual in the Legal Process, 84 Harv. L. Rev. 1329, 1341 (1971) — Eds.

that the "significance, appropriateness and dangers of mathematical proof may depend dramatically on whether such proof is meant to bear upon occurrence, identity, or frame of mind." Do you agree? Is this division useful? Remember that we are talking about the *admissibility* of evidence, not its *sufficiency* to sustain a criminal conviction or civil judgment.

To illustrate this division, Tribe presents several hypothetical uses of mathematical proof (id. at 1339-1343):

1. Occurrence. Consider first the cases in which the existence of the legally significant occurrence or act is itself in question. A barrel falls from the defendant's window onto the plaintiff's head. The question is whether some negligent act or omission by defendant caused the fall. Proof is available to support a finding that, in over sixty percent of all such barrel-falling incidents, a negligent act or omission was the cause. Should such proof be allowed and, if so, to what effect?[33]

A man is found in possession of heroin. The question is whether he is guilty of concealing an illegally imported narcotic drug. Evidence exists to support the finding that ninety-eight percent of all heroin in the United States is illegally imported. What role, if any, may that fact play at the defendant's trial?

A man is charged with overtime parking in a one-hour zone. The question is whether his car had remained in the parking space beyond the time limit. To prove that it had not been moved, the government calls an officer to testify that he recorded the positions of the tire air-valves on one side of the car. Both before and after a period in excess of one hour, the front-wheel valve was pointing at one o'clock; the rear-wheel valve, at eight o'clock. The driver's defense is that he had driven away during the period in question and just happened to return to the same parking place with his tires in approximately the same position. The probability of such a fortunate accident is somewhere between one in twelve and one in one hundred forty-four.[35] Should proof of that fact be allowed and, if so, to what end?[36]

---

33. A sensible, and now quite conventional, approach to this question is "to treat the probability as the fact if the defendant has the power to rebut the inference." Jaffe, Res Ipsa Loquitur Vindicated, 1 Buff. L. Rev. 1, 6 (1951). On this theory, if the defendant produces a reasonably satisfactory explanation consistent with a conclusion of no negligence, and if the plaintiff produces no further evidence, the plaintiff should lose on a directed verdict despite his mathematical proof — unless (1) he can adequately explain his inability to make a more particularized showing (a possibility not adverted to in id.), or (2) no specific explanation is given, but there is some policy reason to ground liability in the area in question on a substantial probability of negligence in the *type* of case rather than to require a reasoned probability in the *particular* case, thereby moving toward a broader basis of liability. It will be noticed that no such policy is likely to operate when the mathematical evidence goes to the question of the defendant's *identity* and the plaintiff does not explain his failure to produce any more particularized evidence, for it will almost always be important to impose liability on the correct party, *whatever* the basis of such liability might be.

35. If tires rotated in complete synchrony with one another, the probability would be 1/12; if independently, $1/12 \times 1/12$, or 1/144.

36. A Swedish court, computing the probability at $1/12 \times 1/12 = 1/144$ on the dubious assumption that car wheels rotate independently, ruled that fraction large enough to

2. *Identity*. Consider next the cases in which the identity of the responsible agent is in doubt. Plaintiff is negligently run down by a blue bus. The question is whether the bus belonged to the defendant. Plaintiff is prepared to prove that defendant operates four-fifths of all the blue buses in town. What effect, if any, should such proof be given?

A policeman is seen assaulting someone at an undetermined time between 7 P.M. and midnight. The question is whether the defendant, whose beat includes the place of the assault, was the particular policeman who committed the crime. It can be shown that the defendant's beat brings him to the place of the assault four times during the relevant five-hour period each night, and that other policemen are there only once during the same period. In what way, if at all, may this evidence be used?[38]

A man is found shot to death in the apartment occupied by his mistress. The question is whether she shot him. Evidence is available to the effect that, in ninety-five percent of all known cases in which a man was killed in his mistress' apartment, the mistress was the killer. How, if at all, may such evidence be used?[39]

A civil rights worker is beaten savagely by a completely bald man with a wooden left leg, wearing a black patch over his right eye and bearing a six-inch scar under his left, who flees from the scene of the crime in a chartreuse Thunderbird with two dented fenders. A man having these six characteristics is charged with criminal battery. The question is whether the defendant is in fact the assailant. Evidence is available to show that less than one person in twenty has any of these six characteristics, and that the six are statistically independent, so that less than one person in sixty-four million shares all six of them. In what ways, if at all, may that calculation be employed?[40]

---

establish reasonable doubt. Parkeringsfragor, II. Tilforlitligheten av det s.k. locksystemet för parkernigskontroll. Svensk Juristidining, 47 (1962) 17-32. The court's mathematical knife cut both ways, however, for it added that, had all four tire-valves been recorded and found in the same position, the probability of $1/12 \times 1/12 \times 1/12 \times 1/12 = 1/20, 736$ would have constituted proof beyond a reasonable doubt. Id.

38. Note that in this criminal case, as in the preceding civil one, *a fact known about the particular defendant* provides reason to believe that the defendant is involved in a certain percentage of all cases (here, cases of being at the crucial place between 7 P.M. and midnight) possessing a characteristic shared by the litigated case.

39. In this case, unlike the preceding two, it is *a fact known about the particular event that underlies the litigation*, not any fact known about the defendant, that triggers the probabilistic showing: a certain percentage of all events in which the crucial fact (here, the killing of a man in his mistress' apartment) is true are supposedly caused by a person with a characteristic (here, being the mistress) shared by the defendant in this case.

40. This is, of course, People v. Collins, 68 Cal. 2d 319, 438 P.2d 33, 66 Cal. Rptr. 497 (1968), minus the specific mathematical errors of *Collins* and without the interracial couple. One special factor that can lead to major mathematical distortions in this type of case is the "selection effect" that may arise from either party's power to choose matching features for quantification while ignoring non-matching features, thereby producing a grossly exaggerated estimate of the improbability that the observed matching would have occurred by chance. See Finkelstein & Fairley 495 n.14. This difficulty may well have been present in People v. Trujillo, 32 Cal. 2d 105, 194 P.2d 681, cert. denied, 335 U.S. 887 (1948), in which an expert examined a large number of fibers taken from clothing worn by the accused and concluded, upon finding eleven matches with fibers taken from the scene of the crime, that there was only a one-in-a-billion probability of such matching occurring by chance.

3. *Intention.* Consider finally the cases in which the issue is one of intent, knowledge, or some other "mental" element of responsibility. A recently insured building burns down. The insured admits causing the fire but insists that it was an accident. On the question of intent to commit arson, what use, if any, may be made of evidence tending to show that less than one such fire out of twenty is in fact accidentally caused?

As in an earlier example, a man is found possessing heroin. This time the heroin is stipulated at trial to have been illegally imported. In his prosecution for concealing the heroin with knowledge that it had been illegally imported, what effect may be given to proof that ninety-eight percent of all heroin in the United States is in fact illegally imported?

A doctor sued for malpractice is accused of having dispensed a drug without adequate warning, knowing of its tendency to cause blindness in pregnant women. Should he be allowed to introduce evidence that ninety-eight percent of all doctors are unaware of the side-effect in question?

Tribe examines and rejects three commonly advanced objections against the use of mathematical proof in such situations: (1) that the use of such techniques are inappropriate for the determination of *past* events as opposed to the prediction of possible *future* events; (2) that it is not possible to transform mathematical information from evidence about the *generality* of cases to evidence about the *particular* case before the court; and (3) that in very few cases can the mathematical evidence *by itself* establish the proposition to which it is directed with sufficient strength for it to prevail. Id. at 1344-1350.

Nonetheless, Tribe cautions against the use of mathematical and probabilistic proof at trials because it "would be very likely to yield wholly inaccurate and misleadingly precise conclusions." One way in which this happens, Tribe argues, is that the probability proof overwhelms and distorts all the other evidence in the case (id. at 1360-1361):

> The problem of the overpowering number, that one hard piece of information, is that it may dwarf all efforts to put it into perspective with more impressionistic sorts of evidence. This problem of acceptably combining the mathematical with the non-mathematical evidence is not touched in these cases by the [probabilistic] approach.
>
> In situations of the sort being examined here, however, when the thrust of the mathematical evidence is to shed light on the probability assessment with which the trier ought rationally to begin, there is at least one way to take the evidence into account at trial without incurring the risk that the jury will give it too much weight when undertaking to combine the mathematical datum with fuzzier information. Let the judge rather than the jury weigh the probabilistic proof in order to determine whether it might not be both equitable and conducive to an accurate outcome to shift to the other side the burden of producing some believable evidence to take the case outside the general rule seemingly established by the probabilities.[101] If one is to avoid a distortion in

---

101. For example, in line with the suggested approach, the judge might decide to employ the doctrine of res ipsa loquitur, or any of a variety of rebuttable presumptions.

results, however, any such proposal must be qualified, at least when the question is one of the defendant's identity, by the principle that a party is not entitled to a jury verdict on statistical evidence alone absent some plausible explanation for his failure to adduce proof of a more individualized character.[102]

Tribe also argues that mathematical proof cannot be accurately integrated with nonmathematical evidence because of the phenomenon of the "dwarfing of the soft variables" (id. at 1361-1362, 1366):

> The syndrome is a familiar one: If you can't count it, it doesn't exist. Equipped with a mathematically powerful intellectual machine, even the most sophisticated user is subject to an overwhelming temptation to feed his pet the food it can most comfortably digest. Readily quantifiable factors are easier to process — and hence more likely to be recognized and then reflected in the outcome — than are factors that resist ready quantification. The result, despite what turns out to be a spurious appearance of accuracy and completeness, is likely to be significantly warped and hence highly suspect. . . .
>
> One consequence of mathematical proof, then, may be to shift the focus away from such elements as volition, knowledge, and intent, and toward such elements as identity and occurrence — for the same reason that the hard variables tend to swamp the soft. It is by no means clear that such marginal gains, if any, as we may make by finding somewhat more precise answers would not be offset by a tendency to emphasize the wrong questions.

Independent of the above criticisms of mathematical models in the trial process, Tribe argues that the "great virtue of mathematical rigor — its demand for precision, completeness, and candor — may be-

---

See, e.g., O'Dea v. Amodeo, 118 Conn. 58, 170 A. 486 (1934) (presumption of father's consent to son's operation of automobile); Hinds v. John Hancock Mut. Life Ins. Co., 155 Me. 349, 354-67, 155 A.2d 721, 725-32 (1959) (presumption against suicide). One of the traditional functions of the use of presumptions, at least those rebuttable by any substantial contrary evidence, is "to make more likely a finding in accord with the balance of probability." Morgan, Instructing the Jury upon Presumptions and Burden of Proof, 47 Harv. L. Rev. 59, 77 (1933).

102. If the statistical evidence standing alone establishes a sufficiently high prior probability of X, and a satisfactory explanation is provided for the failure to adduce more individualized proof, there seems no defensible alternative (absent believable evidence contrary to X) to directing a verdict for the party claiming X, for no factual question remains about which the jury can reason, and directing a verdict the other way would be more likely to lead to an unjust result. If, however, more individualized proof *is* adduced, and if the party opposing X has discharged the burden (created by the statistical evidence) of producing believable evidence to the contrary, the question remains whether the risk of distortion created by informing the trier of fact of the potentially overbearing statistics so outweighs the probative value of such statistics as to compel their judicial exclusion. If this situation arises in a criminal case, see, e.g., the heroin hypotheticals, the police hypothetical, and the mistress hypothetical, the added threats to important values should probably suffice, in combination with the danger of a distorted outcome, to outweigh the probative value of the statistics. But if the situation arises in a civil case, as in the barrel hypothetical, or in the bus hypothetical, all that I am now prepared to say is that the question of admissibility seems to me a very close one.

come its greatest vice, for it may force jurors to articulate propositions whose truth virtually all might already suspect, but whose explicit and repeated expression may interfere with what seems to me the complex symbolic functions of trial procedure and its associated rhetoric." Id. at 1371. Tribe has in mind two problems with the use of a mathematical value in criminal cases: the factual presumption of guilt at the start of a trial, arising solely because of the accused's status as the defendant; and the quantification of the probability of guilt at the conclusion of the trial. Use of these mathematical data and conclusions, Tribe argues, conflicts with values served by the presumption of innocence and the reasonable doubt standard. Id. at 1370-1375. But, again, does this argument run against the *use* of mathematical methods at trial (i.e., admissibility), or does it have more to do with the sufficiency issue?

Finally, Tribe contends that the use of mathematics in the trial process leads to counter-intuitive results and thus may "make the legal system seem even more alien and inhuman than it already does to distressingly many." Id. at 1376. He continues:

> There is at stake not only the further weakening of the confidence of the parties and of their willingness to abide by the result, but also the further erosion of the public's sense that the law's fact-finding apparatus is functioning in a somewhat comprehensible way, on the basis of evidence that speaks, at least in general terms, to the larger community that the processes of adjudication must ultimately serve. The need now is to enhance community comprehension of the trial process, not to exacerbate an already serious problem by shrouding the process in mathematical obscurity.
>
> It would be a terrible mistake to forget that a typical lawsuit, whether civil or criminal, is only in part an objective search for historical truth. It is also, and no less importantly, a ritual — a complex pattern of gestures comprising what Henry Hart and John McNaughton once called "society's last line of defense in the indispensable effort to secure the peaceful settlement of social conflicts."[151]
>
> One element, at least, of that ritual of conflict-settlement is the presence and functioning of the jury — a cumbersome and imperfect institution, to be sure, but an institution well calculated, at least potentially, to mediate between "the law" in the abstract and the human needs of those affected by it. Guided and perhaps intimidated by the seeming inexorability of numbers, induced by the persuasive force of formulas and the precision of decimal points to perceive themselves as performing a largely mechanical and automatic role, few jurors — whether in criminal cases or in civil — could be relied upon to recall,

151. Hart & McNaughton, Evidence and Inference in the Law, in Evidence and Inference 48, 52 (D. Lerner ed. 1958). I do not exclude the possibility that, in extraordinary cases, and especially in cases involving highly technical controversies, the "historical" function may be so dominant and the need for public comprehension so peripheral that a different analysis would be in order, laying greater stress on trial accuracy and less on the elements of drama and ritual.

let alone to perform, this humanizing function, to employ their intuition and their sense of community values to shape their ultimate conclusions.

When one remembers these things, one must acknowledge that there was a wisdom of sorts even in trial by battle — for at least that mode of ascertaining truth and resolving conflict reflected well the deeply-felt beliefs of the times and places in which it was practiced. This is something that can hardly be said of trial by mathematics today.

Michael Saks and Robert Kidd, in Human Information Processing and Adjudication: Trial by Heuristics, 15 Law & Soc. Rev. 123, 125 (1980-81), contend, contrary to Tribe, that "while certain errors and harm may be inherent even in the proper use of probabilistic tools, even more harm may be inherent in not using them." In making this point, Saks and Kidd first apply the research findings of behavioral decision theorists to challenge Tribe's assumptions from an empirical point of view. They conclude that explicit calculation of probabilities will, in most cases, lead a trier of fact closer to the correct conclusion than will reliance on intuitive, commonsense judgments. Id. at 125. This is because most lay decisionmakers employ a number of simplifying strategies, known as "heuristics," to reduce complex information to a point where they can make a decision. Saks and Kidd offer the following examples and analysis of this phenomenon (id. at 127-130):

1. After observing three consecutive red wins, a group of people playing roulette start to switch their bets to black. After red wins on the fourth and fifth spins, more and more players switch to black, and they are increasingly surprised when the roulette wheel produces a red win the sixth, and then the seventh time. In actuality, on each spin the odds of a red win remain constant at $1:1$. The shifting of bets to black was irrational, as was the strong subjective sense that after each successive red win, black became more likely.

2. The following description is of a man selected at random from a group composed of 70 lawyers and 30 engineers. "John is a 39-year-old man. He is married and has two children. He is active in local politics. The hobby that he most enjoys is rare book collecting. He is competitive, argumentative, and articulate." A large group of respondents was asked to estimate the probability that John is a lawyer rather than an engineer. Their median probability estimate was .95. Another group of respondents was asked the same question, except that they were first told that the group from which John was selected consisted of 30 lawyers and 70 engineers. The second group's median estimate of the likelihood that John is a lawyer was also .95. Information about the composition of the group from which John was selected logically should have affected the estimated probability, but it had no effect at all on the decision makers' judgment. (This problem is taken from Kahneman and Tversky, 1973.) Only at the extremes of the distributions, where the group approaches 100 lawyers and 0 engineers (or the converse) do the decision makers become sensitive to the information about group composition.

3. A cab was involved in a hit-and-run accident at night. Two cab com-

panies, the green and the blue, operate in the city. A witness reports that the offending cab was blue, and legal action is brought against the blue cab company. The court learns that 85 percent of the city's cabs are green and 15 percent are blue. Further, the court learns that on a test of ability to identify cabs under appropriate visibility conditions, the witness is correct on 80 percent of the identifications and incorrect on 20 percent. Several hundred persons have been given this problem and asked to estimate the probability that the responsible cab was in fact a blue cab. Their typical probability response was .80. In actuality, the evidence given leads to a probability of .41 that the responsible cab was blue. (This problem is taken from Tversky and Kahneman, 1980.)

The first example illustrates the simplest and best known of errors in human probability judgment, the "Gambler's Fallacy." In a sequence of independent events, outcomes of prior events do not affect the probability of later events. Each event is independent of the other. On the seventh spin, the roulette wheel neither remembers nor cares what it did on the preceding six spins. People know that in the long run, half the wins will be red and half black. They err in believing that a small local sequence of events will be representative of the infinite sequence. "Chance is commonly viewed as a self-correcting process in which a deviation in one direction induces a deviation in the opposite direction to restore the equilibrium. In fact, deviations are not-'corrected' as a chance process unfolds, they are merely diluted" (Tversky and Kahneman, 1974). Although intuition in this context is out of harmony with reality, we all feel it compellingly, and continue to hear that baseball players who have not had a hit in some time are "due" for one, and that lightning will not strike twice in the same place. These common-sense judgments are, nevertheless, dead wrong.

The second example illustrates how human decision making tends to be insensitive to base rates when case-specific information is available. Given only the group base rates — 30 lawyers: 70 engineers — people rely heavily on this information to make their judgments. They correctly say the probability is .30 that the person selected is a lawyer. When descriptive case-specific information is added, they tend to ignore the numerical base rate and rely instead on the degree to which the description of John is representative of their stereotype of lawyers. Subjects base their estimate of the probability that John is a lawyer on the degree of correspondence between his description and their stereotype of lawyers as argumentative, competitive, and politically aware. Given the base-rate data in this example, it is 5.44 times as likely that John is a lawyer when the group is composed of 70 lawyers and 30 engineers than when the opposite membership distribution holds.

The third example also demonstrates insensitivity to base-rate information, this time in a context where both the base-rate and the case-specific information are given numerically. The actual low probability that the cab is blue is due to the fact that the base rate for blue cabs is very low, and the witness is of dubious acuity. Indeed, the base rate is more extreme than the witness is credible. But, fact finders apparently are unable simultaneously to relate the color of the hit-and-run cab to two different concerns, namely, the sampling of cabs from the city's cab population and imperfect color identification by the witness. They ignore the base-rate information and treat

Evd   100 cars   witness 80%
PSB   85%   15 blue   accurate

.8X85   .2X85   .8X15   .2X15
says   says   say   say
says   Blue   blue   green
gr   Blue   blu   green

gr   17   12   3
68

i.e. if say Blue $\frac{12}{29}$ are Blue   41%

17/29 are actually green

the accuracy of the witness as equal to the probability of a correct identification.

These illustrations demonstrate the gap between the judgments people make intuitively and the probabilities yielded by explicit calculation (or by empirical observation of actual outcomes).

Further, Saks and Kidd argue that, contrary to Tribe's assumption, the empirical evidence is that fact-finders *undervalue* quantitative evidence in the face of particularistic or anecdotal information, rather than finding it overpersuasive. The implications of this, they contend, are that statistical data are not so overwhelming as to be prejudicial and that the true problem is getting fact-finders to incorporate statistical evidence into their decisions at all. Id. at 149.

Saks and Kidd acknowledge the symbolic values of the trial process. However, "[t]o accept the dilemma posed by Tribe and adopt his preference for intuition is to choose a comforting ritual over accurate decisions, much like a patient who would rather have a human physician make a wrong diagnosis than allow a computer to make a correct one." Id. at 146. Not surprisingly, Saks and Kidd refuse to accept the "dilemma" (id. at 147-148):

> Moreover, the choice is not really between computers and people. It is between explicitly presented computing and subjective computing, or between more and less accurate computing. This is not to degrade humans. It is merely to recognize, on the one hand, our information processing limitations and, on the other, our capacity to invent tools that can do the job better.[29] After all, many people trust their pocket calculators and the light meters in their cameras, whose workings they do not begin to comprehend; yet their faith is well placed, because these devices make decisions and judgments faster and more accurately than people do.[30] The comparison is not between humans and mathematics, but between humans deciding alone and humans deciding with the help of a tool.
>
> Our suggestion is modest, and most lawyers should find it comfortingly traditional. Namely, experts ought to be permitted to offer their data, their algorithms, and their Bayesian theorems. The errors that may be introduced will be subjected to adversarial cross-examination. Various formal mathematical models do have room for errors — variables omitted, poor measurements, and others that Tribe has cogently presented. But so do intuitive techniques. Properly employed and developed, the former can have fewer. It

29. That people can invent tools that do a better job than the humans who invented them should come as no surprise to people who have used such devices as radios, light meters, or hammers. Indeed, the adversary process is just such a tool. It seems intuitively wrong to many people, but it is capable of accomplishing certain purposes that intuitive individuals cannot.

30. Trust in the pocket calculator is based on experience with it. People who acquire experience with mathematical decision making in management, operations, planning, science, economics, and so on, develop a similar trust in these other computational aids.

is up to opposing counsel to unmask the errors. Moreover, as a matter of developing and introducing new tools from what might be called decision-making technology, the identification of flaws does not imply that the tools ought not be used. The proper question is whether the tool, however imperfect, still aids the decision maker more than no tool at all.

As an example of how a statistical "tool" can aid the decisionmaker, Saks and Kidd describe the use of "aggregate probabilities" or base-rate data in making decisions in specific cases (id. at 149-150):

> The problem usually posed is: how can information about a general state of affairs, background information, legislative facts, base rates, serve as evidence about a specific event? Several examples may help to clarify the question (drawn from Tribe, 1971):
>
> (1) A person is found guilty of heroin possession. The next question is whether the drug was domestic or illegally imported. It can be shown that 98 percent of all illegally possessed heroin is illegally imported. May this fact be used in deciding the question in this case?
>
> (2) A physician sued for malpractice is accused of having dispensed a drug without warning of what he knew to be its tendency to cause blindness in pregnant women. Should he be allowed to introduce evidence that 95 percent of all physicians are unaware of that side effect (as evidence that he did not know)?
>
> (3) A plaintiff is negligently run down by a blue bus. The question is whether the blue bus belonged to the defendant who, it can be shown, owns 85 percent of the blue buses in town. What effect may such evidence be permitted to have?
>
> We know from the research described earlier that when a decision involves only simple base-rate data, people make (approximately) the correct probability estimate. The legal question is whether such evidence may be offered as proof. The argument for admitting it rests largely on the contribution such evidence will make to reaching a correct finding based on available information. The argument against it rests on the premise that base rates are uninformative about specific cases. "[I]t has been held not enough that mathematically the chances somewhat favor a proposition to be proved; for example, the fact that colored automobiles made in the current year outnumber black ones would not warrant a finding that an undescribed automobile of the current year is colored and not black, nor would the fact that only a minority of men die of cancer warrant a finding that a particular man did not die of cancer" (Sargent v. Massachusetts Accident Co., 1940). "[Such cases] are entirely sensible if understood . . . as insisting on the presentation of *some* non-statistical and 'individualized' proof of identity before compelling a party to pay damages, and even before compelling him to come forward with defensive evidence, absent an adequate explanation of the failure to present such individualized proof" (Tribe, 1971: 1344 n.37).
>
> The assumption in these decisions is that somehow particularistic evidence is of greater probative value, that is, is more diagnostic. The studies we have described can be seen as making some enlightening points about such a seem-

ing distinction. If neither case-specific nor base-rate data are available, the fact finder has no real way to evaluate a witness's statement. In the absence of internal or external contradiction, they probably accept it as credible. When only case-specific information is present, the fact finder regards the probability that proposition X is true as equal to the credibility of the witness. This is a condition which exists *only* when the base rate is 50:50. If no base-rate data are available, and this is common, the fact finders are doing the best they can; in essence, placing an even bet.

Now consider what is gained when base-rate information is added. The value of the base-rate information is that it provides a context in which the case-specific information has meaning. Once one knows that 85 percent of the buses are blue, and that the witness is 80 percent accurate in the appropriate color identification task, then one can, with the proper tools, evaluate the probative force of the statement "I saw the bus, and it was blue."[33] Contrary to the speculations of many commentators, the research on heuristics suggests that errors are massively in the direction of being seduced by case-specific information and failing to employ base-rate information to temper belief in a witness's credibility.

Finally, Saks and Kidd challenge Tribe's fundamental distinction between intuitive, anecdotal, or case-specific information on the one hand, and mathematical, aggregate, or base-rate data on the other (id. at 150-154):

Perhaps the most serious error is an epistemological one: the assumption that case-specific information is really *qualitatively* different from base-rate information. The courts, commentators, and we through most of this article have categorized them separately. And, indeed, it seems obvious that background base-rate information is about other cases while particularistic information is about *this* case. Whatever meaning the distinction may have, it is not one that pertains to the probability of an accurate decision on the facts. Much of the testimony that is commonly thought of as particularistic only seems so. It is far more probabilistic than we normally allow jurors (or judges) to realize. This includes eyewitness identification, fingerprints, and anything else we could name. This follows not from the nature (and fallibility) of these particular techniques, but from the nature of the logic of classifying and identifying. All identification techniques place the identified object in a class with others (Tribe, 1971: 1330 n.2). There is little, if any, pinpointed, one-person-only evidence in this world. In fairness to Tribe, he notes this non-distinction, then promptly ignores its implications by saying, "I am, of course, aware that *all* factual evidence is ultimately statistical, and all legal proof ultimately probabilistic, in the epistemological sense that no conclusion can ever be drawn from empirical data without some step of inductive inference — even if only an inference that things are usually what they are perceived to be. . . . My concern, however, is only with types of evidence and modes of proof that

33. If 95 percent of the buses are blue, and the witness is 80 percent accurate, when a witness reports seeing a blue bus, this yields a .98 probability that the bus was, indeed, blue.

bring this 'probabilistic' element of inference to explicit attention in a quantified way. As I hope to show, much turns on whether such explicit quantification is attempted" (Tribe, 1971: 1330 n.2). The problems of probability do not come into existence only when we become aware of them. Making them explicit does not create the problems, it only forces us to recognize them and enables us to begin dealing with them. Burying them in implicitness is no solution; revealing their existence is not the problem.

Suppose we must decide if a person on trial for possession of heroin is guilty also of possessing illegally imported heroin. And suppose we can learn either that 90 percent of all heroin in the U.S. is illegally imported or that a witness whom we judge to be 80 percent credible (e.g., knows and tells the truth 80 percent of the time) asserts that he (or she) observed the delivery and it was an illegal importation.

The usual argument, recall, is that the particularistic evidence tells us something on which we can base a decision, while the base-rate data are all but irrelevant to the case at hand. But, from the viewpoint of a disinterested fact finder, all information is indirect, distant, abstract, and imperfectly credible. The fact finders, in terms of their truth-seeking role, simply have a set of input information on which to base a judgment, and depending on the characteristics of the evidence and the way it is processed, that finding will have a greater or lesser probability of being correct. The simple fact in this example is that the fact finder can be 80 percent sure of being right or 90 percent sure. Consequently, in this instance it is the base-rate information that is more diagnostic, more probative, and more likely to lead to a correct conclusion.

Making this argument with the relatively concrete images of a case hampers our consideration of the concept. Let us try to make the point with one of those concretely abstract statistical anecdotes. Suppose you are at a state fair and approach a kind of shell game. You are presented with two overturned cups, each hiding a marble. One of the marbles is red. Your task is to bet on which cup is covering the red marble. You learn that under one cup is a marble drawn randomly from a bag containing 90 percent red marbles. A bystander, whom you know to tell the truth 80 percent of the time tells you, "I saw the marble placed under the other cup, and it was red." Placing your bet, the base-rate vs. case-specific character of the evidence is irrelevant. The odds of betting correctly, of maximizing the likelihood of winning, are dictated only by the content of the information. The question for the decision maker is which is more informative, an imperfectly credible witness, or an imperfectly pinpointed set of base-rate information. One choice offers a .90 probability of being correct, the other only .80. The diagnostic value of the information is not affected by whether it appears to report background facts or "case-specific" facts. Even so-called particularistic evidence is probabilistic. Invariably, all information is really probability information. Only if we neglect to uncover, or otherwise conceal from a fact finder the base rates of witness (or other evidence) reliability, will the case-specific information seem more informative. Only if we conceal from the bettor the fact that the witness who says "I saw the marble and it was red" is only .80 truthful or .50 accurate in color perception, will the assertion seem to have special probative force. The distinction between what one can learn from case-specific as opposed to base-rate information is more imaginary than real. In terms of accurate fact finding, it is a difference that makes no difference.

Similarly mistaken are distinctions between certain kinds of identifications. Descriptions which lead to a probability of correct classification of a person (e.g., "a completely bald man with a wooden left leg, wearing a black patch over his right eye and bearing a six-inch scar under his left, who flees from the scene of the crime in a chartreuse Thunderbird with two dented fenders") are treated as different from the "particularistic" type where a witness says, "Yes, that's the person." Some have argued that evidence that the above description fits only one person in 64 million ought not to be used in the trial of a person fitting that description, because it merely specifies the class to which he belongs and its size; it does not identify him. The latter identification would be more welcome, because it singles out a unique individual. The identifying witness may be confident that the identification is correct, but the fact finder ought to appreciate the inherently probabilistic nature of perception, storage, recall, and identification. Apparently, fact finders (like legal commentators) fail to appreciate this point. They act as though the eyewitness identification is highly accurate, when in reality it may be far more likely than once in 64 million to be in error. Indeed, the probability of correct eyewitness identification has been found to be far lower than commonly assumed.

The most meaningful difference between these two kinds of identification is that in one we allow the identifying witness to make the decision instead of letting the fact finder do so. But to think we have here evidence that is somehow uniquely diagnostic is only to conceal from ourselves the probabilistic nature and limited accuracy of the identification process. In *both kinds* of identifications we are dealing with classes containing more than one person, and there is no guarantee that the "particularistic" approach yields smaller classes.

Saks and Kidd's point of view has serious implications for our second question, concerning the sufficiency of probability evidence to support a verdict, treated in Chapter IX. For now, the question is simply the admissibility of mathematical proof, devices, and argumentation in the trial process. In the end, Saks and Kidd are outspokenly critical of the traditional, nonquantitative, ritualistic approach (id. at 156):

> Tribe advocates, in short, the maintenance of a fantasyland of apparent certainty in a world of patent uncertainty. Regarded from only a mildly different angle, such a deliberate turning away from reality may serve neither the law nor the defendant. First of all, the symbolism is so at variance with the objective reality as well as with the conceptualizations of legal scholars (certainly including Tribe himself) and the subjective experience of judges and jurors, that this may be one more of the legal fictions that tend to undermine the law's own credibility. An institution that would so deliberately ignore real, measurable doubt and assert not that it has made the best decision it was able

to but that it is "certain" it is correct, is unlikely to keep the masquerade going forever or to fool everyone.

Do you agree?

F. State of Mind of the Person

Problem I-17
Neither a Borrower nor a Lender Be

Action of debt on a note. *D* denied that he owed *P* any money, alleging that the note was a forgery. Several witnesses testified for *P* that the signature on the note was the handwriting of *D*. *D* then introduced several witnesses who testified that he was not in the country on the date of the note and several samples of his signature for the jury to compare with the signature on the note. *P* then called *W*, who offered to testify that *D* asked *W* to loan him money both before and after the date of the note.

Should *W*'s evidence be received? What is the inference that *P* wants the court to draw from *W*'s testimony? How would you articulate this inference in deductive form? Is this evidence "direct" or "circumstantial"? Does it combine elements of both? If it combines elements of both direct and circumstantial evidence, which type of evidence is of concern to us here? Would *W*'s testimony be more or less relevant if he did not lend *D* money? Would the evidence be more or less cogent if *W*'s testimony was that *D* sought to borrow from him the same sum for which the note to *P* was subsequently given? Would *W*'s testimony be more or less relevant if *P* introduced two additional witnesses to testify that *D* also sought to borrow money from them, or that *D* was a pauper?

If the defense offers a receipt for payment of the note, what should plaintiff's response be?

Problem I-18
Flight as Circumstantial Evidence

Charge: murder. The state offers evidence that, prior to her arrest, *D* attempted to flee and conceal her identity. This evidence is offered on the theory that it constitutes proof of *D*'s consciousness of guilt. *D* objects on the ground of irrelevancy and offers to prove that the more plausible inferences to be drawn from her attempted flight were her belief that a nonsupport warrant for her arrest was outstanding, her fear of being arrested for narcotics hidden in her car, and the fact that she had violated her parole.

Disregarding any hearsay problems, which are discussed further in the chapter on hearsay, should the evidence be admitted?

Problem I-19
Non-Flight as Circumstantial Evidence

Charge: robbery. *D* offers evidence that while being transported before trial from one city to another, he and the transporting officer stopped at a restaurant for a meal. *D*'s handcuffs were removed, but he made no attempt to flee. The prosecutor objects on the grounds of irrelevancy. *D* contends that failure to flee when an opportunity is presented is proof of an innocent frame of mind which, in turn, leads to an inference that he had acted in conformity with that state of mind and had not committed the offense charged.

Should the evidence be admitted? Is it relevant? What is the standard of probative worth that evidence must meet to be admissible?

Problem I-20
Toilet Bowl Evidence

Charge: prescribing a narcotic to persons not under treatment for a pathology. The state seeks to introduce evidence that during the preliminary hearing the clerk permitted Dr. *D* to examine the exhibits and later discovered that the prescriptions were missing. Pieces of the prescriptions were subsequently found floating in a toilet bowl in the courthouse rest room. *D* objects on grounds of relevancy.

What ruling and why? What chain of inferences does the prosecution want the jury to create in considering this evidence?

Problem I-21
Double Indemnity

HARTENSTEIN v. NEW YORK LIFE INSURANCE CO., 113 N.E.2d 712 (Ohio Ct. App. 1952): Mrs. Irma L. Hartenstein, as the beneficiary of a life insurance policy issued upon the life of her husband, Alfred D. Hartenstein, sued the New York Life Insurance Company to recover double indemnity provided for in the policy for death .... from bodily injury effected solely through external, violent and accidental means [but not from suicide].

[Plaintiff alleged that on November 16 her husband was in his car at a railroad crossing and was struck and killed by a locomotive. The insurance company claimed that the husband committed suicide.]

The testimony of the several persons who were near the scene of the tragedy and witnessed the conduct and activity of the insured was that the insured drove his automobile on an improved highway to a point several hundred feet from a well-marked main line, four-track railroad crossing and then parked for "fifteen or twenty minutes." . . . Several automobiles at about this time came to the crossing and stopped to give way to a forty-car loaded Baltimore and Ohio freight train, which was approaching at a speed of approximately 40 miles an hour. While the warning lights were flashing, and the train's whistle was blowing, the insured drove his car away from its parked position, passed around the several automobiles ahead, which had been stopped for the train, hesitated momentarily at the boundary of the crossing, and then proceeded slowly to the track upon which the train was approaching, where the automobile came to a stop. In a "matter of seconds" the inevitable collision occurred, and the insured was thrown from his car to the side of the tracks, while the train continued on through the crossing, carrying the automobile on the front of the engine. Death followed quickly. In addition to the warning signals, there is evidence that the train could be plainly seen in the broad light of the day by all who approached the crossing.

After introduction of the above evidence, the defendant moves for a nonsuit at the close of the plaintiff's case. Defendant argues that the evidence shows, as a matter of law, that the insured committed suicide. What ruling and why?

During the trial, additional evidence was offered to show that at the time of his death the insured was the secretary of a local lodge. As secretary he received dues, and it was his duty to deposit this money in a local bank. Several weeks before his death an annual audit of these funds was commenced by the lodge, and it was revealed that while the secretary's books showed $23,401.76 on hand, the reconciliation with the bank indicated $13,607.76 in the account. Should such evidence have been admitted? What is its relevance? Does its relevance require an inference to be piled on another inference?

Should there be a rule against piling an inference on an inference? If not, should each intermediate inference have to be established to some degree of certitude (e.g., a preponderance) before the evidence will be admitted?

G. Probative Value, Prejudicial Effect, and the Effectiveness of Categorical Rules of Exclusion

Many of the preceding problems and cases illustrate the notion embodied in Rule 403 that the trial judge may exclude relevant and otherwise admissible evidence if its probative value is "substantially outweighed by the danger of unfair prejudice, confusion of the issues, or misleading the jury" or by considerations of institutional efficiency.

The frequent recurrence of certain potentially prejudicial situations has prompted the development of a number of categorical exclusionary rules that supplement Rule 403's general and discretionary weighing of prejudicial effect and probative value. For example, Rules 404 and 405 exclude evidence of the character of an accused in a criminal case when offered solely to prove his propensity for criminal acts. These rules are discussed in Chapter II. Rule 407 excludes evidence of subsequent remedial measures when offered to prove negligence; Rule 408 excludes settlement offers and negotiations when offered to prove liability. Rule 409 excludes evidence showing one party's payment of another's medical expenses when offered to prove liability. Rule 410 generally excludes evidence of a subsequently withdrawn guilty plea or of a plea of nolo contendere. Rule 411 excludes evidence of liability insurance to prove negligence. Rule 412 — passed in 1978, several years after the original adoption of the Federal Rules — excludes from most cases evidence of a rape victim's past sexual conduct to prove the elements of a rape charge or defense.

These rules by and large represent policy choices that were previously obscured under the common law concept of "legal relevancy," which has been much criticized and is in general disrepute today. See the excerpt from James, supra. The question remains, however, whether the categorical rules of exclusion may be individually justified on specific policy grounds. To answer this we must explore the policy underlying each rule. Once the possible policy justifications for each rule have been analyzed, the question remains whether these categorical rules are necessary to accomplish their objectives. Is it not possible for all of the policy concerns reflected by these rules to be considered and properly weighed under Rule 403? What are the advantages of having special rules for these situations, in addition to a general prejudice rule? What disadvantages are there? Again, would it be preferable to leave the development of the law in these areas to judicial elaboration in applying Rule 403 rather than have Congress frame detailed rules? Would a middle road be preferable? For example, should the rules specify what types of evidence are generally excluded but permit exceptions when the evidence in a particular case is particularly necessary, probative, or free from prejudice? What factors are relevant in evaluating the efficacy of particular exclusionary rules?

Most of these categorical exclusionary rules exclude evidence if offered for one purpose but do not exclude the evidence if it is offered for other purposes. For example, evidence of subsequent remedial measures, inadmissible to prove negligence, may be introduced to prove "ownership, control, or feasibility of precautionary measures, if controverted, or impeachment." Similarly, evidence of settlement offers, excluded by Rule 408 on the issue of liability, may be used to show that a witness has a stake in the outcome of the case (bias). Even when evidence cannot be introduced for any permissible purpose, attorneys sometimes suggest it to the jury in various ways that are possibly improper and unethical. If evidence within the reach of one of these categorical rules were offered by your opponent under a permissible purpose exception, or if you were aware that it was going to be suggested to the jury improperly, how would you go about keeping it out? If it got in anyhow, how would you attempt to counteract its prejudicial effect? As a judge in this situation, what limiting instructions would you give? How effective are limiting instructions in these situations? Evidence that is purportedly excluded by these rules nevertheless often gets before the jury; to what extent does this affect your view on the wisdom of having these rules?

1.   Subsequent Remedial Measures

FRE 407
Subsequent Remedial Measures

When, after an event, measures are taken which, if taken previously, would have made the event less likely to occur, evidence of the subsequent measures is not admissible to prove negligence or culpable conduct in connection with the event. This rule does not require the exclusion of evidence of subsequent measures when offered for another purpose, such as proving ownership, control, or feasibility of precautionary measures, if controverted, or impeachment.

Problem I-22
Locking the Barn Door

(1) Pedestrian *P1* v. *D* Construction Company for personal injuries sustained when *P1* was struck by *D*'s crane while *P1* was walking on the sidewalk past *D*'s construction site. At trial, *P1* offers evidence that the day after the accident *D*'s superintendent posted a safety rule reading as follows:

EFFECTIVE IMMEDIATELY

When operating a crane or any other equipment on this job within 10 feet of a sidewalk or street, a lookout must be posted to watch for pedestrians and other traffic.

By Order of the Superintendent.

Is this evidence admissible?

(2) Pedestrian *P2* v. *D* Construction Company for personal injuries sustained when *P2* was struck by *D*'s crane while *P2* was walking on the sidewalk past *D*'s construction site, in the same place *P1* had been struck. At trial, *P2* offers evidence of the posted safety policy, which was posted the day *before* his accident. Admissible?

Problem I-23
The Exploding Pinto

In 1969, *P* bought a Ford Pinto. *P* alleged it to be dangerously designed because the location of the rear fuel tank was such that even in a minor rear-end collision the tank would easily be pierced and explode. In 1971 Ford redesigned the car, moving the tank to the front. In 1973, *P*'s car exploded into flames after a rear-end collision, and *P* was badly burned. At the trial of *P*'s action against Ford, *P* offers evidence of Ford's relocation of the fuel tank in the 1971 and later models. Ford objects. What ruling and why?

Problem I-24
The Dismissed Employee

P v. *D* Company for personal injuries sustained by *P* when struck by a *D* Co. truck driven by *D*'s driver, *E*. At trial, *P* offers evidence that *D* fired *E* one month after the accident. Admissible?

Problem I-25
The D-Craft 184 Crash

P v. *D* Aircraft Company for damages for the death of *P*'s husband, *H*, who perished when the plane he was flying — a twin-engine "D-Craft 184" — crashed for no apparent reason on a clear day. The theory of *P*'s case, which she plans to present through expert testimony, is that the fuel tanks on the D-Craft 184, located in the wings, feed fuel to the engines through a "gravitational flow" system that is susceptible to centrifugal force when the fuel tanks are only partially full and the plane is in a steep curve or dive. *P*'s expert will testify that the centrifugal force causes the delivery of fuel to the engine from the tank on the wing on the inside of the curve to be momentarily interrupted. When this happens the inside engine stalls, causing the other engine to jerk the plane around in the opposite direction. The force of this resulting pull reverses the forces on the fuel tanks, causing the second engine to stall. *P*'s expert will testify that when this condition occurs, even an experienced test pilot would be lucky to bring the plane back under control and prevent a crash. *P* has other evidence that tends to suggest that the crash may have happened in this way.

P's attorney learns through pretrial discovery that *D* Aircraft Company plans to call an expert on light plane design to testify that the "gravitational flow" fuel system is safe for twin-engine planes of the "184" series. *P*'s attorney also learns that shortly after the accident, *D* Aircraft Company replaced the gravitational flow fuel system in its 184s with an electronic-pump system.

Is any of this admissible? How should the attorneys for *P* and *D* Aircraft Company structure their examination of the witnesses to put in as much favorable evidence as they can and keep out as much unfavorable evidence as possible?

Problem I-26
Third-Party Repairs

P was injured when his car was struck by *D*'s train while crossing *D*'s railroad tracks. After the accident the State Highway Department installed signal lights at the crossing. *P* sues *D*. At trial, *P* offers evidence of the Highway Department's remedial measures. *D* objects. What ruling and why?

Problem I-27
The Exploding Pinto — A Reprise

(1) Suppose that in Problem I-23 above, *P* offered evidence that Ford knew of accidents in which the fuel tank had exploded under minimum impact but had not changed the design to protect against this. Admissible to prove negligence? Gross negligence?

(2) Suppose, instead, that Ford offers evidence in its defense that it had carefully studied accidents in which the fuel tank had ruptured and had purposefully *not* changed the design of its cars. Further, Ford offers evidence that Chrysler had placed the fuel tank in a similar position in its cars of the same model years as the Pintos that had exploded and that Chrysler had not changed its design either. Admissible?

Problem I-28
The Aluminum Gear Box

P v. *D* Equipment Manufacturing Company for personal injuries sustained by *P* when the vehicle in which she was driving left the road and plunged into a canyon. *P*'s complaint alleged that the aluminum gear box had failed. The claim was based on a theory of strict liability and breach of warranty. At trial, *P* offered evidence that aluminum was inappropriate for the gear box and that after the accident *D* changed from aluminum to malleable iron in producing the gear box. On *D*'s objection, what ruling and why?

ROBBINS v. FARMERS UNION GRAIN TERMINAL ASSOCIATION
552 F.2d 788 (8th Cir. 1977)

LAY, J. Farmers Union Grain Terminal Association (GTA) appeals from the award of $391,908.21 damages in favor of Wayne Robbins, Charles Robbins and James Robbins for the loss or damage to their cattle allegedly caused by a feed supplement, Rum-Liq, manufactured by GTA. The jury found the defendant liable under alternative theories of negligence, breach of implied warranty and strict liability. . . .

FACTUAL BACKGROUND

The plaintiffs are partners in a cattle feeding operation near Watertown, South Dakota. In the fall of 1971 they purchased 3,259 calves with an average weight of 412 pounds. The calves were started on a feeding program which included Rum-Liq, a cattle feed protein supplement advertised as aiding in weight gain and being more economical than other protein sources. The main ingredient of Rum-Liq is urea, a widely used non-protein nitrogen substance which ruminant animals are able to convert into protein.

GTA's product bore a tag which stated: "WARNING — Follow directions on back of tag. . . ." The relevant part of the tag providing the feeding instructions read:

> STARTING CATTLE ON FEED: Cattle coming into feedlot have normally been subjected to considerable stress — shipping, changes in feed, water and environment. Fresh, clean water and medium quality hay should be available in the feedlot when the cattle arrive. The first ten days follow the recommended programs using GTA ROUGHAGE ROUSER MEDICATED or GTA BEEF START MEDICATED. At the close of this period, change to a recommended GTA feedlot feeding program.

The plaintiffs started feeding each calf one-quarter pound of Rum-Liq daily. They gradually increased the dosage so that fourteen days after the calves arrived in the feed lot they were receiving one pound of Rum-Liq per day. After the fourteen-day "conditioning period," the calves were moved to outer pens where they continued to receive one pound of Rum-Liq each day. During the second week in November of

1971 some of the calves died and others were uncoordinated, bloated, urinating frequently, shaking and shivering, showing white foaming saliva, and breathing hard.

The Robbins first suspected that the calves were suffering from a respiratory disease, and they attempted treatment, but the calves did not respond. On December 8, 1971, after 77 animals had died and approximately 600 others were sick, two animals were taken to the diagnostic laboratory at South Dakota State University at Brookings. The lab found that blood of the two calves had a high level of ammonia, and they advised the plaintiffs, on the same day, that this could be the result of urea feeding. The plaintiffs immediately cleaned all the feed containing Rum-Liq out of the feed bunks, and stopped adding Rum-Liq to the feed. The sudden death losses decreased rapidly after December 9 and few animals subsequently developed the above described symptoms.

Beginning on March 7 the plaintiffs shipped their cattle for "finishing" to a commercial feed lot in Nebraska. According to plaintiffs' proof each of the seven shipments of cattle, when sold, weighed less on an average than normally expected and each shipment incurred extra feed and drug costs. An additional 59 head died at the commercial lot and 64 were sold early.

The plaintiffs sought the following damages: $2,000 for the Rum-Liq; $12,000 for extra veterinary expenses; $64,000 for the 342 dead animals (this figure took into account normal or expected deaths); $73,000 for extra feed; and $185,000 for losses on early sales and failure of the cattle to gain weight.

NEGLIGENCE

The thrust of plaintiffs' case is that GTA failed to give adequate warnings for the safe and effective use of its product. Plaintiffs claim that GTA knew or should have known that, although their instructions recommended waiting 10 days before starting calves on a full feeding program, experts recommended a longer delay.

Plaintiffs' animal nutrition experts testified that a manufacturer should warn a feeder to wait 28 to 30 days before starting calves on a high percentage urea feeding program such as Rum-Liq. Furthermore, Dr. Britzman, the Director of Animal Nutrition, Research and Management Services for GTA admitted that he knew of one authority who recommended that urea not be fed to calves within four weeks of weaning and that another authority questioned the feeding of urea to unadapted calves during early feed lot stages. From this evidence a jury could find that GTA's instructions inadequately warned of the danger of feeding urea to unadapted calves and that GTA had or through the exercise of reasonable care should have had knowledge of the dangers of urea. . . .

SUBSEQUENT REMEDIAL WARNING

On December 31, 1971, GTA mailed the following notice to its sales personnel:

File copy distributed to all division personnel 1/12/72

SUPPLEMENTARY DIET FOR "NEWLY ARRIVED"
FEEDLOT CATTLE

It is *not* recommended that high urea supplements (liquid or dry) be fed to cattle which have recently been placed in the feedlot. These cattle should be allowed time to overcome the stresses associated with shipment, vaccination, and adjustment to feedlot conditions. This may involve as long as 28-30 days. During this period, GTA ROUGHAGE ROUSER MEDICATED, or a similar low-urea supplement, should be fed.

Additional recommendation for handling and starting newly arrived feeder cattle are given on the attached sheets.

> *GTA FEEDS*
> Department of Animal Nutrition,
> Research and Management Services.

Plaintiffs offered this letter into evidence as relevant to the strict liability count to show an unreasonably dangerous and defective product. Plaintiffs also sought to show the feasibility of issuing such a warning in 1971 under their negligence theory. GTA objected that the exhibit was inadmissible on both counts under Fed. R. Evid. 407. The trial court ruled that the letter was admissible as substantive evidence since Rule 407 did not apply to strict liability, but that it would not be admissible on the negligence count unless feasibility was "controverted" as required by Rule 407. Plaintiffs then requested GTA to admit feasibility, and when GTA refused the trial court ruled that plaintiff could show that it was feasible to give the remedial instruction prior to the plaintiffs' purchase of the feed supplement.

On appeal GTA asserts that the exhibit should have been excluded under Rule 407 on both the strict liability and negligence counts and urges that the feasibility of giving the precautionary measure was *not properly* controverted. In addition GTA claims that the trial court failed to give any limiting instruction as to the exhibit's admissibility, and that the plaintiffs improperly argued to the jury that the post-remedial measure was evidence of GTA's negligence.

We need not consider whether the issue of feasibility was properly controverted because we find (1) that the exhibit was admissible under strict liability and (2) that GTA failed to object to plaintiffs' argument before the jury and did not request any cautionary instruction, or object to the court's failure to give a limiting instruction.

RULE 407

The trial court in receiving the exhibit relied on Ault v. International Harvester Co., 13 Cal. 3d 113, 117 Cal. Rptr. 812, 528 P.2d 1148 (1974). In the *Ault* decision the Supreme Court of California observed that the exclusionary rule governing subsequent remedial measures (Cal. Evid. Code §1151) is applicable only to negligent or culpable conduct.[9] The court said that while the exclusionary rule "may fulfill this anti-deterrent function in the typical negligence action, the provision plays no comparable role in the products liability field."[10] 13 Cal. 3d at 120, 117 Cal. Rptr. at 815, 528 P.2d at 1151. . . . We have applied the *Ault* rationale in allowing proof of post-occurrence design modification and to a subsequent remedial instruction, and find no reason to bar its applicability to Rule 407 since Rule 407 is, by its terms, confined to cases involving negligence or other culpable conduct. The doctrine of strict liability by its very nature, does not include these elements. See Ault v. International Harvester Co., supra; and Passwaters v. General Motors Corp., 454 F.2d 1270, 1277-79 (8th Cir. 1972).

9. It is noteworthy that the Advisory Committee's Note to Fed. R. Evid. 407 specifically indicates that Rule 407 is patterned after §1151 of the California Evidence Code. 2 J. Weinstein & M. Berger, Weinstein's Evidence, §407 (1975).

10. Justice Mosk writing for the Supreme Court of California offered the following cogent explanation:

"When the context is transformed from a typical negligence setting to the modern products liability field, however, the 'public policy' assumptions justifying this evidentiary rule are no longer valid. The contemporary corporate mass producer of goods, the normal products liability defendant, manufactures tens of thousands of units of goods; it is manifestly unrealistic to suggest that such a producer will forego making improvements in its product, and risk innumerable additional lawsuits and the attendant adverse effect upon its public image, simply because evidence of adoption of such improvement may be admitted in an action founded on strict liability for recovery on an injury that preceded the improvement. In the products liability area, the exclusionary rule of section 1151 does not affect the primary conduct of the mass producer of goods, but serves merely as a shield against potential liability. In short, the purpose of section 1151 is not applicable to a strict liability case and hence its exclusionary rule should not be gratuitously extended to that field.

"This view has been advanced by others. It has been pointed out that not only is the policy of encouraging repairs and improvements of doubtful validity in an action for strict liability since it is in the economic self interest of a manufacturer to improve and repair defective products, but that the application of the rule would be contrary to the public policy of encouraging the distributor of mass-produced goods to market safer products. (Note, Products Liability and Evidence of Subsequent Repairs, 1972 Duke L.J. 837, 845-852.)

"The recent case of Sutkowski v. Universal Marion Corporation (1972), 5 Ill. App. 3d 313, 281 N.E.2d 749, directly supports this conclusion. Noting that in the products liability field 'policy considerations are involved which shift the emphasis from the *defendant manufacturer's conduct to the character of the product*' (emphasis added) (281 N.E.2d at p. 753), the *Sutkowski* court held that the Illinois statutory rule excluding evidence of post-occurrence changes in negligence cases did not apply to products liability cases." Ault v. International Harvester Co.,13 Cal. 3d 113, 121-22, 117 Cal. Rptr. 812, 815-16, 528 P.2d 1148, 1151-52 (1974) (footnote omitted).

RELEVANCY

Relevancy of post-remedial measures in a defective design case have been outlined by the Seventh Circuit:

> [T]he plaintiff must establish that the "product in question has [not] lived up to the required standard of safety." This, of course, requires proof that, inter alia: 1) the product as designed is incapable of preventing the injury complained of; 2) there existed an alternative design which would have prevented the injury; and 3) in terms of cost, practicality and technological possibility, the alternative design was feasible. Evidence of post-occurrence change which tended to satisfy plaintiff's burden on any of these issues would therefore, be relevant.

Lolie v. Ohio Brass Co., 502 F.2d 741, 744 (7th Cir. 1974).

Under the view that "foreseeable danger" is still considered an element of strict liability,[13] evidence of "technological possibility," as related to the feasibility of a manufacturer to provide adequate instructions with its product, implies knowledge that such instructions could have been used to make the product safe or, at least, implies that such knowledge could be obtained through "the application of reasonably developed human skill and foresight." See Restatement (Second) of Torts §402A, Comment j. In the instant case Dr. Britzman of GTA testified that it was "feasible" to give, in 1971, a warning similar to that contained in the exhibit. Although the trial court limited the proof to show that it was feasible "to have sent out the notice," implicit in this admission is that it was technologically possible to have given the instructions in 1971. It would hardly be possible to concede feasibility to send out such cautionary instructions, if the manufacturer did not have either actual or constructive knowledge of the technological information. More relevant is the fact that a remedial instruction may provide substantial evidence that with a different instruction the harm would not have resulted (causation) and that failure to give the instruction created an unreasonably dangerous product (defect).[15] Lolie v. Ohio Brass Co., supra.

---

13. Although we express reservation in using negligence terms in a strict liability case (see n.15 infra), the trial court instructed as follows:

"In order to prevent the product from being unreasonably dangerous, the seller may be required to give directions or warning, on the container, as to its use. Where, however, the product contains an ingredient whose danger is not generally known, or if known is one which the user would reasonably not expect to find in the product, the manufacturer is required to give warning against it, *if said manufacturer has knowledge, or by the application of reasonable, developed human skill and foresight should have knowledge,* of the presence of the ingredient and the danger. Failure to warn of such a danger renders such a product defective, but you are instructed, however, that the defendant is liable only if you find that such failure to warn is a proximate cause of the loss and injury to the plaintiffs' cattle." (Emphasis added.)

15. In product liability cases relating to the alleged failure of a manufacturer to give adequate instructions, the cases are confusing as to whether strict liability (defective prod-

We conclude that the directive was relevant and properly admitted under the strict liability count. The fact that the exhibit was generally admitted and should have been limited to the strict liability count does not require reversal. As we pointed out the defendant did not offer any

---

uct by reason of inadequate instructions) and negligence (failure to exercise reasonable care in instructing) theories of recovery require the same elements of proof as to known or foreseeable dangers. Compare Phillips v. Kimwood Machine Co., 269 Or. 485, 525 P.2d 1033 (1974); and Berkebile v. Brantly Helicopter Corp., 462 Pa. 83, 337 A.2d 893 (1975); with Karjala v. Johns-Manville Prods. Corp., 523 F.2d 155 (8th Cir. 1975); and Borel v. Fibreboard Paper Prods. Corp., 493 F.2d 1076, 1088 (5th Cir. 1973), cert. denied, 419 U.S. 869 (1974).

Since knowledge and culpable fault are not elements in the proof of strict liability in product cases, it is somewhat anomalous to confuse negligence and strict liability by suggesting the same elements of proof. Conceptually, when dealing with a product made unreasonably dangerous by reason of inadequate instructions, to require proof that the manufacturer knew or should have known of the danger ("foreseeable dangers") is a misapplication of the principles underlying strict liability. As stated in Dreisonstok v. Volkswagenwerk, A.G., 489 F.2d 1066 (4th Cir. 1974), discussing the second collision rule set forth in Larsen v. General Motors Corp., 391 F.2d 495 (8th Cir. 1968): "The key phrase in the statement of the *Larsen* rule is '*unreasonable risk* of injury in the event of a collision,' not foreseeability of collision. The *latter circumstance is assumed in collision cases under the Larsen principle*; it is the element of 'unreasonable risk' that is uncertain in such cases and on which the determination of liability or no liability will rest." 489 F.2d at 1071 (emphasis added).

In recognizing this distinction in a product case involving a failure to adequately warn, the Supreme Court of Oregon perhaps says it best:

"In a strict liability case we are talking about the condition (dangerousness) of an article which is sold without any warning, while in negligence we are talking about the reasonableness of the manufacturer's actions in selling the article without a warning. The article can have a degree of dangerousness because of a lack of warning which the law of strict liability will not tolerate even though the actions of the seller were entirely reasonable in selling the article without a warning considering what he knew or should have known at the time he sold it. A way to determine the dangerousness of the article, as distinguished from the seller's culpability, is to assume the seller knew of the product's propensity to injure as it did, and then to ask whether, with such knowledge, he would have been negligent in selling it without a warning.

"It is apparent that the language being used in the discussion of the above problems is largely that which is also used in *negligence* cases, i.e., 'unreasonably dangerous,' 'have reasonably anticipated,' 'reasonably prudent manufacturer,' etc. It is necessary to remember that whether the doctrine of negligence, ultrahazardousness, or strict liability is being used to impose liability, the same process is going on in each instance, i.e., weighing the utility of the article against the risk of its use." Phillips v. Kimwood Machine Co., 269 Or. 485, 525 P.2d 1033, 1039 (1974).

Later in the same opinion the Oregon court referred to Professor Wade's article, On the Nature of Strict Tort Liability for Products, 44 Miss. L.J. 825, 830 (1973), and observed:

"Professor Wade also suggests an appropriate jury instruction which embodies the new standard. We have taken the liberty of modifying his suggestion to a form which seems to us more appropriate for use by a jury. It is as follows:

"'The law imputes to a manufacturer [supplier] knowledge of the harmful character of his product whether he actually knows of it or not. He is presumed to know of the harmful characteristics of that which he makes [supplies]. Therefore, a product is dangerously defective if it is so harmful to persons [or property] that a reasonable prudent manufacturer [supplier] with this knowledge would not have placed it on the market.'" 525 P.2d at 1040-41 n.16. . . .

The relevant issue concerning foreseeability in strict liability relates to intended use. We have previously acknowledged that "intended use" is merely a convenient adaptation of

limiting instruction or object to the failure of the trial court to give such an instruction. The purpose for requiring specific objection to instructions or to any alleged trial error is to provide the trial court the opportunity to correct the error at the time. See, e.g., Sterling Drug, Inc. v. Cornish, 370 F.2d 82 (8th Cir. 1966). This case is exemplary of the rule since it is clear that the trial judge fully intended to give a limiting instruction concerning Exhibit 38 but it was later inadvertently omitted. Under the circumstances the defendant cannot complain. See Griggs v. Firestone Tire & Rubber Co., 513 F.2d 851 (8th Cir.), cert. denied, 423 U.S. 865 (1975).

Is the *Robbins* opinion internally consistent? Insofar as strict liability doctrine employs negligence concepts such as "foreseeable danger" and "unreasonably dangerous," is there a sound basis for the distinction as to proof of subsequent repairs in strict liability cases and in negligence cases? Does the policy on which Rule 407 is based apply to the same extent in strict liability cases as it does in negligence cases? Is the evidence more or less probative in such cases? Does this argue for or against the policy of excluding such evidence generally?

WERNER v. UPJOHN CO.
628 F.2d 848 (4th Cir. 1980)

WIDENER, J. The plaintiff, Jack Werner, brought this action against the Upjohn Co. and Dr. Ralph J. Carbo, an ophthalmologist, to recover damages for injuries Werner received as result of his taking the prescription drug Cleocin which was manufactured by Upjohn and prescribed by Dr. Carbo. Jurisdiction is based on diversity of citizenship and the requisite amount in controversy.

The case was tried to a jury which found that Carbo was negligent in prescribing the drug and that his negligence proximately caused or contributed to plaintiff's injury; that Upjohn was negligent in either marketing or selling Cleocin and such negligence proximately caused or

---

the test of foreseeability. See Polk v. Ford Motor Co., 529 F.2d 259 (8th Cir.), cert. denied, 426 U.S. 907 (1976); and Passwaters v. General Motors Corp., 454 F.2d 1270, 1275 (8th Cir. 1972). Under strict liability the knowledge of the danger is otherwise imputed to the defendant. Proof of a subsequent remedial modification, under these circumstances, therefore becomes relevant to show that a different design or instruction would have prevented the harm and that it was technologically feasible to provide a safer design or give a more adequate instruction before the product was marketed. See Lolie v. Ohio Brass Co., 502 F.2d 741, 744 (7th Cir. 1974).

contributed to plaintiff's injury; that Upjohn was negligent in failing to warn properly of the dangerous side effects of Cleocin; that Upjohn breached either an express or implied warranty in its sale of Cleocin to Carbo; and that Upjohn was not liable in strict liability for marketing an unreasonably dangerous drug. Based on these findings the jury awarded damages of $400,000. The defendants appeal.

Upjohn argues that there is insufficient evidence on which the jury could find that Upjohn was negligent; that the jury verdicts are inconsistent; that a subsequently revised warning was improperly admitted into evidence; that several of the jury instructions were improper; and that it could not be found liable even if the warning was inadequate because Dr. Carbo admitted that he did not read the warning which was given. . . .

We hold that the district court erred in admitting the subsequent warning into evidence. We therefore reverse and remand for a new trial.

The prescription drug at the base of this action is Cleocin (generic name Clindamycin HCl) a broad-spectrum antibiotic. The Food and Drug Administration (FDA) first approved Cleocin for general use in 1970, and it soon became a popular alternative antibiotic for those persons who were allergic to penicillin. As the use of Cleocin increased Upjohn began to receive reports of side effects from Cleocin use, such as diarrhea and colitis. The appearance of these side effects was reported to the FDA and several medical studies were done both independently and by Upjohn which sought to clarify the incidence and extent of these side effects. The plaintiff argued that Upjohn knew of serious side effects in 1974 and failed to act on this information until March 1975. Upjohn argued that its 1974 warning contained all the relevant information available at that time. In any event, as a result of the reported side effects and subsequent studies, the warning information accompanying Cleocin went through several revisions. Throughout this period the central concern over Cleocin was its capacity to cause pseudomembranous colitis (PMC) in some patients. Prior to 1974 the incidence of PMC in Cleocin users was thought to be quite low, but in late 1973 a Dr. Tedesco published a study which found signs of PMC in 10 percent of a test group who took the drug. However, it was not clear that the PMC found in Tedesco's patients was the same as the more commonly known and admittedly extremely serious PMC since Dr. Tedesco's patients recovered without any permanent problems. As a result of Tedesco's study and information provided by Upjohn and others a new warning was issued in the summer of 1974. This new warning was included in the package insert accompanying Cleocin and was the subject of what is called a "Dear Doctor" letter which was mailed to every physician in the United States. The adequacy of this warning at the time it was released is one of the central issues in this case. The 1974 warning stated:

WARNING

Severe and persistent diarrhea, which may be accompanied by blood and mucus, and which may be associated with changes in large bowel mucosa diagnosed as "pseudomembranous colitis," has been reported in association with the administration of Cleocin HCl (clindamycin HCl hydrate).

When significant diarrhea occurs (usually more than 5 bowel movements daily), the drug should be discontinued or, if necessary, continued only with close observation of the patient (large bowel endoscopy has been recommended). Mild cases of colitis may respond to drug discontinuance alone. Moderate to severe cases should be managed promptly with fluid, electrolyte and protein supplementation as indicated. Antiperistaltic agents — opiates, meperidine, and diphinoxylate with atrophine may prolong and/or worsen the condition. Systemic corticoid and corticoid retention enemas may help relieve the colitis. Other causes of colitis should also be considered.

Note: Diarrhea has been observed to begin up to several weeks following cessation of therapy with Cleocin HCl. The physician must be alert to this possibility.

The plaintiff first visited Dr. Carbo in Maryland on December 10, 1974 for treatment of a chalazion on his eyelid. Dr. Carbo prescribed Cleocin for the plaintiff's condition and stated that he advised plaintiff that he might experience some nausea, vomiting or diarrhea, and told him that if he experienced these side effects he should stop using the drug and report to him. The plaintiff testified that Carbo gave him no such warning. Carbo's warning was based on the 1973 package insert. He admitted that he did not read the 1974 Dear Doctor letter before prescribing Cleocin to the plaintiff even though it was available in his office. . . .

As mentioned a central issue in the case against Upjohn and an important collateral issue in the case against Dr. Carbo was the adequacy of the 1974 warning, and both the plaintiff and Upjohn presented a great deal of evidence on the true dangers and incidence of side effects of Cleocin and whether the warning adequately conveyed the facts. . . .

No evidence introduced by the plaintiff was more important on the adequacy of the 1974 warning, than the evidence he introduced, over objection, of a warning published in March 1975 which expanded on the 1974 warning. The 1975 warning stated:

Clindamycin can cause severe colitis which may end fatally. Therefore, it should be reserved for serious infections where less toxic antimicrobial agents are inappropriate, as described in the INDICATIONS section. It should not be used in patients with nonbacterial infections, such as most upper respiratory tract infections. The colitis is usually characterized by severe, persistent diarrhea and severe abdominal cramps and may be associated with the passage of blood and mucus. Endoscopic examination may reveal pseudomembranous colitis.

When significant diarrhea occurs, the drug should be discontinued or, if necessary, continued only with close observation of the patient. Large bowel endoscopy has been recommended.

Antiperistaltic agents such as opiates and diphinoxylate with atrophine (Lomotil) may prolong and/or worsen the condition.

Diarrhea, colitis, and pseudomembranous colitis have been observed to begin up to several weeks following cessation of therapy with clindamycin.

Upjohn moved to exclude all reference to the 1975 warning. The court denied this motion and allowed the plaintiff to introduce the warning into evidence. When the warning was offered into evidence, over objection, the district judge instructed the jury that the warning was not to be used as evidence of negligence or culpable conduct. However, the court did not inform the jury at that time for what purpose it was to be considered. Later, after all evidence was in, the judge instructed the jury that they should only consider the 1975 warning on the issue of feasibility, obviously referring to Federal Rule of Evidence 407.

Federal Rule of Evidence 407, which enacts the common law rule excluding subsequent remedial measures to prove negligence, does, however, permit evidence of subsequent remedial measures to be used to prove the feasibility of such measures, but only if feasibility is controverted by the defendant. But, despite the judge's limiting instruction on this point it is clear that the 1975 warning was used by the plaintiff to prove negligence. The warning was mentioned several times during the course of the trial when expert witnesses were asked whether the information in the 1975 warning should have been included in the 1974 warning if that information had been available to Upjohn at the time the 1974 warning was given. This use of the warning has no conceivable connection to feasibility. The plaintiff's expert witnesses were asked time after time whether Upjohn "should have" included the information in the 1975 warning in the 1974 warning. The obvious inference is that if Upjohn should have used the subsequent warning earlier, then it was negligent for failing to do what it "should have" done. This use of the 1975 warning clearly was impermissible and constitutes reversible error. Columbia & Puget Sound R. Co. v. Hawthorne, 144 U.S. 202 (1892). . . .

Plaintiff also made improper use of the 1975 warning in closing argument to the jury. Plaintiff's counsel stated:

If we were to boil this down to the least common denominator, if you were to be asked tomorrow, after, hopefully, the case is decided and done with, what was the biggest single thing that Upjohn did wrong that impells [sic] you to bring in a verdict for the plaintiff against Upjohn, would you not have to say Upjohn knew of the fatalities and didn't tell the doctors until much later, after this whole episode was over and done? That they knew it should not be used for other than serious, life-threatening infections? That they knew there were other less toxic antibiotics which were appropriate, and they told people that later? That they knew that they had, according to their people, cut off promotion of the drug in the middle of '74, but didn't tell the doctors that? Don't you think, honestly, and you have to answer this to yourselves, don't you think any one of those four things was a violation of a duty which any ethical drug manufacturer owes the public, to keep the public informed, or keep the doctors informed so the public can be informed?

Instead of that, they held it under their belt; they continued the advertising for at least four more months, in many instances. They held off the change until March of '75; [the date the 1975 warning was released] nine months after they knew this, and they cashed in as much as they could. . . .

But, in this delay, from July 1 to March of '75, before they really cut and told the doctors what they should have told them long ago, in that nine month period . . . .

The clear import of this argument is that Upjohn breached its duty of due care by failing to adopt the 1975 warning in 1974. Thus, plaintiff used the substance of the subsequent warning to prove antecedent negligence and thereby violated Rule 407. . . .

Plaintiff also argues that since an instruction was given limiting the use of the 1975 warning to the issue of feasibility that any error caused by plaintiff's departure from this rule is harmless because it was cured by the limiting instruction. This argument is without merit. In the abstract, of course, evidence, may be admissible for one purpose and inadmissible for another. The usual solution for this problem is to admit the evidence to prove the permissible inference, but limit its use by jury instructions. This does not mean, however, that the party offering evidence for a limited purpose is free to use it for a forbidden purpose, over objection, during the course of the trial and insulate reversal by pointing to a limiting instruction given at the close of the case. . . .

Thus, plaintiff's efforts to expand the feasibility exception must fail. Since feasibility was not in issue in the case the evidence should have been excluded. See Advisory Committee Notes to Rule 407. Rule 407 is designed to protect the important policy of encouraging defendants to repair and improve their products and premises without the fear that such actions will be used later against them in a lawsuit. Several exceptions to the rule have developed, but it is clear that they must be narrowly construed if the central policy behind the rule is to be effectuated. If feasibility were to be found at issue in the case at bar, it is difficult to imagine a situation where it would not at least arguably be in issue. As Professor McCormick has said:

[T]he extrinsic policy of encouraging remedial safety measures is the predominant reason for holding evidence of these measures to be privileged. It is apparent that the free admission of such evidence for purposes other than as admissions of negligence is likely to defeat this paramount policy. It is submitted that before admitting the evidence for any of these other purposes, the

> court should be satisfied that the issue on which it is offered is of substantial importance and is actually, and not merely formally in dispute, that the plaintiff cannot establish the fact to be inferred conveniently by other proof, and consequently that the need for the evidence outweighs the danger of its misuse.

McCormick on Evidence, §275, at 668-669 (2d ed. 1972). In sum, feasibility is not in issue in this case, and even if it were, it is clear that the use made by the plaintiff of the 1975 warning was not so limited.

Alternately, plaintiff argues that even if the 1975 warning was not admissible to show feasibility it was admissible on other grounds. It is arguable that this question is not directly before us on appeal because the 1975 warning was in fact used to prove negligence, and thus the fact that the evidence might have been admissible on some other ground not raised at trial should not prevent reversal and a new trial. Especially because this case must be tried again, and we do not believe that the 1975 warning was admissible, we examine plaintiff's other arguments for admitting the evidence.

Plaintiff argues, and we agree, that the exceptions listed in Rule 407 — ownership, control or feasibility of precautionary measures (if controverted), and impeachment, are illustrative and not exhaustive. See Advisory Committee Notes to Rule 407. However, we note once again that Rule 407 promotes an important policy of encouraging subsequent remedial measures. If this policy is to be effectuated we should not be too quick to read new exceptions into the rule because by so doing there is a danger of subverting the policy underlying the rule.

Plaintiff's principal argument along this line is that the 1975 warning is admissible because the suit includes a strict liability claim. The courts have split on this proposition. We suppose, without making a numerical comparison, that the majority of courts would admit the evidence for one reason or another. Compare e.g., Smith v. E. R. Squibb & Sons, Inc., 405 Mich. 79, 273 N.W.2d 476 (1979); Price v. Buckingham Mfg. Co., 110 N.J. Super. 462, 266 A.2d 140 (1970); with Robbins v. Farmers Union Grain Terminal Assn., 552 F.2d 788 (8th Cir. 1977); Ault v. Intl. Harvester, 13 Cal. 3d 113, 117 Cal. Rptr. 812, 528 P.2d 1148 (1974).

In support of his argument to admit the evidence plaintiff first argues that Rule 407 in terms only bars the evidence to prove negligence or culpable conduct and that the rule therefore does not allow for exclusion on the strict liability issue. We disagree. The mere fact that Rule 407 by its terms only excludes evidence of subsequent precautionary measures to prove negligence or culpable conduct does not necessarily mean that the evidence should be admissible to prove strict liability. It is clear that in enacting the Federal Rules of Evidence Congress did not intend to wipe out the years of common law development in the field of evidence, indeed the contrary is true. The new rules contain many gaps and omissions and in order to answer these unresolved questions courts certainly should rely on common law precedent. This is true with respect to Rule 407 which merely enacts the common law rule. Rule 407 bars evidence of subsequent precautionary measures to prove negligence or culpable conduct with exceptions for control, ownership or feasibility (if controverted) and impeachment. The rule simply does not speak in terms to the question of whether the evidence should come in to prove strict liability. To resolve this question we must examine the policy behind Rule 407 and the common law basis for the rule, and then determine if admitting the evidence as evidence of strict liability is more akin to the use of it to prove negligence, or if it is closer to one of the recognized exceptions to the rule. That is to say, would the policy behind the common law rule be served or subverted if evidence of subsequent precautionary measures be admitted to prove strict liability.

We first note that Rule 407 excludes evidence of subsequent precautionary measures to prove negligence or culpable conduct. Culpable conduct normally involves something more than simple negligence and implies conduct which is "blamable; censurable; involving the breach of a legal duty or the commission of a fault. . . . [I]t implies that the act or conduct spoken of is reprehensible or wrong, but not that it involves malice or a guilty purpose." Black's Law Dictionary (4th ed. 1968). Thus, Congress has determined that such evidence should be excluded not only in cases involving negligence but where the defendant is charged with culpable conduct. Strict liability on the other hand involves conduct which is technically less blameworthy than simple negligence, since the plaintiff need not prove a breach of duty by the defendant other than placing the product on the market. From a policy standpoint it follows that if the rule expressly excludes evidence of subsequent repairs to prove culpable conduct that the same should be true for strict liability. Stated another way, if the common law and Congress were willing to exclude the evidence on the issue of culpable conduct, the result should be no different on policy grounds as long as strict liability is not distinguishable on some other ground.

Plaintiff argues that a fundamental distinction exists between negligence and strict liability since in a negligence action it is the reasonableness of the defendant's conduct which is in issue while in a strict liability case the issue is whether the product is unreasonably dangerous. Thus, the argument goes, in a negligence action the focus is on the defendant while in strict liability the focus is on the product. We concede the obvious distinction between negligence and strict liability, but we do not believe that this distinction should produce a different result. The rationale behind Rule 407 is that people in general would be less likely to take subsequent remedial measures if their repairs or improvements would be used against them in a lawsuit arising out of a prior accident. By excluding this evidence defendants are encouraged to make such

improvements. It is difficult to understand why this policy should apply
any differently where the complaint is based on strict liability as well as
negligence. From a defendant's point of view it is the fact that the evidence may be used against him which will inhibit subsequent repairs or
improvement. It makes no difference to the defendant on what theory
the evidence is admitted; his inclination to make subsequent improvements will be similarly repressed. The reasoning behind this asserted distinction we believe to be hypertechnical, for the suit is against
the manufacturer, not against the product. . . .

Our conclusion is supported by the close similarity between negligence and strict liability. The elements of both are the same with the
exception that in negligence plaintiff must show a breach of a duty of
due care by defendant while in strict liability plaintiff must show the
product was unreasonably dangerous. The distinction between the two
lessens considerably in failure to warn cases since it is clear that strict
liability adds little in warning cases. Under a negligence theory the issue
is whether the defendant exercised due care in formulating and updat-
ing the warning, while under a strict liability theory the issue is whether
the lack of a proper warning made the product unreasonably dangerous. Though phrased differently the issue under either theory is essentially the same: was the warning adequate?

Any remaining distinction in theories disappears when a failure to
warn case involves an unavoidably dangerous drug which the product in
this case admittedly was. The Restatement of Torts (2d) §402A, comment k makes it clear that a drug manufacturer is not to be held strictly
liable for injuries caused by an unavoidably dangerous new drug if the
warning is adequate. The standard for liability under strict liability and
negligence is essentially the same. . . .

Plaintiff's final argument on the admissibility of the 1975 warning is
that it was required by the FDA, and that since defendant Upjohn had
no choice in the matter, the policy behind Rule 407 would not be served
by excluding the evidence. While this argument may have a surface
plausibility, we do not believe the evidence should be admitted for this
reason. First, when a third party has required the change the relevance
of the evidence is one more step removed from the central issue in the
case, the adequacy of the warning at the time the product was marketed.
When a third party makes a subsequent change the inference is removed
not only in time but in who made the change. This is especially true in
the case at bar since the FDA itself approved the 1974 warning at the
time it was first used. Thus, it would appear that any separate relevance
of the FDA's actions with regard to the 1975 warning is overridden by
the fact that the FDA approved the 1974 warning as well.

Furthermore, plaintiff's argument overlooks the dual responsibility
for preparing warnings for prescription drugs. The FDA can require

that a warning be changed, but this does not tell the whole story. In addition to its broad regulatory sanctions it is clear that it also relies on voluntary compliance and compromise in determining the content of warnings and advertising for prescription drugs. . . .

If subsequent warnings are admitted to prove antecedent negligence simply because FDA required or might have required the change, then drug companies may be discouraged from taking early action on their own and from participating fully in voluntary compliance procedures. Thus, we think that the FDA's regulatory power should not be read as in conflict with the protective policy of Rule 407. The FDA's regulations and policies encourage early unilateral action by the drug companies to improve their warnings, and Rule 407 promotes the same goal. We therefore hold that FDA regulations in the area of drug labeling do not require a new exception to Rule 407. . . .

The judgment appealed from must be vacated and the case remanded for a new trial.

2.   Settlement Offers and Payment of Medical Expenses

FRE 408
Compromise and Offers to Compromise

Evidence of (1) furnishing or offering or promising to furnish, or (2) accepting or offering or promising to accept, a valuable consideration in compromising or attempting to compromise a claim which was disputed as to either validity or amount, is not admissible to prove liability for or invalidity of the claim or its amount. Evidence of conduct or statements made in compromise negotiations is likewise not admissible. This rule does not require the exclusion of any evidence otherwise discoverable merely because it is presented in the course of compromise negotiations. This rule also does not require exclusion when the evidence is offered for another purpose, such as proving bias or prejudice of a witness, negativing a contention of undue delay, or proving an effort to obstruct a criminal investigation or prosecution.

FRE 409
Payment of Medical and Similar Expenses

Evidence of furnishing or offering or promising to pay medical, hospital, or similar expenses occasioned by an injury is not admissible to prove liability for the injury.

Problem I-29
Mr. Nice Guy

(1) Cars driven by *D* and *P* collide at an intersection controlled by a traffic signal. Each alights from his car, and the following dialogue ensues:

D: Why didn't you stop for the light? See what you've done?

P: What do you mean, "*you* stop for the light"? I had the green. Oh, my car. And my neck is hurt. Ohh. . . .

D: Well, maybe it turned on me in the intersection. Let's not make a big deal of this. Maybe we can handle this ourselves.

P: Ohh, my neck . . . and my back . . . ohhh. . . .

D: Now wait a minute, let's talk this over. I'm sorry I ran the light. Here, how's about if I give you this, ah, $100, for the fender, and, ah, here's another $100 for your neck — go get a massage or something. Let's forget about it — how about it?

P sues *D* for $750,000 for personal injuries and property damage. Is any of the above admissible?

(2) During pretrial discovery, *P*'s lawyer takes *D*'s deposition. After four hours of testimony, *D*, who is represented by counsel, says:

D: Now, look, you guys — I've had enough of this. Let's go off the record. This isn't going anywhere. Even if the case goes to trial it will take five years to get there, and who knows if *P* will get a cent? Even if he wins, he isn't going to get more than my liability coverage provides. How much were *P*'s medical bills? $2,300? Here's a check for that amount plus $1,700 for his time. If he signs this release, it's his.

P rejects these terms. At trial how much of this is admissible?

Problem I-30
Threatening Letters

D Manufacturing Company recently received a letter from *P* Technology, Inc., accusing *D* of infringing three *P* patents on computerized credit authorization systems. *P* has a reputation as a vigorous enforcer of its patents. Indeed, *P* is currently involved in a fierce patent infringement action on the same patents against *C* Manufacturing Company, a competitor of *D*. The letter invited *D* to take a license for future use at a fee ($5,000,000) that might reflect damages for past infringement. *D* makes and sells credit authorization systems but utilizes technology developed by its employees. Nevertheless, *D*'s general counsel asked a patent attorney to look into *P*'s charge and draft a reply. Before he mails the reply, the general counsel would like your advice as to the effect on any subsequent patent infringement litigation of sending such a letter. The draft letter reads as follows:

Dear *P* Technology, Inc.:

This is in response to your letter of February 16 regarding U.S. Patent Nos. 3,212,062, 3,407,388, and 3,498,069.

We have reviewed these patents and considered our need for a license under them in light of our present and future products. We have concluded that we have no need for a license under any of these patents at this time. However, to show our good faith, we would be willing to take a fully paid license of these patents at a nominal rate ($50,000 to $100,000 range), if accompanied by a general release for past acts.

Please let us have your response within 10 days.

> Sincerely,
> (*Signature*)
> General Counsel,
> *D* Manufacturing Company

Problem I-31
The Plot Thickens

P, a passenger in *O*'s car, sues *D* for injuries resulting when *O*'s car collided with *D*'s car. *P* seeks to introduce evidence of a settlement reached between *D* and *Q*, another passenger in *O*'s car. *D* objects. What ruling and why? What other information might be useful in making this ruling?

Problem I-32
Thicker Still

P, a passenger in *O*'s car, was injured when the car collided with a taxi driven by *D*. *P* sues *D*. *D* seeks to introduce evidence of settlements between *D* and *O*, where *O* agreed to pay for damages to *D*'s vehicle, and between *P* and *O*, wherein *O* paid *P* an undisclosed amount for *P*'s injuries. What ruling and why?

Problem I-33
Even Thicker

Plaintiffs sued *D* Manufacturing Company, its accountants, and seven of its officers and employees for various security violations in connection with a public offering of *D*'s stock. Two of the individual defendants, Jones and Smith — corporate officers — cross-claimed against the corporation, seeking indemnification for expenses incurred in defending the action. Under applicable state law a corporate officer is entitled to indemnification for reasonable attorneys' fees and expenses, "to the extent he has been successful on the merits in a proceeding where his action as an officer allegedly violated the law." During the pretrial phase of the case, cross-claimants obtained voluntary dismissals, with prejudice, of the actions against them. As part of the arrangement, Jones made a payment to the plaintiffs of $35,000. Smith made no payment.

At the trial of the indemnification claims the issue is whether Jones and Smith were "successful on the merits" in the main case. On this point the officers offer the dismissals. The corporation offers proof of Jones's $35,000 payment and an affidavit of an attorney for the plaintiffs in the main case regarding the settlement of the plaintiffs' claims against Smith and Jones. Is any of this admissible?

Problem I-34
Civil Settlements and Criminal Cases

D is prosecuted for violation of a Price Control Act in selling *P* a car at a price above the legal limit. The act premises criminal liability on a showing of willfulness, whereas civil liability exists for merely negligent violations. Testimony at trial shows that salesperson *S*, employed by *D*, actually made the sale. Liability therefore turns on whether *D* directed or acquiesced in *S*'s overcharging of *P*, the prosecutrix. The prosecution offers evidence of an offer made by *D* to *P* to refund the overcharge. *D* objects.

What ruling and why? What other information might the judge want to have before making this decision? What other policies besides that in favor of extrajudicial settlement of disputes are relevant in this context?

3. Proof of Insurance

FRE 411
Liability Insurance

Evidence that a person was or was not insured against liability is not admissible upon the issue whether he acted negligently or otherwise wrongfully. This rule does not require the exclusion of evidence of insurance against liability when offered for another purpose, such as proof of agency, ownership, or control, or bias or prejudice of a witness.

Problem I-35
The Deep Pocket Approach

(1) P v. D Company for damages suffered by P while he was working at a pressing machine at D Company, his employer. P's arm became caught in the machine and eventually had to be amputated. P alleges negligence in the maintenance of the press. During P's cross-examination of W, the general manager of the D Company plant, P's attorney asks W if D Company carries insurance against such accidents and, if so, in what amount. The attorney for D Company objects. What ruling and why?

(2) During the cross-examination of Dr. X, another witness for D Company, who is called as an expert to testify on the operation and maintenance of the presses, P's attorney asks X if he has been retained by the Casualty Insurance Company. D Company's attorney objects. P makes an offer of proof that if allowed to testify, Dr. X will state that he has been retained by the Casualty Insurance Company and, further, that Casualty has insured D Company for losses of this sort up to $3,000,000. What ruling and why?

Problem I-36
Hit and Run

D is accused of leaving the scene of an accident. The testimony at his trial shows that, upon leaving work, P discovered her parked car to be dented along the side; W testifies that he saw D's car skid, thump P's parked car, and then drive away. D admits skidding toward P's car but denies striking it. At trial, D offers to prove that he is covered by insurance for such damage. P objects. What ruling and why?

Problem I-37
Absence of Coverage

P v. D Company for damages. While in D Company's employ, P was directing the backing up of a D Company truck which "jerked back" and crushed P's arm against a loading dock. At trial, P's attorney asks P on direct examination whether he received any Worker's Compensation benefits. D objects. During D's case-in-chief, D's attorney askes W, the president of D Company, whether D Company is insured for claims such as these. *P* objects. In each case the answer would be "no." How should the court rule?

4. Pleas and Related Statements

FRE 410
Inadmissibility of Pleas, Offers of Pleas,
Plea Discussions,
and Related Statements

Except as otherwise provided in this rule, evidence of the following is not, in any civil or criminal proceeding, admissible against the defendant who made the plea or was a participant in the plea discussions:

(1) a plea of guilty which was later withdrawn;

(2) a plea of nolo contendere;

(3) any statement made in the course of any proceedings under Rule 11 of the Federal Rules of Criminal Procedure or comparable state procedure regarding either of the foregoing pleas; or

(4) any statement made in the course of plea discussions with an attorney for the prosecuting authority which do not result in a plea of guilty or which result in a plea of guilty later withdrawn.

However, such a statement is admissible (i) in any proceeding wherein another statement made in the course of the same plea or plea discussions has been introduced and the statement ought in fairness be considered contemporaneously with it, or (ii) in a criminal proceeding for perjury or false statement if the statement was made by the defendant under oath, on the record and in the presence of counsel.

Problem I-38
Plea Bargain

D was arrested on heroin distribution charges by DEA Agent *A*, who gave him *Miranda* warnings. *D* then informed *A* that he had cooperated with the government in the past and would be willing to do so in the future. In the course of this conversation *D* made incriminating statements relating to the crime for which he had been arrested. Later that day *D* met in a prearraignment conference with Assistant United States Attorney *B* and had a similar conversation. After his arraignment *D* returned to DEA headquarters with a lawyer to meet with *A*. *D* again offered to cooperate, and *A* suggested that *D* contact Agent *C*. *D* thereafter contacted *C*, offered to cooperate, and made some incriminatory statements. At no time during any of these conversations did *D* explicitly offer to plead guilty or request a concession from the government.

Which parts, if any, of the conversations related above should be excluded under Rule 410? What additional information might assist you in making this determination?

Problem I-39
Is Turnabout Fair Play?

D is charged with the sale of a controlled substance — heroin. At trial, *D* calls *W*, who was formerly the Assistant United States Attorney in charge of the case but is now in private practice. Through *W*, *D*'s attorney seeks to show that *W* offered *D* the opportunity to plead to possession, rather than sale, in exchange for *D*'s testimony against others. The prosecution objects. What ruling and why?

CHAPTER II

Character and Credibility

This chapter explores the rules relating to proof of character. When trying to determine whether a person did something, it is often helpful (relevant) to know whether he or she is the *kind of person* who would do such a thing. This is evidence of character used to prove action "in conformity therewith," in the phrase of Rule 404(a). Although perhaps relevant, evidence about a person's character raises severe problems of prejudice. Learning that a defendant is a confirmed thief, for example, might make it seem more likely that he was guilty of theft in the specific instance being litigated. However, it could also reduce the jury's concern about mistakenly finding the defendant guilty, thereby altering the effective standard of proof.

Opening the subject of character to proof also risks wasting time with marginally relevant evidence. How better to show someone's character (and thereby to show action in conformity therewith) than to introduce evidence about those episodes of the person's past life that most effectively reveal his character? Yet to expand the focus of the trial from the litigated event to include a variety of other factual episodes in the life of the defendant or witness is to vastly expand the scope of inquiry.

These considerations — prejudice and waste of time — leading to constraints on proving character, however, are opposed by considerations of fairness to a defendant who wants to prove his innocence by showing that he is *not* the sort of person who would commit such a crime. Such evidence, it might be argued, could tend to raise the effective standard of proof. But what would this mean in the criminal context, where proof of guilt must be beyond reasonable doubt? Such evidence also might waste some time, but this is a weak objection both from the viewpoint of a defendant trying to prove himself innocent and from that of the state trying to justify incarcerating the defendant.

These cross-currents are typical of those that swirl around the issues of character. The result at common law was an elaborate set of rules that sometimes permitted proof of character and sometimes barred it. The rules drew a major distinction between evidence of character offered to prove action in conformity therewith *on the occasion of the litigated event* (did he do it?) and evidence of the character of a witness to show action in conformity therewith *while testifying at trial* (is he lying?). Moreover, in instances where character could be proved, the common law rules often constrained the method of proof, insisting on time-saving but perhaps ineffective modes of proof in some instances, allowing effective but perhaps inefficient modes in others. Character to show action in conformity therewith could be proved, if at all, only by evidence of reputation, not by evidence of the specific acts in the person's life. By contrast, when a person's character was itself the subject of litigation (for example, in libel suits), proof could be by specific acts.

Justice Jackson, in Michelson v. United States, 335 U.S. 469 (1948), page 115, below, described the character rules as "archaic, paradoxical and full of compromises and compensations by which an irrational advantage to one side is offset by a poorly reasoned counter privilege to the other." But he hesitated to tinker with it. "To pull one misshapen stone out of the grotesque structure," he said, "is more likely simply to upset its present balance between adverse interests than to establish a rational edifice."

The draftsmen of the Federal Rules had the opportunity to propose a complete overhaul; they chose not to. Changes have been made, yet the overall structure remains an elaborate compromise, keyed to considerations of prejudice and remoteness. It is sensitive to the differing functions of civil and criminal litigation, to the differing interests of prosecution and defense, and to the differing contests of direct and cross-examination. Three years after the promulgation of the Federal Rules, Congress did make a major change, specifically with regard to proof of character of the victim in sexual assault cases (Rule 412), but this may have been more a result of changes in social and political outlook than concern for logic in the law of evidence.

As you explore and try to integrate Federal Rules 404, 405, 406, 412, 607, 608, and 609, consider whether Justice Jackson's eloquent description is fair. Is the structure of these rules both grotesque and irrational, or merely grotesque?

A. The Propensity Rule

PEOPLE v. ZACKOWITZ
254 N.Y. 192, 172 N.E. 466 (1930)

CARDOZO, C.J. On November 10, 1929, shortly after midnight, the defendant in Kings county shot Frank Coppola and killed him without justification or excuse. A crime is admitted. What is doubtful is the degree only.

Four young men, of whom Coppola was one, were at work repairing an automobile in a Brooklyn street. A woman, the defendant's wife, walked by on the opposite side. One of the men spoke to her insultingly, or so at least she understood him. The defendant, who had dropped behind to buy a newspaper, came up to find his wife in tears. He was told she had been insulted, though she did not then repeat the words. Enraged, he stepped across the street and upbraided the offenders with words of coarse profanity. He informed them, so the survivors testify, that "if they did not get out of there in five minutes, he would come back and bump them all off." Rejoining his wife, he walked with her to their apartment house located close at hand. He was heated with liquor which he had been drinking at a dance. Within the apartment he induced her to tell him what the insulting words had been. A youth had asked her to lie with him, and had offered her $2. With rage aroused again, the defendant went back to the scene of the insult and found the four young men still working at the car. In a statement to the police, he said that he had armed himself at the apartment with a .25-caliber automatic pistol. In his testimony at the trial he said that this pistol had been in his pocket all the evening. Words and blows followed, and then a shot. The defendant kicked Coppola in the stomach. There is evidence that Coppola went for him with a wrench. The pistol came from the pocket, and from the pistol a single shot, which did its deadly work. The defendant walked away and at the corner met his wife who had followed him from the home. The two took a taxicab to Manhattan, where they spent the rest of the night at the dwelling of a friend. On the way the defendant threw his pistol into the river. He was arrested on January 7, 1930, about two months following the crime.

At the trial the vital question was the defendant's state of mind at the moment of the homicide. Did he shoot with a deliberate and premeditated design to kill? Was he so inflamed by drink or by anger or by both combined that, though he knew the nature of his act, he was the prey to sudden impulse, the fury of the fleeting moment? People v. Caruso, 246 N.Y. 437, 446, 159 N.E. 390. If he went forth from his apartment with a preconceived design to kill, how is it that he failed to shoot at once? How to reconcile such a design with the drawing of the pistol later in the heat and rage of an affray? These and like questions the jurors were to ask themselves and answer before measuring the defendant's guilt. Answers consistent with guilt in its highest grade can reasonably be made. Even so, the line between impulse and deliberation is too narrow and elusive to make the answers wholly clear. The sphygmograph records with graphic certainty the fluctuations of the pulse. There is no instrument yet invented that records with equal certainty the fluctuations of the mind. At least, if such an instrument exists, it was not working at midnight in the Brooklyn street when Coppola and the defendant came together in a chance affray. With only the rough and ready tests supplied by their experience of life, the jurors were to look into the workings of another's mind, and discover its capacities and disabilities, its urges and inhibitions, in moments of intense excitement. Delicate enough and subtle is the inquiry, even in the most favorable conditions, with every warping influence excluded. There must be no blurring of the issues by evidence illegally admitted and carrying with it in its admission an appeal to prejudice and passion.

Evidence charged with that appeal was, we think, admitted here. Not only was it admitted, and this under objection and exception, but the changes were rung upon it by prosecutor and judge. Almost at the opening of the trial the people began the endeavor to load the defendant down with the burden of an evil character. He was to be put before the jury as a man of murderous disposition. To that end they were allowed to prove that at the time of the encounter and at that of his arrest he had in his apartment, kept there in a radio box, three pistols and a tear-gas gun. There was no claim that he had brought these weapons out at the time of the affray, no claim that with any of them he had discharged the fatal shot. He could not have done so, for they were all of different caliber. The end to be served by laying the weapons before the jury was something very different. The end was to bring persuasion that here was a man of vicious and dangerous propensities, who because of those propensities was more likely to kill with deliberate and premeditated design than a man of irreproachable life and amiable manners. Indeed, this is the very ground on which the introduction of the evidence is now explained and defended. The district attorney tells us in his brief that the possession of the weapons characterized the defendant as "a desperate type of criminal," a "person criminally inclined." The dissenting opinion, if it puts the argument less bluntly, leaves the substance of the thought unchanged. "Defendant was presented to the jury as a man having dangerous weapons in his possession, making a selection therefrom and going forth to put into execution his threats to kill." The weapons were not brought by the defendant to the scene of the encounter. They were left in his apartment where they were incapable of harm. In such circumstances, ownership of the weapons, if it has any relevance at all, has relevance only as indicating a general disposition to make use of them thereafter, and a general disposition to make use of them thereafter is without relevance except as indicating a "desperate type of criminal," a criminal affected with a murderous propensity.

We are asked to extenuate the error by calling it an incident; what was proved may have an air of innocence if it is styled the history of the crime. The virus of the ruling is not so easily extracted. Here was no passing reference to something casually brought out in the narrative of the killing, as if an admission had been proved against the defendant that he had picked one weapon out of several. Here in the forefront of the trial, immediately following the statement of the medical examiner, testimony was admitted that weapons, not the instruments of the killing, had been discovered by the police in the apartment of the killer; and the weapons with great display were laid before the jury, marked as exhibits, and thereafter made the subject of animated argument. Room for doubt there is none that in the thought of the jury, as in that of the district attorney, the tendency of the whole performance was to characterize the defendant as a man murderously inclined. The purpose was not disguised. From the opening to the verdict, it was flaunted and avowed.

If a murderous propensity may be proved against a defendant as one of the tokens of his guilt, a rule of criminal evidence, long believed to be of fundamental importance for the protection of the innocent, must be first declared away. Fundamental hitherto has been the rule that character is never an issue in a criminal prosecution unless the defendant chooses to make it one. Wigmore, Evidence, vol. 1, §§55, 192. In a very real sense a defendant starts his life afresh when he stands before a jury, a prisoner at the bar. There has been a homicide in a public place. The killer admits the killing, but urges self-defense and sudden impulse. Inflexibly the law has set its face against the endeavor to fasten guilt upon him by proof of character or experience predisposing to an act of crime. The endeavor has been often made, but always it has failed. At times, when the issue has been self-defense, testimony has been admitted as to the murderous propensity of the deceased, the victim of the homicide, but never of such a propensity on the part of the killer. The principle back of the exclusion is one, not of logic, but of policy. There may be cogency in the argument that a quarrelsome defendant is more likely to start a quarrel than one of milder type, a man of dangerous mode of life more likely than a shy recluse. The law is not blind to this, but equally it is not blind to the peril to the innocent if character is accepted as probative of crime. "The natural and inevitable tendency of the tribunal — whether judge or jury — is to give excessive weight to the vicious record of crime thus exhibited, and either to allow it to bear too strongly on the present charge, or to take the proof of it as justifying a condemnation irrespective of guilt of the present charge." Wigmore, Evidence, vol. 1, §194, and cases cited.

A different question would be here if the pistols had been bought in expectation of this particular encounter. They would then have been admissible as evidence of preparation and design. A different question would be here if they were so connected with the crime as to identify the perpetrator, if he had dropped them, for example, at the scene of the affray. They would then have been admissible as tending to implicate the possessor (if identity was disputed), no matter what the opprobrium attached to his possession. Different, also, would be the question if the defendant had been shown to have gone forth from the apartment with all the weapons on his person. To be armed from head to foot at the very moment of an encounter may be a circumstance worthy to be consid-

ered, like acts of preparation generally, as a proof of preconceived design. There can be no such implication from the ownership of weapons
which one leaves behind at home.

The endeavor was to generate an atmosphere of professional criminality. It was an endeavor the more unfair in that, apart from the suspicion attaching to the possession of these weapons, there is nothing to
mark the defendant as a man of evil life. He was not in crime as a
business. He did not shoot as a bandit shoots in the hope of wrongful
gain. He was engaged in a decent calling, an optician regularly employed, without criminal record, or criminal associates. If his own testimony be true, he had gathered these weapons together as curios, a
collection that interested and amused him. Perhaps his explanation of
their ownership is false. There is nothing stronger than mere suspicion
to guide us to an answer. Whether the explanation be false or true, he
should not have been driven by the people to the necessity of offering it.
Brought to answer a specific charge, and to defend himself against it, he
was placed in a position where he had to defend himself against another,
more general and sweeping. He was made to answer to the charge,
pervasive and poisonous even if insidious and covert, that he was a man
of murderous heart, of criminal disposition. . . .

The judgment of conviction should be reversed, and a new trial ordered.

POUND, J. (dissenting). . . . Nearly two months after the killing of
Coppola, the police entered defendant's home in connection with his
arrest and found there concealed in a box in the radio three revolvers
and a tear-gas bomb, together with a supply of cartridges suitable for use
both in the revolvers and the bomb. Defendant had in his confession,
which was received without objection, admitted that he had these
weapons in his possession at the time of the killing. The .25-caliber
automatic was not among them. Defendant says that he threw it away
after he shot Coppola. The people, as a part of their principal case,
introduced these articles in evidence over defendant's objection and
exception. This is the only ruling by which the question of error in law is
presented on this appeal. No objection was made to the summation by
the district attorney nor to any specific instructions by the court. The
possession of these dangerous weapons was a separate crime. Penal Law,
§1897. The broad question is whether it had any connection with the
crime charged. The substantial rights of the defendant must be protected. Where the penalty is death, we may grant a new trial if justice
requires it, even though no exception was taken in the court below. Code
Cr. Proc. §528.

The people may not prove against a defendant crimes not alleged in
the indictment committed on other occasions than the crime charged as

aiding the proofs that he is guilty of the crime charged unless such proof tends to establish (1) motive; (2) intent; (3) absence of mistake or accident; (4) a common scheme or plan embracing the commission of two or more crimes so related to each other that proof of the one tends to establish the other; (5) the identity of the person charged with the commission of the crime on trial. These exceptions are stated generally and not with categorical precision and may not be all-inclusive. None of them apply here, nor were the weapons offered under an exception to the general rule. They were offered as a part of the transaction itself. The accused was tried only for the crime charged. The real question is whether the matter relied on has such a connection with the crime charged as to be admissible on any ground. If so, the fact that it constitutes another distinct crime does not render it inadmissible. The rule laid down in the *Molineux* case has never been applied to prevent the people from proving all the elements of the offense charged, although separate crimes are included in such proof. Thus in this case no question is made as to the separate crime of illegal possession of the weapon with which the killing was done. It was "a part of the history of the case" having a distinct relation to and bearing upon the facts connected with the killing.

As the district attorney argues in his brief, if defendant had been arrested at the time of the killing, and these weapons had been found on his person, the people would not have been barred from proving the fact, and the further fact that they were near by in his apartment should not preclude the proof as bearing on the entire deed of which the act charged forms a part. Defendant was presented to the jury as a man having dangerous weapons in his possession, making a selection therefrom, and going forth to put into execution his threats to kill; not as a man of a dangerous disposition in general, but as one who, having an opportunity to select a weapon to carry out his threats, proceeded to do so. . . .

The judgment of conviction should be affirmed.

How would you state the general rule, as relied on by Chief Justice Cardozo, regarding proof of character by the prosecution in criminal cases? Is such evidence excluded because it is irrelevant? Would it have made any difference in this case if Zackowitz had taken the other guns with him to the affray? Why? Would it have made any difference if Zackowitz had been convicted of illegally possessing the other guns? Why? How would you state the rule as relied upon by Justice Pound? Would Pound's rationale for admitting the "other guns" evidence annihilate the propensity rule? With which statement and application of the rule do you agree?

FRE 404
Character Evidence Not Admissible to Prove Conduct; Exceptions; Other Crimes

(a) *Character evidence generally.* Evidence of a person's character or a trait of his character is not admissible for the purpose of proving that he acted in conformity therewith on a particular occasion, except:

(1) *Character of accused.* Evidence of a pertinent trait of his character offered by an accused, or by the prosecution to rebut the same;

(2) *Character of victim.* Evidence of a pertinent trait of character of the victim of the crime offered by an accused, or by the prosecution to rebut the same, or evidence of a character trait of peacefulness of the victim offered by the prosecution in a homicide case to rebut evidence that the victim was the first aggressor;

(3) *Character of witness.* Evidence of the character of a witness, as provided in Rules 607, 608, and 609.

(b) *Other crimes, wrongs, or acts.* Evidence of other crimes, wrongs, or acts is not admissible to prove the character of a person in order to show that he acted in conformity therewith. It may, however, be admissible for other purposes, such as proof of motive, opportunity, intent, preparation, plan, knowledge, identity, or absence of mistake or accident.

Problem II-1
A Return to the Scene of the Crime

Charge: theft of valuable documents, coins, and case from the heavy metal safe in Attorney *A*'s office on June 1. Modus operandi: opening the combination lock and absconding with the contents.

At *D*'s trial the state offers to prove that on May 1, *D* broke into Attorney *A*'s office, opened the safe, and stole some bonds from the safe. *D* objects on the basis of the propensity rule.

What ruling and why? If *D*'s objection is overruled, what type of limiting charge should *D* request?   *Admit*

Problem II-2
The Case of the Hidden Observer

On June 1, *D* murdered *V* by shooting him through the head with a .357-caliber magnum, "the most powerful handgun made." Bill and Charles observed this crime. *D* knows that Bill observed the crime, but Charles was a hidden observer and *D* does not know that Charles observed the crime. On July 1 Bill's body is found stuffed in a dumpster in a back alley. On August 1, *D* is charged with the murder of Bill. At *D*'s trial for the murder of Bill, the state offers Charles to testify to *D*'s murder of *V* on June 1.

What should the court's ruling be on *D*'s objection that this evidence is irrelevant, immaterial, and prejudicial and that it violates the propensity rule? If *D*'s objection is overruled, what should be requested?

Problem II-3
"Money or Death"

Charge: robbery of the First National Bank in City *A* on June 1. Modus operandi: handing the teller a note with a death threat on it that says, "Money or death: The choice is yours," accompanied by pictures of a dead body under the word "death" and a live, smiling person under the word "money." At trial the state offers to prove through the teller of the First Federal Bank in City *B* that on February 1 he was robbed in the same manner by *D* — i.e., that he was handed a deposit slip with the very same death threat written on it. The state also offers several other bank tellers from different banks to testify similarly.

D objects to the tellers' testimony. What ruling and why?

UNITED STATES v. DANZEY
594 F.2d 905 (2d Cir.), cert. denied, 441 U.S. 951 (1979)

OAKES, J. . . .

THE BANK ROBBERY

The Community National Bank and Trust Co. is located at the corner of Clove Road and Niagara Street in Staten Island, New York. At about 9:30 A.M. on July 30, 1977, a young woman who was sitting in a car outside the bank waiting for her sister to transact business inside observed two men wearing ski masks and gloves getting out of a white car with a black vinyl top bearing New Jersey license plates. One man carried a bag and a gun while the other, who was "slumped over," wore sneakers and carried a bag. A third man sat in the driver's seat. The two masked men walked into the bank, remained inside about three minutes, rushed out, and re-entered the white car which then sped away from the bank. The young woman's sister, who was in the bank, was ordered to the floor several times by the shorter of the two men from whose voice she concluded that he was black; the man ultimately knocked her to her knees. She also observed the second masked man, the taller of the two, run into the bank, "hunched over like a monkey or an ape," vault the teller's counter carrying a bag, take the entire money trays from two of the tellers, and stuff the booty into a canvas bag. He revaulted the teller's counter and left with the shorter man. None of the bank employees or the two sisters could identify anyone as the bank robbers.

However, another young woman, Sylvia Csuros, a nineteen-year-old college student, had been studying in her mother's bedroom in their second floor apartment located only about two blocks from the bank. The corner apartment overlooked Grand and Dudley Avenues, quiet residential streets in Staten Island. Shortly after 9:00 A.M. on July 30, 1977, a bright and sunny morning, from a window facing Grand Avenue Csuros saw a large gold car followed closely by a smaller white car speed down Grand Avenue and turn right onto Dudley. She left her mother's bedroom and went into the living room which faced both Grand and Dudley Avenues and with her view unobstructed observed the gold car park across the narrow street below the living room window and the white car park directly behind the gold car. She then saw a man emerge from the street side of the gold car carrying a brown paper bag. She watched him walk in the street back to the white car and either toss or pass the brown bag into the front seat of the white car, then return to the gold car. She then saw a taller man exit from the driver's side of the gold car. She described him as black and tall and said that he wore a wig, a bright orange shirt, and elevated shoes. The man walked along the sidewalk to the white car and got into the front seat of the white car on the driver's side, causing the original driver, whom Ms. Csuros never saw, to slide over to the passenger side. Ms. Csuros then saw the first man, who had tossed the brown bag into the front seat of the white car, return from the gold car to the white car and enter it by the rear door. The white car drove off, shortly after returned, and the occupants transferred back to the gold car and drove off at a high rate of speed. . . .

Similar Acts Evidence

Appellant Gore's only argument is that the Government's introduction into evidence of his admissions of fifteen similar criminal acts, consisting of other bank robberies, was highly prejudicial and deprived him of a fair trial. This evidence was admitted under Fed. R. Evid. 404(b) to show identity. The trial court found on the basis of the Government's offer of proof that appellant Gore's similar crimes had such a distinctive modus operandi that the evidence could be so admitted.

Appellant Gore's contention that the evidence was more prejudicial than it was probative borders on the frivolous. Appellant concedes, as he must, that the evidence was relevant. By Gore's own statements he had a modus operandi, practically a signature, to his robberies; according to the testimony at trial of the FBI agent to whom appellant made the statements, "He said that he had a certain trademark in robbing a bank." Cars would be stolen for a bank robbery late the night before or early on the morning of the robbery. If the "getaway" car was dark, the "switch" car would be light and vice versa. The cars would be early 1970's Fords, the easiest to steal. They would be stolen by pulling out the ignition with a "dent puller." The getaway car, used at the bank, was always a stolen car, while the switch car was sometimes legitimate. The robberies occurred early in the morning between 9:00 and 11:00. Gore said that he always wore a ski mask, gloves, and two sets of clothes, one of which he would remove after leaving the bank. Three or four men were always involved in the robbery. Gore himself would run into the bank in a crouched position carrying a paper, plastic, or canvas bag; vault over the counter; remove the entire teller tray along with the money; and put the trays and the money into his bag. One accomplice would be the getaway driver outside; another would stand near the door, brandish a gun or a sawed-off shotgun (at his preference), and order everyone in the bank to lie on the floor. Some of his robberies included a second vaulter, that is to say, a fourth accomplice, although only three were involved in the robbery of the Community National Bank. After taking the teller trays, Gore would vault back over the counter and run from the bank, again in a crouched position. The robbers would drive from the bank a few blocks to where they had previously left the switch car. There they would abandon the getaway car, drive in the switch car to another area, abandon that car, and then split up.

This evidence was so plainly relevant as to be classic similar act evidence admissible under the rule and under our cases to show a modus operandi. United States v. Hayes, 553 F.2d 824, 828-29 (2d Cir.), cert. denied, 434 U.S. 867 (1977) (proof of identity by similar bank robberies). The other bank robberies had so many of the same features as readily to satisfy any requirement of United States v. Corey, 566 F.2d 429, 431 (2d Cir. 1978) (a case involving proof of guilty knowledge), that there be a "close parallel" between the crime charged and the prior act shown; indeed, the proof here went further, since appellant himself admitted he had a "trademark." Corey also stresses the significance of time lapse between the indicted charge and the similar act. Id. at 432. Here the other robberies to which Gore admitted occurred within four months before and three months after the robbery of the Community National Bank; they were thus closely proximate in time.

But appellant Gore argues that, even though the evidence was relevant, the trial court was required to weigh against the probative value of the evidence the possibility of unfair prejudice. Fed. R. Evid. 403. He also objects because the trial court ruled that it would admit the evidence at the very beginning of the trial, before any witnesses had testified. He directs our attention to the cautionary dictum of United States v. Leonard, 524 F.2d 1076, 1092 (2d Cir. 1975), cert. denied, 425 U.S. 958 (1976), that it is usually preferable for the trial court to await the conclusion of the defendant's case before admitting similar act evidence, a suggestion that was stated more imperatively in United States v. Benedetto, 571 F.2d 1246, 1249 (2d Cir. 1978). See also United States v. Halper, 590 F.2d 422, 432 (2d Cir. 1978). The rationale for this limitation is that the court will best be able to judge the prosecutor's need for the evidence after the defense; at that time the court may best weigh the probative value of the evidence against its prejudicial effect. Here, however, it was abundantly clear to the trial judge before the case began that the only major issue was the identity of the robbers, that is, did Gore and/or Danzey commit this robbery. There was no way for Gore to remove the identity issue from the case short of Gore's admitting his participation in the robbery and claiming some other defense such as duress.

Were the *Leonard* dictum applicable, however, the Government would have had no case. Unless this evidence were admissible during the Government's case, the Government might well be without any proof whatsoever of identity, a crucial issue. It was the only proof, and it was surely highly relevant proof, to take the case to the jury since the only other evidence linking Gore to the crime was a fingerprint on a paper bag found in the getaway car, allegedly used to carry money taken in the robbery. Thus in this case, because the defense rested without putting on a case, the evidence of Gore's other crimes, if it could only have been admitted at the close of the defense case, would never have been admitted; the case would have ended with the doing of the act and the defendant's responsibility for it unproven.

Does this mean that we must reject that dictum or that the evidence was inadmissible? We think not, and we believe that we can demonstrate this if we elaborate upon the distinction between admitting similar acts to show intent on the one hand and to show design, system, or plan on the other. Our cases have not expressly made this distinction, one made by the leading text-writers. Wigmore's treatise points out that similar acts are admitted to prove *intent* on the basis that from the point of view of the doctrine of chances, the element of innocence is eliminated by multiplying instances of the same result. That is to say, "similar results do not usually occur through abnormal causes"; and the recurrence of a similar result in the form of an unlawful act tends to negative accident, inadvertence, duress, good faith, self-defense, or other innocent mental state and tends to establish to at least some extent the presence of criminal intent. The act itself is assumed to be done, either because the defendant has conceded doing the act or because the court instructs the jury not to consider the evidence until they find that the defendant did the act and they proceed to determine intent. See generally 2 J. Wigmore, Evidence §302, at 196-201 (3d ed. 1940).

When, however, the very doing of the act charged is still to be proved, one of the evidentiary facts receivable is the person's design, system, or plan to do it as demonstrated by his having committed other acts almost identical to the act charged. See 1 id. §102; 2 id. §304. See also 2 Weinstein's Evidence ¶404[09], at 404-57 to -66. By "a concurrence of common features . . . the various acts are naturally to be explained as caused by a general plan of which they are the individual manifestations." 2 Wigmore, supra, §304, at 202 (emphasis omitted). In this case, for example, there is such a high degree of similarity between the bank robberies admitted to and this one that the other crimes lead to the logical inference, by virtue of the combination of common features, that a common plan or design was at the basis for all the robberies and hence that it was appellant Gore who committed this robbery.

Drawing the distinction that Wigmore and McCormick . . . draw helps explain why the government should ordinarily be permitted to introduce similar act evidence in its case-in-chief if the evidence is relevant to identity (used as a shorthand for referring to proof of the doing of the criminal act by this defendant), but not, see *Leonard*, supra, if the evidence is relevant merely to intent. At a minimum, the Government must prove that this defendant committed the crime for which he is on trial, so that identity evidence may properly constitute part of its case-in-chief even if there will be a defense case. Compare United States v. O'Connor, 580 F.2d 38 (2d Cir. 1978).

Proof of intent on the other hand may be inferable from the act itself. In such case, unless the defense specifically raises lack of intent as a defense, the prejudice to the defendant of evidence of similar acts may outweigh its probative value. And even where the crime requires specific criminal intent not readily inferable, the defendant might not raise lack of intent as a defense, or he might stipulate to the existence of intent if the jury finds the other elements of the offense.

Thus, to sum up, where, as here, similar acts are offered to prove design, from which the jury could infer that appellant Gore committed the particular bank robbery in question, the *Leonard* dictum as to awaiting the conclusion of the defense case is inapplicable.

Of course this evidence is prejudicial — it is highly prejudicial because it both tends to prove the commission of the criminal act in issue, as well as to show the defendant's bad, or criminal, character. But common design evidence is always highly prejudicial. The *undue* prejudice it engenders may be guarded against in only one way: by an instruction — as was given here — to the effect that the jury is not to consider the evidence as going to the character of the accused but only as going to identity. It may well be that the jury cannot make this distinction in its collective mind. If that is so it is unfortunate, but it happens all the time — critical evidence may well be prejudicial, but it is admitted because it is so clearly relevant and so highly critical: Lady MacBeth's "damned spot" would have been admissible. . . .

Problem II-4
Res Gestae

(1) Charge: violation of federal firearms statute by unlawfully receiving a firearm transported interstate after *D* had previously been convicted of a crime punishable by more than one year in prison. At trial, *W*, a druggist, testified for the prosecution that *D* had entered his pharmacy with a prescription that *W* recognized as forged. When *W* asked *D* to remain in the store so the police could check the prescription, *D* bolted, and *W* gave chase. During the chase *D* dropped the drugs and gun over the side of a wall. *D* objected to the evidence of the alleged forged prescription.

(2) Charge: illegal sale of narcotics. At trial a state narcotics agent is offered by the prosecution to testify that he and another agent had visited *D*'s house together and that each had purchased a can containing some substance, which the agents believed was marijuana. *D* objects to the testimony concerning the sale to the other agent.

Is the evidence in either case admissible under Rule 404? 403? Compare the treatment of the "other guns" evidence in *Zackowitz*, supra, with the "other crimes" evidence in this problem. Under what theory would admission of this evidence in these two cases be consistent with the propensity rule? Do you think Justice Cardozo would have held that the admission of the "other crimes" evidence in these cases constituted reversible error?

TUCKER v. STATE
82 Nev. 127, 412 P.2d 970 (1966)

THOMPSON, J. On May 7, 1957, Horace Tucker telephoned the police station and asked a detective to come to the Tucker home in North Las Vegas. Upon arrival the detective observed that Tucker had been drinking, was unshaven, and looked tired. Tucker led the detective to the dining room where one, Earl Kaylor, was dead on the floor. Kaylor had been shot several times. When asked what had happened, Tucker said that he (Tucker) had been sleeping in the bedroom, awakened, and walked to the dining room where he noticed Kaylor lying on the floor. Upon ascertaining that Kaylor was dead, Tucker telephoned the police station. He denied having killed Kaylor. A grand jury conducted an extensive investigation. Fifty-three witnesses were examined. However, an indictment was not returned as the grand jury deemed the evidence inconclusive. No one, including Tucker, has ever been charged with that killing.

On October 8, 1963, Horace Tucker telephoned the police and asked a sergeant to come to the Tucker home in North Las Vegas; that there was an old man dead there. Upon arrival the sergeant noticed that Tucker had been drinking. The body of Omar Evans was dead on the couch in the living room. Evans had been shot. Tucker stated that he (Tucker) had been asleep, awakened, and found Evans dead on the couch. Subsequently Tucker was charged with the murder of Evans. A jury convicted him of second degree murder and the court pronounced judgment and the statutory sentence of imprisonment for a term of "not less than 10 years, which term may be extended to life."

At trial, over vehement objection, the court allowed the state to introduce evidence of the Kaylor homicide. The court reasoned that the circumstances of the deaths of Kaylor and Evans were sufficiently parallel to render admissible evidence of the Kaylor homicide to prove that Tucker intended to kill Evans, that the killing of Evans was part of a common scheme or plan in Tucker's mind, and also to negate any defense of accidental death. These limited purposes, for which the evidence was received and could be considered by the jury, were specified by court instruction as required by case law. See Brown v. State, 81 Nev. 397, 404 P.2d 428 (1965); State v. Monahan, 50 Nev. 27, 249 P. 566 (1926); State v. McFarlin, 41 Nev. 486, 172 P. 371 (1918). We rule that evidence of the Kaylor homicide was not admissible for any purpose and that prejudicial error occurred when the court permitted the jury to hear and consider it. . . .

Whenever the problem of evidence of other offenses confronts a trial court, grave considerations attend. The danger of prejudice to the defendant is ever present, for the jury may convict now because he has escaped punishment in the past. Nor has the defendant been advised that he must be prepared to meet extraneous charges. Indeed, as our system of justice is accusatorial rather than inquisitorial, there is much to be said for the notion that the prosecution must prove the defendant guilty of the specific crime charged without resort to past conduct. Thus when the other offense sought to be introduced falls within an exception to the rule of exclusion, the trial court should be convinced that the probative value of such evidence outweighs its prejudicial effect. Brown v. State, supra; Nester v. State, supra; State v. Nystedt, 79 Nev. 24, 377 P.2d 929 (1963). The reception of such evidence is justified by necessity and, if other evidence has substantially established the element of the crime involved (motive, intent, identity, absence of mistake, etc.), the probative value of showing another offense is diminished, and the trial court should rule it inadmissible even though relevant and within an exception to the rule of exclusion.

In the case at hand we need not consider whether evidence of the Kaylor homicide comes within one of the exceptions to the rule of exclusion, because the first requisite for admissibility is wholly absent — namely, that the defendant on trial committed the independent offense sought to be introduced. There is nothing in this record to establish that Tucker killed Kaylor. Anonymous crimes can have no relevance in deciding whether the defendant committed the crime with which he is charged. Kaylor's assailant remains unknown. A fortiori, evidence of that crime cannot be received in the trial for the murder of Evans.

We have not before had occasion to discuss the quantum of proof needed to establish that the defendant on trial committed the separate offense sought to be introduced. Here there was only conjecture and suspicion, aroused by the fact that Kaylor was found dead in Tucker's home. We now adopt the rule that, before evidence of a collateral offense is admissible for any purpose, the prosecution must first establish by plain, clear and convincing evidence, that the defendant committed that offense. Labiosa v. Govt. of the Canal Zone, 198 F.2d 282 (Cir. 5, 1952); Gart v. United States, 294 F. 66 (Cir. 8, 1923); Paris v. United States, 260 F. 529 (Cir. 8, 1919); cases collected annot., 3 A.L.R. 784. Fundamental fairness demands this standard in order to preclude verdicts which might otherwise rest on false assumptions. . . .

Reversed and remanded for new trial.

What quantum of proof of other crimes should be required when the state seeks to admit such proof under one of the exceptions to the general rule of exclusion? What is "plain, clear and convincing evidence"? Is it more than a preponderance? How much more? As much as proof beyond a reasonable doubt? Is defendant's connection with the other crime a jury question or a question for the judge? Does it matter which exception to the propensity rule is called into play? What do the Federal Rules provide on this question?

What effect should acquittal of a charge of an alleged prior crime have on the admissibility of evidence of that prior crime when it is offered to show a common scheme or plan at a subsequent trial on another offense? Are res judicata or double jeopardy principles applicable? Does it depend on the quantum of proof of the prior crime chosen as the standard for proof of prior crimes under the propensity rule exceptions?

PEOPLE v. MASSEY
196 Cal. App. 2d 230, 16 Cal. Rptr. 402 (1961)

KAUFMAN, J. The record reveals the following facts: about 4:30 A.M. on the morning of May 2, 1960, Mrs. Sarah Finley, who lived alone in a one-room apartment, was awakened when she felt "a terrific jerk." She saw a Negro man hovering over her face and screamed. The intruder hurried to the open window, leaped out and ran off. Mrs. Finley took a pill for her heart condition and telephoned for help. The police arrived and discovered that $13 was missing from her purse, as well as a few other small items from the apartment. A large rectangular piece had been cut out of the sheet on Mrs. Finley's bed, probably with the scissors on the nearby table. Later the same day, Mrs. Finley's apartment was dusted for latent fingerprints by an officer from the crime laboratory. A fingerprint was found on the inside of the window in Mrs. Finley's room and a knife outside the window.

Mrs. Finley had lived for several years in the apartment on the first floor of the Gaylord Hotel at 620 Jones Street in San Francisco. Her apartment had only two windows which overlooked the porch and the hotel next door. On the prior evening, May 1, 1960, she retired about 10:00 P.M.; as the night was very warm, she opened both windows, locked them with the chain, and covered herself only with a sheet.

The above occurrence remained unsolved for several weeks. About 3:00 A.M. on the morning of May 26, 1960, Elsie Cox, who lived alone in a two-room apartment at 757 Sutter Street, awoke and in the large mirror facing her bed, saw the reflection of a man entering the living room where she slept. She could see him very clearly as the living room window extended almost the entire wall and overlooked the brightly lit Trader Vic's parking area next door. The venetian blinds on the window were down but open. She watched the prowler creep around her bed, and noticed that he kept a white cloth over his hand as he flashed a light into the closet and took a leisurely survey. He then turned and lifted up the pillow next to hers and pushed his hand under it. Then he straightened up, proceeded to the end of the bed, and the other side of the room. After he climbed out the kitchen window, she called the police. Later, she discovered that only a dish towel was missing, although several things were awry. Miss Cox's apartment was on the second floor; there was a fire escape and some pipes near the kitchen window. Shortly thereafter, a police officer saw the appellant walking down Post Street near Mason Street, and returned with him to Miss Cox's apartment. Miss Cox positively identified the appellant as the prowler at that time and at the later trial.

On June 9, 1960, while in custody on the Cox matter, the appellant was questioned about the Finley burglary. He denied being at Mrs. Finley's apartment on the morning in question and indicated he did not wish to make any further statements. . . . At the trial, . . . [h]e testified that on May 1, he had gone to bed around 10 o'clock at the home of his sister and brother-in-law at 184 Hoff Street. The appellant's sister and her husband also testified that the appellant was in his bed on the night of May 1 at their home in the Ingleside district. It was also brought out at the trial that one week earlier, the appellant had been tried and acquitted of the Cox burglary. . . .

Appellant . . . argues that the evidence relating to the subsequent burglary of Miss Cox's apartment was not admissible because of his acquittal and because of its prejudicial effect. It is well established, however, that an acquittal does not prevent the admissibility of evidence concerning another wrongful act as conviction of the offense is not a prerequisite to the introduction of such evidence.

As stated in People v. Brown, 168 Cal. App. 2d at pages 552-553, 336 P.2d at page 3:

"The ultimate fact to be proved is the defendant's guilt of the crime with which he is charged and not the other offense. The evidence of the other offense is admissible even though the defendant was not convicted of it, provided such evidence is relevant. Therefore, the rule concerning the admissibility of other offenses . . . must be limited to those circumstances where the proof is relevant and material to the crime for which the defendant is being tried."

Appellant here argues that the Cox burglary is not relevant to the Finley burglary; the attorney general argues that the evidence was relevant and admissible as the Cox burglary was committed in the same neighborhood [about 2 blocks from the Gaylord Hotel where Mrs. Finley lived], was committed within the same month in the early hours of the morning, and both involved the use of a white cloth, Miss Cox's dish cloth, and by inference, the piece cut from Mrs. Finley's sheet.

The general rule of the admissibility of other criminal acts is stated in People v. Sanders, 114 Cal. 216, at page 230, 46 P. 153, at page 157:

"If the evidence of another crime is necessary or pertinent to the proof of the one charged, the law will not thwart justice by excluding that evidence, simply because it involves the commission of another crime. People v. Tucker, 104 Cal. 440, 38 P. 195. The general tests of the admissibility of evidence in a criminal case are: First. Is it a part of the res gestae? Second. If not, does it tend logically, naturally, and by reasonable inference to establish any fact material for the people, or to overcome any material matter sought to be proved by the defense? If it does, then it is admissible, whether it embraces the commission of another crime or does not, whether the other crime be similar in kind or not, whether it be part of a single design or not. . . ."

We think the evidence of the Cox burglary was pertinent to the issue of intent. . . .

OLIPHANT v. KOEHLER

594 F.2d 547 (6th Cir. 1979), cert. denied, 444 U.S. 877 (1979)

WEICK, J. The petitioner Oliphant has appealed from a judgment of the District Court denying his application for a writ of habeas corpus. The District Court's opinion denying the writ is reported in Oliphant v.

Koehler, 451 F. Supp. 1305 (W.D. Mich. 1978). Oliphant had been convicted by a jury, in the Circuit Court of Ingham County, Michigan on
charges of forcible rape, in violation of M.C.L.A. §750.520; M.S.A.
§28.788, and gross indecency, in violation of M.C.L.A. §750.338b;
M.S.A. §28.570(2) of an eighteen year old white girl who was a freshman
at Michigan State University. His conviction followed a second trial on
the above charges. He was sentenced on June 2, 1972 to a term of four to
five years' imprisonment on the gross indecency conviction and twenty
to thirty years' imprisonment on the rape conviction. He served his
sentence on the gross indecency conviction and was discharged on February 19, 1975 and is now serving the unexpired sentence on his rape
conviction. His first trial resulted in a mistrial when the jury was unable
to reach a verdict. His conviction was affirmed by the Michigan Court of
Appeals in People v. Oliphant, 52 Mich. App. 242, 217 N.W.2d 141
(1974), and by the Supreme Court of Michigan in People v. Oliphant,
399 Mich. 472, 250 N.W.2d 443 (1976).

In his appeal from the denial of the writ of habeas corpus, Oliphant
contends that in his trial, the admission of certain evidence under Michigan's "similar acts" statute put him in double jeopardy for the "same"
offense and was barred by collateral estoppel. . . .

We affirm. In our opinion, in his conviction for rape there was no
double jeopardy or any violation of the doctrine of collateral estoppel.
His rape of complainant involved a different person than the young
women complaining in the similar acts shown. . . .

[A description of the rape is omitted.]

At no time was she beaten or were her clothes torn. No weapon was
exhibited. Following the intercourse, complainant replaced her clothing
and was driven directly back to her dormitory. Oliphant advised her not
to endeavor to prosecute him for rape, stating that she could not prove
rape. He further stated that he had a tape recorder in the car although
none was ever found. He asked her to sign an agreement not to prosecute, but could not find a pencil. Oliphant also told complainant that he
was married and had children. As she was getting out of Oliphant's car,
he told her to be sure to get the license plate number of his car. Complainant then returned to her dormitory crying and telling her girl
friend that she had been raped. The campus police were called. She was
taken to the Olin Health Center of Michigan State University where she
was examined by the Center's attending physician. . . .

After Oliphant dropped complainant off, he proceeded to the East
Lansing Police Department. He told officers that he had engaged in sex
with a girl that evening. Oliphant stated that when he complained of her
body odor she became angry with him. Her alleged body odor, however,
did not seem to deter Oliphant from committing the atrocities on her
body. He indicated to the police that he feared she might charge him
with rape. Shortly thereafter a report of her complaint of rape came in
to the police and Oliphant was arrested.

Testifying in his own behalf, Oliphant admitted that he engaged in acts of fellatio and sexual intercourse with complainant. He claimed, however, that all of these acts were consensual. . . . Oliphant denied that he attempted to orchestrate the events and circumstances of the evening in order to make proof of the alleged rape more difficult. Ordinarily a rapist is not cunning enough to devise such an elaborate scheme as was adopted by Oliphant to escape conviction, and he nearly succeeded as is evidenced by the result of the first trial.

In rebuttal, and in an effort to prove that Oliphant carried out such a planned orchestration of events, the people proposed to call three additional witnesses. Testimony was offered pursuant to Michigan's similar acts statute, which read as follows:

> In any criminal case where the defendant's motive, intent, the absence of, mistake or accident on his part, or the defendant's scheme, plan or system in doing an act, is material, any like acts or other acts of the defendant which may tend to show his motive, intent, the absence of, mistake or accident on his part, or the defendant's scheme, plan or system in doing the act, in question, may be proved, whether they are contemporaneous with or prior or subsequent thereto; notwithstanding that such proof may show or tend to show the commission of another or prior or subsequent crime by the defendant. [M.C.L.A. §768.27; M.S.A. §28.1050]

Two of the rebuttal witnesses had been complainants in two prior rape trials involving Oliphant. In both prior trials he had been acquitted. The testimony of these two women is the basis of Oliphant's double jeopardy and collateral estoppel claim.[2]

Before the testimony of the two women was offered the trial judge conducted a hearing in the absence of the jury where the matter was carefully considered and resolved, particularly that its probative value was not substantially outweighed by the potentially unfair prejudicial effect. Immediately prior to the introduction of any of the rebuttal testimony the trial judge advised the jurors of the limited purpose for which the testimony was offered and for which it could be used. The court also advised the jurors of Oliphant's acquittal both before and after the testimony of rebuttal witnesses. In his final instructions to the jury, the trial judge restated the limited purpose for which such evidence could be considered. This point was also made by the prosecutor in his closing argument. . . .

[Descriptions of the three other alleged rapes are omitted.]

Oliphant relies on the decision of the Supreme Court in Ashe v.

---

2. The testimony of a third rebuttal witness was similar to that of the other two except that no charge was ever brought against Oliphant. Oliphant does not now challenge the use of the testimony of this third witness. All three women were white ladies of college age, one of whom attended Michigan State University.

Swenson, 397 U.S. 436 (1970), in support of his claim of double jeopardy and collateral estoppel. Such reliance is misplaced. The Supreme Court of Michigan distinguished *Ashe* stating:

"The keystone of defendant's argument is Ashe v. Swenson, 397 U.S. 436 (1970). *Ashe* involved a conviction for the robbery of a participant in a card game after the defendant had previously been acquitted of robbing another of the players in the same game. The Supreme Court held that the first jury had determined that the state had failed to prove defendant had been one of the robbers in the first trial and was, therefore, precluded from trying to prove the same fact in the second trial which was identical in all aspects except for the named victim. *Ashe* involved a single criminal episode and the relitigation of the same fact after it had been decided in defendant's favor in the first trial.

"In the case at bar, the jury had to decide whether defendant raped complainant on June 1, 1971. The two other incidents testified to which resulted in acquittals were not part of the same criminal episode, nor did they turn on the same crucial fact. An issue of fact in each of the prior trials was whether *B* and *C* consented to the intercourse or submitted as the result of the threat of force. These issues are distinct from the question of whether complainant consented to intercourse or submitted as the result of the threat of force. Assuming the only rational basis for the prior acquittals was a consent determination favorable to defendant, this could in no way bar the people from proving nonconsent on the part of complainant."

In this case the people were endeavoring to prove that Oliphant had engaged in similar, prior acts of "orchestration." The Supreme Court of Michigan held that such proof was "material" under state law. It was also not barred by collateral estoppel. The juries which acquitted Oliphant could easily have concluded both that Oliphant orchestrated the events surrounding the prior sexual encounters and that the women had in fact consented to his ultimate advances. See *Ashe, supra,* 397 U.S. at 444. Since the state prosecutor did not seek to relitigate any issue which had previously been determined in Oliphant's favor, his claim of collateral estoppel is without merit.

EDWARDS, C.J., dissenting. With all respect to my colleagues, I do not think this case can be decided without reference to the important issue of federal constitutional law which it presents. The Fifth Amendment to the United States Constitution says in part, "nor shall any person be subject for the same offence to be twice put in jeopardy of life or limb. . . ."

Here, two witnesses were allowed to testify that appellant (at times and places totally unrelated to the instant charge) performed acts which (if the testimony was believed) constituted the crime of forcible rape. Mich. Comp. Laws Ann. §750.520. The constitutional problem is posed by the fact that in both of these instances that identical charge had been filed by each of these two witnesses, appellant had been subjected to a jury trial, and the jury had found him "not guilty." To allow these same complainants to testify to these same events to buttress another complainant's charge of the same offense committed against her appears to me to allow appellant to be put in jeopardy twice in each such instance. Certainly the state should be estopped from relitigating the forcible rape issue, as was done here. Ashe v. Swenson, 397 U.S. 436 (1970).

I dissent.

Problem II-5
The Brides in the Baths

REX v. SMITH, 11 Cr. App. R. 229, 84 L.J.K.B. 2153 (1915): Appeal on points of law against a conviction for murder before Scrutton, J. at the Central Criminal Court. The appellant was indicted for the murder of Bessie Munday, who was discovered dead in her bath at Herne Bay on the 12th July 1912. The appellant had gone through a ceremony of marriage with the deceased, his own wife being then alive. At the trial of the appellant on the charge of murder evidence was given that subsequent to the death of Bessie Munday two other women named Alice Burnham and Margaret Elizabeth Lofty had both died in their baths under nearly the same circumstances as those which occurred in the case of Bessie Munday. In both of these subsequent cases the appellant had gone through a ceremony of marriage. The appellant was convicted at the Central Criminal Court of the murder of Bessie Munday and sentenced to death. The contention on behalf of the appellant is that the evidence was not admissible on examination in chief. It was admitted as evidence of a system of murder.

Did the trial court err? When, if ever, may evidence of subsequent crimes be introduced for one of the purposes for which it is permissible to show proof of prior crimes? When should such evidence be allowed? What sort of foundation must be laid? What quantum of proof of the subsequent crimes should be required? Consider the opinion of the Lord Chief Justice.

LORD READING, C.J. The principles of law governing the admission of evidence of this nature have been often under the consideration of this court and depend chiefly on the statement of the law in the case of Makin v. Attorney-General for New South Wales (sup.), where Lord Herschell says:

"It is undoubtedly not competent for the prosecution to adduce evidence tending to show that the accused has been guilty of criminal acts other than those covered by the indictment, for the purpose of leading to the conclusion that the accused is a person likely from his criminal conduct or character to have committed the offence for which he is being tried. On the other hand, the mere fact that the evidence adduced tends to show the commission of other crimes does not render it inadmissible if it be relevant to an issue before the jury, and it may be so relevant if it bears upon the question whether the acts alleged to constitute the crime charged in his indictment were designed or accidental, or to rebut a defence which would otherwise be open to the accused."

In the present case the prosecution tendered evidence relating to the other two women, and it was admitted by the judge as tending to show that the act charged was committed with design.

The second point taken is that even assuming that evidence of the other two women was admissible, the prosecution should not have been allowed to give evidence beyond the fact that the two women were found dead in their baths. Obviously for the reasons given in dealing with the first point, it would not have been of any assistance to cut short the evidence in this way. We think that the prosecution were entitled to give, and the judge rightly admitted, evidence of the circumstances relating to the deaths of the two women.

Appeal dismissed.

B. When Can You Prove Character — and How?

MICHELSON v. UNITED STATES
335 U.S. 469 (1948).

JACKSON, J. In 1947 petitioner Michelson was convicted of bribing a federal revenue agent. The Government proved a large payment by accused to the agent for the purpose of influencing his official action. The defendant, as a witness on his own behalf, admitted passing the money but claimed it was done in response to the agent's demands, threats, solicitations, and inducements that amounted to entrapment. It is enough for our purposes to say that determination of the issue turned on whether the jury should believe the agent or the accused.

On direct examination of defendant, his own counsel brought out that, in 1927, he had been convicted of a misdemeanor having to do with trading in counterfeit watch dials. On cross-examination it appeared that in 1930, in executing an application for a license to deal in second-hand jewelry, he answered "No" to the question whether he had theretofore been arrested or summoned for any offense.

Defendant called five witnesses to prove that he enjoyed a good reputation. Two of them testified that their acquaintance with him extended over a period of about thirty years and the others said they had known him at least half that long. A typical examination in chief was as follows:

Q: Do you know the defendant Michelson?
A: Yes.
Q: How long do you know Mr. Michelson?
A: About 30 years.
Q: Do you know other people who know him?
A: Yes.
Q: Have you had occasion to discuss his reputation for honesty and truthfulness and for being a law-abiding citizen?
A: It is very good.
Q: You have talked to others?
A: Yes.
Q: And what is his reputation?
A: Very good.

These are representative of answers by three witnesses; two others replied, in substance, that they never had heard anything against Michelson.

On cross-examination, four of the witnesses were asked, in substance, this question: "Did you ever hear that Mr. Michelson on March 4, 1927, was convicted of a violation of the trademark law in New York City in regard to watches?" This referred to the twenty-year-old conviction about which defendant himself had testified on direct examination. Two of them had heard of it and two had not.

To four of these witnesses the prosecution also addressed the question the allowance of which, over defendant's objection, is claimed to be reversible error: "Did you ever hear that on October 11, 1920, the defendant, Solomon Michelson, was arrested for receiving stolen goods?" None of the witnesses appears to have heard of this.

The trial court asked counsel for the prosecution, out of presence of the jury, "Is it a fact according to the best information in your possession, that Michelson was arrested for receiving stolen goods?" Counsel replied that it was, and to support his good faith exhibited a paper record which defendant's counsel did not challenge.

The judge also on three occasions warned the jury, in terms that are not criticized, of the limited purpose for which this evidence was received.[3]

3. In ruling on the objection when the question was first asked, the Court said:
". . . I instruct the jury that what is happening now is this: the defendant has called character witnesses, and the basis for the evidence given by those character witnesses is the reputation of the defendant in the community, and since the defendant tenders the issue of his reputation the prosecution may ask the witness if she has heard of various incidents in his career. I say to you that regardless of her answer you are not to assume that the

Defendant-petitioner challenges the right of the prosecution so to cross-examine his character witnesses. The Court of Appeals held that it was permissible. The opinion, however, points out that the practice has been severely criticized and invites us, in one respect, to change the rule.[4] Serious and responsible criticism has been aimed, however, not alone at the detail now questioned by the Court of Appeals but at common-law doctrine on the whole subject of proof of reputation or character. It would not be possible to appraise the usefulness and propriety of this cross-examination without consideration of the unique practice con-

---

incidents asked about actually took place. All that is happening is that this witness' standard of opinion of the reputation of the defendant is being tested. Is that clear?"

In overruling the second objection to the question the Court said:

"Again I say to the jury there is no proof that Mr. Michelson was arrested for receiving stolen goods in 1920, there isn't any such proof. All this witness has been asked is whether he had heard of that. There is nothing before you on that issue. Now would you base your decision on the case fairly in spite of the fact that that question has been asked? You would? All right."

The charge included the following:

"In connection with the character evidence in the case I permitted a question whether or not the witness knew that in 1920 this defendant had been arrested for receiving stolen goods. I tried to give you the instruction then that that question was permitted only to test the standards of character evidence that these character witnesses seemed to have. There isn't any proof in the case that could be produced before you legally within the rules of evidence that this defendant was arrested in 1920 for receiving stolen goods, and that fact you are not to hold against him; nor are you to assume what the consequences of that arrest were. You just drive it from your mind so far as he is concerned, and take it into consideration only in weighing the evidence of the character witnesses."

4. Footnote 8 to that court's opinion reads as follows:

"Wigmore, Evidence (3d ed. 1940) §988, after noting that 'such inquiries are almost universally admitted,' not as 'impeachment by extrinsic testimony of particular acts of misconduct,' but as means of testing the character 'witness' grounds of knowledge,' continues with these comments: 'But the serious objection to them is that practically the above distinction — between rumors of such conduct, as affecting reputation, and the fact of it as violating the rule against particular facts — cannot be maintained in the mind of the jury. The rumor of the misconduct, when admitted, goes far, in spite of all theory and of the judge's charge, towards fixing the misconduct as a fact upon the other person, and thus does three improper things, — (1) it violates the fundamental rule of fairness that prohibits the use of such facts, (2) it gets at them by hearsay only, and not by trustworthy testimony, and (3) it leaves the other person no means of defending himself by denial or explanation, such as he would otherwise have had if the rule had allowed that conduct to be made the subject of an issue. Moreover, these are not occurrences of possibility, but of daily practice. This method of inquiry or cross-examination is frequently resorted to by counsel for the very purpose of injuring by indirection a character which they are forbidden directly to attack in that way; they rely upon the mere putting of the question (not caring that it is answered negatively) to convey their covert insinuation. The value of the inquiry for testing purposes is often so small and the opportunities of its abuse by underhand ways are so great that the practice may amount to little more than a mere subterfuge, and should be strictly supervised by forbidding it to counsel who do not use it in good faith.'

"Because, as Wigmore says, the jury almost surely cannot comprehend the judge's limiting instruction, the writer of this opinion wishes that the United States Supreme Court would tell us to follow what appears to be the Illinois rule, i.e., that such questions are improper unless they relate to offenses similar to those for which the defendant is on trial. See Aiken v. People, 183 Ill. 215, 55 N.E. 695; cf. People v. Hannon, 381 Ill. 206, 44 N.E. 2d 923."

cerning character testimony, of which such cross-examination is a minor part.

Courts that follow the common-law tradition almost unanimously have come to disallow resort by the prosecution to any kind of evidence of a defendant's evil character to establish a probability of his guilt. Not that the law invests the defendant with a presumption of good character, Greer v. United States, 245 U.S. 559, but it simply closes the whole matter of character, disposition and reputation on the prosecution's case-in-chief. The state may not show defendant's prior trouble with the law, specific criminal acts, or ill name among his neighbors, even though such facts might logically be persuasive that he is by propensity a probable perpetrator of the crime. The inquiry is not rejected because character is irrelevant; on the contrary, it is said to weigh too much with the jury and to so overpersuade them as to prejudge one with a bad general record and deny him a fair opportunity to defend against a particular charge. The overriding policy of excluding such evidence, despite its admitted probative value, is the practical experience that its disallowance tends to prevent confusion of issues, unfair surprise and undue prejudice.

But this line of inquiry firmly denied to the State is opened to the defendant because character is relevant in resolving probabilities of guilt. He may introduce affirmative testimony that the general estimate of his character is so favorable that the jury may infer that he would not be likely to commit the offense charged. This privilege is sometimes valuable to a defendant for this Court has held that such testimony alone, in some circumstances, may be enough to raise a reasonable doubt of guilt and that in the federal courts a jury in a proper case should be so instructed. Edgington v. United States, 164 U.S. 361.

When the defendant elects to initiate a character inquiry, another anomalous rule comes into play. Not only is he permitted to call witnesses to testify from hearsay, but indeed such a witness is not allowed to base his testimony on anything but hearsay. What commonly is called "character evidence" is only such when "character" is employed as a synonym for "reputation." The witness may not testify about defendant's specific acts or courses of conduct or his possession of a particular disposition or of benign mental and moral traits; nor can he testify that his own acquaintance, observation, and knowledge of defendant leads to his own independent opinion that defendant possesses a good general or specific character, inconsistent with commission of acts charged. The witness is, however, allowed to summarize what he has heard in the community, although much of it may have been said by persons less qualified to judge than himself. The evidence which the law permits is not as to the personality of defendant but only as to the shadow his daily life has cast in his neighborhood. This has been well described in a different connection as "the slow growth of months and years, the resultant picture of forgotten incidents, passing events, habitual and daily conduct, presumably honest because disinterested, and safer to be trusted because prone to suspect. . . . It is for that reason that such general repute is permitted to be proven. It sums up a multitude of trivial details. It compacts into the brief phrase of a verdict the teaching of many incidents and the conduct of years. It is the average intelligence drawing its conclusion." Finch, J., in Badger v. Badger, 88 N.Y. 546, 552.

While courts have recognized logical grounds for criticism of this type of opinion-based-on-hearsay testimony, it is said to be justified by "overwhelming considerations of practical convenience" in avoiding innumerable collateral issues which, if it were attempted to prove character by direct testimony, would complicate and confuse the trial, distract the minds of jurymen and befog the chief issues in the litigation. People v. Van Gaasbeck, 189 N.Y. 408, 419, 82 N.E. 718, 721.

Another paradox in this branch of the law of evidence is that the delicate and responsible task of compacting reputation hearsay into the "brief phrase of a verdict" is one of the few instances in which conclusions are accepted from a witness on a subject in which he is not an expert. However, the witness must qualify to give an opinion by showing such acquaintance with the defendant, the community in which he has lived and the circles in which he has moved, as to speak with authority of the terms in which generally he is regarded. To require affirmative knowledge of the reputation may seem inconsistent with the latitude given to the witness to testify when all he can say of the reputation is that he has "heard nothing against defendant." This is permitted upon assumption that, if no ill is reported of one, his reputation must be good. But this answer is accepted only from a witness whose knowledge of defendant's habitat and surroundings is intimate enough so that his failure to hear of any relevant ill repute is an assurance that no ugly rumors were about.

Thus the law extends helpful but illogical options to a defendant. Experience taught a necessity that they be counterweighted with equally illogical conditions to keep the advantage from becoming an unfair and unreasonable one. The price a defendant must pay for attempting to prove his good name is to throw open the entire subject which the law has kept closed for his benefit and to make himself vulnerable where the law otherwise shields him. The prosecution may pursue the inquiry with contradictory witnesses to show that damaging rumors, whether or not well-grounded, were afloat — for it is not the man that he is, but the name that he has which is put in issue. Another hazard is that his own witness is subject to cross-examination as to the contents and extent of the hearsay on which he bases his conclusions, and he may be required to disclose rumors and reports that are current even if they do not affect his own conclusion. It may test the sufficiency of his knowledge by asking what stories were circulating concerning events, such as one's arrest, about which people normally comment and speculate. Thus, while the law gives defendant the option to show as a fact that his reputation reflects a life and habit incompatible with commission of the offense charged, it subjects his proof to tests of credibility designed to prevent him from profiting by a mere parade of partisans.

To thus digress from evidence as to the offense to hear a contest as to the standing of the accused, at its best opens a tricky line of inquiry as to a shapeless and elusive subject matter. At its worst it opens a veritable Pandora's box of irresponsible gossip, innuendo and smear. In the frontier phase of our law's development, calling friends to vouch for defendant's good character, and its counterpart — calling the rivals and enemies of a witness to impeach him by testifying that his reputation for veracity was so bad that he was unworthy of belief on his oath — were favorite and frequent ways of converting an individual litigation into a community contest and a trial into a spectacle. Growth of urban conditions, where one may never know or hear the name of his next-door neighbor, have tended to limit the use of these techniques and to deprive them of weight with juries. The popularity of both procedures has subsided, but courts of last resort have sought to overcome danger that the true issues will be obscured and confused by investing the trial court with discretion to limit the number of such witnesses and to control cross-examination. Both propriety and abuse of hearsay reputation testimony, on both sides, depend on numerous and subtle considerations difficult to detect or appraise from a cold record, and therefore rarely and only on clear showing of prejudicial abuse of discretion will Courts of Appeals disturb rulings of trial courts on this subject.

Wide discretion is accompanied by heavy responsibility on trial courts to protect the practice from any misuse. The trial judge was scrupulous to so guard it in the case before us. He took pains to ascertain, out of presence of the jury, that the target of the question was an actual event, which would probably result in some comment among acquaintances if not injury to defendant's reputation. He satisfied himself that counsel was not merely taking a random shot at a reputation imprudently exposed or asking a groundless question to waft an unwarranted innuendo into the jury box.

The question permitted by the trial court, however, involves several features that may be worthy of comment. Its form invited hearsay; it asked about an arrest, not a conviction, and for an offense not closely similar to the one on trial; and it concerned an occurrence many years past.

Since the whole inquiry, as we have pointed out, is calculated to ascertain the general talk of people about defendant, rather than the witness' own knowledge of him, the form of inquiry, "Have you heard?" has general approval, and "Do you know?" is not allowed.

A character witness may be cross-examined as to an arrest whether or not it culminated in a conviction, according to the overwhelming weight of authority. This rule is sometimes confused with that which prohibits cross-examination to credibility by asking a witness whether he himself has been arrested.

Arrest without more does not, in law any more than in reason, impeach the integrity or impair the credibility of a witness. It happens to the innocent as well as the guilty. Only a conviction, therefore, may be inquired about to undermine the trustworthiness of a witness.

Arrest without more may nevertheless impair or cloud one's reputation. False arrest may do that. Even to be acquitted may damage one's good name if the community receives the verdict with a wink and chooses to remember defendant as one who ought to have been convicted. A conviction, on the other hand, may be accepted as a misfortune or an injustice, and even enhance the standing of one who mends his ways and lives it down. Reputation is the net balance of so many debits and credits that the law does not attach the finality to a conviction, when the issue is reputation, that is given to it when the issue is the credibility of the convict.

The inquiry as to an arrest is permissible also because the prosecution has a right to test the qualifications of the witness to bespeak the community opinion. If one never heard the speculations and rumors in which even one's friends indulge upon his arrest, the jury may doubt whether he is capable of giving any very reliable conclusions as to his reputation.

In this case the crime inquired about was receiving stolen goods; the trial was for bribery. The Court of Appeals thought this dissimilarity of offenses too great to sustain the inquiry in logic, though conceding that it is authorized by preponderance of authority. It asks us to substitute the Illinois rule which allows inquiry about arrest, but only for very closely similar if not identical charges, in place of the rule more generally adhered to in this country and in England. We think the facts of this case show the proposal to be inexpedient.

The good character which the defendant had sought to establish was broader than the crime charged and included the traits of "honesty and truthfulness" and "being a law-abiding citizen." Possession of these characteristics would seem as incompatible with offering a bribe to a revenue agent as with receiving stolen goods. The crimes may be unlike, but both alike proceed from the same defects of character which the witnesses said this defendant was reputed not to exhibit. It is not only by comparison with the crime on trial but by comparison with the reputation asserted that a court may judge whether the prior arrest should be made subject of inquiry. By this test the inquiry was permissible. It was proper cross-examination because reports of his arrest for receiving stolen goods, if admitted, would tend to weaken the assertion that he was known as an honest and law-abiding citizen. The cross-examination may take in as much ground as the testimony it is designed to verify. To hold otherwise would give defendant the benefit of testimony that he was honest and law-abiding in reputation when such might not be the fact; the refutation was founded on convictions equally persuasive though not for crimes exactly repeated in the present charge.

The inquiry here concerned an arrest twenty-seven years before the trial. Events a generation old are likely to be lived down and dropped from the present thought and talk of the community and to be absent from the knowledge of younger or more recent acquaintances. The court in its discretion may well exclude inquiry about rumors of an event so remote, unless recent misconduct revived them. But two of these witnesses dated their acquaintance with defendant as commencing thirty years before the trial. Defendant, on direct examination, voluntarily called attention to his conviction twenty years before. While the jury might conclude that a matter so old and indecisive as a 1920 arrest would shed little light on the present reputation and hence propensities of the defendant, we cannot say that, in the context of this evidence and in the absence of objection on this specific ground, its admission was an abuse of discretion.

We do not overlook or minimize the consideration that "the jury almost surely cannot comprehend the judge's limiting instruction," which disturbed the Court of Appeals. The refinements of the evidentiary rules on this subject are such that even lawyers and judges, after study and reflection, often are confused, and surely jurors in the hurried and unfamiliar movement of a trial must find them almost unintelligible. However, limiting instructions on this subject are no more difficult to comprehend or apply than those upon various other subjects; for example, instructions that admissions of a co-defendant are to be limited to the question of his guilt and are not to be considered as evidence against other defendants, and instructions as to other problems in the trial of conspiracy charges. A defendant in such a case is powerless to prevent his cause from being irretrievably obscured and confused; but, in cases such as the one before us, the law foreclosed this whole confounding line of inquiry, unless defendant thought the net advantage from opening it up would be with him. Given this option, we think defendants in general and this defendant in particular have no valid complaint at the latitude which existing law allows to the prosecution to meet by cross-examination an issue voluntarily tendered by the defense. See Greer v. United States, 245 U.S. 559.

We end, as we began, with the observation that the law regulating the offering and testing of character testimony may merit many criticisms.

England and some states have overhauled the practice by statute. But the task of modernizing the long-standing rules on the subject is one of magnitude and difficulty which even those dedicated to law reform do not lightly undertake.

The law of evidence relating to proof of reputation in criminal cases has developed almost entirely at the hands of state courts of last resort, which have such questions frequently before them. This Court, on the other hand, has contributed little to this or to any phase of the law of evidence, for the reason, among others, that it has had extremely rare occasion to decide such issues, as the paucity of citations in this opinion to our own writings attests. It is obvious that a court which can make only infrequent sallies into the field cannot recast the body of case law on this subject in many, many years, even if it were clear what the rules should be.

We concur in the general opinion of courts, textwriters and the profession that much of this law is archaic, paradoxical and full of compromises and compensations by which an irrational advantage to one side is offset by a poorly reasoned counterprivilege to the other. But somehow it has proved a workable even if clumsy system when moderated by discretionary controls in the hands of a wise and strong trial court. To pull one misshapen stone out of the grotesque structure is more likely simply to upset its present balance between adverse interests than to establish a rational edifice.

The present suggestion is that we adopt for all federal courts a new rule as to cross-examination about prior arrest, adhered to by the courts of only one state and rejected elsewhere. The confusion and error it would engender would seem too heavy a price to pay for an almost imperceptible logical improvement, if any, in a system which is justified, if at all, by accumulated judicial experience rather than abstract logic.

The judgment is affirmed.

FRE 405
Methods of Proving Character

(a) *Reputation or opinion.* In all cases in which evidence of character or a trait of character of a person is admissible, proof may be made by testimony as to reputation or by testimony in the form of an opinion. On cross-examination, inquiry is allowable into relevant specific instances of conduct.

(b) *Specific instances of conduct.* In cases in which character or a trait of character of a person is an essential element of a charge, claim, or defense, proof may also be made of specific instances of his conduct.

How do Rules 403, 404, and 405 relate to each other? How does the question of *when* proof of character can be made relate to the question of *what form* such proof should take? What form of character evidence — reputation, opinion, or specific prior acts — is most probative? Most prejudicial? Most desirable from an objective viewpoint? Do you feel that the use of such evidence can be confined to its permissible purposes by instructions to the jury?

In federal court what type of character evidence may be introduced for purposes other than impeaching a witness' credibility:

(1) By the prosecution as part of its case-in-chief;

(2) By the accused as part of its case-in-chief;

(3) By the prosecution on cross-examination of defendant's witnesses;

(4) By the prosecution to rebut the accused's case-in-chief;

(5) By the accused to rehabilitate its case after attack by the prosecution; and

(6) In a civil case, by either side?

What are the reasons and policies behind these rules?

Is the "Illinois rule," discussed in the *Michelson* case, an improvement on the federal rule? Why not exclude character evidence — good and bad — regardless of who offers it, when its only purpose is to prove the evil or saintly character of the accused? Or should all the rules of exclusion and exception be replaced with one rule giving the trial judge discretion, similar to Rule 403? What should the standard of review be on appeal of these issues under the present system or a modified system?

Problem II-6
Proof of the Defendant's Good Character

Charge: robbery.

(1) At *D*'s trial the state calls *W1*, a teller at the bank, who identifies *D* as the robber. The state next calls *W2* and proposes that *W2* testify that he is familiar with *D*'s reputation in the community and that *D*'s reputation is one of a thieving, embezzling, bunko artist. On *D*'s timely objection what ruling and why? Does the objection call into play the propensity rule?

(2) Assume that *D*'s objection to *W2*'s testimony is sustained and the prosecution rests. *D* calls witness *W3* to testify to *D*'s reputation in the community as an honest, quiet person. On the district attorney's timely objection, what ruling and why? Does the objection call into play the propensity rule? Should it?

(3) Suppose the district attorney's objection is overruled. *W3* testifies as proposed. On cross-examination may the district attorney ask *W3* — over *D*'s objection — whether *W3* has heard that last year *D* swindled the widow Brown?

(4) After *W3* is through testifying and *D* has presented the rest of her case, should the state be allowed to reopen its case to offer proof of *D*'s prior arrest for armed robbery? Why?

Problem II-7
Proof of the Defendant's Violent Character

Charge: murder by strangulation, bludgeoning, stabbing, and burning.

(1) As part of the state's case-in-chief the district attorney offers the testimony of witness *A* to testify that for the past 20 years she has lived in the same town as *D* and that she knows *D*'s reputation in the community to be that of a vicious bully and troublemaker, prone to violence and breaches of the peace. *D* objects to *A*'s testimony. What ruling and why?

(2) Suppose that *D*'s objection to *A*'s testimony is sustained. The district attorney next offers witness *B* to testify that on May 1, a year ago, *D* committed an armed robbery of *B*. *D* objects to *B*'s testimony. What ruling and why?

(3) Suppose that *D*'s objection to *B*'s testimony is sustained. The district attorney introduces a certified record of *D*'s conviction for armed robbery of *B* one year ago. Should this evidence be admitted over *D*'s objection?

(4) Suppose that *D*'s objection to proof of his prior conviction, on the grounds that the evidence is irrelevant, incompetent, immaterial, and prejudicial, is overruled and the evidence is admitted. *D* is convicted. On appeal the judgment is affirmed by the state supreme court, which holds that such evidence is admissible to show *D*'s propensity as a habitual criminal, thus affecting the degree of punishment. *D*'s petition for a writ of certiorari to the U.S. Supreme Court is granted. Has *D* been deprived of due process of law?

Problem II-8
The Sodomitical Snob

Action against the *D* Tribune for libel, with federal jurisdiction based on diversity of citizenship. *P* alleges that *D* published an article referring to her as "a nattering nabob of negativism, an effete intellectual snob, and a perverted commie."

At trial, *D* offers evidence that *P* has been twice convicted of sex offenses and is a card-carrying member of the Che Guevara Brigade of the Communist Internationale, secret cell 1137. *P* objects. What ruling and why?

C. Proof of Character and Prior Similar Occurrences in Civil Cases

Problem II-9
Mean Guys Finish Fourth

Bully Martin v. Runny Sandle for damage allegedly occurring as a result of Sandle's assault and battery on Martin in the dugout at Yankee Stadium on July 14. Defendant's answer alleges that plaintiff was the aggressor and pleads self-defense.

(1) As part of his case-in-chief Martin offers evidence of his reputation for peacefulness. Admissible?

(2) As part of his case-in-chief Martin offers evidence of Sandle's reputation as a bully, fighter, and all-around troublemaker. Admissible?

(3) Suppose that the evidence offered in (1) and (2) is excluded and that as part of his case-in-chief defendant offers evidence of his good reputation. Admissible? Suppose defendant also offers evidence of plaintiff's bad reputation. Admissible?

(4) Suppose the court excludes all the evidence offered above except defendant's good reputation evidence. On rebuttal may plaintiff offer evidence of defendant's bad reputation or of his own good reputation?

MUTUAL LIFE INSURANCE COMPANY v. KELLY
49 Ohio App. 319, 197 N.E. 235 (1934)

SHERICK, J. The Mutual Life Insurance Company of Baltimore, defendant in the trial court, here seeks reversal of a judgment entered against it and in favor of Blanche Kelly, the beneficiary named in a life policy upon the life of one Harold Farson; and also an additional sum upon an accidental death provision thereof.

The petition avers that the insured was accidentally shot on the 19th of April, 1933, by a trap gun which had been placed on the inside of a cottage located on the banks of the Muskingum river, and that the insured died as a result thereof.

To this petition the insurer interposed three defenses, the first being a general denial; the second averred a condition of the policy of nonliability in the event that "insured dies in consequence of his or her own criminal action," and that insured did die in consequence of his own criminal act; the third defense pleaded a further contractual provision, in that "no accidental death benefit will be paid if the death of the insured resulted . . . from violation of law by the insured," and that he, the insured, did die as a result of violating the law. The reply filed is a general denial.

The facts disclose that the insured and another had purchased a pair of pliers, and had thereafter proceeded to hunt mushrooms, and on their return home entered an inclosed lot belonging to one Brown. It is in evidence that four or five "keep out" notices were posted in conspicuous places about the premises, which notices the companion of the insured says he did not see. There is evidence of the fact that the cottage had a screened-in porch; that a few days prior to the happening the screen door was intact, closed, and hooked in two places with nails bent over the hooks; that after the happening this door was found open, the nails bent and broken, and the screen torn in two places convenient to the hooks. It further appears that the insured called his associate to the porch window to see a canoe that was inside the cottage, and that while he stood there admiring the canoe, he heard a shot and saw the deceased run off the porch; further than this he knows little or nothing of the transaction.

It is affirmatively in evidence as a part of the company's case that a readable sign was glued on the inside of the glass in the door through which the insured was shot. It read "Friendly warning, Keep out." This fact is negatively denied by several of the plaintiff's witnesses who were called in rebuttal. It is further proved and not denied that the gun set upon a tripod near the door had an iron rod attached to the trigger of the gun, which rod extended to within three or four inches from the lower part of the door, and that the door was bolted at the top. The almost conclusive inference is that the insured must have pushed in the door sufficiently at the bottom to spring the door, and thereby caused the gun to be discharged. The further evidence is, from one of the first arrivals on the scene, that the door "burst at the top" when he applied pressure, and that he then entered thereby. There is some evidence pro and con concerning a strip nailed to the floor at the bottom of the door, but whatever the fact may be as to that seems to us to be immaterial. It is further in evidence that a box of fishing tackle that had belonged to Brown, which had reposed on the window ledge inside the porch, was afterwards found in the insured's pocket, along with the recently purchased pliers, which showed jaw marks like those on the nails found broken off at the screen door.

In view of this chain of circumstances we are unable to conceive how the jury could have arrived at the conclusion that the insured's trespass was but a technical trespass, and not a criminal trespass; unless it be that the jury was influenced by certain testimony which we feel was improperly admitted in evidence over objection.

We have painstakingly read every word of the evidence in this case to discover whether the company introduced any evidence which would place in issue the character of the insured. Such was not done by the pleading; nor was it done by the proof offered. No attempt was made to show that the insured had ever done a prior similar act, and the truth is that only facts and circumstances pertaining to this affair were placed in evidence.

In rebuttal the beneficiary was permitted to call a number of character witnesses, who testified that the deceased bore a good reputation and was a peaceable and law-abiding citizen. In this we think the court erred to the prejudice of the plaintiff in error.

The defendant in error asserts that this evidence was admissible and competent because of the fact that the second and third defenses in effect charge that the insured had committed a crime, that thereby his character was questioned and placed in issue, wherefor the rule applicable in criminal cases applied, to wit, that reputation evidence is admissible for the reason that a man with a good reputation is not as likely to commit a criminal act as one with a bad reputation. But the fact is overlooked that this is a civil action based upon a contract, wherein the insured's general character was not involved.

It is the generally accepted rule that in civil actions, even where fraud is imputed or dishonesty is charged, evidence of a party's good or bad character is incompetent in evidence unless it be made an issue by the pleadings or the proof, as in actions for libel and slander, malicious prosecution, or cases of seduction. In these exceptions to the rule, character is generally involved, and the amount of the damages recoverable may be affected thereby. . . .

The reason for the rule is obvious. It is twofold. Administrative policy requires that litigation be kept within bounds, and in order that the real issue of a cause may be tried and not be confused with or beclouded by an irrelevant matter having but a remote bearing on the proof of the act or fact in issue.

We believe the principle determined finds recognition in a slander action found in Sloneker v. Van Ausdall, 106 Ohio St. 320, 325, 140 N.E. 121, 123, 28 A.L.R. 759, 761, wherein it is held that "the good reputation of the plaintiff is presumed only until it is either attacked by the pleading or proof." Applying that rule to the controversy before us, the insured's character must be considered good; and it not having been generally attacked by the pleadings or proof, evidence of that fact was surplusage and irrelevant, for it was but proof of what the law presumed. It confused the real issue before the jury and led them afield.

For the reasons assigned, the judgment is reversed and the cause remanded.

Do you agree that the insured's character had not been attacked? Was not in issue? That the jury would not consider the insured's character in formulating its verdict? When, if ever, would you allow proof of bad or good character in civil cases where the character of a party is not an element of a claim or defense? Compare the following case.

HESS v. MARINARI
81 W. Va. 500, 94 S.E. 968 (1918)

RITZ, J. This suit is prosecuted for the purpose of recovering damages for an assault alleged to have been committed by the defendants upon the plaintiff. The defendant Patsy Marinari owned and conducted a store, and his codefendant Consino Constantino was employed by Marinari as a salesman in the store. On the evening that the assault complained of is alleged to have been committed, there was quite a number of people congregated in Marinari's store, most of whom appear to have been Italians, to which race both Marinari and Constantino belonged. The plaintiff, together with three or four other Americans, entered the store, and according to his contention he purchased some cider, and after paying for it left the parties with whom he had entered the store and went to playing a slot machine on the opposite side of the room. Shortly after he began to play the slot machine, he says he heard a disturbance on the opposite side of the room where he had left his companions, including his brother, and heard somebody present call another a liar. He went across the room to see about the trouble. About that time Marinari, who had theretofore been engaged back of the counter, called Constantino, and after saying something to him which the plaintiff did not understand, inasmuch as it was in the Italian language, picked up the butcher's cleaver which was lying on the meat block, and Constantino picked up a butcher knife, and Marinari commanded the parties in the store to vacate, announcing that he wanted no disturbance in his store; that immediately upon making this announcement he and Constantino passed through a gate or door in the counter; that before the plaintiff had opportunity to get out of the store Marinari struck him across the shoulder with the sharp end of the meat cleaver, and again when he had about reached the door struck him with the cleaver upon the shoulder, and after he had gotten outside Constantino cut him in the back with the butcher knife, making two severe wounds. It appears that a considerable quarrel or row occurred outside of the store after all of the parties had left it, in which at least one shot was fired and a great many stones were thrown. What else transpired is not clear. Marinari on his part admits that he did pick up the cleaver, but contends that he never struck the defendant with it, and it is contended by the defendants that whatever injuries were received by the plaintiff were received in the row outside of the store. There is evidence to support each contention. The jury found for the plaintiff and fixed his damages at the sum of $9,000, upon which verdict judgment was rendered. This writ of error challenges the rulings of the court in the rejection of certain evidence offered by the defendant, in the giving of instructions to the jury, and in the refusal of the court to set aside the verdict of the jury upon the ground that it is excessive.

It is insisted by the defendant Marinari that the court erred in refusing to admit evidence offered by him to show that he was a man of good character for peace and quietude. The general rule is that evidence of the good character of the defendant is not admissible in a civil case, but is this rule of universal application? It must be borne in mind that in this case the plaintiff was seeking to recover and did recover a verdict for very heavy punitive damages. In order for him to recover such damages, it was necessary for the jury to believe that the defendant had acted with malice toward the plaintiff; in other words, the jury would have to believe the very same things that would have to be shown in order to find him guilty of a criminal offense. What good reason is there for admitting evidence of character in a criminal case to overcome the evidence of criminal intent and rejecting it in a civil case in which the very same intent has to be established in order to recover? We can see no good reason for admitting it in the one case that does not exist in the other. Evidence of good character of the defendant is admitted in all criminal cases where the question of criminal intent is one to be found by the jury, upon the theory that it bears upon that question, and, where in a civil case it is necessary that the jury find that the defendant acted with criminal intent, there is no good reason why he should not be allowed to prove his good character in the respect which it is necessarily questioned by charging him with the offense. . . .

[W]e conclude that where it is necessary to the recovery which the plaintiff seeks that he prove against the defendant facts which constitute a crime, and that in order to such recovery the defendant must have had criminal intent when he did the acts complained of, it is proper for the defendant to introduce character evidence such as was offered in this case for the purpose of overcoming the proof offered to show criminal intent.

There is another very good reason why this sort of evidence is admissible in a case like this where punitive damages are sought and recovered. Anything allowed to the plaintiff as damages in addition to what is necessary to compensate him for his injury is purely punishment to the defendant. It is true the damages which are allowed him as compensation are also punishment as far as the defendant is concerned, but whatever is allowed in addition to this is giving the plaintiff something to which he is in no wise entitled, except upon the theory that the defendant ought to be punished, and that the amount allowed as compensation is not sufficient for the purpose. How may the jury arrive at these punitive damages? What would be punishment for one man might be inadequate punishment for another. Surely the jury would not conclude that a man of good character for peace and quietude in the community should be punished by a fine as large as one who is a notorious bully. In fixing the punishment for crime, one of the very important elements to be considered is the subject of the punishment, and no reason is perceived why the jury should not be advised as to the character of a man who committed the acts complained of, not only for the purpose of weighing this evidence upon the question of criminal intent, or the malice charged against him, but upon the question of ascertaining the amount they think necessary to fine him in order to inflict adequate punishment.

_____

How can you reconcile *Hess* and *Mutual Life*? Is the possibility of punitive damages in *Hess* the crucial factor? Why? Do you think the *Hess* court would grant plaintiff's request to charge the jury that proof of defendant's good character is admissible only on the amount of punitive damages? Is such evidence relevant to this issue? When should a party be able to offer evidence of his good character?

see suppl. 357-9

Problem II-10
The Acrobatic Driver

On June 1 at the intersection of Walden and Thoreau Streets *A*, a pedestrian, was hit by *B*'s car and killed. *B* entered Walden Street from the south. There is a stop sign controlling such traffic at the corner. Shortly after the accident *B* died of injuries unrelated to the accident.

P, the executor of *A*'s estate, sued *D*, the executor of *B*'s estate, for damages due to *B*'s alleged negligence. The issue is whether *B* stopped at the stop sign. At trial, *P* proposes to have *W1* testify that he once saw *B* drive the wrong way down a one-way street, that he once saw *B* blow his horn in a hospital quiet zone, and that he once saw *B* steer with his feet in heavy traffic. *P* also proposes to have *W2* testify that he is familiar with *B*'s reputation for driving and that his reputation is that of a reckless daredevil.

Is the proffered testimony of *W1* or *W2* relevant? Is it admissible in a Federal Rules jurisdiction? Should such evidence be admitted? If you were *P*'s attorney, how would you try to get this evidence in?

PHINNEY v. DETROIT UNITED RAILWAY COMPANY
232 Mich. 399, 205 N.W. 124 (1925)

SHARPE, J. A highway, running north and south, crosses the line of defendant's railway almost at right angles at the village of Atlas, in Genesee county. On Sunday, February 20, 1921, about 2 o'clock in the afternoon, John H. Densmore was driving a Ford roadster, going north, on the highway. With him in the car were his wife, his child, Odessa, and Florence Phinney, the wife of plaintiff. Defendant has a small station house at Atlas, located about 50 feet east of the highway. About 1,300 feet east of the crossing, defendant's track makes a long sweeping curve to the south. One of defendant's limited interurban cars, going west, not scheduled to stop at Atlas, collided with the roadster driven by Densmore at the crossing. As a result of the collision, the three adults were killed, and the child was injured.

Plaintiff, as administrator of his wife's estate, brings this action to recover the loss sustained, due to her death. The cause was submitted to the jury, who found for the defendant. Plaintiff reviews the judgment entered by writ of error. . . .

3. Edward Elford, who was in the employ of the defendant as a conductor on an interurban car at the time of the accident, and had been so employed for several years prior thereto, was asked, "What would be the proper thing to do to stop it as quickly as possible in case of an emergency?" An objection to the question asked was sustained. Error is assigned thereon.

Hinkley, called for cross-examination, had testified that he first saw the automobile when his car was 800 or 900 feet from the crossing; that the station house afterwards obstructed his view, and he next saw it when it was about 50 feet from the crossing and his car about 250 or 300 feet therefrom; that he made no special effort to stop until within 100 feet from the crossing, and that he then applied the brakes with full force; that he did "not sound the foot gong, or reverse the motor, nor apply the sand on the wheels"; that he had theretofore sounded the usual crossing whistle; that he considered the application of the air (emergency) brake the safer way to quickly stop his car; that at that time he was going from 35 to 40 miles an hour. He admitted that on a former trial of this case he had testified that he had not applied the brakes until his car was within 35 or 40 feet from the crossing, and, on being asked, "That is right, is it?" answered, "Yes, sir."

Clarence White, a witness for plaintiff, who was formerly a motorman in the employ of the defendant, testified that in case of an emergency the best thing to do in order to stop quickly is to "reverse the car and use the sand on the rails."

Elford had never acted as a motorman. He testified that he had "seen motormen do different things in stopping quick." Hinkley was called upon to do that which in his judgment, based upon his experience and any instructions which might have been given him, would be the most effective to stop his car when the collision seemed imminent. Whether he at that time neglected or failed to perform this duty, in our opinion, could be tested only by the judgment of other motormen or men having special knowledge of the mechanism provided for stopping cars and the most efficient manner of applying it to secure the desired result.

4. Error is assigned on the refusal of court to permit plaintiff's counsel to show by Elford and other employees of the defendant that Hinkley

had the reputation of being a reckless motorman. The authorities cited by counsel in support of his contention that this evidence was admissible are cases in which employees were injured through the negligence of a fellow servant. We think they have no application to the facts here presented. The jury were concerned only with the manner in which Hinkley drove his car and the effort he made to stop it at the time of the collision. Williams v. Edmunds, 75 Mich. 92, 96, 42 N.W. 534; Boick v. Bissell, 80 Mich. 260, 45 N.W. 55; Langworthy v. Green Tp., 88 Mich. 207, 217, 50 N.W. 130.

Why was Elford's testimony as to the motorman's reputation for recklessness excluded? Would evidence of specific acts of recklessness have been admissible?

DALLAS RAILWAY & TERMINAL COMPANY v. FARNSWORTH
148 Tex. 584, 227 S.W.2d 1017 (1950)

Action for damages on account of injuries suffered by respondent, Mrs. Letta M. Farnsworth, when struck by petitioner's streetcar immediately after she had alighted from it.

Respondent, a widow, fifty-two years of age, became a passenger, together with her thirty year old daughter and three year old grandson, on petitioner's streetcar to travel from South Lamar Street to the corner of Elm and St. Paul Streets, a distance estimated by the operator of the streetcar to be approximately one mile and by respondent approximately three or four miles. Traveling east on Elm Street, the car stopped when it arrived at St. Paul Street. At that place the car tracks do not extend farther on Elm Street, but turn to the left and north on St. Paul Street. Although respondent had been a passenger on streetcars in Dallas and in other places oftentimes over many years, she had never been on a streetcar on Elm Street and did not know that the car turned to the left at St. Paul Street, and did not look at the tracks ahead of the car, and she had never observed that the rear end of a streetcar would swing out as the car went around a curve and did not know that it would.

Eight or ten passengers alighted from the streetcar at its front door. According to respondent's testimony all of the others were ahead of respondent, her daughter and grandchild, respondent being the last passenger to alight. She testified that just as she stepped off the streetcar step within the safety zone the traffic light which she was facing and in the direction that she intended to go, that is, to the south, changed to red, and that before she had time to take a step, almost instantaneously, she was struck and knocked down by the streetcar.

The operator of the streetcar testified that as he closed the door of the car immediately before starting he looked to his right, saw that the door was clear, and saw no one within reach of the door or within reach of the overhang of the streetcar, and that there was no one "at the point of my front door within the overswing zone"; and that after he closed the door and started the streetcar he never looked back to his right or to the back of the streetcar, his attention being given to watching the traffic traveling west on Elm Street and the pedestrians who were crossing St. Paul Street. His testimony shows that he knew nothing about the accident until he had traveled to the end of the line and returned to Elm and Ervay Streets, where he was told of it by the company's supervisor.

Respondent was permitted to testify, over objections, that when she entered the streetcar on Lamar Street the operator started the car before she could get to a seat and was in a great hurry, that he stopped at Lamar and Young Streets and passengers "scarcely got off before he started," and that the same was true at Lamar and Main Streets. This testimony when first considered may appear to be forbidden by the general rule that "when the question is whether or not a person has been negligent in doing or in failing to do a particular act, evidence is not admissible to show that he has been guilty of a similar act of negligence or even habitually negligent upon a similar occasion." The reason for the rule is the fundamental principle that evidence must be relevant to the facts in issue in the case on trial and tend to prove or disprove those facts, evidence as to collateral facts not being admissible. There are some modifications of the general rule as applied to particular cases. It has been said that evidence of similar transactions or *conduct on other occasions* is not competent to prove the commission of a particular act charged *"unless the acts are connected in some special way, indicating a relevancy beyond mere similarity in certain particulars."*

Should the evidence of the operator's prior conduct be admitted? Can this case be reconciled with *Phinney*? What does the court have in mind by "unless the acts are connected in some special way, indicating a relevancy beyond mere similarity in certain particulars"? Does the admissibility of evidence of similar occurrences in civil cases depend on the way counsel packages it?

Problem II-11
The Why Concert

On December 1, 1978, Peter, age 15, was killed at the Cincinnati Riverfront Coliseum. Peter had gone to the Coliseum to attend a concert by The Why, a rock-and-roll group. He and 10 others were killed when the crowd trampled them to death.

P, Peter's father, has brought a wrongful death diversity action in federal court against *D1*, the owner of the Coliseum, and *D2*, the promoter of the concert. *P*'s complaint alleges that the defendants were negligent in overselling general admission tickets and in failing to control the crowd of ticketholders waiting to get in and that the defendants' negligence caused Peter's death. Specifically, *P* alleges that the defendants sold more tickets than there were seats, did not admit the gathered crowd of ticketholders in a timely and orderly manner, and failed to provide sufficient access, security, and crowd control. Both defendants have filed general denials and affirmatively pleaded contributory negligence and assumption of the risk.

At trial, *P* calls *W* to testify that she has been to 12 rock concerts at the coliseum in the past year. She says that at every concert there was a mad scramble for general admission tickets, a press of people outside the doors until they opened a half-hour or so before the scheduled starting time of the concert, and once the doors opened a violent rush for the best seats and standing room.

Should *W*'s testimony be accepted?

CLARK v. STEWART
126 Ohio St. 263, 185 N.E. 71 (1933)

STEPHENSON, J. The action was for personal injuries alleged to have been caused by the negligence of the son of the defendant, who at the time was agent for his father, and, while acting within the scope of his employment while operating an automobile, negligently struck plaintiff from the rear, causing the injuries of which he complains.

The first theory of the petition sought to invoke the doctrine of respondeat superior. There were six averments of negligence. There was an additional averment in the petition to the effect that defendant's son at the time of the collision and injury was of about the age of seventeen years and was an inexperienced, careless, reckless and incompetent driver, which fact was well known to the defendant, and that the defendant was careless and negligent in entrusting his motor vehicle to his son on a public highway. This is followed by the averments of earning capacity, injury, damage, and prayer for recovery.

Defendant in answering plaintiff's amended petition admits that, on the date claimed by plaintiff, his son was operating a motor vehicle as his agent and that there was a collision between the motor vehicle and the person of the plaintiff. He proceeds with the affirmative statement that the injuries sustained by plaintiff on said occasion were caused solely by plaintiff's negligence and carelessness, in the particulars therein set out.

It is claimed that error was infused into the case when counsel for plaintiff called the defendant for cross-examination under the statute and propounded the following questions:

Q: Before January 5, 1931, how many automobile accidents had Walter Stewart had? (Defendant objects.)

And thereupon court recessed for a few minutes, the court first admonishing the jury. . . . And thereupon after the jury returned to the court room the objection was sustained. To all of which the plaintiff excepted.

Q: Had you ridden with Walter when he drove the car?

A: Yes, sir.

Q: You have ridden with him when he drove the car sixty miles an hour, haven't you?

A: No, sir.

Q: Ever ride with him when he run into another car?

A: No, sir.

Q: Were you with him when he —

Mr. Elliott: I object and I think this question is for the purpose of getting around the ruling of the court.

Mr. Harlan, in behalf of plaintiff, objected to misconduct of counsel.

Q: Were you riding with Walter in the latter part of May, 1930, when he was traveling very fast and ran into an automobile at Flenner's Corner? (Defendant objects; overruled; defendant excepts.)

A: Why he never ran into anybody at Flenner's Corner.

Q: (Stenographer reads question.)

A: No, I wasn't.

Q: You make the statement he never ran into any one, how do you know?

A: If he broke the machine or damaged the machine I would know it, wouldn't I?

Q: Didn't he break the machine up some at Flenner's Corner in May, 1930? (Defendant objects; overruled; defendant excepts.)

Q: You say you ought to know it if he had damaged the car any — isn't it a matter of fact, don't you know it, that he did? (Defendant objects; overruled; defendant excepts.)

A: No, he didn't.

Q: Didn't he have an accident there and damage your car and didn't David Clark himself bring Walter home?

A: No, he brought the other boy home. This wasn't Walter. This was Roy. The accident didn't happen at Flenner's Corner, either.

Q: It was about at Flenner's Corner, wasn't it?

A: No, the fellows took the machine to Flenner's Corner to have it fixed.

Q: It was in the neighborhood of Flenner's Corner, wasn't it?

A: No.

Q: Where did it happen?

A: In front of Jake Stout's.

Q: That is farther on towards Excello from where you live?

A: Yes, sir.

Q: You say that wasn't Walter?

A: No, it wasn't Walter.

Q: Where is the other boy?

A: At home.

Q: How old is he?

A: Nineteen.

Q: Was that the boy David Clark brought home?

A: Yes, sir.

Q: Wasn't it Walter?

A: No.

Q: Now you say you ought to know if Walter ever had the car broken up, let's see if you know. Didn't he run into somebody at Matson's Corner and have the car broken up? (Defendant objects.)

Court: He may answer if he knows. (Defendant excepts.)

Q: (Stenographer reads question.)

A: Not as I know of.

Q: Not that you know of?

A: Not my car.

Q: Well, whose car was it?

A: I don't know.

Q: Sir?

A: He was driving the milk route for his brother and was coming out of the road and somebody ran into him, that is all.

Q: Were you there?

A: No.

Q: When you say somebody ran into him, then you have no personal knowledge of that, have you — no personal knowledge, have you?

A: Well I heard them talking about it. . . . (Plaintiff moves to strike out answer; answer stricken out.)

Q: Now the automobile that he was driving that you refer to at Matson's Corner, wasn't that yours?

A: No, sir.

Q: That was another son's?

A: Yes, sir.

Q: Was that Roy's?

A: No, sir, William's. . . .

Q: Was Walter driving your car and ran into another car, just outside of Monroe? (Defendant objects; overruled; defendant excepts.) . . .

Q: Don't you know Walter had the reputation of driving fifty or sixty miles an hour? (Defendant objects.)

Court: He may answer yes or no, as to whether he knows. (Defendant excepts.)

A: He did not have that reputation.

Q: Do you have any personal knowledge of his running into other automobiles? (Defendant objects; overruled; defendant excepts.)

A: Well, I know he never ran into any other automobiles."

Was the cross-examination proper? What objections would you make to it? Why? Is proof of character or prior occurrences ever proper in civil cases? When? Compare Rule 405.

D. Character and Habit

FRE 406
Habit; Routine Practice

Evidence of the habit of a person or of the routine practice of an organization, whether corroborated or not and regardless of the presence of eyewitnesses, is relevant to prove that the conduct of the person or organization on a particular occasion was in conformity with the habit or routine practice.

Problem II-12
The Careless Smoker

Action for damages by garage owner *P* against *D*, the administrator of the estate of *S*, who was burned to death in a fire in *P*'s garage. *P*'s complaint claims that *S* went to sleep in his car while smoking a cigarette which ignited the seats in *S*'s car and touched off a general conflagration which burned *P*'s garage to the ground. *S*'s body was found in his car in the smoldering remains of the garage. At trial, *P* offers evidence of three previous fires caused by *S*'s smoking and falling asleep.

Is such evidence relevant? Is it admissible? Is it evidence of habit or character?

Problem II-13
Pothead v. Daredevil

Action for damages and personal injuries received by *P* when the car that *P* was driving collided with *D*'s car at 7:30 p.m. on Saturday, June 1, at an intersection controlled by a traffic light. *P* claims that she was proceeding through a green light when *D*'s car struck her from the right.

D claims that *P* ran a yellow light and that *D* had the green light while in the intersection. There were no eyewitnesses to the accident other than the drivers.

At the trial, *D* offers the testimony of *P*'s roommate, *W*, a hostile witness, that on the night in question, *P* was on her way to a movie and that *P* generally smoked several marijuana cigarettes immediately before or on the way to movies. *P* offers evidence showing that *D* has been cited eight times in the past two years for going through red lights and that three of those citations were given after automobiles driven by *D* had been involved in collisions with other vehicles.

Is any of this evidence admissible? Why?

Problem II-14
The Acrobatic Driver — A Reprise

In the case of the acrobatic but reckless driver, Problem II-10 above, suppose *P* offers *W3* to testify that he worked at a gas station on the corner of Walden and Thoreau Streets, that he has serviced *B*'s car and knows it is a standard-shift automobile, and that in all the times he saw *B* drive through the Walden/Thoreau intersection, he never saw *B* come to a full stop at the stop sign. Rather, *B* always would spurt through the intersection without downshifting to first gear.

Is *W3*'s testimony relevant? Is it admissible? What is the difference between *W3*'s proposed testimony and *W1*'s and *W2*'s proposed testimony? Would your decision as to whether any of the witnesses' testimony should be admitted be affected by the presence or absence of eyewitnesses to the collision between *B*'s car and *A*? Should it be?

MEYER v. UNITED STATES
464 F. Supp. 317 (D. Colo. 1979).

FINESILVER, J. As the wife of a serviceman, plaintiff was an eligible patient at the Family Dental Clinic and on March 29, 1974, she was seen by Kent L. Aitkin, D.D.S. After his examination, Dr. Aitkin advised her that she needed several fillings and recommended extraction of her upper and lower third molars (wisdom teeth). He advised her that the teeth were impacted and absent removal she would have trouble in the future. She was already experiencing distress and pain from the molars. These molars are the end back teeth and generally are not functional either in concert or alone.

Plaintiff returned to the clinic on April 12, 1974, at which time two right third molars were removed by Dr. Aitkin. Packing was placed in the extracted areas. She was allowed to return home with the packing in place, additional replacement packing, medications, prescriptions for pain and infection, and instructions on care at home.

Later that same evening (or in the early morning hours), plaintiff had a coughing spell and was unable to swallow apparently because of residual bloody and boney fragments resulting from the operation. She was seen in the emergency room at Fitzsimons Army Medical Center and received a prescription that offered her relief. She returned home. Shortly thereafter she experienced numbness to the right side of the tongue and right gum line.

On April 26, 1974, she was seen again by Dr. Aitkin at the clinic who noted that healing was proceeding in regular fashion. He informed her that her complaints of numbness to the tongue, right gum and partial impairment of sensation were temporary and would return in a matter of months. He also noted this condition was normal in some molar extractions.

Thereafter she was seen by Dr. Jones, an oral surgeon attached to Lowry Air Force Base. She was advised that the loss of sensation and numbness could dissipate in eighteen months, and failure to do so might mean permanent loss of lingual sensation to the right side of the mouth and, in that event, she should consult a lawyer. This suit was filed in January of 1977, following earlier filing of an administrative claim.

It is unrefuted that at this time plaintiff suffers from numbness, permanent loss of sensation and loss of taste in the right front quadrant of her tongue, and right front gum.

Plaintiff related that her injury as a result of nerve damage manifests itself in her inability to taste bland foods, lack of taste differentiation on the right side of the tongue, numbness to this area and to the right gum, and a tendency to stutter. Anxiety over the condition, she contends, makes her unsure of her speech and this has affected her progress and effectiveness as a banking executive for a savings and loan banking facility.

Dentists agree that the lingual nerve has been damaged. Causation of the nerve damage and question of informed consent are matters in dispute.

II

Dr. Aitkin, a dentist in general practice, had specialized dental surgical experience during his three year military service and surgical rotation at each of three duty stations. He had a three month training period in dental surgery at Fort Hood and like periods in Vietnam and in a V.A. residency dental program in California. He related that he had previously performed numerous extractions of third molars in military service and on a weekly basis at the Family Dental Clinic.

Dr. Aitkin does not recollect the various surgical procedures undertaken by him in treating the plaintiff nor the exact conversation he had with plaintiff prior to surgery. His testimony was based in part on his recollection refreshed by the patient's dental chart. He also based his testimony on his habit, custom, and treating routine followed over a considerable period of time.

III

Prior to the extraction procedure, Dr. Aitkin reviewed the x-rays of the teeth in question and in his opinion they were sufficient for the surgical procedure. He administered three injections of novocaine to deaden the pain. The top molar was removed without incident. The lower third molar presented more difficulty because of its mesial angular impaction. He cut a small flap in the lower right gum proximate to the lower molar, observed the impacted molar, removed the bone over the tooth by use of dental instruments, and sectioned and surgically removed the molar. The flap was sutured and area cleansed. Additional injections of novocaine were administered during the operative period. There is no evidence that the lingual nerve was visible to Dr. Aitkin during the operation. The evidence is clear that the nerve may be located along the gum line or elsewhere in the jaw. The nerve is frequently hidden, and the exact location not discernible. In his opinion, x-rays of the molars and locations of roots are of no assistance in knowing where the lingual nerve is situated. The preponderance of the evidence supports this view.

IV

One issue in the case is that of informed consent. Plaintiff testified that she did not receive advice and warnings by Dr. Aitkin as to potential risks of the surgical procedure including possible nerve damage, and had she been so advised she may have declined to go through with the operation.

Dr. Aitkin testified that his habit and custom since dental school, during his three year military service and extending to his association at the Family Dental Clinic, was to give standard advice to patients about extraction of third molars. He advised patients as to the need for the extraction, potential for nerve damage from extraction of the molars including loss of sensation or taste, and general details of the extraction procedure. He generally gave the advice to the patient when he first diagnosed the need for the extraction, although, from his custom, it could come at any time prior to the surgical procedure.

While the testimony is in conflict, we find (a) that plaintiff was informed that as a result of the extractions there was a possibility of damage to the nerves that were proximately located in the area of the molars and roots, and (b) she fully and voluntarily consented to the extraction and medical procedure.

We find that Dr. Aitkin's habit and custom, and routine of advising patients of potential risk as a result of molar extraction was present with plaintiff and he acted in conformity with that long established habit and custom.

We further find that Dr. Aitkin advised plaintiff in a general way of the common and potential risks of extraction of the lower third molar, as shown by his habit, custom and routine, and corroborated by dental assistants Mugele and Smith. He thus complied with a dentist's or physician's duty under Colorado law to inform a patient in a general way as to procedures to be followed in the operation and potential risks. . . .

In the context of Rule 406, habit is a person's or organization's practice of handling a particular kind of situation with a specific type of conduct. Habit is one's regular response to a repeated specific situation. McCormick on Evidence §195 (2d ed. 1972). In similar fashion, an organization's regularity of action is within the purview of Rule 406.

Habit in modern usage is described as "a tendency to act in a certain way or to do a certain thing; usual way of acting; custom; practice. . . ." World Book Dictionary (1974 ed.).

In the instant action there is substantial evidence establishing that the principal actor (Dr. Aitkin) routinely and regularly informed dental patients of the potential risks involved in extraction of third molars. His testimony is supported by two chair-side dental assistants (Mugele and Smith) neither of whom heard the testimony of the other (sequestration pursuant to Rule 615, Fed. R. Evid. was in force during the trial).

What is the difference between evidence of habit and evidence of prior similar acts? Compare *Meyer* with the case of the reckless motorman, Phinney v. Detroit United Railway Company, above.

E. Character and Credibility

FRE 608
Evidence of Character and Conduct of Witness

(a) *Opinion and reputation evidence of character.* The credibility of a witness may be attacked or supported by evidence in the form of opinion or reputation, but subject to these limitations: (1) the evidence may refer only to character for truthfulness or untruthfulness, and (2) evidence of truthful character is admissible only after the character of the witness for truthfulness has been attacked by opinion or reputation evidence or otherwise.

(b) *Specific instances of conduct.* Specific instances of the conduct of a witness, for the purpose of attacking or supporting his credibility, other than conviction of crime as provided in rule 609, may not be proved by extrinsic evidence. They may, however, in the discretion of the court, if probative of truthfulness or untruthfulness, be inquired into on cross-examination of the witness (1) concerning his character for truthfulness or untruthfulness, or (2) concerning the character for truthfulness or untruthfulness of another witness as to which character the witness being cross-examined has testified.

The giving of testimony, whether by an accused or by any other witness, does not operate as a waiver of his privilege against self-incrimination when examined with respect to matters which relate only to credibility.

FRE 609
Impeachment by Evidence of Conviction of Crime

(a) *General rule.* For the purpose of attacking the credibility of a witness, evidence that he has been convicted of a crime shall be admitted if elicited from him or established by public record during cross-examination but only if the crime (1) was punishable by death or imprisonment in excess of one year under the law under which he was convicted, and the court determines that the probative value of admitting this evidence outweighs its prejudicial effect to the defendant, or (2) involved dishonesty or false statement, regardless of the punishment.

(b) *Time limit.* Evidence of a conviction under this rule is not admissible if a period of more than ten years has elapsed since the date of the conviction or of the release of the witness from the confinement imposed for that conviction, whichever is the later date, unless the court determines, in the interests of justice, that the probative value of the conviction supported by specific facts and circumstances substantially outweighs its prejudicial effect. However, evidence of a conviction more than ten years old as calculated herein, is not admissible unless the proponent gives to the adverse party sufficient advance written notice of intent to use such evidence to provide the adverse party with a fair opportunity to contest the use of such evidence.

(c) *Effect of pardon, annulment, or certificate of rehabilitation.* Evidence of a conviction is not admissible under this rule if (1) the conviction has been the subject of a pardon, annulment, certificate of rehabilitation, or other equivalent procedure based on a finding of the rehabilitation of the person convicted, and that person has not been convicted of a subse-

quent crime which was punishable by death or imprisonment in excess
of one year, or (2) the conviction has been the subject of a pardon,
annulment, or other equivalent procedure based on a finding of innocence.

(d) *Juvenile adjudications.* Evidence of juvenile adjudications is generally not admissible under this rule. The court may, however, in a criminal case allow evidence of a juvenile adjudication of a witness other than
the accused if conviction of the offense would be admissible to attack the
credibility of an adult and the court is satisfied that admission in evidence is necessary for a fair determination of the issue of guilt or innocence.

(e) *Pendency of appeal.* The pendency of an appeal therefrom does not
render evidence of a conviction inadmissible. Evidence of the pendency
of an appeal is admissible.

1.   What Is the Difference Between Character and Credibility?

UNITED STATES v. BEECHUM
582 F.2d 898 (5th Cir. 1978); cert. denied, 440 U.S. 920 (1979)

TJOFLAT, J.   This case comes before the court en banc for reconsideration of this circuit's doctrine on the admissibility of offenses extrinsic to a
defendant's indictment to prove his criminal intent.[1]   That doctrine, deriving in part from the case of United States v. Broadway, 477 F.2d 991
(5th Cir. 1973), requires that the essential physical elements of the extrinsic offense include those of the offense charged and that each of

---

1. We shall use the term "extrinsic offense" to denote an "offense," see infra this note,
for which the defendant is not charged in the indictment that is the subject of the case sub
judice. Commentators and cases have referred to such offenses as "prior" or "similar"
offenses. We choose to avoid the connotations carried by these more commonly used terms
for the following reasons.

The principles governing extrinsic offense evidence are the same whether that offense
occurs before or after the offense charged. See United States v. Pollard, 509 F.2d 601 (5th
Cir.), cert. denied, 421 U.S. 1013 (1975). The term "prior offense" is therefore unnecessarily restrictive and misleading.

"Similar offense" is a phrase that assumes the conclusion that extrinsic offenses are
admissible only if similar to the offense charged. Although in a technical sense this is true,
the common connotations of the word are misleading. The meaning and significance of
similarity depends on the issue to which the extrinsic offense evidence is addressed. Stone,
The Rule of Exclusion of Similar Fact Evidence: England, 46 Harv. L. Rev. 954, 955
(1933). Therefore, to avoid an ambiguous application of the term, we shall speak of
similarity only when its meaning is clear in the context.

We use the term "offense" to include "other crimes, wrongs, or acts," as set forth in Fed.
R. Evid. 404(b). See Part III. C. infra. Our analysis applies whenever the extrinsic activity
reflects adversely on the character of the defendant, regardless whether that activity might
give rise to criminal liability.

these elements be proved by plain, clear, and convincing evidence. We are here called upon to determine the effect of the recently enacted Federal Rules of Evidence on this doctrine, an issue expressly reserved in a number of our cases decided prior to the panel opinion in this case. The panel hearing this case was of the opinion, Judge Gee dissenting, that *Broadway* and its progeny survived intact the enactment of the rules. United States v. Beechum, 555 F.2d 487, 504-08 (5th Cir. 1977). With deference to the panel, we must disagree.

A jury convicted Orange Jell Beechum, a substitute letter carrier for the United States Postal Service, of unlawfully possessing an 1890 silver dollar that he knew to be stolen from the mails, in violation of 18 U.S.C. §1708 (1976). To establish that Beechum intentionally and unlawfully possessed the silver dollar, the Government introduced into evidence two Sears, Roebuck & Co. credit cards found in Beechum's wallet when he was arrested. Neither card was issued to Beechum, and neither was signed. The Government also introduced evidence indicating that the cards had been mailed some ten months prior to Beechum's arrest to two different addresses on routes he had serviced. The propriety of the admission of this evidence is the primary issue in this appeal. . . .

The Government indicted Beechum on one count for unlawfully possessing the silver dollar. Argument at the preliminary hearing indicated that the primary issue in the case would be whether Beechum harbored the requisite intent to possess the silver dollar unlawfully. Defense counsel, by motion in limine heard in the absence of the jury, sought to exclude the credit cards as irrelevant and prejudicial. The court overruled the motion, in part on the basis that the cards were relevant to the issue of intent.

In its case in chief, the Government introduced the credit cards and explained the circumstances surrounding their obtention. . . .

In anticipation that Beechum would claim that he sought to turn in the silver dollar, the Government called to the stand Beechum's supervisor, Mr. Cox. Cox testified that he was in the view of Beechum on several occasions, and, indeed, that he had taken mail directly from Beechum.

At the close of the Government's case in chief, the defense moved for a directed verdict of acquittal, alleging that the Government had failed to come forward with sufficient evidence "to establish that Mr. Bonner [sic] possessed the silver dollar with a requisite specific intent that the government is required to establish in this case."

The defense argued that the Government had failed to demonstrate that the credit cards were unlawfully taken from the mail or that Beechum possessed the cards without authorization. The motion was overruled.

At this time defense counsel indicated to the court that Beechum would take the stand and would testify "as to matters concerning the offense for which he is charged," but that he would invoke the fifth amendment as to any questions concerning the credit cards. The defense sought a ruling that the Government be precluded from asking Beechum any question about the cards; the rationale was that the defendant should not be required to invoke his fifth amendment privilege in the presence of the jury. The court declined so to limit the prosecution and indicated that Beechum would have to invoke the amendment in response to the questions he did not wish to answer.

On direct examination Beechum testified that the silver dollar fell out of the mailbox as he was raking out the mail and that he picked it up and placed it first in his shirt pocket, and later (after it had fallen out) in his hip pocket, where he claimed to keep his change. Beechum also testified that, upon return to the postal station, he intended to turn in the silver dollar to Cox but that he could not find Cox. Beechum also stated that he was not leaving the station when he was arrested. No mention was made of the credit cards.

On cross-examination the Government asked Beechum if the credit cards were in his wallet when he was arrested. Defense counsel objected on the basis that inquiry about the cards was outside the scope of cross-examination, and the court overruled the objection. On reassertion of the question, Beechum invoked his fifth amendment rights, but the prosecutor continued questioning on the subject of the cards. This occasioned repeated invocation of the fifth amendment by Beechum and vehement objection by defense counsel. Eventually, Beechum did admit to stating shortly after his arrest that the inspector could "answer his own questions" when the inspector quizzed him about the cards and that the only credit cards he had were his own. . . .

A. SCOPE OF CROSS-EXAMINATION

Beechum took the stand at trial to explain his possession of the silver dollar. He claimed that he came upon it innocently when he collected the mail from the box in which the test letter was placed. He testified that he placed the coin in his hip pocket, with the rest of his change, after it fell out of his shirt pocket. Beechum explained that he searched for his supervisor, Cox, so that he could properly relinquish the coin but that Cox was nowhere to be found. Clearly, Beechum was saying that he did not intend to possess the coin unlawfully because he obtained it innocently and intended to give it to the proper authority.

At the time of his arrest, however, Beechum was carrying in his wallet the credit cards of two other persons. If Beechum wrongfully possessed these cards, the plausibility of his story about the coin is appreciably diminished. Therefore, assuming that it could be established that the cards were wrongfully possessed by Beechum, they were relevant to the issue of Beechum's intent to commit the crime for which he was charged. Fed. R. Evid. 401, see Part III. C. infra.

The scope of proper cross-examination is set forth in Fed. R. Evid.
611(b), which provides as follows:

> *Scope of cross-examination.* Cross-examination should be limited to the sub-
> ject matter of the direct examination and matters affecting the credibility of
> the witness. The court may, in the exercise of discretion, permit inquiry into
> additional matters as if on direct examination.

Implicit in the rule is that all evidence relevant to the subject matter of
direct examination is within the scope of cross-examination. See McCormick, Evidence §30, at 57-58 (2d ed. 1972). Of course, this is not to say
that all such relevant evidence is admissible, for the rules themselves
embody policies that exclude evidence even though relevant. E.g., Fed.
R. Evid. 403, 404(b). Unless, however, one of these exclusionary policies
acts to prohibit the introduction of the credit cards, they are admissible
as within the scope of cross-examination because they are relevant to the
issue of intent, an issue placed squarely in contention by Beechum's
testimony. Moreover, that Beechum did not refer to the cards on direct
examination does not render inquiry about them irrelevant and therefore does not preclude the Government's inquiries about them.

B. REPEATED INVOCATION OF THE FIFTH AMENDMENT

At the close of the Government's case in chief, defense counsel sought
a ruling that the prosecutor be prohibited from questioning Beechum
about the credit cards because Beechum intended to assert the fifth
amendment as to any such questions. The court denied the motion, but
Beechum took the stand to profess his innocence despite the court's
ruling. As promised, when the prosecutor asked Beechum about the
cards, he invoked the fifth amendment. The prosecutor continued to
question Beechum concerning the cards, and Beechum continued to
assert the privilege. The defense claims this to have created undue prejudice before the jury. We cannot agree.

It is an inveterate principle that a defendant who takes the stand
waives his fifth amendment privilege against self-incrimination at least to
the extent of cross-examination relevant to issues raised by his testimony. E.g., Brown v. United States, 356 U.S. 148, 155-56 (1958); Powers v. United States, 223 U.S. 303 (1912); United States v. Pate, 357 F.2d
911, 915 (7th Cir. 1966). Whether a defendant waives the privilege to
the full scope of cross-examination permissible under the Federal Rules
is an issue we need not determine. As we shall show, however, the cross-
examination in this case comes well within the scope of matters that a
defendant is deemed to waive when he takes the stand. The rationale
behind this waiver rule is of equal pertinence to the extrinsic offense
issue in this case; therefore, we briefly explicate that rationale below.

Truth is the essential objective of our adversary system of justice. Of course, the search for truth is in certain instances subordinated to higher values. Indeed, the privilege against self-incrimination ordinarily represents such a value. But where the defendant takes the stand to offer his version of the facts, "the interests of the [Government] and regard for the function of courts of justice to ascertain the truth become relevant, and prevail in the balance of considerations determining the scope and limits of the privilege against self-incrimination." Brown v. United States, 356 U.S. 148, 156 (1958). To allow a defendant to testify with impunity on matters he chooses and in a manner he chooses is a "positive invitation to mutilate the truth a party offers to tell." Id.; accord, Fitzpatrick v. United States, 178 U.S. 304, 316 (1900). The defendant therefore is deemed to waive the privilege, at least with respect to matters about which he testifies, and the Government is entitled to subject his testimony to the acid test of adverse cross-examination.

Here, Beechum sought to attain precisely what the waiver rule seeks to prohibit. His objective was to testify that he intended to give the silver dollar to his supervisor without having to explain the possession of two credit cards not belonging to him. In this, he was largely successful. Had the Government been allowed to ask Beechum about the credit cards, he would have had to explain why he would turn in the coin but keep the cards. Any answer would have borne directly on the issue of intent, and the jury was entitled to consider such highly probative testimony.

The questions the government sought to ask Beechum concerned matters within the letter and the spirit of the waiver rule. The court below erroneously permitted Beechum to invoke the fifth amendment and avoid response. Not satisfied with this, Beechum contends that he was unduly prejudiced by having to assert the amendment repeatedly. He claims that the prejudice was aggravated because the Government knew that the questions would evoke the assertion of the privilege. We find these contentions without merit.

It is impermissibly prejudicial for the Government to attempt to influence the jury by calling a witness it knows will invoke the fifth amendment. United States v. Ritz, 548 F.2d 510 (5th Cir. 1977); United States v. Maloney, 262 F.2d 535 (2d Cir. 1959). Moreover, where the government witness indicates beforehand that he will invoke the privilege, the court may properly refuse to allow him to testify before the jury. United States v. Lacouture, 495 F.2d 1237 (5th Cir.), cert. denied, 419 U.S. 1053 (1974). But this is not such a case. Here the *defendant* took the stand, knowing full well that the Government would inquire about the cards because the court had refused to prohibit that inquiry. Any prejudice deriving from the invocation of the privilege is therefore attributable to Beechum's decision to testify. Indeed, Beechum can hardly complain: if the court had ruled correctly and not allowed him to invoke the fifth amendment, he could have refused to respond only on peril of contempt. See United States v. Brannon, 546 F.2d 1242, 1247 (5th Cir.

1977). Moreover, in that instance the Government would have been entitled to comment on Beechum's refusal to answer, see Caminetti v. United States, 242 U.S. 470 (1917), notwithstanding the prohibition on such comment where the privilege is properly invoked, Griffin v. California, 380 U.S. 609 (1965). Beechum achieved essentially what he desired, refusal to testify concerning the cards, without subjection to contempt or comment. He surely cannot successfully claim undue prejudice on this basis.

C.   THE EXTRINSIC OFFENSE

At the time of his arrest, Beechum possessed a silver dollar and two credit cards, none of which belonged to him. The only contested issue concerning the silver dollar was whether Beechum intended to turn it in, as he claimed, or to keep it for himself. Apparently, he had possessed the credit cards for some time, perhaps ten months, prior to his arrest. The obvious question is why would Beechum give up the silver dollar if he kept the credit cards. In this case, the Government was entitled to an answer.

It is derogative of the search for truth to allow a defendant to tell his story of innocence without facing him with evidence impeaching that story. A basic premise of our adversary system of justice is that the truth is best attained by requiring a witness to explain contrary evidence if he can. As we have seen, for this reason the defendant who chooses to testify waives his fifth amendment privilege with respect to relevant cross-examination. This is not to say that merely by taking the stand a defendant opens himself to the introduction of evidence that is relevant solely to his propensity to commit bad acts or crimes. But where the defendant testifies to controvert an element of the Government's case, such as intent, to which the extrinsic offense is highly relevant, the integrity of the judicial process commands that the defendant be faced with that offense.

In this case, the jury was entitled to assess the credibility of Beechum's explanation but was deprived of the most effective vehicle for determining the veracity of Beechum's story when the judge erroneously allowed Beechum to invoke the fifth amendment and avoid the critical question on cross-examination. The Government was relegated to the inferences the jury might draw from the credit cards themselves and the additional evidence relating to them. The panel held that the cards and this evidence were insufficient to satisfy the strict standards for admissibility of extrinsic offense evidence established by United States v. Broadway, 477 F.2d 991 (5th Cir. 1973). We agree that *Broadway* dictates that the credit cards should not have been admitted; because this is so, we must reject the *Broadway* standards.

Broadway established two prerequisites to the admissibility of extrinsic offense evidence. First, it required that the physical elements of the extrinsic offense include the essential physical elements of the offense for which the defendant was indicted. Second, the case mandated that each of the physical elements of the extrinsic offense be established by plain, clear, and convincing evidence. The elements of the offense for which Beechum was convicted, violation of 18 U.S.C. §1708 (1976), include the following: (1) that the defendant possessed the item, (2) that the item was stolen from the mail, (3) that the defendant knew that the item was stolen, and (4) that the defendant specifically intended to possess the item unlawfully. The first three elements were not disputed, except to the extent that a denial of the fourth renders the item not stolen for the purposes of the second and third elements. The physical elements of the crime are the first two. The panel held that the Government's proof as to the credit cards failed to establish the second element, that the cards were stolen from the mail, by the plain, clear, and convincing evidence required by the second prong of the *Broadway* test. For the purposes of the following analysis, we accept this conclusion as valid.

We must overrule *Broadway* because a straightforward application of the Federal Rules of Evidence calls for admission of the cards. The directly applicable rule is Fed. R. Evid. 404(b). The rule follows the venerable principle that evidence of extrinsic offenses should not be admitted solely to demonstrate the defendant's bad character. Even though such evidence is relevant, because a man of bad character is more likely to commit a crime than one not, the principle prohibits such evidence because it is inherently prejudicial. See, e.g., Michelson v. United States, 335 U.S. 469, 475-76 (1948). Without an issue other than mere character to which the extrinsic offenses are relevant, the probative value of those offenses is deemed insufficient in all cases to outweigh the inherent prejudice. Where, however, the extrinsic offense evidence is relevant to an issue such as intent, it may well be that the evidence has probative force that is not substantially outweighed by its inherent prejudice. If this is so, the evidence may be admissible.

What the rule calls for is essentially a two-step test. First, it must be determined that the extrinsic offense evidence is relevant to an issue other than the defendant's character. Second, the evidence must possess probative value that is not substantially outweighed by its undue prejudice and must meet the other requirements of rule 403. See Rule 404(b) Other Crimes Evidence: The Need for a Two-Step Analysis, 71 Nw. U.L. Rev. 636 (1976). The test for relevancy under the first step is identical to the one we have already encountered. The standards are established by rule 401, which deems evidence relevant when it has "any tendency to make the existence of any fact that is of consequence to the determination of the action more probable or less probable than it would be without the evidence." Where the evidence sought to be introduced is an extrinsic offense, its relevance is a function of its similarity to the offense charged. In this regard, however, similarity means more than that the extrinsic and charged offense have a common characteristic. For the purposes of determining relevancy, "a fact is similar to another only when the common characteristic is the significant one for the purpose of the inquiry at hand." Stone, The Rule of Exclusion of Similar Fact Evidence: England, 46 Harv. L. Rev. 954, 955 (1933). Therefore, similarity, and hence relevancy, is determined by the inquiry or issue to which the extrinsic offense is addressed.

Where the issue addressed is the defendant's intent to commit the offense charged, the relevancy of the extrinsic offense derives from the defendant's indulging himself in the same state of mind in the perpetration of both the extrinsic and charged offenses. The reasoning is that because the defendant had unlawful intent in the extrinsic offense, it is less likely that he had lawful intent in the present offense. Under *Broadway*, that the defendant had unlawful intent in the commission of the extrinsic offense is established by requiring the Government to prove each physical element of that offense by plain, clear, and convincing evidence. And the extrinsic offense is deemed admissible only if its physical elements include those of the offense charged. We think that *Broadway* runs afoul of the Federal Rules of Evidence by imposing on the Government too strict a standard of proof and by requiring too close an identity of elements.

Obviously, the line of reasoning that deems an extrinsic offense relevant to the issue of intent is valid only if an offense was in fact committed and the defendant in fact committed it. Therefore, as a predicate to a determination that the extrinsic offense is relevant, the Government must offer proof demonstrating that the defendant committed the offense. If the proof is insufficient, the judge must exclude the evidence because it is irrelevant. The issue we must decide is by what standard the trial court is to determine whether the Government has come forward with sufficient proof.

The standard of proof for ruling upon factual conditions to relevancy is supplied by Fed. R. Evid. 104(b), which states as follows:

> *Relevancy conditioned on fact.* When the relevancy of evidence depends upon the fulfillment of a condition of fact, the court shall admit it upon, or subject to, the introduction of evidence sufficient to support a finding of the fulfillment of the condition.

As the rule provides, the task for the trial judge is to determine whether there is sufficient evidence for the jury to find that the defendant in fact committed the extrinsic offense. See Morgan, Functions of Judge and Jury in the Determination of Preliminary Questions of Fact, 43 Harv. L. Rev. 165 (1927). The judge need not be convinced beyond a reasonable doubt that the defendant committed the extrinsic offense, nor need he require the Government to come forward with clear and convincing proof. The standard for the admissibility of extrinsic offense evidence is that of rule 104(b): "the preliminary fact can be decided by the judge against the proponent only where the jury could not reasonably find the preliminary fact to exist." 21 Wright & Graham, Federal Practice and Procedure: Evidence §5054, at 269 (1977).

Once it is determined that the extrinsic offense requires the same intent as the charged offense and that the jury could find that the defendant committed the extrinsic offense, the evidence satisfies the first step under rule 404(b). The extrinsic offense is relevant (assuming the jury finds the defendant to have committed it) to an issue other than propensity because it lessens the likelihood that the defendant committed the charged offense with innocent intent. It is not necessary that the physical elements of the charged and extrinsic offenses concur for this inference to be drawn and relevancy established. If the elements do match, the extrinsic offense may have greater probative value, but this is not an issue of relevancy. Evidence is relevant once it appears "to alter the probabilities of a consequential fact." Weinstein & Berger, Weinstein's Evidence ¶401[06], at 401-18 (1976). The probative value of the evidence is a matter to be weighed against its potential for undue prejudice, and the similarity of the physical elements of the charged and extrinsic offenses figures in at this stage. Therefore, we turn to the second step of the analysis required by rule 404(b), whether the evidence satisfies rule 403.

As we have stated, the central concern of rule 403 is whether the probative value of the evidence sought to be introduced is "substantially outweighed by the danger of unfair prejudice." *Broadway* would reverse this standard by requiring a high degree of similarity between the extrinsic and charged offenses and a stringent standard of proof. In effect, the case attempts to establish a threshold requirement that the evidence possess great probative value before it can be admitted. This requirement not only contravenes rule 403 but also fails to meet its own declared ends. Demanding that the Government prove by excessive evidence each physical element of the extrinsic offense does not necessarily enhance its probative value and may in fact increase its unfair prejudice. One of the dangers inherent in the admission of extrinsic offense evidence is that the jury may convict the defendant not for the offense charged but for the extrinsic offense. . . . The touchstone of the trial judge's analysis in this context should be whether the Government has proved the extrinsic offense sufficiently to allow the jury to determine that the defendant possessed the same state of mind at the time he committed the extrinsic offense as he allegedly possessed when he committed the charged offense. Forcing the Government to "overpersuade" the jury that the defendant committed an offense of substantial similarity engenders excessive and unnecessary prejudice. . . .

Probity in this context is not an absolute; its value must be determined with regard to the extent to which the defendant's unlawful intent is established by other evidence, stipulation, or inference. It is the incremental probity of the evidence that is to be balanced against its potential for undue prejudice. Thus, if the Government has a strong case on the intent issue, the extrinsic offense may add little and consequently will be excluded more readily. See, e.g., United States v. Lawrance, 480 F.2d 688, 691-92 n.6 (5th Cir. 1973). If the defendant's intent is not contested, then the incremental probative value of the extrinsic offense is inconsequential when compared to its prejudice; therefore, in this circumstance the evidence is uniformly excluded. In measuring the probative value of the evidence, the judge should consider the overall similarity of the extrinsic and charged offenses. If they are dissimilar except for the common element of intent, the extrinsic offense may have little probative value to counterbalance the inherent prejudice of this type of evidence. Of course, equivalence of the elements of the charged and extrinsic offenses is not required. But the probative value of the extrinsic offense correlates positively with its likeness to the offense charged.[20] Whether the extrinsic offense is sufficiently similar in its physical elements so that its probative value is not substantially outweighed by its undue prejudice is a matter within the sound discretion of the trial judge. The judge should also consider how much time separates the extrinsic and charged offenses: temporal remoteness depreciates the probity of the extrinsic offense.

As this case demonstrates, a significant consideration in determining the probative value of extrinsic offense evidence is the posture of the case. If at the commencement of trial it is not certain that the defendant will contest the issue of intent, the judge is in a poor position to weigh the probative value against the prejudice of the evidence because he cannot foresee the nature or extent of either the Government's case or the defendant's response. Whether a mere plea of not guilty justifies the Government in introducing extrinsic offense evidence in its case in chief is an open question in this circuit. We need not now answer it. Although the credit cards in this case were introduced by the Government in its case in chief, it was clear before the case went to trial that the crucial issue would be Beechum's intent. In effect all the other elements of the crime for which Beechum was indicted were conceded. Where it is evident that intent will be an issue at trial, we have held the admission of the extrinsic offense as part of the Government's case in chief not to be grounds for reversal. United States v. Adderly, 529 F.2d at 1182. In any

20. It is true as well that the more closely the extrinsic offense resembles the charged offense, the greater the prejudice to the defendant. The likelihood that the jury will convict the defendant because he is the kind of person who commits this particular type of crime or because he was not punished for the extrinsic offense increases with the increasing likeness of the offenses. Of course, it is also true that this prejudice is likely to be less when the extrinsic activity is not of a criminal nature. . . .

event, Beechum waived any objection he might have had to the Government's order of proof when he took the stand and professed the innocence of his intent.

We shall now apply the precepts we have set forth to the facts of this case. As we have demonstrated above, the credit card evidence is relevant to Beechum's intent with respect to the silver dollar. That Beechum possessed the credit cards with illicit intent diminishes the likelihood that at the same moment he intended to turn in the silver dollar. If there is sufficient evidence to establish that Beechum wrongfully possessed the credit cards, the requirement of the first step under rule 404(b), that the evidence be relevant to an issue other than propensity, is met. This is so even if the evidence were insufficient for a finding that the cards were stolen from the mail. As we have said, relevancy is established once the identity of the significant state of mind is established. The similarity of the physical elements of the extrinsic and charged offenses is a measure of probity.

The standard for determining whether the evidence is sufficient for a finding that Beechum wrongfully possessed the credit cards is provided by rule 104(b): whether the evidence would support such a finding by the jury. We think the evidence in the record clearly supports a finding that Beechum possessed the credit cards with the intent not to relinquish them to their rightful owners. Beechum possessed the credit cards of two different individuals. Neither card had been signed by the person to whom it was issued. When asked about the cards, Beechum answered first that the only cards he had were his own. When confronted with the credit cards, which were obviously not his own, Beechum responded that they had never been used. He refused to respond further because the inspector "had all the answers." The logical inference from this statement is that Beechum was attempting to mitigate his culpability, having been caught red-handed. The undisputed evidence indicated that he could have possessed the cards for some ten months. The jury would have been wholly justified in finding that Beechum possessed these cards with the intent permanently to deprive the owners of them. This is all the rules require the court to determine to establish the relevancy of the extrinsic offense evidence.

We move now to the second step of the rule 404(b) analysis, the application of rule 403. The incremental probity of the extrinsic offense evidence in this case approaches its intrinsic value. Indeed, the posture of this case and the nature of the Government's proof with respect to the intent issue present perhaps the most compelling circumstance for the admission of extrinsic offense evidence. From the very inception of trial, it was clear that the crucial issue in the case would be Beechum's intent in possessing the silver dollar. He took the stand to proclaim that he intended to surrender the coin to his supervisor. The issue of intent was therefore clearly drawn, and the policies of justice that require a defendant to explain evidence that impugns his exculpatory testimony were in full force. As we have seen, these policies dictate that a defendant waive his fifth amendment privilege against self-incrimination as to cross-examination relevant to his testimony. Where a privilege so central to our notions of fairness and justice yields to the search for truth, we should not lightly obstruct that quest. The credit card evidence bore directly on the plausibility of Beechum's story; justice called for its admission.

That the posture of this case demanded the admission of the credit card evidence is reinforced by the nature of the Government's proof on the issue of intent apart from that evidence. This proof consisted of the following. The Government called Cox, Beechum's supervisor, who testified that Beechum had had several opportunities to surrender the coin to him. Beechum denied this, and called two fellow employees who testified that Beechum had asked them if they had seen Cox. Absent the credit card evidence, the issue would have been decided wholly by the jury's assessment of the credibility of these witnesses. The Government, therefore, did not make out such a strong case of criminal intent that the credit card evidence would have been of little incremental probity. In fact, the credit card evidence may have been determinative.

Having examined at length the circumstances of this case, we conclude that the credit card evidence meets the requirements of rule 403. Therefore, the conditions imposed by the second step of the analysis under rule 404(b) have been met, and the extrinsic offense evidence in this case was properly admitted at trial.

GOLDBERG, J., with whom GODBOLD, SIMPSON, MORGAN and RONEY, JJ., join, dissenting:

As the lights are being extinguished on Broadway, I feel impelled to light a few candles in requiem.

The majority has gone well out of its way to overrule *Broadway*. In the panel opinion, 555 F.2d 487 (5th Cir. 1977), the panel majority explained why the policies and doctrines of *Broadway* are sound. I affirm those views here. But I must add a few comments because the opinion of the en banc majority leaves the law in this area in such a confused state. In this dissent I make two broad arguments. First I show how the majority misinterpreted Rule 404(b) of the Federal Rules of Evidence. Basically the majority's reading of the rule fails because it reads so broadly the second sentence in Rule 404(b), which makes certain evidence admissible, that it allows the second sentence to swallow up the first sentence of Rule 404(b), which explicitly bars the admissibility of certain evidence. In addition, this too broad reading of Rule 404(b)'s second sentence conflicts with explicit language in other related federal evidence rules, such as Rules 609 and 608. . . . My second broad argument concerns the test with which the majority replaces *Broadway*. I argue that not only is this test little more than a subjective, difficult to apply version of *Broadway,* but that it is even *more* hostile to extrinsic offense evidence than *Broadway* in some respects.

I. THE MAJORITY MISINTERPRETS RULE 404(B)

A. THE MAJORITY'S TOO BROAD READING OF THE SECOND SENTENCE IN RULE 404(B) ALLOWS IT TO SWALLOW UP THE FIRST SENTENCE

Rule 404(b) seems to me to identify two conflicting policies and to require the courts to reconcile them. One policy is that extrinsic acts evidence is sometimes probative of material facts. For that reason, the second sentence authorized us to reason from unrelated past acts and states of mind to current states of mind. But at the same time the drafters of the rule were wary of such reasoning. Thus they wrote the first sentence. Its purpose is to caution us that extrinsic acts evidence is fraught with dangers of prejudice — extraordinary dangers not presented by other types of evidence. Had the drafters not thought the dangers were extraordinary, they would never have given us the first sentence; they would have written only the second sentence and the general balancing test of Rule 403. *Broadway* and similar doctrines were designed precisely to deal with such extraordinary dangers.

The majority reads this rule differently. It thinks that so long as the probative value of extrinsic acts evidence is not "substantially outweighed" by its prejudicial effect, Rule 403, the evidence is to be admitted. How does the majority dispose of the first sentence, then? Here is where, to my mind, it seriously misapprehends the rule. The majority reads the rule to establish two watertight compartments: extrinsic acts evidence which relates "solely to . . . the defendant's character," and that which is relevant for other purposes, including state of mind. Thus the majority thinks the rule unequivocally allows us to reason that because a defendant displayed an improper intent in the past, he is more likely to have had an evil intent in the act for which he is tried. How this differs from reasoning that the defendant has a "propensity" to act with evil intent, is beyond reason; but the majority says the rule prohibits references based on propensity. There simply are no such watertight compartments to be found, unless we engage in subtle and sophisticated metaphysical analysis.

Even the majority implies at one point that extrinsic offense evidence submitted allegedly to show intent is really just bad character evidence in sheep's clothing. . . .

To be sure, I find it nearly impossible to imagine any "extrinsic offense" which would make a jury think that the defendant had a bad character or a criminal propensity, but which did not also have at least *some* tendency to make it less probable than it would be without the evidence that he had a purely innocent, law-abiding intent in the charged offense. But, more importantly, if such "extrinsic offense" evidence were so purely irrelevant to intent and to the other elements of the charged crime, I can not see how it could pass the Rule 401 relevancy test even to necessitate the application of the Rule 404(b) bar to its admission.

The "watertight compartment" view of Rule 404(b) could lead to other peculiarities as well. Constrained by the explicit words of Rule 404(b), the majority concedes that extrinsic offense evidence which relates "solely" to a defendant's propensity to commit the charged crime is barred by the first sentence of Rule 404(b), no matter how much its probative value outweighs its prejudicial effect. But when a judge thinks the extrinsic offense also relates to the defendant's propensity to intend to commit the charged crime, then the question leaps over to the second watertight compartment, where the presumption is heavily in favor of admitting the evidence, unless its probative value is substantially outweighed by prejudice. The alchemy of the majority opinion would radically change the rule from a total bar of the evidence regardless of the probative-prejudice balance to a balancing test substantially weighted in favor of admissibility, simply because a judge metaphysically classifies the question as propensity to intend rather than as propensity to commit. Since propensity is largely a concept of a person's psychological bent or frame of mind, it seems extreme to have so much turn on so little, if any, of a distinction. I respectfully refuse to adopt the majority's Dr. Jekyll-Mr. Hyde interpretation of Rule 404(b). It is a horror fantasy that should pass by the boards of Broadway.

B. THE MAJORITY'S READING OF RULE 404(B) CONFLICTS WITH THE EXPLICIT LANGUAGE IN RULES 609 AND 608

Another problem with the majority's interpretation of the vague language in Rule 404(b) is that it conflicts with the specific language in Rules 608 and 609. Suppose, for example, that Beechum had been convicted of fraudulent use of credit cards 10 years before his trial for the coin theft. Under Rule 609, if Beechum took the stand his credibility could be impeached with evidence of the prior conviction only if the probative value of the prior offense *substantially* outweighed its prejudicial impact on the jury. If the conviction had been more recent than 10 years ago, then the test would be a simple weighing of probativeness and prejudice.

Next, suppose that the evidence of the prior offense were clear and convincing, but that the defendant had never been convicted for it. In this case, Rule 608 would forbid *any* admission of the evidence of the prior offense except for what could be elicited from the defendant on the stand. If the defendant chose to exercise his Fifth Amendment right of silence, then no evidence of the prior offense could reach the jury.

Now, finally, consider the result under the majority's reading of Rule 404(b). Here the evidence of a prior offense is independently admissible to the jury,[6] as long as its probative value is not substantially outweighed by its prejudicial impact. The prior offense need not be proved beyond a reasonable doubt, as in Rule 609, nor even clearly and convincingly, as might be the case under Rule 608, but rather only to the minimal Rule 104 standard, i.e. where a reasonable jury might find the defendant committed the crime. This leads to a bizarre anomaly. According to the majority, the government under Rule 404(b) can submit with ease prejudicial, flimsy evidence of an extrinsic offense, but under Rule 609, where the crime was proved beyond a reasonable doubt, the admissions standards are much stricter. Under Rule 608, the evidence is inadmissible entirely except from the defendant's own mouth, even if the evidence of the other crime is clear and convincing, or established beyond a reasonable doubt.[7] You might say then that, for purposes of admitting extrinsic offense evidence, the majority of this court may at times presume a defendant guilty until he is proven guilty beyond a reasonable doubt, at which point the court may begin presuming him innocent. . . .

II. THE MAJORITY REPLACES *BROADWAY* WITH A WORSE TEST

If Rule 404(b) were no more than the intersection of Rules 104, 401 and 403, as the majority at times implies, then the prosecution of any crime in which intent was an element could include evidence of any extrinsic wrong-doing of the defendant which had *any* tendency to prove that it was less probable he acted with law-abiding intent (Rule 401), and which evidence had a prejudicial effect which might outweigh its probativeness, but not substantially (Rule 403).[17] Instead the majority re-

---

6. That is, the government can submit it directly to the jury, whether or not the defendant takes the stand, and does not have to elicit it from the defendant on the stand, as in Rule 608.

7. The majority might try to explain this by asserting that impeachment evidence of a criminal defendant is generally less probative of guilt than evidence of an element of the crime, such as intent. We find this argument less than convincing. Inferring intent in one crime from the defendant's behavior in a totally unrelated crime seems to us at least as tenuous and unprobative as evidence that a defendant is lying on the stand. The 609/404 distinction is especially flimsy where the defendant is testifying about his intent. Where extremely tenuous evidence is involved, we see little difference between trying to prove that the defendant is lying, and trying to prove that what he is saying is a lie.

Moreover, probativeness is a factor taken into account in the balancing process itself. If impeachment evidence is inherently less probative, then this can be fully reflected by its weight in the balancing test itself without also requiring that the test be weighted specially against the evidence.

17. This standard would be as unfair as it is all encompassing, given that criminal defendants invariably tend to live in the real world, which is not inhabited by saints alone. (Even visitors to Broadway must travel a few paces on 42nd Street before reaching the comfort and safety of their loge seats.) The plain fact is that many people think there is a criminal "type" who not only has a bad "character," but everything that goes with it — bad

stricts this hopelessly broad floodgate for extrinsic offense evidence by building into Rule 401 a "similarity" test reminiscent of *Broadway*. Strictly speaking, the relevance test in Rule 401 is no more than a requirement that the evidence have some "tendency" to change the probability of a consequential fact, such as criminal intent. But the majority adds to this simple, albeit grossly overbroad threshold test, the requirement that the intent of the extrinsic crime be the "same" as the intent of the charged crime. . . .

The majority nowhere explains where it gets this additional test. It is no more stated in Rules 401, 403 and 404 than is *Broadway*. Admittedly it does seem to serve the same critical function of preventing the second sentence in Rule 404(b) from swallowing the first. Nevertheless, it is a poor replacement for *Broadway* for two reasons. First, it replaces *Broadway*'s objective test of similar physical elements with a subjective, psychological test of determining when a defendant was "indulging . . . in the same state of mind in the perpetration of both the . . . offenses." Second, in some situations it could be even more hostile to the admission of extrinsic offense evidence than *Broadway* was.

A.   THE MAJORITY'S NEW SIMILARITY TEST IS A SUBJECTIVE VERSION OF *BROADWAY*

The majority's "psychological indulgence" test seems to call on a district judge to decide whether the defendant "indulged himself" in the "same state of mind" in the preparation of two crimes. It totally escapes me how one would go about making this decision. If a person snatches a purse, cheats on his income taxes, and then steals a coin from the mail, is he "indulging himself in the same state of mind in the perpetration" of the offenses? Would a court say, for example, that the defendant is "indulging himself in the same state of mind in the perpetration" of these offenses because, at some point in each offense, he intends to possess property rightfully belonging or owed to another? Moreover, is this Freudian and ill-defined type of psycho-analysis required, or even suggested, by Rule 401's definition of relevance?

It was precisely this impossibility of comparing psychological states of mind that led *Broadway* to settle on a simple comparison of only the physical elements of the two crimes. As is demonstrated in the next section, the issue of the *strictness* of a test can be kept entirely separate from whether the test turns on subjective or objective factors. Thus I do

---

intentions, bad motives, bad plans, etc. This kind of thinking is inimical to the principles of due process and presumed innocence that dignify our criminal system. In this country our government simply may not deprive one of its citizens of his freedom unless it charges that he committed a specific crime and proves beyond a reasonable doubt that he committed that specific crime.

not see what the majority accomplishes by telling a district judge to match up psychological indulgences rather than physical elements. The new test seems to add little to the effort except hazy uncertainty. One might even say that the majority did not overrule *Broadway* at all; it simply moved it from Times Square to the Bermuda Triangle.

B.   THE MAJORITY'S "PSYCHOLOGICAL INDULGENCE" TEST COULD BE
     EVEN STRICTER THAN *BROADWAY*

Needless to say, turning a test of objective facts into a test of subjective facts does not necessarily make it a looser test. In fact, in this case there is a good chance that the majority's "psychological indulgence" test could be even more hostile to extrinsic offense evidence than was *Broadway*. The majority deludes itself on this point by defining *Broadway* too harshly. Specifically, the majority seems to think that *Broadway* requires a one-to-one correspondence between all the physical elements of the two offenses. This is wrong. In fact, in this case the panel opinion even left open the question whether both thefts had to involve the mails. For example, it might be possible that *Broadway* would be satisfied by an extrinsic offense involving a theft of credit cards from a neighbor's wallet, as long as the essential physical elements of theft were shared and there was "some basis for an inference of similarity between the mental elements of the extrinsic and charged offenses." . . .

We might easily imagine a situation in which two crimes involved the same essential physical elements and in which there was "some basis for an inference of similarity between the mental elements" of the two crimes, but in which there was not enough evidence to support a jury determination that the defendant possessed the *same* state of mind in both cases. For example, imagine a defendant who stole two cars, one for a joy ride around the block and one to resell surreptitiously. *Broadway* might allow in evidence of the joy ride, whereas the "psychological indulgence" test might not.

CONCLUSION

At the heart of the majority's error in this case is its mistaken placement of the spotlight on the Federal Rules of Evidence, instead of where it rightfully belongs — on the criminal trial of a human being. The majority places the vague and uninformed stage hands of the drama — the Federal Rules of Evidence — in the center of the stage, and pushes the principles of a fair criminal trial into weak, whispered supporting roles off to the edge of the proscenium wall. This means the death of *Broadway,* the majority admits. But it is also an assault on the legitimacy of our criminal system. The majority has, and is, misdirected. The Federal Rules can be supporting actors, at most. They must be directed one way in a civil trial and another way altogether in a criminal trial where human freedom is at stake. Rule 404(b), and most of the other federal rules as well, were designed to be broadly applicable to both criminal and civil trials. But evidence is allowed into a civil trial under a much more flexible, utilitarian standard than in a criminal trial. Due process requires extreme vigilance against the contamination of a criminal trial with cheap and mean character slander, and against the conviction of a citizen for improper reasons. The majority cannot possibly think that Rule 404(b) overrules this central principle of justice, or that it collapses the criminal trial into the utilitarianism of civil litigation.

Broadway may not be stylish, it may not be chic, but its old-fashioned virtues should command our reverence. *Broadway* was one more last bastion of judging a man by the specifics of the charged crime, rather than by a vague, undocumented, unauthenticated record of misbehavior. The protective mantle of presumed innocence is under severe attack in some modern-day jurisprudence, but the majority's Cain marks become almost ineradicable. The majority's opinion goes far in making one slip a noose.

At the heart of this dissent is a concern about the proper level of hostility or hospitality to extrinsic offense evidence. But in this dissent I am even more concerned about the practicality and integrity of the analysis this circuit will employ in making these judgments. In this case the majority has obliterated a venerable, well-reasoned body of law for no good reason at all, and has replaced it with a Freudian, difficult to apply subjective test that, outside this and a few other similar cases, will not even accomplish what the majority wants. It is especially ironic that the majority should justify its evisceration of *Broadway* by declaring that the "revolutionary" drafters of Rule 404(b) wanted the old standards cleared from the stage to make room for the free form, uncontrolled balancing-test discretion of the new Theatre of the Absurd. For no sooner were the objective flats and screens of the legitimate *Broadway* stage pulled aside, than the majority brought in the psychological psychedelics of the Theatre of Indulgence. I can only hope that the majority will soon see the error of its ways and return to the Great White Way of *Broadway* with the appreciation and respect that the grand old boulevard deserves. . . .

———————————————

Which view of "other crimes" evidence do you feel is more consistent with the thrust of Rule 404 and the rest of the Federal Rules, the majority's or the dissent's? Does the majority's formulation of the "similarity" requirement of Rule 404(b) open the floodgates to overuse of such evidence? Or as the dissent charges, does the majority's "psychological indulgence" approach impose unnecessarily strict barriers to the use of evidence of other crimes to prove intent?

Do you agree with the majority's use of Rule 104(b)'s standard of proof ("sufficient to support a finding") as the threshold for other crimes evidence? Does this standard afford sufficient protection to defendants?

How does the majority's view of the scope of cross-examination and the breadth of defendant's waiver of his privilege against self-incrimination affect your appraisal of the fairness of Rule 404(b)?

Is this case more appropriately treated under Rules 608 and 609 than under 404 and 405? What was the government really trying to prove with the credit card evidence?

Problem II-15
"A Nice Piece of Change"

Action by a real estate broker, Leon Easerly, for his brokerage commission. New York's statute of frauds excepted real estate brokers' oral agreements for commission from the normal requirement that such contracts be in writing. Easerly claims that Letwin, the defendant, orally commissioned him to negotiate the purchase of a shopping center owned by a Mr. Odessa. At trial Easerly testifies that after he persuaded Odessa to accept Letwin's offer for the property, hence earning his commission, Letwin backed out of the deal. Letwin claims that he never made any arrangement with Easerly. Moreover, Letwin's lawyer has discovered that in the last two years Easerly has brought eight very similar lawsuits against others in the New York area, all based on alleged oral contracts.

During the direct examination, Easerly testifies that Letwin promised him, "Leon, don't worry. Listen, you put that deal over, and there's going to be a nice piece of change for you."

On cross-examination Letwin's lawyer tries to bring out these eight previous lawsuits and in an offer of proof states that the trial transcripts of them show Easerly claiming that at the critical moment the prospective buyer or seller said, "There's a nice piece of change in it for you."

Should defendant's offer of proof be accepted? What factors militate for and against receiving evidence of the eight other lawsuits?

2. Proving Character for Truthfulness

Problem II-16
Murder at the Hash House

Detective Kojak is called to V's Hash House, where he finds V lying on the floor with his stomach open and his intestines splattered over the french frier. The till is open and empty. W is there. Detective Kojak says

"What's happenin', baby?" W says, "D did it. Yesterday he told me he was going to get V."

At D's trial for murder and robbery W testifies to D's alleged statement. Other circumstantial evidence against D is introduced. D defends with an alibi and offers the following evidence concerning W:

(1) The testimony of A that several years ago A was an altar boy at the local church and W was a chorister and that several times A saw W stealing church property, such as sacramental cups and other religious objects;

(2) The testimony of a justice of the peace that on May 1 of the previous year W was tried before him and convicted of forgery;

(3) The testimony of B that he is the butler in W's parents' home, that he has known W for W's entire life, and that, in his personal opinion, W is untruthful;

(4) The testimony of C that he lives in the same neighborhood as W and knows W's reputation in the neighborhood for truth and veracity to be bad; and

(5) The testimony of Dr. Q, a psychiatrist, who has examined W and found him to be, in Dr. Q's opinion, a pathological liar.

Which if any of these offers of proof should be admitted? Why?

Problem II-17
The Case of the Jilted Law Student

D, a third-year law student, is accused of murdering Mr. V, an attractive, wealthy young divorcé, on June 1 between the hours of 9 and 11 P.M. at Mr. V's fashionable home in Cambridge. The alleged M.O. is stabbing Mr. V with the blade of his food processor. The alleged motive is revenge for Mr. V's ending their affair to take up with a medical student. At trial Mr. V's maid, Emma, gives scream-scram testimony for the prosecution: She heard Mr. V scream, she saw D scram. The defense is an alibi. The principal defense witness is W, who testifies that from 9 to 11 P.M. on June 1 she and D were at the law review cite-checking Professor Smith's latest article, Law School Pedagogy — Use of the Socratic Method in a Non-Intimidating Manner. In rebuttal the prosecution offers to prove through C, a cashier at Martin's Liquor Store, that on May 1 he saw W steal a case of Rémy Martin by pretending it had been paid for when in fact it had not. D objects. What ruling and why?

Suppose that the prosecution offers to prove on cross-examination W's conviction for grand larceny for a theft of a case of Rémy Martin from Martin's and D objects. What ruling and why? What reasons are there to treat the two situations differently? If the prosecution introduces evidence of W's prior conviction, should the defense in sur-rebuttal be allowed to elicit from W testimony that she was convicted but was framed and is really innocent?

Problem II-18
Fracas at Fenway Park

Action for damages arising out of *D*'s alleged assault and battery on *P* on June 1, 1979, in the bleachers at Fenway Park. The complaint alleges that *D* struck *P* over the head with a Budweiser bottle while *P* was giving Ron Guidry a standing ovation for striking out Rice, Yaz, and Fisk in order. The defense: self-defense.

(1) At trial, *P* offers the testimony of *A* that he was at the game with *P* and that he saw *D* strike *P* over the head with a Budweiser bottle without any provocation. *P* then offers the testimony of *B* that although he was not at the game with *P* and *A*, he lives on the same street in the Bronx as *A* and know. *A*'s reputation in the community for peace and quietude to be good. *D* objects. What result and why?

(2) Suppose that *B*'s testimony is that he is familiar with *A*'s reputation in the community for truthfulness and veracity and that it is good. *D* objects. What ruling and why?

(3) On cross-examination of *A*, defense counsel asks *A* whether he has ever been convicted of possession of marijuana. *P* objects. What ruling and why?

(4) On cross-examination of *A*, defense counsel asks *A* if he was convicted of perjury on June 1, 1968. *P* objects. What ruling and why?

(5) Suppose that the objection to *B*'s testimony, set forth in (2), above, was overruled. On cross-examination of *B*, defense counsel asks *B* if he knows that *A* was convicted of perjury on June 1, 1968. *P* objects. What ruling and why? What if *B* is asked on cross-examination whether he is aware that *A* was convicted of possession of marijuana?

(6) In rebuttal, *D* offers the testimony of *C* that on May 1, 1969, *A* filed a false 10K statement with the SEC. *P* objects. What ruling and why?

(7) Suppose that after *A* has been asked on cross-examination by defense counsel whether he was previously convicted for perjury, or after *C* testified to the false 10K statement, or after rebuttal reputation testimony that *A*'s reputation in the community for truthfulness is bad, *B* is recalled to the stand to testify to *A*'s reputation for truthfulness. *D* objects. What ruling and why?

(8) Suppose that on cross-examination of *A*, *A* admits that he is *P*'s brother. *P* then calls *B* to testify that *A*'s reputation for truthfulness and veracity is good. *D* objects. What ruling and why?

(9) Suppose that as part of *A*'s direct examination, *A* testifies that in the third inning he saw *D* drink three large beers. In rebuttal, *D* testifies that in the third inning he had two cokes, three hot dogs, a box of popcorn, two bags of peanuts, two pieces of pizza, and an ice cream, but no beer. In surrebuttal, may *B* testify to *A*'s reputation for truthfulness and veracity?

3. The Use of Prior Convictions

Problem II-19
Robbery of the Mom & Pop Spa

Charge: robbery on June 1, 1969 of the Mom & Pop Spa. M.O.: pointing a gun at Pop and absconding with. the contents of the cash register. At trial the state calls *C*, the Clerk of the Superior Court, to testify and authenticate as an exhibit certified records of *D*'s prior convictions as follows:
(1) Armed robbery, June 1, 1968;
(2) Petty larceny, May 1, 1968;
(3) Fraud, June 1, 1967;
(4) Perjury, June 1, 1966; and
(5) Perjury, June 1, 1947.
Which, if any, of these prior convictions are admissible?

The statutory history of Rule 609 is outlined in the Advisory Committee's notes. Which formulation seems more desirable to you? What procedures do you think should be required for proof of prior convictions? How much discretion should the trial judge have to exclude proof of prior criminal convictions? What factors should the judge weigh in the exercise of discretion? Should the rule regarding the use of prior criminal convictions to impeach a witness be different in civil cases? How? Why?

Should the trial judge exercise different standards of discretion and weigh different factors under Rules 609(a), 609(b), and 403? Compare the following cases.

UNITED STATES v. PAIGE
464 F. Supp. 99 (E.D. Pa. 1978)

NEWCOMER, J. The defendant pleaded guilty on October 19, 1970, to violating Title 18, United States Code, Section 659, that is, possession of goods of a value in excess of $100 stolen from a foreign shipment knowing that the goods were stolen. Pursuant to Rule 609(a)(1) of the Federal Rules of Evidence, he moves to prevent the government from impeaching his credibility by use of that conviction in the upcoming criminal trial of the above-captioned matter. Rule 609(a)(1) provides:

> For the purpose of attacking the credibility of a witness, evidence that he has been convicted of a crime shall be admitted if elicited from him or established by public record during cross-examination but only if the crime (1) was pun-

ishable by death or imprisonment in excess of one year under the law under which he was convicted, and the court determines that the probative value of admitting this evidence outweighs its prejudicial effect to the defendant.

It is the government's burden to establish that the probative value of the prior conviction's use outweighs its prejudicial effect. United States v. Hayes, 553 F.2d 824 (2d Cir.), cert. denied, 434 U.S. 867 (1977). In this case, where the defendant is charged with the knowing receipt and concealment of stolen securities in violation of Title 18, United States Code, Section 2315, the government has failed to meet that burden.

To make the necessary determination under Rule 609(a)(1) the Court should take into account certain factors:

> (1) the impeachment value of the prior crime;
> (2) the point in time of the conviction and the witness's subsequent history;
> (3) the similarity between the past crime and the charged crime;
> (4) the importance of the defendant's testimony; and
> (5) the centrality of the credibility issue.

United States v. Mahone, 537 F.2d 922 (7th Cir.), cert. denied, 429 U.S. 1025 (1976). Upon balancing these factors in this case, the Court is convinced that evidence of the prior conviction should be excluded.

Although the defendant's prior crime reflects adversely to his honesty and integrity, the length of time between that conviction and the present trial lessens its probative value. Eight years ago he entered that plea and received a five year sentence which term was suspended but for one month. Since that time, he has not been convicted of any other crimes. Therefore, the defendant's subsequent criminal history and the prior conviction's age diminish its probative value.

On the other hand, the prior conviction's effect on the jury is likely to be extremely prejudicial. The prior crime and the presently charged crime are similar, sharing the common element of possession of stolen goods. Although the government argues that the "similarity in the crimes is the strongest argument in support of the use of this evidence," the law is directly the contrary. Similarity between the crimes weighs strongly in favor of exclusion. United States v. Seamster, 568 F.2d 188 (10th Cir. 1978); United States v. Hawley, 554 F.2d 50, n.6 (2d Cir. 1977); United States v. Hayes, supra. Revealing the prior conviction to the jurors may cause them to believe that if the defendant "did it before he probably did so this time." Gordon v. United States, 127 U.S. App. D.C. 343, 347, 383 F.2d 936, 940 (1967), cert. denied, 390 U.S. 1029 (1968). Because such use of the prior conviction would be highly prejudicial and improper, prior similar crimes generally are not admitted unless strong reasons exist for disclosure.

In this case, it is especially important that the defendant feel free to testify and this also weighs heavily against allowing the impeachment use of the prior similar conviction. The government is likely to ask the Court to instruct the jury that it may infer guilt from proof of the defendant's recent possession of stolen goods, if the defendant has failed to explain such possession to the jury's satisfaction. This instruction is usually given, and it practically shifts the burden to defendant to explain his possession of the goods. For the defendant to do so, he probably will have to testify. Thus, his defense will be prejudiced severely if he is deterred from testifying from fear that he will be convicted on the basis of a prior crime. Suggs v. United States, 129 U.S. App. D.C. 133, 391 F.2d 971 (1968). Therefore, as was recognized in Smith v. United States, 123 U.S. App. D.C. 259, 359 F.2d 243 (1966), justice requires that use of the prior conviction be disallowed unless the government shows strong justification. As the prior conviction's probative value is limited, such justification has not been shown here.

Therefore, the motion will be granted.

UNITED STATES v. FEARWELL
595 F.2d 771 (1978)

WRIGHT, C.J. This appeal comes to us from the United States District Court for the District of Columbia, where appellant Steven Fearwell was convicted under 18 U.S.C. §371 (1976) of conspiracy to violate the Food Stamp Act, 7 U.S.C. §2023 (1976). On February 14, 1978 appellant was sentenced to a prison term of from 20 months to five years to run concurrently with any other sentence he was then serving. Prior to trial the prosecution informed defense counsel that, if appellant chose to testify, it intended to impeach his credibility by introducing evidence of his prior conviction of attempted petit larceny, and the trial court ruled that it would permit the prosecution to proceed with the impeachment as planned. Accordingly, it is argued on appeal, Fearwell, who was to have been the only witness to appear in his own behalf, decided not to testify. Further, the trial court, after making this ruling but before being informed that appellant would not testify, refused to grant a continuance so that counsel could devise a new defense strategy involving other witnesses.

Fearwell appeals from both rulings of the District Court and asks that his conviction be set aside. We agree that, under Federal Rule of Evidence 609(a), impeachment with evidence of the prior conviction involved in this case should not be permitted. Hence the trial judge was incorrect in ruling that the prosecution would be able to proceed, as planned, with its impeachment of Fearwell if he chose to testify. But because we do not know what Fearwell's testimony would have been, we cannot yet determine whether this error requires setting aside the conviction. Hence we remand to the District Court to determine the nature of his testimony. Finally, in our view the trial court did not err by refusing to grant a continuance.

I. BACKGROUND

Appellant's conviction of conspiracy to violate the Food Stamp Act was in connection with an illegal scheme to use Authorization to Purchase (ATP) cards of the federal Food Stamp Program for personal gain. Under the Food Stamp Program the issuing agency — in the District of Columbia, the Department of Human Resources — sends ATP cards each month to all person eligible for food stamps. These cards state that if the recipient pays a specified amount he or she will receive foods stamps valued at a greater amount. For example, the card may say that a payment of $40 will result in receipt of food stamps valued at $100.

There are, of course, a certain number of intended recipients of these cards who have perhaps died or moved, and who are at any event no longer resident at the address to which a card was sent. Cards sent in such cases are returned to the Department of Human Resources. Appellant's brother, Joseph Fearwell, was employed by the Department of Human Resources from September 1974 to July 1975, and one of his assigned tasks was to transport the returned cards from one floor of the Department to another. After terminating employment with the Department in July 1975, Joseph Fearwell regularly visited the Department and began to remove a number of the returned ATP cards on many of his visits. Once having removed the cards, it was quite simple for Joseph Fearwell to translate the stolen cards into food stamps and quite a handsome profit.

After a time, according to the Government's case, Joseph Fearwell started to supply stolen ATP cards to his brother, appellant here, who likewise began redeeming the stolen cards for stamps and then selling the stamps for profit. Joseph and Steven Fearwell were not, however, content to operate alone; they apparently feared that their repeated trips to redeem the ATP cards might arouse suspicion. Consequently, they enlisted the help of Ms. Yvonne Mason, a teller at the Friendship House Federal Credit Union. The agreement struck among the brothers Fearwell and Ms. Mason specified a fixed sum — apparently five dollars — that she would receive from the brothers for each stolen ATP card she redeemed in her capacity as clerk at the Credit Union. She testified that for a period ranging from mid-1976 to early 1977 one of the brothers would present her with a packet of cards two or three times a week, which she was happy to redeem for stamps so long as she was paid the agreed upon amount. Indeed, the record indicates that 99 stolen ATP cards, worth over $10,000, were redeemed through Ms.

Mason in the relevant period, and that the cards bore a certain similarity in signatures. A handwriting expert for the prosecution testified that the similarity on many of the cards was attributable to a single person's having supplied the various signatures, and that that person was Steven Fearwell.

II. IMPEACHMENT

Before introduction of evidence had commenced at Steven Fearwell's trial, and out of the range of the jury, defense counsel informed the trial judge that the prosecution intended, if Fearwell chose to testify, to impeach his testimony with evidence of a prior conviction of attempted petit larceny. Defense counsel asked the judge to rule that the conviction could not be used to impeach because "[i]t is a minor offense and is his only prior conviction to my knowledge." The prosecution, wishing to use the prior conviction "purely for impeachment," argued in response that the crime of attempted petit larceny "involve[s] dishonesty[ ] and, as such, . . . goes to the defendant's credibility." Further, the prosecution reasoned, attempted petit larceny "is not a particularly inflammatory type of conviction," so presumably nothing would be lost and much would be gained by using the conviction for impeachment purposes. Defense counsel retorted, but without elaboration, that Fearwell intended to be the only witness in his own behalf. Yet when the trial judge specifically asked defense counsel whether Fearwell would testify notwithstanding the prospect of being impeached, counsel's only response was that "I believe he intends to. He wants to."

This discussion among the trial judge, the prosecutor, and defense counsel did not, in terms, include a direct reference to the legal rule that governed the perplexity confronting them, Federal Rule of Evidence 609(a), or to this circuit's leading case construing Rule 609(a), United States v. Smith, 179 U.S. App. D.C. 162, 551 F.2d 348 (1976). . . .

To be admitted under Rule 609(a)(1), the prior conviction must have been "punishable by death or imprisonment in excess of one year." There is no indication in the record that Fearwell's prior conviction was anything other than the misdemeanor of attempted petit larceny, and counsel at oral argument suggested that the attempted petit larceny was committed in the District of Columbia. The language of the provision in the District of Columbia Code in which petit larceny is described stipulates that a person convicted under its authority faces punishment of imprisonment "for not more than one year." 22 D.C. Code §2202 (1973). As a general category of crime, moreover, in no matter what jurisdiction, the misdemeanor of attempted petit larceny would not likely be punishable in more severe terms. Indeed, a leading text on criminal law points out that petit larceny is normally classified as "a misdemeanor with a maximum punishment of six months imprisonment." W. LaFave

& A. Scott, Criminal Law 634 (1972). Accordingly, it is clear that Rule 609(a)(1) does not apply, because that subsection of the rule requires, inter alia, that the crime underlying the prior conviction be "punishable by death or imprisonment in excess of one year."

We are left with Rule 609(a)(2). Under this prong the trial judge *must* permit use of the prior conviction for impeachment purposes if the crime underlying the conviction involved "dishonesty or false statement, regardless of the punishment." This court, in United States v. Smith, supra, held that the crime of attempted robbery did not qualify for automatic admission pursuant to Rule 609(a)(2), because that crime involves no "dishonesty or false statement," as required by that subsection of the rule. "[D]ishonesty or false statement," the court concluded, was clearly intended by Congress "to denote a fairly narrow subset of criminal activity." 179 U.S. App. D.C. at 176, 551 F.2d at 362. In reaching this conclusion the court in *Smith* relied on the Conference Committee Report, which described "dishonesty or false statement" in terms of "crimes such as perjury or subornation of perjury, false statement, criminal fraud, embezzlement, or false pretense, or any other offense in the nature of crimen falsi, the commission of which involves some element of deceit, untruthfulness, or falsification bearing on the accused's propensity to testify truthfully."

The *Smith* case, to be sure, involved the crime of attempted robbery, not attempted petit larceny. But since *Smith* was handed down this court has decided United States v. Dorsey, 192 U.S. App. D.C. —, 591 F.2d 922 (D.C. Cir. No. 77-1750, decided December 21, 1978), in which it was held that the crime of shoplifting as defined in Article 27, Section 551A(a)(1) of the Maryland Code did not involve the deceit requisite to meeting Rule 609(a)(2)'s rigid standard. As the court wrote in *Dorsey*, "At worst, this type of shoplifting offense, *like many petty larceny crimes*, involves stealth, which *Smith* makes clear is not the same as deceit." 192 U.S. App. D.C. at —, 591 F.2d at 935 (emphasis added). The District of Columbia Code, relevant to the present case, defines petit larceny as "feloniously tak[ing] and carry[ing] away any property of value of less than $100. . . ." 22 D.C. Code §2202 (1973). Because there is no suggestion of fraud or deceit as an element, this offense would seem to fit *Dorsey*'s distinction between crimes involving stealth and those involving deceit. Indeed, unless specified to the contrary in the controlling statute, it would seem that petit larceny does not involve the requisite deceit to qualify for admission under Rule 609(a)(2).[8]

To understand why attempted petit larceny is outside the scope of Rule 609(a)(2), we must turn, as this court did in *Dorsey*, to the *Smith* case,

---

8. *Smith* and *Dorsey* leave open the possibility "that Rule 609(a)(2) may be operative if the prosecution can show that, although the prior crime was not characterized by an element of fraud or deceit, it nonetheless was committed by such means." United States v. Dorsey, 192 U.S. App. D.C. —, 591 F.2d 935 (1978); see United States v. Smith, supra note 5, 179 U.S. App. D.C. at 174 n.28, 551 F.2d at 364 n.28.

which penetratingly analyzed the nature of Rule 609(a)(2). In that case, as we have pointed out, the court held that attempted robbery did not qualify as a crime involving "dishonesty or false statement." But *Smith* went further by rendering most succinctly the crimes that *could* be used to impeach under Rule 609(a)(2): "those crimes characterized by an element of deceit or deliberate interference with a court's ascertainment of truth." United States v. Smith, supra, 179 U.S. App. D.C. at 177, 551 F.2d at 363. This language penetrates to the core of Rule 609(a)(2) because it closely tracks the intent of Congress as evidenced by language in the Conference Committee Report that describes "dishonesty or false statement." The Report focuses on crimes "bearing on the accused's propensity to testify truthfully."

Building on the solid foundation of *Smith*, and on application of *Smith*'s analysis to the crime of shoplifting in *Dorsey*, we conclude today that the crime of petit larceny does not involve dishonesty or false statement. Thus it is covered by neither Rule 609(a)(1) nor Rule 609(a)(2). This crime, like multifarious others of a similar nature, simply has no bearing whatever on the "accused's propensity to testify truthfully." H.R. Conf. Rep. No. 93-1597, [1974] U.S. Code Cong. & Ad. News at 7103. Accordingly, evidence of a prior conviction for petit larceny may not be admitted for the purpose of attacking the credibility of a witness.

In reaching this conclusion, we do not stray from the collective wisdom of our sister circuits. Indeed, to this date the Second, Third, Fourth, Fifth, Seventh, Ninth, and Tenth Circuits have in varying degrees come to the same conclusion that we reach here today. Thus the import of *Smith*, *Dorsey*, and the present case, in combination with the various decisions of the other circuits, can be described as follows: Rule 609(a)(2) is to be construed narrowly; it is not carte blanche for admission on an undifferentiated basis of all previous convictions for purposes of impeachment; rather, precisely because it involves no discretion on the part of the trial court, in the sense that all crimes meeting its stipulation of dishonesty or false statement must be permitted to be used for impeachment purposes, Rule 609(a)(2) must be confined, in the words of *Smith*, to a "narrow subset of crimes" — those that bear *directly* upon the accused's propensity to testify truthfully. Quite simply, attempted petit larceny is not within this subset. . . .

UNITED STATES v. SIMS
588 F.2d 1145 (1978)

PHILLIPS, C.J. This appeal presents the question of whether the district court abused its discretion by permitting the Government to impeach the appellant by introducing evidence of two prior felony convictions which were more than ten years old, in violation of Rule 609(b) of the Federal Rules of Evidence.

James Dewey Sims appeals from his jury conviction for possession of a firearm as a previously convicted felon in violation of 18 U.S.C. Appendix §1202(a)(1). On March 15, 1977, Sims was arrested in Pulaski County, Kentucky, while driving his automobile. During a search of Sims' vehicle, a Pulaski County deputy sheriff found a .38 caliber revolver underneath the front seat on the driver's side. Sometime in March 1977, that same .38 caliber revolver had been stolen from the home of one of Sims' neighbors. Sims was indicted and convicted on a single count indictment charging him with being a convicted felon in possession of a firearm. The underlying felony conviction recited in the indictment was the conviction of Sims on May 18, 1970, in the McCreary County Circuit Court at Whitley City, Kentucky, of the felony crime of knowingly possessing stolen property.

Sims testified that he had no knowledge of the pistol being in his vehicle. He stated that on Thursday, March 10, 1977, his son and a neighbor boy cleaned out the vehicle, including the space beneath the driver's seat. On the following day Sims traveled from Somerset, Kentucky, to Cincinnati, Ohio, to attend the funeral of a relative. He testified that he was unaware that the pistol was in his car until it was found by the deputy sheriff.

In addition to appellant's 1970 felony conviction, the prosecution introduced, for the purpose of impeachment, evidence of two other prior felony convictions of appellant, both of which were more than ten years old. One was a 21 year old conviction for burglary in 1956. The second was a 12 year old conviction for interstate transportation of a stolen motor vehicle in 1965.

A previous trial of Sims on this indictment resulted in a deadlocked jury. Evidence of his two old convictions, the 1956 conviction for burglary and the 1965 conviction for interstate transportation of a stolen vehicle, were not introduced in the earlier trial.

The sole issue on appeal is whether it was reversible error to allow impeachment of appellant by evidence of the two prior felony convictions, both more than ten years old.

Section 609 of the Federal Rules of Evidence provides as follows: [A discussion of the legislative history of Rule 609(b) is omitted.]

An important purpose of Rule 609(b) is to avoid convicting criminal defendants as a result of prejudice caused by the cumulative effect of old criminal convictions. When stale convictions are offered for the purpose of impeaching a witness, they often shed little light on the present tendency of the witness towards truthfulness and veracity. In United States v. Harding, 525 F.2d 84, 89 (7th Cir. 1975), the court stated:

"When the prior conviction is used to impeach a defendant who elects to take the stand to testify in his own behalf, two inferences, one permissible and the other impermissible, inevitably arise. The fact that the defendant has sinned in the past implies that he is more likely to give false testimony than other witnesses; it also implies that he is more likely to have committed the offense for which he is being tried than if he had previously led a blameless life. The law approves of the former inference but not the latter."

In United States v. Belt, 169 U.S. App. D.C. 1, 9, 514 F.2d 837, 845 (D.C. Cir. 1975), the court stated that Rule 609(b) should be applied "to criminal defendants where impeachment 'presents a danger of improperly influencing the outcome of the trial by persuading the trier of fact to convict the defendant on the basis of his prior criminal record.'" Cf. United States v. Johnson, 542 F.2d 230, 234-35 (5th Cir. 1976). In Abbott Labs., Ross Labs. Division v. N.L.R.B., 540 F.2d 662, 667 (4th Cir. 1976), the Fourth Circuit cited Rule 609(b) as analogous support for its proposition that "Hall's prior criminal record of twenty years earlier did not require that he be disbelieved."

Under Rule 609(b), the district judge must make "an on-the-record finding based on specific facts and circumstances that the probative value of the evidence substantially outweighs the danger of unfair prejudice." United States v. Mahler, 579 F.2d 730, 734 (2d Cir. 1978).

In United States v. Mahone, 537 F.2d 922, 929 (7th Cir.), cert. denied, 429 U.S. 1025 (1976), the court set down the following test for the admission of prior felony convictions under Rule 609:

"In the future, to avoid the unnecessary raising of the issue of whether the judge has meaningfully invoked his discretion under Rule 609, we urge trial judges to make such determinations after a hearing on the record, as the trial judge did in the instant case, and to explicitly find that the prejudicial effect of the evidence to the defendant will be outweighed by its probative value. When such a hearing on the record is held and such an explicit finding is made, the appellate court easily will be able to determine whether the judge followed the strictures of Rule 609 in reaching his decision. 3 J. Weinstein, Evidence ¶609[03] at 609-78 (1975).

"The hearing need not be extensive. Bearing in mind that Rule 609 places the burden of proof on the government, Cong. Rec. 12254, 12257 (daily ed., December 18, 1974) (remarks of House conferees); 3 J. Weinstein, Evidence ¶609[03] at 609-40, 41, 42 (1975), the judge should require a brief recital by the government of the circumstances surrounding the admission of the evidence, and a statement of the date, nature and place of the conviction. The defendant should be permitted to rebut the government's presentation, pointing out to the court the possible prejudicial effect to the defendant if the evidence is admitted.

"Some of the factors which the judge should take into account in making his determination were articulated by then Judge Burger in Gordon v. United States, 127 U.S. App. D.C. 343, 383 F.2d 936, 940 (1967):

" '(1) The impeachment value of the prior crime.

" '(2) The point in time of the conviction and the witness' subsequent history.

" '(3) The similarity between the past crime and the charged crime.

" '(4) The importance of the defendant's testimony.

" '(5) The centrality of the credibility issue.'

"See 3 J. Weinstein, Evidence ¶609[03]. . . ."

In the present case the Government gave the notice required by the Rule. The district court stated the following basis for allowing admission of the two convictions more than ten years old:

"I think based upon Rule 609(b) that the United States has given sufficient advance notice here and that I believe in the interest of justice the probative value of these convictions substantially outweighs its prejudicial effect. I think, one prime factor in that is that I have the benefit of having tried the case before and the case really comes down somewhat to the issue of credibility of the defendant. In the present case, and of course, he might not take the stand, but if he takes the stand as in the previous case, he stated that he knew nothing about the weapon and that's a real issue of credibility. But under different circumstances, of course, the Court might determine that the prejudicial effect outweighs the probative value. But in this case, under these circumstances where his credibility is essentially the whole case, I think that it is certainly probative and I will grant the United States' request to use these two convictions if we get to that point. . . ."

Rule 609(b) creates, in effect, a rebuttable presumption that convictions over ten years old are more prejudicial than helpful and should be excluded. United States v. Johnson, supra, 542 F.2d at 234. As set forth in the legislative history quoted above, evidence of convictions more than ten years old will be admitted "very rarely and only in exceptional circumstances." In *Johnson*, a 16 year old felony conviction was found properly admitted under Rule 609(b) to impeach the defendant where that prior conviction directly contradicted the testimony of the defendant. We conclude that no such "exceptional circumstance" is presented by use of appellant's prior convictions in the instant case.

The previous trial of appellant, when the jury had no knowledge of his two old prior convictions, resulted in a deadlocked jury. At the trial involved in the present appeal, the Government was permitted to introduce evidence of appellant's two prior convictions because appellant's credibility was "essentially the whole case" and because the convictions were probative of that credibility. With the evidence of those two previous convictions before them, the members of the jury discredited the testimony of appellant and returned a guilty verdict.

We cannot agree that the probative value of a 21 year old burglary conviction or a 12 year old conviction for transporting a stolen motor vehicle substantially outweighs their prejudicial effect in the present case. Nor do we find any rare and exceptional circumstances that would justify the admission of the two stale convictions into evidence. Both convictions were remote in time and neither necessarily shed any light upon the credibility of appellant. We conclude that their admission into evidence in the present case outweighed their probative value and violated both the language and purpose of the rule.

The purpose of Rule 609(b) is to prevent the conviction of a defendant on the basis of his old prior criminal record, when evidence of that record is introduced ostensibly for the purpose of impeaching the defendant's credibility, but the stale convictions are not probative of credibility. Therefore, it is contrary to that purpose to permit the Government, after a previous mistrial, to bolster its case by evidence of stale convictions, thereby enabling the prosecution to obtain a conviction on the second trial.

With all deference to the wide discretion of the district judge in overseeing the presentation of evidence to the jury, United States v. Jenkins, 525 F.2d 819, 824 (6th Cir. 1975), we conclude that the obvious prejudice resulting from the admission of appellant's prior conviction substantially outweighed their probative value. The admission of these two old convictions into evidence had precisely the effect which Rule 609(b) is intended to eliminate — prejudicing the jury against the defendant on the basis of his prior criminal record. Accordingly, we conclude that the district court abused its discretion in permitting the two stale convictions to be introduced into evidence in the present case.

The judgment of conviction is reversed and the case is remanded for a new trial.

ENGEL, J. I respectfully dissent. I would hold that Judge Siler's statement of his reasons for admitting the evidence of Sims' earlier convictions met at least the minimum requirements of Rule 609(b).

Since proof of Sims' prior conviction of a felony is an essential element of the crime under 18 U.S.C. §1202(a)(1) (Appendix), the jury was necessarily possessed of this prejudicial information regardless of whether he testified. Likewise, we have held in our circuit that it is not improper for an indictment to charge or the government to prove in such cases that the defendant had been previously convicted of more than one felony. United States v. Burkhart, 545 F.2d 14 (6th Cir. 1976); United States v. Fields, 500 F.2d 69 (6th Cir.), cert. denied, 419 U.S. 1071 (1974). The government is also not obligated to accept a stipulation from the defendant in lieu of presenting proof of prior crimes to the jury. *Burkhart,* supra. Thus it is entirely possible that the government here might have included the other felonies in the indictment and thus have placed them before the jury in any event, without any compliance with Rule 609 being required.

Of course, the government did not do so here, nor do I suggest that it should have. I do suggest, however, that in prosecutions under Section 1202(a)(1), at least, the prejudicial impact of proof of prior convictions is considerably lessened because the jury already knows the defendant had a record. At the same time the value of the evidence to the jury in determining the credibility of the defendant as a witness is somewhat enhanced because a man with a more extensive record is much more likely to know it is unlawful to possess weapons and to guard against the danger. The case hung on whether the jury would believe or disbelieve Sims' story. In such circumstances, the jury should be possessed of as much information as is useful and permissible to assist it in the difficult task of assessing the defendant's credibility.

Although somewhat abbreviated in form, the trial judge's statement here reflects, in my judgment, a conscientious exercise of the discretion vested in him under Rule 609. I would affirm.

4.   Rehabilitation of Credibility of Witnesses

When a witness's credibility has been attacked on cross-examination by other character witnesses, through prior inconsistent statements, or by specific contradiction, how and when may the witness's credibility be supported or restored? Consider the following problems.

Problem II-20
Assault and Battery

Charge: assault and battery on *V*. At trial, *D* takes the stand and denies the assault.

(1) *D* calls *W* to testify that he is familiar with *D*'s reputation for truth and veracity and that *D*'s reputation is good. On the prosecution's objection what ruling and why?

(2) *W* is asked to testify as to *D*'s reputation for peace and quietude. On the prosecution's objection, what ruling and why?

(3) In rebuttal the prosecution shows that *D* was convicted of grand larceny nine years ago. In surrebuttal *D* recalls *W* and puts the same question to him as in (1) about *D*'s reputation for truth and veracity. On the prosecution's objection what ruling and why?

Problem II-21
Impeachment by Specific and Self-Contradiction

(1) Charge: murder in the first degree. M.O.: beating *D*'s father-in-law on November 27 and poisoning him on November 28, with death resulting on December 8. At *D*'s trial the star witness for the prosecution is *S*, the sister of *D*'s husband. *S* testifies that at noon on November 27, in *D*'s house, she saw *D* beat her father over the head with a wrench and that on November 28, in *D*'s house, she saw *D* take pills from a bottle and

give them to her father, who chugged them down. Later at the trial, *D* produces a witness, *J*, who testifies that on November 27 he was with *D* all day hunting, 200 miles away from *D*'s residence. How if at all does *J*'s testimony tend to impeach *S*?

(2) Suppose that *J*'s testimony is that on November 28 *S* told him that the day before she had seen someone beat her father over the head but that it was not *D* — it was someone else. How does the impeachment of *S* in (2) differ from that in (1)?

Problem II-22
Rehabilitation After Contradiction

Action for damages arising out of an automobile collision on June 1. Liability is conceded. The issue is whether *P* sustained neck and back injuries in the accident or whether the injuries are feigned. At trial, on direct examination, *P* testified that he did not go to see a doctor until two months after the collision because he did not have the money to pay a doctor. On cross-examination it was brought out that *P* had a health and accident insurance policy that would have covered the cost of seeing a doctor and also that *P* was receiving a Veterans' Administration pension of $90 a month that could have been used to defray at least some of the cost. In rebuttal, *P* offered the testimony of a witness to testify to *P*'s good reputation for truth and veracity.

Problem II-23
Red Light/Green Light

Action for damages arising out of the collision of *P*'s and *D*'s cars at the intersection of Commonwealth Avenue and Beacon Street. The issue is who had the green light. At trial, *P* calls *W1* who testifies that he saw the accident and that the light was green for *P* and red for *D*. In defense, *D* calls *W2* who testifies that he saw the accident and that the light was red for *P* and green for *D*. In rebuttal, *P* calls *W3* to testify to *W1*'s good reputation for truth and veracity. On *D*'s objection what ruling and why?

F. Using Extrinsic Evidence to Prove Character and Credibility

Proof of character may be elicited through direct and cross-examination of the witness whose character is in question, by means of a document, or through the testimony of other witnesses. Understanding the rules of

the road of direct and cross-examination, the offering of exhibits, and
the making of objections and offers of proof is vital to this process.
These subjects are covered by Rule 103 and the rules in Article VI of the
Federal Rules of Evidence, which are discussed in more detail in the next
chapter. However, proof of character so often involves the issue of
whether and when "extrinsic evidence" (i.e., evidence other than that
obtained by examination of the principal witness) ought to be allowed
that it is dealt with in this chapter on character and credibility. The
extrinsic evidence rule is prominent in this area because of the "collateral" nature of proof of character. In this sense the issues raised in the
introduction to this chapter are simply placed in sharper focus when
extrinsic evidence, rather than cross-examination, is offered to prove
character or credibility.

Problem II-24
Bijou Blues

Charge: violation of Dyer Act (interstate transportation of stolen
vehicle). The principal prosecution witness, W, testifies that on June 1,
1969, D accosted him in Philadelphia, stole his car, and absconded across
the Delaware River Bridge into Camden, New Jersey.

The cross-examination of W is as follows:

Q: Where did you have supper June 1?
A: The Philadelphia Hoagie House.
Q: What did you do after dinner?
A: Went to the movies.
Q: Where?
A: The Bijou.
Q: What did you see?
A: *Trash.*

As part of its case-in-chief, D calls M, the manager of the Bijou, to testify
that on June 1 *The Summer of '42* was playing at the Bijou. On the
prosecution's objection what ruling and why? Is M's testimony relevant
to impeach W's credibility? What sort of impeachment is M's testimony?
What considerations are important in deciding whether to sustain or
overrule the objection? What is the appropriate standard of "collateralness" in deciding whether extrinsic impeachment evidence is admissible? Can any workable standard be articulated? Should there be *any*
limit on the use of extrinsic impeachment evidence?

In Attorney-General v. Hitchcock, 1 Exch. 91, 99 (Eng. 1847), Chief
Baron Pollock laid down the rule as follows:

If the answer of a witness is [about] a matter which you would be allowed on your part to prove in evidence — if it have such a connection with the issue, that you would be allowed to give it in evidence — then it is a matter on which you may contradict him [with extrinsic evidence]. *Collateral fact rule*

Is this a sound rule for determining when contradiction by extrinsic evidence should be allowed? Is it workable?

Problem II-25
The Wind River Ranch

In the ejectment action over the Wind River Ranch, *D*'s attorney asks *W*, *P*'s witness, the following questions on cross-examination and receives the following answers.

Q: Is *W* your correct name?
A: Yes.
Q: Have you ever been known by another name?
A: No.
Q: What is your address?
A: 42 Russell Street.
Q: What do you do for a living now?
A: I am a teller at the Cooperative Bank.

In rebuttal, *D* offers to prove that *W* changed his name from *X* five years ago, lives on Pine Street, and works as a Fuller Brush man. *P* objects on the grounds that such evidence relates to a collateral matter not independently provable and thus is not provable by extrinsic evidence for impeachment purposes.

What ruling under the *Hitchcock* rule? Should this extrinsic evidence be admitted? See Rule 608.

Problem II-26
Harry's Harborside

P, executor of *V*'s estate, v. *D* for damages for an alleged assault and battery by *D* on *V*, on June 1 at 10 P.M. at Harry's Harborside Tavern, a rowdy sailors' bar in Revere, Massachusetts. At trial, *P*'s first witness is Harry. Harry testifies that on June 1 at around 10 P.M. in his bar he saw *D* splash *V*'s face with beer and then break a beer bottle over *V*'s head. On cross-examination the following occurs:

Q: Weren't you bitten by *D*'s dog on May 1?
By P's counsel: Objection — beyond the scope of the direct examination.
   (What ruling and why?)
A: No, I was not bitten by *D*'s dog on May 1.

In rebuttal, *D* offers *W*, who testifies that *D* was out fishing all day and
night on June 1, and the testimony of *D*, Jr., that on May 1 he saw Fang,
the *D* family dog, bite Harry. *P*'s counsel objects to *D*, Jr.'s testimony.
What ruling and why?

Abel case here Supp 359

Problem II-27
Cutting Through an Alibi

Charge: robbing a drug store using a knife. Several employees of the
store identified *D*.

At the conclusion of the government's case, a bench conference is
held in which the government urges that it be allowed to call Coombs, an
undercover agent of the Bureau of Alcohol, Tobacco, and Firearms,
who would testify that *D* had told him three months before the robbery
that he had robbed a drug dealer, using a knife. The government
theory, articulated in a memorandum of law for the court, is that the use
of a knife in a prior crime is probative of appellant's identity under Rule
404(b)(2). The district court and counsel engage in the following colloquy:

Mr. Healy (prosecutor):   Essentially, that is my case. I submitted a
   memo. . . .
The Court: I read the memo and I would say, in the interest of quitting
   while you are ahead, at the present time I will confine you to your
   case. I don't know what George has for a defense. You might try
   and get it in rebuttal, if it gets to that point.
Mr. Higgins (counsel for defendant):   Mine is strictly alibi, your Honor.
The Court: This business — I am sure you have a copy (indicating).
Mr. Higgins: I am going to be eating large chunks of the rug if he starts
   with that stuff.
The Court: It is arguably admissible. If you read the *Heatherton* (sic) and
   Wright cases [United States v. Eatherton, 519 F.2d 603 (1st Cir.
   1975); United States v. Wright, 573 F.2d 681 (1st Cir. 1978)], it is
   arguably admissible. I won't say I won't let it come in, but for your
   direct case I don't think you need it at the moment. You have a
   pretty strong case and I suggest you quit while you are ahead. At the
   end of his case, if you want to take a shot at it and offer it, we will see
   about it then.

D then presents his case, testifying that he had been elsewhere at the

gourmand consumption of carp

time of the robbery. In the course of *D*'s cross-examination by the government, the relevant questions and answers are as follows:

Q: In late 1977, did you commit any robberies by knife?
A: In 1977? By knife? Did I commit any robberies?
Mr. Higgins: I object to that, your Honor.
The Witness: No.
The Court: He said no. All right.
The Witness: No. I didn't, wait a minute. 1977? Did I commit any robberies?
Q: Late 1977, any robberies by knife?
A: I — no. I have not committed any robberies by knife in 1977.

After the defendant presents his case, the government seeks once again to introduce Agent Coombs's testimony. ~~now lets in the evid of mere propensity~~

Mr. Healy: There were certain matters that I had written a memorandum on and I want to put out in my case in chief, and at this time there is one in particular, and that is my recollection of the defendant's testimony was that he denied. . . .
The Court: Conducting a robbery in late 1977 by the use of a knife, and you have a witness that is going to say he admitted that, and that is admissible on the limited issue of his credibility.
Mr. Healy: Yes.
Mr. Higgins: Your Honor, please note my objection. It will be my position that that is so prejudicial as to warrant its exclusion; and, further, that matter was not raised on direct.
The Court: It was raised on cross-examination, and the defendant's credibility is crucial in this case where there is an alibi defense, and there are Court of Appeals opinions indicating that when a defendant's testimony is critical that cross-examination is permissible on the issue of credibility. I will take it with a limiting instruction that I will give to the jury that it is admissible on the defendant's credibility. I will, of course, note your objection.

The prosecution then calls Agent Coombs:

Q: Sir, in what capacity did you meet the defendant?
A: I met him while I was working in an undercover capacity.
Q: Now, sir, did there come a time in September of 1977 when you had a conversation with him concerning the possible robbery of a drug dealer?
A: Yes.
Q: What, if any, conversation was that?
A: In, I believe it was in the beginning of September, he asked me if I would be interested in assisting him in the robbery of a Puerto Rican drug dealer in the City of Somerville.

Q: Did he state the drug dealer's name?
A: No.
Q: November 16, 1977, sir; did you see him on that day?
A: Yes.
Q: Did you have a conversation with him concerning that same drug dealer?
A: Yes.
Q: And, sir, in substance, what did he say?
A: He basically said that he had robbed a Puerto Rican drug dealer by the name of Vincente with a knife.

D is convicted. Was there error?

UNITED STATES v. PISARI
636 F.2d 855 (1981)

COFFIN, C.J. On June 5, 1980 we issued our opinion in this case, reversing appellant's conviction and holding that rebuttal testimony of a government witness, Coombs, was improperly admitted, being admissible neither as independent proof of appellant's identity, Fed. R. Evid. 404(b), nor as impeachment by prior inconsistent statement. On August 4 we granted the government's petition for rehearing and withdrew our opinion. After receiving and considering new briefs from the parties, we arrive at the same result, a reversal, via a different analysis. . . .

The parties, the district court, and this court have been mistaken in various ways in their analysis of the admissibility of agent Coombs' statement. The district court, as noted, admitted the evidence as proof of a prior inconsistent statement relevant to the credibility of the defendant. The government defends the district court's admission of the evidence for impeachment purposes, or as a proper resort to Rule 404(b), the testimony tending to prove that defendant had committed an earlier "strikingly similar" crime and therefore was the person who committed the crime at bar. Appellant has attacked the testimony as constituting extrinsic evidence of specific conduct, in violation of Rule 608(b). He opposes the application of Rule 404(b), arguing that the testimony was not admitted on this basis and that in any event the evidence of misconduct was neither direct nor competent. As for the impeachment ground, appellant argues that defendant's denial of having engaged in robbery by knife is not necessarily inconsistent with his having falsely told the undercover agent that he had committed such an act. In our earlier opinion, we rejected both proffered grounds for admissibility on the rationale now understandably defended on rehearing by appellant.

In our rethinking of the admissibility of the Coombs testimony, we consider first the impeachment ground specifically relied on by the district court. The government has suggested the proper starting point for

analysis by acknowledging that a denial on cross-examination which relates to a collateral matter cannot be disputed by extrinsic evidence,
citing McCormick, Law of Evidence, ch. 56, §36 at 70 (2d ed. 1972). See
also Saltzburg and Redden, Federal Rules of Evidence Manual, 390 (2d
ed. 1977). As one treatise summarizes the test at common law,

> The test for collateralness proposed by Wigmore and endorsed by a num-
> ber of federal courts [footnote omitted] is "Could the fact, as to which the
> prior self-contradiction is predicated, have been shown in evidence for any
> purpose independently of the self-contradiction?" In other words, the [prior
> inconsistent] statement may be proved if it relates to a matter which the
> examiner could have proven even if the witness had said nothing on the
> subject. 3 Weinstein's Evidence, ¶607[06], at 607-69, -70 (1978).

While at common law the test for collateralness was frequently mechanical, we are advised by commentators that: "The better approach —
and one in accord with the structure of the federal rules — would be to
eliminate mechanical application of the 'collateral' test in favor of the
balancing approach mandated by Rule 403. Evidence at which the collateral test is primarily directed, which is relevant solely because it suggests
that the witness may have lied about something in the past would generally be excluded because of its low probative value and its tendency to
prejudice the jury. Evidence of higher probative value would be assessed
in terms of its impact on the jury in light of the particular circumstances
presented." Id. at 607-71 to -72.

The government assumes that the issue of collateralness is easily
hurdled, because "[t]he identity of the perpetrator of a crime is always a
relevant and material issue." That is, the government contends that the
prior robbery of a drug dealer by appellant, having a knife as his
weapon, is so "strikingly similar" to the robbery of the postal installation
in the pharmacy presented in this case that it is probative that the same
person, appellant, committed both crimes.

We think the government has underestimated the similarity necessary
to justify, under Rule 404(b), the admission of evidence of other crimes
to prove identity. Weinstein quotes McCormick as stating that evidence
may be admitted:

> to prove other like crimes by the accused so nearly identical in method as to
> ear-mark them as the handiwork of the accused. Here much more is de-
> manded than the mere repeated commission of crimes of the same class, such
> as repeated burglaries or thefts. *The device used must be so unusual and distinctive
> as to be like a signature.* (Emphasis in original.) Id. at 404-92, quoting McCor-
> mick, Evidence §157 (1954). . . .

Our own precedents allowing "other crimes as signature" evidence
have involved the conjunction of several identifying characteristics or
the presence of some highly distinctive quality. In United States v.

Eatherton, 519 F.2d 603, 611 (1st Cir.), cert. denied, 423 U.S. 987 (1975), a gun and three ski masks taken from defendant corresponded in character and number to accessories used in a robbery a few days earlier. In United States v. Barrett, 539 F.2d 244, 248 (1st Cir. 1976), testimony that defendant possessed expertise in the operation of burglar alarms was admissible where, in the case at bar, a burglary had been facilitated by bypassing an alarm, "so distinctive a feature of the stamp burglary" that defendant's expertise "reinforced the evidence that linked him to the burglary."

In contrast, the only factor common to the postal installation burglary and the robbery about which agent Coombs quoted appellant was a knife. We have no idea whether the knives used on these occasions were either similar or distinctive. We have no clear idea of the propinquity of the events in time. In one case a store is the target of the crime; in the other, an individual is the target. In one case, there were two robbers; in the other, so far as we know, one. In this case the objects taken were drugs and money; we do not know whether drugs or money were taken in the other robbery. . . .

We are, in short, unable to make the determination that the elements of the offense revealed in agent Coombs' testimony and in the case at bar are so distinctive as to give rise to an inference that the same person was involved in both. The single fact that in committing a robbery, one invokes the threat of using a knife falls far short of a sufficient signature or trademark upon which to posit an inference of identity. We therefore conclude that, since agent Coombs' testimony, not being justified as evidence bearing on the identity of appellant, was addressed only to a collateral matter, it was improperly admitted as impeachment evidence. Our analysis also necessarily rules out any invocation of Rule 404(b) as an independent basis of admissibility. No other basis has been suggested, nor does any commend itself to us. . . .

Since we cannot say with certainty that the error was harmless, we must reverse. . . .

Reversed and remanded.

G. Proving Character and Credibility in Sexual Assault Cases

Proof of character and credibility raises especially sensitive issues in sexual assault cases, particularly where sexual conduct is admitted and the defense is consent. In these cases the defendant often desires to offer proof not only of his good character but also of the character of the complaining witness. This may consist of evidence of the complaining witness's sexual predisposition or of the complaining witness's credibility with regard to allegations of improper sexual conduct. In the former case the evidence is offered for the purpose of proving circumstantially that in the case charged the complaining witness acted in conformity with her character to engage in sexual conduct. In the latter situation the evidence is offered to impugn the witness's trustworthiness. In either case the offered evidence could take the form of reputation, opinion, or specific acts; it could be elicited on cross-examination or consist of extrinsic proof. In all cases its admission would subject the complaining witness to public disclosure of her prior sexual history.

When if ever should such evidence be admitted? Why should such evidence not be allowed? Does proof of character and credibility in sexual assault cases differ from proof of character and credibility under Rules 404, 405, 608, and 609 in general? Are restrictions on this sort of proof in sexual assault cases based on considerations of *relevance*, or do the modern rape-victim shield statutes (such as Rule 412, below) create a *privilege* for the sexual assault victim, similar to other privileges, that operates to exclude incontestably relevant evidence? If the rape-victim shield statutes are based on considerations of relevance, does the balance struck by the statutes square either with the definition of relevant evidence in Rule 401 or with the way most people think in the real world? If the rape-victim shield statutes create a privilege, what values does the privilege further? Is the privilege based on a concern for the victim's privacy, or is it designed to encourage victims of sexual assault to come forward in prosecutions of their assailants, thus furthering society's interest in effective law enforcement against this type of crime? How does a privilege for sexual assault victims compare with the treatment afforded victims of other crimes? See, for example, Rule 404(a)(2). Are there reasons why sexual assault victims should be treated differently than victims of other crimes? Do rape-victim shield statutes such as Rule 412 raise sixth amendment confrontation clause problems?

FRE 412
Rape Cases; Relevance of Victim's Past Behavior

(a) Notwithstanding any other provision of law, in a criminal case in which a person is accused of rape or of assault with intent to commit rape, reputation or opinion evidence of the past sexual behavior of an alleged victim of such rape or assault is not admissible.

(b) Notwithstanding any other provision of law, in a criminal case in which a person is accused of rape or of assault with intent to commit rape, evidence of a victim's past sexual behavior other than reputation or opinion evidence is also not admissible, unless such evidence other than reputation or opinion evidence is —

(1) admitted in accordance with subdivisions (c)(1) and (c)(2) and is constitutionally required to be admitted; or

(2) admitted in accordance with subdivision (c) and is evidence of —

(A) past sexual behavior with persons other than the accused, offered by the accused upon the issue of whether the accused was or was not, with respect to the alleged victim, the source of semen or injury; or

(B) past sexual behavior with the accused and is offered by the accused upon the issue of whether the alleged victim consented to the sexual behavior with respect to which rape or assault is alleged.

(c)(1) If the person accused of committing rape or assault with intent to commit rape intends to offer under subdivision (b) evidence of specific instances of the alleged victim's past sexual behavior, the accused shall make a written motion to offer such evidence not later than fifteen days before the date on which the trial in which such evidence is to be offered is scheduled to begin, except that the court may allow the motion to be made at a later date, including during trial, if the court determines either that the evidence is newly discovered and could not have been obtained earlier through the exercise of due diligence or that the issue to which such evidence relates has newly arisen in the case. Any motion made under this paragraph shall be served on all other parties and on the alleged victim.

(2) The motion described in paragraph (1) shall be accompanied by a written offer of proof. If the court determines that the offer of proof contains evidence described in subdivision (b), the court shall order a hearing in chambers to determine if such evidence is admissible. At such hearing the parties may call witnesses, including the alleged victim, and offer relevant evidence. Notwithstanding subdivision (b) of rule 104, if the relevancy of the evidence which the accused seeks to offer in the trial depends upon the fulfillment of a condition of fact, the court, at the hearing in chambers or at a subsequent hearing in chambers scheduled for such purpose, shall accept evidence on the issue of whether such condition of fact is fulfilled and shall determine such issue.

(3) If the court determines on the basis of the hearing described in paragraph (2) that the evidence which the accused seeks to offer is relevant and that the probative value of such evidence outweighs the danger of unfair prejudice, such evidence shall be admissible in the trial to the extent an order made by the court specifies evidence which may be offered and areas with respect to which the alleged victim may be examined or cross-examined.

(d) For purposes of this rule, the term "past sexual behavior" means sexual behavior other than the sexual behavior with respect to which rape or assault with intent to commit rape is alleged.

During the debates on the Privacy Protection for Rape Victims Act of 1978, Pub. L. No. 95-540, 92 Stat. 2046 (1978), which eventually became Rule 412, Representative Mann spoke in support of the bill. 124 Cong. Rec. H11,944-11,945 (daily ed. Oct. 10, 1978). Were his arguments fair or accurate? Under the preexisting rules, when could evidence of specific acts of conduct be admitted?

Mr. Speaker, for many years in this country, evidentiary rules have permitted the introduction of evidence about a rape victim's prior sexual conduct. Defense lawyers were permitted great latitude in bringing out intimate details about a rape victim's life. Such evidence quite often serves no real purpose and only results in embarrassment to the rape victim and unwarranted public intrusion into her private life.

The evidentiary rules that permit such inquiry have in recent years come under question; and the States have taken the lead to change and modernize their evidentiary rules about evidence of a rape victim's prior sexual behavior. The bill before us similarly seeks to modernize the Federal evidentiary rules.

The present Federal Rules of Evidence reflect the traditional approach. If a defendant in a rape case raises the defense of consent, that defendant may then offer evidence about the victim's prior sexual behavior. Such evidence may be in the form of opinion evidence, evidence of reputation, or evidence of specific instances of behavior. Rule 404(a)(2) of the Federal Rules of Evidence permits the introduction of evidence of a "pertinent character trait." The advisory committee note to that rule cites, as an example of what the rule covers, the character of a rape victim when the issue is consent. Rule 405 of the Federal Rules of Evidence permits the use of opinion or reputation evidence or the use of evidence of specific behavior to show a character trait.

Thus, Federal evidentiary rules permit a wide ranging inquiry into the private conduct of a rape victim, even though that conduct may have at best a tenuous connection to the offense for which the defendant is being tried. H.R. 4727 amends the Federal Rules of Evidence to add a new rule, applicable only in criminal cases, to spell out when, and under what conditions, evidence of a rape victim's prior sexual behavior can be admitted. The new rule provides that reputation or opinion evidence about a rape victim's prior sexual behavior is not admissible. The new rule also provides that a court cannot admit evidence of specific instances of a rape victim's prior sexual conduct except in three circumstances. . . .

TANFORD AND BOCCHINO, RAPE VICTIM SHIELD LAWS AND THE SIXTH AMENDMENT
128 U. Pa. L. Rev. 544, 544-549, 550-551 (1980)

In the last few years, forty-six jurisdictions have made efforts to protect rape victims from the humiliation of public disclosure of the details of their prior sexual activities. In most states the legislatures have passed shield laws restricting a criminal defendant's ability to present to the jury evidence of past sexual history. In one instance, the same result has been reached by an appellate court ruling. Late in 1978, the United States Congress followed this trend and enacted rule 412 of the Federal Rules of Evidence. While these laws vary in scope and procedural details, they share the features of declaring an end to the presumptive admissibility of such evidence and of restricting the situations in which a defendant will be allowed to bring the victim's sexual history to the attention of the jury. Almost unanimously, the literature of the last few years has encouraged these laws and attempted to justify any adverse consequences to the defendant by claiming that the state's interest in protecting rape victims is sufficiently important to overcome any constitutional objections. The changing moral climate in this country and the increasing leniency about sexual relationships outside of marriage, it is usually argued, have discredited the old rationale that the unchastity of a woman has a material bearing on whether she has really been raped.

The new laws do not, however, merely end an antiquated rule of evidence; they establish a new rule in some cases as extreme as the old one. Statutes such as rule 412 create a presumption that the sexual history of a rape victim will never be admissible, except when compelled by due process because of overwhelming probative value. It is, of course, difficult to argue with the position that the old rule of automatic admissibility should have been eliminated. It is not as easy to say that it is wise or consistent with the rights of a criminal defendant automatically to prevent introduction of evidence of a rape victim's sexual history.

The premise of the first part of this Article is that evidence of a rape victim's sexual history may be probative of an issue material to determining the guilt of a defendant charged with rape. Later sections of the Article will discuss particular circumstances in which such evidence is relevant and necessary to the effective presentation of the accused's defense. Initially, this Article will evaluate the new rules in light of the sixth amendment rights of a defendant to confront the witnesses against him and to produce witnesses in his favor. An analysis of laws affecting criminal defendants must be approached not from the standpoint of the victim, but from the standpoint of the accused. Whatever indignities are suffered by the complaining witness in any criminal trial, they do not compare with those a convicted defendant must suffer. There is no more serious undertaking of the state than accusing a person of a crime, with the concomitant threat of loss of liberty or life.

We reluctantly conclude that some rape victim shield laws violate the sixth amendment right to defend oneself. In the attempt to protect the sensibilities of rape victims, the defendant's right to present evidence to the jury is infringed. Surely the rights of defendants charged with rape are no less important or protected than the rights of defendants accused of other crimes. To the extent that a defendant in a rape case is categorically prevented from offering types of evidence that other criminal defendants may offer, his sixth amendment rights are violated.

II. HISTORICAL PERSPECTIVES

At common law, the rules governing the use of a rape complainant's sexual history provided that such evidence was always admissible. Three elements combined to create the rule of admissibility. The first was the fear of false charges brought by vindictive women. Sir Matthew Hale, Lord Chief Justice of the King's Bench, stated that rape "is an accusation easily to be made . . . and harder to be defended by the party accused, tho never so innocent." Second was the concept that chastity was a character trait. If a woman could be shown to be unchaste by nature, then it could be inferred that she had consented to sex with the defendant. Third was the belief that premarital sex was immoral. Acts of previous illicit sexual relations, like other acts of moral turpitude, could thus be used to impeach the credibility of the complaining witness in a rape case.

The fear expressed by Sir Matthew Hale, that it is difficult to defend against fabricated rape charges, pervaded the early writings justifying the need for sexual history evidence.

> The unchaste (let us call it) mentality finds . . . expression in the narration of imaginary sex incidents of which the narrator is the heroine or the victim. On the surface the narration is straightforward and convincing. The real victim, however . . . is the innocent man; for the respect and sympathy naturally felt by any tribunal for a wronged female helps to give easy credit to such a plausible tale.

To protect these innocent men, juries were usually instructed to scrutinize closely the testimony of a rape complainant: "Where the complaining witness and the defendant are the only witnesses, a charge of rape is one which, generally speaking, is easily made, and once made, difficult to disprove. Therefore, I charge you that the law requires that you examine the testimony of the prosecuting witness with caution." Dean Wigmore went so far as to urge that all women who brought rape charges undergo psychiatric examination before being allowed to testify in order to weed out charges stemming from sexual fantasy, rather than fact.

Whatever the situation may have been in times past, it is difficult to argue today that the danger of false charges is greater for rape than for any other kind of crime. If anything, the statistics show just the opposite. Rape is one of the most underreported crimes. In addition, rape allegations are carefully screened in most instances to assure that only legitimate cases go to trial. For no other category of crime is the scrutiny by the police and prosecutor closer.

Most states today do *not* have a rule automatically allowing the use in rape trials of testimony about a woman's "character" for chastity. Not long ago, however, courts reasoned that most women were virtuous by nature and that an unchaste woman must therefore have an unusual character flaw. This character trait had caused her to consent in the past (when, obviously, a "normal" woman would never have consented) and made it likely that she would consent repeatedly. Because consent was a defense to rape, evidence that was thought to show a propensity towards sexual relations was always admissible to suggest consent in the particular instance. Courts and legislatures have adapted to the times and have realized that a woman who is unchaste — or in modern parlance, who has had extramarital sexual relationships — is no more likely to consent indiscriminately than is a chaste woman.

Another problem that led to dissatisfaction with viewing sexual history as evidence of character was the manner of proof. Character is usually proved by testimony about a person's reputation and less often by opinion testimony or by evidence of specific acts. Thus, in rape cases, the defendant was entitled to introduce testimony about the sexual reputation of the victim and could often have a witness testify to his opinion of the woman's chastity. Even if there is some probative value in showing that a rape victim is casual in her selection of sexual partners, the least accurate way of doing so is by evidence of her reputation or the opinion of one witness perhaps lacking any personal knowledge.

Sensing the inherent weaknesses of relying on the character-evidence rationale for admitting sexual history evidence, some courts attempted to justify it on the ground that it impeached the complainant's credibility. This reasoning assumes that promiscuity is a form of dishonesty, and that, as in the case of other acts affecting honesty, promiscuity lessens the witness's credibility. This effort to justify admitting evidence of sexual history is seriously flawed. First, the cases offering this explanation limited the inference to women. Promiscuous men could not be similarly impeached. Second, only women who brought rape charges were open to this kind of impeachment. Female prosecuting witnesses who charged defendants with other types of crimes, such as robbery, could never be impeached by their prior sexual history. . . .

Yet even as the old laws were premised on the myths of a male-dominated society, the vituperative attacks and much of the resulting legislation are themselves based on an emotional premise: that the rape victim is unfairly subject to a "second rape" by the criminal justice system. Uniformly, the cry for revision of the rape evidence laws calls for special protections for the rape victim not available to most prosecuting witnesses. Writers have gone so far as to advocate considering a rape victim as a "defendant," entitled to the same protections as defendants charged with crimes.

These authors are undoubtedly correct that the old laws that singled out rape cases for special evidentiary rules were unwarranted. This thesis, however, cuts both ways: just as testimony should not automatically be admissible in rape cases, it should not automatically be inadmissible solely because a trial involves rape instead of some other crime affecting the same people. A basic premise of evidentiary rules is that they focus on issues common to all trials and do not develop differently for each substantive crime and civil cause of action.

III. The Modern Response

Much of the debate about rape victim shield laws has centered on the attempt to define precisely those situations in which fairness and due process demand that the defendant be allowed to introduce sexual history evidence. Professor Berger has written a comprehensive article defining seven particular types of evidence that, subject to judicial findings of relevance and fairness, the defendant ought to be allowed to introduce.[41] Other writers have argued that a man accused of rape may delve into the victim's sexual history in far fewer instances.[42] . . .

VII. Conclusion

A state is constitutionally prohibited from enacting a rape victim shield law that limits a defendant's ability to introduce otherwise admissible evidence. The sixth amendment rights of confrontation and compulsory process guarantee exactly this: no person accused of a crime may be denied the right to introduce evidence when the probative value outweighs the prejudicial effect. The state and federal governments may not legislate to alter the rules of evidence so as to place unusual and new burdens on the accused's ability to defend himself. Testing rape victim shield laws against this federal constitutional standard finds many of them defective.

Because sexual history evidence is potentially relevant in some rape cases, those statutes that contain absolute prohibitions, whether against all such evidence or only certain classes or uses of evidence, certainly cannot be reconciled with the sixth amendment. Shield laws also run

---

41. (1) Evidence of the complainant's sexual conduct with the defendant; (2) evidence of specific instances of conduct to show that someone other than the accused caused the physical condition (semen, pregnancy, disease) allegedly arising from the act; (3) evidence of a distinctive pattern of conduct closely resembling the defendant's version of the encounter, to prove consent; (4) evidence of prior sexual conduct known to the defendant (presumably by reputation) tending to prove that he believed complainant was consenting; (5) evidence showing a motive to fabricate the charge; (6) evidence that rebuts proof offered by the state on victim's sexual conduct; and (7) evidence as the basis for expert testimony that the complainant fantasized the act. Berger, [Man's Trial, Woman's Tribulation: Rape Cases in the Courtroom, 77 Colum. L. Rev. 90,] 98-99 [1977].

42. E.g., Ordover, [Admissibility of Patterns of Similar Sexual Conduct: The Unlamented Death of Character for Chastity, 63 Cornell L. Rev. 90, 110-118 (1979)] (distinctive patterns of behavior under similar circumstances); Note, California Rape Evidence Reform: An Analysis of Senate Bill 1678, 26 Hastings L.J. 1551, 1572 (1975) (only when victim's testimony is sole incriminating evidence); 52 Wash L. Rev. 1011, 1023, 1027-33 (1977) (bias and relations with the defendant only).

afoul of the Constitution when they alter the traditional standard for the admissibility of evidence. The sixth amendment guarantees incorporate a federal constitutional standard for the admission and exclusion of evidence offered by the accused, and the states cannot, therefore, require the evidence offered by rape defendants to satisfy a stricter standard.

There is, however, nothing wrong with requiring that the relevance of sexual history evidence be determined before trial, by employing the traditional standard of probative value weighed against prejudicial effect. To the extent that shield statutes limit the accused from unfairly attacking the morality of a rape victim, they are unobjectionable. To the extent that such statutes require that rape victims be treated no differently from other witnesses and that sexual conduct testimony be treated the same as any other evidence, they are certainly valid. A statute that seeks to correct past abuses and to change the old rule automatically admitting evidence of the rape victim's morality is laudatory. No valid constitutional reason justifies singling out rape complainants for different treatment. But fairness to rape victims and control over potentially prejudicial testimony can also be accomplished by a pretrial determination of the relevance of sexual history evidence. A valid shield law should thus read:

> Evidence of specific instances of the victim's sexual conduct, opinion evidence of the victim's sexual conduct, and reputation evidence of the victim's sexual conduct may be admitted . . . only if, and only to the extent that, the judge finds that the evidence is material to a fact at issue in the case and that its inflammatory or prejudicial nature does not outweigh its probative value.
>
> If the defendant proposes to ask any question concerning [such evidence], either by direct examination or cross-examination of any witness, the defendant must inform the court out of the hearing of the jury prior to asking any such question. After this notice, the court shall conduct an in camera hearing . . . to determine whether the proposed evidence is admissible.

Times change, and the prevailing morality changes with them. The move for equality of women has made us aware of the abuse of rape victims in the criminal justice system. Although steps have appropriately been taken towards protecting them, they have in many instances come at the expense of rights guaranteed the accused. While a rape defendant should have no greater right to present evidence than other defendants and should not be allowed to sidetrack the search for truth by introducing irrelevant testimony about the sexual mores of the complainant, the sixth amendment guarantees that he will not be prevented from eliciting testimony relevant to his defense. Shield laws must be tested against his established rights to confront his accusers and to present his own defense. If these laws are found wanting, they must be struck down and rewritten to assure that the desire to protect rape victims does not unconstitutionally hinder the ability of the accused to defend himself.

COMMONWEALTH v. GOUVEIA
371 Mass. 566, 358 N.E.2d 1001 (1976)

BRAUCHER, J. The defendant appeals from convictions of rape and an unnatural act, and argues two assignments of error: (1) exclusion of evidence of prior sexual intercourse by the victim, and (2) denial of his motion for a mistrial after the prosecutor in his closing argument asserted that there was no evidence to refute the victim's testimony as to what happened when she and the defendant were alone together. We hold that there was no error in excluding evidence of prior sexual acts between the victim and a person other than the defendant. . . . We therefore affirm the convictions.

The case for the Commonwealth consisted almost entirely of the testimony of the victim, which we summarize. She was nineteen years old and lived and worked in Billerica. On the evening of Saturday, August 25, 1973, she drove her automobile to a bar in Lowell and had two or three drinks with friends and with a young man whom she met there and who invited her to a family birthday party. She drove him to the party, a few minutes away, arriving about 11:30 to 12 P.M., and found approximately thirty people there. About a half hour later, she felt sick and she and her escort went out and got into the back seat of her car. He passed out, she vomited, and she discovered that her wallet and car keys were missing. She got out of the car and spoke to others who said they would look for the car keys.

At this point the defendant, whom she did not know, suggested that she could lie down in his van, parked nearby, and she did so. She was there for about two hours, during which time several men looked in, and one made sexual advances which she repulsed. Finally, the defendant got into the van and committed the crimes charged. After ten or fifteen minutes the defendant "gave up"; she put her jeans back on; and she went back to her car, leaving her underwear in the van. She rolled up the windows and locked the doors of her car, and a woman came over and screamed at her. Others were standing around. Later the defendant came back, said the woman was going to beat her up, and offered to give her "a ride to get out of there." They got into the van, and he drove her to within a quarter of a mile of her home. He gave her the wrong name of the street where the party was, and he falsely said the van was not his. She noted the license number and wrote it down when she arrived home about 5:15 A.M.

About 7 or 7:30 A.M. she called a friend, and he drove her to Lowell to look for her car. The same morning, after searching without success, they went to the Lowell police department. She gave the police the license number of the van and learned the defendant's name. About a week later the police recovered her car, and her wallet was found in a mailbox.

The defendant stipulated that he was at the party with his van, and that he drove the victim home. The escort, six women, and the husband of one of them testified for the defendant. All the witnesses were related to the escort by blood or marriage and all but one testified that they had known the defendant for many years. He did not testify.

In September, 1975, the defendant was convicted of both rape and an unnatural act, and was sentenced to nine to twelve years for rape and to a lesser concurrent sentence for an unnatural act. An appeal to the Appellate Division of the Superior Court resulted in concurrent sentences of three to five years. The defendant appealed pursuant to G.L. c. 278, §§33A-33G, and we allowed the parties' joint application for direct appellate review, which focused on the admissibility of evidence of prior sexual acts by a rape victim.

1. *Evidence of prior sexual acts.* The victim testified on direct examination that she was outside in the back seat of her car with her escort about two hours before the crimes took place. On cross-examination she said that she was talking to him, and that he kissed her and "attempted to make a pass" at her, "and that was it." She denied having sexual intercourse with him, but the judge sustained an objection to the question and instructed the jury to disregard it. She denied that she was undressed.

Defense witnesses testified that the victim and her escort were in the back seat of her car, and that he passed out and was carried into the house. They testified that both the victim and her escort were completely undressed, and two of them testified to obscene behavior on her part. Several also testified that she got out of the car wholly or partly undressed and walked down the street. The judge excluded questions whether she and her escort engaged in sexual intercourse.

The defendant accepts our general rule that in a rape case, although evidence of a general reputation for unchastity may be admitted, evidence of instances of prior intercourse of the victim with persons other than the defendant is inadmissible. Commonwealth v. Gardner, 350 Mass. 664, 668, 216 N.E.2d 558 (1966), and cases cited. But he argues that the rule should be limited to cases where it is "justified on the ground that collateral questions relating to those specific events would prolong the trial and divert the attention of the trier of fact from the issues." Commonwealth v. McKay, 363 Mass. 220, 227, 294 N.E.2d 213, 218 (1973). Here, he says, the prior act was close in time and nature to the crimes charged, and it was therefore admissible . . . to prove her consent. . . .

On the issue of consent, we stand by the principle that "the victim's consent to intercourse with one man does not imply her consent in the case of another." Commonwealth v. McKay, supra, 363 Mass. at 227, 294 N.E.2d at 218. At least in the circumstances here, a prior consent close in time and place might negate rather than create such an implication of subsequent consent. We need hardly add that the defendant had no right to appeal to the jury on the basis that by her conduct the victim had forfeited any claim to protection from rape.

The defendant further complains that proof of the victim's "obscene and public actions, short of intercourse, . . . strongly and erroneously implied to the jury that no such intercourse did occur," and that subsequent consent to intercourse with the defendant therefore seemed "most improbable." It is at least equally likely that the jury disbelieved the defense testimony, or that they thought, as we do, that prior consent was irrelevant to subsequent consent. In any event, the evidence of "obscene and public actions" was all introduced by the defendant, and he is in no position to complain.

The defendant argues that if our rule excludes the "demonstrably relevant evidence" offered in this case, "merely to protect the dignity of the witness," it denies the defendant his right to a fair trial and violates the United States Constitution. We have said enough to indicate that no relevant evidence was excluded. We do not regard the protection of the dignity of witnesses as illegitimate. See Commonwealth v. Bailey, 348 N.E.2d 746 (1976). But that is not the purpose of the rule here considered. . . .

When might such evidence of the victim's specific acts be "constitutionally required to be admitted"? With whom is the federal rule concerned when it speaks of "unfair prejudice" — the defendant or the victim?

Problem II-28
The "Woman" Who Cries "Wolf"

Charge: rape. M.O.: victim put in fear of serious bodily harm but no violent assault. Defense: consent. You are defense counsel. In pretrial investigation you learn that in the past two years the victim has accused five other men of rape. In four cases she subsequently withdrew her accusations, and in the other case the accused was acquitted by the jury in one-half hour after a five-day trial. You have been informed by an expert psychologist that the victim is probably either a pathological liar or is suffering from delusions that all men are evil and want to rape her. How would you introduce evidence of the prior false accusations at defendant's trial? Should such evidence be admitted? As a judge how would you rule?

PEOPLE v. SCHOLL
225 Cal. App. 2d 558, 37 Cal. Rptr. 475 (1964)   *out of date?*

KINGSLEY, J. Defendant was convicted by court trial of violation of sections 288 and 288a of the Penal Code, sexual offenses upon a female child 8 years of age. Defendant appeals from the order of the trial court denying a new trial. . . .

The evidence was sufficient to support the judgment. There were no eyewitnesses to the exact sexual offenses, and no evidence of physical harm, nor other corroboration. However, corroboration is not prerequisite to a conviction of a crime of this nature. The apparent conflicts in the testimony about the times, places and circumstances related to the offenses, noted by defendant, are to be deemed to have been properly weighed by the trial court. Stress is laid by defendant upon the child's failure to immediately complain to her mother. The complaint was made about four weeks after the first incident, but it included the second incident, which occurred about nine days before the complaint. However, the child testified that defendant threatened to kill her and her mother and she was scared. Such delay, under such circumstances, was not unreasonable nor the testimony too remote as a matter of law. . . .

Defendant attempted to cross-examine the child's mother by inquiring if she had complained of advances made to her by various men. The court rejected the proffer. We think it was in error. It is well established that such cases as these are fraught with great danger, since the charge rests on the credibility of a child witness against the defendant's denial. Especially where, as here, there is a total lack of corroboration, a belated complaint by the child to her mother, and a marked inconsistency in her testimony, the courts must heed the admonition of our Supreme Court in People v. Adams (1939) 14 Cal. 2d 154, 167 [93 P.2d 146]: "As a matter of practical observation to many judges who have presided over trials of this nature, it is plainly recognized that, notwithstanding the salutary rule that an accused is presumed to be innocent until his guilt has been established beyond a reasonable doubt, nevertheless, to the mind of the average citizen or juror, the mere fact that a person has been accused of the commission of such an offense seems to constitute sufficient evidence to warrant a verdict of 'guilty'; and that — instead of its being necessary for the prosecution to prove his guilt beyond a reasonable doubt — in order to secure an acquittal of the charge, it becomes incumbent upon the accused to completely establish his innocence, and to accomplish that result not only by a preponderance of the evidence but beyond a reasonable doubt." Where, as in the instant case, the charge is of sexual misconduct with a child, the problem is intensified, since we are, as we shall point out, concerned with the reliability of not one but two prosecutrices. The child (the alleged victim) may, as we all know, be motivated by malice against the defendant, based on some real or fancied wrong in punishment, restraint, or the like. Against such false charges, the defendant's sole defense is evidence of bias and cross-examination to show bias. Again, the child may, without malice, be the victim of sexual fantasies. Psychiatric experience tells us that such fantasies are far from uncommon and that, at an age when reality and imagination are frequently indistinguishable, the charge of sexual abuse may flow from the fantasy and not from the reality. For this reason, in California, the child can be cross-examined as to other charges, against other men, of similar acts. (People v. Hurlburt (1958) 166 Cal. App. 2d 334 [333 P.2d 82, 75 A.L.R.2d 500].)

In addition to the problems inherent in the testimony of the child herself, such cases usually involve, also, problems inherent in the testimony of a mother or other relative. Normally, it is from such a person that information of the alleged offense comes to the prosecution. But we know that, for some women, the normal concern for the welfare of their child may take an aggravated form. If the mother is abnormally oriented toward sexual conduct, and has an abnormal fear of and reaction to sexual relations, she may, quite unconsciously, build up, in her own mind, a quite innocent act or caress into a grievous wrong. Young children are especially suggestible. The inquiries put by such a mother to her daughter may, themselves, implant into the child's mind ideas and details which existed only in the fears and fantasies of the adult. Once implanted, they become quite real in the mind of the child witness and are impervious to cross-examination.

In addition, experience has shown that a mother may be motivated by actual malice, fear, retribution, retaliation, jealousy, or other motives of her own toward defendant and either by design, or unintentionally, may have implanted in the child's mind, nonexistent details which convert an innocent act into a heinous one.

For the same reasons that require a broad freedom of exploration of the child's propensities to fabricate or to imagine sexual crimes, we think a defendant should be allowed to explore, within reasonable range, the possibility of similar propensities or motivation on the part of the adult from and through whom the charge to authority emanates in alleged crimes of this nature.

In the instant case, no witness corroborated the child's story; no physical evidence of molestation existed. Under these circumstances, it seems to us error to deny to the defendant a reasonable opportunity to explore the not impossible existence of such a morbid fear of sexual acts in the mind of the mother as to make the charge a creature of that morbidity.

Reasonable latitude in cross-examination is likewise indicated in a case, such as here, where four witnesses, none of whom was acquainted with defendant, testified that the reputation of the mother for truthfulness was not good. In such instances, the possibilities of fabrication are enormous and the resulting detriment to the accused is irreparable.

The order is reversed.

Problem II-29
Impeachment with Prior Inconsistent Statements

V testified against *D* at a preliminary sexual assault hearing. On cross-examination she testified that she had been a virgin prior to the rape, but later at the same preliminary hearing she testified that she had had sexual intercourse some five or six months earlier. At the trial neither *V* nor the prosecutor presents any claim of lack of prior sexual experience on her part. Can *D* impeach *V* with her statements at the preliminary hearing? Can *D* offer extrinsic proof to show that she was sexually experienced? Is the case different if she asserts at trial that she was a virgin?

Problem II-30
Impeachment and Pregnancy

At *D*'s trial for sexual assault of *V*, *V* testifies that *D* raped her and that she became pregnant as a result. *D* seeks to prove *V*'s prior consensual sexual activity with *X* on the theory that *V* became pregnant by *X* and then falsely accused *D* of rape to provide an alternate explanation for the pregnancy. Admissible?

Problem II-31
Occupational Hazards[1]

At *D*'s trial for rape of *V*, *D* testifies that he is an exterminator and that on the day in question he went on a service call to the home of the complaining witness. *D* claims that he arrived late in the afternoon and that *V* consented to — in fact initiated — sexual relations. *D*'s version is

---

1. This problem and the two following ones are adapted from Tanford and Bocchino, Rape Shield Laws and the Sixth Amendment, 128 U. Pa. L. Rev. 544, 581, 586, 588 (1981). — EDS.

that they fell asleep until late evening, at which time *V* panicked because the company truck was parked in front of the house in full view of the neighbors. She started screaming at him to get out, and he later found himself arrested for rape. There is no evidence of injury or weapons. *V* claims that she engaged in sex with *D* because *D* threatened to kill her.

D seeks to prove the complainant's reputation among deliverymen for initiating sex with those who make deliveries to her house. Admissible?

D offers several deliverymen to testify not only to *V*'s reputation but also that she initiated sex with them when they delivered to her house. Admissible?

Problem II-32
The Singles Scene

D and *V* met at a singles bar and after a few drinks returned to *V*'s apartment, where they engaged in sexual intercourse. *D* claims that *V* consented but that they had a fight later and *V* then threw him out. *D* admits hitting *V* during the fight. *V* claims that she invited *D* for coffee and that he hit and raped her. *D* seeks to prove that *V* regularly met men in singles bars, invited them to her apartment, and had consensual sexual relations with them. Admissible?

Problem II-33
"Don't Leave Home Without It"

D and *V* met at a bar, then went to a hotel room and engaged in sexual intercourse. *V* claims that she was raped. *D* claims that *V* is a prostitute and that he made a deal with her for $50, but that when it came time to pay he had only $20 with him. *V* became enraged and accused him of rape. *D* offers proof that *V* is a prostitute. Admissible?

COMMONWEALTH v. BOHANNON
376 Mass. 90, 378 N.E.2d 987 (1978)

ABRAMS, J. The defendant Willard E. Bohannon, Jr. (Bohannon), was convicted after a jury trial of rape, kidnapping, commission of an unnatural act, and assault and battery by means of a dangerous weapon. He appeals these convictions pursuant to G.L. c. 278, §§33A-33G. We conclude that there must be a new trial.

We summarize the evidence presented at the trial. On May 22, 1974, Bohannon, Robert Stonestreet (Stonestreet), and a juvenile picked up the complainant who was hitch-hiking to Brockton. The group went to a liquor store where Stonestreet bought two quarts of beer. They then drove to a sandpit near Brockton. At trial, the complainant and the two codefendants, Bohannon and Stonestreet, agreed that various sexual acts took place at the sandpit, but they disagreed sharply as to which defendant had done what and as to whether the complainant had consented to participate in these acts.

The complainant, the only witness that the Commonwealth presented on the issue of consent, was a thirty-three year old, mildly retarded woman with an I.Q. of 63. She testified that after they arrived at the sandpit Bohannon ordered her out of the car and that she complied. She stated that he then forcibly undressed her and pushed her down on the ground. She maintained that he then penetrated her briefly and forced her to commit fellatio. She testified that he also briefly inserted a bottle and a stick into her vagina. The complainant testified that Stonestreet had also raped her.

The complainant's testimony concerning the events of the night in question was inconsistent and confused. Her allegations concerning Bohannon were inconsistent with testimony she had earlier given in the District Court of Brockton and with her statements to the district attorney two days prior to trial. On these occasions she had stated that Bohannon had not raped her. When she was asked on cross-examination to explain this inconsistency, the complainant stated that she had recently seen "in a mist" that Bohannon had penetrated her. Her testimony concerning Stonestreet was also inconsistent. In the District Court, prior to trial, and at the trial, the complainant had maintained that Stonestreet had raped her. However, after her trial testimony was concluded, she informed the district attorney that she was now uncertain as to whether Stonestreet was involved. When recalled by the district attorney, the complainant testified that Stonestreet had not raped her.

Both Bohannon and Stonestreet testified at the trial. They asserted that the complainant consented to the sexual activities which had occurred. Bohannon testified that he asked her to get out of the car with him and she did. He stated that she then voluntarily performed fellatio on him and undressed. They lay down together outside the car, but he was unable to have intercourse. Bohannon testified that the complainant then became annoyed, and he tried using a beer bottle for a few seconds. Then the complainant handed him a stick and said, "use this." After a while she asked him to bring over his friends. Both Stonestreet and the juvenile then came over. Stonestreet testified that the complainant left the car voluntarily with Bohannon and that she appeared to acquiesce in the acts involved. He stated that the complainant had invited him to participate, but that he had been unwilling. He denied that he engaged in intercourse with her.

Medical evidence of the injuries sustained by the complainant indicated a small cut on the cervix which slowly oozed blood for several hours and a bruise on her eye. No evidence of sperm was found.

The central focus of the trial was the credibility of the complainant, particularly in connection with the issue of consent. During the cross-examination of the complainant, defense counsel requested a bench conference to determine whether it was permissible to ask her the following questions: "[w]hether or not she has prior to this made accusations that other men have raped her, and how many times, if the answer is yes, she has made these accusations." In support of the propriety of these questions, defense counsel made an offer of proof that, according to hospital records, the complainant had made a number of unsubstantiated, and apparently false, accusations of rape. The trial judge concluded that the questions could not be asked. The correctness of this determination is the sole issue presented for review.

In general, evidence of prior bad acts may not be used to impeach a witness's credibility.[3] One clear exception to this general rule is that records of criminal convictions may be used to impeach credibility. Evidence of prior false allegations has been excluded as a consequence of this general rule. Miller v. Curtis, 158 Mass. 127, 32 N.E. 1039 (1893). Commonwealth v. Regan, 105 Mass. 593 (1870).

In the *Miller* opinion, however, we indicated that the rule was not inflexible and that there might be cases presented in which such evidence might be competent. Miller v. Curtis, 158 Mass. at 131, 32 N.E. 1039. We conclude that this is such a case. When evidence concerning a critical issue is excluded and when that evidence might have had a significant impact on the result of the trial, the right to present a full defense has been denied.

The credibility of the complainant was the critical issue in the present case. The central issue in dispute was whether she consented to the acts

---

3. The defendant contends that the purpose of the proposed cross-examination was to demonstrate bias on the part of the witness. If such were the case, the defendant would be entitled as a matter of right to reasonable cross-examination for the purpose of showing this bias. Commonwealth v. Cheek, — Mass. —, —, 373 N.E.2d 1161 (1978) (Mass. Adv. Sh. [1978] 649, 651). Commonwealth v. Ahearn, 370 Mass. —, —, 346 N.E.2d 907 (1976) (Mass. Adv. Sh. [1976] 1256, 1261). Commonwealth v. Graziano, 368 Mass. 325, 330, 331 N.E.2d 808 (1975). Commonwealth v. Michel, 367 Mass. 454, 459, 327 N.E.2d 720 (1975). See Commonwealth v. Ferrara, 368 Mass. 182, 330 N.E.2d 837 (1975); Davis v. Alaska, 415 U.S. 308 (1974). The defendant argues that since the complainant was returned to the hospital each time her mother thought she had sexually misbehaved, she thought she might persuade her mother to allow her to remain at home if she could convince her mother that she was raped. Thus, the defendant maintains that a rape charge and conviction are more in the complainant's personal interest than is generally true. The defendant, however, did not bring the bias aspects of his proposed cross-examination to the attention of the judge and the fact that the purpose of the questions was to demonstrate bias was not clear from the questions themselves. Therefore we consider the cross-examination as directed to credibility only.

involved, and the complainant, as in most cases of this type, was the only Commonwealth witness on the issue of consent.

Evaluations of credibility are, of course, within the exclusive province of the trier of fact. The defendant sought by his questions to bring to the jury's attention the fact that the complainant had made false allegations of rape on several occasions in the past. Evidence of prior false accusations of the specific crime which is the subject of the trial might itself have seriously damaged the complainant's credibility. Moreover, in this case the possibility that this evidence might have had a significant impact on the issue of credibility is enhanced by the fact that the complainant's testimony was inconsistent and confused. See Commonwealth v. Franklin, 366 Mass. at 290, 318 N.E.2d 469. Thus the proffered evidence, if believed, might have had a significant impact on the issue of consent and consequently on the outcome of the trial. In the circumstances of this case, we therefore think the exclusion of the defendant's proposed questions violated his right to present his defense fully.

We wish to stress two features of the present case which are relevant to the decision we have reached. First, the defendant made an offer of proof which indicated that he had a factual basis from independent third party records for concluding that prior allegations of rape had, in fact, been made and were, in fact, untrue. It is particularly important that when a proposed question even remotely connected with sexual conduct is to be asked "the cross-examiner should have a reason for asking any such questions and should be prepared to disclose that reason to the judge." Commonwealth v. White, 367 Mass. 280, 284, 325 N.E.2d 575, 578 (1975).

Second, the proposed questions dealt with prior allegations of rape; they in no way sought to elicit a response concerning the complainant's prior sexual activity or reputation for chastity. We, therefore, do not reach any issues related to the recently enacted "rape-shield" statute, G.L. c. 233, §21B, inserted by St. 1977, c. 110. Nor should this decision be viewed as indicating any adherence to that "part of a legal tradition, established by men, that the complaining woman in a rape case is fair game for character assassination in open court." Commonwealth v. Manning, 367 Mass. 605, 613-614, 328 N.E.2d 496, 501 (1975) (Braucher, J., dissenting). We firmly reject approval of any evidentiary rule which is grounded in a mistrust of women rather than in logic.

The convictions are reversed and the cases are remanded for a new trial.

CHAPTER III

Competency of Witnesses,
Direct and Cross-Examination,
Making and Meeting Objections,
Functions of Judge and Jury —
the Rules of the Road

The preceding chapters already have demonstrated the importance of understanding and being able to use the mechanics of proof — the rules relating to examination of witnesses, introduction of exhibits, making of objections, offers of proof, the record on appeal, and functions of judge, jury, appeals court, and advocate. The evidence rules that govern these functions may be thought of as the courtroom rules of the road. Like the rules of the highway, they tell you *how* to get where you want to go, not *where* you want to go; like driving rules, they should be learned so thoroughly that conforming to them becomes automatic.

The approach we have chosen in this book is to integrate the problems associated with these more mechanical or procedural rules with the substantive subjects of relevancy, hearsay, privileges, experts, and writings. We deliberately have constructed problems and chosen cases in the other chapters to highlight procedural problems as they arise in specific evidentiary contexts. See, for example, the section in Chapter IV on the procedural aspects of admitting evidence under Rule 801(d)(2)(E) (statements of a co-conspirator). This integrated approach emphasizes the connections between the procedural and substantive aspects of evidence and also replicates the world in which such rules are applied.

Nonetheless, it seems worthwhile to focus separately on the rules of the road, as this chapter does, albeit in a somewhat abbreviated manner. Segregating and considering the procedural rules in a variety of substantive contexts reveals that they are not as mechanical as they first seem; they often present important policy choices that implicate fundamental values. Both perspectives — the integrated and the isolated — are valuable.

This chapter takes a closer look at examination of witnesses, introduction of exhibits, use of views, real evidence, and photographic evidence, and the different functions of judge and jury in deciding preliminary questions of fact on which the introduction of other evidence depends. In particular, it examines the purposes of cross-examination, the limits of permissible cross-examination, and the form and scope of both direct and cross-examination.

Cross-examination, as the trial lawyers claim, is an art that the student cannot begin to master in an introductory course in evidence. Our much more modest goal is to impart an understanding of the basic rules and an appreciation for the potential of the method. The same is true for the sections on views, real evidence, and photographic proof, with the additional goal of imparting a sense of how such evidence compares to live-witness testimony. Overlapping all of these concerns is the question of who — of judge, jury, and appellate court — decides what and on what basis. This last question could easily be the sole subject of an advanced seminar on evidence. In an introductory course it is enough to understand the formal division of labor made by the Federal Rules and to identify the principles on which the division is premised.

When considering the specific issues posed by the problems and cases in this chapter, reflect on the larger questions associated with the federal rules of the road. What values do these rules serve? Accuracy? Efficiency? Fairness? Certainty? What do these rules reveal about the drafters' views of the competency and proper role of the jury and the trial judge? What image of the adversary system do these rules reveal? How would you improve the system?

A. The Purposes of Cross-Examination

Problem III-1
The B & G Bar and Grill

Malpractice damage action against surgeon *D* for the alleged negligent performance of a tonsillectomy on *P* on June 1, 1980, at 2 P.M. The specific negligent act alleged is operating while intoxicated. At trial, *P* offers *W*, a waitress at the B & G Bar and Grill, to testify that on June 1 at 1 P.M. *D* entered the bar, occupied the booth, and consumed several drinks. The cross-examination is as follows:

Q: What were the drinks that the defendant ordered?
A: Bloody Marys.
Q: How many drinks did he order?

A: A lot of drinks.

Q: What do you mean by "A lot of drinks"?

A: More than two.

Q: More than five?

A: Maybe — about that many.

Q: Did you see the drinks mixed?

A: No.

Q: Was the defendant alone?

A: No. There were people with him.

Q: How many?

A: Several — three or four.

Q: Men or women?

A: Men and women.

Q: How many men and how many women?

A: I don't know. There were some of each.

Q: Did defendant eat anything when he was there?

A: I don't know.

Q: How many customers were in the B & G while defendant was there?

A: Oh, it's a big place and very busy at that hour.

Q: How many?

A: Probably 50 or so.

Q: How many waitresses were there?

A: Well, there were just two of us on then, I think.

Q: Did you also take money and serve as a cashier?

A: Yes, except Harry at the bar took money there for drinks.

Q: So during the time defendant was in the bar you would be taking money and making change?

A: Yes.

Q: Who paid the tab for the drinks at defendant's table?

A: I can't remember.

Q: Have you ever had a disagreement with defendant over the service or anything else in the B & G?

A: Well, once he claimed to have given me a $20 bill when he had given me only a $10 bill, and we had some words over it.

What is the purpose of this cross-examination? What qualities of the witness are tested? What capacities and skills of the witness are impugned?

Consider the following from Kinsey v. State, 65 P.2d 1141 (Ariz. 1937):

What is the purpose of cross-examination? Obviously it is to convince the triers of fact, in some manner, that the testimony of the witness is untrue, for if the cross-examiner accepts it as true, there will be no need nor desire for cross-examination. How, then, may the truthfulness of the evidence of a

3 attacks

witness be attacked through cross-examination? It seems to us that all attacks thereon must be reduced to one of three classes: (a) Upon the honesty and integrity of the witness; (b) upon his ability to observe accurately at the time the incident occurred; and (c) upon his accuracy of recollection of the past events.

If one of the purposes of cross-examination is to destroy the credibility of the witness, what are the limits of acceptable attack?

BERGER v. UNITED STATES
295 U.S. 78 (1935)

Charge: conspiracy to utter counterfeit notes.

SUTHERLAND, J. . . . . That the United States prosecuting attorney overstepped the bounds of that propriety and fairness which should characterize the conduct of such an officer in the prosecution of a criminal offense is clearly shown by the record. He was guilty of misstating the facts in his cross-examination of witnesses; of putting into the mouths of such witnesses things which they had not said; of suggesting by his questions that statements had been made to him personally out of court, in respect of which no proof was offered; of pretending to understand that a witness had said something which he had not said and persistently cross-examining the witness upon that basis; of assuming prejudicial facts not in evidence; of bullying and arguing with witnesses; and in general, of conducting himself in a thoroughly indecorous and improper manner. We reproduce in the margin[1] a few excerpts from the

---

1. [The defendant (petitioner) was on the stand; cross-examination by the United States attorney]:

Q: The man who didn't have his pants on and was running around the apartment, he wasn't there?

A: No, Mr. Singer. Mr. Godby told me about this, he told me, as long as you ask me about it, if you want it, I will tell you, he told me "If you give this man's name out, I will give you the works."

Q: Give me the works?

A: No, Mr. Godby told me that.

Q: You are going to give me the works?

A: Mr. Singer, you are a gentleman, I have got nothing against you. You are doing your duty.

Mr. Wegman: You are not going to give Mr. Singer the works. Apparently Mr. Singer misunderstood you. Who made that statement?

The Witness: Mr. Godby says that.

Q: Wait a minute. Are you going to give me the works?

A: Mr. Singer, you are absolutely a gentleman, in my opinion, you are doing your duty here.

Q: Thank you very much. But I am only asking you are you going to give me the works?

A: I do not give anybody such things, I never said it.

record illustrating some of the various points of the foregoing summary. It is impossible, however, without reading the testimony at some length, and thereby obtaining a knowledge of the setting in which the objectionable matter occurred, to appreciate fully the extent of the misconduct. The trial judge, it is true, sustained objections to some of the questions, insinuations and misstatements, and instructed the jury to disregard

---

Q: All right. Then do not make the statement.

Mr. Wegman: The witness said that Mr. Godby said that.

The Court: The jury heard what was said. It is not for you or me to interpret the testimony.

Q: I asked you whether the man who was running around this apartment . . . , was he there in the Secret Service office on the morning that you were arrested?

A: I didn't see him.

Q: I wasn't in that apartment, was I?

A: No, Mr. Singer.

Q: I didn't pull the gun on you and stick you up against the wall?

A: No.

Q: I wasn't up in this apartment at any time, as far as you know, was I?

A: As far as I know, you weren't.

Q: You might have an idea that I may have been there?

A: No, I should say not.

Q: I just want to get that part of it straight. . . .

Q: Was I in that apartment that night?

A: No, but Mr. Godby —

Q: Was Mr. Godby in that apartment?

A: No, but he has been there. . . .

Q: Do you include as those who may have been there the Court and all the jurymen and your own counsel?

A: Mr. Singer, you ask me a question. May I answer it?

Mr. Wegman: I object to the question.

The Witness: Are you serious about that?

The Court: I am not going to stop him because the question includes the Court. I will let him answer it.

Mr. Singer: I would like to have an answer to it.

The Witness: Mr. Singer, you asked me the question before —

The Court: You answer this question.

(Question repeated by the reporter.)

A: I should say not; that is ridiculous. . . .

Q: Now Mr. Berger, do you remember yesterday when the court recessed for a few minutes and you saw me out in the hall; do you remember that?

A: I do, Mr. Singer.

Q: You talked to me out in the hall?

A: I talked to you?

Q: Yes.

A: No.

Q: You say you didn't say to me out in the hall yesterday, "You wait until I take the stand and I will take care of you"? You didn't say that yesterday?

A: No; I didn't. Mr. Singer; you are lying.

Q: I am lying, you are right. You didn't say that at all?

A: No.

Q: You didn't speak to me out in the hall?

A: I never did speak to you outside since this case started, except the day I was in your office, when you questioned me.

Q: I said yesterday.

A: No, Mr. Singer.

Q: Do you mean that seriously?

them. But the situation was one which called for stern rebuke and re-
pressive measures and, perhaps, if these were not successful, for the
granting of a mistrial. It is impossible to say that the evil influence upon
the jury of these acts of misconduct was removed by such mild judicial
action as was taken.

A witness by the name of Goldie Goldstein had been called by the
prosecution to identify the petitioner. She apparently had difficulty in
doing so. The prosecuting attorney, in the course of his argument, said
(italics added):

"Mrs. Goldie Goldstein takes the stand. She says she knows Jones, *and
you can bet your bottom dollar she knew Berger.* She stood right where I am
now and looked at him and was afraid to go over there, and when I
waved my arm everybody started to holler, 'Don't point at him.' You
know the rules of law. Well, it is the most complicated game in the world.
I was examining *a woman that I knew knew Berger and could identify him,* she
was standing right here looking at him, and I couldn't say, 'Isn't that the
man?' Now, imagine that! But that is the rules of the game, and I have to
play within those rules."

The jury was thus invited to conclude that the witness Goldstein knew
Berger well but pretended otherwise; and that this was within the personal knowledge of the prosecuting attorney.

Again, at another point in his argument, after suggesting that defendants' counsel had the advantage of being able to charge the district
attorney with being unfair, "of trying to twist a witness," he said:

"But, oh, they can twist the questions, . . . *they can sit up in their offices
and devise ways to pass counterfeit money;* 'but don't let the Government
touch me, that is unfair; please leave my client alone.' "

In what ways did the prosecuting attorney overstep the bounds of
acceptable cross-examination? Would the same behavior by defense

---

A: I said no.
Q: That never happened?
A: No, Mr. Singer, it did not.
Q: You did not say that to me?
A: I did not.
Q: Of course, I have just made that up?
A: What do you want me to answer you?
Q: I want you to tell me I am lying, is that so? . . .
     [No effort was later made to prove that any such statement had ever been made.]
Q: Did she say she was going to meet me for anything except business purposes?
A: No.
Q: If she was to meet me?
A: Just told me that you gave her your home telephone number and told her to call you
     up after nine o'clock in the evening if she found out anything about the case that you
     could help me with, that is what she told me.
Q: Even if that is so, what is wrong about that, that you have been squawking about all
     morning?

counsel be improper? When a lawyer is out to destroy the credibility of an opponent's witness who, let us assume, the lawyer believes is either lying or mistaken, how do you draw the line between permissible and impermissible attack?

B. Competency of Witnesses

The common law had very strict rules about who was qualified to testify in court. Parties were deemed incompetent as witnesses because of the natural inclination of humans to stretch the truth in their own self-interest. Similarly, spouses were held incompetent under the doctrine of *coverture* as a natural extension of the disqualification for *interest*. Felons were disqualified for *infamy* on the grounds that any person convicted of a serious crime was not worthy of belief. Witnesses who could not swear their belief in an omnipotent God who saw and immediately rewarded falsehood with a severe sanction were disqualified for *irreligion*. This requirement was subsequently relaxed to require only a belief in a God who rewarded and punished truth and falsity in the hereafter, and then relaxed further to require only a belief in God.

With all these disqualifications, it was sometimes difficult to find anyone with any first-hand knowledge of the relevant event to testify. A not too far-fetched example:

Time: early nineteenth century. Place: the Four Horseshoes Inn, a country pub at Madingley, Cambridgeshire. Present in the pub are Peter, Peter's wife, Mary, David, Lawrence, and Kevin, the tavern keeper. A brawl breaks out between Peter and David, and Peter later brings an action of assault against David. Lawrence, it develops, is a convicted felon, and when Kevin is called to the witness stand at trial, he states that he is an agnostic.

Who could testify to what happened in the pub? No one. Peter and David were incompetent because of their interest. Mary was incompetent by reason of coverture, Lawrence by reason of infamy, and Kevin on account of his irreligion.

The common law system gradually gave way to the modern approach of Rules 601 and 602:

FRE 601
General Rule of Competency

Every person is competent to be a witness except as otherwise provided in these rules. However, in civil actions and proceedings, with respect to an element of a claim or defense as to which State law supplies the rule of decision, the competency of a witness shall be determined in accordance with State law.

FRE 602
Lack of Personal Knowledge

A witness may not testify to a matter unless evidence is introduced sufficient to support a finding that he has personal knowledge of the matter. Evidence to prove personal knowledge may, but need not, consist of the testimony of the witness himself. This rule is subject to the provisions of rule 703, relating to opinion testimony by expert witnesses.

What, if anything, is left of the common law disqualifications for interest, coverture, infamy, and irreligion? Most of the concerns expressed by these concepts have been relegated to reliance on cross-examination to bring out the infirmities of witness testimony, but some vestiges remain. The "Dead Man's Rule" in some state jurisdictions prevents a party from testifying in a lawsuit when death has stilled the tongue of his opponent. Spouses today have a privilege not to testify against each other. In certain circumstances felons may have their criminal record brought out to impeach their credibility. And witnesses still must swear or affirm that they will testify truthfully:

FRE 603
Oath or Affirmation

Before testifying, every witness shall be required to declare that he will testify truthfully, by oath or affirmation administered in a form calculated to awaken his conscience and impress his mind with his duty to do so.

However, fire and brimstone have officially disappeared:

FRE 610
Religious Beliefs or Opinions

Evidence of the beliefs or opinions of a witness on matters of religion is not admissible for the purpose of showing that by reason of their nature his credibility is impaired or enhanced.

If cross-examination has supplanted the common law's witness qualification rules, does competency now require a minimum opportunity for cross-examination? Consider the following problems.

Problem III-2
The Intoxicated Informer

Charge: sale of a proscribed substance, to wit, heroin, to *I*. The state introduces evidence to show that *I*, a known heroin addict, was given $300 by the police to purchase heroin from *D* at *D*'s barber shop. The state calls *I* as its first witness. *D* objects to any testimony from *I* on the grounds that *I* is incompetent to be a witness by virtue of drug use. The trial court conducts an in-chambers hearing on the question. *D* calls *P*, a psychiatrist, who testifies that the use of LSD may confuse one's perception, thereby impairing the capacity to perceive or remember one's observations. *P*'s opinion is based on her experience with LSD users, whom she has found to have a history of suffering blackouts, although she has not personally interviewed *I*. *I* admits to excessive use of drugs, including LSD, but denies ever passing out, freaking out, or having loss of memory from the use of LSD.

What ruling and why? Is there a minimum threshold of the ability of the witness to observe, remember, relate, and appreciate the obligation of telling the truth that the witness must cross before he will be allowed to testify?

Problem III-3
Little Archie — The Child Witness

On June 1, 1966, a male child is born to Mr. and Mrs. *P*. The child is normal and named Archie. On June 1, 1969, Archie suffers multiple punctures of his leg in a playground injury. No one saw what happened. The punctures could have been made by a dog's teeth, nails in the sandbox board, or any number of other things. Archie's parents claim that *D*'s dog is the culprit. On June 15, 1969, *P* sues *D*. At trial beginning July 15, 1969, Archie is called to testify. *D*'s objection to calling Archie as a witness is sustained. *P* takes a voluntary nonsuit, and the case is dismissed. On December 15, 1969, *P* refiles his complaint. *D* answers. There are many continuances. Finally, the trial is held in 1975 before the same judge who presided at the first trial. Archie is called as the first witness.

D's objection to calling Archie as a witness is overruled. Are the two rulings compatible?

Problem III-4
The Aphasic Witness

Action for damages for personal injuries arising out of a collision between *P*'s car and *D*'s bus. The accident took place in November 1980 at the intersection of Oak Park Avenue and Madison Street. This intersection is controlled by traffic lights. At trial the issue is who ran the traffic light. Prior to the accident, *P* had been a healthy, active 35-year-old policeman. He was taken unconscious from the scene of the accident, suffering from a head injury. When *P* regained consciousness, it was found that he had lost the power of reason and speech; restraints were needed to control him. Two weeks later his condition was slightly improved and he was sent home, but at the time of trial the injuries still affected his ability to speak coherently and intelligently. He could answer only simple questions. On direct examination, *P* gave his name, address, age, and the day and year of the accident but was unable to say the month in which the accident took place. He was able to testify that the accident took place at the Oak Park Avenue and Madison Street intersection and that there were traffic lights there. Further direct testimony was as follows:

Q: What street were you driving on when the accident happened?
A: Oak Park and Madison Street.
Q: Were there any traffic lights at Oak Park and Madison Street?
A: Yes.
Q: What direction were you going?
A: South.
Q: Now what was the color of the light as you approached and reached the intersection?
A: Green.
Q: What happened as you were going over? Tell the jury what happened.
A: Green and amber, amber and bus struck.
Q: What happened as you were going over the crossing?
A: I get hit.
Q: You got hit?
A: Yes.
Q: By what?
A: A bus.
Q: What do you next remember after that?
A: I don't remember.

There was no objection to *P*'s competency at this point.

The cross-examination required 20 pages of transcript. In response to defense counsel's questions *P* could not say where he had been going.

His answers often lacked consistency. He would testify differently to the same question. Sometimes his answers were incoherent and meaningless; however, some answers were corroborated by other credible evidence. At the conclusion of the cross-examination D objected and moved to strike P's direct and cross-examination. The judge conducted a voir dire on the issue. Medical experts testified that P understood the questions put to him but that his speech was impaired and that his mental condition made him unable to repeat simple phrases or frame his responses. The experts testified that P could answer single-word questions correctly for a while but that he would tire and become confused. This condition was diagnosed as "aphasia" — the inability to coordinate thoughts and use words to express them.

How should the judge rule? Should the direct and cross-examination be stricken on the grounds that the witness is incompetent to testify, or should the evidence go to the jury for whatever weight it decides to give it?

Problem III-5
The Knee-Jerk Witness

Charge: theft of personal property from the person in an amount not exceeding $150. M.O.: taking a ring from the finger of the victim while she slept in her bed in a nursing home. At trial the victim of the crime was incompetent to testify. The principal witness against D was the victim's roommate, W, an elderly lady who could not speak but who, according to medical testimony, had normal hearing. W could answer the questions put to her only by raising her right knee if the answer to the question were "yes" and by remaining still if the answer were "no." In this manner W testified that she was the roommate of the victim, that she knew D, and that D was the person who came into the room of the victim and the witness late at night and took the ring from the victim's finger.

Defense counsel objected to W's testimony on grounds of competency. What ruling and why?

Problem III-6
The Medium Is the Message

Should a witness who is unable to speak be permitted to testify if the only way the witness can communicate is through another person, such as a medium, who claims to be able to apprehend in some way the witness's answers to questions and to translate them? If the medium is sworn to interpret the witness's answers correctly, should the mute witness be allowed to testify? See People v. Walker, 69 Cal. App. 475,

231 P. 572 (1924); I. Disraeli, Curiosities of Literature, chapters on "Literary Impostures" and "Literary Forgeries," cited in J. Maguire, J. Weinstein, J. Chadbourn, and J. Mansfield, Evidence 265 (1973). See also Hamisi s/o Salum v. R. (1951) 18 E.A.C.A. 217 (Kenya), discussed in P. Durand, Evidence for Magistrates 94 (1969).

FRE 604
Interpreters

An interpreter is subject to the provisions of these rules relating to qualification as an expert and the administration of an oath or affirmation that he will make a true translation.

Problem III-7
"You Feel Very Sleepy . . ."

Charge: murder in the first degree. Evidence for the state tended to show that Wilma Norris was the operator of a house of prostitution. Linda Lingle was one of her employees. In the late evening of June 24, 1975, the bodies of the two women were found lying on their stomachs on a bed in the house. Both had been dead for a number of hours. A coiled rope lay on the bed. Each body lay in an unnatural position, indicating that the hands had been bound behind the back at the time of death and then released. The cause of death in each instance was a bullet wound in the back of the head.

The principal prosecution witness, Barbara Kiser, testified, "Sometimes I knew that I saw the defendant kill them and sometimes I really knew I hadn't seen him; I just know I couldn't remember." At her request she had been hypnotized a few weeks prior to trial. She testified, "When I was under hypnosis I was able to actually go back to that day five years ago and just relive the whole morning and see the whole day like it was right now, everything was fresh. I remember now that I saw those women being shot by Roger McQueen [the defendant]."

Defense counsel were given a tape of the hypnosis procedure the day before trial. It was not offered in evidence. The hypnotist was not called as a witness either by the state or the defense. The record contains no testimony concerning the hypnotic procedure or what the witness related while under hypnosis.

Defendant contended at trial that Kiser had killed Norris and Lingle and objected to Kiser's testimony on the grounds that it was false and the result of her pretrial hypnosis.

Did the court err in allowing Kiser's testimony? How would you cross-examine or otherwise defend against hypnotically recollected evidence?

What procedural protections would you recommend when such evidence is offered? Should a witness be permitted to testify in court while under hypnosis? Should a pretrial statement made by a witness while under hypnosis be admissible?

C. Form and Scope of Examination of Witnesses

FRE 611
Mode and Order of Interrogation and Presentation

(a) *Control by court.* The court shall exercise reasonable control over the mode and order of interrogating witnesses and presenting evidence so as to (1) make the interrogation and presentation effective for the ascertainment of the truth, (2) avoid needless consumption of time, and (3) protect witnesses from harassment or undue embarrassment.

(b) *Scope of cross-examination.* Cross-examination should be limited to the subject matter of the direct examination and matters affecting the credibility of the witness. The court may, in the exercise of discretion, permit inquiry into additional matters as if on direct examination.

(c) *Leading questions.* Leading questions should not be used on the direct examination of a witness except as may be necessary to develop his testimony. Ordinarily leading questions should be permitted on cross-examination. When a party calls a hostile witness, an adverse party, or a witness identified with an adverse party, interrogation may be by leading questions.

1. Form of Examination of Witnesses

Problem III-8
Direct Examination: Accident

Action for damages for personal injuries that allegedly occurred when *D* ran over *P* on June 1 while *P* was crossing the road. Complaint: See Official Form 9, F.R. Civ. P. *D*'s answer denies the allegations of the complaint and pleads contributory negligence. At trial the jury is sworn, counsel makes a brief opening statement, and *P* is called to the stand as plaintiff's first witness. The first question put to her is, "Where were you on June 1?" *D* objects. What ruling and why?

The next question is, "Did defendant drive his car into you on June 1?" *D* objects. What ruling and why?

Construct a direct examination of *P* that will avoid the mistakes plaintiff's attorney has made.

Problem III-9
Direct Examination: Car Theft

Action for the alleged conversion by *D* on June 1 of a $5,000 car allegedly owned by *P*. *D*'s answer is a general denial of every allegation in the complaint. On direct examination of *P*, the first witness, the preliminary foundational questions are asked and answered, at which point *P*'s counsel asks the witness, "And when you returned from the store, you saw *D* driving your car away, didn't you?" *D* objects.

What ruling and why? What mistake has *P*'s attorney made? Construct a short segment of direct examination that would avoid the problem presented in this example.

Problem III-10
Direct and Cross-Examination — High Sticking

Charge: aggravated assault and battery. Defendant: *D*, a professional hockey player for the Brotherly Bullies. Victim: Kevin O'Casey, a loyal Boston Bruin fan. M.O.: striking O'Casey over the head with a hockey stick in the Boston Garden on February 14, 1980. At *D*'s trial O'Casey is the first prosecution witness and testifies on direct examination as to his name, age, employment, and so forth. The assistant D.A. next has a hockey stick marked as People's Exhibit *A* for identification. The direct examination continues:

Q: I show you what has been marked as People's Exhibit *A* for identification and ask you if you recognize it?
(The witness does not answer.)
Q: Mr. *D* struck you with this, didn't he?
By defense counsel: Objection — leading question.

What ruling and why?
The second witness at *D*'s trial is Brad Pork, a member of the Bruins who has been subpoenaed and called by the defense as its first witness. On cross-examination of Pork by the assistant D.A. the following occurs:

Q: Did you see anyone strike O'Casey?
A: Yes.
Q: Was it you?
A: No.

Q: It was the defendant, *D*, who struck him, wasn't it?
By defense counsel: Objection.

What ruling and why?

What standard should be used in deciding whether a question is an improper leading question? What are the practical or policy considerations for the rule prohibiting leading questions to a friendly witness? What is wrong with leading a friendly witness?

Problem III-11
Cross-Examination — Charles Atlas

Charge: mayhem. Defendant: *D*, a 5'3", 90-pound weakling. Victim: Ali, a 6'4", 230-pound tough dude. At *D*'s trial the first witness for the prosecution is the arresting officer, *O*. On cross-examination, defense counsel elicits facts concerning *D*'s size and weight and then asks, "Isn't it a fact that the evidence shows beyond a reasonable doubt that the defendant is too small to beat up the victim?" *Inference*

The prosecution objects. What ruling and why?

Problem III-12
Cross-Examination — Lover's Quarrel

Charge: murder. Defendant: *D*. Victim: Mr. *D*. M.O.: shotgun wound to the body. Eyewitnesses: none. Defense: alibi. At trial the prosecution makes out a prima facie case and rests. *D* takes the stand and on direct questioning maintains her complete innocence. On cross-examination the following questions are asked by the district attorney:

Q: What had your husband done to cause you to kill him? . . .
Q: Did you have any reason for taking that man's life that you said you loved? . . .
Q: Can you give the jury any reason why you shot your husband and killed him? . . .
Q: Did he threaten you? . . . *all N.G*
Q: Did he draw a gun? Just answer yes or no. . . .

Defense counsel objects to these questions. What ruling and why?

Problem III-13
Opium

Charge: violation of Section 54 of the state penal code, which makes it a crime for any person to manufacture, possess, control, sell, prescribe, administer, or dispense any narcotic drug except as provided therein. The indictment alleges that on June 1 *D* did unlawfully manufacture, possess, and control a narcotic drug — to wit, opium. At trial the D.A. makes his opening statement, in which he says that the prosecution will prove that *D* purchased paregoric and then proceed to reduce it to opium. The first witness for the prosecution is *J.J.* His direct examination is as follows:

Q: What is your name?
A: J.J.
Q: Where do you live?
A: 734 Boylston Street, Boston.
Q: Are you employed?
A: On June 1, 1980, *D* bought paregoric and reduced it to opium.
By defense counsel: Object and move to strike.

What ruling and why?

2. Scope of Cross-Examination

Problem III-14
Hostile Witness

Personal injury action arising out of a collision between a truck owned by *D* Company and operated by *D*'s employee, *S*, and the car in which *P* was riding. At trial, *P*'s first witness is *S*. On direct examination *S* is asked if he was in the employ of *D* and engaged in *D*'s employ at the time of the accident. Upon establishing *S*'s agency *P* has no further questions for *S*. *D* asks *S* questions designed to elicit the following:

(1) That at the time the accident occurred *S* was detouring from his normal route in order to check in with his bookie; *To show not agency*

(2) That *S* came to a full stop and waited for a green light before entering the intersection in which the accident occurred; and *not I of agency*

(3) That *P* ran a red light and hit *S*.
On *P*'s objection, what ruling and why?

oK

no

Problem III-15
Death at the Awahnee

Civil action by *P* against *D* Insurance Company on an insurance policy issued by *D* on the life of *V*, naming *P* as the beneficiary. The policy covers only accidental death, expressly excluding death by suicide. At trial, *P*'s first witness is *C*, the caretaker of the Awahnee Hunting Lodge. *C* testifies that on December 31, 1979, she found *V*'s body near the lodge; *V*'s body was clad in hunting clothes and was warm and supple. Next to the body *C* found a double-barrel shotgun with one barrel discharged; there was a gaping wound in *V*'s chest. *C* is then excused by *P*.

At this point what alternative procedures could be followed by *D* to elicit further testimony from *C* that on December 25, she had Christmas dinner with *V* at the lodge, that *C* and *V* had many strong drinks, that *V* drank a lot but ate nothing, that *V* said he had advanced cancer and remarked, "As the '70s end, so will I"?

Problem III-16
The Powder-Puff Killer

On June 1 at 6 P.M. Mrs. *D*, wife of Dr. *D*, awakens from her nap and begins to dress and apply cosmetics for the opera. She opens her compact and takes out her powder-puff. Suddenly a spider emerges, springs on Mrs. *D*, bites her, and absconds. That night Mrs. *D* is in bed in pain and is feverish. Dr. *D* gives her a hypodermic injection. The injection may be demerol or it may be air bubbles. Shortly after the injection Mrs. *D* dies. Dr. *D* is charged with premeditated murder by spider bite and air bubbles.

(1) At Dr. *D*'s trial the prosecution calls Dr. *T*, a toxicologist, as its first witness. On direct examination Dr. *T* states that upon testing the cadaver of Mrs. *D* for venom he found spider venom. On cross-examination the following occurs:

Q: How much venom did you find?
A: About one-half cc.
Q: What kind?
A: Black widow.
Q: You also found traces of demerol, didn't you?
By the D.A.: Objection.

What is the basis of the district attorney's objection? What ruling should the court make? Why?

(2) Suppose that after Dr. *T* is excused the prosecution calls *M*, Mrs. *D*'s mother. *M* testifies that she saw *D* open his wife's compact and put a spider into it. On cross-examination *M* is asked if she has made a will that disinherits Dr. *D*. The D.A. objects.

What ruling and why? What general rules concerning the scope of cross-examination may be derived from this example?

Problem III-17
Showdown at the W-Q Ranch

Ejectment action by *P* against *D. P*'s complaint avers that he owns the W-Q Ranch and that *D* is wrongfully in possession. *P* prays for judgment giving possession of the W-Q Ranch to *P*. The former owner of the W-Q Ranch was Mr. Quarrels. Mr. Quarrels died New Year's day, 1980. *P* is Mr. Quarrels's nephew; *D* is Mr. Quarrels's son. *D* claims as Mr. Quarrels's heir; *P* claims as Mr. Quarrels's grantee and claims that a document he possesses (Plaintiff's Exhibit *A*) is a deed whereby Mr. Quarrels granted the W-Q Ranch to *P* in fee simple absolute. Exhibit *A* is dated December 23, 1979. *D* has examined Exhibit *A* and claims that Mr. Quarrels's signature is spurious and that even if it is real the document was never delivered to take effect as a deed. At trial, *P* is the first witness. He testifies that on December 24, 1979, he received Exhibit *A* through the mail, was overjoyed, and said to himself, "Hooray for Uncle *Q*!" Plaintiff's second witness is Mr. *M,* the late Mr. Quarrels's secretary and manager of the W-Q Ranch. On direct examination *M* testifies that on December 23 in Mr. Quarrels's study at the W-Q Ranch he saw Mr. Quarrels sign Exhibit *A*. On cross-examination Mr. *M* is asked the following question:

Q: Isn't it true that on January 1, 1980 at the W-Q Ranch, you saw Exhibit *A* among the papers on Mr. Quarrels's desk?

(1) On *P*'s objection what ruling and why? What problem regarding the scope of cross-examination is presented by this example that has not been presented by the previous problems? If there should be a rule of restrictive cross-examination, how should it be applied when multiple witnesses have testified and the question asked on cross-examination of a later witness (*W2*) is within the scope of questions asked on direct examination of a former witness (*W1*) but not within the scope of the direct examination of the witness on the stand (*W2*)?

(2) Suppose *P*'s objection is sustained. *M* then turns to the judge and says that he is most anxious to complete his testimony in the case and leave for Australia, where he has an impending business engagement. *D* proposes that he make *M* his witness and examine *M* then and there on the question of delivery of the deed. *P* objects. What should the court do? If the court accepts defendant's suggestion, how will the procedure differ from allowing *D* to put his questions regarding delivery of the deed to *M* on cross-examination? What types of questions will be permitted, or precluded, by following the procedure suggested by *D*?

Problem III-18
Blind Witness

Action to establish execution and the terms of a will, now lost. The central issues in the case are (1) did *T* sign the document as testator and (2) did Jim and Joe sign as witnesses? At trial, *P* is the first witness. After the usual preliminaries *P* testifies that she saw *T* sign the will by looking over *T*'s shoulder. Cross-examination establishes that *P* uses glasses but did not have them on when she saw *T* purportedly sign the will. On redirect examination *P*'s counsel asks *P*, "Did you see Jim and Joe sign the will as witnesses?"

On objection by defense counsel what ruling and why? What mistake did *P*'s attorney make and what can he do about it?

3. Using Real and Demonstrative Evidence; The Mechanics of Proof

FRE 901
Requirement of Authentication or Identification

(a) *General Provision.* The requirement of authentication or identification as a condition precedent to admissibility is satisfied by evidence sufficient to support a finding that the matter in question is what its proponent claims.

(b) *Illustrations.* By way of illustration only, and not by way of limitation, the following are examples of authentication or identification conforming with the requirements of this rule:

(1) *Testimony of witness with knowledge.* Testimony that a matter is what it is claimed to be. . . .

(9) *Process or system.* Evidence describing a process or system used to produce a result and showing that the process or system produces an accurate result.

Problem III-19
The Case of the Nosy Neighbor

Charge: assault with a deadly weapon. Weapon: baseball bat. M.O.: aiming and swinging the baseball bat at Nosy Neighbor's head.

At *D*'s jury trial the prosecution calls Nosy Neighbor as its first witness. Neighbor testifies to certain background facts, that *D* came up behind him and swung a baseball bat at him, but that he managed to duck just in time to avoid disaster. At this point the judge announces that it is time for the court's lunch recess. Upon reconvening at 2:30 P.M. the district attorney produces a 32-inch Louisville slugger, Roberto Clemente model baseball bat, has the clerk tag the bat for identification as People's Exhibit *A*, and tenders the bat in evidence as the weapon involved in the assault. Defendant objects. What ruling and why?

Problem III-20
The Case of the Careless Cop

Section 909 of the penal code of state *S* provides that it is unlawful to possess in a motor vehicle any alcoholic beverage except those contained in bottles sealed with unbroken state tax stamps. On June 1, 1974, State Police Officer Obie stopped *D* for speeding. While writing out the ticket Obie saw on the seat a half-full bottle of Old Redneck 100 proof sour-mash bourbon with fragments of a torn state tax stamp around the neck of the bottle. Obie confiscated the bottle, and shortly thereafter *D* was charged with violation of Section 909 of the Penal Code.

At *D*'s trial Obie is the star witness. On direct examination Obie testifies to the facts set forth above. The D.A. then produces a half-full bottle of Old Redneck, has the clerk tag the bottle as People's Exhibit *A* for identification, and asks Obie if he recognizes it. Obie says that he recognizes the bottle as the bottle confiscated from *D* on June 1, 1974. The D.A. then offers the bottle into evidence. Defense counsel asks the court for permission to take the witness on voir dire for the purpose of making an objection to the admission of the bottle. The court grants defense counsel's request. On voir dire counsel shows Obie three other identical half-full bottles of Old Redneck (which secretly contain iced tea) and asks Obie how he distinguishes between the offered exhibit and the three other bottles presented to him.

What mistake in police administration has Obie made? What principle of evidence relating to the handling of real evidence has Obie violated?

MILLER v. PATE
386 U.S. 1 (1967)

Mr. Justice STEWART delivered the opinion of the Court.

On November 26, 1955, in Canton, Illinois, an eight-year-old girl died as the result of a brutal sexual attack. The petitioner was charged with her murder.

Prior to his trial in an Illinois court, his counsel filed a motion for an order permitting a scientific inspection of the physical evidence the prosecution intended to introduce. The motion was resisted by the prosecution and denied by the court. The jury trial ended in a verdict of guilty and a sentence of death. On appeal the judgment was affirmed by the Supreme Court of Illinois. On the basis of leads developed at a subsequent unsuccessful state clemency hearing, the petitioner applied to a federal district court for a writ of habeas corpus. After a hearing, the court granted the writ and ordered the petitioner's release or prompt retrial. The Court of Appeals reversed, and we granted certiorari to consider whether the trial that led to the petitioner's conviction was constitutionally valid. We have concluded that it was not.

There were no eyewitnesses to the brutal crime which the petitioner was charged with perpetrating. A vital component of the case against him was a pair of men's underwear shorts covered with large, dark, reddish-brown stains — People's Exhibit 3 in the trial record. These shorts had been found by a Canton policeman in a place known as the Van Buren Flats three days after the murder. The Van Buren Flats were about a mile from the scene of the crime. It was the prosecution's theory that the petitioner had been wearing these shorts when he committed the murder, and that he had afterwards removed and discarded them at the Van Buren Flats.

During the presentation of the prosecution's case, People's Exhibit 3 was variously described by witnesses in such terms as the "bloody shorts" and "a pair of jockey shorts stained with blood." Early in the trial the victim's mother testified that her daughter "had type 'A' positive blood." Evidence was later introduced to show that the petitioner's blood "was of group 'O.'"

Against this background the jury heard the testimony of a chemist for the State Bureau of Crime Identification. The prosecution established his qualifications as an expert, whose "duties include blood identification, grouping and typing both dry and fresh stains," and who had "made approximately one thousand blood typing analyses while at the State Bureau." His crucial testimony was as follows:

> I examined and tested "People's Exhibit 3" to determine the nature of the staining material upon it. The result of the first test was that this material upon the shorts is blood. I made a second examination which disclosed that the blood is of human origin. I made a further examination which disclosed that the blood is of group "A."

The petitioner, testifying in his own behalf, denied that he had ever owned or worn the shorts in evidence as People's Exhibit 3. He himself referred to the shorts as having "dried blood on them."

In argument to the jury the prosecutor made the most of People's Exhibit 3:

> Those shorts were found in the Van Buren Flats, with blood. What type blood? Not "O" blood as the defendant has, but "A" — type "A."

And later in his argument he said to the jury:

> And, if you will recall, it has never been contradicted the blood type of Janice May was blood type "A" positive. Blood type "A." Blood type "A" on these shorts. It wasn't "O" type as the defendant has. It is "A" type, what the little girl had.

Such was the state of the evidence with respect to People's Exhibit 3 as the case went to the jury. And such was the state of the record as the judgment of conviction was reviewed by the Supreme Court of Illinois. The "blood stained shorts" clearly played a vital part in the case for the prosecution. They were an important link in the chain of circumstantial evidence against the petitioner,[8] and, in the context of the revolting crime with which he was charged, their gruesomely emotional impact upon the jury was incalculable.[9]

So matters stood with respect to People's Exhibit 3, until the present habeas corpus proceeding in the Federal District Court.[10] In this proceeding the State was ordered to produce the stained shorts, and they were admitted in evidence. It was established that their appearance was the same as when they had been introduced at the trial as People's Exhibit 3. The petitioner was permitted to have the shorts examined by a chemical microanalyst. What the microanalyst found cast an extraordinary new light on People's Exhibit 3. The reddish-brown stains on the shorts were not blood, but paint.

The witness said that he had tested threads from each of the 10 reddish-brown stained areas on the shorts, and that he had found that all of them were encrusted with mineral pigments ". . . which one commonly uses in the preparation of paints." He found "no traces of human blood."[11] The State did not dispute this testimony, its counsel contenting himself with prevailing upon the witness to concede on cross-examination that he could not swear that there had never been any blood on the shorts.[12] . . .

In argument at the close of the habeas corpus hearing, counsel for the State contended that "[e]verybody" at the trial had known that the shorts

8. In affirming the petitioner's conviction, the Supreme Court of Illinois stated that "it was determined" that the shorts "were stained with human blood from group A," and referred to the petitioner's "bloody shorts." 13 Ill. 2d, at 89 and 106, 148 N.E.2d, at 458 and 467.

9. People's Exhibit 3 was forwarded here as part of the record, and we have accordingly had an opportunity to see it with our own eyes.

10. At the state clemency hearing, some additional evidence was adduced to show that the shorts had not belonged to the petitioner.

11. There were two other discolored areas on the shorts, one black and the other "a kind of yellowish color." A thread from the first of these areas contained material "similar to a particle of carbon." "[N]o particulates showed up" on the thread taken from the other.

12. The witness pointed out, however, that "blood substances are detectable over prolonged periods. That is, there are records of researches in which substances extracted from Egyptian mummies have been identified as blood."

were stained with paint. That contention is totally belied by the record. The microanalyst correctly described the appearance of the shorts when he said, "I assumed I was dealing . . . with a pair of shorts which was heavily stained with blood. . . . [I]t would appear to a layman . . . that what I see before me is a garment heavily stained with blood." The record of the petitioner's trial reflects the prosecution's consistent and repeated misrepresentation that People's Exhibit 3 was, indeed, "a garment heavily stained with blood." The prosecution's whole theory with respect to the exhibit depended upon that misrepresentation. For the theory was that the victim's assailant had discarded the shorts *because* they were stained with blood. A pair of paint-stained shorts, found in an abandoned building a mile away from the scene of the crime, was virtually valueless as evidence against the petitioner.[15] The prosecution deliberately misrepresented the truth. . . .

The judgment of the Court of Appeals is reversed, and the case is remanded for further proceedings consistent with this opinion.

It is so ordered.

What does this case reveal about defense counsel's function when confronted with an item of "real" evidence? What opportunities and options do the Federal Rules provide in these situations? Who has the burden of raising an issue as to the authenticity of an item of real evidence? Who has the burden of proving that an exhibit is authentic?

Problem III-21
Where the Rubber Meets the Road

You represent *P* in a consumer's action for damages arising out of an alleged breach of warranty on two new automobile tires purchased by your client from *D* Tire Co. The alleged defects are loose treads and bulges in the sidewalls of the tires. At trial your first witness is *P*. Draft a short examination of *P* sufficient to establish your case-in-chief.

Problem III-22
Live Exhibits

Action for support payments. The complaint alleges that *D* had sexual intercourse with *P* in late January 1970 and that on September 21, 1970, *P* gave birth to a boy, Snookins, of whom *D* is the father. *D* admits the intercourse but denies paternity.

---

15. The petitioner was not a painter but a taxi driver.

During her preparation of the case *P*'s lawyer observes that Snookins bears a striking resemblance to *D* and decides that she would like the jury to see this with their own eyes. How can she do this? What kind of evidence is involved? If the case is appealed, how could the evidence be transferred to an appellate court for review? When should such evidence be admitted in paternity cases? What procedures should be followed? What instructions should be given?

4. Views

CITY OF COLUMBUS v. CARTER
71 Ohio App. 263, 49 N.E.2d 186 (1943)

GEIGER, J. Rich street and Town street are two east and west streets, immediately adjacent, in Columbus, Ohio. Grant avenue is a north and south avenue, crossing these two east and west streets. The defendant was tried in the police court on an affidavit. . . .

The affidavit, in fact, charges two offenses against the defendant, one based upon the claim that she failed to stop in response to the red light signal; and second, that she proceeded to cross the street before the traffic signal had turned green. . . .

While much of the evidence in this case relates to the condition of the traffic light controlling traffic on Grant avenue on the theory that whatever light is shown on Grant avenue there would be a reverse light on the intersecting Town street, this is not a safe ground for inference as to the relative condition of the light governing traffic on the intersecting streets.

The evidence displayed by the bill of exceptions is to the effect that about 12:45 P.M. on the day named, and at the intersection of Town street and Grant avenue, the defendant's car came into collision with a fire department emergency car, which was then proceeding northwardly, causing the department car to leave the road, jump the curb, cross the sidewalk and break through an iron fence. The evidence, as in most criminal cases, is conflicting. It would be of little value to review the evidence of the several witnesses. . . .

The most interesting witness and one who seems to have testified with great intelligence was Perry H. Mahness who testified that he was a patient at the hospital, which was immediately upon the northwest corner of Town and Grant; that he occupied a room on the fifth floor; that his bed was drawn close to the window, which was open; and that he had a full view of Grant avenue and its intersection with Town street. This witness testified that he could see the intersection; and that it happened that he was talking over the telephone to his mother and heard the siren and remarked to his mother over the telephone that another ambulance was coming, as one had just come in about five minutes before. This witness testified that he could see about 35 or 40 feet beyond the intersection on Grant and Town; that when he saw a car coming into view, he still thought it was an ambulance, but upon discovering that it was not he remarked to his mother, "It's a fire wagon," and said, "oh-oh, he is going to run the red light"; that the light was red north; that at the same time another car was coming from the west, east on Town street, and entered the intersection and really entered it a split second before the car going north; and that the car going north was moving rapidly and the car going east was not going very fast, "They simply progressed in their relative directions until they met with a collision in the center of the street." The witness heard the siren for a second or two before the crash, but said it was not sounding when the car approached some 35 or 40 feet south of the intersection of Town and Grant. The witness states that he noted in the paper that Mrs. Carter had been arrested and that he offered to become a witness in her favor. This witness testified: "*Q.* Red north and south? *A.* Red, north, and I don't know how it showed south."

The trial judge, no doubt being impressed with the importance of the testimony of this witness, went to the hospital a few days after the trial to determine whether a patient lying in bed could see the lights at the intersection. The trial judge, before passing upon the case, stated in the presence of counsel:

> Well, I have heard quite a bit of testimony in this case. Somebody testifying in this case was mistaken and I don't say they were telling a falsehood, but somebody was mistaken as to who had the green light. There were three people down on the street who were all within a block of the light, and they all said it was green for the fire department, except a patient who was up in room 508 overlooking Grant avenue, looking out of the window, and about a week ago the court went up to inspect this room, and from my observation it would be a very difficult angle to see down to the street — the street light can be seen from there, but it is very difficult to see it.
>
> So I can only arrive at one conclusion that the patient in the hospital was mistaken as to what he saw when referring to the light, in view of the testimony of the other witnesses who were down on the street and did see it.
>
> Of course I find the defendant guilty on this charge. . . .

The procedure followed by the judge in the *Carter* case is known as "taking a view." Does the judge's action seem proper to you? When is a view proper? May a view be taken by the jury as well as by the judge? What should be the status of information obtained during a view? Is it evidence? May the judge or jury rely on it as evidence? How may such information be incorporated into the record for appellate review?

Problem III-23
The Case of the Spite Fence

Action for abatement of an alleged spite fence erected by *D* on his property, which abuts and faces *P*'s property. The complaint alleges that *D* has erected a spite fence as defined by Property Code §2022. Section 2022 defines a spite fence as any fence exceeding 15 feet in height or a fence of less than 15 feet that is constructed or decorated in a manner not conforming to prevailing standards.

The case is tried to a jury, and the crucial question is whether the fence erected by *D* is a spite fence within the meaning of the Code. On this issue *P* testifies as to his ownership of his property and that *D* erected a fence on *D*'s adjoining property that faces *P*'s house. On *P*'s motion and on order of the court the jury takes a view and observes the fence. In some spots the fence is 15 feet high, but in other spots it is less than 15 feet. However, along the entire length of the fence on the side facing *P*'s property are paintings that are repulsive by any standard. When court reconvenes, *P* rests.

D moves for a nonsuit. Should it be granted? On what rationale?

What kinds of problems does taking a view create? For example, must a court reporter be present at the view? Must the judge? Must counsel be present? What safeguards should be taken to insure that only the right objects are viewed, that conditions are substantially the same at the time of the view as the time of the occurrence in issue, and that no hearsay or other unsworn evidence is obtained by the viewers at the scene? What if conditions have changed since the time of the incident? Must the accused in a criminal case be present at a view? May a view be taken beyond the jurisdiction of the trial court? Does a defendant in a criminal case have a constitutional or other right to demand that the jury take a view of the scene of the crime or other relevant place? If some members of the jury take an unauthorized view of the scene of the crime, what effect does it have on the defendant's rights?

DOHERTY v. PROVIDENCE JOURNAL CO.
94 R.I. 392, 181 A.2d 105 (1962)

POWERS, J. This is an action of trespass on the case for negligence. It was tried to a superior court justice who reserved decision on the defendant's motion for a directed verdict and submitted the case to a jury, which returned a verdict for the plaintiff in the sum of $5,000. The trial justice thereupon entered his decision denying the defendant's motion and the case is before us on the defendant's bill of exceptions, the sole exception being to the decision.

It is established by the record that at or about ten o'clock on the morning of September 18, 1958, plaintiff, who was a route salesman of bakery products, drove his delivery truck into the building of defendant corporation wherein was located a garage with a loading platform customarily used by defendant's trucks and those of business invitees. The plaintiff delivered bread and rolls five days weekly to defendant's cafeteria which was located on the second floor of the building, and on the day in question was making a regular stop at the regular time. It was raining slightly. He backed the truck to within two feet of the loading platform, leaving room to open its doors. He then filled his basket with bread and rolls, delivered them to the cafeteria, returned, placed his basket back in the truck, and on walking to the driver's seat slipped, fell heavily and sustained personal injuries.

The record further discloses that the garage area in question was fairly large; that some twelve to eighteen trucks could be accommodated simultaneously at the loading platform; that the floor was of cement composition; and that at times the garage was very busy with the trucks of defendant and others moving in and out.

The plaintiff testified that after loading his basket he walked to his right diagonally across an open space large enough for several trucks; and that he walked in front of the parked trucks, climbed the three steps of the loading platform, walked along its length and took the freight elevator to the cafeteria. He further testified that he made delivery and returned to his truck; that on his return he walked down the stairs, not using the elevator; that from the loading platform to his truck he practically retraced his steps; that after placing the basket in the truck he started around the right side, being the same side he had used in getting to the back of the truck; that he was about four feet to the right of his truck when he slipped on "some slimy substance"; and that he was later taken to the hospital.

On cross-examination plaintiff testified that he was familiar with the premises; that the lighting conditions were satisfactory; that he always looked where he was going; and that in going from the cab of his truck to the rear he noticed nothing although he was looking at the floor.

Significantly plaintiff was not asked and neither he nor any other witness gave any estimate as to the period of time required for him to make his delivery and return.

Ralph M. Baker, building superintendent for defendant corporation, was called as a witness by plaintiff. He testified that among his duties was supervision of ten porters who were responsible for cleaning the garage; that each morning between eight and nine o'clock the porters thoroughly swept the garage floor; that if there were any grease or oil a chemical preparation named Zorbal was put on to absorb it and then swept up; that the same operation was repeated in the afternoon; and that no special time was allotted for such cleaning. The witness' exact words in this regard were, "It probably is supposed to be done to the best of their ability, that is the way." . . .

The plaintiff did not contend and made no effort to prove that defendant had actual knowledge of the oil and water on which he allegedly slipped, but tried his case on the theory of constructive notice.

After plaintiff rested, defendant did also and moved for a directed verdict on the grounds that plaintiff had failed to prove that the "slimy substance" consisted of oil and water and that there was no testimony, or reasonable inferences to be drawn therefrom, which would support a finding of constructive notice. The trial justice reserved his decision . . . and submitted the case to the jury.

In support of its contention that plaintiff had failed to prove that the slimy substance on which he had apparently slipped was composed of oil and water as alleged in the declaration, defendant argues that the substance was not analyzed; that there was no evidence whatsoever of what is consisted; and that it might have been cream or jelly from plaintiff's own bakery products with as much likelihood as oil and water.

The trial justice, drawing all inferences adversely to defendant and favorable to plaintiff as he was required to do, concluded from all of the evidence that the substance might reasonably be supposed to have been oil and that some water was present. Whether he was warranted in his conclusion need not be considered in the view we take of defendant's remaining contention.

In reaching his decision on the question of constructive notice the trial justice commented as follows: "It would seem to me that it would be a reasonable and fair inference for the Jury from this evidence to say that this substance was there when this plaintiff backed in and that it was the same situation and continued when he came back from making his deliveries. We don't have any particular time schedule on that, that is, there is no statement in the evidence as to how long it took him to walk up to the delivery place and walk back from there, and what he did there except to make his deliveries, and how long it took to do that and what was involved in that; whether there was any exchange of slips and charges on paper, or anything of that kind, or payment of money, whether there was any consultation, whether there was anything we don't know. The evidence indicates he went up, made his delivery, came down and went back. It seems to me there was a question of fact whether or not that time lapse was sufficient to put the defendant on notice of the existence of this condition. There was sufficient evidence to go to the Jury upon the question of whether or not the defendant had constructive notice of the condition as having existed at the time in question."

The defendant contends in effect that in the absence of any evidence whatsoever as to the time involved, no reasonable inference could be made and that the jury could only speculate. We are of the opinion that there is merit in this contention.

The plaintiff argues, however, that since the jury took a view it was within their powers of deduction reasonably to estimate the time involved. The effect of such an argument is to substitute a view for evidence which, in a long line of cases, we have held to be contrary to the true office of a view. It is to aid the jury to understand the evidence and is not evidence in itself. The plaintiff's argument in this regard as we understand it is that the jury, having covered the same route in taking the view, could fairly approximate the time consumed by plaintiff on the day of his injury. This argument is fallacious. Whether the jury took more or less time is open only to speculation. . . .

The defendant's exception to the denial of its motion for a directed verdict is sustained. . . .

CHOUINARD v. SHAW
99 N.H. 26, 104 A.2d 522 (1954)

Actions of Case, to recover damages resulting from an automobile accident in Boscawen, on August 31, 1951. Trial by jury, with a view, resulted in verdicts for the defendants.

At the view counsel for the defendants made a measurement with a tape measure from a certain culvert cover to a point on the highway nine feet from the edge of the culvert cover. The measurement was made in the presence of the jury and was particularly called to the jury's attention. Before any evidence was received counsel for the plaintiffs called the matter to the attention of the Trial Court by a motion for a mistrial. Thereupon the Presiding Justice went with counsel to the place where the view was taken, heard arguments on the motion for a mistrial but reserved decision on the motion at that time. Before the introduction of evidence the Presiding Justice made the following statement to the foreman and members of the jury:

> At the view yesterday I understand there was some measurement taken by counsel on the road at or near the scene of this accident. I am going to instruct you to disregard that measurement. We don't know what the evidence will show, but you have seen the road and you saw the other things that were pointed out to you by counsel, and you listen to the evidence as it is produced before you and then you come to your final conclusion after all of the evidence is in.

The plaintiffs seasonably excepted to the refusal of the Court to grant their motion for a mistrial. . . .

KENISON, C.J. Information that a jury obtains from a view is evidence which it is authorized to use in reaching a verdict. This is believed to be the better rule and has been the law in this state at least since 1917 when the "leading opinion" of Carpenter v. Carpenter, 78 N.H. 440, was decided. IV Wig. Ev. (3rd ed.) s.1168, p.292. The allowance of a view is determined by the Presiding Justice "under such rules as [he] may prescribe." Once allowed, "the manner and extent of the view" is regulated by the Trial Court. And "it has not been the practice" to disturb the Trial Court's ruling unless it was plainly wrong.

The purpose of a view is to enable the jury to observe "places or objects" (R.L., c.395, s.21) which are pointed out to it by counsel for the parties. "The jury are not sent out to get evidence generally, or to examine physical facts not authorized in the order. They do not hear oral testimony; no witnesses are examined; no arguments are made. They merely see such physical objects as are properly shown to them, and receive impressions therefrom. They get a mental picture of the locality, which as sensible men they carry back to the court room and use in their deliberations as evidence." Carpenter v. Carpenter, 78 N.H. 440, 445. It is not the function of a view to receive comment, discussion, argument or the making of measurements. Tests and experiments are not permissible at a view unless specifically authorized by the court. Such practices are generally considered to be a violation of the hearsay rule. "Here, also, the only question can be whether the impropriety is upon the circumstances sufficient ground for setting aside the verdict." VI Wig. Ev. (3rd ed.) s.1802(4). . . .

The present case is similar to those instances in which a juror at an authorized view takes measurements or steps off distances. If the measurements or distances were not in dispute, it has been held that the conduct of the jurors, although susceptible of criticism, was insufficient to warrant a new trial. . . .

It is presumed that the Court's instruction to the jury to disregard the measurement made by counsel and to confine themselves to the evidence introduced in the case was followed. "It is a cardinal principle of our practice that errors which occur in the course of a trial are not necessarily incurable and that the effect of evidence which comes improperly before a jury may be cured by an order that it be stricken from the record and an instruction to the jury to disregard it." Emerson v. Cobb, 88 N.H. 199, 201. From an examination of the record it cannot be said that the Trial Court abused its discretion in denying the motion for a mistrial under the circumstances of this case.

5.   Pictorial Evidence

Problem III-24
The Spite Fence — A Reprise

Suppose in the spite fence case, Problem III-23, above, *P* testifies to ownership of his property and other background matters. Instead of having the jury take a view of the fence, however, on direct examination *P*'s counsel shows *P* a photograph marked Plaintiff's Exhibit *A* for identification. In response to counsel's questions *P* states that he recognizes the photograph as a fair and accurate representation of *D*'s fence as it appears from the living room of *P*'s house. *P*'s counsel offers the photograph into evidence as Exhibit *A*. *D* moves to examine the witness of voir dire for the purpose of making an objection to this exhibit. The court allows the examination. On voir dire the following colloquy takes place:

Q: Did you take Exhibit *A*?
A: No.
Q: Do you know who did?
A: No.
Q: Well, did you develop or print it?
A: No.
Q: Do you know who did?
A: No.
Q: Have you ever seen this picture before?
A: No.

Defense counsel objects to the photograph on grounds of inadequate foundation. What result and why? What are the general conditions of admissibility of photographic evidence? What is the status of a photograph introduced as an exhibit? Is it evidence in and of itself? Is everything it reveals evidence?

ADAMCZUK v. HOLLOWAY
338 Pa. 263, 13 A.2d 2 (1940)

MAXEY, J. Plaintiffs brought an action in trespass against defendants for personal injuries and property damage arising out of a collision between a car owned and operated by plaintiff, Jack J. Adamczuk, and a car owned by defendant, Morris Cohen, and driven by defendant, Elmer Holloway. . . .

The jury returned a verdict for defendants. Plaintiffs' motion for a new trial was refused and these appeals followed.

The assignment of error which appellant stresses is based upon the refusal of the court to admit in evidence a certain photograph of the locus of the accident and the approach to it on Highway Route 6.

When plaintiff, Jack Adamczuk, was on the stand, he was shown "Exhibit No. 3" and he identified the roads and buildings appearing in the picture and stated, in answer to his counsel, that "the conditions represented by that picture truly represent the conditions of the crossing at the time of this accident except for the fact of daylight or dark." Then the exhibit was offered in evidence. On cross-examination it was disclosed that the witness did not know who took the picture or when it was taken. He stated that when the picture was taken the location of the camera was on route 6 but he did not know at what distance from the intersection. He had no experience in photography. He said he did not know whether the photographer tilted the camera up or down when the picture was taken, and he did not know whether the photographer "endeavored to accentuate certain parts of the picture." The court then sustained the objection to the picture's introduction.

It was offered in evidence again when Herbert C. Dillard, Civil Engineer and County Surveyor, was on the stand. He was asked on cross-examination by defendant's counsel: "If you were taking a picture, and wanted to accentuate the curve of route six to the west, you could accomplish that by taking the picture farther away from the intersection, that is, farther to the east of the intersection, could you not?" He answered: "I think you could, yes." This witness was asked if he took photographs and developed them. He answered: "Very little."

At the close of plaintiff's case the picture was again offered in evidence and was objected to and the objection sustained, and court saying: "There is some mystery about exhibit number three, which is not clear to the court. There is no proof of who took it, or any identity as to the picture, other than the physical view thereon; it isn't shown where the camera was standing, under what conditions it was taken, and whether it was taken with a view to distorting it or not." The court then commented on the fact that plaintiff had two days "since adjournment last Friday, to procure the original taker of this photograph and thus establish it in the legal way with the right of cross-examination to defendants' counsel of the photographer."

The rule is well settled that a photograph may be put in evidence if relevant to the issue and if verified. It does not have to be verified by the taker. Its verification depends on the competency of the verifying witness and as to that the trial judge must in the first instance decide, subject to reversal for substantial error.

Wigmore on Evidence (2d ed.), Vol 2, sec. 792, p.97, says:

> The objection that a photograph may be so made as to misrepresent the object is genuinely directed against its testimonial soundness; but it is of no validity. It is true that a photograph can be deliberately so taken as to convey the most false impression of the object. But so also can any witness lie in his words. A photograph can falsify just as much and no more than the human being who takes it or verifies it. The fallacy of the objection occurs in assuming that the photograph can come in testimonially without a competent person's oath to support it. If a qualified observer is found to say, "This photograph represents the fact as I saw it," there is no more reason to exclude it than if he had said, "The following words represent the fact as I saw it," which is always in effect the tenor of a witness's oath. If no witness has thus

R| TJ may reject pic b/c unnecessary
discretion to admit

attached his credit to the photograph, then it should not come in at all, any more than an anonymous letter should be received as testimony.

Section 793:

> The map or photograph must first, to be admissible, be made a part of some qualified person's testimony. Someone must stand forth as its testimonial sponsor; in other words, it must be verified. There is nothing anomalous or exceptional in this requirement of verification; it is simply the exaction of those testimonial qualities which are required equally of all witnesses; the application merely takes a different form.

In other words, if a witness is familiar with the scene photographed and is competent to testify that the photograph correctly represents it, it should, if relevant, be admitted. . . .

What are the theoretical underpinnings of the pictorial testimony rule advocated by Wigmore (2d ed.), above, and followed by the court in this case? Is it broad enough to cover all cases where photographs should be admitted? Is it too broad?

Problem III-25
The Case of the Hidden Camera

Action for alleged conversion of negotiable bearer bonds. M.O.: rifling P's safe in the wall of her study by turning the combination lock.

At trial, P is the first witness. She testifies that during May she noticed that cash and jewels were apparently being pilfered from her safe. On June 1 she engaged a Pinkerton's detective to install a hidden camera in the wall of her study that would be triggered by the opening of the safe and that would clandestinely take a picture of whoever was opening the safe. P further testified that on June 1, when the camera was installed, 100,000 Big Mac bonds were safely ensconced in her safe and that she did not open the safe thereafter until June 15. P further testifies that on June 15 she noticed that the camera had been triggered. When she opened the safe, the bonds were missing. P removed the film from the camera and turned it over to Pinkerton's. The Pinkerton's detective was the next witness. She testified to her expertise and experience with the camera, the operation of the camera and the triggering mechanism, the development of the film, and the chain of custody of the film. The detective then identified a print of the photograph taken by the camera as Plaintiff's Exhibit A for identification. It is a photograph of D. P offered this exhibit into evidence.

Is Exhibit *A* admissible? Should it be? What basis of proof should suffice for admission of photographs generally when no witness can sponsor the photograph?

SISK v. STATE
232 Md. 155, 192 A.2d 108 (1963)

PRESCOTT, J. After conviction of, and sentence for, obtaining money by means of a false pretense under Code (1962 Cum. Supp.), Article 27, §140, James T. Sisk appeals.

The questions involved are whether a Regiscope photograph was properly admitted into evidence, and if not, was its admission prejudicial.

At the trial below, the State offered a Mr. William Sraver, chief investigator for the Protection Department of Montgomery Ward Company, Inc. (the Company). He stated that his "record" showed that a check was cashed in "our store" on August 1st, 1962, drawn by Talbott & Hanson, Inc., made payable to Charles A. Neubert, Jr., dated August 1st, drawn on the Maryland Trust Company, and signed by Frank G. Hanson and Anna P. Myers. The check was endorsed "Charles A. Neubert, Jr." It was not honored, but returned to the Company.

Sraver explained that when cash is requested for a check, the Company takes a picture with a Regiscope machine. These machines operate in the following manner. A number stamp places numbers in sequence on the checks. After a number is stamped on a check, a picture is taken of the check, the identification used by the person having the check cashed and the individual cashing the check, simultaneously. This is accomplished by means of a two-lens camera, located in the cashier's cage, which takes two pictures at one time, one straight down at the check and identification, and the other pointing out, taking a picture of the individual cashing the check. When five hundred films have been used or there is current need for a picture, whichever first occurs, the film is removed from the camera by Sraver, and sent by mail to the Regiscope Company in Fairfax, Virginia. Upon request, the films are developed and the pictures of individual transactions are sent to the Company. Sraver was not present when the photograph in the instant case was taken by a cashier, or when the film was developed by Regiscope. He, therefore, stated that he was not "in a position to say whether the picture [was] a correct likeness of what was in front of the camera" at the time the picture was taken. He also stated that he supposed it was "within the realm of possibility" that the same check could have been exposed with six different persons in front of the camera, from time to time, if the cashier had so desired. The appellant admitted to the police that the individual on the photograph was he, but he denied cashing the check. Without further authentication, the photograph of appellant, the check he allegedly cashed and the identification purportedly used by him was admitted over his objection. And this was all the evidence produced against him, except, as noted above, his admission to the police that he was the individual pictured on the exhibit.

Although the taking of a picture by the Regiscope operation is more complicated than the taking of an ordinary photograph, we see no reason why the admissibility of a picture taken by such an operation should not be governed by the same principles as those governing ordinary pictures. A photograph, like a map or diagram, is the witness' pictured expression of the data observed by him and therein communicated to the tribunal more accurately than by words says Professor Wigmore. 3 Wigmore, Evidence (3 Ed.) §792. Generally, a photograph's admissibility as evidence is left to the discretion of the trial court, but it is obvious, even if we take at full value appellant's admission that the individual was he, that the portion of the picture taken straight down had no testimonial sponsor. And the rule that the admissibility of photographs is ordinarily left to the discretion of the trial court does not come into play until there is competent extrinsic evidence showing the photograph to be a true representation of the scene or object which it purports to represent at the time when the appearance of such scene or object is relevant to the inquiry in connection with which the photograph is offered. . . . At no time was the exhibit shown by extrinsic evidence to be a fair representation of the scene that it purported to represent; hence it should not have been admitted. And there can be little doubt that its admission was prejudicial. As we pointed out above in our statement of the facts, it was the only evidence that connected him with the alleged offense. Of course, it may be possible for the State in the new trial ordered to authenticate it properly.

STATE v. TATUM
360 P.2d 754 (Wash. 1961)

DONWORTH, J. Ralph Tatum (hereinafter called appellant) was convicted of the crime of first degree forgery and was sentenced to life imprisonment as an habitual criminal.

The essential facts of the case are summarized as follows:

One William Tousin, of Pasco, received monthly welfare checks from the state of Washington. In February, 1960, Tousin did not receive his check (the checks were generally mailed to a rooming house in Pasco where Tousin resided). The mail was normally left on a window ledge in the hallway of the rooming house. Appellant resided at the same place. Tousin's February check for $28.90 was endorsed and cashed at Sherman's Food Store in Pasco by someone other than the payee, Tousin.

An employee of the store, Caroline Pentecost, testified that, although she could not specifically recall the above-mentioned transaction, the initials appearing on the face of the check were hers. She also testified that whenever a check was presented to her for payment at the store, the store manager had instructed her to initial it and then insert it into a "Regiscope" machine. This machine is designed to simultaneously photograph, through two separate lenses, both the check and the person facing the machine.

When it was discovered that the endorsement of the payee was a forgery, the Regiscope film of the transaction was sent to the Regiscope distributor in Portland to be developed. The processed film shows both the check and the person of appellant (from his waist up) with the food store in the background. Upon the trial, both the negative and the print therefrom were admitted in evidence, over appellant's objection. . . .

Were the Regiscope films (the negative and the print) authenticated sufficiently to warrant their admission into evidence? . . .

At the outset, with respect to the question of the admissibility of the Regiscope films, it should be noted that this court has for many years encouraged the admission and use of demonstrative evidence, including photographs. There is equally well-established precedent for the proposition that the admission or rejection of photographs as evidence lies within the sound discretion of the trial court. . . . We have also held that the trial court's discretion extends to the sufficiency of identification.

What quantum of authentication do courts require before a photograph may be admissible in evidence? It is simply this — that some witness (not necessarily the photographer) be able to give some indication as to when, where, and under what circumstances the photograph was taken, and that the photograph accurately portray the subject or subjects illustrated. The photograph need only be sufficiently accurate to be helpful to the court and the jury.

Witness Pentecost testified that she recognized the background shown in the picture as that of the food store, and, as mentioned previously, she also testified as to the store's standard procedure of "regiscoping" each individual who cashed a check at the store. Phillip Dale testified at length concerning the Regiscope process. The testimony of these two witnesses taken together amounted to a sufficient authentication to warrant the admission of the photograph (both the print and the negative) into evidence.

The authentication supplied by the testimony summarized above, of course, did not preclude appellant from attempting to prove that the individual portrayed was someone other than appellant, that the photograph was inaccurate in one or more respects, the appellant was somewhere else at the moment the photograph was taken, or any other such defense. But these arguments go to the weight rather than to the admissibility of the exhibits in question. In our opinion, the Regiscope exhibits, coupled with the other evidence produced by the state, sufficed to establish a prima facie case of first degree forgery. . . .

The judgment of the trial court is affirmed.

Do the *Sisk* and *Tatum* courts apply the same standards to the Regiscope pictures? Do they seem to proceed from the same theoretical basis respecting pictorial evidence? Do they apply the same rules regarding what foundation must be laid for introduction of this type of evidence? Can the cases be reconciled? With which case do you agree?

Do these cases suggest any shortcomings in the "pictorial testimony" theory advocated by Wigmore and followed by the *Adamczuk* court? Under this pictorial testimony theory, would X rays be admissible? What about a chance picture of a crowd that on close examination shows the commission of a crime not seen by anyone at the time? Or a picture taken with a telescopic lens?

PEOPLE v. BOWLEY
59 Cal. 2d 855, 31 Cal. Rptr. 471, 382 P.2d 591 (1963)

PETERS, J. Defendant appeals from a judgment of conviction entered upon a jury verdict finding him guilty of a violation of Penal Code section 288a,[1] and of a prior felony conviction.

The only witness who testified for the prosecution[2] was a woman named Joan. She testified that in April of 1960 the defendant's brother employed her to play a part in a motion picture to be filmed in a San Francisco studio; that she went to the studio; that the picture was taken; that in making this picture, in addition to several other sexual activities, she voluntarily engaged in an act of oral copulation with the sexual organ of defendant.

A film purporting to show these activities was produced by the prosecution. Joan testified that she had seen portions of the film, and that those portions accurately represented what took place during the making of the film. Over objection, it was introduced into evidence and was shown to the jury. In response to the question: "Is that the film of the events in which you participated on this particular date at the Beaumont Studio," Joan said "yes." She also testified that the defendant was the male in the film whose face was covered with a coat of dark grease,

---

1. That section provides, in part: "Any person participating in an act of copulating the mouth of one person with the sexual organ of another is punishable by imprisonment in the state prison. . . ."

2. Defendant did not testify, nor did he offer any evidence in his defense.

whose hair was covered with a cloth turban, and with whom frequent acts in violation of Penal Code section 288a were shown.

Joan was, of course, an accomplice. As such her testimony must be corroborated.[3] This is a strict requirement, much stricter than found in many other states. It is based on the fear that an accomplice may be motivated to falsify his testimony in the hope of securing leniency for himself. . . .

Defendant's main contention is that the film may not be used to corroborate Joan's testimony because its admission into evidence rests solely upon her foundation testimony. Under these circumstances, it is argued, the film is not "other evidence" within the meaning of Penal Code section 1111.

According to Professor Wigmore, a photograph is no more than the nonverbal expression of the witness upon whose foundation testimony its authenticity rests. (3 Wigmore, Evidence (3d ed. 1940) §790, pp. 174-175; ibid. §792, p.178; ibid. §793, p.186.) It is merely that witness' testimony in illustrated form; a "pictorial communication of a qualified witness who uses this method of communication instead of or in addition to some other method." (3 Wigmore, Evidence (3d ed. 1940) §793, p.186.) If this theory were accepted, it would necessarily follow that the film in this case does not fulfill the corroboration requirement. An accomplice cannot, of course, corroborate his own testimony.

Other authorities disagree. They urge that once a *proper foundation* has been established as to the accuracy and authenticity of a photograph, "it speaks with a certain probative force in itself." (Scott, Photographic Evidence (1942) §601, p.476.)

> [P]hotographs may, under proper safeguards, not only be used to illustrate testimony, but also as photographic or silent witnesses who speak for themselves. . . . [A] picture taken with adequate equipment under proper conditions by a skilled photographer is itself substantive evidence to be weighed by the jury. (Gardner, The Camera Goes to Court, (1946) 24 N.C.L. Rev. 233, 245). . . .

Until now, this court has not been called upon to state the theory upon which photographs are admitted into evidence. In doing so we recognize that photographs are useful for different purposes. When admitted merely to aid a witness in explaining his testimony they are, as Wigmore states, nothing more than the illustrated testimony of that witness. But they may also be used as probative evidence of what they

---

3. Section 1111 of the Penal Code provides in part: "A conviction can not be had upon the testimony of an accomplice unless it be corroborated by such other evidence as shall tend to connect the defendant with the commission of the offense; and the corroboration is not sufficient if it merely shows the commission of the offense or the circumstances thereof."

depict. Used in this manner they take on the status of independent "silent" witnesses.

An example of a photograph which is probative in itself is found in People v. Doggett, 83 Cal. App. 2d 405, 188 P.2d 792, in which convictions of violating Penal Code section 288a were affirmed. The only evidence of the crime was a photograph showing the defendants committing an act of sexual perversion. This photograph was introduced into evidence although there was no testimony by any eyewitness that it accurately depicted what it purported to show. There was, however, other evidence of when, in point of time, the picture was taken, the place where it was taken and that the defendants were the persons shown in the picture. Furthermore, there was testimony by a photographic expert that the picture was not a composite and had not been faked but was a true representation of a "pure" negative. Upon this foundation, it was held that the photograph was admissible in evidence.

Since no eyewitness laid the foundation for the picture's admission into evidence in the Doggett case, the picture necessarily was allowed to be a silent witness; to "speak for itself." It was not illustrating the testimony of a witness. This seems to be a sound rule. Similarly, X-ray photographs are admitted into evidence although there is no one who can testify from direct observation inside the body that they accurately represent what they purport to show.[5]

There is no reason why a photograph or film, like an X-ray, may not, in a proper case, be probative in itself. To hold otherwise would illogically limit the use of a device whose memory is without question more accurate and reliable than that of a human witness. It would exclude from evidence the chance picture of a crowd which on close examination shows the commission of a crime that was not seen by the photographer at the time. It would exclude from evidence pictures taken with a telescopic lens. It would exclude from evidence pictures taken by a camera set to go off when a building's door is opened at night. We hold, therefore, that a photograph may, in a proper case, be admitted into evidence not merely as illustrated testimony of a human witness but as probative evidence in itself of what it shows.

But because the film was properly admitted into evidence, and because that film, if properly authenticated is of itself evidence of what it depicts, it does not follow that the film can corroborate the testimony of

---

5. Wigmore recognizes the apparent inconsistency between his pictorial testimony theory of photographs and the introduction of X-rays. He reasons, however, that once the instrument or process is known to be trustworthy, as is the case with X-rays, "it follows that a photograph of its images would always be receivable like any other photograph." (3 Wigmore, Evidence (3d ed. 1940) §795, p.190.) Other writers have not been convinced by this analysis, however, and refer to the admission of X-rays as an example of a photograph speaking for itself. (See Scott, Photographic Evidence (1942) §601, p.476; Gardner, The Camera Goes to Court (1946) 24 N.C.L. Rev. 233, 243-245.)

the sole authenticating witness when she is an accomplice. To satisfy the requirement of Penal Code section 1111,

> [T]he corroborative evidence . . . must be considered without the aid of the testimony which is to be corroborated and . . . it is not sufficient if it requires the interpretation and direction of such testimony in order to give it value.

In other words, the section requires evidence apart from that of the accomplice which tends to instill trust in the inherently suspect testimony of the accomplice.[6] The film in the instant case can fulfill this function only if it is assumed to be authentic. Since the film cannot "speak for itself" as to its own authenticity, reliance must first be placed in the veracity of Joan that it is accurate before it can supply any corroboration. This is the very reliance which section 1111 tells us cannot be assumed but reason for which must be found elsewhere.

No photograph or film has any value in the absence of a proper foundation. It is necessary to know when it was taken and that it is accurate and truly represents what it purports to show. It becomes probative only upon the assumption that it is relevant and accurate. This foundation is usually provided by the testimony of a person who was present at the time the picture was taken, or who is otherwise qualified to state that the representation is accurate. In addition, it may be provided by the aid of expert testimony, as in the Doggett case, although there is no one qualified to authenticate it from personal observation. When authenticated by a witness from personal observation its admission into evidence presumes confidence in that witness' veracity. Although Penal Code section 1111 does not bar the use of accomplice testimony for purposes of admitting the film into evidence, it does fix a stringent standard for purposes of the sufficiency of the evidence to sustain a conviction. Just as we do not question the competency of an accomplice to testify, we do not question his competency to lay the foundation for the admission of a photograph into evidence. But as Penal Code section 1111 prohibits conviction upon the testimony of an accomplice, so it also prohibits conviction upon evidence the foundation for which was supplied by an accomplice. For a photograph to qualify for admission into evidence the source of the authentication is immaterial. But section 1111 requires that to sustain a conviction the source of the authentication of

---

6. If it were necessary for Joan to identify the male participant in the film as the defendant, this test would not have been satisfied and no further discussion of the point would be necessary. But as already pointed out, the disguise was not effective. Comparing the height, weight, build and visible facial features of the man portrayed in the film with those of the defendant, the members of the jury could reasonably make the identification for themselves. In fact, the record shows that the jury relied heavily upon their independent identification of the male in the film. After deliberating for over two hours, the jury requested that the defendant stand before them without his glasses. Following 45 minutes more deliberation, they requested a second viewing of part of the film. It then required only eight minutes more to decide upon a verdict of guilty.

the corroborating evidence must be independent of the accomplice. To hold otherwise would allow the prosecution to pull itself up by its own bootstraps.

It follows that although the film is sufficient corroboration if authenticated by a source independent of the accomplice, it cannot here be used to corroborate Joan's testimony. Since its value rests upon the testimony of the accomplice, it is not "other evidence" within the meaning of Penal Code section 1111. This result is compelled by the code section. The judgment must therefore be reversed.

The judgment is reversed.

Is the California court's approach to photographic evidence an improvement on Wigmore's pictorial testimony theory? Should a photograph be admitted as probative evidence in and of itself, even without a testimonial sponsor to vouch that the picture accurately depicts what she saw? What are the foundational requirements for photographic evidence under the Federal Rules?

D. Making and Meeting Objections: Preserving Issues for Appeal

The law relating to making and meeting objections is not difficult, yet attorneys seem to make more mistakes with these basic procedures than in other areas. This is unfortunate because next to losing a claim for a client by letting the statute of limitations expire, failing to preserve a winning point on appeal is most likely to result in a call to the professional liability insurance carrier. Mistakes are on the transcript, and the Rules are not structured to forgive an appellant who fails to preserve an objection at trial.

When thinking about this problem, consider an offer of proof from three viewpoints:

(1) The proponent's, whose objective is to have the offer accepted and the record preserved for appeal on the issue;

(2) The opponent's, whose objective is to have the offer rejected and the record preserved for appeal on the issue; and

(3) The judge's, who wants to rule correctly and avoid error and who always must consider the possibility of an appeal by the proponent or opponent.

Preserving an issue for appeal has two aspects: (1) The proper offer or objection must be made in the trial court, and (2) a record must adequately present the objection or offer so that the appellate court can consider it months or years later. How is this done? What tactical factors must counsel consider when confronted with objectionable evidence?

Recall the actions of counsel in the *Lopinson* case, Problem I-8 above. Were counsel's actions counterproductive or necessary to preserve his client's rights?

FRE 103
Rulings on Evidence

(a) *Effect of erroneous ruling.* Error may not be predicated upon a ruling which admits or excludes evidence unless a substantial right of the party is affected, and

    (1) *Objection.* In case the ruling is one admitting evidence, a timely objection or motion to strike appears of record, stating the specific ground of objection, if the specific ground was not apparent from the context; or

    (2) *Offer of proof.* In case the ruling is one excluding evidence, the substance of the evidence was made known to the court by offer or was apparent from the context within which questions were asked.

(b) *Record of offer and ruling.* The court may add any other or further statement which shows the character of the evidence, the form in which it was offered, the objection made, and the ruling thereon. It may direct the making of an offer in question and answer form.

(c) *Hearing of jury.* In jury cases, proceedings shall be conducted, to the extent practicable, so as to prevent inadmissible evidence from being suggested to the jury by any means, such as making statements or offers of proof or asking questions in the hearing of the jury.

(d) *Plain error.* Nothing in this rule precludes taking notice of plain errors affecting substantial rights although they were not brought to the attention of the court.

FRE 102
Purpose and Construction

These rules shall be construed to secure fairness in administration, elimination of unjustifiable expense and delay, and promotion of growth and development of the law of evidence to the end that the truth may be ascertained and proceedings justly determined.

Problem III-26
Professional Malpractice

On June 1 Doctor *D*, chief resident at General Hospital, gives her patient, *P*, a shot that is supposed to be sodium chloride and water but that actually is potassium chloride and water. Ivan, an intern, discovers *D*'s error by testing the solution in the needle after he hears of *P*'s sudden death. Ivan files a regular hospital lab report of his test. *P*, by the administrator of his estate, sues *D*. At trial, *P*'s attorney calls *W*, Chief of Records of the hospital, and seeks to introduce Ivan's lab report and other hospital records relating to *P*. These records are hearsay, but under Rule 803(6) they may be admissible as the records of a regularly conducted activity if certain foundational facts are established. Suppose *P*'s attorney skips over these foundational steps, simply asks *W* to identify the records, and then offers them into evidence? *D*'s attorney says, "I object," and sits down. The judge says, "Objection overruled." The evidence is admitted.

What chance is there that the appellate court will reverse on the improper admission of this evidence, assuming that there are good grounds for such an objection?

Problem III-27
The Case of the "Reckless Commie"

On June 1, *P* is hit by a car driven by *D* and injured. Shortly thereafter *P* dies of lung cancer. *P*'s wife sues *D* for *P*'s pain and suffering. *P* makes a prima facie case and calls *W* as a witness. After finishing with the formalities, *P* and *W* engage in the following dialogue:

Q: W, did you know D 10 years ago?
A: Yes.
Q: Was he a communist then?
A: Yes.
D's attorney: I object, your honor.
The Court: Objection overruled.

What chance does *D* have of obtaining a favorable ruling from the appellate court on this objection? What general rule do you derive from the two preceding problems?

Problem III-28
The Converted Corn Crib

(1) Action for conversion of a crib of corn that *P* alleges is his share of the harvest that *P* and *D* had agreed to divide equally. At trial, *P* calls *W* as his first witness to testify that *D* said to *P*, "That there crib of corn is your half of this year's harvest, *P*." *D* objects on grounds of hearsay. The objection is overruled, and the evidence is admitted. On appeal the ruling below is upheld.

(2) Same case as above except that *D* objects generally to *W*'s tes-

timony, silently basing the objection in his own mind on grounds of hearsay. However, the objection is sustained (erroneously — see Problem IV-8), and the evidence is excluded. On appeal *P* argues that *W*'s testimony is not hearsay. *D*, finally seeing the light (i.e., that the statement is *not* hearsay), argues that the objection should be sustained for lack of any foundation showing that *W* had first-hand knowledge of that to which he testified. Suppose this objection is well-founded. What ruling and why? What principles do you derive from these hypotheticals?

TOOLEY v. BACON, 70 N.Y. 34 (1877): When evidence is excluded upon a mere general objection, the ruling will be upheld, if any ground in fact existed for the exclusion. It will be assumed, in the absence of any request by the opposing party or the court to make the objection definite, that it was understood, and that the ruling was placed upon the right ground. If in such a case a ground of objection be specified, the ruling must be sustained upon that ground, unless the evidence excluded was in no aspect of the case competent, or cannot be made so.

How do the Federal Rules treat this problem? Is it better to object with a general objection or a specific objection? Should objections be compound or simple? Disjunctive or conjunctive?

E.   The Functions of Judge and Jury

What are the functions of judge and jury in deciding preliminary questions of fact on which the exclusion or admissibility of evidence depends? Who should decide such questions? Does it make any difference what the preliminary question is or what type of objection is made? For example, should the judge or the jury decide whether (1) a witness is competent to testify (Rule 601), (2) an offered item of evidence is relevant (Rule 401), (3) a document is authentic (Rule 901), (4) an asserted privilege is applicable (Rule 501), (5) a witness has the requisite first-hand knowledge (Rule 602), or (6) an original writing once existed but has been lost, thus allowing proof of the contents of the alleged writing through a copy (Rule 1004)? Should it make any difference if the preliminary question of fact is also one of the ultimate issues of fact in the case? If the judge decides the preliminary question of fact, what standard of proof should apply? A preponderance of the evidence? Substantial evidence? If the judge decides to admit the challenged evidence, should the objecting party be given a "second bite at the apple" — i.e., should the judge instruct the jury to decide the preliminary fact issue itself and to disregard the offered evidence if it decides contrary to the judge?

In connection with these questions and the cases that follow, recall Problem I-5, above (The Rim), and consider Rules 104 and 1008; J. Maguire, Evidence: Common Sense and Common Law 211-231 (1947); Morgan, Functions of the Judge and Jury in the Determination of Preliminary Questions of Fact, 43 Harv. L. Rev. 165 (1929); McGuire and Epstein, Preliminary Questions of Fact in Determining the Admissibility of Evidence, 40 Harv. L. Rev. 392 (1927). On the special problem of ruling on preliminary questions of fact under the co-conspirators' hearsay exception, Rule 801(d)(2)(E), see pages 325-327, below.

FRE 104
Preliminary Questions

(a) *Questions of admissibility generally.* Preliminary questions concerning the qualification of a person to be a witness, the existence of a privilege, or the admissibility of evidence shall be determined by the court, subject to the provisions of subdivision (b). In making its determination it is not bound by the rules of evidence except those with respect to privileges.

(b) *Relevancy conditioned on fact.* When the relevancy of evidence depends upon the fulfillment of a condition of fact, the court shall admit it upon, or subject to, the introduction of evidence sufficient to support a finding of the fulfillment of the condition. . . .

FRE 1008
Functions of Court and Jury

When the admissibility of other evidence of contents of writings, recordings, or photographs under these rules depends upon the fulfillment of a condition of fact, the question whether the condition has been fulfilled is ordinarily for the court to determine in accordance with the provisions of rule 104. However, when an issue is raised (a) whether the asserted writing ever existed, or (b) whether another writing, recording, or photograph produced at the trial is the original, or (c) whether other evidence of contents correctly reflects the contents, the issue is for the trier of fact to determine as in the case of other issues of fact.

Problem III-29
The Dead Deponent

P and *D* make an oral contract in the presence and hearing of *W*. Later, *P* commences a federal diversity action against *D* for breach of the contract. During the pretrial phase of the case, *P* takes *W*'s deposition. At trial, *P* offers *W*'s deposition into evidence together with evidence that *P* claims establishes *W*'s death. Under Rule 804(b)(1) and F.R. Civ. P. 32(a)(3), *W*'s deposition is admissible only if *W* is unavailable as defined therein. Death constitutes unavailability under both rules. *D* objects to the introduction of *W*'s deposition and offers to prove on voir dire that *W* is alive and well and at home one block from the courthouse.

In ruling on this objection the judge states, "There is a conflict in the testimony that must be resolved by the jury. Objection overruled. The deposition may be read to the jury, but the jury will be instructed to disregard the evidence if it finds that *W* is alive and available."

On appeal of the judge's ruling what result and why? Should the judge or the jury decide the preliminary question of fact whether *W* is available? Do Rules 804 and 104 and F.R. Civ. P. 32(a)(3) provide an answer?

Problem III-30
The Case of the Incompetent Child

Charge: murder in the first degree. Defendant: Mrs. *D*. Victim: Mr. *D*. M.O.: gunshot wounds. Present at the crime: Mr. *D*, Mrs. *D*, and *D*, Jr., their three-year-old son. At the trial of *D*, three months after the homicide of Mr. *D*, the prosecution offers the testimony of *D*, Jr., as to what took place on that occasion. *D* objects and in support of her objection offers to have a child psychologist testify that she has tested *D*, Jr., from time to time and in her opinion, *D*, Jr., cannot separate reality from fantasy, especially with regard to the crime in question. In response the district attorney offers to produce a psychologist to testify that *D*, Jr., is of normal if not high intelligence for a child of his age, understands what happened to his father, and can talk truthfully about it.

In ruling on *D*'s objection the judge states, "There's a conflict in the testimony that must be resolved by the jury. The objection is overruled. *D*, Jr., may testify, but the jury will be instructed to disregard his testimony if it finds that *D*, Jr., should be disqualified because of incompetence."

On appeal of the judge's ruling what result and why? What alternative procedures could the judge have followed?

Problem III-31
The Case of the Witness Wife

Charge: grand larceny. Defendant: Mr. *D*. At trial the prosecution offers as its first witness a woman who identifies herself as Ms. *W*. *D* objects to the swearing of Ms. *W* on the grounds that Ms. *W* is really Mrs.

D and that to allow her to testify would violate the husband-wife testimonial privilege, which in this jurisdiction resides in the accused spouse. Evidence is presented on both sides of the issue whether Ms. *W* is Mrs. *D*.

How should this question be resolved? Who should resolve it — the jury or the judge? A combination of the two? What alternative procedures could be followed?

Problem III-32
The Case of the Careless Quack

Action: damages for wrongful death. Deceased: Karl, a 21-year-old man. Plaintiff: *P*, Karl's father. Defendant: Dr. *D*, an alleged specialist in obesity treatment. Cause of death: the accidental injection of potassium chloride instead of the prescribed injection of sodium chloride.

At trial, at the bench and out of the hearing of the jury, *P* makes the following offers of proof:

(1) *W1*, an alleged expert toxicologist, to testify to the effects on a human of injections of potassium chloride and sodium chloride. *D* objects to this offer of proof on the grounds that *W1* is a phoney, a charlatan, and an imposter — i.e., that he is not an expert. There is a dispute on the issue of *W1*'s qualifications as an expert.

(2) *W2* to testify that on the day after the injection in question, Dr. *D* told him that she had administered the wrong medicine to Karl. Dr. *D* objects on the grounds that *W2* is an attorney consulted by her in confidence for legal advice. *P* admits that *W2* is an attorney but disputes that the statement was made in confidence and for the purpose of obtaining legal advice. There is a dispute on the applicability of the attorney-client privilege.

(3) Exhibit *A*, a letter from Dr. *D* to her insurance agent stating in part, "Yesterday I gave one of my patients potassium chloride by mistake. If I get sued, am I covered?" *D* objects on the grounds that the letter is a forgery — that it was never written by her. The authenticity of the letter is disputed.

What procedure should be followed in deciding the preliminary questions of fact upon which the admissibility of these offers of proof depend? How do Rules 104, 901, and 1008 bear on these issues?

Problem III-33
The Case of the Perjurious Policeman

Action: damages for the negligent running down of *P* when the car that *D* was driving on June 1 allegedly hit *P* while he was crossing at the crosswalk at Commonwealth and Massachusetts Avenues. At trial, after

P has completed testifying, *P* calls as his first witness Officer Kojak. Officer Kojak testifies that he observed the accident and starts to tell what he saw. *D* objects and asks the court for permission to call Officer Barretta on voir dire. Permission is granted. Officer Baretta is called and sworn. Officer Barretta testifies that he and Officer Kojak were in Poughkeepsie on the day of the accident, June 1. The judge sustains the objection. Is the ruling correct? See Rules 602 and 104.

Problem III-34
The Coerced Confession

Charge: murder in the first degree. At trial the prosecution offers evidence that *D* made a custodial confession, that the police gave *D* the fourfold *Miranda* warnings, and that the confession was voluntary. *D* objects on the grounds that the *Miranda* warnings were never given and the confession was involuntary. Who decides this preliminary question of fact, the judge or the jury? A combination? Are the procedural alternatives limited by constitutional considerations in this case? In this regard, consider the following three cases.

COMMONWEALTH v. REAGAN
175 Mass. 335, 56 N.E. 577 (1900)

HAMMOND, J. As the result of the voir dire examination of the witness, the judge was of the opinion that she was not competent; but no formal order or ruling was made, and he permitted her to be sworn and to testify, stating that he should leave the question of her competency to the jury. In his charge to them he gave full and careful instructions as to the law material to that issue, and told them that, if they found her competent, they should take her statements as evidence; otherwise, they were to disregard all she had said, and deal with the case as though she had not been called. The evidence as to her competency is not before us, but, from the course taken by the judge, we must assume that in his judgment it would warrant a finding by the jury that she was competent. The defendant excepted to this course, contending that it was the duty of the court alone to decide that question. The jury brought in a verdict of guilty, and, in reply to the question put by the court, said that they found the witness competent, and in reaching their verdict they treated her as such, and relied in part on her testimony. We assume that her testimony was prejudicial to the defendant, and therefore the simple question raised on the report is whether there was error in law in the method of dealing with the question of the competency of the witness.

Speaking generally, the text-books on evidence lay down the proposi-

Commr v Reardon
Mas 1906

duty of the judge to decide
~~competence + to exclude~~
~~inclusion~~ admissability
of evidence eg competency of w
& to reject there for

(& it may further act
jury to reject testimony
notwithstanding)

tion that in a jury trial all questions as to the admissibility of evidence are for the judge. The practice in this commonwealth is stated by Morton, C.J., in Com. v. Preece, 140 Mass. 276, 5 N.E. 494, as follows: "When a confession is offered in evidence, the question whether it is voluntary is to be decided primarily by the presiding justice. If he is satisfied that it is voluntary, it is admissible; otherwise, it should be excluded. When there is conflicting testimony, the humane practice in this commonwealth is for the judge, if he decides that it is admissible, to instruct the jury that they may consider all the evidence, and that they should exclude the confession if, upon the whole evidence in the case, they are satisfied that it was not the voluntary act of the defendant." In Com. v. Culver, 126 Mass. 464, Lord, J., alluding to the practice sometimes followed in a criminal case where an objection to an alleged confession of a defendant is made upon the ground that it was improperly obtained, for the judge to allow the confession, and all the evidence bearing upon the manner in which it was obtained, to be submitted to the jury, either to be rejected wholly by them, or to be allowed such weight as, under all the circumstances, they think proper, says that this is done rather by consent than otherwise, neither party desiring to take the decision of the judge upon the question; but he adds: "The prisoner has always the right to require of the judge a decision of the competency of the evidence; and, even after the judge has decided the evidence to be competent, the prisoner has the right to ask of the jury to disregard and to give no weight to it, because of the circumstances under which the confessions were obtained." And the practice, as thus stated, is well settled in this commonwealth.

The rule conduces to the orderly and efficient conduct of a trial. It is also of the gravest importance in a criminal case that the radical question whether a witness understands the nature of an oath should be considered by itself in the first instance, free from any complication with the nature of the evidence he is expected to give, or its bearing upon the issues of the case. When the decision is to be made by a mind so situated as to be in danger of being influenced by the nature of the story as told by the witness, and the importance of the testimony, and its bearing one way or the other, it is plain that the decision is not so likely to be upon the real merits of the question as it otherwise would be; and it is easy to see (as, indeed, this very case may perhaps show) that, with the whole case before the jury, there is danger that the question of the competency of a witness may be decided according as his testimony may be legally necessary to sustain a view of the case which the emotions of the jury may lead them to take, if they can find evidence enough to justify them.

Upon principle, and by an overwhelming weight of authority in England and in this country, we are satisfied that when a witness is called, and it is objected that by reason of insanity or youthfulness he does not understand the nature of the oath, and is therefore incompetent, it is the duty of the judge to examine into the question of his competency, and to reject him unless he is satisfied that he is competent. Against the objection of the prisoner, a different course was taken in this case. The judge was of the opinion that the witness was not competent. It was the right of the prisoner, upon that finding, to have the witness excluded. The verdict should be set aside. Since it is possible that before another trial the witness, by reason of mental development and instruction, general and special, may have sufficient comprehension of the nature and obligation of an oath to satisfy the court that she is a competent witness, we make no further order. Verdict set aside.

JACKSON v. DENNO
378 U.S. 368 (1964)

Mr. Justice WHITE delivered the opinion of the Court.

Petitioner, Jackson, has filed a petition for habeas corpus in the Federal District Court asserting that his conviction for murder in the New York courts is invalid because it was founded upon a confession not properly determined to be voluntary. The writ was denied, 206 F. Supp. 759 (D.C.S.D.N.Y.), the Court of Appeals affirmed, 309 F.2d 573 (C.A.2d Cir.), and we granted certiorari to consider fundamental questions about the constitutionality of the New York procedure governing the admissibility of a confession alleged to be involuntary.

I

On June 14, 1960, at about 1 A.M., petitioner, Jackson, and Nora Elliott entered a Brooklyn hotel where Miss Elliott registered for both of them. After telling Miss Elliott to leave, which she did, Jackson drew a gun and took money from the room clerk. He ordered the clerk and several other people into an upstairs room and left the hotel, only to encounter Miss Elliott and later a policeman on the street. A struggle with the latter followed, in the course of which both men drew guns. The policeman was fatally wounded and petitioner was shot twice in the body. He managed to hail a cab, however, which took him to the hospital.

A detective questioned Jackson at about 2 A.M., soon after his arrival at the hospital. Jackson, when asked for his name, said, "Nathan Jackson, I shot the colored cop. I got the drop on him." He also admitted the robbery at the hotel. According to the detective, Jackson was in "strong" condition despite his wounds.

Jackson was given 50 milligrams of demerol and 1/50 of a grain of scopolamine at 3:55 A.M. Immediately thereafter an Assistant District Attorney, in the presence of police officers and hospital personnel, questioned Jackson, the interrogation being recorded by a stenographer. Jackson, who had been shot in the liver and lung, had by this time lost about 500 cc. of blood. Jackson again admitted the robbery in the hotel, and then said, "Look, I can't go on." But in response to further questions he admitted shooting the policeman and having fired the first shot.[2] The interview was completed at 4 A.M. An operation upon petitioner was begun at 5 A.M. and completed at 8 A.M.

Jackson and Miss Elliott were indicted for murder in the first degree and were tried together. The statements made by Jackson, both at 2 and 3:55 A.M., were introduced in evidence without objection by Jackson's counsel. Jackson took the stand in his own defense. His account of the robbery and of the shooting of the policeman differed in some important respects from his confession. According to Jackson's testimony, there was a substantial interval of time between his leaving the hotel and the shooting, and the policeman attempted to draw his gun first and fired the first shot. As to the questioning at the hospital, Jackson recalled

---

2. The confession reads in pertinent part as follows:

Q: Where did you meet the officer?
A: On the street.
Q: What happened when you met him?
A: I said, "There was a fight upstairs."
Q: Then what?
A: He insisted I go with him so I got the best of him.
Q: How did you get the best of him?
A: I know Judo.
Q: You threw him over?
A: Yeah.
Q: Where was your gun while you were giving him the Judo?
A: In my holster.
Q: After you threw him to the ground, did you pull your gun? Where was the holster?
A: On my shoulder.
Q: After you threw him to the ground, what did you do about your gun?
A: He went for his gun.
Q: What did you do?
A: I got mine out first.
Q: Did you point the gun at him?
A: Yeah.
Q: What did you say to him?
A: Told him not to be a hero. . . .
Q: How many shots did you fire at the officer?
A: I don't know.
Q: Was it more than one?
A: Yeah.
Q: Who fired first, you or the police officer?
A: I beat him to it.
Q: How many times did you fire at him?
A: I don't know; twice probably.
Q: Did he go down? Did he fall down?
A: Yeah.
Q: What did you do?
A: I shot. I didn't know. I knew I was shot. While I was on the ground he fired the gun.

that he was in pain and gasping for breath at the time and was refused water and told he would not be let alone until the police had the answers they wanted. He knew that he had been interrogated but could remember neither the questions nor the answers.

To counter Jackson's suggestion that he had been pressured into answering questions, the State offered the testimony of the attending physician and of several other persons. They agreed that Jackson was refused water, but because of the impending operation rather than his refusal to answer questions. On cross-examination of the doctor, Jackson's counsel, with the help of the hospital records, elicited the fact that demerol and scopolamine were administered to Jackson immediately before his interrogation. But any effect of these drugs on Jackson during the interrogation was denied.

Although Jackson's counsel did not specifically object to the admission of the confession initially, the trial court indicated its awareness that Jackson's counsel was questioning the circumstances under which Jackson was interrogated.

In his closing argument, Jackson's counsel did not ask for an acquittal but for a verdict of second-degree murder or manslaughter. Counsel's main effort was to negative the premeditation and intent necessary to first-degree murder and to separate the robbery felony from the killing. He made much of the testimony tending to show a substantial interval between leaving the hotel and the beginning of the struggle with the policeman. The details of that struggle and the testimony indicating the policeman fired the first shot were also stressed.

Consistent with the New York practice where a question has been raised about the voluntariness of a confession, the trial court submitted that issue to the jury along with the other issues in the case. The jury was told that if it found the confession involuntary, it was to disregard it entirely, and determine guilt or innocence solely from the other evidence in the case; alternatively, if it found the confession voluntary, it was to determine its truth or reliability and afford it weight accordingly.[5]

---

5. "If you determine that it was a confession, the statement offered here, and if you determine that Jackson made it, and if you determine that it is true; if you determine that it is accurate, before you may use it, the law still says you must find that it is voluntary, and the prosecution has the burden of proving that it was a voluntary confession. The defendant merely comes forward with the suggestion that it was involuntary, but the burden is upon the prosecution to show that it was voluntary.

"Under our law, a confession, even if true and accurate, if involuntary, is not admissible, and if it is left for the jury to determine whether or not it was voluntary, its decision is final. If you say it was involuntarily obtained, it goes out of the case. If you say it was voluntarily made, the weight of it is for you. So I am submitting to you as a question of fact to determine whether or not (a) this statement was made by Jackson, or allegedly made by Jackson, whether it was a voluntary confession, and whether it was true and accurate. That decision is yours.

"Should you decide under the rules that I gave you that it is voluntary, true and accurate, you may use it, and give it the weight you feel that you should give it. If you

The jury found Jackson guilty of murder in the first degree, Miss Elliott of manslaughter in the first degree. Jackson was sentenced to death, Miss Elliott to a prison term. Jackson's conviction was affirmed by the New York Court of Appeals, 10 N.Y.2d 780, 177 N.E.2d 59, its remittitur being amended to show that it had necessarily passed upon the voluntariness of the confession and had found that Jackson's constitutional rights had not been violated. 10 N.Y.2d 816, 178 N.E.2d 234. Certiorari was denied here. 368 U.S. 949. Jackson then filed a petition for habeas corpus, claiming that the New York procedure for determining the voluntariness of a confession was unconstitutional and that in any event his confession was involuntary. After hearing argument and examining the state court record the District Court denied the petition without holding an evidentiary hearing. Indicating that it is the trier of fact who must determine the truth of the testimony of prisoner and official alike and resolve conflicts in the testimony, the court found "no clear and conclusive proof that these statements were extorted from him, or that they were given involuntarily." Nor was any constitutional infirmity found in the New York procedure. 206 F. Supp. 759 (D.C.S.D.N.Y.). The Court of Appeals, after noting the conflicting testimony concerning the coercion issue and apparently accepting the State's version of the facts, affirmed the conviction. 309 F.2d 573 (C.A.2d Cir.).

II

It is now axiomatic that a defendant in a criminal case is deprived of due process of law if his conviction is founded, in whole or in part, upon an involuntary confession, without regard for the truth or falsity of the confession, Rogers v. Richmond, 365 U.S. 534, and even though there is ample evidence aside from the confession to support the conviction. Malinski v. New York, 324 U.S. 401; Stroble v. California, 343 U.S. 181; Payne v. Arkansas, 356 U.S. 560. Equally clear is the defendant's constitutional right at some stage in the proceedings to object to the use of the confession and to have a fair hearing and a reliable determination on

---

should decide that it is involuntary, exclude it from the case. Do not consider it at all. In that event, you must go to the other evidence in the case to see whether or not the guilt of Jackson was established to your satisfaction outside of the confession, beyond a reasonable doubt.

"If you should determine that Jackson made this confession, and that it was a true confession, and you have so determined from the evidence, then if you should decide that it was gotten by influence, of fear produced by threats, and if that is your decision, then reject it.

"I repeat to you again, the burden of proving the accuracy, truth, and the voluntariness of the confession always rests upon the prosecution."

There is no issue raised as to whether these instructions stated an adequate and correct federal standard for determining the voluntariness of Jackson's confession.

the issue of voluntariness, a determination uninfluenced by the truth or falsity of the confession. Rogers v. Richmond, supra. In our view, the New York procedure employed in this case did not afford a reliable determination of the voluntariness of the confession offered in evidence at the trial, did not adequately protect Jackson's right to be free of a conviction based upon a coerced confession and therefore cannot withstand constitutional attack under the Due Process Clause of the Fourteenth Amendment. We therefore reverse the judgment below denying the writ of habeas corpus.

III

Under the New York rule, the trial judge must make a preliminary determination regarding a confession offered by the prosecution and exclude it if in no circumstances could the confession be deemed voluntary. But if the evidence presents a fair question as to its voluntariness, as where certain facts bearing on the issue are in dispute or where reasonable men could differ over the inferences to be drawn from undisputed facts, the judge "must receive the confession and leave to the jury, under proper instructions, the ultimate determination of its voluntary character and also its truthfulness." Stein v. New York, 346 U.S. 156, 172. If an issue of coercion is presented, the judge may not resolve conflicting evidence or arrive at his independent appraisal of the voluntariness of the confession, one way or the other. These matters he must leave to the jury.

This procedure has a significant impact upon the defendant's Fourteenth Amendment rights. In jurisdictions following the orthodox rule, under which the judge himself solely and finally determines the voluntariness of the confession, or those following the Massachusetts procedure,[8] under which the jury passes on voluntariness only after the judge

---

8. We raise no question here concerning the Massachusetts procedure. In jurisdictions following this rule, the judge hears the confession evidence, himself resolves evidentiary conflicts and gives his own answer to the coercion issue, rejecting confessions he deems involuntary and admitting only those he believes voluntary. It is only the latter confessions that are heard by the jury, which may then, under this procedure, disagree with the judge, find the confession involuntary and ignore it. Given the integrity of the preliminary proceedings before the judge, the Massachusetts procedure does not, in our opinion, pose hazards to the rights of a defendant. While no more will be known about the views of the jury than under the New York rule, the jury does not hear all confessions where there is a fair question of voluntariness, but only those which a judge actually and independently determines to be voluntary, based upon all of the evidence. The judge's consideration of voluntariness is carried out separate and aside from issues of the reliability of the confession and the guilt or innocence of the accused and without regard to the fact the issue may again be raised before the jury if decided against the defendant. The record will show the judge's conclusions in this regard and his findings upon the underlying facts may be express or ascertainable from the record.

Once the confession is properly found to be voluntary by the judge, reconsideration of this issue by the jury does not, of course, improperly affect the jury's determination of the credibility or probativeness of the confession or its ultimate determination of guilt or innocence.

has fully and independently resolved the issue against the accused,[9] the judge's conclusions are clearly evident from the record since he either admits the confession into evidence if it is voluntary or rejects it if involuntary. Moreover, his findings upon disputed issues of fact are expressly stated or may be ascertainable from the record. In contrast, the New York jury returns only a general verdict upon the ultimate question of guilt or innocence. It is impossible to discover whether the jury found the confession voluntary and relied upon it, or involuntary and supposedly ignored it. Nor is there any indication of how the jury resolved disputes in the evidence concerning the critical facts underlying the coercion issue. Indeed, there is nothing to show that these matters were resolved at all, one way or the other.

These uncertainties inherent in the New York procedure were aptly described by the Court in Stein v. New York, 346 U.S. 156, 177-178:

"Petitioners suffer a disadvantage inseparable from the issues they raise in that this procedure does not produce any definite, open and separate decision of the confession issue. Being cloaked by the general verdict, petitioners do not know what result they really are attacking here. . . ."

A defendant objecting to the admission of a confession is entitled to a fair hearing in which both the underlying factual issues and the voluntariness of his confession are actually and reliably determined. But did the jury in Jackson's case make these critical determinations, and if it did, what were these determinations?

Notwithstanding these acknowledged difficulties inherent in the New York procedure, the Court in *Stein* found no constitutional deprivation to the defendant. The Court proceeded to this conclusion on the basis of alternative assumptions regarding the manner in which the jury might have resolved the coercion issue. Either the jury determined the disputed issues of fact against the accused, found the confession voluntary and therefore properly relied upon it; or it found the contested facts in favor of the accused and deemed the confession involuntary, in which event it disregarded the confession in accordance with its instructions and adjudicated guilt based solely on the other evidence. On either assumption the Court found no error in the judgment of the state court.

We disagree with the Court in *Stein*; for in addition to sweeping aside its own express doubts that the jury acted at all in the confession matter

---

9. Not all the States and federal judicial circuits can be neatly classified in accordance with the above three procedures. In many cases it is difficult to ascertain from published appellate court opinions whether the New York or Massachusetts procedure, or some variant of either, is being followed. Some jurisdictions apparently leave the matter entirely to the discretion of the trial court; others state the rule differently on different occasions; and still others deal with voluntariness in terms of trustworthiness, which is said to be a matter for the jury, an approach which, in the light of this Court's recent decision in Rogers v. Richmond, 365 U.S. 534, may make these cases of doubtful authority. . . .

the Court, we think, failed to take proper account of the dangers to an accused's rights under either of the alternative assumptions.

On the assumption that the jury found the confession voluntary, the Court concluded that it could properly do so. But this judgment was arrived at only on the further assumptions that the jury had actually found the disputed issues of fact against the accused and that these findings were reliably arrived at in accordance with considerations that are permissible and proper under federal law. These additional assumptions, in our view, were unsound.

The New York jury is at once given both the evidence going to voluntariness and all of the corroborating evidence showing that the confession is true and that the defendant committed the crime. The jury may therefore believe the confession and believe that the defendant has committed the very act with which he is charged, a circumstance which may seriously distort judgment of the credibility of the accused and assessment of the testimony concerning the critical facts surrounding his confession.

In those cases where without the confession the evidence is insufficient, the defendant should not be convicted if the jury believes the confession but finds it to be involuntary. The jury, however, may find it difficult to understand the policy forbidding reliance upon a coerced, but true, confession, a policy which has divided this Court in the past, see Stein v. New York, supra, and an issue which may be reargued in the jury room. That a trustworthy confession must also be voluntary if it is to be used at all, generates natural and potent pressure to find it voluntary. Otherwise the guilty defendant goes free. Objective consideration of the conflicting evidence concerning the circumstances of the confession becomes difficult and the implicit findings become suspect.[10]

10. "It may be urged that the commitment of our system to jury trial presupposes the acceptance of the assumptions that the jury follows its instructions, that it will make a separate determination of the voluntariness issue, and that it will disregard what it is supposed to disregard. But that commitment generally presupposes that the judge will apply the exclusionary rules before permitting evidence to be submitted to the jury." Meltzer, Involuntary Confessions: The Allocation of Responsibility Between Judge and Jury, 21 U. Chi. L. Rev. 317, 327 (1954). See also 9 Wigmore, Evidence (3d ed. 1940), §2550.

"The case of a confession induced by physical or mental coercion deserves special mention. The protection which the orthodox rule or the Massachusetts doctrine affords the accused is of major value to him. A fair consideration of the evidence upon the preliminary question is essential; in this consideration the truth or untruth of the confession is immaterial. Due process of law requires that a coerced confession be excluded from consideration by the jury. It also requires that the issue of coercion be tried by an unprejudiced trier, and, regardless of the pious fictions indulged by the courts, it is useless to contend that a juror who has heard the confession can be uninfluenced by his opinion as to the truth or falsity of it. . . . The rule excluding a coerced confession is more than a rule excluding hearsay. Whatever may be said about the orthodox reasoning that its exclusion is on the ground of its probable falsity, the fact is that the considerations which call for the exclusion of a coerced confession are those which call for the protection of every citizen,

The danger that matters pertaining to the defendant's guilt will infect the jury's findings of fact bearing upon voluntariness, as well as its conclusion upon that issue itself, is sufficiently serious to preclude their unqualified acceptance upon review in this Court, regardless of whether there is or is not sufficient other evidence to sustain a finding of guilt. In Jackson's case, he confessed to having fired the first shot, a matter very relevant to the charge of first degree murder. The jury also heard the evidence of eyewitnesses to the shooting. Jackson's testimony going to his physical and mental condition when he confessed and to the events which took place at that time, bearing upon the issue of voluntariness, was disputed by the prosecution. The obvious and serious danger is that the jury disregarded or disbelieved Jackson's testimony pertaining to the confession because it believed he had done precisely what he was charged with doing. . . .

Under the New York procedure, the evidence given the jury inevitably injects irrelevant and impermissible considerations of truthfulness of the confession into the assessment of voluntariness. Indeed the jury is told to determine the truthfulness of the confession in assessing its probative value.[13] As a consequence, it cannot be assumed, as the *Stein* Court assumed, that the jury reliably found the facts against the accused.[14]

---

whether he be in fact guilty or not guilty. And the rule of exclusion ought not to be emasculated by admitting the evidence and giving to the jury an instruction which, as every judge and lawyer knows, cannot be obeyed." Morgan, Some Problems of Proof Under the Anglo-American System of Litigation (1956), 104-105.

13. The question of the credibility of a confession, as distinguished from its admissibility, is submitted to the jury in jurisdictions following the orthodox, Massachusetts, or New York procedure. Since the evidence surrounding the making of a confession bears on its credibility, such evidence is presented to the jury under the orthodox rule not on the issue of voluntariness or competency of the confession, but on the issue of its weight. Just as questions of admissibility of evidence are traditionally for the court, questions of credibility, whether of a witness or a confession, are for the jury. This is so because trial courts do not direct a verdict against the defendant on issues involving credibility. Nothing in this opinion, of course, touches upon these ordinary rules of evidence relating to impeachment.

A finding that the confession is voluntary prior to admission no more affects the instructions on or the jury's view of the reliability of the confession than a finding in a preliminary hearing that evidence was not obtained by an illegal search affects the instruction on or the jury's view of the probativeness of this evidence.

The failure to distinguish between the discrete issues of voluntariness and credibility is frequently reflected in opinions which declare that it is the province of the court to resolve questions of admissibility of confessions, as with all other questions of admissibility of evidence, the province of the jury to determine issues of credibility, but which then approve the trial court's submission of the voluntariness question to the jury. Meltzer, Involuntary Confessions: The Allocation of Responsibility Between Judge and Jury, 21 U. Chi. L. Rev. 317, 320-321 (1954).

14. Another assumption of *Stein* — that a criminal conviction can stand despite the introduction of a coerced confession if there is sufficient other evidence to sustain a finding of guilt and if the confession is only tentatively submitted to the jury — an assumption also related to the view that the use of involuntary confessions is constitutionally proscribed solely because of their illusory trustworthiness, has also been rejected in the decisions of

This unsound assumption undermines *Stein*'s authority as a precedent and its view on the constitutionality of the New York procedure. The admixture of reliability and voluntariness in the considerations of the jury would itself entitle a defendant to further proceedings in any case in which the essential facts are disputed, for we cannot determine how the jury resolved these issues and will not assume that they were reliably and properly resolved against the accused. And it is only a reliable determination on the voluntariness issue which satisfies the constitutional rights of the defendant and which would permit the jury to consider the confession in adjudicating guilt or innocence.

But we do not rest on this ground alone, for the other alternative hypothesized in *Stein* — that the jury found the confession involuntary and disregarded it — is equally unacceptable. Under the New York procedure, the fact of a defendant's confession is solidly implanted in the jury's mind, for it has not only heard the confession, but it has been instructed to consider and judge its voluntariness and is in position to assess whether it is true or false. If it finds the confession involuntary, does the jury — indeed, can it — then disregard the confession in accordance with its instructions? If there are lingering doubts about the sufficiency of the other evidence, does the jury unconsciously lay them to rest by resort to the confession? Will uncertainty about the sufficiency of the other evidence to prove guilt beyond a reasonable doubt actually result in acquittal when the jury knows the defendant has given a truthful confession?

It is difficult, if not impossible, to prove that a confession which a jury has found to be involuntary has nevertheless influenced the verdict or that its finding of voluntariness, if this is the course it took, was affected by the other evidence showing the confession was true. But the New York procedure poses substantial threats to a defendant's constitutional rights to have an involuntary confession entirely disregarded and to have the coercion issue fairly and reliably determined. These hazards we cannot ignore.[16]

---

this Court. It is now clear that reversal follows if the confession admitted in evidence is found to be involuntary in this Court regardless of the possibility that the jury correctly followed instructions and determined the confession to be involuntary.

16. Further obstacles to a reliable and fair determination of voluntariness under the New York procedure result from the ordinary rules relating to cross-examination and impeachment. Although not the case here, an accused may well be deterred from testifying on the voluntariness issue when the jury is present because of his vulnerability to impeachment by proof of prior convictions and broad cross-examination, both of whose prejudicial effects are familiar. The fear of such impeachment and extensive cross-examination in the presence of the jury that is to pass on guilt or innocence as well as voluntariness may induce a defendant to remain silent, although he is perhaps the only source of testimony of the facts underlying the claim of coercion. Where this occurs the determination of voluntariness is made upon less than all of the relevant evidence. Cf. United States v. Carignan, 342 U.S. 36.

IV

We turn to consideration of the disposition of this case. Since Jackson has not been given an adequate hearing upon the voluntariness of his confession he must be given one, the remaining inquiry being the scope of that hearing and the court which should provide it.

As we have already said, Jackson is entitled to a reliable resolution of these evidentiary conflicts. If this case were here upon direct review of Jackson's conviction, we could not proceed with review on the assumption that these disputes had been resolved in favor of the State for as we have held we are not only unable to tell how the jury resolved these matters but, even if the jury did resolve them against Jackson, its findings were infected with impermissible considerations and accordingly cannot be controlling here. Cf. Rogers v. Richmond, supra. Likewise, a federal habeas corpus court, in the face of the unreliable state court procedure, would not be justified in disposing of the petition solely upon the basis of the undisputed portions of the record. At the very least, Townsend v. Sain, 372 U.S. 293, would require a full evidentiary hearing to determine the factual context in which Jackson's confession was given. . . .

Reversed and remanded.

Mr. Justice BLACK, with whom Mr. Justice CLARK joins as to Part I of this opinion, dissenting in part and concurring in part.

I

In Stein v. New York, 346 U.S. 156, 177-179, this Court sustained the constitutionality of New York's procedure under which the jury, rather than the trial judge, resolves disputed questions of fact as to the voluntariness of confessions offered against defendants charged with crime. I think this holding was correct and would adhere to it. While I dissented from affirmance of the convictions in *Stein*, my dissent went to other points; I most assuredly did not dissent because of any doubts about a State's constitutional power in a criminal case to let the jury, as it does in New York, decide the question of a confession's voluntariness. In fact, I would be far more troubled about constitutionality should either a State or the Federal Government declare that a jury in trying a defendant charged with crime is compelled to accept without question a trial court's factual finding that a confession was voluntarily given. Whatever might be a judge's view of the voluntariness of a confession, the jury in passing on a defendant's guilt or innocence is, in my judgment, entitled to hear and determine voluntariness of a confession along with other factual issues on which its verdict must rest. . . .

Another reason given by the Court for invalidating the New York rule is that it is inherently unfair and therefore unconstitutional to permit the jury to pass on voluntariness, since the jury, even though finding a confession to have been coerced, may nevertheless be unwilling to follow the court's instruction to disregard it, because it may also believe the confession is true, the defendant is guilty, and a guilty person ought not be allowed to escape punishment. This is a possibility, of a nature that is inherent in any confession fact-finding by human fact-finders — a possibility present perhaps as much in judges as in jurors. There are, of course, no statistics available, and probably none could be gathered, accurately reporting whether and to what extent fact-finders (judges or juries) are affected as the Court says they may be. . . .

The Court in note 8 of its opinion indicates that a State may still, under the new constitutional rule announced today, permit a trial jury to determine voluntariness if first the trial judge has "fully and independently resolved the issue against the accused," In other words, the Constitution now requires the judge to make this finding, and the jury's power to pass on voluntariness is a mere matter of grace, not something constitutionally required. If, as the Court assumes, allowing the jury to pass on the voluntariness of a confession before the judge has done so will "seriously distort" the jury's judgment, I fail to understand why its judgment would not be similarly distorted by its being allowed to pass on voluntariness after the judge has decided that question. Yet, of course, the jury passing on guilt or innocence must, under any fair system of criminal procedure, be allowed to consider and decide whether an offered confession is voluntary in order to pass on its credibility. But it should be obvious that, under the Court's new rule, when a confession does come before a jury it will have the judge's explicit or implicit stamp of approval on it. This Court will find it hard to say that the jury will not be greatly influenced, if not actually coerced, when what the trial judge does is the same as saying "I am convinced that this confession is voluntary, but, of course, you may decide otherwise if you like."[7]

Another disadvantage to the defendant under the Court's new rule is the failure to say anything about the burden of proving voluntariness. The New York rule does now and apparently always has put on the State the burden of convincing the jury beyond a reasonable doubt that a confession is voluntary. See Stein v. New York, supra, 346 U.S. at 173 and note 17; People v. Valletutti, 297 N.Y. 226, 229, 78 N.E.2d 485, 486. The Court has not said that its new constitutional rule, which requires the judge to decide voluntariness, also imposes on the State the burden of proving this fact beyond a reasonable doubt. Does the Court's new

---

7. The Court's opinion indicates that the judge will not make any such statement to the jury. If the Court here is holding that it is constitutionally impermissible for the judge to tell the jury that he himself has decided that the confession is voluntary, that is one thing. As I read the decisions in this field, however, I am far from persuaded that there are not many States in which the judge does admit the confession along with his statement that it is voluntary.

rule allow the judge to decide voluntariness merely on a preponderance of the evidence? If so, this is a distinct disadvantage to the defendant. In fashioning its new constitutional rule, the Court should not leave this important question in doubt.

Finally, and even more important, the Court's new constitutional doctrine is, it seems to me, a strange one when we consider that both the United States Constitution and the New York Constitution (Art I, §2) establish trial by jury of criminal charges as a bedrock safeguard of the people's liberties. The reasons given by the Court for this downgrading of trial by jury appear to me to challenge the soundness of the Founders' great faith in jury trials. Implicit in these constitutional requirements of jury trial is a belief that juries can be trusted to decide factual issues. Stating the obvious fact that "it is only a *reliable* determination on the voluntariness issue which satisfies the constitutional rights of the defendant . . . ," (emphasis supplied), the Court concludes, however, that a jury's finding on this question is tainted by inherent unreliability. In making this judgment about the unreliability of juries, the Court, I believe, overlooks the fact that the Constitution itself long ago made the decision that juries *are* to be trusted. . . .

Separate dissents by CLARK, J., and HARLAN, J., are omitted.

An important issue in *Jackson* is the effectiveness of jury instructions in connection with use of a defendant's confession. The Court registers serious doubts about the jury's ability to follow such instructions in this context. The same issue arises in connection with confrontation-clause claims in joint trials of alleged co-conspirators. See the *Harrington, Bruton,* and *Parker* cases in Chapter V, pages 440-445 and 476-485.

Eight years later the Supreme Court addressed the burden-of-proof question raised by Justice Black.

LEGO v. TWOMEY
404 U.S. 477 (1972)

Mr. Justice WHITE delivered the opinion of the Court.

In 1964 this Court held that a criminal defendant who challenges the voluntariness of a confession made to officials and sought to be used against him at his trial has a due process right to a reliable determination that the confession was in fact voluntarily given and not the outcome of coercion which the Constitution forbids. Jackson v. Denno, 378 U.S. 368. While our decision made plain that only voluntary confessions may be admitted at the trial of guilt or innocence, we did not then announce, or even suggest, that the factfinder at a coercion hearing need judge voluntariness with reference to an especially severe standard of proof. Nevertheless, since *Jackson*, state and federal courts have addressed themselves to the issue with a considerable variety of opinions. We granted certiorari in this case to resolve the question.

Petitioner Lego was convicted of armed robbery in 1961 after a jury trial in Superior Court, Cook County, Illinois. The court sentenced him to prison for 25 to 50 years. The evidence introduced against Lego at trial included a confession he had made to police after arrest and while in custody at the station house. Prior to trial Lego sought to have the confession suppressed. He did not deny making it but did challenge that he had done so voluntarily. The trial judge conducted a hearing, out of the presence of the jury, at which Lego testified that police had beaten him about the head and neck with a gun butt. His explanation of this treatment was that the local police chief, a neighbor and former classmate of the robbery victim, had sought revenge upon him. Lego introduced into evidence a photograph that had been taken of him at the county jail on the day after his arrest. The photograph showed that petitioner's face had been swollen and had traces of blood on it. Lego admitted that his face had been scratched in a scuffle with the robbery victim but maintained that the encounter did not explain the condition shown in the photograph. The police chief and four officers also testified. They denied either beating or threatening petitioner and disclaimed knowledge that any other officer had done so. The trial judge resolved this credibility problem in favor of the police and ruled the confession admissible.[2] At trial, Lego testified in his own behalf. Although he did not dispute the truth of the confession directly, he did tell his version of the events that had transpired at the police station. The trial judge instructed the jury as to the prosecution's burden of proving guilt. He did not instruct that the jury was required to find the confession voluntary before it could be used in judging guilt or innocence.[3] On direct appeal the Illinois Supreme Court affirmed the conviction.

Four years later petitioner challenged his conviction by seeking a writ of habeas corpus in the United States District Court for the Northern District of Illinois. He maintained that the trial judge should have found the confession voluntary beyond a reasonable doubt before admitting it into evidence. Although the judge had made no mention of the standard he used, Illinois law provided that a confession challenged as involun-

---

2. In ruling the confession admissible, the judge stated:

"The petitioner has admitted under oath he had a struggle with the complaining witness over the gun; he was wounded, obtained a facial wound. The Officers testified he was bloody at the time he was arrested.

"I don't believe the defendant's testimony at all that he was beaten up by the Police. The condition he is in is well explained by the defendant himself."

3. Illinois followed what we described in Jackson v. Denno, 378 U.S. 368 (1964), as "the orthodox rule, under which the judge himself solely and finally determines the voluntariness of the confession. . . ."

tary could be admitted into evidence if, at a hearing outside the presence of the jury, the judge found it voluntary by a preponderance of the evidence. In the alternative petitioner argued that the voluntariness question should also have been submitted to the jury for its separate consideration. After first denying the writ for failure to exhaust state remedies, the District Court granted a rehearing motion, concluded that Lego had no state remedy then available to him and denied relief on the merits. The Court of Appeals for the Seventh Circuit affirmed.

I

Petitioner challenges the judgment of the Court of Appeals on three grounds. The first is that he was not proved guilty beyond a reasonable doubt as required by In re Winship, 397 U.S. 358 (1970), because the confession used against him at his trial had been proved voluntary only by a preponderance of the evidence. Implicit in the claim is an assumption that a voluntariness hearing is designed to enhance the reliability of jury verdicts. To judge whether that is so we must return to Jackson v. Denno, 378 U.S. 368. . . .

We did not think it necessary, or even appropriate, in *Jackson* to announce that prosecutors would be required to meet a particular burden of proof in a *Jackson* hearing held before the trial judge.[9] Indeed, the then-established duty to determine voluntariness had not been framed in terms of a burden of proof, nor has it been since *Jackson* was decided. We could fairly assume then, as we can now, that a judge would admit into evidence only those confessions that he reliably found, at least by a preponderance of the evidence, had been made voluntarily.

We noted in *Jackson* that there may be a relationship between the involuntariness of a confession and its unreliability. But our decision was not based in the slightest on the fear that juries might misjudge the accuracy of confessions and arrive at erroneous determinations of guilt or innocence. That case was not aimed at reducing the possibility of convicting innocent men.

Quite the contrary, we feared that the reliability and truthfulness of even coerced confessions could impermissibly influence a jury's judgment as to voluntariness. The use of coerced confessions, whether true or false, is forbidden because the method used to extract them offends constitutional principles. Rogers v. Richmond, 365 U.S. 534, 540-541 (1961). The procedure we established in *Jackson* was designed to safeguard the right of an individual, entirely apart from his guilt or inno-

---

9. "Judge" is used here and throughout the opinion to mean a fact-finder, whether trial judge or jury, at a voluntariness hearing. The proscription against permitting the jury that passes upon guilt or innocence to judge voluntariness in the same proceeding does not preclude the States from impaneling a separate jury to determine voluntariness. Jackson v. Denno, 378 U.S., at 391 n.19.

cence, not to be compelled to condemn himself by his own utterances. Nothing in *Jackson* questioned the province or capacity of juries to assess the truthfulness of confessions. Nothing in that opinion took from the jury any evidence relating to the accuracy or weight of confessions admitted into evidence. A defendant has been as free since *Jackson* as he was before to familiarize a jury with circumstances that attend the taking of his confession, including facts bearing upon its weight and voluntariness. In like measure, of course, juries have been at liberty to disregard confessions that are insufficiently corroborated or otherwise deemed unworthy of belief.

Since the purpose that a voluntariness hearing is designed to serve has nothing whatever to do with improving the reliability of jury verdicts, we cannot accept the charge that judging the admissibility of a confession by a preponderance of the evidence undermines the mandate of In re Winship, 397 U.S. 358 (1970). Our decision in *Winship* was not concerned with standards for determining the admissibility of evidence or with the prosecution's burden of proof at a suppression hearing when evidence is challenged on constitutional grounds. *Winship* went no further than to confirm the fundamental right that protects "the accused against conviction except upon proof beyond a reasonable doubt of every fact necessary to constitute the crime with which he is charged." Id., at 364. A high standard of proof is necessary, we said, to ensure against unjust convictions by giving substance to the presumption of innocence. Id., at 363. A guilty verdict is not rendered less reliable or less consonant with *Winship* simply because the admissibility of a confession is determined by a less stringent standard. Petitioner does not maintain that either his confession or its voluntariness is an element of the crime with which he was charged. He does not challenge the constitutionality of the standard by which the jury was instructed to decide his guilt or innocence; nor does he question the sufficiency of the evidence that reached the jury to satisfy the proper standard of proof. Petitioner's rights under *Winship* have not been violated.

II

Even conceding that *Winship* is inapplicable because the purpose of a voluntariness hearing is not to implement the presumption of innocence, petitioner presses for reversal on the alternative ground that evidence offered against a defendant at a criminal trial and challenged on constitutional grounds must be determined admissible beyond a reasonable doubt in order to give adequate protection to those values that exclusionary rules are designed to serve. . . .

The argument is straightforward and has appeal. But we are unconvinced that merely emphasizing the importance of the values served by exclusionary rules is itself sufficient demonstration that the Constitution also requires admissibility to be proved beyond reasonable doubt. Evidence obtained in violation of the Fourth Amendment has been excluded from federal criminal trials for many years. Weeks v. United States, supra. The same is true of coerced confessions offered in either federal or state trials. Bram v. United States, 168 U.S. 532 (1897); Brown v. Mississippi, supra. But, from our experience over this period of time no substantial evidence has accumulated that federal rights have suffered from determining admissibility by a preponderance of the evidence. Petitioner offers nothing to suggest that admissibility rulings have been unreliable or otherwise wanting in quality because not based on some higher standard. Without good cause, we are unwilling to expand currently applicable exclusionary rules by erecting additional barriers to placing truthful and probative evidence before state juries and by revising the standards applicable in collateral proceedings. Sound reason for moving further in this direction has not been offered here nor do we discern any at the present time. This is particularly true since the exclusionary rules are very much aimed at deterring lawless conduct by police and prosecution and it is very doubtful that escalating the prosecution's burden of proof in Fourth and Fifth Amendment suppression hearings would be sufficiently productive in this respect to outweigh the public interest in placing probative evidence before juries for the purpose of arriving at truthful decisions about guilt or innocence.

To reiterate what we said in *Jackson*: when a confession challenged as involuntary is sought to be used against a criminal defendant at this trial, he is entitled to a reliable and clear-cut determination that the confession was in fact voluntarily rendered. Thus, the prosecution must prove at least by a preponderance of the evidence that the confession was voluntary. Of course, the States are free, pursuant to their own law, to adopt a higher standard. They may indeed differ as to the appropriate resolution of the values they find at stake.

III

We also reject petitioner's final contention that, even though the trial judge ruled on his coercion claim, he was entitled to have the jury decide the claim anew. To the extent this argument asserts that the judge's determination was insufficiently reliable, it is no more persuasive than petitioner's other contentions. To the extent the position assumes that a jury is better suited than a judge to determine voluntariness, it questions the basic assumptions of Jackson v. Denno; it also ignores that *Jackson* neither raised any question about the constitutional validity of the so-called orthodox rule for judging the admissibility of confessions nor even suggested that the Constitution requires submission of voluntariness claims to a jury as well as a judge. Finally, Duncan v. Louisiana, 391 U.S. 145 (1968), which made the Sixth Amendment right to trial by jury applicable to the States, did not purport to change the normal rule that the admissibility of evidence is a question for the court rather than the jury. Nor did that decision require that both judge and jury pass upon the admissibility of evidence when constitutional grounds are asserted for excluding it. We are not disposed to impose as a constitutional requirement a procedure we have found wanting merely to afford petitioner a second forum for litigating his claim.

The decision of the Court of Appeals is affirmed.

Mr. Justice POWELL and Mr. Justice REHNQUIST took no part in the consideration or decision of this case.

Mr. Justice BRENNAN, with whom Mr. Justice DOUGLAS and Mr. Justice MARSHALL join, dissenting.

When the prosecution, state or federal, seeks to put in evidence an allegedly involuntary confession, its admissibility is determined by the command of the Fifth Amendment that "[n]o person . . . shall be compelled in any criminal case to be a witness against himself." . . .

Ideally, of course, a defendant's compelled utterance would never be admitted into evidence against him. As we said in Jackson v. Denno, 378 U.S. 368, 376 (1964), it is "axiomatic" that a criminal conviction cannot stand if it "is founded, in whole or in part, upon an involuntary confession . . . even though there is ample evidence aside from the confession to support the conviction." Yet I doubt that informed observers of the criminal process would deny that at least some compelled utterances slip through, even assuming scrupulous adherence to constitutional standards and the most rigorous procedural protections. *Jackson* was an attempt to move that reality somewhat closer to the ideal. We there rejected the New York rule because it "did not afford a reliable determination of the voluntariness of the confession offered in evidence at the trial" and consequently "did not adequately protect [a defendant's] right to be free of a conviction based upon a coerced confession." . . .

In my view, the rationale of *Jackson* requires the conclusion that the preponderance standard does not provide sufficient protection against the danger that involuntary confessions will be employed in criminal trials.

A *Jackson* hearing normally presents the factfinder with conflicting testimony from the defendant and law enforcement officers about what occurred during the officers' interrogation of the defendant. The factfinder's resolution of this conflict is often, as a practical matter, the final resolution of the voluntariness issue. *Jackson*, supra, at 390-391. This case is a typical example. Petitioner testified that he confessed because the police had beaten him; the police testified that there was no beating. As the Court notes, "[t]he trial judge resolved this credibility problem in favor of the police and ruled the confession admissible." When the question before the factfinder is whether to believe one or the other of two self-serving accounts of what has happened, it is apparent that the standard of persuasion will in many instances be of controlling significance. Although the Court suggests "that federal rights have [not] suffered from determining admissibility by a preponderance of the evidence" and that there has been no showing "that admissibility rulings have been unreliable . . . because not based on some higher standard," I do not think it can be denied, given the factual nature of the ordinary voluntariness determination, that permitting a lower standard of proof will necessarily result in the admission of more involuntary confessions than would be admitted were the prosecution required to meet a higher standard. The converse, of course, is also true. Requiring the higher standard means that some voluntary confessions will be excluded as involuntary even though they would have been found voluntary under the lower standard.

The standard of proof required for a criminal conviction presents a similar situation, yet we have held that guilt must be established by proof beyond a reasonable doubt. In re Winship, 397 U.S. 358, 361-364. Permitting proof by a preponderance of the evidence would necessarily result in the conviction of more defendants who are in fact innocent. Conversely, imposing the burden of proof beyond a reasonable doubt means that more defendants who are in fact guilty are found innocent. It seems to me that the same considerations that demand the reasonable-doubt standard when guilt or innocence is at stake also demand that standard when the question is the admissibility of an allegedly involuntary confession.

We permit proof by a preponderance of the evidence in civil litigation because "we view it as no more serious in general for there to be an erroneous verdict in the defendant's favor than for there to be an erroneous verdict in the plaintiff's favor." Id., at 371 (Harlan, J., concurring). We do not take that view in criminal cases. We said in *Winship* that the reasonable-doubt standard "is a prime instrument for reducing the risk of convictions resting on factual error. The standard provides concrete substance for the presumption of innocence. . . ." Id., at 363. As Mr. Justice Harlan put it in his concurring opinion, the requirement of proof beyond a reasonable doubt is "bottomed on a fundamental value determination of our society that it is far worse to convict an innocent man than to let a guilty man go free." Id., at 372.

If we permit the prosecution to prove by a preponderance of the evidence that a confession was voluntary, then, to paraphrase Mr. Justice Harlan, we must be prepared to justify the view that it is no more serious in general to admit involuntary confessions than it is to exclude voluntary confessions. I am not prepared to justify that view. Compelled self-incrimination is so alien to the American sense of justice that I see no way that such a view could ever be justified. . . .

CHAPTER IV

The Rule Against Hearsay and Its Exceptions

The rule against hearsay is a historical product of the Anglo-American system of judicial resolution of disputes. Continental systems of adjudication seem to do nicely without this complex and difficult doctrine. What accounts for its development and persistence in Anglo-American jurisprudence? Traditional justifications for the rule usually focus on some of the peculiar characteristics of the Anglo-American trial system: (1) the adversarial presentation of proof (2) by live witnesses (3) before a lay fact-finder. These justifications view the rule against hearsay as simply another device to promote reliable fact-finding in a system of this design. The big question is, do the rule and its exceptions effectively and consistently fulfill this function?

As the preceding chapters indicate, the device most heavily relied upon to promote reliable fact-finding at trial is cross-examination. Other devices, rules, and limitations that are relied upon to a lesser extent to promote accuracy include: the oath and sanctions for its violation, competency limitations, the rule requiring first-hand knowledge, the confrontation clause of the Constitution, the relevancy rule, the prejudice rule, and the categorical rules of exclusion primarily found in Rules 404 through 412. These devices are designed to promote fair and accurate fact-finding by deterring, excluding, or exposing false testimony of witnesses about *their own* perceptions of events relevant to the inquiry.

A conceptual problem is posed by the traditional explanation for the rule against hearsay and its exceptions: When, if ever, may these other truth-promoting devices, rules, and limitations safely be dispensed with? Put another way, when should an in-court witness (or document) be allowed to relate the observation, statements, or beliefs of someone who is not in court and thus not subject to the normal truth-promoting rules, policies, and procedures (especially cross-examination)? This is the realm of the rule against hearsay.

As Professor Morgan observed, consistency would require that the answer to the previous questions be "never." "Consistency, however, is

271

not a characteristic of common law procedure. History, policy, and experience render impractical the application of the rules of formal logic." Morgan, Hearsay Dangers and the Application of the Hearsay Concept, 62 Harv. L. Rev. 177, 179 (1948). Moreover, some evidence that cannot be subjected to the normal truth-promoting devices may be superior to evidence that is subject to these devices. Furthermore, the choice is often between taking evidence as it is found — absent the normal safeguards applied to in-court testimony — or doing without it altogether. Thus, history, policy, experience, necessity, and perhaps logic convert the clearcut "never" into a confusing "sometimes."

Given the origins of the rule and the bases for its exceptions, application to concrete cases sometimes seems as much art as science. Nevertheless, it should be possible for students to develop an analytical approach to hearsay that (1) usually makes sense and (2) provides a methodology by which most hearsay problems can be quickly identified and resolved. The materials in this chapter are organized along the lines of the following suggested structure for dealing with hearsay problems:

(1) Decide if the offered evidence raises a hearsay issue;

(2) Decide if the offered evidence is hearsay. This involves consideration of

(a) What the evidence is offered to prove (relevancy);

(b) Whether the evidence is a "statement," i.e., an oral or written assertion or nonverbal conduct intended as an assertion;

(c) Whether the statement was made by someone other than the witness testifying at the hearing;

(d) Whether the statement is offered to prove the truth of the matter asserted;

(3) Decide if the evidence may be admitted for another, nonhearsay purpose;

(4) If the evidence is hearsay, decide if the evidence fits within one of the many hearsay exceptions; and

(5) Decide whether the evidence, even if it is not hearsay, ought to be excluded because of prejudice or constitutional considerations related to the policy behind the rule against hearsay.

The following problems and materials should stimulate students to consider the larger jurisprudential and policy questions raised by the hearsay doctrine. Does the hearsay doctrine promote the values it purports to serve? Is it based on valid assumptions about juror competence? Does it reflect a paternalistic, elitist view of society? Has the rule become so bulky and complex that it creates more problems than it solves? Is the doctrine merely a "glass-bead game" for trial lawyers or a self-protective mechanism for courts? Should the rule and exceptions be replaced by a unitary rule that gives the trial judge discretion to admit hearsay for whatever it is worth if, on balance, the evidence is more probative than prejudicial? For a provocative attempt to "rationalize the rule against hearsay" and a critique of the modern approach to hearsay contained in

the Federal Rules, see Note, The Theoretical Foundation of the Hearsay
Rules, 93 Harv. L. Rev. 1786 (1980), at page 412, below.

A. The Rule Against Hearsay

NOTE: THE TREASON TRIAL OF SIR WALTER RALEIGH

In a celebrated trial in 1603 Sir Walter Raleigh was accused of conspiracy to commit treason against the Crown by attempting to establish
Arabella Stuart as queen of England. At his trial the evidence consisted
primarily of a sworn "confession" by Lord Cobham, Raleigh's alleged co-
conspirator, before the Privy Council and a letter by Cobham. Raleigh
asserted that Cobham had recanted his confession and protested its
introduction:

> But it is strange to see how you press me still with my Lord Cobham, and yet
> will not produce him; . . . [H]e is in the house hard by, and may soon be
> brought hither; let him be produced, and if he will yet accuse me or avow this
> confession of his, it shall convict me and ease you of further proof.

Raleigh's Trial, 2 How. St. Tr. 16 (1603); 1 Jardine's Crim. Trials 418
(1832). The prosecution responded not by producing Cobham but by
calling a boat pilot named Dyer, who testified that while in Lisbon a
Portuguese gentleman told him, "Your king [James] shall never be
crowned for Don Cobham and Don Raleigh will cut his throat before he
come to be crowned." Raleigh protested this evidence on the ground
that, "This is the saying of some wild Jesuit or beggarly priest; but what
proof is it against me?" The prosecutor, Lord Coke, responded, "It must
perforce arise out of some preceding intelligence and shews that your
treason had wings." On this evidence Raleigh was convicted and executed. See 1 J. Stephen, A History of the Criminal Law of England 333-
336 (1883); 9 Holdsworth, A History of English Law 216-217, 226-228
(1926). J. G. Phillimore, History and Principles of the Law of Evidence
157 (1850).

What do the testimonies of Lord Cobham and Dyer have in common?
What infirmities, if any, does such evidence contain? Should such evidence be admissible in criminal or civil cases? Does it make a difference
whether other probative, corroborative evidence is introduced by live
witnesses who testify from their own observations? What values are implicated by the use of such evidence? Fairness? Reliability? Necessity?
Individual integrity?

Outrage at the injustice done to Raleigh contributed to the development of the hearsay rules and the constitutional rights of confrontation
and compulsory process. One of the puzzles of this subject is how hear-

say, confrontation, and compulsory process interrelate. For more on this, see Chapter V.

FRE 801(a), (b), (c)
Definitions

The following definitions apply under this article:

(a) *Statement.* A "statement" is (1) an oral or written assertion or (2) nonverbal conduct of a person, if it is intended by him as an assertion.

(b) *Declarant.* A "declarant" is a person who makes a statement.

(c) *Hearsay.* "Hearsay" is a statement, other than one made by the declarant while testifying at the trial or hearing, offered in evidence to prove the truth of the matter asserted.

Problem IV-1
Arsenic and Hors d'Oeuvres

Time: Christmas Eve. Place: the *D* family house. The *D* family consists of Mr. and Mrs. *D* and Mrs. *D*'s aged, invalid father. As usual *D* prepares pre-dinner drinks — martinis for his wife and father-in-law and a high-ball for himself. Since it is a special occasion, *D* also prepares hors d'oeuvres. But *D* does not eat any hors d'oeuvres himself. The next day his wife and father-in-law are found dead. An autopsy of the bodies and a chemical analysis of the martinis and hors d'oeuvres reveal traces of arsenic poisoning in the bodies, drinks, and food. *D* is charged with two counts of first-degree murder.

(1) At *D*'s trial suppose that the prosecution proves the above and then calls *W*, a salesman in the local drugstore, to testify that on December 24 he sold *D* a tube of rat poison. On *D*'s objection, what ruling and why?

(2) Suppose that *W* is alive and in court but the prosecution calls *S*, *W*'s sister, to testify that *W* told her on December 25 that *D* bought rat poison. On *D*'s objection, what ruling and why?

Problem IV-2
Murder at the Seaside Bistro

Charge: first-degree murder. M.O.: blowing *V*'s head off with a shotgun. Time: 10 A.M., June 1. The day after the murder Officer Kojak interviews *H*, the owner of the Seaside Bistro, in which the shooting occurred. In Kojak's presence *H* prepares and signs a statement that says, "I saw *D* shoot *V*."

At *D*'s trial the first witness is Kojak. Kojak identifies *H*'s written statement and says, "*H* is dead." *H*'s statement is offered. *D* objects. What ruling and why? Is *H*'s statement hearsay? If it is hearsay, should it be admitted nonetheless? If it is not hearsay, should it be excluded anyhow?

Problem IV-3
Assault on Massachusetts Avenue

Action for damages for assault. At trial, *P* testifies that she was driving down Massachusetts Avenue at 6 P.M. on June 1, and while she was stopped at a street light someone threw a brick through her car window. Although *P* did not see who hurled the brick, Andy, Bob, Cindy, and Dora were the only ones on the street at the time.

(1) *P* proposes to testify further that she stopped her car and Andy walked over to her and said, "*D* threw it, Lady." *D* objects. What ruling and why?

(2) Suppose that *P* proposes to testify that she stopped her car and asked Andy who threw the brick and Andy pointed to *D*. *D* objects. What ruling and why?

Problem IV-4
Murder in the Ajax Building

Time: June 1, 11:55 A.M. Place: room 1601 on the sixteenth floor of the Ajax Building. Room 1601 is a one-room office with one window. Outside the window on the ledge is a pigeon's nest containing freshly laid pigeon eggs. Several feet to the left of the window in room 1601 are two desks with typewriters and swivel chairs. There is also a copying machine several feet to the right of the window. At 11:59 A.M. there are four people in room 1601: Agnes, Belle, Claire, and David. Agnes and Belle are sitting in the swivel chairs at the two desks. Claire is standing on a chair at point *C*, leaning out the open window. David is at the copying machine. A schematic drawing of the noon scene looks like this:

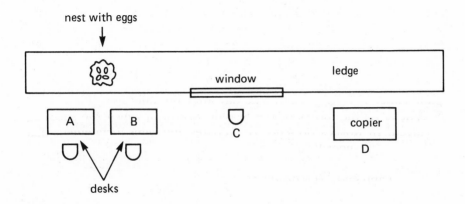

At 12:01 P.M. Claire's bruised, crushed, and dead body is in the street, lying face down in the gutter.

There are three possible explanations for Claire's change in position: (1) There was an accident; (2) she committed suicide; or (3) a homicide has occurred. The state decides that the third explanation is the most likely and indicts and tries David for Claire's murder.

(1) At David's trial the first witness for the prosecution is Scalpel, the coroner. Scalpel testifies that she took possession of Claire's body shortly after arriving on the scene. Scalpel then describes the condition of the body including the results of an autopsy. Among other things, the autopsy revealed that Claire was not pregnant at the time of her death.

(2) The second witness for the prosecution is Nosey. Nosey testifies that she works in room 1500 in the Babbo Building, which is directly across the street from the Ajax Building. Room 1500 is on the fifteenth floor of the Babbo Building, which puts it slightly below room 1601 of the Ajax Building. Nosey testifies that from room 1500 of the Babbo Building she has a good view of the window of room 1601 of the Ajax Building. Nosey further testifies that shortly before noon on June 1 she had her back to the window of room 1500 of the Babbo Building. She heard a scream, turned, and saw a body falling. She looked up at the window and saw what appeared to be the face of a man at the window of room 1601 of the Ajax Building. If you were defense counsel in this case, what type of questions would you want to ask Nosey on cross-examination?

(3) The third witness for the prosecution at David's trial is Officer Kojak. Kojak testifies that he is a member of the municipal homicide squad. He was assigned to investigate Claire's death. As part of his investigation, Kojak spoke to Agnes at 6 P.M. on June 1. Kojak proposes to testify that during this conversation Agnes told him that David shoved Claire, who then fell to her death. Defendant objects. What ruling and why? Is Kojak's proposed testimony hearsay? Should it be admitted anyhow? If it is not hearsay, should it nonetheless be excluded?

(4) The fourth witness for the prosecution is Belle. Belle testifies that she was in room 1601 at the time Claire fell to her death and that she saw what happened. Belle further testifies that she was interviewed by Kojak at her home at 7 P.M. on June 1. Belle testifies that during that interview she told Kojak that David pushed Claire out the window. Defendant objects and moves to strike. What ruling and why? Is Belle's testimony hearsay? If it is hearsay, should it be admitted anyhow? If it is not hearsay, should it nonetheless be excluded?

(5) The prosecution offers as People's Exhibit A a document found face up on the copying machine in room 1601 immediately after Claire's fall. The document is identified and authenticated as being in Claire's handwriting. It states:

Dear David,

I am three months pregnant by you. I will not place myself in the hands of a back-alley butcher. I will have the baby and sue you for support.

                                                              Love,
                                                              Claire   o k no t
                                                                                          H5
David objects to the admission of the exhibit. What ruling and why? Is   *no t for*
Exhibit *A* hearsay? If it is hearsay, should it be admitted anyhow? If it is   *trv/th*
not hearsay, should it nonetheless be excluded?

PARK, McCORMICK ON EVIDENCE AND THE CONCEPT OF HEARSAY: A CRITICAL ANALYSIS FOLLOWED BY SUGGESTIONS TO LAW TEACHERS
65 Minn. L. Rev. 423 (1981)

Definitions of hearsay are commonly either assertion-oriented or declarant-oriented. An assertion-oriented definition focuses on whether an out-of-court assertion will be used to prove the truth of what it asserts, while a declarant-oriented definition focuses on whether the use of the utterance will require reliance on the credibility of the out-of-court declarant.

The exposition of the concept of hearsay in *McCormick* draws on both of these traditions. The book defines hearsay as follows:

> Hearsay evidence is testimony in court, or written evidence, of a statement made out of court, the statement being offered as an assertion to show the truth of matters asserted therein, and thus resting for its value upon the credibility of the out-of-court asserter.

Although this definition is essentially assertion-oriented, the final clause introduces a declarant-oriented aspect by stating that when an utterance is offered for its truth, then it rests for value on the declarant's credibility. The text immediately following the definition goes further, and indicates that when an assertion is *not* offered for its truth, then it does not depend for value on the declarant's credibility. Taken together, these passages in *McCormick* suggest that the assertion-oriented and declarant-oriented definitions are functionally equivalent.

This suggestion is misleading, since choice of one definition over the other can lead to different results. An utterance offered as a falsehood provides the most vivid example. Suppose that *X* is charged with committing a crime in Boston. The police talk to *X*'s wife, who tells them that

X was with her in Denver on the day in question. The wife's statement is demonstrably false, and the prosecution seeks to use it against X for the inference that X's wife lied because she knew him to be guilty. Under an assertion-oriented definition, the wife's statement is not hearsay because it is not offered to prove the truth of the matter asserted. Under a declarant-oriented definition, however, the statement would be hearsay because the trier's use of it requires reliance on the wife's powers of memory, perception, and narration.[11]

McCormick itself deems certain utterances nonhearsay even though they depend for value upon the declarant's credibility. For example, the book states that the utterance "Harold is the finest of my sons," offered to prove that the declarant was fond of Harold, is nonhearsay because it is not offered to show the truth of its assertion. Under a declarant-oriented definition, however, the utterance would be hearsay because it rests on the declarant's sincerity and narrative ability.[13]

Problem IV-5
Hot Goods

Charge: knowingly receiving stolen goods (two diamond earrings) by D from Jenkens on June 1. At trial the prosecution makes out a prima facie case and rests. D proposes to testify that Jenkens gave him the diamond earrings on June 1, told D that he had bought them as an anniversary gift for his wife, and asked him to keep them until Mr. and Mrs. Jenkens's anniversary on June 7, so that Jenkens could surprise his wife. D further testifies that he believed Jenkens. The D.A. objects. What ruling and why? Is D's proposed testimony hearsay? If it is hearsay,

11. The wife might not have intended a cover-up; she may simply have been mistaken about the date of her husband's presence in Denver. Even if she intended to mislead the police because she believed her husband was guilty, her belief may have been based on a bare suspicion or an insane delusion. Alternatively, she may have misspoken, saying "June first" when she meant "July first." Thus, substantial reliance on her memory, perception, and narrative ability are required in order to reach the final inference that her husband is guilty. For examples of declarant-oriented definitions that would seem to classify the wife's utterance as hearsay, see R. Lempert & S. Saltzburg [A Modern Approach to Evidence 340-341 (1977)], at 340-45; Tribe [Triangulating Hearsay, 87 Harv. L. Rev. 957, 959 (1974)], at 959-60. See also Morgan [Hearsay Dangers and the Application of the Hearsay Concept, 62 Harv. L. Rev. 196-212 (1948)], at 218-19.

13. The utterance rests on the declarant's narrative ability because it loses value if the declarant meant to say "Arnold is the finest of my sons" or "Harold is the first of my sons." It rests on the declarant's sincerity because a deliberate lie about Harold's character, for example to his prospective employer, would undercut the inference that the declarant was especially fond of Harold. Another hearsay danger, ambiguity of inference, is also present because the declarant might genuinely believe that Harold is the finest, but might nevertheless be more fond of his youngest son Joe.

should it be admitted anyhow? If it is not hearsay, should it nonetheless be excluded?

Problem IV-6
The Case of the Loathsome Leper

Action for defamation. At trial, *P* is the first witness. *P* proposes to testify that *D* said, in the presence of several people, "*P* is now and has always been a loathsome leper." *D* objects. What ruling and why? Is *P* proposed testimony hearsay? If it is hearsay, should it be admitted anyhow? If it is not hearsay, should it nonetheless be excluded?

Problem IV-7
Deep Throat

Federal court action against Los Angeles Police Department officers for an injunction and declaratory relief arising out of the search and seizure of certain items from the plaintiff, the Hollywood Free Paper and Adult Cinema Cooperative. Plaintiff alleges that defendants' search and seizure violated the first and fourth amendments to the U.S. Constitution and the qualified journalist's privilege recognized by some members of the Supreme Court in Branzburg v. Hayes. In support of its motion for summary judgment, plaintiff submits an affidavit from Robert Woodstein, a reporter for the Washington Boast. Woodstein's affidavit states that press searches tend to chill confidential news sources in and out of government. The affidavit contains several examples in which Woodstein allegedly lost sources of his own after he was subpoenaed by the Attorney General and forced to disclose the identity of Deep Throat, a source for a particularly sensitive story that died when the Attorney General's subpoena was served. Defendants object and move to strike the affidavits on the grounds of hearsay. What ruling and why?

TRIBE, TRIANGULATING HEARSAY
87 Harv. L. Rev. 957, 957-961 (1974)

While another elaborate argument for the reform of hearsay law might be in order, the purpose of this Comment is a more modest one. It will present a heuristic device which I believe can aid in the analysis of the hearsay rule and its exceptions by exposing the rule's structure and the underlying values at stake. The goal, in the first instance, is to assist students of the law in understanding an otherwise complex area. No less important, by directing the attention of students, practitioners, and judges toward structure and policy and away from cookbook formulas of rule and exception, the device may dramatize the inconsistencies and oddities that pervade hearsay law. And that may be a first step to future reform.

I. THE TESTIMONIAL TRIANGLE

The basic hearsay problem is that of forging a reliable chain of inferences, from an act or utterance of a person not subject to contemporaneous in-court cross-examination about that act or utterance, to an event that the act or utterance is supposed to reflect. Typically, the first link in the required chain of inferences is the link from the act or utterance to the belief it is thought to express or indicate. It is helpful to think of this link as involving a "trip" into the head of the person responsible for the act or utterance (the declarant) to see what he or she was really thinking when the act occurred. The second link is the one from the declarant's assumed belief to a conclusion about some external event that is supposed to have triggered the belief, or that is linked to the belief in some other way. This link involves a trip out of the head of the declarant, in order to match the declarant's assumed belief with the external reality sought to be demonstrated.

The trier must obviously employ such a chain of inferences whenever a witness testifies in court. But the process has long been regarded as particularly suspect when the act or utterance is not one made in court, under oath, by a person whose demeanor at the time is witnessed by the trier, and under circumstances permitting immediate cross-examination by counsel in order to probe possible inaccuracies in the inferential chain. These inaccuracies are usually attributed to the four testimonial infirmities of ambiguity, insincerity, faulty perception, and erroneous memory. In the absence of special reasons, the perceived untrustworthiness of such an out-of-court act or utterance has led the Anglo-Saxon legal system to exclude it as hearsay despite its potentially probative value.

There exists a rather simple way of schematizing all of this in terms of an elementary geometric construct that serves to structure its several related elements. The construct might be called "the testimonial triangle." By making graphic the path of inferences, and by functionally grouping problems encountered along the path, the triangle makes it easier both to identify when a hearsay problem exists and to structure consideration of the appropriateness of exceptions to the rule that bars hearsay inferences.

The diagram is as follows:

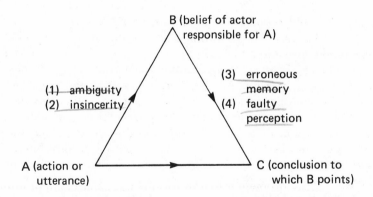

If we use the diagram to trace the inferential path the trier must follow, we begin at the lower left vertex of the triangle (*A*), which represents the declarant's (*X*'s) act or assertion. The path first takes us to the upper vertex (*B*), representing *X*'s belief in what his or her act or assertion suggests, and then takes us to the lower right vertex (*C*), representing the external reality suggested by *X*'s belief. When "A" is used to prove "C" along the path through "B," a traditional hearsay problem exists and the use of the act or assertion as evidence is disallowed upon proper objection in the absence of some special reason to permit it.

It is of course a simple matter to locate the four testimonial infirmities on the triangle to show where and how they might impede the process of inference. To go from "A" to "B," the declarant's belief, one must remove the obstacles of (1) ambiguity and (2) insincerity. To go from "B" to "C," the external fact, one must further remove the obstacles of (3) erroneous memory and (4) faulty perception.

When it is possible to go directly from "A" to "C" with no detour through "B," there is no hearsay problem unless the validity of the trier's conclusion depends upon an implicit path through "B."[9] Suppose, for example, that the issue in a lawsuit is whether the Government took adequate safety precautions in connection with the nuclear test at Amchitka in 1971. James Schlesinger, then Chairman of the Atomic Energy

ex

9. An uncompromising behaviorist might insist that no detour through mental states is ever necessary because every trip from an act or utterance "A" to a conclusion "C" is reducible to a circumstantial inference about the statistical frequency with which "C" is present when "A" is present. There are difficulties with accepting the behaviorist perspective as a coherent one. See Chomsky, A Review of B. F. Skinner's Verbal Behavior, 35 Language 26 (1959); Chomsky, The Case Against B. F. Skinner, New York Review of Books, Dec. 30, 1971, at 18. But even if one does adopt such a perspective, it does not follow that the trier's way of using the evidence "A" will in fact mirror that perspective, for the trier is likely to reason about states of mind even if it is in some sense incorrect or unnecessary to do so. Moreover, the connection between "A" and "C" may well be such that the frequency with which the latter accompanies the former depends upon the actor's testimonial capacities so that, even from a behaviorist perspective, information about a declarant's use of language, tendency to lie, eyesight, and so forth, may increase or decrease the statistical correlation between the utterance and the fact reported.

Commission, "told reporters at Elmendorf Air Force Base outside Anchorage that he was taking his wife . . . and daughters . . . with him [to the site of the Amchitka blast] in response to Alaska Gov. William E. Egan's invitation. Egan strongly disapprove[d] of the test." In these circumstances, the trip from "A," the Chairman's proposed travel with his family to the site of the blast, to "C," the conclusion that the blast was reasonably safe, may appear at first to be purely "circumstantial," but in fact that trip requires a journey into the Chairman's head and out again — a journey through the belief "B" suggested by his willingness to be near the blast with his family. The journey from "A" to "B" involves problems of possible ambiguity and of insincerity in that the Chairman was apparently seeking to dispel fears of danger, so that his act may not bespeak an actual belief in the test's safety. And the journey from "B" to "C" involves problems of memory and perception in that he may not have recalled all the relevant data and may have misperceived such data in the first instance, so that his belief in the test's safety, even if we assume the journey from "A" to "B" safely completed, may not correspond to the facts sought to be demonstrated. On both legs of the triangle, therefore, there are testimonial infirmities that cross-examination contemporaneous with the act "A" could help to expose.

By contrast, when the trier's inference can proceed from "A" directly to "C," the infirmities of hearsay do not arise. . . .

Problem IV-8
The "Corn-Crib" Case

Plaintiff Hanson owned and leased a farm to Schrik. Under the lease, Schrik was to pay Hanson 2/5 of the corn grown in return for the use of the land. In other words, Schrik was a sharecropper. To obtain money for seed and fertilizer, Schrik gave a mortgage to defendant bank on his share of the crops. The bottom fell out of the corn market, and Schrik's tenant's mortgaged property was sold at auction by the bank with his permission. At this sale a crib of corn containing 393 bushels was sold by the bank to defendant Johnson. Hanson contended that this corn was his share of the crop and thus that it had been converted by defendants.

In an effort to prove that the corn was part of his share, Hanson testified, over the objection of hearsay and self-serving, that when Schrik was about through husking corn he was on the farm and the tenant pointed out the corn in question and said: "Mr. Hanson, here is your corn for this year, this double crib here and this single crib here is your share for this year's corn; this belongs to you, Mr. Hanson." A bystander was called and against the same objection testified to having heard the talk in substantially the same language.

(1) Is plaintiff's proposed testimony hearsay? If it is, should it be admitted anyhow? If it is not, should it nonetheless be excluded?

(2) What if plaintiff called another bystander to testify that after the tenant had husked the corn, tenant said to the second bystander, out of the presence of Hanson, "This double crib here and this single crib here is Mr. Hanson's share for this year's corn; this belongs to him." Would this testimony be hearsay?

Problem IV-9
Contractual Terms as Hearsay

Action for the purchase price of a television set bought by D from the Acme TV Company. P's complaint alleges the following:

(1) Acme sold and delivered a television to D on June 1 on credit;

(2) D has failed to pay for the television in breach of the credit agreement;

(3) Acme assigned its claim to P on September 1;

(4) On September 15 P demanded payment from D; D refused; and

(5) P's claim is now due and unpaid, whereby P demands judgment for the purchase price.

D's answer alleges that P is not the real party in interest. At trial, P testifies that on September 1 he proposed to Acme that Acme assign its claim to him and that Acme then executed a document marked Plaintiff's Exhibit 1 for identification. Exhibit 1 states: "Acme TV Company hereby assigns its claim against D to P for good and valuable consideration." D objects and moves to strike P's testimony and to exclude Exhibit 1. What ruling and why?

Problem IV-10
Assault of V

Charge: assault of V on June 1. At D's trial for this offense, three years later, the state calls Officer Friday to testify that he arrived on the scene shortly after the assault and that V pointed out D from among a group of men on the other side of the street and said, "D is your man." D objects on grounds of hearsay. What ruling and why?

Compare this case with the corn-crib case, Problem IV-8 above. For purposes of hearsay analysis, how does the evidence in this case differ from the evidence in the corn-crib case? If this evidence is hearsay, should it be admitted anyhow?

Problem IV-11
Trespass Per Quod Servitium

Action for damages to P's child, C, which allegedly occurred when D struck C, causing C to suffer permanent paralysis of her vocal chords. D's answer is a general denial. In the second week of trial, D offers W to testify that the day before he heard C say, "I can speak." P objects. What ruling and why? What if W proposes to testify that he heard C say, "Don't step on a crack or you'll break your mother's back"?

not offered for truth OK

Problem IV-12
The Dissatisfied Purchaser

P, administrator of Sucker's estate, v. Desert Land Co. for a return of the down payment made by Sucker on real estate located in the Mojave Desert, California, and sold by Desert. At trial, P offers two exhibits:

(1) *P1*, an advertisement from the New York Times for Mojave Garden Lots. The ad says, "Make a down payment to reserve your lot and pay later by installments. If you inspect your lot within 90 days and state your dissatisfaction to us and ask for your down payment back, it will be returned, no questions asked."

(2) *P2*, a letter from Sucker to Desert Land that says, "I have inspected my lot. I am dissatisfied. I demand my money back."

Defendant objects to the introduction of the exhibits. Are they hearsay? If so, should they be admitted anyhow? If not, should they be excluded anyhow?   *also not for truth*

Problem IV-13
Captain Cook and Davey Jones

Action for loss of P's goods when D Shipping Company's ship went down in calm waters off Liverpool. P alleges that D's ship was not seaworthy. D generally denies. At trial, D offers evidence that Captain Cook, a sea captain with 30-years' experience, inspected every part of its ship before setting sail on it with his own family on board. P objects. What ruling and why? Is this evidence hearsay? If so, should it be admitted anyhow? If not, should it nonetheless be excluded?

like Schlesinger N6

FALKNOR, THE "HEAR-SAY" RULE AS A "SEE-DO" RULE: EVIDENCE OF CONDUCT
33 Rocky Mt. L. Rev. 133-138 (1960)

It is time to go to lunch. When you left home for the office in the morning it was raining and you brought your umbrella. Will you need it at lunchtime? You consult your secretary, she looks out the window, and tells you that you had better take your umbrella. If, in some subsequent litigation, the question should arise whether it was raining when you went out to lunch, would the secretary be permitted to testify that when she looked out she saw a number of passers-by with their umbrellas up? More precisely, would her testimony as to what she *saw* these people *do* ~~not~~ be equated to what she would have *heard* them *say*, had she called out, ~~asserne~~ asked them whether it was raining, and they had replied that it was?

Uggh

Or, take another one: You drive up to signal-controlled intersection and pull up behind a large truck and trailer which has stopped at the near side of the intersection. The truck and trailer block your view of the traffic light. In a moment or so the truck moves ahead and you follow it. If, in subsequent litigation, the question arises whether the light had changed to green when you started up, may you testify, as tending to show that the light had changed, that the truck driver had moved ahead *No* before you did? More precisely, would your testimony as to what you *saw* the truck driver *do*, be equated to what you would have *heard* him *say* had he, before moving ahead, called back to tell you that the light had changed?

Of course, if, in either of these supposititious situations, the conduct proposed to be shown is to be treated as merely equivalent to an assertion of the fact the evidence is offered to establish, we are in trouble with the hearsay rule. And by many cases (probably in most of those where the hearsay question has been identified and raised) evidence of extra-judicial conduct, relevant only as an "implied assertion" of the fact the evidence is offered to prove, is within the hearsay ban. Put otherwise, where evidence of non-verbal conduct is relevant only as supporting inferences from the conduct to the belief of the actor and thence to the truth of his belief, prevailing doctrine stigmatizes the evidence as hearsay, inadmissible unless accommodated within one of the exceptions to the rule. Thus, it seems quite correct to say that in situations of this sort, the "hear-say" rule actually operates as a "see-do" rule.

In the instances supposed, the conduct offered to be proven was completely "non-verbal"; but an identical problem arises where the conduct, although "verbal," is relevant, not as tending to prove the truth of what was said, but circumstantially, that is, as manifesting a belief in the existence of the fact the evidence is offered to prove. As a matter of fact the leading case equating an "implied" to an "express" assertion and thus stigmatizing the evidence as hearsay, concerned the admissibility, in a will contest, of evidence of the writing of a letter to the testator by the vicar of the parish about a matter of consequence, relevant not as evidence of the truth of anything in the letter, but as manifesting the vicar's apparent belief in the testator's mental competency as tending to prove competency.

And in a Texas case, where defendant was charged with stealing his grandmother's cow which he admittedly sold while she was away, his defense being that she had authorized him to sell the cow, evidence (offered by the prosecution) that on her return home she demanded of the purchaser the cow rather than the balance of the purchase price, was

ex

held inadmissible as hearsay; it amounted merely to her extra-judicial "implied" assertion that she had not authorized the sale. A similar question has arisen in prosecutions for the maintenance of a betting establishment when the prosecution has offered to prove incoming telephone calls, during the raid, by callers seeking to place bets. Here again, while the conduct sought to be shown is "verbal," relevancy does not depend on a direct hearsay use of the utterances but only upon acceptance of the calls as "implied" assertions of the character of the place to which the calls were directed.

The same problem arises with respect to evidence of "non-action" or "silence" when relevant as justifying inferences from the non-action of the individual to his apparent belief and thence to the truth of that belief. While there is a division of authority with respect to the applicability of the hearsay rule to evidence of this sort, it is undoubtedly correct to say that in most cases where the hearsay objection has been urged, it has been sustained. The typical case has to do with the admissibility, on an issue of the quality of goods, of evidence of the failure of other purchasers to complain.

In any of these situations, the hearsay objection is likely to be overlooked. This is especially so when the evidence concerns "nonverbal" conduct because the hearsay rule is almost always, in the abstract, phrased in terms of "statements" or "utterances" and the possible application of the rule to "conduct" may not be immediately apparent. And the same is true, although perhaps to a lesser degree, when the evidence is of "verbal" conduct relevant only circumstantially. Cases are legion consequently where the hearsay objection, with strong supporting authority, might have been raised but was not.

But ought the hearsay rule be deemed applicable to evidence of conduct? As McCormick has observed, the problem "has only once received any adequate discussion in any decided case," i.e., in Wright v. Tatham, already referred to. And even in that case the court did not pursue its inquiry beyond the point of concluding that evidence of an "implied" assertion would be inadmissible. But as has been pointed out more than once (although I find no *judicial* recognition of the difference), the "implied" assertion is, from the hearsay standpoint, not nearly as vulnerable as an express assertion of the fact which the evidence is offered to establish.

This is on the assumption that the conduct was "non-assertive"; that the passers-by had their umbrellas up for the sake of keeping dry, not for the purpose of telling anyone it was raining; that the truck driver started up for the sake of resuming his journey, not for the purpose of telling anyone that the light had changed; that the vicar wrote the letter to the testator for the purpose of settling the dispute with the latter, rather than with any idea of expressing his opinion of the testator's sanity. And in the typical "conduct as hearsay" case this assumption will be quite justifiable.

On this assumption, it is clear that evidence of conduct must be taken as freed from at least one of the hearsay dangers, i.e., mendacity. A man does not lie to himself. Put otherwise, if in doing what he does a man has no intention of asserting the existence or non-existence of a fact, it would appear that the trustworthiness of evidence of this conduct is the same whether he is an egregious liar or a paragon of veracity. Accordingly, the lack of opportunity for cross-examination in relation to his veracity or lack of it, would seem to be of no substantial importance. Accordingly, the usual judicial disposition to equate the "implied" to the "express" assertion is very questionable.

This is not to say that the "implied" assertion is completely free of hearsay infirmities or that cross-examination of the individual would not be helpful. His opportunity to observe the event or condition in question, the quality of the sense-impressions which he received, and of his recollection, are all matters which bear upon the trustworthiness of his conduct, and, ideally, these ought to be subject to being probed by cross-examination. Nonetheless, the absence of the danger of misrepresentation does work strongly in favor of by-passing the hearsay objection, at least where the evidence of conduct is cogently probative. And it will be, where the action taken was important to the individual in his own affairs, e.g., the action of the vicar in communicating with the testator, the action of the truck driver in moving ahead. . . .

Accordingly, it has sometimes been suggested, that the admissibility of evidence of non-assertive conduct should depend on a preliminary finding by the judge that the conduct was of a sort "as to give reasonable assurance of trustworthiness," that is to say, that it was of substantial importance to the actor in his own affairs. But for application in the "heat and hurry" of the trial, such a solution leaves a good deal to be desired. As Thayer observed, "we should have a system of evidence, simple, aiming straight at the substance of justice, not nice or refined in its details, not too rigid, easily grasped and easily applied."

The "simple, easily grasped and easily applied" rule, "not nice or refined in its details," would seem to be one which would eliminate completely the hearsay stigma from evidence of non-assertive conduct. Because such conduct is evidently more dependable than an assertion, there is rational basis for the differentiation. And there is a cogent practical argument for such a rule in the circumstance that experience has shown that very often, probably more often than not, and understandably, the hearsay objection to evidence of non-assertive conduct is overlooked in practice with the result that the present doctrine operates very unevenly.

Such is the solution proposed by the [Federal] Rules of Evidence. . . . Non-assertive conduct is excluded from the definition of hearsay. Precisely, a statement (so as to be subject to the hearsay ban) would include only "non-verbal conduct of a person intended by him as a substitute for words in expressing the matter stated." This, it seems clear, would operate to eliminate the hearsay stigma from evidence of conduct unless it appeared to the judge that what was done was done for the sake of asserting the fact the evidence is now offered to establish.

This does not mean that all non-assertive conduct would be provable. There would remain the question of relevancy; and even though the evidence appeared to possess some slight probative value, it would be subject to exclusion under Uniform Rule 45 if the judge concluded that probative value was "substantially out-weighed" by the "counter-factors" enumerated in that rule: that to receive the evidence would take more time than it is worth, that it would confuse the issues, mislead the jury, create undue prejudice or unfairly surprise the opponent. . . .

Problem IV-14
Hot Pursuit?

At 11:30 P.M. Dr. and Mrs. David Alberstrom returned to their suburban Washington home from a night at the opera. As Dr. Alberstrom entered the living room, he was attacked by a knife-wielding man coming from the dining room. Dr. Alberstrom and the stranger struggled for some minutes, but the intruder escaped, leaving the doctor wounded on the floor. Mrs. Alberstrom rushed to help her husband. She noticed that he had been stabbed and was bleeding. They got into their car to go to the hospital, with the doctor behind the steering wheel. Proceeding down the country road leading from the Alberstrom house, the doctor noticed a man running along the side of the road. As the car drew even with the man, it swerved sharply to the right, striking the man and coming to rest in a ditch at the side of the road. Dr. Alberstrom was slumped over the wheel unconscious. An ambulance called to the scene took both Dr. Alberstrom and the injured pedestrian to the hospital. Dr. Alberstrom died of his knife wounds without regaining consciousness. The pedestrian recovered from his injuries and was subsequently charged with attempted robbery and the murder of Dr. Alberstrom.

At defendant's trial the prosecution offers Mrs. Alberstrom's testimony to the above on the issue of the identity of the knife-wielding intruder. Defendant objects. What ruling and why? What result if Mrs. Alberstrom's proffered testimony included Dr. Alberstrom's exclaiming "That's him!" just before the car swerved into the defendant?

Problem IV-15
Black Crepe

(1) Action against *D* Insurance Company to recover on a life insurance policy on Howard's life. The policy expired midnight May 31. Howard's death occurred the week of May 31, but there is a disputed

issue of fact as to whether death occurred prior to or after May 31. At trial, P calls White to testify that on the afternoon of May 31 he saw the doorway to Howard's house hung with black crepe and bedecked with white lilies.

(2) At trial, P calls Weir to testify that he saw Dr. Munroe, Howard's attending physician, examine Howard on May 31 and then pull the bed sheet up over Howard's head.

Problem IV-16
More Conduct as Hearsay

(1) If it becomes important in a lawsuit to prove that the first serve in a tennis tournament was "in" rather than a "fault," would evidence that the receiver of the serve moved to the other side of the court to receive the next serve be hearsay?

(2) If an issue in a lawsuit were whether Charles was insane, would it be hearsay to offer evidence that Charles was committed to an insane asylum?

(3) If the issue in a lawsuit were whether Testator was sane, would evidence that A, B, and C had written business letters to Testator be hearsay? If the issue in a lawsuit were whether Patient had cancer, would evidence that Patient was receiving cobalt treatments be hearsay?

(4) If the issue in a lawsuit were Testator's sanity, would evidence that Testator said "I am the Pope" be hearsay? See E. Morgan, Basic Problems of Evidence 248-249.

(5) Without regard to whether the evidence in any of the above cases technically is hearsay, *should* such evidence be admitted?

Problem IV-17
The Fertilizer Case

Action for breach of contract. P alleges that he put fertilizer on D's land and that D has refused to pay. D denies he contracted with P for the fertilizer; rather, the contract was with S. At trial, D offers to prove that S demanded payment from him for application of the fertilizer. Hearsay?

Problem IV-18
The Devoted Wife's Will

Action for wrongful death of P's wife, W. Defense: Liability is admitted, but the probability that P would have received any pecuniary benefits from *W* is in issue on damages. At trial, *D* offers *W*'s will, executed by *W* four months prior to her death. *W*'s will states in part:

> Whereas I have been a loving and devoted wife to my husband and he has returned my love with acts of infidelity, cruelty and indifference, I leave him one cent.

Is *W*'s will admissible?

Problem IV-19
Ptomaine Poisoning at the Greasy Spoon

Action against the Greasy Spoon Restaurant. *P* claims she was served spoiled baked beans by the Greasy Spoon on June 1 and got ptomaine poisoning as a result. At trial defendant offers to prove that the Greasy Spoon had a large pot of beans in the kitchen on June 1, that *P* was served from this pot, that at least 20 other Greasy Spoon patrons were served from the same pot, and that the Greasy Spoon received no other complaints. *P* objects. What ruling and why? What is the nature of the hearsay problem presented by this case? What result under the Federal Rules?

SILVER v. NEW YORK CENTRAL RAILROAD COMPANY
329 Mass. 14 (1952)

WILKINS, J. On January 14, 1948, Frances Silver became a passenger, bound from Boston to Cincinnati, on a train operated by the defendant railroad. The following morning the Pullman car in which she had a berth was detached at Cleveland and stood for nearly four hours in the yard to await connection with the next train to Cincinnati. She was suffering from a circulatory ailment known as Raynaud's disease. The temperature in the car became too cold for her, and she experienced ill effects. Mrs. Silver, who will be referred to as the plaintiff, brought this action against the defendant railroad and The Pullman Company. . . .

Certain basic facts are not in dispute. The plaintiff, who was 58 years of age, boarded the train at Boston, on January 14, 1948, at 4:50 P.M. She occupied a lower berth in the rear car, which was the only through car to Cincinnati. The train was scheduled to arrive in Cleveland at 6:20 A.M. the following day, but did not do so until 8:40 A.M., too late for the intended connection for Cincinnati. This necessitated a lay-over in Cleveland until the next train for Cincinnati, which left at 12:30 P.M. In Cleveland the weather bureau records show that the temperature at 5:35 A.M. was one degree below zero Fahrenheit and 26 degrees above zero at

Silver v NYCRR   C13290
              NY 1952

evid that other pax
did not complain that
car was too cold
properly admitted

R / reasonable inference
based on common experience

9 P.M. The plaintiff reached Cincinnati without further event, but because of her tendency to develop Raynaud's syndrome and the exposure to cold in Cleveland the condition of her hands required that she be hospitalized. . . .

Findings as to the plaintiff's experience at Cleveland could have been based upon statements she had made before suit was brought. She woke up about 9 A.M. because she was cold. She rang for the porter but no one came. She was alone in the car, which was standing in the yard and not at a platform. The station was inaccessible. She went to the washroom and got dressed. She "had to bundle up with her coat and furs," and put on a pair of woolen gloves. She rang twice more. Still no one came. She thought that the temperature was below freezing. She was extremely cold. She went back to her berth. The car remained in the same condition until connected with the Cincinnati train after 12 P.M. At that time the temperature outside was 10 to 15 degrees, and the car had been "without any heat whatsoever" for about three hours with that temperature outside. . . .

As part of its obligation to furnish suitable accommodations, it is the undoubted duty of a common carrier to provide the heat necessary for the health, comfort, and safety of passengers during the performance of the transportation contract. . . .

The porter in the plaintiff's car was rightly allowed to testify as to the temperature conditions in that car. He was giving at first hand his experience with the same conditions which confronted the plaintiff. But he was not permitted to give evidence that eleven other passengers in that car made no complaint to him as to the temperature while at Cleveland. This is a somewhat different proposition, as it was sought to draw from the silence of those passengers a deduction that the car was not too cold, otherwise they would have spoken. In certain courts evidence of absence of complaints by customers has been excluded on the issue of defective quality of goods sold, and the hearsay rule has been relied upon or referred to. . . .

Evidence as to absence of complaints from customers other than the plaintiff has been admitted in . . . cases, . . . relating to breach of warranty in the sale of food, in this Commonwealth. . . . In Landfield v. Albiani Lunch Co., 268 Mass. 528, the plaintiff alleged that he had been made ill by eating beans purchased at the defendant's restaurant. Subject to his exception, evidence was admitted that on that day and on the day preceding no complaint as to the beans was made by any other customer. In upholding the ruling on evidence, it was said, "The fact that others than the plaintiff ate the food complained of without . . effects is competent evidence that it was not unwholesome. . . . There is a reasonable inference based on common experience that one who ate and suffered as he believed in consequence would make complaint. There is a further reasonable inference, based on logic, that if no one complained no one suffered. Obviously, the latter conclusion is not convincing that the food was wholesome, unless one is satisfied that both plaintiff and others ate of it. Evidence of no complaint is too remote and should not be admitted unless, in addition to the fact that no complaints were made, there is evidence of circumstances indicating that others similarly situated ate and had opportunity for complaining." . . .

In the case at bar, should the circumstances of the plaintiff and of the other passengers as to exposure to the cold be shown to be substantially the same, the negative evidence that none of the others spoke of it to the porter might properly be admitted. The evidence would not be equivocal, and would then be offered on the basis of a common condition which all in the car encountered. The porter's duties should be shown to include the receipt of that sort of complaints from those passengers. It should appear that he was present and available to be spoken to, and that it was not likely that complaints were made by these passengers to other employees of the railroad or the sleeping car company. This would not seem to be a situation where one might prefer to remain silent rather than to make any statement. Indeed, if the car was too cold, ordinary prudence might seem to require that one speak out. There would be no ambiguity of inference. There would be at least as strong a case for admissibility as in the food cases, and a far stronger one than those relating to the sale of allegedly defective goods in which little may be known of the terms of sale to the noncomplaining buyers. Unlike the unknown users of a stairway in a business block, the uniform result of silence in the cases of a large number of passengers, here apparently eleven, would not be inconclusive. See Falknor, Silence as Hearsay, 89 U. of Pa. L. Rev. 192. Exceptions sustained.

Problem IV-20
"Palming Off"

P Knife Manufacturing Company v. *D* Knife Manufacturing Company for *D*'s alleged unfair methods of competition in "palming off" a knife made by *D* to look like *P*'s knife. *D* denies generally. At trial, *P* offers a letter it received from the National Business Gifts Company, a jobber of pocket knives, which states, "We did not find this knife in the catalogue but are sure you made it." The enclosed knife was manufactured by *D*. Admissible?

Problem IV-21
"Thieves Will Out"

Charge: murder in the first degree. M.O.: shotgun blast in the face. Defense: alibi. At *D*'s trial the government calls *W* to testify that just before the shooting, the victim, *V*, handed him a slip of paper with *D*'s nickname and telephone number on it. *V* told *W* to call the police if *V* were not home by 3 P.M. the next day and give the police the slip of paper. *D* objects to *W*'s proposed testimony and to the introduction of the slip of paper. What ruling and why? Would the case for admission be stronger or weaker if the defense were self-defense or accident?

skip

UNITED STATES v. DAY
591 F.2d 861 (D.C. Cir. 1978)

MACKINNON, C.J. On appeal, the Government challenges the district court's ruling insofar as it applied to three items relative to this series of events, all of which were excluded by the court:

(1) The fact that decedent gave Mason a slip of paper upon which he had written "Beanny, Eric, 635-3135" and told Mason "if he [Williams] wasn't back home by three the next day to call the police and tell them what he had told me and give them the number."

(2) Decedent's statement to Mason the decedent and "Beanny" (i.e., Day) had a fight over guns and coats and that Beanny and "his boy" were trying to "get out on him" over the guns and leather coats. . . .

We note at the outset that the district court expressed concern on the question of whether Mason was a credible witness. . . . However, the court plainly did not find that this witness was *incompetent* to testify. Rather, the court appears simply to have been giving its own views on the credibility of the witness. The opinions which the trial court holds as to credibility do not constitute valid reason for withholding otherwise admissible evidence. While the competency of a witness to testify before a jury is a threshold question of law committed to the trial court's discretion, and which will not be set aside unless clear error appears, it remains for the jury to assess the credibility of the witness and the weight to be given his testimony. We are satisfied that the district court did not exclude this evidence *because* it thought the witness lacked credibility. Rather, the court was principally concerned with hearsay problems and questions of relevancy and prejudice, and it is on those issues that the proper resolution of this phase of the case depends. . . .

B. WILLIAMS' STATEMENT ACCOMPANYING DELIVERY OF THE SLIP OF PAPER

We turn first to the Government's contention in their brief and at oral argument that the following testimony should be admitted: the fact that Williams gave Mason a slip of paper, the writing on that paper, and the contemporaneous statement that if he (Williams) was not home by 3:00 o'clock the next day, Mason should call the police, tell them what he had said, and give the number.

The Government, in arguing this point, does not seek to have admitted the content of "what he (Williams) had said," concerning the statements made prior to giving Mason the slip of paper about the fight and the dispute between him and Day, the robbery, and the location of the guns.

In arguing that the statement which immediately accompanied the delivery of the slip of paper is not hearsay, the Government states: "All that is sought to be proven in connection with the statement now under consideration is that it was *in fact* made." But in actuality, the Government seeks to have something more inferred from the content of the statement. The jury is being asked to infer from Williams' words that Day bore ill will toward Williams and had reason to cause him harm. Because this inference attaches to Williams' statement, the Government is seeking to use the statement for more than the mere fact that it was made.

The Government also contends that this statement is admissible as an utterance contemporaneous with a non-verbal act which relates to and elucidates that event, i.e., the giving of the piece of paper. Professor Wigmore has described the limitations which attended the use of utterances forming the verbal part of an act. The first limitation is:

> [T]he conduct that is to be made definite must be independently material and provable under the issues, either as a fact directly in issue or as incidentally or evidentially relevant to the issue. The use of the words is wholly subsidiary and appurtenant to the use of the conduct. The former without the latter have no place in the case, and could only serve as a hearsay assertion in direct violation of the rule. . . .

VI Wigmore on Evidence, §1773, at 268 (Chadbourn rev. 1976). In this case, the conduct to be made definite is that Williams gave Mason a slip of paper. Had Williams said "take this slip," that utterance would have been "wholly subsidiary and appurtenant" to the conduct. Here, Williams said more, and the inference from those words is not wholly incidental to the conduct. We conclude that the statement accompanying the delivery of the paper is inadmissible hearsay.

Our analysis does not end here, as Rule 803(3) provides an exception for evidence of state of mind. That rule provides:

> The following are not excluded by the hearsay rule, even though the declarant is available as witness: . . .
>
> (3) *Then existing mental, emotional or physical condition.* A statement of the declarant's then existing *state of mind*, emotion, sensation, or physical condition (such as intent, plan, motive, design, *mental feeling*, pain and bodily health), but not including a statement of memory or belief to prove the fact remembered or believed unless it relates to the execution, revocation, identification, or terms of declarant's will. [Emphasis added.]

We briefly summarized the purpose of the exception in United States v. Brown, 160 U.S. App. D.C. 190, 490 F.2d 758 (1970): "[T]he state of mind exception to the hearsay rule allows the admission of extrajudicial statements to show the state of mind of the declarant at that time *if that is the issue in the case*. . . . It also allows such statements to show a future intent of the declarant to perform an act if the occurrence of that act is at issue." 160 U.S. App. D.C. at 194, 490 F.2d at 762 (emphasis added). We noted that such statements invariably contain some extraneous factual elements which necessitate limiting instructions to ensure that the statements are considered solely on the issue of the declarant's mental state and not for the truth of the matters contained therein. 160 U.S. App. D.C. at 195, 490 F.2d at 763. We also noted that whether such evidence is admissible is subject to the rule of extrinsic policy, which is now embodied in Rule 403: "[S]ome evidence, while bearing some *logical* relevance to the case, may in the discretion of the judge nevertheless be excluded where its probative value is substantially outweighed by the danger of *unfair* prejudice, confusion or delay." Id. (emphasis in original except "unfair").[40] While Williams' statements to Mason are some indication of his state of mind, i.e. to fear of the future, there is a danger that the jury would misuse such evidence. . . .

We think that the inference to be drawn from Williams' statement to Mason which accompanied his handing over of the slip of paper, involving as it did somewhat of a prophecy of what might happen to him, has too great a potential for *unfair* prejudice, and we do not think that a limiting instruction can correct that deficiency. As was the case in *Brown*, the prejudicial dangers in the statement in question are substantial. Had Williams referred to prior harmful acts or threats by Day, such statements would be even more unfairly prejudicial, but even here "a palpable danger exists" that the jury will infer from the statement, "if anything happens to me, call the police and give them the names on this slip [i.e., Day and Sheffey]," that Day and Sheffey were capable of murder, or that they had done things in the past to justify Williams' apprehension. Such inferences insofar as they reflect on defendants' intentions or past conduct would be improperly drawn. See 160 U.S. App. D.C. at 210, 490 F.2d at 778. In fact, on the present record,

---

40. We elaborated upon these dangers later in the opinion: "Quite a number of courts have confronted facts similar to those here involving hearsay statements made by the victim of a homicide which inferentially implicate the defendant. Such statements by the victims often include previous threats made by the defendant towards the victim, narrations of past incidents of violence on the part of the defendant or general verbalizations of fear of the defendant. While such statements are admittedly of some value in presenting to the jury a complete picture of all of the facts and circumstances surrounding the homicide, it is generally agreed that their admissibility must be determined by a careful balancing of their probative value against their prejudicial effect. Courts have recognized that such statements are fraught with inherent dangers and require the imposition of rigid limitations." 160 U.S. App. D.C. at 197-98, 490 F.2d at 765-66.

Williams' state of mind, from which such inferences would be drawn, is immaterial. Of course, the situation will be different if the defendant seeks to adduce evidence tending to show self-defense or accident. Under the present circumstances of this case, we find the proffered evidence in this regard to be inadmissible at the outset of the Government's case in chief, and we would doubt the efficacy of a limiting instruction.

Even though we affirm the district court's ruling that the statement accompanying the delivery of the slip cannot be admitted, the slip of paper itself is admissible and Mason can testify that sometime in the hour before the shooting Williams gave him the slip of paper, that he telephoned the police after witnessing the shooting, and that he gave the police the information on the slip.

No hearsay problem is presented by the slip of paper and the writing on it ("Beanny, Eric, 635-3135"). Written assertions are not immune from the hearsay rule, Fed. R. Evid. 801(a)(1). However, the information on the slip was not hearsay. The words themselves do not assert anything except that Beanny and/or Eric might have a particular telephone number. The statement is not being offered as proof that Beanny and/or Eric had that telephone number, and hence, we conclude that the statement is not within the definition of hearsay evidence, Fed. R. Evid. 801(c).

The dissent contends that if the information on the slip means no more than that two individuals might have a particular telephone number, there can be no justification for allowing the slip to be admitted into evidence. We disagree, as we believe the slip nevertheless has relevance to the issues in the case. The slip itself, when coupled with the fact that Williams wrote it, tends to show a current *association* between Williams and individuals named "Beanny" and "Eric."[42] When statements by an

---

42. It is this fact, among others, which distinguishes this case from United States v. Barash, 365 F.2d 395 (2d Cir. 1966), after remand, 412 F.2d 26 (2d Cir.) cert. denied, 396 U.S. 832 (1969), cited by the dissent in note 47. In *Barash*, defendant had been convicted of various counts relating to improper payments to internal revenue agents in connection with their office audit examinations of income tax returns of certain of defendant's (an attorney and CPA) clients. An agent testifying for the Government was permitted to state at trial that he had expected a payoff because defendant had been introduced to him by a fellow employee who "never introduced me to anyone except someone who was going to pay me off." 365 F.2d at 399. The court said this testimony was hearsay, as the fellow employee was asserting in effect that Barash was an accountant of the paying kind. Id. The court recognized that evidence admissible for one purpose is not rendered wholly inadmissible simply because it fails to satisfy the rules in its other use; under such circumstances, the opponent of the evidence is entitled only to a limiting instruction on timely request. 365 F.2d at 400. But in that case, the court could not find another purpose: the evidence was relevant because its only purpose was to show the agent's state of mind, and state of mind was irrelevant unless induced by the fellow employee, a fact as to which the employee's statement was hearsay. Id. Even if the statements and acts in the present case were hearsay, the existence of the other purpose would distinguish our facts from *Barash*.

out-of-court declarant which are neutral (not assertive of direct complicity in crime)[43] are offered to show association and not to show the truth of the matters contained therein, and the evidence is not otherwise unfairly prejudicial, the weight of the decided cases allows admission. For example, in United States v. Ruiz, 477 F.2d 918 (2d Cir.), cert. denied, 414 U.S. 1004 (1973), appellant had been convicted of conspiracy to distribute heroin. On appeal, he argued that a slip of paper bearing his nickname and a telephone number, seized from the person of an alleged coconspirator after that individual's arrest, was inadmissible hearsay and was therefore not relevant on the threshold question of conspiracy. The court disagreed, holding: "The paper was not introduced to prove the truth or falsity of its contents. It was merely evidence supporting the inference that Torres [the alleged coconspirator] knew Ruiz and anticipated calling him on the telephone." 477 F.2d at 919. In Brown v. United States, 403 F.2d 489 (5th Cir. 1968), cert. denied, 397 U.S. 927 (1970), appellant had been convicted of numerous drug charges along with three other persons. On appeal, he argued that a slip of paper found on appellant bearing the handwritten information "Ramon" and a telephone number was inadmissible hearsay. The court disagreed, stating that the writing on the note was not hearsay, as it was offered to show knowledge by appellant of one "Ramon" who may or may not have been an associate of the alleged supplier of the drugs. 403 F.2d at 491.[44]

43. In describing this information as "neutral," we distinguish the information on the slip from other types of statements. For example, if the slip contained in writing the statements made orally by Williams when he delivered the slip, we would not characterize the information as "neutral." Similarly, if the writing on the slip contained a statement to the effect that, "I am afraid I will be killed by [Eric and Beanny]," see United States v. Brown, 160 U.S. App. D.C. 190, 210, 490 F.2d 758, 778 (1973), we would not characterize the information as neutral.

44. There are many other reported cases which draw these analytical distinctions in related contexts. In United States v. Ellis, 461 F.2d 962 (2d Cir.), cert. denied, 409 U.S. 866 (1972), appellant had been convicted of three counts of violating the federal bank robbery statute. On appeal, he raised several challenges, including that the trial court received inadmissible hearsay into evidence. Appellant argued that address books belonging to his codefendants and which contained his name and a driver's license in the name of one codefendant found in one of the address books were hearsay. The court held that the address books were not hearsay and were "admissible as circumstantial evidence showing association." 461 F.2d at 970. Also, the court found the driver's license not to be hearsay, since it was not "offered for the truth of the matter asserted therein, but rather as circumstantial evidence to show that [the codefendant] was the owner of the address book and the coat in which the book and the license were found." Id.

In United States v. Canieso, 470 F.2d 1224 (2d Cir. 1972), defendants had been convicted of conspiring to import heroin and of possessing it with intent to distribute. Chou, one defendant, claimed that a letter from Canieso's person, the codefendant, was erroneously admitted against him under the hearsay rule. Two letters were found in Chou's pockets. The letter found in Canieso's wallet to which Chou objected dovetailed into the two letters found in Chou's pockets. The court stated: "The only way in which the letter can be deemed hearsay is by inserting in it a statement that the writer had entrusted Chou with the task of making the needed contacts in New York. We see no particular reason for doing this simply to create a hearsay problem that would not otherwise exist — even

These cases as well as the instant case are to be distinguished from those such as United States v. Watkins, 171 U.S. App. D.C. 158, 519 F.2d 294 (1975), where the proffered written statements are being used to prove the truth of the matters contained therein.[45] In short, we conclude that the "Beanny, Eric" slip itself is not inadmissible hearsay and is not inadmissible for lack of relevancy. Likewise it is not inadmissible because of the availability of some oral testimony to prove some association of the parties named on the slip and the victim. The slip of paper is stronger evidence of association and it indicates that such association was continuing almost up to the moment of the murder. There is no reason to deny the Government such proof. Together with other evidence it tends to prove that defendants were not killing a stranger.

No hearsay problem is presented by Mason's testimony that he received the slip from Williams. In so testifying, Mason is simply a witness to an act performed by another in his presence. While we must be sensitive to the possible communicative content of the act of handing over the slip of paper, we believe that the act of handing this slip of

---

though the jury would doubtless draw exactly this inference. Here the resemblance of the letter found in Canieso's wallet to the one found on Chou's person affords a considerably stronger basis for a conclusion that the Canieso letter was receivable '*circumstantially*, as giving rise to indirect inferences, but not as assertions to prove the matter asserted.' 6 Wigmore, Evidence §1766, at 180 (3d ed. 1940). . . ." 470 F.2d at 1232. Without expressing approval or disapproval for the results in the particular cases above, we follow the reasoning in these cases by not inserting content into the presently neutral information on the slip, which is to be viewed apart from the prejudicial statement made upon delivery that we excise from the evidence to be given to the jury.

See United States v. Snow, 517 F.2d 441, 443-44 (9th Cir. 1975) (name tape which was affixed to case in which gun was found and which bore defendant's name was not hearsay and was properly admitted to show that defendant knowingly possessed the unregistered weapon; name tape treated as circumstantial evidence and deemed relevant); Hiram v. United States, 354 F.2d 4, 7 (9th Cir. 1965) (newspaper article describing bank robbery and naming certain person as robber was not inadmissible as hearsay in prosecution on charge of being accessory after the fact to bank robbery, where article was not offered for truth of matter stated therein but only to show notice to defendant of the robbery and of named person's alleged participation therein); United States v. Mishkin, 317 F.2d 634, 637 (2d Cir.), cert. denied, 375 U.S. 827 (1963) (slips of paper, which had unpublished telephone number of defendant and his first name on them, and which were found in wallet of alleged coconspirator when he attempted to pick up obscene books from subway locker, were not inadmissible hearsay, since slips were admitted not to prove defendant's telephone number and connection with the bookstore, but as part of proof that codefendant had received the key to subway locker from defendant).

45. In *Watkins*, appellant was charged with various drug violations. A search of a room in which appellant and others were present at the time turned up drugs, drug-related paraphernalia, large amounts of cash, and three receipts indicating that appellant had paid the rent on the apartment for two months and had paid for utility service in another month. 171 U.S. App. D.C. at 159-60, 519 F.2d at 295-96. Against the Government's contention that the documents were tendered not for the truth of their contents but rather to show they were found in the bedroom occupied by appellant on the day in question, the court noted the rule that "receipts are hearsay as independent evidence of the making of payment" and found the receipts inadmissible, as "a principal, if not the primary, purpose of the introduction . . . was . . . to show 'who was living there.' " 171 U.S. App. D.C. at 160-61, 519 F.2d at 296-97.

paper to Mason — when the accompanying oral statement made by Williams is excised from the proffered testimony — is virtually neutral (no assertive of direct complicity in crime). But the act of delivery is not without relevance, for it tends to show association between the decedent and the individuals whose names appear on the slip. It is a relevant circumstance from which reasonable inferences can be drawn. If Mason is asked whether a statement accompanied the handing over of the slip, he may not testify as to the content of the statement but he may answer the question by indicating in the affirmative or negative whether a statement was made, *unless* the district court rules, on grounds not apparent in the present record that such an answer would be unfairly prejudicial. Normally, an answer to such a question is admissible. The mere fact that a statement was made is not the same as offering the statement for the truth of the matter contained therein. See VI Wigmore on Evidence §1766, at 250 (Chadbourn rev. 1976).

No hearsay problem is presented by Mason's testimony that after he witnessed the shooting, he called the police and gave them the information on the slip. In so testifying, Mason is simply relating his own conduct after the murder. Such testimony is not unfairly prejudicial: while Mason's actions were carrying out Williams' instructions, calling the police would have been normal conduct if Williams had made no statements to him. Mason's testimony is not irrelevant, for it shows why the defendants were immediately suspects in the murder and why a search for them was undertaken immediately with such incriminating results.

We do not believe that the evidence we are admitting encourages unfairly prejudicial inferences by the jury. The reason Williams' statement accompanying the handing over of the slip is excluded is that it is hearsay. The hearsay danger posed is that the jury might conclude from the statement that Day bore ill will toward Williams and had reason to cause him harm. The jury might infer from the slip, apart from the statement, that Williams was *associated* with defendants. That is a permissible inference since there is nothing in the slip of the paper itself that would lead the jury to conclude that defendants had a reason to kill Williams. It is only from the connection with other admissible evidence that such conclusion might emerge. The evidence that we rule may be admitted is circumstantial, non-hearsay evidence, and we perceive no unfair prejudice in its admission.[47] Given the relevance of the evidence

47. The dissent suggests with respect to the testimony relating to the slip of paper bearing the names and telephone numbers that because the hearsay rule requires the exclusion of some of the attendant statements that the paper should thereby be excluded entirely (dissent at 893). However, if that were to be the outcome, the rule itself would provide for the complete exclusion of such evidence, but it does not so provide — only the accompanying hearsay statements must be excluded. The exhibit may still be introduced and its circumstantial effect argued to the jury. The timing of the delivery of the paper, and the fact that it bore the names of Day and Sheffey and their telephone numbers,

and the fact that it is not unfairly prejudicial, the mere fact that the Government might have other witnesses who could testify that Williams was associated with Day and Sheffey before the murder does not provide a reason to exclude the testimony that we hold to be properly admissible. No other witness can testify — directly or indirectly — to the *immediacy* of the association of Williams with "Beanny & Eric" that flows from the writing on the paper and its delivery at the time it was delivered. The prosecution is entitled to such probative evidence — not because it is innocuous as the dissent characterizes our position — but because there is strong proof of its veracity and it is not *unfairly* prejudicial. And it is probative of the association and relationship of the parties. Thus, the potential for jury misuse does not exist as an *independent* factor and the writing is admissible. Fed. R. Evid. 403. . . .

ROBINSON, J., dissenting in part.

I am in complete accord with the court's application of Judge Mac-Kinnon's perceptive opinion in *Brown* to the bulk of the statements made by Williams to Mason. I cannot, however, reconcile *Brown* with admission of (a) the slip bearing appellees' names and a telephone number, (b) testimony by Mason that when Williams turned the slip over he made a statement or (c) evidence that Mason called the police after the shooting and gave them the information on the slip — when it is combined with the first two.

To begin with, if testimony averring the mere delivery of the slip is as "neutral" as the court labels it, then by the same token it is also quite irrelevant. And if the writing on the slip does "not assert anything except that Beanny and/or Eric might have a particular telephone number" and "is not being offered as proof that Beanny and/or Eric had that telephone number," what possible justification is there for allowing its admission? If as the court holds, Mason cannot reveal to the jury the content of Williams' statement accompanying the delivery, what is accomplished by showing simply that a statement was made? And if Mason's post-homicide call to the police conveyed nothing but valueless

---

circumstantially linked them to the victim at the critical time. The jury was entitled to weigh these circumstances along with the rest of the evidence. The dissent contends that such evidence is valueless, but it is not. It was one of the material pieces of evidence that led the police to the bloody gun, bloody pants, and keys to the bloody car, containing the discharged shotgun shell, parked around the corner from Day's house. All bore blood of the victim's type. Because the slip's relevance and probative effect must be restricted by excluding the accompanying statement does not mean that the paper must be entirely excluded. The dissent's argument for the exclusion of the evidence would coin a new exclusionary rule. The delivery of the paper by Williams tends to prove his contemporaneous association with Day and Sheffey and the bloody exhibits (which the paper assisted in producing) tend to prove Day and Sheffey's contemporaneous association with Williams. These are strong circumstances that justice requires be laid before the jury for their evaluation.

data on the slip, what importance would it have to the issues? Regardless of hearsay analysis, . . . the "evidence is admissible only if it is relevant and fairly probative on a material issue in the case."

The court suggests that this evidence "tends to show a current *association* between Williams and individuals named 'Beanny' and 'Eric.' " This theory was never mentioned by the Government in any of its lengthy pretrial filings, probably because it has a long line of witnesses, including Mason himself, who could testify *directly* to the undisputed fact that Williams knew Day and Sheffey and had been in contact with them shortly before the murder. The simple fact is that "in actuality, the Government seeks to have something more inferred"[42]: that Williams feared Day and Sheffey.

Thus, I cannot subscribe to my colleagues' theory that these items of evidence are innocuous. On the contrary, I have no difficulty in recognizing the implications they are apt to have for lay jurors. The only consequence thus far emerging toward which these evidentiary items could contribute is that the jury will infer that Williams told Mason something about Day and Sheffey that would indicate that they were the parties who shot Williams an hour later. Thus, not from the *content* of Williams' statement to Mason but simply from its *making*, and from the turnover of a slip of paper naming both Day and Sheffey coupled with transmittal of that information to the police, "[t]he jury is being asked to infer . . . that Day," and Sheffey as well, "bore ill will toward Williams and had reason to cause him harm."

That the inference arising from Williams' delivery of the note is somewhat less obvious than that which would spring from the excluded content of his concomitant statement — his instruction to Mason to communicate with the police if he had not returned to his home by the following afternoon — does not mean that it is appreciably less potent. The urgent and threatening circumstances surrounding the episode are enough to demonstrate that Williams intended the utterance of the statement, as well as its content, as an assertion that he feared Day and Sheffey, and thus it can be no more reliable than the words themselves. Consequently, even assuming that Mason's description of the physical events would not be hearsay when viewed completely in isolation, it does not follow that the inferences the jury may well draw,[46] and that the

---

42. The court suggests that the Government's access to direct evidence of the fact that Williams associated with Day and Sheffey "does not provide a reason to exclude the testimony [the slip and testimony concerning its delivery and Mason's call to the police] that we hold to be properly admissible." As one distinguished work on this subject has put it however, "where the danger of the jury's misuse of the evidence for the incompetent purpose is great, and its value for the legitimate purpose is slight *or the point for which it is competent can readily be proved by other evidence,* the judge's power to exclude the evidence altogether [should] be recognized." McCormick, Evidence 136 (2d ed. 1972) (emphasis supplied).

46. In *Brown,* supra note 34, there was only one level of inference to deal with because

Government patently wants drawn, from Williams' behavior are unburdened by the dangers of hearsay.[48]

I submit that, in the milieu in which it was made, the fact of Williams' statement does not qualify under the hearsay-rule exception for nonassertive nonverbal conduct. I say, too, that the text of Williams' note — plainly intended as a message from Williams to the police, through the medium of transmittal by Mason — deserves the usual fate of unmitigated hearsay. I think, in sum, that each of the evidentiary items under discussion is inadmissible even if accompanied by a limiting instruction. Since Williams cannot be confronted nor his perception, memory, narrative-accuracy and sincerity tested,[50] I would exclude not only the statement but also all its behavioral trappings. Because the court refuses to uphold the District Judge on this score and on his rejection of the other crimes evidence implicating Day, I must respectfully dissent.

B.   Statements of a Party Opponent

This and the following sections explore the application of the rule against hearsay in situations where an out-of-court statement is offered for the truth of the matter it asserts. In this section, the out-of-court statement is that of a party or its agents; cross-examination of the declarant sometimes is not possible or practical, but if other conditions are satisfied, the statement is admitted. Why? Is it because such statements are inherently reliable? Because there is no "right" to cross-examination in such circumstances, or because there is no "need" to cross-examine?

---

the victim had expressly stated that he was afraid of the accused. We were concerned, however, that the jury might infer that Brown "had done things in the past to [the victim] to justify this fear, or that Brown had explicitly threatened [the victim's] life in the past." 160 U.S. App. D.C. at 200, 490 F.2d at 778. Here we have two levels of inference. From Williams' strange conduct the jury may conclude that he dreaded Day, and then it may draw the *Brown* inference that Day had done something to warrant Williams' apprehension. The first inference is so strongly compelled by the evidence the court rules admissible that this situation cannot possibly be distinguished from that in *Brown* on the basis of the purposes of the hearsay rule.

48. . . . Conduct may often be less dangerous than statements because it frequently entails the declarant's reliance upon the veracity of the assertion implied, and thus removes the declarant's possible lack of sincerity. No such reliance is to be found where, as here, the conduct is consciously assertive in nature. Williams' actions here, even if not consciously intended as an assertion themselves, were merely necessary accompaniment to the oral statement excluded by the court, and thus cannot possibly be any more reliable.

50. See Moore v. United States, 429 U.S. 20, 22 (1976). "No liberalization of evidentiary rules can circumscribe the fundamental right to confrontation and cross-examination." United States v. Rogers, 549 F.2d 490, 499 n.11 (8th Cir. 1976), cert. denied, 431 U.S. 918 (1977). Because I believe admission of this evidence is improper under the Federal Rules of Evidence, I have no need to reach the constitutional issue.

Note that many admissions are self-serving; also, that in many of these cases where the statement is that of a party's agent, the agent may not be available at trial to explain or deny the statement. Is an estoppel-like "game" theory of litigation at work in this area? What values would such a theory further?

FRE 801(d)(2)
Definitions

(d) *Statements which are not hearsay.* A statement is not hearsay if — . . .
   (2) *Admissions by party-opponent.* The statement is offered against a party and is (A) his own statement, in either his individual or a representative capacity, or (B) a statement of which he has manifested his adoption or belief in its truth, or (C) a statement by a person authorized by him to make a statement concerning the subject, or (D) a statement by his agent or servant concerning a matter within the scope of his agency or employment, made during the existence of the relationship, or (E) a statement by a co-conspirator of a party during the course and in furtherance of the conspiracy.

Problem IV-22
He Who Laughs Last . . .

City *A* taxes real property on the basis of 100 percent of value. The city tax collector appraises Cheat's property at $100,000 and taxes it accordingly. Cheat files an abatement request stating that his property is worth only $50,000. Later, the state condemns Cheat's property under its power of eminent domain. The value of the property is disputed. The state claims the property is worth $50,000; Cheat claims it is worth $100,000.
   (1) At the trial of this issue the state offers Cheat's abatement request filing. Cheat objects. What ruling and why? If admitted, what is the reasoning on which the decision rests?
   (2) Suppose the state claims the value of the property is $30,000. Cheat offers the abatement request filing. The state objects. What ruling and why?
   (3) At trial Cheat offers the city tax assessment. The state objects. What ruling and why?

Problem IV-23
"If You're Gonna Get Hit, Get Hit by a Rolls"

D's Rolls-Royce strikes *P* while *P* is crossing the street in a crosswalk with the light. *D*'s chauffeur, *C*, who was in the Rolls at the time, and *P* are the only eyewitnesses. *P* has amnesia as a result of the accident and cannot remember what occurred. *P*, by his guardian, *G*, sues *D* for damages. The issue is *C*'s negligence *vel non*.

(1) At trial, *P* offers a letter by *D* properly authenticated, which says in part, "*C*'s negligence caused *P*'s injuries." *D* objects. What ruling and why?

(2) If *P* rests after the above and *D* moves for a nonsuit, what ruling and why?

(3) *P* also calls *W*, a bystander who witnessed the accident, to testify that *C* said to *P*, "I'm *D*'s chauffeur. It was all my fault. Don't worry, I'm sure that *D* will make this good." *D* objects. What ruling and why?

What indicia of reliability inhere in admissions? What justifications are there for permitting the use of hearsay admissions? Are these justifications sufficiently strong to override even nonhearsay limitations on the admission of evidence, such as the firsthand knowledge rule (Rule 602), the opinion rule (Rule 701), and the rule requiring the production of the original document (Rule 1002)? Why?

Problem IV-24
Silence as Statement

(1) *D*, the executor of *E*'s estate, is charged with secreting *E*'s assets, to wit, fifty $1,000 bills. *D* denies the existence of this money.

At *D*'s trial the state calls *W* to testify that he was present at the meeting of *E*'s heirs on June 1 when *D* opened *E*'s wall safe. *W* will testify that he saw *D* rummage around in the safe and announce, "Nothing of value — just some one-dollar bills." *W* will further testify that *E*'s son, *S*, who was peering over *D*'s shoulder, responded, "Hey, those aren't one-dollar bills; they're one thousand-dollar bills" and that *D* was silent. *S* is dead. May *W* testify to *S*'s statement? If so, how should the court charge the jury?

(2) At trial, *O* is called to testify that on June 2 he arrested *D* for theft; on the way down to the station in the police cruiser *O* said to *D*, "So you thought you would get away with an easy 50 grand, did you?" *D* was silent. Is *O*'s testimony admissible? Why?

(3) Charge: first-degree murder. Defense: self-defense. At trial the prosecution seeks to elicit testimony on cross-examination of *D* that *D* did not come forward to report the incident or his involvement in it to the police for two weeks. Would such evidence be hearsay? Would its introduction violate the confrontation clause, the self-incrimination clause, the due process clause, or the doctrine of Griffin v. California, 380 U.S. 609 (1965)? Should such evidence be admitted even if *D* does not take the stand?

JENKINS v. ANDERSON
447 U.S. 231 (1980)

Mr. Justice POWELL delivered the opinion of the Court.

The question in this case is whether the use of prearrest silence to impeach a defendant's credibility violates either the Fifth or the Fourteenth Amendments to the Constitution.

On August 13, 1974, the petitioner stabbed and killed Doyle Redding. The petitioner was not apprehended until he turned himself in to governmental authorities about two weeks later. At his state trial for first-degree murder, the petitioner contended that the killing was in self-defense.

The petitioner testified that his sister and her boyfriend were robbed by Redding and another man during the evening of August 12, 1974. The petitioner, who was nearby when the robbery occurred, followed the thieves a short distance and reported their whereabouts to the police. According to the petitioner's testimony, the next day he encountered Redding, who accused him of informing the police of the robbery. The petitioner stated that Redding attacked him with a knife, that the two men struggled briefly, and that the petitioner broke away. On cross-examination, the petitioner admitted that during the struggle he had tried "[t]o push that knife into [Redding] as far as [he] could," App., at 36, but maintained that he had acted solely in self-defense.

During the cross-examination, the prosecutor questioned the petitioner about his actions after the stabbing:

Q: And I suppose you waited for the Police to tell them what happened?
A: No, I didn't.
Q: You didn't?
A: No.
Q: I see. And how long was it after this day that you were arrested, or that you were taken into custody?

App., at 33. After some discussion of the date on which petitioner surrendered, the prosecutor continued:

Q: When was the first time that you reported the things that you have told us in Court today to anybody?
A: Two days after it happened.
Q: And who did you report it to?
A: To my probation officer.
Q: Well, apart from him?
A: No one.
Q: Who?

A: No one but my —
Q: (Interposing):   Did you ever go to a Police Officer or to anyone else?
A: No, I didn't.
Q: As a matter of fact, it was two weeks later, wasn't it?
A: Yes. . . .

At trial the prosecutor attempted to impeach the petitioner's credibility by suggesting that the petitioner would have spoken out if he had killed in self-defense. The petitioner contends that the prosecutor's actions violated the Fifth Amendment as applied to the States through the Fourteenth Amendment. The Fifth Amendment guarantees an accused the right to remain silent during his criminal trial and prevents the prosecution for commenting on the silence of a defendant who asserts the right. Griffin v. California, 380 U.S. 609, 614 (1965). In this case, of course, the petitioner did not remain silent throughout the criminal proceedings. Instead, he voluntarily took the witness stand in his own defense.

This Court's decision in Raffel v. United States, 271 U.S. 494 (1926), recognized that the Fifth Amendment is not violated when a defendant who testifies in his own defense is impeached with his prior silence. [T]he *Raffel* Court concluded that the defendant was "subject to cross-examination impeaching his credibility just like any other witness." Grunewald v. United States, 353 U.S. 391, 420 (1957).

It can be argued that a person facing arrest will not remain silent if his failure to speak later can be used to impeach him. But the Constitution does not forbid "every government-imposed choice in the criminal process that has the effect of discouraging the exercise of constitutional rights." The " 'threshold question is whether compelling the election impairs to an appreciable extent any of the policies behind the rights involved.' " Chaffin v. Stynchcombe, 412 U.S., at 32, quoting Crampton v. Ohio, decided with McGautha v. California, 402 U.S. 183, 213 (1971). The *Raffel* Court explicitly rejected the contention that the possibility of impeachment by prior silence is an impermissible burden upon the exercise of Fifth Amendment rights. "We are unable to see that the rule that [an accused who] testified . . . must testify fully, adds in any substantial manner to the inescapable embarrassment which the accused must experience in determining whether he shall testify or not." 271 U.S., at 499.

This Court similarly defined the scope of the Fifth Amendment protection in Harris v. New York, 401 U.S. 222 (1971). There the Court held that a statement taken in violation of *Miranda* may be used to impeach a defendant's credibility. Rejecting the contention that such impeachment violates the Fifth Amendment, the Court said: "Every criminal defendant is privileged to testify in his own defense, or to refuse to do so. But that privilege cannot be construed to include the right to commit perjury. . . . Having voluntarily taken the stand, petitioner was under an obligation to speak truthfully and accurately, and the prosecution here did no more than utilize the traditional truth-testing devices of the adversary process." Id., at 225.

In determining whether a constitutional right has been burdened impermissibly, it also is appropriate to consider the legitimacy of the challenged governmental practice. Attempted impeachment on cross-examination of a defendant, the practice at issue here, may enhance the reliability of the criminal process. Use of such impeachment on cross-examination allows prosecutors to test the credibility of witnesses by asking them to explain prior inconsistent statements and acts. A defendant may decide not to take the witness stand because of the risk of cross-examination. But this is a choice of litigation tactics. Once a defendant decides to testify, "[t]he interests of the other party and regard for the function of the courts of justice to ascertain the truth become relevant, and prevail in the balance of considerations determining the scope and limits of the privilege against self-incrimination." Brown v. United States, 356 U.S. 148, 156 (1958).

Thus, impeachment follows the defendant's own decision to cast aside his cloak of silence and advances the truth-finding function of the criminal trial. We conclude that the Fifth Amendment is not violated by the use of prearrest silence to impeach a criminal defendant's credibility.

The petitioner also contends that use of prearrest silence to impeach his credibility denied him the fundamental fairness guaranteed by the Fourteenth Amendment. We do not agree. Common law traditionally has allowed witnesses to be impeached by their previous failure to state a fact in circumstances in which that fact naturally would have been asserted. 3A Wigmore, Evidence §1042, at 1056 (Chadbourn rev. 1970). Each jurisdiction may formulate its own rules of evidence to determine when prior silence is so inconsistent with present statements that impeachment by reference to such silence is probative. For example, this Court has exercised its supervisory powers over federal courts to hold that prior silence cannot be used for impeachment where silence is not probative of a defendant's credibility and where prejudice to the defendant might result.[5]

Only in Doyle v. Ohio, 426 U.S. 610, did we find that impeachment by silence violated the Constitution. In that case, a defendant received the warnings required by Miranda v. Arizona, 384 U.S. 436, 467-473, when he was arrested for selling marihuana. At that time, he made no statements to the police. During his subsequent trial, the defendant testified

---

5. Mr. Justice Marshall contends that the petitioner's prearrest silence is not probative of his credibility. In this case, that is a question of state evidentiary law. In federal criminal proceeding the relevance of such silence, of course, would be a matter of federal law. See United States v. Hale, supra, 422 U.S., at 181.

that he had been framed. The prosecutor impeached the defendant's credibility on cross-examination by revealing that the defendant remained silent after his arrest. The State argued that the prosecutor's actions were permissible, but we concluded that "the *Miranda* decision compels rejection of the State's position." *Miranda* warnings inform a person that he has the right to remain silent and assure him, at least implicitly, that his subsequent decision to remain silent cannot be used against him. Accordingly, " 'it does not comport with due process to permit the prosecution during the trial to call attention to his silence at the time of arrest and to insist that because he did not speak about the facts of the case at that time, as he was told he need not do, an unfavorable inference might be drawn as to the truth of his trial testimony.' "

In this case, no governmental action induced petitioner to remain silent before arrest. The failure to speak occurred before the petitioner was taken into custody and given *Miranda* warnings. Consequently, the fundamental unfairness present in *Doyle* is not present in this case. We hold that impeachment by use of prearrest silence does not violate the Fourteenth Amendment.

Our decision today does not force any state court to allow impeachment through the use of prearrest silence. Each jurisdiction remains free to formulate evidentiary rules defining the situations in which silence is viewed as more probative than prejudicial. We merely conclude that the use of prearrest silence to impeach a defendant's credibility does not violate the Constitution. The judgment of the Court of Appeals is affirmed.

Mr. Justice MARSHALL, with whom Mr. Justice BRENNAN joins, dissenting.

Today the Court holds that a criminal defendant's testimony in his own behalf may be impeached by the fact that he did not go to the authorities before his arrest and confess his part in the offense. The decision thus strikes a blow at two of the foundation stones of our constitutional system: the privilege against self-incrimination and the right to present a defense.

The Court's decision today is extraordinarily broad. It goes far beyond a simple holding that the common-law rule permitting introduction of evidence of silence in the face of accusation or in circumstances calling for a response does not violate the privilege against self-incrimination. For in this case the prosecution was allowed to cast doubt on an accused's testimony that he acted in self-defense by forcing him to testify that he did not go to the police of his own volition, before he had been indicted, charged, or even accused of any offense, and volunteer his version of the events.

The Court's holding that a criminal defendant's testimony may be impeached by his prearrest silence has three patent — and, in my view, fatal — defects. First, the mere fact of prearrest silence is so unlikely to be probative of the falsity of the defendant's trial testimony that its use for impeachment purposes is contrary to the Due Process Clause of the Fourteenth Amendment. Second, the drawing of an adverse inference from the failure to volunteer incriminating statements impermissibly infringes the privilege against self-incrimination. Third, the availability of the inference for impeachment purposes impermissibly burdens the decision to exercise the constitutional right to testify in one's own defense.

The use of prior silence for impeachment purposes depends, as the majority recognizes, on the reasonableness of an inference that it is inconsistent with the statements that are to be impeached. If the defendant's prior silence does not make it more likely that his trial testimony was false, the evidence is simply irrelevant. Such an inference cannot fairly be drawn from petitioner's failure to go to the police before any charges were brought, admit that he had committed a homicide, and offer an exculpatory explanation.

In order for petitioner to offer his explanation of self-defense, he would necessarily have had to admit that it was he who fatally stabbed the victim, thereby supplying against himself the strongest possible proof of an essential element of criminal homicide. It is hard to imagine a purer case of self-incrimination. Since we cannot assume that in the absence of official warnings individuals are ignorant of or oblivious to their constitutional rights, we must recognize that petitioner may have acted in reliance on the constitutional guarantee. In fact, petitioner had most likely been informed previously of his privilege against self-incrimination, since he had two prior felony convictions. One who has at least twice before been given the *Miranda* warnings, which carry the implied promise that silence will not be penalized by use for impeachment purposes, Doyle v. Ohio, 426 U.S. 610 (1976), may well remember the rights of which he has been informed, and believe that the promise is still in force. Accordingly, the inference that petitioner's conduct was inconsistent with his exculpatory trial testimony is precluded. . . .

Moreover, other possible explanations for silence spring readily to mind. It is conceivable that a person who had acted in self-defense might believe that he had committed no crime and therefore had no call to explain himself to the police. Indeed, all the witnesses agreed that after the stabbing the victim ran across the street and climbed a flight of stairs before collapsing. Initially, at least, then, petitioner might not have known that there was a homicide to explain. Moreover, petitioner testified that he feared retaliation if he went to the police. One need not be persuaded that any of these possible explanations represents the true reason for petitioner's conduct to recognize that the availability of other plausible hypotheses vitiates the inference on which the admissibility of the evidence depends. . . .

The Court implies that its decision is consistent with the practice at common law; but at common law silence is admissible to contradict subsequent statements only if the circumstances would naturally have called for a response. For example, silence was traditionally considered a tacit admission if a statement made in the party's presence was heard and understood by the party, who was at liberty to respond, in circumstances naturally calling for a response, and the party failed to respond.[2] Silence was not considered an admission if any of the prerequisites were absent, for in such a case the failure to speak could be explained other than as assent. Similarly, failure to assert a fact could be used for impeachment if it would have been natural, under the circumstances, to assert the fact. But the authority cited by the majority in support of this proposition, makes it clear that the rule cannot be invoked unless the facts affirmatively show that the witness was called on to speak, circumstances which are not present in this case.[3] As we have previously observed, "[i]n most circumstances silence is so ambiguous that it is of little probative force." United States v. Hale, supra, at 176.

Since petitioner's failure to report and explain his actions prior to his arrest was not probative of the falsity of his testimony at trial, it was fundamentally unfair and a deprivation of due process to allow the jury to draw from that silence an inference that his trial testimony was false. . . .

The use of prearrest silence for impeachment purposes also violates the privilege against self-incrimination secured by the Fifth and Fourteenth Amendments.

[Separate opinions by Justices STEWART and STEVENS are omitted.]

Problem IV-25
Omar the Disappearing Cat

Action for negligence of D, a veterinarian who owns the Deluxe Cat and Dog Sanitarium. P's complaint alleges that his prize Persian cat,

---

2. See, e.g., McCormick supra n.2, §§161, 270; 4 J. Wigmore, Evidence §§1071, 1072 (J. Chadbourn rev. 1970); Gamble, The Tacit Admission Rule: Unreliable and Unconstitutional, 14 Ga. L. Rev. 27 (1979); Brody, Admissions Implied from Silence, Evasion and Equivocation in Massachusetts Criminal Cases, 42 B.U.L. Rev. 46 (1962); Heller, Admissions by Acquiescence, 15 U. Miami L. Rev. 161 (1960); Note, Tacit Criminal Admissions, 112 U. Pa. L. Rev. 210 (1963).

3. The Wigmore treatise lists three categories of cases in which silence may be used for impeachment:

"(1) Omissions *in legal proceedings* to assert what would naturally have been asserted under the circumstances.

"(2) Omissions to assert anything . . . when *formerly narrating*, on the stand or elsewhere, the matter now dealt with.

"(3) Failure to take the stand at all. . . ." 3A Wigmore, Evidence §1042, at 1056-1058 (J. Chadbourn rev. 1972) (footnotes omitted, emphasis in original).

Plainly, the omission to seek out an opportunity to speak is not included within these categories. Of all the cases cited by Wigmore involving silence by a criminal defendant, not one involves prearrest silence by a suspect not in the presence of law enforcement officers.

Omar, developed a neurosis in his declining years, so *P* sent him to *D*'s hospital on June 1 where *D* accepted Omar as a patient. *P*'s complaint further alleges that on June 2, as a result of *D*'s employees' negligence, Omar escaped and has not been seen since. *P* seeks $1 million in damages. *D*'s answer denies that he ever received Omar.

(1) At trial, *P* calls *M*, who testifies that she is now and was on June 1 the manager of *D*'s hospital. *M* is excused. *P* then testifies that Omar was his cat; that on June 1 he instructed his chauffeur, *C*, whose whereabouts are now unknown, to take Omar to *D*'s hospital; that on the evening of June 1 *P* stopped at *D*'s office and asked *M* if Omar had been checked in; that *M* replied, "Yes, and we are honored to have him." *D* objects. What ruling and why?

OK agent

(2) Suppose that *M* does not testify as in (1) above but that *P* testifies that when he went by *D*'s hospital on the evening of June 1, the office was locked so he went across the street to a restaurant for dinner. At dinner *P* told his tablemate about Omar and his tablemate said, "Don't worry about Omar; he's snug in the cat hospital." *P* then said, "How do you know?" His tablemate replied, "It's my business to know; I'm *D*'s manager." *D* objects. What ruling and why?

OK

Problem IV-26
P v. Greed Power & Light Company

On June 1st at 4 A.M., following two days of heavy rain, a flood wiped out the housing development at Rancho Mudslide. The cause of the flood was the collapse of the dam five miles upstream from the development. The dam was built and owned by the Greed Power & Light Company. *P*, individually and on behalf of the class of residents of Rancho Mudslide, has sued Greed for $5 million in actual property damages and $50 million in punitive damages, alleging that Greed was negligent in building and maintaining the dam.

The following evidentiary problems came to light at the pretrial conference. How would you resolve each of them?

(1) *P* proposes to call Meyer, the president of the Rancho Mudslide Homeowner's Association, to testify that on May 25 he was at the dam site and that an engineer who had been sent to repair a sluice said to him, "This repair won't do much good if there is a heavy rain. The whole system is bad."

OK agent

(2) *P* proposes to call Harry, the engineer's husband, to testify that his wife told him that when she came home from work on May 25 "the repairs she had made would not do any good if there was a heavy rain because the whole system was bad."

OK agent

(3) *P* proposes to call Clark Kent, a reporter for the Mudslide Muckraker, to testify that, upon learning of the catastrophe, he called up

OK

Rockeyfellow, the president of Greed, at 5 A.M. on June 1 for a reaction. Kent will testify that upon hearing what had happened, Rockeyfellow said, "Oh my God, the sluice system must have failed. We were negligent in maintaining it."

OK

(4) *P* proposes to call Stoole, a Greed employee, to testify that a report by the Rancid Corporation, an outside consulting firm, prepared for the company 10 years ago when the decision to build the dam was being made, states, "The soil at the suggested dam site is too porous. In case of heavy rain, there would be danger of collapse and flooding of the land downstream."

no.
must be
used
against
a party

(5) *D* proposes to call Harbinger, its vice-president for public relations, to testify that eight years ago he sent a letter to all owners of land in the then-proposed Rancho Mudslide development, informing them that the proposed development lay in the path of any water discharge from the dam and that a property owner would be foolish and negligent to build a residence in that location.

MAHLANDT v. WILD CANID SURVIVAL & RESEARCH CENTER, INC.
588 F.2d 626 (8th Cir. 1979)

VAN SICKLE, J. This is a civil action for damages arising out of an alleged attack by a wolf on a child. The sole issues on appeal are as to the correctness of three rulings which excluded conclusionary statements against interest. Two of them were made by a defendant, who was also an employee of the corporate defendant; and the third was in the form of a statement appearing in the records of a board meeting of the corporate defendant.

On March 23, 1973, Daniel Mahlandt, then 3 years, 10 months, and 8 days old, was sent by his mother to a neighbor's home on an adjoining street to get his older brother, Donald. Daniel's mother watched him cross the street, and then turned into the house to get her car keys. Daniel's path took him along a walkway adjacent to the Poos' residence. Next to the walkway was a five foot chain link fence to which Sophie had been chained with a six foot chain. In other words, Sophie was free to move in a half circle having a six foot radius on the side of the fence opposite from Daniel.

Sophie was a bitch wolf, 11 months and 28 days old, who had been born at the St. Louis Zoo, and kept there until she reached 6 months of age, at which time she was given to the Wild Canid Survival and Research Center, Inc. It was the policy of the Zoo to remove wolves from the Children's Zoo after they reached the age of 5 or 6 months. Sophie was supposed to be kept at the Tyson Research Center, but Kenneth Poos, as Director of Education for the Wild Canid Survival and Research

Center, Inc., had been keeping her at his home because he was taking Sophie to schools and institutions where he showed films and gave programs with respect to the nature of wolves. Sophie was known as a very gentle wolf who had proved herself to be good natured and stable during her contacts with thousands of children, while she was in the St. Louis Children's Zoo.

Sophie was chained because the evening before she had jumped the fence and attacked a beagle who was running along the fence and yapping at her.

A neighbor who was ill in bed in the second floor of his home heard a child's screams and went to his window, where he saw a boy lying on his back within the enclosure, with a wolf straddling him. The wolf's face was near Daniel's face, but the distance was so great that he could not see what the wolf was doing and did not see any biting. Within about 15 seconds the neighbor saw Clarke Poos, about seventeen, run around the house, get the wolf off of the boy, and disappear with the child in his arms to the back of the house. Clarke took the boy in and laid him on the kitchen floor.

Clarke had been returning from his friend's home immediately west when he heard a child's cries and ran around to the enclosure. He found Daniel lying within the enclosure, about three feet from the fence, and Sophie standing back from the boy the length of her chain, and wailing. An expert in the behavior of wolves stated that when a wolf licks a child's face that it is a sign of care, and not a sign of attack; that a wolf's wail is a sign of compassion, and an effort to get attention, not a sign of attack. No witness saw or knew how Daniel was injured. Clarke and his sister ran over to get Daniel's mother. She says that Clarke told her, "a wolf got Danny and he is dying." Clarke denies that statement. The defendant, Mr. Poos, arrived home while Daniel and his mother were in the kitchen. After Daniel was taken in an ambulance, Mr. Poos talked to everyone present, including a neighbor who came in. Within an hour after he arrived home, Mr. Poos went to Washington University to inform Owen Sexton, President of Wild Canid Survival and Research Center, Inc., of the incident. Mr. Sexton was not in his office so Mr. Poos left the following note on his door:

> Owen, would call me at home, 727-5080? Sophie bit a child that came in our back yard. All has been taken care of. I need to convey what happened to you. [Exhibit 11]

Denial of admission of this note is one of the issues on appeal.

Later that day, Mr. Poos found Mr. Sexton at the Tyson Research Center and told him what had happened. Denial of plaintiff's offer to prove that Mr. Poos told Mr. Sexton that, "Sophie had bit a child that day," is the second issue on appeal.

A meeting of the Directors of the Wild Canid Survival and Research Center, Inc., was held on April 4, 1973. Mr. Poos was not present at that meeting. The minutes of that meeting reflect that there was a "great deal of discussion . . . about the legal aspects of the incident of Sophie biting the child." Plaintiff offered an abstract of the minutes containing that reference. Denial of the offer of that abstract is the third issue on appeal.

Daniel had lacerations of the face, left thigh, left calf, and right thigh, and abrasions and bruises of the abdomen and chest. Mr. Mahlandt was permitted to state that Daniel had indicated that he had gone under the fence. Mr. Mahlandt and Mr. Poos, about a month after the incident, examined the fence to determine what caused Daniel's lacerations. Mr. Mahlandt felt that they did not look like animal bites. The parallel scars on Daniel's thigh appeared to match the configuration of the barbs or tines on the fence. The expert as to the behavior of wolves opined that the lacerations were not wolf bites or wounds caused by wolf claws. Wolves have powerful jaws and a wolf bite will result in massive crushing or severing of a limb. He stated that if Sophie had bitten Daniel there would have been clear apposition of teeth and massive crushing of Daniel's hands and arms which were not injured. Also, if Sophie had pulled Daniel under the fence, tooth marks on the foot or leg would have been present, although Sophie possessed enough strength to pull the boy under the fence.

The jury brought in a verdict for the defense.

The trial judge's rationale for excluding the note, the statement, and the corporate minutes, was the same in each case. He reasoned that Mr. Poos did not have any personal knowledge of the facts, and accordingly, the first two admissions were based on hearsay; and the third admission contained in the minutes of the board meeting was subject to the same objection of hearsay, and unreliability because of lack of personal knowledge. . . .

[T]he statement in the note pinned on the door is not hearsay, and is admissible against Mr. Poos. It was his own statement, and as such was clearly different from the reported statement of another. Example, "I was told that. . . ." It was also a statement of which he had manifested his adoption or belief in its truth. And the same observations may be made of the statement made later in the day to Mr. Sexton that, "Sophie had bit a child. . . ."

Are these statements admissible against Wild Canid Survival and Research Center, Inc.? They were made by Mr. Poos when he was an agent or servant of the Wild Canid Survival and Research Center, Inc., and they concerned a matter within the scope of his agency, or employment, i.e., his custody of Sophie, and were made during the existence of that relationship.

Defendant argues that Rule 801(d)(2) does not provide for the admission of "in house" statements; that is, it allows only admissions made to third parties.

The notes of the Advisory Committee on the Proposed Rules discuss the problem of "in house" admissions with reference to Rule 801(d)(2)(C) situations. This is not a (C) situation because Mr. Poos was not authorized or directed to make a statement on the matter by anyone. But the rationale developed in that comment does apply to this (D) situation. Mr. Poos had actual physical custody of Sophie. His conclusions, his opinions, were obviously accepted as a basis for action by his principal. See minutes of corporate meeting. As the Advisory Committee points out in its note on (C) situations:

> communication to an outsider has not generally been thought to be an essential characteristic of an admission. Thus a party's books or records are usable against him, without regard to any intent to disclose to third persons. V Wigmore on Evidence §1557.

Weinstein's discussion of Rule 801(d)(2)(D), states that:

> Rule 801(d)(2)(D) adopts the approach . . . which, as a general proposition, makes statement made by agents within the scope of their employment admissible. . . . Once agency, and the making of the statement while the relationship continues, are established, the statement is exempt from the hearsay rule so long as it relates to a matter within the scope of the agency.

After reciting a lengthy quotation which justifies the rule as necessary, and suggests that such admissions are trustworthy and reliable, Weinstein states categorically that although an express requirement of personal knowledge on the part of the declarant of the facts underlying his statement is not written into the rule, it should be. He feels that is mandated by Rules 805 and 403.

Rule 805 recites, in effect, that a statement containing hearsay within hearsay is admissible if each part of the statement falls within an exception to the hearsay rule. Rule 805, however, deals only with hearsay exceptions. A statement based on the personal knowledge of the declarant of facts underlying his statement is not the repetition of the statement of another, thus not hearsay. It is merely opinion testimony. Rule 805 cannot mandate the implied condition desired by Judge Weinstein.

Rule 403 provides for the exclusion of relevant evidence if its probative value is substantially outweighed by the danger of unfair prejudice, confusion of the issues, or misleading the jury, or by consideration of undue delay, waste of time, or needless presentation of cumulative evidence. Nor does Rule 403 mandate the implied condition desired by Judge Weinstein.

Thus, while both Rule 805 and Rule 403 provide additional bases for excluding otherwise acceptable evidence, neither rule mandates the introduction into Rule 801(d)(2)(D) of an implied requirement that the

declarant have personal knowledge of the facts underlying his statement. So we conclude that the two statements made by Mr. Poos were
admissible against Wild Canid Survival and Research Center, Inc.

As to the entry in the records of a corporate meeting, the directors as
primary officers of the corporation had the authority to include their
conclusions in the record of the meeting. So the evidence would fall
within 801(d)(2)(C) as to Wild Canid Survival and Research Center, Inc.,
and be admissible. The "in house" aspect of this admission has already
been discussed, Rule 801(d)(2)(D), supra.

But there was no servant, or agency, relationship which justified admitting the evidence of the board minutes as against Mr. Poos.

None of the conditions of 801(d)(2) cover the claim that minutes of a
corporate board meeting can be used against a non-attending, non-
participating employee of that corporation. The evidence was not admissible as against Mr. Poos.

There is left only the question of whether the trial court's rulings
which excluded all three items of evidence are justified under Rule 403.
He clearly found that the evidence was not reliable, pointing out that
none of the statements were based on the personal knowledge of the
declarant.

Again, that problem was faced by the Advisory Committee on Proposed Rules. In its discussion of 801(d)(2) exceptions to the hearsay rule,
the Committee said:

> The freedom which admissions have enjoyed from technical demands of
> searching for an assurance of trustworthiness in some against-interest circum-
> stances, and from the restrictive influences of the opinion rule and the rule
> requiring first hand knowledge, when taken with the apparently prevalent
> satisfaction with the results, calls for generous treatment of this avenue to
> admissibility. 28 U.S.C.A., Volume of Federal Rules of Evidence, Rule 801,
> p.527, at p.530.

So here, remembering that relevant evidence is usually prejudicial to
the cause of the side against which it is presented, and that the prejudice
which concerns us is unreasonable prejudice; and applying the spirit of
Rule 801(d)(2), we hold that Rule 403 does not warrant the exclusion of
the evidence of Mr. Poos' statements as against himself or Wild Canid
Survival and Research Center, Inc.

But the limited admissibility of the corporate minutes, coupled with
the repetitive nature of the evidence and the low probative value of the
minute record, all justify supporting the judgment of the trial court
under Rule 403.

The judgment of the District Court is reversed and the matter remanded to the District Court for a new trial consistent with this opinion.

Problem IV-27
The Exploding Remington

Action for personal injuries, based on both negligence and breach of warranty. *P* lost almost total eyesight in one eye when he fired an old rifle using ammunition salvaged from the Spanish-American War and subsequently sold to *P* by *D* Company.

The evidence showed that *P* was something of a gun buff. He already owned two rifles and a shotgun when he saw an advertisement in a gun magazine for a .43-caliber Remington Rolling Block rifle. He ordered the rifle, which had been manufactured in 1879 and used by an Argentine police force until shortly before its resale. Several months later, in response to *D* Company's advertisement in American Rifleman Magazine, he purchased 200 rounds of .43-caliber ammunition. He fired a number of rounds without mishap, but on July 17 *P* and a friend visited a target practice area near Tacoma. When *P* fired the second round of the day, something hit the right side of his face. Although the surrounding facial area was not harmed, he suffered extremely serious injury to his right eye.

The lengthy history of the .43-caliber ammunition supplied by *D* Company gradually unfolded at trial. It had been manufactured in Spain in the last two decades of the nineteenth century, sent to Cuba, and eventually captured by the United States during the Spanish-American War. For years it was kept in a damp concrete storage bunker on an island in the middle of the Hudson River. Six years before *P*'s

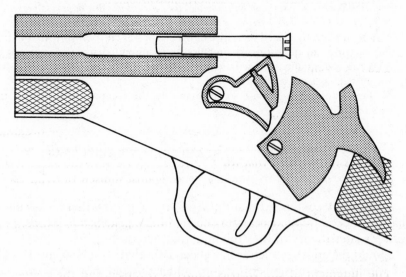

REMINGTON ROLLING BLOCK

purchase, *D* Company obtained about 200,000 rounds of the ammunition for $200. Much of the ammunition was so badly corroded that it was not salable and was scrapped. Some of the remaining ammunition was resized to fit the rolling block .43-caliber rifle. No notice was given to customers of the age of the powder and primers, the possibility of corrosion, or the reprocessing rather than reloading of the shells.

Error was assigned to the refusal of the trial court to admit as evidence a letter written by *P*'s counsel that gave notice of breach of warranty.

D Company contended that the letter written by *P*'s attorney shortly after the accident should have been accepted by the trial judge as an admission. The letter read as follows:

August 2

D Company
38 Pistol Road
Richfield, New Jersey 07657

    Re: Mr. *P*

Gentlemen:

We are the attorneys for Mr. *P* of Kent, Washington. On March 8 Mr. *P* sent you an order for 200 rounds of .43-caliber Spanish ammunition and paid for the same. The ammunition was received by him on or about May 28. Thereafter, on July 17, while using this ammunition in a Remington Rolling-Block rifle (Spanish .43-caliber rifle), the cartridge, while exploding, left the chamber, striking his right eye and permanently injured the vision of his right eye. *Preliminary investigation indicates that the accident was due in part to premature firing of the primer and defective cartridge.*

You are hereby placed on notice of breach of warranty on your part in that the cartridge in question was not fit for its intended use and was not of merchantable quality. Please be advised that Mr. *P* will hold you responsible for all damages caused thereby.

Would you please advise us the name of the company who loaded the cartridges in question.

Very truly yours,

STAHL, DELAY & OBFUSCATE
Attorney for Mr. P

D Company contended that the sentence suggesting that the accident may have been due to premature firing of the primer was inconsistent with *P*'s later theory of how the injury occurred.

Should the attorney's letter have been admitted? Is it hearsay? Does it fall within the admissions provisions under the Federal Rules?

Problem IV-28
Recall Letters

Action initiated by Mrs. *P*, administrator of Mr. *P*'s estate, for wrongful death of *P* allegedly caused by Dbilt Truck Company's negligence in the design, testing, and manufacture of the truck that *P* was driving when he died. The complaint also contains a count in strict liability based on Dbilt Truck Company's failure to give *P* timely warning as to the unsafe condition of the suspension system of the truck. Sixteen weeks after the accident, Mrs. *P* received the following letter, addressed to her deceased husband, from Dbilt Truck Company:

> This letter is sent to you pursuant to the requirement of the National Traffic and Motor Vehicle Safety Act. The rear suspension of your Dbilt truck/tractor . . . may contain a potentially hazardous condition.
>
> We have discovered that the combination of spring misalignment, improper maintenance, and pressure imbalance can cause overstressing of one spring resulting in a premature spring failure that can seriously affect vehicle control. You should make a simple visual inspection at once and have broken springs replaced immediately (at no charge). Regardless of the condition of these springs, federal law requires that an authorized Dbilt distributor perform certain adjustments and modifications to prevent the development of a hazardous condition.
>
> We apologize for the inconvenience this will cause you, but the seriousness of this situation cannot be overstated. We urge you to contact any authorized Dbilt distributor and make your vehicle available for this rework at the earliest possible time.

Dbilt Truck Company objects to the introduction of the recall letter on the grounds of hearsay and prejudice, pointing out that the recall campaign was instituted under the compulsion of the National Traffic and Motor Vehicle Safety Act, 15 U.S.C. §1401, et seq. What ruling and why?

Problem IV-29
"The Rat Roommate"

Charge: murder. On the issue of *D*'s intention to kill *V*, the prosecution, in rebuttal, puts a police officer, *W*, on the stand to testify that *R*, *D*'s roommate, after being fully warned of his rights, told *W*, "The night before the killing *D* said something about his planning to get *V*." *D* objects. What ruling and why?

Co-conspirator

Problem IV-30
"Incident"

Harry is robbed at knifepoint by two muggers as he leaves his favorite tavern one summer evening. After giving up his money, he and his buddies jump into a car and cruise the neighborhood, looking for the culprits. They spot some people in a vacant lot. Harry says, "That's them." The men pile out of the car and grab a young man and woman. During the struggle, the man says, "The girl made me do it." The woman says something that could be construed as a denial. Harry says, "He already told us you put him up to it."

If the state attempts to call Harry to testify to the man's statement at a trial of the woman, is the statement admissible? Why? Is the woman's response? Is Harry's response to the woman's statement?

UNITED STATES v. FLOYD
555 F.2d 45 (2d Cir. 1977), cert. denied, 434 U.S. 851 (1977)

COFFRIN, J. Lamont Floyd and Peter Olivo appeal from judgments of conviction in the United States District Court for the Eastern District of New York after a five day jury trial. . . . They were convicted of the armed robbery of the Chase Manhattan Bank on Rutland Road, in Brooklyn, New York, on October 31, 1975, in violation of 18 U.S.C. §§2113(a), (d), and 2. Appellant Floyd challenges the admission of certain testimony as hearsay. . . .

I

The evidence at trial indicates that on October 31, 1975, at approximately 10:25 A.M. the Chase Manhattan Bank on Rutland Road in Brooklyn, was robbed by three armed men wearing Halloween masks. The bank's records showed that $8,591.00 had been stolen. Because the men wore masks, there was no positive identification of the robbers. The bank guard was able to describe the perpetrators generally but was unable to specifically identify the appellants. Photographs taken by a security camera were introduced into evidence. One of the pictures showed a portion of the side of one robber's face. Through a courtroom demonstration the jury was afforded an opportunity to compare the appearance of the person in that picture with appellant Floyd.

The Government's principal witness was Xavier King, who was involved in the bank robbery as the driver of the getaway car. According to the testimony of King, the robbery was planned during the early morning hours of October 31, 1975 at an apartment on Saratoga Avenue in Brooklyn. King testified in detail as to the participants, their roles in the crime, the weapons used and the particulars of the robbery, its planning and aftermath. King's testimony indicated that Beverly Boston, Olivo's girlfriend was present in the apartment on the morning of the robbery, and that when King and the others returned to the apartment after the robbery, Suqulia Vantessa "Van" Manning (Floyd's girlfriend), "Debbie," Barry "Tuba" McDaniels and "Little Mike" were there.

The government also called James Duffin as a witness. Duffin testified that on the morning after the robbery Olivo asked him to take a walk. In the course of the walk Duffin agreed to help Olivo set fire to the getaway car, which had been parked on the street behind the Saratoga Avenue apartment building in which the robbers had headquartered their criminal activities. Duffin testified that a man standing on the stoop of a nearby building witnessed the arson of the automobile. The testimony further indicated that Olivo told Duffin that he, Floyd and others had robbed a bank.[3]

Olivo and Floyd each presented alibi defenses, claiming to have been at places other than the bank at the time of the robbery. Evidence of their respective defenses was presented through the testimony of the appellants and through the testimony of their girlfriends. . . .

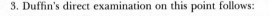

Should Duffin's testimony have been admitted? Was the conspiracy continuing or had it terminated?

Under Grunewald v. United States, 353 U.S. 391, 401 (1957), the test for whether a conspiracy had been terminated is whether the "central criminal purposes" of the conspiracy had been attained. Applying this standard is not always easy. Suppose, for example, several defendants conspire to rob a bank. How would you characterize the central criminal purpose of the conspiracy? Is it merely to rob the bank? To rob the bank and not get caught? To obtain money illegally? To obtain money illegally and use it for a particular purpose? To obtain money illegally and live the good life? Does your answer to when a conspiracy terminates depend

---

3. Duffin's direct examination on this point follows:

Q: Did he say where he wanted to go?
A: No, just we was walking, walking toward Key Food, and he [Olivo] told me he robbed a bank.
Q: Did he say who he had robbed the bank with?
A: Yes, with Lamont, him and some other people I don't know who they were.

on how close in time such events occur? See United States v. Hickey, 596 F.2d 1082, 1089-1090 (1st Cir.) cert. denied, 100 S. Ct. 107 (1979).

NOTE: THE PROCEDURE OF ADMITTING EVIDENCE UNDER RULE 801(d)(2)(E) — CO-CONSPIRATORS' STATEMENTS

Difficult procedural questions arise when statements of an alleged co-conspirator are offered against a defendant under Rule 801(d)(2)(E). Under the rule such statements are admissible only if made during and in furtherance of the conspiracy. Thus, a preliminary question that must be answered before the exception becomes applicable is whether a conspiracy existed at the time the statement was made.

Is this a question for the judge to determine under Rule 104(a), or is it a 104(b) question of conditional relevancy for the jury to determine like any other issue of conditional relevancy? If this question is a 104(b) issue, is the standard of proof of a conspiracy that must be satisfied before the hearsay is allowed any different from the standard of proof of conspiracy that the judge must apply if this is a 104(a) question? Regardless of whether this is a 104(a) or 104(b) issue, may the hearsay statement itself be considered on the preliminary issue of whether a conspiracy existed? If the court decides that the existence of a conspiracy is a 104(a) question, must it hear *all* the proof regarding existence or nonexistence of the conspiracy and make its decision as to whether a conspiracy existed before allowing in the hearsay statement whose admissibility depends on a finding of a conspiracy? If the court concludes that the existence of a conspiracy is a 104(b) issue, or if the court concludes it is a 104(a) issue but allows the hearsay evidence in before ruling on the preliminary issue of the existence of a conspiracy, and it turns out that the proof of the existence of a conspiracy is insufficient, what corrective options are available to the court?

UNITED STATES v. VINSON
606 F.2d 149 (6th Cir. 1979)

MERRIT, J. After a jury trial in the United States District Court for the Eastern District of Kentucky, Vinson, Sheriff of Lawrence County, and Thompson, a county magistrate, were convicted of extorting money from a coal company and of conspiring to do so. 18 U.S.C. §1951 (1976). We affirm the defendants' convictions. The major issue on appeal is whether the District Judge followed proper procedures governing admission of co-conspirator hearsay evidence. We address questions left unanswered by our recent decision in United States v. Enright, 579 F.2d

980 (6th Cir. 1978), and establish guidelines for administering the co-conspirator exception to the hearsay rule, Fed. R. Evid. 801(d)(2)(E).

I

During the government's case-in-chief, the District Court admitted testimony describing out-of-court statements of Sheriff Vinson which tended to incriminate Magistrate Thompson in both the conspiracy and the substantive offenses. An officer of the coal company who was the target of the extortion plan testified that the Sheriff told him that the Magistrate was his agent in the extortion scheme and would pick up the extortion payments. Upon timely objection, the District Judge instructed the jury as follows:

> That [hearsay] will not be considered by you, ladies and gentlemen, as any evidence against [the Magistrate] until you are satisfied or the Court makes a ruling of a prima facie case of conspiracy.

Further along in the government's case, the District Judge made a preliminary finding that the government had proved a conspiracy involving the Sheriff and Magistrate by a preponderance of the evidence. He then ruled that the out-of-court statements of the Sheriff, made in the course of and in furtherance of the conspiracy, could be used as evidence against the Magistrate. He instructed the jury:

> Ladies and gentlemen . . . let me advise you that the admonition that I have given you earlier in the case about not considering certain testimony as to [the Magistrate] is now withdrawn.

Both defendants objected to the judge's second statement on the ground that it amounted to an improper comment on the sufficiency of the evidence. Although we believe that the judge should have made neither statement, we find that no prejudice resulted to defendants. The government's proof of the conspiracy as well as of the substantive offense rested on strong non-hearsay evidence which showed that the Sheriff, the Magistrate and an unindicted third person conspired to and, in fact, did extort money from the coal company. Sheriff Vinson was the principal in the scheme, and the Magistrate and the third person were his agents. The three threatened to harass the coal company's trucks which operated on county roads unless extortion payments were made. Two such payments were made before authorities apprehended the defendants. There was relatively little co-conspirator hearsay admitted both before and after the District Judge made his preliminary finding, and the jury had abundant, non-hearsay evidence on which to base its verdict. Moreover, any confusion which might have been caused by the trial judge's comments to the jury was cured by his final conspiracy instruction in which the elements of a criminal conspiracy and the government's burden of proof were clearly and correctly stated.

In *Enright* we held that, before the government can take advantage of the co-conspirator exception to the hearsay rule, it must show by a preponderance of the evidence (1) that a conspiracy existed, (2) that the defendant against whom the hearsay is offered was a member of the conspiracy, and (3) that the hearsay statement was made in the course and in furtherance of the conspiracy. We also held that this preliminary finding is the sole province of the trial judge. Fed. R. Evid. 104(a). In *Enright*, however, we did not decide whether, before the judge has made his finding on the preliminary question, he may admit the hearsay subject to connection later in the trial, as did the trial judge here. We also did not decide whether the trial judge may consider the hearsay itself in making his preliminary finding.

A trial judge must have considerable discretion in controlling the mode and order of proof at trial and his rulings should not cause reversal of a criminal conviction unless they "affect substantial rights." Thus, we do not believe that it is appropriate to set forth hard and fast procedures. Rather, we set forth alternative means for District Judges to structure conspiracy trials, that will allow the government to present its proof while at the same time protecting defendants from inadmissible hearsay evidence.

One acceptable method is the so-called "mini-hearing" in which the court, without a jury, hears the government's proof of conspiracy and makes the preliminary *Enright* finding. If the hearsay is found admissible, the case, including co-conspirator hearsay, is presented to the jury. Although this procedure has been criticized as burdensome, time-consuming and uneconomic, a trial judge, in the exercise of his discretion, may choose to order the proof in this manner if the circumstances warrant.

The judge may also require the government to meet its initial burden by producing the non-hearsay evidence of conspiracy first prior to making the *Enright* finding concerning the hearsay's admissibility. This procedure clearly avoids "the danger . . . of injecting the record with inadmissible hearsay in anticipation of proof of a conspiracy which never materializes."

The judge may also, as was done here, admit the hearsay statements subject to later demonstration of their admissibility by a preponderance of the evidence. If this practice is followed, the court should stress to counsel that the statements are admitted subject to defendant's continuing objection and that the prosecution will be required to show by a preponderance of the evidence that a conspiracy existed, that the defendant against whom the statements are hearsay was a participant and that the statement was made in the course and in furtherance thereof. At the conclusion of the government's case-in-chief, the court should rule on the defendant's hearsay objection. If the court finds that the government has met the burden of proof described in *Enright*, it should overrule the objection and let all the evidence, hearsay included, go to the jury, subject, of course, to instructions regarding the government's ultimate burden of proof beyond a reasonable doubt and the weight and credibility to be given to co-conspirators' statements. If, on the other hand, the court finds that the government has failed to carry its burden, it should, on defendant's motion, declare a mistrial unless convinced that a cautionary jury instruction would shield the defendant from prejudice.

If the trial judge does choose to admit the hearsay (a) after the government has established the conspiracy by a preponderance at the trial, or (b) at a "mini-hearing," or (c) conditionally subject to connection, he should refrain from advising the jury of his findings that the government has satisfactorily proved the conspiracy. The judge should not describe to the jury the government's burden of proof on the preliminary question. Such an instruction can serve only to alert the jury that the judge has determined that a conspiracy involving the defendant has been proven by a preponderance of the evidence. This may adversely affect the defendant's right to trial by jury. The judge's opinion is likely to influence strongly the opinion of individual jurors when they come to consider their verdict and judge the credibility of witnesses.

Finally, we believe that, whatever procedure a District Judge uses, the hearsay statements themselves may be considered by the judge in deciding the preliminary question of admissibility. The preliminary finding of conspiracy for purposes of the co-conspirator exception to the hearsay rule is a "question concerning . . . the admissibility of evidence" governed by Fed. R. Evid. 104(a), and we believe that the final sentence of Rule 104(a) — stating that the judge "is not bound by the rules of evidence" — modifies prior law to the contrary. The fact that the judge may consider under Rule 104(a) hearsay evidence which the jury could not consider is an added reason the judge should refrain from advising the jury of his findings. . . .

C. Prior Statements

FRE 801(d)(1)
Definitions

(d) *Statements which are not hearsay.* A statement is not hearsay if —

   (1) *Prior statements by witness.* The declarant testifies at the trial or hearing and is subject to cross-examination concerning the statement,

and the statement is (A) inconsistent with his testimony, and was given under oath subject to the penalty of perjury at a trial, hearing, or other proceeding, or in a deposition, or (B) consistent with his testimony and is offered to rebut an express or implied charge against him of recent fabrication or improper influence or motive, or (C) one of identification of a person made after perceiving him.

FRE 613
Prior Statements of Witnesses

(a) *Examining witness concerning prior statement.* In examining a witness concerning a prior statement made by him, whether written or not, the statement need not be shown nor its contents disclosed to him at that time, but on request the same shall be shown or disclosed to opposing counsel.

(b) *Extrinsic evidence of prior inconsistent statement of witness.* Extrinsic evidence of a prior inconsistent statement by a witness is not admissible unless the witness is afforded an opportunity to explain or deny the same and the opposite party is afforded an opportunity to interrogate him thereon, or the interests of justice otherwise require. This provision does not apply to admissions of a party-opponent as defined in Rule 801(d)(2).

FRE 804
Hearsay Exceptions: Declarant Unavailable

(a) *Definition of unavailability.* "Unavailability as a witness" includes situations in which the declarant —

(1) is exempted by ruling of the court on the ground of privilege from testifying concerning the subject matter of his statement; or

(2) persists in refusing to testify concerning the subject matter of his statement despite an order of the court to do so; or

(3) testifies to a lack of memory of the subject matter of his statement; or

(4) is unable to be present or to testify at the hearing because of death or then existing physical or mental illness or infirmity; or

(5) is absent from the hearing and the proponent of his statement has been unable to procure his attendance (or in the case of a hearsay exception under subdivision (b)(2), (3), or (4), his attendance or testimony) by process or other reasonable means.

A declarant is not unavailable as a witness if his exemption, refusal, claim of lack of memory, inability, or absence is due to the procurement or wrongdoing of the proponent of his statement for the purpose of preventing the witness from attending or testifying.

I/A

Problem IV-31
The Stolen BMW

P drives her new BMW home from the BMW dealer on June 1. She parks it in front of her house with the motor running while she goes in to pick up her running shoes. *P* notices some acquaintances — *W*, *D*, and *T* — standing on the sidewalk. *P* shouts to them to keep an eye on her new car. When *P* comes out of her house a minute later the BMW is gone and so are *D* and *T*. *P* asks *W* where the car is. W says, "*D* took it."

P sues *D* for conversion of the BMW. *D*'s answer generally denies *P*'s allegations. At trial, *P* calls *W* and asks him if he saw who took the BMW. W says, "Yes, *T* took it." *P* then questions *W* about his June 1 statement to *P* that *D* took the BMW. *D*'s objection is overruled. *W* denies making the statement. *P* takes the stand and over *D*'s objection testifies to *W*'s June 1 statement. *P* rests her case. *D* moves for a nonsuit. If *D*'s motion is granted, what is the rationale for overruling his objections to the evidence but granting his motion? Compare Rules 607, 613, and 801(d)(1).

prob allowed under 801 ∴ subst ∴ no nonsuit

Problem IV-32
The "Forgetful" Witness

Charge: conspiracy to commit mail fraud. *D* was indicted with two alleged co-conspirators who pled guilty before defendant's trial. *W*, one of these co-conspirators, was called at *D*'s trial by the prosecution to testify to the details of *D*'s participation in the alleged mail fraud. But *W* testified that he could not remember these details. At this point the prosecution sought to introduce *W*'s grand jury testimony on these points. *D* objected. On voir dire *W* states that he does not remember making the statements attributed to him before the grand jury nor does he now remember the details of the alleged mail fraud.

(1) Are *W*'s prior statements before the grand jury "inconsistent"?

(2) Does testimony before the grand jury fall within 801(d)(1)(A)? Should it? Compare the limitations on the use of former testimony in Rule 804(b)(1). What does "other proceeding," as used in Rule 801(d)(1)(A), include?

(3) Would it make any difference to the admissibility of *W*'s grand jury testimony if *W* were present in the courtroom but was not called by the prosecution to testify? Should it?

(4) Is *W* "subject to cross-examination" concerning the grand jury testimony?

(5) Have *D*'s sixth amendment rights been violated?

(6) Would your analysis of any of the above questions be any different if instead of grand jury testimony the prosecution sought to introduce in this situation:

(a) *W*'s testimony at a preliminary hearing at which he was actually cross-examined by *D*'s attorney; or

(b) *W*'s statements to the arresting officer while in custody prior to indictment?

MORGAN, HEARSAY DANGERS AND THE APPLICATION OF THE HEARSAY CONCEPT
62 Harv. L. Rev. 177, 192-196 (1948)

There is one situation where the courts are prone to call hearsay what does not in fact involve in any substantial degree any of the hearsay risks. When the declarant is also a witness, it is difficult to justify classifying as hearsay evidence of his own prior statements. This is especially true where declarant as a witness is giving as part of his testimony his own prior statement. . . . The courts declare the prior statement to be hearsay because it was not made under oath, subject to the penalty for perjury or to the test of cross-examination. To which the answer might well be: "The declarant as a witness is now under oath and now purports to remember and narrate accurately. The adversary can now expose every element that may carry a danger of misleading the trier of fact both in the previous statement and in the present testimony, and the trier can judge whether both the previous declaration and the present testimony are reliable in whole or in part." To this Mr. Justice Stone of the Minnesota Supreme Court, speaking of evidence of prior contradictory statements, has framed this reply:

> The chief merit of cross-examination is not that at some future time it gives the party opponent the right to dissect adverse testimony. Its principal virtue is in its immediate application of the testing process. Its strokes fall while the iron is hot. False testimony is apt to harden and become unyielding to the blows of truth in proportion as the witness has opportunity for reconsideration and influence by the suggestions of others, whose interest may be, and often is, to maintain falsehood rather than truth.

He adds the "practical reasons" that receipt of such evidence would create temptation and opportunity to manufacture evidence and entrap witnesses, and would require admission of prior consistent statements. Why does falsehood harden any more quickly or unyieldingly than truth? What has become of the idea that truth is eternal and, though crushed to earth, will rise again? Isn't the opportunity for reconsideration and for baneful influence by others even more likely to color the later testimony than the prior statement? Furthermore, it must be remembered that the trier of fact is often permitted to hear these prior statements to impeach or rehabilitate the declarant-witness. In such event, of course, the trier will be told that he must not treat the statement as evidence of the truth of the matter stated. But to what practical effect? Wasn't Judge Swan right in saying, "Practically, men will often believe that if a witness has earlier sworn to the opposite of what he now swears to, he was speaking the truth when he first testified"? Do the judges deceive themselves or do they realize that they are indulging in a pious fraud? . . .

In these situations it is unquestionably true that the trier is being asked to treat the former utterance as if it were now being made by the witness on the stand. But whether or not the declarant at the time of the utterance was subject to all the conditions usually imposed upon witnesses should be immaterial, for the declarant is now present as a witness. If his prior statement is consistent with his present testimony, he now affirms it under oath subject to all sanctions and to cross-examination in the presence of the trier who is to value it. Perhaps it ought not to be received because unnecessary, but surely the rejection should not be on the ground that the statement involves any danger inherent in hearsay. If the witness testifies that all the statements he made were true . . . , then the only debatable question is whether he made the statement; and as to that the trier has all the witnesses before him, and has also the benefit of thorough cross-examination as to the facts which are the subject matter of the statement. If the witness denies having made any statement at all, the situation is but little different, for he will usually swear that he tried to tell the truth in anything that he may have said. If he concedes that he made the statement but now swears that it wasn't true, the experience in human affairs which the average trier brings to a controversy will enable him to decide which story represents the truth in the light of all the facts, such as the demeanor of the witness, the matter brought out on his direct and cross-examination, and the testimony of others. In any of these situations Proponent is not asking Trier to rely upon the credibility of any one who is not present and subject to all the conditions imposed upon a witness. Adversary has all the protection which oath and cross-examination can give him. Trier is in a position to consider the evidence impartially and to give it no more than its reasonable persuasive effect. Consequently there is no real reason for classifying the evidence as hearsay. . . .

RUHALA v. ROBY
379 Mich. 102, 150 N.W.2d 146 (1967)

[Ruhala, the administrator of the estate of the deceased, Mrs. Kingsley, brought a wrongful death action against Roby and Burditt. The plaintiff claimed that Kingsley was killed when her car, which was allegedly being driven by Roby, collided with a truck driven by Burditt. The trial judge directed a verdict for Burditt from which the plaintiff did not appeal. Plaintiff appealed from the jury verdict for Roby and from the trial judge's denial of a motion for a new trial. At trial the issue was whether Roby or Mrs. Kingsley was driving the car at the time of the accident. Burditt testified that Kingsley and not Roby was the driver of the car. The issue on appeal was the admissibility of prior inconsistent statements admittedly made by Burditt soon after the accident to the effect that Roby was driving the car. The Michigan supreme court found the prior statements inadmissible as substantive evidence, reasoning as follows:]

The status of the law regarding the admissibility of prior inconsistent statements is relatively settled. Such statements are generally admissible for impeachment purposes and are also admissible when they constitute an admission by a party opponent. The effect of such prior inconsistent statements when admitted in evidence is not so clear in the law, and in many cases it becomes important to determine whether the prior inconsistent statement is in fact substantive evidence or whether it is admissible merely to impeach. In his handbook on the law of evidence, Professor Charles T. McCormick states the problem as follows:

> When a witness has changed sides and altered his story or forgets or claims to forget some fact, and his previous statement is received for impeachment purposes, what effect shall be given to the statement as evidence? Under the generally accepted doctrine the statement is not usable as substantive evidence of the facts stated. The adversary if he so is entitled to an instruction to that effect, and, more important, if the only evidence of some essential fact is the rule such a previous statement, the party's case fails.
>
> Only two escapes from the lethal effect of this doctrine, where the sole witness to a vital fact has turned coat, are revealed by the cases. The first is the rule that when the hostile witness is an adverse party to the present action, his former inconsistent statement has two faces. As an impeaching statement it would not be substantive evidence, but as the admission of a party opponent it comes in under an exception to the rule excluding hearsay and as such is evidence of its truth.

McCormick on Evidence, Ch. 5, §39, pp. 73, 74.

The second escape from the doctrine as described by Professor McCormick is the case wherein the witness adopts his prior statement as true, making his prior statement and his present testimony one and the same.

Before we can consider the effect of the two prior inconsistent statements when offered for the purpose of impeaching Burditt, we must first grapple with the problem of whether the two prior inconsistent statements represented admissions of a party opponent, within the rule holding such admissions to be substantive evidence which can be considered by the jury. The problem here is that the admissions of one defendant are not admissible in evidence against a co-defendant. Thus, even if Burditt's prior inconsistent statements were admissions, a matter we need not decide, and thus admissible as substantive evidence against Burditt, they were totally inadmissible as to Roby, and where the appeal is taken only against Roby, the plaintiff cannot be said to have been harmed because the extrajudicial statements of Burditt were not received in evidence against Roby. . . .

If the extrajudicial statements of Burditt were inadmissible against Roby as admissions of Burditt, what was their evidentiary effect when offered for impeachment purposes? As has already been indicated, the general rule followed in this State for many years is that evidence of prior inconsistent statements when offered for impeachment purposes does not constitute substantive evidence unless the truth of the prior inconsistent statements is admitted when the witness is confronted with them on the stand. This rule has been called the orthodox view and is founded on the reason that such statements are hearsay, that their value rests on the credibility of the declarant who was not under oath and not subject to cross-examination when the statement was made. The rule is one of general acceptance. Nevertheless, there has been some criticism of the rule. Judge Learned Hand in his opinion in Di Carlo v. United States, 6 F.2d 364 (C.C.A. 2, 1925) says:

"The possibility that the jury may accept as the truth the earlier statements in preference to those made upon the stand is indeed real, but we find no difficulty in it. If, from all that the jury see of the witness, they conclude that what he says now is not the truth, but what he said before, they are nonetheless deciding from what they see and hear of that person and in court. There is no mythical necessity that the case must be decided only in accordance with the truth of words uttered under oath in court."

Mr. Justice Otis Smith, writing for the Court in the *Schratt* case, states, 371 Mich. at page 245, 123 N.W.2d at page 784, as follows:

"We agree with the view stated in McCormick on Evidence, §39, p. 75:

> If the prior statement of the witness is contradictory of his present story on the stand, the opportunity for testing the veracity of the two stories by the two parties through cross-examination and re-examination is ideal. Too often the cross-examiner of a dubious witness is faced by a smooth, blank wall. The witness has been able throughout to present a narrative which may be false, yet is consistent with itself and offers no foothold for the climber who would look beyond. But the witness who has told one story aforetime and another today has opened the gates to all the vistas of truth which the common-law practice of cross-examination and re-examination was invented to explore. It will go hard, but the two questioners will lay bare the sources of the change of face, in forgetfulness, carelessness, pity, terror or greed, and thus reveal which is the true story and which the false. *It is hard to escape the view that*

evidence of a previous inconsistent statement, when the declarant is on the stand to explain it if he can, has in high degree the safeguards of examined testimony.

This quotation from Professor McCormick represents an excerpt from a lengthy and most interesting discussion. The substance of the balance of Professor McCormick's remarks is that he believes that the rule which prohibits the use of impeachment testimony as substantive evidence is not a reasonable one. He is not talking about prior inconsistent statements which are adopted by the witness as he concedes that these are already generally held to be substantive evidence. He points out that the prior inconsistent statement because made closer in time to the fact is based upon a fresher memory and for that reason may even be more reliable than the testimony of the witness in court. . . .

Those who argue for the use of such statements as substantive evidence, that is, as tending to prove the truth of the thing said, reason in this fashion: since the principal reason for the hearsay rule lies in the absence of an opportunity to cross-examine the declarant on his statement, the reason for the rule fails whenever the declarant is available for cross-examination. Under this line of reasoning, prior consistent statements, as well as prior inconsistent statements, would be admissible substantive evidence whenever the declarant was on the witness stand.

The difficulty with this argument is that it does not recognize the real nature of cross-examination. Cross-examination presupposes a witness who affirms a thing being examined by a lawyer who would have him deny it, or a witness who denies a thing being examined by a lawyer who would have him affirm it. Cross-examination is in its essence an adversary proceeding. The extent to which the cross-examiner is able to shake the witness, or induce him to equivocate is the very measure of the cross-examiner's success.

Bearing in mind that when the witness adopts the prior statement his prior statement becomes his present testimony, and becomes admissible substantive evidence by settled law, it is readily apparent that the present discussion only relates to those cases where the witness does not adopt his prior statement as true. If he refuses to adopt his prior statement as true, there can be no adversary cross-examination upon it. If he refuses to affirm, no question can be put to him which would shake his own confidence in his affirmation. . . .

The would-be cross-examiner is not only denied the right to be the declarant's adversary, he is left with no choice but to become the witness' friend, protector and savior. Though he may be permitted to ask questions in the form of cross-examination, the substance of his effort will be re-direct examination and rehabilitation. The reason is simple. The witness cannot recant! Every cross-examiner tries to bring the witness to the point where he changes his story — literally eats his words — in the presence of the jury.

A statement made from the witness stand is not beyond total recall by the witness. Stale friendly cross-examination "with respect to" a prior extrajudicial statement is no substitute for timely, adversary cross-examination "upon" a statement. The importance of this distinction is clearly seen when we analyze the case before us. The statement Burditt gave to the police officer, and which plaintiff would have the jury consider as substantive evidence, was as follows:

Q: William, you said earlier that a woman was on your side when you hit, so would you say that the man in the car was driving?

A: He had to have been, there was a man driving.

Trial lawyers are keenly aware of the vulnerability of "hadda" witnesses and "musta" witnesses. When a witness says that the driver *had to have been* speeding, or *must have* swerved this way or that way, his very choice of verbs betrays that he is stating his conclusions rather than his observations. For the purpose of demonstrating the difference between timely and stale cross-examination, let us suppose that a cross-examiner had been present at the time Burditt made his statement to the police officer. And let us suppose, for the sake of discussion, that the following had taken place:

Q: William, you say that the man had to have been driving, is that right?

A: Yes.

Q: Did you see the man behind the wheel before the accident?

A: No.

Q: Did you see the man behind the wheel after the accident?

A: No.

Q: Did you ever see the man in the car?

A: No.

Q: Why then, do you say that the man had to have been driving?

A: Because when I first looked over there after the accident, the woman was lying out of the door on the passenger's side, and if she was on the passenger's side, she must have been the passenger and the man had to have been the driver.

Q: Isn't it possible that the man was thrown out of the car from the passenger's side and the woman was thrown across the front seat from the driver's seat?

A: Yes, that's possible.

Q: *Do you still say that the man had to have been driving?*

A: *No, I guess not.*

Now let us see whether the stale cross-examination of Burditt "*with respect to*" his statement, as ... advocated by Professor McCormick, would have the same effect:

Q: William, you say that the man had to have been driving, is that right?

A: No, I'm not saying that.

Q: Well, that's what you told the police officer, isn't it?

A: Yes.

Q: Did you see the man behind the wheel before the accident?

A: No.

Q: Did you see the man behind the wheel after the accident?

A: No.

Q: Did you ever see the man in the car?

A: No.

Q: Why then did you tell the police officer that the man had to have been driving?

A: Because when I first looked over there after the accident, the woman was lying out of the door on the passenger's side, and if she was on the passenger's side, she must have been the passenger and the man had to have been the driver.

Q: Isn't it possible that the man was thrown out of the car from the passenger's side and the woman was thrown across the front seat from the driver's side?

A: Yes, that's possible.

At this point, the cross-examiner is stymied. The crucial question which would give the witness a chance to change his story, *"Do you still say that the man had to have been driving?"* is meaningless. The witness has already testified that he is not still saying that the man had to have been driving. Instead of a plunge to the jugular, the examiner will have to be satisfied with applying a bandage. It would sound something like this:

Q: And isn't this the reason why the story you are telling us today is different from the story you told the police officer?

or,

Q: And isn't it true that if you had thought of that possibility at the time, you never would have told the police officer that the man had to have been driving the car?

By these hypothetical examples we have tried to show the windmill-fighting nature of stale cross-examination with respect to the prior statement. No matter how deadly the thrust of the cross-examiner, the ghost of the prior statement stands. His questions will always sound like attempts to permit the witness to explain *why* he changed his story before coming to court, with the jury being left to infer that he might have been induced to change his story in the intervening months or years, for some unrevealed and sinister reason.

When a cross-examiner on timely cross-examination *succeeds* in getting the witness to change his story, the integrity of the recantation is apparent, and *his original, recanted version no longer stands as substantive evidence*. If the only evidence of an essential fact in a lawsuit were a statement made from the witness stand which the witness himself completely recanted and repudiated before he left the witness stand, no one would seriously urge that a jury question had been made out.

Scholarly legal writings are useful and necessary. When they challenge the established rules, the courts have an obligation to re-examine those rules and measure the theoretical criticism against the hard facts of a living system of justice. This Opinion has been longer than we would have liked, but there seemed to be a need. . . .

Do you agree that to make cross-examination effective the witness must affirm his present belief in the truth of the prior statement? How could the imaginary cross-examination with respect to the prior statements be improved upon?

Problem IV-33
The Dishonest Employee

P owns a gas station and motel. In September he goes to Florida, leaving *W*, a relatively new employee, in charge. Before leaving, *P* secures a fidelity bond from *D* in the sum of $5,000. When *P* returns from Florida in May, he discovers shortages in the bank accounts of the business. *P* files a claim with *D*, who investigates the affair. During the investigation, *W* makes a series of contradictory statements concerning his responsibility for the shortages. Some of these are inculpatory. *P* sues *D* on the bond. At trial, *W* denies any responsibility for the shortages. *P*'s only proof on this crucial point is *W*'s prior inconsistent statement to *D* during the investigation. Are these prior statements sufficient to withstand a directed verdict under the federal rules? Should they be admitted as substantive evidence? Are they reliable? What additional guarantees of trustworthiness would one desire in this situation?

not admission b/c not party opponent
admitted for impeachment

WHITEHURST v. WRIGHT
592 F.2d 834 (5th Cir. 1979)

[Civil rights action under 42 U.S.C. §1983 against defendant city police officers.]

VANCE, J. Bernard Whitehurst was gunned down by Montgomery,

Alabama police who mistook him for a suspect in a local robbery. The fatal shot was fired by police officer Donald Foster, who claims that Whitehurst shot first. Although none of the officers in the vicinity found a gun near the body, a detective subsequently called to the scene spotted a gun twenty-seven inches from the victim. It was later discovered that the gun had been confiscated by police in a drug raid occurring over one year prior to the Whitehurst shooting. . . .

IMPEACHMENT OF PLAINTIFF'S WITNESS

Mrs. Whitehurst contends that the trial court erroneously refused to allow her to impeach her own witness, in violation of Fed. R. Evid. 607. The witness, Detective Cecil Humphrey of the Montgomery Police Department, was called solely to establish whether he had fired the single spent round in the gun found next to Whitehurst's body. Humphrey denied that he had fired the gun, and Mrs. Whitehurst was aware that he would so testify. Nevertheless, she called him to the stand with the express purpose of impeaching him with an out of court statement made by Humphrey to his friend, Lt. J.G. Cunningham, to the effect that he had fired the gun.[6]

While it is now proper for a party to impeach his own witness, Fed. R. Evid. 607, "impeachment by prior inconsistent statement may not be permitted where employed as a mere subterfuge to get before the jury evidence not otherwise admissible." Here the statement made to Cunningham is hearsay and is generally inadmissible for substantive purposes. Fed. R. Evid. 801(c), 802.[7] Mrs. Whitehurst asserts on appeal that she would have called Lt. Cunningham "to establish Humphrey's role concerning the pistol firing. . . ." To use a prior inconsistent statement in that manner exceeds the scope of impeachment, and is an attempt to use hearsay evidence for substantive purposes. We do not believe that the rules of evidence espouse such a revolutionary approach to circumvent the traditional principles of hearsay. . . .

---

6. The following colloquy took place prior to the direct examination of Humphrey:

Mr. Watkins: . . . we expect the evidence to show that Mr. Humphrey actually retrieved the gun from the scene and has reported to a J. C. Cunningham that he checked the gun at that point, saw that it had not been fired and fired the gun, one round, so that the gun would appear to have been fired at some point between the time he retrieved the gun at the scene and the time he arrived with the gun at police headquarters.
Mr. Black [defense counsel]:   You deny that, don't you?
Mr. Humphrey: That's right, I don't know what he is talking about.
Mr. Watkins: Then we would like to call J. C. Cunningham behind him.

7. Because the statement was offered only for impeachment purposes, we make no determination as to its admissibility under Fed. R. Evid. §803(24). But cf. Fed. R. Evid. 801(d)(1)(A). . . .

Do you agree with the court's conclusion? What arguments could you make for admissibility?

Problem IV-34
The Perjurious Performer

Charge: extortion. At trial, *W1* testifies to having made extortionary payments to *D*. *D*'s cross-examination reveals that *W1* testified before the grand jury that he had no knowledge of *D*'s extortionary scheme. The cross-examination further suggests that *W1*'s trial testimony is fabricated in order to gain leniency in *W1*'s perjury prosecution, which is based on *W1*'s grand jury testimony. In rebuttal the government calls *W2* to testify that prior to *W1*'s grand jury appearance, *W1* told him that he (*W2*) could obtain a job from *D* through the payment of extortion money. *D* objects. What ruling and why?

Problem IV-35
The Prosecution's Patsy

Charge: possession with intent to distribute heroin. At trial, *W*, who has pled guilty to a lesser charge in return for her cooperation, testifies against *D*. Her testimony includes references to *D*'s nephew's participation in the narcotics distribution scheme. On cross-examination *D* is permitted to impeach *W* by introducing evidence that *W*'s grand jury testimony and her testimony at the trial of two other members of the ring did not include any reference to *D*'s nephew. On redirect the government seeks to read portions of *W*'s prior grand jury testimony and the testimony from the two other trials that are consistent with his present testimony implicating *D* but that do not contain any references to *D*'s nephew. *D* objects. What ruling and why? Has *D* expressly or impliedly charged *W* with recent fabrication or improper influence or motive? If so, has the prosecution rebutted that charge?

Problem IV-36
The Colombian Mule

D, a citizen of Colombia, flies from Guatemala to Los Angeles. At Los Angeles International Airport he is stopped for questioning by customs agents. *D* invites the officers to search his baggage and voluntarily submits to a full body search. The officers find a white powder in the lining of his suitcase. *D* expresses great surprise at the discovery of the white powder. Later, at his trial for illegally and knowingly importing cocaine, *D* testifies that he was loaned the suitcase by an American he met in Colombia who was helping him immigrate to America and that he had no knowledge of the hidden cocaine. *D* offers a tape recording of the airport search and interview to show that his testimony was not a recent fabrication. The government objects. What ruling and why?

Problem IV-37
The Erring Eyewitness

Charge: armed robbery. At trial, *W*, an eyewitness, is asked to pick out the robber. She points to a U.S. Marshal seated in the courtroom. After the prosecutor recovers he elicits testimony from *W* concerning *W*'s selection of a photograph of the alleged robber from a display of photographs conducted shortly after the robbery. The photograph was of the defendant. Defendant objects. What ruling and why? Does Rule 801(d)(1)(C) apply to photographic as well as corporeal out-of-court identifications? Does Rule 801(d)(1)(A)'s "under oath" limitation apply to prior identifications inconsistent with a later in-court identification? Is this a case of "inconsistency"? Should third-party testimony concerning an out-of-court identification by a witness be admissible if the witness cannot recall the prior identification?

D. Former Testimony

FRE 804(b)(1)
Hearsay Exceptions: Declarant Unavailable

(b) *Hearsay exceptions.* The following are not excluded by the hearsay rule if the declarant is unavailable as a witness:

(1) *Former testimony.* Testimony given as a witness at another hearing of the same or a different proceeding, or in a deposition taken in compliance with law in the course of the same or another proceeding, if the party against whom the testimony is now offered, or, in a civil action or proceeding, a predecessor in interest, had an opportunity and similar motive to develop the testimony by direct, cross, or redirect examination. . . .

Problem IV-38
Speaking from the Grave — The Dead Witness, I

Action against *D* Supermarket for injuries allegedly sustained when *P* slipped and fell while shopping in the *D* store. *P* claims he slipped on ketchup from a broken bottle. *D* claims *P* slipped on a wad of tobacco from *P*'s mouth. *W*, a customer in the store who rushed to *P*'s aid while *P* was lying unconscious on the floor, is *P*'s first witness at trial. *W* testifies that she saw ketchup on the soles of *P*'s shoes after the fall. On cross-examination defense counsel questions *W*'s perception, memory, and veracity but fails to make much progress. Verdict is for *P*, but when the jury is polled it is discovered that the panel consists of only 11 people. A mistrial is declared. On retrial, *P* introduces evidence that *W* is dead and calls *R*, the court reporter from the first trial, to testify that he remembers *W*'s former testimony and to relate it. *D* objects. What ruling and why?

What policies justify the use of former testimony of an unavailable witness? What are the dangers and drawbacks of the use of this type of evidence? What limitations should be imposed on the use of former testimony?

Problem IV-39
The Dead Witness, II

P's car collides with *D*'s car. *G* was a guest in *P*'s car. *W* witnessed the collision. At the trial of *P*'s action against *D*, *W* testifies for *P*. Later, at the trial of *G*'s action against *D*, *G* proves *W*'s death and offers a transcript of *W*'s former testimony from the first trial. *D* objects. What rulings and why?

Problem IV-40
The Dead Witness, III

P is tried on a charge of arson. *W* testifies for the prosecution. Later, *P* sues *D* Insurance Company to recover for losses sustained in the fire. *D* Insurance Company proves *W*'s death and offers a transcript of *W*'s former testimony. *P* objects. What ruling and why?

What result if *W* had first testified in the civil action and his testimony was offered at a subsequent criminal trial?

Problem IV-41
The Dead Witness, IV

P is injured while alighting from the *D* Bus Company's bus. *P*'s husband, *H*, sues *D* for loss of his wife's services, claiming that *D*'s driver started driving the bus before *P* had completely alighted. At trial, *W* testifies for *D* that the bus did not move but that *P* tripped over her own feet. Later, *P* sues *D* for personal injuries. *D* proves *W*'s death and offers the transcript of *W*'s former testimony. *P* objects. What ruling and why?

Under the approach adopted in Rule 804(b)(1), what factors should a court consider in determining whether a party in a later case is a "predecessor in interest" to a party in a former case who "had an opportunity and similar motive to develop the testimony" as the present party? Compare In re Master Key Antitrust Litigation, 72 F.R.D. 108 (D. Conn.), aff'd per curiam, 551 F.2d 300 (2d Cir. 1976) (the special relationship between government antitrust suits and subsequent private actions justifies allowing the defendant to use testimony elicited from a now unavailable witness at the former government action in the later private action), with In re IBM Peripheral EDP Devices Antitrust Litigation, 444 F. Supp. 110 (N.D. Cal. 1978) (former testimony elicited in previous government and private antitrust cases inadmissible against plaintiff who was not a party in those proceedings because "predecessor in interest" defined by substantive law).

Problem IV-42
The Dead Witness, V

P's car collides with *D*'s car, injuring bystander *W*. At the trial of *P*'s action against *D, D* testifies. Later, at the trial of *W*'s action against *P, W* proves *D*'s death and offers a transcript of *D*'s former testimony. *P* objects. What ruling and why?

Compare this problem with the Dead Witness, II, above. What additional information would you like to have in deciding this problem? In determining the admissibility of former testimony, should the trial judge place greater weight on similarity of factual issues in the two proceedings or on similarity of legal issues? To what extent should former testimony be excluded on the grounds that it related only to a collateral issue in the earlier proceeding?

E. Statements Against Interest

FRE 804(b)(3)
Hearsay Exceptions: Declarant Unavailable

(b) *Hearsay exceptions.* The following are not excluded by the hearsay rule if the declarant is unavailable as a witness: . . .

(3) *Statement against interest.* A statement which was at the time of its making so far contrary to the declarant's pecuniary or proprietary interest, or so far tended to subject him to civil or criminal liability, or to render invalid a claim by him against another, that a reasonable man in his position would not have made the statement unless he believed it to be true. A statement tending to expose the declarant to criminal liability and offered to exculpate the accused is not admissible unless corroborating circumstances clearly indicate the trustworthiness of the statement. . . .

Problem IV-43
The Fraudulent Transfers

Action on a promissory note and for fraudulent transfer of *D*'s assets, allegedly rendering him insolvent. *P*'s complaint seeks a money judgment for $10,000, the amount of the note, interest, and costs, and an order against *D* and *E*, setting aside a purported conveyance of Brownacre from *D* to *E*. *D*'s answer admits the debt to *P* and the conveyance to *E* but denies that the conveyance was made with any fraudulent intent or effect. At trial, *D* offers two witnesses:

(1) *W1*, Jr., to testify that his father, *W1*, Sr., is dead, that *W1*, Sr.'s estate is not yet settled, and that just before *W1*, Sr. died he said that he owed *D* $5,000.

(2) *W2*, Jr., to testify that his father, *W2*, Sr., is dead, that *W2*, Sr.'s estate is not yet settled, and that just before *W2*, Sr. died he said that he had secretly conveyed Goldacre to *D*.

What ruling and why on these offers? What policy considerations support admissibility? What policy considerations militate against admitting such evidence? What types of statements are covered by the exception for statements against interest? Where would you draw the line? What other elements must exist to invoke the exception?

Problem IV-44
The Speeding Chauffeur

Action for damages that allegedly occurred when *D*'s car collided with *B*'s car, swerved up on the sidewalk, and struck *P*, who was walking on the sidewalk. *D*'s car was driven by *D*, but *B*'s car was driven by his chauffeur, Jeeves, who was alone in the car. *D*'s answer denies he was negligent and alleges the accident was totally Jeeves' fault. At trial, *B* is unavailable. *D* offers *W* to testify that a month before trial *W* heard *B* say that Jeeves was driving so fast at the time of the accident, that he ran a stop sign. *P* objects. What ruling and why?

TAGUE, PERILS OF THE RULEMAKING PROCESS: THE DEVELOPMENT, APPLICATION, AND UNCONSTITUTIONALITY OF RULE 804(B)(3)'S PENAL INTEREST EXCEPTION

69 Geo. L.J. 851, 862-863, 971 (1981)

The penal interest exception rests on the assumption that no one would knowingly implicate himself falsely in criminal conduct. Testing the validity of that assumption in a particular case involves at least six evidentiary questions. . . .

First, is a statement against a declarant's penal interest because of the "plain" meaning of the words spoken, the litigation effect of the statement, or the declarant's motivation to tell the truth? If a court concentrates on the words spoken, it probably will limit admissibility to confessions ("I am guilty of murdering Smith") or to explicit factual assertions ("I shot Smith"). If, however, the court analyzes the litigation effect of the statement, it might permit the introduction of opinions ("The defendant is not guilty"), statements whose relevance depends upon an inference ("I was present when Smith was shot"), or comments about the defendant's complicity related to the statement ("X and I, but not the defendant, committed the crime").

Second, must the statement have been "against interest" at the time the declarant made it? If a court admits only statements that are confessional in nature, it would focus on when the declarant made the statement. If, however, the court analyzes the litigation effect of the statement, its inquiry could encompass a greater time period.

Third, must the declarant have understood that his statement was "against interest"? Courts usually use a "reasonable man" inquiry because they condition admission on the declarant's unavailability to testify. If, however, at the moment he spoke or at some later point the declarant says that he understood the "against interest" nature of his statement, should a court reject the "reasonable man" test and focus instead on the declarant's apparent subjective understanding?

Fourth, must the statement substitute the declarant for the defendant as the culprit? If so, a court should exclude the statement if it is relevant only to the defendant's degree of culpability, not his innocence. A statement that exonerated the defendant of complicity in a crime committed by more than one person is similarly inadmissible because this kind of statement provides the Government with a reason to charge the declarant as well as the defendant.

Fifth, may the Government use the exception to introduce a statement that implicates both the declarant and the defendant? A Government-offered statement presents the same "collateral statement" problem as does the defense-offered statement in the fourth issue.

Sixth, must the proponent introduce other evidence to support the truthfulness of either the witness' report of the statement or the statement itself? Demanding corroborating evidence of either sort suggests uncertainty about the declarant's motivation or his sincerity. . . .

Five mechanical questions arise when the defendant offers a penal interest statement. First, should the judge or the jury decide if the statement satisfies the "against interest" tests of the rule's first sentence and the corroboration test of the rule's second sentence? Second, may the judge consider the trustworthiness of the reporting witness in deciding whether to admit the statement? Third, what is the defendant's burden of proof under the separate tests of the rule's first and second sentences? Fourth, what evidence may the judge consider in deciding whether to admit the statement? Finally, what evidence may the jury consider in deciding how to evaluate the declarant's statement? . . .

Problem IV-45
Thick as Thieves

Charge: murder of *V* on June 1 at the intersection of Boylston Street and Massachusetts Avenue.

(1) At *D*'s trial, *D* offers, through *W*, the statement of Joe (now dead), "I killed *V*." Is Joe's statement admissible? Under what circumstances?

(2) Suppose instead that *D* offers a letter signed by Joe, dated June 5, stating "I killed *V*." After objection and on voir dire the prosecution offers the coroner to testify that on June 5 Joe committed suicide. Is the letter admissible?

(3) Suppose instead that *D* offers, through *W*, Joe's statement, "*D* is not guilty of killing *V*." Admissible?

(4) Suppose instead that *D* offers, through *W*, Joe's statement, "Frank and I killed *V*. *D* did not have anything to do with it." Admissible?

(5) Suppose the prosecution offers, through *W*, Joe's statement, "*D* and I killed *V*." Admissible?

The Supreme Court has indicated that there are constitutional limitations on a state's application of the declaration against interest exception to the hearsay rule in criminal cases when the declaration is offered by the defendant. See Green v. Georgia, 442 U.S. 95 (1979), page 514, below.

F. Dying Declarations

FRE 804(b)(2)
Hearsay Exceptions: Declarant Unavailable

(b) *Hearsay exceptions.* The following are not excluded by the hearsay rule if the declarant is unavailable as a witness: . . .

(2) *Statement under belief of impending death.* In a prosecution for homicide or in a civil action or proceeding, a statement made by a declarant while believing that his death was imminent, concerning the cause or circumstances of what he believed to be his impending death. . . .

Problem IV-46
The Voice from the Grave

[handwritten: Fo und must show she thought death imminent   admit as DD]

Charge: femicide, first-degree. M.O.: shooting *V* with a handgun on June 1 and then escaping unseen. *V* is taken to the hospital and her condition deteriorates over the next five days. On June 6, in agony and gasping for breath, *V* says that her sister, *D*, shot her. *V* then dies. At *D*'s trial the D.A. offers *W*, who heard *V*'s declaration, to testify to its contents. *D* objects. What ruling and why?

What policy considerations generally support admitting such statements? In what respects are such statements similar to or different from admissions, declarations against interest, or excited utterances? Are they more or less reliable than declarations admitted under these other exceptions?

Problem IV-47
Dying Like Flies

Charge: homicide, first-degree. M.O.: striking *V* on the head with a tire iron at noon on June 1. *D* and *E* were the only two present at the scene of the crime. One of them did it. At 12:55 *V* is dying and knows it. Before he dies, *V* says that it was *D* who struck him. At noon on June 2, *E* has a heart attack. At 12:55, *E* is dying and knows it. Before he dies *E* says that it was he who struck *V* on June 1. At trial the D.A. offers proof of *V*'s statement, and *D* offers proof of *E*'s statement. What rulings and why to timely objections to both offers?

Problem IV-48
Common Sense and Common Law

Charge: felony murder of *V*, Sr. At trial the state proves that *V* and his son, *V*, Jr., were killed by a robber during a hold-up of their South End liquor store on June 1. *V*, Sr., died instantly, but before *V*, Jr., croaked, he told Kojak, a homicide detective on the scene, "It was *D*."

The state offers Kojak to testify to V, Jr.'s statement. On D's objection what ruling and why?

Problem IV-49
Double Death

Action by P, executor of V's estate, against D for V's wrongful death. Evidence is introduced to show that V was struck in a crosswalk by a hit-and-run driver. V was taken to a hospital and her condition worsened. V knew death was imminent and shouted out, "It was that bastard D who hit me." The only auditor of this statement was A, another patient in the room with V. After V's body was wheeled out of the room, the doctor told A his death was imminent. A then said to the doctor, "Before I die I must unburden myself. V told me that it was D who hit her." A then dies. At trial, P calls the doctor to testify to A's statement. D objects. What ruling and why?

What rule would you propose for dying declarations? Would it be the same for civil and criminal cases? Should the admissibility of hearsay dying declarations depend upon the declarant's belief in an afterlife?

Problem IV-50
Hesitation at the Door to the Void

Action by P, by his guardian, G, against D for damages allegedly caused by D's striking P with a hockey stick in the Boston Arena on February 14. After the incident P is taken to the hospital, told it is hopeless, and given the last rites. P then says to O, an orderly, "I'll die happy as long as my executor sues that son of a bitch D who hit me." P lapses into a coma, in which he remains. At trial plaintiff's first witness is O, who is asked to recount P's statement. On D's objection what ruling and why?

SHEPARD v. UNITED STATES   *very dubious reliability*
290 U.S. 96 (1933)

Mr. Justice CARDOZO delivered the opinion of the Court.

The petitioner, Charles A. Shepard, a major in the medical corps of the United States army, has been convicted of the murder of his wife, Zenana Shepard, at Fort Riley, Kansas, a United States military reservation. The jury having qualified their verdict by adding thereto the words "without capital punishment" (U.S.C. title 18, §567), the defendant was sentenced to imprisonment for life. The judgment of the United States

District Court has been affirmed by the Circuit Court of Appeals for the Tenth Circuit, one of the judges of that court dissenting. 62 F.2d 683, 64 F.2d 641. A writ of certiorari brings the case here.

The crime is charged to have been committed by poisoning the victim with bichloride of mercury. The defendant was in love with another woman, and wished to make her his wife. There is circumstantial evidence to sustain a finding by the jury that to win himself his freedom he turned to poison and murder. Even so, guilt was contested and conflicting inferences are possible. The defendant asks us to hold that by the acceptance of incompetent evidence the scales were weighted to his prejudice and in the end to his undoing.

The evidence complained of was offered by the Government in rebuttal when the trial was nearly over. On May 22, 1929, there was a conversation in the absence of the defendant between Mrs. Shepard, then ill in bed, and Clara Brown, her nurse. The patient asked the nurse to go to the closet in the defendant's room and bring a bottle of whisky that would be found upon a shelf. When the bottle was produced, she said that this was the liquor she had taken just before collapsing. She asked whether enough was left to make a test for the presence of poison, insisting that the smell and taste were strange. And then she added the words, "Dr. Shepard has poisoned me."

The conversation was proved twice. After the first proof of it, the Government asked to strike it out, being doubtful of its competence, and this request was granted. A little later, however, the offer was renewed, the nurse having then testified to statements by Mrs. Shepard as to the prospect of recovery. "She said she was not going to get well; she was going to die." With the aid of this new evidence, the conversation already summarized was proved a second time. There was a timely challenge of the ruling.

She said, "Dr. Shepard has poisoned me." The admission of this declaration, if erroneous, was more than unsubstantial error. As to that the parties are agreed. The voice of the dead wife was heard in accusation of her husband, and the accusation was accepted as evidence of guilt. If the evidence was incompetent, the verdict may not stand.

Upon the hearing in this court the Government finds its main prop in the position that what was said by Mrs. Shepard was admissible as a dying declaration. This is manifestly the theory upon which it was offered and received. The prop, however, is a broken reed. To make out a dying declaration the declarant must have spoken without hope of recovery and in the shadow of impending death. The record furnishes no proof of that indispensable condition. So, indeed, it was ruled by all the judges of the court below, though the majority held the view that the testimony was competent for quite another purpose, which will be considered later on.

We have said that the declarant was not shown to have spoken without hope of recovery and in the shadow of impending death. Her illness began on May 20. She was found in a state of collapse, delirious, in pain, the pupils of her eyes dilated, and the retina suffused with blood. The conversation with the nurse occurred two days later. At that time her mind had cleared up, and her speech was rational and orderly. There was as yet no thought by any of her physicians that she was dangerously ill, still less that her case was hopeless. To all seeming she had greatly improved, and was moving forward to recovery. There had been no diagnosis of poison as the cause of her distress. Not till about a week afterwards was there a relapse, accompanied by an infection of the mouth, renewed congestion of the eyes, and later hemorrhages of the bowels. Death followed on June 15.

Nothing in the condition of the patient on May 22 gives fair support to the conclusion that hope had then been lost. She may have thought she was going to die and have said so to her nurse, but this was consistent with hope, which could not have been put aside without more to quench it. Indeed, a fortnight later, she said to one of her physicians, though her condition was then grave, "You will get me well, won't you?" Fear or even belief that illness will end in death will not avail of itself to make a dying declaration. There must be "a settled hopeless expectation" that death is near at hand, and what is said must have been spoken in the hush of its impending presence. . . .

The petitioner insists that the form of the declaration exhibits other defects that call for its exclusion, apart from the objection that death was not imminent and that hope was still alive. Homicide may not be imputed to a defendant on the basis of mere suspicions, though they are the suspicions of the dying. To let the declaration in, the inference must be permissible that there was knowledge or the opportunity for knowledge as to the acts that are declared. . . . The form is not decisive, though it be that of a conclusion, a statement of the result with the antecedent steps omitted. Wigmore, §1447. "He murdered me," does not cease to be competent as a dying declaration because in the statement of the act there is also an appraisal of the crime. State v. Mace, 118 N.C. 1244, 24 S.E. 798; State v. Kuhn, [117 Iowa, 216, 90 N.W. 733]. One does not hold the dying to the observance of all the niceties of speech to which conformity is exacted from a witness on the stand. What is decisive is something deeper and more fundamental than any difference of form. The declaration is kept out if the setting of the occasion satisfies the judge, or in reason ought to satisfy him, that the speaker is giving expression to suspicion or conjecture, and not to known facts. The difficulty is not so much in respect of the governing principle as in its application to varying and equivocal conditions. In this case, the ruling that there was a failure to make out the imminence of death and the

abandonment of hope relieves us of the duty of determining whether it
is a legitimate inference that there was the opportunity for knowledge.
We leave that question open. . . .

Con't p 360

Problem IV-51
"Speak Up, Please"

Charge: murder of *V*. Dr. Jones is called to the stand by the prosecution. At *D*'s request the judge first listens to Dr. Jones's testimony out of
the presence of the jury. Jones states that just before *V* died, Jones said
to her, "You are very badly wounded," and that shortly thereafter *V*
mumbled, "*D* did it." The judge thinks that *V* probably knew she was
dying but recognized that reasonable people might differ on that question. The judge also thinks that *V* probably did not say, "*D* did it," but
rather mumbled something else which the doctor misunderstood, but
the judge recognizes that reasonable persons might also differ on that.
Defense counsel objects to Jones's being allowed to testify before the
jury. What ruling and why?

G. Statements of Present Sense Impressions, Then-Existing Mental, Emotional, Physical, or Medical Condition, and Excited Utterances

FRE 803
Hearsay Exceptions: Availability of Declarant Immaterial

The following are not excluded by the hearsay rule, even though the
declarant is available as a witness:

(1) *Present sense impression.* A statement describing or explaining an
event or condition made while the declarant was perceiving the event or
condition or immediately thereafter.

(2) *Excited utterance.* A statement relating to a startling event or condition made while the declarant was under the stress of excitement caused
by the event or condition.

(3) *Then existing mental, emotional, or physical condition.* A statement of
the declarant's then existing state of mind, emotion, sensation, or physical condition (such as intent, plan, motive, design, mental feeling, pain,
and bodily health), but not including a statement of memory or belief to
prove the fact remembered or believed unless it relates to the execution,
revocation, identification, or terms of declarant's will.

(4) *Statements for purposes of medical diagnosis or treatment.* Statements made for purposes of medical diagnosis or treatment and describing medical history, or past or present symptoms, pain, or sensations, or the inception or general character of the cause or external source thereof insofar as reasonably pertinent to diagnosis or treatment.

Problem IV-52
Stage Fright

(1) Action for wrongful death of *V. D* denies generally. At trial, *P* calls *V*'s daughter, *G*, to testify that on June 1 she and *V* were riding in *V*'s carriage along a narrow country road, that she saw *D* come up behind the carriage on horseback, that she did not see anything thereafter because she ducked down on the floor of the carriage, and that after the carriage turned over *V* said to her, "That no good *D* hit our horse with his whip." On *D*'s objection what ruling and why?

(2) *P* also calls *B*, *V*'s butler, to testify that when *G* arrived home on June 1 she was distraught and speechless. *B* immediately gave her a brandy and made her lie down. Two hours later *G* awoke and told *B* that *D* had whipped the horse and caused the carriage to turn over, killing *V*. On *D*'s objection what ruling and why?

What considerations of reliability militate for admission of such statements? What considerations militate against admission? How would you frame a rule of law applicable generally to such declarations?

Problem IV-53
Stagger P

Action for damages allegedly sustained when *P* was struck by a car driven by *D*. Defense: contributory negligence. At trial, *D* calls *W* to testify that 10 minutes before the accident *W* was at a bar with *P* and *Q*, that *P* got up to leave, and that *Q* said to *W*, "Look at *P* stagger. Man, is he smashed." *P* objects. What ruling and why? What factors militate for and against admission of this evidence?

Problem IV-54
Husband Harry

Action for damages arising out of a collision between cars driven by *P* and *D*. At trial, *P* calls *W*, a passenger in *D*'s car, to testify that just after the accident she called *D*'s husband, Harry to inform him of the accident and that Harry said, "Oh, my goodness. It must have been our fault.

We've known those brakes were bad for two weeks." On D's objection, what ruling and why?

Problem IV-55
Snowmobile Slaughter

Action for damages P allegedly sustained on January 1 when D ran over P with his snowmobile while P was cross-country skiing. D denies hitting P and also that P suffered any injuries.

no

(1) At trial, P calls W to testify that he was a patient in the same room of the hospital to which P was taken and that the day after P was brought in P said to W, "D ran over me with his snowmobile. I was in agony out on the trail, couldn't sleep last night, and now my legs are really throbbing." D objects. What ruling and why?

(2) Suppose that P's statement was made to the attending hospital physician while P was being examined. May W testify to the statement? May the physician?

yes

(3) Suppose that P's statement was made to a second physician retained specially by P's brother, a personal injury plaintiff's lawyer, to examine P in anticipation of his testifying against D at a future trial. May W testify to the statement? May this physician?

Problem IV-56
"Well, Doc, This Is How It Happened . . ."

Action against D Railway Company for personal injuries suffered by P when struck by one of D's trains. P called Dr. W to the witness stand and through her offered a statement of history given by P to her four days after the injuries were sustained. Dr. W stated that the notes as to the history were given to her in the presence of an intern, taken down by the intern, and typed 18 days later. The notes indicate that P told Dr. W that he was walking beside the train and that a projection from the train struck him and caused him to fall under the train. Dr. W stated that this information was not necessary for the treatment of P.

not adm

Are the notes or Dr. W's testimony about this interview admissible?

yes

GOLDSTEIN v. SKLAR
216 A.2d 298 (Me. 1966)

Dufresne, J. . . . . There is much conflict on the subject. The apparent weight of authority however seems to uphold the rule that statements made to a physician by a patient, as to the cause and manner of the happening of an injury, which statements cannot qualify as part of the res gestae, are not admissible in evidence.

But the current trend of the authorities seems to recognize that such part of the history of the case given by the patient to the doctor as describes the general character of the cause or the general manner of happening of the injury when relevant to his diagnosis, treatment, or medical opinion, may be admitted into evidence, if not as evidence of the facts stated, than at least in support or explanation of the medical conclusions.

As we have seen, our Court in Ross' case [Ross' Case, 124 Me. 107, 126 A. 484 (1924)] aligned itself with the exclusionary rule jurisdictions. But Ross' case involved a history of the place of the accident, to wit, the employer's finishing room, and such was not relevant or necessary for proper medical diagnosis, treatment or opinion, and therefor the history was inadmissible on that ground. In our present case, the history of plaintiff being thrown to the left as a result of the impact or automobile accident was relevant material evidence for consideration of the doctor for purposes of intelligent diagnosis and treatment and in support or explanation of his ultimate medical expert opinion. It did not have, as in Ross' case, the fatal feature of tending to prove responsibility for the injury.

It was factually similar on this portion of the case history to that in Johnson [Johnson v. Bangor Railway and Electric Company, 125 Me. 88, 131 A. 1 (1925)], where our Court held it admissible in aid to the examining physician's opinion.

The presiding justice instructed the jury that this type of evidence as contained in the history of the case given by the plaintiff to the doctor could not be considered as evidence of the facts stated, but only as it might support or explain the doctor's diagnosis and opinion of the nature of the injury. This was not error.

The history given by the plaintiff to the doctor, objected to by the defendant, recited plaintiff's past condition, symptoms, sensations and feelings.

> . . . his head snapped at the impact. He noted immediate soreness involving the left side of the neck, the left shoulder, and the left side of the body. He complained further that within 24 hours after this injury, he noted numbness on the outer aspect of the hand and forearm, which we call the ulna area of the hand and forearm named after the nerve that supplies that area of the hand and arm.
>
> He also complained of pain in the left shoulder shortly after the injury. He then gave me further history as to what took place from that time until the time I saw him.

This evidence was received subject to the court's limitative instruction as previously indicated, that the jury was not to consider the same as *very dubious*

evidence of the facts stated, but only in its bearing on the doctor's diagnosis and opinion.

Dr. Chodosh was consulted by the plaintiff for purposes of treatment. As testified to by him, the examining physician customarily takes a case history from his patient as to what happened, because the history of complaints goes a long way in determining diagnosis.

It is common knowledge that examining physicians inquire into the history of the development of the sickness or the event of the injury, its duration, its symptoms, whether the patient suffers pain, what remedies or treatment have been employed, and every other circumstance which the patient can reveal which may aid in the recognition of the real nature of the disease or injury to be treated.

All these declarations made by the patient to the examining physician as to his present or past symptoms are known by the patient who is seeking medical assistance to be required for proper diagnosis and treatment and by reason thereof, are viewed as highly reliable and apt to state true facts.

These statements of past bodily condition, pain and suffering made by the plaintiff to the attending physician for the purpose of securing diagnosis and treatment, were admitted through the medical witness, not to establish the truth of the facts stated, but to show the basis upon which he had formed his professional opinion as to the nature and extent of the plaintiff's injury. In this, there was no error.

Defendant also objected to the case history, because it contained a recital of the past treatment of the plaintiff by a previous treating physician.

> Doctor Goldstein told me that he was receiving diathermy treatment to the neck, traction treatments to the neck and injections of vitamin B-12.

We do recognize that previous treatment of an injury or illness may be material in diagnosing a physical condition and in determining the proper treatment thereafter. We further appreciate that the plaintiff could have testified to the same, if the defendant's testate were living.

Where this evidence, although relevant and beneficial, is perhaps not absolutely necessary to the attending physician's approach to this diagnosis and treatment, we would not sanction under the guise of case history, even to the limited extent allowed in this case, a lengthy recital of past treatment with all the minute details thereof. Such evidence must be kept within reasonable legal orbit under the discretion of the presiding justice, so that the jury will not get the impression that the history of past treatment is substantive evidence in the case.

There was no abuse of discretion in admitting this short history of past treatment under the restrictive instruction of the court below. No prejudicial error appears. . . .

MEANEY v. UNITED STATES
112 F.2d 538 (2d Cir. 1940)

L. HAND, J. . . . The utterances of a patient in the course of his examination, so far as they are spontaneous, may be merely ejaculatory — as when he emits a cry upon palpation — or they may be truly narrative; and it will often be impossible to distinguish rationally between the two; between an inarticulate cry, for example, and a statement such as: "That hurts." The warrant for the admission of both is the same; the lack of opportunity or motive for fabrication upon an unexpected occasion to which the declarant responds immediately, and without reflection. But most of what he tells will not ordinarily be of this kind at all; there may be, and there is in fact, good reason to receive it, but it is a very different reason. A man goes to his physician expecting to recount all that he feels, and often he has with some care searched his consciousness to be sure that he will leave out nothing. If his narrative of present symptoms is to be received as evidence of the facts, as distinguished from mere support for the physician's opinion, these parts of it can only rest upon his motive to disclose the truth because his treatment will in part depend upon what he says. That justification is not necessary in the case of his spontaneous declarations, even when they are narrative; but it is necessary for those we are now considering. . . .

The same reasoning applies with exactly the same force to a narrative of past symptoms, and so the Supreme Court of Massachusetts declared obiter in Roosa v. Boston Loan Co., 132 Mass. 439. A patient has an equal motive to speak the truth; what he has felt in the past is as apt to be important in his treatment as what he feels at the moment. Thus, in spite of the dicta in Northern Pacific R.R. v. Urlin, 158 U.S. 271, and Boston & Albany R.R. v. O'Reilly, 158 U.S. 334, that only declarations of present symptoms are competent, several federal courts have seemed not to take the distinction between declarations of present and past symptoms, provided the patient is consulting the physician for treatment, and Professor Wigmore appears to assent. Wigmore §1722. This situation is quite different from United States v. Balance, 61 App. D.C. 226, 59 F.2d 1040, where the declarations were made by a veteran to physicians of the Veterans' Administration; and it is obviously different from declarations of facts irrelevant to the declarant's treatment, such as what was the cause of his injury. It is true that this body of authority is not impressive as such, but it appears to us that if there is to be any consistency in doctrine, either declarations of all symptoms, present or past, should be competent, or only those which fall within the exception of spontaneous utterances. Nobody would choose the second, particularly as the substance of the declarations can usually be got before the jury as parts of the basis on which the physician's opinion was formed. It is indeed always possible that a patient may not really consult his physician for treatment; the consultation may be colorable. The judge has power to prevent an abuse in such cases, and here as elsewhere, when the competency of evidence depends upon the question of fact, his conclusion is final. He must decide before admitting the declarations whether the patient was consulting the physician for treatment and for that alone. Unless he is so satisfied, he must exclude them, though it is true that if he admits them, the defendant may still argue that they are untrustworthy. They will be evidence, but in estimating their truth the jury may have to decide for themselves the very issue on which the judge himself passed before he admitted them; the competency of evidence is always independent of its weight.

We hold that the insured's "history of the case" as narrated to the physician was competent and that its exclusion was error.

Judgment reversed; new trial ordered.

Problem IV-57
The Full-Service Lawyer

Action against D Company for back injuries suffered on the job by P on July 29, 1954. P immediately reported the injury to his superior and went to the company hospital where Dr. A examined him, taped his back, and gave him pills to relieve his pain.

In the middle of August 1954, while still being treated by the company doctor, P went to Dr. B, who ordered a brace for his back, gave him pills to relieve his pain, and had him use a heat pad and a bed board. At the request of Dr. B, Dr. C X-rayed P's back. P saw Dr. B about 15 times, the last visit being on June 7, 1955. Suit had been filed on January 6, 1955.

In August 1955 P went to Dr. D at the suggestion of one of his attorneys and not at the suggestion or with the knowledge of Dr. B. P knew that Dr. D was to make a report to his lawyer. Dr. D knew the patient had been referred to her by the lawyer and assumed that a suit was pending and that she might be called to testify.

Dr. D performed Nafziger, Fabere, and Lesegue tests on P. Dr. D did not use a myelogram to ascertain whether the patient had a ruptured disc because she said it is generally used only as a preparation for surgical intervention. She did not give him any treatment, never had him go to a hospital, and never had his back X-rayed.

Dr. D testified that as a consultant she leaves the treatment of the patient to the doctor who sends the patient, unless she herself operates on the patient, and that in this case she did not prescribe the pain medication, physical therapy, or corset for P but merely suggested it to Dr. B.

Dr. D admitted that her diagnosis of a possible ruptured disc was based on subjective symptoms elicited from the patient but stated that unless the patient is a good actor, an experienced observer would not be fooled.

At this point D Company objected to P's attempt to have Dr. D testify to statements concerning the medical history of the patient, the cause of the injury, and her diagnosis. What ruling and why?

Problem IV-58
Strong Feelings and Future Plans

(1) Action for alienation of affections of P's wife, A. At trial, P calls W, a former friend of A, to testify that A told her, "After one night with D, I realized how much I despise P." D objects. What ruling and why? If testimony is admitted, what should D do?

(2) Worker's Compensation action by W seeking recovery against D for the death of her husband, H. The issue is whether the accident in which H perished occurred during the course of H's employment. At trial, W offers evidence that shortly before going to the airport H made several statements that he had to go away on business. D objects. What ruling and why?

What difference do you see between these two problems in terms of the purposes for which the evidence is offered? What considerations support and militate against admitting the evidence in these situations? How would you frame a rule of law to cover both situations?

MUTUAL LIFE INSURANCE COMPANY v. HILLMON
145 U.S. 285 (1892)

GRAY, J. On July 13, 1880, Sallie E. Hillmon, a citizen of Kansas, brought an action against the Mutual Life Insurance Company, a corporation of New York, on a policy of insurance, dated December 10, 1878, on the life of her husband, John W. Hillmon, in the sum of $10,000, payable to her within sixty days after notice and proof of his death. On the same day the plaintiff brought two other actions, the one against the New York Life Insurance Company, a corporation of New York, on two similar policies of life insurance, dated respectively November 30, 1878, and December 10, 1878, for the sum of $5,000 each; and the other against the Connecticut Mutual Life Insurance Company, a corporation of Connecticut, on a similar policy, dated March 4, 1879, for the sum of $5,000.

In each case, the declaration alleged that Hillmon died on March 17, 1879, during the continuance of the policy, but that the defendant, though duly notified of the fact, had refused to pay the amount of the policy, or any part thereof; and the answer denied the death of Hillmon, and alleged that he, together with John H. Brown and divers other persons, on or before November 30, 1878, conspiring to defraud the defendant, procured the issue of all the policies, and afterwards, in March and April, 1879, falsely pretended and represented that Hillmon was dead, and that a dead body which they had procured was his, whereas in reality he was alive and hiding. . . .

At the trial the plaintiff introduced evidence tending to show that on or about March 5, 1879, Hillmon and Brown left Wichita in the State of Kansas in search of a site for a cattle ranch; that on the night of March 18 while they were in camp at a place called Crooked Creek, Hillmon was killed by the accidental discharge of a gun; that Brown at once notified persons living in the neighborhood; and that the body was thereupon taken to a neighboring town, where, after an inquest, it was buried. The defendants introduced evidence tending to show that the body found in the camp at Crooked Creek on the night of March 18 was not the body of Hillmon, but was the body of one Frederick Adolph Walters. Upon the question whose body this was, there was much conflicting evidence, including photographs and descriptions of the corpse, and of the marks and scars upon it, and testimony to its likeness to Hillmon and to Walters.

The defendants introduced testimony that Walters left his home at Fort Madison in the State of Iowa in March, 1878, and was afterwards in Kansas in 1878, and in January and February, 1879; that during that time his family frequently received letters from him, the last of which was written from Wichita; and that he had not been heard from since March, 1879. The defendants also offered the following evidence:

Elizabeth Rieffenach testified that she was a sister of Frederick Adolph Walters, and lived at Fort Madison; and thereupon, as shown by the bill of exceptions, the following proceedings took place:

> Witness further testified that she had received a letter written from Wichita, Kansas, about the 4th or 5th day of March, 1879, by her brother Frederick Adolph; that the letter was dated at Wichita, and was in the handwriting of her brother; that she had searched for the letter, but could not find the same, it being lost; that she remembered and could state the contents of the letter.
>
> Thereupon the defendants' counsel asked the question: "State the contents of that letter." To which the plaintiff objected, on the ground that the same is incompetent, irrelevant, and hearsay. The objection was sustained, and the defendants duly excepted. The following is the letter as stated by witness:
>
> Wichita, Kansas
>
> March 4th or 5th or 3d or 4th — I don't know — 1879.
>
> Dear Sister and all: I now in my usual style drop you a few lines to let you know that I expect to leave Wichita on or about March the 5th, with a certain Mr. Hillmon, a sheep-trader, for Colorado or parts unknown to me. I expect

to see the country now. News are of no interest to you, as you are not acquainted here. I will close with compliments to all inquiring friends. Love to
all.

> I am truly your brother,
> Fred. Adolph Walters.

Alvina D. Kasten testified that she was twenty-one years of age and
resided in Fort Madison; that she was engaged to be married to Frederick Adolph Walters; that she last saw him on March 24, 1878, at Fort
Madison; that he left there at that time and had not returned; that she
corresponded regularly with him, and received a letter from him about
every two weeks until March 3, 1879, which was the last time she received a letter from him; that this letter was dated at Wichita, March 1,
1879, and was addressed to her at Fort Madison, and the envelope was
postmarked "Wichita, Kansas, March 2, 1879"; and that she had never
heard from or seen him since that time.

The defendants put in evidence the envelope with the postmark and
address; and thereupon offered to read the letter in evidence. The
plaintiff objected to the reading of the letter, the court sustained the
objection, and the defendants excepted.

This letter was dated "Wichita, March 1, 1879," was signed by Walters, and began as follows: *letters excluded*

> Dearest Alvina: Your kind and ever welcome letter was received yesterday
> afternoon about an hour before I left Emporia. I will stay here until the fore
> part of next week, and then will leave here to see a part of the country that I
> never expected to see when I left home, as I am going with a man by the name
> of Hillmon, who intends to start a sheep ranch, and as he promised me more
> wages than I could make at anything else I concluded to take it, for a while at
> least, until I strike something better. There is so many folks in this country
> that have got the Leadville fever, and if I could not of got the situation that I
> have now I would have went there myself; but as it is at present I get to see the
> best portion of Kansas, Indian Territory, Colorado, and Mexico. The route
> that we intend to take would cost a man to travel from $150 to $200, but it will
> not cost me a cent; besides, I get good wages. I will drop you a letter occasion-
> ally until I get settled down; then I want you to answer it. . . .

The court, after recapitulating some of the testimony introduced,
instructed the jury as follows:

> You have perceived from the very beginning of the trial that the conclusion to
> be reached must practically turn upon the question of fact, and all the large
> volume of evidence, with its graphic and varied details, has no actual
> significance, save as the facts established thereby may throw light upon and
> aid you in answering the question, whose body was it that on the evening of
> March 18, 1879, lay dead by the camp-fire on Crooked Creek? The decision
> of that question decides the verdict you should render.

The jury, being instructed by the court to return a separate verdict in each case, returned verdicts for the plaintiff against the three defendants respectively for the amounts of their policies, and interest, upon which separate judgments were rendered. The defendants sued out four writs of error, one jointly in the three cases as consolidated, and one in each case separately. . . .

The matter chiefly contested at the trial was the death of John W. Hillmon, the insured; and that depended upon the question whether the body found at Crooked Creek on the night of March 18, 1879, was his body, or the body of one Walters. . . .

A man's state of mind or feeling can only be manifested to others by countenance, attitude or gesture, or by sounds or words, spoken or written. The nature of the fact to be proved is the same, and evidence of its proper tokens is equally competent to prove it, whether expressed by aspect or conduct, by voice or pen. When the intention to be proved is important only as qualifying an act, its connection with that act must be shown, in order to warrant the admission of declarations of the intention. But whenever the intention is of itself a distinct and material fact in a chain of circumstances, it may be proved by contemporaneous oral or written declarations of the party.

The existence of a particular intention in a certain person at a certain time being a material fact to be proved, evidence that he expressed that intention at that time is as direct evidence of the fact, as his own testimony that he then had that intention would be. After his death, there can hardly be any other way of proving it; and while he is still alive, his own memory of his state of mind at a former time is no more likely to be clear and true than a bystander's recollection of what he then said, and is less trustworthy than letters written by him at the very time and under circumstances precluding a suspicion of misrepresentation.

The letters in question were competent, not as narratives of facts communicated to the writer by others, nor yet as proof that he actually went away from Wichita, but as evidence that, shortly before the time when other evidence tended to show that he went away, he had the intention of going, and of going with Hillmon, which made it more probably both that he did go and that he went with Hillmon, than if there had been no proof of such intention. In view of the mass of conflicting testimony introduced upon the question whether it was the body of Walters that was found in Hillmon's camp, this evidence might properly influence the jury in determining that question.

The rule applicable to this case has been thus stated by this court: "Wherever the bodily or mental feelings of an individual are material to be proved, the usual expression of such feelings are original and competent evidence. Those expressions are the natural reflexes of what it might be impossible to show by other testimony. If there be such other testimony, this may be necessary to set the facts thus developed in their true light, and to give them their proper effect. As independent, explanatory or corroborative evidence, it is often indispensable to the due administration of justice. Such declarations are regarded as verbal acts, and are as competent as any other testimony, when relevant to the issue. Their truth or falsity is an inquiry for the jury." Teachers Ins. Co. v. Mosley, 8 Wall. 397, 404, 405. . . .

Upon principle and authority, therefore we are of opinion that the two letters were competent evidence of the intention of Walters at the time of writing them, which was a material fact bearing upon the question in controversy; and that for the exclusion of these letters, as well as for the undue restriction of the defendants' challenges, the verdicts must be set aside, and a new trial had.

Should statements of a declarant that he intended to do a certain act be admissible to prove that another person did a subsequent act? For example, should *V*'s statement that she was going out with defendant the night she was murdered be admissible to prove that the defendant went out with her?

Or in the *Hillmon* case, if it were disputed whether Hillmon went to Crooked Creek (which it was not), should Walters' letters be admissible on this issue? A more recent example is United States v. Pheaster, 544 F.2d 353 (9th Cir. 1976), where evidence was offered in a kidnapping prosecution that shortly before he disappeared the victim said he was going to meet the defendant. Should such evidence be admitted to prove the defendant went to meet the victim? Compare the Advisory Committee Notes and the Report of the House Committee on the Judiciary, S. Rep. No. 1277, 93d Cong., 2d Sess., 120 Cong. Rec. 40069 (1974). Should the availability of the declarant be a factor in these situations?

Problem IV-59
Threats

Charge: murder of *V*. Defense: alibi. At trial, *D* calls *W* to testify that a week before *V*'s death, *O* told *W*, "I hate *V*. Someday I'll kick *V* from here to Timbuktu." The prosecution objects. What ruling and why?

Problem IV-60
The Accusing Hand

Charge: murder. M.O.: poisoning patients in a Veterans' Administration hospital where *D* was a nurse. At *D*'s trial the prosecution seeks to introduce a note written by a patient, now deceased, two hours after suffering a respiratory arrest allegedly caused by *D*. The patient's doctor testified that about two hours after the arrest he ascertained that the patient was resting comfortably and assured the patient he was out of danger. The doctor then asked if anyone had given him any medication just before the arrest. The patient responded by writing *D*'s name. On *D*'s objection, what ruling and why?

Problem IV-61
The Time Dimension of State-of-Mind

Should out-of-court statements of present memory or facts believed by the declarant ever be admitted to show that the remembered or believed fact previously existed? In other words should the *Hillmon* exception, incorporated in Rule 803(3), point backward in time as well as forward?

In the *Shepard* case, discussed above on another point, the prosecution sought to introduce testimony through a nurse that the defendant's wife, the victim, had told her, "Dr. Shepard [the deceased's husband] has poisoned me." Admissible?

SHEPARD v. UNITED STATES
290 U.S. 96 (1933)

CARDOZO, J. . . . We pass to the question whether the statements to the nurse, though incompetent as dying declarations, were admissible on other grounds.

The Circuit Court of Appeals determined that they were. Witnesses for the defendant had testified to declarations by Mrs. Shepard which suggested a mind bent upon suicide, or at any rate were thought by the defendant to carry that suggestion. More than once before her illness she had stated in the hearing of these witnesses that she had no wish to live, and had nothing to live for, and on one occasion she added that she expected some day to make an end to her life. This testimony opened the door, so it is argued, to declarations in rebuttal that she had been poisoned by her husband. They were admissible, in that view, not as evidence of the truth of what was said, but as betokening a state of mind inconsistent with the presence of suicidal intent.

(a) The testimony was neither offered nor received for the strained and narrow purpose now suggested as legitimate. . . .

(b) Aside, however, from this objection, the accusatory declaration must have been rejected as evidence of a state of mind, though the purpose thus to limit it had been brought to light upon the trial. The defendant had tried to show by Mrs. Shepard's declarations to her friends that she had exhibited a weariness of life and a readiness to end it, the testimony giving plausibility to the hypothesis of suicide. Wigmore, Evidence §1726; Commonwealth v. Trefethen, 157 Mass. 180, 31 N.E. 961. By the proof of these declarations evincing an unhappy state of mind the defendant opened the door to the offer by the Government of declarations evincing a different state of mind, declarations consistent with the persistence of a will to live. The defendant would have no grievance if the testimony in rebuttal had been narrowed to that point. What the Government put in evidence, however, was something very different. It did not use the declarations by Mrs. Shepard to prove her present thoughts and feelings, or even her thoughts and feelings in times past. It used the declarations as proof of an act committed by someone else, as evidence that she was dying of poison given by her husband. This fact, if fact it was, the Government was free to prove, but not by hearsay declarations. It will not do to say that the jury might accept the declarations for any light that they cast upon the existence of a vital urge, and reject them to the extent that they charged the death to someone else. Discrimination so subtle is a feat beyond the compass of ordinary minds. The reverberating clang of those accusatory words would drown all weaker sounds. It is for ordinary minds, and not for psychoanalysts, that our rules of evidence are framed. They have their source very often in considerations of administrative convenience, of practical expediency, and not in rules of logic. When the risk of confusion is so great as to upset the balance of advantage, the evidence goes out. Thayer, Preliminary Treatise on the Law of Evidence, 266, 516; Wigmore, Evidence, §§1421, 1422, 1714.

These precepts of caution are a guide to judgment here. There are times when a state of mind, if relevant, may be proved by contemporaneous declarations of feeling or intent. Mutual Life Ins. Co. v. Hillmon, 145 U.S. 285, 295. . . .

The ruling in that case marks the high water line beyond which courts have been unwilling to go. It has developed a substantial body of criticism and commentary.* Declarations of intention, casting light upon the future, have been sharply distinguished from declarations of memory, pointing backwards to the past. There would be an end, or nearly that, to the rule against hearsay if the distinction were ignored.

The testimony now questioned faced backward and not forward. This at least it did in its most obvious implications. What is even more important, it spoke to a past act, and more than that, to an act by some one not the speaker. Other tendency, if it had any, was a filament too fine to be disentangled by a jury.

The judgment should be reversed and the cause remanded to the

---

*Maguire, The Hillmon Case, 38 Harvard L. Rev. 709, 721, 727; Seligman, An Exception to the Hearsay Rule, 26 Harvard L. Rev. 146; Chaffee, Review of Wigmore's Treatise, 37 Harvard L. Rev. 513, 519.

District Court for further proceedings in accordance with this opinion. Reversed.

———————

Is the *Shepard* rule logically persuasive? Should there be a general exception for the declaration of any unavailable or dead declarant? If the declaration is made prior to the commencement of the action in which it is offered? If the statement concerns a condition or event that had been recently perceived by the declarant and the declarant's recollection is shown to have been clear at the time? If the declaration is also shown to have been made in good faith, not in contemplation of pending or anticipated litigation, and not in response to the instigation of a person engaged in litigation? If the declaration relates to declarant's will? Various exceptions to the hearsay rule along this line have been proposed. Some have even been adopted. Compare Rule 803(1); deleted Rule 804(b)(2) and Advisory Committee Notes following. See generally McCormick on Evidence, §296 at 701-704 and Supplement page 87.

H.   Two Processes of Proof: Refreshing Recollection and Past Recollection Recorded

FRE 803(5)
Hearsay Exceptions: Availability of Declarant Immaterial

The following are not excluded by the hearsay rule, even though the declarant is available as a witness: . . .

(5) *Recorded recollection.* A memorandum or record concerning a matter about which a witness once had knowledge but now has insufficient recollection to enable him to testify fully and accurately, shown to have been made or adopted by the witness when the matter was fresh in his memory and to reflect that knowledge correctly. If admitted, the memorandum or record may be read into evidence but may not itself be received as an exhibit unless offered by an adverse party.

FRE 612
Writing Used to Refresh Memory

Except as otherwise provided in criminal proceedings by Section 3500 of title 18, United States Code, if a witness uses a writing to refresh his memory for the purposes of testifying, either —

(1) while testifying, or

(2) before testifying, if the court in its discretion determines it is necessary in the interests of justice, an adverse party is entitled to have the writing produced at the hearing, to inspect it, to cross-examine the witness thereon, and to introduce in evidence those portions which relate to the testimony of the witness. If it is claimed that the writing contains matters not related to the subject matter of the testimony the court shall examine the writing in camera, excise any portions not so related, and order delivery of the remainder to the party entitled thereto. Any portion withheld over objections shall be preserved and made available to the appellate court in the event of an appeal. If a writing is not produced or delivered pursuant to order under this rule, the court shall make any order justice requires, except that in criminal cases when the prosecution elects not to comply, the order shall be one striking the testimony or, if the court in its discretion determines that the interests of justice so require, declaring a mistrial.

Problem IV-62
Negligent Entrustment

Action against D Warehouse Company for negligence. In June 1971 Mrs. P prepared to sell her Cambridge house and move to Palo Alto. She decided to sell some of her household furnishings, take some with her, and store the rest. Mrs. P's maid, M, is put in charge of selecting things to be sold at a garage sale and packing what is not sold for storage. After the garage sale M packs the unsold items in sealed boxes and makes a handwritten list of the contents of each box. The boxes are then delivered to the D Warehouse Company for storage. Ten years later Mrs. P returns to Cambridge, claims the boxes, and is told they were destroyed by termites. At trial the only issue is the contents of the boxes. Compare these methods of proof:

(1) Mrs. P takes the stand and testifies to her 1971 instructions to M, her employee, and authenticates the handwriting on the lists as M's. The lists are then offered in evidence. D objects.

(2) M takes the stand and testifies to the instructions she received in 1971 from Mrs. P, her employer, and how she carried out those instructions. When asked to specify the contents of the boxes, however, M says that she cannot remember what was put into the boxes. P's attorney then shows M the lists. M studies the lists, testifies that she now remembers the contents of the boxes, and proceeds to specify the contents. D objects and moves to strike.

(3) The same as in (2) except that M testifies that even after looking at the lists she cannot remember what she put into the boxes. However, she does remember making the lists when she did the packing and that they

were made accurately. The lists are then offered in evidence. *D* objects.

(4) Suppose that instead of *M*'s doing all the packing alone, Mrs. *P* helped her by packing each item in the boxes, stating orally what each item was and in which box it was put while *M* recorded the items on the lists. However, *M*, being fully occupied with making the lists, did not observe Mrs. *P* pack the items. At trial, Mrs. *P* and *M* testify to the above. Mrs. *P* cannot remember the items packed but does remember making the oral statements, which were accurate. *M* cannot remember what Mrs. *P* said but does remember taking down her statements and that her notes were accurate. *M* identifies the lists, and *P*'s attorney then reads the lists. *D* objects.

Which of these methods of proof will work? What reasons underlie the rules governing the use of past recollection recorded and refreshing recollection? What are the elements and procedures of each method? Compare Rules 803(5) and 612.

I. Recorded Recollection and Business Records

FRE 803(6) and (7)
Hearsay Exceptions: Availability of Declarant Immaterial

The following are not excluded by the hearsay rule, even though the declarant is available as a witness: . . .

(6) *Records of regularly conducted activity.* A memorandum, report, record, or data compilation, in any form, of acts, events, conditions, opinions or diagnoses, made at or near the time by, or from information transmitted by, a person with knowledge, if kept in the course of a regularly conducted business activity, and if it was the regular practice of that business activity to make the memorandum, report, record, or data compilation, all as shown by the testimony of the custodian or other qualified witness, unless the source of information or the method or circumstances of preparation indicate lack of trustworthiness. The term "business" as used in this paragraph includes business, institution, association, profession, occupation, and calling of every kind, whether or not conducted for profit.

(7) *Absence of entry in records kept in accordance with the provisions of paragraph (6).* Evidence that a matter is not included in the memoranda reports, records, or data compilations, in any form, kept in accordance with the provisions of paragraph (6), to prove the nonoccurrence or nonexistence of the matter, if the matter was of a kind of which a memorandum, report, record, or data compilation was regularly made

and preserved, unless the sources of information or other circumstances indicate lack of trustworthiness.

Problem IV-63
The Window Washers' Witnesses

Action by the P Window Washing Company against the D Tower Company for money allegedly due P for washing the windows on D's 100-story skyscraper, the D Tower. D denies it owes P anything and disputes that the work was ever done.

As P's attorney you have found out that for a large tower like the D Tower, P assigns a window washing foreman to each floor. Several window washers, grade one, and window washers' assistants, grade two, are assigned to each foreman. As the washers and assistants wash a window, they "tick-off" a square representing the washed window on a form that depicts the window arrangement for the floor on which they are working. At the end of the day the foreman collects the forms and delivers them to the area supervisor. There is usually an area supervisor for every 10 floors. The area supervisors tally the number of windows washed and report this information to P's building manager. The manager turns this information over to P's bookkeeping office, where the information is fed into P's data processing equipment. For billing purposes P's computer provides a biweekly printout of the number of windows washed during that period.

You want to prove that P Window Washing Company washed 97,873 windows (the total shown by the computer printouts) on the D Tower during the period in question. How do you go about it? What foundational and procedural considerations are there? Try preparing direct examination(s) to get the proof in.

Compare Rule 803(5) and (6). How does the exception for business records relate to the exception for recorded recollection? What are the differences between the various formulations of the business records exception to the hearsay rule? Why is an exception made for such records in the first place? Do these reasons suggest limits to the exception based on type of business or record? Should the routineness of the report or the motivations of the reporter affect the admissibility of such records?

Problem IV-64
Accident Reports

Action by P Plumbing & Heating Company for property damages to P's vehicle, driven by its employee E, allegedly sustained in an accident with a D Bus Company bus driven by D's employee, F. At trial, P offers a memo made by *E* one hour after the accident and filed at *P*'s office. The memo says that *F*'s bus ran a red light and struck *E*'s car broadside. *D* objects.

In its case *D* offers an accident report on its standard form made out by *F* three hours after the accident, which claims *E* ran the light. *P* objects. What rulings and why?

PALMER v. HOFFMAN
318 U.S. 109 (1943)

Mr. Justice DOUGLAS delivered the opinion of the Court.

This case arose out of a grade crossing accident which occurred in Massachusetts. . . .

I

The accident occurred on the night of December 25, 1940. On December 27, 1940 the engineer of the train who died before the trial, made a statement at a freight office of petitioners where he was interviewed by an assistant superintendent of the road and by a representative of the Massachusetts Public Utilities Commission. See Mass. Gen. L. (1932) c.159, §29. This statement was offered in evidence by petitioners under the Act of June 20, 1936, 49 Stat. 1561, 28 U.S.C. §695. They offered to prove (in the language of the Act) that the statement was signed in the regular course of business, it being the regular course of such business to make such a statement. Respondent's objection to its introduction was sustained.

We agree with the majority view below that it was properly excluded. We may assume that if the statement was made "in the regular course" of business, it would satisfy the other provisions of the Act. But we do not think that it was made "in the regular course" of business within the meaning of the Act. The business of the petitioners is the railroad business. That business like other enterprises entails the keeping of numerous books and records essential to its conduct or useful in its efficient operation. Though such books and records were considered reliable and trustworthy for major decisions in the industrial and business world, their use in litigation was greatly circumscribed or hedged about by the hearsay rule — restrictions which greatly increased the time and cost of making the proof where those who made the records were numerous. 5 Wigmore, Evidence (3d ed., 1940) §1530. It was that problem which started the movement towards adoption of legislation embodying the principles of the present Act. See Morgan et al., The Law of Evidence, Some Proposals for its Reform (1927) c.V. And the legislative history of the Act indicates the same purpose.

The engineer's statement which was held inadmissible in this case falls into quite a different category. It is not a record made for the systematic conduct of the business as a business. An accident report may affect that business in the sense that it affords information on which the management may act. It is not, however, typical of entries made systematically or as a matter of routine to record events or occurrences, to reflect transactions with others, or to provide internal controls. The conduct of a business commonly entails the payment of tort claims incurred by the negligence of its employees. But the fact that a company makes a business out of recording its employees' versions of their accidents does not put those statements in the class of records made "in the regular course" of the business within the meaning of the Act. If it did, then any law office in the land could follow the same course, since business as defined in the Act includes the professions. We would then have a real perversion of a rule designed to facilitate admission of records which experience has shown to be quite trustworthy. Any business by installing a regular system for recording and preserving its version of accidents for which it was potentially liable could qualify those reports under the Act. The result would be that the Act would cover any system of recording events or occurrences provided it was "regular" and though it had little or nothing to do with the management or operation of the business as such. Preparation of cases for trial by virtue of being a "business" or incidental thereto would obtain the benefits of this liberalized version of the early shop book rule. The probability of trustworthiness of records because they were routine reflections of the day to day operations of a business would be forgotten as the basis of the rule. Regularity of preparation would become the test rather than the character of the records and their earmarks of reliability acquired from their source and origin and the nature of their compilation. We cannot so completely empty the words of the Act of their historic meaning. If the Act is to be extended to apply not only to a "regular course" of a business but also to any "regular course" of conduct which may have some relationship to business, Congress not this Court must extend it. Such a major change which opens wide the door to avoidance of cross-examination should not be left to implication. Nor is it any answer to say that Congress has provided in the Act that the various circumstances of the making of the record should affect its weight not its admissibility. That provision comes into play only in case the other requirements of the Act are met.

In short, it is manifest that in this case those reports are not for the systematic conduct of the enterprise as a railroad business. Unlike payrolls, accounts receivable, accounts payable, bills of lading and the like these reports are calculated for use essentially in the court, not in the business. Their primary utility is in litigating, not in railroading.

It is, of course, not for us to take these reports out of the Act if Congress has put them in. But there is nothing in the background of the law on which this Act was built or in its legislative history which suggests for a moment that the business of preparing cases for trial should be included. In this connection it should be noted that the Act of May 6, 1910, 36 Stat. 350, 45 U.S.C. §38, requires officers of common carriers by rail to make under oath monthly reports of railroad accidents to the Interstate Commerce Commission, setting forth the nature and causes of the accidents and the circumstances connected therewith. And the same Act, 45 U.S.C. §40, gives the Commission authority to investigate and to make reports upon such accidents. It is provided, however, that

> Neither the report required by section 38 of this title nor any report of the investigation provided for in section 40 of this title nor any part thereof shall be admitted as evidence or used for any purpose in any suit or action for damages growing out of any matter mentioned in said report or investigation.

45 U.S.C. §41. A similar provision, 36 Stat. 916, 54 Stat. 148, 45 U.S.C. §33, bars the use in litigation of reports concerning accidents resulting from the failure of a locomotive boiler or its appurtenances. 45 U.S.C. §§32, 33. The legislation reveals an explicit Congressional policy to rule out reports of accidents which certainly have as great a claim to objectivity as the statement sought to be admitted in the present case. We can hardly suppose that Congress modified or qualified by implication these long standing statutes when it permitted records made "in the regular course" of business to be introduced. Nor can we assume that Congress having expressly prohibited the use of the company's reports on its accidents impliedly altered that policy when it came to reports by its employees to their superiors. The inference is wholly the other way.

The several hundred years of history behind the Act (Wigmore, supra, §§1517-1520) indicate the nature of the reforms which it was designed to effect. It should of course be liberally interpreted so as to do away with the anachronistic rules which gave rise to its need and at which it was aimed. But "regular course" of business must find its meaning in the inherent nature of the business in question and in the methods systematically employed for the conduct of the business as a business. . . .

Problem IV-65
Hospital Reports

D hit P, a small boy, when P ran out into the street. D picked up P and rushed him to A Hospital. In a suit for negligence by P against D arising from the accident, P's lawyer calls the custodian of records of A Hospital and through him seeks to introduce a hospital report dated the day of the accident, reading as follows:

D brought *P* to the emergency room stating that *D* had struck *P* with his car when *P* ran into the street. *D* stated that he tried to stop in time but his brakes were bad and he could not.

D's lawyer objects. What ruling and why?

Problem IV-66
Loss Memos

Action by *P*, franchisee, against *D*, franchisor and supplier, for credit for inventory returned by *P* after termination of *P*'s franchise. At trial, *P* offers a list of inventory parts and their value which was compiled by *P* after the termination. *D* objects. What ruling and why?

Problem IV-67
Computer Records

Action by *P* Insurance Company against *D* Trucking Company for premiums allegedly owed under a retrospective liability policy. Under such a policy the premium for each year is calculated on the basis of the loss experience for that year according to an elaborate, agreed-upon formula. A computer in *P*'s office stores this formula and the claims history for the year on its magnetic disc memory. At trial, *P* offers a printout of the computer's data and calculations to prove the amount due it. *D* objects. What ruling and why? What are the foundational requirements? Try preparing a direct examination to admit this evidence.

J. Public Records and Reports

FRE 803(8), (9), (10)
Hearsay Exceptions: Availability of Declarant Immaterial

The following are not excluded by the hearsay rule, even though the declarant is available as a witness: . . .

(8) *Public records and reports.* Records, reports, statements, or data compilations, in any form, of public offices or agencies, setting forth (A) the activities of the office or agency, or (B) matters observed pursuant to duty imposed by law as to which matters there was a duty to report,

excluding, however, in criminal cases matters observed by police officers and other law enforcement personnel, or (C) in civil actions and proceedings and against the Government in criminal cases, factual findings resulting from an investigation made pursuant to authority granted by law, unless the sources of information or other circumstances indicate lack of trustworthiness.

(9) *Records of vital statistics.* Records or data compilations, in any form, of births, fetal deaths, deaths, or marriages, if the report thereof was made to a public office pursuant to requirements of law.

(10) *Absence of public record or entry.* To prove the absence of a record, report, statement, or data compilation, in any form, or the nonoccurrence or nonexistence of a matter of which a record, report, statement, or data compilation, in any form, was regularly made and preserved by a public office or agency, evidence in the form of a certification in accordance with rule 902, or testimony, that diligent search failed to disclose the record, report, statement, or data compilation, or entry.

Problem IV-68
Police Reports

Action for wrongful death of *P*'s intestate, killed when the bicycle the deceased was riding collided with *D*'s car. At trial, *D* offers an official report of the accident, filed by the first officer on the scene, which contains the observations of witnesses interviewed by the officer at the scene. *P* objects. What ruling and why?

JOHNSON v. LUTZ
253 N.Y. 124, 170 N.E. 517 (1930)

HUBBS, J. This action is to recover damages for the wrongful death of the plaintiff's intestate, who was killed when his motorcycle came into a collision with the defendants' truck at a street intersection. There was a sharp conflict in the testimony in regard to the circumstances under which the collision took place. A policeman's report of the accident filed by him in the station house was offered in evidence by the defendants under section 374-a of the Civil Practice Act, and was excluded. The sole ground for reversal urged by the appellants is that said report was erroneously excluded. That section reads:

Any writing or record, whether in the form of an entry in a book or otherwise, made as a memorandum or record of any act, transaction, occurrence or event, shall be admissible in evidence in proof of said act, transaction, occurrence or event, if the trial judge shall find that it was made in the regular course of any business, and that it was the regular course of such business to make such memorandum or record at the time of such act, transaction occurrence or event, or within a reasonable time thereafter. All other circumstances of the making of such writing or record, including lack of personal knowledge by the entrant or maker, may be shown to effect its weight, but they shall not affect its admissibility. The term "business" shall include business, profession, occupation and calling of every kind.

Prior to the decision in the well-known case of Vosburgh v. Thayer, 12 Johns. 461, decided in 1815, shopbooks could not be introduced in evidence to prove an account. The decision in that case established that they were admissible where preliminary proof could be made that there were regular dealings between the parties; that the plaintiff kept honest and fair books; that some of the articles charged had been delivered; and that the plaintiff kept no clerk. At that time it might not have been a hardship to require a shopkeeper who sued to recover an account to furnish the preliminary proof required by that decision. Business was transacted in a comparatively small way, with few, if any, clerks. Since the decision in that case, it has remained the substantial basis of all decisions upon the question in this jurisdiction prior to the enactment in 1928 of section 374-a, Civil Practice Act.

Under modern conditions, the limitations upon the right to use books of account, memoranda, or records, made in the regular course of business, often resulted in a denial of justice, and usually in annoyance, expense, and waste of time and energy. A rule of evidence that was practical a century ago had become obsolete. The situation was appreciated, and attention was called to it by the courts and text-writers. Woods Practice Evidence (2d Ed.) 377; 3 Wigmore on Evidence (1923) §1530. . . .

In view of the history of section 374-a and the purpose for which it was enacted, it is apparent that it was never intended to apply to a situation like that in the case at bar. The memorandum in question was not made in the regular course of any business, profession, occupation, or calling. The policeman who made it was not present at the time of the accident. The memorandum was made from hearsay statements of third persons who happened to be present at the scene of the accident when he arrived. It does not appear when they saw the accident and stated to him what they knew, or stated what some other persons had told them.

The purpose of the Legislature in enacting section 374-a was to permit a writing or record, made in the regular course of business, to be received in evidence, without the necessity of calling as witnesses all of the persons who had any part in making it, provided the record was made as a part of the duty of the person making it, or on information imparted by persons who were under a duty to impart such information. The amendment permits the introduction of shopbooks without the necessity of calling all clerks who may have sold different items of account. It was not intended to permit the receipt in evidence of entries based upon voluntary hearsay statements made by third parties not engaged in the business or under any duty in relation thereto. It was said, in Mayor, etc., of New York City v. Second Ave. R. Co., 102 N.Y. 572, at page 581, 7 N.E. 905, 909, 55 Am. Rep. 839: "It is a proper qualification of the rule admitting such evidence that the account must have been made in the ordinary course of business, and that it should not be extended so as to admit a mere private memorandum, not made in pursuance of any duty owing by the person making it, or when made upon information derived from another who made the communication casually and voluntarily, and not under the sanction of duty or other obligation."

An important consideration leading to the amendment was the fact that in the business world credit is given to records made in the course of business by persons who are engaged in the business upon information given by others engaged in the same business as part of their duty.

> Such entries are dealt with in that way in the most important undertakings of mercantile and industrial life. They are the ultimate basis of calculation, investment, and general confidence in every business enterprise. Nor does the practical impossibility of obtaining constantly and permanently the verification of every employee affect the trust that is given to such books. It would seem that expedients which the entire commercial world recognizes as safe could be sanctioned, and not discredited, by courts of justice. When it is a mere question of whether provisional confidence can be placed in a certain class of statements, there cannot profitably and sensibly be one rule for the business world and another for the court-room. The merchant and the manufacturer must not be turned away remediless because the methods in which the entire community places a just confidence are a little difficult to reconcile with technical judicial scruples on the part of the same persons who as attorneys have already employed and relied upon the same methods. In short, courts must here cease to be pedantic and endeavor to be practical.

3 Wigmore on Evidence (1923) §1530, p.278.

The Legislature has sought by the amendment to make the courts practical. It would be unfortunate not to give the amendment a construction which will enable it to cure the evil complained of and accomplish the purpose for which it was enacted. In constructing it, we should not, however, permit it to be applied in a case for which it was never intended.

The judgment should be affirmed, with costs.

UNITED STATES v. OATES
560 F.2d 45 (1977)

WATERMAN, J. This is an appeal from a judgment of the United States District Court for the Eastern District of New York convicting appellant, following a six-day jury trial, of possession of heroin with intent to distribute, and of conspiracy to commit that substantive offense. In seeking reversals of his convictions, appellant urges upon us three unrelated claims of error. . . .

Appellant's second claim of error is that the trial court incorrectly admitted into evidence at trial the official report and worksheet of the chemist who analyzed the substance seized from Daniels. Appellant contends that the introduction of this evidence was impermissible for the evidence was inadmissible hearsay under the new Federal Rules of Evidence, and, also, that under the circumstances of this case, the introduction of the report and the worksheet violated appellant's right under the Sixth Amendment to the United States Constitution to confront the witnesses against him. . . .

Appellant next claims that the trial court committed error by admitting into evidence at trial two documentary exhibits purporting to be the official report and accompanying worksheet of the United States Customs Service chemist who analyzed the white powdery substance seized from Isaac Daniels. The documents, the crucial nature of which is beyond cavil, concluded that the powder examined was heroin. Appellant contends, first of all, that under the new Federal Rules of Evidence (hereinafter "FRE") the documents should have been excluded as hearsay and, alternatively, that, even if they were not inadmissible on that basis, their exclusion was nonetheless required because their admission into evidence over appellant's objection would have violated and did violate appellant's right under the Sixth Amendment to the United States Constitution to confront the witnesses against him. . . .

At trial the government had planned upon calling as one of its final witnesses a Mr. Milton Weinberg, a retired United States Customs Service chemist who allegedly had analyzed the white powder seized from Isaac Daniels. It seems that Mr. Weinberg had been present on the day the trial had been scheduled to commence but he was not able to testify then because of a delay occasioned by the unexpected length of the pretrial suppression hearing. The government claims that by the time Weinberg was rescheduled to testify he had become "unavailable." The Assistant United States Attorney explained the circumstances of this unavailability as follows: "I am told by his wife [he is] very sick. Apparently he has some type of bronchial infection." . . .

Before the onset of Weinberg's bronchial condition, the prosecutor had planned to call Weinberg for the purpose of eliciting from him testimony that Weinberg had analyzed the powder seized from Daniels and found it to be heroin. When Weinberg became "unavailable," the government decided to call another Customs chemist, Shirley Harrington, who, although she did not know Weinberg personally, was able to testify concerning the regular practices and procedures used by Customs Service chemists in analyzing unknown substances. Through Mrs. Harrington the government was successful in introducing Exhibits 13 and 12 which purported to be, respectively, the handwritten worksheet used by the chemist analyzing the substance seized from Daniels and the official typewritten report of the chemical analysis. The report summarizes salient features of the worksheet. Mrs. Harrington claimed to be able to ascertain from the face of the worksheet the various steps taken by Weinberg to determine whether the unknown substance was, as suspected, heroin. When the defense voiced vigorous objection to the attempt to introduce the documents through Mrs. Harrington, the government relied upon three different hearsay exceptions contained in the new Federal Rules of Evidence to support its position that the documents were admissible. While principal reliance was placed on the modified "business records" exception found in FRE 803(6), the evidence was also claimed to be admissible under FRE 803(8) as a "public record" or under FRE 803(24). The defense was primarily concerned that the defendant was being denied his Sixth Amendment right to confront his accusers, in this case, the missing chemist Weinberg.

Mrs. Harrington was obviously an experienced chemist, having conducted thousands of tests while working for the Customs Service, including hundreds designed to identify heroin. She was also an experienced witness, having testified "probably a hundred or so" times in the course of her duties with the Customs Service. She had never worked with Weinberg personally and had never observed him perform any chemical tests. She had never received any notes or letters from him, but she identified Weinberg's writing on Exhibit 13 and his signature on Exhibit 12, presumably because she had, in accordance with Customs Service practices, reanalyzed, prior to destruction, substances Weinberg had previously analyzed shortly after the substances were seized.

The defense, in addition to having no opportunity to cross-examine Weinberg, the chemist who had performed the analysis, was also disturbed about two other circumstances surrounding the introduction of Exhibits 12 and 13. In particular, the defense was surprised that Exhibit 12, the official typewritten report, contained Weinberg's signature, for no such signature had appeared on the copy of this exhibit given to the defense beforehand. Moreover, the defense was particularly, and understandably, distressed about the absence of Weinberg in view of the fact that the two exhibits differed in one important particular, a particular in which they certainly should have been identical. A notation per-

taining to the chain of custody of the powder within the agency
appeared on both exhibits, in typewritten form on the official report and
in handwriting, presumably Weinberg's, on the worksheet. The notation
read "Received from and returned to CSO Fromkin." On the typewritten official report, however, this statement had been crossed out, although it still was legible beneath the scribbling. Mrs. Harrington knew
nothing about this deletion. There is nothing in the exhibits themselves
or in the testimony of any witnesses that would explain why, when and
by whom this deletion was made. . . .

It is eminently clear that the report and worksheet were "written
assertions" constituting "statements," FRE 801(a)(1), which were "offered [by the prosecution] in evidence [at trial] to prove the truth of the
matters asserted [in them]." FRE 801(c). As such, they were hearsay and,
for our present purposes, under FRE 802 were inadmissible "except as
[otherwise] provided by" other provisions of the Federal Rules of Evidence. The so-called "exceptions" to the hearsay rule are delineated in
FRE 803 and 804. What immediately catches one's attention upon referring to these sections is the prefatory language of each: "The following *are not excluded* by the hearsay rule. . . ." (Emphasis supplied.) These
two rules enumerating the exceptions to the hearsay rule are thus *not*
designed to insure *admissibility* of the questioned evidence but only designed to prevent automatic exclusion on hearsay grounds. Why this
language was drafted in this fashion, and why, as we shall see, other
specific language, either contained in the rules as proposed to and approved by Congress or inserted by Congress itself during the legislative
process, was drafted with comparable circumspection, is succinctly explained by the Advisory Committee. . . .

The reason for "the exceptions set forth in Rules 803 and 804 [being]
stated in terms of exemption from the general exclusionary mandate of
the hearsay rule, rather than in positive terms of admissibility," is the
Advisory Committee's "recognition of the separateness of the confrontation clause [of the Sixth Amendment to the United States Constitution]
and the hearsay rule" and its desire "to avoid inviting collisions between"
the two. Id. Indeed, although "[u]nder the earlier cases, the confrontation clause may have been little more than a constitutional embodiment
of the hearsay rule, even including traditional exceptions but with some
room for expanding them along similar lines . . . , under the recent
[court] cases the impact of the clause clearly extends beyond the confines
of the hearsay rule." These remarks leave absolutely no doubt, of course,
that the draftsmen were fully aware of the "significant recent developments," see, e.g., 5 Wigmore, Evidence §1397, at 155 (Chadbourn rev.
1974), concerning the right to confrontation which had occurred and
were likely to occur in the future. The remarks also evince a clear intention to draft the rules in such a way as to eliminate, if possible, any

tension between the hearsay rule as embodied in Article VIII of the Federal Rules of Evidence and the confrontation clause.

These efforts to avert the possibility of conflict between the hearsay exceptions and the confrontation clause find their most emphatic expression in FRE 803(8) and it is to that provision that we now turn. On this appeal the government and the appellant are in complete disagreement over the materiality of FRE 803(8) to the issue of whether the chemist's report and worksheet were excludable as hearsay. Although at trial the government placed some reliance on FRE 803(8), the so-called "public records and reports" exception to exclusion, in its brief in this court it completely ignores the provision, apparently abandoning any reliance on it for reasons we shall discuss below. Instead, it urges us to find that the challenged evidence falls easily within the scope of what has traditionally been labeled the "business records exception" to the hearsay exclusionary rule, the codification of which in the Federal Rules of Evidence is found in FRE 803(6). Appellant, on the other hand, vigorously asserts that the issue of whether the chemist's report and worksheet were fatal hearsay can be correctly evaluated only by a careful study of the precise wording of FRE 803(8) and the legislative intent underlying the enactment of that rule.

While the problem presented is not susceptible of any facile solution, we believe that, on balance, appellant's emphasis on the importance of FRE 803(8) is well-founded. It would certainly seem to be the exception which would logically come to mind if a question arose as to the admissibility of reports of the kind we are considering in this case. Moreover, although as a general rule there is no question that hearsay evidence failing to meet the requirements of one exception may nonetheless satisfy the standards of another exception, see, e.g., United States v. Smith, 172 U.S. App. D.C. 297, 521 F.2d 957, 964 (D.C. Cir. 1975), and there thus might be no need to examine FRE 803(8) at all, we agree with appellant that both the language of Rule 803(8) and the congressional intent, as gleaned from the explicit language of the rule and from independent sources, which impelled that language have impact that extends beyond the immediate confines of exception (8) itself. We therefore regard FRE 803(8) as the proper starting point for our evidentiary analysis.

That the chemist's report and worksheet could not satisfy the requirements of the "public records and reports" exception seems evident merely from examining, on its face, the language of FRE 803(8). . . . While there may be no sharp demarcation between the records covered by exception 8(B) and those referenced in exception 8(C), see, e.g., United States v. Smith, supra, 521 F.2d at 968 n.24, and indeed there may in some cases be actual overlap, we conclude without hesitation that surely the language of item (C) is applicable to render the chemist's documents inadmissible as evidence in this case, and they might also be within the ambit of the terminology of item (B), a claim appellant argues to us persuasively.

It is manifest from the face of item (C) that "factual findings resulting from an investigation made pursuant to authority granted by law" are not shielded from the exclusionary effect of the hearsay rule by "the public records exception" if the government seeks to have those "factual findings" admitted *against* the accused in a criminal case. It seems indisputable to us that the chemist's official report and worksheet in the case at bar can be characterized as reports of "factual findings resulting from an investigation made pursuant to authority granted by law." The "factual finding" in each instance, the conclusion of the chemist that the substance analyzed was heroin, obviously is the product of an "investigation," see, e.g., Martin v. Reynolds Metal Corp., 297 F.2d 49, 57 (9th Cir. 1961) (" 'investigation,' when liberally construed, includes the sampling and *testing* here contemplated") (emphasis supplied), supposedly involving on the part of the chemist employment of various techniques of scientific analysis. Furthermore, in view of its reliance on the chemist's report at trial and its representation to the district court that "chemical analys[e]s of unidentified substances are indeed a regularly conducted activity of the Customs laboratory of Customs chemists," the government here is surely in no position to dispute the fact that the analyses regularly performed by United States Customs Service chemists on substances lawfully seized by Customs officers are performed pursuant to authority granted by law.

Though with less confidence, we believe that the chemist's documents might also fail to achieve status as public records under FRE 803(8)(B) because they are records of "matters observed by police officers and other law enforcement personnel." Although in characterizing the chemist's report and worksheet here it is quite accurate to designate those reports as the reports of factual findings made pursuant to an investigation, the reports in this case conceivably could also be susceptible of the characterization that they are "reports . . . setting forth . . . (B) matters observed pursuant to duty imposed by law as to which matters there was a duty to report." If this characterization is justified, the difficult question would be whether the chemists making the observations could be regarded as "other law enforcement personnel." We think this phraseology must be read broadly enough to make its prohibitions against the use of government-generated reports in criminal cases coterminous with the analogous prohibitions contained in FRE 803(8)(C). See United States v. Smith, supra, 521 F.2d at 968-69 n.24. We would thus construe "other law enforcement personnel" to include, at the least, any officer or employee of a governmental agency which has law enforcement responsibilities. Applying such a standard to the case at bar, we

easily conclude that full-time chemists of the United States Customs
Service are "law enforcement personnel." The chemist in this case was
employed by the Customs Service, a governmental agency which had
clearly defined law enforcement authority in the field of illegal narcotics
trafficking; the officers who actually seized the suspected contraband
were employed by the Customs Service, and the unidentified substance
was delivered by them to a laboratory operated by the Customs Service.
The unidentified substance was then subjected to analysis by a chemist,
one of whose regular functions is to test substances seized from suspected narcotics violators. Chemists at the laboratory are, without question, important participants in the prosecutorial effort. As well as
analyzing substances for the express purpose of ascertaining whether
the substances are contraband, and if so, participating in eventual prosecution of narcotics offenders, the chemists are also expected to be familiar with the need for establishing the whereabouts of confiscated drugs
at all times from seizure until trial. Moreover, the role of the chemist
typically does not terminate upon completion of the chemical analysis
and submission of the resulting report but participation continues until
the chemist has testified as an important prosecution witness at trial.
Indeed, Mrs. Harrington had herself testified "probably a hundred or
so" times. Also of some interest perhaps is a remark made by Mrs.
Harrington which indicates that the Customs chemists do not mentally
disassociate themselves from those who undoubtedly are law enforcement personnel. After chemical analyses are performed, according to
Mrs. Harrington, "the material [is] returned to the agent or *our* Customs
officer." In short, these reports are not "made by persons and for purposes unconnected with a criminal case [but rather they are a direct]
result of a test made for the specific purpose of convicting the defendant
and conducted by agents of the executive branch, the very department
of government which seeks defendant's conviction." State v. Larochelle,
112 N.H. 392, 400, 297 A.2d 223, 228 (1972) (dissenting opinion). It
would therefore seem that if the chemist's report and worksheet here
can be deemed to set forth "matters observed," the documents would fail
to satisfy the requirements of exception FRE 803(8) for the chemist must
be included within the category of "other law enforcement personnel."

Our conclusion that the chemist's report and worksheet do not satisfy
the standards of FRE 803(8) comports perfectly with what we discern to
be clear legislative intent not only to exclude such documents from the
scope of FRE 803(8) but from the scope of FRE 803(6) as well. The
reason why such a restrictive approach was adopted can be established
by referring to the Advisory Committee's Notes and by examining the
way in which Congress revised the draft legislation proposed by the
Advisory Committee and which the Supreme Court submitted to Congress. As already explained, an overriding concern of the Advisory

Committee was that the rules be formulated so as to avoid impinging upon a criminal defendant's right to confront the witnesses against him. The Advisory Committee, in unequivocal language, offers the specter of collision with the confrontation clause as the explanation for the presence of FRE 803(8)(C) in its proposed (and, since FRE 803(8)(C) was unaltered during the legislative process, final) form:

> In one respect, however, the rule with respect to evaluative reports under [FRE 803(8)(C)] is very specific: they are admissible only in civil cases and against the government in criminal cases in view of the *almost certain collision with confrontation rights which would result from their use against an accused in a criminal case.* . . .

Despite what we perceive to be clear congressional intent that reports not qualifying under FRE 803(8)(B) or (C) should, and would, be inadmissible against defendants in criminal cases, the government completely ignores those provisions, as well as FRE 803(24), another hearsay exception upon which it relied at trial, and argues instead that the chemist's report and worksheet in the case at bar fall clearly within the literal terms of the modified business records exception to the hearsay rule contained in FRE 803(6), entitled *"Records of regularly conducted activity."* . . . [T]he government's argument that the documents in this case satisfy the requirements of the modified "business records" exception is not altogether unappealing if it is assessed strictly on the basis of the literal language of FRE 803(6) and without reference to either the legislative history or the language of FRE 803(8)(B) and (C). For instance, it is true that, traditionally, a proponent's inability to satisfy the requirements of one hearsay exception does not deny him the opportunity to attempt to meet the standards of another. See, e.g., United States v. Smith, supra, 521 F.2d at 964. Secondly, it is clear from the explicit inclusion of the words "opinions" and "diagnoses" in FRE 803(6) that, in one sense anyway, Congress intended to expand, or at least ratify, the view of prior court cases that had expanded the concept of what constitutes a "business record." The Advisory Committee's Notes confirm this. Advisory Committee's Notes, Note to Paragraph (6) of Rule 803. It is reasonable to assume that a laboratory analysis may well be an "opinion." Thirdly, the testimony of Mrs. Harrington, a "qualified witness," established that it was a regular practice of the Customs laboratory to make written reports of their analyses and that these particular written reports were made in the regular course of the laboratory's activities. However, not nearly as clear is whether under the facts here the "method or circumstances of preparation" might not "indicate lack of trustworthiness." . . . Here there are some "circumstances of preparation [which tend to] indicate lack of trustworthiness." As already noted, Exhibits 12 and 13 differ from each other in one significant respect in which they should be identical. On both, in handwriting on the worksheet and in typewritten form on the official report, the notation "Received from and returned to CSO Fromkin" appears. Yet, on the report this notation has been crossed out. Nothing indicates who deleted the notation, when it was deleted, or why it was deleted and, as it relates to the issue of chain of custody, it is a matter of some importance. Moreover, before trial defense counsel was given what was purported to be a copy of the official chemist's report. Yet, this document did not contain the signature of the certifying chemist Weinberg. At trial the official report the government offered *was* signed. Assuming that Weinberg did sign the document the government offered, there is obviously a question as to *when* this document was signed, it not being unreasonable to assume that it was signed after the government had already given the defense a copy of an originally unsigned report. However, while we are troubled by these concededly unusual circumstances, and it may well be that they raise ample doubts to require exclusion on the face of FRE 803(6) alone, we prefer not to predicate our decision on a finding that the "circumstances of preparation indicate lack of trustworthiness." Instead, we assume for purposes of argument here, that, as sedulously asserted by the government, the chemist's report and worksheet might fall within the literal language of FRE 803(6).

For purposes of our present analysis, we thus consider the situation to be that the chemist's documents might appear to be within the literal language of FRE 803(6) although there is clear congressional intent that such documents be deemed inadmissible against a defendant in a criminal case. This would not be the first time that a court has encountered a situation pitting some literal language of a statute against a legislative intent that flies in the face of that literal language. Our function as an interpretive body is, of course, to construe legislative enactments in such a way that the intent of the legislature is carried out. . . . [W]e shall now attempt to ascertain the legislative intent underlying FRE 803(6). . . .

As already mentioned, Representative William Hungate, in presenting the report of the Committee of Conference to the House of Representatives, left no doubt that it was the belief of the Committee of Conference that under the new Federal Rules of Evidence the *effect* of FRE 803(8)(B) and (C) was to render law enforcement reports and evaluative reports inadmissible against defendants in criminal cases. It is thus clear that the only way to construe FRE 803(6) so that it is reconcilable with this intended effect is to interpret FRE 803(6) and the other hearsay exceptions in such a way that police and evaluative reports not satisfying the standards of FRE 803(8)(B) and (C) may not qualify for admission under FRE 803(6) or any of the other exceptions to the hearsay rule. . . . [T]he pervasive fear of the draftsmen and of Congress that interference with an accused's right to confrontation would occur was the reason why in criminal cases evaluative reports of government agencies and law enforcement reports were expressly denied the benefit to which they might otherwise be entitled under FRE 803(8). It follows that this explanation of the reason for the special treatment of evaluative and law enforcement reports under FRE 803(8) applies with equal force to the treatment of such reports under *any* of the other exceptions to the hearsay rule. The prosecution's utilization of any hearsay exception to achieve admission of evaluative and law enforcement reports would serve to deprive the accused of the opportunity to confront his accusers as effectively as would reliance on a "public records" exception. Thus, there being no apparent reason why Congress would tolerate the admission of evaluative and law enforcement reports by use of some other exception to the hearsay rule (for example, the "business records" exception of FRE 803(6) or the "open-ended" exceptions of FRE 803(24) or 804(b)(5)), it simply makes no sense to surmise that Congress ever intended that these records could be admissible against a defendant in a criminal case under *any* of the Federal Rules of Evidence's exceptions to the hearsay rule. . . .

[S]erious questions of constitutional dimension reinforce our belief that we are correct in holding, as we hold here, that in criminal cases reports of public agencies setting forth matters observed by police officers and other law enforcement personnel and reports of public agencies setting forth factual findings resulting from investigations made pursuant to authority granted by law cannot satisfy the standards of any hearsay exception if those reports are sought to be introduced against the accused. Inasmuch as the chemist's documents here can be characterized as governmental reports which set forth matters observed by law enforcement personnel or which set forth factual findings resulting from an authorized investigation, they were incapable of qualifying under any of the exceptions to the hearsay rule specified in FRE 803 and 804. The documents were crucial to the government's case, they were, of course, hearsay, and, inasmuch as they were ineligible to qualify for any exception to the hearsay rule, their admission at trial against appellant was prejudicial error. . . .

Problem IV-69
Aircrash

Action against *D* Airline Company for wrongful death of plaintiff's intestate, who perished in a crash of one of *D*'s planes. At trial, *P* offers the following on the issue of *D*'s negligence:

(1) The policy manual of the air traffic control tower at the airport controlling the plane at the time of the crash;

(2) The U.S. Meteorological Service records of the weather on the night of the crash; and

(3) The report of the FAA investigational team assigned to investigate and report on the cause of the crash. The report contains 356 pages of detailed findings and 56 pages of conclusions and recommendations. One of the report's conclusions is that the failure of the plane's operator to properly maintain the plane's radar equipment was a primary cause of the crash.

D objects to these offers. What rulings and why? What factors justify the receipt of such evidence or argue against its use?

K.   "Other Exceptions"

FRE 803(24)
Hearsay Exceptions: Availability of Declarant Immaterial

The following are not excluded by the hearsay rule, even though the declarant is available as a witness: . . .

(24) *Other exceptions.* A statement not specifically covered by any of the foregoing exceptions but having equivalent circumstantial guarantees of trustworthiness, if the court determines that (A) the statement is offered as evidence of a material fact; (B) the statement is more probative on the point for which it is offered than any other evidence which the proponent can procure through reasonable efforts; and (C) the general purposes of these rules and the interests of justice will best be served by admission of the statement into evidence. However, a statement may not be admitted under this exception unless the proponent of it makes known to the adverse party sufficiently in advance of the trial or hearing to provide the adverse party with a fair opportunity to prepare to meet it, his intention to offer the statement and the particulars of it, including the name and address of the declarant.

FRE 804(b)(5)
Hearsay Exceptions: Declarant Unavailable

(b) *Hearsay exceptions.* The following are not excluded by the hearsay rule if the declarant is unavailable as a witness: . . .

(5) *Other exceptions.* A statement not specifically covered by any of the foregoing exceptions but having equivalent circumstantial guarantees of

trustworthiness, if the court determines that (A) the statement is offered
as evidence of a material fact; (B) the statement is more probative on the
point for which it is offered than any other evidence which the proponent can procure through reasonable effort; and (C) the general purposes of these rules and the interests of justice will best be served by
admission of the statement into evidence. However, a statement may not
be admitted under this exception unless the proponent of it makes
known to the adverse party sufficiently in advance of the trial or hearing
to provide the adverse party with a fair opportunity to prepare to meet
it, his intention to offer the statement and the particulars of it, including
the name and address of the declarant.

DALLAS COUNTY v. COMMERCIAL UNION
ASSURANCE COMPANY
286 F.2d 388 (5th Cir. 1961)

Wisdom, J. This appeal presents a single question — the admissibility
in evidence of a newspaper to show that the Dallas County Courthouse
in Selma, Alabama, was damaged by fire in 1901. We hold that the
newspaper was admissible, and affirm the judgment below.

On a bright, sunny morning, July 7, 1957, the clock tower of the
Dallas County Courthouse at Selma, Alabama, commenced to lean,
made loud cracking and popping noises, then fell, and telescoped into
the courtroom. Fortunately, the collapse of the tower took place on a
Sunday morning; no one was injured, but damage to the courthouse
exceeded $100,000. An examination of the tower debris showed the
presence of charcoal and charred timbers. The State Toxicologist, called
in by Dallas County, reported the char was evidence that lightning struck
the courthouse. Later, several residents of Selma reported that a bolt of
lightning struck the courthouse July 2, 1957. On this information, Dallas
County concluded that a lightning bolt had hit the building causing the
collapse of the clock tower five days later. Dallas County carried insurance for loss to its courthouse caused by fire or lightning. The insurers'
engineers and investigators found that the courthouse collapsed of its
own weight. They reported that the courthouse had not been struck by
lightning; that lightning could not have caused the collapse of the tower;
that the collapse of the tower was caused by structural weaknesses attributable to a faulty design, poor construction, gradual deterioration of
the structure, and overloading brought about by remodeling and the
recent installation of an air-conditioning system, part of which was constructed over the courtroom trusses. In their opinion, the char was the
result of a fire in the courthouse tower and roof that must have occurred
many, many years before July 2, 1957. The insurers denied liability.

The County sued its insurers in the Circuit Court of Dallas County.

As many of the suits as could be removed, seven, were removed to the United States District Court for the Southern District of Alabama, and were consolidated for trial. The case went to the jury on one issue: did lightning cause the collapse of the clock tower?

The record contains ample evidence to support a jury verdict either way. The County produced witnesses who testified they saw lightning strike the clock tower; the insurers produced witnesses who testified an examination of the debris showed that lightning did not strike the clock tower. Some witnesses said the char was fresh and smelled smoky; other witnesses said it was obviously old and had no fresh smoky smell at all. Both sides presented a great mass of engineering testimony bearing on the design, construction, overload or lack of overload. All of this was for the jury to evaluate. The jury chose to believe the insurers' witnesses and brought in a verdict for the defendants.

During the trial the defendants introduced a copy of the Morning Times of Selma for June 9, 1901. This issue carried an unsigned article describing a fire that occurred at two in the morning of June 9, 1901, while the courthouse was still under construction. The article stated, in part: "The unfinished dome of the County's new courthouse was in flames at the top, and . . . soon fell in. The fire was soon under control and the main building was saved. . . ." The insurers do not contend that the collapse of the tower resulted from unsound charred timbers used in the repair of the building after the fire; they offered the newspaper account to show there had been a fire long before 1957 that would account for charred timber in the clock tower.

As a predicate for introducing the newspaper in evidence, the defendants called to the stand the editor of the Selma Times-Journal who testified that his publishing company maintains archives of the published issues of the Times-Journal and of the Morning Times, its predecessor, and that the archives contain the issue of the Morning Times of Selma for June 9, 1901, offered in evidence. The plaintiff objected that the newspaper article was hearsay; that it was not a business record nor an ancient document, nor was it admissible under any recognized exception to the hearsay doctrine. The trial judge admitted the newspaper as part of the records of the Selma Times-Journal. The sole error Dallas County specifies on appeal is the admission of the newspaper in evidence.

In the Anglo-American adversary system of law, courts usually will not admit evidence unless its accuracy and trustworthiness may be tested by cross-examination. Here, therefore, the plaintiff argues that the newspaper should not be admitted: "You cannot cross-examine a newspaper."[1] Of course, a newspaper article *is* hearsay, and in almost all

---

1. This argument, a familiar one, rests on a misunderstanding of its origin and the nature of the hearsay rule. The rule is not an ancient principle of English law recognized at Runnymede. And, gone is its odor of sanctity.

circumstances is inadmissible. However, the law governing hearsay is somewhat less than pellucid. And, as with most rules, the hearsay rule is not absolute; it is replete with exceptions. Witnesses die, documents are lost, deeds are destroyed, memories fade. All too often, primary evidence is not available and courts and lawyers must rely on secondary evidence. . . .

We turn now to a case, decided long before the Federal Rules were adopted, in which the court used an approach we consider appropriate for the solution of the problem before us. G. & C. Merriam Co. v. Syndicate Pub. Co., 2 Cir., 1913, 207 F. 515, 518, concerned a con-

---

Wigmore is often quoted for the statement that "cross-examination is beyond my doubt the greatest legal engine ever invented for the discovery of truth." 5 Wigmore §1367 (3d ed.) In over 1200 pages devoted to the hearsay rule, however, he makes it very clear that:

"[T]he rule aims to insist on testing all statements by cross-examination, *if they can be*. . . . No one could defend a rule which pronounced that all statements thus untested are worthless; for all historical truth is based on uncross-examined assertions; and every day's experience of life gives denial to such an exaggeration. What the Hearsay Rule implies — and with profound verity — is that all testimonial assertions *ought to be* tested by cross-examination, as the best attainable measure; and it should not be burdened with the pedantic implication that they must be rejected as worthless if the test is unavailable." 1 Wigmore §8c. In this connection see Falknor, The Hearsay Rule and its Exceptions, 2 U.C.L.A.L. Rev. 43 (1954).

In The Introductory Note to Chapter VI, Hearsay Evidence, American Law Institute Model Code of Evidence (1942), Edmund M. Morgan, Reporter, it is pointed out that "the hearsay rule is the child of the adversary system." The Note continues:

"During the first centuries of the jury system, the jury based its decision upon what the jurors themselves knew of the matter in dispute and what they learned through the words of their fathers and through such words of these persons whom they are bound to trust as worthy. . . . Until the end of the sixteenth century hearsay was received without question.

". . . The opportunity for cross-examination is not a necessary element of a jury system, while it is the very heart of the adversary system.

". . . As the judges began their attempts to rationalize the results of the decisions dealing with evidence, they first relied upon the general notion that a party was obliged to produce the best evidence available, but no more. Had they applied this generally, hearsay would have been received whenever better evidence could not be obtained. Therefore the judges discovered a special sort of necessity in . . . exceptional cases . . . [making] the admissible hearsay less unreliable than hearsay in general. . . . [By 1840] it became the fashion to attribute the exclusion of hearsay to the incapacity of the jury to evaluate, and in the development of exceptions to the rule, courts have doubtless been influenced by this notion. . . . Modern textwriters and judges have purported to find for each exception some sort of necessity for resort to hearsay and some condition attending the making of the excepted statement which will enable the jury to put a fair value upon it and will thus serve as a substitute for cross-examination. A careful examination of the eighteen or nineteen classes of utterances, each of which is now recognized as an exception to the hearsay rule by some respectable authority, will reveal that in many of them the necessity resolves itself into mere convenience and the substitute for cross-examination is imperceptible. . . . In most of the exceptions, however, the adversary theory is disregarded. There is nothing in any of the situations to warrant depriving the adversary of an opportunity to cross-examine; but those rationalizing the results purport to find some substitute for cross-examination. In most instances one will look in vain for anything more than a situation in which an ordinary man making such a statement would positively desire to tell the truth; and in some the most that can be claimed is the absence of a motive to falsify." For the history of the rule see 5 Wigmore, Evidence, §1364 (3rd ed.); 9 Holdsworth's History of English Law, 214 (1926).

troversy between dictionary publishers over the use of the title "Webster's Dictionary" when the defendant's dictionary allegedly was not based upon Webster's Dictionary at all. The bone of contention was whether a statement in the preface to the dictionary was admissible as evidence of the facts it recited. Ogilvie, the compiler of the dictionary, stated in his preface that he used Webster's Dictionary as the basis for his own publication. The dictionary, with its preface, was published in 1850, sixty-three years before the trial of the case. Ogilvie's published statement was challenged as hearsay. Judge Learned Hand, then a district judge, unable, as we are here, to find a case in point, for authority relied solely on Wigmore on Evidence (then a recent publication), particularly on Wigmore's analysis that "the requisites of an exception of the hearsay rule are necessity and circumstantial guaranty of trustworthiness." Wigmore on Evidence, §§1421, 1422, 1690 (1st ed. 1913). Applying these criteria, Judge Hand held that the statement was admissible as an exception to the hearsay rule:

"Ogilvie's preface is of course an unsworn statement and as such only hearsay testimony, which may be admitted only as an exception to the general rule. The question is whether there is such an exception. I have been unable to find any express authority in point and must decide the question upon principle. In the first place, I think it fair to insist that to reject such a statement is to refuse evidence about the truth of which no reasonable person should have any doubt whatever, because it fulfills both the requisites of an exception to the hearsay rule, necessity and circumstantial guaranty of trustworthiness. Wigmore, §§1421, 1422, 1906. . . . Besides Ogilvie, everyone else is dead who ever knew anything about the matter and could intelligently tell us what the fact is. . . . As to the trustworthiness of the testimony, it has the guaranty of the occasion, at which there was no motive for fabrication." 207 F. 515, 518.

The Court of Appeals adopted the district court's opinion in its entirety.

The first of the two requisites is necessity. As to necessity, Wigmore points out this requisite means that unless the hearsay statement is admitted, the facts it brings out may otherwise be lost, either because the person whose assertion is offered may be dead or unavailable, or because the assertion is of such a nature that one could not expect to obtain evidence of the same value from the same person or from other sources. Wigmore, §1421 (3rd ed.). "In effect, Wigmore says that, as the word necessary is here used, it is not to be interpreted as uniformly demanding a showing of total inaccessibility of firsthand evidence as a condition precedent to the acceptance of a particular piece of hearsay, but that necessity exists where otherwise great practical inconvenience would be experienced in making the desired proof. (Wigmore, 3d Ed., Vol. V, sec. 1421; Vol. VI, sec. 1702). . . . If it were otherwise, the result would be that the exception created to the hearsay rule would thereby be mostly, if not completely, destroyed." United States v. Aluminum Co. of America, D.C. 1940, 35 F. Supp. 820, 823.

The fire referred to in the newspaper account occurred fifty-eight years before the trial of this case. Any witness who saw that fire with sufficient understanding to observe it and describe it accurately, would have been older than a young child at the time of the fire. We may reasonably assume that at the time of the trial he was either dead or his faculties were dimmed by the passage of fifty-eight years. It would have been burdensome, but not impossible, for the defendant to have discovered the name of the author of the article (although it has no by-line) and, perhaps, to have found an eyewitness to the fire. But it is improbable — so it seems to us — that any witness could have been found whose recollection would have been accurate at the time of the trial of this case. And it seems impossible that the testimony of any witness would have been as accurate and as reliable as the statement of facts in the contemporary newspaper article.

The rationale behind the "ancient documents" exception is applicable here: after a long lapse of time, ordinary evidence regarding signatures or handwriting is virtually unavailable, and it is therefore permissible to resort to circumstantial evidence. Thus, in Trustees of German Township, Montgomery County v. Farmers & Citizens Savings Bank Co., Ohio Com. Pl. 1953, 113 N.E.2d 409, 412, affirmed Ohio App., 115 N.E.2d 690, the court admitted as ancient documents newspapers eighty years old containing notices of advertisements for bids relating to the town hall: "Such exhibits, by reason of age, alone, and unquestioned authenticity, qualify as ancient documents." The ancient documents rule applies to documents a generation or more in age. Here, the Selma Times-Journal article is almost two generations old. The principle of necessity, not requiring absolute impossibility of total inaccessibility of first-hand knowledge, is satisfied by the practicalities of the situation before us.

The second requisite for admission of hearsay evidence is trustworthiness. According to Wigmore, there are three sets of circumstances when hearsay is trustworthy enough to serve as a practicable substitute for the ordinary test of cross-examination:

> Where the circumstances are such that a sincere and accurate statement would naturally be uttered, and no plan of falsification be formed; where, even though a desire to falsify might present itself, other considerations, such as the danger of easy detection or the fear of punishment, would probably counteract its force; where the statement was made under such conditions of publicity that an error, if it had occurred, would probably have been detected and corrected.

5 Wigmore, Evidence, §1422 (3rd ed.). These circumstances fit the instant case.

There is no procedural canon against the exercise of common sense in deciding the admissibility of hearsay evidence. In 1901 Selma, Alabama was a small town. Taking a common sense view of this case, it is inconceivable to us that a newspaper reporter in a small town would report there was a fire in the dome of the new courthouse — if there had been no fire. He is without motive to falsify, and a false report would have subjected the newspaper and him to embarrassment in the community. The usual dangers inherent in hearsay evidence, such as lack of memory, faulty narration, intent to influence the court proceedings, and plain lack of truthfulness are not present here. To our minds, the article published in the Selma Morning-Times on the day of the fire is more reliable, more trustworthy, more competent evidence than the testimony of a witness called to the stand fifty-eight years later.

We hold, that in matters of local interest, when the fact in question is of such a public nature it would be generally known throughout the community, and when the questioned fact occurred so long ago that the testimony of an eye-witness would probably be less trustworthy than a contemporary newspaper account, a federal court, under Rule 43(a), may relax the exclusionary rules to the extent of admitting the newspaper article in evidence. We do not characterize this newspaper as a "business record," nor as an "ancient document," nor as any other readily identifiable and happily tagged species of hearsay exception. It is admissible because it is necessary and trustworthy, relevant and material, and its admission is within the trial judge's exercise of discretion in holding the hearing within reasonable bounds.

Judgment is affirmed.

Problem IV-70
An Accusing Finger

The state offers the following picture (The Boston Globe, November 17, 1981, p. 1) into evidence at a trial of the handcuffed man in the dark sweater for armed robbery. Is it hearsay? If so, does it fall within any exception of the hearsay rule? Does this depend on whether the guard lying on the stretcher is available? If the picture does not fall within any specific exception to the hearsay rule, should it nonetheless be admitted under either of the residual exceptions, Rule 803(24) or 804(b)(5)?

Compare this case to the *Dallas County* case. Is this a stronger or weaker case for admission? Would admitting this picture violate the defendant's rights under the confrontation clause?

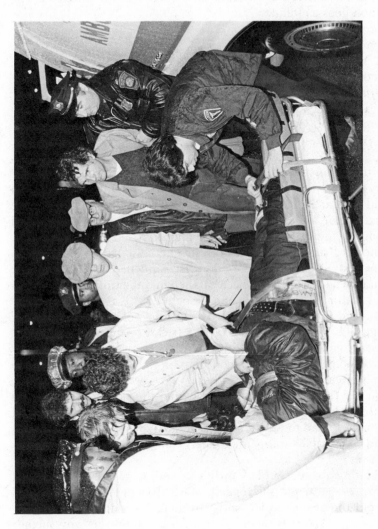

AN ACCUSING FINGER — While ambulance attendant straps him to stretcher, Brink's guard John McCann identifies John McGrath (hatless, second right) as man involved in $150,000 holdup in which McCann suffered gunshot wound. Suspect was arrested near scene of robbery outside First National Bank's Fields Corner office in Dorchester. Second suspect is sought. Page 20. GLOBE PHOTO BY GEORGE RIZER

Copyright © 1981 by The Boston Globe

389

Problem IV-71
Emergency Evidence

Charge: rape-murder. Defense: alibi. At *D*'s trial the prosecution offers a tape recording of a telephone call received by the Boston Police
Department 911 emergency operator at 1:09:40 P.M. on March 14. The
conversation goes as follows:

Police operator: Police emergency.
Woman: Yes, please. Emergency at 295 Commonwealth Avenue,
    Apartment 2B.
Police operator: What's going on?
Woman: I was just stabbed.
Police operator: Do you need an ambulance?
Woman: Yes.

The prosecution also offers the testimony of *W*, a registered nurse. *W*
will testify that he was apartment-hunting with a friend on March 14 on
the second floor at 295 Commonwealth Avenue when he heard someone
say, "Get a doctor." *W* looked into a room through a door left ajar and
saw a woman lying face down on the floor with her knees slightly bent.
She had nothing on from the waist down. There was clothing on the top
half of her body. *W* asked the woman what happened, and she replied,
"I've been raped. I've been stabbed." *W* then told the woman that he was
going to call for help. The woman responded, "I've already called."
After he called the police, *W* went back to the woman and asked her
name. She said, "*V*." *W* then checked *V*'s back to determine if she had
any injuries to her spine before turning her over and straightening her
legs. At that point he could see bloodstains on the clothes. He pulled up
the victim's sweater and blouse and exposed a wound just under her
ribcage on her right side. *W* inquired whether the victim suffered from
any health problems or allergies, and she answered "migraines" and
"mushrooms." *W* had to repeat his questions. *V*'s responses were getting
slower and weaker. She was getting paler. Her pulse was getting thread-
ier and faster.

After getting a towel to place on *V*'s wound, *W* asked *V* if she could
identify the assailant, and she replied, "Two black men." Then *W* asked
her how old they were, and *V* said, "In their 20s." *W* asked her their
height. *V* said, "About 6 feet, 2 inches." *W* couldn't get any further
information from *V*.

Shortly thereafter, a nurse and a doctor arrived at the apartment. *V*
was lifted to a chair and a sheet was wrapped around her. *V*'s head
flopped forward. At that point *W* felt that *V* would not make it. *V* died
two hours later.

Is either the tape recording or *W*'s testimony admissible? If so, on
what theory?

UNITED STATES v. BAILEY
439 F. Supp. 1303 (W.D. Pa. 1977)

TEITELBAUM, J. On June 9, 1976, the defendant, Milton Edward Bailey, was indicted by a Federal Grand Jury sitting in the Western District of Pennsylvania. The two-count indictment, alleging violations of Sections 2, 2113(a) and 2113(d) of Title 18, United States Code, charged the defendant with the February 6, 1975, armed robbery of the branch office of the Colony Federal Savings and Loan Office in Aliquippa, Pennsylvania.

Palm prints taken from the teller's counter at the bank were determined to be those of John Bernard Stewart. Stewart was indicted and on April 29, 1976, pursuant to a plea bargain, gave a written statement to the Federal Bureau of Investigation detailing the robbery and naming Milton Edward Bailey as his accomplice.[1]

A major issue at trial was identification. Four of the eyewitnesses to the robbery did not identify the defendant at trial and had made no pretrial photographic identification.[2] Two other eyewitnesses testified that they had picked the defendant's picture out of a pretrial photographic display and, in Court, they were only able to make a qualified identification of the defendant.

John Bernard Stewart, who at the time of his guilty plea to the instant robbery had agreed to testify for the government, was called, out of the presence of the jury, as a witness. However, Stewart refused to testify despite an order of the Court to do so. In view of Stewart's refusal, the government moved, pursuant to Rule 804 of the Federal Rules of Evidence, to have Stewart's written statement admitted into evidence. The Court granted both counsel a day's recess to research the question of admissibility. After argument, the Court admitted the statement under Rule 804(b)(5). Thereafter, a defense counsel, having previously been given a copy of the statement, was given a three-day recess to prepare to meet the statement and was told additional time would be given if needed.

The detailed statement of John Bernard Stewart, which was read into evidence by Special Agent Preston of the Federal Bureau of Investigation, alleged that Stewart and the defendant, Bailey, using the defendant's girlfriend's car, drove to Aliquippa from Washington, D.C., the morning of the robbery, searched Aliquippa for an opportune bank to rob, drove to Pittsburgh, Pa. where they split up and met again in Washington, D.C., to divide the proceeds of the robbery.

---

1. Ms. Caroline Thomas and Mrs. Regina Dorsey both testified that John Bernard Stewart was a friend of Milton Bailey.

2. Tellers Farinelli and Cavender were ordered to lie face down on the floor and they never even glimpsed the robber standing near the manager's desk. Likewise, the customer, Mr. Sylvester, was struck on the head from behind and had only the briefest opportunity, as he fell from his chair onto the floor, to see his assailant's face.

Counsel, on cross-examination, was permitted to impeach Stewart by questioning Agent Preston about Stewart's prior criminal record and motive to lie.

Upon the foregoing testimony, the jury returned a verdict of guilty as to both counts of the indictment. Defendant has now moved for a new trial and/or judgment of acquittal.

ISSUE

The issue to be decided is whether the out-of-court statement of Stewart was properly admitted into evidence as a hearsay exception under Rule 804(b)(5) of the Federal Rules of Evidence, and, if so, whether its admissibility comports with the Sixth Amendment right to confront one's accusers.

EVIDENTIARY ADMISSIBILITY

Rule 804(b)(5) formulates a new "trustworthiness" exception to the hearsay rule. . . .

The first question to be asked is whether Stewart was "unavailable" within the ambit of 804(b)(5). The answer to this question is easily provided by 804(a)(2) which states:

(a) *Definition of unavailability.* "Unavailability as a witness" includes situations in which the declarant (2) persists in refusing to testify concerning the subject matter of his statement despite an order of the court to do so.

In the case sub judice, Stewart refused to testify in spite of an order of Court. Stewart, therefore, was clearly unavailable for purposes of application of the Federal Rules of Evidence in general and 804(b)(5) in particular.

We now turn to an examination of the specific requirements of admissibility under 804(b)(5).

The first requirement is that the statement offered be evidence of a material fact. All parties concede that identity was a material issue at trial.

The second requirement is that the statement be more probative on the point for which it is offered than any other evidence which the proponent can procure through reasonable efforts. This requirement was satisfied because no other person was able to provide the specific evidence as to identity that was furnished via Stewart's statement.

The third requirement is that the general purpose of the Rules and the interests of justice will be best served by admission of the statement into evidence. Stewart testified in his statement that defendant and he were driving the car that belonged to the mother of defendant's girlfriend. That particular car was in Aliquippa at the time of the robbery and those persons who robbed the bank used that car to flee.[5] Such a corroborating circumstance serves to guarantee the trustworthiness of the statement and mandates its admission in the interests of justice.

Additionally, the statement cannot be admitted under 804(b)(5) unless the adverse party knows of it sufficiently in advance of trial to be provided with a fair opportunity to meet it. The purpose of this notice requirement is to give the adverse party an adequate opportunity to prepare to contest the use of the statement. H. Conf. Rep. No. 93-1597, 93rd Cong. 2d Sess. (1974). Although notice was not given to defense counsel prior to trial, the trial was recessed for three days to enable counsel to prepare to meet Stewart's statement and additional time was made available to him if necessary. The failure of pretrial disclosure occurred because Stewart's "unavailability" did not arise until trial when he refused to testify in defiance of this Court's Order. The government could not know whether Stewart would be unavailable to testify until after his refusal during trial. Thus, the notice requirement of 804(b)(5) was fulfilled in both spirit and purpose by recessing the proceedings. It is significant to note that defendant does not claim three days was insufficient for investigation or that he was prejudiced in any manner by the procedure utilized. Under the circumstances sub judice, Stewart's statement was properly admitted under Rule 804(b)(5).

SIXTH AMENDMENT RIGHT OF CONFRONTATION

The Confrontation Clause of the Sixth Amendment provides "that in all criminal prosecutions, the accused shall enjoy the right . . . to be confronted with the witnesses against him."

The Constitutional Right of Confrontation is distinct from the hearsay rules of the Federal Rules of Evidence. As stated in California v. Green, 399 U.S. 149:

"While it may readily be conceded that hearsay rules and the Confrontation Clause are generally designed to protect similar values, it is quite a different thing to suggest that the overlap is complete and that the Confrontation Clause is nothing more or less than a codification of the rules of hearsay and their exceptions as they existed historically at common law. Our decisions have never established such a congruence; indeed, we have more than once found a violation of confrontation values even though the statements in issue were admitted under an arguably recognized hearsay exception."

---

5. One of the witnesses made a positive identification of the car as being the getaway vehicle.

Thus, admissibility under 804(b)(5) does not ipso facto satisfy the Confrontation Clause. Measurement must be by the separate Constitutional yardstick of the Sixth Amendment.

"The particular vice that gave impetus to the confrontation claim was the practice of trying defendants on 'evidence' which consisted solely of ex parte affidavits or depositions secured by the examining magistrates, thus denying the defendant the opportunity to challenge his accuser in a face-to-face encounter in front of the trier of fact. Prosecuting attorneys 'would frequently allege matters which the prisoner denied and called upon them to prove. The proof was usually given by reading depositions, confessions of accomplices, letters, and the like; and this occasioned frequent demands by the prisoner to have his "accusers," i.e., the witnesses against him, brought before him face to face.' " California v. Green, supra, at 156-57.

Thus, the central theme of the Confrontation Clause is that a witness be available at trial for cross-examination by the defendant.[6]

"Availability" for cross-examination is impliedly codified by Rule 804(a) of the Federal Rules of Evidence. However, as previously indicated, the Confrontation Clause and evidentiary hearsay rules are not completely symmetrical. Therefore the issue arises whether under the circumstances of this case Stewart can be deemed available to testify for purposes of the Constitution even though the Federal Rules view Stewart as being unavailable. In other words, do the Federal Rules articulate a standard of availability which is of Constitutional dimension?

The first factor to be considered is that Stewart's refusal to testify on behalf of the government was motivated by a desire to help the defendant.[7] Stewart had already pled guilty to the instant robbery and therefore no longer retained a Fifth Amendment Privilege.[8] There can be no

6. The right of Confrontation is limited where there has been a prior opportunity for cross-examination by the defendant. California v. Green, supra; Mattox v. United States, 156 U.S. 237 (1895); United States ex rel. Oliver v. Rundle, 417 F.2d 305 (3d Cir. 1969). However, in the case sub judice defendant at no point in time had an opportunity to cross-examine Stewart. While Brookhart v. Janis, 384 U.S. 1 (1966), recognized that the Confrontation Clause was violated by the introduction of a confession against the defendant made out of court by one of his codefendants who did not testify in Court and was not previously cross-examined by defendant, that decision is not presently controlling. First, the parties in Brookhart had stipulated to a Confrontation Clause violation and therefore the Court focused almost completely on whether or not defendant had waived his Constitutional right. Thus, the adversary process was not utilized to arduously contest the premise of a violation. Secondly, the government in Brookhart had not made as exhaustive an attempt to present the codefendant in Court as was done by the government sub judice. Although lodged in an Ohio reformatory at the time of trial, the codefendant in Brookhart, who had previously entered a guilty plea after being indicted with defendant, was not called to testify in person at the Ohio Court of Common Pleas trial. Brookhart, supra at 2.

7. Stewart and the defendant were friends.

8. This Court was cognizant at trial of the possibility that Stewart might incriminate himself in other crimes and intended to restrict the scope of questioning accordingly.

other conclusion but that Stewart's refusal to testify despite an Order of Court was prompted by a desire to protect the defendant. Cf. Motes v. United States, 178 U.S. 458 (1900).

A second factor to be considered is the potential efficacy of any cross-examination. Such examination would have been detrimental to defendant's case. This fact was admitted by counsel for defendant at trial when he stated: "If I call him for cross examination, I am making out the case for the government." The only possible effective cross-examination would have had to focus on impeachment. Impeachment as to Stewart's prior criminal record was permitted during the cross-examination of Agent Preston. Therefore, defendant had the benefit of cross-examination in substance to the extent that it could have reasonably aided his cause.

Under this factual mosaic, defendant's right of confrontation was satisfied. The government made every effort to have Stewart testify at trial. The Court ordered Stewart to testify. Stewart was plainly protecting his friend, the defendant. Even had he taken the stand, Stewart's testimony would have reinforced the government's case to the detriment of the defendant. To the extent that cross-examination of Stewart could reasonably have been beneficial to the defendant, the benefit was obtained by the questioning of Agent Preston as to Stewart's plea bargain and prior criminal record. The framers of the Constitution could not have envisioned carrying the Sixth Amendment to the unwarranted extent disclosed by these circumstances.

Even were the Federal Rules definition of unavailability constitutionally mandated, this is the type of situation where reliability is so firmly established as to satisfy the Confrontation Clause via the policy basis of the hearsay exception itself.

Although the Confrontation Clause and hearsay rules are conceptually distinct, the Supreme Court has refused to render an opinion indicting all forms of hearsay as violative of the Confrontation Clause. The Court in Bruton v. United States, 390 U.S. 123, 128 (1968) stated: "There is not before us, therefore, any recognized exception to the hearsay rule insofar as petitioner is concerned and we intimate no view whatever that such exceptions necessarily raise questions under the Confrontation Clause."

The hearsay exception sub judice is clearly as reliable as other forms of hearsay which satisfy the Confrontation Clause absent any opportunity for cross-examination. Mattox v. United States, 156 U.S. 237 (1895) (Dying Declaration); United States v. Kelly, 349 F.2d 720, 770 (2d Cir. 1965) (Past Recollection Recorded). If dying declarations may be admitted despite the Confrontation Clause, so should the reliable hearsay of Stewart, especially where Stewart would be deemed "unavailable." See Vol. 4. J. Weinstein, Evidence, 800-24 & 25.

CONCLUSION

We have examined defendant's other contentions and find them to be without merit. Defendant's motion for a new trial and/or judgment of acquittal is therefore denied. An appropriate Order will issue.

Do you agree with the District Court's use of Rule 804(b)(5) in *Bailey*? If you represented the defendant, what counter arguments would you make to the Court of Appeals?

UNITED STATES v. BAILEY, 581 F.2d 341 (3d Cir. 1978): There is no doubt that Stewart's confession was a "written assertion," and thus a "statement" by Stewart, which the government offered at trial to prove the truth of the matters asserted in it. Thus it was hearsay under F.R. Evid. 801(c), and as such was inadmissible unless other rules permitted the statement to be admitted. F.R. Evid. 802.

At trial, the government argued that the confession of Stewart was admissible as a declaration against penal interest, pursuant to Fed. R. Evid. 804(b)(3). The court determined that the requirements of that section had not been met, since the statement had been made by Stewart while he was in custody and after he had been offered a bargain involving dismissal of one count of the indictment against him. The government has not pressed its argument on this point here, and we do not disagree with the trial court.

The trial court grounded the admissibility of the Stewart confession on rule 804(b)(5) of the Federal Rules of Evidence. That rule is one of two "residual" exceptions to the hearsay rule, providing for the admission of evidence even when the traditional requirements for the admission of hearsay are not met.

Prior to the adoption of the Federal Rules of Evidence, the out-of-court confession involved in this case could not have been used against Bailey. Thus we must determine the extent to which the addition of the residual rule of 804(b)(5) has broadened the trial court's discretion in admitting evidence.

The trial court is vested with discretion in its determination whether hearsay evidence afforded by a party meets the requirements of an exception set forth in the Federal Rules of Evidence. Our role, therefore, is to decide whether the trial court abused its discretion in determining that Stewart's confession met all requirements of Rule 804(b)(5).

To be admissible under Rule 804(b)(5), an out-of-court statement must meet the following requirements:

The declarant must be unavailable;

The statement must have circumstantial guarantees of trustworthiness equivalent to the first four exceptions in Rule 804(b);

The statement must be offered as evidence of a material fact;

The statement must be more probative on the point for which it is offered than any other evidence that the proponent reasonably can procure;

Introduction of the statement must serve the interests of justice and the purposes of the Federal Rules;

The proponent of the evidence to be offered must have given his adversary the notice required by the rule.

The history of Rule 804(b)(5) and its counterpart, Rule 803(24), indicates a congressional intention that the rules have a narrow focus. The initial "residual" rule for the introduction of hearsay not covered by one of the specific exceptions to the hearsay rule was phrased by the Advisory Committee as follows:

> A statement not specifically covered by any of the foregoing exceptions, but having comparable circumstantial guarantees of trustworthiness.

56 F.R.D. 183, 322 (1972).

After the rules were submitted to Congress, the House Judiciary Committee removed from both Rules 803 and 804 the residual exceptions on the grounds that the rules added too much uncertainty to the law of evidence.[7] The Senate Judiciary Committee reinstated the deleted Advisory Committee residual exceptions in a modified form. S. Rep. No. 1277, 93d Cong., 2d Sess. (1974), reprinted in [1974] U.S. Code Cong. & Admin. News, pp. 7051, 7056. The Senate Committee noted its fear that without residual rules of admissibility for hearsay in certain instances, the established exceptions would be tortured in order to allow reliable evidence to be introduced. Further, the new proposed residual rules were drafted to apply only when certain exceptional guarantees of trustworthiness exist and when high degrees of probativeness and necessity are present.[8] The Senate Committee further stated that the residual

---

7. The committee noted that some leeway was provided for the courts by Rule 102, which could cover the anomalous situation calling for admission of hearsay not covered by an enumerated exception. Rule 102 states:

"These rules shall be construed to secure fairness in administration, elimination of unjustifiable expense and delay, and promotion of growth and development of the law of evidence to the end that the truth may be ascertained and proceedings justly determined."

The House Committee also stated that "if additional hearsay exceptions are to be created, they should be by amendments to the Rules, not on a case-by-case basis." H.R. Rep. No. 650, 93d Cong. 2d Sess. (1973), reprinted in [1974] U.S. Code Cong. & Admin. News, pp. 7051, 7079.

8. The Committee cited as an appropriate example the case of Dallas County v. Commercial Union Assoc. Co., Ltd., 286 F.2d 388 (5th Cir. 1961). In that case, the court allowed into evidence a copy of a newspaper article describing a fire in a county courthouse fifty years prior to the collapse of the courthouse tower. The insurer offered this evidence in order to show that certain charred wood found in the ruins might not have been the product of lightning striking the courthouse and causing its collapse, as the county con-

exceptions were to be used only rarely, and in exceptional circumstances. The Senate Report cautioned that "[t]he residual exceptions are not meant to authorize major judicial revisions of the hearsay rules, including its present exceptions."

The House-Senate Conference Committee agreed to include the Senate residual rule with further modifications. H. Conf. Rep. No. 1597, 93d Cong., 2d Sess. (1974), reprinted in [1974] U.S. Code Cong. & Admin. News pp. 7051, 7106. Representative Dennis, one of the floor managers of the Federal Rules of Evidence bill, stated in the House debate preceding passage of the bill, that the residual rules applied to situations "comparable to the ordinary hearsay exceptions." 120 Cong. Rec. 40894 (1974). In his view, the residual rule did not purport to accomplish much at all regarding expansion of traditional rules of evidence. Thus, in reviewing the admissibility of evidence under Rule 804(b)(5), we must keep in mind its limited scope as intended by Congress.

Defendant does not contest the trial judge's finding that Stewart was unavailable,[10] or that the confession was evidence of a material fact — Bailey's identification as one of the bank robbers. Bailey contends, however, that other elements of Rule 804(b)(5) were not satisfied.[11] Initially, he argues that the statement cannot be used against him since it was not until after trial had commenced that the government informed him that it would seek to have Stewart's statement introduced.

Before an out-of-court statement can be admitted pursuant to Rule 804(b)(5), the proponent of it must advise the adverse party his intention to use the statement, as well as the "particulars of it, including the name and address of the declarant." The proponent must give notice "sufficiently before trial . . . to provide the adverse party with a fair opportunity to meet [the statement]. . . ." The advance notice provision came into being during the House-Senate Conference on the proposed

---

tended. The article, however, would have supported the insurer's proposition that the tower collapsed because of deterioration and disrepair. In allowing the evidence to be admitted, the court considered the inconceivability of the unknown reporter fifty years previously writing about a fire if one had not in fact occurred. See S. Rep. No. 1277, 93d Cong. 2d Sess. (1974) reprinted in [1974] U.S. Code Cong. & Admin. News at 7065-66.

10. Rule 804(a) defines "unavailability" in part as including situations in which the declarant "persists in refusing to testify concerning the subject matter of his statement despite an order of the court to do so." F.R. Evid. 804(a)(2). See United States v. Gonzalez, 559 F.2d 1271 (5th Cir. 1977); United States v. Carlson, 547 F.2d 1346 (8th Cir. 1976); cert. denied, 431 U.S. 914 (1977).

11. One of Bailey's contentions is that Stewart's statement was not "more probative on the point for which it is offered than any other evidence which the proponent can procure through reasonable efforts," F.R. Evid. 804(b)(5)(B). We disagree. Although the government made an effort to place Bailey in the bank during the robbery through the identification testimony of prosecution witnesses, none were able to state positively that they recognized Bailey at trial as the second bank robber. We feel the trial judge did not abuse his discretion in resolving this issue.

rules. H. Conf. Rep. No. 1597, 93d Cong., 2d Sess. (1974), reprinted in [1974] U.S. Code Cong. & Admin. News pp. 7051, 7106.

The debates in Congress and the statements of Rep. William Hungate (Chairman of the House Judiciary Committee Subcommittee on Criminal Justice) indicate some understanding that the requirement of advance notice was to be strictly followed. See 120 Cong. Rec. 40893 (1974). A number of courts of appeals have held that the purpose of the advance notice provision of the rule is satisfied even though notice is given after the trial begins, as long as there is sufficient opportunity provided for the adverse party to prepare for and contest the admission of the evidence offered pursuant to the rule. United States v. Carlson, supra; United States v. Medico, 557 F.2d 309 (2d Cir. 1977); see Weinstein's Evidence ¶803(24)[01] at 803-243. But see United States v. Oates, 560 F.2d 45, 72-73 n.30 (2d Cir. 1977) (dictum) (finds legislative history to require an "undeviating adherence to the requirement that notice be given in advance of trial").

We believe that the purpose of the rules and requirement of fairness to an adversary contained in the advance notice requirement of Rule 803(24) and Rule 804(b)(5) are satisfied when, as here, the proponent of the evidence is without fault in failing to notify his adversary prior to trial and the trial judge has offered sufficient time, by means of granting a continuance, for the party against whom the evidence is to be offered to prepare to meet and contest its admission. Since the government was unable to notify Bailey's counsel prior to trial of Stewart's refusal to testify, and since the trial judge offered counsel time to conduct interviews as well as to research the evidentiary question, we feel that Bailey was not prejudiced by the lack of notice before trial. By examining the adequacy of the notice and the time allowed to prepare to meet a statement offered pursuant to these rules, a reviewing court may determine whether the adverse party has had "a fair opportunity to prepare to contest the use of the statement." H. Conf. Rep. No. 1597, 93d Cong., 2d Sess. (1974), reprinted in [1974] U.S. Code Cong. & Admin. News at 7106.

Bailey also argues that Stewart's confession failed to meet the requirement that the evidence to be admitted pursuant to Rule 804(b)(5) must possess "guarantees of trustworthiness" equivalent to the other enumerated exceptions under Rule 804(b). We find this contention convincing.

The specific hearsay exceptions of Rule 804(b) include those for former testimony, dying declarations, statements against interest, and statements of family background or history. Each of these kinds of statements is admissible, though hearsay, because the circumstances in which the statements are made are indicative of a strong propensity for truthfulness (dying declarations), because there has been a previous opportunity for cross-examination (former testimony), or because the contents of the statements themselves are of such a nature that one reasonably would conclude that the speaker was telling the truth (statements against interest, statements of family history).[12]

The trial judge determined the reliability of the hearsay statement on the evidence that the bank robbers fled the crime in Bailey's girlfriend's car. Since the statement mentioned that Stewart and Bailey traveled to Aliquippa in the car, the trial judge held that Stewart's statement possessed sufficient indicia of reliability to justify its admission pursuant to 804(b)(5). We believe that the recitation of this single factor does not satisfy the requirement that the statement to be offered in evidence have "circumstantial guarantees of trustworthiness" equivalent to the other 804(b) exceptions. Indeed, if Stewart had borrowed the car from Bailey and had committed the robbery with another, the bargain he struck with the authorities provided him with the opportunity to sidetrack the investigation and protect his accomplice by naming Bailey, a plausible suspect, as his partner in the robbery.

We do not feel that the trustworthiness of a statement offered pursuant to the rule should be analyzed solely on the basis on the facts corroborating the authenticity of the statement. Since the rule is designed to come into play when there is a need for the evidence in order to ascertain the truth in a case, it would make little sense for a judge, in determining whether the hearsay is admissible, to examine only facts corroborating the substance of the declaration. Such an analysis in effect might increase the likelihood of admissibility when corroborating circumstances indicate a reduced need for the introduction of the hearsay statement. We do not believe that Congress intended that "trustworthiness" be analyzed in this manner. Rather, the trustworthiness of a statement should be analyzed by evaluating not only the facts corroborating the veracity of the statement, but also the circumstances in which the declarant made the statement and the incentive he had to speak truthfully or falsely. Further, consideration should be given to factors bearing on the reliability of the reporting of the hearsay by the witness.

In United States v. Medico, 557 F.2d 309 (2d Cir. 1977), the court held that circumstantial degrees of trustworthiness justified the admission of an unknown bystander's report of the license plate of a fleeing automobile used by escaping bankrobbers. The bystander shouted the

---

12. As originally submitted to Congress, the proposed Federal Rules contained an additional exception for statements of recent perception. The House Committee, however, deleted this rule on the grounds that statements of the type encompassed within this exception did not bear "sufficient guarantees of trustworthiness to justify admissibility." H.R. Rep. No. 650, 93d Cong., 2d Sess., reprinted in [1974] U.S. Code Cong. & Admin. News at 7079-80. We think that an awareness of Congress' deletion of proposed Rule 804(b)(2) provides some guidance in determining whether a statement offered under Rule 804(b)(5) possesses guarantees of trustworthiness equivalent to those 804(b) exceptions included in the final version of the federal rules.

numbers out from the street to another bystander, who was stationed next to the locked door of the bank. The bystander near the door relayed the information into the bank to an employee who transcribed the description and tag number of the car. In assessing the reliability of the hearsay, the court looked to the opportunity of the declarants to observe, the amount of time for the information to be relayed to the bank employee, and the potential for misidentification or fabrication, determining that the situation in which the statements were offered provided a guarantee of trustworthiness on a par with the enumerated 804(b) exceptions.

In United States v. Gomez, 559 F.2d 1271 (5th Cir. 1977), the court held that the grand jury testimony of a witness who had refused to take the stand at trial was not admissible, because the circumstances in which he gave his grand jury testimony did not measure up to the trustworthiness requirement of Rule 804(b)(5). In that case, the witness had been convicted and had been granted immunity in order to compel him to testify before the grand jury. Since the government had made the witness aware that he could be subjected an unlimited number of contempt proceedings if he failed to testify, and since the witness was in fear of retaliation against himself and his family if he did testify, the court found that his responses to leading questions before the grand jury failed to pass the trustworthiness test of Rule 804(b)(5).[13]

In this case, the circumstances under which Stewart provided his statement implicating Bailey do not inspire confidence in its reliability. First, as we have discussed, the statement was made during negotiations for reduction of charges lodged against Stewart. Secondly, the statements were made in a face-to-face meeting with two FBI agents. Further, the statement was not made under oath and its veracity had not been tested, certainly not by cross-examination. Finally, the fact relied upon by the trial judge as corroborating Stewart's confession, the identification of the car, does not provide a sufficient degree of reliability to justify the statement's introduction. Thus we feel that the trial judge's determination as to the trustworthiness of the statement was an abuse of his discretion, since the assertions in the statement and the circumstances in which the statement was given do not provide guarantees of trustworthiness equivalent to the other Rule 804(b) exceptions that serve as a benchmark for Rule 804(b)(5).

---

13. In United States v. Carlson, supra, the Eighth Circuit held admissible statements by a grand jury witness who refused to testify at trial. There the court focused on the fact that the declarant had been under oath at the time of making the statements, and that when informing the trial judge of his refusal to testify later, the declarant stated that he had told the truth to the grand jury. See also United States v. West, 574 F.2d 1131 (4th Cir. 1978) (trustworthiness found in deceased declarant's grand jury testimony because close supervision of his activities as undercover informant rendered deception of agents "substantially impossible").

We also have grave doubts about the propriety of introducing Stewart's confession in light of clause (C) of 804(b)(5), which requires that "the general purpose of [the Federal Rules of Evidence] and the interests of justice will best be served by [the] admission of the statement into evidence." Although we do not reach the constitutional issue raised in this case, we are concerned with the relationship between the Confrontation Clause of the Sixth Amendment and the admissibility of this evidence under the Federal Rules of Evidence. In drafting the proposed rules submitted to Congress, the Advisory Committee provided leeway in order to insure that the rules did not collide with the Confrontation Clause.[14] Thus, in analyzing the admissibility of evidence pursuant to Rule 804(b)(5), a court should exercise its discretion in order to avoid potential conflicts between confrontation rights and this hearsay exception.

The use of Stewart's confession at Bailey's trial raises difficult constitutional issues, and we have doubts whether, in light of the lack of cross-examination, the questionable reliability of the statement on the record before us, and the devastating impact of the statement, admission of this statement could pass constitutional muster. Thus, in evaluating the purpose of the rules under 804(b)(5)(C), the better course would have been for the trial judge to have exercised his discretion under the rules not to admit the evidence.

Although we have mentioned the values protected by the Confrontation Clause, we expressly do not base our decision to reverse Bailey's conviction on constitutional grounds. At present, the state of this aspect of the Sixth Amendment is unsettled, and its future path has been a matter of some commentary. Our decision is based on the failure of Stewart's statement implicating Bailey to satisfy the requirements of Rule 804(b)(5).

The judgment of the district court will be reversed and remanded for a new trial.

---

14. In its introductory note to Article VIII of the proposed Federal Rules, the Advisory Committee discussed the relationship of the rules to developing law related to the right of confrontation as follows:

"Under the earlier cases, the confrontation clause may have been little more than a constitutional embodiment of the hearsay rule, even including traditional exceptions but with some room for expanding them along similar lines. But under the recent cases the impact of the clause clearly extends beyond the confines of the hearsay rule. These considerations have led the Advisory Committee to conclude that a hearsay rule can function usefully as an adjunct to the confrontation right in constitutional areas and independently in nonconstitutional areas. In recognition of the separateness of the confrontation clause and the hearsay rule, and to avoid inviting collisions between them or between the hearsay rule and other exclusionary principles, the exceptions set forth in Rules 803 and 804 are stated in terms of exemption from the general exclusionary mandate of the hearsay rule, rather than in positive terms of admissibility. See Uniform Rule 63(1) to (31) and California Evidence Code §§1200-1340." 56 F.R.D. 183, 292 (1972).

UNITED STATES v. WEST
574 F.2d 1131 (4th Cir. 1978)

HAYNSWORTH, C.J. Calvin W. West, Floyd Lee Davis and Joseph Lee Dempsey appeal their convictions for distributing heroin and possessing heroin with the intent to distribute it. The most significant question presented is whether the admission of the grand jury testimony of Michael Victor Brown, who was slain prior to trial, was permissible under Rule 804(b)(5) of the Federal Rules of Evidence and the Confrontation Clause of the Sixth Amendment. We hold that it was.

The convictions challenged here are the product of an extensive Drug Enforcement Agency (DEA) investigation in which Brown played a vital role. Brown volunteered his assistance to the DEA while he was in jail on a drug charge and under a detainer for parole violation. He agreed to purchase heroin under police surveillance.

Each purchase was similar. Brown would contact West or Davis and arrange to purchase heroin. Twice the DEA monitored Brown's calls to West arranging heroin deals. It also monitored one phone call to Davis. On other occasions it seems that Brown simply notified the DEA that he had arranged a purchase.

Each time that the DEA agents received notice that Brown was about to make a purchase, they made arrangements for extensive surveillance. Before each purchase, DEA agents strip-searched Brown to make sure that he had no drugs, and they concealed a transmitter on him. They then searched his vehicle to be sure that it contained no drugs and gave Brown the money required for the anticipated purchase.

According to the government's evidence, on three occasions, Brown went to West, gave West money, and obtained heroin. Twice Brown went to Davis, gave Davis money and obtained heroin. On another occasion, Brown gave West money then accompanied him to meet Dempsey. West then gave Dempsey money and told Brown that they were to meet Dempsey at Griffin's home. Brown and West went to Griffin's home. Dempsey arrived, went to the open window of Brown's car and then entered Griffin's home and told Brown that everything was all right. Brown then returned to his car to find 30 capsules of heroin.

Each time, law enforcement officials observed Brown's movements and obtained photographs of Brown as he met with West and with Davis. After each transaction Brown returned to the DEA office and surrendered the heroin that he had purchased and any money remaining. Each time the agents searched Brown and his car to be sure that he retained no contraband. Agent Scott then discussed with Brown the events that had taken place and composed a detailed summary of what had occurred, which Brown read, corrected and signed. After one of the purchases Brown himself prepared a statement which Agent Scott revised before Brown read, corrected and signed it. Each time, Scott and

Brown listened to the tapes from the body transmitter for audibility and voice identification. By reviewing the tapes with Brown, Scott independently became able to identify the voices of the defendants.

On March 8, 1976, the defendants and others were indicted by a grand jury, apparently without Brown's testimony. On March 16, Brown appeared before a grand jury and testified under oath regarding his knowledge of the drug traffic in Virginia's Tidewater area. The government attorney read the statements that Brown had signed and periodically asked Brown if they were correct.

As a result of his cooperation, Brown was released from jail, the pending drug charge against him was nol prossed, and the detainer for parole violation was lifted. The DEA also gave Brown $855 for his personal use so that he would not arouse suspicion and jeopardize his cover by being without funds immediately after supposedly selling a large amount of heroin.

On March 19 Brown was murdered in a manner suggestive of contract killers. Four bullets were fired into the back of his head while he was driving his car. According to the government, at least four potential government witnesses in this and related narcotics investigations have been murdered after they had agreed to cooperate. But these defendants have not been charged with Brown's murder, and the government did not offer any evidence to show that they were responsible for it.

On April 22, a week before the scheduled trial date, the government notified the defendants, pursuant to Rule 804(b)(5) of the Federal Rules of Evidence, that it intended to introduce Brown's grand jury testimony at trial. It agreed to give defense counsel all of its evidence, including Brown's arrest record, and transcripts of the tapes of Brown's conversations with the defendants.

After a pre-trial hearing, the district court ruled that the grand jury testimony was admissible under Rule 804(b)(5) because, under the circumstances, it was essential and trustworthy. It also gave the defense a week's continuance after it announced that it would admit Brown's grand jury testimony.

During the trial the government introduced the transcript of Brown's grand jury testimony, the photographs, an expert on voice identification and the heroin. It also played the tapes of Brown's conversations with the defendants. Law enforcement agents testified about their observation of Brown's activities and corroborated Brown's highly detailed grand jury testimony. The government sought to introduce transcripts which it had prepared from the tapes from Brown's body transmitter. Although the district judge found that the transcripts were a fair representation of the taped conversations, he permitted the jury to see the transcripts only while they listened to the tapes and instructed the jurors to decide for themselves what the tapes said.

I

The defendants contend that the district judge erred in concluding that the transcript of Brown's grand jury testimony was admissible under Rule 804(b)(5). . . .

The defendants do not contend that the grand jury transcript fails to meet the criteria of clauses (A), (B) and (C). Instead, they focus upon the general requirement that the statement have "equivalent circumstantial guarantees of trustworthiness" as statements the admission of which is authorized by any of the preceding four paragraphs. They find a lack of trustworthiness in Brown's criminal record and their lack of any opportunity to cross-examine him. They point to legislative history indicating that Rule 804(b)(5) applies only where "exceptional circumstances" lend to the extra-judicial statement a degree of trustworthiness equivalent to that of evidence admissible under other §804(b) exceptions.

There were present very exceptional circumstances providing substantial guarantees of trustworthiness of Brown's grand jury testimony probably exceeding by far the substantial guarantees of trustworthiness of some of the other §804(b) hearsay exceptions. Before each contact by Brown with West, Davis or Dempsey, the agents took elaborate steps to assure themselves that Brown possessed no drugs or money other than the money supplied by the agents to effect the purchases. Except when he entered a building and became concealed from their view he was under constant surveillance, and photographs were taken when he was with one of the defendants. Moreover, his transmitter was broadcasting his conversations with the defendants, and a tape recorder preserved those conversations. Moreover, immediately after each purchase, he and one of the agents reviewed what Brown had done, said and observed, and a statement of it was prepared and corrected. The immediate transcription and verification of Brown's statements provide an additional guarantee other admissible hearsay statements lack. But the most impressive assurance of trustworthiness comes from the corroboration provided by the observations of the agents, the pictures they took and their recordings of the conversations. Brown had a criminal record, and he was seeking favors to avoid further incarceration, but the circumstances make deception of the agents inconceivable. The agents simply followed, photographed and recorded conversations to such an extent that deception by Brown was substantially impossible. Moreover, his interest in gaining favors to avoid further imprisonment gave him every incentive to be extremely accurate in his reports. He knew what the agents were doing to corroborate and verify his reports, and any attempted deception would only have been calculated to arouse the suspicion of the agents and to lose for Brown their favor.

The substantially contemporaneous sworn written statements by

Brown were the basis of Brown's grand jury testimony. The corroborative circumstances and verification procedures lend to his grand jury testimony a degree of trustworthiness probably substantially exceeding that inherent in dying declarations, statements against interest, and statements of personal or family history, all of which are routinely admitted under §804(b)(2), (3) and (4).

Although Brown's grand jury testimony was not subject to immediate cross-examination, to a large extent what Brown said was corroborated by the observations of the agents. The agents did appear as witnesses and were subject to cross-examination about what they observed, including the possibility of mistake or prevarication by Brown, and their own roles in preparing Brown's statements. Moreover, defense counsel had Brown's criminal record and knew of his interest in gaining favor with the agents. They could, and did, present those bases of impeachment of Brown which might have been developed on cross-examination if Brown had been present to testify.

Under all of these circumstances, the absence of an opportunity to cross-examine Brown himself is of considerable less significance than in those cases involving statements against interest, statements of family history, or dying declarations.

Whether the circumstantial guarantees of trustworthiness of Brown's grand jury testimony are equivalent to those which arise from cross or direct examination which underlies the former testimony exception of §804(b)(1), we need not determine. In this unusual case, those guarantees were probably greater, but the equivalent guarantee of trustworthiness requirement of §804(b)(5) is met if there is equivalency of any one of the preceding §804(b) exceptions. Clearly there is such equivalency with the exceptions we find in paragraphs 2, 3, and 4.

The defense lawyers were given every opportunity to attack Brown's credibility, and they fully utilized their opportunities. It may be of passing significance that the jury did not accept all that Brown said, for it acquitted two of the defendants implicated by him. That it convicted West, Davis and Dempsey suggests that it carefully considered the very substantial extent to which the corroborative evidence established their guilt, either directly or through strong demonstration of the trustworthiness of Brown's testimony as to them. . . .

UNITED STATES v. GARNER
574 F.2d 1141 (4th Cir. 1978)

HAYNSWORTH, C.J. Convicted of drug related offenses arising out of the alleged importation of substantial quantities of heroin from West Germany and Holland, the defendants complain primarily of the admission in evidence of the grand jury testimony of an alleged co-conspirator who declined to testify at the trial despite the best efforts of the trial judge and his own lawyer to get him to do so.

I

Warren Robinson, the grand jury witness, had been indicted for offenses committed by him in connection with the importation of the heroin. He had previously commenced serving a six year sentence imposed upon him for unrelated offenses, and he was under indictment in New York for still other unrelated offenses. Faced with the possibility that very heavy penalties might be imposed upon him if convicted under this indictment, he entered into a plea agreement. The agreement was that he would enter a plea of guilty to a two-count information, would testify fully before a grand jury and in any ensuing criminal proceedings, in exchange for which the government would dismiss the indictment. There was no agreement respecting the disposition of the New York charges.

Robinson entered his guilty pleas to the two counts in the information, and was sentenced to two successive five year terms to commence upon completion of his earlier six year sentence. He then appeared as a seemingly willing witness before a grand jury.

He told the grand jury that Garner had approached him with information that McKethan, an airline employee, had a source for large quantities of heroin in West Germany. Garner sought to enlist Robinson's participation in the importation of heroin from western Europe and its distribution in the metropolitan Washington area.

There followed a number of trips to West Germany and to Holland, where another source of supply had been developed with the assistance of their first contact. Robinson did not get his passport in time to make Garner's first trip, but he and Garner traveled together on two later ones, and he was told by the defendants of still later trips that they took. On one of the trips Garner and Robinson were accompanied by two young women who, traveling separately on the return trip, brought the heroin into the United States concealed in their girdles.

Before Garner and McKethan were brought to trial, Robinson indicated reluctance to testify at trial. This occasioned inquiry of him in an *in camera* proceeding before the trial opened. He then stated that in the absence of his lawyer he would not testify. His lawyer was summoned and advised him to testify, but to no avail. After the trial opened, though the court had granted him use immunity, and threatened him with a contempt citation if he refused, he persisted in his refusal to testify. In another *in camera* proceeding, Robinson indicated that he might answer questions put by defense counsel. The district court then ruled that, though he was "unavailable" as a witness within the meaning of Rule 804(b)(5) of the F.R. Evid., he was "available" for cross-examination by defense counsel. In the presence of the jury, Robinson stated that he knew Garner and McKethan and that his grand jury testimony was inaccurate. He answered some questions about European travel with answers which seemed to say that he knew nothing of any drug trafficking by Garner or McKethan. At other times he declined to answer, and his seeming disclaimers of knowledge may have been understood by the jury to be the equivalent of a refusal to testify. The transcript gives one the general impression not that the grand jury testimony was false but that, whatever pressures were brought upon him, the defendant was unwilling to testify, and particularly unwilling to say anything which would incriminate either of these defendants.

There is no explanation of this unwillingness. Cooperating former co-conspirators have sometimes been the victims of threats by their former associates facing trials. That Robinson was the victim of threats by either Garner or McKethan, however, can be no more than speculation. Robinson was in prison at the time, and he may have been the victim of the code that condemns a conspirator for testifying against his former associates.

II

In United States v. West, 4th Cir., 574 F.2d 1131, we have upheld the admission of sworn grand jury testimony, though not subject to cross-examination, when the witness was murdered in the interim between his grand jury testimony and the trial of the drug offenders. In that case, there was extraordinary corroboration of the grand jury testimony, for he had been wired for sound; his conversations had been recorded; he had been kept under close surveillance when not within buildings, and the officers who had watched and recorded his conversations were witnesses available for cross-examination.

In United States v. Carlson, 8th Cir., 547 F.2d 1346, a grand jury witness refused to testify at Carlson's trial because, he said, of threats directed to him by Carlson. That, too, was a drug offense case. There was substantial circumstantial corroboration of the grand jury testimony. Because of that, and a general affirmation by the witness at trial of his grand jury testimony, the Eighth Circuit held the grand jury testimony admissible under Rule 804(b)(5). As to the Confrontation Clause, it held that Carlson had waived his right, reasoning that Carlson should not be allowed to complain of the silence of the witness when he was the procurer of the silence. See Motes v. U.S., 178 U.S. 458.

On the other hand, in United States v. Gonzalez, 5th Cir., 559 F.2d 1271, the Fifth Circuit, in another drug offense case, held that the testimony of the grand jury witness was inadmissible. There the grand jury witness had been most reluctant to testify during his appearance before the grand jury, apparently torn between the possibility of injury to himself or his family if he testified and further imprisonment for contempt if he refused. Faced with these unpleasant alternatives, the pressure to testify may have prompted the witness falsely to identify the defendant as his employer, and the identity of the employer was entirely dependent upon the testimony of the witness.

Since we have canvassed this scene in *West*, we need not repeat it here. It is enough to recite that sworn grand jury testimony may be admitted under Rule 804(b)(5) when there are substantial guarantees of trustworthiness equivalent to those which warrant recognized exceptions to the hearsay rule. The admission of such sworn testimony is not a violation of the Confrontation Clause of the Constitution if it bears sufficient guarantees of reliability and the circumstances contain a sufficient basis upon which the jury may assess its trustworthiness. The distinction is illustrated by the strong indicators of reliability found in *West* and the absence of such indicators in *Gonzalez*. See also U.S. v. Rogers, 549 F.2d 490 (8th Cir. 1976), cert. denied, 431 U.S. 918 (1977).

Here there are strong indicators of reliability, and the jury had an ample basis upon which to determine the trustworthiness of the testimony.

One of the two young women who, according to Robinson's grand jury testimony, had accompanied Garner and him on their trip to Amsterdam beginning on October 15, 1974, was produced as a witness at the trial. She fully confirmed Robinson's grand jury testimony about the trip. She, Miss McKee, and a Miss Hallums, had accompanied Garner and Robinson to Amsterdam for the purpose of serving as couriers. While in Amsterdam, Miss McKee shared a hotel room with Robinson, while Miss Hallums shared another nearby room with Garner. After Garner and Robinson had procured the heroin, she testified, Robinson "blended" it into powder form and packaged it into two packages. This was done in a hotel room in which Garner and the two women were also present. Miss McKee "snorted" some of the heroin, and the men showed the girls how to conceal one package each in her girdle. The two girls then flew to Dulles, while the two men took another plane to New York, just as Robinson had testified. When the men got to Washington, Miss McKee testified she delivered the two packages of heroin to Garner, who was sitting on the passenger side of a car being driving by Robinson.

Moreover, there was irrefutable evidence of their travels. The United States introduced records of airline tickets, customs declarations, passport endorsements, and European hotel registrations. They show that McKethan made five trips to western Europe between mid-July 1974 and mid-March 1975. Garner made seven such trips in the same period. These records show that McKethan was in Amsterdam in early September 1974 when Robinson testified that he and Garner met him there and made their first contact with the Chinese supplier. McKethan and Garner were also in Copenhagen at the same time in December 1974 and apparently were traveling on the same flights to Copenhagen and Amsterdam in March 1975.

Moreover, the records show that Henry Thompson arrived at Dulles from Europe on September 4, 1974. Thompson was a member of the United States Armed Forces stationed in West Germany. He was McKethan's cousin. On his entry form he noted that he would be staying with McKethan and that McKethan was a person who would know his whereabouts. Robinson had testified that Garner had used Thompson, their initial heroin contact in Europe, as a courier after Garner's first trip, although the available records indicate that Thompson was on the same flight with Garner and Robinson returning from their first joint trip. Testifying from his recollection more than a year later, Robinson may have been confused about which trip Thompson made, but the record of Thompson's flight provides general corroboration of Robinson's testimony that he was used as a courier.

These travel records would contain no implication of guilt if the record contained any reasonable explanation of them consistent with innocence. If the defendants were stewards employed by Pan American Air Lines in international flights, their frequent European travels would contain no suggestion of wrong doing. Suspicion would not attach if they were reputable international businessmen with branches in Holland, Denmark and the United States. For others of us, however, having no patent occasion for frequent European travel, the sudden onset of successive trips of short duration alone can raise suspicion as long as any reasonable explanation is lacking. As to Garner, there is no suggestion of any such explanation. McKethan testified, however, and attempted to offer one but, as a description of it will indicate, it may fairly be regarded as preposterous. The only believable explanation of the frequent trips is that offered by Robinson in his grand jury testimony, and the record of the trips strongly tends to corroborate the testimony.

McKethan was employed as a cargo handler by United Airlines in Washington National Airport. His airline employment, he testified, entitled him to very large discounts on airline fares, and he made his frequent trips to Frankfurt, Copenhagen, Amsterdam, and London mostly for pleasure. For a while he had a girlfriend in Copenhagen, a fact that Robinson had mentioned. He was also learning the "language of the pyramids" from a black African in Europe,[1] and he was busy making inquiries in Germany and Sweden about the importation into the United States of Mercedes-Benz automobiles and Swedish sheepskin jackets. He did not suggest how an airline cargo handler might finance such businesses, nor was any such business developed.

Robinson, in his grand jury testimony, did not suggest that McKethan

---

1. According to McKethan, knowledge of this "lost language of the pyramids" would enable him to arrive eventually at "logical procedures of understanding." McKethan sought in Copenhagen "rhythm[s] of understanding."

skip 389-42

was a part of the distribution business conducted jointly by Garner and Robinson for a number of months, and later separately by each, but did testify that McKethan was the one who initially suggested that he could put them in touch with Henry Thompson in Frankfurt as a source of supply. According to Robinson, he agreed to meet them in Frankfurt in September, but by the time Garner and Robinson arrived at Thompson's house, they were told by Thompson's girlfriend that she was to take them to Amsterdam. In Amsterdam they did meet McKethan and Thompson, who put them in touch with a Chinese supplier. According to Robinson, McKethan was paid some $10,000 for his part in arranging this source of supply for them. Later, Robinson had testified, McKethan agreed to meet Garner in Amsterdam, for the purpose of showing Garner how to avoid the thorough searches made of passengers flying out of Amsterdam to the United States. This turned out to be no more than taking a train from Amsterdam to Copenhagen and flying from there to the United States. Afterwards McKethan complained to Robinson that Garner had not paid him the $7,000 he promised. Moreover, the joint trip by Garner and McKethan in March 1975, against this background, does not suggest that McKethan was off on an independent lark of his own.

McKethan did admit having received a payment of $3,500 from Robinson on one occasion, but he claimed that he had set up a grocery business for Robinson, though none of the stock was issued in Robinson's name, and the $3,500 was in payment for his services in setting up the grocery business.

McKethan's testimony does not tarnish the badges of reliability for Robinson's grand jury testimony. He offered innocent explanations of his frequent trips to Europe, but the jury was entitled to find the explanation incredible. The fact remains that the truthfulness of Robinson's grand jury testimony is strengthened by the testimony of Miss McKee and, particularly, by the airline tickets, customs declarations, passport endorsements, and hotel records. This is enough to satisfy the requirements of Rule 804(b)(5) and to avoid the bar of the hearsay rule. It also satisfies the requirements of the Confrontation Clause.

In this case, of course, Robinson did appear on the witness stand. Indeed, the defendants complain that this prejudiced their cases in the minds of the jurors, but the judge ordered the initial examination of Robinson in the presence of the jury in order that the jury would not be left with speculation about the reason for Robinson's absence, speculation which might have suggested inferences more hurtful to the defendants than Robinson's refusal to testify. He was presented for cross-examination only after Robinson had stated in an *in camera* hearing that he might answer the questions of defense counsel, and that he could not tell whether he would respond until they asked the questions. Though, as we have indicated earlier, the jurors may have taken Robinson's earlier disclaimers of knowledge as equivalent to a later explicit refusal to testify, they also may have received such disclaimers, with Robinson's statement that his grand jury testimony was inaccurate, as exculpatory. In any event, the jury saw and heard Robinson on the witness stand. What they saw and heard may have been of substantial assistance to the jury in assessing the truthfulness of his grand jury testimony. We do not hold, however, that this cross-examination under these difficult circumstances was adequate to meet the requirements of the Confrontation Clause. Cf. U.S. v. Insana, 423 F.2d 1165 (2d Cir.), cert. denied, 400 U.S. 841 (1970); U.S. v. Mingoia, 424 F.2d 710 (2d Cir. 1970). It is enough that the grand jury testimony was admissible because of its strong corroboration by the testimony of Miss McKee and the undeniable records. . . .

Problem IV-72
The Mystery of the Available Declarant

Charge: mail fraud and racketeering. Part of the prosecution's case is that D, the mayor of A, received bribes in exchange for favoring B Bus Company in its bid for the contract to bus A school children to and from school. The prosecution presented the testimony of C, a member of the city council, which had to recommend the contractor, that certain unidentified councilors had told them that the Mayor "would not mind" if the council recommended B Bus Company. D objects. The prosecution argues that the evidence is admissible under 803(24). What ruling and why?

Consider the different approaches advocated by the House and Senate committees to a residual hearsay exception (Rules 803(24); 804(b)(5)). Compare these views to the pre-Federal Rules view expressed by the court in *Dallas County* above and the results in *Bailey*, *West*, and *Garner*, above. Have these open-ended provisions "emasculated" the hearsay rules and undermined the rationale of codification? Have they introduced too much uncertainty in civil cases and exposed the defendant in criminal cases to confrontation clause violations? Or on the other hand, are these exceptions an appropriate attempt to prevent ossification of the rules consistently with the policies on which the rules are based? Should the rule against hearsay, and its exceptions, be abolished?

NOTE, THE THEORETICAL FOUNDATION OF THE HEARSAY RULES
93 Harv. L. Rev. 1786, 1786-1807 (1980)

Why have centuries of jurisprudence given rise to a rule known mostly by its exceptions, a rule that allows many avenues of circumvention and whose violation is rarely cause for concern by appellate courts? For decades, a fierce polemic has raged over the rule against hearsay and its exceptions. . . . [T]his debate is totally misdirected because the participants appeal to principles that have never been critically examined and that are incapable of rationalizing the rule against hearsay in any form.

I. RATIONALIZING THE RULE AGAINST HEARSAY

A. A GENERAL MODEL FOR EXCLUSION

Motivated by the assumption that a primary goal of our legal system is to achieve accurate case results, this Section will develop a framework that premises the exclusion of a relevant piece of evidence upon an expectation that the jury will erroneously assess the credibility of that evidence. To determine the extent to which the jury's assessment is erroneous, that assessment must be measured against some standard. Although ideally one would choose a standard of "truth," such a standard is, of course, impossible in principle to ascertain in the context of a trial. Instead, the framework will use the best alternative: the credibility that would be assigned to the evidence by "experts" — judges, attorneys, and academicians. This criterion will be referred to as "absolute reliability." Any relevant evidence, including hearsay, has at least some absolute reliability because the existence of infirmities and uncertainties of a piece of evidence only justifies *discounting* the weight given to the evidence rather than *ignoring* the evidence through exclusion. For example, even a statement by one known to be biased should not be ignored completely. With respect to hearsay, the existence of bias may be uncertain because there is no opportunity to cross-examine the declarant. Yet exclusion of such evidence would be inappropriate since the effect is to discount the evidence even more than if we were certain that the witness was biased.

If the jury's assessment is accurate by the standard of absolute reliability — that is, if the jury and the "expert" assessments coincide — the evidence should be admitted. When the jury cannot accurately assess the credibility of a piece of evidence, the error results in a gap between the jury's perception of the evidence and the absolute reliability of the evidence. Were the jury expected to *under*assess reliability, the controversy would not be over exclusion but over methods designed to increase the jury's reliance on the evidence. Exclusion is premised upon jury *over*assessment.

Any error that the jury commits in using the evidence to arrive at its verdict will depend upon the gap that remains at the conclusion of the trial — the residual gap — and not on the gap that existed after direct examination. Cross-examination and closing argument present opportunities to expose the weaknesses of testimony, improving the accuracy of the jury's assessment. Although with hearsay evidence cross-examination must be of the in-court witness instead of the declarant, there are still opportunities to expose weaknesses in the evidence. For example, if the evidence is ambiguous, cross-examination designed to reveal each of the possible meanings of the hearsay declaration would bring the weakness to the jury's attention. After these "remedies," the residual gap presumably would be smaller than the gap that existed immediately after direct examination. Such remedies vary, however, in their effectiveness and are limited in their range of potential application and by their strategic costs.

The concept of residual gap measures the expected jury error — the cost of admitting evidence. Credibility, judged by the standard of absolute reliability, measures the expected value of the evidence — the expected benefit from admission. A cost-benefit decision rule aimed at maximizing the accuracy of the result in a given case would exclude evidence when the expected error exceeds the expected value. This formula is analogous to rule 403 of the Federal Rules of Evidence which provides for the exclusion of relevant evidence when its prejudicial effect outweighs its probative value.

One way to examine the amount of error required to outweigh value, in order to justify exclusion, is to imagine a scale for recording assessments of the credibility of evidence. Zero would correspond to evidence given no credibility whatsoever; 100 to evidence believed with absolute certainty. Suppose the expert assessment (absolute reliability) of the evidence is above 50 — for example, 51. Since the greatest value the jury could assign to the evidence is 100, the largest possible gap is 49. Thus, the expected value (51) exceeds the gap (at most 49) and the evidence should be admitted under the decision rule. Alternatively, consider a case where the expert assessment of value was 30 and the jury assessment was 61. The resulting gap of 31 exceeds the value of 30, barely justifying exclusion. Exclusion requires that the gap exceed the value of the evidence, and, as this second example indicates, this condition is fulfilled only if the jury assessment exceeds twice the value of the evidence.[13] The occurrence of this condition is unlikely since it requires the existence of factors that indicate to the experts in the legal profession

---

13. More formally:

$$\text{Gap} = \text{Jury Perception} - \text{Absolute Reliability}.$$
$$\text{Absolute Reliability} = \text{Value}.$$

This implies $\text{Gap} = \text{Jury Perception} - \text{Value}.$

Therefore $\text{Gap} > \text{Value}$

is equivalent to $\text{Jury Perception} - \text{Value} > \text{Value},$

which yields $\text{Jury Perception} > 2 \times \text{Value}$

as an equivalent condition.

that the credibility of some evidence is very low but that are so far beyond the comprehension of laypersons that juries still would assess the credibility as being quite high.[14]

B. EXCLUSION ON THE GROUND THAT EVIDENCE IS HEARSAY

The process of determining the admissibility of a relevant piece of evidence by balancing its value against the residual gap between expected jury perception and absolute reliability is applicable to all types of evidence, and not just hearsay. Hearsay is distinguished from other evidence by the absence of the declarant. To justify the exclusion of evidence *because it is hearsay*, two conditions must be satisfied: (1) In the absence of the declarant (or when testimony is offered of the witness' own past statements), the gap must exceed value. (2) If the declarant is present (testifying to a current recollection of the events), the value must exceed the gap. If the first condition fails, there would be no reason to exclude. Without the second, exclusion would be justified even if the evidence were not hearsay. The second condition might fail, for example, when the exclusion of excited utterances is defended on the ground that the jury is not sufficiently aware of possible flaws in the declarant's perception. It is not, however, the hearsay character of this evidence that causes jury overassessment. Thus, that the evidence is an out-of-court declaration could not be asserted as the ground for exclusion.

Positions taken by those advocating reform of the rule against hearsay can readily be evaluated in the context of the framework just developed. For example, Judge Weinstein's well-known argument for more liberal admission of hearsay emphasizes the probative force (value) of hearsay, but provides no explicit analysis of the gap against which probative force must be balanced.[19] The implicit assumption necessary to justify his

---

14. Many commentators reject the claim that there is any significant jury misperception at all. . . . No attempt has been made to quantify the degree of overevaluation.

Given the range of efforts over the decades attempting merely to explain the hearsay rules and the difficulties in teaching the intricacies of the hearsay rules to law students, one might question the ability of the jury to evaluate hearsay evidence accurately. See Blackmore, Some Things About Hearsay: Article VIII, 6 Cap. U.L. Rev. 597, 597 (1977). It would be a mistake, however, to infer from the complexity of the hearsay *rules* that evaluation of most hearsay *evidence* is beyond the competence of a jury.

One qualification is necessary in the case of exceptionally unreliable hearsay evidence (for example, with a value of one on the 100 point scale) where it may be plausible that the jury assessment would exceed twice the value (in this example, an assessment of three). Such evidence may be excluded because of the waste of time, Fed. R. Evid. 403, and in any event the impact of such slight error would be de minimis. Moreover, for evidence of such low credibility, it is not clear that the jury will usually overassess the evidence instead of giving it too little weight or ignoring it completely.

19. Weinstein, Alternatives [to the Present Hearsay Rules, 44 F.R.D. 375 (1967)] at 379-80; Weinstein, Probative Force [of Hearsay, 46 Iowa L. Rev. 331 (1961)] at 338-42. He only analogizes loosely to a balance similar to considerations of prejudice, Fed. R. Evid. 403;

approach is that the reliability of hearsay is usually high enough (over 50 on the scale)[20] that insufficient room remains for a gap large enough to outweigh the value of the hearsay. Some favor abolishing the rule against hearsay on the ground that juries comprehend the shortcomings of hearsay as well as the "experts" do, a challenge to the existence of any initial gap. Others supporting abolition believe that cross-examination or other techniques will alert the jury to the weaknesses of hearsay, an assertion that any initial gap is remediable. Unfortunately, one feature common to most discourse on hearsay is the absence of any in-depth examination of these assumptions concerning the characteristics of evidence and how they are perceived by jurors.

It is not surprising that neither abolition nor extensive liberalization has occurred since few in the legal profession believe that juries are fully as aware of hearsay dangers as "experts," few believe that remedies are completely effective in all cases, and few believe that the value of evidence is always so high that all prospects of jury error can be ignored. But what apparently has gone unnoticed is that justifying retention of the rule against hearsay simultaneously requires that juries are generally unaware of hearsay dangers, that remedies usually fail to reveal dangers to the jury, and that the value of hearsay rarely approaches an intermediate level of credibility (50 on the scale) — a level that would make it impossible for the jury's assessment of hearsay to exceed twice the expert assessment (value) of the evidence.

II.   MISDIRECTION OF THE HEARSAY RULES: FAILURE ON THEIR OWN TERMS

A.   THE MYSTERY OF THE AVAILABLE DECLARANT

Admissibility of hearsay where the declarant is available has received much attention in the literature and is addressed explicitly in the Federal Rules of Evidence.[27] In the context of considering the accuracy of the

---

Weinstein, Probative Force, supra, at 338-39. Since the prejudice rule is already applicable to all evidence, his position for all practical purposes supports abolition of the rule against hearsay. However, his comment that "[t]he circumstantial proof of credibility which gave rise to the class exception may continue to be utilized in the particular case in assessing probative force," id. at 339, implies that his intention falls short of abolition. In any event, he provides no framework for the required balancing of value and jury overassessment. . . .

20. Actually, Judge Weinstein's approach could be justified if reliability were *near or above* 50. For example, if some evidence had only an absolute reliability of 45, admission would be proper for any jury perception below 90 — which arguably includes most cases — and the greatest possible net loss would be limited to 10, in the case where the jury gave full weight to the evidence (an assessment of 100). However, once these subtleties are combined with the argument of probative force, the justification for Judge Weinstein's approach should be more properly viewed as derived from the entire framework presented in this Note.

27. The Federal Rules have two sets of exceptions — those for which availability of the declarant is immaterial and those for unavailable declarants. Fed. R. Evid. 803, 804. There

result in a given case, arguments over the admission of the hearsay of available declarants make little sense because in any given case application of either of the two extreme approaches (always exclude or always admit) leads to the same result. If the declarant is available, (1) exclusion would be of little consequence to the party needing the evidence since the declarant can be called directly, and (2) admission would not damage the position of a party fearing jury overvaluation of the hearsay since the declarant can be called for cross-examination, which allows the same impeachment possibilities that would have existed were the opponent to have called the declarant for direct examination. If exclusion is the general rule, some special treatment of hearsay of available declarants may be justified on grounds unrelated to fears of jury overvaluation. For example, business records might be admitted to save the time and expense of calling the five employees who each had a hand in processing the data. Nonetheless, the traditional discussion claiming to address the accuracy of case results persists with full force despite the fact that it has no bearing upon whether the hearsay of an available declarant should be admitted.[30] The remainder of this Part therefore implicitly considers only the unavailable declarant.

B.   TRADITIONAL JUSTIFICATION FOR HEARSAY EXCEPTIONS

Exceptions to the rule against hearsay are traditionally justified on the grounds that some hearsay is particularly reliable or necessary. This Section will address the prominence of each criterion in the hearsay polemic, question the possibility and practicality of applying each consistently, and analyze shortcomings revealed by application of the framework developed in Part I.

1.   *Reliability.* The most common and accepted characterization of the hearsay problem is that such evidence is not sufficiently reliable and that exceptions are made for categories of hearsay that exhibit additional guarantees of trustworthiness. This approach permeates the ma-

---

is no across-the-board rule admitting the hearsay of available declarants. Thus, the Federal Rules go to great lengths to differentiate among the hearsay of available declarants in determining admissibility. See Advisory Comm. Note, Fed. R. Evid. 803.

The existence of rule 803(24) of the Federal Rules of Evidence is difficult to explain. If the declarant is *unavailable,* identical exception 804(b)(5) may be used; if the declarant is *available,* the criteria of the exception seem impossible to meet since "the statement [must be] more probative on the point for which it is offered than any other evidence which the proponent can procure through reasonable efforts." Fed. R. Evid. 803(24).

30. Exclusion serves to minimize the potential for manipulation when the decision not to call the available declarant may provide some strategic benefit. Also, it avoids disruption that might result from allowing the opponent to cross-examine the declarant immediately after direct examination of the witness testifying to the hearsay statement, possible surprise to the opponent if no notice is required, and placing burdens on the opponent to procure the declarant. . . .

jor treatises on evidence. The Federal Rules of Evidence demonstrate adherence to this view through the requirements for an exception under the residual clauses and more generally through the supporting analysis provided by the Advisory Committee. Perhaps the most famous of hearsay decisions, Dallas County v. Commercial Union Assurance Co., recognizes this principle, as does Chambers v. Mississippi, in which the Supreme Court examined the constitutional implications of the hearsay rules in criminal procedure. This view is pervasive in the contemporary debate over hearsay issues.

Focusing on reliability as a justification for admission ignores all but the first element (absolute reliability) of the framework developed in Part I. First, this traditional approach errs by failing to consider the jury's perception of reliability.[39] For example, a piece of hearsay evidence may be fairly reliable, yet the jury may still significantly overassess its credibility; on the other hand, some hearsay may have no circumstantial indicia of reliability, but all its defects may be obvious to any juror. The traditional approach would admit the former evidence, despite the danger of overassessment, and exclude the latter, though it poses no real threat. Second, Part I demonstrated the need for examining the potential to remedy defects in jury evaluation of hearsay and the likelihood that such defects would not arise had the declaration been testimony subject to cross-examination. It is not surprising that one overlooks these factors when focusing solely upon reliability since the importance of both factors becomes apparent only upon recognition that the central emphasis should be on jury perception. Most investigations look to the reliability of hearsay in a vacuum instead of focusing upon the reliability *gap*. Finally, examinations of the exceptions often ignore the value lost whenever evidence is excluded, against which the reliability gap must be balanced.

Current analyses are unpersuasive even in their attempts to identify which categories of hearsay are reliable. The reliability of hearsay is usually determined by examining the degree to which believing the evidence requires unsupported reliance upon the declarant's four testimonial capacities: narration, sincerity, memory, and perception. If circumstances indicate that no danger would result from reliance upon

39. In other words, focus is upon absolute reliability instead of upon the reliability gap.

For analysis of the absolute reliability in isolation to provide the same result as a complete examination of the residual hearsay gap, the jury must always give full weight to hearsay evidence. In that event, any unreliability contributes to the reliability gap. But, if the jury gives the hearsay anything less than full weight, including the possibility of giving too little weight, the unreliability of the evidence overstates the warrant for exclusion. It is impossible for the jury always to give hearsay full weight when conflicting hearsay is presented by opposing parties. Similarly, it seems unlikely that it would give hearsay full weight when conflicting nonhearsay evidence on the issue is present since this implicitly assumes that the jury gives full weight to the dubious hearsay evidence while giving no weight to the other evidence, which may be of greater reliability. This makes the full weight assumption implausible regardless of how able one thinks jurors are. . . .

one or more of these capacities, an exception is sometimes said to be warranted. Yet it is not clear why the hearsay problem is "solved" when only one or two of the four defects have been removed. Analysis of an exception justified on the basis of circumstantial guarantees as to one capacity suggests that the three that remain unchecked present no significant ground for worry. After examination of several exceptions, each justified by guarantees as to a different capacity, one would conclude that *none* of the four capacities found wanting in circumstantial guarantees presents a significant problem. One might respond to this criticism by assuming that the degree to which the reliability gap exceeded the value of the evidence was small enough that the incremental decrease in the gap provided by the removal of one of the defects is sufficient to swing the balance in favor of admission. If that is the case, however, it seems curious that those implicitly making this assumption devote so much attention to determining which categories of hearsay should be admitted and which should be excluded. The assumption itself suggests that most questions regarding the admissibility of hearsay are nearly a tossup.

The above criticism would not prove embarrassing to those wishing to inquire into the reliability of hearsay if one capacity could be isolated as the most important, with exceptions being made solely when there exist circumstantial guarantees for that capacity. In fact, most advocates of exceptions do emphasize circumstantial guarantees for one capacity — the sincerity of the out-of-court declarant. Acceptance of the principle that only appeals to sincerity can justify exceptions renders meaningless all current discussion of the other three capacities. More important, analysis within the framework of the first Part reveals how this justification backfires. Distinguishing hearsay from other evidence depends upon the testability of the hearsay declaration, assuming that it was offered as testimony in court. Few would doubt that cross-examination effectively remedies defects in the other three capacities: it exposes and resolves ambiguity, it tests or refreshes memory, and it brings into question possible defects in perception. By contrast, cross-examination may be less well suited to exposing insincerity. Studies of jury reaction to eyewitness testimony indicate that the jury does not function as an effective lie detector. Focus upon sincerity as the pivotal element could be justified if it is the most testable capacity; in fact, it may be the least. Alternatively, one might justify this focus on the ground that, although sincerity is less testable, sincerity problems occur far more frequently in the underlying population of potential hearsay evidence than do weaknesses in the other three capacities. This empirical assertion has not even been stated, much less proved, by those who appeal to circumstantial indications of sincerity when arguing for exceptions. Without facing such empirical questions and defending one particular position, it is impossible to rationalize singling out sincerity as the most important capacity. The current approach of justifying hearsay exceptions by appeals to the circumstantial guarantees of testimonial capacities cannot be defended by isolating sincerity, in terms of testability or frequency of occurrence. Thus, the traditional formulation is without rational foundation. . . .

[T]he current method of justifying hearsay exceptions is the opposite of the proper approach. Instead of considering those testimonial capacities for which there are circumstantial guarantees of trustworthiness, one should focus upon those capacities for which there are *not* such guarantees. For example, the current approach allows a hearsay exception for excited utterances because of their alleged sincerity. The reliability of such utterances is dubious, however, because the declarant's perception and narration may be impaired. Regardless of strong guarantees as to sincerity, the evidence may remain unreliable.

2. *Necessity.* Although Wigmore puts forth the principle of necessity as coequal with the principle of reliability for the purpose of justifying exceptions to the rule against hearsay, necessity is addressed far less frequently in specific analyses of exceptions, and its prominence in the literature seems to exceed its impact upon the rules of evidence. In the Federal Rules of Evidence, it is one of the many requirements for admission under the residual exceptions but does not appear explicitly elsewhere. Even though the principle seems central to the justification for some exceptions, such as dying declarations, the rules make no distinction between "necessary" and other uses of the evidence. . . .

Since necessity is a function of the other evidence available in a given case, it will be difficult to identify, a priori, any categories of hearsay — with the possible exception of dying declarations — that will be "necessary." Therefore, implementing the necessity principle involves according broad discretion to the trial judge. Even then, a circulatory problem arises within a single trial because the necessity of any evidence depends upon what other evidence is admitted. This difficulty is compounded by problems raised by the order of presentation, the difficulty of changing previous rulings, the potential for parties to manipulate the judge by failing to investigate or present other sources of evidence, and the sheer complexity of making rulings that depend upon the variety of possible configurations of other evidence in a given case. . . .

[T]wo polar cases reveal how the principle of necessity may be just as likely to favor exclusion as admission. First, where much other evidence or far more credible evidence is available, there is no *need* to let in hearsay that may mislead the jury. The very existence of the other or better evidence, however, implies that, even if the jury's error in evaluating the hearsay is large, its error in deciding the case will be small since that decision reflects its consideration of all the other evidence in combination with the hearsay. By contrast, in the second case, where there is little or no other evidence probative of the issue, the evidence is most valuable to the case as a whole. Assume that a significant reliability gap initially exists. Since that gap arises from the jury's overvaluation of the evidence in question, one would expect significant error to remain in the jury's determination of the ultimate issue because no other information intervened in its decision process. It is precisely when the unreliable evidence is highly probative and little other evidence is available that the greatest danger appears. Thus, the greater the need, the greater the danger, and the less the need, the less the danger.

The principle of necessity thus directs attention away from the individual piece of evidence and towards its impact on the case as a whole. The correlation between necessity and the value of evidence to the case as a whole has always been recognized. What is generally ignored is the correlation between necessity and the impact of jury error upon its ultimate decision; the less other evidence is available, the less will be the opportunity to remedy or mitigate the impact of jury error in evaluating the given piece of evidence.

A formal analysis of how the necessity of the evidence affects both its value and its danger reveals that, a priori, the implications of the necessity criterion for determining the admissibility of evidence are indeterminate. The expected jury error in processing the evidence to reach its ultimate decision and the value of the evidence both increase as necessity increases. This is illustrated in Figure 1. The amount and quality of other evidence is measured along the horizontal axis. The value of the evidence to the case as a whole — "Value" — and the expected error in the jury's decision resulting from admission — "Error" — are both measured along the vertical axis. For any category of hearsay, there are four possible cases. First, it is possible that error exceeds value for all degrees of necessity, justifying exclusion in all cases (illustrated in Figure 1). Second, value might exceed error for all degrees of necessity, justifying admission in all cases (Figure 2). In both cases the necessity of the evidence is irrelevant to the decision to admit or exclude. A third possibility is that value declines more rapidly than does error as the amount and quality of other available evidence increases (i.e., as the necessity of the evidence in question decreases). In other words, where little other evidence is available, value outweighs error, and the evidence should be admitted; where much is available, error exceeds value, and the evidence should be excluded (Figure 3). The standard argument that necessity justifies the admission of hearsay assumes that this case is an accurate description of the world. The existence of a fourth case, however, indicates that the opposite result is equally plausible. This would occur if error is above value when little other evidence is available, justifying exclusion, but that error falls below value as more evidence is available, justifying admission (Figure 4). In both case three and case four, the admissibility decision when little other evidence is available will

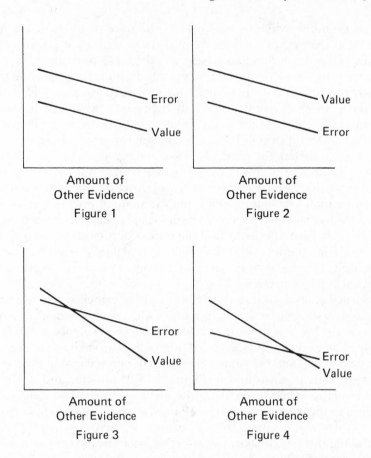

be the opposite of the ruling when much other evidence is available. Neither case is complete without specification of where that reversal occurs. For example, Figure 3 portrays a crossover where little other evidence on the issue is available, and in Figure 4 the crossover does not occur until far more evidence is available. In other words, one must determine how much other evidence must be available to change the decision. Asserting that the reversal occurs at *some* point is only a first step toward a workable principle either for discretionary implementation by judges or for application to the debate over the delineation of hearsay exceptions. No attempt has been made to support the implicit empirical judgment reflected by adherence to case three, to specify the location of the switching point, or to examine the significance of the gap between error and value for any given level of necessity.[66]

66. A priori, one can predict only that error and value decline as the quantity of other evidence increases; these declining functions need not be linear, as portrayed in Figures 1 to 4. Thus, combinations of cases three and four in general are possible, wherein the proper ruling alternates between admitting and excluding the hearsay evidence as the amount and quality of other available evidence increases.

III. INCONSISTENCY OF THE HEARSAY RULES WITH JUDGE-JURY RELATIONS

Both the traditional analysis of hearsay examined in Part II and the framework presented in Part I take maximizing the accuracy of case results as the objective, thereby assuming the legitimacy of excluding hearsay on the grounds that it is unreliable or likely to be misperceived by juries. Yet one could use the same grounds to justify the exclusion of nonhearsay evidence, a result directly contrary to "the time-honored formula [that] credibility is a matter of fact for the jury, not a matter of law for the court."[67]

The Federal Rules of Evidence provide that "[a]lthough relevant, evidence may be excluded if its probative value is substantially outweighed by the danger of unfair prejudice." Under this structure, exclusion is justified by fears of how the jury will be influenced by the evidence. However, it is not traditional to think of hearsay as merely a subdivision of this structure, and the Federal Rules do not conceive of hearsay in that manner. Prejudice refers to the jury's use of evidence for inferences other than those for which the evidence is legally relevant; by contrast, the rule against hearsay questions the jury's ability to evaluate the strength of a *legitimate* inference to be drawn from the evidence. For example, were a judge to exclude testimony because a witness was particularly smooth or convincing, there would be no doubt as to the usurpation of the jury's function. Thus, unlike prejudices recognized by the evidence rules, such as those stemming from racial or religious biases or from the introduction of photographs of a victim's final state, the exclusion of hearsay on the basis of misperception strikes at the root of the jury's function by usurping its power to process quite ordinary evidence, the type of information routinely encountered by jurors in their everyday lives.

Even if one were to accept the coherence of the two principles of reliability and necessity, hearsay provisions based on them would remain inconsistent with the common understanding of the role played by the rules of evidence in our system of adjudication. Outside the hearsay context, it is not generally required that evidence be necessary in order to be admissible. Furthermore, exclusion of evidence because it is unreliable is grossly inconsistent with our usual view of the jury's ability to

---

67. Chadbourn, Bentham and the Hearsay Rule — A Benthamic View of Rule 63(4)(c) of the Uniform Rules of Evidence, 75 Harv. L. Rev. 932, 947 (1962); cf. Advisory Comm. Note, Fed. R. Evid. 104(b) ("If preliminary questions of conditional relevancy were determined solely by the judge, as provided in subdivision (a), the functioning of the jury as trier of fact would be greatly restricted and in some cases virtually destroyed.").

One condition argued to be necessary to rationalize the exclusion of evidence because it is hearsay was that the reliability gap would not exceed value had the evidence been in-court testimony. But acceptance of the legitimacy of the reliability gap/value balancing test formulation in fact suggests that any evidence that could not be effectively tested before the jury should be excluded.

process evidence and to make inferences. In considering absolute reliability, which is germane to the weight that should be given to evidence, the rulemakers and treatise writers approach to the hearsay problems from the wrong perspective; they exclude evidence that they would discount or disbelieve if *they* were sitting as trier of fact rather than considering which evidence should be kept from a trier of fact.

The practice of regularly admitting hearsay evidence for nonhearsay purposes further illustrates the inconsistency of the hearsay rules with traditional conceptions of the role of the jury. Even if the jury is instructed that such evidence may only be used for nonhearsay purposes, the result will be little different than if the jury had been permitted to evaluate the evidence for the hearsay purpose as well. To have justified excluding the evidence as hearsay, the reliability gap must have exceeded the value of the evidence in its hearsay use. To justify reversal of that judgment, the value of the evidence in its nonhearsay use must be greater than the amount by which the gap had exceeded the value in its hearsay use. Yet this assumption is unwarranted since any nonhearsay use is considered sufficient to admit any evidence otherwise excluded by the rule against hearsay. Thus, when focusing upon nonhearsay uses of evidence, courts implicitly ignore the original justifications for the exclusion of hearsay, a result that is not surprising since those justifications conflict with the usual view of the role of the jury.

Though the rule against hearsay is formally applicable to bench trials, it is in fact little used in the absence of a jury. The appropriateness of applying the hearsay prohibition to bench trials has been questioned on the ground that the hearsay rules reflect a concern with attributes peculiar to the jury, a position flowing comfortably from the analysis that focuses on jury perception. A variety of techniques are employed that, in effect, permit the admission of hearsay in nonjury trials. It is not surprising that these techniques arose given that judges presiding without a jury undoubtedly found the inconsistency between the treatment of hearsay and other evidence too glaring to tolerate, reinforcing the conclusion that the hearsay rules and debate are in fact directed more toward issues of evaluation than toward questions of admission. These practices also demonstrate that exclusion cannot rationally be premised on the traditional ground of unreliability because this rationale makes no distinction between whether a jury or a judge is the trier of fact. De facto *consistency* within the nonjury setting highlights the *inconsistency* of the hearsay rules with other rules of evidence when the jury is present.

IV. The Hearsay Rules as a Means of Enhancing the Social Acceptance of Our System of Adjudication

Some explanation is necessary for the continued reliance upon the traditional hearsay analysis given that all justifications for the rules both fail on their own terms and conflict with accepted notions of the role of the jury. This Part offers one possible explanation of how the traditional approach came to be and why it tends to survive.

Society needs to have confidence in the outcomes produced by its system of adjudication. Criminal law most clearly dramatizes this need; when we contemplate punishment that deprives one of liberty, property, or even life, the *perception* of fairness is essential to quiet our collective conscience. Social acceptance is a function of how the system is perceived, and not of how it actually performs. The hearsay rules, though incoherent when viewed from the [traditional] perspective, might seem more comprehensible when viewed from a cynical perspective, . . . as aimed at enhancing social acceptance by directly addressing society's perception of the system rather than the system's performance.

First, hearsay rules shield the system from possible embarrassment. Admitting hearsay generally creates the possibility that the declarant might later come forward to reveal that injustice resulted from the trier of fact's reliance on such evidence. Second, hearsay is distinctive in that its deficiencies can be observed readily by anyone outside the system. With other evidence, the jury functions as a "black box": its ability to observe demeanor, though limited in revealing truth, "justifies" deference to the jury's decision because the jury ostensibly has additional information that those absent could not possibly duplicate and those present could not fully communicate.

These two considerations indicate how a rule against hearsay enhances social acceptance by excluding evidence. Yet extensive exclusion of hearsay may itself diminish acceptance since we like to believe that the trier considers all relevant information in reaching its decision. Therefore, maximizing social acceptance implies that hearsay exceptions are appropriate where the danger of *exposing* error is less, whereas the Part I framework justifies exceptions where the danger of jury misperception is less.

The danger of exposing error is minimized by creating exceptions to the rule against hearsay when later contradictory statements from the declarant are unlikely to arise or would not prove embarrassing. The clearest illustration is the exception for dying declarations, the classic example of an exception of dubious validity by traditionally accepted criteria. Admissions by a party opponent would be allowed in evidence since "[a] party can hardly object that he had no opportunity to cross-examine himself or that he is unworthy of credence save when speaking under sanction of an oath." With respect to present sense impressions, excited utterances, and indications of the declarant's state of mind, the declarant's recollection of the events presented after a trial is no more and possibly less credible than the extrinsic (hearsay) evidence of the declarant's knowledge at the time of the incident. For business records and official public reports, the body responsible for the existence of the information is unlikely to surprise us later. Similarly, the admission of statements against interest by an unavailable declarant does not risk future embarrassment because declarants typically will not become available, and, even if one does, later contrary statements will not prove embarrassing. As these examples illustrate, the current pattern of hearsay exceptions seems quite rational as a reflection of the desire to enhance social acceptance by shielding the system from possible embarrassment.

The retention of rules excluding hearsay in non-jury trials despite widespread admission of hearsay in actual practice may also reflect the desire to promote social acceptance. Improperly admitted hearsay endangers the appearances of the system only if it appears that the trial court actually relied on the hearsay in making its decision. Current appellate practice, by invoking "the time-honored presumption that a trial judge does not utilize erroneously admitted evidence in rendering his verdict," preserves the appearance that such evidence was not a factor in the decision. The public's view of the courts may similarly decline if it appears that the trial judge is not considering admissible evidence. Appellate courts avoid this danger by inviting the trial judge to admit this evidence into the record. If the evidence in the record is disregarded by the trial judge, who believed it to be inadmissible,[100] the appellate court will still uphold the decision although the evidence was admissible, implicitly presuming that the evidence was considered in the decision.[101] This appellate procedure is supplemented by a veritable arsenal of weapons that increase the likelihood of upholding the admission of hearsay (and other evidence) by lower courts in both jury and nonjury settings. Since reliance on the hearsay is not explicit when any of these methods is used, the system's appearances are protected.

If this rationalization of the hearsay structure were the true explanation for its existence, one still would not expect it to be explicitly advanced in support of the hearsay rules since stating this rationalization is self-defeating; rules cannot successfully protect the appearances of a system if the rules are openly presented as serving that end. It seems implausible that the hearsay rules were consciously designed and subse-

---

100. The use of such evidence in reaching the decision would be contrary to the trial judge's belief that the evidence was inadmissible. This practice is inconsistent with conscientious judicial behavior and, in any event, will not be imputed by the appellate court; an error in fact may result though no error in law is admitted. Furthermore, if inadmissible evidence is to be entered into the record, trial judges will give less thought to questions of admissibility in the first instance, making ultimate reliance upon improper evidence more likely.

101. The result is effectively to exclude admissible evidence since the judge as trier of fact ignores it, but, as a consequence of the act of admitting the evidence into record, the judge's erroneous belief is insulated from review. In fact, an appellate ruling might be unnecessary since the evidence would have been admitted and there would not be any ruling by the lower court that the evidence was ignored. For example, the lower court may admit the evidence and simply make no mention of it in a finding of fact, directed verdict, or judgment notwithstanding the verdict. See, Note, Improper Evidence in Nonjury Trials: Basis for Reversal?, 79 Harv. L. Rev. 407, 409-11 (1965).

quently modified to shelter the system from embarrassment and to preserve the jury's ability to function as a "black box." It seems plausible, however, that those operating within our system of adjudication would be motivated by a desire, perhaps subconscious, to feel that the system to which they have devoted their energy is worthy of society's acceptance as a system of justice.

Since the underlying purposes may remain subconscious and, in any event, could not be openly expressed, other justifications would be offered in their place. These surrogate justifications would give rise to a set of rules that only approximately mirror the rules that would result if the actual objectives were openly admitted. After the process of adjusting and amending the proffered justifications to fit the desired objectives more closely, one would expect the resultant patchwork of rules to appear confused and complex, much as the hearsay rules are today.

The hypothesis that the hearsay rules are designed to protect appearances explains the prominence in the hearsay debate of absolute reliability instead of the reliability gap. Keeping hearsay evidence from the jury because it is unreliable both seems necessary to avoid exposure of error, since nothing prevents outside observers from perceiving the deficiency, and lends additional external credibility to trials by giving the impression that the process is cleansed of such questionable evidence. Because the broad interpretations given to hearsay exceptions and the limited appellate scrutiny are not readily apparent to those outside the system, they do not seriously threaten the appearance afforded by appealing to reliability. The strong superficial appeal of reliability as a criterion makes it easy to understand how dependence upon it might have arisen during the evolution of our rules of evidence and why this dependence continues even now. By contrast, suggesting that one focus upon jury error . . . directly presents the problem of the jury's inability to assess hearsay accurately, undermining any attempt to defend the system's appearances.

The principle of necessity is similarly attractive. Assurances that there is no other evidence probative on the issue shield the system from all sources of potential future embarrassment except from the hearsay declarant. Appeals to the criterion of necessity implicitly recognize the decline in value of the evidence as more evidence is available but overlook the decline in jury error. Both recognition of this shortcoming and attempts to rectify it necessarily direct attention to the jury's inability to evaluate hearsay.

This open recognition, which careful analysis of the reliability or the necessity criterion makes inevitable, engenders not merely suspicion about hearsay evidence but also a deep skepticism about the institution of trial by jury. Without the jury to insulate us from observing the inherent limitations upon factfinding, our system of adjudication is called into question. . . .

The social acceptance rationale should be rejected as a normative basis for the hearsay rules for another more compelling reason. . . . [W]e tend to hide the limitations of the jury as a trier of fact while promoting an almost mystic view of our system of justice. To accept that such an approach produces sound results entails unwarranted optimism — a belief that what exists, although we never examine it or admit its nature even to ourselves, is either for the best or will improve if left to itself, perhaps for another century of incoherent evolution. Even if the legal profession is fully aware of what is at issue, contrary to the indications, . . . there remain serious questions concerning whether it is appropriate for the profession to aim directly at social acceptance when making decisions about the course of adjudication on behalf of society at large. This secrecy also limits the range of our imagination when considering problems that continue to arise in the law of evidence and elsewhere. Finally, there are moral questions raised by acceptance of the framework of the current polemic: Can we continue to call our system "just" when we allow the signs of injustice to remain hidden from our own view?

V. CONCLUSION . . .

Since virtually all criteria seeking to distinguish between good and bad hearsay are either incoherent, inconsistent, or indeterminate, the only alternative to a general rule of admission would be an absolute rule of exclusion, which is surely inferior. More important, the assumptions necessary to justify a rule against hearsay — requiring that the jury's assessment of hearsay evidence, after possible remedies, generally exceed twice the value of the evidence — seem insupportable and, in any event, are inconsistent with accepted notions of the function of the jury. Therefore, the hearsay rules should be abolished.

CHAPTER V

Confrontation and Compulsory Process

Most of the material to this point has been concerned with alternative formulations of evidence rules, particularly the rule against hearsay and its exceptions, in light of policies of promoting fairness and accuracy of factfinding. This section examines constitutional restrictions on these state and federal policy choices. The issue at its extreme is: In a criminal trial what limitations do the due process clause and the sixth amendment guarantees of confrontation and compulsory process place on the admissibility of prosecution evidence and the exclusion of evidence offered by the accused? In considering the cases that bear on this issue, one should be sensitive to the relationship between rules of evidence — particularly the rule excluding hearsay and its exceptions — and constitutional doctrine. To what extent have the hearsay rules been constitutionalized? Should they be? On this point, see generally The Advisory Committee's Introductory Note to Federal Rules of Evidence, Article 8.

The cases in this chapter demonstrate that the meaning of the confrontation clause has puzzled and continues to puzzle the Supreme Court. As Justice Harlan said in California v. Green, "The Confrontation Clause comes to us on faded parchment." There are at least six meanings that can be attributed to the clause, and it will be useful to consider which of these informs the cases or might retrospectively rationalize the cases:

(1) A rule of history: The clause endorses whatever procedure prevailed in 1789;

(2) A rule requiring that any witness who testifies against a defendant be subject to cross-examination by him;

(3) A rule requiring cross-examination of the declarant of any statement that is offered against an accused for the truth of the matter it asserts;

(4) A rule requiring that all statements offered against an accused be reliable to some foundational degree (with such reliability always attainable if the declarant is or has been subject to cross-examination);

(5) A rule of preference requiring that prosecutors produce the declarant if available but permitting hearsay if the declarant is not available; or

(6) A rule of sufficiency requiring that uncross-examined statements not comprise too heavy a proportion of the totality of the evidence against the accused.

A. Confrontation — The Search for Theory

MATTOX v. UNITED STATES
156 U.S. 237 (1895)

[Plaintiff was convicted in 1894 for murder on federal land. He had previously been tried and convicted for this offense, but his first conviction had been reversed.]

Mr. Justice BROWN delivered the opinion of the court.

Error is assigned to the action of the court below . . . in admitting to the jury the reporter's notes of the testimony of two witnesses at the former trial, who had since died. . . .

Upon the trial it was shown by the government that two of its witnesses on the former trial, namely, Thomas Whitman and George Thornton, had since died, whereupon a transcribed copy of the reporter's stenographic notes of their testimony upon such trial, supported by his testimony that it was correct, was admitted to be read in evidence, and constituted the strongest proof against the accused. Both these witnesses were present and were fully examined and cross-examined on the former trial. It is claimed, however, that the constitutional provision that the accused shall "be confronted with the witnesses against him" was infringed, by permitting the testimony of witnesses sworn upon the former trial to be read against him. No question is made that this may not be done in a civil case, but it is insisted that the reasons of convenience and necessity which excuse a departure from the ordinary course of procedure in civil cases cannot override the constitutional provision in question. . . .

The primary object of the constitutional provision in question was to prevent depositions or ex parte affidavits, such as were sometimes admitted in civil cases, being used against the prisoner in lieu of a personal examination and cross-examination of the witness in which the accused has an opportunity, not only of testing the recollection and sifting the conscience of the witness, but of compelling him to stand face to face with the jury in order that they may look at him, and judge by his

demeanor upon the stand and the manner in which he gives his testimony whether he is worthy of belief. There is doubtless reason for
saying that the accused should never lose the benefit of any of these
safeguards even by the death of the witness; and that, if notes of his
testimony are permitted to be read, he is deprived of the advantage of
that personal presence of the witness before the jury which the law has
designed for his protection. But general rules of law of this kind, however beneficent in their operation and valuable to the accused, must
occasionally give way to considerations of public policy and the necessities of the case. To say that a criminal, after having once been convicted
by the testimony of a certain witness, should go scot free simply because
death has closed the mouth of that witness, would be carrying his constitutional protection to an unwarrantable extent. The law in its wisdom
declares that the rights of the public shall not be wholly sacrificed in
order that an incidental benefit may be preserved to the accused.

We are bound to interpret the Constitution in the light of the law as it
existed at the time it was adopted, not as reaching out for new guaranties
of the rights of the citizen, but as securing to every individual such as he
already possessed as a British subject — such as his ancestors had inher-
ited and defended since the days of Magna Charta. Many of its provisions in the nature of a Bill of Rights are subject to exceptions,
recognized long before the adoption of the Constitution, and not inter-
fering at all with its spirit. Such exceptions were obviously intended to be
respected. A technical adherence to the letter of a constitutional provision may occasionally be carried farther than is necessary to the just
protection of the accused, and farther than the safety of the public will
warrant. For instance, there could be nothing more directly contrary to
the letter of the provision in question than the admission of dying declarations. They are rarely made in the presence of the accused; they are
made without any opportunity for examination or cross-examination;
nor is the witness brought face to face with the jury; yet from time
immemorial they have been treated as competent testimony, and no one
would have the hardihood at this day to question their admissibility.
They are admitted not in conformity with any general rule regarding
the admission of testimony, but as an exception to such rules, simply
from the necessities of the case, and to prevent a manifest failure of
justice. As was said by the Chief Justice when this case was here upon the
first writ of error, (146 U.S. 140, 152), the sense of impending death is
presumed to remove all temptation to falsehood, and to enforce as strict
an adherence to the truth as would the obligation of an oath. If such
declarations are admitted, because made by a person then dead, under
circumstances which give his statements the same weight as if made
under oath, there is equal if not greater reason for admitting testimony
of his statements which were made under oath. . . .

The substance of the constitutional protection is preserved to the prisoner in the advantage he has once had of seeing the witness face to face, and of subjecting him to the ordeal of a cross-examination. . . .

———————

Which confrontation rule does the Court apply in this case? Does the Court adequately explain why the confrontation clause was not violated? Would the evidence have been admissible under the Federal Rules? Does argument by analogy to dying declarations prove too much? Does *Mattox* stand for the principle that all statements that are as reliable as dying declarations are admissible without violating the confrontation clause, at least if the witness is unavailable?

KIRBY v. UNITED STATES
174 U.S. 47 (1899)

Mr. Justice HARLAN delivered the opinion of the court. . . .

[T]he charge against Kirby was that on a named day he feloniously received and had in his possession with intent to convert to his own use and gain certain personal property of the United States, theretofore feloniously stolen, taken and carried away by Wallace, Baxter and King, who had been indicted and convicted of the offence alleged to have been committed by them. . . .

How did the Government attempt to prove the essential fact that the property was stolen from the United States? In no other way than by the production of a record showing the conviction under a separate indictment of Wallace, Baxter and King — the judgments against Wallace and Baxter resting wholly upon their respective pleas of guilty, while the judgment against King rested upon a trial and verdict of guilty. With the record of those convictions out of the present case, there was no evidence whatever to show that the property alleged to have been received by Kirby was stolen from the United States.

We are of the opinion that the trial court erred in admitting in evidence the record of the convictions of Wallace, Baxter and King, and then in its charge saying that in the absence of proof to the contrary, the fact that the property was stolen from the United States was sufficiently established against Kirby by the mere production of the record showing the conviction of the principal felons. Where the statute makes the conviction of the principal thief a condition precedent to the trial and punishment of a receiver of the stolen property, the record of the trial of the former would be evidence in the prosecution against the receiver to show that the principal felon had been convicted; for a fact of that nature could only be established by a record. The record of the conviction of the principals could not however be used to establish, against the alleged receiver, charged with the commission of another and substantive crime, the essential fact that the property alleged to have been feloniously received by him was actually stolen from the United States. Kirby was not present when Wallace and Baxter confessed their crime by pleas of guilty, nor when King was proved to be guilty by witnesses who personally testified before the jury. Nor was Kirby entitled of right to participate in the trial of the principal felons. If present at that trial he would not have been permitted to examine Wallace and Baxter upon their pleas of guilty, nor cross-examine the witnesses introduced against King, nor introduce witnesses to prove that they were not in fact guilty of the offence charged against them. If he had sought to do either of those things — even upon the ground that the conviction of the principal felons might be taken as establishing prima facie a vital fact in the separate prosecution against himself as the receiver of the property — the court would have informed him that he was not being tried and could not be permitted in anywise to interfere with the trial of the principal felons. And yet the court below instructed the jury that the conviction of the principal felons upon an indictment against them alone was sufficient prima facie to show, as against Kirby, indicted for another offence, the existence of the fact that the property was stolen — a fact which, it is conceded, the United States was bound to establish beyond a reasonable doubt in order to obtain a verdict of guilty against him.

One of the fundamental guarantees of life and liberty is found in the Sixth Amendment of the Constitution of the United States, which provides that "in all criminal prosecutions the accused shall . . . be confronted with the witnesses against him." Instead of confronting Kirby with witnesses to establish the vital fact that the property alleged to have been received by him had been stolen from the United States, he was confronted only with the record of another criminal prosecution, with which he had no connection and the evidence in which was not given in his presence. . . .

Which confrontation rule does the Court apply in *Kirby*? Would the evidence be admissible under the Federal Rules? Is Justice Harlan's constitutional problem one of admissibility or of sufficiency?

POINTER v. TEXAS
380 U.S. 400 (1965)

Mr. Justice BLACK delivered the opinion of the Court. . . .

The petitioner Pointer and one Dillard were arrested in Texas and taken before a state judge for a preliminary hearing (in Texas called the "examining trial") on a charge of having robbed Kenneth W. Phillips of $375 "by assault, or violence, or by putting in fear of life or bodily injury," in violation of Texas Penal Code Art. 1408. At this hearing an Assistant District Attorney conducted the prosecution and examined witnesses, but neither of the defendants, both of whom were laymen, had a lawyer. Phillips as chief witness for the State gave his version of the alleged robbery in detail, identifying petitioner as the man who had robbed him at gunpoint. Apparently Dillard tried to cross-examine Phillips but Pointer did not, although Pointer was said to have tried to cross-examine some other witnesses at the hearing. Petitioner was subsequently indicted on a charge of having committed the robbery. Some time before the trial was held, Phillips moved to California. After putting in evidence to show that Phillips had moved and did not intend to return to Texas, the State at the trial offered the transcript of Phillips' testimony given at the preliminary hearing as evidence against petitioner. Petitioner's counsel immediately objected to introduction of the transcript, stating, "Your Honor, we will object to that, as it is a denial of the confrontment of the witnesses against the Defendant." Similar objections were repeatedly made by petitioner's counsel but were overruled by the trial judge, apparently in part because, as the judge viewed it, petitioner had been present at the preliminary hearing and therefore had been "accorded the opportunity of cross examining the witnesses there against him." The Texas Court of Criminal Appeals, the highest state court to which the case could be taken, affirmed petitioner's conviction, rejecting his contention that use of the transcript to convict him denied him rights guaranteed by the Sixth and Fourteenth Amendments. . . .

The Sixth Amendment is a part of what is called our Bill of Rights. In Gideon v. Wainwright, supra, in which this Court held that the Sixth Amendment's right to the assistance of counsel is obligatory upon the States, we did so on the ground that "a provision of the Bill of Rights which is 'fundamental and essential to a fair trial' is made obligatory upon the States by the Fourteenth Amendment." 372 U.S., at 342. . . . We hold today that the Sixth Amendment's right of an accused to confront the witnesses against him is likewise a fundamental right and is made obligatory on the States by the Fourteenth Amendment.

It cannot seriously be doubted at this late date that the right of cross-examination is included in the right of an accused in a criminal case to confront the witnesses against him. And probably no one, certainly no one experienced in the trial of lawsuits, would deny the value of cross-examination in exposing falsehood and bringing out the truth in the trial of a criminal case. See, e.g., 5 Wigmore, Evidence §1367 (3d ed. 1940). The fact that this right appears in the Sixth Amendment of our Bill of Rights reflects the belief of the Framers of those liberties and safeguards that confrontation was a fundamental right essential to a fair trial in a criminal prosecution. Moreover, the decisions of this Court and other courts throughout the years have constantly emphasized the necessity for cross-examination as a protection for defendants in criminal cases. . . .

This Court has recognized the admissibility against an accused of dying declarations, Mattox v. United States, 146 U.S. 140, 151, and of testimony of a deceased witness who has testified at a former trial. Mattox v. United States, 156 U.S. 237, 240-244. Nothing we hold here is to the contrary. The case before us would be quite a different one had Phillips' statement been taken at a full-fledged hearing at which petitioner had been represented by counsel who had been given a complete and adequate opportunity to cross-examine. Compare Motes v. United States, supra, 178 U.S., at 474. There are other analogous situations which might not fall within the scope of the constitutional rule requiring confrontation of witnesses. The case before us, however, does not present any situation like those mentioned above or others analogous to them. Because the transcript of Phillips' statement offered against petitioner at his trial had not been taken at a time and under circumstances affording petitioner through counsel an adequate opportunity to cross-examine Phillips, its introduction in a federal court in a criminal case against Pointer would have amounted to denial of the privilege of confrontation guaranteed by the Sixth Amendment. Since we hold that the right of an accused to be confronted with the witnesses against him must be determined by the same standards whether the right is denied in a federal or state proceeding, it follows that use of the transcript to convict petitioner denied him a constitutional right, and that his conviction must be reversed.

Reversed and remanded.

Which confrontation rule does the court apply in *Pointer*? This case frames the confrontation clause as a rule of admissibility; could it have been framed equally well as a rule of sufficiency? If cross-examination is the touchstone of confrontation, as it seems here, how can the use of dying declarations be rationalized? Were Phillips's statements under oath at the preliminary hearing less reliable than dying declarations?

DOUGLAS v. ALABAMA
380 U.S. 415 (1965)

Mr. Justice BRENNAN delivered the opinion of the Court.

The petitioner and one Loyd were tried separately in Alabama's Circuit Court on charges of assault with intent to murder. Loyd was tried first and was found guilty. The State then called Loyd as a witness at petitioner's trial. Because Loyd planned to appeal his conviction, his lawyer, who also represented petitioner, advised Loyd to rely on the privilege against self-incrimination and not to answer any questions. When Loyd was sworn, the lawyer objected, on self-incrimination grounds, "to this witness appearing on the stand," but the objection was overruled. Loyd gave his name and address but, invoking the privilege, refused to answer any questions concerning the alleged crime. The trial judge ruled that Loyd could not rely on the privilege because of his conviction, and ordered him to answer, but Loyd persisted in his refusal. The judge thereupon granted the State Solicitor's motion "to declare [Loyd] a hostile witness and give me the privilege of cross-examination." The Solicitor then produced a document said to be a confession signed by Loyd. Under the guise of cross-examination to refresh Loyd's recollection, the Solicitor purported to read from the document, pausing after every few sentences to ask Loyd, in the presence of the jury, "Did you make that statement?" Each time, Loyd asserted the privilege and refused to answer, but the Solicitor continued this form of questioning until the entire document had been read. The Solicitor then called three law enforcement officers who identified the document as embodying a confession made and signed by Loyd. Although marked as an exhibit for identification, the document was not offered in evidence.

This procedure, petitioner argues, violated his rights under the Confrontation Clause of the Sixth Amendment as applied to the States. The statements from the document as read by the Solicitor recited in considerable detail the circumstances leading to and surrounding the alleged crime; of crucial importance, they named the petitioner as the person who fired the shotgun blast which wounded the victim.[3] The jury found

---

3. Two of the Solicitor's questions were as follows:

"Did you make the further statement, 'We intended to shoot these trucks before they got to Centreville, but when we turned and went back north and passed the trucks again I was unable to bring myself to the point of shooting the trucks. After we passed the trucks this time we turned around and went south again toward Centreville, Alabama. These trucks were both stopped at a truck stop in Centreville where we passed them again and we proceeded on south on No. 5 about twenty miles. We sat alongside of the highway waiting for the trucks to come on and several trucks passed us, so we thought we ought to move before someone recognized us. We went back north again and saw a station wagon that looked suspicious so we turned off No. 5 onto 16. We drove over this route about six or eight miles and pulled in behind a church. We sat there for about five minutes and then heard what sounded like two trucks together going south on No. 5. We thought this was the two trucks and we went back to No. 5. When we got to No. 5 I told Douglas that I would drive and he said that was fine because I knew the car better than he. I drove on until we caught these trucks about five or eight miles above the junction of No. 5 and No. 80 and we passed them proceeding on to the junction where we turned around and headed back north to meet these trucks. Jesse Douglas was in the back seat with the automatic shotgun that belongs to B. F. Jackson and had it loaded with buckshot. He rolled down the window and when we passed these trucks he shot the lead truck as we passed them heading back north as they were coming south. We then went on to Highway 14, turned left and went into Greensboro, Alabama. We turned left in Greensboro on No. 69, drove south about five miles and realised we were going the wrong direction to go to Tuscaloosa, Alabama.

petitioner guilty. The Court of Appeals of Alabama affirmed, 42 Ala. App. 314, 163 So. 2d 477. . . .

In the circumstances of this case, petitioner's inability to cross-examine Loyd as to the alleged confession plainly denied him the right of cross-examination secured by the Confrontation Clause. Loyd's alleged statement that the petitioner fired the shotgun constituted the only direct evidence that he had done so; coupled with the description of the circumstances surrounding the shooting, this formed a crucial link in the proof both of petitioner's act and of the requisite intent to murder. Although the Solicitor's reading of Loyd's alleged statement, and Loyd's refusals to answer, were not technically testimony, the Solicitor's reading may well have been the equivalent in the jury's mind of testimony that Loyd in fact made the statement; and Loyd's reliance upon the privilege created a situation in which the jury might improperly infer both that the statement had been made and that it was true. Since the Solicitor was not a witness, the inference from his reading that Loyd made the statement could not be tested by cross-examination. Similarly, Loyd could not be cross-examined on a statement imputed to but not admitted by him. Nor was the opportunity to cross-examine the law enforcement officers adequate to redress this denial of the essential right secured by the Confrontation Clause. Indeed, their testimony enhanced the danger that the jury would treat the Solicitor's questioning of Loyd and Loyd's refusal to answer as proving the truth of Loyd's alleged confession. But since their evidence tended to show only that Loyd made the confession, cross-examination of them as to its genuineness could not substitute for cross-examination of Loyd to test the truth of the statement itself. Motes v. United States, 178 U.S. 458; cf. Kirby v. United States, 174 U.S. 47.

Hence, effective confrontation of Loyd was possible only if Loyd affirmed the statement as his. However, Loyd did not do so, but relied on his privilege to refuse to answer. We need not decide whether Loyd properly invoked the privilege in light of his conviction. It is sufficient for the purposes of deciding petitioner's claim under the Confrontation Clause that no suggestion is made that Loyd's refusal to answer was procured by the petitioner, see Motes v. United States, supra, at 471; on this record it appears that Loyd was acting entirely in his own interests in doing so. . . .

Would this evidence be admissible under the Federal Rules? What is the prosecution impeaching? Without Loyd's confession, is there

---

We turned around and went back up to No. 69 to Tuscaloosa.' Did you make that statement?"

"Were you asked the question, 'How many shots were fired at the truck?' And your answer, 'Only one.' Did you say that?"

sufficient evidence to sustain Douglas's conviction? What theory of the confrontation clause does Justice Brennan seem to adopt?

BARBER v. PAGE, WARDEN
390 U.S. 719 (1968)

Mr. Justice MARSHALL delivered the opinion of the Court.

The question presented is whether petitioner was deprived of his Sixth and Fourteenth Amendment right to be confronted with the witnesses against him at his trial in Oklahoma for armed robbery, at which the principal evidence against him consisted of the reading of a transcript of the preliminary hearing testimony of a witness who at the time of trial was incarcerated in a federal prison in Texas.

Petitioner and one Woods were jointly charged with the robbery, and at the preliminary hearing were represented by the same retained counsel, a Mr. Parks. During the course of the hearing, Woods agreed to waive his privilege against self-incrimination. Parks then withdrew as Woods' attorney but continued to represent petitioner. Thereupon Woods proceeded to give testimony that incriminated petitioner. Parks did not cross-examine Woods, although an attorney for another codefendant did.

By the time petitioner was brought to trial some seven months later, Woods was incarcerated in a federal penitentiary in Texarkana, Texas, about 225 miles from the trial court in Oklahoma. The State proposed to introduce against petitioner the transcript of Woods' testimony at the preliminary hearing on the ground that Woods was unavailable to testify because he was outside the jurisdiction. Petitioner objected to that course on the ground that it would deprive him of his right to be confronted with the witnesses against him. His objection was overruled and the transcript was admitted and read to the jury, which found him guilty. On appeal the Oklahoma Court of Criminal Appeals affirmed his conviction. . . .

Many years ago this Court stated that "[t]he primary object of the [Confrontation Clause of the Sixth Amendment] . . . was to prevent depositions or ex parte affidavits . . . being used against the prisoner in lieu of a personal examination and cross-examination of the witness in which the accused has an opportunity, not only of testing the recollection and sifting the conscience of the witness, but of compelling him to stand face to face with the jury in order that they may look at him, and judge by his demeanor upon the stand and the manner in which he gives his testimony whether he is worthy of belief." Mattox v. United States, 156 U.S. 237, 242-243 (1895). More recently, in holding the Sixth Amendment right of confrontation applicable to the States through the Fourteenth Amendment, this Court said, "There are few subjects, perhaps, upon which this Court and other courts have been more nearly unanimous than in their expressions of belief that the right of confrontation and cross-examination is an essential and fundamental requirement for the kind of fair trial which is this country's constitutional goal." Pointer v. Texas, 380 U.S. 400, 405 (1965).

It is true that there has traditionally been an exception to the confrontation requirement where a witness is unavailable and has given testimony at previous judicial proceedings against the same defendant which was subject to cross-examination by that defendant. E.g., Mattox v. United States, supra (witnesses who testified in original trial died prior to the second trial). This exception has been explained as arising from necessity and has been justified on the ground that the right of cross-examination initially afforded provides substantial compliance with the purposes behind the confrontation requirement. See 5 Wigmore, Evidence §§1395-1396, 1402 (3d ed. 1940); C. McCormick, Evidence §§231, 234 (1954).

Here the State argues that the introduction of the transcript is within that exception on the grounds that Woods was outside the jurisdiction and therefore "unavailable" at the time of trial, and that the right of cross-examination was afforded petitioner at the preliminary hearing, although not utilized then by him. For the purpose of this decision we shall assume that petitioner made a valid waiver of his right to cross-examine Woods at the preliminary hearing. . . .

We start with the fact that the State made absolutely no effort to obtain the presence of Woods at trial other than to ascertain that he was in a federal prison outside Oklahoma. It must be acknowledged that various courts and commentators have heretofore assumed that the mere absence of a witness from the jurisdiction was sufficient ground for dispensing with confrontation on the theory that "it is impossible to compel his attendance, because the process of the trial Court is of no force without the jurisdiction, and the party desiring his testimony is therefore helpless." 5 Wigmore, Evidence §1404 (3d ed. 1940).

Whatever may have been the accuracy of that theory at one time, it is clear that at the present time increased cooperation between the States themselves and between the States and the Federal Government has largely deprived it of any continuing validity in the criminal law. . . .

The Court of Appeals majority appears to have reasoned that because the State would have had to request an exercise of discretion on the part of federal authorities, it was under no obligation to make any such request. Yet as Judge Aldrich, sitting by designation, pointed out in dissent below, "the possibility of a refusal is not the equivalent of asking and receiving a rebuff." 381 F.2d, at 481. In short, a witness is not "unavailable" for purposes of the foregoing exception to the confrontation requirement unless the prosecutorial authorities have made a good-faith effort to obtain his presence at trial. The State made no such effort here, and, so far as this record reveals, the sole reason why Woods was not present to testify in person was because the State did not attempt to seek his presence. The right of confrontation may not be dispensed with so lightly. . . .

Moreover, we would reach the same result on the facts of this case had petitioner's counsel actually cross-examined Woods at the preliminary hearing. See Motes v. United States, 178 U.S. 458 (1900). The right to confrontation is basically a trial right. It includes both the opportunity to cross-examine and the occasion for the jury to weigh the demeanor of the witness. A preliminary hearing is ordinarily a much less searching exploration into the merits of a case than a trial, simply because its function is the more limited one of determining whether probable cause exists to hold the accused for trial. While there may be some justification for holding that the opportunity for cross-examination of a witness at a preliminary hearing satisfies the demands of the confrontation clause where the witness is shown to be actually unavailable, this is not, as we have pointed out, such a case. . . .

––––––––––––––

Should it make any difference that the defendant also made no effort to obtain Woods's presence at trial? How does the defendant's right to compulsory process relate to the confrontation clause? Does this case depend on the prosecution's *peculiar* ability to obtain cooperation from federal authority? Would the case be stronger or weaker if Woods were in Oklahoma and easily available to either side but simply not called?

BRUTON v. UNITED STATES
391 U.S. 123 (1968)

Mr. Justice BRENNAN delivered the opinion of the Court.

This case presents the question, last considered in Delli Paoli v. United States, 352 U.S. 232, whether the conviction of a defendant at a joint trial should be set aside although the jury was instructed that a codefendant's confession inculpating the defendant had to be disregarded in determining his guilt or innocence.

A joint trial of petitioner and one Evans in the District Court for the Eastern District of Missouri resulted in the conviction of both by a jury on a federal charge of armed postal robbery, 18 U.S.C. §2114. A postal inspector testified that Evans orally confessed to him that Evans and petitioner committed the armed robbery. The postal inspector obtained the oral confession, and another in which Evans admitted he had an accomplice whom he would not name, in the course of two interrogations of Evans at the city jail in St. Louis, Missouri, where Evans was held in custody on state criminal charges. Both petitioner and Evans appealed their convictions to the Court of Appeals for the Eighth Circuit. That court set aside Evans' conviction on the ground that his oral confessions to the postal inspector should not have been received in evidence against him. 375 F.2d 355, 361. However, the court, relying upon *Delli Paoli*, affirmed petitioner's conviction because the trial judge instructed the jury that although Evans' confession was competent evidence against Evans it was inadmissible hearsay against petitioner and therefore had to be disregarded in determining petitioner's guilt or innocence. 375 F.2d, at 361-363.[2] We granted certiorari to reconsider *Delli Paoli*. 389 U.S. 818. The Solicitor General has since submitted a memorandum stating that "in the light of the record in this particular case and in the interests of justice, the judgment below should be reversed and the cause remanded for a new trial." The Solicitor General states that this disposition is urged in part because "[h]ere it has been determined that the confession was wrongly admitted against [Evans] and his conviction has been reversed, leading to a new trial at which he was acquitted. To argue, in this situation, that [petitioner's] conviction should nevertheless stand may be to place too great a strain upon the [*Delli Paoli*] rule — at least, where, as here, the other evidence against [petitioner] is not strong." We have concluded, however, that *Delli Paoli* should be overruled. We hold that, because of the substantial risk that the jury, despite instructions to the contrary, looked to the incriminating extrajudicial statements in determining petitioner's guilt, admission of Evans' confession in this joint trial violated petitioner's right of cross-examination secured by the Confrontation Clause of the Sixth Amendment. We therefore overrule *Delli Paoli* and reverse. . . .

Delli Paoli assumed that . . . encroachment on the right to confrontation could be avoided by the instruction to the jury to disregard the inadmissible hearsay evidence. But . . . that assumption has since been

---

2. At the close of the Government's direct case, the trial judge cautioned the jury that Evans' admission implicating petitioner "if used, can only be used against the defendant Evans. It is hearsay insofar as the defendant George William Bruton is concerned, and you are not to consider it in any respect to the defendant Bruton, because insofar as he is concerned it is hearsay."

The instructions to the jury included the following:

"A confession made outside of court by one defendant may not be considered as evidence against the other defendant, who was not present and in no way a party to the confession. Therefore, if you find that a confession was in fact voluntarily and intentionally made by the defendant Evans, you should consider it as evidence in the case against Evans, but you must not consider it, and should disregard it, in considering the evidence in the case against the defendant Bruton. . . .

"It is your duty to give separate, personal consideration to the cause of each individual defendant. When you do so, you should analyze what the evidence shows with respect to that individual, leaving out of consideration entirely any evidence admitted solely against some other defendant. Each defendant is entitled to have his case determined from his own acts and statements and the other evidence in the case which may be applicable to him."

effectively repudiated. True, the repudiation was not in the context of the admission of a confession inculpating a codefendant but in the context of a New York rule which submitted to the jury the question of the voluntariness of the confession itself. Jackson v. Denno, 378 U.S. 368. Nonetheless the message of *Jackson* for *Delli Paoli* was clear. We there held that a defendant is constitutionally entitled at least to have the trial judge first determine whether a confession was made voluntarily before submitting it to the jury for an assessment of its credibility. More specifically, we expressly rejected the proposition that a jury, when determining the confessor's guilt, could be relied on to ignore his confession of guilt should it find the confession involuntary. Id. at 388-389. Significantly, we supported that conclusion in part by reliance upon the dissenting opinion of Mr. Justice Frankfurter for the four Justices who dissented in Delli Paoli. . . .

We, of course, acknowledge the impossibility of determining whether in fact the jury did or did not ignore Evans' statement inculpating petitioner in determining petitioner's guilt. But that was also true in the analogous situation in Jackson v. Denno, and was not regarded as militating against striking down the New York procedure there involved. It was enough that that procedure posed "substantial threats to a defendant's constitutional rights to have an involuntary confession entirely disregarded and to have the coercion issue fairly and reliably determined. These hazards we cannot ignore." 378 U.S., at 389. Here the introduction of Evans' confession posed a substantial threat to petitioner's right to confront the witnesses against him, and this is a hazard we cannot ignore. Despite the concededly clear instructions to the jury to disregard Evans' inadmissible hearsay evidence inculpating petitioner, in the context of a joint trial we cannot accept limiting instructions as an adequate substitute for petitioner's constitutional right of cross-examination. The effect is the same as if there had been no instruction at all.

Reversed.

Mr. Justice WHITE, dissenting. . . .

The defendant's own confession may not be used against him if coerced, not because it is untrue but to protect other constitutional values. The jury may have great difficulty understanding such a rule and following an instruction to disregard the confession. In contrast, the codefendant's admissions cannot enter into the determination of the defendant's guilt or innocence because they are unreliable. This the jury can be told and can understand. Just as the Court believes that juries can reasonably be expected to disregard ordinary hearsay or other inadmissible evidence when instructed to do so, I believe juries will disregard the portions of a codefendant's confession implicating the defendant when so instructed. Indeed, if we must pick and choose between hearsay as to which limiting instructions will be deemed effective and hearsay the admission of which cannot be cured by instructions, codefendants' admissions belong in the former category rather than the latter, for they are not only hearsay but hearsay which is doubly suspect. If the Court is right in believing that a jury can be counted on to ignore a wide range of hearsay statements which it is told to ignore, it seems very odd to me to question its ability to put aside the codefendant's hearsay statements about what the defendant did. . . .

Why was Evans's confession inadmissible against Bruton? Does the sixth amendment require exclusion of Evans's statement against Bruton? Why?

Besides the *Bruton* situation, what other contexts exist in which "the risk that the jury will not, or cannot, follow instructions is so great, and the consequences of failure so vital to the defendant, that the practical limitations of the jury system cannot be ignored"? Or to use Justice Stewart's phraseology, what kinds of hearsay are "at once so damaging, so suspect, and yet so difficult to discount, that jurors cannot be trusted to give such evidence the minimal weight it logically deserves, *whatever* instructions the trial judge might give," 391 U.S. at 138 (Stewart, J., concurring), and thus barred by the confrontation clause? Do not dangers of jury misuse of evidence exist whenever evidence that would be hearsay if admitted to prove the truth of its content is admitted for a nonhearsay purpose, such as proving knowledge? What principles would you apply to "pick and choose" between hearsay which may be admitted with curative instructions and that which cannot be cured with instructions? 391 U.S. at 142 (White, J., dissenting).

Does *Bruton* cast doubt on the constitutionality of the admissibility of all co-conspirators' statements under Rule 801(d)(2)(E)? Or does the existence of Rule 801(d)(2)(E) lend support to the notion that it was the unreliability of the particular evidence in *Bruton* (i.e., its self-serving, after-the-fact, finger-pointing quality), rather than the unavailability of the declarant, that was crucial in *Bruton*?

HARRINGTON v. CALIFORNIA
395 U.S. 250 (1969)

Mr. Justice Douglas delivered the opinion of the Court.

We held in Chapman v. California, 386 U.S. 18, that "before a federal constitutional error can be held harmless, the court must be able to declare a belief that it was harmless beyond a reasonable doubt." Id., at 24. We said that, although "there are some constitutional rights so basic to a fair trial that their infraction can never be treated as harmless error" (id., at 23), not all "trial errors which violate the Constitution automatically call for reversal." Ibid.

The question whether the alleged error in the present case was "harmless" under the rule of *Chapman* arose in a state trial for attempted robbery and first-degree murder. Four men were tried together — Harrington, a Caucasian, and Bosby, Rhone, and Cooper, Negroes — over an objection by Harrington that his trial should be severed. Each of his three codefendants confessed and their confessions were introduced at the trial with limiting instructions that the jury was to consider each confession only against the confessor. Rhone took the stand and Harrington's counsel cross-examined him. The other two did not take the stand.[1]

In Bruton v. United States, 391 U.S. 123, a confession of a codefendant who did not take the stand was used against Bruton in a federal prosecution. We held that Bruton had been denied his rights under the Confrontation Clause of the Sixth Amendment. Since the Confrontation Clause is applicable as well in state trials by reason of the Due Process Clause of the Fourteenth Amendment (Pointer v. Texas, 380 U.S. 400), the rule of *Bruton* applies here.

The California Court of Appeal affirmed the convictions, 256 Cal. App. 2d 209, 64 Cal. Rptr. 159, and the Supreme Court denied a petition for a hearing. We granted the petition for certiorari to consider whether the violation of *Bruton* was on these special facts harmless error under *Chapman*.

Petitioner made statements which fell short of a confession but which placed him at the scene of the crime. He admitted that Bosby was the trigger man; that he fled with the other three; and that after the murder he dyed his hair black and shaved off his moustache. Several eyewitnesses placed petitioner at the scene of the crime. But two of them had previously told the police that four Negroes committed the crime. Rhone's confession, however, placed Harrington inside the store with a gun at the time of the attempted robbery and murder.

Cooper's confession did not refer to Harrington by name. He referred to the fourth man as "the white boy" or "this white guy." And he described him by age, height, and weight.

Bosby's confession likewise did not mention Harrington by name but referred to him as a blond-headed fellow or "the white guy" or "the Patty."

Both Cooper and Bosby said in their confessions that they did not see "the white guy" with a gun, which is at variance with the testimony of the prosecution witnesses.

---

1. All four were found to have participated in an attempted robbery in the course of which a store employee was killed. Each was found guilty of felony murder and sentenced to life imprisonment.

Petitioner argues that it is irrelevant that he was not named in Cooper's and Bosby's confessions, that reference to "the white guy" made it as clear as pointing and shouting that the person referred to was the white man in the dock with the three Negroes. We make the same assumption. But we conclude that on these special facts the lack of opportunity to cross-examine Cooper and Bosby constituted harmless error under the rule of *Chapman*.

Rhone, whom Harrington's counsel cross-examined, placed him in the store with a gun at the time of the murder. Harrington himself agreed he was there. Others testified he had a gun and was an active participant. Cooper and Bosby did not put a gun in his hands when he denied it. They did place him at the scene of the crime. But others, including Harrington himself, did the same. Their evidence, supplied through their confessions, was of course cumulative. But apart from them the case against Harrington was so overwhelming that we conclude that this violation of *Bruton* was harmless beyond a reasonable doubt, unless we adopt the minority view in *Chapman* (386 U.S., at 42-45) that a departure from constitutional procedures should result in an automatic reversal, regardless of the weight of the evidence.

It is argued that we must reverse if we can imagine a single juror whose mind might have been made up because of Cooper's and Bosby's confessions and who otherwise would have remained in doubt and unconvinced. We of course do not know the jurors who sat. Our judgment must be based on our own reading of the record and on what seems to us to have been the probable impact of the two confessions on the minds of an average jury. We admonished in *Chapman*, 386 U.S., at 23, against giving too much emphasis to "overwhelming evidence" of guilt, stating that constitutional errors affecting the substantial rights of the aggrieved party could not be considered to be harmless. By that test we cannot impute reversible weight to the two confessions.

We do not depart from *Chapman*; nor do we dilute it by inference. We reaffirm it. We do not suggest that, if evidence bearing on all the ingredients of the crime is tendered, the use of cumulative evidence, though tainted, is harmless error. Our decision is based on the evidence in this record. The case against Harrington was not woven from circumstantial evidence. It is so overwhelming that unless we say that no violation of *Bruton* can constitute harmless error, we must leave this state conviction undisturbed.

Affirmed.

Despite the Court's disclaimer in the last paragraph of the opinion, has the Court effectively announced a sufficiency rule? Is harmless error really error at all?

CALIFORNIA v. GREEN
399 U.S. 149 (1970)

Mr. Justice WHITE delivered the opinion of the Court.

Section 1235 of the California Evidence Code, effective as of January 1, 1967, provides that "[e]vidence of a statement made by a witness is not made inadmissible by the hearsay rule if the statement is inconsistent with his testimony at the hearing and is offered in compliance with Section 770."[1] In People v. Johnson, 68 Cal. 2d 646, 441 P.2d 111 (1968), cert. denied, 393 U.S. 1051 (1969), the California Supreme Court held that prior statements of a witness that were not subject to cross-examination when originally made, could not be introduced under this section to prove the charges against a defendant without violating the defendant's right of confrontation guaranteed by the Sixth Amendment and made applicable to the States by the Fourteenth Amendment. In the case now before us the California Supreme Court applied the same ban to a prior statement of a witness made at a preliminary hearing, under oath and subject to full cross-examination by an adequately counseled defendant. We cannot agree with the California court for two reasons, one of which involves rejection of the holding in People v. Johnson.

I

In January 1967, one Melvin Porter, a 16-year-old minor, was arrested for selling marihuana to an undercover police officer. Four days after his arrest, while in the custody of juvenile authorities, Porter named respondent Green as his supplier. As recounted later by one Officer Wade, Porter claimed that Green had called him earlier that month, had asked him to sell some "stuff" or grass, and had that same afternoon personally delivered a shopping bag containing 29 "baggies" of marihuana. It was from this supply that Porter had made his sale to the undercover officer. A week later, Porter testified at respondent's preliminary hearing. He again named respondent as his supplier, although he now claimed that instead of personally delivering the marihuana, Green had showed him where to pick up the shopping bag, hidden in the bushes at Green's parents' house. Porter's story at the preliminary hearing was subjected to extensive cross-examination by respondent's counsel — the same counsel who represented respondent at his subsequent trial. At the conclusion of the hearing, respondent was charged with furnishing marihuana to a minor in violation of California law.

1. Cal. Evid. Code §1235 (1966). Section 770 merely requires that the witness be given an opportunity to explain or deny the prior statement at some point in the trial. See Cal. Evid. Code §770 (1966).

Respondent's trial took place some two months later before a court sitting without a jury. The State's chief witness was again young Porter. But this time Porter, in the words of the California Supreme Court, proved to be "markedly evasive and uncooperative on the stand." People v. Green, 70 Cal. 2d 654, 657, 451 P.2d 422, 423 (1969). He testified that respondent had called him in January 1967, and asked him to sell some unidentified "stuff." He admitted obtaining shortly thereafter 29 plastic "baggies" of marihuana, some of which he sold. But when pressed as to whether respondent had been his supplier, Porter claimed that he was uncertain how he obtained the marihuana, primarily because he was at the time on "acid" (LSD), which he had taken 20 minutes before respondent phoned. Porter claimed that he was unable to remember the events that followed the phone call, and that the drugs he had taken prevented his distinguishing fact from fantasy.

At various points during Porter's direct examination, the prosecutor read excerpts from Porter's preliminary hearing testimony. This evidence was admitted under §1235 for the truth of the matter contained therein. With his memory "refreshed" by his preliminary hearing testimony, Porter "guessed" that he had indeed obtained the marihuana from the backyard of respondent's parents' home, and had given the money from its sale to respondent. On cross-examination, however, Porter indicated that it was his memory of the preliminary testimony which was "mostly" refreshed, rather than his memory of the events themselves, and he was still unsure of the actual episode. Later in the trial, Officer Wade testified, relating Porter's earlier statement that respondent had personally delivered the marihuana. This statement was also admitted as substantive evidence. Porter admitted making the statement, and insisted that he had been telling the truth as he then believed it both to Officer Wade and at the preliminary hearing; but he insisted that he was also telling the truth now in claiming inability to remember the actual events.

Respondent was convicted. The District Court of Appeal reversed, holding that the use of Porter's prior statements for the truth of the matter asserted therein, denied respondent his right of confrontation under the California Supreme Court's recent decision in People v. Johnson, supra. The California Supreme Court affirmed, finding itself "impelled" by recent decisions of this Court to hold §1235 unconstitutional insofar as it permitted the substantive use of prior inconsistent statements of a witness, even though the statements were subject to cross-examination at a prior hearing. We granted the State's petition for certiorari, 396 U.S. 1001 (1970).

II

The California Supreme Court construed the Confrontation Clause of the Sixth Amendment to require the exclusion of Porter's prior testimony offered in evidence to prove the State's case against Green because, in the court's view, neither the right to cross-examine Porter at the trial concerning his current and prior testimony, nor the opportunity to cross-examine Porter at the preliminary hearing satisfied the commands of the Confrontation Clause. We think the California court was wrong on both counts. . . .

Section 1235 of the California Evidence Code represents a considered choice by the California Legislature between two opposing positions concerning the extent to which a witness' prior statements may be introduced at trial without violating hearsay rules of evidence. The orthodox view, adopted in most jurisdictions, has been that the out-of-court statements are inadmissible for the usual reasons that have led to the exclusion of hearsay statements: the statement may not have been made under oath; the declarant may not have been subjected to cross-examination when he made the statement; and the jury cannot observe the declarant's demeanor at the time he made the statement. Accordingly, under this view, the statement may not be offered to show the truth of the matters asserted therein, but can be introduced under appropriate limiting instructions to impeach the credibility of the witness who has changed his story at trial.

In contrast, the minority view adopted in some jurisdictions and supported by most legal commentators and by recent proposals to codify the law of evidence would permit the substantive use of prior inconsistent statements on the theory that the usual dangers of hearsay are largely nonexistent where the witness testifies at trial. "The whole purpose of the Hearsay rule has been already satisfied [because] the witness is present and subject to cross-examination [and] [t]here is ample opportunity to test him as to the basis for his former statement."

Our task in this case is not to decide which of these positions, purely as a matter of the law of evidence, is the sounder. The issue before us is the considerably narrower one of whether a defendant's constitutional right "to be confronted with the witnesses against him" is necessarily inconsistent with a State's decision to change its hearsay rules to reflect the minority view described above. While it may readily be conceded that hearsay rules and the Confrontation Clause are generally designed to protect similar values, it is quite a different thing to suggest that the overlap is complete and that the Confrontation Clause is nothing more or less than a codification of the rules of hearsay and their exceptions as they existed historically at common law. Our decisions have never established such a congruency; indeed, we have more than once found a violation of confrontation values even though the statements in issue were admitted under an arguably recognized hearsay exception. See Barber v. Page, 390 U.S. 719 (1968); Pointer v. Texas, 380 U.S. 400 (1965). The converse is equally true: merely because evidence is admitted in violation of a long-established hearsay rule does not lead to the automatic conclusion that confrontation rights have been denied.

Given the similarity of the values protected, however, the modification of a State's hearsay rules to create new exceptions for the admission of evidence against a defendant, will often raise questions of compatibility with the defendant's constitutional right to confrontation. Such questions require attention to the reasons for, and the basic scope of, the protections offered by the Confrontation Clause.

The origin and development of the hearsay rules and of the Confrontation Clause have been traced by others and need not be recounted in detail here. It is sufficient to note that the particular vice that gave impetus to the confrontation claim was the practice of trying defendants on "evidence" which consisted solely of ex parte affidavits or depositions secured by the examining magistrates, thus denying the defendant the opportunity to challenge his accuser in a face-to-face encounter in front of the trier of fact. Prosecuting attorneys "would frequently allege matters which the prisoner denied and called upon them to prove. The proof was usually given by reading depositions, confessions of accomplices, letters, and the like; and this occasioned frequent demands by the prisoner to have his 'accusers,' i.e. the witnesses against him, brought before him face to face. . . ."[10]

But objections occasioned by this practice appear primarily to have been aimed at the failure to call the witness to confront personally the defendant at his trial. So far as appears, in claiming confrontation rights no objection was made against receiving a witness' out-of-court depositions or statements, so long as the witness was present at trial to repeat his story and to explain or repudiate any conflicting prior stories before the trier of fact.

Our own decisions seem to have recognized at an early date that it is this literal right to "confront" the witness at the time of trial that forms the core of the values furthered by the Confrontation Clause:

"The primary object of the constitutional provision in question was to prevent depositions or ex parte affidavits, such as were sometimes admitted in civil cases, being used against the prisoner in lieu of a personal examination and cross-examination of the witness in which the accused has an opportunity, not only of testing the recollection and sifting the conscience of the witness, but of compelling him to stand face to face with the jury in order that they may look at him, and judge by his demeanor upon the stand and the manner in which he gives his testimony whether he is worthy of belief." Mattox v. United States, 156 U.S. 237, 242-243 (1895). Viewed historically, then, there is good reason to conclude that the Confrontation Clause is not violated by admitting a

---

10. 1 J. Stephen, A History of the Criminal Law of England 326 (1883). See also [9 W. Holdsworth, A History of English Law 225-228 n.9 (3d ed. 1944)].

A famous example is provided by the trial of Sir Walter Raleigh for treason in 1603. At least one author traces the Confrontation Clause to the common-law reaction against these abuses of the Raleigh trial. See F. Heller, The Sixth Amendment 104 (1951).

declarant's out-of-court statements, as long as the declarant is testifying as a witness and subject to full and effective cross-examination.

This conclusion is supported by comparing the purposes of confrontation with the alleged dangers in admitting an out-of-court statement. Confrontation: (1) insures that the witness will give his statements under oath — thus impressing him with the seriousness of the matter and guarding against the lie by the possibility of a penalty for perjury; (2) forces the witness to submit to cross-examination, the "greatest legal engine ever invented for the discovery of truth"; (3) permits the jury that is to decide the defendant's fate to observe the demeanor of the witness in making his statement, thus aiding the jury in assessing his credibility.

It is, of course, true that the out-of-court statement may have been made under circumstances subject to none of these protections. But if the declarant is present and testifying at trial, the out-of-court statement for all practical purposes regains most of the lost protections. If the witness admits the prior statement is his, or if there is other evidence to show the statement is his, the danger of faulty reproduction is negligible and the jury can be confident that it has before it two conflicting statements by the same witness. Thus, as far as the oath is concerned, the witness must now affirm, deny, or qualify the truth of the prior statement under the penalty of perjury; indeed, the very fact that the prior statement was not given under a similar circumstance may become the witness' explanation for its inaccuracy — an explanation a jury may be expected to understand and take into account in deciding which, if either, of the statements represents the truth.

Second, the inability to cross-examine the witness at the time he made his prior statement cannot easily be shown to be of crucial significance as long as the defendant is assured of full and effective cross-examination at the time of trial. The most successful cross-examination at the time the prior statement was made could hardly hope to accomplish more than has already been accomplished by the fact that the witness is now telling a different, inconsistent story, and — in this case — one that is favorable to the defendant. We cannot share the California Supreme Court's view that belated cross-examination can never serve as a constitutionally adequate substitute for cross-examination contemporaneous with the original statement. The main danger in substituting subsequent for timely cross-examination seems to lie in the possibility that the witness' "[f]alse testimony is apt to harden and become unyielding to the blows of truth in proportion as the witness has opportunity for reconsideration and influence by the suggestions of others, whose interest may be, and often is, to maintain falsehood rather than truth." State v. Saporen, 205 Minn. 358, 362, 285 N.W. 898, 901 (1939). That danger, however, disappears when the witness has changed his testimony so that, far from "hardening," his prior statement has softened to the point where he now repudiates it.

The defendant's task in cross-examination is, of course, no longer identical to the task that he would have faced if the witness had not changed his story and hence had to be examined as a "hostile" witness giving evidence for the prosecution. This difference, however, far from lessening, may actually enhance the defendant's ability to attack the prior statement. For the witness, favorable to the defendant, should be more than willing to give the usual suggested explanations for the inaccuracy of his prior statement, such as faulty perception or undue haste in recounting the event. Under such circumstances, the defendant is not likely to be hampered in effectively attacking the prior statement, solely because his attack comes later in time.

Similar reasons lead us to discount as a constitutional matter the fact that the jury at trial is foreclosed from viewing the declarant's demeanor when he first made his out-of-court statement. The witness who now relates a different story about the events in question must necessarily assume a position as to the truth value of his prior statement, thus giving the jury a chance to observe and evaluate his demeanor as he either disavows or qualifies his earlier statement. The jury is alerted by the inconsistency in the stories, and its attention is sharply focused on determining either that one of the stories reflects the truth or that the witness who has apparently lied once, is simply too lacking in credibility to warrant its believing either story. The defendant's confrontation rights are not violated, even though some demeanor evidence that would have been relevant in resolving this credibility issue is forever lost.

It may be true that a jury would be in a better position to evaluate the truth of the prior statement if it could somehow be whisked magically back in time to witness a gruelling cross-examination of the declarant as he first gives his statement. But the question as we see it must be not whether one can somehow imagine the jury in "a better position," but whether subsequent cross-examination at the defendant's trial will still afford the trier of fact a satisfactory basis for evaluating the truth of the prior statement. On that issue, neither evidence nor reason convinces us that contemporaneous cross-examination before the ultimate trier of fact is so much more effective than subsequent examination that it must be made the touchstone of the Confrontation Clause.

Finally, we note that none of our decisions interpreting the Confrontation Clause requires excluding the out-of-court statements of a witness who is available and testifying at trial. The concern of most of our cases has been focused on precisely the opposite situation — situations where statements have been admitted in the absence of the declarant and without any chance to cross-examine him at trial. These situations have arisen through application of a number of traditional "exceptions" to the hearsay rule, which permit the introduction of evidence despite the absence of the declarant usually on the theory that the evidence possesses other indicia of "reliability" and is incapable of being admitted, despite good-faith efforts of the State, in any way that will secure confrontation with the declarant. Such exceptions, dispensing altogether with the literal right to "confrontation" and cross-examination, have been subjected on several occasions to careful scrutiny by this Court. . . .

We have no occasion in the present case to map out a theory of the Confrontation Clause that would determine the validity of all such hearsay "exceptions" permitting the introduction of an absent declarant's statements. For where the declarant is not absent, but is present to testify and to submit to cross-examination, our cases, if anything, support the conclusion that the admission of his out-of-court statements does not create a confrontation problem. . . .

. . . [I]n Bruton v. United States, 391 U.S. 123 (1968), the Court found a violation of confrontation rights in the admission of a co-defendant's confession, implicating Bruton, where the co-defendant did not take the stand. The Court again emphasized that the error arose because the declarant "does not testify and cannot be tested by cross-examination," 391 U.S., at 136, suggesting that no confrontation problem would have existed if Bruton had been able to cross-examine his co-defendant. Cf. Harrington v. California, 395 U.S. 250, 252-253 (1969). Indeed, *Bruton*'s refusal to regard limiting instructions as capable of curing the error, suggests that there is little difference as far as the Constitution is concerned between permitting prior inconsistent statements to be used only for impeachment purposes, and permitting them to be used for substantive purposes as well.

We find nothing, then, in either the history or the purposes of the Confrontation Clause, or in the prior decisions of this Court, that compels the conclusion reached by the California Supreme Court concerning the validity of California's §1235. Contrary to the judgment of that court, the Confrontation Clause does not require excluding from evidence the prior statements of a witness who concedes making the statements, and who may be asked to defend or otherwise explain the inconsistency between his prior and his present version of the events in question, thus opening himself to full cross-examination at trial as to both stories.

III

We also think that Porter's preliminary hearing testimony was admissible as far as the Constitution is concerned wholly apart from the question of whether respondent had an effective opportunity for confrontation at the subsequent trial. For Porter's statement at the preliminary hearing had already been given under circumstances closely approximating those that surround the typical trial. Porter was under oath; respondent was represented by counsel — the same counsel in fact who later represented him at the trial; respondent had every opportunity to cross-examine Porter as to his statement; and the proceedings were conducted before a judicial tribunal, equipped to provide a judicial record of the hearings. Under these circumstances, Porter's statement would, we think, have been admissible at trial even in Porter's absence if Porter had been actually unavailable, despite good-faith efforts of the State to produce him. That being the case, we do not think a different result should follow where the witness is actually produced.

This Court long ago held that admitting the prior testimony of an unavailable witness does not violate the Confrontation Clause. Mattox v. United States, 156 U.S. 237 (1895). That case involved testimony given at the defendant's first trial by a witness who had died by the time of the second trial, but we do not find the instant preliminary hearing significantly different from an actual trial to warrant distinguishing the two cases for purposes of the Confrontation Clause. Indeed, we indicated as much in Pointer v. Texas, 380 U.S. 400, 407 (1965), where we noted that "[t]he case before us would be quite a different one had Phillips' statement been taken at a full-fledged hearing at which petitioner had been represented by counsel who had been given a complete and adequate opportunity to cross-examine." And in Barber v. Page, 390 U.S. 719, 725-726 (1968), although noting that the preliminary hearing is ordinarily a less searching exploration into the merits of a case than a trial, we recognized that "there may be some justification for holding that the opportunity for cross-examination of a witness at a preliminary hearing satisfies the demands of the confrontation clause where the witness is shown to be actually unavailable. . . ." In the present case respondent's counsel does not appear to have been significantly limited in any way in the scope or nature of his cross-examination of the witness Porter at the preliminary hearing. If Porter had died or was otherwise unavailable, the Confrontation Clause would not have been violated by admitting his testimony given at the preliminary hearing — the right of cross-examination then afforded provides substantial compliance with the purposes behind the confrontation requirement, as long as the declarant's inability to give live testimony is in no way the fault of the State. Compare Barber v. Page, supra, with Motes v. United States, 178 U.S. 458 (1900).

But nothing in Barber v. Page or in other cases in this Court indicates that a different result must follow where the State produces the declarant and swears him as a witness at the trial. It may be that the rules of evidence applicable in state or federal courts would restrict resort to prior sworn testimony where the declarant is present at the trial. But as a constitutional matter, it is untenable to construe the Confrontation Clause to permit the use of prior testimony to prove the State's case where the declarant never appears, but to bar that testimony where the declarant is present at the trial, exposed to the defendant and the trier of fact, and subject to cross-examination. As in the case where the witness is physically unproducible, the State here has made every effort to introduce its evidence through the live testimony of the witness; it produced Porter at trial, swore him as a witness, and tendered him for cross-examination. Whether Porter then testified in a manner consistent or inconsistent with his preliminary hearing testimony, claimed a loss of memory, claimed his privilege against compulsory self-incrimination, or simply refused to answer, nothing in the Confrontation Clause prohibited the State from also relying on his prior testimony to prove its case against Green.

IV

There is a narrow question lurking in this case concerning the admissibility of Porter's statements to Officer Wade. In the typical case to which the California court addressed itself, the witness at trial gives a version of the ultimate events different from that given on a prior occasion. In such a case, as our holding in Part II makes clear, we find little reason to distinguish among prior inconsistent statements on the basis of the circumstances under which the prior statements were given. The subsequent opportunity for cross-examination at trial with respect to both present and past versions of the event, is adequate to make equally admissible, as far as the Confrontation Clause is concerned, both the casual, off-hand remark to a stranger, and the carefully recorded testimony at a prior hearing. Here, however, Porter claimed at trial that he could not remember the events that occurred after respondent telephoned him and hence failed to give any current version of the more important events described in his earlier statement.

Whether Porter's apparent lapse of memory so affected Green's right to cross-examine as to make a critical difference in the application of the Confrontation Clause in this case is an issue which is not ripe for decision at this juncture. The state court did not focus on this precise question, which was irrelevant given its broader and erroneous premise that an out-of-court statement of a witness is inadmissible as substantive evidence, whatever the nature of the opportunity to cross-examine at the trial. Nor has either party addressed itself to the question. Its resolution depends much upon the unique facts in this record, and we are reluctant to proceed without the state court's views of what the record actually discloses relevant to this particular issue.

We therefore vacate the judgment of the California Supreme Court and remand the case to that court for further proceedings not inconsistent with this opinion.

It is so ordered.

Mr. Justice HARLAN, concurring.

The precise holding of the court today is that the Confrontation Clause of the Sixth Amendment does not preclude the introduction of an out-of-court declaration, taken under oath and subject to cross-examination, to prove the truth of the matters asserted therein, when the declarant is available as a witness at trial. With this I agree.

The California decision that we today reverse demonstrates, however, the need to approach this case more broadly than the Court has seen fit to do, and to confront squarely the Confrontation Clause because the holding of the California Supreme Court is the result of an understandable misconception, as I see things, of numerous decisions of this Court, old and recent, that have indiscriminately equated "confrontation" with "cross-examination."

These decisions have, in my view, left ambiguous whether and to what extent the Sixth Amendment "constitutionalizes" the hearsay rule of the common law.

If "confrontation" is to be equated with the right to cross-examine, it would transplant the ganglia of hearsay rules and their exceptions into the body of constitutional protections. The stultifying effect of such a course upon this aspect of the law of evidence in both state and federal systems need hardly be labored, and it is good that the Court today, as I read its opinion, firmly eschews that course.

Since, in my opinion, this state decision imperatively demonstrates the need for taking a fresh look at the constitutional concept of "confrontation," I do not think that stare decisis should be allowed to stand in the way, albeit the presently controlling cases are of recent vintage. As the Court's opinion suggests, the Confrontation Clause comes to us on faded parchment. History seems to give us very little insight into the intended scope of the Sixth Amendment Confrontation Clause. Commentators have been prone to slide too easily from confrontation to cross-examination.

Against this amorphous backdrop I reach two conclusions. First, the Confrontation Clause of the Sixth Amendment reaches no farther than to require the prosecution to *produce* any *available* witness whose declarations it seeks to use in a criminal trial. Second, even were this conclusion deemed untenable as a matter of Sixth Amendment law, it is surely agreeable to Fourteenth Amendment "due process," which, in my view, is the constitutional framework in which state cases of this kind should be judged. For it could scarcely be suggested that the Fourteenth Amendment takes under its umbrella all common-law hearsay rules and their exceptions.

The text of the Sixth Amendment reads: "In all criminal prosecutions, the accused shall enjoy the right . . . to be confronted with the witnesses against him." Simply as a matter of English the clause may be read to confer nothing more than a right to meet face to face all those who appear and give evidence at trial. Since, however, an extrajudicial declarant is no less a "witness," the clause is equally susceptible of being interpreted as a blanket prohibition on the use of any hearsay testimony.

Neither of these polar readings is wholly satisfactory, still less compelling. Similar guarantees to those of the Sixth Amendment are found in a number of the colonial constitutions and it appears to have been assumed that a confrontation provision would be included in the Bill of Rights that was to be added to the Constitution after ratification. The Congressmen who drafted the Bill of Rights amendments were primarily concerned with the political consequences of the new clauses and paid scant attention to the definition and meaning of particular guarantees. Thus, the Confrontation Clause was apparently included without debate along with the rest of the Sixth Amendment package of rights — to notice, counsel, and compulsory process — all incidents of the adversarial proceeding before a jury as evolved during the 17th and 18th centuries.

The early decisions that consider the confrontation right at any length all involved ex parte testimony submitted by deposition and affidavit. See Reynolds v. United States, 98 U.S. 145 (1879); Mattox v. United States, 156 U.S. 237 (1895); Motes v. United States, 178 U.S. 458 (1900); Kirby v. United States, 174 U.S. 47 (1899). It was in this context that Mr. Justice Brown in an oft-quoted passage from Mattox v. United States set forth as the primary objective of the constitutional guarantee, the prevention of "depositions or ex parte affidavits, such as were sometimes admitted in civil cases, being used against the prisoner in lieu of a personal examination and cross-examination of the witness in which the accused has an opportunity, not only of testing the recollection and sifting the conscience of the witness, but also of compelling him to stand face to face with the jury in order that they may look at him, and judge by his demeanor upon the stand and the manner in which he gives his testimony whether he is worthy of belief." 156 U.S., at 242-243.

This restricted reading of the clause cannot be defended — taking, as it does, a metaphysical approach, one that attempts to differentiate between affidavits, as a substitute for first-hand testimony, and extrajudicial testimonial utterances.

Notwithstanding language that appears to equate the Confrontation Clause with a right to cross-examine, and, by implication, exclude hearsay, the early holdings and dicta can, I think, only be harmonized by viewing the confrontation guarantee as being confined to an availability rule, one that requires the production of a witness when he is available to testify. This view explains the recognition of the dying declaration exception, which dispenses with any requirement of cross-examination, and the refusal to make an exception for prior recorded statements, taken subject to cross-examination by the accused, when the witness is still available to testify. Compare Mattox v. United States, supra, with Motes v. United States, supra.

II

Recent decisions have, in my view, fallen into error on two scores. As a matter of jurisprudence I think it unsound, for reasons I have often elaborated to incorporate *as such* the guarantees of the Bill of Rights into the Due Process Clause. While, in this particular instance, this would be of little practical consequence if the Court had confined the Sixth Amendment guarantee to an "availability" requirement, some decisions have, unfortunately, failed to separate, even as a federal matter, restrictions on the abuse of hearsay testimony, part of the due process right of a reliable and trustworthy conviction, and the right to confront an available witness.

By incorporating into the Fourteenth Amendment its misinterpretation of the Sixth Amendment these decisions have in one blow created the present dilemma, that of bringing about a potential for a constitutional rule of hearsay for both state and federal courts. However ill-advised would be the constitutionalization of hearsay rules in federal courts, the undesirability of imposing those brittle rules on the States is manifest. Given the ambulatory fortunes of the hearsay doctrine, evidenced by the disagreement among scholars over the value of excluding hearsay and the trend toward liberalization of the exceptions, it would be most unfortunate for this Court to limit the flexibility of the States and choke experimentation in this evolving area of the law. Cf. Baldwin v. New York, supra. I adhere to what I consider to be the sound view expressed in Stein v. New York, 346 U.S. 156, 196 (1953): "The hearsay-evidence rule, with all its subtleties, anomalies and ramifications, [should] not be read into the Fourteenth Amendment."

What I would hold binding on the States as a matter of due process is what I also deem the correct meaning of the Sixth Amendment's Confrontation Clause — that a State may not in a criminal case use hearsay when the declarant is available. There is no reason in fairness why a State should not, as long as it retains a traditional adversarial trial, produce a witness and afford the accused an opportunity to cross-examine him when he can be made available. That this principle is an essential element of fairness is attested to not only by precedent, Motes v. United States, supra; Barber v. Page, supra; but also by the traditional and present exceptions to the hearsay rule which recognize greater flexibility for receiving evidence when the witness is not available. Furthermore it accommodates the interest of the State in making a case, yet recognizes the obligation to accord the accused the fullest opportunity to present his best defense. For those rare cases where a conviction occurs after a trial where no credible evidence could be said to justify the result, there remains the broader due process requirement that a conviction cannot be founded on no evidence.

Putting aside for the moment the "due process" aspect of this case, it follows, in my view, that there is no "confrontation" reason why the prosecution should not use a witness' prior inconsistent statement for the truth of the matters therein asserted. Here the prosecution has produced its witness, Porter, and made him available for trial confrontation. That, in my judgment, perforce satisfies the Sixth Amendment. . . .

The fact that the witness, though physically available, cannot recall either the underlying events that are the subject of an extra-judicial statement or previous testimony or recollect the circumstances under which the statement was given, does not have Sixth Amendment consequence. The prosecution has no less fulfilled its obligation simply because a witness has a lapse of memory. The witness is, in my view, available. To the extent that the witness is, in a practical sense, unavailable for cross-examination on the relevant facts, . . . I think confrontation is nonetheless satisfied. . . .

What confrontation rule does the Court apply in *Green*? What rule does Justice Harlan apply?

Suppose, under the Federal Rules, that Porter were deemed to be an unavailable witness as a result of either failure of memory or refusal to testify and that defense counsel had chosen not to cross-examine him thoroughly at the preliminary hearing. Would Porter's prior testimony have been admissible? Compare Rule 804(b)(1), providing for the admissibility of former testimony of unavailable witnesses, with Rule 801(d)(1), governing the admissibility of prior statements by a witness. To what extent are the specific limitations of the Federal Rules constitutionally mandated by California v. Green? Are they constitutionally adequate under *Green*? In *Green* what facts must the state court find on remand in order to render Porter's statements to Officer Wade constitutionally admissible? How does *Bruton* bear on this question? What are the respective roles of availability and reliability in sixth amendment analysis? Do you agree with Justice Harlan that the confrontation clause is only a rule of preference mandating the use of live, in-court testimony when the witness is available? For a scholarly endorsement and extrapolation of this view, see Westen, Confrontation and Compulsory Process: A Unified Theory of Evidence for Criminal Cases, 91 Harv. L. Rev. 567 (1978).

DUTTON v. EVANS
400 U.S. 74 (1970)

Mr. Justice STEWART announced the judgment of the Court and an opinion in which THE CHIEF JUSTICE, Mr. Justice WHITE, and Mr. Justice BLACKMUN join.

Early on an April morning in 1964, three police officers were brutally murdered in Gwinnett County, Georgia. Their bodies were found a few hours later, handcuffed together in a pine thicket, each with multiple gunshot wounds in the back of the head. After many months of investigation, Georgia authorities charged the appellee, Evans, and two other men, Wade Truett and Venson Williams, with the officers' murders. Evans and Williams were indicted by a grand jury; Truett was granted immunity from prosecution in return for his testimony.

Evans pleaded not guilty and exercised his right under Georgia law to be tried separately. After a jury trial, he was convicted of murder and sentenced to death. The judgment of conviction was affirmed by the Supreme Court of Georgia, and this Court denied certiorari. Evans then brought the present habeas corpus proceeding in a federal district court, alleging, among other things, that he had been denied the constitutional right of confrontation at his trial. The District Court denied the writ, but the Court of Appeals for the Fifth Circuit reversed, holding that Georgia had, indeed, denied Evans the right, guaranteed by the Sixth and Fourteenth Amendments, "to be confronted by the witnesses against him." From that judgment an appeal was brought to this Court, and we noted probable jurisdiction. The case was originally argued last Term, but was set for reargument. 397 U.S. 1060.

In order to understand the context of the constitutional question before us, a brief review of the proceedings at Evans' trial is necessary. The principal prosecution witness at the trial was Truett, the alleged accomplice who had been granted immunity. Truett described at length and in detail the circumstances surrounding the murder of the police officers. He testified that he, along with Evans and Williams, had been engaged in switching the license plates on a stolen car parked on a back road in Gwinnett County when they were accosted by the three police officers. As the youngest of the officers leaned in front of Evans to inspect the ignition switch on the car, Evans grabbed the officer's gun from its holster. Evans and Williams then disarmed the other officers at gunpoint, and handcuffed the three of them together. They then took the officers into the woods and killed them by firing several bullets into their bodies at extremely close range. In addition to Truett, 19 other witnesses testified for the prosecution. Defense counsel was given full opportunity to cross-examine each witness, and he exercised that opportunity with respect to most of them.

One of the 20 prosecution witnesses was a man named Shaw. He testified that he and Williams had been fellow prisoners in the federal penitentiary in Atlanta, Georgia, at the time Williams was brought to Gwinnett County to be arraigned on the charges of murdering the police officers. Shaw said that when Williams was returned to the penitentiary from the arraignment, he had asked Williams: "How did you make out in court?" and that Williams had responded, "If it hadn't been for that dirty son-of-a-bitch Alex Evans, we wouldn't be in this now." Defense counsel objected to the introduction of this testimony upon the ground that it was hearsay and thus violative of Evans' right of confrontation.

After the objection was overruled, counsel cross-examined Shaw at length.

The testimony of Shaw relating what he said Williams had told him was admitted by the Georgia trial court, and its admission upheld by the Georgia Supreme Court, upon the basis of a Georgia statute that provides: "After the fact of conspiracy shall be proved, the declarations by any one of the conspirators during the pendency of the criminal project shall be admissible against all." As the appellate court put it:

" 'The rule is that so long as the conspiracy to conceal the fact that a crime has been committed or the identity of the perpetrators of the offense continues, the parties to such conspiracy are to be considered so much a unit that the declarations of either are admissible against the other.' The defendant, and his co-conspirator, Williams, at the time this statement was made, were still concealing their identity, keeping secret the fact that they had killed the deceased, if they had, and denying their guilt. There was evidence sufficient to establish a prima facie case of conspiracy to steal the automobile and the killing of the deceased by the conspirators while carrying out the conspiracy, and the statement by Williams made after the actual commission of the crime, but while the conspiracy continued was admissible." (Citations omitted.)

This holding was in accord with a consistent line of Georgia decisions construing the state statute.

It was the admission of this testimony of the witness Shaw that formed the basis for the appellee's claim in the present habeas corpus proceeding that he had been denied the constitutional right of confrontation in the Georgia trial court. In upholding that claim, the Court of Appeals for the Fifth Circuit regarded its duty to be "not only to interpret the framers' original concept in light of historical developments, but also to translate into due-process terms the constitutional boundaries of the hearsay rule." (Footnotes omitted.) The court upheld the appellee's constitutional claim because it could find no "salient and cogent reasons" for the exception to the hearsay rule Georgia applied in the present case, an exception that the court pointed out was broader than that applicable to conspiracy trials in the federal courts.

The question before us, then, is whether in the circumstances of this case the Court of Appeals was correct in holding that Evans' murder conviction had to be set aside because of the admission of Shaw's testimony. In considering this question, we start by recognizing that this Court has squarely held that "the Sixth Amendment's right of an accused to confront the witnesses against him is . . . a fundamental right . . . made obligatory on the States by the Fourteenth Amendment." Pointer v. Texas, 380 U.S. 400, 403. But that is no more than the beginning of our inquiry. . . .

It seems apparent that the Sixth Amendment's Confrontation Clause and the evidentiary hearsay rule stem from the same roots. But this

Court has never equated the two, and we decline to do so now. We confine ourselves, instead, to deciding the case before us.

This case does not involve evidence in any sense "crucial" or "devastating." . . . It does not involve the use, or misuse, of a confession made in the coercive atmosphere of official interrogation, as did *Douglas* [and] *Bruton*. . . . It does not involve any suggestion of prosecutorial misconduct or even negligence, as did *Pointer*, *Douglas* and *Barber*. It does not involve the use by the prosecution of a paper transcript, as did *Pointer* . . . and *Barber*. It does not involve a joint trial, as did *Bruton*. . . .

In the trial of this case no less than 20 witnesses appeared and testified for the prosecution. Evans' counsel was given full opportunity to cross-examine every one of them. The most important witness, by far, was the eyewitness who described all the details of the triple murder and who was cross-examined at great length. Of the 19 other witnesses, the testimony of but a single one is at issue here. That one witness testified to a brief conversation about Evans he had had with a fellow prisoner in the Atlanta Penitentiary. The witness was vigorously and effectively cross-examined by defense counsel. His testimony, which was of peripheral significance at most, was admitted in evidence under a co-conspirator exception to the hearsay rule long established under state statutory law. The Georgia statute can obviously have many applications consistent with the Confrontation Clause, and we conclude that its application in the circumstances of this case did not violate the Constitution.

Evans was not deprived of any right of confrontation on the issue of whether Williams actually made the statement related by Shaw. Neither a hearsay nor a confrontation question would arise had Shaw's testimony been used to prove merely that the statement had been made. The hearsay rule does not prevent a witness from testifying as to what he has heard; it is rather a restriction on the proof of fact through extrajudicial statements. From the viewpoint of the Confrontation Clause, a witness under oath, subject to cross-examination, and whose demeanor can be observed by the trier of fact, is a reliable informant not only as to what he has seen but also as to what he has heard.[19]

The confrontation issue arises because the jury was being invited to infer that Williams had implicitly identified Evans as the perpetrator of the murder when he blamed Evans for his predicament. But we conclude that there was no denial of the right of confrontation as to this question of identity. First, the statement contained no express assertion about past fact, and consequently it carried on its face a warning to the jury against giving the statement undue weight. Second, Williams' per-

---

19. Of course Evans had the right to subpoena witnesses, including Williams, whose testimony might show that the statement had not been made. Counsel for Evans informed us at oral argument that he could have subpoenaed Williams but had concluded that this course would not be in the best interests of his client.

sonal knowledge of the identity and role of the other participants in the triple murder is abundantly established by Truett's testimony and by Williams' prior conviction. It is inconceivable that cross-examination could have shown that Williams was not in a position to know whether or not Evans was involved in the murder. Third, the possibility that Williams' statement was founded on faulty recollection is remote in the extreme. Fourth, the circumstances under which Williams made the statement were such as to give reason to suppose that Williams did not misrepresent Evans' involvement in the crime. These circumstances go beyond a showing that Williams had no apparent reason to lie to Shaw. His statement was spontaneous, and it was against his penal interest to make it. These are indicia of reliability which have been widely viewed as determinative of whether a statement may be placed before the jury though there is no confrontation of the declarant.

The decisions of this Court make it clear that the mission of the Confrontation Clause is to advance a practical concern for the accuracy of the truth-determining process in criminal trials by assuring that "the trier of fact [has] a satisfactory basis for evaluating the truth of the prior statement." California v. Green, 399 U.S., at 161. Evans exercised, and exercised effectively, his right to confrontation on the factual question whether Shaw had actually heard Williams make the statement Shaw related. And the possibility that cross-examination of Williams could conceivably have shown the jury that the statement, though made, might have been unreliable was wholly unreal.

Almost 40 years ago, in Snyder v. Massachusetts, 291 U.S. 97, Mr. Justice Cardozo wrote an opinion for this Court refusing to set aside a state criminal conviction because of the claimed denial of the right of confrontation. The closing words of that opinion are worth repeating here: "There is danger that the criminal law will be brought into contempt — that discredit will even touch the great immunities assured by the Fourteenth Amendment — if gossamer possibilities of prejudice to a defendant are to nullify a sentence pronounced by a court of competent jurisdiction in obedience to local law, and set the guilty free." 291 U.S., at 122.

The judgment of the Court of Appeals is reversed, and the case is remanded to that court for consideration of the other issues presented in this habeas corpus proceeding.

It is so ordered.

Mr. Justice BLACKMUN, whom THE CHIEF JUSTICE joins, concurring.

I join Mr. Justice Stewart's opinion. For me, however, there is an additional reason for the result.

The single sentence attributed in testimony by Shaw to Williams about Evans, and which has prolonged this litigation, was, in my view and in the light of the entire record, harmless error if it was error at all. Furthermore, the claimed circumstances of its utterance are so incredible that the testimony must have hurt, rather than helped, the prosecution's case. On this ground alone, I could be persuaded to reverse and remand.

Shaw testified that Williams made the remark at issue when Shaw "went to his room in the hospital" and asked Williams how he made out at a court hearing on the preceding day. On cross-examination, Shaw stated that he was then in custody at the federal penitentiary in Atlanta; that he worked as a clerk in the prison hospital; that Williams was lying on the bed in his room and facing the wall; that he, Shaw, was in the hall and not in the room when he spoke with Williams; that the door to the room "was closed"; that he spoke through an opening about 10 inches square; that the opening "has a piece of plate glass, window glass, just ordinary window glass, and a piece of steel mesh"; that this does not impede talking through the door; and that one talks in a normal voice when he talks through that door. Shaw conceded that when he had testified at Williams' earlier trial, he made no reference to the glass in the opening in the door. . . .

I add an observation about corroboration. . . . Lawrence H. Hartman, testified that his 1963 red Oldsmobile hardtop was stolen from his home in Atlanta the night of April 16, 1964 (the murders took place on the early morning of April 17). He went on to testify that the 1963 Oldsmobile found burning near the scene of the tragedy was his automobile. There is testimony in the record as to the earlier acquisition by Evans and Williams of another wrecked Oldsmobile of like model and color; as to the towing of that damaged car by a wrecker manned by Williams and Evans; and as to the replacement of good tires on a Chevrolet occupied by Williams, Evans, and Truett, with recapped tires then purchased by them.

This record testimony, it seems to me, bears directly and positively on the Williams-Evans-Truett car-stealing conspiracy and accomplishments and provides indisputable confirmation of Evans' role. The requirements of the Georgia corroboration rule were fully satisfied and Shaw's incredible remark fades into practical and legal insignificance.

The error here, if one exists, is harmless beyond a reasonable doubt. Chapman v. California, 386 U.S. 18, 21-25; Harrington v. California, 395 U.S. 250.

Mr. Justice HARLAN, concurring in the result.

Not surprisingly the difficult constitutional issue presented by this case has produced multiple opinions. Mr. Justice Stewart finds Shaw's testimony admissible because it is "wholly unreal" to suggest that cross-examination would have weakened the effect of Williams' statement on the jury's mind. Mr. Justice Blackmun, while concurring in this view, finds admission of the statement to be harmless, seemingly because he deems Shaw's testimony so obviously fabricated that no normal jury would have given it credence. Mr. Justice Marshall answers both suggestions to my satisfaction, but he then adopts a position that I cannot accept. He apparently would prevent the prosecution from introducing any out-of-court statement of an accomplice unless there is an opportunity for cross-examination, and this regardless of the circumstances in which the statement was made and regardless of whether it is even hearsay.

The difficulty of this case arises from the assumption that the core purpose of the Confrontation Clause of the Sixth Amendment is to prevent overly broad exceptions to the hearsay rule. I believe this assumption to be wrong. Contrary to things as they appeared to me last Term when I wrote in California v. Green, 399 U.S. 149, 172 (1970), I have since become convinced that Wigmore states the correct view when he says:

> The Constitution does not prescribe what kinds of testimonial statements (dying declarations, or the like) shall be given infra-judicially, — this depends on the law of Evidence for the time being, — but only what mode of procedure shall be followed — i.e. a cross-examining procedure — in the case of such testimony as is required by the ordinary law of Evidence to be given infra-judicially.

5 J. Wigmore, Evidence §1397, at 131 (3d ed. 1940) (footnote omitted). The conversion of a clause intended to regulate trial procedure into a threat to much of the existing law of evidence and to future developments in that field is not an unnatural shift, for the paradigmatic evil the Confrontation Clause was aimed at — trial by affidavit — can be viewed almost equally well as a gross violation of the rule against hearsay and as the giving of evidence by the affiant out of the presence of the accused and not subject to cross-examination by him. But however natural the shift may be, once made it carries the seeds of great mischief for enlightened development in the law of evidence.

If one were to translate the Confrontation Clause into language in more common use today, it would read: "In all criminal prosecutions, the accused shall enjoy the right to be present and to cross-examine the witnesses against him." Nothing in this language or in its 18th-century equivalent would connote a purpose to control the scope of the rules of evidence. The language is particularly ill-chosen if what was intended was a prohibition on the use of any hearsay — the position toward which my Brother Marshall is being driven, although he does not quite yet embrace it.

Nor am I now content with the position I took in concurrence in California v. Green, supra, that the Confrontation Clause was designed to establish a preferential rule, requiring the prosecutor to avoid the use of hearsay where it is reasonably possible for him to do so — in other words, to produce available witnesses. Further consideration in the light of facts squarely presenting the issue, as *Green* did not, has led me to conclude that this is not a happy intent to be attributed to the Framers absent compelling linguistic or historical evidence pointing in that direction. It is common ground that the historical understanding of the clause furnishes no solid guide to adjudication.

A rule requiring production of available witnesses would significantly curtail development of the law of evidence to eliminate the necessity for production of declarants where production would be unduly inconvenient and of small utility to a defendant. Examples which come to mind are the Business Records Act, 28 U.S.C. §§1732-1733, and the exceptions to the hearsay rule for official statements, learned treatises, and trade reports. If the hearsay exception involved in a given case is such as to commend itself to reasonable men, production of the declarant is likely to be difficult, unavailing, or pointless. . . .

Regardless of the interpretation one puts on the words of the Confrontation Clause, the clause is simply not well designed for taking into account the numerous factors that must be weighed in passing on the appropriateness of rules of evidence. The failure of Mr. Justice Stewart's opinion to explain the standard by which it tests Shaw's statement, or how this standard can be squared with the seemingly absolute command of the clause, bears witness to the fact that the clause is being set a task for which it is not suited. The task is far more appropriately performed under the aegis of the Fifth and Fourteenth Amendments' commands that federal and state trials, respectively, must be conducted in accordance with due process of law. It is by this standard that I would test federal and state rules of evidence. . . .

Judging the Georgia statute here challenged by the standards of due process, I conclude that it must be sustained. Accomplishment of the main object of a conspiracy will seldom terminate the community of interest of the conspirators. Declarations against that interest evince some likelihood of trustworthiness. The jury, with the guidance of defense counsel, should be alert to the obvious dangers of crediting such testimony. As a practical matter, unless the out-of-court declaration can be proved by hearsay evidence, the facts it reveals are likely to remain hidden from the jury by the declarant's invocation of the privilege against self-incrimination. In light of such considerations, a person weighing the necessity for hearsay evidence of the type here involved against the danger that a jury will give it undue credit might reasonably conclude that admission of the evidence would increase the likelihood of just determinations of truth. Appellee has not suggested that Shaw's testimony possessed any peculiar characteristic that would lessen the force of these general considerations and require, as a constitutional matter, that the trial judge exercise residual discretion to exclude the evidence as unduly inflammatory. Exclusion of such statements, as is done in the federal courts, commends itself to me, but I cannot say that it is essential to a fair trial. The Due Process Clause requires no more.

On the premises discussed in this opinion, I concur in the reversal of the judgment below.

Mr. Justice MARSHALL, whom Mr. Justice BLACK, Mr. Justice DOUGLAS, and Mr. Justice BRENNAN join, dissenting. . . .

[T]he Court today concludes that admission of the extrajudicial statement attributed to an alleged partner in crime did not deny Evans the right "to be confronted with the witnesses against him" guaranteed by the Sixth and Fourteenth Amendments to the Constitution. In so doing, the majority reaches a result completely inconsistent with recent opinions of this Court, especially Douglas v. Alabama, 380 U.S. 415 (1965), and Bruton v. United States, 391 U.S. 123 (1968). In my view, those cases fully apply here and establish a clear violation of Evans' constitutional rights. . . .

In Douglas v. Alabama, supra, this Court applied the principles of *Pointer* to a case strikingly similar to this one. There, as here, the State charged two defendants with a crime and tried them in separate trials. There, as here, the State first prosecuted one defendant (Loyd) and then used a statement by him in the trial of the second defendant (Douglas). . . .

[T]he Court held that the prosecutor's reading of Loyd's statement in a purported attempt to refresh his memory denied Douglas' right to confrontation. "Loyd could not be cross-examined on a statement imputed to but not admitted by him." 380 U.S., at 419. Of course, Douglas was provided the opportunity to cross-examine the officers who testified regarding Loyd's statement. "But since their evidence tended to show only that Loyd made the confession, cross-examination of them . . . could not substitute for cross-examination of Loyd to test the truth of the statement itself." Surely, the same reasoning compels the exclusion of Shaw's testimony here. Indeed, the only significant difference between *Douglas* and this case, insofar as the denial of the opportunity to cross-examine is concerned, is that here the State did not even attempt to call Williams to testify in Evans' trial. He was plainly available to the State, and for all we know he would have willingly testified, at least with regard to his alleged conversation with Shaw.[4] . . .

Mr. Justice Stewart's opinion for reversal characterizes as "wholly unreal" the possibility that cross-examination of Williams himself would

4. My Brother Stewart comments that Evans might have brought Williams to the courthouse by subpoena. Defense counsel did not do so, believing that Williams would stand on his right not to incriminate himself. Be that as it may, it remains that the duty to confront a criminal defendant with witnesses against him falls upon the *State,* and here the State was allowed to introduce damaging evidence without running the risks of trial confrontation.

change the picture presented by Shaw's account. A trial lawyer might well doubt, as an article of the skeptical faith of that profession, such a categorical prophecy about the likely results of careful cross-examination. Indeed, the facts of this case clearly demonstrate the necessity for fuller factual development which the corrective test of cross-examination makes possible. The plurality for reversal pigeonholes the out-of-court statement that was admitted in evidence as a "spontaneous" utterance, hence to be believed. As the Court of Appeals concluded, however, there is great doubt that Williams even made the statement attributed to him. Moreover, there remains the further question what, if anything, Williams might have meant by the remark that Shaw recounted. Mr. Justice Stewart's opinion concedes that the remark is ambiguous. Plainly it stands as an accusation of some sort: "If it hadn't been for . . . Evans," said Williams, according to Shaw, "we wouldn't be in this now." At his trial Evans himself gave unsworn testimony to the effect that the murder prosecution might have arisen from enmities that Evans' own law enforcement activities had stirred up in the locality. Did Williams' accusation relate to Evans as a man with powerful and unscrupulous enemies, or Evans as a murderer? Mr. Justice Stewart's opinion opts for the latter interpretation, for it concludes that Williams' remark was "against his penal interest" and hence to be believed. But at this great distance from events, no one can be certain. The point is that absent cross-examination of Williams himself, the jury was left with only the unelucidated, apparently damning, and patently damaging accusation as told by Shaw.

Thus we have a case with all the unanswered questions that the confrontation of witnesses through cross-examination is meant to aid in answering: What did the declarant say, and what did he mean, and was it the truth? If Williams had testified and been cross-examined, Evans' counsel could have fully explored these and other matters. The jury then could have evaluated the statement in the light of Williams' testimony and demeanor. As it was, however, the State was able to use Shaw to present the damaging evidence and thus to avoid confronting Evans with the person who allegedly gave witness against him. I had thought that this was precisely what the Confrontation Clause as applied to the States in *Pointer* and our other cases prevented.

Although Mr. Justice Stewart's opinion for reversal concludes that there was no violation of Evans' right of confrontation, it does so in the complete absence of authority or reasoning to explain that result. For example, such facts as that Williams' alleged statement was not made during official interrogation, was not in transcript form, and was not introduced in a joint trial — though they differentiate some of the cases — are surely irrelevant. Other cases have presented each of these factors, and no reason is offered why the right of confrontation could be so limited.

Nor can it be enough that the statement was admitted in evidence "under a long-established and well-recognized rule of state law." Mr. Justice Stewart's opinion surely does not mean that a defendant's constitutional right of confrontation must give way to a state evidentiary rule. That much is established by our decision in Barber v. Page, supra, which held unconstitutional the admission of testimony in accordance with a rule similarly well recognized and long established. However, the plurality for reversal neither succeeds in distinguishing that case nor considers generally that there are inevitably conflicts between *Pointer* and state evidentiary rules. Rather, it attempts to buttress its conclusion merely by announcing a reluctance to equate evidentiary hearsay rules and the Confrontation Clause.[7] . . .

Finally, the plurality for reversal apparently distinguishes the present case on the ground that it "does not involve evidence in any sense 'crucial' or 'devastating.' " Despite the characterization of Shaw's testimony as "of peripheral significance at most," however, the possibility of its prejudice to Evans was very real. The outcome of Evans' trial rested, in essence, on whether the jury would believe the testimony of Truett with regard to Evans' role in the murder. Truett spoke as an admitted accomplice who had been immunized from prosecution. Relying on Georgia law, not federal constitutional law, the trial judge instructed the jury that "you cannot lawfully convict upon the testimony of an accomplice alone. . . . [T]he testimony of an accomplice must be corroborated. . . . [T]he corroboration . . . must be such as to connect the defendant with the criminal act." The State presented the testimony of a number of other witnesses, in addition to that of the alleged accomplice that tended to corroborate Evans' guilt. But Shaw's account of what Williams supposedly said to him was undoubtedly a part of that corroborating evidence.

Indeed, Mr. Justice Stewart's opinion does not itself upset the Court of Appeals' finding that the admission of Shaw's testimony, if erroneous, could not be considered harmless. Beyond and apart from the question of harmless error, Mr. Justice Stewart undertakes an inquiry, the purpose of which I do not understand, into whether the evidence admitted is "crucial" or "devastating." The view is, apparently, that to require the

---

7. Constitutionalization of "all common-law hearsay rules and their exceptions," California v. Green, 399 U.S., at 174 (concurring opinion), would seem to be a prospect more frightening than real. Much of the complexity afflicting hearsay rules comes from the definition of hearsay as an out-of-court statement presented for the truth of the matter stated — a definition nowhere adopted by this Court for confrontation purposes. Rather, the decisions, while looking to availability of a declarant, Barber v. Page, supra, recognize that "cross-examination is included in the right of an accused in a criminal case to confront the witnesses against him," Pointer v. Texas, 380 U.S., at 404, and that admission in the absence of cross-examination of certain types of suspect and highly damaging statements is one of the "threats to a fair trial" against which "the Confrontation Clause was directed," Bruton v. United States, 391 U.S., at 136.

exclusion of evidence falling short of that high standard of prejudice would bring a moment of clamor against the Bill of Rights. I would eschew such worries and confine the inquiry to the traditional questions: Was the defendant afforded the right to confront the witnesses against him? And, if not, was the denial of his constitutional right harmless beyond a reasonable doubt? . . .

I am troubled by the fact that the plurality for reversal, unable when all is said to place this case beyond the principled reach of our prior decisions, shifts its ground and begins a hunt for whatever "indicia of reliability" may cling to Williams' remark, as told by Shaw. Whether Williams made a "spontaneous" statement "against his penal interest" is the very question that should have been tested by cross-examination of Williams himself. If "indicia of reliability" are so easy to come by, and prove so much, then it is only reasonable to ask whether the Confrontation Clause has any independent vitality at all in protecting a criminal defendant against the use of extrajudicial statements not subject to cross-examination and not exposed to a jury assessment of the declarant's demeanor at trial.[11] I believe the Confrontation Clause has been sunk if any out-of-court statement bearing an indicium of a probative likelihood can come in, no matter how damaging the statement may be or how great the need for the truth-discovering test of cross-examination. . . . The incriminatory extrajudicial statement of an alleged accomplice is so inherently prejudicial that it cannot be introduced unless there is an opportunity to cross-examine the declarant, whether or not his statement falls within a genuine exception to the hearsay rule.

In my view, Evans is entitled to a trial in which he is fully accorded his constitutional guarantee of the right to confront and cross-examine all the witnesses against him. I would affirm the judgment of the Court of Appeals and let this case go back to the Georgia courts to be tried without the use of this out-of-court statement attributed by Shaw to Williams.

Does the *Dutton* court adequately distinguish *Bruton, Green,* and other earlier confrontation clause cases? Is the Court's reasoning persuasive? Internally consistent? Compare the views expressed in the plurality opinion concerning the reliability of the evidence with the concurring opinion of Justice Blackmun. How reliable would you judge the evidence? How valuable would cross-examination of the declarant have

---

11. Mr. Justice Harlan answers this question with directness by adopting, to decide this case, his view of due process which apparently makes no distinction between civil and criminal trials, and which would prohibit only irrational or unreasonable evidentiary rulings. Needless to say, I cannot accept the view that Evans' constitutional rights should be measured by a standard concededly having nothing to do with the Confrontation Clause.

been? How likely was the jury to overestimate the probative value of the statement? Do you agree with the suggestion made in the concurrence that *Dutton* would be more appropriately analyzed under a harmless error approach? How do you explain Justice Harlan's abandonment of the "availability" standard in the context of this case?

NELSON, WARDEN v. O'NEIL
402 U.S. 622 (1971)

Mr. Justice STEWART delivered the opinion of the Court.

The respondent, Joe O'Neil, was arrested along with a man named Runnels when the police of Culver City, California, answered a midnight call from a liquor store reporting that two men in a white Cadillac were suspiciously cruising about in the neighborhood. The police responded to the call, spotted the Cadillac, and followed it into an alley where a gun was thrown from one of its windows. They then stopped the car and apprehended the respondent and Runnels. Further investigation revealed that the car had been stolen about 10:30 that night in Los Angeles by two men who had forced its owner at gunpoint to drive them a distance of a few blocks and then had robbed him of $8 and driven off. The victim subsequently picked Runnels and the respondent from a lineup, positively identifying them as the men who had kidnaped and robbed him.

Arraigned on charges of kidnaping, robbery, and vehicle theft, both the respondent and Runnels pleaded not guilty, and at their joint trial they offered an alibi defense. Each told the same story: they had spent the evening at the respondent's home until about 11 P.M., when they had left together. While waiting at a bus stop they were picked up by a friend driving a white Cadillac, and he offered to lend them the car for a few hours while he went into a nightclub. They accepted the offer, and once on their way discovered that there was a gun in the glove compartment. They entered an alley in search of a place to dispose of the gun, since they were afraid of being stopped with it in the car. Soon after throwing the gun out of the window they were stopped by the police and arrested. The supposed friend was not called as a witness and was not shown to be unavailable, but other witnesses corroborated parts of their alibi testimony.

The owner of the white Cadillac made a positive in-court identification of the defendants, and a police officer testified to the facts of the arrest. Another police officer testified that after the arrest Runnels had made an unsworn oral statement admitting the crimes and implicating the respondent as his confederate. The trial judge ruled the officer's testimony as to the substance of the alleged statement admissible against

Runnels, but instructed the jury that it could not consider it against the respondent. When Runnels took the stand in his own defense, he was asked on direct examination whether he had made the statement, and he flatly denied having done so. He also vigorously asserted that the substance of the statement imputed to him was false. He was then intensively cross-examined by the prosecutor, but stuck to his story in every particular. The respondent's counsel did not cross-examine Runnels, although he was, of course, fully free to do so. The respondent took the stand on his own behalf and told a story identical to that of Runnels as to the activities of the two on the night in question. Both the prosecutor and Runnels' counsel discussed the alleged confession in their closing arguments to the jury, and the trial judge repeated his instruction that it could be considered only against Runnels.

The jury found both defendants guilty as charged. . . .

Runnels' out-of-court confession implicating the respondent was hearsay as to the latter, and therefore inadmissible against him under state evidence law. The trial judge so ruled, and instructed the jury that it must not consider any part of the statement in deciding whether or not the respondent was guilty. In *Bruton*, however, we held that, quite apart from the law of evidence, such a cautionary instruction to the jury is not an adequate protection for the defendant where the codefendant does not take the witness stand. We held that where the jury hears the codefendant's confession implicating the defendant, the codefendant becomes in substance, if not in form, a "witness" against the defendant. The defendant must constitutionally have an opportunity to "confront" such a witness. This the defendant cannot do if the codefendant refuses to take the stand.

It was clear in *Bruton* that the "confrontation" guaranteed by the Sixth and Fourteenth Amendments is confrontation *at trial* — that is, that the absence of the defendant at the time the codefendant allegedly made the out-of-court statement is immaterial, so long as the declarant can be cross-examined on the witness stand at trial. This was confirmed in California v. Green, 399 U.S. 149, where we said that "[v]iewed historically . . . there is good reason to conclude that the Confrontation Clause is not violated by admitting a declarant's out-of-court statements, as long as the declarant is testifying as a witness and subject to full and effective cross-examination." Id., at 158. Moreover, "where the declarant is not absent, but is present to testify and to submit to cross-examination, our cases, if anything, support the conclusion that the admission of his out-of-court statements does not create a confrontation problem." Id., at 162. This is true, of course, even though the declarant's out-of-court statement is hearsay as to the defendant, so that its admission against him, in the absence of a cautionary instruction, would be reversible error under state law. The Constitution as construed in *Bruton*, in other words, is violated *only* where the out-of-court hearsay statement is that of a declarant who is unavailable at the trial for "full and effective" cross-examination.

The question presented by this case, then, is whether cross-examination can be full and effective where the declarant is present at the trial, takes the witness stand, testifies fully as to his activities during the period described in his alleged out-of-court statement, but denies that he made the statement and claims that its substance is false.

In affirming the District Court, the Court of Appeals relied heavily on the dictum of this Court in Douglas v. Alabama, 380 U.S. 415, 420, that "effective confrontation" of a witness who has allegedly made an out-of-court statement implicating the defendant "was possible only if [the witness] affirmed the statement as his." The Court in that case also remarked that the witness "could not be cross-examined on a statement imputed to but not admitted by him." Id., at 419. Of course, a witness *can* be cross-examined concerning a statement not "affirmed" by him, but this dictum from *Douglas* was repeated in *Bruton,* supra, at 127. In *Douglas* and *Bruton* (and in the other confrontation cases before *Green*) there was in fact no question of the effect of an affirmance or denial of the incriminating statement, since the witness or codefendant was in each case totally unavailable at the trial for any kind of cross-examination. . . .

The circumstances of *Green* are inverted in this case. There, the witness affirmed the out-of-court statement but was unable to testify in court as to the underlying facts; here, the witness, Runnels, denied ever making an out-of-court statement but testified at length, and favorably to the defendant, concerning the underlying facts.

Had Runnels in this case "affirmed the statement as his," the respondent would certainly have been in far worse straits than those in which he found himself when Runnels testified as he did. For then counsel for the respondent could only have attempted to show through cross-examination that Runnels had confessed to a crime he had not committed, or, slightly more plausibly, that those parts of the confession implicating the respondent were fabricated. This would, moreover, have required an abandonment of the joint alibi defense, and the production of a new explanation for the respondent's presence with Runnels in the white Cadillac at the time of their arrest. To be sure, Runnels might have "affirmed the statement" but denied its truthfulness, claiming, for example, that it had been coerced, or made as part of a plea bargain. But cross-examination by the respondent's counsel would have been futile in that event as well. For once Runnels had testified that the statement was false, it could hardly have profited the respondent for his counsel through cross-examination to try to shake that testimony. If the jury were to believe that the statement was false as to Runnels, it could hardly conclude that it was not false as to the respondent as well.

The short of the matter is that, given a joint trial and a common defense, Runnels' testimony respecting his alleged out-of-court statement was more favorable to the respondent than any that cross-examination by counsel could possibly have produced, had Runnels "affirmed the statement as his." It would be unrealistic in the extreme in the circumstances here presented to hold that the respondent was denied either the opportunity or the benefit of full and effective cross-examination of Runnels.

We conclude that where a codefendant takes the stand in his own defense, denies making an alleged out-of-court statement implicating the defendant, and proceeds to testify favorably to the defendant concerning the underlying facts, the defendant has been denied no rights protected by the Sixth and Fourteenth Amendments. Accordingly, the judgment is reversed and the case is remanded to the Court of Appeals for further proceedings consistent with this opinion.

It is so ordered.

Mr. Justice BRENNAN, with whom Mr. Justice DOUGLAS and Mr. Justice MARSHALL join, dissenting.

With all deference, I think the Court asks and answers the wrong question in this case. Under the law of California at the time of respondent's trial, admissions to a police officer by a criminal defendant after his arrest could not be used as substantive evidence against other defendants, whether or not the declarant testified at trial.[1] The question with which we are faced is not, therefore, whether the Sixth Amendment would forbid California from using Runnels' statement as substantive evidence against respondent O'Neil if it chose to do so. California rejected that choice: the jury in the present case was explicitly instructed that Runnels' statement could not be considered as evidence against O'Neil. The question, therefore, is whether California, having determined for whatever reason that the statement involved in this case was inadmissible against respondent, may nevertheless present the statement to the jury that was to decide respondent's guilt, and instruct that jury that it should not be considered against respondent. I think our cases compel the conclusion that it may not. . . .

Bruton and *Roberts* compel the conclusion that the Federal Constitution forbids the States to assume that juries can follow instructions that tell them to wipe their minds of highly damaging, incriminating admissions of one defendant that simultaneously incriminate another defendant whose guilt or innocence the jury is told to decide. In the present case, California itself has made the judgment that, although Runnels did take the stand, his extrajudicial statements could not be considered by

---

1. The California Evidence Code, presently in effect, did not become operative until January 1, 1967.

the jury as evidence against respondent. Under *Bruton* and *Roberts,* California having made the determination that Runnels' statement could not be considered as evidence against O'Neil may not subvert its own judgment in some but not all cases by presenting the inadmissible evidence to the jury and telling the jury to disregard it. For the inevitable result of this procedure is that, in fact, different rules of evidence will be applied to different defendants depending solely upon the fortuity of whether they are jointly or separately tried. This is a discrimination that the Constitution forbids. . . .

———————————

What confrontation rule does the *Nelson* court apply? What is left of *Douglas* and *Bruton* after *O'Neil?*

MANCUSI v. STUBBS
408 U.S. 204 (1972)

Mr. Justice REHNQUIST delivered the opinion of the Court.

Respondent Stubbs was convicted of a felony in a New York State court and sentenced as a second offender under the laws of that State by reason of a prior Tennessee murder conviction obtained in 1964. He thereafter sought federal habeas corpus, claiming that the Tennessee conviction was had in violation of his Sixth and Fourteenth Amendment right to confront witnesses against him, and thus could not be used by New York as the predicate for a stiffer punishment. The District Court denied habeas corpus, but the Court of Appeals reversed, 442 F.2d 561 (C.A.2 1971). We granted certiorari, 404 U.S. 1014, and reverse for the reasons hereinafter stated. . . .

In July 1954, respondent was convicted in the Tennessee trial court of murder in the first degree, assault with intent to murder, and two counts of kidnaping. The jury impaneled for that trial could have concluded from the evidence presented to it that respondent, a few days after his release from a Texas penitentiary in June 1954, kidnaped Mr. and Mrs. Alex Holm and forced them at gunpoint to accompany him in their car. Stubbs drove the car and sat in the front seat, while the Holms sat in the back seat. Mr. Holm testified that somewhere east of Blountville, Tennessee, Stubbs, without saying anything, shot him twice in the head and shot and killed Mrs. Holm. Stubbs then left the car, obtained a ride as a hitchhiker, and was ultimately arrested at a roadblock. At the time of his arrest, Stubbs explained the blood on his clothing as having resulted from his having fallen off a cliff while fishing. . . .

Nine years after his state court trial for murder, Stubbs sought release on federal habeas corpus from the United States District Court for the Middle District of Tennessee.

He successfully urged upon that court the contention that he had been denied the effective assistance of counsel in this 1954 trial because counsel had been appointed for him only four days before the trial took place. Stubbs v. Bomar, Civil Action No. 3585 (M.D. Tenn. 1964). The State of Tennessee then elected to retry him, and did so in 1964. By that time Holm, who had been born in Sweden but had become a naturalized American citizen, had returned to Sweden and taken up permanent residence there. Tennessee issued a subpoena that was sent to Texas authorities in an attempt to serve Holm at his last known United States address. No service having been obtained, the State at trial called Holm's son as a witness and elicited from him the fact that his father now resided in Sweden. Over appropriate objection on constitutional grounds, the Tennessee trial judge then permitted Holm's testimony at the earlier trial to be read to the jury. Stubbs . . . was again convicted. This conviction was in due course affirmed by the Supreme Court of Tennessee. Stubbs v. State, 216 Tenn. 567, 393 S.W.2d 150 (1965).

Respondent has challenged the present second-offender sentence that was imposed upon him by the New York courts on the ground that his 1964 conviction upon retrial was constitutionally infirm because he was denied his Sixth and Fourteenth Amendment right to confront the witness Holm. The Court of Appeals sustained this contention, relying on this Court's opinion in Barber v. Page, 390 U.S. 719 (1968).

In *Barber,* a prospective witness for the prosecution in an Oklahoma felony trial was incarcerated in a federal prison in Texas. . . . In this case, of course, Holm was not merely absent from the State of Tennessee; he was a permanent resident of Sweden. Respondent argues that Tennessee might have obtained Holm as a trial witness by attempting to invoke 28 U.S.C. §1783(a), which provided as of the time here relevant that:

> A court of the United States may subpoena, *for appearance before it,* a citizen or resident of the United States who . . . is beyond the jurisdiction of the United States and whose testimony in a criminal proceeding is desired by the Attorney General. . . .

(1958 ed.) (Emphasis supplied.)

We have been cited to no authority applying this section to permit subpoena by a federal court for testimony in a state felony trial, and certainly the statute on its face does not appear to be designed for that purpose.

The Uniform Act to secure the attendance of witnesses from without a State, the availability of federal writs of habeas corpus ad testificandum, and the established practice of the United States Bureau of Prisons to honor state writs of habeas corpus ad testificandum, all supported the Court's conclusion in *Barber* that the State had not met its obligations to make a good-faith effort to obtain the presence of the witness merely by showing that he was beyond the boundaries of the prosecuting State. There have been, however, no corresponding developments in the area of obtaining witnesses between this country and foreign nations. Upon discovering that Holm resided in a foreign nation, the State of Tennessee, so far as this record shows, was powerless to compel his attendance at the second trial, either through its own process or through established procedures depending on the voluntary assistance of another government. We therefore hold that the predicate of unavailability was sufficiently stronger here than in *Barber* that a federal habeas court was not warranted in upsetting the determination of the state trial court as to Holm's unavailability. . . .

Stubbs also contends that even though the prior determination may not be binding upon subsequent review, the fact that counsel was appointed only four days before trial necessarily requires a finding that the cross-examination of Holm was constitutionally inadequate. Counsel for Stubbs at the 1964 trial placed in the record a list of 12 questions not asked of Holm in 1954, which he said he would have asked had the witness been present at the second trial. With one exception these were directed to the events leading up to and surrounding the shooting. Though not asked in haec verba in 1954, they were nonetheless adverted to in the earlier cross-examination. No one defense counsel will ever develop precisely the same lines of inquiry or frame his questions in exactly the words of another, but from this record counsel at the retrial did not in his proffer show any new and significantly material line of cross-examination that was not at least touched upon in the first trial. . . .

Since there was an adequate opportunity to cross-examine Holm at the first trial, and counsel for Stubbs availed himself of that opportunity, the transcript of Holm's testimony in the first trial bore sufficient "indicia of reliability" and afforded " 'the trier of fact a satisfactory basis for evaluating the truth of the prior statement,' " Dutton v. Evans, 400 U.S., at 89. The witness Holm, consistently with the requirement of the Confrontation Clause, could have been and was found by the trial court to be unavailable at the time of the second trial. There was, therefore, no constitutional error in permitting his prior-recorded testimony to be read to the jury at that trial, and no constitutional infirmity in the judgment of conviction resulting from that trial that would prevent the New York courts from considering that conviction in sentencing Stubbs as a second offender. The judgment of the Court of Appeals is therefore reversed.

PARKER v. RANDOLPH
442 U.S. 62 (1979)

Mr. Justice REHNQUIST announced the Court's judgment and delivered an opinion of the Court with respect to Parts I and III, in which BURGER, C.J., and STEWART, WHITE, and BLACKMUN, JJ., joined, and an opinion (Part II), in which BURGER, C.J., and STEWART and WHITE, JJ., joined.

In Bruton v. United States, 391 U.S. 123 (1968), this Court reversed the robbery conviction of a defendant who had been implicated in the crime by his codefendant's extrajudicial confession. Because the codefendant had not taken the stand at the joint trial and thus could not be cross-examined, the Court held that admission of the codefendant's confession had deprived the defendant of his rights under the Confrontation Clause of the Sixth Amendment. The issue before us in this case is whether *Bruton* requires reversal of a defendant's conviction when the defendant himself has confessed and his confession "interlocks" with and supports the confession of his codefendant. We hold that it does not.

I

Respondents were convicted of murder committed during the commission of a robbery and were sentenced to life imprisonment. The cast of characters playing out the scenes that led up to the fatal shooting could have come from the pen of Bret Harte. The story began in June 1970, when one William Douglas, a professional gambler from Las Vegas, Nev., arrived in Memphis, Tenn., calling himself Ray Blaylock and carrying a gun and a deck of cards. It ended on the evening of July 6, 1970, when Douglas was shot and killed in a Memphis apartment.

Testimony at the trial in the Tennessee state court showed that one Woppy Gaddy, who was promised a cut of Douglas' take, arranged a game of chance between Douglas and Robert Wood, a sometime Memphis gambler. Unwilling to trust the outcome of the contest entirely to luck or skill, Douglas marked the cards, and by game's end Robert Wood and his money had been separated. A second encounter between the two men yielded similar results, and Wood grew suspicious of Douglas' good fortune. In order to determine whether and how Douglas was cheating, Wood brought to the third game an acquaintance named Tommy Thomas, who had a reputation of being a "pretty good poker player." Unknown to Wood, however, Thomas' father and Douglas had been close friends; Thomas, predictably, threw in his lot with Douglas, purposefully lost some $1,000, and reported to Wood that the game was clean. Wood nonetheless left the third game convinced that he was being cheated and intent on recouping his now considerable losses. He explained the situation to his brother, Joe E. Wood, and the two men decided to relieve Douglas of his ill-gotten gains by staging a robbery of the upcoming fourth game.

At this juncture respondents Randolph, Pickens, and Hamilton entered the picture. To carry out the staged robbery, Joe Wood enlisted respondent Hamilton, who was one of his employees, and the latter in turn associated respondents Randolph and Pickens. Douglas and Robert Wood sat down to the fourth and final contest on the evening of July 6, 1970. Joe Wood and Thomas were present in the room as spectators. During the course of the game, Douglas armed himself with a .38-caliber pistol and an automatic shotgun; in response to this unexpected development Joe Wood pulled a derringer pistol on Douglas and Thomas, gave the gun to Robert Wood, and left to tell respondents to move in on the game. Before respondents arrived, however, Douglas reached for his pistol and was shot and killed by Robert Wood. Moments later, respondents and Joe Wood broke down the apartment door, Robert Wood gathered up the cash left on the table, and the gang of five fled into the night. Respondents were subsequently apprehended by the police and confessed to their involvement in the crime.

Respondents and the Wood brothers were jointly tried and convicted of murder during the commission of a robbery. Tenn. Code Ann. §39-2402 (1975). Each defendant was sentenced to life imprisonment. Robert Wood took the stand at trial, admitting that he had killed Douglas, but claiming that the shooting was in self-defense. Thomas described Douglas' method of cheating at cards and admitted his complicity in the fraud on Robert Wood. He also testified in substance that he was present in the room when Joe Wood produced the derringer and when Robert Wood shot and killed Douglas.

None of the respondents took the stand. Thomas could not positively identify any of them, and although Robert Wood named Hamilton as one of the three men involved in the staged robbery, he did not clearly identify Randolph and Pickens as the other two. The State's case against respondents thus rested primarily on their oral confessions, found by the trial court to have been freely and voluntarily given, which were admitted into evidence through the testimony of several officers of the Memphis Police Department.[3] A written confession signed by Pickens was also admitted into evidence over his objection that it had been obtained in violation of his rights under Miranda v. Arizona, 384 U.S. 436 (1966). The trial court instructed the jury that each confession could be used only against the defendant who gave it and could not be considered as evidence of a codefendant's guilt.

The Tennessee Court of Criminal Appeals reversed respondents' convictions, holding . . . that admission of their confessions at the joint trial violated this Court's decision in *Bruton.* The Tennessee Supreme Court in turn reversed the Court of Criminal Appeals and reinstated the

---

3. Each of the confessions was subjected to a process of redaction in which references by the confessing defendant to other defendants were replaced with the words "blank" or "another person." As the Court of Appeals for the Sixth Circuit observed below, the confessions were nevertheless "such as to leave no possible doubt in the jurors' minds concerning the 'person[s]' referred to." 575 F.2d, at 1180.

convictions. Because "each and every defendant either through words or actions demonstrated his knowledge that 'killing may be necessary,' " the court held that respondents' agreement to participate in the robbery rendered them liable under the Tennessee felony-murder statute for Douglas' death. The Tennessee Supreme Court also disagreed with the Court of Criminal Appeals that *Bruton* had been violated, emphasizing that the confession at issue in *Bruton* had inculpated a *nonconfessing* defendant in a joint trial at which neither defendant took the stand. Here, in contrast, the "interlocking inculpatory confessions" of respondents Randolph, Pickens, and Hamilton, "clearly demonstrated the involvement of each, as to crucial facts such as time, location, felonious activity, and awareness of the overall plan or scheme." Accordingly, the Tennessee Supreme Court concluded: "The fact that jointly tried codefendants have confessed precludes a violation of the *Bruton* rule where the confessions are similar in material aspects." Ibid.

The United States District Court for the Western District of Tennessee thereafter granted respondents' applications for writs of habeas corpus, ruling that their rights under *Bruton* had been violated and that introduction of respondent Pickens' uncounseled written confession had violated his rights under Miranda v. Arizona, supra. The Court of Appeals for the Sixth Circuit affirmed, holding that admission of the confessions violated the rule announced in *Bruton* and that the error was not harmless since the evidence against each respondent, even considering his confession, was "not so overwhelming as to compel the jury verdict of guilty. . . ." 575 F.2d 1178, 1182. . . .

Petitioner urges us . . . to hold that the *Bruton* rule does not apply in the context of interlocking confessions. Alternatively, he contends that if introduction of interlocking confessions at a joint trial does violate *Bruton,* the error is all but automatically to be deemed harmless beyond a reasonable doubt. We agree with petitioner that admission at the joint trial of respondents' interlocking confessions did not infringe respondents' right of confrontation secured by the Sixth and Fourteenth Amendments to the United States Constitution, but prefer to cast the issue in a slightly broader form than that posed by petitioner.

Bruton recognized that admission at a joint trial of the incriminating extrajudicial statements of a nontestifying codefendant can have "devastating" consequences to a nonconfessing defendant, adding "substantial, perhaps even critical, weight to the Government's case." 391 U.S., at 128. Such statements go to the jury untested by cross-examination and, indeed, perhaps unanswered altogether unless the defendant waives his Fifth Amendment privilege and takes the stand. The prejudicial impact of a codefendant's confession upon an incriminated defendant who has, insofar as the jury is concerned, maintained his innocence from the beginning is simply too great in such cases to be cured by a limiting instruction. The same cannot be said, however, when the defendant's own confession — "probably the most probative and damaging evidence that can be admitted against him," id., at 139 (White, J., dissenting) — is properly introduced at trial. The defendant is "the most knowledgeable and unimpeachable source of information about his past conduct," id., at 140 (White, J., dissenting), and one can scarcely imagine evidence more damaging to his defense than his own admission of guilt. Thus, the incriminating statements of a codefendant will seldom, if ever, be of the "devastating" character referred to in *Bruton* when the incriminated defendant has admitted his own guilt. The right protected by *Bruton* — the "constitutional right of cross-examination," id., at 137 — has far less practical value to a defendant who has confessed to the crime than to one who has consistently maintained his innocence. Successfully impeaching a codefendant's confession on cross-examination would likely yield small advantage to the defendant whose own admission of guilt stands before the jury unchallenged. Nor does the natural "motivation to shift blame onto others," recognized by the *Bruton* Court to render the incriminating statements of codefendants "inevitably suspect," id., at 136, require application of the *Bruton* rule when the incriminated defendant has corroborated his codefendant's statements by heaping blame onto himself.

The right of confrontation conferred by the Sixth Amendment is a safeguard to ensure the fairness and accuracy of criminal trials, see Dutton v. Evans, 400 U.S. 74, 89 (1970), and its reach cannot be divorced from the system of trial by jury contemplated by the Constitution. A crucial assumption underlying that system is that juries will follow the instructions given them by the trial judge. Were this not so, it would be pointless for a trial court to instruct a jury, and even more pointless for an appellate court to reverse a criminal conviction because the jury was improperly instructed. The Confrontation Clause has never been held to bar the admission into evidence of every relevant extrajudicial statement made by a nontestifying declarant simply because it in some way incriminates the defendant. See, e.g., id., at 80; Mattox v. United States, 156 U.S. 237, 240-244 (1895). And an instruction directing the jury to consider a codefendant's extrajudicial statement only against its source has been found sufficient to avoid offending the confrontation right of the implicated defendant in numerous decisions of this Court.

When, as in *Bruton,* the confessing codefendant has chosen not to take the stand and the implicated defendant has made no extrajudicial admission of guilt, limiting instructions cannot be accepted as adequate to safeguard the defendant's rights under the Confrontation Clause. Under such circumstances, the "practical and human limitations of the jury system," Bruton v. United States, supra, at 135, override the theoretically sound premise that a jury will follow the trial court's instructions. But when the defendant's own confession is properly before the jury, we believe that the constitutional scales tip the other way. The possible prejudice resulting from the failure of the jury to follow the trial court's instructions is not so "devastating" or "vital" to the confessing defendant to require departure from the general rule allowing admission of evidence with limiting instructions. We therefore hold that admission of interlocking confessions with proper limiting instructions conforms to the requirements of the Sixth and Fourteenth Amendments to the United States Constitution. Accordingly, the judgment of the Court of Appeals as to respondents Hamilton and Randolph is reversed. . . .

Mr. Justice POWELL took no part in the consideration or decision of this case.

Mr. Justice BLACKMUN, concurring in part. . . .

For me, any error that existed in the admission of the confessions of the codefendants, in violation of Bruton v. United States, 391 U.S. 123 (1968), was, on the facts of this case, clearly harmless beyond a reasonable doubt. I refrain from joining Part II of the principal opinion because, as I read it, it abandons the harmless-error analysis the Court previously has applied in similar circumstances and now adopts a per se rule to the effect that *Bruton* is inapplicable in an interlocking confession situation. . . .

It is possible, of course, that the new approach will result in no more than a shift in analysis. Instead of focusing on whether the error was harmless, defendants and courts will be forced, instead, to inquire whether the confessions were sufficiently interlocking so as to permit a conclusion that *Bruton* does not apply. And I suppose that after making a determination that the confessions did not interlock to a sufficient degree, the court then would have to make a harmless-error determination anyway, thus adding another step to the process.

Unfortunately, it is not clear that the new approach mandates even an inquiry whether the confessions interlock. Respondents have argued that the confessions in this case, in fact, did not interlock. The principal opinion, however, simply assumes the interlock. It thus comes close to saying that so long as all the defendants have made some type of confession which is placed in evidence, *Bruton* is inapplicable without inquiry into whether the confessions actually interlock and the extent thereof. If it is willing to abandon the factual inquiry that accompanies a harmless-error determination, it should be ready, at least, to substitute an inquiry into whether there is genuine interlocking before it casts the application of *Bruton,* and the underlying Confrontation Clause right, completely aside. . . .

Mr. Justice STEVENS, with whom Mr. Justice BRENNAN and Mr. Justice MARSHALL join, dissenting.

As Mr. Justice Blackmun makes clear, proper analysis of this case requires that we differentiate between (1) a conclusion that there was no error under the rule of Bruton v. United States, 391 U.S. 123, and (2) a conclusion that even if constitutional error was committed, the possibility that inadmissible evidence contributed to the conviction is so remote that we may characterize the error as harmless. Because Mr. Justice Blackmun properly rejects the first conclusion, my area of disagreement with him is narrow. In my view, but not in his, the concurrent findings of the District Court and the Court of Appeals that the error here was not harmless preclude this Court from reaching a different result on this kind of issue.

My area of disagreement with the plurality opinion is far wider and prompts more extended remarks. The plurality adopts the first conclusion above — that no constitutional error was committed when the confessions of all three respondents were admitted into evidence at their joint trial. Without purporting to modify the *Bruton* rule precluding the use of a nontestifying codefendant's extrajudicial admissions against a defendant in a joint trial, the plurality reaches this conclusion by attempting to create a vaguely defined exception for cases in which there is evidence that the defendant has also made inculpatory statements which he does not repudiate at trial. . . .

Evidence that a defendant has made an "extrajudicial admission of guilt" which "stands before the jury unchallenged," *ante,* is not an acceptable reason for depriving him of his constitutional right to confront the witnesses against him. In arguing to the contrary, and in striving "to cast the issue" presented "in a . . . broader form" than any of the parties felt necessary to dispose of the case, *ante,* the plurality necessarily relies on two assumptions. Both are erroneous. First, it assumes that the jury's ability to disregard a codefendant's inadmissible and highly prejudicial confession is invariably increased by the existence of a corroborating statement by the defendant. Second, it assumes that all unchallenged confessions by a defendant are equally reliable. Aside from two quotations from the dissent in *Bruton,* however, the plurality supports these assumptions with nothing more than the force of its own assertions. But the infinite variability of inculpatory statements (whether made by defendants or codefendants), and of their likely effect on juries, makes those assertions untenable. A hypothetical example is instructive.

Suppose a prosecutor has 10 items of evidence tending to prove that defendant X and codefendant Y are guilty of assassinating a public figure. The first is the tape of a televised interview with Y describing in detail how he and X planned and executed the crime. Items two through nine involve circumstantial evidence of a past association between X and Y, a shared hostility for the victim, and an expressed wish for his early demise — evidence that in itself might very well be insufficient to convict X. Item 10 is the testimony of a drinking partner, a former cellmate, or a divorced spouse of X who vaguely recalls X saying that he had been with Y at the approximate time of the killing. Neither X nor Y takes the stand.

If Y's televised confession were placed before the jury while Y was immunized from cross-examination, it would undoubtedly have the "devastating" effect on X that the *Bruton* rule was designed to avoid. 391 U.S., at 128. As Mr. Justice Stewart's characteristically concise explanation of the underlying rationale in that case demonstrates, it would also plainly violate X's Sixth Amendment right to confront his accuser. Nevertheless, under the plurality's first remarkable assumption, the prejudice to X — and the violation of his constitutional right — would be entirely cured by the subsequent use of evidence of his own ambiguous statement. In my judgment, such dubious corroboration would enhance, rather than reduce, the danger that the jury would rely on Y's televised confession when evaluating X's guilt. Even if I am wrong, however, there is no reason to conclude that the prosecutor's reliance on item 10 would obviate the harm flowing from the use of item 1.

The dubiousness of X's confession in this example — as in any case in which the defendant's inculpatory statement is ambiguous, incomplete, the result of coercive influences, or simply the product of the well-recognized and often untrustworthy "urge to confess" — illustrates the inaccuracy of the plurality's second crucial assumption. It is no doubt true that in some cases a defendant's confession will constitute such convincing evidence of his guilt that the violation of his constitutional rights is harmless beyond a reasonable doubt. E.g., Brown v. United States, 411 U.S. 223; Schneble v. Florida, 405 U.S. 427. But in many cases, it is not so convincing. Moreover, such evidence is not inherently more incriminating or more reliable than other kinds of evidence such as fingerprints, photographs, or eyewitness testimony. Yet, if these types of corroboration are given the same absolute effect that the plurality would accord confessions, the *Bruton* rule would almost never apply. . . .

In short, I see no logic to commend the proposed exception to the rule of *Bruton* save, perhaps, a purpose to limit the effect of that rule to the largely irrelevant set of facts in the case that announced it. If relevant at all in the present context, the factors relied on by the plurality support a proposition no one has even remotely advocated in this case — that the corroborated evidence used in this case was so trustworthy that it should have been fully admissible against all of the defendants, and the jury instructed as much. Conceivably, corroborating or other circumstances surrounding otherwise inadmissible hearsay may so enhance its reliability that its admission in evidence is justified in some situations. But before allowing such a rule to defeat a defendant's fundamental right to confront his accusers, this Court surely should insist upon a strong showing not only of the reliability of the hearsay in the particular case but also of the impossibility, or at least difficulty, of making the accusers available for cross-examination. And, in most cases the prosecution will be hard pressed to make the latter showing in light of its ability to try the defendant and codefendant separately and to afford each immunity from the use against him of his testimony at the other's trial. See Kastigar v. United States, 406 U.S. 441.

Absent admissibility of the codefendants' confessions against respondents, therefore, the controlling question must be whether it is realistic to assume that the jury followed the judge's instructions to disregard those confessions when it was evaluating respondents' guilt. The plurality would answer this question affirmatively. . . .

I prefer to stand by the observations about this sort of question by jurists like Felix Frankfurter, Learned Hand, Wiley Rutledge, Robert Jackson, and Henry Friendly, and by scholars like Wigmore and Morgan. In my judgment, as I think in theirs, the odds that a jury will obey a command to ignore a codefendant's confession — whether or not the defendant has himself confessed — are no less stacked against the defendant than was the deck of cards that William Douglas used to Robert Wood's, and ultimately to his own, downfall in the game of chance arranged by Woppy Gaddy. In contests like this, the risk that one player may be confused with another is not insubstantial.

I respectfully dissent.

Which confrontation rule does the plurality apply? How does the plurality opinion distinguish *Bruton*? Does it do so convincingly? Is there a divergence between theory and practice in the jury's ability to follow limiting instructions? If so, how should this be reconciled? Is Justice Rehnquist's opinion internally consistent in upholding the limited admissibility of this evidence with cautionary instructions? Are juries more or less likely to follow instructions in this type of case than in the *Bruton* situation? To what extent must confessions "interlock" to satisfy the plurality's test? How should a trial court handle a case in which the codefendants have given confessions that do not interlock but in fact contradict each other's in important respects?

Is the harmless error approach advocated by Justice Blackmun and the dissenters a preferable ground of decision in *Parker*? Taking up the challenge posed by the dissenting opinion, was the corroborated evidence in this case so trustworthy that the co-defendants' confessions should have been fully admissible against all the defendants, and the jury instructed as much?

What positions do the Justices take in *Parker* on the importance of reliability and availability in confrontation clause analysis? Did the prosecution, by deciding to try Randolph, Pickens, Hamilton, and the Wood brothers together, "procure" the unavailability of the declarants within the meaning of Rule 804(a)? How should this factor affect confrontation clause analysis?

OHIO v. ROBERTS
448 U.S. 56 (1980)

Mr. Justice BLACKMUN delivered the opinion of the Court.

This case presents issues concerning the constitutional propriety of the introduction in evidence of the preliminary hearing testimony of a witness not produced at the defendant's subsequent state criminal trial.

I

Local police arrested respondent, Herschel Roberts, on January 7, 1975, in Lake County, Ohio. Roberts was charged with forgery of a check in the name of Bernard Isaacs, and with possession of stolen credit cards belonging to Isaacs and his wife Amy.

A preliminary hearing was held in Municipal Court on January 10. The prosecution called several witnesses, including Mr. Isaacs. Respondent's appointed counsel had seen the Isaacs' daughter, Anita, in the courthouse hallway, and called her as the defense's only witness. Anita Isaacs testified that she knew respondent, and that she had permitted him to use her apartment for several days while she was away. Defense counsel questioned Anita at some length and attempted to elicit from her an admission that she had given respondent checks and the credit cards without informing him that she did not have permission to use them. Anita, however, denied this. Respondent's attorney did not ask to have the witness declared hostile and did not request permission to place her on cross-examination. The prosecutor did not question Anita.

A county grand jury subsequently indicted respondent for forgery, for receiving stolen property (including the credit cards), and for possession of heroin. The attorney who represented respondent at the preliminary hearing withdrew upon becoming a Municipal Court Judge, and new counsel was appointed for Roberts.

Between November 1975 and March 1976, five subpoenas for four different trial dates were issued to Anita at her parents' Ohio residence. The last three carried a written instruction that Anita should "call before appearing." She was not at the residence when these were executed. She did not telephone and she did not appear at trial.

In March 1976, the case went to trial before a jury in the Court of Common Pleas. Respondent took the stand and testified that Anita Isaacs had given him her parents' checkbook and credit cards with the understanding that he could use them. Relying on Ohio Rev. Code Ann. §2945.49 (1975), which permits the use of preliminary examination testimony of a witness who "cannot for any reason be produced at the trial," the State, on rebuttal, offered the transcript of Anita's testimony.

Asserting a violation of the Confrontation Clause and, indeed, the unconstitutionality thereunder of §2945.49, the defense objected to the use of the transcript. The trial court conducted a voir dire hearing as to its admissibility. Amy Isaacs, the sole witness at voir dire, was questioned by both the prosecutor and defense counsel concerning her daughter's whereabouts. Anita, according to her mother, left home for Tucson, Ariz., soon after the preliminary hearing. About a year before the trial, a San Francisco social worker was in communication with the Isaacs about a welfare application Anita had filed there. Through the social worker, the Isaacs reached their daughter once by telephone. Since then, however, Anita had called her parents only one other time and had not been in touch with her two sisters. When Anita called, some seven or eight months before trial, she told her parents that she "was traveling" outside Ohio, but did not reveal the place from which she called. Mrs. Isaacs stated that she knew of no way to reach Anita in case of an emergency. Nor did she "know of anybody who knows where she is." The trial court admitted the transcript into evidence. Respondent was convicted on all counts.

The Court of Appeals of Ohio reversed. After reviewing the voir dire, that court concluded that the prosecution had failed to make a showing of a "good-faith effort" to secure the absent witness' attendance, as required by Barber v. Page, 390 U.S. 719, 722-725 (1968). The court noted that "we have no witness from the prosecution to testify . . . that no one on behalf of the State could determine Anita's whereabouts, [or] that anyone had exhausted contact with the San Francisco social worker." Unavailability would have been established, the court said, "[h]ad the State demonstrated that its subpoenas were never actually served on the witness and that they were unable to make contact in any way with the witness. . . . Until the Isaacs' voir dire, requested by the defense, the State had done nothing, absolutely nothing, to show the Court that Anita would be absent because of unavailability, and they showed no effort having been made to seek out her whereabouts for purpose of trial."

The Supreme Court of Ohio, by a 4-3 vote, affirmed, but did so on other grounds. It first held that the Court of Appeals had erred in concluding that Anita was not unavailable. Barber v. Page was distinguished as a case in which "the government knew where the absent witness was," whereas Anita's "whereabouts were entirely unknown." "[T]he trial judge could reasonably have concluded from Mrs. Isaacs' voir dire testimony that due diligence could not have procured the attendance of Anita Isaacs"; he "could reasonably infer that Anita had left San Francisco"; and he "could properly hold that the witness was unavailable to testify in person."

The court, nonetheless, held that the transcript was inadmissible. Reasoning that normally there is little incentive to cross-examine a witness at a preliminary hearing, where the "ultimate issue" is only probable cause, and citing the dissenting opinion in California v. Green, 399 U.S. 149, 189 (1970), the court held that the mere opportunity to cross-examine at a preliminary hearing did not afford constitutional confrontation for purposes of trial. The court distinguished *Green,* where this Court had ruled admissible the preliminary hearing testimony of a declarant who was present at trial, but claimed forgetfulness. The Ohio court perceived a "dictum" in *Green* that suggested that the mere opportunity to cross-examine renders preliminary hearing testimony admissible. But the court concluded that *Green* "goes no further than to suggest that cross-examination actually conducted at preliminary hearing *may* afford adequate confrontation for purposes of a later trial." Since Anita had not been cross-examined at the preliminary hearing and was absent at trial, the introduction of the transcript of her testimony was held to have violated respondent's confrontation right. The three dissenting Justices would have ruled that "'the test is the opportunity for full and complete cross-examination rather than the use which is made of that opportunity.'" . . .

The Confrontation Clause operates in two separate ways to restrict the range of admissible hearsay. First, in conformance with the Framers' preference for face-to-face accusation, the Sixth Amendment establishes a rule of necessity. In the usual case (including cases where prior cross-examination has occurred), the prosecution must either produce, or demonstrate the unavailability of, the declarant whose statement it wishes to use against the defendant.[7]

The second aspect operates once a witness is shown to be unavailable. Reflecting its underlying purpose to augment accuracy in the factfinding process by ensuring the defendant an effective means to test adverse evidence, the Clause countenances only hearsay marked with such trustworthiness that "there is no material departure from the reason of the general rule." Snyder v. Massachusetts, 291 U.S., at 107. . . . "It is clear from these statements, and from numerous prior decisions of this Court, that even though the witness be unavailable his prior testimony must bear some of these 'indicia of reliability.'" [Mancusi v. Stubbs], 408 U.S., at 213.

The Court has applied this "indicia of reliability" requirement principally by concluding that certain hearsay exceptions rest upon such solid foundations that admission of virtually any evidence within them comports with the "substance of the constitutional protection." Mattox v.

---

7. A demonstration of unavailability, however, is not always required. In Dutton v. Evans, 400 U.S. 74 (1970), for example, the Court found the utility of trial confrontation so remote that it did not require the prosecution to produce a seemingly available witness.

United States, 156 U.S., at 244.[8] This reflects the truism that "hearsay rules and the Confrontation Clause are generally designed to protect similar values," California v. Green, 399 U.S., at 155, and "stem from the same roots," Dutton v. Evans, 400 U.S. 74, 86 (1970). It also responds to the need for certainty in the workaday world of conducting criminal trials.

In sum, when a hearsay declarant is not present for cross-examination at trial, the Confrontation Clause normally requires a showing that he is unavailable. Even then, his statement is admissible only if it bears adequate "indicia of reliability." Reliability can be inferred without more in a case where the evidence falls within a firmly rooted hearsay exception. In other cases, the evidence must be excluded, at least absent a showing of particularized guarantees of trustworthiness.[9]

III

We turn first to that aspect of confrontation analysis deemed dispositive by the Supreme Court of Ohio, and answered by it in the negative — whether Anita Isaacs' prior testimony at the preliminary hearing bore sufficient "indicia of reliability." Resolution of this issue requires a careful comparison of this case to California v. Green, supra.

A

In *Green,* at the preliminary hearing, a youth named Porter identified Green as a drug supplier. When called to the stand at Green's trial, however, Porter professed a lapse of memory. Frustrated in its attempt to adduce live testimony, the prosecution offered Porter's prior statements. The trial judge ruled the evidence admissible, and substantial portions of the preliminary hearing transcript were read to the jury.

---

8. See, e.g., Pointer v. Texas, 380 U.S., at 407 (dying declarations); Mattox v. United States, 156 U.S., at 243-244 (same); Mancusi v. Stubbs, 408 U.S. 204, 213-216 (1972) (cross-examined prior-trial testimony); Comment, 30 La. L. Rev. 651, 668 (1970) ("Properly administered the business and public records exceptions would seem to be among the safest of the hearsay exceptions").

9. The complexity of reconciling the Confrontation Clause and the hearsay rules has triggered an outpouring of scholarly commentary. Few observers have commented without proposing, roughly or in detail, a basic approach. . . .

Notwithstanding this divergence of critical opinion, we have found no commentary suggesting that the Court has misidentified the basic interests to be accommodated. Nor has any commentator demonstrated that prevailing analysis is out of line with the intentions of the Framers of the Sixth Amendment. Convinced that "no rule will perfectly resolve all possible problems," Natali, 7 Rutgers-Camden L.J., at 73, we reject the invitation to overrule a near-century of jurisprudence. Our reluctance to begin anew is heightened by the Court's implicit prior rejection of principal alternative proposals, see Dutton v. Evans, 400 U.S., at 93-100 (concurring opinion), and California v. Green, 399 U.S., at 172-189 (concurring opinion); the mutually critical character of the commentary; and the Court's demonstrated success in steering a middle course among proposed alternatives.

This Court found no error. Citing the established rule that prior trial testimony is admissible upon retrial if the declarant becomes unavailable, and recent dicta suggesting the admissibility of preliminary hearing testimony under proper circumstances, the Court rejected Green's Confrontation Clause attack. It reasoned:

"Porter's statement at the preliminary hearing had already been given under circumstances closely approximating those that surround the typical trial. Porter was under oath; respondent was represented by counsel — the same counsel in fact who later represented him at the trial; respondent had every opportunity to cross-examine Porter as to his statement; and the proceedings were conducted before a judicial tribunal, equipped to provide a judicial record of the hearings." 399 U.S., at 165.

These factors, the Court concluded, provided all that the Sixth Amendment demands: "substantial compliance with the purposes behind the confrontation requirement." Id., at 166.[10]

This passage and others in the *Green* opinion suggest that the *opportunity* to cross-examine at the preliminary hearing — even absent actual cross-examination — satisfies the Confrontation Clause. Yet the record showed, and the Court recognized, that defense counsel in fact had cross-examined Porter at the earlier proceeding. Thus, Mr. Justice Brennan, writing in dissent, could conclude only that "[p]erhaps" "the mere opportunity for face-to-face encounter [is] sufficient."

We need not decide whether the Supreme Court of Ohio correctly dismissed statements in *Green* suggesting that the mere opportunity to

_____

10. This reasoning appears in Part III of *Green*, the only section of that opinion directly relevant to the issue raised here. The Ohio court in the present case appears to have dismissed Part III as "dictum." The United States has suggested that Part III properly is viewed as an "alternative holding." Either view, perhaps, would diminish *Green*'s precedential significance. We accept neither.

In Part II of *Green*, the Court held that use of a trial witness' prior inconsistent statements as substantive evidence did not, as a general rule, violate the Confrontation Clause. In Part III, the Court went further and held: "Porter's preliminary hearing testimony was admissible . . . wholly apart from the question of whether respondent had an effective opportunity for confrontation at the subsequent trial. For Porter's statement at the preliminary hearing had already been given under circumstances closely approximating those that surround the typical trial." In Part IV, the Court returned to the general rule articulated in Part II. The Court contrasted cases in which the declarant testifies at trial that he has forgotten the underlying events, rather than claiming recollection but advancing an inconsistent story. The Court noted that commentators disagreed over whether the former class of cases should be brought within the general rule articulated in Part II. Given the difficulty of the issue, which was neither briefed in this Court nor addressed below, the Court remanded the case for a determination of whether assertedly inconsistent remarks made by Porter to a police officer could be admitted under the rule of Part II. Since the critical reason for this disposition was Porter's asserted forgetfulness at trial, the same result clearly would have obtained in regard to Porter's preliminary hearing testimony were it not for the Court's holding in Part III. It follows that Part III was not an alternative holding, and certainly was not dictum. That portion of the opinion alone dispositively established the admissibility of Porter's preliminary hearing testimony.

cross-examine rendered the prior testimony admissible. Nor need we decide whether de minimis questioning is sufficient, for defense counsel in this case tested Anita's testimony with the equivalent of significant cross-examination.

B

Counsel's questioning clearly partook of cross-examination as a matter of *form*. His presentation was replete with leading questions, the principal tool and hallmark of cross-examination. In addition, counsel's questioning comported with the principal *purpose* of cross-examination: to challenge "whether the declarant was sincerely telling what he believed to be the truth, whether the declarant accurately perceived and remembered the matter he related, and whether the declarant's intended meaning is adequately conveyed by the language he employed." Davenport, The Confrontation Clause and the Co-Conspirator Exception in Criminal Prosecutions: A Functional Analysis, 85 Harv. L. Rev. 1378 (1972). Anita's unwillingness to shift the blame away from respondent became discernible early in her testimony. Yet counsel continued to explore the underlying events in detail. He attempted, for example, to establish that Anita and the defendant were sharing an apartment, an assertion that was critical to respondent's defense at trial and that might have suggested ulterior personal reasons for unfairly casting blame on the defendant. At another point, he directly challenged Anita's veracity by seeking to have her admit that she had given the credit cards to respondent to obtain a television. When Anita denied this, defense counsel elicited the fact that the only television she owned was a "Twenty Dollar . . . old model."

Respondent argues that, because defense counsel never asked the court to declare Anita hostile, his questioning necessarily occurred on direct examination. But however state law might formally characterize the questioning of Anita, it afforded "substantial compliance with the purposes behind the confrontation requirement," Green, 399 U.S., at 166, no less so than classic cross-examination. Although Ohio law may have authorized objection by the prosecutor or intervention by the court, this did not happen. As in Green, respondent's counsel was not "significantly limited in any way in the scope or nature of his cross-examination." Ibid.

We are also unpersuaded that Green is distinguishable on the ground that Anita Isaacs — unlike the declarant Porter in Green — was not personally available for questioning at trial. This argument ignores the language and logic of Green: "Porter's statement would, we think, have been admissible at trial even in Porter's absence if Porter had been actually unavailable. . . . That being the case, we do not think a different result should follow where the witness is actually produced." Id., at 165.

Nor does it matter that, unlike Green, respondent had a different lawyer at trial from the one at the preliminary hearing. Although one might strain one's reading of *Green* to assign this factor some significance, respondent advances no reason of substance supporting the distinction. Indeed, if we were to accept this suggestion, *Green* would carry the seeds of its own demise; under a "same attorney" rule, a defendant could nullify the effect of *Green* by obtaining new counsel after the preliminary hearing was concluded.

Finally, we reject respondent's attempt to fall back on general principles of confrontation, and his argument that this case falls among those in which the Court must undertake a particularized search for "indicia of reliability." Under this theory, the factors previously cited — absence of face-to-face contact at trial, presence of a new attorney, and the lack of classic cross-examination — combine with considerations uniquely tied to Anita to mandate exclusion of her statements. Anita, respondent says, had every reason to lie to avoid prosecution or parental reprobation. Her unknown whereabouts is explicable as an effort to avoid punishment, perjury, or self-incrimination. Given these facts, her prior testimony falls on the unreliable side, and should have been excluded.

In making this argument, respondent in effect asks us to disassociate preliminary hearing testimony previously subjected to cross-examination from previously cross-examined prior-trial testimony, which the Court has deemed generally immune from subsequent confrontation attack. Precedent requires us to decline this invitation. In *Green* the Court found guarantees of trustworthiness in the accouterments of the preliminary hearing itself; there was no mention of the inherent reliability or unreliability of Porter and his story.

In sum, we perceive no reason to resolve the reliability issue differently here than the Court did in *Green*. "Since there was an adequate opportunity to cross-examine [the witness], and counsel . . . availed himself of that opportunity, the transcript . . . bore sufficient 'indicia of reliability' and afforded ' "the trier of fact a satisfactory basis for evaluating the truth of the prior statement." ' " 408 U.S., at 216.

IV

Our holding that the Supreme Court of Ohio erred in its "indicia of reliability" analysis does not fully dispose of the case, for respondent would defend the judgment on an alternative ground. The State, he contends, failed to lay a proper predicate for admission of the preliminary hearing transcript by its failure to demonstrate that Anita Isaacs was not available to testify in person at the trial. All the justices of the Supreme Court of Ohio rejected this argument.

A

The basic litmus of Sixth Amendment unavailability is established: "[A] witness is not 'unavailable' for purposes of . . . the exception to the confrontation requirement unless the prosecutorial authorities have made a *good-faith effort* to obtain his presence at trial." Barber v. Page, 390 U.S., at 724-725.

Although it might be said that the Court's prior cases provide no further refinement of this statement of the rule, certain general propositions safely emerge. The law does not require the doing of a futile act. Thus, if no possibility of procuring the witness exists (as, for example, the witness' intervening death), "good faith" demands nothing of the prosecution. But if there is a possibility, albeit remote, that affirmative measures might produce the declarant, the obligation of good faith *may* demand their effectuation. "The lengths to which the prosecution must go to produce a witness . . . is a question of reasonableness." California v. Green, 399 U.S., at 189, n.22 (concurring opinion, citing Barber v. Page, supra). The ultimate question is whether the witness is unavailable despite good-faith efforts undertaken prior to trial to locate and present that witness. As with other evidentiary proponents, the prosecution bears the burden of establishing this predicate.

B

On the facts presented we hold that the trial court and the Supreme Court of Ohio correctly concluded that Anita's unavailability, in the constitutional sense, was established.

At the voir dire hearing, called for by the defense, it was shown that some four months prior to the trial the prosecutor was in touch with Amy Isaacs and discussed with her Anita's whereabouts. It may appropriately be inferred that Mrs. Isaacs told the prosecutor essentially the same facts to which she testified at voir dire: that the Isaacs had last heard from Anita during the preceding summer; that she was not then in San Francisco, but was traveling outside Ohio; and that the Isaacs and their other children knew of no way to reach Anita even in an emergency. This last fact takes on added significance when it is recalled that Anita's parents earlier had undertaken affirmative efforts to reach their daughter when the social worker's inquiry came in from San Francisco. This is not a case of parents abandoning all interest in an absent daughter.

The evidence of record demonstrates that the prosecutor issued a subpoena to Anita at her parents' home, not only once, but on five separate occasions over a period of several months. In addition, at the voir dire argument, the prosecutor stated to the court that respondent "witnessed that I have attempted to locate, I have subpoenaed, there has been a voir dire of the witness' parents, and they have not been able to locate her for over a year."

Given these facts, the prosecution did not breach its duty of good-faith effort. To be sure, the prosecutor might have tried to locate by telephone the San Francisco social worker with whom Mrs. Isaacs had spoken many months before and might have undertaken other steps in an effort to find Anita. One, in hindsight, may always think of other things. Nevertheless, the great improbability that such efforts would have resulted in locating the witness, and would have led to her production at trial, neutralizes any intimation that a concept of reasonableness required their execution. We accept as a general rule, of course, the proposition that "the possibility of a refusal is not the equivalent of asking and receiving a rebuff." But the service and ineffectiveness of the five subpoenas and the conversation with Anita's mother were far more than mere reluctance to face the possibility of a refusal. It was investigation at the last-known real address, and it was conversation with a parent who was concerned about her daughter's whereabouts.

Barber and Mancusi v. Stubbs, supra, are the cases in which this Court has explored the issue of constitutional unavailability. Although each is factually distinguishable from this case, *Mancusi* provides significant support for a conclusion of good-faith effort here, and *Barber* has no contrary significance. Insofar as this record discloses no basis for concluding that Anita was abroad, the case is factually weaker than *Mancusi*; but it is stronger than *Mancusi* in the sense that the Ohio prosecutor, unlike the prosecutor in *Mancusi*, had no clear indication, if any at all, of Anita's whereabouts. In *Barber*, the Court found an absence of good-faith effort where the prosecution made no attempt to secure the presence of a declarant incarcerated in a federal penitentiary in a neighboring State. There, the prosecution knew where the witness was, procedures existed whereby the witness could be brought to the trial, and the witness was not in a position to frustrate efforts to secure his production. Here, Anita's whereabouts were not known, and there was no assurance that she would be found in a place from which she could be forced to return to Ohio.

We conclude that the prosecution carried its burden of demonstrating that Anita was constitutionally unavailable for purposes of respondent's trial.

The judgment of the Supreme Court of Ohio is reversed. . . .

Mr. Justice BRENNAN, with whom Mr. Justice MARSHALL and Mr. Justice STEVENS join, dissenting.

The Court concludes that because Anita Isaacs' testimony at respondent's preliminary hearing was subjected to the equivalent of significant cross-examination, such hearsay evidence bore sufficient "indicia of reliability" to permit its introduction at respondent's trial without offending the Confrontation Clause of the Sixth Amendment. As the Court recognizes, however, the Constitution imposes the threshold requirement that the prosecution must demonstrate the unavailability of the witness whose prerecorded testimony it wishes to use against the defendant. Because I cannot agree that the State has met its burden of establishing this predicate, I dissent.[1] . . .

From all that appears in the record — and there has been no suggestion that the record is incomplete in this respect — the State's *total* effort to secure Anita's attendance at respondent's trial consisted of the delivery of five subpoenas in her name to her parents' residence, and three of those were issued after the authorities had learned that she was no longer living there. At least four months before the trial began, the prosecution was aware that Anita had moved away; yet during that entire interval it did nothing whatsoever to try to make contact with her. It is difficult to believe that the State would have been so derelict in attempting to secure the witness' presence at trial had it not had her favorable preliminary hearing testimony upon which to rely in the event of her "unavailability." The perfunctory steps which the State took in this case can hardly qualify as a "good-faith effort." In point of fact, it was no effort at all.

The Court, however, is apparently willing to excuse the prosecution's inaction on the ground that any endeavor to locate Anita Isaacs was unlikely to bear fruit. I not only take issue with the premise underlying that reasoning — that the improbability of success can condone a refusal to conduct even a cursory investigation into the witness' whereabouts — but I also seriously question the Court's conclusion that a bona fide search in the present case would inevitably have come to naught.

Surely the prosecution's mere speculation about the difficulty of locating Anita Isaacs cannot relieve it of the obligation to attempt to find her. Although the rigor of the undertaking might serve to palliate a failure to prevail, it cannot justify a failure even to try. . . .

Nor do I concur in the Court's bleak prognosis of the likelihood of procuring Anita Isaacs' attendance at respondent's trial.[4]

---

1. Because I am convinced that the State failed to lay a proper foundation for the admission of Anita Isaacs' preliminary hearing testimony, I have no occasion to consider whether that testimony had in fact been subjected to full and effective adverse questioning and whether, even conceding the adequacy of the prior cross-examination, the significant differences in the nature and objectives of the preliminary hearing and the trial preclude substituting confrontation at the former proceeding for the constitutional requirement of confrontation at the latter. See California v. Green, 399 U.S. 149, 195-203 (1970) (Brennan, J., dissenting).

4. In attempting to distinguish this case from Barber v. Page, and demonstrate the reasonableness of the State's conduct, the Court states that "there was no assurance that [Anita] would be found in a place from which she could be forced to return to Ohio." Once located, however, it is extremely unlikely that Anita could have resisted the State's efforts to secure her return. The Uniform Act to Secure the Attendance of Witnesses from Without a State in Criminal Proceedings enables prosecuting authorities in one State to obtain an order from a court in another State compelling the witness' appearance to testify in court in the first State. The Uniform Act has been adopted in the District of Columbia,

Which approach to the confrontation clause does the Court follow in *Roberts*? Are the "necessity" and "reliability" justifications for the use of hearsay evidence in criminal cases complementary or contradictory? What strategic problems at the preliminary hearing does *Roberts* raise for defense counsel?

With regard to Anita Isaacs's unavailability at trial, is *Roberts* closer to Barber v. Page or Mancusi v. Stubbs? What is the prosecution's burden of proof on this issue? What is a reviewing court's standard of review?

B.   Confrontation, Compulsory Process, and the Bridge to Privileges

DAVIS v. ALASKA
415 U.S. 308 (1974)

Mr. Chief Justice BURGER delivered the opinion of the Court.

We granted certiorari in this case to consider whether the Confrontation Clause requires that a defendant in a criminal case be allowed to impeach the credibility of a prosecution witness by cross-examination directed at possible bias deriving from the witness' probationary status as a juvenile delinquent when such an impeachment would conflict with a State's asserted interest in preserving the confidentiality of juvenile adjudications of delinquency.

I

When the Polar Bar in Anchorage closed in the early morning hours of February 16, 1970, well over a thousand dollars in cash and checks was in the bar's Mosler safe. About midday, February 16, it was discovered that the bar had been broken into and the safe, about two feet square and weighing several hundred pounds, had been removed from the premises.

Later that afternoon the Alaska State Troopers received word that a safe had been discovered about 26 miles outside Anchorage near the home of Jess Straight and his family. The safe, which was subsequently determined to be the one stolen from the Polar Bar, had been pried open and the contents removed. Richard Green, Jess Straight's stepson, told investigating troopers on the scene that at about noon on February 16 he had seen and spoken with two Negro men standing alongside a

---

the Panama Canal Zone, Puerto Rico, the Virgin Islands, and every State in the Union except Alabama. 11 U.L.A. 1 (Supp. 1980).

late-model metallic blue Chevrolet sedan near where the safe was later discovered. The next day Anchorage police investigators brought him to the police station where Green was given six photographs of adult Negro males. After examining the photographs for 30 seconds to a minute, Green identified the photograph of petitioner as that of one of the men he had encountered the day before and described to the police. Petitioner was arrested the next day, February 18. On February 19, Green picked petitioner out of a lineup of seven Negro males.

At trial, evidence was introduced to the effect that paint chips found in the trunk of petitioner's rented blue Chevrolet could have originated from the surface of the stolen safe. Further, the trunk of the car contained particles which were identified as safe insulation characteristic of that found in Mosler safes. The insulation found in the trunk matched that of the stolen safe.

Richard Green was a crucial witness for the prosecution. He testified at trial that while on an errand for his mother he confronted two men standing beside a late-model metallic blue Chevrolet, parked on a road near his family's house. The man standing at the rear of the car spoke to Green asking if Green lived nearby and if his father was home. Green offered the men help, but his offer was rejected. On his return from the errand Green again passed the two men and he saw the man with whom he had had the conversation standing at the rear of the car with "something like a crowbar" in his hands. Green identified petitioner at the trial as the man with the "crowbar." The safe was discovered later that afternoon at the point, according to Green, where the Chevrolet had been parked.

Before testimony was taken at the trial of petitioner, the prosecutor moved for a protective order to prevent any reference to Green's juvenile record by the defense in the course of cross-examination. At the time of the trial and at the time of the events Green testified to, Green was on probation by order of a juvenile court after having been adjudicated a delinquent for burglarizing two cabins. Green was 16 years of age at the time of the Polar Bar burglary, but had turned 17 prior to trial.

In opposing the protective order, petitioner's counsel made it clear that he would not introduce Green's juvenile adjudication as a general impeachment of Green's character as a truthful person but, rather, to show specifically that at the same time Green was assisting the police in identifying petitioner he was on probation for burglary. From this petitioner would seek to show — or at least argue — that Green acted out of fear or concern of possible jeopardy to his probation. Not only might Green have made a hasty and faulty identification of petitioner to shift suspicion away from himself as one who robbed the Polar Bar, but Green might have been subject to undue pressure from the police and made his identifications under fear of possible probation revocation.

Green's record would be revealed only as necessary to probe Green for bias and prejudice and not generally to call Green's good character into question.

The trial court granted the motion for a protective order, relying on Alaska Rule of Children's Procedure 23,[1] and Alaska Stat. §47.10.080(g) (1971).[2]

Although prevented from revealing that Green had been on probation for the juvenile delinquency adjudication for burglary at the same time that he originally identified petitioner, counsel for petitioner did his best to expose Green's state of mind at the time Green discovered that a stolen safe had been discovered near his home. Green denied that he was upset or uncomfortable about the discovery of the safe. He claimed not to have been worried about any suspicions the police might have been expected to harbor against him, though Green did admit that it crossed his mind that the police might have thought he had something to do with the crime.

Defense counsel cross-examined Green in part as follows:

Q: Were you upset at all by the fact that this safe was found on your property?

A: No, sir.

Q: Did you feel that they might in some way suspect you of this?

A: No.

Q: Did you feel uncomfortable about this though?

A: No, not really.

Q: The fact that a safe was found on your property?

A: No.

Q: Did you suspect for a moment that the police might somehow think that you were involved in this?

A: I thought they might ask a few questions is all.

Q: Did that thought ever enter your mind that you — that the police might think that you were somehow connected with this? . . .

A: No, it didn't really bother me, no.

Q: Well, but . . . .

A: I mean, you know, it didn't — it didn't come into my mind as worrying me, you know.

---

1. Rule 23 provides:

"No adjudication, order, or disposition of a juvenile case shall be admissible in a court not acting in the exercise of juvenile jurisdiction except for use in a presentencing procedure in a criminal case where the superior court, in its discretion, determines that such use is appropriate."

2. Section 47.10.080(g) provides in pertinent part:

"The commitment and placement of a child and evidence given in the court are not admissible as evidence against the minor in a subsequent case or proceedings in any other court. . . ."

Q: That really wasn't — wasn't my question, Mr. Green. Did you think
that — not whether it worried you so much or not, but did you feel
that there was a possibility that the police might somehow think that
you had something to do with this, that they might have that in their
mind, not that you . . . .

A: That came across my mind, yes, sir.

Q: That did cross your mind?

A: Yes.

Q: So as I understand it you went down to the — you drove in with the
police in — in their car from mile 25, Glenn Highway down to the
city police station?

A: Yes, sir.

Q: And then went into the investigators' room with Investigator Gray
and Investigator Weaver?

A: Yeah.

Q: And they started asking you questions about — about the incident,
is that correct?

A: Yeah.

Q: Had you ever been questioned like that before by any law enforcement officers?

A: No.

Mr. Ripley: I'm going to object to this. Your Honor, it's a carry-on with
rehash of the same thing. He's attempting to raise in the jury's
mind . . . .

The court: I'll sustain the objection.

Since defense counsel was prohibited from making inquiry as to the
witness' being on probation under a juvenile court adjudication, Green's
protestations of unconcern over possible police suspicion that he might
have had a part in the Polar Bar burglary and his categorical denial of
ever having been the subject of any similar law-enforcement interrogation went unchallenged. The tension between the right of confrontation
and the State's policy of protecting the witness with a juvenile record is
particularly evident in the final answer given by the witness. Since it is
probable that Green underwent some questioning by police when he was
arrested for the burglaries on which his juvenile adjudication of delinquency rested, the answer can be regarded as highly suspect at the very
least. The witness was in effect asserting, under protection of the trial
court's ruling, a right to give a questionably truthful answer to a cross-
examiner pursuing a relevant line of inquiry; it is doubtful whether the
bold "No" answer would have been given by Green absent a belief that
he was shielded from traditional cross-examination. It would be difficult
to conceive of a situation more clearly illustrating the need for cross-
examination. The remainder of the cross-examination was devoted to an
attempt to prove that Green was making his identification at trial on the

basis of what he remembered from his earlier identifications at the photographic display and lineup, and not on the basis of his February 16 confrontation with the two men on the road.

The Alaska Supreme Court affirmed petitioner's conviction, concluding that it did not have to resolve the potential conflict in this case between a defendant's right to a meaningful confrontation with adverse witnesses and the State's interest in protecting the anonymity of a juvenile offender since "our reading of the trial transcript convinces us that counsel for the defendant was able adequately to question the youth in considerable detail concerning the possibility of bias or motive." 499 P.2d 1025, 1036 (1972). Although the court admitted that Green's denials of any sense of anxiety or apprehension upon the safe's being found close to his home were possibly self-serving, "the suggestion was nonetheless brought to the attention of the jury, and that body was afforded the opportunity to observe the demeanor of the youth and pass on his credibility." Ibid. The court concluded that, in light of the indirect references permitted, there was no error.

Since we granted certiorari limited to the question of whether petitioner was denied his right under the Confrontation Clause to adequately cross-examine Green, 410 U.S. 925 (1973), the essential question turns on the correctness of the Alaska court's evaluation of the "adequacy" of the scope of cross-examination permitted. We disagree with that court's interpretation of the Confrontation Clause and we reverse.

II

The Sixth Amendment to the Constitution guarantees the right of an accused in a criminal prosecution "to be confronted with the witnesses against him." This right is secured for defendants in state as well as federal criminal proceedings under Pointer v. Texas, 380 U.S. 400 (1965). Confrontation means more than being allowed to confront the witness physically. "Our cases construing the [confrontation] clause hold that a primary interest secured by it is the right of cross-examination." Douglas v. Alabama, 380 U.S. 415, 418 (1965). Professor Wigmore stated:

> The main and essential purpose of confrontation is *to secure for the opponent the opportunity of cross-examination.* The opponent demands confrontation, not for the idle purpose of gazing upon the witness, or of being gazed upon by him, but for the purpose of cross-examination, which cannot be had except by the direct and personal putting of questions and obtaining immediate answers.

5 J. Wigmore, Evidence §1395, p.123 (3d ed. 1940). (Emphasis in original.)

Cross-examination is the principal means by which the believability of a witness and the truth of his testimony are tested. Subject always to the broad discretion of a trial judge to preclude repetitive and unduly harassing interrogation, the cross-examiner is not only permitted to delve into the witness' story to test the witness' perceptions and memory, but the cross-examiner has traditionally been allowed to impeach, i.e., discredit, the witness. One way of discrediting the witness is to introduce evidence of a prior criminal conviction of that witness. By so doing the cross-examiner intends to afford the jury a basis to infer that the witness' character is such that he would be less likely than the average trustworthy citizen to be truthful in his testimony. The introduction of evidence of a prior crime is thus a general attack on the credibility of the witness. A more particular attack on the witness' credibility is effected by means of cross-examination directed toward revealing possible biases, prejudices, or ulterior motives of the witness as they may relate directly to issues or personalities in the case at hand. The partiality of a witness is subject to exploration at trial, and is "always relevant as discrediting the witness and affecting the weight of his testimony." 3A J. Wigmore, Evidence §940, p.775 (Chadbourn rev. 1970). We have recognized that the exposure of a witness' motivation in testifying is a proper and important function of the constitutionally protected right of cross-examination. Greene v. McElroy, 360 U.S. 474, 496 (1959).

In the instant case, defense counsel sought to show the existence of possible bias and prejudice of Green, causing him to make a faulty initial identification of petitioner, which in turn could have affected his later in-court identification of petitioner.[5]

We cannot speculate as to whether the jury, as sole judge of the credibility of a witness, would have accepted this line of reasoning had counsel been permitted to fully present it. But we do conclude that the jurors were entitled to have the benefit of the defense theory before them so that they could make an informed judgment as to the weight to place on Green's testimony which provided "a crucial link in the proof . . . of petitioner's act." Douglas v. Alabama, 380 U.S., at 419. The accuracy and truthfulness of Green's testimony were key elements in the State's case against petitioner. The claim of bias which the defense sought to develop was admissible to afford a basis for an inference of undue pressure because of Green's vulnerable status as a probationer, cf. Alford v. United States, 282 U.S. 687 (1931), as well as of Green's possible concern that he might be a suspect in the investigation.

---

5. "[A] *partiality* of mind at some *former time* may be used as the basis of an argument to the same state at the time of testifying; though the ultimate object is to establish partiality at the time of testifying." 3A J. Wigmore, Evidence §940, p.776 (Chadbourn rev. 1970). (Emphasis in original; footnotes omitted.)

We cannot accept the Alaska Supreme Court's conclusion that the cross-examination that was permitted defense counsel was adequate to develop the issue of bias properly to the jury. While counsel was permitted to ask Green *whether* he was biased, counsel was unable to make a record from which to argue *why* Green might have been biased or otherwise lacked that degree of impartiality expected of a witness at trial. On the basis of the limited cross-examination that was permitted, the jury might well have thought that defense counsel was engaged in a speculative and baseless line of attack on the credibility of an apparently blameless witness or, as the prosecutor's objection put it, a "rehash" of prior cross-examination. On these facts it seems clear to us that to make any such inquiry effective, defense counsel should have been permitted to expose to the jury the facts from which jurors, as the sole triers of fact and credibility, could appropriately draw inferences relating to the reliability of the witness. Petitioner was thus denied the right of effective cross-examination which " 'would be constitutional error of the first magnitude and no amount of showing of want of prejudice would cure it.' Brookhart v. Janis, 384 U.S. 1, 3." Smith v. Illinois, 390 U.S. 129, 131 (1968).

III

The claim is made that the State has an important interest in protecting the anonymity of juvenile offenders and that this interest outweighs any competing interest this petitioner might have in cross-examining Green about his being on probation. The State argues that exposure of a juvenile's record of delinquency would likely cause impairment of rehabilitative goals of the juvenile correctional procedures. This exposure, it is argued, might encourage the juvenile offender to commit further acts of delinquency, or cause the juvenile offender to lose employment opportunities or otherwise suffer unnecessarily for his youthful transgression.

We do not and need not challenge the State's interest as a matter of its own policy in the administration of criminal justice to seek to preserve the anonymity of a juvenile offender. Cf. In re Gault, 387 U.S. 1, 25 (1967). Here, however, petitioner sought to introduce evidence of Green's probation for the purpose of suggesting that Green was biased and, therefore, that his testimony was either not to be believed in his identification of petitioner or at least very carefully considered in that light. Serious damage to the strength of the State's case would have been a real possibility had petitioner been allowed to pursue this line of inquiry. In this setting we conclude that the right of confrontation is paramount to the State's policy of protecting a juvenile offender. Whatever temporary embarrassment might result to Green or his family by disclosure of his juvenile record — if the prosecution insisted on using him to make its case — is outweighed by petitioner's right to probe into the influence of possible bias in the testimony of a crucial identification witness.

In Alford v. United States, supra, we upheld the right of defense counsel to impeach a witness by showing that because of the witness' incarceration in federal prison at the time of trial, the witness' testimony was biased as "given under promise or expectation of immunity, or under the coercive effect of his detention by officers of the United States." 282 U.S., at 693. In response to the argument that the witness had a right to be protected from exposure of his criminal record, the Court stated: "[N]o obligation is imposed on the court, such as that suggested below, to protect a witness from being discredited on cross-examination, short of an attempted invasion of his constitutional protection from self incrimination, properly invoked. There is a duty to protect him from questions which go beyond the bounds of proper cross-examination merely to harass, annoy or humiliate him." Id., at 694. As in *Alford,* we conclude that the state's desire that Green fulfill his public duty to testify free from embarrassment and with his reputation unblemished must fall before the right of petitioner to seek out the truth in the process of defending himself.

The State's policy interest in protecting the confidentiality of a juvenile offender's record cannot require yielding of so vital a constitutional right as the effective cross-examination for bias of an adverse witness. The State could have protected Green from exposure of his juvenile adjudication in these circumstances by refraining from using him to make out its case; the State cannot, consistent with the right of confrontation, require the petitioner to bear the full burden of vindicating the State's interest in the secrecy of juvenile criminal records. The judgment affirming petitioner's convictions of burglary and grand larceny is reversed and the case is remanded for further proceedings not inconsistent with this opinion.

It is so ordered.

Mr. Justice STEWART, concurring.

The Court holds that, in the circumstances of this case, the Sixth and Fourteenth Amendments conferred the right to cross-examine a particular prosecution witness about his delinquency adjudication for burglary and his status as a probationer. Such cross-examination was necessary in this case in order "to show the existence of possible bias and prejudice ...," ante, at 317. In joining the Court's opinion, I would emphasize that the Court neither holds nor suggests that the Constitution confers a right in every case to impeach the general credibility of a witness through cross-examination about his past delinquency adjudications or criminal convictions.

Mr. Justice WHITE, with whom Mr. Justice REHNQUIST joins, dissenting.

As I see it, there is no constitutional principle at stake here. This is nothing more than a typical instance of a trial court exercising its discretion to control or limit cross-examination, followed by a typical decision of a state appellate court refusing to disturb the judgment of the trial court and itself concluding that limiting cross-examination had done no substantial harm to the defense. Yet the Court insists on second-guessing the state courts and in effect inviting federal review of every ruling of a state trial judge who believes cross-examination has gone far enough. I would not undertake this task, if for no other reason than that I have little faith in our ability, in fact-bound cases and on a cold record, to improve on the judgment of trial judges and of the state appellate courts who agree with them. I would affirm the judgment.

What confrontation rule does the *Davis* court apply? To what extent is the *Davis* rationale capable of application to nonbias situations? To what extent does the decision turn upon the fact that Green's testimony was crucial to the prosecution's case? Does *Davis* cast doubt upon the constitutionality of the constraints of Rules 608 and 609 on the presentation of evidence bearing generally on a witness's credibility? For example, suppose that in *Davis*, Green had been suspended from high school for cheating and later expelled from college for having falsified a high school transcript. Rule 608(b) would bar the admission of extrinsic evidence to prove these specific instances of conduct for the purpose of attacking Green's credibility and would permit inquiry into them, in the discretion of the court, only on cross-examination of Green (or under *Michelson* and Rule 608(b)(2), on cross-examination of a witness testifying about Green's good character, which could happen only after attack on Green's credibility through reputation or opinion evidence). Would Davis's sixth amendment rights be violated by the judge's refusal to permit such impeachment? Would Davis's rights be violated if on cross-examination Green denied that these incidents occurred and the state did not produce any character witnesses on his behalf so as to permit *Michelson*-type impeachment?

To what extent are questions of constitutional dimension raised by the application of Rule 609 to restrict use by the defendant of evidence of criminal convictions for impeachment purposes? To what extent are questions of constitutional dimension raised by the recognition of privileges that restrict evidence sought to be introduced by the defendant? How does the rape-victim's shield privilege, Rule 412, deal with this problem? To what extent does Rule 611 raise problems of constitutional dimensions?

Problem V-1
Cross-Examination and Confrontation

D is tried in federal court for arson. The principal prosecution witness, *W*, lives next to the building that burned and testifies that he saw *D* carrying a can of gasoline into the building in question on the day of the fire. *D* seeks to cross-examine *W* concerning his conviction 11 years ago for selling marijuana, a crime punishable by more than one year in prison. The prosecution objects to this line of questioning on the grounds that the evidence is irrelevant to credibility and, in the alternative, that its probative value is outweighed by its prejudicial effect. What ruling and why?

Problem V-2
Other Extortion

D, a union official, is tried for extortion. *W*, the supervisor at a nonunion construction project, testifies that *D* threatened harm to his company's employees and equipment if the company did not agree either to hire union workers or to pay protection money. *W* testifies that payments were made to *D* out of fear that these threats might be carried out. On cross-examination of *W*, *D* seeks to question *W* concerning payments made to other local unions for the purpose of showing that the payments to *D* were not made out of fear (an element of the crime) but were part of the company's routine business practices. The prosecution objects under Rule 611(b) to this line of questioning on the grounds that evidence of prior similar acts is not relevant to the particular crime charged. The trial court sustains the objection under Rule 403. On appeal, what result and why?

CHAMBERS v. MISSISSIPPI
410 U.S. 284 (1973)

Mr. Justice POWELL delivered the opinion of the Court. . . .

I

The events that led to petitioner's prosecution for murder occurred in the small town of Woodville in southern Mississippi. On Saturday evening, June 14, 1969, two Woodville policemen, James Forman and Aaron "Sonny" Liberty, entered a local bar and pool hall to execute a warrant for the arrest of a youth named C. C. Jackson. Jackson resisted and a hostile crowd of some 50 or 60 persons gathered. The officers' first attempt to handcuff Jackson was frustrated when 20 or 25 men in the crowd intervened and wrestled him free. Forman then radioed for assistance and Liberty removed his riot gun, a 12-gauge sawed-off shotgun, from the car. Three deputy sheriffs arrived shortly thereafter and the officers again attempted to make their arrest. Once more, the officers were attacked by the onlookers and during the commotion five or six pistol shots were fired. Forman was looking in a different direction when the shooting began, but immediately saw that Liberty had been shot several times in the back. Before Liberty died, he turned around and fired both barrels of his riot gun into an alley in the area from which the shots appeared to have come. The first shot was wild and high and scattered the crowd standing at the face of the alley. Liberty appeared, however, to take more deliberate aim before the second shot and hit one of the men in the crowd in the back of the head and neck as he ran down the alley. That man was Leon Chambers.

Officer Forman could not see from his vantage point who shot Liberty or whether Liberty's shots hit anyone. One of the deputy sheriffs testified at trial that he was standing several feet from Liberty and that he saw Chambers shoot him. Another deputy sheriff stated that, although he could not see whether Chambers had a gun in his hand, he did see Chambers "break his arm down" shortly before the shots were fired. The officers who saw Chambers fall testified that they thought he was dead but they made no effort at that time either to examine him or to search for the murder weapon. Instead, they attended to Liberty, who was placed in the police car and taken to a hospital where he was declared dead on arrival. A subsequent autopsy showed that he had been hit with four bullets from a .22-caliber revolver.

Shortly after the shooting, three of Chambers' friends discovered that he was not yet dead. James Williams, Berkley Turner, and Gable McDonald loaded him into a car and transported him to the same hospital. Later that night, when the county sheriff discovered that Chambers was still alive, a guard was placed outside his room. Chambers was subsequently charged with Liberty's murder. He pleaded not guilty and has asserted his innocence throughout.

The story of Leon Chambers is intertwined with the story of another man, Gable McDonald. McDonald, a lifelong resident of Woodville, was in the crowd on the evening of Liberty's death. Sometime shortly after that day, he left his wife in Woodville and moved to Louisiana and found a job at a sugar mill. In November of that same year, he returned to Woodville when his wife informed him that an acquaintance of his, known as Reverend Stokes, wanted to see him. Stokes owned a gas station in Natchez, Mississippi, several miles north of Woodville, and upon his return McDonald went to see him. After talking to Stokes, McDonald agreed to make a statement to Chambers' attorneys, who maintained offices in Natchez. Two days later, he appeared at the attorneys' offices and gave a sworn confession that he shot Officer Liberty. He also stated that he had already told a friend of his, James Williams, that he shot Liberty. He said that he used his own pistol, a nine-shot .22-caliber revolver, which he had discarded shortly after the shooting. In response to questions from Chambers' attorneys, McDonald affirmed that his confession was voluntary and that no one had compelled him to come to them. Once the confession had been transcribed, signed, and witnessed, McDonald was turned over to the local police authorities and was placed in jail.

One month later, at a preliminary hearing, McDonald repudiated his prior sworn confession. He testified that Stokes had persuaded him to confess that he shot Liberty. He claimed that Stokes had promised that he would not go to jail and that he would share in the proceeds of a lawsuit that Chambers would bring against the town of Woodville. On examination by his own attorney and on cross-examination by the State, McDonald swore that he had not been at the scene when Liberty was shot but had been down the street drinking beer in a cafe with a friend, Berkley Turner. When he and Turner heard the shooting, he testified, they walked up the street and found Chambers lying in the alley. He, Turner, and Williams took Chambers to the hospital. McDonald further testified at the preliminary hearing that he did not know what had happened, that there was no discussion about the shooting either going to or coming back from the hospital, and that it was not until the next day that he learned that Chambers had been felled by a blast from Liberty's riot gun. In addition, McDonald stated that while he once owned a .22-caliber pistol he had lost it many months before the shooting and did not own or possess a weapon at that time. The local justice of the peace accepted McDonald's repudiation and released him from custody. The local authorities undertook no further investigation of his possible involvement.

Chambers' case came on for trial in October of the next year. At trial, he endeavored to develop two grounds of defense. He first attempted to show that he did not shoot Liberty. Only one officer testified that he actually saw Chambers fire the shots. Although three officers saw Liberty shoot Chambers and testified that they assumed he was shooting his attacker, none of them examined Chambers to see whether he was still alive or whether he possessed a gun. Indeed, no weapon was ever recovered from the scene and there was no proof that Chambers had ever owned a .22-caliber pistol. One witness testified that he was standing in the street near where Liberty was shot, that he was looking at Chambers when the shooting began, and that he was sure that Chambers did not fire the shots.

Petitioner's second defense was that Gable McDonald had shot Officer Liberty. He was only partially successful, however, in his efforts to bring before the jury the testimony supporting this defense. Sam

Hardin, a lifelong friend of McDonald's, testified that he saw McDonald shoot Liberty. A second witness, one of Liberty's cousins, testified that he saw McDonald immediately after the shooting with a pistol in his hand. In addition to the testimony of these two witnesses, Chambers endeavored to show the jury that McDonald had repeatedly confessed to the crime. Chambers attempted to prove that McDonald had admitted responsibility for the murder on four separate occasions, once when he gave the sworn statement to Chambers' counsel and three other times prior to that occasion in private conversations with friends.

In large measure, he was thwarted in his attempt to present this portion of his defense by the strict application of certain Mississippi rules of evidence. Chambers asserts in this Court, as he did unsuccessfully in his motion for new trial and on appeal to the State Supreme Court, that the application of these evidentiary rules rendered his trial fundamentally unfair and deprived him of due process of law. It is necessary, therefore, to examine carefully the rulings made during the trial.

II

Chambers filed a pretrial motion requesting the court to order McDonald to appear. Chambers also sought a ruling at that time that if the State itself chose not to call McDonald, he be allowed to call him as an adverse witness. Attached to the motion were copies of McDonald's sworn confession and of the transcript of his preliminary hearing at which he repudiated that confession. The trial court granted the motion requiring McDonald to appear but reserved ruling on the adverse-witness motion. At trial, after the State failed to put McDonald on the stand, Chambers called McDonald, laid a predicate for the introduction of his sworn out-of-court confession, had it admitted into evidence, and read it to the jury. The State, upon cross-examination, elicited from McDonald the fact that he had repudiated his prior confession. McDonald further testified, as he had at the preliminary hearing, that he did not shoot Liberty, and that he confessed to the crime only on the promise of Reverend Stokes that he would not go to jail and would share in a sizable tort recovery from the town. He also retold his own story of his actions on the evening of the shooting, including his visit to the cafe down the street, his absence from the scene during the critical period, and his subsequent trip to the hospital with Chambers.

At the conclusion of the State's cross-examination, Chambers renewed his motion to examine McDonald as an adverse witness. The trial court denied the motion, stating: "He may be hostile, but he is not adverse in the sense of the word, so your request will be overruled." On appeal, the State Supreme Court upheld the trial court's ruling, finding that "McDonald's testimony was not adverse to appellant" because "[n]owhere did he point the finger at Chambers." 252 So. 2d, at 220.

Defeated in his attempt to challenge directly McDonald's renunciation of his prior confession, Chambers sought to introduce the testimony of the three witnesses to whom McDonald had admitted that he shot the officer. The first of these, Sam Hardin, would have testified that, on the night of the shooting, he spent the late evening hours with McDonald at a friend's house after their return from the hospital and that, while driving McDonald home later that night, McDonald stated that he shot Liberty. The State objected to the admission of this testimony on the ground that it was hearsay. The trial court sustained the objection.

Berkley Turner, the friend with whom McDonald said he was drinking beer when the shooting occurred, was then called to testify. In the jury's presence, and without objection, he testified that he had not been in the cafe that Saturday and had not had any beers with McDonald. The jury was then excused. In the absence of the jury, Turner recounted his conversations with McDonald while they were riding with James Williams to take Chambers to the hospital. When asked whether McDonald said anything regarding the shooting of Liberty, Turner testified that McDonald told him that he "shot him." Turner further stated that one week later, when he met McDonald at a friend's house, McDonald reminded him of their prior conversation and urged Turner not to "mess him up." Petitioner argued to the court that, especially where there was other proof in the case that was corroborative of these out-of-court statements, Turner's testimony as to McDonald's self-incriminating remarks should have been admitted as an exception to the hearsay rule. Again, the trial court sustained the State's objection.

The third witness, Albert Carter, was McDonald's neighbor. They had been friends for about 25 years. Although Carter had not been in Woodville on the evening of the shooting, he stated that he learned about it the next morning from McDonald. That same day, he and McDonald walked out to a well near McDonald's house and there McDonald told him that he was the one who shot Officer Liberty. Carter testified that McDonald also told him that he had disposed of the .22-caliber revolver later that night. He further testified that several weeks after the shooting, he accompanied McDonald to Natchez where McDonald purchased another .22 pistol to replace the one he had discarded. The jury was not allowed to hear Carter's testimony. Chambers urged that these statements were admissible, the State objected, and the court sustained the objection. On appeal, the State Supreme Court approved the lower court's exclusion of these witnesses' testimony on hearsay grounds. 252 So. 2d, at 220.

In sum, then, this was Chambers' predicament. As a consequence of the combination of Mississippi's "party witness" or "voucher" rule and its hearsay rule, he was unable either to cross-examine McDonald or to present witnesses in his own behalf who would have discredited McDonald's repudiation and demonstrated his complicity. Chambers had, however, chipped away at the fringes of McDonald's story by introducing admissible testimony from other sources indicating that he had not been seen in the cafe where he said he was when the shooting started, that he had not been having beer with Turner, and that he possessed a .22 pistol at the time of the crime. But all that remained from McDonald's own testimony was a single written confession countered by an arguably acceptable renunciation. Chambers' defense was far less persuasive than it might have been had he been given an opportunity to subject McDonald's statements to cross-examination or had the other confessions been admitted.

III

The right of an accused in a criminal trial to due process is, in essence, the right to a fair opportunity to defend against the State's accusations. The rights to confront and cross-examine witnesses and to call witnesses in one's own behalf have long been recognized as essential to due process. Mr. Justice Black, writing for the Court in In re Oliver, 333 U.S. 257, 273 (1948), identified these rights as among the minimum essentials of a fair trial: "A person's right to reasonable notice of a charge against him, and an opportunity to be heard in his defense — a right to his day in court — are basic in our system of jurisprudence; and these rights include, as a minimum, a right to examine the witnesses against him, to offer testimony, and to be represented by counsel." See also Morrissey v. Brewer, 408 U.S. 471, 488-489 (1972); Jenkins v. McKeithen, 395 U.S. 411, 428-429 (1969); Specht v. Patterson, 386 U.S. 605, 610 (1967). Both of these elements of a fair trial are implicated in the present case.

A

Chambers was denied an opportunity to subject McDonald's damning repudiation and alibi to cross-examination. He was not allowed to test the witness' recollection, to probe into the details of his alibi, or to "sift" his conscience so that the jury might judge for itself whether McDonald's testimony was worthy of belief. Mattox v. United States, 156 U.S. 237, 242-243 (1895). The right of cross-examination is more than a desirable rule of trial procedure. It is implicit in the constitutional right of confrontation, and helps assure the "accuracy of the truth-determining process." Dutton v. Evans, 400 U.S. 74, 89 (1970); Bruton v. United States, 391 U.S. 123, 135-137 (1968). It is, indeed, "an essential and fundamental requirement for the kind of fair trial which is this country's constitutional goal." Pointer v. Texas, 380 U.S. 400, 405 (1965). Of course, the right to confront and to cross-examine is not absolute and may, in appropriate cases, bow to accommodate other legitimate interests in the criminal trial process. E.g., Mancusi v. Stubbs, 408 U.S. 204 (1972). But its denial or significant diminution calls into question the ultimate " 'integrity of the fact-finding process' " and requires that the competing interest be closely examined. Berger v. California, 393 U.S. 314, 315 (1969).

In this case, petitioner's request to cross-examine McDonald was denied on the basis of a Mississippi common-law rule that a party may not impeach his own witness. The rule rests on the presumption — without regard to the circumstances of the particular case — that a party who calls a witness "vouches for his credibility." Clark v. Lansford, 191 So. 2d 123, 125 (Miss. 1966). Although the historical origins of the "voucher" rule are uncertain, it appears to be a remnant of primitive English trial practice in which "oath-takers" or "compurgators" were called to stand behind a particular party's position in any controversy. Their assertions were strictly partisan and, quite unlike witnesses in criminal trials today, their role bore little relation to the impartial ascertainment of the facts.

Whatever validity the "voucher" rule may have once enjoyed, and apart from whatever usefulness it retains today in the civil trial process, it bears little present relationship to the realities of the criminal process. It might have been logical for the early common law to require a party to vouch for the credibility of witnesses he brought before the jury to affirm his veracity. Having selected them especially for that purpose, the party might reasonably be expected to stand firmly behind their testimony. But in modern criminal trials, defendants are rarely able to select their witnesses: they must take them where they find them. Moreover, as applied in this case, the "voucher" rule's impact was doubly harmful to Chambers' efforts to develop his defense. Not only was he precluded from cross-examining McDonald, but, as the State conceded at oral argument, he was also restricted in the scope of his direct examination by the rule's corollary requirement that the party calling the witness is bound by anything he might say. He was, therefore, effectively prevented from exploring the circumstances of McDonald's three prior oral confessions and from challenging the renunciation of the written confession.

In this Court, Mississippi has not sought to defend the rule or explain its underlying rationale. Nor has it contended that its rule should override the accused's right of confrontation. Instead, it argues that there is no incompatibility between the rule and Chambers' rights because no right of confrontation exists unless the testifying witness is "adverse" to the accused. The state's brief asserts that the "right of confrontation applies to witnesses *'against'* an accused." Relying on the trial court's determination that McDonald was not "adverse," and on the State Supreme Court's holding that McDonald did not "point the finger at Chambers," the State contends that Chambers' constitutional right was not involved.

The argument that McDonald's testimony was not "adverse" to, or "against," Chambers is not convincing. The State's proof at trial excluded the theory that more than one person participated in the shooting of Liberty. To the extent that McDonald's sworn confession tended to incriminate him, it tended also to exculpate Chambers. And, in the circumstances of this case, McDonald's retraction inculpated Chambers to the same extent that it exculpated McDonald. It can hardly be disputed that McDonald's testimony was in fact seriously adverse to Chambers. The availability of the right to confront and to cross-examine those who give damaging testimony against the accused has never been held to depend on whether the witness was initially put on the stand by the accused or by the State. We reject the notion that a right of such substance in the criminal process may be governed by that technicality or by any narrow and unrealistic definition of the word "against." The "voucher" rule, as applied in this case, plainly interfered with Chambers' right to defend against the State's charges.

B

We need not decide, however, whether this error alone would occasion reversal since Chambers' claimed denial of due process rests on the ultimate impact of that error when viewed in conjunction with the trial court's refusal to permit him to call other witnesses. The trial court refused to allow him to introduce the testimony of Hardin, Turner, and Carter. Each would have testified to the statements purportedly made by McDonald, on three separate occasions shortly after the crime, naming himself as the murderer. The State Supreme Court approved the exclusion of this evidence on the ground that it was hearsay.

The hearsay rule, which has long been recognized and respected by virtually every State, is based on experience and grounded in the notion that untrustworthy evidence should not be presented to the triers of fact. Out-of-court statements are traditionally excluded because they lack the conventional indicia of reliability: they are usually not made under oath or other circumstances that impress the speaker with the solemnity of his statements; the declarant's word is not subject to cross-examination; and he is not available in order that his demeanor and credibility may be assessed by the jury. California v. Green, 399 U.S. 149, 158 (1970). A number of exceptions have developed over the years to allow admission of hearsay statements made under circumstances that tend to assure reliability and thereby compensate for the absence of the oath and opportunity for cross-examination. Among the most prevalent of these exceptions is the one applicable to declarations against interest — an exception founded on the assumption that a person is unlikely to fabricate a statement against his own interest at the time it is made. Mississippi recognizes this exception but applies it only to declarations against pecuniary interest. It recognizes no such exception for declarations, like

McDonald's in this case, that are against the penal interest of the declarant. Brown v. State, 99 Miss. 719, 55 So. 961 (1911).

This materialistic limitation on the declaration-against-interest hearsay exception appears to be accepted by most States in their criminal trial processes, although a number of States have discarded it. Declarations against penal interest have also been excluded in federal courts under the authority of Donnelly v. United States, 228 U.S. 243, 272-273 (1913), although exclusion would not be required under the newly proposed Federal Rules of Evidence. Exclusion, where the limitation prevails, is usually premised on the view that admission would lead to the frequent presentation of perjured testimony to the jury. It is believed that confessions of criminal activity are often motivated by extraneous considerations and, therefore, are not as inherently reliable as statements against pecuniary or proprietary interest. While that rationale has been the subject of considerable scholarly criticism, we need not decide in this case whether, under other circumstances, it might serve some valid state purpose by excluding untrustworthy testimony.

The hearsay statements involved in this case were originally made and subsequently offered at trial under circumstances that provided considerable assurance of their reliability. First, each of McDonald's confessions was made spontaneously to a close acquaintance shortly after the murder had occurred. Second, each one was corroborated by some other evidence in the case — McDonald's sworn confession, the testimony of an eyewitness to the shooting, the testimony that McDonald was seen with a gun immediately after the shooting, and proof of his prior ownership of a .22-caliber revolver and subsequent purchase of a new weapon. The sheer number of independent confessions provided additional corroboration for each. Third, whatever may be the parameters of the penal-interest rationale,[20] each confession here was in a very real sense self-incriminatory and unquestionably against interest. See United States v. Harris, 403 U.S. 573, 584 (1971); Dutton v. Evans, 400 U.S., at 89. McDonald stood to benefit nothing by disclosing his role in the shooting to any of his three friends and he must have been aware of the possibility that disclosure would lead to criminal prosecution. Indeed, after telling Turner of his involvement, he subsequently urged Turner not to "mess him up." Finally, if there was any question about the truthfulness of the extrajudicial statements, McDonald was present

20. The Mississippi case which refused to adopt a hearsay exception for declarations against penal interest concerned an out-of-court declarant who purportedly stated that he had committed the murder with which his brother had been charged. The Mississippi Supreme Court believed that the declarant might have been motivated by a desire to free his brother rather than by any compulsion of guilt. The Court also noted that the declarant had fled, was unavailable for cross-examination, and might well have known at the time he made the statement that he would not suffer for it. Brown v. State, 99 Miss. 719, 55 So. 961 (1911). There is, in the present case, no such basis for doubting McDonald's statements.

in the courtroom and was under oath. He could have been cross-examined by the State, and his demeanor and responses weighed by the jury. See California v. Green, 399 U.S. 149 (1970). The availability of McDonald significantly distinguishes this case from the prior Mississippi precedent, Brown v. State, supra, and from the *Donnelly*-type situation, since in both cases the declarant was unavailable at the time of trial.[21]

Few rights are more fundamental than that of an accused to present witnesses in his own defense. E.g., Webb v. Texas, 409 U.S. 95 (1972); Washington v. Texas, 388 U.S. 14, 19 (1967); In re Oliver, 333 U.S. 257 (1948). In the exercise of this right, the accused, as is required of the State, must comply with established rules of procedure and evidence designed to assure both fairness and reliability in the ascertainment of guilt and innocence. Although perhaps no rule of evidence has been more respected or more frequently applied in jury trials than that applicable to the exclusion of hearsay, exceptions tailored to allow the introduction of evidence which in fact is likely to be trustworthy have long existed. The testimony rejected by the trial court here bore persuasive assurances of trustworthiness and thus was well within the basic rationale of the exception for declarations against interest. That testimony also was critical to Chambers' defense. In these circumstances, where constitutional rights directly affecting the ascertainment of guilt are implicated, the hearsay rule may not be applied mechanistically to defeat the ends of justice.

We conclude that the exclusion of this critical evidence, coupled with the State's refusal to permit Chambers to cross-examine McDonald, denied him a trial in accord with traditional and fundamental standards of due process. In reaching this judgment, we establish no new principles of constitutional law. Nor does our holding signal any diminution in the respect traditionally accorded to the States in the establishment and implementation of their own criminal trial rules and procedures. Rather, we hold quite simply that under the facts and circumstances of this case the rulings of the trial court deprived Chambers of a fair trial.

The judgment is reversed and the case is remanded to the Supreme

21. McDonald's presence also deprives the State's argument for retention of the penal-interest rule of much of its force. In claiming that "[t]o change the rule would work a travesty on justice," the State posited the following hypothetical: "If the rule were changed, A could be charged with the crime; B could tell C and D that he committed the crime; B *could go into hiding* and at A's trial C and D would testify as to B's admission of guilt; A could be acquitted and B would return to stand trial; B could then provide several witnesses to testify as to his whereabouts at the time of the crime. The testimony of those witnesses along with A's statement that he really committed the crime could result in B's acquittal. A would be barred from further prosecution because of the protection against double jeopardy. No one could be convicted of perjury as A did not testify at his first trial, B did not lie under oath, and C and D were truthful in their testimony." Brief for Respondent 7 n.3 (emphasis supplied). Obviously, B's absence at trial is critical to the success of the justice-subverting ploy.

Court of Mississippi for further proceedings not inconsistent with this opinion.

It is so ordered.

Would the statements of McDonald, Hardin, Turner, and Carter in *Chambers* be admissible under the Federal Rules? Would they be admissible as substantive evidence or only for impeachment? Would they be admissible if offered by the prosecution at a trial of McDonald?

Which confrontation rule does Justice Powell apply in *Chambers*? What is the relationship between the confrontation and compulsory process clauses? Reconsider the trial of Sir Walter Raleigh, page 273, above. If that trial took place in federal court today, would its conduct violate the Federal Rules, the confrontation clause, or the compulsory process clause? Which of the six possible confrontation clause formulations would Raleigh's trial violate?

What are the practical implications of Justice Powell's statement in *Chambers* that, "where constitutional rights directly affecting the ascertainment of guilt are implicated, the hearsay rule may not be applied mechanistically to defeat the ends of justice"? What is the status of Mississippi's declarations-against-interest exception after *Chambers*? Of its "party witness" or "voucher" rule? Of any state's exception? Of any rules or exceptions of any jurisdiction that exclude evidence offered by an accused? Does *Chambers* signal the "federalization" of the laws of evidence? Do you agree with Justice Powell that, "[i]n reaching this judgment, [the Court] establishes no new principles of constitutional law. Nor does our holding signal any diminution in the respect traditionally accorded to the States in the establishment and implementation of their own criminal trial rules and procedures"?

GREEN v. GEORGIA
442 U.S. 95 (1979)

PER CURIAM. Petitioner and Carzell Moore were indicted together for the rape and murder of Teresa Carol Allen. Moore was tried separately, was convicted of both crimes, and has been sentenced to death. Petitioner subsequently was convicted of murder, and also received a capital sentence. The Supreme Court of Georgia upheld the conviction and sentence, 242 Ga. 261, 249 S.E.2d 1 (1978), and petitioner has sought review of so much of the judgment as affirmed the capital sentence. We grant the motion for leave to proceed in forma pauperis and the petition for certiorari and vacate the sentence.

The evidence at trial tended to show that petitioner and Moore abducted Allen from the store where she was working alone and, acting either in concert or separately, raped and murdered her. After the jury determined that petitioner was guilty of murder, a second trial was held to decide whether capital punishment would be imposed. See Ga. Code §27-2503 (1978). At this second proceeding, petitioner sought to prove he was not present when Allen was killed and had not participated in her death. He attempted to introduce the testimony of Thomas Pasby, who had testified for the State at Moore's trial. According to Pasby, Moore had confided to him that he had killed Allen, shooting her twice after ordering petitioner to run an errand. The trial court refused to allow introduction of this evidence, ruling that Pasby's testimony constituted hearsay that was inadmissible under Ga. Code §38-301 (1978).[1] The State then argued to the jury that in the absence of direct evidence as to the circumstances of the crime, it could infer that petitioner participated directly in Allen's murder from the fact that more than one bullet was fired into her body.

Regardless of whether the proffered testimony comes within Georgia's hearsay rule, under the facts of this case its exclusion constituted a violation of the Due Process Clause of the Fourteenth Amendment. The excluded testimony was highly relevant to a critical issue in the punishment phase of the trial, see Lockett v. Ohio, 438 U.S. 586, 604-605 (opinion of Blackmun, J.), and substantial reasons existed to assume its reliability. Moore made his statement spontaneously to a close friend. The evidence corroborating the confession was ample, and indeed sufficient to procure a conviction of Moore and a capital sentence. The statement was against interest, and there was no reason to believe that Moore had any ulterior motive in making it. Perhaps most important, the State considered the testimony sufficiently reliable to use it against Moore, and to base a sentence of death upon it. In these unique circumstances, "the hearsay rule may not be applied mechanistically to defeat the ends of justice." Chambers v. Mississippi, 410 U.S. 284, 302 (1973). Because the exclusion of Pasby's testimony denied petitioner a fair trial on the issue of punishment, the sentence is vacated and the case is remanded for further proceedings not inconsistent with this opinion.

Reversed and remanded.

Mr. Justice REHNQUIST dissenting.

The Court today takes another step toward embalming the law of evidence in the Due Process Clause of the Fourteenth Amendment to the United States Constitution. I think it impossible to find any justification in the Constitution for today's ruling, and take comfort only from the fact that since this is a capital case, it is perhaps an example of the maxim that "hard cases make bad law."

The Georgia trial court refused to allow in evidence certain testimony

---

1. Georgia recognizes an exception to the hearsay rule for declarations against pecuniary interest, but not for declarations against penal interest.

at petitioner's sentencing trial on the ground that it constituted inadmissible hearsay under Ga. Code §38-301 (1978). This Court does not, and could not, dispute the propriety of that ruling. Instead, it marshals a number of ad hoc reasons why Georgia should adopt a code of evidence that would allow this particular testimony to be admitted, and concludes that "[i]n these unique circumstances, 'the hearsay rule may not be applied mechanistically to defeat the ends of justice.' "

Nothing in the United States Constitution gives this Court any authority to supersede a State's code of evidence because its application in a particular situation would defeat what this Court conceives to be "the ends of justice." The Court does not disagree that the testimony at issue is hearsay or that it fails to come within any of the exceptions to the hearsay rule provided by Georgia's rules of evidence. The Court obviously is troubled by the fact that the same testimony was admissible at the separate trial of petitioner's codefendant at the behest of the State. But this fact by no means demonstrates that the Georgia courts have not evenhandedly applied their code of evidence, with its various hearsay exceptions, so as to deny petitioner a fair trial. No practicing lawyer can have failed to note that Georgia's evidentiary rules, like those of every other State and of the United States, are such that certain items of evidence may be introduced by one party, but not by another. This is a fact of trial life, embodied throughout the hearsay rule and its exceptions. This being the case, the United States Constitution must be strained to or beyond the breaking point to conclude that all capital defendants who are unable to introduce all of the evidence which they seek to admit are denied a fair trial. I therefore dissent from the vacation of petitioner's sentence.

Problem V-3
Confrontation and Privacy

State S's statutes contain a broad physician-patient privilege that can be waived only by the patient. Defendant D is charged with the crime of false imprisonment. D's defense of necessity is grounded upon his assertion that his actions were necessary to prevent the complaining witness, W, from committing suicide. D testifies that although he was not previously acquainted with W, he believed that his actions were necessary because W told him of previous suicide attempts. On cross-examination W denies having told D of any suicide attempts and denies having tried to kill himself in the past. D moves to have W's medical records, which show prior suicide attempts, admitted to impeach his testimony. The prosecution objects on the grounds that the information is privileged. What ruling and why?

Problem V-4
Confrontation and Privilege

D is charged with possession of marijuana, found by the police in a jacket hanging in D's room in an apartment shared by D and W. D was out of town when the police executed the search warrant. The prosecution, in order to establish D's knowing and intentional possession of the marijuana, relies on W's testimony that she had seen D wear the jacket. On cross-examination W testifies that guests had occupied D's room during her absence, that D made leather jackets to order, and that D obtained jackets from her customers to aid her in fitting the leather jackets. However, W invokes her fifth amendment privilege in response to questions concerning who actually owned the particular jacket, whether D and W borrowed each other's clothes, and whether W had ever worn the jacket. If the claim of privilege is upheld and D is convicted, have her constitutional rights been violated?

CHAPTER VI

Privileges

A. Privileges in General

In Chapter I we explored the fundamental rule of evidence that all relevant evidence is admissible and all irrelevant evidence is inadmissible. The premise on which this primary rule is based is that accurate fact-finding in an adversary system of justice is promoted when the fact-finder has all the information that bears on the issues in dispute. As we have seen, there are many exceptions to the primary rule. But virtually all the exceptions we have examined to this point have been justified on the grounds that the excluded evidence is likely to undermine the fact-finding process because of the unreliability or prejudicial nature of the evidence or its capacity to mislead or confuse the fact-finder. Concededly, some of the categorical rules of exclusion, such as Rules 407 to 412 (evidence of subsequent repairs, compromise offers, payment of medical expenses, pleas, liability insurance, and prior sexual history), are based at least in part on policy considerations not directly connected to the truth-promoting principle, but, as seen, the legitimacy of these rules is a matter of controversy, and there is strong pressure to eliminate some of them.

The evidentiary privileges are the most important set of rules that operate to exclude relevant, nonprejudicial, and non-confusing evidence for reasons completely unrelated to the truth-promoting principle. Is there a unifying principle that justifies departure from the quest for truth in these instances? Or does the existing system of privileges simply reflect ad hoc policy judgments on specific issues or, more cynically, the relative power of various economic or social interests?

Our examination of this and other issues begins by considering some general philosophical questions raised by the nature and justification of privileges. These issues are explored more specifically in connection with the assertion of a reporter's privilege in the *Farber* case and juxtaposed with the privileges applicable to communications to clergymen, psychotherapists, and lawyers. The remainder of the chapter pursues issues raised in the introductory section while treating in greater detail the two most frequently encountered privileges — lawyer-client and husband-wife.

On the conceptual level, it is interesting to observe how commentators' and judges' views on specific privileges seem to be colored by the underlying philosophical approach they take to the subject. These approaches range from the utilitarian, instrumental, or pragmatic view to the humanistic.

The classic utilitarian approach is Wigmore's. Starting from the premise that "the public is entitled to every man's evidence" and that exemptions from this rule are exceptional and to be discountenanced, Wigmore posits four conditions that must be fulfilled to justify a privilege:

> (1) The communications must originate in a *confidence* that they will not be disclosed.
>
> (2) This element of *confidentiality must be essential* to the full and satisfactory maintenance of the relation between the parties.
>
> (3) The *relation* must be one which in the opinion of the community ought to be sedulously *fostered*.
>
> (4) The *injury* that would inure to the relation by the disclosure of the communications must be *greater than the benefit* thereby gained for the correct disposal of litigation.

8 Wigmore, Evidence, §§2191, 2192, 2285 (McNaughton rev. 1961). Note the dual focus in Wigmore's formula on the instrumental purpose of the communication and the cost/benefit effect on the litigation process.

In the *Nixon* tapes case, United States v. Nixon, 418 U.S. 683 (1974), the Supreme Court applied this utilitarian approach to the president's claim of a privilege for confidential presidential communications. In rejecting the President's claim of privilege in the specific case before it, the Court took pains to highlight the fundamental inconsistency between privileges and accuracy in the judicial process:

> But this presumptive privilege [for Presidential communications] must be considered in light of our historic commitment to the rule of law. This is nowhere more profoundly manifest than in our view that "the twofold aim [of criminal justice] is that guilt shall not escape or innocence suffer." Berger v. United States, 295 U.S., at 88. We have elected to employ an adversary system of criminal justice in which the parties contest all issues before a court of law. The need to develop all relevant facts in the adversary system is both fundamental and comprehensive. The ends of criminal justice would be defeated if judgments were to be founded on a partial or speculative presentation of the facts. The very integrity of the judicial system and public confidence in the system depend on full disclosure of all the facts, within the framework of

the rules of evidence. To ensure that justice is done, it is imperative to the function of courts that compulsory process be available for the production of evidence needed either by the prosecution or by the defense.

Only recently the Court restated the ancient proposition of law, albeit in the context of a grand jury inquiry rather than a trial, "That 'the public . . . has a right to every man's evidence,' except for those persons protected by a constitutional, common-law, or statutory privilege, United States v. Bryan, 339 U.S. [323, 331 (1950)]; Blackmer v. United States, 284 U.S. 421, 438 (1932). . . ." Branzburg v. Hayes, 408 U.S. 665, 688 (1972). The privileges referred to by the Court are designed to protect weighty and legitimate competing interests. Thus, the Fifth Amendment to the Constitution provides that no man "shall be compelled in any criminal case to be a witness against himself." And, generally, an attorney or a priest may not be required to disclose what has been revealed in professional confidence. . . . [T]hese exceptions to the demand for every man's evidence are not lightly created nor expansively construed, for they are in derogation of the search for truth. . . .

Nowhere in the Constitution, as we have noted earlier, is there any explicit reference to a privilege of confidentiality, yet to the extent this interest relates to the effective discharge of a President's powers, it is constitutionally based.

The right to the production of all evidence at a criminal trial similarly has constitutional dimensions. The Sixth Amendment explicitly confers upon every defendant in a criminal trial the right "to be confronted with the witnesses against him" and "to have compulsory process for obtaining witnesses in his favor." Moreover, the Fifth Amendment also guarantees that no person shall be deprived of liberty without due process of law. It is the manifest duty of the courts to vindicate those guarantees, and to accomplish that it is essential that all relevant and admissible evidence be produced.

In this case we must weigh the importance of the general privilege of confidentiality of Presidential communications in performance of the President's responsibilities against the inroads of such a privilege on the fair administration of criminal justice. The interest in preserving confidentiality is weighty indeed and entitled to great respect. However, we cannot conclude that advisers will be moved to temper the candor of their remarks by the infrequent occasions of disclosure because of the possibility that such conversations will be called for in the context of a prosecution.

On the other hand, the allowance of the privilege to withhold evidence that is demonstrably relevant in a criminal trial would cut deeply into the guarantee of due process of law and gravely impair the basic function of the courts. A President's acknowledged need for confidentiality in the communications of his office is general in nature, whereas the constitutional need for production of relevant evidence in a criminal proceeding is specific and central to the fair adjudication of a particular criminal case in the administration of justice. Without access to specific facts a criminal prosecution may be totally frustrated. The President's broad interest in confidentiality of communications will not be vitiated by disclosure of a limited number of conversations preliminarily shown to have some bearing on the pending criminal cases.

We conclude that when the ground for asserting privilege as to subpoenaed materials sought for use in a criminal trial is based only on the generalized interest in confidentiality, it cannot prevail over the fundamental demands of due process of law in the fair administration of criminal justice. The generalized assertion of privilege must yield to the demonstrated, specific need for evidence in a pending criminal trial.

Some modern commentators have criticized Wigmore and the Supreme Court's approach as too narrowly based on an instrumental calculus that overvalues accuracy in the judicial process while undervaluing other important human values such as privacy, dignity, intimacy, anonymity, and individuality. Focusing on these humanistic values, Professor Alan Westin, Privacy and Freedom 31-39 (1967), has identified the following important functions furthered by privacy in communications in modern democratic societies:

> *personal autonomy:* privacy preserves social processes that safeguard one's "sacred individuality" . . . and permits "sheltered experimentation and testing of ideas";
> *emotional release:* privacy affords "relaxation . . . from the pressure of playing social roles, [creates an opportunity for people] to lay their masks aside for a rest [and obtain] respite from the emotional stimulation of daily life, [grants] protection . . . to minor non-compliance with social norms, [and allows one] to give vent to . . . anger at the system . . . without fear of being held responsible for such comments";
> *self-evaluation:* privacy is essential if one is to fulfill the individual's need "to integrate his experiences into a meaningful pattern and to exert his individuality on events" . . . and "process the information that is constantly bombarding [him]"; privacy also furthers "the proper timing of the decision to move from private reflection or intimate conversations to a more general publication of acts and thoughts";
> *limited and protected communications:* privacy is necessary for psychic self-preservation for men in the metropolis, "[providing] the opportunities . . . for sharing confidences and intimacies with those he trusts — spouse; the family; personal friends; and close associates at work."

Professor Thomas Krattenmaker, building mostly on Westin's catalogue of functions served by privacy in communications, is severely critical of the modern trend toward an instrumentalist view of privileges. In an analysis of the federal privilege rules proposed by the Supreme Court, Krattenmaker states:

> [I]n circumscribing personal testimonial privileges, the Rules would intrude severely and unwarrantably upon personal privacy and the individual's interest in freedom of expression. . . .
> It is imperative to ascertain precisely what is meant by the concept of privacy in twentieth century America, what individual and societal benefits flow from public protections accorded privacy, whether recognition of interpersonal testimonial privileges does, indeed, substantially contribute to these ends, and whether less drastic means might produce whatever benefits

privileges yield. In short, the central question is whether the simple device of excluding evidence at trial can be viewed as an important, well-designed adjunct of the right of privacy.

Privacy, in the sense that term is employed here, is not merely secrecy but also involves the voluntary and secure control one possesses over communication of information about oneself; a person locked in a closet against his will may have secrecy but is unlikely to be enjoying privacy. Simple secrecy is in no sense a valuable right. What makes privacy both a distinct concept and a valuable right is the fact that it is voluntary and that it includes a secured ability to control by oneself how much information about oneself is disseminated and the scope and circumstances of its communication.

The rejection of a claim of privilege destroys the claimant's control over the breadth of the audience receiving personal information as well as his control over the timing and conditions of its release. Clearly then, limitations on testimonial privileges are invasions of privacy.

Not every deprivation of privacy, of course, is socially deplorable or constitutionally objectionable. For example, mandatory examination of restaurant workers for the presence of communicable diseases robs such persons of voluntary control over information concerning one aspect of themselves, but that probably would not lead thoughtful people to conclude that such examinations should be abolished. Most people would agree that such a limited intrusion is outweighed by other social needs.

The question whether to protect an interest in privacy, then, necessarily must involve weighing matters of degree. Therefore, whether society should tolerate either a lesser intrusion upon privacy or an intrusion for certain weighty countervailing reasons must depend, in large measure, upon the importance to individuals and American society of the right of personal privacy as well as the precise nature of that right. At bottom it appears the Rules implicitly adopt an incredible topsy-turvy ranking of the relative strengths of governmental, corporate and individual claims to the right of privacy. . . .

The right of privacy is not simply a very important means to highly valued but distinct ends. Rather, privacy is further an end in itself — an essential condition of political liberty and our very humanity. Without the opportunities privacy provides for personal autonomy, emotional release, self-evaluation and limited and protected communications, individual political freedom as we know it would not flourish. Democracy requires both individual growth, creativity and responsibility, and an inner zone of personal security which the state cannot penetrate. Privacy provides both that zone of impenetrable individuality and the means by which public contributions can flow from responsible individual control over oneself. Privacy both protects private citizens from state control and permits full development of their public selves. . . .

Once care is taken to analyze the concept of privacy, its relationship to personal testimonial privileges is quite striking. Indeed, it is not a farfetched view that personal evidentiary privileges go to the heart of the modern American citizen's need for a right of privacy. For, to repeat, the essence of that right is control over, not the absence of, information. In this regard, privacy is a two-sided concept. People in society constantly are seeking a balance between personal secrecy and social participation. The principal contribution of this right of privacy is that it permits individuals to seek their own balance without being forced to choose between the extremes of total secrecy and total openness. For this reason, it is even more important to the preservation of a useful right of privacy that limited communication be possible than that full secrecy be available.

Testimonial privileges, through fostering this control, help to provide a context for the development of personal autonomy, emotional release, self-evaluation, and limited and protected communication. None of these ends is attainable solely by oneself; successful pursuit of any one of them apparently requires at least some disclosure to another, but that must occur in a situation which permits individual control over the breadth of disclosure. And, as further noted above, providing a means for attaining these ends is essential to the maintenance of democracy and the human condition.

Indeed, this need for controlled disclosure such as by privileged communication, touching as it does upon such fundamental conditions of our society, is supported not simply by considerations of privacy, but by similar and perhaps more familiar principles respecting the function of freedom of speech. For the social policies furthered by recognition of a right of personal privacy are in many instances similar to those protected by the theoretical underpinnings of freedom of speech. . . .

Proponents of testimonial privileges need not carry the burden of proving what factors influence behavior. Privileges also are important for other reasons as well. For in protecting those relatively few confidential utterances that do bear upon concrete litigation, the law protects all those that may. Moreover, the societal recognition of the right of privacy entailed in permitting a claim of personal privilege serves as an embodiment of the fundamental regard in which society does, and should, hold that right. Most important, however, is the simple fact that when a particular confidant's claim of privilege is upheld, so is his very right of privacy. That society cannot protect against all abridgments of that right makes it more, not less, imperative that privacy be preserved whenever possible. That we cannot guarantee the inviolability of every man's every attempt to strike his own balance between secrecy and participation does not mean judges should be unleashed to compel divulgence of every confidence they can discover. In short, our security and privacy is enriched substantially when a testimonial privilege, properly invoked, is given societal approval. . . .

The confidential communication that is part and parcel of the right of privacy may pass between parent and child or counsellor and client or roommate and roommate, as well as husband and wife or doctor and patient. Not only attorneys and their clients, but also judges and their clerks and legislators or administrators and their aides, may need the privilege if law is to be freely and fairly administered. Like the corporation's trade secret, such matters deserve a finer, more discriminating treatment than wholesale rejection in advance of every such claim of privilege, without regard to the necessity for the testimony or the availability of other techniques to better protect the interests of all litigants. Accordingly, a general, qualified privilege for confidential communications that pass between individuals intimately related or in a position of close personal trust should be adopted, modeled upon the trade secrets provision of rule 508.

Krattenmaker, Testimonial Privileges in Federal Courts: An Alternative to the Proposed Federal Rules of Evidence, 62 Geo. L.J. 61, 85-94 (1973). See also Louisell, Confidentiality, Conformity and Confusions: Privileges in Federal Court Today, 31 Tul. L. Rev. 101 (1956).

Krattenmaker's response was a typical reaction at one extreme to the Supreme Court's proposed rules on privileges, the most controversial of the proposed federal rules. Some of the criticism was based on clear-cut policy differences and focused on specific proposed privileges or the absence of others — for example, the lack of a reporter's privilege. Other criticism was more broadly based on separation of powers and federalism grounds, contending that it was for the legislature and not the courts to create rules of privilege and that in diversity cases state rather than federal rules should apply.

To prevent the controversy over the privilege rules from delaying the entire Federal Rules, Congress decided to delete all 13 of the Court's proposed privilege rules (nine privileges and four ancillary rules) and to substitute a single rule, Rule 501, which did two things:

(1) It adopted the approach of Erie Railroad Co. v. Tompkins, 304 U.S. 64 (1938), by mandating that in federal court cases governed by state substantive law, state law as to privileges shall apply; and

(2) It provided that in cases governed by federal substantive law, the principles of the common law shall apply, "as they may be interpreted by the courts of the United States in the light of reason and experience."

In short, the final version of the Federal Rules left the whole matter of privileges up in the air and the philosophical debate over the underlying justification for the recognition and nonrecognition of certain privileges no closer to a resolution.

Must one choose sides in this debate? Does either the instrumentalist or the humanistic approach by itself provide a satisfactory explanation for the recognized privileges and for the nonrecognition of seemingly similar but unprotected relationships? If not, perhaps it is because there is more than one type of privilege designed to accomplish more than one purpose.

Indeed, there seem to be at least two distinct types of privileges. A rudimentary binary classification of privileges could be made on the basis of the relationship between the holder of the privilege and the other communicant. The first class or group of privileges includes those in which a professional counseling relationship exists between the holder of the privilege and the "other." Privileges of this sort include the well-recognized ones of lawyer-client, physician-patient, and communications-to-clergy and the generally unrecognized ones of accountant-client, social worker, and stockbroker. The most obvious purpose of recognizing these privileges is to foster the effective rendering of the professional service offered by the counselor.

The second group of privileges includes those that are designed simply to throw a veil of secrecy around specific zones of privacy in order to protect individual autonomy and human dignity. No professional relationship is involved and no furthering of any service need be demonstrated. Examples of these privileges include the marital privilege and the privilege against self-incrimination.

These categories necessarily overlap. The reporter's privilege is one example of a privilege that falls into both categories, and there may be others. Nonetheless, it may be helpful to try to sort the privileges in this fashion to see whether more than one test should be applied to determine if a putative privilege should be recognized. For example, perhaps only the privileges in the first group — those based on the existence of a professional relationship — should be subjected to an instrumentalist or pragmatic test; those in the second group may not be susceptible to the same analysis. If this is true, then on what basis might they be justified? And why do these justifications fail to justify privileges for communications between "best friends" and "grandma-grandson" as well?

Despite all the effort that has been devoted to rationalizing the law of privileges, it is possible that neither the instrumentalist-utilitarian approach nor the humanistic approach can justify either the present system of privileges as a whole or even any particular privilege. For the professional privileges, for example, what data would suffice to prove that the utilitarian calculus justifies the various privileges? Is it possible to obtain such data? What data justifies the nonprofessional privileges? How would a social scientist go about testing the assumptions or assertions that underlie most thinking about these privileges? If it is not possible to demonstrate under either the utilitarian or humanistic approach that the various established privileges should exist and that other asserted privileges should not, what else explains the present system of privileges?

Does an alternate thesis that privileges rest on relative power and influence exercised by certain segments of society better explain the present system of privileges? After all, we are talking about *privilege*.

IN RE FARBER (STATE v. JASCALEVICH)
78 N.J. 259, 394 A.2d 330, cert. denied, 439 U.S. 997 (1978)

MOUNTAIN, J. In these consolidated appeals The New York Times Company and Myron Farber, a reporter employed by the newspaper, challenge judgments entered against them in two related matters — one a proceeding in aid of a litigant (civil contempt), the other for criminal contempt of court. The proceedings were instituted in an ongoing murder trial now in its seventh month, as a result of the appellants' failure to comply with two subpoenas duces tecum, directing them to produce certain documents and materials compiled by one or both of these appellants in the course of Farber's investigative reporting of certain allegedly criminal activities. Farber's investigations and reporting are said to have contributed largely to the indictment and prosecution of Dr. Mario E. Jascalevich for murder. Appellants moved unsuccessfully before Judge William J. Arnold, the trial judge in State v. Jascalevich, to quash the two subpoenas; an order was entered directing that the subpoenaed material be produced for in camera inspection by the court. . . .

Impelled by appellants' persistent refusal to produce the subpoenaed materials for in camera inspection, Judge Arnold issued an order returnable before Judge Theodore W. Trautwein, directing appellants to show cause why they should not be deemed in contempt of court. . . .

Judge Trautwein determined that both appellants had wilfully contemned Judge Arnold's order directing that materials be produced for in camera inspection and found them guilty as charged. A fine of $100,000 was imposed on The New York Times and Farber was ordered to serve six months in the Bergen County jail and to pay a fine of $1,000. Additionally, in order to compel production of the materials subpoenaed on behalf of Jascalevich, a fine of $5,000 per day for every day that elapsed until compliance with Judge Arnold's order was imposed upon The Times; Farber was fined $1,000 and sentenced to confinement in the county jail until he complied with the order. . . .

I. The First Amendment

Appellants claim a privilege to refrain from revealing information sought by the subpoenas duces tecum essentially for the reason that were they to divulge this material, confidential sources of such information would be made public. Were this to occur, they argue, newsgathering and the dissemination of news would be seriously impaired, because much information would never be forthcoming to the news media unless the persons who were the sources of such information could be entirely certain that their identities would remain secret. The final result, appellants claim, would be a substantial lessening in the supply of available news on a variety of important and sensitive issues, all to the detriment of the public interest. They contend further that this privilege to remain silent with respect to confidential information and the sources of such information emanates from the "free speech" and "free press" clauses of the First Amendment.

In our view the Supreme Court of the United States has clearly rejected this claim and has squarely held that no such First Amendment right exists. In Branzburg v. Hayes, 408 U.S. 665 (1972), three news media representatives argued that, for the same reason here advanced, they should not be required to appear and testify before grand juries, and that this privilege to refrain from divulging information, asserted to have been received from confidential sources, derived from the First

Amendment. Justice White, noting that there was no common law privilege, stated the issue and gave the Court's answer in the first paragraph of his opinion:

"The issue in these cases is whether requiring newsmen to appear and testify before state or federal grand juries abridges the freedom of speech and press guaranteed by the First Amendment. We hold that it does not." Branzburg v. Hayes, supra, 408 U.S. at 667 (1972).

In that case one reporter, from Frankfort, Kentucky, had witnessed individuals making hashish from marijuana and had made a rather comprehensive survey of the drug scene in Frankfort. He had written an article in the Louisville Courier-Journal describing this illegal activity. Another, a newsman-photographer employed by a New Bedford, Massachusetts television station, had met with members of the Black Panther movement at the time that certain riots and disorders occurred in New Bedford. The material he assembled formed the basis for a television program that followed. The third investigative reporter had met with members of the Black Panthers in northern California and had written an article about the nature and activities of the movement. In each instance there had been a commitment on the part of the media representative that he would not divulge the source of his article or story.

By a vote of 5 to 4 the Supreme Court held that newspaper reporters or other media representatives have no privilege deriving from the First Amendment to refrain from divulging confidential information and the sources of such information when properly subpoenaed to appear before a grand jury. The three media representatives were directed to appear and testify. The holding was later underscored and applied directly to this case by Justice White in a brief opinion filed in this cause upon the occasion of his denial of a stay sought by these appellants. He said,

"There is no present authority in this Court either that newsmen are constitutionally privileged to withhold duly subpoenaed documents material to the prosecution or defense of a criminal case or that a defendant seeking the subpoena must show extraordinary circumstances before enforcement against newsmen will be had." New York Times and Farber v. Jascalevich, — U.S. — (1978). . . .

[A]mong the many First Amendment protections that may be invoked by the press, there is not to be found the privilege of refusing to reveal relevant confidential information and its sources to a grand jury which is engaged in the fundamental governmental function of "[f]air and effective law enforcement aimed at providing security for the person and property of the individual . . ." 408 U.S. at 690. The reason this is so is that a majority of the members of the United States Supreme Court have so determined. . . .

Thus we do no weighing or balancing of societal interests in reaching our determination that the First Amendment does not afford appellants the privilege they claim. The weighing and balancing has been done by a higher court. Our conclusion that appellants cannot derive the protection they seek from the First Amendment rests upon the fact that the ruling in *Branzburg* is binding upon us and we interpret it as applicable to, and clearly including, the particular issue framed here. It follows that the obligation to appear at a criminal trial on behalf of a defendant who is enforcing his Sixth Amendment rights is at least as compelling as the duty to appear before a grand jury.

II. The Shield Law[2]

In Branzburg v. Hayes, supra, the Court dealt with a newsman's claim of privilege based solely upon the First Amendment. As we have seen,

2. The term "shield law" is commonly and widely applied to statutes granting newsmen and other media representatives the privilege of declining to reveal confidential sources of information. The New Jersey shield law reads as follows:

"Subject to Rule 37, a person engaged on, engaged in, connected with, or employed by news media for the purpose of gathering, procuring, transmitting, compiling, editing or disseminating news for the general public or on whose behalf news is so gathered, procured, transmitted, compiled, edited or disseminated has a privilege to refuse to disclose, in any legal or quasi-legal proceeding or before any investigative body, including, but not limited to, any court, grand jury, petit jury, administrative agency, the Legislature or legislative committee, or elsewhere:

"a. The source, author, means, agency or persons from or through whom any information was procured, obtained, supplied, furnished, gathered, transmitted, compiled, edited, disseminated, or delivered; and

"b. Any news or information obtained in the course of pursuing his professional activities whether or not it is disseminated. . . .

"Unless a different meaning clearly appears from the context of this act, as used in this act:

"a. 'News media' means newspapers, magazines, press associations, news agencies, wire services, radio, television or other similar printed, photographic, mechanical or electronic means of disseminating news to the general public.

"b. 'News' means any written, oral or pictorial information gathered, procured, transmitted, compiled, edited or disseminated by, or on behalf of any person engaged in, engaged on, connected with or employed by a news media and so procured or obtained while such required relationship is in effect.

"c. 'Newspaper' means a paper that is printed and distributed ordinarily not less frequently than once a week and that contains news, articles of opinion, editorials, features, advertising, or other matter regarded as of current interest, has a paid circulation and has been entered at a United States post office as second class matter.

"d. 'Magazine' means a publication containing news which is published and distributed periodically, has a paid circulation and has been entered at a United States post office as second class matter.

"e. 'News agency' means a commercial organization that collects and supplies news to subscribing newspapers, magazines, periodicals and news broadcasters.

"f. 'Press association' means an association of newspapers or magazines formed to gather and distribute news to its members.

"g. 'Wire service' means a news agency that sends out syndicated news copy by wire to subscribing newspapers, magazines, periodicals or news broadcasters.

"h. 'In the course of pursuing his professional activities' means any situation, including a social gathering, in which a reporter obtains information for the purpose of disseminating it to the public, but does not include any situation in which a reporter intentionally this claim of privilege failed. In *Branzburg* no shield law was involved. Here we have a shield law, said to be as strongly worded as any in the country.

We read the legislative intent in adopting this statute in its present form as seeking to protect the confidential sources of the press as well as information so obtained by reporters and other news media representatives to the greatest extent permitted by the Constitution of the United States and that of the State of New Jersey. It is abundantly clear that appellants come fully within the literal language of the enactment. . . .

III. THE SIXTH AMENDMENT AND ITS NEW JERSEY COUNTERPART

Viewed on its face, considered solely as a reflection of legislative intent to bestow upon the press as broad a shield as possible to protect against forced revelation of confidential source materials, this legislation is entirely constitutional. Indeed, no one appears to have attacked its facial constitutionality.

It is, however, argued, and argued very strenuously, that if enforced under the facts of this case, the Shield Law violates the Sixth Amendment of the Federal Constitution as well as Article 1, ¶10 of the New Jersey Constitution. . . . Essentially the argument is this: The Federal and State Constitutions each provide that in all criminal prosecutions the accused shall have the right "to have compulsory process for obtaining witnesses in his favor." Dr. Jascalevich seeks to obtain evidence to use in preparing and presenting his defense in the ongoing criminal trial in which he has been accused of multiple murders. He claims to come within the favor of these constitutional provisions — which he surely does. Finally, when faced with the Shield Law, he invokes the rather elementary but entirely sound proposition that where Constitution and statute collide, the latter must yield. Subject to what is said below, we find this argument unassailable.

The compulsory process clause of the Sixth Amendment has never been elaborately explicated by the Supreme Court. Not until 1967, when it decided Washington v. Texas, 388 U.S. 14, had the clause been directly construed. Westen, Confrontation and Compulsory Process: A Unified Theory of Evidence for Criminal Cases, 91 Harv. L. Rev. 567, 586 (1978). In *Washington* the petitioner sought the reversal of his conviction for murder. A Texas statute at the time provided that persons charged or convicted as co-participants in the same crime could not testify for one another. One Fuller, who had already been convicted of the murder, was prevented from testifying by virtue of the statute. The

---

conceals from the source the fact that he is a reporter, and does not include any situation in which a reporter is an eyewitness to, or participant in, any act involving physical violence or property damage." N.J.S.A. 2A:84A-21 and 21a.

record indicated that had he testified his testimony would have been favorable to petitioner. The Court reversed the conviction on the ground that petitioner's Sixth Amendment right to compulsory process had been denied. At the same time it determined that the compulsory process clause in the Sixth Amendment was binding on state courts by virtue of the due process clause of the Fourteenth Amendment. It will be seen that *Washington* is like the present case in a significant respect. The Texas statute and the Sixth Amendment could not both stand. The latter of course prevailed. So must it be here.

Quite recently, in United States v. Nixon, 418 U.S. 683 (1974), the Court dealt with another compulsory process issue. There the Special Prosecutor, Leon Jaworski, subpoenaed various tape recordings and documents in the possession of President Nixon. The latter claimed an executive privilege and refused to deliver the tapes. The Supreme Court conceded that indeed there was an executive privilege and that although "[n]owhere in the Constitution . . . is there any explicit reference to a privilege of confidentiality, yet to the extent this interest relates to the effective discharge of a President's powers, it is constitutionally based." 418 U.S. at 711. Despite this conclusion that at least to some extent a president's executive privilege derives from the Constitution, the Court nonetheless concluded that the demands of our criminal justice system required that the privilege must yield. . . .

It is important to note that the Supreme Court in this case compelled the production of privileged material — the privilege acknowledged to rest in part upon the Constitution — even though there was no Sixth Amendment compulsion to do so. The Sixth Amendment affords rights to an accused but not to a prosecutor. The compulsion to require the production of the privileged material derived from the necessities of our system of administering criminal justice.

Article I, ¶10 of the Constitution of the State of New Jersey contains, as we have seen, exactly the same language with respect to compulsory process as that found in the Sixth Amendment. There exists no authoritative explication of this constitutional provision. Indeed it has rarely been mentioned in our reported decisions. We interpret it as affording a defendant in a criminal prosecution the right to compel the attendance of witnesses and the production of documents and other material for which he may have, or may believe he has, a legitimate need in preparing or undertaking his defense. It also means that witnesses properly summoned will be required to testify and that material demanded by a properly phrased subpoena duces tecum will be forthcoming and available for appropriate examination and use.

Testimonial privileges, whether they derive from common law or from statute, which allow witnesses to withhold evidence seem to conflict with this provision. This conflict may arise in a variety of factual contexts with respect to different privileges. We confine our consideration here to the single privilege before us — that set forth in the Shield Law. We hold that Article 1, ¶10 of our Constitution prevails over this statute. . . .

IV. PROCEDURAL MECHANISM

Appellants insist that they are entitled to a full hearing on the issues of relevance, materiality and overbreadth of the subpoena. We agree. The trial court recognized its obligation to conduct such a hearing, but the appellants have aborted that hearing by refusing to submit the material subpoenaed for an in camera inspection by the court to assist it in determining the motion to quash. That inspection is no more than a procedural tool, a device to be used to ascertain the relevancy and materiality of that material. Such an in camera inspection is not in itself an invasion of the statutory privilege. Rather it is a preliminary step to determine whether, and if so to what extent, the statutory privilege must yield to the defendant's constitutional rights.

Appellants' position is that there must be a full showing and definitive judicial determination of relevance, materiality, absence of less intrusive access, and need, prior to any in camera inspection. The obvious objection to such a rule, however, is that it would, in many cases, effectively stultify the judicial criminal process. It might well do so here. The defendant properly recognizes Myron Farber as a unique repository of pertinent information. But he does not know the extent of this information nor is it possible for him to specify all of it with particularity, nor to tailor his subpoena to precise materials of which he is ignorant. Well aware of this, Judge Arnold refused to give ultimate rulings with respect to relevance and other preliminary matters until he had examined the material. We think he had no other course. It is not rational to ask a judge to ponder the relevance of the unknown.

The same objection applies with equal force to the contention that the subpoena is overbroad. Appellants do not assert that the subpoena is vague and uncertain, but that the data requested may not be relevant and material. To deal effectively with this assertion it is not only appropriate but absolutely necessary for the trial court to inspect in camera the subpoenaed items so that it can make its determinations on the basis of concrete materials rather than in a vacuum. . . .

While we agree, then, that appellants should be afforded the hearing they are seeking, one procedural aspect of which calls for their compliance with the order for in camera inspection, we are also of the view that they, and those who in the future may be similarly situated, are entitled to a preliminary determination before being compelled to submit the subpoenaed materials to a trial judge for such inspection. Our decision in this regard is not, contrary to the suggestion in some of the briefs filed with us, mandated by the First Amendment; for in addition to ruling generally against the representatives of the press in *Branzburg*, the Court particularly and rather vigorously, rejected the claims there asserted that before going before the grand jury, each of the reporters, at the very least, was entitled to a preliminary hearing to establish a number of threshold issues. Branzburg v. Hayes, supra, 408 U.S. at 701-07. Rather, our insistence upon such a threshold determination springs from our obligation to give as much effect as possible, within ever-present constitutional limitations, to the very positively expressed legislative intent to protect the confidentiality and secrecy of sources from which the media derive information. To this end such a determination would seem a necessity.

PASHMAN, J., dissenting. . . . This case is the first major test of New Jersey's new "Shield Law." There is no reason to accord this statute an unfriendly reception in any court of this State. There should be no eagerness to narrow or circumvent it. The Shield Law is not an irritation. It is an act of the Legislature.

This law was passed in the aftermath of the Supreme Court's decision in Branzburg v. Hayes, 408 U.S. 665 (1972). In *Branzburg*, the Court held that the First Amendment will not always prevent forced disclosure of a reporter's confidential sources and information. More specifically, it ruled that the reporters there involved had no privilege under the First Amendment against being compelled, on pain of contempt, to reveal such confidential data to an investigating grand jury. In its view, the resulting infringement upon the reporters' investigating abilities was outweighed by the grand jury's need to have everyman's evidence.

The Court emphasized, however, that state legislatures were not powerless to alter the result reached in *Branzburg*. As Justice White stated:

"At the federal level, Congress has freedom to determine whether a statutory newsman's privilege is necessary and desirable and to fashion standards and rules as narrow or broad as deemed necessary to deal with the evil discerned and, equally important, to refashion those rules as experience from time to time may dictate. *There is also merit in leaving state legislatures free, within First Amendment limits, to fashion their own standards in light of the conditions and problems with respect to the relations between law enforcement officials and press in their own areas.* It goes without saying, of course, that we are powerless to bar state courts from responding in their own way and construing their own constitutions so as to recognize a newsman's privilege, either qualified or absolute." [408 U.S. at 706, emphasis supplied].

The News Media Privilege Act was New Jersey's response to the Court's invitation. This Act reflects our Legislature's judgment that an uninhibited news media is more important to the proper functioning of our society than is the ability of either law enforcement agencies, the courts or criminal defendants to gain access to confidential news data. . . .

A reporter's ability to obtain sensitive information depends on his reputation for keeping confidences. Once breached — that reputation is destroyed. Potential sources of information can no longer rest secure that their identities and confidences will remain free from disclosure.

Realizing that strict confidentiality is essential to the workings of a free press, our Legislature, through the News Media Privilege Act, has granted reporters an immunity from disclosure which is both absolute and comprehensive. *Any* person connected with *any* news media for the purpose of gathering or disseminating news is granted the privilege of refusing to disclose, in *any* legal or quasi-legal proceeding or before *any* investigative body, both the source of and any information acquired.

Courts are thus given no discretion to determine on a case-by-case basis whether the societal importance of a free and robust press is "outweighed" by other assertedly compelling interests. The Legislature has done the weighing and balancing and has determined that in every case the right to non-disclosure is paramount. If a reporter falls within the ambit of the statute, he has a privilege of non-disclosure.

This privilege exists not only with respect to public disclosures; it encompasses revelations to any legal or quasi-legal body, including "any court." Even forced in camera disclosures are thus prohibited.

[A concurring opinion by Chief Judge Hughes and a dissenting opinion by Judge Handler are omitted.]

What arguments may be advanced in support of a reporter's privilege? Does a reporter's privilege satisfy Wigmore's four conditions? Can such a privilege be defended on purely utilitarian grounds or on the basis of other values extrinsic to the litigation process? What data would support a reporter's privilege on either basis? Is such data obtainable? If not, is a reporter's privilege justifiable? Do the majority and dissenting opinions in the *Farber* case reflect fundamentally different philosophical approaches to privileges in general or only different conceptions of the impact that such a privilege would have on the judicial process?

What institutional issues do you see in the *Farber* case? What are the appropriate respective roles of the legislature and the judiciary in establishing privileges? Again, does this question depend upon the approach taken to the subject of privileges — the instrumentalist-utilitarian, the humanistic, or the perquisite of power?

Problem VI-1
Clergymen, Psychiatrists, Lawyers — The Farber Variations

In the *Farber* case, the defendant in the criminal prosecution, Dr. Jascalevich, subpoenaed documents and solicited testimony that he alleged was relevant, material, and unavailable from any other source, including the prosecution. Dr. Jascalevich's lawyers alleged that the reporter, Myron Farber, had obtained this material in the course of his 1975 investigation into the 1965-1966 deaths in Dr. Jascalevich's hospital, which subsequently led to the reopening of the police investigation and the indictment of Dr. Jascalevich. Among the evidence sought by the defense counsel were Farber's notes and his recollections of interviews with Dr. Stanley Harris, a surgeon at the hospital where the criminal activities are said to have occurred. Dr. Harris admitted having spoken to Farber five times before the New York Times articles appeared in 1975 and before his reinterview by the prosecutor's office in 1976. In his interview with the prosecutor, Dr. Harris stated that his suspicions of Dr. Jascalevich were originally aroused by the unexplained deaths of some of his patients. The defense characterized Dr. Harris as Dr. Jascalevich's principal accusor.

(1) Suppose that Dr. Harris's communications were made to his clergyman or to his psychiatrist rather than to Myron Farber. If defense counsel subpoenaed the clergyman or psychiatrist, how would the court be likely to treat a claim of privilege asserted on Dr. Harris's behalf by the clergyman or doctor under a state common law privilege for communications to clergymen or psychiatrists similar to proposed Rules 504 and 506?

(2) Suppose Dr. Harris's communications were with Martin Ferber, Esq., his attorney. If defense counsel subpoenaed Attorney Ferber, how would the court be likely to treat a claim of privilege asserted by the lawyer on Dr. Harris's behalf under a state common law lawyer-client privilege similar to proposed Rule 503?

To the extent that you feel that the court would react differently to a claim of clergyman, psychiatrist, or lawyer-client privilege than it did to Farber's claim of reporter's privilege, what explains the difference?

B.   The Lawyer-Client Privilege

Of all the privileges, the lawyer-client privilege is undoubtedly the most solidly entrenched. Not surprisingly, it is also the privilege with which lawyers — litigators and nonlitigators alike — are most often concerned. Indeed, on a daily basis, most practicing lawyers find themselves in situations in which the existence or nonexistence of the privilege is a vital consideration. Fortunately, at its core and in routine cases, the privilege is relatively easy to understand and apply. At the edges, however, for example, when the attorney is communicating with corporate employees about possible unlawful payments to public officials or is handed a smoking gun by an out-of-breath client, the privilege is both murky and controversial. For lawyers in these situations, a correct understanding of the privilege and their professional responsibilities is all that stands between them and the possibility of malpractice, contempt of court, or disciplinary sanctions.

This section takes a quick look at the basic elements of the privilege and the mechanisms for asserting it. It then focuses on two specific and very real problems that highlight the difficult policy judgments underlying the privilege:

(1) How does a lawyer handle "hot stuff" — in the business context, tax records; in the criminal law context, weapons, evidence, or contraband?

(2) How well does current privilege doctrine recognize and provide for the conflicting interests of lawyer, client, and others, especially in the context of the modern business enterprise?

Before taking on the complex policy and ethical issues that emerge at the frontiers of the privilege when these problems are considered, it may be helpful to try to formulate possible reasons for recognizing a lawyer-client privilege in the simplest case; that is, where the lawyer is explicitly retained by an individual to furnish confidential legal advice to that person concerning a lawful course of conduct contemplated or previously taken by that person. The following arguments have been advanced to support the privilege in this and more complex situations.

(1) It is necessary for the effective rendering of legal services that the client communicate every relevant detail to the lawyer. No stone can be left unturned if the client is to receive effective legal advice. The client may not feel free to reveal damaging, embarrassing, or tentative details unless she is assured that her confidence will be protected. In the criminal context it may be asserted that the lawyer-client privilege is necessary to protect the accused's fifth and sixth amendment rights to the effective assistance of counsel.

(2) Without the privilege, lawyers would become witnesses in almost every lawsuit, creating intolerable problems in the administration of trials.

(3) The adversary system and the professional role of the lawyer/counselor require that a zone of privacy surround the lawyer-client relationship.

(4) The privilege promotes justice. In fact, very little evidence is suppressed that cannot be obtained by other means. And the existence of the privilege causes information to come to the attention of the attorney which is used to counsel the client toward the "correct" course of conduct.

Which of these arguments do you find persuasive in the simple core situation described above? Are they equally applicable in all situations to which the privilege might arguably be extended, such as communications to a corporate attorney by mid-level corporate employees or communications by an individual to an attorney concerning the location of a weapon or a body? Which of these arguments rest on untested or untestable assumptions about human behavior? What data support these assumptions? Is the case for a broad lawyer-client privilege stronger than the case for a similarly broad privilege for communications with other professionals and counselors, such as accountants, social workers, stock brokers, show business agents, trustees, partners, or other fiduciaries, or between employees or even "best friends"? As long ago as 1827, one observer was skeptical that the lawyer-client privilege could be justified on *any* basis.

J. BENTHAM, RATIONALE OF JUDICIAL EVIDENCE
from The Works of Jeremy Bentham 473-479 (Browning ed. 1842), as quoted in 8 Wigmore, Evidence §2291, pp. 549-551 (McNaughton rev. 1961)

When in consulting with a law adviser, attorney or advocate, a man has confessed his delinquency, or disclosed some fact which, if stated in court, might tend to operate in proof of it, such law adviser is not to be suffered to be examined as to any such point. The law adviser is neither to be compelled, nor so much as suffered, to betray the trust thus reposed in him. Not suffered? Why not?

Oh, because to betray a trust is treachery; and an act of treachery is an immoral act.

But if such confidence, when reposed, is permitted to be violated, and if this be known, (which, if such be the law, it will be), the consequence will be, that no such confidence will be reposed. Not reposed? — Well: and if it be not, wherein will consist the mischief? The man by the supposition is guilty; if not, by the supposition there is nothing to betray: let the law adviser say every thing he has heard, every thing he can have heard from his client, the client cannot have any thing to fear from it. That it will often happen that in the case supposed no such confidence will be reposed, is natural enough: the first thing the advocate or attorney will say to his client, will be, — Remember that, whatever you say to me, I shall be obliged to tell, if asked about it. What, then, will be the consequence? That a guilty person will not in general be able to derive quite so much assistance from his law adviser, in the way of concerting a false defence, as he may do at present. . . .

A counsel, solicitor, or attorney, cannot conduct the cause of his client (it has been observed) "if he is not fully instructed in the circumstances attending it: but the client" (it is added) "could not give the instructions with safety, if the facts confided to his advocate were to be disclosed." Not with safety? So much the better. To what object is the whole system of penal law directed, if it be not that no man shall have it in his power to flatter himself with the hope of safety, in the event of his engaging in the commission of an act which the law, on account of its supposed mischievousness, has thought fit to prohibit? The argument employed as a reason against the compelling such disclosure, is the very argument that pleads in favour of it. . . .

Thus much in vindication of the proposed rule. As for its disadvantages, they are to be sought for not so much in its direct, as in its indirect, operation. The party himself having been, as he ought to be, previously subjected to interrogation; his lawyer's evidence, which, though good of its kind, is not better than hearsay evidence, would not often add any new facts to those which had already been extracted from the lips of the client. The benefit which would arise from the abolition of the exclusionary rule, would consist rather in the higher tone of morality which would be introduced into the profession itself. A rule of law which, in the case of the lawyer, gives an express license to that wilful concealment of the criminal's guilt, which would have constituted any other person an accessory in the crime, plainly declares that the practice of knowingly engaging one's self as the hired advocate of an unjust cause, is, in the eye of the law, or (to speak intelligibly) in that of the law-makers, an innocent, if not a virtuous practice. But for this implied declaration, the man who in this way hires himself out to do injustice or frustrate justice with his tongue, would be viewed in exactly the same light as he who frustrates justice or does injustice with any other instrument.

Proposed FRE 503
Lawyer-Client Privilege

(a) *Definitions.* As used in this rule:

(1) A "client" is a person, public officer, or corporation, association, or other organization or entity, either public or private, who is rendered professional legal services by a lawyer, or who consults a lawyer with a view to obtaining professional legal services from him.

(2) A "lawyer" is a person authorized, or reasonably believed by the client to be authorized, to practice law in any state or nation.

(3) A "representative of the lawyer" is one employed to assist the lawyer in the rendition of professional legal services.

(4) A communication is "confidential" if not intended to be disclosed to third persons other than those whom disclosure is in furtherance of the rendition of professional legal services to the client or those reasonably necessary for the transmission of the communication.

(b) *General Rule of Privilege.* A client has a privilege to refuse to disclose and to prevent any other person from disclosing confidential communications made for the purpose of facilitating the rendition of professional legal services to the client, (1) between himself or his representative and his lawyer or his lawyer's representative, or (2) between his lawyer and the lawyer's representative, or (3) by him or his lawyer to a lawyer representing another in a matter of common interest, or (4) between representatives of the client or between the client and a representative of the client, or (5) between lawyers representing the client.

(c) *Who May Claim the Privilege.* The privilege may be claimed by the client, his guardian or conservator, the personal representative of a deceased client, or the successor, trustee, or similar representative of a corporation, association, or other organization, whether or not in existence. The person who was the lawyer at the time of the communication may claim the privilege but only on behalf of the client. His authority to do so is presumed in the absence of evidence to the contrary.

(d) *Exceptions.* There is no privilege under this rule:

(1) *Furtherance of Crime or Fraud.* If the services of the lawyer were sought or obtained to enable or aid anyone to commit or plan to commit what the client knew or reasonably should have known to be a crime or fraud; or

(2) *Claimants Through Same Deceased Client.* As to a communication relevant to an issue between parties who claim through the same deceased client, regardless of whether the claims are by testate or intestate succession or by inter vivos transaction; or

(3) *Breach of Duty by Lawyer or Client.* As to a communication relevant to an issue of breach of duty by the lawyer to his client or by the client to his lawyer; or

(4) *Document Attested by Lawyer.* As to a communication relevant to an issue concerning an attested document to which the lawyer is an attesting witness; or

(5) *Joint Clients.* As to a communication relevant to a matter of common interest between two or more clients if the communication was made by any of them to a lawyer retained or consulted in common, when offered in an action between any of the clients.

Problem VI-2
The Blackacre Fraud

(1) Action to enjoin *D* from recording a deed to Blackacre allegedly procured by fraud from the trustee of the Widow Brown Trust. While the first witness is testifying for *P* at trial, *P*'s attorney notices that *D* is whispering to his attorney. After the first witness stands down, *P*'s attorney calls *D*'s attorney and asks him to repeat his conversation with *D*. On *D*'s attorney's objection, what ruling and why?

(2) Instead of calling *D*'s attorney, *P* calls *D* to testify as to what he said to his attorney. On *D*'s attorney's objection, what ruling and why?

(3) Suppose, instead, that *D* is asked, "What did you tell the trustee of

the Widow Brown Trust?" *D* replies, "I object. I just told that to my attorney." What ruling and why?

(4) Suppose that *D* is asked to hand over to *P*'s attorney notes that he has been writing to his attorney during the trial. On *D*'s objection, what ruling and why? What result if *D* is asked to produce notes and letters to his attorney sent prior to the trial?

(5) Before trial, at a preliminary hearing, *P*'s attorney moves for an order directing *D*'s attorney, if he has possession of the deed or any document purporting to be the deed, to deliver it to the clerk to be marked as Plaintiff's Exhibit 1 for identification. *D*'s attorney objects on the grounds that the deed was given to him in private by *D*. What ruling and why?

Problem VI-3
The Eavesdropper

Action for breach of promise of marriage. At trial, *P* called *W* to testify that a few days before the action was commenced, *W* was at the office of *D*'s attorney. *W* observed *D* enter and through a closed door overheard a muted conversation between *D* and his attorney in which *D* said he was afraid a woman would sue him for breach of a promise of marriage. *D* objects to *W*'s proposed testimony on grounds of the lawyer-client privilege. What ruling and why? See the answer of the Massachusetts Supreme Court in a venerable case.

HOY v. MORRIS, 79 Mass. 519 (1859): [A]ssuming that the interview between Mr. Todd [the attorney] and the defendant was strictly of a privileged character, and that all the communications of the latter during its continuance were made by him as a client to his counsel and professional adviser, still the testimony of the witness Aldrich was admissible, and was properly allowed to be used before the jury.

The privilege of exemption from testifying to facts actually known is extended only to an attorney or legal adviser who derives his knowledge from the communications of a client who applies and makes disclosures to him in his professional character, and to those other persons whose intervention is strictly necessary to enable the parties to communicate with each other. This is the rule which . . . seems uniformly to have been recognized as a correct statement of the law upon this subject. . . . Applying this rule to the facts in the present case, the conclusion is inevitable that the statement of [defendant] to his counsel Mr. Todd was overheard and became known to Aldrich under circumstances which entitled the plaintiff to the benefit of his testimony concerning it. Aldrich was not an attorney, nor in any way connected with Mr. Todd; and certainly in no situation where he was either necessary or useful to the parties to enable them to understand each other. On the contrary, he was a mere bystander, and casually overheard conversation not addressed to him nor intended for his ear, but which the client and attorney meant to have respected as private and confidential. Mr. Todd could not lawfully have revealed it. But, in consequence of a want of proper precaution, the communications between him and his client were overheard by a mere stranger. As the latter stood in no relation of confidence to either of the parties, he was clearly not within the rule of exemption from giving testimony; and he might therefore, when summoned as a witness, be compelled to testify to what he overheard, so far as it was pertinent to the subject matter of inquiry upon the trial this is all that was allowed by the court.

Do you agree with the Massachusetts court? Does Hoy *reflect an objective or subjective approach to the issue of the existence of the conditions necessary for the lawyer-client privilege? Which approach would you adopt? Which approach does the proposed Federal Rule adopt?*

PRICHARD v. UNITED STATES
181 F.2d 326 (6th Cir. 1950), aff'd 339 U.S. 974 (1950)

SIMONS, J. The appellant and his law partner, A. E. Funk, Jr., were indicted under §241, Title 18 U.S.C.A. for conspiracy to stuff ballot boxes in certain precincts of Bourbon County, Kentucky, at the general election in November, 1948, which was, of course, a national election. . . .

The principal ground for the appeal as argued and briefed, relates to the testimony of Judge Ardery as to an interview solicited from him by Prichard, and this necessitates a recital of the circumstances which led to the conversation and the status of the parties at the time. Prichard is a lawyer with a career of marked distinction. Graduated from college and with a law degree from Harvard Law School, admitted to the bar in 1939, he had been research secretary to one and probably two of the present Justices of the Supreme Court, to the Attorney General of the United States and the Secretary of the Treasury, and was, at one time, general counsel of the Democratic National Committee. Returning from Washington to Kentucky a number of years before the incidents here involved, he practiced law in the Circuit Court of his county and in the Court of Appeals of the Commonwealth of Kentucky. He became a man of great influence in the politics of his state and county. Judge Ardery is a judge of the 14th Judicial Circuit of the State of Kentucky, had known Prichard all his life, especially since Prichard had been a school mate and later a law partner of his son, Philip. At the election 254 forged ballots had been placed in the ballot boxes of a number of the precincts in Bourbon County prior to the opening of the polls. On the night that the appellant, accompanied by Philip Ardery, sought the interview with the judge, the latter had already called a grand jury to investigate election frauds in the county. The grand jury was to meet the following morning at which time Judge Ardery was expected to instruct the grand jurors as to their duties and the scope of the investigation, as required by Kentucky law.

Prichard had gone to Philip Ardery, his former law partner, on Sunday evening, November 7, 1948, for legal advice. Whatever conversation there was between them at that time was held by the district judge to be within the attorney-client relationship, so privileged, and is not here involved. Prichard and Philip Ardery, however, decided to consult Judge Ardery and drove to the judge's house, arriving there about 11 o'clock. Being advised that the interview which then transpired would be met by the claim of privilege on behalf of Prichard, the district judge heard evidence and argument in camera as to the nature of the evidence expected to be solicited from the judge, and limited interrogation with scrupulous concern for Prichard's rights. In view of Judge Ardery's official position, the duties he was then engaged upon in reference to the grand jury, the command of Kentucky statutes and the public interest, he concluded that one who seeks the advice of the judge of the court in which his case is to be tried is not entitled to the privilege accorded by law to confidential communications between an attorney and client. To allow the privilege under such circumstances would invite frustration of the administration of the courts by their duly elected and qualified judges. Such application would seem inimical to the public interest and a perversion of the purpose and spirit of the rule. He decided that Judge Ardery's testimony was admissible and would be received by the jury with caution as to its lack of bearing upon the guilt of the co-defendant.

At the preliminary hearing the judge had told the court that when Mr. Prichard appeared at his door that night he said, "Judge, I am in deep trouble and I want your advice." He then invited him into his home. To the jury the judge testified, "Mr. Prichard told me that he and two other young men prepared the ballots here in issue and put them in the ballot boxes before the election began." He said that he felt he could give Prichard legal advice and that if anything transpired later he would not sit in the case. Prichard gave him two details in regard to it. He said one of the young men wrote the names of the election officers on the ballots and that he stamped the ballot which scratched Senator Chapman. Prichard appeared greatly disturbed, both mentally and emotionally. His mind was not on the past. It was on the future, at what it might hold for him. "He asked me if I had a suggestion which would help him. I had none at that time." Asked whether Prichard had requested suggestions at any other time, the judge testified that he had on the following Wednesday. At this point the court excused the jury for the purpose of considering the competency of this additional evidence. Judge Ardery then explained, "I suggested to him that he go to his pastor and talk over the matter he had told me of. He didn't seem inclined to receive that suggestion favorably, and then I told him that in my opinion the sooner he got this question over and disposed of, the better it would be. My grand jury was then in session. . . . We understood each other as to what my words meant." While this second conversation was not permitted to go to the jury it has bearing upon the problem here involved. . . .

Judge Ardery was not merely a judge giving, as a lawyer, legal advice to a client — he was the presiding circuit judge of Bourbon County and as such had impaneled a grand jury which he was about to instruct concerning reported infractions of law upon which his advice was sought. By all standards of ethical conduct which govern the conduct of a judge it was morally, if not legally, impossible for Judge Ardery to enter into an attorney-client relationship with one whose conduct was to be investigated by a grand jury already called and about to be instructed, and this Prichard knew or must have known. It is true that no indictment against Prichard was returned by the local grand jury, but this was because the Federal Bureau of Investigation had taken over the inquiry and the state grand jury investigation was never completed. Prichard testified in camera that he knew Judge Ardery would be disqualified in sitting upon his case if an indictment against him were returned. By all the modern concepts of judicial ethics, the judge was not only disqualified from sitting on Prichard's case, but doubtless was also disqualified from organizing and instructing the grand jury once he was advised that the investigation would likely bring within the ambit of the inquest matters bearing upon the conduct of one who, upon the eve of inquiry, had already discussed with him participation in the very alleged unlawful conduct about to be investigated. . . .

Canon 31 of Judicial Ethics promulgated by the American Bar Association on July 9, 1924, Reports of American Bar Association, Vol. 62, 1937, recites: "In many states the practice of law by one holding judicial position is forbidden. In superior courts of general jurisdiction, it should never be permitted." Canon 24 provides: "A judge should not accept inconsistent duties; nor incur obligations, pecuniary or otherwise, which will in any way interfere or appear to interfere with his devotion to the expeditious and proper administration of his official functions." Rule 209(B) of the American Law Institute's Model Code of Evidence, defines "lawyer" for the purpose of the sections dealing with privilege as "a person authorized, or reasonably believed by the client to be authorized, to practice law in any state or nation the law of which recognizes a privilege against disclosure of confidential communications between client and lawyer." These concepts of propriety must have been known to a lawyer of the attainments and experience of Prichard. In our view they prohibit the possibility of existence between Prichard and the judge of an attorney-client relationship. To this may perhaps be added the

general understanding of an informed laity that judges, at least those of
appellate and the higher trial courts, should not and do not practice law.

While Prichard asserts he went to the judge for legal advice, and while
the judge thought he might give such advice and then withdraw from
any case that might result from the grand jury investigation, there is no
suggestion in the record as to any advice sought or given that would
constitute legal advice. Rather is there strong inference that Prichard
sought the interview to ease a troubled conscience and sought it of Judge
Ardery not in his professional capacity as a lawyer capable of giving legal
counsel but as a wise and valued friend who had known him all his life.
"I am in deep trouble and I want your advice," and so the judge seemingly interpreted it. "I suggested to him that he go to his pastor and talk
over the matter he had told me of. . . . We understood each other as to
what my words meant." . . .

Finally, Prichard's request for advice was robbed of the element of
good faith once he knew, as know he did, that the judge was about to
charge a grand jury in respect to election frauds. Whether we conceive
the function of the judge in organizing and instructing a grand jury to
be judicial or administrative is immaterial. In either capacity, knowledge
of law violation may not be reposed in him under the cloak of privilege.
As Wigmore puts it, [5 Wigmore on Evidence, 2d ed.] §2300, "A consultation with a judge, in his capacity as such, falls unquestionably outside
the present privilege." Judge Ardery was currently engaged in ferreting
out election frauds under the authority and command of the laws of his
state. Knowledge that came to him while exercising this function could
not be received by him in confidence. Whether judges of superior courts
may ever enter into an attorney-client relationship, we need not presently decide, even though voicing our doubts. It is sufficient to say for
purpose of present decision, that a judge circumstanced as was Judge
Ardery, may not enter into such relationship with a lawyer who may not
deny knowledge of accepted notions of judicial propriety. There was no
error in receiving Judge Ardery's evidence.

Is the result in *Prichard* consistent with proposed Rule 503? Does the
Prichard court utilize an objective, subjective, or strict liability approach
to the question of the existence of a confidential lawyer-client relationship?

Problem VI-4
The Energetic Investigator

Action for damages for assault and battery. *D*'s attorney, Silvertongue, has been trying to arrange an interview with *P* for some time but

with no success. Silvertongue sends Archie Goodwind, his private investigator, over to *P*'s counsel's office to try to arrange for an interview. Archie is cooling his heels in opposing counsel's waiting room when he observes *P* entering the office. Seizing the initiative, Archie rises to his feet and introduces himself to *P* as "a private investigator on the *P* v. *D* case." Archie explains that the lawyer is busy. At this point, *P* starts to discuss the facts of the case with Archie. Pleased with this opportunity to talk to *P* about the case, Archie directs him into an empty conference room off the waiting room, where he interrogates *P* in detail for 35 minutes.

At trial, *D* calls Archie to testify to statements made by *P* during this interview. *P*'s attorney objects on grounds of lawyer-client privilege. What ruling and why?

Problem VI-5
Tania's Tale

Patty sues Lee, an attorney who represented her in a criminal case, for malpractice after he lost her case and she was sent to jail. Her complaint alleges that Lee advised her to assert her fifth amendment privilege against self-incrimination as to some events with which she was charged and that this constituted malpractice because she was put in the position of frequently invoking the privilege in front of the jury. Lee counterclaims for $250,000, representing the amount allegedly still due him on his fee, which Patty has refused to pay on the grounds of incompetent assistance of counsel. At the trial of these actions, Lee takes the stand to testify to various communications between himself and Patty regarding the events about which she asserted the privilege against self-incrimination. Patty's present lawyer objects on grounds of privilege. What ruling and why?

Problem VI-6
The Evanescent Privilege

D was convicted of armed robbery. At the sentencing hearing, he told the judge that he had not committed the armed robbery but that he had been prevented from so testifying because his court-appointed counsel, Louis Bender, had advised him that all or virtually all of his extensive prior criminal record would be introduced to impeach his credibility. Under questioning by the judge, it became apparent that Mr. Bender was not completely familiar with Rule 609. In particular, it was unclear whether Mr. Bender understood that under Rule 609 some of the defendant's prior crimes could be excluded by the judge because of their prejudicial impact. The court scheduled a hearing to consider whether D should be granted a new trial because of incompetent assistance of counsel.

At the hearing on the motion for a new trial, D represented himself with the assistance of an attorney-adviser appointed by the court. Mr. Bender, who had been subpoenaed by the prosecution, was also represented by counsel. D called himself as his first witness. Before taking the stand, he attempted to obtain from the court a ruling limiting cross-examination to Mr. Bender's advice to him concerning the admissibility of his prior criminal record at his original trial if he had taken the stand. The court refused to so limit the scope of cross-examination.

D changed his mind and decided not to testify. Instead, he called Mr. Bender. After eliciting some preliminary testimony, D asked Mr. Bender to relate the substance of conversations he had with him in D's prison cell and during trial concerning the admissibility of D's prior criminal record. Mr. Bender objected to such questions on the ground that they were covered by the attorney-client privilege and that there was no evidence that D had made a knowing and intelligent waiver of the privilege. The judge stated that he had had lengthy discussions with D and was satisfied that D was making a knowing and intelligent waiver, overruled the objection, and ordered Mr. Bender to answer. Mr. Bender then related the substance of several conversations between himself and D concerning his advice as to the admissibility of D's prior convictions at the original trial. On cross-examination, the assistant U.S. Attorney asked Mr. Bender to relate the entirety of the conversations concerning D's decision whether to take the stand. Both D and Mr. Bender objected to this line of questioning, attempting to assert the attorney-client privilege to everything except the portions of the conversations concerning the admissibility of the prior convictions.

How should the court rule?

Problem VI-7
Name That Client

At a grand jury probe into conspiracy to commit income tax violations, the state calls three persons, each of whom is a duly licensed and practicing attorney. The purpose of calling them is to obtain the names of certain unknown conspirators who, among other things, met with the attorneys to secure representation for the named and indicted conspirators.

The U.S. Attorney asks each attorney the following questions:

(1) Did any of the named defendants employ you to represent him?

(2) Did any third party make arrangements for you to represent a named defendant? If so, who?

(3) If you posted bond for a named defendant, who furnished the bond money?

(4) If you have been paid any attorney's fees on behalf of a named defendant, who paid them?

Which, if any, of these questions may be successfully resisted on grounds of privilege? When the attorney-client privilege is asserted and contested, where does the burden of proof lie?

UNITED STATES v. PAPE
144 F.2d 778 (2d Cir. 1944)

CLARK, J. Pape appeals from a judgment of conviction under an indictment for transporting a woman in interstate commerce "for the purpose of prostitution, debauchery and other immoral purposes." . . .

[T]he attorney, Buckley, . . . appeared for the woman in Washington when she was first taken up by the police, and she was discharged in his custody. On preliminary examination the judge developed that he was retained by the accused about July 15, 1942, to represent the woman as well as the accused — for what purpose, so far as the latter was concerned, never appeared. . . . [The judge] proceeded to make his ruling explicit by saying that the lawyer could be asked who retained him to appear for the woman on the occasion in question and who paid his fee, identifying the persons if they were in court. . . . The lawyer did, therefore, testify that the accused retained him to represent the woman and paid his fee, also that he saw the defendant in Washington and that he had a Packard automobile. Of course, practically all this was merely cumulative; the court records were produced and showed that the woman was indeed released to the attorney; and the only additional fact brought out was that the accused's clearly proved interest in the woman went to the point of retaining and paying for a lawyer to secure her release.

The authorities are substantially uniform against any privilege as applied to the fact of retainer or identity of the client. The privilege is limited to confidential communications, and a retainer is not a confidential communication, although it cannot come into existence without some communication between the attorney and the — at that stage prospective — client. . . . [T]here may be situations in which so much has already appeared of the actual communications between an attorney and a client, that the disclosure of the client will result in a breach of the privilege; but nothing of the sort occurred here. . . .

It seems clear on the authorities, therefore, that the evidence actually brought out before the jury was not privileged. There seems nothing in the preliminary disclosure to the judge that the attorney was also to represent the accused to change this result. . . . Generally speaking, relevant evidence is freely admissible, except as it is privileged; and the privilege extends only so far as the policy behind it demands. Here, as Mr. Justice Shientag shows with his usual felicity, People ex rel. Vogelstein v. Warden of County Jail, supra, 150 Misc. 714, 270 N.Y.S. at page 367, "it was not the purpose of the privilege to shield guilt. Its primary object was to secure the orderly administration of justice by insuring frank revelation by the client to the attorney without fear of a forced disclosure; in other words, to promote freedom of consultation. To be sure the exercise of the privilege may at times result in concealing the truth and allowing the guilty to escape. That is an evil, however, which is considered to be outweighed by the benefit which results to the administration of justice generally."

He adds, "There is nothing in the books to show that the privilege was to extend to the fact of the retention of counsel. No point is made that the employment of counsel should be shrouded with secrecy." Hence when the narrow exclusionary rule ceases to apply, then the more general and pervasive rule of free disclosure to ascertain the truth and prevent the guilty from escaping furnishes the governing principle.

Conviction affirmed.

L. HAND, J. (dissenting). The evidence of the accused's guilt was so strong that I feel some compunction in voting to reverse, yet there are two errors which I think require the case to be retried. Pape retained Buckley as his own lawyer at the same time that he retained him for the woman. I agree that this retainer of an attorney for himself involved no privileged communication; I have nothing to add to, or subtract from, what my brothers say on that. Moreover, it goes without saying that Pape's retainer of Buckley for the woman would not have been privileged, had he not retained him as his own attorney. On the other hand I attach no importance to the fact that he retained him in both capacities at the same time; the case stands as it would, if he had retained him for himself first. Yet if he had done that, when he told him to appear for her, I think it was a communication between attorney and client, a step in his own defence; it may have been also a step in hers but that, I submit, is irrelevant. That direction to his own attorney in his own interest was as much a privileged communication as any direction would have been, made in the course of preparing for a trial; as much, for example, as to tell one's attorney to interview a witness. That it was an important step in connecting him with the woman's prostitution, admits of no debate.

Problem VI-8
On the Waterfront

Blumfeld, attorney for the United Importers Association, Inc., an organization of merchants who import produce from abroad, testified before the Commissioner of Investigation that a member of the association had retained him in an effort to work out certain problems he was having on the waterfront with racketeers trying to extort protection money from the importers. In response to questioning, Blumfeld also testified that this anonymous member told him that he had learned that two powerful city politicians were involved in the protection racket and shared in its proceeds. The Commissioner asked the name of the member. Blumfeld refused to give it on grounds of lawyer-client privilege and was cited for contempt. On appeal, what ruling and why?

COUCH v. UNITED STATES
409 U.S. 322 (1973)

Mr. Justice POWELL delivered the opinion of the Court.

On January 7, 1970, the Government filed a petition in the United States District Court for the Western District of Virginia, pursuant to 26 U.S.C. §§7402(b) and 7604(a), seeking enforcement of an Internal Revenue summons in connection with an investigation of petitioner's tax liability from 1964-1968. The summons was directed to petitioner's accountant for the production of:

All books, records, bank statements, cancelled checks, deposit ticket copies, workpapers and all other pertinent documents pertaining to the tax liability of the above taxpayer.

The question is whether the taxpayer may invoke her Fifth Amendment privilege against compulsory self-incrimination to prevent the production of her business and tax records in the possession of her accountant. Both the District Court[3] and the Court of Appeals for the Fourth Circuit[4] held the privilege unavailable. We granted certiorari, 405 U.S. 1038.

Petitioner is the sole proprietress of a restaurant. Since 1955 she had given bank statements, payroll records, and reports of sales and expenditures to her accountant, Harold Shaffer, for the purpose of preparing her income tax returns. The accountant was not petitioner's personal employee but an independent contractor with his own office and numerous other clients who compensated him on a piecework basis. When

---

3. The District Court held that "[s]ince, at the time the summons was served, the taxpayer, Lillian V. Couch, was not in possession of the books, records and documents described in the summons, she may not assert any Fifth Amendment privilege against self-incrimination as a bar to the enforcement of the summons."

4. The Court of Appeals also noted that the answer to petitioner's Fifth Amendment contentions lay in the fact that "the records were not in the intervenor's [taxpayer's] possession but were in the custody of her accountant," 449 F.2d 141, 143 (1971).

petitioner surrendered possession of the records to Shaffer, she, of course, retained title in herself.

During the summer of 1969, Internal Revenue Agent Dennis Groves commenced an investigation of petitioner's tax returns.

Special Agent Jennings of the Intelligence Division next commenced a joint investigation with Groves to determine petitioner's correct tax liability, the possibility of income tax fraud and the imposition of tax fraud penalties, and, lastly, the possibility of a recommendation of a criminal tax violation. Jennings first introduced himself to petitioner, gave her Miranda warnings as required by IRS directive, and then issued the summons to Shaffer[5] after the latter refused to let him see, remove, or microfilm petitioner's records.

When Jennings arrived at Shaffer's office on September 2, 1969, the return day of the summons, to view the records, he found that Shaffer, at petitioner's request, had delivered the documents to petitioner's attorney. Jennings thereupon petitioned the District Court for enforcement of the summons, and petitioner intervened, asserting that the ownership of the records warranted a Fifth Amendment privilege to bar their production.[6]

II

The importance of preserving inviolate the privilege against compulsory self-incrimination has often been stated by this Court and need not be elaborated. Counselman v. Hitchcock, 142 U.S. 547 (1892); Malloy v. Hogan, 378 U.S. 1 (1964); Miranda v. Arizona, 384 U.S. 436 (1966). By

5. The summons . . . was issued on August 18, 1969, pursuant to 26 U.S.C. §7602, which provides:

"EXAMINATION OF BOOKS AND WITNESSES.

"For the purpose of ascertaining the correctness of any return, making a return where none has been made, determining the liability of any person for any internal revenue tax or the liability at law or in equity of any transferee or fiduciary of any person in respect of any internal revenue tax, or collecting any such liability, the Secretary or his delegate is authorized —

"(1) To examine any books, papers, records, or other data which may be relevant or material to such inquiry;

"(2) To summon the person liable for tax or required to perform the act, or any officer or employee of such person, or any person having possession, custody, or care of books of account containing entries relating to the business of the person liable for tax or required to perform the act, or any other person the Secretary or his delegate may deem proper, to appear before the Secretary or his delegate at a time and place named in the summons and to produce such books, papers, records, or other data, and to give such testimony, under oath, as may be relevant or material to such inquiry; and

"(3) To take such testimony of the person concerned, under oath, as may be relevant or material to such inquiry."

6. Petitioner also claimed that enforcement of the summons would violate her Fourth Amendment right to be secure from unreasonable searches and seizures. We agree with the Government, however, that "this claim is not further articulated and does not appear to be independent of her Fifth Amendment argument."

its very nature, the privilege is an intimate and personal one. It respects a private inner sanctum of individual feeling and thought and proscribes state intrusion to extract self-condemnation. Historically, the privilege sprang from an abhorrence of governmental assault against the single individual accused of crime and the temptation on the part of the State to resort to the expedient of compelling incriminating evidence from one's own mouth. United States v. White, 322 U.S. 694, 698 (1944). The Court has thought the privilege necessary to prevent any "recurrence of the Inquisition and the Star Chamber, even if not in their stark brutality." Ullmann v. United States, 350 U.S. 422, 428 (1956).

In Murphy v. Waterfront Comm'n, 378 U.S. 52, 55 (1964), the Court articulated the policies and purposes of the privilege: "[O]ur unwillingness to subject those suspected of crime to the cruel trilemma of self-accusation, perjury or contempt; our preference for an accusatorial rather than an inquisitorial system of criminal justice; our fear that self-incriminating statements will be elicited by inhumane treatment and abuses; our sense of fair play which dictates 'a fair state-individual balance by requiring the government . . . in its contest with the individual to shoulder the entire load,' . . . our respect for the inviolability of the human personality and of the right of each individual 'to a private enclave where he may lead a private life.' . . ."

It is important to reiterate that the Fifth Amendment privilege is a personal privilege: it adheres basically to the person, not to information that may incriminate him. As Mr. Justice Holmes put it: "A party is privileged from producing the evidence but not from its production." Johnson v. United States, 228 U.S. 457, 458 (1913). The Constitution explicitly prohibits compelling an accused to bear witness "against himself"; it necessarily does not proscribe incriminating statements elicited from another. Compulsion upon the person asserting it is an important element of the privilege, and "prohibition of compelling a man . . . to be witness against himself is a prohibition of the use of physical or moral compulsion to extort communications from *him*," Holt v. United States, 218 U.S. 245, 252-253 (1910) (emphasis added). It is extortion of information from the accused himself that offends our sense of justice.

In the case before us the ingredient of personal compulsion against an accused is lacking. The summons and the order of the District Court enforcing it are directed against the accountant.[9] He, not the taxpayer, is the only one compelled to do anything. And the accountant makes no

---

9. Technically the order to produce the records was directed to petitioner's attorney since, after the summons was served upon the accountant, he ignored it and surrendered the records to the attorney. But constitutional rights obviously cannot be enlarged by this kind of action. The rights and obligations of the parties became fixed when the summons was served, and the transfer did not alter them. See United States v. Zakutansky, 401 F.2d 68, 72 (C.A.7 1968), cert. denied, 393 U.S. 1021 (1969); United States v. Lyons, 442 F.2d 1144 (C.A.1 1971).

claim that he may tend to be incriminated by the production. Inquisitorial pressure or coercion against a potentially accused person, compelling her, against her will, to utter self-condemning words or produce incriminating documents is absent. In the present case, no "shadow of testimonial compulsion upon or enforced communication by the accused" is involved. Schmerber v. California, 384 U.S. 757, 765 (1966).

The divulgence of potentially incriminating evidence against petitioner is naturally unwelcome. But petitioner's distress would be no less if the divulgence came not from her accountant but from some other third party with whom she was connected and who possessed substantially equivalent knowledge of her business affairs. The basic complaint of petitioner stems from the fact of divulgence of the possibly incriminating information, not from the manner in which or the person from whom it was extracted. Yet such divulgence, where it does not result from coercion of the suspect herself, is a necessary part of the process of law enforcement and tax investigation.

III

Petitioner's reliance on Boyd v. United States, 116 U.S. 616 (1886), is misplaced. In Boyd, the person asserting the privilege was in possession of the written statements in question. The Court in Boyd did hold that "any forcible and compulsory extortion of a man's own testimony or of his private papers to be used as evidence to convict him of crime," violated the Fourth and Fifth Amendments. Id., at 630. That case did not, however, address or contemplate the divergence of ownership and possession, and petitioner concedes that court decisions applying Boyd have largely been in instances where possession and ownership conjoined. . . . In Boyd, the production order was directed against the owner of the property who, by responding, would have been forced "to produce and authenticate any personal documents or effects that might incriminate him." United States v. White, 322 U.S., at 698. But we reiterate that in the instant case there was no enforced communication of any kind from any accused or potential accused.

Petitioner would, in effect, have us read Boyd to mark ownership, not possession, as the bounds of the privilege, despite the fact that possession bears the closest relationship to the personal compulsion forbidden by the Fifth Amendment. To tie the privilege against self-incrimination to a concept of ownership would be to draw a meaningless line. It would hold here that the business records which petitioner actually owned would be protected in the hands of her accountant, while business information communicated to her accountant by letter and conversations in which the accountant took notes, in addition to the accountant's own workpapers and photocopies of petitioner's records, would not be subject to a claim of privilege since title rested in the accountant. Such a holding would thus place unnecessary emphasis on the form of communication to an accountant and the accountant's own working methods, while diverting the inquiry from the basic purposes of the Fifth Amendment's protections.

Petitioner argues, nevertheless, that grave prejudice will result from a denial of her claim to equate ownership and the scope of the privilege. She alleges that "[i]f the IRS is able to reach her records the instant those records leave her hands and are deposited in the hands of her retainer whom she has hired for a special purpose then the meaning of the privilege is lost." That is not, however, the import of today's decision. We do indeed believe that actual possession of documents bears the most significant relationship to Fifth Amendment protections against governmental compulsions upon the individual accused of crime. Yet situations may well arise where constructive possession is so clear or the relinquishment of possession is so temporary and insignificant as to leave the personal compulsions upon the accused substantially intact. But this is not the case before us. Here there was no mere fleeting divestment of possession: the records had been given to this accountant regularly since 1955 and remained in his continuous possession until the summer of 1969 when the summons was issued. Moreover, the accountant himself worked neither in petitioner's office nor as her employee.[18] The length of his possession of petitioner's records and his independent status confirm the belief that petitioner's divestment of possession was of such a character as to disqualify her entirely as an object of any impermissible Fifth Amendment compulsion.

IV

Petitioner further argues that the confidential nature of the accountant-client relationship and her resulting expectation of privacy in delivering the records protect her, under the Fourth and Fifth Amendments, from their production. Although not in itself controlling, we note that no confidential accountant-client privilege exists under federal law, and no state-created privilege has been recognized in federal cases, Falsone v. United States, 205 F.2d 734 (C.A.5 1953), cert. denied, 346 U.S. 864;

---

18. As we noted, . . . his status is that of an independent contractor. He actually did "very little work for the petitioner," had many other clients, and was compensated by the job. . . .

This is a significant point. The Government noted in oral argument: "In the Internal Revenue Service practice, so long as the taxpayer has retained possession of the records and they are being used only by his full-time employees or others on the taxpayer's premises, without the taxpayer having relinquished possession and control of the records, we ordinarily in those situations issue the summons to the taxpayer, because it is the taxpayer who has the dominion over the records and the authority to return the summons. And if the taxpayer chooses to plead the privilege against self-incrimination, that is up to the taxpayer."

Gariepy v. United States, 189 F.2d 459, 463-464 (C.A.6 1951); Himmel-
farb v. United States, 175 F.2d 924, 939 (C.A.9 1949), cert. denied, 338
U.S. 860; Olender v. United States, 210 F.2d 795, 806 (C.A.9 1954). Nor
is there justification for such a privilege where records relevant to income tax returns are involved in a criminal investigation or prosecution.
In *Boyd*, a pre-income tax case, the Court spoke of protection of privacy,
116 U.S., at 630, but there can be little expectation of privacy where
records are handed to an accountant, knowing that mandatory disclosure of much of the information therein is required in an income tax
return. What information is not disclosed is largely in the accountant's
discretion, not petitioner's. Indeed, the accountant himself risks criminal
prosecution if he willfully assists in the preparation of a false return. 26
U.S.C. §7206(2). His own need for self-protection would often require
the right to disclose the information given him. Petitioner seeks exten-
sions of constitutional protections against self-incrimination in the very
situation where obligations of disclosure exist and under a system largely
dependent upon hònest self-reporting even to survive. Accordingly, petitioner here cannot reasonably claim, either for Fourth or Fifth Amendment purposes, an expectation of protected privacy or confidentiality.

V

The criterion for Fifth Amendment immunity remains not the ownership of property but the " 'physical or moral compulsion' exerted."
Perlman, 247 U.S., at 15. We hold today that no Fourth or Fifth Amendment claim can prevail where, as in this case, there exists no legitimate
expectation of privacy and no semblance of governmental compulsion
against the person of the accused. It is important, in applying constitutional principles, to interpret them in light of the fundamental interests
of personal liberty they were meant to serve. Respect for these principles
is eroded when they leap their proper bounds to interfere with the
legitimate interest of society in enforcement of its laws and collection of
the revenues. . . .

[A concurring opinion by Justice Brennan and dissenting opinions by
Justices Douglas and Marshall are omitted.]

Why is there no accountant-client privilege corresponding to the
lawyer-client privilege? Is the claim for an accountant-client privilege
significantly weaker than the claim for the lawyer-client privilege under
either Wigmore's instrumental approach or the humanistic approach to
privileges? Why did Mrs. Couch not have a "legitimate expectation of
privacy"? Does this concept have any intrinsic meaning in this context or
is it a tautology?

If, after *Couch*, a client came to you for advice on how she should handle her tax records to enhance their confidentiality, how would you advise her? In *Couch*, would the taxpayer have been in a stronger position to claim a privilege if she had kept possession of the documents herself? If she had sent the documents to her attorney in the first instance and the attorney had then hired the accountant? To what extent does the nature of the thing sought to be disclosed — e.g., thoughts, business records, personal diary, weapons — affect the scope of privilege protection? To what extent is the scope of privilege protection dependent on *why* the claimant of the privilege conveyed the records to a third person, such as an accountant or lawyer?

UNITED STATES v. SCHMIDT
343 F. Supp. 444 (M.D. Pa. 1972)

SHERIDAN, C.J. This is an action in which petitioners, the United States of America and James W. Meade, Jr., Special Agent of the Internal Revenue Service, seek judicial enforcement of an Internal Revenue summons pursuant to 26 U.S.C.A. §§7402(b) and 7604(a).

On April 1, 1971, Special Agent James W. Meade, Jr., of the Internal Revenue Service, issued an Internal Revenue summons requiring respondent, J. Donald Schmidt, a Certified Public Accountant, to appear and to testify concerning the tax liabilities of Vincent C. McCue for the taxable years 1966, 1967, 1968 and 1969, and with respect to the preparation of the joint tax return of Vincent C. McCue and Elizabeth A. McCue for the taxable year 1969. Respondent, J. Donald Schmidt, refused to answer certain questions propounded to him by Special Agent Meade; he has continued to refuse to answer, asserting both the attorney-client privilege and the privilege against self-incrimination. Petitioners moved the court for enforcement of the summons. . . .

The sole question to which the court presently addresses itself is the applicability of the attorney-client privilege. On the record before the court, the uncontroverted facts are as follows: respondent-taxpayers, Vincent C. McCue and Elizabeth A. McCue, retained respondent-attorneys, Shumaker, Williams & Placey, in August 1969; Shumaker, Williams & Placey employed J. Donald Schmidt, a Certified Public Accountant, on April 1, 1970, subsequent to the establishment of the attorney-client relationship; an agreement was entered into between said attorneys and accountant on April 1, 1970, setting forth the terms and conditions of Schmidt's employment. Pursuant to the aforementioned agreement, all accountant's services were to be performed at the written request of counsel; it was made explicit that Vincent and Elizabeth McCue were the clients of the law firm, and not of the accountant; it was stated that Schmidt's services were required to facilitate an accurate and complete legal consultation between the law firm and its taxpayer-clients in the interest of allowing counsel to furnish informed legal advice; all bookkeeping and accounting records, work papers, schedules and reports relating to the taxpayers were made the exclusive property of the law firm, even if they had been prepared by the accountant and even if they were in the accountant's possession; all billings for accounting services were to be made to the law firm; all information obtained by the accountant while performing accounting services was to be confidential, and the accountant was prohibited from disclosing same without the prior written consent of the law firm or an order of court, the only exception to the confidentiality requirement being the information which actually appeared on the tax return.

It is respondents' contention that the establishment of the foregoing is sufficient in itself to bring the subject matter of the questions propounded to Schmidt within the scope of the attorney-client privilege. . . .

What result and why? Have the taxpayers successfully circumvented *Couch*? Why should it make any difference to the existence of a privilege whether the taxpayer hires an accountant or hires an attorney who hires an accountant?

Is there any privilege that protects the taxpayer from forced disclosure of tax preparation material prepared by his accountant but turned over to his attorney *prior* to the issuance of any government subpoena?

FISHER v. UNITED STATES
425 U.S. 391 (1976)

Mr. Justice WHITE delivered the opinion of the Court.

In these two cases we are called upon to decide whether a summons directing an attorney to produce documents delivered to him by his client in connection with the attorney-client relationship is enforceable over claims that the documents were constitutionally immune from summons in the hands of the client and retained that immunity in the hands of the attorney.

I

In each case, an Internal Revenue agent visited the taxpayer or taxpayers and interviewed them in connection with an investigation of possible civil or criminal liability under the federal income tax laws. Shortly after the interviews — one day later in No. 74-611 and a week or two later in No. 74-18 — the taxpayers obtained from their respective accountants certain documents relating to the preparation by the accountants of their tax returns. Shortly after obtaining the documents — later the same day in No. 74-611 and a few weeks later in No. 74-18 — the taxpayers transferred the documents to their lawyers — respondent Kasmir and petitioner Fisher, respectively — each of whom was retained to assist the taxpayer in connection with the investigation. Upon learning of the whereabouts of the documents, the Internal Revenue Service served summonses on the attorneys directing them to produce documents listed therein. In No. 74-611, the documents were described as

> the following records of Tannebaum Bindler & Lewis [the accounting firm].
> 1. Accountant's work papers pertaining to Dr. E. J. Mason's books and records of 1969, 1970 and 1971.[2]
> 2. Retained copies of E. J. Mason's income tax returns for 1969, 1970 and 1971.
> 3. Retained copies of reports and other correspondence between Tannebaum Bindler & Lewis and Dr. E. J. Mason during 1969, 1970 and 1971.

In No. 74-18, the documents demanded were analyses by the accountant of the taxpayers' income and expenses which had been copied by the accountant from the taxpayers' canceled checks and deposit receipts.[3] In No. 74-611, a summons was also served on the accountant directing him to appear and testify concerning the documents to be produced by the lawyer. In each case, the lawyer declined to comply with the summons directing production of the documents, and enforcement actions were commenced by the Government under 26 U.S.C. §§7402(b) and 7604(a). In No. 74-611, the attorney raised in defense of the enforcement action the taxpayer's accountant-client privilege, his attorney-client privilege, and his Fourth and Fifth Amendment rights. In No. 74-18, the attorney claimed that enforcement would involve compulsory self-incrimination of the taxpayers in violation of their Fifth Amendment privilege, would involve a seizure of the papers without necessary compliance with the Fourth Amendment, and would violate the taxpayers' right to communicate in confidence with their attorney. In No. 74-18 the taxpayers intervened and made similar claims. . . .

II

All of the parties in these cases and the Court of Appeals for the Fifth Circuit have concurred in the proposition that if the Fifth Amendment would have excused a *taxpayer* from turning over the accountant's papers

---

2. The "books and records" concerned the taxpayer's large medical practice.
3. The husband taxpayer's checks and deposit receipts related to his textile waste business. The wife's related to her women's wear shop.

had he possessed them, the *attorney* to whom they are delivered for the purpose of obtaining legal advice should also be immune from subpoena. Although we agree with this proposition for the reasons set forth in Part III, infra, we are convinced that, under our decision in Couch v. United States, 409 U.S. 322 (1973), it is not the taxpayer's Fifth Amendment privilege that would excuse the *attorney* from production.

The relevant part of that Amendment provides:

> No person . . . shall be *compelled* in any criminal case to be a *witness against himself.* (Emphasis added by the Court.)

The taxpayer's privilege under this Amendment is not violated by enforcement of the summonses involved in these cases because enforcement against a taxpayer's lawyer would not "compel" the taxpayer to do anything — and certainly would not compel him to be a "witness" against himself. The Court has held repeatedly that the Fifth Amendment is limited to prohibiting the use of "physical or moral compulsion" exerted on the person asserting the privilege. In Couch v. United States, supra, we recently ruled that the Fifth Amendment rights of a taxpayer were not violated by the enforcement of a documentary summons directed to her accountant and requiring production of the taxpayer's own records in the possession of the accountant. We did so on the ground that in such a case "the ingredient of personal compulsion against an accused is lacking." 409 U.S., at 329.

Here, the taxpayers are compelled to do no more than was the taxpayer in *Couch.* The taxpayers' Fifth Amendment privilege is therefore not violated by enforcement of the summonses directed toward their attorneys. This is true whether or not the Amendment would have barred a subpoena directing the taxpayer to produce the documents while they were in his hands.

The fact that the attorneys are agents of the taxpayers does not change this result. *Couch* held as much, since the accountant there was also the taxpayer's agent, and in this respect reflected a longstanding view. In Hale v. Henkel, 201 U.S. 43, 69-70 (1906), the Court said that the privilege "was never intended to permit [a person] to plead the fact that some third person might be incriminated by his testimony, even though he were the agent of such person. . . . [T]he Amendment is limited to a person who shall be compelled in any criminal case to be a witness against *himself.*" (Emphasis in original.) "It is extortion of information from the accused himself that offends our sense of justice." Couch v. United States, supra, at 328. Agent or no, the lawyer is not the taxpayer. The taxpayer is the "accused," and nothing is being extorted from him.

Nor is this one of those situations, which *Couch* suggested might exist, where constructive possession is so clear or relinquishment of possession so temporary and insignificant as to leave the personal compulsion upon the taxpayer substantially intact. 409 U.S., at 333. In this respect we see no difference between the delivery to the attorneys in these cases and delivery to the accountant in the *Couch* case. As was true in *Couch*, the documents sought were obtainable without personal compulsion on the accused.

Respondents in No. 74-611 and petitioners in No. 74-18 argue, and the Court of Appeals for the Fifth Circuit apparently agreed that if the summons was enforced, the taxpayers' Fifth Amendment privilege would be, but should not be, lost solely because they gave their documents to their lawyers in order to obtain legal advice. But this misconceives the nature of the constitutional privilege. The Amendment protects a person from being compelled to be a witness against himself. Here, the taxpayers retained any privilege they ever had not to be compelled to testify against themselves and not to be compelled themselves to produce private papers in their possession. *This* personal privilege was in no way decreased by the transfer. It is simply that by reason of the transfer of the documents to the attorneys, those papers may be subpoenaed without compulsion on the taxpayer. The protection of the Fifth Amendment is therefore not available. "A party is privileged from producing evidence but not from its production." Johnson v. United States, supra, at 458.

The Court of Appeals for the Fifth Circuit suggested that because legally and ethically the attorney was required to respect the confidences of his client, the latter had a reasonable expectation of privacy for the records in the hands of the attorney and therefore did not forfeit his Fifth Amendment privilege with respect to the records by transferring them in order to obtain legal advice. It is true that the Court has often stated that one of the several purposes served by the constitutional privilege against compelled testimonial self-incrimination is that of protecting personal privacy. . . . But the Court has never suggested that every invasion of privacy violates the privilege. Within the limits imposed by the language of the Fifth Amendment, which we necessarily observe, the privilege truly serves privacy interests; but the Court has never on any ground, personal privacy included, applied the Fifth Amendment to prevent the otherwise proper acquisition or use of evidence which, in the Court's view, did not involve compelled testimonial self-incrimination of some sort.

The proposition that the Fifth Amendment protects private information obtained without compelling self-incriminating testimony is contrary to the clear statements of this Court that under appropriate safeguards private incriminating statements of an accused may be overheard and used in evidence, if they are not compelled at the time they were uttered, and that disclosure of private information may be compelled if immunity removes the risk of incrimination. If the Fifth

Amendment protected generally against the obtaining of private information from a man's mouth or pen or house, its protections would presumably not be lifted by probable cause and a warrant or by immunity. The privacy invasion is not mitigated by immunity; and the Fifth Amendment's strictures, unlike the Fourth's, are not removed by showing reasonableness. The Framers addressed the subject of personal privacy directly in the Fourth Amendment. They struck a balance so that when the State's reason to believe incriminating evidence will be found becomes sufficiently great, the invasion of privacy becomes justified and a warrant to search and seize will issue. They did not seek in still another Amendment — the Fifth — to achieve a general protection of privacy but to deal with the more specific issue of compelled self-incrimination.

We cannot cut the Fifth Amendment completely loose from the moorings of its language, and make it serve as a general protector of privacy — a word not mentioned in its text and a concept directly addressed in the Fourth Amendment. We adhere to the view that the Fifth Amendment protects against "compelled self-incrimination, not [the disclosure of] private information."

Insofar as private information not obtained through compelled self-incriminating testimony is legally protected, its protection stems from other sources — the Fourth Amendment's protection against seizures without warrant or probable cause and against subpoenas which suffer from "too much indefiniteness or breadth in the things required to be 'particularly described,'" the First Amendment, or evidentiary privileges such as the attorney-client privilege.[7]

III

Our above holding is that compelled production of documents from an attorney does not implicate whatever Fifth Amendment privilege the taxpayer might have enjoyed from being compelled to produce them himself. . . . In this posture of the case, we feel obliged to inquire whether the attorney-client privilege applies to documents in the hands of an attorney which would have been privileged in the hands of the client by reason of the Fifth Amendment.

Confidential disclosures by a client to an attorney made in order to obtain legal assistance are privileged. 8 J. Wigmore, Evidence §2292 (McNaughton rev. 1961) (hereinafter Wigmore); McCormick §87, p.175. The purpose of the privilege is to encourage clients to make full disclosure to their attorneys. As a practical matter, if the client knows

---

7. . . . Special problems of privacy which might be presented by subpoena of a personal diary, United States v. Bennett, 409 F.2d 888, 897 (C.A.2 1969) (Friendly, J.) are not involved here.

First Amendment values are also plainly not implicated in these cases.

that damaging information could more readily be obtained from the attorney following disclosure than from himself in the absence of disclosure, the client would be reluctant to confide in his lawyer and it would be difficult to obtain fully informed legal advice. However, since the privilege has the effect of withholding relevant information from the factfinder, it applies only where necessary to achieve its purpose. Accordingly it protects only those disclosures — necessary to obtain informed legal advice — which might not have been made absent the privilege. This court and the lower courts have thus uniformly held that pre-existing documents which could have been obtained by court process from the client when he was in possession may also be obtained from the attorney by similar process following transfer by the client in order to obtain more informed legal advice. The purpose of the privilege requires no broader rule. Pre-existing documents obtainable from the client are not appreciably easier to obtain from the attorney after transfer to him. Thus, even absent the attorney-client privilege, clients will not be discouraged from disclosing the documents to the attorney, and their ability to obtain informed legal advice will remain unfettered. It is otherwise if the documents are not obtainable by subpoena duces tecum or summons while in the exclusive possession of the client, for the client will then be reluctant to transfer possession to the lawyer unless the documents are also privileged in the latter's hands. Where the transfer is made for the purpose of obtaining legal advice, the purposes of the attorney-client privilege would be defeated unless the privilege is applicable. "It follows, then, that *when the client himself would be privileged* from production of the documents, either as party at common law . . . or as exempt from self-incrimination, the attorney having possession of the document is not bound to produce." 8 Wigmore §2307, p.592. . . . United States v. Judson, 322 F.2d 460, 466 (C.A.9 1963). This proposition was accepted by the Court of Appeals for the Fifth Circuit below, is asserted by petitioners in No. 74-18 and respondents in No. 74-611, and was conceded by the Government in its brief and at oral argument. Where the transfer to the attorney is for the purpose of obtaining legal advice, we agree with it.

Since each taxpayer transferred possession of the documents in question from himself to his attorney in order to obtain legal assistance in the tax investigations in question, the papers, if unobtainable by summons from the client, are unobtainable by summons directed to the attorney by reason of the attorney-client privilege. We accordingly proceed to the question whether the documents could have been obtained by summons addressed to the taxpayer while the documents were in his possession. The only bar to enforcement of such summons asserted by the parties or the courts below is the Fifth Amendment's privilege against self-incrimination. . . .

IV

The proposition that the Fifth Amendment prevents compelled production of documents over objection that such production might incriminate stems from Boyd v. United States, 116 U.S. 616 (1886). *Boyd* involved a civil forfeiture proceeding brought by the Government against two partners for fraudulently attempting to import 35 cases of glass without paying the prescribed duty. The partnership had contracted with the Government to furnish the glass needed in the construction of a Government building. The glass specified was foreign glass, it being understood that if part or all of the glass was furnished from the partnership's existing duty-paid inventory, it could be replaced by duty-free imports. Pursuant to this arrangement, 29 cases of glass were imported by the partnership duty free. The partners then represented that they were entitled to duty-free entry of an additional 35 cases which were soon to arrive. The forfeiture action concerned these 35 cases. The Government's position was that the partnership had replaced all of the glass used in construction of the Government building when it imported the 29 cases. At trial, the Government obtained a court order directing the partners to produce an invoice the partnership had received from the shipper covering the previous 29-case shipment. The invoice was disclosed, offered in evidence, and used, over the Fifth Amendment objection of the partners, to establish that the partners were fraudulently claiming a greater exemption from duty than they were entitled to under the contract. This Court held that the invoice was inadmissible and reversed the judgment in favor of the Government. The Court ruled that the Fourth Amendment applied to court orders in the nature of subpoenas duces tecum in the same manner in which it applies to search warrants, id., at 622; and that the Government may not, consistent with the Fourth Amendment, seize a person's documents or other property as evidence unless it can claim a proprietary interest in the property superior to that of the person from whom the property is obtained. Id., at 623-624. The invoice in question was thus held to have been obtained in violation of the Fourth Amendment. The Court went on to hold that the accused in a criminal case or the defendant in a forfeiture action could not be forced to produce evidentiary items without violating the Fifth Amendment as well as the Fourth. More specifically, the Court declared, "a compulsory production of the private books and papers of the owner of goods sought to be forfeited . . . is compelling him to be a witness against himself, within the meaning of the Fifth Amendment to the Constitution." Id., at 634-635. Admitting the partnership invoice into evidence had violated both the Fifth and Fourth Amendments.

Among its several pronouncements, *Boyd* was understood to declare that the seizure, under warrant or otherwise, of any purely evidentiary materials violated the Fourth Amendment and that the Fifth Amendment rendered these seized materials inadmissible. That rule applied to documents as well as to other evidentiary items — "[t]here is no special sanctity in papers, as distinguished from other forms of property, to render them immune from search and seizure, if only they fall within the scope of the principles of the cases in which other property may be seized. . . ." Private papers taken from the taxpayer, like other "mere evidence," could not be used against the accused over his Fourth and Fifth Amendment objections.

Several of *Boyd*'s express or implicit declarations have not stood the test of time. The application of the Fourth Amendment to subpoenas was limited by Hale v. Henkel, 201 U.S. 43 (1906), and more recent cases. See, e.g., Oklahoma Press Pub. Co. v. Walling, 327 U.S. 186 (1946). Purely evidentiary (but "nontestimonial") materials, as well as contraband and fruits and instrumentalities of crime, may now be searched for and seized under proper circumstances, Warden v. Hayden, 387 U.S. 294 (1967). Also, any notion that "testimonial" evidence may never be seized and used in evidence is inconsistent with Katz v. United States, 389 U.S. 347 (1967); Osborn v. United States, 385 U.S. 323 (1966); and Berger v. New York, 388 U.S. 41 (1967), approving the seizure under appropriate circumstances of conversations of a person suspected of crime. See also Marron v. United States, 275 U.S. 192 (1927).

It is also clear that the Fifth Amendment does not independently proscribe the compelled production of every sort of incriminating evidence but applies only when the accused is compelled to make a *testimonial* communication that is incriminating. We have, accordingly, declined to extend the protection of the privilege to the giving of blood samples, Schmerber v. California, 384 U.S. 757, 763-764 (1966)[10]; to the giving of handwriting exemplars, Gilbert v. California, 388 U.S. 263, 265-267 (1967); voice exemplars, United States v. Wade, 388 U.S. 218, 222-223 (1967); or the donning of a blouse worn by the perpetrator, Holt v. United States, 218 U.S. 245 (1910). Furthermore, despite *Boyd*, neither a partnership nor the individual partners are shielded from compelled production of partnership records on self-incrimination grounds. Bellis v. United States, 417 U.S. 85 (1974). It would appear that under that case the precise claim sustained in *Boyd* would now be rejected for reasons not there considered.

The pronouncement in *Boyd* that a person may not be forced to produce his private papers has nonetheless often appeared as dictum in later opinions of this Court. To the extent, however, that the rule against

10. The Court's holding was: "Since the blood test evidence, although an incriminating product of compulsion, was neither petitioner's testimony nor evidence relating to some communicative act or writing by petitioner, it was not inadmissible on privilege grounds." 384 U.S., at 765.

compelling production of private papers rested on the proposition that seizures of or subpoenas for "mere evidence," including documents, violated the Fourth Amendment and therefore also transgressed the Fifth, the foundations for the rule have been washed away. In consequence, the prohibition against forcing the production of private papers has long been a rule searching for a rationale consistent with the proscriptions of the Fifth Amendment against compelling a person to give "testimony" that incriminates him. Accordingly, we turn to the question of what, if any, incriminating testimony within the Fifth Amendment's protection, is compelled by a documentary summons.

A subpoena served on a taxpayer requiring him to produce an accountant's workpapers in his possession without doubt involves substantial compulsion. But it does not compel oral testimony; nor would it ordinarily compel the taxpayer to restate, repeat, or affirm the truth of the contents of the documents sought. Therefore, the Fifth Amendment would not be violated by the fact alone that the papers on their face might incriminate the taxpayer, for the privilege protects a person only against being incriminated by his own compelled testimonial communications. Schmerber v. California, supra; United States v. Wade, supra; and Gilbert v. California, supra. The accountant's workpapers are not the taxpayer's. They were not prepared by the taxpayer, and they contain no testimonial declarations by him. Furthermore, as far as this record demonstrates, the preparation of all of the papers sought in these cases was wholly voluntary, and they cannot be said to contain compelled testimonial evidence, either of the taxpayers or of anyone else.[11] The taxpayer cannot avoid compliance with the subpoena merely by asserting that the item of evidence which he is required to produce contains incriminating writing, whether his own or that of someone else.

The act of producing evidence in response to a subpoena nevertheless has communicative aspects of its own, wholly aside from the contents of the papers produced. Compliance with the subpoena tacitly concedes the existence of the papers demanded and their possession or control by the taxpayer. It also would indicate the taxpayer's belief that the papers are those described in the subpoena. Curcio v. United States, 354 U.S. 118, 125 (1957). The elements of compulsion are clearly present,

11. The fact that the documents may have been written by the person asserting the privilege is insufficient to trigger the privilege, Wilson v. United States, 221 U.S. 361, 378 (1911). And, unless the Government has compelled the subpoenaed person to write the document, cf. Marchetti v. United States, 390 U.S. 39 (1968); Grosso v. United States, 390 U.S. 62 (1968), the fact that it was written by him is not controlling with respect to the Fifth Amendment issue. Conversations may be seized and introduced in evidence under proper safeguards, Katz v. United States, 389 U.S. 347 (1967); Osborn v. United States, 385 U.S. 323 (1966); Berger v. New York, 388 U.S. 41 (1967); United States v. Bennett, 409 F.2d, at 897 n.9, if not compelled. In the case of a documentary subpoena the only thing compelled is the act of producing the document and the compelled act is the same as the one performed when a chattel or document not authored by the producer is demanded. McCormick §128, p.269.

but the more difficult issues are whether the tacit averments of the taxpayer are both "testimonial" and "incriminating" for purposes of applying the Fifth Amendment. These questions perhaps do not lend themselves to categorical answers; their resolution may instead depend on the facts and circumstances of particular cases or classes thereof. In light of the records now before us, we are confident that however incriminating the contents of the accountant's workpapers might be, the act of producing them — the only thing which the taxpayer is compelled to do — would not itself involve testimonial self-incrimination.

It is doubtful that implicitly admitting the existence and possession of the papers rises to the level of testimony within the protection of the Fifth Amendment. The papers belong to the accountant, were prepared by him, and are the kind usually prepared by an accountant working on the tax returns of his client. Surely the Government is in no way relying on the "truthtelling" of the taxpayer to prove the existence of or his access to the documents. 8 Wigmore §2264, p.380. The existence and location of the papers are a foregone conclusion and the taxpayer adds little or nothing to the sum total of the Government's information by conceding that he in fact has the papers. Under these circumstances by enforcement of the summons "no constitutional rights are touched. The question is not of testimony but of surrender." In re Harris, 221 U.S. 274, 279 (1911).

When an accused is required to submit a handwriting exemplar he admits his ability to write and impliedly asserts that the exemplar is his writing. But in common experience, the first would be a near truism and the latter self-evident. In any event, although the exemplar may be incriminating to the accused and although he is compelled to furnish it, his Fifth Amendment privilege is not violated because nothing he has said or done is deemed to be sufficiently testimonial for purposes of the privilege. This Court has also time and again allowed subpoenas against the custodian of corporate documents or those belonging to other collective entities such as unions and partnerships and those of bankrupt businesses over claims that the documents will incriminate the custodian despite the fact that producing the documents tacitly admits their existence and their location in the hands of their possessor. The existence and possession or control of the subpoenaed documents being no more in issue here than in the above cases, the summons is equally enforceable.

Moreover, assuming that these aspects of producing the accountant's papers have some minimal testimonial significance, surely it is not illegal to seek accounting help in connection with one's tax returns or for the accountant to prepare workpapers and deliver them to the taxpayer. At this juncture, we are quite unprepared to hold that either the fact of existence of the papers or of their possession by the taxpayer poses any realistic threat of incrimination to the taxpayer.

As for the possibility that responding to the subpoena would authenticate the workpapers, production would express nothing more than the taxpayer's belief that the papers are those described in the subpoena. The taxpayer would be no more competent to authenticate the accountant's workpapers or reports by producing them than he would be to authenticate them if testifying orally. The taxpayer did not prepare the papers and could not vouch for their accuracy. The documents would not be admissible in evidence against the taxpayer without authenticating testimony. Without more, responding to the subpoena in the circumstances before us would not appear to represent a substantial threat of self-incrimination. . . .

Whether the Fifth Amendment would shield the taxpayer from producing his own tax records in his possession is a question not involved here; for the papers demanded here are not his "private papers," see Boyd v. United States, 116 U.S., at 634-635. We do hold that compliance with a summons directing the taxpayer to produce the accountant's documents involved in these cases would involve no incriminating testimony within the protection of the Fifth Amendment. . . .

[Concurring opinions by Justices BRENNAN and MARSHALL are omitted.]

After *Fisher*, how would you advise a client seeking both sound tax advice and full confidentiality of his business records? Are there any arrangements that will ensure that *both* objectives are met, or must the taxpayer choose between them?

In his concurring opinion in *Fisher*, Justice Brennan states:

> The common-law and constitutional extension of the privilege to testimonial materials, such as books and papers, was inevitable. An individual's books and papers are generally little more than an extension of his person. They reveal no less than he could reveal upon being questioned directly. Many of the matters within an individual's knowledge may as easily be retained within his head as set down on a scrap of paper. I perceive no principle which does not permit compelling one to disclose the contents of one's mind but does permit compelling the disclosure of the contents of that scrap of paper by compelling its production. Under a contrary view, the constitutional protection would turn on fortuity, and persons would, at their peril, record their thoughts and the events of their lives. The ability to think private thoughts, facilitated as it is by pen and paper, and the ability to preserve intimate memories would be curtailed through fear that those thoughts or the events of those memories would become the subjects of criminal sanctions however invalidly imposed.

425 U.S. at 420.

Should all types of books and papers be regarded equally for purposes of privilege? For example, in an investigation into alleged fraud on the government in the furnishing of supplies, suppose the government seeks a search warrant for the premises of the target company. Assuming there is probable cause, can a warrant lawfully be executed to obtain each of the following items?

(1) A copy of the invoice allegedly used to double-bill the government for the supplies in question;

(2) A memorandum to the file by the company's president summarizing his view of the facts relevant to the investigation;

(3) The company president's personal diary; and

(4) A copy of a letter from the company's president to his attorney including a copy of the memorandum described above.

To the extent that any of these documents could be lawfully seized during a search of the company's premises, if the documents were delivered to the company's lawyer prior to the search, could the government obtain them by means of a subpoena directed to the attorney?

What advice can the attorney in a *Fisher* situation give his clients about retention of tax preparation documents? Can she advise them to destroy such documents? How do the accessory-after-the-fact and obstruction-of-justice statutes, the spoliation doctrine, and the ethical obligations of counsel limit the attorney's options?

BRONSTON v. UNITED STATES, 409 U.S. 352 (1973): Petitioner is the sole owner of Samuel Bronston Productions, Inc., a company that between 1958 and 1964, produced motion pictures in various European locations. For these enterprises, Bronston Productions opened bank accounts in a number of foreign countries; in 1962, for example, it had 37 accounts in five countries. As president of Bronston Productions, petitioner supervised transactions involving the foreign bank accounts.

In June 1964, Bronston Productions petitioned for an arrangement with creditors under Chapter XI of the Bankruptcy Act, 11 U.S.C. §701 et seq. On June 10, 1966, a referee in bankruptcy held a §21(a) hearing to determine, for the benefit of creditors, the extent and location of the company's assets. . . .

[A]t that bankruptcy hearing, . . . the following colloquy with a lawyer for a creditor of Bronston Productions [took place]:

Q: Do you have any bank accounts in Swiss banks, Mr. Bronston?
A: No, sir.
Q: Have you ever?
A: The company had an account there for about six months, in Zurich.
Q: Have you any nominees who have bank accounts in Swiss banks?
A: No, sir.
Q: Have you ever?
A: No, sir."

It is undisputed that for a period of nearly five years, between October 1959 and June 1964, petitioner had a personal bank account at the

International Credit Bank in Geneva, Switzerland, into which he made deposits and upon which he drew checks totaling more than $180,000. It is likewise undisputed that petitioner's answers were literally truthful. (a) Petitioner did not at the time of questioning have a Swiss bank account. (b) Bronston Productions, Inc., did have the account in Zurich described by petitioner. (c) Neither at the time of questioning nor before did petitioner have nominees who had Swiss accounts.

---

(1) If you represented Bronston in the bankruptcy proceeding and were aware of the personal Swiss bank account, what would your professional obligations be upon hearing Bronston's testimony? In advance of the hearing, how would you counsel Bronston to answer questions similar to the ones actually asked? If you counseled Bronston to answer how he did, knowing it would mislead Bronston's creditors, would you be risking violation of 18 U.S.C. §1503 (the federal obstruction of justice statute), below? If you did not counsel Bronston as to how he should answer questions to avoid disclosing what was not strictly asked for, would you risk violating your ethical and professional responsibilities as outlined in the ABA Considerations and Standards, below?

(2) What error did the creditor's lawyer make in his interrogation?

(3) Has Bronston violated 18 U.S.C. §1621, the federal perjury statute?

> Whoever, having taken an oath before a competent tribunal, officer, or person, in any case in which a law of the United States authorizes an oath to be administered, that he will testify, declare, depose, or certify truly, or that any written testimony, declaration, deposition, or certificate by him subscribes any material matter which he does not believe to be true, is guilty of perjury, and shall, except as otherwise expressly provided by law, be fined not more than $2,000 or imprisoned not more than five years, or both.

18 U.S.C. §3
Accessory After the Fact

Whoever, knowing that an offense against the United States has been committed, receives, relieves, comforts or assists the offender in order to hinder or prevent his apprehension, trial or punishment, is an accessory after the fact.

Except as otherwise expressly provided by any Act of Congress, an accessory after the fact shall be imprisoned not more than one-half the maximum term of imprisonment or fined not more than one-half the maximum fine prescribed for the punishment of the principal, or both; or if the principal is punishable by death, the accessory shall be imprisoned not more than ten years.

18 U.S.C. §1503
Obstruction of Justice

Whoever corruptly . . . influences, obstructs, or impedes, or endeavors to influence, obstruct, or impede, the due administration of justice, shall be fined not more than $5,000 or imprisoned not more than five years, or both.

AMERICAN BAR ASSOCIATION STANDARDS FOR CRIMINAL JUSTICE, THE DEFENSE FUNCTION
(2d ed. 1980)

4-1.1. The defense counsel, in protecting the rights of the defendant, may resist the wishes of the judge on some matters, and though such resistance should never lead to disrespectful behavior, defense counsel may appear unyielding and uncooperative at times. In so doing, defense counsel is not contradicting his or her duty to the administration of justice but is fulfilling a function within the adversary system. The adversary system requires defense counsel's presence and zealous professional advocacy just as it requires the presence and zealous advocacy of the prosecutor and the constant neutrality of the judge. Defense counsel should not be viewed as impeding the administration of justice simply because he or she challenges the prosecution, but as an indispensable part of its fulfillment.

The role of counsel for the accused is difficult because it is complex, involving multiple obligations. Toward the client the lawyer is a counselor and an advocate; toward the prosecutor the lawyer is a professional adversary; toward the court the lawyer is both advocate for the client and counselor to the court. The lawyer is obliged to counsel the client against any unlawful future conduct and to refuse to implement any illegal conduct. But included in defense counsel's obligations to the client is the responsibility of furthering the defendant's interest to the fullest extent that the law and the standards of professional conduct permit.

Advocacy is not for the timid, the meek, or the retiring. Our system of justice is inherently contentious, albeit bounded by the rules of professional ethics and decorum, and it demands that the lawyer be inclined toward vigorous advocacy. Nor can a lawyer be half-hearted in the application of his or her energies to a case. Once a case has been undertaken, a lawyer is obliged not to omit any essential honorable step in the defense, without regard to compensation or the nature of the appointment. . . .

The "alter ego" concept of a defense lawyer, which regards the lawyer as a "mouthpiece" for the client, is fundamentally wrong, unethical, and destructive of the lawyer's image; more important to the accused, perhaps, this pernicious idea is destructive of the lawyer's usefulness. The lawyer's value to each client stems in large part from the lawyer's independent stance, as a professional representative rather than as an ordinary agent. What the lawyer can accomplish for any one client depends heavily on his or her reputation for professional integrity. Court and opposing counsel will treat the lawyer with the respect that facilitates furthering the client's interests only if the lawyer maintains proper professional detachment and conduct in accord with accepted professional standards.

It is fundamental that in relations with the court, defense counsel must be scrupulously candid and truthful in representations of any matter before the court. This is not only a basic ethical requirement, but it is essential if the lawyer is to be effective in the role of advocate, for if the lawyer's reputation for veracity is suspect, he or she will lack the confidence of the court when it is needed most to serve the client. . . .

[The 1974 Approved Draft of this standard contained the following specific advice to defense lawyers concerning confidential communications.

> He can [bring to bear on the problems of defense the skill, experience, and judgment he possesses] only if he knows all that his client knows concerning the facts. The client is not competent to evaluate the relevance or significance of facts; hence the lawyer must insist on complete and candid disclosure. Secondly, he must be able to conduct the case free from interference. These two factors explain the rule of leading criminal defense lawyers that they have complete disclosure of all facts and entire control of the technical and legal aspects of the litigation.]

LAWYER-CLIENT RELATIONSHIP

4-3.1. Establishment of relationship.

(a) Defense counsel should seek to establish a relationship of trust and confidence with the accused. The lawyer should explain the necessity of full disclosure of all facts known to the client for an effective defense, and the lawyer should explain the obligation of confidentiality which makes privileged the accused's disclosures relating to the case. . . .

4-3.2. Interviewing the client.

(a) As soon as practicable the lawyer should seek to determine all relevant facts known to the accused. In so doing, the lawyer should probe for all legally relevant information without seeking to influence the direction of the client's responses.

(b) It is unprofessional conduct for the lawyer to instruct the client or to intimate to him in any way that the client should not be candid in revealing facts so as to afford the lawyer free rein to take action which would be precluded by the lawyer's knowing of such facts.

4-3.7. Advice and service on anticipated unlawful conduct.

(a) It is a lawyer's duty to advise a client to comply with the law but the lawyer may advise concerning the meaning, scope and validity of a law.

(b) It is unprofessional conduct for a lawyer to counsel a client in or knowingly assist a client to engage in conduct which the lawyer knows to be illegal or fraudulent.

(c) It is unprofessional conduct for a lawyer to agree in advance of the commission of a crime that the lawyer will serve as counsel for the defendant, except as part of a bona fide effort to determine the validity, scope, meaning or application of the law, or where the defense is incident to a general retainer for legal services to a person or enterprise engaged in legitimate activity.

(d) A lawyer may reveal the expressed intention of a client to commit a crime and the information necessary to prevent the crime; and the lawyer must do so if the contemplated crime is one which would seriously endanger the life or safety of any person or corrupt the processes of the courts and the lawyer believes such action on his or her part is necessary to prevent it.

AMERICAN BAR ASSOCIATION MODEL CODE OF PROFESSIONAL RESPONSIBILITY, ETHICAL CONSIDERATION EC4-1
(1980)

Both the fiduciary relationship existing between lawyer and client and the proper functioning of the legal system require the preservation by the lawyer of confidences and secrets of one who has employed or sought to employ him. A client must feel free to discuss whatever he wishes with his lawyer and a lawyer must be equally free to obtain information beyond that volunteered by his client. A lawyer should be fully informed of all the facts of the matter he is handling in order for his client to obtain the full advantage of our legal system. It is for the lawyer in the exercise of his independent professional judgment to separate the relevant and important from the irrelevant and unimportant. The observance of the ethical obligation of a lawyer to hold inviolate the confidences and secrets of his client not only facilitates the full development of facts essential to proper representation of the client but also encourages laymen to seek early legal assistance.

Problem VI-9
The Smoking Gun

Hombre, a regular client, walks into your office with a .32 magnum Special, the barrel still smoking, and says, "I have just shot *V* and here is the gun." What parts of this transaction are privileged? What advice should you give Hombre about the gun? What are your professional responsibilities?

If Hombre tells you where he has hidden his gun, is that information privileged? If he tells you where he has hidden V's corpse, is that information privileged? What, if anything, should you do with either piece of information? Do the application of the privilege and the lawyer's professional or personal responsibilities vary depending on whether the client discloses to the lawyer evidence, instrumentalities or fruits of the crime or information concerning them?

CLARK v. STATE
159 Tex. Cr. R. 187, 261 S.W.2d 339, cert. denied, 346 U.S. 855 (1953)

MORRISON, J. The offense is murder; the punishment, death.

The deceased secured a divorce from appellant on March 25, 1952. That night she was killed, as she lay at home in her bed, as the result of a gunshot wound. From the mattress on her bed, as well as from the bed of her daughter, were recovered bullets which were shown by a firearms expert to have been fired by a .38 special revolver having Colt characteristics. Appellant was shown to have purchased a Colt .38 Detective Special some ten months prior to the homicide.

The State relied in main upon three witnesses to establish its case. . . .

Marjorie Bartz, a telephone operator in the City of San Angelo, testified that at 2:49 in the morning of March 26, 1952, while on duty, she received a call from the Golden Spur Hotel; that at first she thought the person placing the call was a Mr. Cox and so made out the slip; but that she then recognized appellant's voice, scratched out the word "Cox" and wrote "Clark." She stated that appellant told her he wanted to speak to his lawyer, Jimmy Martin in Dallas, and that she placed the call to him at telephone number Victor 1942 in that city and made a record thereof, which record was admitted in evidence. Miss Bartz testified that, contrary to company rules, she listened to the entire conversation that ensued, and that it went as follows:

The appellant: Hello, Jimmy I went to the extremes.
The voice in Dallas: What did you do?
The appellant: I just went to the extremes.
The voice in Dallas: You got to tell me what you did before I can help.
The appellant: Well, I killed her.
The voice in Dallas: Who did you kill; the driver?
The appellant: No, I killed her.
The voice in Dallas: Did you get rid of the weapon?
The appellant: No, I still got the weapon.

The voice in Dallas: Get rid of the weapon and sit tight and don't talk to
anyone, and I will fly down in the morning.

It was stipulated that the Dallas telephone number of appellant's
attorney was Victor 1942. . . .

We now discuss the question of the privileged nature of the conversation. Wigmore on Evidence (Third Edition), Section 2326, reads as follows:

> The law provides subjective freedom for the client by assuring him of
> exemption from its processes of disclosure against himself or the attorney or
> their agents of communication. This much, but not a whit more, is necessary
> for the maintenance of the privilege. Since the means of preserving secrecy of
> communication are entirely in the client's hands, and since the privilege is a
> derogation from the general testimonial duty and should be strictly con-
> strued, it would be improper to extend its prohibition to third persons who
> obtain knowledge of the communications.

The precise question here presented does not appear to have been
passed upon in this or other jurisdictions.

In Hoy v. Morris, 13 Gray 519, 79 Mass. 519, a conversation between
a client and his attorney was overheard by Aldrich, who was in the
adjoining room. The Court therein said:

"Aldrich was not an attorney, not in any way connected with Mr.
Todd; and certainly in no situation where he was either necessary or
useful to the parties to enable them to understand each other. On the
contrary, he was a mere bystander, and casually overheard conversation
not addressed to him nor intended for his ear, but which the client and
attorney meant to have respected as private and confidential. Mr. Todd
could not lawfully have revealed it. But, in consequence of a want of
proper precaution, the communications between him and his client were
overheard by a mere stranger. As the latter stood in no relation of
confidence to either of the parties, he was clearly not within the rule of
exemption from giving testimony; and he might therefore, when summoned as a witness, be compelled to testify as to what he overheard, so
far as it was pertinent to the subject matter of inquiry upon the trial. . . ."

In Walker v. State, 19 Tex. App. 176, we find the following:

"Mrs. Bridges was not incompetent or disqualified because she was
present and heard the confessions made by defendant, even assuming
that the relation of attorney and client subsisted in fact between him and
Culberson."

The above holding is in conformity with our statute, Article 713,
Code Cr. Proc.:

> All other persons, except those enumerated in articles 708 and 714, what-
> ever may be the relationship between the defendant and witness, are compe-

tent to testify, except that an attorney at law shall not disclose a communication made to him by his client during the existence of that relationship, nor disclose any other fact which came to the knowledge of such attorney by reason of such relationship.

Attention is also called to Russel v. State, 38 Tex. Cr. R. 590, 44 S.W. 159.

Appellant relies upon Gross v. State, 61 Tex. Cr. R. 176, 135 S.W. 373, 376, 33 L.R.A., N.S., 477, wherein we held that a letter written by the accused to his wife remained privileged even though it had fallen into the hands of a third party. We think that such opinion is not authority herein, because therein we said:

"There is a broad distinction between the introduction of conversations overheard by third parties occurring between husband and wife and the introduction of letters written by one to the other, as shown by practically, if not all, the authorities. It is unnecessary to take up or discuss the question as to conversations going on between husband and wife which are overheard by other parties. That question is not in the case, and it is unnecessary to discuss it. We hold that the introduction of the contents of the letter through the witness Mrs. Maud Coleman was inadmissible. It was a privileged communication under the statute, and therefore interdicted. Article 774, Code of Criminal Procedure."

And, further on in the opinion, we find the following:

"Not minimizing the same relation of client and attorney, but we do say that the relation between husband and wife is far more sacred, and to be the more strongly guarded, than that of relation between attorney and client."

We hold that the trial court properly admitted the evidence of the telephone operator. . . .

ON APPELLANT'S MOTION FOR REHEARING

WOODLEY, J. We are favored with masterful briefs and arguments in support of appellant's motion for rehearing, including amicus curiae brief by an eminent and able Texas lawyer addressed to the question of privileged communications between attorney and client. . . .

As to the testimony of the telephone operator regarding the conversation between appellant and Mr. Martin, the conversation is set forth in full in our original opinion. Our holding as to the admissibility of the testimony of the operator is not to be considered as authority except in comparable fact situations.

For the purpose of this opinion we assume that the Dallas voice was that of Mr. Martin, appellant's attorney. If it was not appellant's attorney the conversation was not privileged.

It is in the interest of public justice that the client be able to make a full disclosure to his attorney of all facts that are material to his defense or that go to substantiate his claim. The purpose of the privilege is to encourage such disclosure of the facts. But the interests of public justice further require that no shield such as the protection afforded to communications between attorney and client shall be interposed to protect a person who takes counsel on how he can safely commit a crime.

We think this latter rule must extend to one who, having committed a crime, seeks or takes counsel as to how he shall escape arrest and punishment, such as advice regarding the destruction or disposition of the murder weapon or of the body following a murder.

One who knowing that an offense has been committed conceals the offender or aids him to evade arrest or trial becomes an accessory. The fact that the aider may be a member of the bar and the attorney for the offender will not prevent his becoming an accessory.

Art. 77, P.C. defining an accessory contains the exception "One who aids an offender in making or preparing his defense at law" is not an accessory.

The conversation as testified to by the telephone operator is not within the exception found in Art. 77, P.C. When the Dallas voice advised appellant to "get rid of the weapon" (which advice the evidence shows was followed) such aid cannot be said to constitute aid "in making or preparing his defense at law." It was aid to the perpetrator of the crime "in order that he may evade an arrest or trial."

Is such a conversation privileged as a communication between attorney and client?

If the adviser had been called to testify as to the conversation, would it not have been more appropriate for him to claim his privilege against self-incrimination rather than that the communication was privileged because it was between attorney and client?

Appellant, when he conversed with Mr. Martin, was not under arrest nor was he charged with a crime. He had just inflicted mortal wounds on his former wife and apparently had shot her daughter. Mr. Martin had acted as his attorney in the divorce suit which had been tried that day and had secured a satisfactory property settlement. Appellant called him and told him that he had gone to extremes and had killed "her," not "the driver." Mr. Martin appeared to understand these references and told appellant to get rid of "the weapon."

We are unwilling to subscribe to the theory that such counsel and advice should be privileged because of the attorney-client relationship which existed between the parties in the divorce suit. We think, on the other hand, that the conversation was admissible as not within the realm of legitimate professional counsel and employment.

The rule of public policy which calls for the privileged character of the communication between attorney and client, we think, demands that the rule be confined to the legitimate course of professional employment. It cannot consistent with the high purpose and policy supporting the rule be here applied.

The murder weapon was not found. The evidence indicates that appellant disposed of it as advised in the telephone conversation. Such advice or counsel was not such as merits protection because given by an attorney. It was not in the legitimate course of professional employment in making or preparing a defense at law.

Nothing is found in the record to indicate that appellant sought any advice from Mr. Martin other than that given in the conversation testified to by the telephone operator. We are not therefore dealing with a situation where the accused sought legitimate advice from his attorney in preparing his legal defense. . . .

Appellant's motion for rehearing is overruled.

STATE v. OLWELL
64 Wash. 2d 828, 394 P.2d 681 (1964)

DONWORTH, J. May an attorney refuse to produce, at a coroner's inquest, material evidence of a crime by asserting the attorney-client privilege or by claiming the privilege against self-incrimination on behalf of his client? These are the issues raised in this appeal.

September 18, 1962, a coroner's inquest was held for the purpose of investigating the circumstances surrounding the death of John W. Warren. Several days prior to the date of the inquest, appellant was served with a subpoena duces tecum, which said, in part:

> [B]ring with you all knives in your possession and under your control relating to Henry LeRoy Gray, Gloria Pugh or John W. Warren.

Thereafter, at the coroner's inquest the following exchange took place between a deputy prosecutor and appellant:

Q: Now, Mr. Olwell, did you comply with that? [Subpoena]
A: I do not have any knives in my possession that belong to Gloria Pugh, or to John W. Warren, and I did not comply with it as to the question of whether or not I have a knife belonging to Henry LeRoy Gray.
Q: Now, I would ask you, do you have a knife in your possession or under your control relating to or belonging to Henry LeRoy Gray?
A: I decline to answer that because of the confidential relationship of attorney and client; and to answer the question would be a violation of my oath as an attorney. . . .
Q: And for the record, Mr. Olwell, in the event you do have in your possession a knife or knives that would be called for under the

subpoena duces tecum, I take it your answer would be that you received these at the time you were acting as the attorney for Mr. Gray, is that correct?

A: That is correct.

Further, on examination by the coroner, the following occurred:

Mr. Sowers: . . . As the Coroner of King County I order you to do so [answer] under the provisions of the law set forth in the legislature under RCW 36.24.050.

Mr. Olwell: I decline to surrender any of my client's possessions, if any, because of the confidential relationship of attorney and client because under the law I cannot give evidence which under the law cannot be compelled from my client himself.

The events preceding the issuance of the subpoena and the coroner's inquest (as shown by the record as supplemented by some undisputed statements in the parties' briefs) are substantially as follows: Henry LeRoy Gray and John W. Warren engaged in a fight on September 7, 1962, which resulted in Warren's being mortally injured by knife wounds. On or about September 8, 1962, Gray was taken into custody by the Seattle Police Department and placed in jail. During his incarceration, Gray admitted the stabbing of Warren and was willing to cooperate and to aid in the investigation of the homicide. According to a detective of the police department, Gray was not sure what became of the knife he had used in the fight with Warren.

September 10, 1962, David H. Olwell, appellant, was retained as attorney for Gray, who was still confined in jail. Mr. Olwell conferred with his client and then, between the time of that conference and the issuance of the subpoena duces tecum, he came into possession of certain evidence (a knife). It is not clear whether appellant came into possession of this knife through his own investigation while acting as attorney for Gray or whether possession of it was obtained as the result of some communication made by Gray to Olwell during the existence of their attorney and client relationship. This factor is important in determining whether the evidence could be considered as a privileged communication (which is discussed below.)

Therefore, at the time of the inquest, appellant was in possession of a knife that, at that time, was considered as a possible murder weapon.[1] Thereafter, the coroner issued the subpoena duces tecum previously quoted.

---

1. It is stated in respondent's brief that, on April 25, 1963, Henry LeRoy Gray was tried and convicted of murder and is now serving a life sentence for the crime. Furthermore, a knife other than the one involved in this proceeding was subsequently discovered to be the weapon used by Gray in the fight.

Appellant appeared at the coroner's inquest and the exchange between appellant, the deputy prosecutor, and the coroner took place as described above. At that time, appellant refused to comply with the subpoena duces tecum and raised the issues presented in this appeal. Thereafter, appellant was cited to appear in the Superior Court of King County, where he was found to be in contempt because of his actions at the coroner's inquest on September 18, 1962. Appellant was given 10 days within which to purge himself of contempt, and, upon his failure to do so, an order was entered adjudging him to be in contempt and directing that he serve two days in the county jail. From that order finding him in contempt, Mr. Olwell appeals.

The attorney-client privilege is codified in RCW 5.60.060, which provides, in part:

> The following persons shall not be examined as witnesses: . . .
>
> (2) An attorney or counselor shall not, without the consent of his client, be examined as to any communication made by the client to him, or his advice given thereon in the course of professional employment.

To be protected as a privileged communication, information or objects acquired by an attorney must have been communicated or delivered to him by the client, and not merely obtained by the attorney while acting in that capacity for the client. This means that the securing of the knife in this case must have been the direct result of information given to Mr. Olwell by his client at the time they conferred in order to come within the attorney-client privilege. Although there is no evidence relating thereto, we think it reasonable to infer from the record that appellant did, in fact, obtain the evidence as the result of information received from his client during their conference. Therefore, for the purposes of this opinion and the questions to be answered, we assume that the evidence in appellant's possession was obtained through a confidential communication from his client. If the knife were obtained from a third person with whom there was no attorney-client relationship, the communication would not be privileged, and the third person could be questioned concerning the transaction.[3]

Further, communications concerning an alleged crime or fraud, which are made by a client to the attorney after the crime or the fraudulent transaction has been completed, are within the attorney-client privilege, as long as the relationship of attorney and client has been established. Therefore, we find nothing significant in the fact that the communication was made after and concerned the events of a homicide.

---

3. The state suggests that the knife was obtained from Gray's ex-wife, but it failed to offer any proof of this alleged fact to show that a privileged communication did not, in fact, exist.

In the present case we do not have a situation that readily lends itself to the application of one of the general rules applicable to the attorney-client privilege. Here, we enter a balancing process which requires us to weigh that privilege (which is based on statute and common law), and, as discussed later herein, the privilege against self-incrimination (which is constitutional), against the public's interest in the criminal investigation process. Generally speaking, the public interest at times must yield to protect the individual. State v. Kociolek, 23 N.J. 400, 129 A.2d 417, 425 (1956). Also, we must not lose sight of the policy behind the attorney-client privilege, which is to afford the client freedom from fear of compulsory disclosure after consulting his legal adviser.

We must remember, also, that the attorney-client privilege is not absolute, for it can be waived by the client.

On the basis of the attorney-client privilege, the subpoena duces tecum issued by the coroner is defective on its face because it requires the attorney to give testimony concerning information received by him from his client in the course of their conferences. The subpoena names the client and requires his attorney to produce, in an open hearing, physical evidence allegedly received from his client. This is tantamount to requiring the attorney to testify against the client without the latter's consent. RCW 36.24.080 makes testifying in a coroner's inquest similar to testifying in a superior court, and, therefore, the attorney-client privilege should be equally applicable to witnesses at a coroner's inquest. We, therefore, hold that appellant's refusal to testify at the inquest for the first reason stated by him was not contemptuous.

We do not, however, by so holding, mean to imply that evidence can be permanently withheld by the attorney under the claim of the attorney-client privilege. Here, we must consider the balancing process between the attorney-client privilege and the public interest in criminal investigation. We are in agreement that the attorney-client privilege is applicable to the knife held by appellant, but do not agree that the privilege warrants the attorney, as an officer of the court, from withholding it after being properly requested to produce the same. The attorney should not be a depository for criminal evidence (such as a knife, other weapons, stolen property, etc.), which in itself has little, if any, material value for the purposes of aiding counsel in the preparation of the defense of his client's case. Such evidence given the attorney during legal consultation for information purposes and used by the attorney in preparing the defense of his client's case, whether or not the case ever goes to trial, could clearly be withheld for a reasonable period of time. It follows that the attorney, after a reasonable period, should, as an officer of the court, on his own motion turn the same over to the prosecution.

We think the attorney-client privilege should and can be preserved even though the attorney surrenders the evidence he has in his possession. The prosecution, upon receipt of such evidence from an attorney, where charge against the attorney's client is contemplated (presently or in the future), should be well aware of the existence of the attorney-client privilege. Therefore, the state, when attempting to introduce such evidence at the trial, should take extreme precautions to make certain that the source of the evidence is not disclosed in the presence of the jury and prejudicial error is not committed. By thus allowing the prosecution to recover such evidence, the public interest is served, and by refusing the prosecution an opportunity to disclose the source of the evidence, the client's privilege is preserved and a balance is reached between these conflicting interests. The burden of introducing such evidence at a trial would continue to be upon the prosecution.

The other question raised by appellant is the claim that he could assert the privilege against self-incrimination on behalf of his client, and therefore could also refuse to answer the subpoena duces tecum for that reason. This is the result reached in United States v. Judson, 322 F.2d 460 (C.A. 9th), relied upon by appellant. The holding in that case was that, if the client could raise the privilege himself, his attorney could claim it for him. The court placed emphasis on the fact that the evidence there was for the defense of an income-tax investigation and that an attorney must rely heavily on evidence obtained from his client.

A search of the authorities reveals to us that the question does not have a standard answer. Traditionally, the privilege is said to be personal and must be claimed by the witness or party. In 8 Wigmore, Evidence (McNaughton rev. 1961) §2270, p.416, the following is observed:

> May the witness — party or non-party — make the claim through his *counsel*? The rule is that the privilege must be claimed personally; however, the courts, especially when the witness is a party or when the situation otherwise demands, frequently permit counsel for the witness to call the witness' attention to the privilege or to plead it in his behalf.

Later, in 8 Wigmore, Evidence (McNaughton rev. 1961) §2307, p.592, the following is stated:

> It follows, then, that *when the client himself would be privileged* from production of the document, either as a party at common law or as a third person claiming title or as exempt from self-incrimination, the attorney having possession of the document is not bound to produce. Such has invariably been the ruling. On the other hand, if the *client would be compellable* to produce, either by motion or by subpoena or by bill of discovery, then the attorney is equally compellable, if the document is in his custody, to produce under the appropriate procedure.

This quotation is cited in United States v. Judson, supra, p.467, and relied upon in reaching the result that the privilege can be asserted by the attorney as applied to cancelled checks and bank statements which did not come within the attorney-client privilege.

We find numerous cases which support the position that the privilege against self-incrimination is personal and cannot be asserted by counsel.

One might conclude that a personal privilege of the client could be asserted by his attorney. This does not take into consideration the different principles on which the two privileges are based: (1) The attorney-client privilege is to insure free consultation by the client with the attorney, and (2) the privilege against self-incrimination is to keep the individual free from intimidation. The client, in his relations with the attorney, is protected from compulsory disclosure by his attorney as to communications which come within the attorney-client privilege. The evidence in the present case would be protected for a reasonable period of time if it is of value to counsel in the preparation of the defense of the client's case. There is no reason to extend the privilege against self-incrimination to the attorney because the client is already protected in his relations with his attorney by the attorney-client privilege.

As was previously stated, the attorney should not be a depository for the suppression of such criminal evidence. If the attorney is given such evidence by his client, he should not be able to assert the privilege against self-incrimination which is personal to the client and must be claimed by the client alone. The attorney can aid in its preservation by informing the client of his right to claim the privilege against self-incrimination.

Because the subpoena duces tecum in this case is invalid, since it required the attorney to testify without the client's consent regarding matters arising out of the attorney-client relationship, the order of the trial court finding appellant to be in contempt and punishing him therefor is hereby reversed with directions to dismiss this proceeding.

IN RE RYDER

263 F. Supp. 360 (E.D.Va.), aff'd, 381 F.2d 713 (4th Cir. 1967)

PER CURIAM. This proceeding was instituted to determine whether Richard R. Ryder should be removed from the roll of attorneys qualified to practice before this court. Ryder was admitted to this bar in 1953. He formerly served five years as an Assistant United States Attorney. He has an active trial practice, including both civil and criminal cases.

In proceedings of this kind the charges must be sustained by clear and convincing proof, the misconduct must be fraudulent, intentional, and the result of improper motives. We conclude that these strict requirements have been satisfied. Ryder took possession of stolen money and a sawed-off shotgun, knowing that the money had been stolen and that the gun had been used in an armed robbery. He intended to retain this property pending his client's trial unless the government discovered it. He intended by his possession to destroy the chain of evidence that linked the contraband to his client and to prevent its use to establish his client's guilt.

On August 24, 1966 a man armed with a sawed-off shotgun robbed the Varina Branch of the Bank of Virginia of $7,583. Included in the currency taken were $10 bills known as "bait money," the serial numbers of which had been recorded.

On August 26, 1966 Charles Richard Cook rented safety deposit box 14 at a branch of the Richmond National Bank. Later in the day Cook was interviewed at his home by agents of the Federal Bureau of Investigation, who obtained $348 from him. Cook telephoned Ryder, who had represented him in civil litigation. Ryder came to the house and advised the agents that he represented Cook. He said that if Cook were not to be placed under arrest, he intended to take him to his office for an interview. The agents left. Cook insisted to Ryder that he had not robbed the bank. He told Ryder that he had won the money, which the agents had taken from him, in a crap game. At this time Ryder believed Cook.

Later that afternoon Ryder telephoned one of the agents and asked whether any of the bills obtained from Cook had been identified as a part of the money taken in the bank robbery. The agent told him that some bills had been identified. Ryder made inquiries about the number of bills taken and their denominations. The agent declined to give him specific information but indicated that several of the bills were recorded as bait money.

The next morning, Saturday, August 27, 1966, Ryder conferred with Cook again. He urged Cook to tell the truth, and Cook answered that a man, whose name he would not divulge, offered him $500 on the day of the robbery to put a package in a bank lockbox. Ryder did not believe this story. Ryder told Cook that if the government could trace the money in the box to him, it would be almost conclusive evidence of his guilt. He knew that Cook was under surveillance and he suspected that Cook might try to dispose of the money.

That afternoon Ryder telephoned a former officer of the Richmond Bar Association to discuss his course of action. He had known this attorney for many years and respected his judgment. The lawyer was at home and had no library available to him when Ryder telephoned. In their casual conversation Ryder told what he knew about the case, omitting names. He explained that he thought he would take the money from Cook's safety deposit box and place it in a box in his own name. This, he believed, would prevent Cook from attempting to dispose of the money. The lawyers thought that eventually F.B.I. agents would locate the money and that since it was in Ryder's possession, he could claim a privilege and thus effectively exclude it from evidence. This would prevent the government from linking Ryder's client with the bait money and would also destroy any presumption of guilt that might exist arising out of the client's exclusive possession of the evidence.

Ryder testified:

> I had sense enough to know, one, at that time that apparently the F.B.I. did have the serial numbers on the bills. I had sense enough to know, from many, many years of experience in this court and in working with the F.B.I. and, in fact, in directing the F.B.I. on some occasions, to know that eventually the bank — that the F.B.I. would find that money if I left that money in the bank. There was no doubt in my mind that eventually they would find it. The only thing I could think of to do was to get the money out of Mr. Cook's possession. . . . [T]he idea was that I assumed that if anybody tried to go into a safety deposit box in my name, the bank officials would notify me and that I would get an opportunity to come in this court and argue a question of whether or not they could use that money as evidence.

The lawyers discussed and rejected alternatives, including having a third party get the money. At the conclusion of the conversation Ryder was advised, "Don't do it surreptitiously and to be sure that you let your client know that it is going back to the rightful owners."

On Monday morning Ryder asked Cook to come by his office. He prepared a power of attorney, which Cook signed:

> KNOW YOU ALL MEN BY THESE PRESENTS, that I, CHARLES RICHARD COOK do hereby make, constitute and appoint, R. R. RYDER as my attorney at Law and in fact and do authorize my said Attorney to enter a safety deposit box rented by me at the Richmond National Bank and Trust Company, 2604 Hull Street, Richmond, Virginia, said box requiring Mosler Key Number 30 to open the same and I further authorize the said Attorney to remove the contents of the said box and so dispose of the said contents as he sees fit and I direct the officials of the said bank to cooperate with my said attorney towards the accomplishment of this my stated purpose.

Ryder did not follow the advice he had received on Saturday. He did not let his client know the money was going back to the rightful owners. He testified about his omission:

> I prepared it myself and told Mr. Cook to sign it. In the power of attorney, I did not specifically say that Mr. Cook authorized me to deliver that money to the appropriate authorities at any time because for a number of reasons. One, in representing a man under these circumstances, you've got to keep the man's confidence, but I also put in that power of attorney that Mr. Cook authorized me to dispose of that money as I saw fit, and the reason for that being that I was going to turn the money over to the proper authorities at whatever time I deemed that it wouldn't hurt Mr. Cook.

Ryder took the power of attorney which Cook had signed to the Richmond National Bank. He rented box 13 in his name with his office address, presented the power of attorney, entered Cook's box, took both boxes into a booth, where he found a bag of money and a sawed-off shotgun in Cook's box. The box also contained miscellaneous items which are not pertinent to this proceeding. He transferred the contents of Cook's box to his own and returned the boxes to the vault. He left the bank, and neither he nor Cook returned.

Ryder testified that he had some slight hesitation about the propriety of what he was doing. Within a half-hour after he left the bank, he talked to a retired judge and distinguished professor of law. He told this person that he wanted to discuss something in confidence. Ryder then stated that he represented a man suspected of bank robbery. The judge recalled the main part of the conversation:

> . . . And that he had received from this client, under a power of attorney, a sum [of] money which he, Mr. Ryder, suspected was proceeds of the robbery, although he didn't know it, but he had a suspicion that it was; that he had placed this money in a safety deposit vault at a bank; that he had received it with the intention of returning it to the rightful owner after the case against his client had been finally disposed of one way or the other; that he considered that he had received it under the privilege of attorney and client and that he wanted responsible people in the community to know of that fact and that he was telling me in confidence of that as one of these people that he wanted to know of it.
>
> Q: Did he say anything to you about a sawed-off shotgun?
> A: I don't recall. If Mr. Ryder says he did, I would not deny it, but I do not recall it, because the — my main attention in what he was saying was certainly drawn to the fact that the money was involved, but I just cannot answer the question emphatically, but if Mr. Ryder says he told me, why, I certainly wouldn't deny it.

Ryder testified that he told about the shotgun. The judge also testified that Ryder certainly would not have been under the impression that he — the judge — thought that he was guilty of unethical conduct.

The same day Ryder also talked with other prominent persons in Richmond — a judge of a court of record and an attorney for the Commonwealth. Again, he stated that what he intended to say was confidential. He related the circumstances and was advised that a lawyer could not receive the property and if he had received it he could not retain possession of it.

On September 7, 1966 Cook was indicted for robbing the Varina Branch of the Bank of Virginia. A bench warrant was issued and the next day Ryder represented Cook at a bond hearing. Cook was identified as the robber by employees of the bank. He was released on bond. Cook was arraigned on a plea of not guilty on September 9, 1966.

On September 12, 1966 F.B.I. agents procured search warrants for Cook's and Ryder's safety deposit boxes in the Richmond National Bank. They found Cook's box empty. In Ryder's box they discovered $5,920 of the $7,583 taken in the bank robbery and the sawed-off shotgun used in the robbery.

On September 23, 1966 Ryder filed a motion to suppress the money obtained from Cook by the agents on August 26, 1966. The motion did not involve items taken from Ryder's safety deposit box. The motion came on to be heard October 6, 1966. Ryder called Cook as a witness for examination on matters limited to the motion to suppress. The court called to Ryder's attention papers pertaining to the search of the safety deposit boxes. Ryder moved for a continuance, stating that he intended to file a motion with respect to the seizure of the contents of the lockbox.

On October 14, 1966 the three judges of this court removed Ryder as an attorney for Cook; suspended him from practice before the court until further order; referred the matter to the United States Attorney, who was requested to file charges within five days; set the matter for hearing November 11, 1966; and granted Ryder leave to move for vacation or modification of its order pending hearing.

The United States Attorney charged Ryder with violations of Canons 15 and 32 of the Canons of Professional Ethics of the Virginia State Bar. Ryder did not move for vacation or modification of the order, and the case was heard as scheduled by the court en banc. After the transcript was prepared and the case briefed, the court heard the argument of counsel on December 27, 1966.

At the outset, we reject the suggestion that Ryder did not know the money which he transferred from Cook's box to his was stolen. We find that on August 29 when Ryder opened Cook's box and saw a bag of money and a sawed-off shotgun, he then knew Cook was involved in the bank robbery and that the money was stolen. The evidence clearly establishes this. Ryder knew that the man who had robbed the bank used a sawed-off shotgun. He disbelieved Cook's story about the source of the money in the lockbox. He knew that some of the bills in Cook's possession were bait money.

Judge Learned Hand observed in United States v. Werner, 160 F.2d 438, 441 (2d Cir. 1947):

"The defendants ask us to distinguish between 'knowing' that goods are stolen and merely being put upon an inquiry which would have led to discovery; but they have misconceived the distinction which the decisions have made. The receivers of stolen goods almost never 'know' that they have been stolen, in the sense that they could testify to it in a court room."

Judge Hand then went on to say (160 F.2d 442): "But that the jury must find that the receiver did more than infer the theft from the circumstances has never been demanded, so far as we know; and to demand more would emasculate the statute. . . ."

In Melson v. United States, 207 F.2d 558, 559 (4th Cir. 1953), the court said: "It is well settled that knowledge that goods have been stolen may be inferred from circumstances that would convince a man of ordinary intelligence that this is the fact."

We also find that Ryder was not motivated solely by certain expectation the government would discover the contents of his lockbox. He believed discovery was probable. In this event he intended to argue to the court that the contents of his box could not be revealed, and even if the contents were identified, his possession made the stolen money and the shotgun inadmissible against his client. He also recognized that discovery was not inevitable. His intention in this event, we find, was to assist Cook by keeping the stolen money and the shotgun concealed in his lockbox until after the trial. His conversations, and the secrecy he enjoined, immediately after he put the money and the gun in his box, show that he realized the government might not find the property.

We accept his statement that he intended eventually to return the money to its rightful owner, but we pause to say that no attorney should ever place himself in such a position. Matters involving the possible termination of an attorney-client relationship, or possible subsequent proceedings in the event of an acquittal, are too delicate to permit such a practice.

We reject the argument that Ryder's conduct was no more than the exercise of the attorney-client privilege. The fact that Cook had not been arrested or indicted at the time Ryder took possession of the gun and money is immaterial. Cook was Ryder's client and was entitled to the protection of the lawyer-client privilege. . . .

It was Ryder, not his client, who took the initiative in transferring the incriminating possession of the stolen money and the shotgun from Cook. Ryder's conduct went far beyond the receipt and retention of a confidential communication from his client. Counsel for Ryder conceded, at the time of argument, that the acts of Ryder were not within the attorney-client privilege. . . .

The money in Cook's box belonged to the Bank of Virginia. The law did not authorize Cook to conceal this money or withhold it from the bank. His larceny was a continuing offense. Cook had no title or property interest in the money that he lawfully could pass to Ryder. The Act of Assembly authorizing the promulgation of the Canons of Ethics in Virginia forbids inconsistency with §18.1-107 Code of Virginia, 1950, which provides:

> If any person buy or receive from another person, or aid in concealing, any stolen goods or other thing, knowing the same to have been stolen, he shall be deemed guilty of larceny thereof, and may be proceeded against, although the principal offender be not convicted.

No canon of ethics or law permitted Ryder to conceal from the Bank of Virginia its money to gain his client's acquittal.

Cook's possession of the sawed-off shotgun was illegal. 26 U.S.C. §5851. Ryder could not lawfully receive the gun from Cook to assist Cook to avoid conviction of robbery. Cook had never mentioned the shotgun to Ryder. When Ryder discovered it in Cook's box, he took possession of it to hinder the government in the prosecution of its case, and he intended not to reveal it pending trial unless the government discovered it and a court compelled its production. No statute or canon of ethics authorized Ryder to take possession of the gun for this purpose.

Canon 15 states in part:

> [T]he great trust of the lawyer is to be performed within and not without the bounds of law. The office of attorney does not permit, much less does it demand of him for any client, violation of law or any manner of fraud or chicane. He must obey his own conscience and not that of his client.

In helping Cook to conceal the shotgun and stolen money, Ryder acted without the bounds of law. He allowed the office of attorney to be used in violation of law. The scheme which he devised was a deceptive, legalistic subterfuge — rightfully denounced by the canon [15] as chicane.

Ryder's testimony that he intended to have the court rule on the admissibility of the evidence and the extent of the lawyer-client privilege does not afford justification for his action. He intended to do this only if the government discovered the shotgun and stolen money in his lockbox. If the government did not discover it, he had no intention of submitting any legal question about it to the court. If there were no discovery, he would continue to conceal the shotgun and money for Cook's benefit pending trial.

Ryder's action is not justified because he thought he was acting in the best interests of his client. To allow the individual lawyer's belief to determine the standards of professional conduct will in time reduce the ethics of the profession to the practices of the most unscrupulous. Moreover, Ryder knew that the law against concealing stolen property and the law forbidding receipt and possession of a sawed-off shotgun contain no exemptions for a lawyer who takes possession with the intent of protecting a criminal from the consequences of his crime.

Canon 15 warns against the reasoning urged in support of Ryder:

> Nothing operates more certainly to create or to foster popular prejudice against lawyers as a class and to deprive the profession of that full measure of esteem and confidence which belongs to the proper discharge of its duties than does the false claim, often set up by the unscrupulous in defense of questionable transactions, that it is the duty of the lawyer to do whatever may enable him to succeed in winning his client's cause.

We find it difficult to accept the argument that Ryder's action is excusable because if the government found Cook's box, Ryder's would easily be found, and if the government failed to find both Cook's and Ryder's boxes, no more harm would be done than if the agents failed to find only Cook's. Cook's concealment of the items in his box cannot be cited to excuse Ryder. Cook's conduct is not the measure of Ryder's ethics. The conduct of a lawyer should be above reproach. Concealment of the stolen money and the sawed-off shotgun to secure Cook's acquittal was wrong whether the property was in Cook's or Ryder's possession.

There is much to be said, however, for mitigation of the discipline to be imposed. Ryder intended to return the bank's money after his client was tried. He consulted reputable persons before and after he placed the property in his lockbox, although he did not precisely follow their advice. Were it not for these facts, we would deem proper his permanent exclusion from practice before this court. In view of the mitigating circumstances, he will be suspended from practice in this court for eighteen months effective October 14, 1966. . . .

Problem VI-10
The Corporate Client

Class action for injuries allegedly resulting when tires negligently manufactured by the D Tire Company blew out. Prior to trial, D's attorney interviewed several company employees in connection with the case. Employees interviewed included the chairman of the board, the executive vice-president, the chief of operations, the director of quality control, the foreman of the afternoon tire-molding shift gang, and an employee in the tire-molding crew. The class action's lawyer seeks to discover what was said in these interviews. D claims the talks were privileged. What ruling and why?

Problem VI-11
The Assiduous Attorney

A bus owned and operated by the D Bus Company hits and injures pedestrian P. Fearing a lawsuit, D's in-house counsel, Fleegal, interviews the driver of the bus, C, and the only eyewitness to the accident, W. C describes the relevant events to Fleegal, who takes notes, goes back to his office, and files them. W describes the relevant events to Fleegal, who has his secretary take down W's comments verbatim and transcribe them in typewritten form. W signs the transcript, and Fleegal files it.

Fleegal also has his associate, Cratchet, gather up all the maintenance and driver records and other pertinent D Co. documents. Fleegal has Cratchet prepare a memorandum analyzing these records and an index to them, all of which he files. Fleegal also reviews a memorandum he had

Cratchet prepare some time ago on *D*'s maintenance and driver-training programs and has that filed with the other material.

P sues the *D* Bus Company. During discovery, *P*'s attorney files an FRCP 34 Request for Production of Documents asking for production of "all books, documents, papers, records, reports and things pertinent to, relating to or mentioning the subject accident, the maintenance of Company buses or its training of operating personnel."

What response should Fleegal make to this request? If *P* sends interrogatories to *D* pursuant to FRCP 33 seeking to elicit facts about the accident that Fleegal learned only from *C*, *W*, and Cratchet, what response should Fleegal make?

See the *Hickman* case, FRCP 26, and the *Radiant Burners* and *Upjohn* cases, which follow.

HICKMAN v. TAYLOR
329 U.S. 495 (1947)

Mr. Justice MURPHY delivered the opinion of the Court.

This case presents an important problem under the Federal Rules of Civil Procedure as to the extent to which a party may inquire into oral and written statements of witnesses, or other information, secured by an adverse party's counsel in the course of preparation for possible litigation after a claim has arisen. Examination into a person's files and records, including those resulting from the professional activities of an attorney, must be judged with care. It is not without reason that various safeguards have been established to preclude unwarranted excursions into the privacy of a man's work. At the same time, public policy supports reasonable and necessary inquiries. Properly to balance these competing interests is a delicate and difficult task.

On February 7, 1943, the tug "J. M. Taylor" sank while engaged in helping to tow a car float of the Baltimore & Ohio Railroad across the Delaware River at Philadelphia. The accident was apparently unusual in nature, the cause of it still being unknown. Five of the nine crew members were drowned. Three days later the tug owners and the underwriters employed a law firm, of which respondent Fortenbaugh is a member, to defend them against potential suits by representatives of the deceased crew members and to sue the railroad for damages to the tug.

A public hearing was held on March 4, 1943, before the United States Steamboat Inspectors, at which the four survivors were examined. This testimony was recorded and made available to all interested parties. Shortly thereafter, Fortenbaugh privately interviewed the survivors and took statements from them with an eye toward the anticipated litigation; the survivors signed these statements on March 29. Fortenbaugh also interviewed other persons believed to have some information relating to

the accident and in some cases he made memoranda of what they told
him. At the time when Fortenbaugh secured the statements of the survivors, representatives of two of the deceased crew members had been in
communication with him. Ultimately claims were presented by representatives of all five of the deceased; four of the claims, however, were
settled without litigation. The fifth claimant, petitioner herein, brought
suit in a federal court under the Jones Act on November 26, 1943,
naming as defendants the two tug owners, individually and as partners,
and the railroad.

One year later, petitioner filed 39 interrogatories directed to the tug
owners. The 38th interrogatory read:

> State whether any statements of the members of the crews of the Tugs "J. M.
> Taylor" and "Philadelphia" or of any other vessel were taken in connection
> with the towing of the car float and the sinking of the Tug "John M. Taylor."
> Attach hereto exact copies of all such statements if in writing, and if oral, set
> forth in detail the exact provisions of any such oral statements or reports.

Supplemental interrogatories asked whether any oral or written statements, records, reports or other memoranda had been made concerning
any matter relative to the towing operation, the sinking of the tug, the
salvaging and repair of the tug, and the death of the deceased. If the
answer was in the affirmative, the tug owners were then requested to set
forth the nature of all such records, reports, statements or other memoranda.

The tug owners, through Fortenbaugh, answered all of the interrogatories except No. 38 and the supplemental ones just described.
While admitting that statements of the survivors had been taken, they
declined to summarize or set forth the contents. They did so on the
ground that such requests called "for privileged matter obtained in
preparation for litigation" and constituted "an attempt to obtain directly
counsel's private files." It was claimed that answering these requests
"would involve practically turning over not only the complete files, but
also the telephone records and, almost, the thoughts of counsel."

In connection with the hearing on these objections, Fortenbaugh
made a written statement and gave an informal oral deposition explaining the circumstances under which he had taken the statements.
But he was not expressly asked in the deposition to produce the statements. The District Court for the Eastern District of Pennsylvania, sitting en banc, held that the requested matters were not privileged. 4
F.R.D. 479. The court then decreed that the tug owners and Fortenbaugh, as counsel and agent for the tug owners, forthwith

> answer Plaintiff's 38th interrogatory and supplementary interrogatories;
> produce all written statements of witnesses obtained by Mr. Fortenbaugh, as
> counsel and agent for Defendants; state in substance any fact concerning this

case which Defendants learned through oral statements made by witnesses to Mr. Fortenbaugh whether or not included in his private memoranda and produce Mr. Fortenbaugh's memoranda containing statements of fact by witnesses or to submit these memoranda to the Court for determination of those portions which should be revealed to Plaintiff.

Upon their refusal, the court adjudged them in contempt and ordered them imprisoned until they complied. . . .

The pre-trial deposition-discovery mechanism established by Rules 26 to 37 is one of the most significant innovations of the Federal Rules of Civil Procedure. Under the prior federal practice, the pre-trial functions of notice-giving, issue-formulation and fact-revelation were performed primarily and inadequately by the pleadings. Inquiry into the issues and the facts before trial was narrowly confined and was often cumbersome in method. The new rules, however, restrict the pleadings to the task of general notice-giving and invest the deposition-discovery process with a vital role in the preparation for trial. . . .

We agree, of course, that the deposition-discovery rules are to be accorded a broad and liberal treatment. No longer can the time-honored cry of "fishing expedition" serve to preclude a party from inquiring into the facts underlying his opponent's case.[8] Mutual knowledge of all the relevant facts gathered by both parties is essential to proper litigation. To that end, either party may compel the other to disgorge whatever facts he has in his possession. The deposition-discovery procedure simply advances the stage at which the disclosure can be compelled from the time of trial to the period preceding it, thus reducing the possibility of surprise. But discovery, like all matters of procedure, has ultimate and necessary boundaries. As indicated by Rules 30(b) and (d) and 31(d), limitations inevitably arise when it can be shown that the examination is being conducted in bad faith or in such a manner as to annoy, embarrass or oppress the person subject to the inquiry. And as Rule 26(b) provides, further limitations come into existence when the inquiry touches upon the irrelevant or encroaches upon the recognized domains of privilege.

We also agree that the memoranda, statements and mental impressions in issue in this case fall outside the scope of the attorney-client privilege and hence are not protected from discovery on that basis. It is unnecessary here to delineate the content and scope of that privilege as recognized in the federal courts. For present purposes, it suffices to note that the protective cloak of this privilege does not extend to information which an attorney secures from a witness while acting for his client in

---

8. "One of the chief arguments against the 'fishing expedition' objection is the idea that discovery is mutual — that while a party may have to disclose his case, he can at the same time tie his opponent down to a definite position." Pike and Willis, Federal Discovery in Operation, 7 U. Chi. L. Rev. 297, 303.

anticipation of litigation. Nor does this privilege concern the memoranda, briefs, communications and other writings prepared by counsel
for his own use in prosecuting his client's case; and it is equally unrelated
to writings which reflect an attorney's mental impressions, conclusions,
opinions or legal theories.

But the impropriety of invoking that privilege does not provide an
answer to the problem before us. Petitioner has made more than an
ordinary request for relevant, non-privileged facts in the possession of
his adversaries or their counsel. He has sought discovery as of right of
oral and written statements of witnesses whose identity is well known
and whose availability to petitioner appears unimpaired. He has sought
production of these matters after making the most searching inquiries of
his opponents as to the circumstances surrounding the fatal accident,
which inquiries were sworn to have been answered to the best of their
information and belief. Interrogatories were directed toward all the
events prior to, during and subsequent to the sinking of the tug. Full and
honest answers to such broad inquiries would necessarily have included
all pertinent information gleaned by Fortenbaugh through his interviews with the witnesses. Petitioner makes no suggestion, and we cannot
assume, that the tug owners or Fortenbaugh were incomplete or dishon-
est in the framing of their answers. In addition, petitioner was free to
examine the public testimony of the witnesses taken before the United
States Steamboat Inspectors. We are thus dealing with an attempt to
secure the production of written statements and mental impressions
contained in the files and the mind of the attorney Fortenbaugh without
any showing of necessity or any indication or claim that denial of such
production would unduly prejudice the preparation of petitioner's case
or cause him any hardship or injustice. For aught that appears, the
essence of what petitioner seeks either has been revealed to him already
through the interrogatories or is readily available to him direct from the
witnesses for the asking.

The District Court, after hearing objections to petitioner's request,
commanded Fortenbaugh to produce all written statements of witnesses
and to state in substance any facts learned through oral statements of
witnesses to him. Fortenbaugh was to submit any memoranda he had
made of the oral statements so that the court might determine what
portions should be revealed to petitioner. All of this was ordered without any showing by petitioner, or any requirement that he make a
proper showing, of the necessity for the production of any of this material or any demonstration that denial of production would cause hardship or injustice. The court simply ordered production on the theory
that the facts sought were material and were not privileged as constituting attorney-client communications.

In our opinion, neither Rule 26 nor any other rule dealing with
discovery contemplates production under such circumstances. That is

not because the subject matter is privileged or irrelevant, as those concepts are used in these rules. Here is simply an attempt, without purported necessity or justification, to secure written statements, private memoranda and personal recollections prepared or formed by an adverse party's counsel in the course of his legal duties. As such, it falls outside the arena of discovery and contravenes the public policy underlying the orderly prosecution and defense of legal claims. Not even the most liberal of discovery theories can justify unwarranted inquiries into the files and the mental impressions of an attorney.

Historically, a lawyer is an officer of the court and is bound to work for the advancement of justice while faithfully protecting the rightful interests of his clients. In performing his various duties, however, it is essential that a lawyer work with a certain degree of privacy, free from unnecessary intrusion by opposing parties and their counsel. Proper preparation of a client's case demands that he assemble information, sift what he considers to be the relevant from the irrelevant facts, prepare his legal theories and plan his strategy without undue and needless interference. That is the historical and the necessary way in which lawyers act within the framework of our system of jurisprudence to promote justice and to protect their clients' interests. This work is reflected, of course, in interviews, statements, memoranda, correspondence, briefs, mental impressions, personal beliefs, and countless other tangible and intangible ways — aptly though roughly termed by the Circuit Court of Appeals in this case as the "work product of the lawyer." Were such materials open to opposing counsel on mere demand, much of what is now put down in writing would remain unwritten. An attorney's thoughts, heretofore inviolate, would not be his own. Inefficiency, unfairness and sharp practices would inevitably develop in the giving of legal advice and in the preparation of cases for trial. The effect on the legal profession would be demoralizing. And the interests of the clients and the cause of justice would be poorly served.

We do not mean to say that all written materials obtained or prepared by an adversary's counsel with an eye toward litigation are necessarily free from discovery in all cases. Where relevant and non-privileged facts remain hidden in an attorney's file and where production of those facts is essential to the preparation of one's case, discovery may properly be had. Such written statements and documents might, under certain circumstances, be admissible in evidence or give clues as to the existence or location of relevant facts. Or they might be useful for purposes of impeachment or corroboration. And production might be justified where the witnesses are no longer available or can be reached only with difficulty. Were production of written statements and documents to be precluded under such circumstances, the liberal ideals of the deposition-discovery portions of the Federal Rules of Civil Procedure would be stripped of much of their meaning. But the general policy against invading the privacy of an attorney's course of preparation is so well recognized and so essential to an orderly working of our system of legal procedure that a burden rests on the one who would invade that privacy to establish adequate reasons to justify production through a subpoena or court order. That burden, we believe, is necessarily implicit in the rules as now constituted.

Rule 30(b), as presently written, gives the trial judge the requisite discretion to make a judgment as to whether discovery should be allowed as to written statements secured from witnesses. But in the instant case there was no room for that discretion to operate in favor of the petitioner. No attempt was made to establish any reason why Fortenbaugh should be forced to produce the written statements. There was only a naked, general demand for these materials as of right and a finding by the District Court that no recognizable privilege was involved. That was insufficient to justify discovery under these circumstances and the court should have sustained the refusal of the tug owners and Fortenbaugh to produce.

But as to oral statements made by the witnesses to Fortenbaugh, whether presently in the form of his mental impressions or memoranda, we do not believe that any showing of necessity can be made under the circumstances of this case so as to justify production. Under ordinary conditions, forcing an attorney to repeat or write out all that witnesses have told him and to deliver this account to his adversary gives rise to grave dangers of inaccuracy and untrustworthiness. No legitimate purpose is served by such production. The practice forces the attorney to testify as to what he remembers or what he saw fit to write down regarding witnesses' remarks. Such testimony could not qualify as evidence; and to use it for impeachment or corroborative purposes would make the attorney much less an officer of the court and much more an ordinary witness. The standards of the profession would thereby suffer.

Denial of production of this nature does not mean that any material, non-privileged facts can be hidden from the petitioner in this case. He need not be unduly hindered in the preparation of his case, in the discovery of facts or in his anticipation of his opponents' position. Searching interrogatories directed to Fortenbaugh and the tug owners, production of written documents and the statements upon a proper showing and direct interviews with the witnesses themselves all serve to reveal the facts in Fortenbaugh's possession to the fullest possible extent consistent with public policy. Petitioner's counsel frankly admits that he wants the oral statements only to help prepare himself to examine witnesses and to make sure that he has overlooked nothing. That is insufficient under the circumstances to permit him an exception to the policy underlying the privacy of Fortenbaugh's professional activities. If there should be a rare situation justifying production of these matters, petitioner's case is not of that type.

We fully appreciate the wide-spread controversy among the members of the legal profession over the problem raised by this case. It is a problem that rests on what has been one of the most hazy frontiers of the discovery process. But until some rule or statute definitely prescribes otherwise, we are not justified in permitting discovery in a situation of this nature as a matter of unqualified right. When Rule 26 and the other discovery rules were adopted, this Court and the members of the bar in general certainly did not believe or contemplate that all the files and mental processes of lawyers were thereby opened to the free scrutiny of their adversaries. And we refuse to interpret the rules at this time so as to reach so harsh and unwarranted a result.

We therefore affirm the judgment of the Circuit Court of Appeals. Affirmed.

RULE 26(b)(3), FEDERAL RULES OF CIVIL PROCEDURE
Trial Preparation — Materials

Subject to the provisions of subdivision (b)(4) of this rule [trial preparation: Experts], a party may obtain discovery of documents and tangible things otherwise discoverable under subdivision (b)(1) of this rule and prepared in anticipation of litigation or for trial by or for another party or by or for that other party's representative (including his attorney, consultant, surety, indemnitor, insurer, or agent) only upon a showing that the party seeking discovery has substantial need of the materials in the preparation of his case and that he is unable without undue hardship to obtain the substantial equivalent of the materials by other means. In ordering discovery of such materials when the required showing has been made, the court shall protect against disclosure of the mental impressions, conclusions, opinions, or legal theories of an attorney or other representative of a party concerning the litigation.

A party may obtain without the required showing a statement concerning the action or its subject matter previously made by that party. Upon request, a person not a party may obtain without the required showing a statement concerning the action or its subject matter previously made by that person. . . .

RADIANT BURNERS v. AMERICAN GAS ASSOCIATION
207 F. Supp. 771 (N.D. Ill. 1962), rev'd, 320 F.2d 314 (7th Cir. 1963)

CAMPBELL, C.J. . . . [H]aving after much study and consideration personally come to the point of questioning the application of the attorney-client privilege to a corporate client, I now suggest to the profession and adopt as the law of this case that a corporation is not entitled to make claim to the privilege for the following reasons.

The attorney-client privilege, analogous to the privilege against self-incrimination, is historically and fundamentally personal in nature. Both privileges have their genesis in the common law, and both still exist independently of statute. (The 5th Amendment to the Constitution merely guarantees the self-incrimination privilege against legislative action). Although at earliest common law the attorney-client privilege was solely that of the attorney, since the eighteenth century, and as it now exists, the privilege rests entirely with the client. It logically follows that this personal privilege of the client must, as in the case of the personal privilege against self-incrimination, be claimed only by natural individuals and not by mere corporate entities. As to denying corporations the privilege against self-incrimination see Wilson v. United States, 221 U.S. 361; and Essgee Co. v. United States, 262 U.S. 151. A fortiori, a corporation which is a mere creature of the state and not a natural entity should not, without legislation, be afforded a privilege historically created only for natural persons.

Still another reason exists for denying the attorney-client privilege to corporations. One of the fundamental, universally accepted and most generally stated common law elements necessarily required properly to claim the attorney-client privilege is that the communication be completely confidential between the attorney and the client. Accordingly, if any of the attorney's or client's documents or verbal statements are subject to being disclosed to third parties, anyone other than the attorney or the client, then those documents or statements can no longer be regarded as confidential, the confidence having in the language of the common law been "profaned" and the privilege terminated. Such "profanity" could occur either at the source or point of origin of the information, or, it could take place at the intended repository of the information, should at either place a third party stranger have access to it.

Were we to assume, as obviously many of us have heretofore, that a corporation may claim the privilege, then we are immediately presented with the anomalous situation of determining what persons within the corporate structure hold its confidence and may properly be considered as its alter ego and therefore the "client." In making such a determination should we include within the scope of the term "client" the corporation's president? What then of other officers, members of the board of directors, executive committee members, supervisory personnel, office workers, or for that matter any employee, and finally what about the individual stockholders? If an individual is not permitted to make an agent of still another individual, or more accurately of large groups of individuals, and thus increase the scope of the protection afforded to him through the attorney-client privilege and "profane" its confidence why permit a corporation to do the same thing through normal corporate operations? Clearly, even at common law the client's necessity and the attorney's of having immediate office personnel permitted access to documents without destroying their confidential nature is accepted and approved. (The solicitor or the barrister's clerk for example.) However, it is obvious that there is no comparison between this accepted extension of the scope of the terms "attorney" and "client," and an attempted extension of the term to encompass all those persons who constitute a corporate entity. This is well illustrated by considering the boards of directors and executive committees of most large corporations. Such groups are often made up of dominant and influential individuals of other corporations and organizations, with many of which the corporation has business dealings. . . . Information from or in the hands of these individuals would unquestionably be information from or in the hands of persons outside the scope of the term "client," as this term is intended with reference to the attorney-client privilege. It is most unrealistic to presume that such communications are made with the intention of confidentiality or could possibly avoid the "profanation" so clearly condemned by the Rule as created at common law. As Wigmore states (Sec. 2291), "It (the attorney-client privilege) ought to be strictly confined within the narrowest possible limits consistent with the logic of its principle." Another and later commentary is in my opinion salient to this issue:

> Where corporations are involved, with their large number of agents, masses of documents and frequent dealings with lawyers, the zone of silence grows large. Few judges — or legislators either, for that matter — would long tolerate any common law privilege that allowed corporations to insulate all their activities by discussing them with legal advisors.

Simon, "The Attorney-Client Privilege As Applied to Corporations," 65 Yale L.J. 953, 955 (1956).

It seems to me that the corporate entity is best exemplified for the purpose of claiming this privilege by those who actually share in its ownership, the shareholders, it being only for their benefit that a corporation could make claim to the privilege. Since, then, the privilege is being asserted for their benefit it would seem that they best qualify as the "client." Thus the term "client" is in many instances extended to include literally thousands of persons in a single corporation. Both at common law, and in many instances also by statute the shareholders have the right always to inspect corporate files and records. As owners they of course have the right to inspect property held by their agents. Although some jurisdictions might place minor restrictions aimed at protecting the interest of other owners upon it, the basic right to reasonable inspection always exists and cannot be abrogated even by the articles of incorporation. Once again it becomes apparent that the confidential nature of communications and documents so vital an element of the attorney-client privilege could never exist when such documents and information are readily available to so many thousand persons, whose qualifications for the most part are solely a monetary interest. Indeed, since all of the activities of every corporation are only for the common or group interest, it can never assert a reasonable or proper claim of secrecy. The Supreme Court has recently alluded to this fact in citing the members' right to inspect as grounds for denying a union the privilege against self-incrimination. United States v. White, 322 U.S. 694, 699-700.

An additional third party or "stranger" to a corporation "profaning" any possible confidential nature of corporate books and records is its State of incorporation with its proper visitatorial power over such records. Once a group of individuals elect to form a corporate entity there can be no overriding desire of secrecy, and the circumstances would argue against any desire to keep documents confidential from all others excluding themselves. Wilson v. United States, 221 U.S. 361. One of the prices one pays for the limitation of personal liability through incorporation is the loss of personal privileges one might otherwise have in individual business transactions.

The basic rationale of the attorney-client privilege and the reason prompting its creation apparently is the compelling desire to promote genuine freedom of communication between an individual and his attorney. In its historic genesis in the common law it is so intimately entwined with its great partner the privilege against self incrimination that a person reading its history begins to doubt that two separate privileges ever were originally intended. Rather the one seems to be but an extension and outgrowth of the other, both being limited to a purely personal application and both being restricted as obviously is the one, solely to the field of criminal law. Usage thereafter however has definitely established at common law the application of the attorney-client privilege to civil litigation although always retaining its purely personal character.

Although the same basic rationale would in my opinion warrant extending a similar privilege to a corporation dealing with its attorney this is impossible at common law because of the secrecy element of the privilege as heretofore pointed out herein. Thus nowhere can a corporation's right to the privilege be found in the common law. Neither can I find any legislative or judicial fiat extending the privilege beyond its historic common law limitations.

Since the primary element of secrecy essential to any claim of the attorney-client privilege is not possible in the case of a corporation and since in any event the privilege is purely personal, I hold that it is not available to any of the corporate parties to this suit.

I should point out in conclusion that, although not yet placed in issue here, certain valid claims of privilege do exist and may properly be asserted to protect a corporation against unbridled discovery. See Wigmore on Evidence, Volume VII, Sections 2212, 2219 and 2219(c) in re "trade secrets" and "statutory protections." Another claim of privilege exists — that of an attorney to protect his "work product" from discovery. In many instances this and the attorney-client privilege seem to overlap, their cognate natures often causing basic misapplications. My finding that the attorney-client privilege cannot be claimed by these corporations has no relation to any possible withholding of documents from the plaintiff in light of the "work product" privilege.

The attorney "work product" privilege, to be distinguished from the attorney-client privilege, is historically and traditionally a privilege of the attorney and not that of the client. Its rationale is based upon the right of lawyers to enjoy privacy in the course of their preparations for suit. Consequently, the fact that the client is a corporation would in no way affect the claim of an attorney to his "work product" privilege. . . .

UPJOHN COMPANY v. UNITED STATES
449 U.S. 383 (1981)

Mr. Justice REHNQUIST delivered the opinion of the Court.

Petitioner Upjohn manufactures and sells pharmaceuticals here and abroad. In January 1976 independent accountants conducting an audit of one of petitioner's foreign subsidiaries discovered that the subsidiary made payments to or for the benefit of foreign government officials in order to secure government business. The accountants so informed Mr. Gerard Thomas, petitioner's Vice-President, Secretary, and General Counsel. Thomas is a member of the Michigan and New York bars, and has been petitioner's General Counsel for 20 years. He consulted with outside counsel and R. T. Parfet, Jr., petitioner's Chairman of the Board. It was decided that the company would conduct an internal investigation of what were termed "questionable payments." As part of this investigation the attorneys prepared a letter containing a questionnaire which was sent to "all foreign general and area managers" over the Chairman's signature. The letter began by noting recent disclosures that several American companies made "possibly illegal" payments to foreign government officials and emphasized that the management needed full information concerning any such payments made by Upjohn. The letter indicated that the Chairman had asked Thomas, identified as "the company's General Counsel," "to conduct an investigation for the purpose of determining the nature and magnitude of any payments made by the Upjohn Company or any of its subsidiaries to any employee or official of a foreign government." The questionnaire sought detailed information concerning such payments. Managers were instructed to treat the investigation as "highly confidential" and not to discuss it with anyone other than Upjohn employees who might be helpful in providing the requested information. Responses were to be sent directly to Thomas. Thomas and outside counsel also interviewed the recipients of the questionnaire and some 33 other Upjohn officers or employees as part of the investigation.

On March 26, 1976, the company voluntarily submitted a preliminary report to the Securities and Exchange Commission on Form 8-K disclosing certain questionable payments. A copy of the report was simultaneously submitted to the Internal Revenue Service, which immediately began an investigation to determine the tax consequences of the payments. Special agents conducting the investigation were given lists by Upjohn of all those interviewed and all who had responded to the questionnaire. On November 23, 1976, the Service issued a summons pursuant to 26 U.S.C. §7602 demanding production of:

> All files relative to the investigation conducted under the supervision of Gerard Thomas to identify payments to employees of foreign governments and any political contributions made by the Upjohn Company or any of its affiliates since January 1, 1971 and to determine whether any funds of the Upjohn Company had been improperly accounted for on the corporate books during the same period.
>
> The records should include but not be limited to written questionnaires sent to managers of the Upjohn Company's foreign affiliates, and memoranda or notes of the interviews conducted in the United States and abroad with officers and employees of the Upjohn Company and its subsidiaries.

The company declined to produce the documents specified in the second paragraph on the grounds that they were protected from disclosure by the attorney-client privilege and constituted the work product of attorneys prepared in anticipation of litigation. On August 31, 1977, the United States filed a petition seeking enforcement of the summons under 26 U.S.C. §§7402(b) and 7604(a) in the United States District Court for the Western District of Michigan. That court adopted the recommendation of a magistrate who concluded that the summons should be enforced. Petitioner appealed to the Court of Appeals for the Sixth Circuit which rejected the magistrate's finding of a waiver of the attorney-client privilege, 600 F.2d 1223, 1227, n.12, but agreed that the privilege did not apply "to the extent the communications were made by officers and agents not responsible for directing Upjohn's actions in response to legal advice . . . for the simple reason that the communications were not the 'client's.' " Id., at 1225. The court reasoned that accepting petitioner's claim for a broader application of the privilege would encourage upper-echelon management to ignore unpleasant facts and create too broad a "zone of silence." Noting that petitioner's counsel had interviewed officials such as the Chairman and President, the Court of Appeals remanded to the District Court so that a determination of who was within the "control group" could be made. In a concluding footnote the court stated that the work-product doctrine "is not applicable to administrative summonses issued under 26 U.S.C. §7602." Id., at 1228, n.13.

II

Federal Rule of Evidence 501 provides that "the privilege of a witness . . . shall be governed by the principles of the common law as they may be interpreted by the courts of the United States in light of reason and experience." The attorney-client privilege is the oldest of the privileges for confidential communications known to the common law. 8 Wigmore, Evidence §2290 (McNaughton rev. 1961). Its purpose is to encourage full and frank communication between attorneys and their clients and thereby promote broader public interests in the observance of law and administration of justice. The privilege recognizes that sound legal advice or advocacy serves public ends and that such advice or advocacy depends upon the lawyer being fully informed by the client. As we stated last Term in Trammel v. United States, 445 U.S. 40, 51 (1980), "The attorney-client privilege rests on the need for the advocate and counselor to know all that relates to the client's reasons for seeking representation if the professional mission is to be carried out." And in Fisher v. United States, 425 U.S. 391, 403 (1976), we recognized the purpose of the privilege to be "to encourage clients to make full disclosures to their attorneys." This rationale for the privilege has long been recognized by the Court, see Hunt v. Blackburn, 128 U.S. 464, 470 (1888) (privilege "is founded upon the necessity, in the interest and administration of justice, of the aid of persons having knowledge of the law and skilled in its practice, which assistance can only be safely and readily availed of when free from the consequences or the apprehension of disclosure"). Admittedly complications in the application of the privilege arise when the client is a corporation, which in theory is an artificial creature of the law, and not an individual; but this Court has assumed that the privilege applies when the client is a corporation. United States v. Louisville & Nashville R. Co., 236 U.S. 318, 336 (1915), and the Government does not contest the general proposition.

The Court of Appeals, however, considered the application of the privilege in the corporate context to present a "different problem," since the client was an inanimate entity and "only the senior management, guiding and integrating the several operations, . . . can be said to possess an identity analogous to the corporation as a whole." 600 F.2d at 1226. The first case to articulate the so-called "control group test" adopted by the court below, City of Philadelphia v. Westinghouse Electric Corp., 210 F. Supp. 483, 485 (E.D. Pa.), petition for mandamus and prohibition denied, General Electric Company v. Kirkpatrick, 312 F.2d 742 (C.A.3 1962), cert. denied, 372 U.S. 943 (1963), reflected a similar conceptual approach: "Keeping in mind that the question is, Is it the corporation which is seeking the lawyer's advice when the asserted privileged communication is made?, the most satisfactory solution, I think, is that if the employee making the communication, of whatever rank he may be, is in a position to control or even to take a substantial part in a decision about any action which the corporation may take upon the advice of the attorney, . . . then, in effect, *he is (or personifies) the corporation* when he makes his disclosure to the lawyer and the privilege would apply." (Emphasis supplied by the Court.) Such a view, we think, overlooks the fact that the privilege exists to protect not only the giving of professional advice to those who can act on it but also the giving of information to the lawyer to enable him to give sound and informed advice. See *Trammel*, 445 U.S., at 51; *Fisher*, 425 U.S., at 403. The first step in the resolution of any legal problem is ascertaining the factual background and sifting through the facts with an eye to the legally relevant. See ABA Code of Professional Responsibility, Ethical Consideration 4-1:

> A lawyer should be fully informed of all the facts of the matter he is handling in order for his client to obtain the full advantage of our legal system. It is for the lawyer in the exercise of his independent professional judgment to separate the relevant and important from the irrelevant and unimportant. The observance of the ethical obligation of a lawyer to hold inviolate the confidences and secrets of his client not only facilitates the full development of facts essential to proper representation of the client but also encourages laymen to seek early legal assistance.

See also Hickman v. Taylor, 329 U.S. 495, 511 (1947).

In the case of the individual client the provider of information and the person who acts on the lawyer's advice are one and the same. In the corporate context, however, it will frequently be employees beyond the control group as defined by the court below — "officers and agents . . . responsible for directing [the company's] actions in response to legal advice" — who will possess the information needed by the corporation's lawyers. Middle-level — and indeed lower-level — employees can, by actions within the scope of their employment, embroil the corporation in serious legal difficulties, and it is only natural that these employees would have the relevant information needed by corporate counsel if he is adequately to advise the client with respect to such actual or potential difficulties. This fact was noted in Diversified Industries, Inc. v. Meredith, 572 F.2d 596 (C.A.8 1978) (en banc):

"In a corporation, it may be necessary to glean information relevant to a legal problem from middle management or non-management personnel as well as from top executives. The attorney dealing with a complex legal problem is thus faced with a 'Hobson's choice.' If he interviews employees not having 'the very highest authority' their communications to him will not be privileged. If, on the other hand, he interviews *only* those employees with the 'very highest authority,' he may find it extremely difficult, if not impossible, to determine what happened." Id., at 608-609 (quoting Weinschel, Corporate Employee Interviews and the Attorney-Client Privilege, 12 B.C. Ind. & Comm. L. Rev. 873, 876 (1970)).

The control group test adopted by the court below thus frustrates the very purpose of the privilege by discouraging the communication of relevant information by employees of the client to attorneys seeking to render legal advice to the client corporation. The attorney's advice will also frequently be more significant to noncontrol group members than to those who officially sanction the advice, and the control group test makes it more difficult to convey full and frank legal advice to the employees who will put into effect the client corporation's policy. See, e.g., Duplan Corp. v. Deering Milliken, Inc., 397 F. Supp. 1146, 1164 (D.S.C. 1974) ("After the lawyer forms his or her opinion, it is of no immediate benefit to the Chairman of the Board or the President. It must be given to the corporate personnel who will apply it.").

The narrow scope given the attorney-client privilege by the court below not only makes it difficult for corporate attorneys to formulate sound advice when their client is faced with a specific legal problem but also threatens to limit the valuable effort of corporate counsel to ensure their client's compliance with the law. In light of the vast and complicated array of regulatory legislation confronting the modern corporation, corporations, unlike most individuals, "constantly go to lawyers to find out how to obey the law," Burnham, The Attorney-Client Privilege in the Corporate Arena, 24 Bus. Law. 901, 913 (1969), particularly since compliance with the law in this area is hardly an instinctive matter, see, e.g., United States v. United States Gypsum Co. 438 U.S. 422, 440-441 (1978) ("the behavior proscribed by the [Sherman] Act is often difficult to distinguish from the gray zone of socially acceptable and economically justifiable business conduct").[2] The test adopted by the court below is difficult to apply in practice, though no abstractly formulated and unvarying "test" will necessarily enable courts to decide questions such as this with mathematical precision. But if the purpose of the attorney-client privilege is to be served, the attorney and client must be able to predict with some degree of certainty whether particular discussions will

---

2. The Government argues that the risk of civil or criminal liability suffices to ensure that corporations will seek legal advice in the absence of the protection of the privilege. This response ignores the fact that the depth and quality of any investigations, to ensure compliance with the law would suffer, even were they undertaken. The response also proves too much, since it applies to all communications covered by the privilege: an individual trying to comply with the law or faced with a legal problem also has strong incentive to disclose information to his lawyer, yet the common law has recognized the value of the privilege in further facilitating communications.

be protected. An uncertain privilege, or one which purports to be certain but results in widely varying applications by the courts, is little better than no privilege at all. The very terms of the test adopted by the court below suggest the unpredictability of its application. The test restricts the availability of the privilege to those officers who play a "substantial role" in deciding and directing a corporation's legal response. Disparate decisions in cases applying this test illustrate its unpredictability.

The communications at issue were made by Upjohn employees[3] to counsel for Upjohn acting as such, at the direction of corporate superiors in order to secure legal advice from counsel. As the magistrate found, "Mr. Thomas consulted with the Chairman of the Board and outside counsel and thereafter conducted a factual investigation to determine the nature and extent of the questionable payments *and to be in a position to give legal advice to the company with respect to the payments.*" (Emphasis supplied.) Information, not available from upper-echelon management, was needed to supply a basis for legal advice concerning compliance with securities and tax laws, foreign laws, currency regulations, duties to shareholders, and potential litigation in each of these areas. The communications concerned matters within the scope of the employees' corporate duties, and the employees themselves were sufficiently aware that they were being questioned in order that the corporation could obtain legal advice. The questionnaire identified Thomas as "the company's General Counsel" and referred in its opening sentence to the possible illegality of payments such as the ones on which information was sought. A statement of policy accompanying the questionnaire clearly indicated the legal implications of the investigation. The policy statement was issued "in order that there be no uncertainty in the future as to the policy with respect to the practices which are the subject of this investigation." It began "Upjohn will comply with all laws and regulations," and stated that commissions or payments "will not be used as a subterfuge for bribes or illegal payments" and that all payments must be "proper and legal." Any future agreements with foreign distributors or agents were to be approved "by a company attorney" and any questions concerning the policy were to be referred "to the company's General Counsel." This statement was issued to Upjohn employees worldwide, so that even those interviewees not receiving a questionnaire were aware of the legal implications of the interviews. Pursuant to explicit instructions from the Chairman of the Board, the communications were considered "highly confidential" when made, and

3. Seven of the 86 employees interviewed by counsel had terminated their employment with Upjohn at the time of the interview. Petitioner argues that the privilege should nonetheless apply to communications by these former employees concerning activities during their period of employment. Neither the District Court nor the Court of Appeals had occasion to address this issue, and we decline to decide it without the benefit of treatment below.

have been kept confidential by the company. Consistent with the underlying purposes of the attorney-client privilege, these communications must be protected against compelled disclosure.

The Court of Appeals declined to extend the attorney-client privilege beyond the limits of the control group test for fear that doing so would entail severe burdens on discovery and create a broad "zone of silence" over corporate affairs. Application of the attorney-client privilege to communications such as those involved here, however, puts the adversary in no worse position than if the communications had never taken place. The privilege only protects disclosure of communications; it does not protect disclosure of the underlying facts by those who communicated with the attorney:

"The protection of the privilege extends only to *communications* and not to facts. A fact is one thing and a communication concerning that fact is an entirely different thing. The client cannot be compelled to answer the question, 'What did you say or write to the attorney?' but may not refuse to disclose any relevant fact within his knowledge merely because he incorporated a statement of such fact into his communication to his attorney." City of Philadelphia v. Westinghouse Electric Corp., 205 F. Supp. 830, 831 (E.D. Pa. 1962). See also *Diversified Industries*, 572 F.2d., at 611; State v. Circuit Court, 34 Wis.2d 559, 580, 150 N.W.2d 387, 399 (1967) ("the courts have noted that a party cannot conceal a fact merely by revealing it to his lawyer"). Here the Government was free to question the employees who communicated with Thomas and outside counsel. Upjohn has provided the IRS with a list of such employees, and the IRS has already interviewed some 25 of them. While it would probably be more convenient for the Government to secure the results of petitioner's internal investigation by simply subpoenaing the questionnaires and notes taken by petitioner's attorneys, such considerations of convenience do not overcome the policies served by the attorney-client privilege. As Justice Jackson noted in his concurring opinion in Hickman v. Taylor, 329 U.S., at 516: "Discovery was hardly intended to enable a learned profession to perform its functions . . . on wits borrowed from the adversary." . . .

III

Our decision that the communications by Upjohn employees to counsel are covered by the attorney-client privilege disposes of the case so far as the responses to the questionnaire and any notes reflecting responses to interview questions are concerned. The summons reaches further, however, and Thomas has testified that his notes and memoranda of interviews go beyond recording responses to his questions. To the extent that the material subject to the summons is not protected by the attorney-client privilege as disclosing communications between an employee and counsel, we must reach the ruling by the Court of Appeals that the work-product doctrine does not apply to summonses issued under 26 U.S.C. §7602.

The Government concedes, wisely, that the Court of Appeals erred and that the work-product doctrine does apply to IRS summonses. . . .

While conceding the applicability of the work-product doctrine, the Government asserts that it has made a sufficient showing of necessity to overcome its protections. The magistrate apparently so found. The Government relies on the following language in *Hickman*: "We do not mean to say that all written materials obtained or prepared by an adversary's counsel with an eye toward litigation are necessarily free from discovery in all cases. Where relevant and nonprivileged facts remain hidden in an attorney's file and where production of those facts is essential to the preparation of one's case, discovery may properly be had . . . And production might be justified where the witnesses are no longer available or may be reached only with difficulty." 329 U.S., at 511. The Government stresses that interviewees are scattered across the globe and that Upjohn has forbidden its employees to answer questions it considers irrelevant. The above-quoted language from *Hickman*, however, did not apply to "oral statements made by witnesses . . . whether presently in the form of [the attorney's] mental impressions or memoranda." Id., at 512. As to such material the Court did "not believe that any showing of necessity can be made under the circumstances of this case so as to justify production. . . . If there should be a rare situation justifying production of these matters petitioner's case is not of that type." Id., at 512-513. Forcing an attorney to disclose notes and memoranda of witnesses' oral statements is particularly disfavored because it tends to reveal the attorney's mental processes, 329 U.S., at 513 ("what he saw fit to write down regarding witnesses' remarks"); id., at 516-517 ("the statement would be his [the attorney's] language, permeated with his inferences") (Jackson, J., concurring).[8]

Rule 26 accords special protection to work product revealing the attorney's mental processes. The Rule permits disclosure of documents and tangible things constituting attorney work product upon a showing of substantial need and inability to obtain the equivalent without undue hardship. This was the standard applied by the magistrate. Rule 26 goes on, however, to state that "[i]n ordering discovery of such materials when the required showing has been made, the court shall protect against disclosure of the mental impressions, conclusions, opinions or legal theories of an attorney or other representative of a party concern-

---

8. Thomas described his notes of the interviews as containing "what I consider to be the important questions, the substance of the responses to them, my beliefs as to the importance of these, my beliefs as to how they related to the inquiry, my thoughts as to how they related to other questions. In some instances they might even suggest other questions that I would have to ask or things that I needed to find elsewhere."

ing the litigation." Although this language does not specifically refer to memoranda based on oral statements of witnesses, the *Hickman* court stressed the danger that compelled disclosure of such memoranda would reveal the attorney's mental process. It is clear that this is the sort of material the draftsmen of the Rule had in mind as deserving special protection. See Notes of Advisory Committee on 1970 Amendment to Rules, reprinted in 48 F.R.D. 487, 502 ("The subdivision . . . goes on to protect against disclosure the mental impressions, conclusions, opinions, or legal theories . . . of an attorney or other representative of a party. The *Hickman* opinion drew special attention to the need for protecting an attorney against discovery of memoranda prepared from recollection of oral interviews. The courts have steadfastly safeguarded against disclosure of lawyers' mental impressions and legal theories . . .").

Based on the foregoing, some courts have concluded that *no* showing of necessity can overcome protection of work product which is based on oral statements from witnesses. Those courts declining to adopt an absolute rule have nonetheless recognized that such material is entitled to special protection.

We do not decide the issue at this time. It is clear that the magistrate applied the wrong standard when he concluded that the Government had made a sufficient showing of necessity to overcome the protections of the work-product doctrine. The magistrate applied the "substantial need" and "without undue hardship" standard articulated in the first part of Rule 26(b)(3). The notes and memoranda sought by the Government here, however, are work product based on oral statements. If they reveal communications, they are, in this case, protected by the attorney-client privilege. To the extent they do not reveal communications, they reveal the attorneys' mental processes in evaluating the communications. As Rule 26 and *Hickman* make clear, such work product cannot be disclosed simply on a showing of substantial need and inability to obtain the equivalent without undue hardship.

While we are not prepared at this juncture to say that such material is always protected by the work-product rule, we think a far stronger showing of necessity and unavailability by other means than was made by the Government or applied by the magistrate in this case would be necessary to compel disclosure. . . .

Does Justice Rehnquist's opinion in *Upjohn* overcome the counter arguments put forth by Chief Judge Campbell in *Radiant Burners*, page 595, above? Is application of the lawyer-client privilege to communications from corporate employees justified under the Wigmore formula for privileges or on humanistic grounds?

What data does the Court cite to support the proposition that the "control group" test discourages the communication of relevant information by employees of the client to the corporation's attorneys? Is this claim logically persuasive in the abstract? Is this "relevant information" protected by any privilege that would prevent the government or a private party in a civil action from forcing its disclosure directly from the employees? What data supports the hypothesis that the quality of corporate compliance investigations will suffer unless the lawyer-client privilege is extended to communications from lower level employees?

Could any of the Upjohn employees who responded to the company's "questionable payments questionnaire" or who furnished interviews to the outside counsel claim the lawyer-client privilege with respect to those questionnaires or interviews? Could they claim their fifth amendment privilege against self-incrimination?

If consulted independently, how would you advise a corporate employee facing an *"Upjohn* interview" concerning the privileged nature of his communications to the investigating outside counsel? How should investigating outside counsel advise corporate employees concerning the privileged nature of their interview? What ethical obligations do counsel in this situation have to warn the employees of a possible conflict of interest?

If outside counsel does not warn an employee that the employee has no privilege to prevent disclosure of the information imparted in the interview, could the employee's subjective belief that a privilege *does* exist nonetheless bring the privilege into existence for the employee? If so, what effect will this "rabbit-under-the-hat" privilege have on the ability of outside counsel to disseminate the results of its investigation to corporate officers, the Board of Directors, or enforcement agencies?

In this respect, consider American Bar Association Standards for Criminal Justice, The Defense Function 4.56 (2d ed. 1980):

> *4-4.3 Relations with prospective witnesses. . . .*
> (b) It is not necessary for the lawyer or the lawyer's investigator, in interviewing a prospective witness, to caution the witness concerning possible self-incrimination and the need for counsel.

Given the holding of *Upjohn* that the lawyer-client privilege applies to communications between lower level employees and corporate counsel, should the privilege cover communication between counsel and *former* employees concerning activities during their period of employment? See footnote 3 of the Court's opinion.

UNITED STATES v. ARTHUR YOUNG & CO.
677 F.2d 211 (1982)

FEINBERG, C.J. This is an appeal from an order of the United States District Court for the Southern District of New York, Kevin T. Duffy, J., enforcing an Internal Revenue Service (IRS) summons to Arthur Young & Co. (AY). The summons, issued pursuant to 26 U.S.C. §7602,[1] directed AY to produce all files related to its client, Amerada Hess Corp. (Amerada), for whom AY served as independent auditor. In response to an enforcement proceeding initiated by the IRS, Judge Duffy, in a decision reported at 496 F. Supp. 1152 (S.D.N.Y. 1980), ordered the production of all the items requested by the IRS with two exceptions discussed below. The parties consented to a stay of production pending resolution of this appeal. In this court, AY challenges the district court's order, objecting primarily to the request for its audit workpapers file and for its tax pool (tax accrual workpapers) file. Amerada, utilizing the procedure available under 26 U.S.C. §7609, has intervened to challenge production of the tax accrual workpapers file. Because we find that the audit workpapers are relevant to determining Amerada's tax liability and thus fall within the scope of the IRS summons power, we affirm that part of Judge Duffy's order requiring their production. However, we reverse that part of the district court order enforcing the summons of the tax accrual workpapers. Although we find that this material is also relevant to the determination of tax liability, we believe that these documents should remain confidential in order to protect the reliability of the independent audit process.

I

The involvement of Arthur Young & Co., a firm of certified public accountants, with Amerada Hess Corp. began in November 1971, when AY was retained as Amerada's independent auditor. Among its other duties, AY was responsible for reviewing the financial statements prepared by Amerada in satisfaction of the disclosure requirements of the federal securities law. An AY partner also signed Amerada's tax returns, even though AY did not prepare the returns.

In April 1976, AY became further enmeshed in Amerada's affairs. Around that time, it became known that many American companies had

---

1. 26 U.S.C. §7602 provides in relevant part that:

"For the purpose of ascertaining the correctness of any return, making a return where none has been made, determining the liability of any person for any internal revenue tax or the liability at law or in equity of any transferee or fiduciary of any person in respect of any internal revenue tax, or collecting any such liability, the Secretary or his delegate is authorized —

"(1) To examine any books, papers, records, or other data which may be relevant or material to such inquiry;

"(2) To summon the person liable for tax or required to perform the act, or any officer or employee of such person, or any person having possession, custody, or care of books of account containing entries relating to the business of the person liable for tax or required to perform the act, or any other person the Secretary or his delegate may deem proper, to appear before the Secretary or his delegate at a time and place named in the summons and to produce such books, papers, records, or other data, and to give such testimony, under oath, as may be relevant or material to such inquiry. . . ."

made illegal payments abroad. In response to this publicity, Amerada's board of directors formed a special committee to investigate the possibility of Amerada wrongdoing. The law firm of Milbank, Tweed, Hadley & McCloy, and AY were engaged as independent investigators to assist the committee. This inquiry apparently, and despite the minor nature of the improprieties it uncovered, prompted the IRS in August 1977 to institute a criminal investigation of Amerada's tax returns for the years 1972, 1973, and 1974. Because a regular audit was then in progress, the IRS and Amerada designed a procedure in September 1977 to apprise the corporation of the progress of the criminal investigation. According to their agreement, Special Agent Kenneth Kalemba, who was in charge of the criminal investigation, would issue all summonses relating to that inquiry. In April 1978, a summons signed by Kalemba was issued to AY, requiring it to make all its Amerada files available to the IRS.[4] A quarter of a million pages of documents are involved in this request.

The IRS sought to enforce this summons by an order to show cause, dated October 9, 1979. Judge Duffy tested the summons against the four criteria set forth in United States v. Powell, 379 U.S. 48, 57-58 (1964): "[The Commissioner] must show that the investigation will be conducted pursuant to a legitimate purpose, that the inquiry may be relevant to the purpose, that the information sought is not already

---

4. The summons requested the following documents relating to Amerada's tax liability for the years 1972-74:

"1. Engagement letter(s)
"2. Management letter(s)
"3. Representation letter(s)
"4. History file(s)
"5. Standard workpaper index(es)
"6. Administrative file(s)
"7. Workpaper review file(s)
"8. Engagement planning file(s)
"9. Confirmation control file(s)
"10. Significant events file(s)
"11. Audit program file(s)
"12. Audit workpaper's file(s)
"13. Tax pool analysis file(s)
"14. File(s) prepared during the course of work performed for the 'special committee,' including agreed procedures, selection process, reports, schedules and other workpapers.
"15. The name of the partner in charge, engagement partner and/or senior auditor who directed the Amerada . . .
"16. Any other information pertinent to the audit of Amerada . . . covering the years 1972, 1973 and 1974.
"17. All workpapers, reports, records, correspondence, reconciliations and information relative to the United States Corporate Income Tax Returns (Forms 1120) of Amerada . . . that were prepared by [AY] or under the supervision of [AY] for the calendar years 1972, 1973 and 1974."

At about the same time, a summons was issued to Amerada directly. Enforcement of this summons was also litigated, see United States v. Amerada Hess Corp., 619 F.2d 980 (3d Cir. 1980), but none of the parties here contends that the different issues resolved there control the disposition of this appeal.

within the Commissioner's possession, and that the administrative steps required by the Code have been followed. . . ." He found that with the exception of two types of documents, the summons satisfied all the prongs of the *Powell* test and, accordingly, enforced it. The exceptions related to AY's audit program and to the documents prepared by the special committee that investigated Amerada's questionable payments. Judge Duffy held that the audit program was irrelevant because it "stands many steps removed from the question of the actual tax liability." United States v. Arthur Young & Co., 496 F. Supp. at 1157. He found that the committee report was protected by the work-product privilege under the doctrine of Hickman v. Taylor, 329 U.S. 495 (1947), since the material was prepared under the auspices of Milbank, Tweed in anticipation of litigation, id. at 1157-58. The IRS does not appeal this portion of the district court's order. Among the documents that Judge Duffy did order turned over are AY's audit workpapers and tax accrual workpapers. The challenges advanced on appeal relate to these two categories.

II

AY alone objects to the production of its audit workpapers. These documents consist almost entirely of factual data generated from the books when accountants verify the financial statements prepared by Amerada's own personnel by spot-checking selected bookkeeping entries and records. They include third-party confirmations of transactions, as well as the auditor's own judgments about the implications of the company's transactions. Some of the workpapers contain material learned during confidential discussions between Amerada and AY employees. This material is not used in preparing Amerada's tax returns.

AY makes two objections to disclosure of these documents. First, it focuses on the second *Powell* criterion — relevance — and it claims that the IRS bears an enhanced burden of showing relevance when it seeks documents from a third-party, that is from an entity other than the taxpayer whose return it is auditing. Thus, AY attempts to distinguish our holding in United States v. Noall, 587 F.2d 123 (2d Cir. 1978), cert. denied, 441 U.S. 923 (1979), where a summons forcing a taxpayer to produce its own internal audit workpapers was enforced, on the ground that *Noall* did not involve a third-party. Where, as here, a stranger to the audit is involved, AY argues that this court's opinion in United States v. Harrington, 388 F.2d 520, 524 (2d Cir. 1968), controls and it is insufficient for the IRS merely to allege that some chance of relevance exists.

In *Harrington*, the target of the summons was a lawyer who had as his client the ex-wife of the taxpayer in whom the IRS was interested. In the course of enforcing the IRS summons, the court did point out that it was

"particularly appropriate" that the lawyer and his client receive "judicial
protection against . . . sweeping or irrelevant order[s] . . ." because the
demand was "directed not to the taxpayer but to a third-party who may
have had some dealing with the person under investigation." Id. at 523.
But AY is not a stranger to Amerada's concerns in the same way that
lawyer Harrington was to the husband taxpayer in *Harrington*. AY was
hired to investigate Amerada's financial affairs, and to involve itself in
matters that were likely to be the object of governmental inquiry. We do
not believe that *Harrington* dictates the result sought by AY.

Moreover, we do not understand whose interests AY seeks to protect
by this claim of an enhanced burden. Amerada does not need this protection: it can intervene in its own behalf under §7609. And, in fact, it
has done so. Since Amerada does not object to production of the audit
workpapers, it would be anomalous to deny enforcement on the
strength of its accountant's objection. Nor can AY assert any particular
burden on it. Judge Duffy carefully protected AY from such possibilities
by requiring the IRS to shoulder the costs and to inspect on site, United
States v. Arthur Young & Co., 496 F. Supp. at 1160.

Once it is accepted that the usual threshold of relevance applies, it is
clear that the audit workpapers pass the *Powell* test. In *Noall*, we rejected
a simplistic equation of relevance with use in tax return preparation, and
recognized that "the purposes of the internal audit include the detection
of overstatements or understatements of revenues or expenses, and of
identifying accounting procedures that would lead to these. If the internal auditors have ascertained an understatement of revenues or an over-
statement of expenses, this plainly might throw light on the correctness
of the returns." 587 F.2d at 126. AY has advanced no persuasive argument to distinguish between the usefulness of the internal audit procedure at issue in *Noall* and the external audit at issue here. The
intervening decision in Thor Power Tool Co. v. Commissioner, 439 U.S.
522 (1979), does not change this result. There the Supreme Court held
that the accounting methods that a taxpayer uses for his own financial
records cannot be dispositive of the accounting method used for tax
purposes. But that does not mean that the reliability of the taxpayer's
records is not legitimately of interest to the IRS. Tax liability depends on
a taxpayer's actual revenue and expenses, not on his bookkeeping. The
IRS has an appropriate interest in ensuring that the latter accurately
reflects the former. . . .

III

AY is joined by Amerada and a host of amici curiae in challenging the
power of the IRS to compel the disclosure of tax accrual workpapers.
These documents are generated when an auditor verifies whether the
taxpayer has accurately determined its contingent tax liability. Under

the federal securities laws, a registrant must file a financial statement of its potential liabilities. Furthermore, the amici tell us that generally accepted auditing standards require an auditor to determine whether his client has put aside enough reserves to cover the contingency that, upon audit, it will owe the government more taxes than originally remitted. To make this assessment, the auditor must not only determine how the taxpayer treated his income and expenses in his tax return; he must also decide whether that treatment comports favorably with the Internal Revenue Code, the Regulations, and the case law. In areas where the law is unclear, he must predict the chances that the taxpayer's position will be upheld by the courts — a judgment based on his knowledge of the law and his opinion of where the law is headed. The auditor must also take into account the likelihood that the client will settle the dispute — a judgment based on the auditor's confidential and intimate knowledge of the client. This process frequently requires the auditor to elicit and engage in speculation as to positions that might be taken by the IRS and taxpayer, theoretical analysis, and opinions bearing on the fairness and reasonableness of the parties' positions (as distinguished from factual transactional data), which, if revealed to the IRS, could seriously prejudice the taxpayer in negotiations with it. If the auditor were required to disclose this material, which is not used in preparation of the taxpayer's return and is not needed by the IRS to determine the correctness of the taxpayer's return, the auditor would probably be inhibited from creating or maintaining such papers as part of a full and frank exchange useful in complying with the taxpayer's obligations under federal securities laws.

The Service's emerging practice of requesting tax accrual workpapers has aroused considerable controversy in the accounting and legal professions, as well as sharp disagreement among the courts that have considered the issue. In this appeal, appellants advance three arguments for denying enforcement to this facet of the summons. . . .

[The court then considered and rejected arguments advanced by AY and Amerada that the summons violated Amerada's agreement with Agent Kalemba and called for irrelevant evidence.]

The foregoing reasoning does not mean that the IRS summons in dispute here must now be mechanically enforced, for other considerations also bear on our decision. The Supreme Court has recognized that "contrary legislative purposes" can undercut the "broad latitude" otherwise provided to the IRS, United States v. Euge, 444 U.S. at 716 & n.9. It has also recognized that common law privileges serve to limit the scope of the IRS's power, Upjohn v. United States, 449 U.S. 383 (1981); United States v. Euge, 444 U.S. at 714. We think that the countervailing policies at issue in the case before us require us to fashion protection for the work that independent auditors, retained by publicly owned companies to comply with the federal securities laws, put into preparation of tax accrual workpapers.

Our starting point is Hickman v. Taylor, supra. In that case, the Supreme Court announced a policy of shielding "written statements, private memoranda and personal recollections prepared or formed by an adverse party's counsel in the course of his legal duties . . . ," 329 U.S. at 510, not because the documents were "privileged or irrelevant," id. at 509, but because their "[p]roper preparation . . . is the historical and necessary way in which lawyers act within the framework of our system of jurisprudence to promote justice and to protect their clients' interests." Id. at 511. *Hickman* was decided in the context of discovery under the Federal Rules of Civil Procedure, and the doctrine enunciated there has since been incorporated into Fed. R. Civ. P. 26(b)(3). But neither the Court nor Congress expressed an intent to limit the doctrine to the discovery context, Upjohn Co. v. United States, 101 S. Ct. at 689. Rather, we read both *Hickman* and Rule 26 as requiring us to balance strong public policies against a party's need for information whenever a conflict between the two arises.

The conflict in this case is between "the legitimate interest of society in enforcement of its laws and collection of the revenues," Couch v. United States, 409 U.S. 322, 336 (1973), and the "national public interest [in] insur[ing] the maintenance of fair and honest markets in [securities] transactions," 15 U.S.C. §78b. Congress has protected the former interest by vesting the Service with "the extensive powers granted . . . by the Internal Revenue Code," United States v. Powell, 379 U.S. at 56, including the summons power of §7602. The latter interest has been vindicated by extensively regulating the securities industry. Foremost among these regulations is the Securities Exchange Act of 1934, 15 U.S.C. §78a et seq., which requires public companies such as Amerada Hess to file financial statements, 15 U.S.C. §78l, verified by independent accountants "in accordance with generally accepted auditing standards," 17 C.F.R. §210.1-02(d). The verification procedure envisioned by the Act requires, in turn, that management feel free to cooperate with their auditors, and to disclose to them confidential information, such as the questionable positions taken on tax returns, and willingness to settle rather than litigate when these positions are challenged by the IRS. The procedure recognizes that since tax laws must be general enough to treat complex and diverse factual situations, they are necessarily drafted with a great deal of flexibility. The Code's requirements are therefore not always clear, and people of good faith can often take different positions as to the correct answer in a particular circumstance. While it is quite possible that a corporation motivated to save its shareholders' money might take a favorable — i.e. "minimum tax" — position on a debatable item, it is equally true that the Service, which is also composed of mortals, might, in its zeal to maximize revenues, take an equally incorrect "maximum tax" position. We do not agree with the dissent's statement that in the end, the corporation "pay[s] only what the tax laws required it to pay in the first place." This would be true if every difference of opinion were litigated. But the fact is that very few controversies reach that stage. In reality, at the end of an audit, the IRS and the taxpayers frequently compromise out their differences, each giving in a little. Such negotiations strike an appropriate balance between collecting revenue and conserving judicial resources, but requiring the taxpayer alone to disclose settlement positions would improperly weight the balance.

The result of working with a tax code that is not cast in black and white is that the independent auditor is faced with a very sensitive inquiry. In order to assess whether the corporation has set aside enough reserves to pay contingent liabilities, the auditor must pinpoint possibly vulnerable areas in his client's tax return and then predict how the corporation will handle the Service and vice versa, if these areas are questioned on audit. The inquiry necessarily lays bare not only the auditor's thoughts but also the taxpayer's basic thinking, including decisions not to litigate that are based on considerations wholly apart from the inherent legality of what the taxpayer has done, e.g., the cost of litigation and the possibility that confidential information may be disclosed to competitors. Divulging this information necessarily puts the taxpayer-corporation at a substantial disadvantage when it is audited. The prejudice involved in exposing to the Service appraisals of a taxpayer's weaknesses and settlement positions on audit is of such proportions that a prudent organization might not be perfectly candid with independent auditors once it knew that the information revealed would be reachable under §7602.[9]

The case at bar therefore involves much more than delineating the scope of the IRS's authority under §7602. When the IRS chooses to regularly summon tax accrual workpapers, it creates a clash between two important congressional policies. No matter how we decide this issue, one policy has to bend a bit. Giving the complete latitude to the summons power that the IRS seeks here compromises the procedure designed by Congress to protect the investing public from inaccurate financial information. Protecting the accuracy of the securities laws dilutes the power of the Service to summon a roadmap of the thoughts and theories of a taxpayer and its independent auditor. However, so long as a case does not involve allegations of fraud, the Service does not need to know taxpayer's thoughts. The corporation's own books and the

---

9. The government contends that taxpayer's independent duty to comply with the SEC laws is assured by the risk of SEC prosecution, and exposure to civil suit. The full answer to this contention is provided in Upjohn Co. v. United States, [449 U.S. at 393 n.2]: "This response ignores the fact that the depth and quality of any investigations . . . would suffer. . . . The response also proves too much, since it applies to all communications covered by the privilege: an individual trying to comply with the law or faced with a legal problem also has strong incentive to disclose information to his lawyer, yet the common law has recognized the value of the privilege in further facilitating communications.

audit workpapers furnish the IRS with all the raw data that it needs to calculate the taxpayer's tax liability. A roadmap would merely save the IRS some time in finding the best arguments for asserting a deficiency. The investing public, on the other hand, relies most exclusively on the data generated as a result of the SEC laws. It therefore seems to us that this collision requires that some form of privilege be carved out to protect the independent auditing process. A work-product privilege, similar to the privilege fashioned in *Hickman*, seems to us appropriate. It protects those who benefit from enforcement of the securities laws from the "grave dangers of inaccuracy and untrustworthiness," *Hickman*, 329 U.S. at 513, that would result if tax accrual workpapers were routinely revealed to the Service. At the same time, it allows the IRS to procure these documents when the rare situation arises where it can make a sufficient showing of need to adequately justify invading the integrity of the auditing process, cf. *Hickman*, 329 U.S. at 512-13, Fed. R. Civ. P. 26(b)(3). In reaching this conclusion, we are comforted by the knowledge that if Congress feels that this privilege unduly restricts the IRS's authority, it can require that this material be made available, or that taxpayers flag their questionable positions directly on their returns, in line with the suggestions of former Commissioner Kurtz, 32 Tax Law. at 15-16; Cooper, The Avoidance Dynamic: A Tale of Tax Planning, Tax Ethics, and Tax Reform, 80 Colum. L. Rev. 1553, 1612 (1980). Procuring tax accrual workpapers under §7602 seems to us to effectuate Commissioner Kurtz's proposals through the back door.

In the case at hand, the IRS has not made a sufficient showing of need to override the privilege. Presumably, Amerada has made its own books available pursuant to the Third Circuit's decision in United States v. Amerada Hess Corp., supra. In addition, this decision directs AY to release its audit workpapers, along with the other papers that the district court required it to turn over. Since the IRS is not attempting to prove that Amerada is guilty of fraud, the documents released should be sufficient for its purpose of determining the accuracy of Amerada's returns.

For the foregoing reasons, the judgment of the district court is affirmed in part and reversed in part.

NEWMAN, J., concurring in part and dissenting in part.

The Court today creates a form of accountant's work-product privilege to shield from scrutiny by the Internal Revenue Service an accountant's tax accrual work papers. These papers, reflecting the accountant's identification of doubtful items on the income tax return of the accountant's corporate client, would be examined by the I.R.S. pursuant to its summons authority, 26 U.S.C. §7602 (1976), but for today's judicially-created exception. I respectfully dissent from this aspect of the

Court's decision,[1] believing that Congress has legislated in favor of such examination, that if Congress has left the question open, the decision to create an accountant's work-product privilege should be made by Congress and not by a court, and that if the merits of such a privilege are to be weighed by a court, we should reject it.

1. In enacting §7602, Congress has given the I.R.S. a broad summons authority to seek all information "relevant to a legitimate investigative purpose," United States v. Bisceglia, 420 U.S. 141, 146 (1975). The majority agrees that Arthur Young's tax accrual work papers are relevant to the legitimate investigative purpose of determining the correctness of the tax returns of its client, Amerada Hess Corporation. In the absence of a preexisting privilege, such as the privilege against self-incrimination or the attorney-client privilege, this determination that §7602 applies should result in enforcement of the summons. The majority does not purport to find anything in the text or legislative history of §7602 to support an exception for an accountant's tax accrual work papers. I do not find anything in Hickman v. Taylor, 329 U.S. 495 (1947), or Rule 26 of the Federal Rules of Civil Procedure that requires or even permits this Court to depart from the broad command of §7602.

The Supreme Court has observed that §7602 is subject to the " 'traditional privileges and limitations,' " Upjohn Co. v. United States, 449 U.S. 383, 398 (1981), quoting United States v. Euge, 444 U.S. 707, 714 (1980), which do not include a privilege for either client communications to an accountant, e.g., United States v. Wainwright, 413 F.2d 796, 803 (10th Cir. 1969), cert. denied, 396 U.S. 1009 (1970); United States v. Bowman, 358 F.2d 421, 423 (3d Cir. 1966), or an accountant's work product, e.g., United States v. Kelly, 311 F. Supp. 1216, 1217 (E.D. Pa. 1969); In re Rashba & Pokart, 271 F. Supp. 946, 948 (S.D.N.Y. 1967).[2] In United States v. Noall, 587 F.2d 123 (2d Cir. 1978), cert. denied, 441 U.S. 923 (1979), we were asked to create an exception for a corporation's own internal audit reports and related work papers on the ground that their disclosure to the I.R.S. would run counter to public policy by inhibiting frank disclosure from corporate employees to internal auditors. In rejecting that argument, we stated, "With respect to enforcement of the tax laws, Congress itself has decided the policy issue, and it is not for the courts to challenge that determination." Id. at 126. I would accept Congress' judgment and enforce the summons fully.

---

1. I concur in those portions of Chief Judge Feinberg's opinion upholding enforcement of the summons for Arthur Young's audit work papers and determining that its tax accrual work papers are relevant to the I.R.S.'s civil audit of Amerada Hess Corporation.

2. Federal law does not recognize accountant privileges even when the law of the forum state accords protection. William T. Thompson Co. v. General Nutrition Corp., 671 F.2d 100 (3d Cir. 1982); FDIC v. Mercantile National Bank of Chicago, 84 F.R.D. 345, 349 (N.D. Ill. 1979).

2. If it were thought that the broad command of §7602 leaves open the issue of whether to create an accountant's work-product privilege for tax accrual work papers, the decision to create such a privilege should be made by Congress. We have been authoritatively instructed not to place restrictions on the scope of §7602 "absent unambiguous directions from Congress." United States v. Bisceglia, supra, 420 U.S. at 150. I do not share the majority's comfort in knowing that if Congress prefers *not* to maintain an accountant's work-product privilege, it remains free to abolish it. That approach inverts the proper relationship between courts and Congress in this area. Congress has already legislated on the subject of the I.R.S.'s authority to examine relevant information, and it has thus far refrained from restricting the summons authority with any privileges unknown to the common law. If there is to be recognition of new privileges, we should leave that task to Congress. Cf. City of Milwaukee v. Illinois, 451 U.S. 304 (1981) (presumption of preemption of federal courts' common law role as to subjects on which Congress has legislated). Especially is this the proper approach in matters concerning the tax laws, perhaps the one area of all national legislation in which Congress is most alert to remedy perceived inequities.

3. If we were to enter the policy debate as to whether to create a privilege to protect an accountant's tax accrual work papers, the privilege should be rejected. The majority suggests the privilege is needed to ensure that public corporations will be truthful with their accountants in fulfilling their statutory obligations to file financial statements verified by independent accountants. See 15 U.S.C. §781 (1976); 17 C.F.R. §210.1-02(d) (1981). Analogy is drawn to the work-product privilege of attorneys. I am not persuaded by either the argument or the analogy.

The policy argument rests on an indictment of corporate America that I do not accept. The premise is that some corporations are so anxious to minimize their tax payments that they are willing to deceive their accountants concerning the existence of debatable tax items and thereby violate their obligations under the securities laws.[5] Doubtless all corporations are anxious to pay only the minimum taxes required, and, toward that end, many will take favorable positions on debatable items, some of which the I.R.S. will successfully challenge. But even when the I.R.S. prevails, the corporation ends up paying only what the tax laws required it to pay in the first place.[6] I doubt that many corporations will be so anxious to avoid that result that they will conceal these debatable items

---

5. To the extent that the majority is creating a privilege to encourage communication from the client to the accountant, it is creating a testimonial privilege for the corporation, not a work-product protection for the work of the accountant.

6. I assume the majority's privilege will protect an accountant's analysis of potential liability only of a civil nature. An accountant's privilege, no more than the attorney-client or attorney work-product privileges, should surely not insulate on-going attempts by the corporation or its accountants to carry out criminal evasion of taxes.

from their accountants in violation of the securities laws. But if a few are so tempted, courts should not afford them any shield behind which they can increase their chances of avoiding detection that they have not paid either the amount of taxes a court might rule was lawfully required or whatever adjustment might result from a post-audit settlement. In *Noall* we declined to give corporations an opportunity to shield their own audit work papers from I.R.S. scrutiny, despite the argument that employees would be tempted to deceive internal auditors. I see no reason to be more solicitous of corporations when they elect to enter public capital markets where they are obliged to accept the requirements of complete and honest financial disclosure.

Moreover, the argument that corporate taxpayers will be reluctant to assist in creating records accurately reflecting their contingent tax liabilities proves too much. If that premise were followed, we should insulate from §7602 all the taxpayer's records supporting his claimed tax liabilities, since their inspection by the I.R.S. frequently results in an upward adjustment of tax payments and the taxpayer therefore has an incentive not to maintain them. It is entirely speculative whether the statutory disclosure obligations of the securities laws present a greater need to create new privileges than do the record maintenance obligations of the tax laws themselves. See, e.g., 26 U.S.C. §7203 (1976).

Arguably, it is more important to protect the investing public with contingent-tax-liability disclosure obligations than to protect the public revenues with tax-record maintenance obligations and undiminished summons authority, but that is precisely the sort of policy choice to be made by Congress. A legislative hearing is a better forum than this appeal to determine how realistic is the threat that occasional instances of understated contingent tax liabilities that result in additional tax payments will prejudice investor decisions and whether such a threat justifies diminution of tax revenues by preventing the I.R.S. from focusing its limited auditing resources on identified questionable items.

Furthermore, it is far from clear that the absence of an accountant's work-product privilege increases the risk that a corporation would have much success even if it were tempted to default on its disclosure obligations in the area of contingent tax liabilities. The corporation's independent public accountant has public obligations in the area of contingent tax liabilities. The corporation's independent public accountant has public obligations to assure himself that contingent tax liabilities have been accurately reflected. If the corporation blocks the efforts of the accountant to ascertain the true state of the company's contingent tax liabilities, the accountant would be obliged to decline to certify the financial statements.

This last consideration indicates why the work-product privilege of the attorney is not analogous. The attorney is retained by the client in a completely private relationship, frequently to protect his client against claims of the Government. The work-product privilege assures legitimate privacy to the activity of the attorney in discharging his obligations to the client in vindication of a constitutional right to effective counsel. If the client elects not to make full disclosure to his attorney, the attorney may still undertake the defense; though he may not knowingly abet perjury, he has no obligation to the public to elicit and disclose the true state of his client's affairs. The certified public accountant, however, especially when he certifies financial statements of public corporations, has responsibilities to the public that far transcend his private employment relationship. In preparing and certifying such statements, he is not retained to defend his client against the Government; he is retained to assist his client in complying with government obligations to inform the investing public.

Finally, it is worth noting that privileges generally are created to serve some policy, independent of lawful obligations, that is thought to be impaired in the absence of the privilege. The law does not require spouses to confide in each other, but it nonetheless accords a marital privilege to promote family harmony. Similarly, the law does not require a client to confide in his attorney, but it nonetheless accords an attorney-client privilege to promote the effective assistance of counsel. The majority's privilege for accountants may be the first instance of a court creating a privilege to facilitate compliance with duties already imposed by law.[7]

For all of these reasons,[8] I respectfully dissent from the judicial creation of an accountant's work-product privilege to insulate tax accrual work papers from the scope of §7602.

---

1. Why did Amerada not object to the production of the Arthur Young audit workpapers?

7. The majority suggests that the Supreme Court in Upjohn Co. v. United States, supra, 449 U.S. at 393 n.2, has discounted the significance of a legal obligation of communication and disclosure in determining the scope or existence of a privilege. The footnote in *Upjohn* replied to the argument that the corporate client had an incentive to consult with its attorney and therefore did not need an attorney-client privilege broader than the "control group" test. In declining to restrict an existing privilege because the client had an *incentive* to communicate, the Court had no occasion to assess whether a *legal obligation* to disclose conclusions (here, contingent liabilities) should be ignored in determining whether to create a new privilege to protect underlying details (here, questionable tax items).

8. An additional reason advanced by the majority for favoring an accountant's work-product privilege is to prevent the I.R.S. from obtaining "back door" implementation of the suggestion of former I.R.S. Commissioner Jerome Kurtz that taxpayers should flag their questionable tax items. Kurtz, et al., Discussion on "Questionable Positions," 32 Tax Law. 13, 15-16 (1978). Whether or not the I.R.S. can or should add such a sweeping self-questioning feature to the self-reporting tax system is fairly debatable. But once the I.R.S. has decided to devote its limited resources to an audit or investigation of a particular taxpayer, it should not be obstructed from concentrating its efforts on questionable items nor barred from identifying such items either by inquiry of the taxpayer and his accountant or, more profitably, by inspection of relevant documents.

2. How would the world have changed if Amerada and Arthur Young had lost?

3. The following appearances of counsel are reported in this case:

Leona Sharpe, Asst. U.S. Atty., New York City (William M. Tendy, Acting U.S. Atty., S.D.N.Y., David M. Jones, Michael H. Dolinger, Asst. U.S. Attys., New York City, of counsel), for petitioner-appellee.

Carl D. Liggio, Gen. Counsel, New York City (John E. Matson, Richard I. Janvey, Associate Gen. Counsel, New York City, of counsel), for respondent-appellant Arthur Young & Co.

Robert G. Morvillo, New York City (Obermaier, Morvillo, Abramowitz, Milbank, Tweed, Hadley & McCloy, Roger B. Oresman, Russell E. Brooks, John C. Maloney, Jr., New York City, of counsel), for intervenor-respondent-appellant Amerada Hess Corp.

Willkie Farr & Gallagher, New York City (Kenneth J. Bialkin, Louis A. Craco, Howard C. Buschman, III, Diane K. G. Weeks, New York City, of counsel), for amicus curiae American Institute of Certified Public Accountants.

Donald Dreyfus, Chicago, Ill., for amicus curiae Arthur Andersen & Co.

James F. Strother, Chicago, Ill., for amicus curiae Alexander Grant & Co.

Harris J. Amhowitz, New York City, for amicus curiae Coopers & Lybrand.

Allan Kramer, New York City, for amicus curiae Deloitte Haskins & Sells.

Kenneth H. Lang, Cleveland, Ohio, for amicus curiae Ernst & Whinney.

Barry S. Augenbraun, Philadelphia, Pa., for amicus curiae Laventhol & Horwath.

Victor M. Earle, III, New York City, for amicus curiae Peat, Marwick, Mitchell & Co.

Eldon Olson, New York City, for amicus curiae Price Waterhouse & Co.

Richard A. Meyer, New York City, for amicus curiae Seidman & Seidman.

Richard H. Murray, New York City, for amicus curiae Touche Ross & Co.

What outcome in this case would you think was most desired by the upper-crust corporate bar of New York City?

4. To what extent should audit rules and practices for purposes of SEC regulation be made an affirmative part of the enforcement strategy of the IRS?

5. So what is privilege anyway?

Problem VI-12
Common Defense

Action against *D* Company and *E* Company for infringement of a *P* Company patent by a machine manufactured by *D* and used by *E*. *D*'s attorney submits a report to the *D* Company Executive Committee analyzing the patent and pertinent prior art and setting forth the strengths and weaknesses of *D*'s defense. May *D*'s lawyer share this and other privileged memoranda with *E*'s lawyer without waiving the privilege?

C. The Husband-Wife Privilege

Proposed FRE 505
Husband-Wife Privilege

(a) *General Rule of Privilege.* An accused in a criminal proceeding has a privilege to prevent his spouse from testifying against him.

(b) *Who May Claim the Privilege.* The privilege may be claimed by the accused or by the spouse on his behalf. The authority of the spouse to do so is presumed in the absence of evidence to the contrary.

(c) *Exceptions.* There is no privilege under this rule (1) in proceedings in which one spouse is charged with a crime against the person or property of the other or of a child of either, or with a crime against the person or property of a third person committed in the course of committing a crime against the other, or (2) as to matters occurring prior to the marriage, or (3) in proceedings in which a spouse is charged with importing an alien for prostitution or other immoral purpose in violation of 8 U.S.C. §1328, with transporting a female in interstate commerce for immoral purposes or other offense in violation of 18 U.S.C. §§2421-2424, or with violation of other similar statutes.

Problem VI-13
The Eternal Triangle

H and *W* have been married for seven years, but lately the grapes have begun to wither on the vine. In fact, *W* believes (correctly) that *H* is having an affair with *V*. *W* decides she must erase *V* from the picture. On the night of May 1, with the secret intention of confronting *V* about the affair, *W* tells *H* she is stepping out for a few hours to go to a friend's house. The next day, *V*'s body is found in a muddy field near her apartment. The body is riddled with stab wounds. An autopsy indicates *V* was killed the previous night.

At *W*'s trial for first-degree murder of *V*, *W* asserts that she was home during the night of the crime. The prosecution then calls *H* to testify that *W* had gone out alone that night and returned two hours later with a torn blouse and muddy shoes.

(1) Suppose *H* is more than happy to testify because he believes that *W* killed the woman he loves. The trial takes place in a jurisdiction that has

adopted Proposed Rule 505. W objects to H's testifying against her. What ruling and why? What rule of privilege would you favor in this situation? What social policies are involved in formulating a privilege rule for husband-wife testimony?

(2) Suppose the jurisdiction has adopted a spousal privilege that places the privilege in the hands of the witness spouse. Again, H is happy to testify. Does this change the result? What social policies militate for and against placing the privilege in the hands of the witness spouse rather than the accused? In this connection, see Trammel v. United States, 445 U.S. 40 (1980), which follows.

TRAMMEL v. UNITED STATES
445 U.S. 40 (1980)

Mr. Chief Justice BURGER delivered the opinion of the Court.

We granted certiorari to consider whether an accused may invoke the privilege against adverse spousal testimony so as to exclude the voluntary testimony of his wife. This calls for re-examination of Hawkins v. United States, 358 U.S. 74 (1958).

I

On March 10, 1976, petitioner Otis Trammel was indicted with two others, Edwin Lee Roberts and Joseph Freeman, for importing heroin into the United States from Thailand and the Philippine Islands and for conspiracy to import heroin in violation of 21 U.S.C. §§952(a), 962(a), and 963. The indictment also named six unindicted co-conspirators, including petitioner's wife Elizabeth Ann Trammel.

According to the indictment, petitioner and his wife flew from the Philippines to California in August 1975, carrying with them a quantity of heroin. Freeman and Roberts assisted them in its distribution. Elizabeth Trammel then travelled to Thailand where she purchased another supply of the drug. On November 3, 1975, with four ounces of heroin on her person, she boarded a plane for the United States. During a routine customs search in Hawaii, she was searched, the heroin was discovered, and she was arrested. After discussions with Drug Enforcement Administration agents, she agreed to cooperate with the Government.

Prior to trial on this indictment, petitioner moved to sever his case from that of Roberts and Freeman. He advised the court that the Government intended to call his wife as an adverse witness and asserted his claim to a privilege to prevent her from testifying against him. At a hearing on the motion, Mrs. Trammel was called as a Government witness under a grant of use immunity. She testified that she and petitioner were married in May 1975 and that they remained married.[1] She explained that her cooperation with the Government was based on assurances that she would be given lenient treatment.[2] She then described, in considerable detail, her role and that of her husband in the heroin distribution conspiracy.

After hearing this testimony, the District Court ruled that Mrs. Trammel could testify in support of the Government's case to any act she observed during the marriage and to any communication "made in the presence of a third person"; however, confidential communications between petitioner and his wife were held to be privileged and inadmissible. The motion to sever was denied.

At trial, Elizabeth Trammel testified within the limits of the court's pretrial ruling; her testimony, as the Government concedes, constituted virtually its entire case against petitioner. He was found guilty on both the substantive and conspiracy charges and sentenced to an indeterminate term of years pursuant to the Federal Youth Corrections Act, 18 U.S.C. §5010(b).

In the Court of Appeals petitioner's only claim of error was that the admission of the adverse testimony of his wife, over his objection, contravened this Court's teaching in Hawkins v. United States [358 U.S. 74 (1958)], supra, and therefore constituted reversible error. The Court of Appeals rejected this contention. It concluded that *Hawkins* did not prohibit "the voluntary testimony of a spouse who appears as an unindicted co-conspirator under grant of immunity from the Government in return for her testimony." 583 F.2d 1166, 1168 (C.A.10 1978).

II

The privilege claimed by petitioner has ancient roots. Writing in 1628, Lord Coke observed that "it hath beene resolved by the Justices that a wife cannot be produced either against or for her husband." 1 E. Coke, A Commentarie upon Littleton 6b (1628). See, generally, 8 J. Wigmore, Evidence §2227 (McNaughton rev. 1961). This spousal disqualification sprang from two canons of medieval jurisprudence: first, the rule that an accused was not permitted to testify in his own behalf because of his interest in the proceeding; second, the concept that husband and wife were one, and that since the woman had no recognized separate legal existence, the husband was that one. From those two now long-abandoned doctrines, it followed that what was inadmissible from the lips of the defendant husband was also inadmissible from his wife.

---

1. In response to the question whether divorce was contemplated, Mrs. Trammel testified that her husband had said that "I would go my way and he would go his."

2. The Government represents to the Court that Elizabeth Trammel has not been prosecuted for her role in the conspiracy.

Despite its medieval origins, this rule of spousal disqualification remained intact in most common-law jurisdictions well into the 19th century. See, 8 Wigmore, §2333. . . . [I]t was deemed so well established a proposition as to "hardly requir[e] mention." Indeed, it was not until 1933, in Funk v. United States, 290 U.S. 371, that this Court abolished the testimonial disqualification in the federal courts, so as to permit the spouse of a defendant to testify in the defendant's behalf. *Funk,* however, left undisturbed the rule that either spouse could prevent the other from giving adverse testimony. Id., at 373. The rule thus evolved into one of privilege rather than one of absolute disqualification. See J. Maguire, Evidence, Common Sense and Common Law, 78-92 (1947).

The modern justification for this privilege against adverse spousal testimony is its perceived role in fostering the harmony and sanctity of the marriage relationship. Notwithstanding this benign purpose, the rule was sharply criticized. Professor Wigmore termed it "the merest anachronism in legal theory and an indefensible obstruction to truth in practice." 8 Wigmore, §2228, at 221. The Committee on the Improvements in the Law of Evidence of the American Bar Association called for its abolition. 63 American Bar Association Reports, at 594-595 (1938). In its place, Wigmore, and others suggested a privilege protecting only private marital communications, modeled on the privilege between priest and penitent, attorney and client, and physician and patient. See 8 Wigmore, §2332 et seq.[5]

These criticisms influenced the American Law Institute, which, in its 1942 Model Code of Evidence advocated a privilege for marital confidences, but expressly rejected a rule vesting in the defendant the right to exclude all adverse testimony of his spouse. See American Law Institute, Model Code of Evidence, Rule 215 (1942). In 1953 the Uniform Rules of Evidence, drafted by the National Conference of Commissioners on Uniform State Laws, followed a similar course; it limited the privilege to confidential communications and "abolishe[d] the rule, still existing in some states, and largely a sentimental relic, of not requiring one spouse to testify against the other in a criminal action." See Rule 23(2) and comments. Several state legislatures enacted similarly patterned provisions into law.

In Hawkins v. United States, 358 U.S. 74 (1958), this Court considered the continued vitality of the privilege against adverse spousal testimony in the federal courts. There the District Court had permitted petitioner's wife, over his objection, to testify against him. With one questioning concurring opinion, the Court held the wife's testimony

---

5. This Court recognized just such a confidential marital communications privilege in Wolfle v. United States, 291 U.S. 7 (1934), and in Blau v. United States, 340 U.S. 332 (1951). In neither case, however, did the Court adopt the Wigmore view that the communications privilege be substituted *in place of* the privilege against adverse spousal testimony. The privilege as to confidential marital communications is not at issue in the instant case; accordingly, our holding today does not disturb *Wolfle* and *Blau.*

inadmissible; it took note of the critical comments that the common-law rule had engendered, id., at 76, and n.4, but chose not to abandon it. Also rejected was the Government's suggestion that the Court modify the privilege by vesting it in the witness-spouse, with freedom to testify or not independent of the defendant's control. The Court viewed this proposed modification as antithetical to the widespread belief, evidenced in the rules then in effect in a majority of the States and in England, "that the law should not force or encourage testimony which might alienate husband and wife, or further inflame existing domestic differences." Id., at 79.

Hawkins, then, left the federal privilege for adverse spousal testimony where it found it, continuing "a rule which bars the testimony of one spouse against the other unless both consent." Id., at 78. Accord, Wyatt v. United States, 362 U.S. 525, 528 (1960).[7] However, in so doing, the Court made clear that its decision was not meant to "foreclose whatever changes in the rule may eventually be dictated by 'reason and experience.' " 358 U.S., at 79.

III

A

The Federal Rules of Evidence acknowledge the authority of the federal courts to continue the evolutionary development of testimonial privileges in federal criminal trials "governed by the principles of the common law as they may be interpreted . . . in the light of reason and experience." Fed. Rul. Evid. 501. Cf. Wolfle v. United States, 291 U.S. 7, 12 (1934). The general mandate of Rule 501 was substituted by the Congress for a set of privilege rules drafted by the Judicial Conference Advisory Committee on Rules of Evidence and approved by the Judicial Conference of the United States and by this Court. That proposal defined nine specific privileges, including a husband-wife privilege which would have codified the *Hawkins* rule and eliminated the privilege for confidential marital communications. See proposed Fed. Rule Evid. 505. In rejecting the proposed rules and enacting Rule 501, Congress manifested an affirmative intention not to freeze the law of privilege. Its purpose rather was to "provide the courts with the flexibility to develop

7. The decision in *Wyatt* recognized an exception to *Hawkins* for cases in which one spouse commits a crime against the other. 362 U.S., at 526. This exception, placed on the ground of necessity, was a longstanding one at common law. See Lord Audley's Case, 123 Eng. Rep. 1140 (1931); 8 Wigmore §2239. It has been expanded since then to include crimes against the spouse's property, see Herman v. United States, 220 F.2d 219, 226 (C.A.4 1955), and in recent years crimes against children of either spouse. United States v. Allery, 526 F.2d 1362 (C.A.8 1975). Similar exceptions have been found to the confidential marital communications privilege. See 8 Wigmore, §2338.

rules of privilege on a case-by-case basis," 120 Cong. Rec. 40891 (1974) (statement of Rep. Hungate), and to leave the door open to change.

Although Rule 501 confirms the authority of the federal courts to reconsider the continued validity of the *Hawkins* rule, the long history of the privilege suggests that it ought not to be casually cast aside. That the privilege is one affecting marriage, home, and family relationships — already subject to much erosion in our day — also counsels caution. At the same time, we cannot escape the reality that the law on occasion adheres to doctrinal concepts long after the reasons which gave them birth have disappeared and after experience suggests the need for change. This was recognized in *Funk* where the Court "decline[d] to enforce . . . ancient rule[s] of the common law under conditions as they now exist." 290 U.S., at 382. For, as Mr. Justice Black admonished in another setting, "[w]hen precedent and precedent alone is all the argument that can be made to support a court-fashioned rule, it is time for the rule's creator to destroy it." Francis v. Southern Pacific Co., 333 U.S. 445, 471 (1948) (dissenting opinion).

B

Since 1958, when *Hawkins* was decided, support for the privilege against adverse spousal testimony has been eroded further. Thirty-one jurisdictions, including Alaska and Hawaii, then allowed an accused a privilege to prevent adverse spousal testimony, 358 U.S., at 81, n.3 (Stewart, J., concurring). The number has now declined to 24. In 1974, the National Conference on Uniform State Laws revised its Uniform Rules of Evidence, but again rejected the *Hawkins* rule in favor of a limited privilege for confidential communications. See Uniform Rules of Evidence, Rule 504. That proposed rule has been enacted in Arkansas, North Dakota, and Oklahoma — each of which in 1958 permitted an accused to exclude adverse spousal testimony. The trend in state law toward divesting the accused of the privilege to bar adverse spousal testimony has special relevance because the laws of marriage and domestic relations are concerns traditionally reserved to the states. See Sosna v. Iowa, 419 U.S. 393, 404 (1975). Scholarly criticism of the *Hawkins* rule has also continued unabated.

C

Testimonial exclusionary rules and privileges contravene the fundamental principle that "the public . . . has a right to every man's evidence." United States v. Bryan, 339 U.S. 323, 331 (1950). As such, they must be strictly construed and accepted "only to the very limited extent that permitting a refusal to testify or excluding relevant evidence has a public good transcending the normally predominant principle of utilizing all rational means for ascertaining truth." Elkins v. United States, 364 U.S. 206, 234 (1960) (Frankfurter, J., dissenting). Accord, United States v. Nixon, 418 U.S. 683, 709-710 (1974). Here we must decide whether the privilege against adverse spousal testimony promotes sufficiently important interests to outweigh the need for probative evidence in the administration of criminal justice.

It is essential to remember that the *Hawkins* privilege is not needed to protect information privately disclosed between husband and wife in the confidence of the marital relationship — once described by this Court as "the best solace of human existence." Stein v. Bowman 13 Pet., at 223. Those confidences are privileged under the independent rule protecting confidential marital communications. Blau v. United States, 340 U.S. 332 (1951); see n.5, supra. The *Hawkins* privilege is invoked, not to exclude private marital communications, but rather to exclude evidence of criminal acts and of communications made in the presence of third persons.

No other testimonial privilege sweeps so broadly. The privileges between priest and penitent, attorney and client, and physician and patient limit protection to private communications. These privileges are rooted in the imperative need for confidence and trust. The priest-penitent privilege recognizes the human need to disclose to a spiritual counselor, in total and absolute confidence, what are believed to be flawed acts or thoughts and to receive priestly consolation and guidance in return. The lawyer-client privilege rests on the need for the advocate and counselor to know all that relates to the client's reasons for seeking representation if the professional mission is to be carried out. Similarly, the physician must know all that a patient can articulate in order to identify and to treat disease; barriers to full disclosure would impair diagnosis and treatment.

The *Hawkins* rule stands in marked contrast to these three privileges. Its protection is not limited to confidential communications; rather it permits an accused to exclude all adverse spousal testimony. As Jeremy Bentham observed more than a century and a half ago, such a privilege goes far beyond making "every man's house his castle," and permits a person to convert his house into "a den of thieves." 5 Rationale of Judicial Evidence 340 (1827). It "secures, to every man, one safe and unquestionable and every ready [sic] accomplice for every imaginable crime." Id., at 338.

The ancient foundations for so sweeping a privilege have long since disappeared. Nowhere in the common-law world — indeed in any modern society — is a woman regarded as chattel or demeaned by denial of a separate legal identity and the dignity associated with recognition as a whole human being. Chip by chip, over the years those archaic notions have been cast aside so that "[n]o longer is the female destined solely for the home and the rearing of the family, and only the male for the marketplace and the world of ideas." Stanton v. Stanton, 421 U.S. 7, 14, 15 (1975).

The contemporary justification for affording an accused such a privilege is also unpersuasive. When one spouse is willing to testify against the other in a criminal proceeding — whatever the motivation — their relationship is almost certainly in disrepair; there is probably little in the way of marital harmony for the privilege to preserve. In these circumstances, a rule of evidence that permits an accused to prevent adverse spousal testimony seems far more likely to frustrate justice than to foster family peace. Indeed, there is reason to believe that vesting the privilege in the accused could actually undermine the marital relationship. For example, in a case such as this the Government is unlikely to offer a wife immunity and lenient treatment if it knows that her husband can prevent her from giving adverse testimony. If the Government is dissuaded from making such an offer, the privilege can have the untoward effect of permitting one spouse to escape justice at the expense of the other. It hardly seems conducive to the preservation of the marital relation to place a wife in jeopardy solely by virtue of her husband's control over her testimony.

IV

Our consideration of the foundations for the privilege and its history satisfy us that "reason and experience" no longer justify so sweeping a rule as that found acceptable by the Court in *Hawkins*. Accordingly, we conclude that the existing rule should be modified so that the witness spouse alone has a privilege to refuse to testify adversely; the witness may be neither compelled to testify nor foreclosed from testifying. This modification — vesting the privilege in the witness-spouse — furthers the important public interest in marital harmony without unduly burdening legitimate law enforcement needs.

Here, petitioner's spouse chose to testify against him. That she did so after a grant of immunity and assurances of lenient treatment does not render her testimony involuntary. Cf. Bordenkircher v. Hayes, 434 U.S. 357 (1978). Accordingly, the District Court and the Court of Appeals were correct in rejecting petitioner's claim of privilege, and the judgment of the Court of Appeals is affirmed.

Affirmed.

What justifications for the discarded *Hawkins* rule of spousal exclusion can you articulate that are not discussed by the Court in *Trammel*? Are they persuasive enough to support retention of the *Hawkins* rule? Should the Court have gone further and abolished completely the testimonial spousal privilege, rather than merely shifting it to the witness spouse, thus limiting the spousal privilege to one covering confidential communications?

Should the husband-wife testimonial privilege be expanded to embrace other members of the family? When, if ever, should a father be forced to testify against his child, for example? What values support the privilege recognized in *Trammel*? What is their generative power? Should the *Trammel* privilege be extended to common law marriages, homosexual relationships, and best friends?

Problem VI-14
Home, Sweet Home

Leo and Mickie have been living together in Beverly Hills for 10 years. They have a seven-year-old daughter, Elissa. Leo is charged with assault and battery on Elissa on June 1. On June 30 Leo and Mickie are married by a justice of the peace in Las Vegas, Nevada. At Leo's trial on July 30 the state calls Mickie to testify as to what she witnessed on June 1.

(1) Leo objects. Under proposed Rule 505, what ruling and why?

(2) Mickie objects. Under *Trammel*, what ruling and why?

Problem VI-15
Bits and Pieces

Charge: murder of *V*, *D*'s father-in-law, on June 1. M.O.: bludgeoning with a blunt instrument, dismemberment with a sharp one, and burial in the backyard of her home. The jurisdiction's spousal privilege states that "in every case, the husband or wife of either party shall be deemed a competent witness, provided that neither shall be permitted to disclose any private communication made to him or her by the other during their marriage, except on trials of petitions for divorce between them or trials between them involving their respective property rights."

(1) At trial, the district attorney proposes that *D*'s husband, *H*, testify for the prosecution, over *D*'s objection, that he asked *D* on June 2 where his father was and *D* said, "I killed him and chopped him up into a hundred pieces." Admissible?

(2) *H* testifies that *D*, in response to his question, "Where is Poppa?," showed *H* the 100 pieces of his father that *D* had hidden in a trunk. Admissible?

(3) *H* testifies that on June 1 he was reading in the living room. *D* carried a trunk up from the basement, said "Hi, dear," proceeded to drag the trunk through the living room and out to the backyard, and buried it. Admissible?

(4) *H* testifies that he was asleep in bed the night of June 1. He woke up and noticed that *D* was not beside him. He got out of bed and as he passed the bedroom window saw *D* in the moonlight furtively digging in the backyard. *H* got back into bed and pretended he was asleep. About a half hour later, *D* crept back to bed. *D* never mentioned the matter to *H*, and *H* never raised it with *D*. Admissible?

Problem VI-16
The Set-Up

Section 2054 of State S's penal code prohibits carrying concealed weapons unless one reasonably fears an attack from an enemy. *D* is charged with violating §2054 by carrying a derringer pistol. At trial, *D* proposes to testify that *W*, his wife, told him confidentially before he armed himself that she was having an affair with *X* who loved her so much he was going to kill *D*.

The prosecution objects to *D*'s testimony. *W*, in court, objects as well. Is the testimony admissible?

CHAPTER VII

Opinions, Scientific Proof, and Expert Testimony

Expert opinion poses special problems for courts because it deals with problems of factual inquiry that exceed the ordinary competence of the tribunal and therefore threaten its credibility and control. But as long as our system depends on lay juries and judges, the use of experts will require nonexperts to judge experts and define the boundaries of their expertise.

This chapter presents the range of issues that this problem raises. First, the specificity with which a lay witness must testify is examined. Testimony at either too great a level of generality or too great a level of detail can carry the witness into the domain in which he must be qualified as an expert. Next examined are the questions of what makes a subject appropriate for expert testimony and what makes a witness an expert in the subject. New fields of expertise such as polygraphy (lie detection), spectrography (voiceprint identification), and hypnotic memory enhancement pose serious conceptual and practical problems for courts and juries. Next, the problem of examining expert witnesses is addressed — how they may testify on direct and what weapons may be used against them on cross. Unlike other witnesses, experts are teachers; there is art in being a good teacher, and art in destroying one. The chapter ends with a discussion of court-appointed experts, a remarkably underutilized instrument of judicial administration considering the tremendous problems that adversarial experts pose for factfinders.

How well suited is our court system to the task of resolving disputes involving complex technical or scientific issues, given its present focus on adversarial presentation to lay jurors and judges? What reforms would you suggest to promote efficiency, fairness, and rationality in the resolution of such cases? What dangers lurk in increased use of experts at trial?

A. Lay Opinions

FRE 701
Opinion Testimony by Lay Witnesses

If the witness is not testifying as an expert, his testimony in the form of opinions or inferences is limited to those opinions or inferences which are (a) rationally based on the perception of the witness and (b) helpful to a clear understanding of his testimony or the determination of a fact in issue.

NOTE: THE CONVERGENCE OF FACT AND OPINION

Note that FRE 701 does not require a lay witness to limit himself to statements of fact, as opposed to statements of opinion or inference. The following excerpt from W. King and D. Pillinger, Opinion Evidence in Illinois 3-4 (1942), an article that was highly influential with the draftsmen, explains why.

> When you look at the object on which you are sitting and say "chair" the sound "chair" is obviously not the object "chair." You can't sit on the noise "chair." The word is only your racial and individual response to the pressure of the object on your buttocks and the light beams from the object upon your optic nerves when you look down at it. The word "chair" isn't the fact "chair."
>
> You can perceive a simple thing like a chair in many aspects. You can see it as a piece of furniture constituting with other pieces the furnishings in your room, or as an article of wood and upholstering designed to accommodate a person in a sitting position. A close examination might disclose to the expert that it was a Grand Rapids chair made since 1910. A microscopic examination would disclose the cellular character of the material from which it was made and possibly the locality where that wood was grown, the age of the trees from which it was cut, and (if you were sufficiently interested) the particular tools which have been used in cutting it and which have left their marks upon it. In a sense, however, the ultimate reality of this chair is far beyond your perceptions even with a microscope. Submicroscopically, you know from what science has told you that this chair consists of a mad dance of electrons which you cannot see just as you cannot see the blades of your electric fan when it is running. But which of these various perceptions of the chair is The Fact? Obviously any one of them is just as much (and just as little) a fact as the others. Each of us sees different "facts" in everything we look at. We are surrounded by a world of objective reality which we call facts. But as soon as we try to translate any part of that world into language it ceases to be facts and becomes thoughts.
>
> So, when our judge instructs the witness to state the facts it is as though we demanded that the witness fly by flapping his arms. The witness can't state

facts and neither can the judge — facts are unspeakable and unstatable. We can't reproduce in language either reality or our perception of reality. All statements in language are statements of opinion, i.e., statements of mental processes or perceptions. So-called "statements of fact" are only more specific statements of opinion. What the judge means to say, when he asks the witness to state the facts, is: The nature of this case requires you to be more specific, if you can, in your description of what you saw.

Just how specific a judge should require a witness to be will depend greatly on how central the matter about which the witness is testifying is to the resolution of the case:

> Ordinarily, in a law suit, you would be permitted to testify that this object was a chair. But if the suit were an action to collect a tax on chairs, if the kernel of the controversy was whether the object was a chair, your statement that this was a chair would be rejected as your opinion and you would be asked to "state the facts" regarding the object. In other words, the legal concept of what is a statement of fact and what is a statement of opinion varies with the issues in the case. Id.

The rule, then, is meant to encourage witnesses to speak in a natural way at a level of specificity helpful to the fact finder. For example, witnesses anxious not to overstate their testimony often qualify what they are saying by adding, "I think," or "I believe." Does this indicate that their statements are impermissible opinions under Rule 701 or not based on first-hand knowledge as required by FRE 602? The question cannot be answered dogmatically. As the rule indicates, the judge must decide whether the witness is speaking from personal knowledge, and whether the testimony, as qualified, will be helpful. As Dean Ladd states:

> Closely associated with expression of facts in terms of inference is the statement of facts as the impression of the witness. Illustrative of these expressions are, "I think," "I believe," "my impression is," "I cannot be positive, but I think," "to the best of my recollection," or "it is my understanding." The admissibility of testimony accompanied by such limitations involves the same fundamental issue to be considered when permitting the witness to testify in terms of inference, namely, is the witness speaking from his personal knowledge or is his testimony only a mental speculation. Not infrequently such precautionary statements may strengthen the testimony because they indicate that the witness does not want to overstate the facts. On the other hand, such statements may indicate that his recollection is poor which would weaken the testimony but not exclude it. Only when it appears that the witness has not personally perceived the matter about which he testifies will the testimony be excluded.

Ladd, Expert and Other Opinion Testimony, 40 Minn. L. Rev. 437, 440 (1956). See 3 Weinstein and Berger, Weinstein's Evidence 701-15 to 701-18 at ¶710[02] (1981).

Problem VII-1
Mrs. Jones's Baby

W testifies, "I saw Mrs. Jones about three hundred yards away walking with her baby in her arms." Opposing counsel objects on the grounds of opinion testimony. What ruling and why? Would the ruling be any different if *W* were unavailable at trial and her statement were offered through another witness under an applicable exception to the hearsay rule, such as Rule 804(b)(1) (former testimony)?

Problem VII-2
Presidential Debate

Suppose that you were asked to watch and then testify about a presidential debate. What could you say about how each candidate looked and sounded without violating Rule 701?

Problem VII-3
Murder at the Hotel Thoreau

Action by *P*, executor of *I*'s estate, against *D* Insurance Company, to recover on *I*'s life insurance policy. At trial evidence is introduced to show that *I* was behind in his premium payments and the policy was due to lapse at midnight, May 31. *I*'s body was found in shallow waters of the Concord River the morning of June 1. The crucial issue at trial is the time of *I*'s death.

(1) *P* calls *W*, the night clerk at the Hotel Thoreau, an inn near the Concord River. *W* testifies that *I* checked in on May 31 at 10 P.M., went to his room, and reappeared in the lobby at 11 P.M. The following dialogue then ensues:

Q: Did you observe *I*'s expression?
A: Yes.
Q: What was it?
A: An expression of ineffable sadness.
By defense counsel: Objection. Move to strike. The witness is giving an opinion.
Court: Denied.
Q: Did you observe *I*'s conduct at that time?
A: Yes.
Q: What was it?
A: *I* acted disoriented.
By defense counsel: Objection. Move to strike. The witness is giving an opinion.

Court: Sustained.

Q: What did *I* do?

A: He paced up and down the room, twirled the revolving door, went out, and walked up and down the sidewalk several times, bumping into two or three people when they came by.

How can you reconcile the two rulings by the court?

(2) *Y* is called by *D* and testifies to discovering *I*'s body at 7 A.M. on June 1. The following dialogue then ensues:

Q: Please describe the appearance of the body when you found it.

A: The stomach was bloated, the skin blue, there was blood coming from the nose and froth coming from the mouth. The whole body was stiff as a board.

Q: How long would you say the person had been dead?

A: About eight hours.

By plaintiff's counsel: Objection. Move to strike. The witness is giving an opinion.

What ruling and why?

COMMONWEALTH v. CAVALIER
284 Pa. 311, 131 A. 229 (1925)

SCHAFFER, J. Counsel for appellant, prosecuting this appeal from a conviction of murder of the first degree, call to our attention the fact that at the time of the commission of the crime their client was a boy not quite six months past the age of fourteen years, and contend that he was not mentally responsible for his crime; also that the record discloses trial errors which should cause us to set the verdict aside. The killing was cold-blooded, premeditated and atrocious, as the confession of the defendant discloses. Telling of its circumstances, he said:

I was sitting out on the back porch when I first thought about killing my grandmother; she was out in the yard. I then went upstairs and got the 22 calibre rifle out of her room, also some cartridges. I then went downstairs and sat down in a rocking chair until she came in and went upstairs, then I followed her up about five minutes later. The door of her room was open and she was standing at the foot of the bed, sort of sideways. She did not see me as I didn't make any noise going up the stairs. I was standing in the room next to hers in the doorway when I shot her the first time; I aimed for her head; she fell over on the floor. I stood there for a few minutes, then I walked into her room and fired another shot into her body as she was lying on the floor. I then searched her clothes and found her pocketbook in the pocket of her dress, I took the money out and threw the pocketbook in the closet of the room. I put the rifle back in the corner where she always kept it, went downstairs, locking the door of her room when I left it, putting the key in a little bowl on the shelf in the room next to hers. I put some toilet paper in her mouth, as she was lying on the floor, because she was moaning. She was taking off her shoes when I shot her. After I went downstairs I cut the screen in the kitchen window. After cutting the screen I shook the blood off my right hand onto the wall near the door, then I washed my hands and went out on the porch and sat down until my grandfather came home. I told him that grandmother went away. I left the house about half past four and went to my mother's home on First Street and had supper and then went to the movies and after the movies went home and went to bed. Before going to bed I put the money in a pillow under the mattress. . . .

The defense attempted to be made for appellant is that he was mentally incompetent and insane at the time of the killing. To meet this defense, the Commonwealth called, among other witnesses, Dr. Albert P. Knight, who in answer to a hypothetical question gave it as his professional opinion that the defendant knew the nature and quality of his act and could distinguish between right and wrong. It is urged that this doctor was not competent to express an opinion. The witness was a practicing physician, a graduate of the University of Pennsylvania, and at the time of the trial had been engaged in the practice of his profession for some four or five years. He was at no time connected with an institution having for its main purpose the treatment of mental diseases and had not seen very many cases of insanity. He had, as a part of his medical education, studied the subject of insanity and would appear to have at least the general knowledge of the subject that the ordinary medical practitioner has.

The question of the competency of a witness to testify as an expert is usually for the discretion of the trial court, and we are not convinced that there was an abuse of discretion in receiving the testimony. "It is not necessary that one should be a professed psychiatrist or alienist, in order that his expert opinion may be received. A physician and surgeon who has come in contact with a number of cases of insanity in his general practice may express an opinion as to the sanity of the defendant." Trickett's Criminal Law (1908), vol. 2, p.721. "A general family practitioner may be received to give an opinion, whatever may be its weight, as to whatever comes within the range of such practice." Wharton's Criminal Evidence (10th ed., 1912), vol. 1, p.841. It would be an impracticable thing to lay down a hard and fast rule as to how much experience a practicing physician must have had with insane persons to qualify him to speak as an expert. We think the determination of this question is wisely left with the trial judge, who has the witness before him and is better competent than we are to judge of his capacity to express an opinion. 22 Corpus Juris, p.526. The weight to be given his opinion is, of course, for the jury.

Challenge is made in the third assignment of error of the ruling of the court against the admissibility of the opinion of Carrie Walker, a witness called by the defense, as to the sanity or mental condition of appellant. This witness was the matron of the House of Detention, where defendant was kept, following the commission of the crime, and she had observed him daily during that period. She testified to certain facts concerning his conduct; that he would whistle, but never in tune, that he fought constantly with the other children in the Detention House, including those who were younger than himself, that if she said anything to him, he would not disobey, but would walk upstairs and would not eat, that he did not show any remorse for his act, that he made faces at himself constantly in the mirror and made faces at her, that he told her he saw a ghost, which turned out to be a white garment in a closet. The court excluded her testimony as to the mental condition of the defendant on the ground that the facts to which she testified were not sufficient upon which to base an opinion as to the mental condition of the defendant, that none of them, nor all of them together, indicated insanity. While the cases in this jurisdiction may not be in accord on the question of the admissibility of the opinion of a nonexpert witness as to insanity or mental condition and there are cases like Taylor v. Com., 109 Pa. 262, where it is said, at page 270, that the evidence of such witnesses is receivable after they have testified to acts and conversations which they deem sufficient to found an opinion upon, and that it is for the jury to decide whether the acts and conversations justified the conclusions, nevertheless we think the wise and proper rule is that such opinion testimony should not be received unless, in the opinion of the trial judge, the facts testified to were sufficient upon which to base an opinion. "But when a [lay] witness is offered to express the opinion that the prisoner was sane or insane, he must state facts observed by him, that, in the judgment of the court, tend to justify the opinion which he is about to express. Having done this, he may say whether, in his opinion, the defendant was conscious of his purposes, but until he does it, his opinion is properly excluded." The facts testified to by this witness did not to the trial judge and do not to us indicate insanity in the defendant, but rather the actions of a bad boy; therefore the court properly excluded the opinion testimony of this witness. The ruling of the court as to another witness, Robert Walker, husband of the preceding one, who testified to having observed the same acts of the defendant which were testified to by the wife, was proper for the reasons given in disposing of the contention relative to his wife's testimony.

We think possibly that much of the confusion in the cases may be ascribed to the failure to distinguish between different situations obtaining when witnesses are called to testify, on the one hand, that they have noticed nothing which leads them to believe that a person was of unsound mind, and, on the other, that in their opinion a person was insane. A lay witness, who has had contact with one whose mental state is the subject of inquiry, may testify, after stating his opportunities for observation but without first stating all the facts justifying his conclusion, that he has observed nothing in the conduct or speech of the individual which would lead to the opinion that he is not of normal mind. It is one thing to have lay witnesses thus testify and quite a different situation to have them give an opinion, after the recital of facts coming under their observation, that a person was insane. In the latter case, if the facts testified to would not warrant the conclusion of insanity, it would be irrational to permit the witness to pronounce the conclusion. The jury, having the facts before them indicating no insanity, could not, except perversely, come to the conclusion that the given individual was insane.

JOHN HANCOCK MUTUAL LIFE INSURANCE CO. v. DUTTON
585 F.2d 1289 (5th Cir. 1978)

CLARK, J. As a result of a domestic quarrel between Wensley Sheley and his wife Mamie Ann, Mr. Sheley was fatally wounded. John Hancock Mutual Life Insurance Company insured Sheley's life. John Hancock disputed its liability under an accidental death provision of the policy in the portion of the action tried to a jury. . . .

I.   THE LIABILITY OF JOHN HANCOCK

A.   THE FACTS

Wensley Sheley married Mamie Ann Sheley on September 7, 1974. Their relationship was characterized by frequent violent quarrels. Prior to their marriage, Mr. Sheley had held a gun to Mrs. Sheley's head, while she, then his landlady, was trying to collect rent. During the marriage, Mrs. Sheley was the victim of a number of beatings at the hands of Mr. Sheley, and, on various occasions, he threatened and attempted to shoot her and to run over her with a car. The Sheleys decided their differences could not be resolved and sought a divorce. Mr. Sheley demanded that Mrs. Sheley return his rings and, when she refused, he threatened to cut off her finger with his Boy Scout knife. Their divorce became final on January 7, 1975.

Subsequently, Mrs. Sheley entered a hospital because of injuries received in an automobile accident. During her convalescence, Mr. Sheley visited her daily. The Sheleys were remarried on March 3, 1975.

The series of events that culminated in Mr. Sheley's death occurred on March 15, 1975, just twelve days after the second marriage. On that evening, the Sheleys left their home in Claxton, Georgia, to attend a motion picture theater. Mr. Sheley had been drinking heavily that afternoon and continued to drink during the movie. On the return trip, Mr. Sheley stopped and bought some french fried potatoes for Mrs. Sheley. He became angry when Mrs. Sheley refused to eat them, and the argument continued after the Sheleys had arrived at their home. Mrs. Sheley's daughters heard the quarreling and entered the Sheleys' bedroom to check on their mother. The daughters became involved in the argument, and Mr. Sheley made a threatening remark to one of them. He then removed a gun case from under his bed and began unsheathing a shotgun which Mrs. Sheley knew was loaded. Already fearful because of Mr. Sheley's prior assaults, she had acquired a pistol. Mr. Sheley knew she possessed the pistol. As he removed the shotgun, Mrs. Sheley took her pistol from her purse and shot him. A policeman called to the scene testified that Mr. Sheley, before his death, said, "I didn't think she'd shoot me."

John Hancock had issued two policies of ordinary life insurance on Mr. Sheley's life in the total amount of $26,000. The policies also provided for the payment of double indemnity benefits in the event of accidental death. . . . The jury found John Hancock liable for the accidental death proceeds. John Hancock then moved for judgment notwithstanding the verdict and, in the alternative, for a new trial. The district court denied these motions. John Hancock appeals these rulings.

B. THE ACCIDENTAL DEATH ISSUE

John Hancock urges that . . . the substantive law of Georgia requires that reasonable men must find that Mr. Sheley's death was not accidental. In Georgia, in order to recover on an accidental death policy, a claimant must show that the act causing the insured's death was "unforeseen, unexpected, or unusual." Even when the insured is the aggressor in a situation, a claimant can still recover under an accidental death clause if he can show that the insured reasonably believed that the victim of his aggression would not kill him. . . . The Georgia courts have applied this rule in domestic quarrels. . . .

John Hancock contends that Mr. Sheley must have anticipated that Mrs. Sheley might shoot him since (1) it was the first quarrel in which Mrs. Sheley was armed, (2) Mr. Sheley knew that she was armed, and (3) it was the first time Mr. Sheley had threatened one of Mrs. Sheley's daughters.

We reject John Hancock's arguments. . . . The Georgia cases clearly establish that in determining whether the insured's death is accidental, the controlling fact is the husband's reasonable beliefs concerning his wife's reaction to his aggression. In light of the Georgia law, reasonable men might have concluded from the facts in this case that Mr. Sheley's death was accidental. The district court was correct in denying John Hancock's motion for judgment notwithstanding the verdict.

C.   GAIL BELL'S TESTIMONY

John Hancock contends that the district judge erred in admitting the testimony of one of Mrs. Sheley's daughters, Gail Bell, to the effect that she did not believe that Mr. Sheley thought that Mrs. Sheley would ever shoot him. John Hancock urges that (1) the testimony was irrelevant, and (2) in any event, Bell was unqualified to testify as to Mr. Sheley's subjective feelings. . . .

Under Georgia law, a claimant must, in order to receive benefits under an accidental death policy, show that the insured believed that his victim would not kill him and that this belief was reasonable. Thus, Bell's testimony was relevant to an issue of consequence in this case.

John Hancock also urges that the admission of Bell's testimony violates Federal Rules of Evidence 602 and 701. Rule 602 requires that "a witness may not testify to a matter unless evidence is introduced sufficient to support a finding that he has personal knowledge of the matter." Rule 701 limits the opinion testimony of lay witnesses to "those opinions or inferences which are (a) rationally based on the perception of the witness and (b) helpful to a clear understanding of his testimony or the determination of a fact in issue." John Hancock contends that Bell could not have had personal knowledge of Mr. Sheley's subjective state of mind and that Bell's opinions were therefore not rationally based upon her perceptions.

We reject John Hancock's views concerning Rules 602 and 701. Under John Hancock's construction, a witness could never testify to his views concerning the feelings of another person. As Dean Wigmore has stated:

> The argument has been made that, because we cannot directly see, hear, or feel the state of another person's mind, therefore testimony to another person's state of mind is based on merely conjectural and therefore inadequate data. This argument is finical enough; and it proves too much, for if valid it would forbid the jury to find a verdict upon the supposed state of a person's mind. If they are required and allowed to find such a fact, it is not too much to hear such testimony from a witness who has observed the person exhibiting in his conduct the operations of his mind.

2 J. Wigmore, Wigmore on Evidence, §661 at 773-74 (3d ed. 1940). When, as here, the witness observes first hand the altercation in question, her opinions on the feelings of the parties are based on her personal knowledge and rational perceptions and are helpful to the jury.

The Rules require nothing more for admission of the testimony. The district court did not abuse its discretion in admitting Bell's testimony.

B. Law Opinions

MARX & CO., INC. v. DINERS CLUB, INC.
550 F.2d 505 (2nd Cir. 1977)

GURFEIN, J. This appeal by the Diners' Club, Inc. and Diners/Fugazy Travel, Inc. (collectively "Diners") arises out of a series of transactions whereby the Fugazys sold the assets of their company, Fugazy Travel Bureau, Inc. ("Fugazy Travel") to Diners Club in return for unregistered stock in the latter company. The Fugazys, plaintiffs below, allege that the defendants fraudulently induced the sale, in violation of §10(b) of the Securities Exchange Act of 1934 and Rule 10b-5 thereunder, by representing that defendant Continental Corporation was about to "take over" Diners and that the failure of Diners to use its best efforts to make effective a registration of plaintiffs' shares was part of a manipulative device to induce the plaintiffs not to offer their shares for sale from October 10, 1967 to February 6, 1970. The court ultimately submitted to the jury whether Diners breached *its contractual obligation* to use its best efforts to register the plaintiffs' stock. . . .

The jury found against Diners on these contentions. We agree with Judge Ward that there was sufficient evidence to support the verdict. Marx & Co., Inc. v. Diners Club, Inc., 400 F. Supp. 581 (S.D.N.Y. 1975). The crucial issue, sufficiently posed by objection below, is whether, notwithstanding the general discretion allowed to trial judges respecting expert testimony, the admission of the testimony of a securities law expert, Stanley Friedman, was, in the circumstances, an error of law and highly prejudicial. His testimony construed the contract, as a matter of law, and includes his opinion that the defenses of Diners were unacceptable as a matter of law. . . .

We hold that the District Court erred in permitting Friedman, an expert witness called by plaintiffs, to give his opinion as to the legal obligations of the parties under the contract. Mr. Friedman, a lawyer and a witness not named in the pretrial order, was called as a rebuttal witness on the last day of a three-week trial. Friedman was qualified as an expert in securities regulation, and therefore was competent to explain to the jury the step-by-step practices ordinarily followed by lawyers and corporations in shepherding a registration statement through the SEC. Indeed, Friedman had done so as an expert witness on previous occasions. In Republic Technology Fund, Inc. v. Lionel Corp., 483 F.2d 540,

552 (2d Cir. 1973), this Circuit reversed the dismissal of a breach of contract claim that the defendant had failed to cause a registration statement to become effective within a reasonable time. 483 F.2d at 552. The issue there was whether a delay of one year before the S-1 became effective was a result of an originally misleading interim statement accompanying the S-1, in which event, "the delay may well have been unreasonable." Id. Mr. Friedman gave expert testimony that six to eight weeks was all that should have been necessary to effectuate a registration statement because "much of the work going into it had already been done" in the preparation of a proxy solicitation filed by the surviving corporation in a merger. This testimony concerned the practices of lawyers and others engaged in the securities business.[10] Testimony concerning the ordinary practices of those engaged in the securities business is admissible under the same theory as testimony concerning the ordinary practices of physicians or concerning other trade customs: to enable the jury to evaluate the conduct of the parties against the standards of ordinary practice in the industry. See VII Wigmore on Evidence §1949, at 66 (3d ed. 1940).

In the case at bar, however, witness Friedman's objectionable testimony did *not* concern only the customary practices of a trade or business. Rather, he gave his opinion as to the legal standards which he believed to be derived from the contract and which should have governed Diners' conduct. He testified not so much as to common practice as to what was necessary "to fulfill the covenant" [of the contract]. For example, over the objection of defense counsel, he said that:

> I construe "best efforts" in the context of a covenant to register shares as the assumption on the part of the person who gives the covenant *an absolute, unconditional responsibility,* to set to work promptly and diligently to do everything that would have to be done to make the registration statement effective . . . (emphasis added).

Counsel made timely objection — "that's a legal conclusion." Similarly, the witness opined that "the best efforts obligations requires you to pursue the registration statement unless there is cause beyond your control." This testimony did not concern practices in the securities business, on which Friedman was qualified as an expert, but were rather legal opinions as to the meaning of the contract terms at issue. It was testimony concerning matters outside his area of expertise. See Federal

---

10. In the *Republic Technology* case Mr. Friedman gave testimony concerning the practices of people engaged in this business: that it would be the practice of a prudent lawyer to research blue sky laws prior to the issuance of securities, that it would be unprofitable business practice to cause a registration statement to become effective prior to an imminent merger, and that the ordinary practice of the SEC would be to refer the registration statement to the same SEC staff that had handled the proxy solicitations of the company.

Rule of Evidence 702. Moreover, it would not have been possible to render this testimony admissible by qualifying Friedman as an "expert in contract law." It is not for witnesses to instruct the jury as to applicable principles of law, but for the judge. As Professor Wigmore has observed, expert testimony on law is excluded because "the tribunal does not need the witness' judgment. . . . [T]he *judge* (or the jury as instructed by the judge) can determine equally well. . . ." The special legal knowledge of the judge makes the witness' testimony superfluous. VII Wigmore on Evidence §1952, at 81. . . .

Not only did Friedman construe the contract, but he also repeatedly gave his conclusions as to the legal significance of various facts adduced at trial. He testified on direct examination that, pursuant to its contractual obligation, Diners Club "should have" filed its registration on or about June 20, 1969, and not at the end of August, and therefore concluded that Diners Club did *not* use its best efforts promptly to file. He asserted that it would not be a *legal* excuse (1) that Diners' employees may have been occupied in other activities, or (2) that the parties to the contract were simultaneously attempting to renegotiate the contract, — "Therefore, I don't see that it excuses performance" — or (3) that plaintiffs had failed to advance one-half of the costs of the registration. He also gave it as his legal opinion that the fact that the parties were exploring alternatives was not a *legal* waiver by the plaintiffs of the requirement that Diners go forward.

Friedman was also permitted to testify, over objection, that correspondence between the litigants relating to the payment of one-half the cost of registration by the plaintiffs, including a letter to plaintiff Marx dated July 15, was irrelevant "because the registration statement would have been filed by approximately June 20th and therefore this question comes up very much after the fact." Friedman himself conceded that his opinions were based in part on his "experience and use of the English language." His conclusion that Diners Club had no *legal* excuses for nonperformance was based merely on his examination of documents and correspondence, which were equally before the judge and jury. Thus Friedman's opinion testimony was superfluous. See VII Wigmore on Evidence, §1918. As Professor McCormick notes, such testimony "amounts to no more than an expression of the [witness'] general belief as to how the case should be decided." McCormick on Evidence, §12 at 26-27. The admission of such testimony would give the appearance that the court was shifting to witnesses the responsibility to decide the case. McCormick on Evidence §12, at 27. It is for the jury to evaluate the facts in the light of the applicable rules of law, and it is therefore erroneous for a witness to state his opinion on the law of the forum. Loeb v. Hammond, supra. . . . The applicable law, not being foreign law, could, in no sense, be a question of fact to be decided by the jury.

The limits of expert testimony in securities cases should not be too difficult to draw. While the able trial judge below recognized that "testimony in the form of an opinion or inference otherwise admissible is not objectionable because it embraces an ultimate issue to be decided by the trier of fact," Fed. R. Ev. 704, he failed, in our view, sufficiently to emphasize "otherwise admissible." With the growth of intricate securities litigation over the past forty years, we must be especially careful not to allow trials before juries to become battles of paid advocates posing as experts on the respective sides concerning matters of domestic law. See La Chemise Lacoste v. Alligator Company, Inc., 59 F.R.D. 332, 333 (D. Del. 1973).

The basis of expert capacity, according to Wigmore (§555), may "be summed up in the term 'experience.'" But experience is hardly a qualification for construing a document for its legal effect when there is a knowledgeable gentleman in a robe whose exclusive province it is to instruct the jury on the law. The danger is that the jury may think that the "expert" in the particular branch of the law knows more than the judge — surely an inadmissible inference in our system of law.

Recognizing that an expert may testify to an ultimate fact, and to the practices and usage of a trade, we think care must be taken lest, in the field of securities law, he be allowed to usurp the function of the judge. In our view, the practice of using experts in securities cases must not be permitted to expand to such a point, and hence we must reluctantly conclude that the leeway allowed Friedman was highly prejudicial to the appellant.

———————

If jurors are regarded capable of determining conflicts in expert testimony in all other recognized areas of knowledge, e.g., medicine, statistics, literature, physics, why should law be different? The *Marx* court says: "The danger is that the jury may think that the 'expert' in the particular branch of the law knows more than the judge — surely an inadmissible inference in our system of law." Why is the inference inadmissible? Whom is the court kidding?

Problem VII-4
Wolfman's Law

Consider the facts of the following case, drawn from Sharp v. Coopers & Lybrand, 457 F. Supp. 879 (E.D. Pa., 1978):

> Plaintiffs, investors in an oil drilling venture, alleged in this class action that the defendant, a major accounting firm, is liable to them for misstatements in several opinion letters which advised them as to the supposed tax consequences of those investments. . . .

We certified a class consisting of all persons who purchased these securities after July 22, 1971, 70 F.R.D. 544 (E.D. Pa. 1976). There ensued an apparent novelty in our jurisprudence: a jury trial of issues common to the class under the Rule 10b-5, §20(a) and pendent claims. These issues included foreseeability of damages, the exercise of reasonable care, whether there were misrepresentations and omissions and, if so, their materiality and scienter, and whether the defendant controlled an employee for §20(a) purposes and adequately supervised him. . . .

Plaintiffs are persons who purchased limited partnership interests in oil wells to be drilled in Kansas and Ohio, of which Westland Minerals Corporation (WMC) was general partner and promoter. As a result of criminal fraud by WMC, many of these wells were never drilled and much of the invested money was diverted to WMC's own use. Economic Concepts, Inc. (ECI), the selling agent for these limited partnerships, and WMC sought to engage in April 1971 the services of defendant in rendering opinions as to the federal income tax consequences of these limited partnerships. In July the defendant decided to write such opinion letters, and on July 22, 1971, an opinion letter signed by a Coopers & Lybrand partner in its name was sent to Charles Raymond, president of WMC, stating that "based solely on the facts contained [in the WMC Limited Partnership Agreement] and without verification by us" a limited partner who contributed $65,000 in cash could deduct approximately $128,000 on his 1971 tax return. That letter was drafted by defendant's employee Herman Higgins, who was at that time a tax supervisor working directly under the supervision of four partners of defendant. The letter was written specifically for the use of one Muhammed Ali, a potential WMC investor, with regard to reducing the amount of taxes that would be withheld from a fight purse. In early October 1971 Higgins told David Wright, a partner in the defendant firm, that copies of the July 22 letter had been shown to individual investors besides Ali, and Wright determined that a letter which would be seen by other investors should be more complete. Higgins redrafted the opinion letter, and on October 11, 1971, defendant sent another opinion letter, signed in defendant's name by Wright, and a covering letter to Raymond.

The jury found that the October 11 letter contained both material misrepresentations and material omissions, and that Higgins acted either recklessly or with intent to defraud in preparing the letters. Much of the evidence concerning those misrepresentations and omissions and their recklessness came from plaintiffs' expert witness, Professor Bernard Wolfman of the Harvard Law School, a specialist in federal income taxation. Most of his testimony was not rebutted by the defendant. Professor Wolfman explained the principles behind this tax shelter: a taxpayer who in 1971 contributed $25,000 to a partnership involved in a bona fide oil drilling venture, which then obtained for each $25,000 contribution an additional $25,000 bona fide bank loan that was fully secured by partnership property (the as yet undrilled wells) and then expended all of that $50,000 for drilling, could under the law applicable in 1971 deduct the full $50,000 from his taxable income. The effect would be to accelerate the tax deduction available to the investor in 1971. Professor Wolfman's expert testimony in concert with other evidence provided the basis for the jury's findings that the October 11 letter misrepresented or omitted to state material facts in at least three ways.

First, Professor Wolfman testified that writing such a letter was reckless on its face in that it omitted to state that the non-recourse loan which the letter assumed lending institutions would make to WMC, the value of which loan would be deductible by the taxpayer according to the opinion letter, would have to be secured by collateral (i.e., the oil wells) whose value was equal to or greater than the amount of that loan. Non-recourse loans of the type contemplated by the opinion letter (i.e., with no personal liability to the limited partners) are very rarely entered into by banks for oil drilling ventures, according to Professor Wolfman, because it is hard to secure them fully by undrilled wells, whose value is not known. Unless the value of the property used by the partnership to secure the loan were equal to the amount of the loan, Professor Wolfman explained, the amount of the loan would not be deductible to the limited partner under §752(c) of the Internal Revenue Code. To assume this unlikely fact that the loans would be thus secured without stating the assumption was itself reckless, he said.

Second, the plaintiffs introduced evidence, principally through Higgins' testimony before a grand jury, that at the time Higgins drafted the October 11 letter he was aware of a number of facts because of his close relationship with ECI and WMC. In particular, this evidence suggested that Higgins as of October 11: (a) had recommended to WMC that it take the bank loans through mere bookkeeping transactions "without having to make a bank loan in the normal sense that we think of," (b) knew that WMC had acquired a bank, International Bank & Trust of the Bahamas (IBT), (c) knew that IBT was insolvent, or at least unable to make the loans necessary to fund the oil drilling ventures contemplated by the WMC limited partnership agreements and (d) knew that the actual drilling costs for each limited partnership would be less than $140,000. Higgins testified at his deposition that, while under the transaction contemplated by this "paper loan" WMC would not have access to the money it would "borrow" from IBT, that was "not a difference . . . that in my opinion would be that critical from the tax point of view." As it turned out, many of these facts were untrue as a result of WMC's fraud.

Professor Wolfman stated that if the writer had made such a recommendation and was aware of these facts, the October 11 letter contained a number of misstatements: that the driller would receive $140,000 in cash, that there would be partnership borrowing and that such borrowing would be from a suitable bank or other lending agency. These misrepresentations, which the jury could have found were intentional or at least reckless, in turn rendered the opinion as to tax consequences a misrepresentation, again at best recklessly made, because it was based on assumptions known to be false.

Third, the plaintiffs established that as of October 11 Higgins had decided to leave defendant's employ and that he had as of October 8 taken a leave of absence and was remaining there only to finish the opinion letter. There was evidence that by October 6 Higgins was working closely with ECI, WMC's selling agent, and on October 16 he got powers of attorney from Raymond to execute and file papers for WMC, of which Raymond was president, and for IBT, of which he was board chairman. Professor Wolfman testified that it was improper for an employee of an accounting firm who was employed by ECI to write a tax opinion letter and that the failure to disclose his relationship with the selling agent would be a material omission which would appear to have been intentional or reckless.

(1) Should Professor Wolfman have been allowed to testify as he did?

(2) Suppose the case were criminal. Should the prosecutor be allowed to call Professor Wolfman to explain to the jury why what the defendant did was criminal? (That sort of "explanation" is called "teaching" in Professor Wolfman's regular line of work.)

(3) Would it make more sense for Professor Wolfman to be called as a court appointed expert under Rule 706?

(4) If Wolfman is allowed to testify, what sort of evidence should the defendant be allowed to introduce to counter it? Who resolves any conflicts between Wolfman's testimony and the rebuttal evidence?

(5) Would it be better for judges simply to instruct jurors on the law after considering the arguments of counsel on proposed instructions?

C. Scientific Proof and Expert Testimony

FRE 702
Testimony by Experts

If scientific, technical, or other specialized knowledge will assist the trier of fact to understand the evidence or to determine a fact in issue, a witness qualified as an expert by knowledge, skill, experience, training, or education, may testify thereto in the form of an opinion or otherwise.

1. The "General Acceptance" Test for "Scientific" Proof

Who decides whether specialized knowledge will assist the trier of fact, and by what standard — Rule 104(a) or 104(b)? When is expert testimony based on scientific proof admissible?

The original and most widely used standard for the admissibility of expert testimony and scientific evidence is found in Frye v. United States, a 1923 decision of the U.S. Court of Appeals for the District of Columbia Circuit. In *Frye* the court upheld the exclusion of results of a primitive form of polygraph test that was offered by the defense in a murder trial.

FRYE v. UNITED STATES
293 F. 1013 (D.C. Cir. 1923)

VAN ORSDEL, J. Appellant, defendant below, was convicted of the crime of murder in the second degree, and from the judgment prosecutes this appeal.

A single assignment of error is presented for our consideration. In the course of the trial counsel for defendant offered an expert witness to testify to the result of a deception test made upon defendant. The test is described as the systolic blood pressure deception test. It is asserted that blood pressure is influenced by change in the emotions of the witness, and that the systolic blood pressure rises are brought about by nervous impulses sent to the sympathetic branch of the autonomic nervous system. Scientific experiments, it is claimed, have demonstrated that fear, rage, and pain always produce a rise of systolic blood pressure, and that conscious deception or falsehood, concealment of facts, or guilt of crime, accompanied by fear of detection when the person is under examination, raises the systolic blood pressure in a curve, which corresponds exactly to the struggle going on in the subject's mind, between fear and attempted control of that fear, as the examination touches the vital points in respect of which he is attempting to deceive the examiner.

In other words, the theory seems to be that truth is spontaneous, and comes without conscious effort, while the utterance of a falsehood requires a conscious effort, which is reflected in the blood pressure. The rise thus produced is easily detected and distinguished from the rise produced by mere fear of the examination itself. In the former instance, the pressure rises higher than in the latter, and is more pronounced as the examination proceeds, while in the latter case, if the subject is telling the truth, the pressure registers highest at the beginning of the examination, and gradually diminishes as the examination proceeds.

Prior to the trial defendant was subjected to this deception test, and counsel offered the scientist who conducted the test as an expert to testify to the results obtained. The offer was objected to by counsel for the government, and the court sustained the objection. Counsel for defendant then offered to have the proffered witness conduct a test in the presence of the jury. This also was denied.

Counsel for defendant, in their able presentation of the novel question involved, correctly state in their brief that no cases directly in point have been found. The broad ground, however, upon which they plant their case, is succinctly stated in their brief as follows:

> The rule is that the opinions of experts or skilled witnesses are admissible in evidence in those cases in which the matter of inquiry is such that inexperienced persons are unlikely to prove capable of forming a correct judgment upon it, for the reason that the subject-matter so far partakes of a science, art, or trade as to require a previous habit or experience or study in it, in order to acquire a knowledge of it. When the question involved does not lie within the range of common experience or common knowledge, but requires special experience or special knowledge, then the opinions of witnesses skilled in that particular science, art, or trade to which the question relates are admissible in evidence.

Numerous cases are cited in support of this rule. Just when a scientific principle or discovery crosses the line between the experimental and demonstrable stages is difficult to define. Somewhere in this twilight zone the evidential force of the principle must be recognized, and while courts will go a long way in admitting expert testimony deduced from a well-recognized scientific principle or discovery, the thing from which the deduction is made must be sufficiently established to have gained general acceptance in the particular field in which it belongs.

We think the systolic blood pressure deception test has not yet gained such standing and scientific recognition among physiological and psychological authorities as would justify the courts in admitting expert testimony deduced from the discovery, development, and experiments thus far made.

The judgment is affirmed.

According to Giannelli, The Admissibility of Novel Scientific Evidence: *Frye v. United States*, A Half-Century Later, 80 Colum. L. Rev. 1197 (1980), on which the following discussion is based, the *Frye* test originally envisioned a process whereby the admissibility of a scientific technique would be decided by reference to the stages of its evolution. The technique, after being invented or discovered within a particular field, would be first subjected to rigorous analysis by the scientific community during its "experimental stage." Only after this community "agreed" that the technique was valid ("demonstrable") would evidence of its use be admissible in court. Thus, the way in which the *Frye* test determined when evidence had reached the point of admissibility was to see if the technique was generally accepted by the relevant scientific community. In the last half century the *Frye* test was used for determining the admissibility of many types of scientific evidence besides the polygraph. For example, the test was used with voice prints,[1] neutron activation,[2] gunshot residue tests,[3] bitemark comparisons,[4] sodium pentothal,[5] ion microprobic analysis,[6] and blood grouping tests.[7] See Gianelli, supra, at 1205-1206.

According to Giannelli, the primary argument raised in favor of the *Frye* test is that it "assures that those most qualified to assess the general validity of a scientific method will have the determinative voice." United

1. See, e.g., Reed v. State, 283 Md. 374, 386, 391 A.2d 364, 381 (1978).
2. See, e.g., United States v. Stifel, 433 F.2d 431, 436, 438, 441 (6th Cir. 1970).
3. See, e.g., State v. Smith, 50 Ohio App. 2d 183, 193, 362 N.E.2d 1239, 1246 (1976).
4. See, e.g., People v. Slone, 76 Cal. App. 3d 611, 623, 143 Cal. Rptr. 61, 68 (1978).
5. See, e.g., Lindsey v. United States, 237 F.2d 893, 896 (9th Cir. 1956).
6. See, e.g., United States v. Brown, 557 F.2d 541, 556-557, 558 (6th Cir. 1977).
7. See, e.g., People v. Alston, 79 Misc. 2d 1077, 1085, 362 N.Y.S.2d 356, 362 (Sup. Ct. 1974).

States v. Addison, 498 F.2d 741, 743-744 (D.C. Cir. 1974). Thus, the *Frye* test assigns to experts the task of determining a test's reliability.

> It is therefore best to adhere to a standard which in effect permits the experts who know the most about a procedure to experiment and to study it. In effect, they form a kind of technical jury, which must first pass on the scientific status of a procedure before the lay jury utilizes it in making its findings of fact.

People v. Barbara, 400 Mich. 352, 405, 255 N.W.2d 171, 194 (1977).

Courts have also cited less substantive rationales for the *Frye* test: The "general acceptance standard" guarantees that "a minimal reserve of experts exists who can critically examine the validity of a scientific determination in a particular case." United States v. Addison, supra, 498 F.2d at 744. By requiring general acceptance by the relevant scientific community, *Frye* implicitly requires that such a community exists. Another court has suggested that the *Frye* test "may well promote a degree of uniformity of decision," People v. Kelly, infra, 17 Cal. 3d 24, 31 (1976), because "[i]ndividual judges whose particular conclusions may differ regarding the reliability of particular scientific evidence, may discover substantial agreement and consensus in the scientific community." Id. Another has suggested that "[w]ithout the *Frye* test or something similar, the reliability of an experimental scientific technique is likely to become a central issue in each trial in which it is introduced, as long as there remains serious disagreement in the scientific community over its reliability." Reed v. State, 283 Md. 374, 388, 391 A.2d 364, 371-372 (1978). Finally, some courts have used the "general acceptance" standard as a check against new techniques because "scientific proof may in some instances assume a posture of mystic infallibility in the eyes of a jury of laymen." United States v. Addison, supra, 498 F.2d at 741; United States v. Wilson, 361 F. Supp. 510, 513 (D. Md. 1973).

Consider the application of the *Frye* test in the following two cases, United States v. Tranowski, as reported by The National Law Journal, and People v. Kelly. Are the values supposedly furthered by the *Frye* test promoted in these cases? If so, at what cost to other values?

TYBOR, PERJURY CASE GOES TO DOGS AFTER SHADOW CAST ON WITNESS
The National Law Journal, Sept. 14, 1980, p.4

CHICAGO — Government attorneys would do better to quit stargazing and talk to the animals, according to a recent appellate opinion here.

After listening to what one clerk said was some of the most "entertaining" oral argument it ever heard, the 7th U.S. Circuit Court of Appeals

reversed a perjury conviction based on the expert testimony of an astronomer. The forensic skywatcher attempted to determine the date of a
family photo by measuring the angle of shadow cast by a pet dog named
Jerry.

The case stemmed from the purchase with a phony $5 bill of what the
court described as "two so-called Burger King 'Whoppers' " on Mothers'
Day, May 12, 1974.

Stanley Tranowski was convicted of passing the phony bill and sentenced to six years in prison.

At Stanley's trial, however, Walter Tranowski, his brother, testified
that he was in the defendant's presence for much of the day in question
and insisted that Stanley couldn't have committed the crime.

To support his testimony, Walter produced at trial a family photo he
said was taken in his mother's backyard between 2 P.M. and 3 P.M. that
day — not long before Stanley was alleged to have bought the burgers
with the funny money. It showed Stanley, their mother, Cecilia
Kniebusch, and Jerry the dog.

The jury rejected Stanley's alibi defense, however, and found him
guilty on Dec. 16, 1977.

Then Walter was indicted for perjury on June 29, 1979.

At the perjury trial, the government's key witness was an astronomer,
Larry Ciupik, of the Adler Planetarium here. He said he measured from
an enlargement of the photo the shadows cast by the dog and by the
chimney at the rear of the house and made mathematical and astronomical calculations using a sun chart that ordinarily is used to measure
"lunar mountains."

Based on these calculations, Mr. Ciupik testified that the photo could
only have been taken on the morning of one of two days — April 13 or
Aug. 31, 1974.

In an opinion written by Senior Judge John R. Bartels of the Eastern
District of New York, who was sitting by designation, the majority decision described Mr. Ciupik's testimony as "a novel application of untested
mathematical and astronomical theories" and said that the "trial court
should not be used as a testing ground for theories supported neither by
prior control experiments nor by calculations with [necessary] indicia of
reliability." U.S. v. Tranowski, 80-1413.

It reversed Walter's perjury conviction outright without remand for a
new trial.

PEOPLE v. KELLY
17 Cal. 3d 24, 130 Cal. Rptr. 144, 549 P.2d 1240 (1976)

RICHARDSON, J. In this case we examine the new and emerging technique of speaker identification by spectrographic analysis, commonly

described as "voiceprint." Particularly we inquire whether it has achieved that degree of general scientific acceptance as a reliable identification device which will permit the introduction of voiceprint evidence in California courts.

We have concluded that, on the record before us, the People's showing on this important issue was insufficient, and that since the voiceprint evidence at issue herein was the primary evidence of defendant's guilt, the judgment of conviction must be reversed. Although voiceprint analysis may indeed constitute a reliable and valuable tool in either identifying or eliminating suspects in criminal cases, that fact was not satisfactorily demonstrated in this case.

Defendant was convicted of extortion (Pen. Code, §§518-520) arising out of a series of anonymous, threatening telephone calls to Terry Waskin. The police, acting with Waskin's consent, tape recorded two of these calls (the extortion tapes). An informant familiar with defendant's voice subsequently listened to these tapes and tentatively identified defendant as the caller. Thereafter, the officers obtained a tape recording of defendant's voice during a telephone call (the control tape). Copies of the extortion tapes and the control tape were then sent to Lieutenant Ernest Nash of the Michigan State Police for spectrographic analysis. On the basis of his examination, Nash concluded that the voices on these tapes were those of the same person.

Defendant was indicted by the grand jury and brought to trial. The case was submitted to the trial court, sitting without a jury, on the grand jury transcript and the testimony at a pretrial hearing on the issue of the admissibility of the voiceprint evidence. The People had sought to introduce Nash's testimony, and had asked the trial court to order that an evidentiary hearing be held to determine the admissibility of this evidence. (See Evid. Code, §405.) Initially, the trial court on the authority of Hodo v. Superior Court (1973) 30 Cal. App. 3d 778, 106 Cal. Rptr. 547, held that California now recognized that the scientific community generally accepted voiceprint analysis as a reliable identification technique. Subsequently the trial court reconsidered its order, however, and ruled that the People would be required to present evidence on the issue of general acceptance. Accordingly, Nash was called and testified that among those who were familiar with and used voice identification analysis the technique was considered reliable. No other expert testimony was presented by either side.

Considering Nash's testimony and relying on Hodo v. Superior Court, supra, and United States v. Raymond (D.D.C. 1972) 337 F. Supp. 641, affd. sub nom. United States v. Addison (1974) 162 U.S. App. D.C. 199, 498 F.2d 741, the trial court ruled that voiceprint analysis had attained sufficient scientific approval, and that Nash's testimony identifying defendant as the extortionist was properly admissible.

Defendant attacks his conviction arguing that (1) the People failed to establish that voiceprint techniques have reached the requisite degree of general acceptance in the scientific community, (2) Nash was not qualified to express an expert opinion regarding the judgment of scholars and experts and (3) the testing procedures employed in identifying defendant's voice were not conducted in a fair and impartial manner. Finding ourselves in general agreement with defendant's first two contentions, we do not reach the third. . . .

2. GENERAL PRINCIPLES OF ADMISSIBILITY

The parties agree generally that admissibility of expert testimony based upon the application of a new scientific technique traditionally involves a two-step process: (1) the *reliability of the method* must be established, usually by expert testimony, and (2) the witness furnishing such testimony must be properly *qualified as an expert to give an opinion* on the subject. (See Evid. Code, §§720, 801; Jones, Danger — Voiceprints Ahead (1973) 11 Am. Crim. L. Rev. 549, 554.) Additionally, the proponent of the evidence must demonstrate that correct scientific procedures were used in the particular case. (See People v. Adams (1975) 53 Cal. App. 3d 109, 115-116, 125 Cal. Rptr. 518 [polygraph tests]; United States v. Ridling (E.D. Mich. 1972) 350 F. Supp. 90, 94 [same]; Comment, 56 Minn. L. Rev. at p.1244.)

The test for determining the underlying reliability of a new scientific technique was described in the germinal case of Frye v. United States (1923) 54 App. D.C. 46, 293 F. 1013, 1014, involving the admissibility of polygraph tests: "Just when a scientific principle or discovery crosses the line between the experimental and demonstrable stages is difficult to define. Somewhere in this twilight zone the evidential force of the principle must be recognized, and while courts will go a long way in admitting expert testimony deduced from a well-recognized scientific principle or discovery, the thing from which the deduction is made must be *sufficiently established to have gained general acceptance in the particular field in which it belongs.*" (Italics added.)

We have expressly adopted the foregoing *Frye* test and California courts, when faced with a novel method of proof, have required a preliminary showing of general acceptance of the new technique in the relevant scientific community. (Huntingdon v. Crowley (1966) 64 Cal. 2d 647, 653-654, 51 Cal. Rptr. 254, 414 P.2d 382 [blood tests]; People v. Law, 40 Cal. App. 3d 69, 74, 114 Cal. Rptr. 708 [voiceprints]; People v. Spigno (1957) 156 Cal. App. 2d 279, 290, 319 P.2d 458 [polygraph tests].) Some criticism has been directed at the *Frye* standard, primarily on the ground that the test is too conservative, often resulting in the prevention of the admission of relevant evidence (see United States v. Sample (E.D. Pa. 1974) 378 F. Supp. 43, 53 [voiceprints admissible in probation revocation proceeding]; McCormick, Evidence (2d ed. 1972)

§203, pp. 490-491). As indicated below, we are satisfied that there is ample justification for the exercise of considerable judicial caution in the acceptance of evidence developed by new scientific techniques.

Arguably, the admission of such evidence could be left, in the first instance, to the sound discretion of the trial court, in which event objections, if any, to the reliability of the evidence (or of the underlying scientific technique on which it is based) might lessen the weight of the evidence but would not necessarily prevent its admissibility. This has not been the direction taken by the California courts or by those of most states. *Frye,* and the decisions which have followed it, rather than turning to the trial judge have assigned the task of determining reliability of the evolving technique to members of the scientific community from which the new method emerges. As stated in a recent voiceprint case, United States v. Addison, supra, 498 F.2d 741, 743-744: "The requirement of general acceptance in the scientific community assures that *those most qualified to assess the general validity of a scientific method will have the determinative voice.* Additionally, the *Frye* test protects prosecution and defense alike by assuring that a minimal reserve of experts exists who can critically examine the validity of a scientific determination in a particular case." (Italics added.)

Moreover, a beneficial consequence of the *Frye* test is that it may well promote a degree of uniformity of decision. Individual judges whose particular conclusions may differ regarding the reliability of particular scientific evidence, may discover substantial agreement and consensus in the scientific community. (See Comment, 35 Md. L. Rev. 267, at p.290.)

The primary advantage, however, of the *Frye* test lies in its essentially conservative nature. For a variety of reasons, *Frye* was deliberately intended to interpose a substantial obstacle to the unrestrained admission of evidence based upon new scientific principles. "There has always existed a considerable lag between advances and discoveries in scientific fields and their acceptance as evidence in a court proceeding." (People v. Spigno, supra, 156 Cal. App. 2d at p.289, 319 P.2d at p.464.) Several reasons founded in logic and common sense support a posture of judicial caution in this area. Lay jurors tend to give considerable weight to "scientific" evidence when presented by "experts" with impressive credentials. We have acknowledged the existence of a ". . . misleading aura of certainty which often envelops a new scientific process, obscuring its currently experimental nature." (Huntingdon v. Crowley, supra, 64 Cal. 2d at p.656, 51 Cal. Rptr. at p.262, 414 P.2d at p.390; see People v. King, 266 Cal. App. 2d at p.461, 72 Cal. Rptr. 478.) As stated in *Addison,* supra, in the course of rejecting the admissibility of voiceprint testimony, "scientific proof may in some instances assume a posture of mystic infallibility in the eyes of a jury. . . ." (United States v. Addison, supra, 498 F.2d at p.744.)

Exercise of restraint is especially warranted when the identification technique is offered to identify the perpetrator of a crime. " 'When identification is chiefly founded upon an opinion which is derived from utilization of an unproven process or technique, the court must be particularly careful to scrutinize the general acceptance of the technique.' " (People v. Law, supra, 40 Cal. App. 3d at p.85, 114 Cal. Rptr. at p.719; see People v. King, supra, 266 Cal. App. 2d at p.459, 72 Cal. Rptr. 478.) Moreover, once a trial court has admitted evidence based upon a new scientific technique, and that decision is affirmed on appeal by a published appellate decision, the precedent so established may control subsequent trials, at least until new evidence is presented reflecting a change in the attitude of the scientific community.

For all the foregoing reasons, we are persuaded by the wisdom of, and reaffirm our allegiance to, the *Frye* decision and the "general acceptance" rule which that case mandates. In the matter before us, the People attempted to satisfy the *Frye* test by reliance upon prior decisions of the courts of this state and sister states, and upon Lieutenant Nash's testimony. Yet, as discussed below, none of these sources provide satisfactory proof of the reliability of voiceprint evidence. . . .

The foregoing review of cases from California and other jurisdictions satisfies us that the admissibility of voiceprint testimony remains unresolved. Certainly these cases do not establish, as a matter of law, the reliability of the voiceprint technique. Moreover, amici have cited a number of scientific and legal articles containing differing forms of opposition to the admissibility of voiceprint evidence. Such writings may be considered by courts in evaluating the reliability of new scientific methodology. (See Huntingdon v. Crowley, supra, 64 Cal. 2d at p.656, 51 Cal. Rptr. 254, 414 P.2d 382; People v. Law, supra, 40 Cal. App. 3d at pp. 75-83, 114 Cal. Rptr. 708; United States v. Addison, supra, 498 F.2d at pp. 744-745.) Some of the voiceprint literature is considered in such recent cases as People v. Law, supra, 40 Cal. App. 3d at pages 81-83, 114 Cal. Rptr. 708, and Commonwealth v. Lykus, 327 N.E.2d at pages 675-682. No useful purpose would be served by an extended discussion of it. We make specific note, however, of a recent article submitted to us by the Attorney General, in which Dr. Tosi observes that "Possibly, no combination of [voiceprint] methods may ever produce absolutely positive identification or eliminations in 100% of the cases submitted," and that the reliability of the voiceprint technique may vary depending upon such factors as the quality and extension of available voice samples, the qualifications of the examiner, and the comprehensiveness of the methods used. Dr. Tosi also notes the need for continuing research and practical forensic experience in this area. (Tosi, The Problem of Speaker Identification and Elimination, in Measurement Procedures in Speech, Language and Hearing (Singh edit. 1975) pp. 428-429.)

4. LIEUTENANT NASH'S TESTIMONY

Finding the case authority on the issue before us conflicting and inconclusive, we turn to the record in the present case to determine whether, as the trial court concluded, the prosecution established the reliability of the voiceprint technique. In so doing, we bear in mind the admonition of People v. Law, supra, 40 Cal. App. 3d 69, 85, 114 Cal. Rptr. 708, 718, that "It is our duty . . . , where the life or liberty of a defendant is at stake, to be particularly careful that there is not only substantial evidence to support the implied finding of [defendant's] identity but that the finding is based upon admissible and nonprejudicial evidence."

As indicated, Lieutenant Nash was *the sole witness* testifying on the reliability issue. The record discloses that Nash has been associated with the voiceprint technique since 1967, having been trained in voiceprint analysis by Kersta, the pioneer in this field. At the time of trial, Nash was employed by the Michigan State Police as head of its voice identification unit. Nash studied audiology and speech sciences at Michigan State University, and completed courses in anatomy and the physiology of speech. Although Nash had received approximately 50 hours of college credit in these subjects, he had not attained a formal degree.

Lieutenant Nash testified that since 1967 he has prepared or reviewed 180,000 voice spectrograms. As noted above, he worked with Dr. Tosi in preparing the design for the 1968-1970 Michigan State University study which Dr. Tosi conducted, and he assisted Tosi in drafting the final report of the study. According to Nash, the Tosi study demonstrated a high degree of reliability. It was a "controlled experimental situation" based on examination and identification of the voices of students and other nonsuspect persons, rather than a forensic, in-the-field, study of the reliability of voiceprint analysis in identifying criminals.

Lieutenant Nash stated that among members of the scientific community involved in voiceprint analysis there is general acceptance of the technique as "extremely" reliable. Nash admitted, however, that those persons who are actually involved in voiceprint work are primarily voiceprint examiners "connected with a government agency of some kind," i.e., law enforcement officers such as Nash himself.

Our analysis of Nash's testimony discloses at least three infirmities which, in combination, are fatal to the People's claim that they established that voiceprint analysis is generally accepted as reliable by the scientific community. First, we think it questionable whether the testimony of a single witness alone is ever sufficient to represent, or attest to, the views of an entire scientific community regarding the reliability of a new technique. Ideally, resolution of the general acceptance issue would require consideration of the views of a typical cross-section of the scientific community, including representatives, if there are such, of those who oppose or question the new technique. Several courts have thus concluded that, before evidence based upon a new scientific method may be introduced, " *'something more than the bare opinion of one man, however qualified, is required.'* " (People v. King, supra, 266 Cal. App. 2d at p.453, 72 Cal. Rptr. at p.488, quoting from another voiceprint case, State v. Cary (1967) 49 N.J. 343, 230 A.2d 384, 389; italics added by *King*.) In *King*, for example, the trial court heard the views of three prosecution experts and seven defense experts on the issue of general acceptance. (See also Huntingdon v. Crowley, supra, 64 Cal. 2d 647, 654, 51 Cal. Rptr. 254, 414 P.2d 382, wherein the trial court had considered the opinions of two opposing experts on the issue of blood test reliability, as well as numerous articles from relevant literature on the subject.)

One commentator has suggested that in an appropriate case trial courts should take affirmative steps to assure that an accurate description of the views of the scientific community is placed before the court.

> "After deciding which are the relevant fields, the court must see that the appropriate experts testify. Where only proponents of a technique appear, the court should sua sponte take the responsibility of inquiring not just whether the experts believe the scientific community is generally in agreement, but whether they are in fact aware of any opposing sentiment in the relevant scientific community. *The court should then make an effort to ascertain the extent of any opposition so identified, calling its spokesmen as court-appointed experts if necessary.*"

(Comment, supra, 35 Md. L. Rev. 267, at p.293; fn. omitted, italics added.) In California, the trial court's authority to appoint an expert is set forth in Evidence Code section 730. As the scientific literature referred to above makes clear, in the area of voiceprint analysis there exist several persons whose qualifications would enable them to testify knowledgeably, and critically.

We are troubled by a second feature of the evidentiary record before us. In addition to the trial court's reliance solely upon Nash's testimony to the exclusion of other, possibly adverse, expert witnesses, a serious question existed regarding Nash's ability fairly and impartially to assess the position of the scientific community. Nash has had a long association with the development and promotion of voiceprint analysis. His qualifications in this somewhat limited area cannot be doubted. In addition to his work with Dr. Tosi, Nash was the chief of the Michigan State Police Voice Identification Unit, a position which led him to testify as a voiceprint expert in numerous cases throughout the country. Further, Nash is either a founder or member of four other organizations which promote the use of voiceprint analysis.

Nash's background thus discloses that he is one of the leading propo-

nents of voiceprint analysis; he has virtually built his career on the reliability of the technique. This situation is closely akin to that in People v.
King, supra, 266 Cal. App. 2d 437, 72 Cal. Rptr. 478, in which Kersta, a
pioneer in the field, was the chief prosecution witness supporting the
admissibility of voiceprint evidence. The court in *King* rejected Kersta's
testimony regarding the scientific basis of voiceprint analysis and warned
that "[b]efore a technique or process is generally accepted in the
scientific community, self-serving opinions should not be received which
invade the province of the trier of fact." (Id., at p.458, 72 Cal. Rptr. at
p.491.) Likewise, Nash, a strong advocate of the voiceprint technique,
may be too closely identified with the endorsement of voiceprint analysis
to assess fairly and impartially the nature and extent of any opposing
scientific views. A more detached and neutral observer might more
fairly do so. In the absence of additional and impartial evidence regarding general acceptance, the trial court was in a similar position to that
presented in *King*, in which "a court could only receive Kersta's opinion
on faith." (People v. King, supra, 266 Cal. App. 2d at p.456, 72 Cal.
Rptr. at p.490.)

A third objection to Nash's testimony pertains to his qualifications as
an expert in the field of voiceprint analysis. Substantial doubt exists
whether Nash possessed the necessary academic qualifications which
would have enabled him to express a competent opinion on the issue of
the general acceptance of the voiceprint technique in the scientific community.

"A person is qualified to testify as an expert if he has special knowledge, skill, experience, training, or education sufficient to qualify him as
an expert on the subject to which his testimony relates." (Evid. Code,
§720, subd. (a).) The trial court is given considerable latitude in determining the qualifications of an expert and its ruling will not be disturbed
on appeal unless a manifest abuse of discretion is shown. (Pfingsten v.
Westenhaver (1952) 39 Cal. 2d 12, 20, 244 P.2d 395; Huffman v. Lind-
quist (1951) 37 Cal. 2d 465, 476, 234 P.2d 34; People v. King, supra, 266
Cal. App. 2d at p.443, 72 Cal. Rptr. 478; Witkin, Cal. Evidence (1966)
§1175, p.1088.)

However, whether a person qualifies as an expert in a particular case
depends upon the facts of that case and the witness' qualifications. (People v. Davis (1965) 62 Cal. 2d 791, 801, 44 Cal. Rptr. 454, 402 P.2d 142.)
"The competency of an expert is relative to the topic and fields of knowledge about which the person is asked to make a statement. In considering whether a person qualifies as an expert, the field of expertise must
be carefully distinguished and limited." (People v. King, supra, 266 Cal.
App. 2d at p.445, 72 Cal. Rptr. at p.483.)

The record in the instant case reveals that Nash has an impressive list
of credentials in the field of voiceprint analysis. However, these
qualifications are those of *a technician and law enforcement officer, not a*

scientist. Neither his training under Kersta, his association with the Tosi study, his limited college study in certain speech sciences, his membership in organizations promoting the use of voiceprints, nor his former position as head of the Michigan State Police Voice Identification Unit, necessarily qualifies Nash to express an informed opinion on the view of the scientific community toward voiceprint analysis. This area may be one in which only another scientist, in regular communication with other colleagues in the field, is competent to express such an opinion.

Nash was allowed to testify in a dual role, both as a technician and a scientist, in order to show both that the voiceprint technique is reliable and that it has gained general acceptance in the scientific community. From the demonstrably wide technical experience of Nash, it does not necessarily follow that academic and scientific knowledge are present as well. As expressed in *King*: "Kersta's engineering abilities must not be confused with or made a substitute for learning and training in the fields of anatomy, medicine, physiology, psychology, phonetics or linguistics." (People v. King, supra, 266 Cal. App. 2d at p.458, 72 Cal. Rptr. at p.491.) In considering the position of the scientific community, a court is bound to let scientists speak for themselves. Nash's undoubted qualifications as a technician, like Kersta's, do not necessarily qualify him as a scientist to express an opinion on the question of general scientific acceptance.

Indeed, it is both noteworthy and commendable that Nash was careful and fair in not claiming that he represented the views of the general scientific community on the subject of the reliability of the voiceprint technique. Instead, he expressed the opinion of those persons engaged in the actual use of the spectrogram, persons who were primarily engaged in law enforcement activities. Although the *Frye* test may be satisfied by a showing of general acceptance by those scientists who are most familiar with the use of a new technique (People v. Williams (1958) 164 Cal. App. 2d Supp. 858, 862, 331 P.2d 251; Commonwealth v. Lykus, supra, 327 N.E.2d at pp. 677-678), such a showing, ordinarily, should be presented by those who are engaged in the scientific fields. . . .

The judgment is reversed.

WRIGHT, C.J., and McCOMB, TOBRINER, MOSK, SULLIVAN and CLARK, JJ., concur.

Criticism of the *Frye* rule has focused on the problems of identifying the portion of the scientific community that must accept the scientific principle and procedure, establishing general acceptance in the field, and determining when the *Frye* rule should be applied. Giannelli, supra, at 1208-1221. Critics contend that the *Frye* approach operates (1) to exclude reliable evidence by introducing a conservative "cultural lag" in the acceptance of reliable proof and (2) to include unreliable evidence by depending too heavily on continued acceptance of outmoded techniques by the scientific community. Id. at 1223-1225. McCormick has long advocated abolition of the *Frye* standard:

> "General scientific acceptance" is a proper criterion for taking judicial notice of scientific facts, but not a criterion for the admissibility of scientific evidence. Any relevant conclusions which are supported by a qualified expert witness should be received unless there are other reasons for exclusion. Particularly, its probative value may be overborne by the familiar dangers of prejudicing or misleading the jury, unfair surprise and undue consumption of time. If the courts used this approach, instead of repeating a supposed requirement of "general acceptance" not elsewhere imposed, they would arrive at a practical way of utilizing the results of scientific advances.

McCormick, Evidence 491 (2d ed. 1972). Under this view, evidence of scientific disagreements regarding the reliability of a particular technique should go to the weight, not the admissibility, of the evidence, and disputes regarding the validity of scientific evidence are simply aspects of relevancy. See United States v. Baller, 519 F.2d 463, 466 (4th Cir.), cert. denied, 423 U.S. 1019 (1975).

Under the Federal Rules what is left of *Frye*? Compare the treatment of spectrographic voice-identification by the Second Circuit in the following case with that of the California Supreme Court in *Kelly*, above. Did the reliability of spectrography change in the two years between *Kelly* and *Williams*, or is the different result attributable to different views regarding the applicable rule of evidence? Did the Federal Rules incorporate or abolish the *Frye* test? Did the Federal Rules adopt the McCormick relevancy test? Would it be desirable to infer the relevancy test from the structure of the rules? Does it adequately protect against the misuse of scientific evidence? What safeguards would you apply to the relevancy approach to enhance the reliability of scientific proof?

UNITED STATES v. WILLIAMS
583 F.2d 1194 (2d Cir. 1978), cert. denied, 439 U.S. 1117 (1979)

MARKEY, C.J. Isiah Williams and Michael Manning were convicted of violating federal narcotics laws, 21 U.S.C. §846 (1972) and 21 U.S.C. §841 (1972). The admission of spectrographic voice-identification evidence is challenged for the first time in this circuit. We affirm.

FACTS

On November 12, 1976, an undercover police officer attempted unsuccessfully to purchase heroin from a man introduced to him as "Biggie," an event witnessed by three surveillance officers, including

Detective Copeland, who followed "Biggie" into a bar four days later. Copeland asked "Biggie" for identification, pretending he was investigating a complaint that a man named "Biggie" was taking numbers. "Biggie" admitted that his name was Isiah Williams, and that he was called "Biggie," but denied taking numbers. Explaining his unemployment, Williams showed Copeland a support truss he was wearing. Surveillance officers also observed these events.

On November 30, 1976, Officer Lopez arranged to purchase heroin from "Biggie." The two drove to a building. "Biggie" entered the building. He emerged with another man and both joined Lopez in the car. "Biggie" introduced the other man as "Red." Lopez handed "Biggie" money and "Red" gave the heroin to Lopez. "Red" was later identified as Manning. Except for the transactions in the car, these events were observed by the same surveillance officers.

On December 10, 1976, Lopez purchased additional heroin from "Biggie," in a similar transaction observed by the same surveillance officers.

On December 13, 1976, "Biggie" telephoned Lopez concerning another heroin sale. Lopez taped the call. The proposed sale never materialized. Two days later Lopez called "Biggie" to arrange another date, and taped that conversation. Two more meetings between Lopez and "Biggie" were observed by the same surveillance team.

At trial, Lopez and the surveillance officers unequivocally identified Manning as "Red." Lopez was unable to make an in-court identification of Williams as "Biggie" upon viewing Williams and his arrest photo, a difficulty apparently caused by Williams' having drastically altered his appearance. Lopez did identify a 1972 photo of Williams as "Biggie." All three surveillance officers identified Williams as "Biggie." At the time of his arrest, Williams recognized Copeland from the "numbers complaint ruse," and was found to be wearing a truss.

After his arrest, Williams gave telephone voice exemplars which were taped. After a pre-trial hearing, voice analysis evidence was ruled admissible.[1] At the trial spectrographic voice identification expert Frank Lundgren made aural and spectrographic comparisons of Williams' voice in the exemplars and of "Biggie's" voice in the taped conversations with Lopez. . . .

ISSUES

The sole issue in Williams' appeal is whether it was error to admit a spectrographic voice analysis as identification evidence. . . .

1. Judge Broderick's Memorandum Order of December 20, 1977, included: "That the voice identification by aural comparison and spectrographic analysis has probative value; that the govt's proposed expert in this field, Mr. F. Lundgren, is qualified; and that the jury will not be misled by such evidence, I have therefore ruled that evidence of spectrographic voice analysis and identification will be admitted in this case. . . ."

THE MECHANICS OF SPEECH

Sound consists essentially of pressure waves of varying frequencies
and amplitudes. The pressure waves associated with speech are initiated
when air is exhaled past the vocal cords. The resulting vibration of the
vocal cords produces the pressure waves. . . .

Voice analysis . . . rests on the non-likelihood that two individuals
would have identical vocal cavities and identical dynamic patterns of
articulator manipulation, and on the inability of an individual to change
or disguise the particular voice characteristics created by his unique
combination of cavities and articulator manipulative patterns. Spectrographic voice analysis involves the reflection of voice characteristics in
a "spectrogram" produced by a "spectrograph."[4]

THE SPECTROGRAPH AND SPECTROGRAM

The spectrograph is an electromagnetic instrument which analyzes
sound and disperses it into an array of its time, frequency and intensity
components. The array is graphically displayed in a spectrogram.[5] . . .

The spectrograms of the same words and phrases are . . . compared
visually, to determine whether they were made by the same speaker. The
bar spectrogram indicates time along the horizontal axis, frequency
along the vertical axis, and intensity by varying shades of darkness in the
pattern. The unique speech characteristics of the individual whose voice
is being analyzed produce unique spectrogram patterns of vocal energy
at the various frequency levels. Though it is not necessary that two
spectrograms be identical, there must be exhibited a sufficient number
of similar spectrogram patterns, called "matches," to warrant a conclusion that they were produced by the same person.

ADMISSIBILITY

Though the weight of authority supports the admissibility of spectrographic voice identification evidence, we rest our decision on an independent evaluation.

There is no clearly defined, universal, litmus test for the general
admissibility of all "scientific" evidence.

An oft-cited test, first laid down in Frye v. United States, 54 App. D.C.
46, 293 F. 1013 (1923), requires "general acceptance in the particular

4. Opponents of courtroom use of spectrographic evidence claim that insufficient tests
have been conducted to establish that spectrograms of the same voice cannot differ more
than spectrograms of two different voices, and to establish the inability of an individual to
change his voice. Courts, however, must decide admissibility issues in the light of the
current state of the art.

5. A spectrogram has been often called a "voice-print." We avoid the term as potentially
leading to an unwarranted association with fingerprint evidence.

field to which it belongs." The *Frye* test is usually construed as necessitating a survey and categorization of the subjective views of a number of scientists, assuring thereby a reserve of experts available to testify. Difficulty in applying the *Frye* test has led a number of courts to its implicit modification.

We deal here with the admissibility or non-admissibility of a particular type of scientific evidence, not with the truth or falsity of an alleged scientific "fact" or "truth."[7] Hence the established considerations applicable to the admissibility of evidence come into play, and the probativeness, materiality, and reliability of the evidence, on the one side, and any tendency to mislead, prejudice, or confuse the jury on the other, must be the focal points of inquiry.

In the present case, probativeness and materiality present little difficulty. If the "unknown" voice be established as having been employed in the commission of, or in relation to, the crime alleged, i.e., a proper foundation has been laid, evidence that the voice is that of the accused is both probative and material. Our concern is therefore directed to (a) reliability, and (b) tendency to mislead.

(A) RELIABILITY

A determination of reliability cannot rest solely on a process of "counting (scientific) noses." In the present case, Williams presents a list of 10 scientists classified as favoring use of spectrographic analysis in the courtroom and 17 scientists classified as opposed. Williams admits, however, that there are differing shades of opinion within each classification, and that many names could be added to each. Selection of the "relevant scientific community," appears to influence the result. Acceptance of the technique appeared strong among scientists who had worked with spectrograms and weak among those who had not. Further, some of the scientists now classified as favoring had previously been opposed. Lastly, unanimity of opinion in the scientific community, on virtually any scientific question, is extremely rare. Only slightly less rare is a strong majority. Doubtless, a technique unable to garner *any* support, or only minuscule support, within the scientific community would be found unreliable by a court. In testing for admissibility of a particular type of scientific evidence, whatever the scientific "voting" pattern may be, the courts cannot in any event surrender to scientists the responsibility for determining the reliability of that evidence.

7. McCormick suggests that the *Frye* test "is a proper condition for taking judicial notice of scientific facts, but not a criterion for the admissibility of scientific evidence."

A distinction is required, also, between founding broad legal principles on current scientific "truths," see generally, Buck v. Bell, 274 U.S. 200 (1972); Brown v. Board of Education, 347 U.S. 483 (1954), and admitting particular scientific evidence as probative of an element of a crime.

Nor need it be found that spectrographic evidence is infallible. The sole question is whether spectrographic analysis has reached a level of reliability sufficient to warrant its use in the courtroom.

One indicator of evidential reliability is the potential rate of error. In the most comprehensive study of spectrography made to date, involving experiments at Michigan State University with voices recorded directly and over the telephone, with and without background noise, with words spoken in context and in isolation, and with recordings made contemporaneously and at different times, Dr. Tosi arrived at a false identification rate of 6.3%, a rate reduced to 2.4% when doubtful comparisons were eliminated.[8]

Another reliability indicia is the existence and maintenance of standards. The International Association of Voice Identification, an organization concerned with training and certification of spectrograph examiners and with procedures, requires that ten matches be found before a positive identification can be made.

A third reliability factor can be the care and concern with which a scientific technique has been employed, and whether it appears to lend itself to abuse. In spectrogram analysis only five possible conclusions are permitted. The two voices are: (1) the same; (2) different; (3) probably the same; (4) probably different; and (5) no conclusion is possible. Lundgren, the expert who testified in this case, has rendered a positive identification in only 8% of the 200 cases in which he has been involved. He found the voices different in 6%, and reported an inability to reach any conclusion in 76% of the cases.

A further indication of the reliability of spectrographic analysis is its analogous relationship with other types of scientific techniques, and their results, routinely admitted into evidence. Like handwriting exemplars and gun barrel striations, spectrograms are variable, but contain sufficient points of similarity or dissimilarity to enable a trained expert to reach a conclusion.[9]

Lastly, a convincing element in determining reliability is the presence of "fail-safe" characteristics. A poor quality in the original tapes, poor recording conditions, deterioration of the tapes over time, and changes in mental or physical state of the speaker, can affect spectrogram comparisons, but such factors are more likely to result in different rather

8. Dr. Tosi testified at the preliminary hearing.

9. Spectrography is qualitatively different from polygraph evidence. In spectrography, the examiner merely compares spectrograms reflecting the purely physical characteristics of a voice. In polygraph analysis, the examiner must go on, to extrapolate a judgment of something not directly measured by the machine, i.e., the credibility of the person examined. Commonwealth v. Lykus, 367 Mass. 191, 327 N.E.2d 671 (1975). The skill of the polygraph examiner, the kinds of questions asked, natural variations in blood pressure among individuals, and in how accustomed they are to lying, are unpredictable variables that make the polygraph technique far more speculative than is spectrographic analysis.

than in similar spectrograms. The result would then more likely be that no conclusion is possible, or an erroneous conclusion that two voices are different when they are the same, rather than vice-versa. Thus, inaccuracies in the spectrograms, or failure to accurately reflect the voice of the accused, is more likely to redound to his benefit than to his detriment. Moreover, the listed factors affecting spectrogram accuracy are subject to exposition at the trial, or in a preliminary hearing. If the attack on accuracy goes only to the weight to be given the evidence, admission to jury consideration would appear proper. If the attack establishes such fundamental inaccuracy as to render the particular spectrographic evidence of no assistance to the jury, the potential to mislead may be so great as to warrant an exclusion order.

(B) TENDENCY TO MISLEAD

Williams says there is a tendency of spectrographic voice analysis evidence to mislead or confuse the jury because lay jurors are awed by an "aura of mystic infallibility" surrounding "scientific techniques," "experts," and the "fancy devices" employed. The objection is raisable, of course, whenever an expert witness in any field of science gives conclusions based on his expertise, and on scientific test results produced with technological equipment. It has less force, however, in respect of spectrographic voice analysis evidence than it might in some other fields. As above discussed, the critical step in spectrographic voice analysis is the simple step of visual pattern-matching, a step easily comprehended and evaluated by a jury.

Moreover, in the consideration of spectrographic voice analysis evidence, it is not expected that the jury will participate only as passive listeners. The objective components supplied by spectrography are subject to direct evaluation by the jury. The tapes can be played, and, if need be, replayed for the jury. The spectrograms themselves can be examined and compared by the jury. In addition, the normal safeguards are fully available. The expert's qualifications, the reliability of his equipment, the reliability of the technique itself, and in essence the accuracy and reliability of the spectrograms, are all subject to challenge and attack through cross-examination and the testimony of opposing experts. Finally, the jury can be instructed that the expert's opinion is solely for their assistance, and subject to their complete rejection if they consider it unreliable.

It bears reiteration that admissibility alone is under consideration. The jury remains at liberty to reject voice analysis evidence for any of a number of reasons, including a view that the spectrographic voice analysis technique itself is either unreliable or misleading. We hold only that spectrographic voice analysis evidence is not so inherently unreliable or misleading as to require its exclusion from the jury's consideration in every case.[11]

THE PRESENT CASE

The record in this case demonstrates that virtually all of the safeguards designed to assure reliability, and to prevent a misleading of the jury, were employed. The exemplar tape of Williams' voice was recorded over a telephone line, duplicating as closely as possible the conditions under which the questioned tape, i.e., the tape of the unknown voice, was made. In making the exemplar tape, Williams read from a transcript of the questioned tape. The opinion of spectrograph expert Lundgren was based on both an aural comparison of the voices on the two tapes and on a visual comparison of the spectrograms. The tapes were played for the jury. The spectrograms were shown to the jury. Lundgren's opinion was based on thirteen matches between spectrograms of corresponding words and phrases on the questioned and exemplar tapes, three more than the established standard for identity. A "consistency" was found among the remaining spectrograms. The expert took all the time necessary to make a complete analysis. He was subject to cross-examination concerning his qualifications, his methods, and his equipment. The expert was knowledgeable, his equipment was accurate and reliable, and the spectrograms were proper subjects for comparison. The jury was instructed that the expert's opinion was for their assistance only and could be rejected if found unreliable.[13]

---

11. Fed. R. Evid. 702 provides that a qualified expert having "scientific, technical, or other specialized knowledge" may give an opinion based on that knowledge if it will "assist the trier of fact to understand the evidence or to determine a fact in issue." The advisory committee notes suggest that "[w]hether the situation is a proper one for the use of expert testimony is to be determined on the basis of assisting the trier." Advisory Committee's Note to Fed. R. Evid. 702. No reason appears for keeping from a jury evidence capable of passing that test.

13. Judge Broderick's excellent instruction read: "The government has offered the testimony of Frederick Lundgren as an expert in voice identification, through the technique of spectrographic analysis. You will recall that he testified with respect to a comparison which he made between the voice on an exemplar made by Mr. Williams and a voice that appeared on the tape recording of a telephone conversation which Mr. Lopez testified he recorded. You may consider Mr. Lundgren's opinion on this matter. You may give that opinion whatever weight you feel it deserves, taking into account Mr. Lundgren's qualifications, his methods, and the reasons he gave for his opinion. But I want to stress again that you are the finders of fact in this case. It is you who must determine whether the known voice and the questioned voice are the same or different. You may listen to the tapes yourselves and reach a different conclusion than did Mr. Lundgren. You may conclude that his opinion is not based on adequate education, training, or experience. You may decide that the technique of spectrographic analysis is not reliable. You may conclude that however reliable the technique, Mr. Lundgren has not had sufficient education, training, or experience to be relied upon as a practitioner of that technique. Or you may decide that the technique is reliable and that Mr. Lundgren is a reliable practitioner of the technique, but that you disagree with his conclusion. You may also decide that you agree with his conclusion."

Williams' attack here on Lundgren's qualifications, and on the quality of his equipment, are without merit. All of the experts testifying at the evidentiary hearing, including those presented by Williams, attested to Lundgren's qualifications. Lundgren is certified as an examiner by the International Association of Voice Indentification and has extensive practical experience. No evidence supports the assertion that the spectrograph equipment was defective at the time Lundgren made his analysis, Williams' assertion being based entirely on speculative inferences drawn from past difficulties with the machine. Nor is there evidence to support a finding that the tapes were in any manner defective. On the contrary, all of the experts attested at the hearing to the high quality of the tapes. . . .

Does *Williams* reject the *Frye* standard, or does it hold that it has been satisfied with respect to voice-print analysis? If the latter, how does the *Williams* court treat the issues of defining the relevant scientific community and establishing general acceptance within that community?

Once a test or process has gained general acceptance and thereby satisfied the *Frye* standard, may an opponent of its use in a particular case introduce scientific evidence challenging the basic validity of the test or process and the general admissibility of its results?

STATE v. AQUILERA

25 Crim. L. Rep. (BNA) 2189, 47 U.S.L.W. 2737 (Dade County Ct., May 7, 1979)

NESBITT, J. These consolidated cases involve motions to suppress or exclude the results of radar speed measuring devices in prosecution of traffic violations. Numerous defendants cited for traffic violations and the state presented expert testimony and exhibits to support their respective positions. I believe this is the first case in which any court has been presented so much testimony and so many exhibits from highly qualified experts from all parts of the country.

The court has heard evidence from expert witnesses in the fields of mathematics, electrical engineering, and the design, construction, and testing of radar devices. There has been no argument with the Doppler system itself, but only as to the current use of radar by police as speed measuring devices. The voluminous testimony contained in-depth studies of many of the errors alleged to be inherent in most radar units in present use. The evidence considered the cosine error; batching error; panning and scanning errors; shadowing error; errors due to outside interferences such as billboards, overpasses, passing C.B. radios and many other similar causes; errors due to inside interferences such as heater and air conditioning fans, and police radios; errors due to improper mounting of radar units; errors due to heat build ups; errors due to power surge by shutting off and turning on the radar at the last minute to avoid radar detection devices; errors due to the auto lock system; errors due to reliance on the auto alarm system; errors due to mirror switch aiming; and errors in the identification of target vehicles. Although some of these problems are minimal in degree, their potential for error has been attested to by these witnesses in both theory and actual tests. The state's witnesses, in denying these problems, have sought to rely on adequately trained officers who recognize these errors and do not issue tickets accordingly.

On the basis of all the testimony, exhibits, and arguments, I find that the reliability of radar speed measuring devices as currently used has not been established beyond every reasonable doubt. I therefore grant the motions to suppress in these cases.

How should *Aquilera* have been decided under the Federal Rules? What constitutional limits are there to application of the *Frye* test?

Problem VII-5
Fried by Frye

Charge: murder. Defense: self-defense. The state's version is that *D* had his knife in his hand when he approached *V*. *D*'s version is that he did not draw the knife until *V* wrapped his belt around his hand with the buckle dangling and approached *D*. There is a conflict over who struck the first blow. *D*'s credibility is crucial to his defense.

At trial, *D* offers the testimony of a polygraph examiner to testify that he administered a lie-detector test to *D*. Tendered questions and answers from the test were to the effect that *D* did not intend to use his knife when he stopped his car near *V*, that he did not pull his knife before he got out of the car, that *V* had his belt in his hand when *D* pulled his knife, and that *V* struck the first blow. The polygraph examiner would have testified that *D* was telling the truth when he gave these answers.

The trial judge finds that the polygraph examiner is trained, experienced, and qualified and that the test was well conducted under controlled circumstances and therefore generally reliable. However, the trial judge sustains the state's objection to the polygraph examiner's testimony on the grounds that polygraphy "has not gained sufficient standing and scientific recognition among physiological and psychological authorities and therefore has not gained general acceptance in the particular field in which it belongs."

D is convicted and sentenced to death. Have his constitutional rights been violated?

Two proposed alternatives to the *Frye* "general acceptance test" and the McCormick relevancy approach are (1) creating permanent or ad hoc forensic commissions to advise the courts on the validity of specific scientific procedures and certify their validity (see, for example, Commonwealth v. A Juvenile, 365 Mass. 421, 452, 313 N.E.2d 120, 139 (Kaplan, J., dissenting); Maletskos and Spielman, Introduction of New Scientific Methods in Court, in Law Enforcement Science and Technology 957, 962 (Yefsky ed. 1967) and (2) imposing an enhanced burden of proof on the proponent of scientific evidence so that the prosecution in a criminal case must establish the validity of a novel scientific technique beyond a reasonable doubt and civil litigants and criminal defendants must establish validity to a preponderance of the evidence (see Giannelli, supra, at 1245-1250).

What advantages and disadvantages do these proposals have over the *Frye* and McCormick approaches? Is either approach contemplated or authorized by the Federal Rules?

2. Scientific Proof, the Proper Subjects of Expert Opinion, and the Qualifications of Experts

According to Wigmore, the question to ask with respect to scientific evidence from an expert is: "On *this subject* can a jury from *this person* receive appreciable help?" 7 Wigmore, Evidence §1923 at 21 (3d ed. 1940). Would framing the question in this way have helped in *Tranowski, Kelly, Aquilera,* and *Williams*? Does it help in resolving the following problems and cases?

Problem VII-6
The Dowser

To determine whether there is water within 400 feet of the surface of a piece of land, *P* offers a dowser to testify that she has dowsed the land and that there is no water. Is the testimony admissible?

Problem VII-7
Good Buddy

P wants to show that the load in the back of a truck shifted when the truck going 30 MPH hit a bump in the road. *W* is offered to testify that he is a trucker who often drives the type of truck in question, that he drove over the bump at 30 MPH, and that the bump was big enough to cause a load to shift. Is his testimony admissible? How should the judge decide whether to rule under 701 or 702? Does it matter?

EEN v. CONSOLIDATED FREIGHTWAYS
120 F. Supp. 289 (D.C.N.D. 1954), aff'd, 220 F.2d 82 (8th Cir. 1955)

VOGEL, J. This is an action for damages for personal injuries arising out of a collision between a car driven by the plaintiff Clarence O. Een, now an incompetent, and a truck driven by the defendant Dulski and owned by the defendant Consolidated Freightways. The jury returned a verdict for the defendants. The Court is now presented with plaintiffs' motion for a new trial. Such motion is based principally upon the grounds that the Court erred in allowing a defendants' witness, one John Holcomb, to testify, over objection, that from his observations he believed the collision had occurred on the west (defendants') side of the highway.

Holcomb was a deputy sheriff and former city policeman with over 17 years' experience investigating accidents as a law enforcement officer. He arrived at the scene of the accident approximately an hour and twenty minutes after its occurrence but before the damaged vehicles had been moved from the positions in which they had come to rest after the impact, and before the highway had been opened to other traffic. He was accompanied by a patrolman who also testified in the case, first at the instance of the plaintiffs, later being called by the defendants, but who was not asked by either party concerning his opinion as to where the collision took place. These two were the first police officials to arrive at the scene of the accident. Immediately after arriving, Holcomb took charge of unblocking the road and then in directing traffic past the stalled truck which he had had pulled to one side of the road. Holcomb also visited the scene of the accident on the morning after its occurrence.

After establishing Holcomb's qualifications and having him describe what he found and what he did, defendants' counsel asked him if, from his observations, he had formed an opinion as to where the impact occurred. Upon receiving an affirmative answer, he was asked to state the opinion. Plaintiffs' counsel objected on the grounds that it was incompetent, irrelevant and immaterial, calling for speculation, guess and conjecture, invading the province of the jury and called for a conclusion. The objections were overruled and the witness was allowed to state that in his opinion the impact occurred in the west lane of traffic. There was no objection to the qualifications of the witness and plaintiffs make no point of this in the motion for a new trial. . . . The issue, then, seems to be whether the matter was a proper subject for opinion testimony. . . .

UNITED STATES v. FOSHER
590 F.2d 381 (1st Cir. 1979)

COFFIN, C.J. This is the second appeal arising from the prosecution of appellant for bank robbery and assaulting bank employees. Appellant's first conviction was reversed and remanded for a new trial. United States v. Fosher, 568 F.2d 207 (1st Cir. 1978). The jury in appellant's first retrial was unable to reach a verdict. A second retrial resulted in conviction, from which this appeal arises. The facts and evidence involved are set out in our first opinion in this case.

As noted in our first opinion, the government's case depended almost entirely upon the testimony of two eyewitnesses who placed appellant in the vicinity of the bank at the time of the robbery. The instant appeal arises from appellant's unsuccessful attempt to introduce purportedly expert testimony on the unreliability of eyewitness identification at the second retrial. Specifically, appellant challenges the trial court's rejection of a written offer of proof and of a request for government funds under 18 U.S.C. §3006A(e) to pay for preparation of a testimonial offer on the subject of scientific evidence relating to perception and memory of eyewitnesses. See United States v. Fosher, 449 F. Supp. 76 (D. Mass. 1978). Given the broad discretion allowed a trial court in determining the admissibility of expert testimony, we affirm the decisions to exclude such testimony on the basis of the written offer, forego a testimonial offer, and refuse funds under the Criminal Justice Act.

We begin with the issue of admissibility and with the fundamental proposition that the propriety of receiving expert testimony rests within the sound discretion of the trial court. Salem v. United States Lines Co., 370 U.S. 31 (1962); 3 Weinstein's Evidence ¶702[01], at 702-9. In the instant case, the trial court held that the proffered testimony would not assist the jury in determining the fact at issue; that the jury was fully capable of assessing the eyewitnesses' ability to perceive and remember, given the help of cross-examination and cautionary instructions, without the aid of expert testimony; that expert testimony would raise a substantial danger of unfair prejudice, given the aura of reliability that surrounds scientific evidence; and that the limited probative value of the proof offered was outweighed by its potential for prejudice. We think that these conclusions were supported by the facts and provided a sound basis for the exercise of discretion. Or, to describe our ruling in terms that underscore the burden on appellant, we cannot say that the described testimony must be admitted as matter of law.

First, the written offer of proof did not make clear the relationship between the scientific evidence offered and the specific testimony of the eyewitnesses. Rather, the offer proclaimed that the expert "will not comment at all . . . on the testimony of any named witness in this or any other trial." Although the offer also represented that the expert would not expound in general on the unreliability of eyewitness testimony but would rather confine his recitation to such scientific facts as limited perception given limited opportunity to observe, rate of memory decay, and the source of memory given limited opportunity to observe followed by review of mug shots, the offer never explained how the expert's information would help the jury analyze the particular witnesses' ability to perceive and remember. In short, the offer supported the trial court's discretionary conclusion that the testimony would have limited, if any, relevance.

Second, the offer did not make clear that the testimony, even if relevant to the particular witnesses involved, would be based upon a mode of scientific analysis that meets any of the standards of reliability applicable to scientific evidence. See Frye v. United States, 54 App. D.C. 46, 293 F. 1013 (1923) (applying "general acceptance" standard); United States v. Williams, 583 F.2d 1194 (2d Cir. 1978) (applying "flexible" standard). The trial court's ruling that the eyewitnesses' perceptions and memory were within the ken of a lay jury and that the expert would not assist their evaluation of the quality of the identification, as required by F.R. Evid. 702, reflects this weakness in the offer of proof. As Professor Weinstein explains, a trial court can, in its discretion, conclude that scientific evaluation either has not reached, or perhaps cannot reach a level of reliability such that scientific analysis of a question of fact surpasses the quality of common sense evaluation inherent in jury deliberations.[1] 3 Weinstein, supra, at 702-6.

In the same vein, we are not troubled by appellant's arguments that F.R. Evid. 702 required admission of the expert testimony because it could "assist" the trier of fact. We recognize that the Advisory Committee's Note accompanying Rule 702 suggests that science will "assist" the jury so long as the untrained layman would not be able "to the best possible degree" to determine the issue by himself. See 3 Weinstein, supra, at 702-2. Admittedly, lay jurors may not have the best possible knowledge of the organic and behavioral mechanisms of perception and memory. But to be a proper subject of expert testimony, proof offered to add to their knowledge must present them with a system of analysis that the court, in its discretion, can find reasonably likely to add to common understanding of the particular issue before the jury. We are

---

1. We read the trial court's statement that the expert testimony would "invade the province of the jury" as reflecting its conclusion that the proffered science could not add to common sense evaluation. Contrary to appellant's argument, we do not read the trial court's statement as transgressing the spirit of F.R. Evid. 704. Rule 704 allows an expert to testify about specific facts in issue, and the Advisory Committee's Note on the Rule rejects former doctrine which excluded expert testimony on so-called ultimate issues of fact. See 3 Weinstein, supra, at 704-1. In saying that the expert would invade the province of the jury, we think the trial court was stating that the issue was not a proper subject of expert testimony under F.R. Evid. 702, that is, a subject beyond the ken of the ordinary juror and reliably analyzed by modern science.

satisfied that the trial court was within its discretion when it found the offer in this case neither sufficiently focussed on the issue nor sufficiently beyond the ken of lay jurors to satisfy Rule 702. See United States v. Amaral, 488 F.2d 1148, 1153 (9th Cir. 1973) (reciting requirements of proper subject and accepted scientific analysis and rejecting expert testimony on eyewitness abilities).

Quite apart from questions of limited relevance and reliability, the trial court also feared that the proffered expert testimony would create a substantial danger of undue prejudice and confusion because of its aura of special reliability and trustworthiness. Other courts have expressed the same concern about just this sort of expert testimony. The balancing of prejudice and probative value under F.R. Evid. 403 rests with the sound discretion of the trial court. United States v. Fosher, 568 F.2d 207 (1st Cir. 1978). We can add to the trial court's articulated concerns our own conviction that a trial court has the discretion to avoid imposing upon the parties the time and expense involved in a battle of experts. We cannot say that the balance of prejudice and probative value reached by the trial court was an abuse of discretion. . . .

On the second issue raised in *Fosher,* see also United States v. Watson, 587 F.2d 369 (7th Cir. 1978), where the court excluded the testimony of a psychologist who opined that cross-racial and cross-ethnic eyewitness identifications were unreliable. The court reasoned that the work in the field was inadequate and thus inadmissible. Should such evidence be admitted under FRE 702?

Problem VII-8
Abortion or Manslaughter?

P calls *W,* a pathologist, to give his medical opinion that based on his examination of slides of fetal tissue, the fetus drew a breath of air before it died. Is *D* entitled to cross-examine *W* about his qualifications as a pathologist before he gives his opinion? What is the material issue to which such examination would be directed? Would *D* be entitled, before the doctor gave his opinion, to call witnesses of his own to prove that the doctor is not qualified?

Problem VII-9
The Expert Moralist

In Roe v. Wade, 410 U.S. 113 (1973), the U.S. Supreme Court struck down as unconstitutional a Texas statute prohibiting abortions unless performed to save the mother's life. The Court held that a state has no compelling interest to justify any restrictions on abortions during the first trimester of pregnancy, that restrictions on abortions during the second trimester could be justified only on the grounds of protecting the mother's health, but that the state could restrict — even proscribe — abortions during the third trimester (after "viability") to protect fetal life. Crucial issues argued by both sides were whether a fetus constitutes "life" and, in any event, whether a state may make it a crime to terminate the potential life of a fetus.

(1) At the trial of the *Roe* case, should the court have considered expert testimony by clergymen or philosophers on the issue of the morality of abortion?

(2) Should the trial court have heard expert testimony from qualified sociologists or pollsters on the prevailing social thought about the morality of abortion?

(3) In *Roe*, despite extensive amicus briefs by experts in medicine, philosophy, and theology, the Supreme Court refused to decide the question of when life begins. Should expert testimony have been admitted on this issue? If this is the type of question to which expert testimony is appropriate, why then did the Court refuse to decide the issue?

In connection with the issue of whether expert testimony on questions of morality is appropriate, consider Hart v. Brown, 29 Conn. Supp. 368, 289 A.2d 386 (1972), in which the Connecticut court was faced with the issue of whether parental consent is sufficient to proceed with a kidney transplant between siblings. In *Hart*, should a clergyman have been allowed to testify on the morality of the parents' decision to consent to the procedure?

UNITED STATES v. JOHNSON
575 F.2d 1347 (5th Cir. 1978), cert. denied, 440 U.S. 907 (1979)

[Defendant was charged with conspiracy to import marijuana.]

The next appellant, Dennis Lipper, raises four points in his brief on appeal. He first argues that it was improper to permit de Pianelli to testify as an expert concerning the origin of the marijuana. Appellants concede that the substance with which they were dealing was marijuana. They contend, however, that there was no objective evidence showing that the marijuana was imported from outside the customs territory of the United States. Since no marijuana was ever seized, the only nonhearsay evidence concerning the origin of this marijuana came from de Pianelli. When de Pianelli was first asked to state whether the marijuana had come from Colombia, counsel for defendants objected. The jury was then excused and de Pianelli was examined on voir dire and cross-examined by defense counsel. During voir dire, he admitted that he had smoked marijuana over a thousand times and that he had dealt in marijuana as many as twenty times. He also said that he had been asked to identify marijuana over a hundred times and had done so without making a mistake. He based his identification upon the plant's appearance, its leaf, buds, stems, and other physical characteristics, as well as upon the smell and the effect of smoking it. On cross-examination he stated that he had been called upon to identify the source of various types of marijuana. He explained that characteristics such as the packaging, the physical appearance, the smell, the taste, and the effect could all be used in identifying the source of the marijuana. It was stipulated that he had no special training or education for such identification. Instead, his qualifications came entirely from "the experience of being around a great deal and smoking it." He also said that he had compared Colombian marijuana with marijuana from other places as many as twenty times. Moreover, he had seen Colombian marijuana that had been grown in the United States and had found that it was different from marijuana grown in Colombia.

After the voir dire examination, the defendants objected to de Pianelli's expertise for lack of authentication that he had actually smoked it, touched it, or correctly identified it. Despite the objection, the trial court permitted de Pianelli to give opinion evidence. Before the jury he related his experiences with marijuana and explained that he had tested a sample of marijuana from each importation and had verified that it came from Colombia.

Lipper contends that the source of marijuana is not a matter requiring expert opinion and that there was no foundation for de Pianelli's testimony. Lipper further contends that it was an error to qualify de Pianelli as an expert because he had never been to South America and, of course, had never smoked marijuana there or seen it growing in South America. Finally, Lipper contends that de Pianelli's testimony was conclusively rebutted by an associate professor of biological science at Florida State University, Loren C. Anderson.

In Crawford v. Worth, 447 F.2d 738, 740-41 (5th Cir. 1971), we stated the principle which guides appellate review of trial court determinations concerning expert testimony:

"The federal rule regarding review standards of trial court rulings on expert opinion evidence is stringent. . . . '[T]he trial judge has broad discretion in the matter of the admission or exclusion of expert evidence, and his action is to be sustained unless manifestly erroneous.' Salem v. United States Lines Co., 370 U.S. 31. In this Circuit's terms: 'The expert qualification of a witness is a question for the trial judge, whose discretion is conclusive unless clearly erroneous as a matter of law.' United States v. 41 Cases, More or Less, 420 F.2d 1126 (5th Cir. 1970). . . ."

Here the subject of the inference, the source of the marijuana, is related to the occupation of selling illegal drugs and to the science of botany, neither of which is likely to be within the knowledge of an average juror. For the government to obtain a conviction it was necessary that it prove that the marijuana came from outside the customs territory of the United States. See 21 U.S.C. §952. Testimony which would identify the source of the marijuana would be of obvious assistance to the jury. It was therefore proper for the trial court to consider whether de Pianelli was qualified to provide such testimony.

Rule 702 of the Federal Rules of Evidence provides that expertise may be obtained by experience as well as from formal training or education. de Pianelli's testimony during voir dire revealed that his substantial experience in dealing with marijuana included identification of Colombian marijuana. In light of that testimony, the trial court was within its discretion in deciding to admit the testimony for the jury's consideration.

The introduction of testimony from an expert witness does not foreclose the issue from consideration by the jury, which need not accept the expert's testimony. A defendant is free to introduce his own expert to challenge the prosecution's witness. Here the defense introduced the testimony of Professor Anderson, who said that it was impossible to determine the origin of a particular sample of marijuana by examining its physical characteristics. The trial court instructed the jury in general terms concerning the weight it should give to testimony. In addition, it specifically instructed the jury regarding expert witnesses and concluded with this admonition: "You should consider such expert opinion received in this case and give it such weight as you think it deserves." Thus the conflict between the experts was correctly presented to the jury for resolution. . . .

The only remaining challenge to de Pianelli's status as an expert is the argument that no one can acquire the skill which he professed to have. That objection may be rephrased in the words of this court in International Paper Company v. United States, 227 F.2d 201, 205 (5th Cir. 1955): "an opinion is no better than the hypothesis or the assumption upon which it is based." If the hypothesis is proved to be flawed, the witness should not be allowed to testify. This type of objection would be directed at, for example, the testimony of someone purporting to tell the color of a person's hair from fingerprints or the use of a testing device that had not been generally accepted by the scientific community. For a discussion of the latter problem, see United States v. Brown, 557 F.2d 541, 554-59 (6th Cir. 1977). Neither at trial nor on appeal have the appellants directly argued that no one can distinguish marijuana that has been grown in Colombia from other marijuana. They have, however, done so implicitly; and we believe that they tried to do so through the testimony of Professor Anderson. We shall therefore briefly consider that objection as well. Cf. United States v. Brown, supra, 557 F.2d at 557 n.17.

On the record before us we cannot say that the claim of an ability to identify Colombian marijuana is so inherently implausible that, as a matter of law, a jury should not be permitted to hear testimony on the identification. de Pianelli claimed that he could identify Colombian marijuana. Professor Anderson disputed that claim. But Professor Anderson admitted that climatological differences could produce differences in the marijuana plants. Professor Anderson's testimony was based upon the lack of scientific tests which would demonstrate that marijuana grown in Colombia differed from that grown elsewhere. Tests had shown, however, that marijuana grown in Canada differed from marijuana grown in other locations. Thus, there was some ambiguity in Professor Anderson's testimony. The issue was one that could have been resolved by the jury. In allowing the jury to consider the question and to hear the same arguments counsel now make to us, the court did not err.

KNIGHT v. OTIS ELEVATOR CO.
596 F.2d 84 (3d Cir. 1979)

HIGGINBOTHAM, J. . . . . This is a products liability case in which the plaintiff alleges she was injured when the door of a freight elevator in her employer's workplace prematurely closed and struck her. The plaintiff instituted an action against Otis Elevator Company, the designer, manufacturer and installer of the elevator; Hartford Insurance Group, which, as the insurer of the premises, had the statutory obligation either to inspect the elevator or to choose a licensed firm to perform such inspections; and Atwell, Vogel & Sterling, Inc. ("AVS"), which had been hired by the Hartford Insurance Group to perform the inspections. The plaintiff's employer, Western Electric Company, was joined as a third-party defendant.

The central thesis of the plaintiff's case was that the freight elevator was in a defective condition because, by reason of improper design, manufacture and installation, the buttons or switches controlling the doors could be activated inadvertently and "they protruded beyond the wall and had no guards to prevent . . . accidental pushing. . . ." She thus claimed liability against Otis on the grounds of strict liability, breach of warranty and negligence and against Hartford and AVS on the grounds of negligence. At the close of the plaintiff's case on liability, defendants' motions for directed verdicts were granted. The plaintiff appeals from the orders directing verdicts for each defendant and also challenges two evidentiary rulings by the district court. . . .

1. EXPERT TESTIMONY ISSUE

Knight assigns as error the district court's refusal to permit Emerson Venable to testify as an expert on whether unguarded elevator control buttons constituted a design defect. Absent an abuse of discretion, we will not interfere with the district court's decision on an expert's competence to testify. Universal Athletic Sales Co. v. American Gym, Recreational & Athletic Equipment Corp., 546 F.2d 530, 537 (3d Cir. 1976), cert. denied, 430 U.S. 984 (1977). We must nevertheless assess the district court's ruling in light of the liberal policy of permitting expert testimony which will "probably aid" the trier of fact. Id.

When making his ruling to preclude certain aspects of proffered testimony by Venable, the trial judge commented as follows:

> Direct and extended cross-examination regarding the witness' qualifications establish a background in engineering with special reference to chemistry and safety, including machine guarding, toxicology, and industrial hygiene.
>
> He has designed machine guards on occasions which he cannot detail, and in at least one instance had designed guard buttons in connection with the operation of a punch press.
>
> While he contends he has been consulted on certain elevator claims, he has been unable to relate any precise details as to the nature of the claims, their time frame, or his personal participation therein.
>
> On the contrary, he has never examined the elevator here in question, has examined no plans or sketches thereof, has not operated or otherwise had any contact with a freight elevator for more than twenty-six years.
>
> He has never designed an elevator or any part thereof, although something of his creation may have been used in the insulation, electrical equipment, relays, or coils of elevators without his knowledge.
>
> His activities as a consulting engineer have primarily and principally involved safety as related to fires, explosions, chemical poisoning, failure of materials, and failure of structural and hydraulic parts.
>
> He is not a design engineer, has had no background or experience in that area, has no specific background or experience with respect to elevators, and no knowledge of this specific elevator.
>
> Accordingly, because of his qualifications in the field of safety and machine guards, and his actual design of certain of such guards, he may testify as to the effect of unguarded elevator control buttons as related to safety, but *because of his lack of expertise as to elevators and elevator design, may not express an opinion as to whether such condition constitutes or constituted a design defect in the construction and installation of said elevator.*
>
> Likewise, because of his lack of familiarity with elevators generally, and this elevator in particular, he may not testify as to the operating sequence of

the inner gate and outer doors, the boot on the inner gate, inadequate inspections, and violation of statutory and departmental regulations.

Therefore, as to the five-part offer heretofore detailed, as to all of which the defendants object, it is the ruling of the Court, that, one, as to Item (1), unguarded control buttons, the objection is sustained in part and denied in part.

As to Item (2), operating sequence of inner gate and outer doors, Item (3), defective boot, Item (4), inadequate inspections, Item (5), violation of statutory and departmental regulations, the objection is sustained.

Appellant's Appendix at 611a-614a (emphasis added).

We recognize that the experienced trial judge was confronted with a shotgun approach in that plaintiff's counsel peppered the court with several contentions as to areas in which Venable's testimony was admissible. The trial judge tried valiantly to sort out these issues, and we conclude his rulings were correct as to all aspects except one. That one error, however, requires a reversal. When he ruled that Venable could not express an opinion on whether "unguarded elevator control buttons . . . constituted a design defect in the construction and installation of said elevator," id. at 613a, the trial judge invaded the arena reserved exclusively for the fact finder and thus he erred. While the ultimate fact finders — the jury — could decide that Venable's testimony was not credible and therefore attach no weight to it, this aspect of credibility was nevertheless within the exclusive province of the jury.

From Venable's testimony it appears that he was a consulting chemist and engineer specializing in materials engineering and safety. Since 1947, he has been a registered engineer in Pennsylvania, having studied physics at Carnegie Institute of Technology and safety engineering at the University of Pittsburgh. He later taught a course at the University of Pittsburgh's engineering school, one of the topics of which was "machine guarding." We note further his testimony that his interests were in the guarding and safety elements of machinery, that he had designed safety equipment from 1933 to 1951 and that he had been retained by manufacturers of machinery and had been involved in many investigations of problems on guarding machines. He has designed button guards to prevent inadvertent activation of machinery.

The district court refused to allow Venable to testify as an expert on whether unguarded elevator control buttons were a design defect because it believed that such testimony would require some background in the design and manufacture of elevators. We disagree.

Candidly, we are concerned with an increasing number of trial court rulings which seem to require an expert in a products liability case to be intimately familiar with all aspects of the total machine rather than the particular part in issue. An expert on tires need not be knowledgeable about automobile carburetors and roofs where the claim is a defective tire. Similarly a purported expert on the guarding of buttons need not be a specialist on elevators generally. The words of the late Judge Staley still ring true as he asserted in Trowbridge v. Abrasive Company of Philadelphia, 190 F.2d 825, 829 n.9 (3d Cir. 1951): "If we were to declare as a rule of law that one must actually have practical experience in a given industry in order to qualify as an expert in litigation involving its products, we might very well place an onerous burden on plaintiffs in some cases. Where the industry is small and tightly knit, it may be very difficult for the plaintiff to obtain the services of an expert currently employed therein, and it might be equally difficult to find someone who was formerly employed in the industry. But the key experts of an industry would normally be available to the defendant." Venable's inexperience in the areas of design and manufacturing should go to the weight, and not to the admissibility, of his opinion. See Bundie v. Skil Corporation, 591 F.2d 1334 (3d Cir. 1979). We think the pertinent art here was machine guarding, upon which Venable was competent to testify. The weight to be accorded the opinion on the absence of a guard was for the jury. In *Bundie,* this Court reiterated its reluctance to require highly particularized, subspecialization on the part of experts. We conclude, therefore, that the district court's refusal to accept Venable as an expert on the question of defective design was not consistent with the sound exercise of its discretion. . . .

Do you agree with the trial court's decision excluding the expert's testimony on design defects? Do you agree with the Court of Appeal's action in reversing the trial court?

3.   Examining Expert Witnesses

FRE 703
Bases of Opinion Testimony by Experts

The facts or data in the particular case upon which an expert bases an opinion or inference may be those perceived by or made known to him at or before the hearing. If of a type reasonably relied upon by experts in the particular field in forming opinions or inferences upon the subject, the facts or data need not be admissible in evidence.

ADVISORY COMMITTEE'S NOTE ON RULE 703

Facts or data upon which expert opinions are based may, under the rule, be derived from three possible sources. The first is the firsthand observation of the witness, with opinions based thereon traditionally allowed. A treating physician affords an example. Rheingold, The Basis of Medical Testimony, 15 Vand. L. Rev. 473, 489 (1962). Whether he must first relate his observations is treated in Rule 705. The second source, presentation at the trial, also reflects existing practice. The technique may be the familiar hypothetical question or having the expert attend the trial and hear the testimony establishing the facts. Problems of determining what testimony the expert relied upon, when the latter technique is employed and the testimony is in conflict, may be resolved by resort to Rule 705. The third source contemplated by the rule consists of presentation of data to the expert outside of court and other than by his own perception. In this respect the rule is designed to broaden the basis for expert opinions beyond that current in many jurisdictions and to bring the judicial practice into line with the practice of the experts themselves when not in court. Thus a physician in his own practice bases his diagnosis on information from numerous sources and of considerable variety, including statements by patients and relatives, reports and opinions from nurses, technicians and other doctors, hospital records, and X rays. Most of them are admissible in evidence, but only with the expenditure of substantial time in producing and examining various authenticating witnesses. The physician makes life-and-death decisions in reliance upon them. His validation, expertly performed and subject to cross-examination, ought to suffice for judicial purposes. . . .

FRE 705
Disclosure of Facts or Data Underlying Expert Opinion

The expert may testify in terms of opinion or inference and give his reasons therefor without prior disclosure of the underlying facts or data, unless the court requires otherwise. The expert may in any event be required to disclose the underlying facts or data on cross-examination.

ADVISORY COMMITTEE'S NOTE ON RULE 705

The hypothetical question has been the target of a great deal of criticism as encouraging partisan bias, affording an opportunity for summing up in the middle of the case, and as complex and time consuming. Ladd, Expert Testimony, 5 Vand. L. Rev. 414, 426-427 (1952). While the rule allows counsel to make disclosure of the underlying facts or data as a preliminary to the giving of an expert opinion, if he chooses, the instances in which he is required to do so are reduced. This is true whether the expert bases his opinion on data furnished him at secondhand or observed by him at firsthand. . . .

NOTE: THE BASES OF EXPERT OPINIONS

Rule 703 recognizes four distinct ways for an expert to acquire the data on which he bases his opinion: (1) by supposition at the trial (the hypothetical question); (2) by listening to the testimony of other witnesses at trial; (3) by personal experience before the trial, as in the case of a doctor testifying about a patient whom she has treated personally; or (4) by being informed of data by others before the trial (hearsay).

Hypothetical Questions. The hypothetical question has the potential for carefully delineating the basis of an expert's opinion and for allowing precisely formed cross-examination. The question typically takes a form such as:

Q: Doctor, assume that the following facts are true: fact A, fact B, . . . fact N. (Counsel poses all the relevant facts of *his* case as facts to be assumed.)

    Now, doctor, based on those assumed facts, do you have an opinion whether . . . ?

A: Yes.

Q: What is your opinion?

A: My opinion is that . . . .

On cross-examination opposing counsel can then test the opinion by changing one or more facts, or adding or deleting facts, and asking how (or whether) the doctor's opinion is affected. For example:

Q: Doctor, assume that the car was travelling at 10 MPH instead of 30 MPH at the moment of impact. What then would be your opinion as to . . . ?

One problem with hypothetical questions is that while they may be used constructively, they also may be abused. With each statement of a hypothetical question counsel has an opportunity to reiterate the facts of his case, order them, and indicate their significance — in effect, to make a closing argument. Another problem is their potential complexity. One hypothetical question consumed nearly one hundred pages of transcript. What are the chances that the jury understood the question, or even kept awake through it?

Do the Federal Rules leave the option with counsel to use or not to use hypothetical questions? If so, have the rules failed to deal with the problem of abuse? What power does a federal trial judge have to stop a lawyer from using hypothetical questions in a manner that the judge considers abusive?

Other Witnesses. The difficulties with this method of data acquisition are both practical and theoretical. To acquire data by listening to other witnesses requires the expert to sit in court while the others testify, an expensive proposition. Moreover, if there is any conflict or ambiguity in the testimony of the other witnesses, the expert's data-base will be ambiguous and will require clarification.

Personal Experience. This, typically, is the most effective basis for testimony. A ballistics expert will be most effective if he has test-fired the weapon himself and made microscopic photos of the resulting grooves and comparison photos with the bullet. The problem is that with some forms of expertise it is neither efficient nor sensible for the expert to perform all tests or analyses himself. Unless the expert could rely on the work of others, those who actually performed the tests would have to be called to testify before the expert could give his opinion based on the tests. This problem led to recognition of hearsay as a fourth legitimate form of data base.

Hearsay. As indicated by the Advisory Committee's notes to Rule 703 the most radical extension of this rule is its authorization for experts to rely on facts or data "made known to him" before the hearing, e.g., hearsay. The hearsay must be of a type reasonably relied upon by experts in the particular field in forming opinions or inferences upon the subject; but who is to make *this* determination and how?

Would the following reformulation of Rule 703 be an improvement on the present version or an unwise retreat from a useful reform?

> An expert's opinion may be based on a hypothetical question, facts or data perceived by the expert at or before the hearing, or facts or data in evidence. If of a type reasonably and customarily relied upon by experts in the particular field in forming opinions upon the subject, the underlying facts or data shall be admissible without testimony from the primary source.

Problem VII-10
Engineer's Investigation

(1) *P* offers an engineer to give her opinion that the steering wheel of *P*'s car was defective prior to the accident. She bases her opinion on her post-accident examination of the wreck and on the statement of the driver, reported to the engineer, that the auto lost its steering control before it crashed. How should the trial judge decide whether the engineer's opinion is admissible?

(2) Could the engineer state her opinion without revealing the information on which she based it? If so, how would opposing counsel probe to find out what the basis of the opinion was and what would happen if and when the arguably impermissible basis for the opinion emerged?

(3) Would the situation be materially different if the case were criminal instead of civil?

Problem VII-11
Pediatric Poison

In January, P gives birth to a child five weeks prematurely. The child is blue, weak, and sickly. By February 22 the child shows little improvement and little weight gain and is even more fretful. On March 1, P's pediatrician prescribes a mild dosage of elixir of phenobarbital, one teaspoon every six hours. The prescription is delivered to pharmacist D. D fills a bottle with a solution, labels it, and puts on the label instructions to give the child one teaspoon every six hours. On March 2 the prescription is delivered to P. P gives the child one teaspoon of the medicine. Two hours later the child suffers convulsions and dies. An examination of the contents of bottle reveals that it contained morphine acetate in a one-thirtieth of a grain solution rather than phenobarbital. P sues D for wrongful death of her child caused by D's negligence in filling the doctor's prescription. D admits all of the above facts but denies that his negligence proximately caused the child's death. At trial, P offers to prove that section 904 of Taylor's Medical Jurisprudence (a concededly standard treatise) states that for infants less than one year of age, the maximum safe dosage of morphine acetate is one-fortieth of a grain per teaspoon every six hours and that any greater concentration is likely to cause convulsions and death. D objects. What ruling and why at common law?

Suppose D's objection to P's offer of section 904 is sustained. P then calls Dr. Kildare to the witness stand. Through questioning, P adduces Dr. Kildare's education, internship, professional affiliations, and practice as an expert endocrinologist with 12 years on the staff of a major metropolitan hospital. P then examines Dr. Kildare as follows:

Q: Doctor, what in your opinion is the maximum safe dosage of morphine acetate for an infant less than one year?
A: One-fortieth of a grain per teaspoon every six hours.
Q: That is all. Thank you, Dr. Kildare.

The cross-examination is as follows:

Q: Doctor, have you ever prescribed morphine acetate?
A: No.
Q: Have you ever observed a patient under the influence of morphine acetate?
A: No.
Q: Doctor, have you ever taken morphine acetate yourself?
A: No.
Q: Your opinion, then, is simply a guess, isn't it?
A: No. It is based on section 904 of Taylor's Treatise on Medical Jurisprudence.

D moves to strike Dr. Kildare's entire testimony, including the direct examination. *P* responds, citing Finnegan v. Fall River Gas Works Co., 159 Mass. 311, 312-313, 34 N.E. 523 (1893) (Holmes, J.):

> Although it might not be admissible merely to repeat what a witness had read in a book not itself admissible, still, when one who is competent on the general subject accepts from his reading as probably true a matter of detail which he has not verified, the fact gains an authority which it would not have had from the printed page alone, and, subject perhaps to the exercise of some discretion, may be admitted.

Do you agree with Holmes? What should be the limits, if any, to the license given experts to base their opinions on inadmissible hearsay?

"Is this really necessary, Your Honor? I'm an expert."

Drawing by Levin. Copyright © 1979 by The New Yorker Magazine, Inc.

Problem VII-12
Diminished Capacity

D, being prosecuted for murder, does not want to take the stand but does want the jury to hear her story. Her defense is "diminished capacity." She offers a psychiatrist, who will testify that in his expert opinion, *D* did not have the mental capacity at the time of the killing to premeditate. He bases his opinion on (1) extensive interviews with *D* during which *D* has related her life history and her version of the killing; (2) correspondence with *D*'s family about some of the psychologically formative events of *D*'s life; (3) a report of a neurological examination by another doctor; and (4) a treatise on psychiatry, with a section on diminished capacity written by Dr. Green, Professor of Law and Psychiatry at Ames University.

What can the expert say in his direct examination? Can he testify that in his opinion the defendant lacked the mental capacity to premeditate the crime? On cross-examination can the prosecutor confront the witness with a treatise written by Dr. Brown of Langdell University whose views are contrary to those of Dr. Green? Has the defendant waived her fifth amendment privilege by offering the expert to testify based on the interviews with her?

PEOPLE v. GORSHEN
51 Cal. 2d 716, 336 P.2d 492 (1959)

SCHAUER, J. Defendant pleaded not guilty to a charge of murder. Trial by jury was waived and the court found defendant guilty of second degree murder. Defendant appeals from the ensuing judgment. He urges that uncontradicted psychiatric testimony, accepted by the trial court, establishes that defendant did not intend to take human life or, at least, that he did not act with malice aforethought, and that therefore he should be acquitted or, as a minimum of relief, that the offense should be reduced to manslaughter. We have concluded: (1) that the evidence as to the objective circumstances of the killing supports all findings essentially implied by the judgment; (2) that the record does not support defendant's position that the trial court believed the evidence that defendant did not have the state of mind which was required as an element of second degree murder yet found defendant guilty of that crime; and (3) that, accordingly, the judgment should be affirmed.

Defendant, a longshoreman, shot and killed his foreman, Joseph O'Leary, at about 2:30 A.M. on March 9, 1957. The record discloses the following events leading up to the homicide: At 5 P.M. on March 8 defendant reported to the dispatching hall. Between 6 and 7 o'clock he and a fellow worker ate and consumed a fifth of a gallon of sloe gin.

Defendant worked until 11 P.M. Between 11 and 12 o'clock defendant and the fellow worker ate and consumed a pint of sloe gin. Shortly after 12 midnight O'Leary saw defendant standing on the deck of the ship drinking a glass of coffee. O'Leary told defendant to go to work. Defendant threw the glass to the deck, exchanged "a few words" with O'Leary, and went to work. Thereafter O'Leary told defendant that he was drunk and was not doing his work properly and directed defendant to go home. They argued, defendant spat in O'Leary's face, and O'Leary knocked defendant down and kicked him. At the request of other workers O'Leary walked away from defendant. Defendant threw a piece of dunnage and brandished a carton at O'Leary.

Paul Baker, a "walking boss," took defendant to a hospital. Defendant was bleeding and bruised; his left eye was swollen shut and a deep cut under it required five or six stitches. Defendant was discharged at 1:45 A.M. The hospital records bear the notation, "Alcoholic Breath." As Baker drove defendant back to the pier where they worked, defendant said "that he was going to go home and get a gun and kill this fellow."

When he reached the pier defendant said that he wished to return to work but his superiors insisted that he go home. Defendant said, "I'll go home and get my gun. I'll come back and take care of him." Defendant drove to his home, got a .25 caliber automatic pistol which contained two bullets, fired one shot in his living room, put the gun in his apron, and drove back to the pier. He arrived there about 30 minutes after he had been sent home and went onto the ship looking for O'Leary.

O'Leary and Nelson, a union business agent, had followed defendant to his house and, when they saw defendant leave his house, had driven to a police station. Police officers went to the pier. They searched defendant but did not find his gun. Defendant told the officers that he "had a fight with Mr. O'Leary, and . . . that he couldn't forget about the eye that he had obtained during the fight." One of the officers described defendant as "angry," "almost tearsome," "emotional," but not incoherent or boisterous.

O'Leary and Nelson then appeared. Defendant said, "My buddy. Hah, my buddy," and produced the gun. O'Leary shouted, "Look out, he's got the gun." Defendant shot. The single bullet entered O'Leary's abdomen, killing him; it also wounded Nelson's arm. The officers subdued defendant after a brief struggle. Defendant told the authorities, shortly after the homicide, that O'Leary was "looking at me, smiling, so I just let him have it. . . . Nelson was standing by, I had to take chance to hit him, because I had only one bullet."

Defendant had a very good reputation for peace and quiet and did not usually drink to excess. He testified as follows: During the 15 years he had known O'Leary prior to the night of the homicide they had been friends and had had no trouble. Defendant's recollection of the events of that night was "kind of hazy." He considered it unfair of O'Leary to order him to go home but to retain the fellow worker with whom defendant had been drinking.

> The argument starts about he wants me to go home and I . . . tell him that I intend to wait until business agent comes in, so apparently he, he hit me and knocked me off, off the floor and when I jumped up, he got on and hit me again, and that's — then I tried to defend myself. I, I didn't hit him . . . ; he was apparently too fast for me or stronger, bigger.

Defendant did not recall throwing a piece of dunnage or brandishing a carton or threatening to go home and get a gun. When he discharged the gun in his home, "I didn't know it was on the safety or not, I was shaky, I didn't know what I was doing." Defendant recalled little of his return to the pier, but did recall that the police searched him. Then he saw O'Leary "grinning, looking at me. I don't know what, what become of me. I just grabbed the gun and shot."

Dr. Bernard L. Diamond, a psychiatrist who examined defendant, testified as follows:[2]

After described examinations and tests of defendant, the doctor concluded that defendant suffers from chronic paranoiac schizophrenia, a disintegration of mind and personality. For 20 years defendant has had trances during which he hears voices and experiences visions, particularly of devils in disguise committing abnormal sexual acts, sometimes upon defendant. Defendant recognizes that these experiences are "not real" but believes that they are forced upon him by the devil. Apparently defendant, prior to his examination by Dr. Diamond, had not disclosed these experiences to anyone.

A year before the shooting defendant (who was 56 years of age at the time of trial) became concerned about loss of sexual power. With this concern his sexual hallucinations occurred with increased frequency and his ability in his work became increasingly important to him as a proof of manhood.

On the night of the shooting, O'Leary's statement that defendant was drunk and should leave his work was to defendant the psychological equivalent of the statement that "You're not a man, you're impotent, . . . you're a sexual pervert." Then, according to defendant's statements to Dr. Diamond, O'Leary applied to defendant an epithet which indicated sexual perversion. At this point, according to Dr. Diamond's opinion, defendant was confronted with

> the imminent possibility of complete loss of his sanity. . . . [A]s an alternate to total disintegration . . . , it's possible for . . . an individual of this kind, to develop an obsessive murderous rage, an unappeasable anger. . . . The

---

2. It should be noted that no question of legal insanity is here involved.

strength of this obsession is proportioned not to the reality danger but to the danger of the insanity. . . . [F]or this man to go insane, means to be permanently in the world of these visions and under the influence of the devil. . . . [A]n individual in this state of crisis will do anything to avoid the threatened insanity, and it's this element which lends strength to his compulsive behavior so that he could think of nothing else but to get O'Leary, so he went home and got the gun and shot him; and [as] is usually the case in this type of event, the shooting itself released the danger of [defendant's complete mental disintegration].

Defendant told Dr. Diamond that from the time he was taken to the emergency hospital until the time of the shooting

That is all I was thinking about all of this time is to shoot O'Leary. I forgot about my family, I forgot about God's laws and human's laws and everything else. The only thing was to get that guy, get that guy, get that guy, like a hammer in the head.

In the opinion of the doctor, defendant acted almost as an automaton;

even the fact that policemen were right at his elbow and there was no possibility of getting away with this, still it couldn't stop the train of obsessive thoughts which resulted in the killing. . . . [H]e did not have the mental state which is required for malice aforethought or premeditation or anything which implies intention, deliberation or premeditation.

Dr. Diamond quoted section 188 of the Penal Code, which provides that the "malice aforethought" which is an essential element of murder

may be express or implied. It is express when there is manifested a deliberate intention unlawfully to take away the life of a fellow-creature. It is implied, when no considerable provocation appears, or when the circumstances attending the killing show an abandoned and malignant heart.

He then gave his opinion of the "medical essence" of "malice aforethought"; i.e.,

whether an individual performs an act as a result of his own free will or intentionality or . . . whether the action is directly attributable to some abnormal compulsion or force, or symptom or diseased process from within the individual.[3]

3. The trial court correctly overruled the People's objection that by this testimony the doctor gave "a medical interpretation of a legal principle." The court did not permit the doctor to usurp the judicial function of interpreting legislative language; rather, it properly permitted him to explain what he meant by his opinion that defendant lacked malice aforethought.

The doctor further explained that in his opinion "actions, like the threat to kill, the going home to get the gun and so forth" — actions which "in an ordinary individual" would be evidence "that he intended to do what he did do, and that this was an act of free will and deliberation" — in defendant's case were, rather, "just as much symptoms of his mental illness as the visions and these trances that he goes into." . . .

The trial court stated at some length the matters which it considered in reaching its decision. It said,

> up till the time that Dr. Diamond testified in this case, there was no explanation of why this crime was committed. . . . [The doctor is] the first person that has any reasonable explanation. Whether it's correct or not, I don't know. . . . [I]f I would follow Diamond's testimony in toto, I should acquit this man. . . .
>
> I'm willing to go on the record, that in all probability his theories are correct . . . that he had no particular intent to commit this crime.
>
> I like to be advanced. But it seems to me that my hands are tied with the legal jurisprudence as it stands today, and that's why I'm saying this for the purposes of the record. The Appellate Court might say that my hands are not tied, but I think they are. . . . [E]ven accepting in part the testimony of Dr. Diamond, I still feel that this man is guilty of second degree murder.

In reply to defense counsel's assertion that "There is not one scintilla of malice," the court said,

> it all depends on how you view it. . . . Some other person or another Judge, might say, "Malice, why, it's full of it. He planned it. He said he was going to do it, he went home, he had an hour."

Again defense counsel asked, "Does your Honor feel that there is malice here?" The court replied,

> there was some intent. Now, whether you have free will or not free will, that's so advanced, we're not prepared for that. . . . There's plenty, plenty of malice as far as statements are concerned, and plenty of malice as far as actions are concerned. Now, whether he was compelled to do this because of some mental condition, that is so advanced and so far from us that we don't understand it. . . . [I]t would be a perfect first degree if it wasn't for the fact that he's never been in trouble and because of the statement of the Psychiatrist.

Dr. Diamond's testimony was properly received in accord with the holding of People v. Wells (1949), 33 Cal. 2d 330, 346-357 [202 P.2d 53], that on the trial of the issues raised by a plea of not guilty to a charge of a crime which requires proof of a specific mental state, competent evidence that because of mental abnormality not amounting to legal insanity[5] defendant did not possess the essential specific mental state is

5. I.e., insanity measured by the familiar test restated in M'Naughton's Case (1843), 10

admissible. The admission of testimony such as that of the expert here, for the purpose of consideration by the trier of fact upon issues of particular essential mental state, does not, as it has been suggested, imply acceptance (on the general issue) of the defense of irresistible impulse (which is rejected in this state as a test of the defense of legal insanity); nor does it imply rejection of the criminal law's postulate of free will. It has been said that "Whatever may be the abstract truth, the law has never recognized an impulse as uncontrollable which yet leaves the reasoning powers — including the capacity to appreciate the nature and quality of the particular act — unaffected by mental disease." But this statement must be considered in its context; it was made in the course of an opinion which holds that irresistible impulse does not constitute the insanity which is a complete defense; i.e., which is exculpatory of all penal responsibility for any otherwise criminal act. So considered, statements such as that . . . do not preclude the admission and consideration, on the issue of specific intent or other particular mental state, of expert testimony which includes such concepts as the uncontrollable compulsion described by the expert here (described, it may be added, not as an "abstract truth" but as arising upon the specific facts, objective and subjective, of this particular killing).

Such expert evidence, like evidence of unconsciousness resulting from voluntary intoxication, is received not as a "complete defense" negating capacity to commit any crime but as a "partial defense" negating specific mental state essential to a particular crime. . . .

Section 1962 of the Code of Civil Procedure declares that "A malicious and guilty intent" is conclusively presumed "from the deliberate commission of an unlawful act, for the purpose of injuring another." This "conclusive presumption" has little meaning, either as a rule of substantive law or as a rule of evidence, for the facts of deliberation and purpose which must be established to bring the presumption into operation are just as subjective as the presumed fact of malicious and guilty intent.

A further problem arises as to whether evidence of defendant's abnormal mental or physical condition (whether caused by intoxication, by trauma, or by disease, but not amounting to legal insanity or unconsciousness) can be considered to rebut malice aforethought and intent to kill in a case such as the one at bar, where the prosecution evidence shows infliction of a mortal wound for the purpose of killing and the evidence does not show provocation which would meet the law's

---

Clark & Fin. 200, 8 Eng. Rep. 718, and long accepted in this state (People v. Coffman (1864), 24 Cal. 230, 235; People v. Wells, supra, pp. 350, 351 [20] of 33 Cal.2d): that at the time defendant committed the act, he was laboring under such a defect of reason, from disease of the mind, that he did not know the nature and quality of his act or, if he did know it, that he did not know that he was doing what was wrong. . . .

definition of voluntary manslaughter, an unlawful killing upon a sudden
quarrel or in a heat of passion such as would naturally be aroused in the
mind of an *ordinary reasonable person* under the circumstances. . . .

Section 22 of the Penal Code says that

> whenever the actual existence of *any particular purpose, motive, or intent* is a
> necessary element to constitute any particular *species* or degree of crime, the
> jury may take into consideration the fact that the accused was intoxicated at
> the time, in determining the purpose, motive, or intent with which he com-
> mitted the act.

(Italics added.) The section refers to any "species" (kind) of crime as well
as to any "degree" of crime. The state of mind known as "malice
aforethought" comes within the meaning of the phrase "any particular
purpose, motive, or intent." "Malice aforethought" is a "necessary
[statutorily prescribed] element" of both degrees of murder ("Murder is
the unlawful killing of a human being, with malice aforethought"; Pen.
Code, §187). Specific intent to kill is not a "necessary [statutorily pre-
scribed] element" of second degree murder but is a necessary element of
the kind of first degree murder which we are here considering (a "will-
ful, deliberate, and premeditated killing"; Pen. Code, §189) and is implicit in the statutory description of the kind of manslaughter which we
are here discussing ("the unlawful killing of a human being . . . Voluntary"; Pen. Cod, §192).

It would seem elementary that a plea of not guilty to a charge of
murder puts in issue the existence of the particular mental states which
are essential elements of the two degrees of murder and of manslaughter (a crime traditionally regarded as necessarily included in murder
although in some cases the mental element of manslaughter may be
more accurately described as differing from, rather than included in,
the mental element of murder). Accordingly, it appears only fair and
reasonable that defendant should be allowed to show that in fact, subjec-
tively, he did not possess the mental state or states in issue.

Some cases have recognized the propriety of considering evidence of
subjective mental condition for this purpose. Thus, People v. Selph
(1930), 106 Cal. App. 704, 707 [289 P. 918], in discussing the effect of
evidence of voluntary intoxication in a homicide case, says that "while
the insanity of the defendant is not in issue under the general plea, yet
this does not preclude the introduction of evidence tending to establish
the mental condition of the accused at the time the offense was committed for the purpose of showing a lack of criminal intent, malice or
premeditation." . . .

We conclude that the Selph (1930) case represents a correct view of
the consideration which the trier of fact should give to relevant evidence

of mental condition upon the issues of malice aforethought and intent to kill. . . .

Defendant and amici curiae urge that in the present case statements of the trial court affirmatively show that it believed the expert testimony that defendant, because of the concurrence of mental disease and the objective circumstances with which he was confronted, in fact lacked intent to kill and malice aforethought, yet erroneously concluded that the law required it to find that those elements were present. Defendant would attribute to selected portions of the trial court's remarks the force of findings of fact and conclusions of law. But those remarks when read as a whole set forth reflections and reasoning pro and con, matters which tend to support the judgment and matters which tend to suggest a contrary conclusion, but all proper to be considered by the fair, impartial, conscientious, and able judge in resolving the several issues and reaching his ultimate conclusion.

In accord with the normal process of appellate review, we accept those statements which support the judgment as representing the court's final determinations, and interpret favorable to the judgment those statements which are susceptible of such interpretation. When the statements are so viewed, it is apparent that this is a case where the trial court considered all the conflicting evidence and resolved it in support of its judgment, not a case where the trial court admitted evidence but because of a misapprehension of law refused to consider and weigh it upon the erroneous theory that it could not be considered.

The trial court's informally expressed opinion was that defendant's threats and actions evidenced intent to kill and malice aforethought, but that "whether he was compelled to do this because of some mental condition, that is so advanced and so far from us that we don't understand it." A fair interpretation of the quoted statement is, not that the expert testimony was as a matter of law incomprehensible or unacceptable to the court as a finder of fact or as a judge of the law, but rather that the court as a trier of fact did not have a reasonable doubt that this particular defendant, when he killed, lacked intent to kill and malice aforethought. This interpretation of the quoted statement is borne out by the trial court's further statement that "it would be a perfect first degree [murder] if it wasn't for the fact that he's never been in trouble and because of the statement of the Psychiatrist"; from this statement of the court it affirmatively appears that the implied finding of lack of deliberation and premeditation was based in part upon acceptance of the doctor's testimony.

Thus it is apparent that whatever the trial judge may have had in mind when he stated in the course of his pro and con deliberations that "I like to be advanced. But it seems to me that my hands are tied with the legal jurisprudence as it stands today," he did in truth finally decide that his fact finding hands were not tied; he must have so concluded because he received, considered and gave effect to the expert's testimony on the issues to which it was pertinent. Some of those issues he resolved in favor of the prosecution (he found the defendant guilty of murder), but others he determined in favor of the defendant (he found that the murder was *not* of the first degree). In other words, within the area of culpability for the crime charged the testimony of the expert apparently created a reasonable doubt that the homicide was murder of the first degree but not that it was murder. The differences between the degrees of murder and between murder and voluntary manslaughter have been carefully spelled out and need not be reviewed here. In the light of the cited cases and the record before us, we conclude that the judgment of conviction reached by the trial court is based on a reasonable view of the evidence and a correct understanding and application of the law.

For the reasons above stated, the judgment is affirmed.

NOTE: DISCOVERY OF EXPERT'S OPINIONS

Rule 705 leaves the tactical option with counsel whether or not to have the expert witness lay out the data base. Often counsel wants the expert to function much like a teacher and so is anxious to have the witness fully elaborate the basis and reasoning underlying the opinion. Under what circumstances might counsel make the other tactical choice? Are there circumstances in which counsel could set a trap for the cross-examiner?

Rule 26(b)(4) of the Federal Rules of Civil Procedure gives *well prepared* counsel a means of discovering the bases of the expert's opinion in advance. The comparable discovery rules for criminal cases are much narrower. Compare the two rules.

RULE 26(b)(4)
Federal Rules of Civil Procedure

(4) Trial Preparation: Experts. Discovery of facts known and opinions held by experts, otherwise discoverable under the provisions of subdivision (b)(1) of this rule and acquired or developed in anticipation of litigation or for trial, may be obtained only as follows:

(A)(i) A party may through interrogatories require any other party to identify each person whom the other party expects to call as an expert witness at trial, to state the subject matter on which the expert is expected to testify, and to state the substance of the facts and opinions to which the expert is expected to testify and a summary of the grounds for each opinion. (ii) Upon motion, the court may order further discovery by other means, subject to such restrictions as to scope and such provisions, pursuant to subdivision (b)(4)(C) of this rule, concerning fees and expenses as the court may deem appropriate.

(C) Unless manifest injustice would result, (i) the court shall require that the party seeking discovery pay the expert a reasonable fee for time spent in responding to discovery under subdivisions (b)(4)(A)(ii) and (b)(4)(B) of this rule; and (ii) with respect to discovery obtained under subdivision (b)(4)(A)(ii) of this rule the court may require, and with respect to discovery obtained under subdivision (b)(4)(B) of this rule the court shall require, the party seeking discovery to pay the other party a fair portion of the fees and expenses reasonably incurred by the latter party in obtaining facts and opinions from the expert.

RULE 16
Federal Rules of Criminal Procedure

(a) Disclosure of evidence by the government. . . .

(D) Reports of examinations and tests. Upon request of a defendant the government shall permit the defendant to inspect and copy or photograph any results or reports of physical or mental examinations, and of scientific tests or experiments, or copies thereof, which are within the possession, custody, or control of the government, the existence of which is known, or by the exercise of due diligence may become known, to the attorney for the government, and which are material to the preparation of the defense or are intended for use by the government as evidence in chief at the trial.

(b) Disclosure of evidence by the defendant.

(1) Information subject to disclosure.

(A) Documents and tangible objects. If the defendant requests disclosure under subdivision (a)(1)(C) or (D) of this rule, upon compliance with such request by the government, the defendant, on request of the government, shall permit the government to inspect and copy or photograph books, papers, documents, photographs, tangible objects, or copies or portions thereof, which are within the possession, custody, or control of the defendant and which the defendant intends to introduce as evidence in chief at the trial.

(B) Reports of examinations and tests. If the defendant requests disclosure under subdivision (a)(1)(C) or (D) of this rule, upon compliance with such request by the government, the defendant, on request of the government, shall permit the government to inspect and copy or photograph any results or reports of physical or mental examinations and of scientific tests or experiments made in connection with the particular case, or copies thereof, within the possession or control of the defendant, which the defendant intends to introduce as evidence in chief at

the trial or which were prepared by a witness whom the defendant intends to call at the trial when the results or reports relate to his testimony.

Do these provisions seem adequate to prepare to meet expert testimony at trial?

There are some special discovery problems with scientific evidence. As Professor Giannelli points out, many laboratory reports reveal only the end results of a test, and in some tests the actual evidence is consumed in the testing. Moreover, in criminal cases there is likely to be an imbalance in the expert and laboratory resources available to the prosecution and defense. This can lead to a deficiency in preparation for and rebuttal of the prosecution's experts. See, Giannelli, supra, 80 Colum. L. Rev. at 1242-1243.

What solutions to these problems would you propose?

4.   Court-Appointed Experts

Problem VII-13
Medical Malpractice

In 1979, *P,* a 61-year-old man, is operated on by Dr. *D* for removal of his appendix and gall bladder. On February 18, 1979, *P* suffers severe abdominal pains. An X ray taken that day reveals a hemostat inside *P*'s side. *P* dies February 22, 1979. Doctors *A* and *B* perform an autopsy on *P* prior to interment. *P*'s executor sues Dr. *D* for malpractice and wrongful death. Dr. *D*'s negligence is conceded, but the cause of death is contested. *A* testifies for the plaintiff that the hemostat killed *P. B* testifies for the defendant that *D* died of other causes. What is the role of the experts, judge, and jury in this situation?

FRE 706
Court Appointed Experts

(a) Appointment. The court may on its own motion or on the motion of any party enter an order to show cause why expert witnesses should not be appointed, and may request the parties to submit nominations. The court may appoint any expert witnesses agreed upon by the parties, and may appoint expert witnesses of its own selection. An expert witness shall not be appointed by the court unless he consents to act. A witness so appointed shall be informed of his duties by the court in writing, a copy

of which shall be filed with the clerk, or at a conference in which the parties shall have opportunity to participate. A witness so appointed shall advise the parties of his findings, if any; his deposition may be taken by any party; and he may be called to testify by the court or any party. He shall be subject to cross-examination by each party, including a party calling him as a witness.

(b) *Compensation.* Expert witnesses so appointed are entitled to reasonable compensation in whatever sum the court may allow. The compensation thus fixed is payable from funds which may be provided by law in criminal cases and civil actions and proceedings involving just compensation under the fifth amendment. In other civil actions and proceedings the compensation shall be paid by the parties in such proportion and at such time as the court directs, and thereafter charged in like manner as other costs.

(c) *Disclosure of appointment.* In the exercise of its discretion, the court may authorize disclosure to the jury of the fact that the court appointed the expert witness.

(d) *Parties' experts of own selection.* Nothing in this rule limits the parties in calling expert witnesses of their own selection.

NOTE: NEUTRAL EXPERTS

Use of court-appointed experts is a highly desirable method of assisting juries in cases in which they would otherwise be confused by a barrage of contradictory expert opinions. In addition to assisting the jury in choosing between conflicting opinions, the neutral expert may "exert a sobering effect on the expert witness of a party. . . ." Advisory Committee Notes to Rule 706. Yet many judges have been reluctant to appoint experts. They fear that the court-appointed expert acquires an "aura of infallibility" and becomes too dominant. Despite the fact that the trial judge had "unquestioned inherent power," even before the adoption of Rule 706, to appoint a neutral expert, a survey of all federal district judges reveals that few have done so.

Rule 706 is designed to encourage greater use of court-appointed experts. In an effort to dispel qualms about the expert's dominance, Judge Weinstein writes:

> The fact of the appointment need not be divulged to the jury if the court fears it would be overimpressed by the status of the witness; the judge may ask the parties for their recommendations and act upon them; a court expert's lack of neutrality can be readily exposed because the parties must be furnished with his report and have an absolute right to call their own experts, thus enabling them to prepare for cross-examination; provision is made for compensation; and many procedural aspects surrounding the use of expert testimony are consolidated.

3 Weinstein and Berger, Weinstein's Evidence 706-11-102 (1981).

When should the court exercise its power to appoint an expert? In addition to the more obvious instances in which the appointment of a neutral expert seems appropriate, such as in criminal cases where the prosecution offers novel scientific evidence and the defense is without resources to mount an adversary examination of its reliability, see, for example, Rule 28, F.R. Crim. P., Professor Green has suggested that the court should consider appointing a neutral expert early in a complex civil case where the crucial issue is highly technical. Green believes that a court-appointed expert in such cases may have a powerful dispute-narrowing and settling influence. Under his proposal, the parties would be encouraged to nominate and select a mutually acceptable neutral expert to be appointed by the court. The expert would then conduct an inquiry into the issues within the scope of his appointment. This inquiry could include examination of documents, inspections, experiments, and interviews with witnesses, including the parties' own experts. Green goes so far as to suggest that in certain cases the court-appointed neutral expert conduct a "mini-trial" among the parties and their experts on the crucial technical issues. Green, Expanded Use of the Mini-Trial, Private Judging, Neutral-Expert Fact-Finding, Patent Arbitration and Industry Self-Regulation, Dispute Management (1981).

In many cases, Green suggests, this process will result in a narrowing of the disputed issues and sometimes in complete settlement of the dispute. If the case does not settle during the expert's inquiry, the neutral expert would then "advise the parties of his findings" by submitting to them his written report, as provided in Rule 706. Green argues that since the expert may testify at trial with the imprimatur of the court, the expert's findings will have a persuasive influence on the parties and very often facilitate informal resolution. The danger with this use of neutral experts is that a party may feel unduly coerced by the prospect of a court-appointed expert's adverse testimony. Some critics of this proposal take the position that the deliberate use of a court-appointed expert for this purpose would violate the parties' rights to trial by jury. Green counters that the expert's opinion is "just coercive enough" and that the parties' rights to a fair trial are fully protected by their right to call their own witnesses, including experts, and to cross-examine the court-appointed expert. What do you think?

CHAPTER VIII

Writings

A document is a particularly powerful piece of evidence. In contrast to the testimony of an in-court witness that is developed through interrogation, subject to change upon further interrogation and dependent throughout on the credibility of the witness, documentary proof generally predates the litigation, is permanent, and is not dependent on the perceived credibility of a witness. Once authenticated (the documentary corollary to credibility), a document speaks directly to the trier-of-fact and may travel into the jury room.

A document is also a versatile piece of evidence. In the hands of a skilled trial lawyer, the same document may be used to refresh a witness's memory (Rule 612); to impeach a witness's testimony (Rule 613); as the basis for expert opinion (Rule 703); as recorded recollection or as a business, public, or similar type of record (Rule 803(5) to (18)). Yet a document may be no more reliable than testimonial evidence and much more difficult to discredit.

Appreciation of the great persuasive potential of documents has led to the creation of two sets of special rules of evidence for documentary proof. The first of these implements the foundational requirements of authentication. The second specifies whether the original of a document will be required or if a copy or another form of proof will be accepted as a substitute for the original; this is the so-called best evidence rule. This chapter is organized around the concepts of authentication and best evidence, but it should be kept in mind that effective use of documents in trial requires an appreciation of the many ways in which a document can be used and an understanding of all the rules that apply to them.

A. Authentication

Treatment of the authentication of documents and identification of real evidence formerly comprised a major portion of a course in evidence. At common law, the foundational requirements for admitting a document or a physical object into evidence were complex and unforgiving. The Advisory Committee Notes to the Federal Rules on authentication (Rules 901 to 903) incorporate the scholarly criticism that the common law approach reflected an "attitude of agnosticism" that "departs sharply from men's customs in ordinary affairs" and presents "only a slight obstacle to the introduction of forgeries in comparison to the time and expense devoted to proving genuine writings which correctly show their origin on their face." Advisory Committee Notes to Rule 901, quoting McCormick, Cases on Evidence 388 n.4 (3d ed. 1956), and McCormick, Evidence §185, pp. 395-396.

The Federal Rules greatly simplify the foundational requirements. Authentication and identification are treated as "a special aspect of relevancy" and "an inherent logical necessity." Advisory Committee Notes to Rule 901(a), quoting Michael and Adler, Real Proof, 5 Vand. L. Rev. 344, 362 (1952), and 7 Wigmore, Evidence §2129, p.564. Thus, the Committee Notes take the position that "the requirement of showing authenticity or identity falls into the category of relevancy dependent upon fulfillment of a condition of fact and is governed by the procedure set forth in Rule 104(b)."

In implementing this approach, the Federal Rules contain a general provision that the requirement of authentication or identification is satisfied "by evidence sufficient to support a finding that the matter in question is what its proponent claims." Rule 901(a). This single provision is supplemented — "by way of illustration only" — with 10 examples of authentication or identification conforming with the requirements of the rule. Rule 901(b). These 10 examples may be classified into three general categories:

(1) Testimony of a witness with knowledge — in the case of a document, either the writer or an observer;

(2) Testimony of an expert; and

(3) Circumstantial proof.

The general provision of Rule 901 is also supplemented by 10 categories of "self-authenticated" evidence for which "extrinsic evidence of authenticity as a condition precedent to admissibility is not required." Rule 902. Finally, as the Advisory Committee Notes make clear, at least in civil cases, modern procedural devices such as Requests for Admission, F.R. Civ. P. 36, and Pre-Trial Conferences, F.R. Civ. P. 16, obviate the need for much proof of authenticity at trial.

Despite the attempt by the Federal Rules to simplify and modernize the common law approach, many difficult authentication questions remain. For example, may inadmissible evidence (such as hearsay) be used to authenticate a document? Do the Federal Rules retain the common law chain-of-custody requirement? Does Rule 901 require a showing that an offered document tends to prove the issue on which it is offered, or only that the offered document is "genuine"? Beyond the examples listed in 901(b), what other types of proof will satisfy Rule 901(a)'s general provision? How does Rule 901 relate to Rule 703, which permits an expert to base his opinion on facts or data reasonably relied upon by experts in that field? Should voice identification be treated more like eyewitness identification or authentication of handwriting?

More generally, what rationale justifies the distinction between the categories of self-authenticated evidence in Rule 902 and all other evidence subject to Rule 901's authentication requirement? What are the operative effects of self-authentication? For example, may the opposing party contest the authenticity of a self-authenticated item of evidence? How may it do this? If self-authenticated evidence is challenged, how is the issue resolved and by whom?

Since identification of real evidence already was treated in Chapter III, the problems and cases in this section are discussed within the context of documentary proof and voice identification. As can be seen from these materials, particularly the extended excerpt at the end of this section from the Japanese Electronic Products Antitrust Litigation pretrial orders, authentication and identification issues are still very much alive under the Federal Rules.

FRE 901
Requirement of Authentication or Identification

(a) *General provision.* The requirement of authentication or identification as a condition precedent to admissibility is satisfied by evidence sufficient to support a finding that the matter in question is what its proponent claims.

(b) *Illustrations.* By way of illustration only, and not by way of limitation, the following are examples of authentication or identification conforming with the requirements of this rule:

(1) *Testimony of witness with knowledge.* Testimony that a matter is what it is claimed to be.

(2) *Nonexpert opinion on handwriting.* Nonexpert opinion as to the genuineness of handwriting, based upon familiarity not acquired for purposes of the litigation.

(3) *Comparison by trier or expert witness.* Comparison by the trier of fact or by expert witnesses with specimens which have been authenticated.

(4) *Distinctive characteristics and the like.* Appearance, contents, substance, internal patterns, or other distinctive characteristics, taken in conjunction with circumstances.

(5) *Voice identification.* Identification of a voice, whether heard first-hand or through mechanical or electronic transmission or recording, by opinion based upon hearing the voice at any time under circumstances connecting it with the alleged speaker.

(6) *Telephone conversations.* Telephone conversations, by evidence that a call was made to the number assigned at the time by the telephone company to a particular person or business, if (A) in the case of a person, circumstances, including self-identification, show the person answering to be the one called, or (B) in the case of a business, the call was made to a place of business and the conversation related to business reasonably transacted over the telephone.

(7) *Public records or reports.* Evidence that a writing authorized by law to be recorded or filed and in fact recorded or filed in a public office, or a purported public record, report, statement, or data compilation, in any form, is from the public office where items of this nature are kept.

(8) *Ancient documents or data compilation.* Evidence that a document or data compilation, in any form, (A) is in such condition as to create no suspicion concerning its authenticity, (B) was in a place where it, if authentic, would likely be, and (C) has been in existence 20 years or more at the time it is offered.

(9) *Process or system.* Evidence describing a process or system used to produce a result and showing that the process or system produces an accurate result.

(10) *Methods provided by statute or rule.* Any method of authentication or identification provided by Act of Congress or by other rules prescribed by the Supreme Court pursuant to statutory authority.

FRE 902
Self-Authentication

Extrinsic evidence of authenticity as a condition precedent to admissibility is not required with respect to the following:

(1) *Domestic public documents under seal.* A document bearing a seal purporting to be that of the United States, or of any State, district, Commonwealth, territory, or insular possession thereof, or the Panama Canal Zone, or the Trust Territory of the Pacific Islands, or of a political subdivision, department, officer, or agency thereof, and a signature purporting to be an attestation or execution.

(2) *Domestic public documents not under seal.* A document purporting to bear the signature in his official capacity of an officer or employee of any entity included in paragraph (1) hereof, having no seal, if a public officer

having a seal and having official duties in the district or political subdivision of the officer or employee certifies under seal that the signer has the official capacity and that the signature is genuine.

(3) *Foreign public documents.* A document purporting to be executed or attested in his official capacity by a person authorized by the laws of a foreign country to make the execution or attestation, and accompanied by a final certification as to the genuineness of the signature and official position (A) of the executing or attesting person, or (B) of any foreign official whose certificate of genuineness of signature and official position relates to the execution or attestation or is in a chain of certificates of genuineness of signature and official position relating to the execution or attestation. A final certification may be made by a secretary of embassy or legation, consul general, consul, vice consul, or consular agent of the United States, or a diplomatic or consular official of the foreign country assigned or accredited to the United States. If reasonable opportunity has been given to all parties to investigate the authenticity and accuracy of official documents, the court may, for good cause shown, order that they be treated as presumptively authentic without final certification or permit them to be evidenced by an attested summary with or without final certification.

(4) *Certified copies of public records.* A copy of an official record or report or entry therein, or of a document authorized by law to be recorded or filed and actually recorded or filed in a public office, including data compilations in any form, certified as correct by the custodian or other person authorized to make the certification, by certificate complying with paragraph (1), (2), or (3) of this rule or complying with any Act of Congress or rule prescribed by the Supreme Court pursuant to statutory authority.

(5) *Official publications.* Books, pamphlets, or other publications purporting to be issued by public authority.

(6) *Newspapers and periodicals.* Printed materials purporting to be newspapers or periodicals.

(7) *Trade inscriptions and the like.* Inscriptions, signs, tags, or labels purporting to have been affixed in the course of business and indicating ownership, control, or origin.

(8) *Acknowledged documents.* Documents accompanied by a certificate of acknowledgement executed in the manner provided by law by a notary public or other officer authorized by law to take acknowledgements.

(9) *Commercial paper and related documents.* Commercial paper, signatures thereon, and documents relating thereto to the extent provided by general commercial law.

(10) *Presumptions under Acts of Congress.* Any signature, document, or other matter declared by Act of Congress to be presumptively or prima facie genuine or authentic.

FRE 903
Subscribing Witness's Testimony Unnecessary

The testimony of a subscribing witness is not necessary to authenticate a writing unless required by the laws of the jurisdiction whose laws govern the validity of the writing.

Rule 44
Federal Rules of Civil Procedure
Proof of Official Record

(a) *Authentication*

(1) *Domestic.* An official record kept within the United States, or any state, district, commonwealth, territory, or insular possession thereof, or within the Panama Canal Zone, the Trust Territory of the Pacific Islands, or the Ryukyu Islands, or an entry therein, when admissible for any purpose, may be evidenced by an official publication thereof or by a copy attested by the officer having the legal custody of the record, or by his deputy, and accompanied by a certificate that such officer has the custody. The certificate may be made by a judge of a court of record of the district or political subdivision in which the record is kept, authenticated by the seal of the court, or may be made by any public officer having a seal of office and having official duties in the district or political subdivision in which the record is kept, authenticated by the seal of his office.

(2) *Foreign.* A foreign official record, or an entry therein, when admissible for any purpose, may be evidenced by an official publication thereof; or a copy thereof, attested by a person authorized to make the attestation, and accompanied by a final certification as to the genuineness of the signature and official position (i) of the attesting person, or (ii) of any foreign official whose certificate of genuineness of signature and official position relates to the attestation or is in a chain of certificates of genuineness of signature and official position relating to the attestation. A final certification may be made by a secretary of embassy or legation, consul general, consul, vice consul, or consular agent of the United States, or a diplomatic or consular official of the foreign country assigned or accredited to the United States. If reasonable opportunity has been given to all parties to investigate the authenticity and accuracy of the documents, the court may, for good cause shown, (i) admit an attested copy without final certification or (ii) permit the foreign official record to be evidenced by an attested summary with or without a final certification.

(b) *Lack of Record.* A written statement that after diligent search no record or entry of a specified tenor is found to exist in the records designated by the statement, authenticated as provided in subdivision (a)(1) of this rule in the case of a domestic record, or complying with the requirements of subdivision (a)(2) of this rule for a summary in the case of a foreign record, is admissible as evidence that the records contain no such record or entry.

Rule 27
Federal Rules of Criminal Procedure
Proof of Official Record

An official record or an entry therein or the lack of such a record or entry may be proved in the same manner as in civil actions.

Problem VIII-1
Blackacre

Action to determine title to Blackacre. *P* traces her title through an unrecorded 1972 deed from *G*, now dead. *D* claims by adverse possession for more than 21 years. *P* and *D* dispute the validity of the other's claim. At trial, how may the following evidence be authenticated by the proponent:

(1) The unrecorded deed from *G* to *P*?

(2) The 1944 recorded deed from *G*'s grantor to *G*?

(3) A list of expenditures and receipts relating to the upkeep of Blackacre, going back to 1955, offered by *D*?

(4) A copy of the local newspaper from July 5, 1968, describing a Fourth of July picnic at "*D*'s ranch, Blackacre," offered by *D*?

(5) Tax records and receipts offered by *D*?

(6) Cancelled checks by *D* for utilities for Blackacre over the past 25 years?

(7) A letter from *G* to *D*, offered by *D*, that states, "In reply to your letter of March 3, 1976, I have not executed any deeds to Blackacre."

(8) A telephone conversation a witness allegedly had with *G* on November 10, 1973, in which *G* reportedly denied making any deeds to Blackacre?

Problem VIII-2
The Problematic Promissory Note

Charge: income tax evasion for the year 1971. Using the net worth method the government seeks to prove that *D* substantially understated his income in 1971 and owed approximately $13,000 more in taxes than he paid. In defense, *D* offers in evidence a 1970 promissory note signed by his brother, *B,* to prove that part of the unreported income the government claims he received was actually a nontaxable loan repayment. What foundational proof will suffice to admit the note:

(1) Testimony of a witness that he was familiar with *B*'s handwriting and that the signature on the note appeared to be *B*'s?

(2) Testimony of a witness that he had represented *B* for several years, had seen him sign hundreds of documents, was able to recognize *B*'s handwriting, and identified the signature on the note as *B*'s?

(3) Testimony of *D* that he had seen *B* sign the note?

(4) Testimony of a witness that, in preparation for the trial, he had examined several exemplars of *B*'s signature, conceded to be valid, and that in his opinion the note was signed by *B*?

(5) An offer by *D*'s attorney to submit the note and the concededly valid exemplars to the jury for its comparison?

Suppose the authenticity of the exemplars of *B*'s signature was challenged. Who resolves the issue of their admissibility and on what basis? If none of the above testimony is offered, may the note nonetheless be admitted? Before the note is admissible, must *D* offer testimony by the maker, the payee, or someone who prepared the note to testify as to the transaction of which it was a part?

Problem VIII-3
The International Bank of Commerce Mail Scam

Charge: 11 counts of mail fraud and 2 counts of use of wire communications to defraud. At trial the government seeks to introduce over *D*'s objection 22 letters that on their face purported to come from *D*, "President and Senior Counsel of the International Bank of Commerce," with an address at 8 Creswell Road, Worcester, Massachusetts, and a telephone number of (617) 754-5000. *D* contends that there is no direct evidence that he signed or authorized the sending of any of the documents that purported to come from him. In support of its offer of proof, the government introduces evidence that (1) *D* had a residence at 8 Creswell Road and a telephone number of 754-5000, (2) *D* received, retained, and used at trial replies from 7 of the 22 addressees of these letters, and (3) all 22 letters were on the same stationery, referred to the same type of transaction, and otherwise indicated a common authorship.

Should the letters be admitted?

Problem VIII-4
Viva Card

Collection action against *D* by Bank *P*, owner of the Viva Card credit service. Viva Card's computerized billing service billed *D* on his January statement for $75 for two tickets to an Opera Company December 18 production of *Rigoletto. D* denies ordering the tickets. At trial, *P* offers proof through the opera's business manager that the opera's ticket office contains a computer terminal connected to a data storage system, that telephone charge orders for tickets are taken by operators in the ticket office, and that the operators enter the caller's credit-card number into the computer terminal, causing that number and the amount of the charge to be recorded on tape in the data-storage system. This tape is then sent to *P,* which runs it through its computer system, thereby picking up the opera's charges on its central file of account charges. Each month this central file, containing all charges at any location in that month for all card holders, is "unloaded" to create the monthly statements sent to each card holder. *P* offers:

(1) A printout of Opera Company's December tape;

(2) A printout of the portion of *P*'s central file tape showing *D*'s December account; and

(3) A copy of *D*'s January statement produced for trial by *P* by causing the central file tape for December for his account to be reprinted in statement format.

How may such evidence be authenticated?

Problem VIII-5
The Cudia City Wash

Action by a group of Phoenix, Arizona, homeowners against the Salt River Valley Water Users' Association when their homes were damaged by water escaping from the Arizona Canal. The Arizona Canal is operated by the association as agent for the Salt River Valley Agricultural Improvement and Power District.

The canal traverses the valley in which the homeowners live and intersects at least four major natural washes, including the Cudia City Wash. During normal rainfall, surface runoff collects in these washes and then flows through the canal. However, during extremely severe storms, the washes overflow and flood the surrounding ground. When a storm is anticipated, the association follows storm control procedures designed to enable the canal system to accept and safely carry off as much excess runoff as possible. Ordinarily, these procedures are sufficient to prevent dangerous overflow. However, several of the valley's brief, high-intensity summer storms have been severe enough to cause major breaches in the canal. The records of the association showed that in 1939 and 1943 a desert storm produced runoff that broke the canal banks in several places.

On June 22, 1972, a severe rainstorm occurred in the Cudia City Wash area. The storm was one having a 100-year return frequency, that is, a storm so severe that it could be expected to occur, on the average, only once in 100 years. During the storm the association went into its storm-control procedures. Nonetheless, when the water from the Cudia City Wash hit the canal, there was so much water in the canal and the wash that it created a backflow, causing water in the canal to flow up-stream, overtopping the south bank of the canal, eroding the bank in three places, and causing a wall of water to hit the area in which the plaintiffs reside. The water traveled swiftly, carrying great amounts of mud and debris and possessing sufficient kinetic force to knock down houses and carry away automobiles and horses. The flood waters caused serious damage to the plaintiffs' homes and other property.

Plaintiffs' complaint alleged that the association owed the home-owners a duty to use reasonable care in operating the canal to minimize the destructive effect of desert storms and that the association was neg-ligent in designing and following procedures in the event of severe storms.

At trial, plaintiffs seek to introduce a two-page document that pur-ports to show in graph form the amounts of rain that fell at various points in the Salt River Valley during the storms of 1939 and 1943. This document was found in the association's files and was produced upon plaintiffs' request. The purpose of offering this document is to show that the association knew, or should have known, that storms similar to the June 1972 storm have occurred with some frequency in the Valley. The document is unsigned and undated. Is the document admissible?

UNITED STATES v. STONE
604 F.2d 922 (5th Cir. 1979)

THORNBERRY, J. In this appeal from a conviction for possession of stolen mail we must decide whether the government violated the hearsay rule and the defendant's right of confrontation when the government used an affidavit instead of live testimony for the purpose of explaining how an official record demonstrated that the Treasury Department mailed a check that the defendant later had in his possession. . . .

I

Stone was convicted in a jury trial under 18 U.S.C. §1708 for posses-sion of an item, in this case a United States Treasury check, stolen from the mails. . . .

To prove that the check was in the mail, the government presented as a witness Gwendolyn G. Howard, the payee of the check in question. Howard testified that she was employed by a Veterans Administration Hospital in Florida during 1975, and that she received her paycheck in the mail every two weeks at her residence. She identified a check dated

June 30, 1975 as her payroll check for that period, and testified that she never received it. When she failed to receive her check in the mail on June 30, 1975, she obtained a duplicate check at the hospital. Her original check dated June 30, 1975, and numbered 69,137,606 was found to have been in Stone's possession, and was introduced into evidence.

The government also presented a progress sheet from the Treasury Department's Regional Disbursing Center in Austin, Texas, for the purpose of showing that the check had been placed in the mail. The sheet was an official disbursement form that was marked in part as follows: "PAYMENT DATE: 6-30-75," "OBJECT: SALARY," and "AGENCY: VA: COMPOSITE-BULK-DIRECT." The sheet specified that 99,625 "checks or bonds" were disbursed on that date in a total amount of $65,751,002.39. Checks or bonds numbered 69,108,660 to 69,205,121 were under the category "Direct." The sheet was marked to show the various stages of processing checks. In particular, the checks were marked "mailed or delivered" and "Date and time released: 6/27/75 4:00." The government authenticated this document by attaching an affidavit from staff assistant Alan Ford, the officer with legal custody and direct supervision of the progress sheets. Ford's affidavit identified his position in the first paragraph, then stated that

> I further certify that the attached document is a true copy of Treasury Department disbursing records related to check number 69,137,626, dated June 30, 1975, payable to Gwendolyn G. Howard, 2120 E University AV, NO 14, Gainesville, FL 32601, in the amount of $219.91, issued by G. Clark, Regional Disbursing Officer, over symbol 2205. It consists of a photographic copy of the Progress Sheet used to control the issuance and mailing of the check indicating that such check was individually inserted in an envelope and was mailed on June 27, 1975 with a group of other individually enclosed checks bearing the serial numbers 69,019,681 to 69,205,121.

Counsel for Stone made proper objections against the admission of the affidavit with these explanatory sentences. The judge overruled the objections, and allowed the full affidavit into evidence. Neither the government nor Stone called Ford to testify in person, although no evidence suggests he was unavailable for the trial. The hearsay and confrontation issues are the only points raised on appeal.

Stone does not challenge the admissibility of the progress sheet itself. This sheet was properly admitted under the hearsay exceptions in Fed. R. Evid. 803(6) for records of regularly conducted activity and Fed. R. Evid. 803(8) for public records and reports. The sheet was properly authenticated under Fed. R. Evid. 902(4) by Ford's attached affidavit.

Stone challenges the admission only of the extraneous explanatory statements in Ford's affidavit. To satisfy the requirements of Fed. R. Evid. 902(4), Ford's authenticating affidavit needed only to identify his position of authority and to state that the copy was correct. Ford's affidavit includes these items. Ford's affidavit goes on, however, to explain in detail that the progress sheet refers to Howard's particular check, and that the sheet shows that Howard's check was actually placed in the mail, although the sheet itself only states that certain numbered checks were "mailed or delivered." The admission of these statements without Ford's actual testimony prevented Stone from cross-examining Ford about his explanation of the form.

At oral argument counsel for the government displayed little concern for Stone's need to cross-examine Ford. Government counsel asserted that they typically use such ex parte affidavits to explain the meaning of office records in litigation. The government's frequent and flagrant use of this method for proving an essential element of a crime does not justify its impropriety. When an ex parte affidavit presents evidence beyond the simple authentication requirements of Fed. R. Evid. 902(4), the extraneous portions of the affidavit constitute inadmissible hearsay under Fed. R. Evid. 801. The government relied upon Whiteside v. United States, 346 F.2d 500 (8 Cir. 1965), cert. denied, 384 U.S. 1023 (1966), to show that an affidavit and progress sheet can be used to prove that a check was mailed under 18 U.S.C. §1708. In *Whiteside*, however, the regional disbursing officer actually appeared and testified in the case; the defendant's right to cross-examine the witness was preserved.

The government contends that Ford's statements in the affidavit should be admissible under the hearsay exception for public reports in Fed. R. Evid. 803(8)(A). . . . This hearsay exception is designed to allow admission of official records and reports prepared by an agency or government office for purposes independent of specific litigation. This exception for an agency's official records does not apply to Ford's personal statements prepared solely for purposes of this litigation. Ford's statements are likely to reflect the same lack of trustworthiness that prevents admission of litigation-oriented statements in cases such as Palmer v. Hoffman, 318 U.S. 109 (1943).

The trial judge erred in not striking out those portions of Ford's affidavit that exceed the simple authentication requirements of Fed. R. Evid. 902(4). This error does not require reversal of Stone's conviction, however, because under the circumstances of this case the hearsay violation was harmless. . . .

Stone contends that the admission of Ford's hearsay statement violates his sixth amendment right to confront the witness against him. Although a violation of the evidentiary hearsay rule does not establish that the constitutional right of confrontation has been denied, prevention of ex parte affidavits, like the extraneous statements in Ford's affidavit, is the primary purpose for the constitutional right of confrontation. California v. Green, 399 U.S. 149, 156-59 (1970). When the government introduced into evidence the explanatory statements in Ford's affidavit, and did not present Ford as a witness or show that he was unavailable, Stone's sixth amendment right of confrontation was denied. Although the government's method of presenting testimony cannot be justified, we find that, under the circumstances of this case, the error was harmless beyond a reasonable doubt, and that the conviction should be affirmed according to Chapman v. California, 386 U.S. 18 (1967). Howard's testimony that she always received her paychecks in the mail and the language on the progress sheet itself provide such overwhelming proof of mailing that the denial of Stone's confrontation right is harmless beyond a reasonable doubt. See Harrington v. California, 395 U.S. 250 (1969) (denial of confrontation rights constitutes error harmless beyond a reasonable doubt on record showing overwhelming evidence of guilt). . . .

We hold that the admission into evidence of explanatory statements on an authenticating affidavit constitutes inadmissible hearsay when the person making the statements is available, but does not testify at the trial. Because the defendant had no opportunity to cross-examine the person making the statement, admission of the explanatory statements also violates the defendant's sixth amendment right to confront the witnesses against him. The government's practice of using explanatory affidavits as a substitute for live testimony cannot be tolerated. We find in this case, however, that the admission of these statements was not a substantial influence upon the result, and was harmless beyond a reasonable doubt. For this reason, we affirm appellant's conviction in the court below.

Affirmed.

Could the admissibility of the progress sheet be attacked on confrontational grounds? Is Rule 902(4) constitutional when applied in criminal cases to authenticate an important item of inculpatory evidence?

Problem VIII-6
The Unregistered Gun

D is charged with violating the National Firearms Act by possessing an unregistered firearm in violation of U.S.C.A. §5861(d). At trial the government offers the testimony of W, a special agent of the Alcohol, Tobacco, and Firearms Division of the Internal Revenue Service. Through W the government then seeks to introduce a document bearing a government seal and the signature of the assistant chief of the division's Operations-Coordination Section, stating that the assistant chief has custody of the National Firearms Registration and Transfer record and that after a diligent search of said record she has found no evidence that the gun seized from *D* was registered. *D* objects on the grounds of Rules 901 to 902, the sixth amendment to the Constitution, and Rule 27 of the Federal Rules of Criminal Procedure.

What ruling and why?

Problem VIII-7
"Reach Out, Reach Out and Touch Someone"

D was charged on two counts of violating 26 U.S.C. §7203 by failing to file timely income tax returns for the calendar years 1971 and 1972. At trial an agent of the Internal Revenue Service was called to testify that in September of 1973 she obtained *D*'s telephone number from *D*'s husband and that pursuant to her routine practice, she attempted to contact *D* by telephone. The agent further testified that when she called the telephone number given her by *D*'s husband, *D* stated that the income tax returns for 1971 and 1972 had been filed, which was false. This evidence was offered on the theory that a defendant's false, out-of-court, exculpatory statements may be taken as evidence of guilt. *D* objected to the introduction of this evidence on the grounds that the telephone conversation was not properly authenticated.

What ruling and why?

Problem VIII-8
The Set-Up

D is charged with 10 counts of possession of U.S. Treasury checks stolen from the mails in violation of 18 U.S.C. §1708. The prosecution's evidence indicates that postal inspector Wilson was approached by an informant who arranged a "check buy" from *D*. Wilson arranged to meet the informant and *D* at a restaurant. After preliminary discussions *D* left briefly, returning with 10 U.S. Treasury checks made out to various payees. Five of the checks had forged endorsements, and five were unendorsed. Wilson offered to pay *D* 25 percent of the face value of the checks. *D* accepted this offer. Wilson then left the car, presumably to obtain the cash, and government agents arrested *D*, feigning the arrest of Wilson and the informant.

At trial, *D* acknowledges that he sold treasury checks to Wilson but claims that his arrest was a product of entrapment. He asserts that he had met the informant, "Jimmy," at the home of a friend and that Jimmy asked him if he "did checks" or "could get checks." *D* testifies that he told Jimmy that he was not interested but that Jimmy was not satisfied with this initial rebuff and continued to pursue him both by visiting and telephoning him on numerous occasions. *D* asserts that he obtained checks solely in order to pass them on to Jimmy and satisfy him. *D* also testifies that when Jimmy told him about the proposed check buy, *D* protested but finally agreed to go ahead with the deal only under duress.

D seeks to introduce the testimony of his co-defendant's mother that she received several telephone calls from someone named "Jimmy" who said that he was looking for *D*. The proposed witness was not acquainted with the informant and there was no evidence offered that she could recognize his voice at the time. Is the evidence admissible?

Would it make a difference if the witness testified that although she did not recognize Jimmy's voice at the time, after hearing the informant testify at trial she recognized the voice on the telephone as belonging to him?

Problem VIII-9
Four Unknown, Named Narcotics Agents

P brought an action for damages pursuant to 42 U.S.C. §1983 alleging that the defendants, four New York City police officers, violated his civil rights by falsely arresting him, beating him, and failing to provide him with prompt and adequate medical care.

At trial, *P* testified that he had assisted several officers of the narcotics division of the New York City Police Department in investigating narcotics trafficking in Jamaica, Queens, and that he had applied to become a paid informer. On March 4, 1978, the date of the events in question, at approximately 10:00 P.M., *P* entered a vacant building in Jamaica, which he knew to be a drug "shooting gallery," in an effort to obtain information. While he was there, he observed two hypodermic needles abandoned on the floor and a person receiving a drug injection from the operator of the shooting gallery. Moments later, a contingent of police officers arrived, causing the other people at the scene to flee the premises. *P* testified that he was seized, arrested, and handcuffed, and then placed in an unmarked car with the four defendants. During the ride to the station house, he attempted to convince the officers that he was a police informant and that he had been on the premises attempting to collect information for the police. *P* further testified that if allowed to make a telephone call he could clear up the misunderstanding but that the defendants reacted by punching him in the face with their fists and a hand-held police radio until he lost consciousness, bleeding from his mouth, the left side of his face, and his left ear. At the precinct house he was booked on charges of burglary in the second degree, unlawful possession of a hypodermic needle, and resisting arrest.

P's second witness at trial was New York City Detective Wayne Carrington, who had worked with *P* prior to the incident. Carrington testified that he had asked *P* to gather information concerning drug trafficking in the city and that at the time of *P*'s arrest, he was processing *P*'s application to become a paid informer. Carrington also testified that when he learned of *P*'s arrest, he visited him in the detention center and that *P* told him that the defendants had beaten him after placing him under arrest. Carrington then testified that he contacted the assistant district attorney handling the case to ask if he could check the records to see exactly what the officers said compared to what *P* said. The following colloquy then took place:

Q: Now, after you spoke to the Assistant District Attorney, what did you do if anything next in regard to the case?
A: I attempted to contact the arresting officer.
Q: And how did you do that?
A: I called Mr. Meel.
Q: What happened when you made that phone call? What command are you talking about?
A: I believe it was the Street Crime Unit.
Q: When you called the Street Crime Unit, what happened?
A: I asked for the arresting officer, and he wasn't available, and whoever answered the phone said they'd put me in contact with his partner and I spoke to —
Defendants' counsel: Objection.
Q: Did you seek [sic] his partner?
A: I —
Court: Sustained.
Q: Did you seek [sic] his partner?
Court: Yes, or no. That is all.
Defendants' counsel: Objection.
Court: Just yes or no whether he spoke to him or not.
Q: Did you speak to his partner? Would you please answer that yes or no?
Defendants' counsel: Objection.
Court: I didn't hear that last part.
Plaintiff's counsel: He objected to what you said. I asked — I asked if he spoke to his partner, yes or no.
Court: He may answer it only yes or no. Period. Nothing else.
A: I don't know.
Q: Well did somebody take the phone call — the person — when they said they were going to put you in touch with his partner, did they transfer you to another officer?
A: Another officer got on the phone.
Q: Did that officer tell you he was his partner?
A: Yes, he did.
Q: And did you ask that officer if he was present on the night of the arrest of Tyrone O'Neal at the scene?

A: Yes, I did.

Q: What did he say?

Defendants' counsel: Objection. May we approach the bench?

(Whereupon, the following discussion was held at the side bar:)

Defendants' counsel: Your honor, we contend that any of this —

Court: None of this is relevant.

Plaintiff's counsel: Your honor, can I say one thing? I can't say it?

Court: The only issue in this case is whether the policemen were there, had probable cause or reasonable cause to make the arrest and believed that a crime had been committed. That is it. That is where we are at, not what he thinks or what he said or what somebody told him.

Plaintiff's counsel: Can I say one thing, your honor? He stated his officer told him he was the partner of the arresting officer, and he was present at the arrest which makes him one of the defendants in this case.

Court: No it doesn't.

Defendants' counsel: No foundation.

Court: It does not help.

Plaintiff's counsel: That was my point. Then there is an admission. I am going to ask him about that. That was my point.

Court: Is he a defendant in this case?

Plaintiff's counsel: I beg your pardon?

Court: Is he a defendant in this case?

Plaintiff's counsel: I beg your pardon?

Court: Is he a defendant in this case?

Defendants' counsel: Who?

Plaintiff's counsel: Yes, that is my contention.

Defendants' counsel: There has been no foundation for the question.

Court: Yes.

Plaintiff's counsel: Respectfully except.

Court: Okay.

Defendants contend that the exclusion of the conversation was proper because *P* failed to satisfy the authentication or identification requirements of Rule 901(a). Was the trial judge's ruling correct?

Problem VIII-10
"Joe Sent Me"

Charge: conspiracy to transport in interstate commerce obscene films and magazines concerning and involving children in violation of 18 U.S.C. §1465.

At the trial of *D*, former president of J-E, Inc., of California, *K*, the owner-operator of Kip's Discount, a West Virginia retail outlet dealing in sexually explicit matter, testified that in 1976 he had placed an order for kiddi-porn in a telephone conversation with "Joe" at J-E's place of business in California. Following the telephone conversation, the items of child pornography mentioned in the indictment, consisting of magazines and films, were shipped from J-E in California to Kip's Discount in West Virginia by Greyhound bus. Upon receipt, *K* turned them over to an agent of the FBI.

D contended that he could not be guilty of the charges because during the period in question he was not involved extensively enough in or with J-E's business operations to have been implicated in, or even aware of, those violations if they did in fact occur. *D* admitted incorporating J-E and being its president until 1975 but alleged that he resigned in that year to attend to other business and was succeeded by others who continued to manage and operate J-E.

D objected to permitting the witness to testify to the contents of the telephone conversations, arguing that since the witness had never met him, he could not identify him as the person with whom he had spoken at J-E. The witness testified that he had communicated by telephone with J-E on at least four occasions, always speaking with "Joe," concerning ordering, pricing, and shipping adult materials and kiddi-porn, some of those conversations having been initiated by him and some by J-E. The witness could not pinpoint the exact dates upon which he talked with "Joe" but identified and dated two of the J-E invoices forwarded to Kip's Discount, several of which corresponded to merchandise actually received by Kip's Discount and found to be child pornography. An FBI agent testified that during a search of J-E's premises shortly after these telephone calls, he saw a sign on the door of *D*'s office reading "Joe Espinoza." Are the telephone conversations admissible?

If the criminal action were against J-E, Inc., and *K* still could not identify the voice of "Joe," would the case for admission be stronger or weaker than in the criminal action against *D*?

ZENITH RADIO CORP. v. MATSUSHITA ELECTRIC INDUSTRIAL CO., LTD.
494 F. Supp. 1161 (E.D. Pa. 1980), 505 F. Supp. 1190 (E.D. Pa. 1980), et seq.

[Touching off one of the greatest paper avalanches and lawyers' bonanzas in the history of American litigation, in 1970 National Union Electric Corporation (NUE), the successor to Emerson Radio Co., filed the first of several lawsuits against 24 Japanese manufacturers of consumer electronic products, including Matsushita, Toshiba, Hitachi, Sony, and Mitsubishi Electric (MELSO), and two American companies, Sears, Roebuck & Co. and Motorola. The Japanese Electronic Products

Antitrust Litigation suits alleged that the Japanese defendants and others had conspired to take over the American consumer electronic products industry and thereby to drive NUE out of business. In 1974 Zenith filed an action making similar allegations. The NUE action was consolidated for pretrial proceedings with the Zenith action, and the lawsuits progressed through the discovery process under the Manual for Complex Litigation. The following excerpt from the first of many pretrial orders describes the lawsuit.]

In capsule form, plaintiffs' complaints allege that the Japanese defendants and their coconspirators have been participants in a conspiracy which, by artificially lowering export prices, has for more than twenty years sought the methodical destruction of the United States domestic consumer electronic products industry. The defendants are accused of carrying out the aims of this conspiracy by flooding the United States market with imported goods at prices so attractive to consumers that domestic producers suffered serious losses, and were either unable to compete or able to do so only by moving some or all of their own production facilities to Mexico and the Far East.

The particular offenses charged in the complaints span the entire range of the antitrust laws. The overall conspiracy is alleged to violate §§1 and 2 of the Sherman Act, 15 U.S.C. §§1 and 2, and §73 of the Wilson Tariff Act, 15 U.S.C. §8. Plaintiffs also allege actual and attempted monopolization under §2 of the Sherman Act. Additionally, they allege that the Japanese defendants have violated the 1916 Antidumping Act, 15 U.S.C. §72, by "commonly and systematically," with predatory intent, selling their products in this country for substantially less than their actual market value or wholesale price in Japan. The defendants are also charged with violating the Robinson-Patman Act, 15 U.S.C. §13(a), by discriminating in price among American purchasers. Finally, Zenith charges that Sears, Motorola, and the Matsushita and Sanyo defendants violated §7 of the Clayton Act, 15 U.S.C. §18, in connection with the Japanese companies' acquisitions of interests in domestic consumer electronic products manufacturers. The plaintiffs' papers seek to portray a unitary worldwide conspiracy said to have lasted over a period of some thirty years and to have involved approximately one hundred manufacturers, exporters, and importers of consumer electronic products of various national origins.

The defendants maintain that, notwithstanding their voluminous submissions, plaintiffs have failed to elucidate their claims with any degree of precision. They also deny both the legal and factual validity of the plaintiffs' claims. Additionally, certain of the defendants have asserted counterclaims against Zenith, attacking Zenith on two fronts. First, they allege that Zenith, acting alone and in combination and conspiracy with others, engaged in territorial allocations, price discrimination, and horizontal and vertical price fixing arrangements, and effected certain "key dealer preferences" in violation of the Robinson-Patman Act and §§1 and 2 of the Sherman Act. Second, they accuse Zenith and its coconspirators of seeking to interfere with its competitors, including the counterclaimants, "by every means available, including the submission of complaints, petitions, testimony and other information to various federal governmental agencies and officials, federal courts, and the United States Congress which were based upon sham, false and misleading allegations and information, without regard to the truth or merits of the claims made." The counterclaiming defendants thus invoke the "sham litigation" theory of antitrust liability recognized in Otter Tail Power Co. v. United States, 410 U.S. 366 (1973).

Pending before us currently are motions by all defendants seeking summary judgment against both Zenith and NUE. Some are joint motions; others are motions by individual defendants, some of which are joined by other defendants; some motions are addressed to discrete legal issues; others are omnibus motions addressed to several issues. These motions, which number several dozen, raise a wide variety of issues, both factual and legal. . . .

As the foregoing description suggests, this is a case of considerable complexity. It is also a case of monumental proportions. The document production has run to twenty million documents; deposition transcripts run to over 100,000 pages; interrogatories have come in wave after wave — the plaintiffs' answer to one interrogatory ran to 750 pages. Plaintiffs' final pretrial statement, filed with preclusive effect, consumes over 17,000 pages. And yet not even the foregoing description can adequately portray the character of this litigation. It is only when the matrices of complexity and magnitude are superimposed upon the ambience of this case, which has been conducted throughout in the highest of dudgeon and rhetoric and attended by constant acrimony, that its incredible and burdensome nature can be truly assayed. We will have more to say on this point later.

Rather than waiting to file a comprehensive opinion addressing each motion, we have chosen to write separately on each discrete legal issue, whether raised by one motion or by several. Such an approach will be valuable in terms of case management, for it will permit us to narrow the issues in advance of trial, saving further preparation time for the parties. Furthermore, it will allow us to address in a single opinion those legal issues which are common to several motions. . . .

[In this opinion, the district court held that the Sherman Act could be applied in this case against Japanese manufacturers. Defendants' motion for summary judgment was granted in part and denied in part. 494 F. Supp. at 1245. In subsequent pretrial hearings, lasting over a month, the court considered a myriad of evidentiary issues *in limine* preliminary to ruling on other summary judgment motions. In a series of orders, the court handed down detailed rulings concerning the admissibility of documents under the business records, public reports, and other exceptions to the hearsay rule, as well as the rules relating to relevancy. See, e.g., 505 F. Supp. 1125, below. The court was faced with ruling on over 250,000 documents (many in Japanese) listed in the parties' Final Pretrial Statement (FPS). Conceding that this was a hopeless task, the court was able to identify the crucial documents and categorize them as follows:]

1. Documents, including certain findings, promulgated by the U.S. Treasury Department and U.S. Tariff Commission in connection with proceedings under the 1921 Antidumping Act.

2. Documents, including certain findings, promulgated by the U.S. Tariff Commission and its successor, the U.S. International Trade Commission (I.T.C.) as well as the Secretary of Labor under §§301(b)(1) and (c)(1) and (2) of the Trade Expansion Act of 1962 and §§201(b) and 221 of the Trade Act of 1974.

3. Certain purported findings and related documents of the Japanese Fair Trade Commission (JFTC) arising out of proceedings in two cases before the JFTC, one, in 1957, brought against the Home Electric Appliance Market Stabilization Council, some of whose members are defendants in this action, alleging industry-wide price-fixing, and the second, brought in 1967, alleging retail price maintenance against defendant Matsushita Electric Industries Co., Ltd.

4. The findings of Judge A. Leon Higginbotham, Jr., our predecessor in this case, regarding personal jurisdiction and venue, found at 402 F. Supp. 262 (1975).

5. Statistical data from the statistical office of the United Nations and a report of the Organization for Economic Cooperation and Development.

6. Diaries of officials of several of the Japanese defendants, alleged to contain evidence of the conspiracy referenced in plaintiffs' complaint, which were seized in 1966 and utilized in the course of JFTC Case No. 6 of 1966 (the so-called "Six Company Case"). That case was an investigation and proceedings against six of the defendants, Sanyo Electric Corp., Tokyo Shibaura Electric Corp. (Toshiba), Hayakawa Electrical Industry Corp. (now Sharp Corporation), Hitachi Industry Corp., Matsushita Electric Industry Corp. (MEI), and Mitsubishi Electric Corp. (MELCO). The six companies were charged with a conspiracy to fix prices and to engage in a variety of activities in violation of the Japanese Anti-Monopoly Law. The eight diaries in dispute have been attributed to a Mr. Yajima, an employee of Toshiba (3 diaries); Messrs. Yamamoto (2 diaries) and Yamada, both employees of Hitachi; a Mr. Okuma, an employee of MELCO; and Mr. Tokizane, an employee of MEI. Also included in this category are a number of internal company memoranda also seized by the JFTC.

7. Transcripts of testimony and of protocols by witnesses in the Six-Company case. A protocol is a written statement outlining the substance of oral discussions between a JFTC staff member and a witness, which

the witness signs to indicate that the contents comport with his statement.

8. Various agreements and rules of certain Japanese manufacturers' associations relating to export practices.

9. Various documents alleged to be minutes or memoranda of meetings of committees of certain manufacturers' associations.

10. A purported internal memorandum of the Japan Victor Company, 51% of which is owned by MEI, allegedly reflecting the decision made by the Electronic Industries Association of Japan (EIAJ) to conceal from the Japanese Ministry of International Trade and Industry (MITI) the discrepancy between domestic and export prices and suggesting changes in accounting methods by which such concealment could be accomplished.

11. Various memoranda, letters, telexes, and transactional documents produced by the defendants in discovery and involving the Japanese manufacturers, their trading companies, their American sales subsidiaries and various U.S. customers, which, in plaintiffs' submission, show a pattern of "under the table" or concealed rebates that reduced the price of Japanese TVs to American customers below the so-called check price that was reported to U.S. Customs, and which also reveal a "cover-up" of what plaintiffs describe as a predatory export scheme.

[In a second pretrial evidentiary opinion *in limine*, 505 F. Supp. 1190, the court ruled on objections to the admissibility of some of these documents based on lack of proof of their authenticity. Excerpts (heavily edited) from this opinion follow.]

This opinion will consider admissibility of three major groups of documents: (1) materials seized by the Japanese Fair Trade Commission (JFTC) in "raids" on the offices of several of the defendants here who were respondents in the so-called "Six Company Case"; (2) testimony and statements or "protocols" given by officials of the respondent companies during the course of the JFTC proceedings in the "Six Company Case"; and (3) materials produced in discovery from the files of the Japanese defendants and others relating to activities in Japan of Japanese manufacturers of consumer electronic products or of associations of manufacturers. There were virtually no documents in these categories whose admissibility was agreed upon, and all of the documents were the subject of heated dispute about their admissibility. . . .

Even before the FPS was filed, the emanations from the JFTC proceedings pervaded the case. During the course of many pretrial conferences, and in the initial summary judgment briefs, we were constantly confronted with plaintiffs' allegations that the documents seized by the JFTC during the course of the Six Company Case were laden with evidence of conspiratorial activities by the defendants, in both the domestic Japanese and the export markets. The most frequently cited sources were the three diaries of Seiichi Yajima, an official of Toshiba Corp. The significance of Yajima's diaries was underscored when the

FPS was finally filed, for it contained no less than 600 references to them.

The FPS was similarly suffused with references to other documents which had their source in the JFTC proceedings, many of which were likewise represented as demonstrating the existence of a broad based unitary conspiracy to destroy the American consumer electronic products industry by a low price predatory export conspiracy funded or "war-chested" by conspiratorial high prices in Japan. Because of the extremely broad and allegedly damning implications of the JFTC material as portrayed in the FPS, it became evident to us that the intensive scrutiny of all of the critical documents was a condition precedent to any full and fair decision on the summary judgment motions. . . .

We will thus consider — and at some length because of its importance — the admissibility of Mr. Yajima's diary. Also to be considered at some length, because they are alleged to be of similarly great import are the diaries of Messrs. Yamamoto and Yamada, both employees of Hitachi; Mr. Okuma, an employee of MELCO; and Mr. Tokizane, an employee of Matsushita. During the course of the Six Company Case proceedings, Mr. Yajima and a number of other officials of Japanese companies were interviewed and gave statements, referred to herein as "protocols." They also gave formal testimony at hearings before the JFTC. In plaintiffs' submission, the protocols and testimony contain significant evidence of conspiratorial activity by defendants, and also authenticate the diaries under Federal Rule of Evidence 901 and qualify them as business records within the meaning of Federal Rule of Evidence 803(6). These matters will also be treated at length, as will certain of the materials produced in discovery relating to the activities in Japan of Japanese manufacturers or manufacturers' associations.

The evidence whose admissibility is treated in this opinion is not only of critical importance to plaintiffs' case in chief, but it also forms a major part of the factual basis for the opinions of their expert witnesses, the admissibility of which we will consider in a subsequent opinion. In plaintiffs' submission, the documents coming from Japan demonstrate that the Japanese consumer electronic products manufacturers, including the seven manufacturing defendants, Matsushita (MEI), Toshiba, Hitachi, Sanyo, MELCO, Sharp, and Sony, entered into conspiratorial arrangements, effectuated through a series of monthly meetings involving mid-level to top-level management, the purpose of which was to fix prices in Japan at a high level in order to finance the predatory export campaign to destroy the American consumer electronics products industry to which we have referred. The documents themselves, for the most part, are said to set forth accounts in a variety of forms of what transpired at the meetings of the various "conspiratorial groups," principally the so-called "Tenth Day Group," but including higher echelon groups as well.

Textually, the protocols, testimony and other writings indicate that there were meetings of Japanese consumer electronics products executives, and that at those meetings they discussed predictions of domestic demand, the establishment of domestic "bottom prices," i.e. minimum suggested retail sales prices, and appropriate domestic wholesale profit, retail profit, and "rebate" margins in the retail distribution chain. There are scattered references in the documents to "export," though, for the most part, the executives attending the meetings had no responsibility for export matters.

The protocols, which were prepared by JFTC investigators and signed by the witnesses, are straightforward, readily comprehensible, narrative statements. The testimony is similarly clear, and is developed through question and answer in a manner which is generally similar to that employed to develop testimony in the U.S. legal system.[6] The diaries and memoranda are another matter. The diaries all appear to have been written solely for the diarist, with the notations written in a kind of shorthand or code which the writer presumably himself can understand, but which no one else could fully understand except for occasional excerpts. As defendants correctly note, they are a "hodge podge" of notes in which the author has not explained with any degree of clarity what he meant, to what he was referring, or even where he was when he wrote them. While plaintiffs have clarified a few of the references in the diaries by cross reference to JFTC testimony or protocols, only an infinitesimal part has been thus explained. One would have to engage in the rankest of speculation to make sense out of the vast bulk of the diaries.

One cannot tell with any certainty where entries begin and end. There are many time gaps in the notebooks or diaries, and only a portion of the "conspiratorial meetings" otherwise demonstrated to have taken place are recorded in them. There are all kinds of arrows and innumerable symbols and notations and references which are unintelligible to the translators, who report those references as "illegible." Many of them are written in a code which only a cryptographer could solve.

There is both intrinsic and extrinsic evidence that many of the diary entries reflect occurrences at meetings which the diarists did not attend, but rather about which they were informed by others. The diaries plainly contain numerous instances of second and third level hearsay. Because of the manner in which the diaries are kept, however, it is not possible to sort out which entries are based upon the diarists' personal knowledge and which are based upon hearsay. There is no evidence of regular or continuous habit on the part of any of the diarists in making their notebook entries or checking them systematically. There is no evi-

6. As will be seen, however, portions of the protocols and testimony are not based on the witnesses' personal knowledge. Plaintiffs' and defendants' experts agree that the Japanese legal system does not exclude hearsay evidence in civil cases or in JFTC proceedings.

dence that the diaries were ever communicated (or intended to be communicated) to anyone else. Given this general description, it is obvious that the admissibility of the diaries would be in sharp dispute. . . .

The admissibility of the referenced JFTC materials has been fought on a number of battlegrounds. First, the defendants have challenged the authenticity of much of the proffered material, asserting that the plaintiffs have failed to meet their burden of establishing authentication under F.R.E. 901 and 902. Defendants urge that the notion of authentication does not implicate merely the genuineness of the subject document, but also involves additional layers of foundation. In order for a diary to be authenticated within the meaning of Rule 901, for example, defendants argue that plaintiffs must not only establish its genuineness, but also, to the extent that it is proffered as a faithful account of what transpired at meetings attended by the diarist, must establish personal knowledge by the diarist of the recorded events. . . .

In connection with each of our determinations, whether under the authentication rules or the hearsay rules, we must determine whether admissible evidence is required to support the factual findings which are the underpinnings of the ruling on the admissibility of the evidence proffered. Rule 104(a) provides that in making determinations of preliminary questions concerning the admissibility of evidence, the court is not bound by the Rules of Evidence, except with respect to privileges. Under Rule 104(b), entitled "Conditional Relevancy," however, the jury rather than the court makes the ultimate determination of admissibility, hence admissible evidence is required. The parties dispute the need for admissible evidence in the qualification process not just in connection with authentication, but also at the subsequent levels, e.g., qualification as a business record. The plaintiffs argue that admissible evidence is not required in the qualification process, relying principally on 104(a), while the defendants maintain that it is.

The foregoing is a catalog of the more significant legal questions which have arisen during the course of our hearings over the JFTC and cognate materials. As we have noted, similar questions have arisen in connection with the materials produced in discovery in connection with import transactions. Still other interesting legal questions have arisen which we shall enumerate as we proceed through our discussion. Because virtually all of these questions have been raised with respect to each document, the discussion of each will perforce be many layered, though we hope not labyrinthine.

We have observed about the diaries the difficulty that anyone other than the diarist would have in understanding them. It is of course obvious that there are indeed persons who could eliminate that difficulty and decipher any code-like references in any diary: either the diarist himself, or, in his absence, someone present at the meeting whose proceedings are supposedly recorded in the diary, or someone contemporaneously

familiar with the content of the diary or memo and the diarist's recording practices. However, the plaintiffs, despite their role as proponents of
the documents, hence bearers of the burden to qualify them, have not
proffered the testimony in any form of any such person. Moreover, they
have made it clear that they have no intention of doing so, before or at
trial. Rather, they prefer to qualify the documents circumstantially and
to offer selected (though voluminous) excerpts therefrom in connection
with the summary judgment motions and at trial. . . .

This litigation strategy was maintained in the face of repeated warning from the defendants that they intended to challenge the admissibility
of the diaries, memoranda, protocols, and testimony. This warning came
not only during the course of our numerous pretrial conferences, but
even in MELCO's motion for summary judgment, filed April 1978, well
before the close of discovery. In that motion, MELCO spent many pages
detailing the kinds of evidentiary foundational deficiencies we deal with
herein. Yet the plaintiffs, all the while insisting they were ready for trial,
declined to take depositions of those who might shed light upon the
documents. . . .

Indeed, the plaintiffs were challenged on several occasions by the
Court as to why, having proceeded with this case for close to a decade,
and having inspected literally millions of documents, they had failed to
take depositions for the purpose of laying foundation for the admissibility of the challenged JFTC materials. It was pointed out that such foundational depositions are regular fare in complex cases, i.e., it is the
custom for counsel to take them. Mr. Rome consistently responded that
it was his considered decision not to do so. The plaintiffs did take depositions of some Japanese executives in connection with the motions relative to personal jurisdiction and venue.

The defendants' explanation for plaintiffs' litigation strategy is not
gentle. They state it in their "Memorandum of Certain Defendants in
Support of their Position that Materials from the JFTC Proceeding Are
Not Admissible in Evidence" (pp. 3-4) as follows:

> Indeed, it seems clear that it was precisely because the Japanese materials
> do not constitute records of the only two matters that could make them
> properly probative in this case, that plaintiffs chose not to follow the normal
> route of taking depositions to lay a proper foundation for their introduction.
> Plaintiffs knew that such depositions would not be helpful to their case and
> that, at the end of such discovery, while they might have come up with
> admissible evidence regarding discussions of "bottom prices" by six com-
> panies for two years (1965-1966), they would not come up with any admissible
> evidence of the creation of a U.S. export invasion fund or of a United States
> predatory price agreement. They, therefore, seized upon the ploy of attempt-
> ing to introduce the materials without proper foundations — and without
> any opportunity by the other side to cross examine — and arguing to the jury
> that all kinds of wild inferences can be drawn from a handful of cryptic and

basically incomprehensible "export references" found in materials which were obviously not written to record export activities. Since plaintiffs' direct case will last for some months, the jury will be hopelessly prejudiced by such tactics before the first of the defendants could even be heard.

In furtherance of this approach, plaintiffs adopted the tactic of piling into the FPS hundreds of thousands of materials and spuriously arguing that they are all evidence of conspiracy, so that they could create the argument that it would be extremely burdensome for them to lay foundations in the normal way, even though their PPTM and summary judgment briefs show that they are, in fact, relying on a relatively small number of such Japanese materials.

Defendants conclude with a little homily:

> Fortunately, as we will demonstrate below, our Rules and evidentiary precedents, which are rooted in basic fairness and due process, do not allow for such a result. Evidence must be shown — through the establishment of a foundation in prescribed ways — to be proper and reliable before it can be thrown before a jury and begin to affect that jury's mind.

Of course, the legal aspect of their homily is quite correctly stated. And while we do not endorse defendants' rhetoric, we do note that we find a kernel of truth in defendants' evaluation of plaintiffs' litigation strategy.

The volume of material before us for consideration is staggering. We refer not only to the large number of documents (and the large volume of document pages), but also the extensive briefs and other submissions of the parties. It was represented to us during the hearings that, at that juncture, some 85 or more lawyers and paralegals were working close to full time on the case (75 for the defendants). Scores of memoranda relating to admissibility were filed during the hearings, and it is difficult to digest all of that material so as to write a worthy opinion. We shall do our best.

Because the plaintiffs have not produced the conventional evidentiary foundation, i.e. testimony of a custodian or other qualified witness, it is necessary that we evaluate the subject documents on the basis of the circumstantial factors called to our attention by plaintiffs' counsel at our evidentiary hearings. Doing so will be a tedious process, requiring us, in the case of each document, to review plaintiffs' foundation and defendants' response and then to apply the applicable legal standards to determine admissibility. We are aided materially in this regard by the post-hearing submissions of the parties which summarize the plaintiffs' foundation and defendants' response on each document, and we draw heavily upon those submissions. After a point there will be some degree of repetition in the factual patterns, enabling us to simply incorporate earlier discussion by reference. However, because of the importance plaintiffs attributed to each of the critical documents taken up in this opinion, we cannot, in fairness, unduly truncate or abbreviate our description of plantiffs' foundational proffer or defendants' response. All of this makes for a very long opinion for which we apologize but which we cannot avoid. This is because of our obligation to the parties in this very important case to which they have devoted so much time and expense, and also to the Court of Appeals which will ultimately review it and will need a full statement of the reasons for our major rulings.

For the variety of reasons which follow, we conclude that neither the diaries, memoranda or "minutes of meetings" nor discrete portions thereof are admissible in evidence; that the JFTC testimony is admissible against the defendants in the Six Company Case only, except for any so-called "export" and war-chesting "references," which are, with minor exceptions, inadmissible; and that the protocols are admissible against the employer of the maker of the protocol.

In terms of opinion structure, we shall follow the same course here as we did in the first opinion in this series. In Part II, we shall set out the legal principles applicable to the evidentiary questions we must decide, resolving the disputes between plaintiffs and defendants on legal issues. We shall take up all of the sections of the F.R.E. claimed by the parties to have bearing upon whether any of the documents were authenticated or admissible under one of the exceptions to the hearsay rules. As will be seen, there is hardly a section or subsection of Article VIII (hearsay) or Article IX (authentication) of the F.R.E. that escaped their advocacy. The number of rules invoked is largely a function of plaintiffs' circumstantial mode of laying foundation, as opposed to doing so by direct testimony. Because of these myriad issues and the fact that some of them are of first impression, this discussion will be extremely detailed. Then, in Part III, we shall describe the documents at issue and then apply the legal principles to the documents, determining their admissibility vel non. . . .

II.   RULINGS ON CONTESTED LEGAL ISSUES CONCERNING INTERPRETATION OF THE FEDERAL RULES OF EVIDENCE

A.   AUTHENTICATION . . .

1.   *The Standard for a Preliminary Ruling on Authentication Under Rule 104; Will Inadmissible Evidence Suffice?*

Plaintiffs and defendants differ as to whether admissible evidence is necessary to authenticate evidence. Defendants say "yes" and plaintiffs say "no." We begin with the Advisory Committee's Note to Rule 901, which states expressly that the requirement of showing authentication falls in the category of "relevancy dependent upon fulfillment of a condition of fact," and is thus governed by the procedure set forth in Rule 104(b), and not that set forth in Rule 104(a). . . .

The Advisory Committee Note to Rule 104(b) makes plain that preliminary questions of *conditional relevancy* are not determined solely by the judge, for to do so would greatly restrict the function of the jury as the trier of fact. If, for instance, there were serious questions in this case as to whether Mr. Yajima's diary was a forgery, it is obvious that a question of evidence so critical could not be decided solely by the court. Under the aegis of Rule 104(b), the judge makes a preliminary determination whether the foundation evidence is sufficient to permit a factfinder to conclude that the condition in question has been fulfilled. If so, according to the Advisory Committee Note:

> . . . the item is admitted. If after all of the evidence on the issue is in, pro and con, the jury could reasonably conclude that fulfillment of the condition is not established the issue is for them. If the evidence is not such as to allow a finding, the judge withdraws the matter from their consideration.

In United States v. Goichman, 547 F.2d 778, 784 (3d Cir. 1976), the Court of Appeals formulated this principle as follows: "[T]he showing of authenticity is not on a par with more technical evidentiary rules, such as hearsay exceptions, governing admissibility. Rather, there need be only a prima facie showing, to the court, of authenticity, not a full argument on admissibility." Thus, once a prima facie showing has been made to the court that a document is what its proponent claims, it should be admitted. At that point the burden of going forward with respect to authentication shifts to the opponent to rebut the prima facie showing by presenting evidence to the trier of fact which would raise questions as to the genuineness of the document.[16] The required prima facie showing of authentication need not consist of a preponderance of the evidence. Rather, all that is required is substantial evidence from which the trier of fact might conclude that a document is authentic. As the court in *Goichman,* supra, stated: "[I]t is the jury who will ultimately determine the authenticity of the evidence, not the court. The only requirement is that there has been *substantial evidence* from which they could infer that the document was authentic." Id. (emphasis added).[17]

---

16. Much is made by the plaintiffs of the fact that defendants, despite the "hard line" taken by some of them on matters of authentication, have not come forward with any evidence to refute plaintiffs' showing with respect to various documents. It is in fact true that defendants have come forward with no evidence countering plaintiffs' claim of authentication of the various documents. However, that does not alter the plaintiffs' burden.

17. Although the defendants have offered no evidence to rebut the authenticity of the documents, we need not consider any such evidence at the preliminary stage. The substantial evidence standard, unlike a preponderance standard, requires no balancing of the evidence. The Court must only conclude that a prima facie showing has been made in

The plaintiffs contend that in determining whether an adequate prima facie showing has been made, the court may consider inadmissible evidence. We disagree. Under Rule 104(b), authentication must be established by the "introduction of evidence." By using this language, the Rule plainly contemplates that the jury's determination of authenticity will be made only on the basis of admissible evidence. We find nothing in either Rule 104 or the Advisory Committee Notes to suggest that the jury may consider inadmissible evidence in this regard, except to the extent that evidence may be admitted "subject to" the introduction of subsequent (admissible) evidence of its authenticity.

So then, while the court's power to "consider" inadmissible evidence under Rule 104(a) is clear, the substantive determination which the court is required to make on the issue of authentication is whether *admissible* evidence exists which is sufficient to support a jury finding of authenticity. For it would be a pointless exercise for a judge to rely upon inadmissible evidence to fulfill the substantial evidence requirement when the trier of fact can only consider *admissible* evidence that a proffered document is authentic. Accordingly, we hold that under Rule 104(a), Rule 104(b), and *Goichman,* our task in ruling on authenticity is limited to determining whether there is *substantial admissible evidence* to support a finding of authentication by the trier of fact.[19]

Since only admissible evidence can form the basis for the determination of authentication, the degree to which plaintiffs rely on using some of the documents they have submitted to authenticate other documents creates problems of circularity, and in some cases it is more logical to determine other aspects of admissibility before reaching the 901 determination. This will be considered infra with regard to specific categories of documents.

2. *The Notion of Authentication and the Scope of Rule 901(a); Is Authenticity More than Mere Genuineness?*

Another important issue addressed in argument and briefs is the intended scope of Rule 901(a) and, in particular, the meaning of the last phrase which defines authentication as a finding "that the matter in question is what its proponent claims." In contrast to the position of the plaintiffs, who equate authentication with genuineness, the defendants contend that the scope of authentication is determined by the claims

---

order to admit the documents. It is for the trier of fact to consider the rebuttal evidence and balance it against the authenticating evidence in order to arrive at a final determination on authentication.

19. As a corollary of this holding, we acknowledge that some documents may be authenticated only as against certain parties, since the authenticating evidence for those documents may be admissible only against certain parties.

made by the proponent of a document and encompasses all of what the
proponent "*must* claim it is in order to use it as he wishes to" (emphasis in
original). They argue that the subject documents' "logical status as evidence, and hence their authenticity, could be established only by showing that they are accurate and reliable accounts . . ." (of the allegedly
conspiratorial meetings reported), otherwise "they are not probative"
and thus not what their proponent claims. Since authentication is but a
"special aspect of relevancy," Advisory Committee Note to Rule 901(a),
this is an appealing argument. After all, the plaintiffs claim that Yajima's
diary should be admitted to portray the agreements made at certain
meetings. What does it matter then that the diary is not a forgery, if it is
not an accurate and reliable account of what transpired at the meetings
Yajima purported to record?

The problem with defendants' argument is that it reads the language
of 901 to subsume nearly all of the issues involved in many cases in which
the issue may arise. For example, the proponent claims that many of the
documents under consideration here are "business records." As the Advisory Committee Notes to 901 make clear, however, this is a completely
separate determination which must be addressed outside the scope of
the authentication inquiry. While the Advisory Committee Notes state
specifically that authentication is an aspect of conditional relevancy, they
are also quite clear that it is but one kind of conditional relevancy, and
does not subsume all of the evidentiary foundation which must be established in order to show that a document is relevant evidence:

> Authentication and identification represent a *special aspect* of relevancy. Thus
> a telephone conversation may be irrelevant because on an unrelated topic or
> because the speaker is not identified. The *latter aspect* is the one here involved.

(emphasis added) (citations omitted).

The specific illustrations under subsection (b) further support a narrow interpretation of authentication. For example, authentication can be
established by expert or non-expert opinions on handwriting, F.R.E.
901(b)(2), a method which would do nothing to establish a document as
the "accurate and reliable account" that defendants claim it must be in
order to authenticate it.

While, as defendants urge, different showings are required in accordance with the *type* of evidence presented, in all of the cases and examples which they have cited authentication involves establishing the origin
or authorship of an item, or the connection of an item to a particular
individual or party. In Rhoads v. Virginia-Florida Corporation, 476 F.2d
82 (5th Cir. 1973), upon which defendants place their strongest reliance,
the authenticity of the drawings at issue had been conceded by the
opposing party. The court there pointed out that: "authentication of the
documents *merely established* their authorship, the proof of some human's

'personal connection with a corporal object.' 7 Wigmore On Evidence §2129, at 564 (3d ed. 1940)." 476 F.2d at 85 (emphasis added). The court then proceeded to discuss additional requirements for admissibility and suggested that the drawings must either be "verified" by testimony of a witness, citing 3 Wigmore On Evidence §790, at 218, or must qualify as an exception to the hearsay rule. As we have noted supra, a finding of authentication does not establish admissibility, and any other applicable requirements must also be met.

We conclude that, notwithstanding the apparent sweep of 901, created by its use of a rather expansive locution; i.e., the prescription that authentication is satisfied by evidence sufficient to support a finding that the matter in question is "what its proponent claims," the notion of authentication is a narrow one, akin to the notion of genuineness. The other foundation requirements should not be simply subsumed under the authenticity terminology, but should remain analytically distinct. We find other support for this conclusion. First, the Advisory Committee Note, subdivision (a) provides:

> Also, significant inroads upon the traditional insistence on authentication and identification have been made by accepting as at least prima facie *genuine* items of the kind treated in Rule 902, infra.

(emphasis added). Moreover, a review of the annotations under Rule 901 confirms this view, for the cases discussing the Rule have a similarly limited scope. See S. Saltzburg & K. Redden, Federal Rules of Evidence Manual 651-52 (1977) and 245-47 (1980 supp.) [hereinafter cited as "Saltzburg"]. Thus such foundation issues as personal knowledge of the declarant, which defendants urge us to treat as authentication issues, will be dealt with separately under the appropriate rules.

3. *Methods of Authentication*

Rule 901(b) lists several examples of methods of authentication which would meet the requirements of 901(a). The Advisory Committee Notes for this subsection state that these examples are not intended to exhaust all the possibilities, "but are meant to guide and suggest, leaving room for growth and development in this area of the law."

In their endeavors to authenticate the matters before us, the plaintiffs place primary emphasis on 901(b)(4), Distinctive Characteristics. They also assert, however, that the testimony and protocols from the JFTC proceedings may provide evidence of authenticity under 901(b)(1) (Testimony of a Witness with Knowledge), and that since some of the documents fall just short of the age requirements under 901(b)(8) (Ancient Documents), this subsection in conjunction with other circumstances would be sufficient to fulfill the 901(a) requirements. Once authenticity has been established for one document, 901(b)(3) may be used to authenticate other documents of a similar type.

Rule 903 (Subscribing Witness' Testimony Unnecessary) and the illustrations given under 901(b) make it clear that *testimony* is not essential to establish authenticity, and, as McCormick states, "authentication by circumstantial evidence is uniformly recognized as permissible." Elements which tend to establish authenticity may be found both in Rule 901 itself, in the Advisory Committee Notes, and in the cases which we will outline in the following discussion. One such element is the source of a particular document, i.e., the method or place of its discovery.

    a. *Source of the Document.* Plaintiffs urge that the defendants' production of certain of the documents in answer to interrogatories under Rule 33(c) is itself sufficient to establish them ipso facto as authentic. We disagree with this reading of the Rule. Given the breadth of the discovery rules and the broad requirements for production, we feel it would undermine the liberal intent of those rules to interpret such production as an admission of authenticity in the absence of a specific assertion by the producing party regarding the nature or authorship of the documents produced.

The production of the documents by the defendants may, however, provide circumstantial evidence of authenticity. McCormick notes that a prima facie showing of authenticity is made by the emergence of a document from public custody. He concludes that, while the circumstances of private custody are too varied to warrant an expansion of the rule in every case, "proof of private custody, together with other circumstances, is frequently strong circumstantial evidence of authenticity."

In Alexander Dawson, Inc. v. N.L.R.B., 586 F.2d 1300 (9th Cir. 1978), the Ninth Circuit upheld the decision of an administrative law judge admitting job application forms even though there had been no testimony regarding who had filled out the particular applications, and no witness could testify to a specific chain of custody. The circumstances surrounding their discovery, considered along with their contents was held adequate to authenticate the forms. In United States v. Natale, 526 F.2d 1160, 1173 (2d Cir. 1975), cert. denied, 425 U.S. 950 (1976), a notebook that had been seized during the defendants' arrest for extortion was admitted at trial. The Court of Appeals enumerated among the facts supporting its authenticity: (1) the presence of the defendants at the office where the notebook was discovered; (2) that defendants had held numerous meetings with a witness in that office; and (3) that one of the defendants admitted that the office was his. This, together, with evidence supplied by the notebook's contents, see infra, was sufficient to allow its admission into evidence. We will follow the *Dawson* and *Natale* courts by treating the circumstances of their production as one element of circumstantial evidence which tends to authenticate the documents produced by the defendants.

b. *Characteristics of the Document Itself.* The characteristics of the document itself are also a basis for establishing authentication, Rule 901(b)(4). The last phrase of the rule indicates, however, that characteristics of a document must be considered "in conjunction with circumstances." Although Weinstein states that a document "can be authenticated by its contents alone," it is clear, from the examples used, that he "means in light of surrounding circumstances." ¶901(b)(4)[01] at 901-46. All of the characteristics mentioned in 901(b)(4) are also subject to the overriding requirement of "distinctiveness" under that example.

The first characteristic mentioned in 901(b)(4) is "appearance." Weinstein gives as examples of the types of appearance the courts may wish to consider: a postmark, a return address, a letterhead, a signature even where affixed by a rubber stamp, typing or form which corresponds to usual practice. The aspect of the document's appearance which is most relevant with respect to the JFTC documents is the fact that many of them are marked with a particular person's name in the form of a "chop," a Japanese seal which contains a stylized rendition of a person's name and is sometimes used in lieu of a signature. During the discussion of authenticity of the so-called MITI statement, proffered by defendants, they urged that the "chop" affixed to the document made it the legal equivalent of a signed document. Though this contention was resisted at that time by plaintiffs, we conclude that a "chop" should be given weight equivalent to a signature. We recognize that a "chop," like a signature, may not always be genuine. Furthermore, many people with the same surname may have a common "chop," hence the "chop" does not in every case indicate authorship. The particular use of a "chop" will be considered with respect to the individual document upon which it appears. Many of the import transaction documents also have distinguishing characteristics, particularly letterheads.

A second characteristic mentioned in 901(b)(4), again subject to the distinctiveness requirement, is the contents, or substance, of the document. Contents have been used to establish authentication in a variety of ways. In United States v. Smith, 609 F.2d 1294 (9th Cir. 1979), hotel records of defendant's registration and charges incurred were introduced. Included in the evidence linking the defendant to the records were independent corroboration of his presence at meetings in the hotel, the use of names used by defendant in signing records, and the use of the address which appeared on defendant's business card. In *Natale,* supra, the court similarly relied upon the corroboration of the contents of the notebook involved by independent evidence. One of the entries referred to a loan made to a witness in the case, and served to authenticate the document.

In *Goichman,* supra, 547 F.2d at 783, an unsigned document entitled "History of Children's Assets," which listed the defendants' expenditures, had been produced as part of the docket record in a prior (domestic relations) proceeding. The contents of the document were corroborated by defendant's complaint in that proceeding, and the words "I" and "my" were used in conjunction with the first names of the defendant's three children. The Third Circuit held that this evidence of contents was sufficient to establish a prima facie showing of authentication.

If the subject matter of a document refers to knowledge which only one individual would have had, it is sufficient to authenticate the document. 7 Wigmore on Evidence §2148 (3d ed. 1940). Weinstein disagrees with the insistence on knowledge by only a single person, however, as he states, "the force of the inference decreases as the number of people who know the details . . . increases." Weinstein, ¶901(b)(4)[01] at 901-46 and 47. In United States v. Wilson, 532 F.2d 641 (8th Cir.), cert. denied, 429 U.S. 846 (1976), the prosecution sought to introduce a notebook which contained records of drug transactions. Though it was admitted that the author was unknown, the Court of Appeals upheld the authentication of the notebook on the grounds that only those persons acquainted with the particular transactions involved could have written the entries.

Some of the documents involved are said to contain information allegedly known only to a limited number of individuals who attended various meetings. The plaintiffs' own showing demonstrates that the number was not all that limited. However, to the extent that information contained in documents is corroborated by other admissible evidence, and is known to a limited number of individuals, these factors may be considered in determining whether sufficient evidence exists to authenticate it.

c. *Testimony and Interrogatory Answers.* Testimony before the JFTC, to the extent that it is found admissible, may also be used to authenticate other documents. Rule 901(b)(1) specifically holds testimony sufficient to establish authenticity. Where the testimony does not deal directly with any particular document offered, it may still be helpful in proving authenticity circumstantially. Weinstein ¶901(b)(1)[01] at 901-22. We will have occasion below to consider JFTC testimony both as circumstantial and as direct evidence of authenticity.

The answers to interrogatories may also be considered as "testimony" where they directly identify a document's source or author, corroborate the contents of particular documents, indicate the presence of a purported author at a meeting or a meeting's limited attendance, or otherwise establish the document's authenticity. While Weinstein notes that Interrogatories, Requests for Admissions and Stipulations "should be relied upon to dispose of most authentication problems before trial," ¶901(b)(2)[01] at 901-23, the questions and answers in most of the interrogatories here are not specific enough to constitute a concession of authenticity.

Since we have ruled that documents must be authenticated by admissible evidence, the admissibility of former testimony and the interrogatory answers themselves is an additional issue to be determined. Since the interrogatories may not be admissible against all defendants unless the plaintiffs' conspiracy theory is accepted, this presents a particularly difficult situation.[40] Where authentication depends on the admissibility of an interrogatory, which itself depends on the plaintiffs' establishment of a conspiracy, the documents may be admitted "subject to" such a showing.

d.   *Similarity to Other Authenticated Documents.* The example in 901(b)(3) allows the trier of fact to compare a document to another authenticated document in order to establish its authentication. In *Dawson*, supra, the employment applications involved were "on the same form" as applications whose authenticity was conceded. This, in conjunction with the circumstances of production, was considered sufficient to establish their authenticity, 586 F.2d at 1303. Many of the documents involved here are members of "groups" of documents, sharing similar characteristics. The authentication of one such document may serve as the basis for authenticating the others in a group on the basis of comparison, initially by the court, and ultimately by the trier of fact.

e.   *Age of the Document.* A final element to be considered in our determination of authenticity is the age of the document. Rule 901(b)(8)(C) sets twenty years as the age requirement for "Ancient Documents." None of the documents now before us is twenty years old, although some may reach that age by the time of trial. While Weinstein urges that this figure should not be regarded as an absolute necessity, it is itself ten years shorter than the period under common law. This is explained in the Advisory Committee Notes as being due to a shift in the underlying rationale for the rule from an emphasis on the unavailability of witnesses to an emphasis on the unlikeliness of a fraud over such an extended time period. While the Notes state that any time period is bound to be arbitrary, we feel that in the present case some additional indicia of authenticity are needed where all of the documents fall short of the twenty year limit.

4.   *Self-Authentication Under Rule 902*

Rule 902 provides that certain documents are "self-authenticating" to the extent that no extrinsic evidence of authenticity is needed. Although

---

40. Under F.R.E. 801(c), an interrogatory answer is hearsay except as to the party furnishing the answer, as to whom it is not hearsay under Rule 801(d)(2). While a deposition by written questions under F.R. Civ. P. 31 may be used against all parties present or represented or with reasonable notice, under F.R. Civ. P. 32(a), no such depositions were taken here.

902(3) lists Foreign Public Documents as being of this type, the Advisory Committee Notes to 902(4) make it clear that 902(3) applies to the originals of documents and that 902(4) is the section applicable to copies. Under this section the copy must be certified as correct by either the custodian or other authorized person, and this certification must itself conform to Rule 902(3) in order to be received.

None of the documents involved here were obtained by plaintiffs from official custody or were accompanied by this type of official certification, and thus none are "self-authenticating" under Rule 902. Since the method of authentication provided in Rule 902 is not exclusive, however, plaintiffs' failure to procure certified copies does not bar authentication of the documents under Rule 901. . . .

III. THE YAJIMA DIARIES, DSS-48-50

A. INTRODUCTION

The Yajima diaries, DSS-48-50,[96] are three notebooks which the Japanese Fair Trade Commission ("JFTC") seized during the course of its investigation in the "Six Company Case." Plaintiffs contend that the notebooks were authored by a Toshiba official named Seiichi Yajima, who during 1965 and 1966, the period covered by the diaries, attended on Toshiba's behalf meetings of the so-called "Tenth Day Group," one of a number of groups allegedly engaged in price fixing activities within Japan. The diaries were marked as exhibits during the course of the "Six Company Case." Toshiba Corporation produced these notebooks to plaintiffs during the summer of 1972 in response to a Request for the Production of Documents which had been served by plaintiff NUE at the outset of the litigation and which called for all documents relating to the Six Company Case. . . .

Plaintiffs offer the diaries in evidence against all the defendants in this action. More specifically, plaintiffs offer these diaries as business records under F.R.E. 803(6), as admissions of Toshiba Corporation under F.R.E. 801(d)(2), as a declaration against the interest of Mr. Yajima under F.R.E. 804(b)(3) and as admissible under F.R.E. 804(b)(5), one of the residual hearsay exceptions. Plaintiffs' overriding proffer is that the diaries are an authentic account of what took place at the meetings of the Tenth Day Group and other groups mentioned therein.

Our modus procedendi in dealing with these diaries shall be first to set forth the plaintiffs' and then the defendants' contentions as to matters of foundation or qualification, i.e., we shall set forth the factual and to some extent the legal basis for the parties' contentions that the proffered documents are (or are not) authenticated under F.R.E. 901 and

---

96. Each document considered at the evidentiary hearings was accompanied by a "Document Submission Sheet" or "DSS."

that they are (or are not) admissible under one of the exceptions to the hearsay rules. . . .

B. PLAINTIFFS' FOUNDATION FOR AUTHENTICATION AND ADMISSIBILITY UNDER ONE OF THE EXCEPTIONS TO THE HEARSAY RULES

(1) The diaries are specifically cited, indeed incorporated by reference, in Toshiba's answers to interrogatory numbers 8 and 42-44 to NUE's second set of interrogatories to defendants. In plaintiffs' submission, by this reference, Toshiba has, in effect, conceded authentication, business records status, and other necessary foundation for the diaries.

(2) The three diaries were lawfully seized by the JFTC from Toshiba's offices and turned over to the JFTC by Mr. Kono, then the manager of the TV division. Upon their return, Toshiba made copies of the diaries and produced them to the plaintiffs.

(3) One of the diaries, DSS-48, contains the Toshiba logo in Japanese and English at the top of the page.

(4) During the Six Company Case Mr. Yajima gave the JFTC investigators four protocols (DSS-75, DSS-76, DSS-77, and DSS-78) during which Mr. Yajima identified the diaries. The protocols, which bear a seal, have a recognized legal status in Japan.

(5) During the course of his formal testimony before the JFTC, Mr. Yajima identified the diaries, testified to certain entries, and said that they were accurate and reflected meetings of the six defendants.

(6) Yajima's protocols and testimony also include statements that show that he was present at the meetings he recorded in his diary.

(7) The notebooks appear in the JFTC "investigator's list of evidence" (DSS-93) which plaintiffs claim is an official record of the JFTC.

(8) Testimony of defendants' other employees at the JFTC hearing and statements by defendants' other employees in their protocols referred to one of Yajima's notebooks to confirm what occurred at a meeting.

(9) Mr. Kamakura's protocol makes reference to Yajima's presence at the meetings.

(10) Mr. Yajima allegedly reported to his superiors at Toshiba after returning from certain meetings, passing on information on which they relied.

(11) The diary is on its face a business record; i.e. it pertains purely to business matters which are of importance to Toshiba, and it looks and reads like a business record (the "res ipsa loquitur" contention).

(12) Yajima's obligation to attend meetings and to make reports to Narita suggests that the information that he entered in the diaries was maintained by him as his regular practice; moreover, the entries (about the Tenth Day meetings) occur at fairly regular intervals.

(13) The secretary company of the Tenth Day Group meeting would take down information for production, shipment and inventory, and since Yajima testified that Toshiba was the secretary company from March 1966 to June 1966, when Yajima was recording Tenth Day Group information, he was acting on behalf of the Group and his own company.

(14) Entries were made periodically relating to regular subject matters. They covered basically the same type of information month after month. These topics were continually discussed, and it was part of the practice at these meetings and part of Yajima's practice to record this type of information.

(15) When Yajima was shown the diary during the taking of the JFTC protocol, Yajima said "This notebook is mine and what was written in it deals with the events of this year and was written on the spot."

C. DEFENDANTS' RESPONSE

(1) There is no testimony on the record of this case by a "custodian or other qualified witness," F.R.E. 803(6), or in fact by anyone authenticating or establishing the foundation required by the admission of any of these diaries into evidence. Indeed, plaintiffs took no deposition of any person who (i) had knowledge of the manner in which the notebooks were kept and (ii) could confirm the contents of the notebooks. Rather, plaintiffs rely for foundation completely upon their counsel's presentation to the court.

(2) The Toshiba logo appears on only one of the diaries (DSS-48), and in any event, the fact that Toshiba stationery was used is of no significance.

(3) There are time gaps in the notebooks: DSS-48 refers to November 1965 to December 1965; DSS-49 refers to the period January 1965 to June 1965; DSS-50 refers to the period January 1966 to November 1966. There is no notebook for the period July through October 1965.

(4) The "Yajima Protocols" cited by plaintiffs as places where Mr. Yajima identified the diaries are simply brief passing references to only two of the diaries which, in fact, do not establish that the diaries are admissible under any of the exceptions to the hearsay rules.

(5) The Yajima testimony also does not establish the foundation for the admission of the diaries into evidence. Only one of the diaries is referred to during Mr. Yajima's testimony and only in passing references which do not establish the foundation for the admissibility of the documents.

(6) Toshiba's interrogatory answers do not establish the necessary foundation for the admissibility of the diaries, since the diaries were produced in response to a Request for the Production of Documents, not as answers to Interrogatories. At all events, the interrogatories did

not request information relating to the substance of the meetings or the necessary foundation for the admissibility of the diaries. Moreover, Toshiba, in its interrogatory answers, specifically disclaimed any knowledge concerning the accuracy of the Yajima diaries or concerning what took place at any of the meetings of the groups about which the interrogatories inquired. See Toshiba's Answers to Interrogatories 8, 42, 43, and 44 of Plaintiff's [NUE] Interrogatories Set No. 2.

(7) The testimony and protocols of Messrs. Adachi, Narita, Tsurata, and Kamakura also do not establish the foundation for the admissibility of the diaries since these references to the diaries do not establish any of the requirements of any of the exceptions to the hearsay rules, and are merely passing references to diaries which were being used merely to refresh the recollection of the witness.

(8) While the protocols and testimony contain some statements to the effect that Mr. Yajima reported to his superiors after attending meetings, there is nothing in the record establishing that he utilized his diary for this purpose. Further, there is nothing in the record of this case establishing that Mr. Yajima was under a business duty to keep his diary; nor is there anything in the record of this case to show that Mr. Yajima systematically checked his diary or that it was his continuous habit to keep the diary.

(9) The diaries themselves are a "hodge podge" of notes which are pointless without the testimony of some person who was present at the meetings. One cannot even tell with any certainty where accounts of meetings begin and end; whether the accounts are what the author thought or surmised, or what someone else said, and if so, who said it. Further, there are at least 28 separate entries which the translators noted as "illegible."

(10) The diaries contain double and triple hearsay, and because of the manner in which the entries were kept, it is impossible to sort out what is based upon Yajima's personal knowledge and what is based upon hearsay. Further, Mr. Yajima stated in his protocol that the information he obtained from other companies at meetings was in large part based upon "guesses" and "hunches." Therefore, it is impossible to sort out what part of his diary is guesswork and what part was actually heard by Mr. Yajima.

Against this background of contentions, we now apply our discussion of law to the Yajima diaries on the basis of the developed record.

D. AUTHENTICATION (FRE 901)

Although the question is a close one, especially as against defendants other than Mr. Yajima's employer, Toshiba Corp., we find, pursuant to the applicable Rule (F.R.E. 104(b)), that the diaries have been authenticated under the prima facie standard of United States v. Goichman, supra, as the genuine diaries of Mr. Yajima. Put differently, there is sufficient admissible evidence from which the trier of fact could conclude that the diaries are what their proponents claim (i.e., Mr. Yajima's diaries). In this regard, we rely upon the items of evidence hereinafter enumerated, making shorthand reference to the evidence that has been more fully described, supra, in one or the other of the parties' contentions.

(1) The Toshiba logo. See Part II-A-3(b), supra.

(2) The protocols, which we find admissible against Toshiba only, see infra, but which identify the diaries.

(3) Yajima's testimony, which we find admissible against all defendants in its authentication aspect only, see Part VIII-C-4, infra, and which identifies the diaries.

(4) Toshiba's production of the diaries and reference to them in its Rule 33(c) interrogatory answers.

(5) The cross-reference to Mr. Yajima in the other defendants' interrogatory answers and JFTC testimony.

(6) The similarity to other authenticated documents. While there has been no testimony by any custodian or "subscribing witness," such is unnecessary under Rule 903.

E. BUSINESS RECORD STATUS (FRE 803(6))

For the reasons which follow, we conclude that the plaintiffs have not qualified the Yajima diary as a record of regularly conducted activity under Rule 803(6). Furthermore, we conclude that defendants have shown a lack of trustworthiness under the 803(6) trustworthiness proviso. . . .

IV. THE YAMADA DIARY, DSS-51

A. INTRODUCTION

The Yamada Diary is a notebook into which Noboru Yamada, Department Manager of the Electric Appliance Department, Consumer Products Division of Hitachi, Limited, made certain entries during the period from (approximately) August 1965 to November 1965. It was seized during the JFTC raid upon the offices of Hitachi Ltd. on November 8, 1966. Hitachi produced this notebook to plaintiffs in the course of discovery in these proceedings. . . .

Plaintiffs offer the Yamada diary in evidence against all defendants. Plaintiffs claim that it is authenticated under F.R.E. 901(a), 901(b)(4), 901(b)(9), and 902. They offer it as a business record under F.R.E. 803(6), as an admission of Hitachi, Limited, under F.R.E. 801(d)(2), as a present sense impression under F.R.E. 803(1), as a declaration against interest under F.R.E. 804(b)(3) and as admissible under the residual hearsay exceptions F.R.E. 803(24) and 804(b)(5). In general terms plaintiffs offer the Yamada notebook as an authentic account of what took place at the group meetings which Mr. Yamada purportedly attended.

B.   PLAINTIFFS' FOUNDATION FOR AUTHENTICATION AND
     ADMISSIBILITY UNDER ONE OF THE EXCEPTIONS TO THE
     HEARSAY RULES

Plaintiffs' proffer of Yamada's notebook, as well as those of Yamamoto, Okuma, and Tokizane, considered infra, is based upon the same types of matters that they offered to lay foundation for the Yajima • notebooks. Plaintiffs describe the common bases as follows:

(1) Identification of the diaries in the (respective) interrogatory answers of the diarist's employer as its response to those interrogatories.

(2) The "pattern of cross-authentication" which exist among the DSS-48-98, in which various persons identify entries in documents.

(3) The "confirming testimony" which establishes the trustworthiness of the JFTC material.

Plaintiffs also rely across the board upon "a pattern of reporting the conduct of the meetings to both superiors and subordinates," the fact that the notebooks are "business-related" and upon the lawful JFTC seizure of the diary from the Hitachi premises.

In addition to these factors, plaintiffs also rely upon the following:

(1) Counsel for the Hitachi defendants have indicated that there was "no reason to believe that it was not Mr. Yamada's diary."

(2) The "chop" or seal of Mr. Yamada has been affixed to one of the pages of the diary.

(3) The Yamada diary appears in the JFTC investigator's list of evidence (DSS-93), which plaintiffs claim is an official record of the JFTC.

(4) One or more individuals named Yamada are identified in Hitachi, Toshiba, and Sanyo Answers to Interrogatories (Plaintiffs' FPS, App. A at 423, 480, 485) as having attended meetings of the MD Group and the Market Stabilization Council.

(5) Entries in the Yamada diary are of the sort which might be expected by one in Mr. Yamada's high position, (i.e., general manager of the Yokohama works and later Department Manager, Electronic Appliance Department Consumer Products Division), thus indicating the authenticity of the diary.

(6) There is a pattern of reporting in the notebook congruent with that of other diaries.

C.   DEFENDANTS' RESPONSE

(1) The document was produced to plaintiffs in response to a Rule 34 request, not a Rule 33(c) proffer.

(2) Hitachi's interrogatory answers do not establish in any way either its authenticity or business record status.

(3) Other than a reference in the JFTC list of evidentiary materials (DSS-93), which is of dubious admissibility, there is no information in the record regarding the document.

(4) No evidence has been presented as to when or for what purpose Mr. Yamada's seal was attached to *one* page of the Yamada document.

(5) Entries are essentially illegible and unintelligible.

(6) Mr. Adachi's testimony before the JFTC merely elucidates a few figures in the Yamada diary and does nothing to authenticate the diary.

(7) Validation of the Yamada diary by comparison of certain entries therein to certain entries in the Yamamoto diaries is impermissible unless the Yamamoto diaries have first been authenticated, and even if the Yamamoto diaries were authenticated, similarity in entries could have resulted from information which was derived from a common third-party source.

(8) Yamada is a common Japanese surname and the persons named "Yamada" who are identified in various defendants' answers to interrogatories as having attended various group meetings are not necessarily the same as Noboru Yamada of Hitachi, Ltd., since at least four other persons named "Yamada" are mentioned in the record.

(9) No evidence is in the record to indicate that Noboru Yamada attended any of the meetings noted in the Yamada diary.

(10) Plaintiffs have presented no evidence to demonstrate that Mr. Yamada acted under a duty to record any of the information in the diary.

(11) Plaintiffs have presented no evidence as to what periods of time may have elapsed between when Mr. Yamada learned certain information and when he recorded it in his diary.

(12) There is no evidence of systematic checking or of a regular or continuous habit on Mr. Yamamoto's part in marking entries in his notebooks relating to group meetings.

(13) Mr. Yamada is alive and well and still employed by Hitachi and available for depositions, but has not been deposed by plaintiffs.

D. AUTHENTICATION

Although the point is very close, we find Mr. Yamada's diary to be authenticated for much the same reason as we found Yajima's diaries authenticated. We rely in this regard on the identification of the documents in answers to interrogatories and its production by Hitachi [112]; the

---

112. Defendants have asserted that the document was produced in response to a Rule 34 request, not a Rule 33(c) proffer. This would make some difference on the question of authentication but not enough to affect the outcome here.

presence of Mr. Yamada's "chop" on one of the pages of the diaries; the apparent acknowledgement of the authenticity of the diary in Mr. Adachi's testimony before the JFTC, and the circumstances of seizure of the diary. We believe that these factors taken together satisfy the *Goichman* standard.

E. THE BUSINESS RECORDS EXCEPTION

Yamada's diary does not qualify as a business record under F.R.E. 803(6) for the reasons set forth at length in our discussion of Yajima's diaries. We shall not burden the record by rescribing virtually all of the reasons for nonadmissibility advanced there, and we simply incorporate by reference our rulings. In capsule form, we note the following. First, the plaintiffs have failed to adduce any evidence of routine practice or systematic checking or of any habit of precision or regularity on Mr. Yamada's part in connection with his diary entries. Second, this diary is worse than a "hodge podge." We have read it in its entirety (in English translation of course) and can certify that there is hardly a line much less a page which is intelligible — that is to anyone other than Mr. Yamada, assuming *he* could understand it. To call this document cryptic would be extremely charitable. Third, there are the same problems of lack of evidence of first hand knowledge and a duty to report. Fourth, there is no evidence in the record as to what periods of time may have elapsed between when Mr. Yamada learned certain information and when he recorded it in his diary. Moreover, for the foregoing reasons and because of the character of the diary there are trustworthiness problems of such dimension as to render the diary inadmissible under the 803(6) proviso. To repeat what we said in discussing Yajima's diaries, a document which is unintelligible cannot be trustworthy. We have thus essentially accepted defendants' contentions about the Yamada diary and its admissibility under Rule 803(6).

In addition to the reasons akin to those which required exclusion of Yajima's diaries, there are other reasons preventing the Yamada diary from coming in as business records. There is no evidence in the record as to Yamada's presence at any of the Tenth Day Group meetings. Plaintiffs seem to believe that the congruence between entries in Yamada's diary and entries in the other diaries is sufficient to establish such a presence and also to establish the admissibility of the diary as a business record under 803(6). For the reasons explained above that is incorrrect. Moreover, unlike Yajima, Yamada is alive and well and available for depositions but they have never been taken. Plaintiffs have had an opportunity to lay foundation for admissibility — that is what lawyers usually do in cases before us — but have passed it by. . . .

V. THE YAMAMOTO DIARIES, DSS-52-54

A. INTRODUCTION

The Yamamoto diaries, into which Mr. Mamoru Yamamoto of Hitachi, Limited, purportedly made certain entries during the period of approximately October of 1964 to July of 1966, were seized by JFTC during the course of the Six Company Case. Hitachi Ltd. produced these notebooks to plaintiffs during discovery in these proceedings.

Plaintiffs offer these diaries in evidence against all defendants. More specifically, plaintiffs claim these diaries are authentic under F.R.E. 901(a), 901(b)(4), and 901(b)(9). They are offered as admissions of Hitachi, Limited, under F.R.E. 801(d)(2), as present sense impressions under F.R.E. 803(1), as business records under F.R.E. 803(6), as declarations against Mr. Yamamoto's interest under F.R.E. 804(b)(3) and under the residual exceptions, F.R.E. 803(24) and 804(b)(5). Plaintiffs offer the diaries as authentic accounts of what took place at the group meetings which Mr. Yamamoto purportedly attended.

B. PLAINTIFFS' FOUNDATION FOR AUTHENTICATION AND ADMISSIBILITY UNDER ONE OF THE EXCEPTIONS TO THE HEARSAY RULES

(1) The Yamamoto notebooks were identified in answers to the interrogatories filed by Hitachi Ltd.

(2) In his protocol before the JFTC (DSS-86), Mr. Yamamoto identified the notebooks, which are in turn identified in the JFTC investigator's list of evidence (DSS-93) as his own.

(3) In his testimony before the JFTC (DSS-64), Mr. Adachi testified concerning two entries in the Yamamoto notebooks, and raised no challenge to the authenticity of the notebooks at that time.

(4) Mr. Yamamoto put his business address into his notebooks, and kept his notebooks at his desk, for that is where the JFTC investigators found (and lawfully seized) them.

(5) In his protocol before the JFTC (DSS-64), Mr. Yamamoto stated that he went to some meetings of the Tenth Day Group.

(6) As to group meetings which he did not attend, Mr. Yamamoto states in his protocol before the JFTC (DSS-64) that Mr. Adachi would communicate information concerning these meetings to Mr. Yamamoto within a week of occurrence of the meetings, and that Mr. Yamamoto would promptly record all information relevant to his business responsibilities.

(7) It can be assumed from the corporate structure of Hitachi, Ltd. that Mr. Yamamoto was receiving regular timely reports concerning group meetings which he did not personally attend.

(8) Dates of group meetings noted by Mr. Yamamoto correspond with dates of which plaintiffs are aware from other evidence in this litigation, thus corroborating the accuracy of Mr. Yamamoto's notes.

(9) Mr. Adachi did not "embellish" any of the reports he made to Mr. Yamamoto concerning meetings which Mr. Yamamoto did not attend because he knew the information had to be reliable enough for Mr. Yamamoto to act upon it.

(10) All entries in the Yamamoto notebooks are business-related.

(11) The contents of the Yamamoto notebooks must have been communicated at least at Mr. Ueno, for he signed the receipt when the JFTC investigators seized the notebooks.

(12) Mr. Adachi ratified the contents of the Yamamoto notebooks because, if Mr. Yamamoto's practice in writing this information down were against company policy, Mr. Adachi would have stopped him from acting as he did.

(13) One diary (DSS-53) bears the Hitachi logo, with the legend "1964 Diary" and under that "Hitachi Kaden, Inc." and under that "Hitachi Installment Sales, Inc." Yamamoto gives his name and for his address he gives "TV Dept., TV. SEC," which identifies the diary as a business notebook, not a personal notebook.

C. DEFENDANTS' RESPONSE

(1) The Yamamoto notebooks were produced to plaintiffs in response to a Rule 34 request, not a Rule 33(c) proffer;

(2) The authenticity of the Yamamoto notebooks was not challenged before the JFTC because the notebooks were not introduced as substantive evidence.

(3) Mr. Adachi's testimony before the JFTC relating to entries in the Yamamoto notebooks relates not to the authenticity of the notebooks, but to the inaccuracy of figures recorded in the notebooks.

(4) Correlation of dates recorded for group meetings recorded in the Yamamoto notebooks with dates noted in other items of proffered evidence does nothing to satisfy the requirements of the Federal Rules of Evidence.

(5) Many dates of group meetings which took place in the period covered by the Yamamoto notebooks are not noted therein, which fact indicates a lack of regularity in creation of these entries.

(6) Plaintiffs have presented no evidence that Mr. Yamamoto regularly put into his notebook information concerning group meetings that Mr. Adachi had personally attended, as opposed to meetings which Mr. Yamamoto or Mr. Adachi may have learned of from unidentified third persons.

(7) There is no evidence of systematic checking or of a regular or continuous habit on Mr. Yamamoto's part in making entries in his notebooks relating to group meetings.

(8) Mr. Yamamoto states in his protocol before the JFTC (DSS-86) that Mr. Adachi added his own ideas and accounts of Tenth Day Group meetings to Mr. Yamamoto's.

(9) There is no evidence indicating what Mr. Yamamoto's source was for information regarding meetings of any group other than the Tenth Day Group, and neither Mr. Yamamoto nor Mr. Adachi ever attended a single meeting of some of the groups referenced in the Yamamoto notebooks.

(10) The supposition that a document is found in a business office does not establish it as a business record, nor does the fact that portions of the document are business-related.

(11) There is no evidence that the contents of these notebooks were ever communicated to anyone, and the fact that Mr. Ueno signed the JFTC receipt does not establish that he read the notebooks.

(12) Entries in the Yamamoto notebooks are essentially unintelligible, and it is impossible to determine where opinion stops and the information, if any, begins.

D. DISCUSSION

We need not dwell long on the Yamamoto diaries because we agree essentially with defendants' contentions. Accordingly, the diaries must be excluded for the reasons set forth in our discussion of the Yajima and Yamada diaries. They are authenticated by virtue of their mode of seizure and production, by Mr. Adachi's brief testimony, by Mr. Yamamoto's act of putting his business address in the notebooks, and by his reference to the diaries in his protocol. However, they must be excluded as hearsay because they have not satisfied any of the exceptions. . . .

VII. THE TOKIZANE DIARY, DSS-56-57

A. INTRODUCTION

The Tokizane diary is a notebook of approximately 80 pages, comprising entries purportedly made by Hayata Tokizane, an employee of Matsushita Electric Industrial Co., Ltd. ("MEI"). At the time that the diary entries were allegedly made (between March and April, 1965) Mr. Tokizane was the Director of the Television Division of MEI. He was also a director of MEI from 1967 to 1971 and Managing Director from

1971 to 1974. Only two pages of the diary were submitted to the Court, document numbers MJ3972 and MIH20080.

Plaintiffs offer the Tokizane diary in evidence against all defendants. More specifically, plaintiffs offer this diary as a business record under F.R.E. 803(6), as an admission of MEI under F.R.E. 801(d)(2), as a declaration against the interest of Mr. Tokizane under F.R.E. 804(b)(3), and under the residual hearsay exceptions, F.R.E. 803(24) and F.R.E. 804(b)(5). Substantively, plaintiffs offer the diary as evidence that Matsushita and Sony conspired to fix the price of 9″ color transistor TV sets at 39,800 yen, and that there was a meeting of the Palace Group on March 23, 1965, where a decision was made concerning the price of color TV's.

B. PLAINTIFFS' FOUNDATION FOR AUTHENTICATION AND ADMISSIBILITY UNDER ONE OF THE HEARSAY RULES

(1) MEI answers to interrogatories identify Mr. Tokizane as the director of the television division of MEI from 1964 to 1968; as such, he was the direct superior of the general manager of the television department of MEI, the immediate superior of the general manager of the transistor department of MEI, and the immediate superior of the general manager of the color television department of MEI.

(2) The first part of the diary was produced by the Matsushita defendants, and is referred to by them in their correspondence and in their Answers to Interrogatories Set No. 2, Interrogatories 8, 42, and 44.

(3) The diary contains entries about employee's wages, new employees, and a meeting concerning a press release for new products, i.e. business related matters.

(4) The diary was an exhibit in the "Six Company Case," and part of the record in that proceeding (DSS-93).

(5) The diary contains a March 31 entry about a meeting at the "Head Office" involving the President, Vice President and Managing Director who discussed color TV prices, transistor TV's, that the price of a 9″ television receiver would be 39,800 yen, and that the president would inform Sony to that effect. The diary also contains an April 1 entry indicating "telephone from President about the Sony matter." Plaintiffs claim that this entry, in conjunction with the March 31 entries, indicates that Matsushita and Sony set the price of 9″ transistor color TV's at 39,800 yen.

(6) The April 5 entry refers to a phone call from the "Chairman" (but does not specify which chairman) concerning the decision of the Palace Group on color prices. This decision was purportedly made at a Palace Group meeting on March 23, 1965, since Appendix B to Plaintiffs' FPS

and document MJ2823 (the JFTC investigator's statement of the case, DSS-94) lists a Palace Group Meeting on March 23, 1965.

(7) Despite the fact that the diary entries do not mention the year, they do indicate that April 5 was on a Monday, and an examination of a perpetual calendar reveals that the year must be 1965.

C. DEFENDANTS' RESPONSE

(1) There was no testimony or protocol by Mr. Tokizane in the Six Company Case record. No one else in the Six Company case referred to Mr. Tokizane's diary. The present case has no deposition dealing with Mr. Tokizane. There was no foundation laid for admissibility of the diary in the JFTC proceeding. Consequently, other than the bare diary itself, there is no explanation of what the diary means, how it was prepared, and for what it was used.

(2) Since no other source sheds light on the meaning of the diary, it is impossible to relate any individual entry in the diary to any other entry. For example, nothing in the diary indicates that the 9″ T.R. price of 39,800 yen in the March 31 entry relates to the "telephone from president" entry of April 1, or the "Chairman phone call entry" of April 5, or any other entry. The attempted connection between the 9″ television receiver price of 39,800 yen, in the March 31 entry, with the April 5 entry concerning the Palace Group decision on color prices is impossible, since 39,800 yen is too low a price for a color TV.

(3) The entries do not purport to have anything to do with an export conspiracy, nor do they say that there was any agreement reached in the sense of parallel pricing conduct. Consequently, the jury cannot be permitted to speculate as to what these meaningless entries refer to.

(4) Plaintiffs' contention that the March 31 and the April 1 entries indicate that Sony and Matsushita together set the price of 9″ color transistor TV sets at 39,800 yen is clearly erroneous, since at the alleged time of the diary entries (April 1965) Sony was not exporting color TV sets. Also, the price of 39,800 yen was not comparable to Sony's prices for those models. Furthermore, the diary entries nowhere state that Sony and Matsushita fixed prices, merely that the president will inform Sony about *something*, and it is impossible to infer a price-fixing agreement involving Sony from these cryptic comments in the diary.

(5) It is uncontested that Mr. Tokizane never attended any of the various group meetings. Thus, any references to discussions at the Palace Group meetings are, at best, multiple hearsay.

(6) There is no showing in the diary as to what year the entries were made. References in other documents that meetings took place in 1965 does not shed light on the year that *this* diary was made.

(7) If the diary was necessary to Mr. Tokizane's business, it would have been written in a comprehensible manner.

D.   DISCUSSION

We have spent much time in dealing with the diaries. This has been necessary because of the great scaffolding which plaintiffs have erected on the basis of random entries therein, a scaffolding which collapses because of the non-existence of foundation. It is time to move on to other matters and so we shall simply note that we agree with defendants' contentions and conclude that the Tokizane diary is not admissible under any of the exceptions to the hearsay rules for essentially the same reasons as the other diaries. Plaintiffs make much of Mr. Tokizane's high position within Matsushita. That does not affect admissibility. This document is as cryptic as can be and we are not about to let the trier of the fact (aided of course by some helpful suggestions of their friendly plaintiffs' counsel) speculate as to what it means on the basis of selected bits and pieces.

At the hearing plaintiffs' counsel argued that even if the document was inadmissible, it would still be relied upon for "corroboration." We know of no authority for such a proposition, and suggest that it reflects the bankruptcy of plaintiffs' evidentiary case.

VIII.   JFTC TESTIMONY, DSS-58-74

A.   INTRODUCTION

During the Six Company proceedings, a total of 17 different witnesses testified before the JFTC Hearing Examiners. . . . The six defendants were jointly represented by three counsel, identified in the translations as "surrogates." The vast bulk of the interrogation of the witnesses was conducted by these counsel. Some questions were also put to the witnesses by the JFTC Hearing Examiners and occasionally questions were put by the investigators. The subject matter of the testimony related to business practices of the six companies, with emphasis upon their pricing policies, and to activities at meetings of the Tenth Day Group at which there were discussions of "bottom prices," predicted consumer demand, and of the wholesale, retail, and rebate margins operative in the manufacturers' distribution chains. Virtually all of the testimony concerned the Japanese domestic market, although there is an occasional random reference to exports. . . .

B.   AUTHENTICATION

The proffered documents are copies of the notes of the testimony taken before the JFTC, but without any kind of seal, or certification from the JFTC or its court reporter of its correctness, and without testimony by a witness who has compared the copies with the original. While most of the defendants have not asserted the point, and although plaintiffs express understandable chagrin at the apparent hypertechnicality of the contention, MELCO, correctly noting that it is the plaintiffs' burden to authenticate its evidence regardless of what the defendants come forward with, objects to the admission of the JFTC testimony on the grounds of lack of authentication. The MELCO objections are based on the lack of:

1) certification by the JFTC that the proffered copy is a genuine copy of the original;

2) testimony or certification that the typed copy is an accurate transcript of the original handwritten copy;

3) testimony or certification that the examiner accurately reported his notes of the witness' statements;

4) signature or oath by the witness; and

5) certification of a "public document" as required under F.R.E. 902(3) relating to "foreign public documents." . . .

The plaintiffs have responded to these objections in several ways. First, they point out that defendants identified the notes of testimony in their answer to "Plaintiffs' [NUE] Interrogatories to Defendant, Set No. 2, Interrogatories Nos. 8, 42-44." Secondly, the plaintiffs note that the transcripts were produced by the defendants in response to plaintiffs' Request for the Production of Documents. Thirdly, the plaintiffs observe that all of the witnesses were called to testify by an attorney who represented all respondents to the JFTC case, and that the witnesses were sworn. Fourth, they note that there is a stenographer's seal on the (copy of the) transcript. Fifth, they point out that the format of all the notes of testimony is the same. Finally, they argue that all the witnesses were employed by the various defendants.

We are satisfied that the plaintiffs have made a sufficient prima facie showing of authentication under Rule 901 by virtue of the factors they have noted, and by virtue of the contents and substance of the transcripts themselves taken in conjunction with circumstances. F.R.E. 901(b)(4). . . .

XII. "MINUTES" OF THE EIAJ OFFICERS' MEETINGS, DSS-1027 and DSS-1028

A. INTRODUCTION

The EIAJ Officers' Meeting "Minutes" were produced to plaintiffs during the course of this litigation by the Electronic Industries Association of Japan (EIAJ) at its offices in Japan. DSS-1027 refers to a February 16, 1963, meeting and is identified by document identification numbers EIAJ 318-321. DSS-1028 refers to a January 18, 1964, meeting and is identified by document identification number EIAJ 286.

Although plaintiffs had the opportunity to take the deposition of an EIAJ person with knowledge about the identity of the preparer or the method of preparation of the minutes or the sources of information therefor, they elected not to do so, satisfying themselves with mere production. The "minutes" purport to show attendance at the meetings of representatives of some 24 companies other than the defendants.

Plaintiffs offer the EIAJ Officers' Meeting "Minutes" in evidence against all of the defendants. The documents are offered as admissions of the EIAJ and the defendants who were attendees of the meetings under F.R.E. 801(d)(2), (C) and (D), as business records under F.R.E. 803(6), as present sense impressions under F.R.E. 803(1), as statements against interest of defendants who were attendees of the meetings under F.R.E. 804(d)(3), and as admissible under the residual hearsay exceptions, F.R.E. 803(24) and F.R.E. 804(b)(5).

B. PLAINTIFFS' FOUNDATION FOR AUTHENTICATION AND FOR ADMISSION UNDER ONE OF THE EXCEPTIONS TO THE HEARSAY RULE

(1) The rules of the EIAJ entitle each of the EIAJ members to "peruse" records of the EIAJ and to receive materials published and distributed by the EIAJ. The EIAJ Officers' Meeting Minutes are typewritten and not handwritten, which indicates that they were distributed among the EIAJ members. The Japanese defendants in this litigation who are EIAJ members have access to these minutes and, therefore, have control over these minutes.

(2) The Japanese defendants form the standing board of directors of EIAJ. Accordingly, they control positions of authority in EIAJ.

(3) Various defendants' answers to interrogatories identify the two officers' meetings referred to in DSS-1027 and DSS-1028 as having been held. The interrogatory answers also state that the Japanese defendants were represented at those meetings.

(4) Judge Higginbotham in the transcript of February 26, 1976, at 280, directed that a good faith effort be made to make EIAJ documents available to plaintiffs and that some responsible person be present when plaintiffs searched for such documents. DSS-1027 and DSS-1028 were produced in accordance with Judge Higginbotham's direction, and Hoken Seki, Esquire, counsel for MELCO, was present at that production.

(5) The meetings were held monthly. Minutes were made for every meeting, and were kept at the offices of EIAJ. The format of the minutes follows a consistent pattern. Accordingly, the minutes alone show completeness and accuracy. The meetings for which the minutes were kept conform to the list of the meetings contained in Exhibit P of plain-

tiffs' FPS. DSS-1027 and DSS-1028 were pulled from a stack of other minutes.

(6) None of the defendants has ever withdrawn as a member of the EIAJ throughout the entire period covered in this litigation.

(7) There is no indication in the minutes that any defendant attendee left a meeting during the course of deliberations. There is also no indication in the minutes that there were any disputes or objections concerning the decisions made at the meetings. The attendees allegedly had an opportunity to object to the minutes. Accordingly, the minutes show that there was consistent unanimity among the attendees. The minutes are thus admissions by all the attendees.

(8) Defendants were receiving information concerning U.S. law, i.e. "the problem of duty appraisement," DSS-1027 [apparently a reference to the 1921 Antidumping Act] from their attorney in the United States, Mr. Tanaka. Therefore, they had knowledge of the United States laws.

C. DEFENDANTS' RESPONSE

(1) Plaintiffs did not depose anyone from the EIAJ.

(2) Neither DSS-1027 nor DSS-1028 was signed or indicates its author.

(3) The minutes do not show completeness nor accuracy. There is no indication of the methodology of the anonymous authors to guarantee the reliability of the minutes.

(4) There has been no testimony by any keeper or custodian of the minutes or other witness to establish the foundation for admission of the documents.

(5) There is no indication in the minutes as to who said what at the meetings or what the votes were, if any. There has been no showing that the attendees had authority to act or speak on behalf of their employers. Accordingly, the minutes are not admissions by any defendant.

(6) There has been no showing that the author or custodian of the minutes or any of the attendees at the meetings are unavailable, as required under F.R.E. 804(a)(5).

(7) There is nothing to indicate that the by-laws of the EIAJ on which plaintiffs rely were the by-laws that were effective in 1963.

(8) Judge Higginbotham's direction that some defense lawyers be present when plaintiffs search for documents does not catapult the EIAJ documents to admissible status.

(9) There has been no foundation laid for the admission of the minutes against any of the defendants who were not members of EIAJ.

(10) Nothing is shown in the minutes that would be contrary to anyone's pecuniary or penal interest. Application to a governmental agency for assistance regarding receiving tubes (that is one matter mentioned) is

not a crime in Japan or the United States, nor does it subject anyone to civil liability. Regarding the check price agreements, the United States Department of Justice has reviewed them on at least two occasions and has not found anything objectionable.

(11) The minutes contain double hearsay.

D.   AUTHENTICATION

Although no one has contended that they are specious, and although the task of qualification might not have been difficult had plaintiffs bothered to take a deposition for use at trial, the fact is that plaintiffs have failed to authenticate DSS-1027-1028. As we have explained in Part II supra, mere production of a document from an organization's files does not authenticate it. Defendants neither produced nor vouched for the "minutes" in connection with their interrogatory answers. Rather, the "minutes" were produced by an organization which is not a party in this litigation. Unlike some of the diaries, protocols, or testimony, there is no distinguishing feature of the documents that marks them as genuine "minutes" of meetings. We, of course, cannot read the original Japanese, but we certainly cannot say that the English translation bears some indelible imprint that smacks of genuineness. In short, the plaintiffs have done nothing to establish the genuineness of these documents so as to meet the test of U.S. v. Goichman, supra. . . .

XIII.   The EIAJ Statistics Committee 1966 (or Japan Victor Document), DSS-1029

A.   INTRODUCTION

DSS-1029 is an internal memorandum produced from the files of Japan Victor Company ("JVC"), which is not a party in this litigation. It refers to the December 26, 1966 meeting of the Statistics Committee of the EIAJ. It was produced to plaintiffs during the course of this litigation by Victor Company of Japan, Limited at its offices in Japan, and was designated with document identification number V 3747. In plaintiffs' submission, the document shows that the manufacturers who attended a meeting of the EIAJ Statistics Committee, including defendants, agreed to modify their accounting practices to cover up the disparity between home market and export practices.

Plaintiffs offer the Japan Victor document in evidence against all of the defendants in this action. Plaintiffs offer the document as a business record under F.R.E. 803(6), as admissions of JVC and MEI under F.R.E. 801(d)(2), as present sense impressions under F.R.E. 803(1), see n.48, supra, as a then existing mental, emotional, or physical condition under F.R.E. 803(3), see n.48, supra, and as admissible under the residual hearsay exceptions, F.R.E. 803(24). Plaintiffs offer the Japan Victor document as a non hearsay verbal act, in which the author reported his understanding of what had been discussed and agreed upon at the December 26, 1966 meeting of the EIAJ Statistics Committee, and in which the author gave a direction to the manager of the accounting department in order to effectuate internally an agreement reached at said meeting.

Because of the great reliance which plaintiffs place on the Japan Victor document, and the amount of time devoted thereto (plaintiffs alone have filed a 46 page brief relating to its admissibility) we shall deal with it in detail.

B. PLAINTIFFS' FOUNDATION FOR AUTHENTICATION AND
   ADMISSIBILITY UNDER ONE OF THE EXCEPTIONS TO THE
   HEARSAY RULE

(1) This document was produced pursuant to a subpoena served on and accepted by MEI's counsel on behalf of Japan Victor Company. It was produced at the offices of Japan Victor Company in Tokyo.

(2) The Answers of the Matsushita Defendants to Plaintiffs' Supplemental Interrogatories to Defendants, Set No. 2, dated May 29, 1979, listed JVC as a member of the EIAJ Statistics Committee. The same answers stated in Answer to Interrogatory No. 33 that the December 26, 1966 meeting of the EIAJ Statistics Committee had actually taken place, that MEI's representative had attended the meeting, and that there had been a discussion of the subject referred to in the Japan Victor document. The Answers of the Hitachi Defendants to Plaintiffs' Supplemental Interrogatories, Set No. 2, Relating to Consumer Electronic Products, dated May 25, 1979, Answer to Interrogatory No. 33, stated that the December 26, 1966 meeting had taken place, that Hitachi had been represented at the meeting, and that the subject referred to in the Japan Victor document had been discussed. The Answers of Sony Corporation to Plaintiffs' Supplemental Interrogatories to Defendants, Set No. 2, dated May 22, 1979, Answer to Interrogatory No. 33, stated that Sony's representative had attended the same meeting of the EIAJ Statistics Committee.

(3) Matsushita's Answers to Plaintiffs' Supplemental Interrogatories as mentioned above identified Mr. Oguri as one of the representatives of Japan Victor Company to attend the December 26, 1966 meeting of the EIAJ Statistics Committee. Mr. Oguri's chop appears on DSS-1029. The author of this document is Mr. Oguri, or, at the very least, if he is not the author, he reviewed the document and adopted its correctness.

(4) The document itself identifies the recipient of the document as the manager of the accounting department of the plant. "Common sense"

tells the Court that the accounting department is the appropriate place for this document to be sent.

(5) This document contains the directive from the sales promotion section to the accounting department of the plant. "Common sense" tells the Court that an endorsement by the chief of a section where such directive was issued would in fact be needed in order to effectuate such a directive to the accounting department. Mr. Shiokawa was the chief of the sales promotion section. His chop appears on the document, showing this endorsement.

(6) Defendants in their answers to plaintiffs' interrogatories denied the accuracy of what was reflected in DSS-1029. Their denials amount to defendants' admissions of the fact that there was a December 26, 1966 meeting of the EIAJ Statistics Committee. The answers circumstantially evidence the authenticity of the Japan Victor document.

(7) The content of the document shows the obvious knowledge of the document's author regarding what transpired at the meeting and how JVC records the particular information.

(8) "Common sense" dictates that Mr. Oguri, who had represented JVC at the December 26, 1966 meeting, would have to report back to his superiors after the meeting in order to relay the agreement and information which resulted from the meeting. This document is an internal memo of JVC to serve this reporting purpose.

(9) The document bears the legend "confidential outside the company."

(10) The document indicates that it was prepared on January 6, 1967. This was eleven days after the December 26, 1966 meeting. The document was thus prepared in a timely fashion within the time period for effectuating the reduction of the domestic shipment price which would as agreed begin with the shipments for January 1967.

(11) MEI controls JVC by owning at least 51 percent of its shares of stock. JVC is the "alter-ego" of MEI. Accordingly, an admission of JVC which is the subsidiary of MEI is also an admission of MEI.

(12) "Common sense" tells the Court the import, probative value and high relevancy of the document.

C.   DEFENDANTS' RESPONSE

(1) Notwithstanding plaintiffs' proffer of this document as evidence against all defendants, the document could even if admissible constitute evidence *aliunde* only against JVC (which is not a party).

(2) There has been no evidence of the author or recipient of the document. There has been no showing of the file where this document originated. There has been no testimony or even an affidavit of a custodian or any other witness about the author, recipient or content of this document, or the practice of preparation of this kind of document. Plaintiffs consciously and willfully refused to take a deposition of Mr.

Oguri or Mr. Shiokawa or any other personnel of JVC. Both Mr. Oguri and Mr. Shiokawa are still in the employ of JVC.

(3) Two chops appear on the document, Mr. Oguri's and Mr. Shiokawa's. Part of the alleged chop of Oguri is not even on the document. There has been no evidence that could show the meaning of these chops. There has been no evidence showing that Mr. Oguri, and not Mr. Shiokawa, authored this document. There has been no showing of Oguri's or Shiokawa's practice of putting their chops on a document. Chops are sometimes used to show receipt of a document as well as who authored it.

(4) There has been no showing of the meaning of the Japanese word "Kokeicho," the title of the alleged recipient. Even on the basis of the plaintiffs' translation of the document, there has been no identification of either the "Manager," the "Accounting Department" or the "plant."

(5) The document does not make sense on its face. The agreement allegedly entered into at the EIAJ Statistics Committee meeting and the measures to implement such agreement do not correlate.

(6) All defendants whose answers to interrogatories identified the December 26, 1966 meeting as actually taking place, denied the accuracy of what was stated in the document as a decision of that meeting. Plaintiffs' argument that defendants' denials that they followed the plan described in the document amount to admissions that there was a plan or agreement of the EIAJ Statistics Committee is pure sophistry.

(7) Plaintiffs failed to take any depositions of Japan Victor Company personnel.

(8) DSS 1029 is the only document produced by JVC relating to a meeting of the EIAJ Statistics Committee. The conent of the document does not show anything about whether it was a regularly-prepared document.

(9) Japan Victor Company is a separate company from MEI. It is separately operated, separately managed and has separate product lines, separate distribution and separate brands, and the products are sold in competition with MEI's products both in Japan and in the United States. A 51 percent subsidiary does not make admissions that are ipso facto admissible as to the parent company.

(10) There has been no showing as to who made the statement contained in the Japan Victor document, whether he had authority to make such statement, or whether he had knowledge of the subject matter. The Japan Victor document constitutes hearsay within hearsay under F.R.E. 805.

D.   AUTHENTICATION AND BUSINESS RECORD STATUS

Because of the manner in which plaintiffs have approached this matter, we shall address authentication and business record status together. Much of what is said with respect to the "minutes" of the EIAJ Officers'

Meetings applies to the Japan Victor document. We have no notion of who wrote the document, or where or on what basis. In fact, we know nothing about the document except that it was in Japan Victor's files. No defendant, including Matsushita, whose counsel was present when the document was produced, has itself either produced it (or a copy thereof) or vouched for it in answers to interrogatories or otherwise. Matsushita has disclaimed any knowledge about it and sharply disputed its accuracy.

In the absence of some documented explanation, and notwithstanding plaintiffs' hortatory references to "common sense," plaintiffs' claims about Mr. Oguri and Mr. Shiokawa, and the manager of the Accounting Department, are not only unsupported but are sheer speculation. Yet, while the plaintiffs might have taken the deposition of someone from Japan Victor when their counsel was in Tokyo to receive production of the document and thus shed some light on its origin and its genuineness, they elected not to do so.

Notwithstanding some 46 pages of argument, plaintiffs' position as to authentication and business record status of the Japan Victor document is best characterized by the following passage at pp. 40-41 of their brief:

> If a corporation's own documents are not business records, admissions, evidence of corporate knowledge and state of mind or evidence of their nonverbal conduct, then there was absolutely no reason for those documents to exist and be maintained in the first instance. . . . *Any document created and maintained by a corporation is sufficiently trustworthy as to that corporation to make it admissible at an absolute minimum against that corporation.*
>
> The only reason that a corporation would maintain a document in its files is because of that corporation's reliance on that document.

That this formulation is an ipse dixit and without any basis in law is plain from our discussion in Parts II-A-3 and II-B-4, supra, where we explained that, particularly in light of the broad sweep of the federal discovery rules, no such inference can be drawn from mere production of a document.

Unwilling to rest solely upon this proposition, plaintiffs advance what Matsushita's counsel appropriately calls several "imaginative but unavailing excuses" for their failure to make any attempt at all to establish a foundation for admission of the document. Plaintiffs' first such contention is that depositions would have been "fruitless" since such questions as who wrote the document and who received it "could never be answered" (p.16). The possibility that no one at Japan Victor may be able to identify this document does not advance plaintiffs' cause, for it does not follow that because plaintiffs may be unable to authenticate the document they therefore should not be required to do so, or at least to attempt to do so.

Plaintiffs next argue that the Japan Victor document should be admitted because the defendants supposedly do not recall what happened at the meeting in question. This is irrelevant, because the question whether or not defendants recall this specific meeting has no bearing whatsoever on the admissibility of the document. In the next breath, plaintiffs argue that it does not matter whether or not anyone can recall the meeting or identify the document because, in their view, where a witness "repudiates" a contemporaneous document the document must be believed, and not the witness. However, the cases cited by plaintiffs have nothing to do with the refusal or inability of a witness to authenticate a document. Rather, they deal with the weight to be given to a document which has been properly authenticated and admitted into evidence, where a witness disputes the accuracy of the *contents* of the document. None of these cases holds that a document is admissible even if no one can authenticate it or lay any sort of foundation for its admissibility. Plaintiffs thus have failed to meet the *Goichman* standard of authentication.

The notion that the Japan Victor document qualifies as a business record does not merit extended discussion. Not only do we know nothing of its author, but we know nothing of the circumstances of its preparation, of its source or origin or when it was prepared. Thus, we do not know if there was any habit of regularity or precision or systematic checking attendant to its preparation, or whether it was maintained in the ordinary course of business, nor do we know whether the author had first hand knowledge or received information from someone with such and with a duty to report.

Plaintiffs point to the "obvious knowledge of the author." Such an argument is characteristic of the kind of bootstrapping they have used throughout these proceedings as a substitute for foundation. Plaintiffs also rejoin that: (1) the document was not thrown out, but remained in Japan Victor's files for 10 years; and (2) although Japan Victor produced no other documents purporting to describe the meetings of the EIAJ Statistics Committee — which plaintiffs claim met *every month* — Japan Victor did produce memoranda pertaining to other meetings of other groups (specifically, the MD group), which, plaintiffs contend, are similar in "form, content, structure and purpose" to the Japan Victor document.

As to point (1), we note that plaintiffs cite no case which holds that the failure to dispose of a document establishes that it is a business record. There is no such case, and the argument is without merit. As to point (2), the obvious rejoinder is that, using plaintiffs' own criteria, the fact that Japan Victor allegedly attended monthly meetings of the EIAJ Statistics Committee, but had only one memorandum about all these meetings, hardly suggests that Japan Victor had a regular practice of making such memoranda. Nor does the alleged similarity of the document with three other MD Group memoranda prove anything. Although we cannot read

Japanese, the documents do not look all that similar to us. The fact that they all have dates on them, and a beginning, middle and end, and (according to the translations) look like memoranda, is hardly startling. Finally, even if there were some similarity, that would be irrelevant, since the MD Group memoranda are as lacking in foundation as the Japan Victor document itself.

In sum, plaintiffs have not met their burden of showing that the Japan Victor document is authentic, U.S. v. Goichman, supra, or that it is a business record. . . .

B.   The "Best Evidence" Rule

One of the larger questions raised by the Anglo-American system of evidence is who should be responsible for selecting the evidence to be presented to the trier-of-fact. The range of possible answers to this question is very broad. At one end of the spectrum, the rules could dictate very rigidly that certain types of evidence will not be accepted in lieu of other types of available "superior" evidence. For example, in a dispute over a defective auto part, there could be rules of evidence that provide that, if available, the part must be produced and that photographs of the part or in-court witness testimony describing the part are inadmissible. One could justify such a system with the argument that (1) reliability is the primary concern of the fact-finding process, (2) certain kinds of evidence (for example, "real" evidence) are inherently more reliable than other kinds (for example, testimonial evidence), and (3) the rules of evidence should specify evidentiary choices so as to promote reliability. If one accepted all three parts of this argument, it might be possible to construct a detailed typology of kinds of evidence, from the most to the least favored variety, to apply to all situations. If nothing else, such a catalogue would provide an easily accessible guide to the advocate planning a litigation strategy and to judges ruling on objections at trial.

At the other end of the spectrum would be a system in which there were no rules limiting the kinds of evidence the parties may present at trial. Under this approach, the decision to offer real evidence, documents, in-court witness testimony, views, photographs, affidavits, or what-have-you would be left to the parties. The justification for this approach would be that it is impossible to construct a typology of evidence along reliability lines that is valid for all situations and that it is preferable to permit the parties to select the evidence that they feel best proves their case. An obvious advantage of this "free market" approach is its greater flexibility. Another advantage is that the court need not decide whether in the particular case before it an item of evidence is the best available type of evidence according to the relevant ranking of evidence. On the other hand, if there is no control over the kind of proof offered, might not accuracy in fact-finding suffer? Somewhat, perhaps, but probably not a great deal. To the extent that the most *reliable* evidence is also the most *persuasive,* applying the free market approach ordinarily should result in the use of the most reliable evidence. The tendency to utilize the best evidence is reinforced by the adversarial nature of our justice system. If the best available evidence is not offered, the opposing party is permitted to draw the attention of the jury or judge to the fact that a particular item of evidence has *not* been introduced and to suggest that this was done for strategic reasons. Nonetheless, there may still be situations in which a party deliberately chooses a less reliable and possibly unfair type of evidence. Judicial discretion to exclude in these circumstances would be a necessary component of the free market approach.

What kind of system do we have? A look at the Federal Rules reveals a mixed approach. In the main, there are very few restrictions on what kinds of proof parties must offer. By and large, parties are free to prove their case with whatever evidence they choose, so long as the foundational requirements are satisfied. On the other hand, as discussed in Chapter I, the categorical rules of exclusion found in Rules 404 to 412 can be seen as expressing preferences for certain kinds of proof as well as reflecting social policy. Also, the rule against hearsay and its exceptions, especially those of Rule 804, may be seen as incorporating a rule of preference for live, in-court testimony whenever the truth of an assertion is in issue. But aside from these rules (usually justified on different grounds), with one major exception there are no master lists arranging evidence in hierarchical fashion from the "best" to the "next best" and down through the "worst" and no rules dictating that the best available evidence be offered.

The exception is the rule that requires that in certain cases the original of a document be produced and that other forms of proof of its contents, such as copies or witness testimony, be excluded. This is the so-called best evidence rule of Rules 1001 to 1008 — "so-called" because its familiar appellation implies an application far broader than its terms. Examination of the rule reveals that it does not apply to all evidence but only to "writings" and similar things, such as photographs and recordings. Also, it applies only when the proponent is seeking to prove the "contents" of a writing.

The material in this section explores what "writing" means in this context (Rule 1001) and when the "contents" of a writing are being proved (Rule 1002). Next, the problems and cases examine the issue of what is an "original" for purposes of the rule (Rule 1001) and when a "duplicate" is admissible in lieu of the original (Rule 1003). Finally, the material addresses the acceptable excuses for not producing the original or a duplicate (Rule 1004) and the use of public records (Rule 1005), admissions (Rule 1007), and summaries (Rule 1006). In considering each of these issues, the problems also examine the respective roles of judge and jury in this particular area (Rule 1008).

The mechanics of complying with the requirements of this rule have been greatly simplified by the Federal Rules and by modern discovery and pretrial procedures. Yet the flow of cases under the Federal Rules indicates that many problems remain. Students should consider whether, on balance, the rule requiring the production of original documents is worth preserving as one corner of the system of evidence in which the "best evidence" is supposedly required.

FRE 1001
Definitions

For purposes of this article the following definitions are applicable:

(1) *Writings and recordings.* "Writings" and "recordings" consist of letters, words, or numbers, or their equivalent, set down by handwriting, typewriting, printing, photostating, photographing, magnetic impulse, mechanical or electronic recording, or other form of data compilation.

(2) *Photographs.* "Photographs" include still photographs, X-ray films, video tapes, and motion pictures.

(3) *Original.* An "original" of a writing or recording is the writing or recording itself or any counterpart intended to have the same effect by a person executing or issuing it. An "original" of a photograph includes the negative or any print therefrom. If data are stored in a computer or similar device, any printout or other output readable by sight, shown to reflect the data accurately, is an "original."

(4) *Duplicate.* A "duplicate" is a counterpart produced by the same impression as the original, or from the same matrix, or by means of photography, including enlargements and miniatures, or by mechanical or electronic re-recording, or by chemical reproduction, or by other equivalent techniques which accurately reproduces the original.

FRE 1002
Requirement of Original

To prove the content of a writing, recording, or photograph, the original writing, recording, or photograph is required, except as otherwise provided in these rules or by Act of Congress.

FRE 1003
Admissibility of Duplicates

A duplicate is admissible to the same extent as an original unless (1) a genuine question is raised as to the authenticity of the original or (2) in the circumstances it would be unfair to admit the duplicate in lieu of the original.

FRE 1004
Admissibility of Other Evidence of Contents

The original is not required, and other evidence of the contents of a writing, recording, or photograph is admissible if —

(1) *Originals lost or destroyed.* All originals are lost or have been destroyed, unless the proponent lost or destroyed them in bad faith; or

(2) *Original not obtainable.* No original can be obtained by any available judicial process or procedure; or

(3) *Original in possession of opponent.* At a time when an original was under the control of the party against whom offered, he was put on notice, by the pleadings or otherwise, that the content would be a subject of proof at the hearing, and he does not produce the original at the hearing; or

(4) *Collateral matters.* The writing, recording, or photograph is not closely related to a controlling issue.

FRE 1007
Testimony or Written Admission of Party

Contents of writings, recordings, or photographs may be proved by the testimony or deposition of the party against whom offered or by his written admission, without accounting for the nonproduction of the original.

FRE 1008
Functions of Court and Jury

When the admissibility of other evidence of contents of writings, recordings, or photographs under these rules depends upon the fulfillment of a condition of fact, the question whether the condition has been fulfilled is ordinarily for the court to determine in accordance with the provisions of rule 104. However, when an issue is raised (a) whether the asserted writing ever existed, or (b) whether another writing, recording, or photograph produced at the trial is the original, or (c) whether other evidence of contents correctly reflects the contents, the issue is for the trier of fact to determine as in the case of other issues of fact.

Problem VIII-11
Whiteacre

Action of ejectment to recover possession of Whiteacre. P claims to be the owner entitled to possession. D admits his possession but denies P's ownership. At trial, P proposes to testify that D executed a deed by which he conveyed title in fee simple absolute to P. D objects on best evidence grounds.

What ruling and why? What is so special about writings that there exists a special rule of preference for them?

Problem VIII-12
Sparkplugs

P, the owner and operator of a Piper Cub airplane, placed an order with D, the owner and operator of an airport service station, to fill the fuel tank of her plane with gas. D filled the tank, and P took off. After being airborne for a short time, P's airplane experienced motor failure, requiring a crash landing. P sues D for property damage and personal injuries, alleging that D put automotive rather than aviation gas in the plane, causing the motor failure.

At trial, P's first witness is an aeronautics expert who testifies that one can tell the type of gasoline used in an airplane by the appearance of the sparkplugs and describes the appearance of sparkplugs when automotive gas has been used. P then testifies that following the crash landing she removed the sparkplugs and kept them in her safe deposit box, where they now repose. P's attorney asks her to describe the appearance of the plugs. D objects on grounds of the best evidence rule.

What ruling and why?

Problem VIII-13
Accident Report Forms

(1) Action for personal injuries arising out of an automobile accident. D fills out an accident report form. At trial, P objects to D's testifying to the details of the collision, on the grounds that the accident report form exists and that D is testifying to the contents of a document in violation of Rule 1002. What ruling and why?

(2) On cross-examination, *D* is charged with recent fabrication. On redirect, *D* is asked what he said on the accident report form. *P* objects. What ruling and why?

Problem VIII-14
No Ticket, No Laundry

(1) *D* owns and operates a hand laundry. *P* brings seven shirts to the laundry for cleaning ("boxed, no starch"). *D* fills out a laundry slip and after negotiations with *P* marks on the slip, "Pick-up Tuesday the 12th," and gives the slip to *P*. Later, *P* sues *D* for breach of contract, alleging that the shirts were not ready until Friday the fifteenth. The first witness is *P*, who attempts to testify to the terms of the contract. *D* objects. What ruling and why?

(2) Suppose *D* used a laundry ticket book that contained a series of two identically numbered slips separated by carbon papers. *D* would write up the order and due date and give the carbon to the customer. If *P* offers the carbon and *D* objects, what ruling and why?

Problem VIII-15
Barnyard Justice

Civil action for libel. The complaint alleges that *P* is a general surgeon and *D* is a photographer specializing in novelty photos. *D* refused to pay *P* for a vasectomy after the incision went awry when *P* sneezed. In addition, *D* threatened other retaliatory measures, and when *P* returned to his office in downtown Philadelphia one day, he was greeted by a huge photograph on a billboard depicting a barnyard scene that included *P*'s head attached to the body of a jackass. At trial, *P* is the first witness. He is asked to describe the photograph. *D* objects.

What ruling and why?

Problem VIII-16
The Dangerous Druggist

Action against *D*, a druggist, for the alleged negligent filling of a prescription. At trial, *P*'s first witness is *W*, her family physician. *W* testifies that on January 1, in response to a call from *P*, she phoned *D* and prescribed for *P* a solution of paraldehyde, $C_6H_6O_3$, as a sedative and hangover relief. Unfortunately, *D* delivered a solution of formaldehyde, HCHO, a colorless compound used to manufacture fertilizers, dyes, embalming fluids, preservatives, and disinfectants. Formaldehyde is highly toxic to humans, and *P* was badly hurt when she gulped down half the bottle delivered by *D*.

In defense, *D* claims that *W* ordered formaldehyde. On cross-examination, *D* is asked whether he made a written record of the order. *D* replies that he did but that he threw it away. *P*'s counsel moves to strike *D*'s direct testimony.

What ruling and why?

Problem VIII-17
Arson Interrogation

Charge: arson. At trial the prosecution calls the arresting officer, *A*, to testify that after *D* was read his *Miranda* rights at the station, *D* told *A* that he "knew they had him" and that he wanted to tell *A* the whole story. *A* stopped *D* only long enough to find a secretary to transcribe *D*'s statement.

D objects to *A*'s testimony on grounds that the transcript of *D*'s statement must be introduced as the "best evidence." What ruling and why? Does it make any difference if *D*'s statement is signed? Is your analysis the same (1) if a tape recording instead of a written transcription of *D*'s statement is available, or (2) if *D* never delivers his statement orally but transcribes it himself and asks *A* to read it?

MEYERS v. UNITED STATES, 171 F.2d 800 (D.C. Cir.), cert. denied, 336 U.S. 912 (1949): [In *Meyers,* an appeal from a perjury conviction, the Court of Appeals for the District of Columbia upheld the trial court's admission of a witness's testimony of his recollection of proceedings for which a written transcript was available, against a challenge that it was not the "best evidence." The court noted that:]

As applied generally in federal courts, the [best evidence] rule is limited to cases where the contents of a writing are to be proved. Here there was no attempt to prove the contents of a writing; the issue was what [the defendant] had said, not what the transcript contained. The transcript made from shorthand notes of his testimony was, to be sure, evidence of what he had said, but it was not the only admissible evidence concerning it. [The witness's] testimony was equally competent, and was admissible whether given before or after the transcript was received in evidence. Statements alleged to be perjurious may be proved by any person who heard them, as well as by a reporter who recorded them in shorthand.

[Judge Prettyman delivered a lengthy dissent:]

The testimony given by Lamarre before the Senate Committee was presented to the jury upon the trial in so unfair and prejudicial a fashion as to constitute reversible error. . . .

When the trial began, the principal witness called by the Government . . . was asked by the United States Attorney, "Now, will you tell the Court and the jury in substance what the testimony was that the defendant Lamarre gave before the Committee concerning the Cadillac automobile?" . . .

The court at once called counsel to the bench and said to the prosecutor: "Of course, technically, you have the right to proceed the way you are doing. . . . I do not think that is hearsay under the hearsay rule, but it seems to me . . . that, after all, when you have a prosecution based on perjury, and you have a transcript of particular testimony on which the indictment is based, that you ought to lay a foundation for it or ought to put the transcript in evidence, instead of proving what the testimony was by someone who happens to be present, who has to depend on his memory as to what was said."

Counsel for the defense, objecting, insisted that the procedure was "preposterously unfair." The trial judge said that it seemed to him that the transcript ought to be made available to defense counsel. That was then done, but the prosecutor insisted upon proceeding as he had planned with the witness.

Mr. Rogers then testified: "I will try to give the substance of the testimony. . . . I am sure your Honor appreciates that I do not remember exactly the substance of the testimony. The substance of testimony was this. . . ."

The notable characteristics of this testimony of Rogers are important. In each instance, the "substance" was a short summation, about half a printed page in length. The witness did not purport to be absolute in his reproduction but merely recited his unrefreshed recollection, and his recollection on each of the three matters bears a striking resemblance to the succinct summations of the indictment. It is obvious that what the witness gave as "substance" was an essence of his own distillation and not an attempt to reproduce the whole of Lamarre's testimony. . . .

The difference between the presentation of elemental facts and the piecing of them together so as to reach a conclusion is basic. One is evidence and the other argument. The principle runs through much of the law of evidence.

I doubt that anyone would say that the prosecutor could first have put into evidence the transcript of Lamarre's testimony and thereafter have produced Rogers to give to the jury from the witness box his own summation of it. He would have been met with a ruling that "the transcript speaks for itself." Indeed, exactly that developed. The prosecutor first produced the oral summation, and it was admitted. Then he produced the transcript. Then, when defense counsel attempted to cross-examine as to "the substance," he was blocked because of the presence of the transcript. Can a prosecutor do by so simple and obvious a maneuver that which the law otherwise forbids as unfair? Can he thus transform into sworn evidence from the box that which is otherwise only argument from the rail? I do not think so. In the presence of the unimpeached transcript, even though it was temporarily on counsel table and not yet in the clerk's hands, summation and interpretation was argument and not evidence.

Nor was the prejudice cured by the availability of the transcript to defense counsel for cross-examination. If that were so in this case, the same doctrine would admit in evidence any opinion, or description, or summation of elemental facts otherwise provable in precise accuracy. The impression given by a succinct summation by a live witness on the stand cannot be corrected or offset by the later reading of a long, cold record. It is my view that for this exceedingly practical reason the reception of Rogers' summation in evidence was not permissible. . . .

The rationale of the so-called "best evidence rule" requires that a party having available evidence which is relatively certain may not submit evidence which is far less certain. The law is concerned with the true fact, and with that alone; its procedures are directed to that objective, and to that alone. It should permit no procedure the sole use of which is to obscure and confuse that which is otherwise plain and certain. . . .

To be sure, the writing may be attacked for forgery, alteration or some such circumstance. But absent such impeachment, the writing is immutable evidence from the date of the event, whereas human recollection is subject to many infirmities and human recitation is subject to the vices of prejudice and interest. Presented with that choice, the law accepts the certain and rejects the uncertain. The repeated statement in cases and elsewhere that the best evidence rule applies only to documents is a description of practice and not a pronouncement of principle. The principle is that as between human recollections the law makes no conclusive choice; it makes a conclusive choice only as between evidence which is certain and that which is uncertain. . . .

In my view, the court iterates an error when it says that the best evidence rule is limited to cases where the contents of a writing are to be proved. The purpose of offering in evidence a "written contract" is not to prove the contents of the writing. The writing is not the contract; it is merely evidence of the contract. The contract itself is the agreement between the parties. Statutes such as the statute of frauds do not provide that a contract be in writing; they provide that the contract be evidenced by a writing, or that a written memorandum of it be made. The writing is offered as evidence of an agreement, not for the purpose of proving its own contents. A deed to real estate is different, being actually the instrument of conveyance, although there is authority that it too is merely evidence of the agreement between the parties.

The doctrine that stenographic notes are not the best evidence of testimony was established when stenography was not an accurate science. . . .

But we have before us no such situation. Stenographic reporting has become highly developed, and official stenographic reports are relied upon in many of the most important affairs of life. Even as early as 1909, a court referred to "Experience having demonstrated the impartiality and almost absolute accuracy of the notes of court stenographers" as the reason for legislation making admissible as evidence a court stenographer's report. In the present instance, at least, no one has disputed the correctness of the transcript.

From the theoretical point of view, the case poses this question: Given both (1) an accurate stenographic transcription of a witness' testimony during a two-day hearing and (2) the recollection of one of the complainants as to the substance of that testimony, is the latter admissible as evidence in a trial of the witness for perjury? I think not. To say that it is, is to apply a meaningless formula and ignore crystal-clear actualities. The transcript is, as a matter of simple, indisputable fact, the best evidence. The principle and not the rote of the law ought to be applied. . . .

Problem VIII-18
The Tapes Case

D and others are charged under the federal gambling statute with running a bookmaking operation that took bets on sporting events, primarily over the telephone. The evidence used to secure the indictment was derived from court-ordered electronic surveillance of some 3,000 telephone calls. The statute requires, among other things, a volume of at least $2,000 per day. At the trial an FBI agent with considerable experience in telephone interceptions testifies as to the mechanics of the wiretaps, the accuracy of the equipment, and the training of the monitoring agents. The prosecution then offers the testimony of an expert to the effect that the total daily dollar volume based on an analysis of the 3,000 calls was $899,855, with the lowest daily total being $8,395. D objects on best evidence grounds, arguing that it is necessary to play the tapes to the jury.

What ruling and why?

Problem VIII-19
The Unlisted Number

Charge: knowingly transporting in interstate commerce a stolen vehicle in violation of 18 U.S.C. §2312. At trial, D concedes that the automobile was stolen at the time of interstate transport but denies that he knew it was stolen. The government's first witness, W, an FBI agent, testified that at the time of arrest, D told him that he had bought the automobile from "Bill Holt" of "Bill Holt's Body Shop" on the west side of Chicago. The agent also attempted to testify that he had checked the Chicago telephone directory for the area and that there was no listing for "Bill Holt," "Bill Holt's Body Shop," "Bill Holdt," "Bill Hult," or any other reasonable spelling variation of those names. *D* objected to the agent's testimony on grounds of Rule 1002. The court ruled that the rule does not apply to testimony that books or records have been examined and found *not* to contain any reference to a designated matter.

Is the court's ruling correct?

Recall Problem VIII-6, The Unregistered Gun. Would a best evidence rule objection lie to oral testimony or the introduction of an affidavit that a search of the National Firearms Registration and Transfer Record did not reveal any registration of the defendant's firearm? How does the evidence in that problem differ from the evidence of no telephone number in this case?

UNITED STATES v. RATLIFF
623 F.2d 1293 (8th Cir. 1980), cert. denied, 449 U.S. 876 (1980)

PER CURIAM. Malcolm Eugene Ratliff was convicted pursuant to a jury trial in the United States District Court for the Eastern District of Arkansas of five counts of an eight-count indictment. The jury convicted Ratliff of four counts of making false statements to a bank in violation of 18 U.S.C. §1014 (1976) and of one count of conspiracy to make false statements in violation of 18 U.S.C. §371 (1976). Ratliff misrepresented the collateral value and history of pre-World War II German corporate bonds in order to obtain bank loans. . . .

Ratliff challenges the admission into evidence of the expert testimony of a German banker and bond examiner, Mintken, with regard to the value of the bonds. Ratliff claims Mintken's testimony was hearsay, in violation of the best evidence rule and of Ratliff's constitutional right to compulsory process. The District Court fully considered this issue in its post-trial memorandum. The question presented was whether the unavailability of a master list of redeemable bonds,[7] compiled by the Ger-

---

7. The bonds were issued and sold prior to the outbreak of World War II. These bonds were due and payable in 1950, but prior to World War II many of the bonds had been purchased by or on behalf of the issuer and held for conservation. During the war, the New York selling agent was precluded from cancelling the German obligations. The German authorities, however, repurchased a considerable amount of the bonds. These uncancelled bonds were stored, among others, in the Reichsbank until they would be redeemed by the issuing corporation. When Berlin was invaded at the end of the war, the Russians plundered the bank, resulting in the recirculation of the bonds. The German government set up an examining system to determine which bonds were valid and redeemable. Only a relative few of the bonds (29 with face value of $29,000) were valid and outstanding obligations as of the date of this trial. The bonds now are redeemable only in Germany.

man government after the war, precluded Mintken's testimony of his valuation of the bonds supplied by Ratliff. The District Court admitted Mintken's testimony, finding:

"The primary factor in this Court's decision to admit Mr. Mintken's testimony despite the absence of the master list is the unique relationship of the list, Mr. Mintken's conclusions regarding potential validity, and the value of the bonds. The issue in the case is the value of the bonds — not their value in some abstract sense, but the value they have in a normal commercial context. It is the Court's perception that the value is determined by Mr. Mintken's conclusions as to underlying validity, not by investigation of the master list or other background records. . . .

"This perception leads the Court to conclude that the relevant inquiry concerning a bond's validity ends with a thorough investigation of Mr. Mintken's conclusion and the processes behind it, which may be accomplished by his cross-examination without production of the master list. In this case, . . . the witness who testified to his conclusions was vigorously cross-examined about the background and process behind his conclusions, as well as about the reliability and accuracy of the master list and other records. His testimony regarding background was relevant to the weight and credibility assigned by the jury to his testimony regarding his conclusions, but it did not undermine the admissibility of that testimony. . . ."

We agree with the District Court that Mintken's testimony was not a mere reiteration that Ratliff's bonds were not included on the master list as being valid and outstanding. To the extent that Mintken did testify to the bonds' status on the list, the testimony was admissible under the "catch-all" exception to the hearsay rule. See Fed. R. Evid. 803(24); United States v. Friedman, 593 F.2d 109, 118-19 (9th Cir. 1979). Mintken was subjected to extensive cross-examination, thus satisfying Ratliff's constitutional right of cross-examination.

Ratliff also contends that the District Court erred in not striking Mintken's testimony on the basis that it violated the best evidence rule. See Fed. R. Evid. 1002. Since Mintken did not attempt to "prove the content of a writing [the master list]" the rule does not apply herein. In addition, the District Court found the list to be "unavailable" and "not amenable to court processes in this country."[8] The best evidence rule does not apply to the list under these conditions. See Fed. R. Evid. 1004(2).

Affirmed.

Proof of source, right to possession, and validity must be supplied by those seeking redemption. Mintken is the examiner for the issue of bonds involved in Ratliff's case.

8. On appeal, Ratliff does not challenge this factual finding. He does claim that the court erred in not ruling on whether the list was privileged. Whether the master list was privileged or not is but one possible reason for its unavailability. Ratliff has not demonstrated that it is the only reason. The court, in fact, believed that it had no subpoena power over the documents in Germany. In the absence of such a demonstration, we cannot find the court's finding to be clearly erroneous.

Problem VIII-20
The Electronic Scrivener

Action for breach of contract, the terms of which are allegedly contained in a telex from buyer D to seller P. D refused to go through with the deal when a dispute arose over the price and number of units ordered.

At trial, P offers as Plaintiff's Exhibit 1 a photocopy of the telex. No explanation was offered for P's failure to produce the original telex. D disputes the accuracy of the copy and objects to its introduction under Rule 1003.

Is the photocopy admissible? Who decides, judge or jury? In what situations would it be "unfair to admit the duplicate in lieu of the original"?

Problem VIII-21
The Guarantor

(1) Action for breach of contract. P Bank contends that the alleged contract was contained in a typewritten letter from D to the bank authorizing the bank to pay checks to X, which D would cover. D admits sending the letter but disputes the terms.

At trial the bank's attorney calls C, the head cashier, to testify that he received the letter, read it, and filed it but that a new file clerk, S, mistakenly threw out the file during a regular purge of old files. C is asked what the letter said. D objects. What ruling and why?

(2) As part of his rebuttal case, D attempts to testify to the terms of the letter. P objects. On voir dire it is disclosed that D made a longhand copy of the letter before he sent it and that this copy is in his office in Chicago. D testifies that he did not bring it with him to the trial because he thought that P would bring its original. What ruling and why?

Problem VIII-22
The Cocaine Connection

Charge: conspiracy to distribute a controlled substance, to wit, cocaine. At D's trial, the government calls W, an FBI agent, to testify to the contents of a piece of paper with a telephone number on it found in D's possession at the time of arrest. The agent testified that she had lost the paper and had no independent recollection of the telephone number but that she had accurately transcribed the number onto a telephone company form at the time of arrest. The court overruled D's objection on grounds of hearsay, citing Rule 803(5) (recorded recollection).

Does *D* have other grounds to object to *W*'s testimony? How do Rule 803(5) and the rules governing the admissibility of writings relate?

UNITED STATES v. MARCANTONI
590 F.2d 1324 (5th Cir. 1979), cert. denied, 441 U.S. 937 (1979)

TJOFLAT, J. [Defendant was charged with armed bank robbery.] . . . On Friday, August 6, 1976, at approximately 9:10 A.M., a white male, standing 5'9"-5'10", weighing 170-180 pounds, and wearing a motorcycle helmet with tinted brown sun visor, entered the Tampa Federal Savings & Loan Association (the Bank), Tampa, Florida, and went to the only teller window open at that time. The teller, Tina Brown, looked up into the barrel of a shotgun, screamed and ducked to the floor. The head teller, Debra Beckerink, realizing the situation, walked to Ms. Brown's window and began pulling bills of small denominations out of the money drawer and placing them in a bag. The gunman nervously commanded Beckerink to "give [him] the big bills." Record, vol. 3, at 10. She complied, supplying him in the process with $3,791.00, including ten $10 bills of bait money.[2] The gunman than ran out of the Bank, firing a shot at the sidewalk as he left, and jumped into the back seat of a waiting getaway car being driven by a white, blond-haired female. The getaway car and its occupants were observed by various witnesses. When the Tampa police arrived on the scene moments later, the witnesses gave the officers a description of the vehicle, a 1966 light green Rambler station wagon with luggage racks on the top, and its Florida license tag number. A search of the Florida vehicle registration records disclosed that the tag had been issued to Helen Suzanne Tune Marcantoni for a 1966 Rambler station wagon.

Detectives from the Tampa police department and agents of the Federal Bureau of Investigation went immediately to the residence indicated for Mrs. Marcantoni on the registration but found that she and her husband had moved. The investigation led to her parents' house where the officers learned that the Marcantonis had moved to a house at 3416 Rogers Avenue, in Tampa, which was owned by Mr. Marcantoni's mother. . . .

The following Monday morning, August 9, 1976, Charlie Marcantoni consented to and assisted in a search of his Rogers Avenue residence by the Tampa police. During the search, Detective Edward Brodesser examined several hundred dollars in currency and recorded the serial

2. Bait money was kept in each teller's money drawer. When the bait money in question was removed, a silent alarm to the Tampa Police Department activated. The denominations, serial numbers, series years, and the bank of issue of each bait money bill had been recorded by the Bank.

numbers from the faces of the $10 bills he found, but he did not seize the bills. . . .

On August 13, 1976, Detective Brodesser returned to the Marcantoni residence on Rogers Avenue with a search warrant authorizing the seizure of any of the bait money that might be there. Following his August 9 search of the residence Brodesser had learned that the serial numbers he had recorded from two of the $10 bills he had uncovered during the search matched the serial numbers of two $10 bills on the Bank's list of the bait money taken in the robbery. Brodesser was unable to find these bills on August 13, however, when he returned with the search warrant. Six days later the Marcantonis were indicted. . . .

The argument advanced by the Marcantonis in the court below and on appeal in support of their objection to Detective Brodesser's testimony concerning the two $10 bills has been articulated inartfully at best. Giving the Marcantonis the benefit of every doubt, we read their argument as posing alternative objections to admissibility: (1) Detective Brodesser's testimony was irrelevant because it lacked probative value; (2) his testimony violated the best evidence policy embraced by Fed. R. Evid. 1004.

When Brodesser copied the serial numbers of the two $10 bills, he neglected to record all of the essential identifying data printed on the face of each of the bills — he omitted the series year. Knowledge of the series year was necessary, according to the Government's expert from the Bureau of Printing and Engraving, William Holland, to resolve any possible doubt whether the two bills Brodesser saw were bait money. Holland explained that each of the serial numbers Brodesser copied from the bills had been used by the Bureau on $10 bills in three separate series or years: series 1934A, 1950A, and 1969C. The $10 bills used as bait money were of the 1969C series.

The Marcantonis first objected to Brodesser's testimony about the serial numbers he had seen on the ground that the testimony would prove absolutely nothing; without the series year, they claimed, the jury could not find that either of the $10 bills found at their residence actually came from the Bank. The Government's response to this attack lies in the balance of Holland's testimony, considered in the unique circumstances of this case. Holland explained that the average life of a $10 bill is three and one-half years; thus there is very little chance that any of the series 1934A or 1950A bills were in circulation at the time of the robbery. Record, vol. 4, at 116-18. He further pointed out that series 1934A bills are so rare that they are worth four to five times their face value and are collectors' items, making it extremely unlikely that any of those bills were still in active circulation in 1976. Id., at 118. And chances are not much better that any of the series 1950A bills were then in circulation either. Holland's opinion was, therefore, that the two $10 bills Detective Brodesser uncovered were of the 1969C series and part of the Bank's bait money. He reinforced his opinion by observing that the odds are "extremely remote," id., at 116, that a $10 bill from the 1934A or 1950A series with the same serial number as one of the bait bills could have found its way to the Tampa Bay area at the same time as the bait bills; the odds were "hundreds of times greater" that two sets of such bills could have been in the Tampa Bay vicinity at once. Id. Given Holland's opinion and the independent evidence establishing that Charlie Marcantoni left the Bank with bait money of the same serial numbers and denominations as those found in his home a short time later, the trial judge properly concluded that Brodesser's testimony concerning the serial numbers had probative value.

The Marcantonis' alternative objection to the reception of Brodesser's testimony is that rule 1004 required the Government to introduce the two bills in evidence. Brodesser's testimony, they argue, was secondary evidence of the contents of the bills and not admissible because the Government failed to establish any of the conditions to the admissibility of secondary evidence specified by Fed. R. Evid. 1004. . . .

The Government made no formal attempt to qualify Brodesser's recital of the incriminating serial numbers as secondary evidence admissible under the rule. First, as the Government concedes, it did not undertake to show that the two bills were lost or destroyed. Second, it was not established that the Marcantonis were served notice that the contents of the bills would be a subject of proof at trial, and no process was directed to them to produce the bills in court. Finally, the Government did not, and in our opinion could not, contend that the evidence was "not closely related to a controlling issue."

There was little if anything in the argument of counsel that even addressed the qualifications of rule 1004 or, much less, whether they had been met in this instance. In overruling the Marcantonis' objection, the trial judge, quite understandably we think, gave no reasons for his decision. Consequently, we cannot determine whether the court treated Brodesser's statements about the serial numbers as secondary evidence,[4] and, if so, which of the conditions to admissibility prescribed by the rule it found to be fulfilled.

If, in truth, the court considered Brodesser's testimony to be secondary evidence, we must assume that the court was satisfied that at least one of those conditions had been established. It should have been obvious after Detective Brodesser's return to the Marcantoni residence with a search warrant failed to produce the two $10 bills in question that the bills would not be available to the prosecution for trial. We have no difficulty in concluding that, under the circumstances of this case, the

---

4. It is conceivable that the court viewed Brodesser's statements as present recollection refreshed or as past recollection recorded. Fed. R. Evid. 803(5).

trial judge would have been authorized to find, under section (1) of the rule, that the two bills were "lost or [had] been destroyed." Surely, the Marcantonis could not have contended that the unavailability of the bills was the product of Government "bad faith." The trial judge could also have found, under section (2) of the rule, that "[n]o original [could] be obtained by any available judicial process or procedure." Even assuming that the Marcantonis were amenable to a subpoena directing the production of the bills at trial,[5] we think it unrealistic to expect that they would have readily produced the two instruments that would have made the Government's case against them complete. In short, the Government was not required to go through the motion of having a subpoena issued, served and returned unexecuted in order to establish, under section (2), that the bills were unobtainable.

As for section (3) of the rule, a legitimate argument can be made on this record that the Marcantonis were "put on notice" that the serial numbers of the two $10 bills "would be a subject of proof" at the trial, and that, having not produced them at trial, the Marcantonis could not object to the use of Brodesser's notes. In sum, although the trial judge, in overruling the Marcantonis' best evidence objection, should have announced the predicate to admissibility he found to have been established under rule 1004, his decision to receive the evidence was correct.[6]

---

5. We think it fairly debatable whether the Marcantonis could have been compelled, in the face of the fifth amendment privilege against self-incrimination, to produce the two $10 bills for use by the prosecution at trial. See generally Bellis v. United States, 417 U.S. 85 (1974); United States v. Hankins, 565 F.2d 1344 (5th Cir. 1978).

6. An argument can be advanced that the admissibility of Detective Brodesser's statements about the serial numbers is not controlled by rule 1004. Although these statements have all the indicia of mere secondary evidence, it might be said that they constitute something more; Brodesser was testifying about what he had observed first hand during the course of his search of the Marcantoni residence. Whether he was testifying from present recollection refreshed or past recollection recorded, see Fed. R. Evid. 803(5), however, cannot be determined with certainty from the record. In questioning Brodesser about the serial numbers on direct examination, the prosecutor did not undertake to establish, as a preliminary matter, whether the witness was actually able to remember the precise serial numbers he had noted on the two $10 bills in issue; instead, he went straight to the heart of the matter, simply asking Brodesser to repeat the serial numbers he had seen and recorded. The likelihood is, of course, that even with the benefit of his notes, Brodesser could not recall the precise serial numbers and that his testimony was strictly a recital of what he had recorded.

We think it not far fetched to say that Brodesser's notes constituted, in the language of rule 803(5), "[a] memorandum or record concerning a matter about which a witness once had knowledge but now has insufficient recollection to enable him to testify fully and accurately, shown to have been made. . . by the witness when the matter was fresh in his memory and to reflect that knowledge correctly." We should point out, however, that if Rule 803(5) is considered the *sole* basis of admissibility, the notes themselves, as distinguished from a recital thereof, should not have been received as an evidentiary exhibit in the Government's case-in-chief. As the rule states, "[i]f admitted, the memorandum or record may be read into evidence but may not itself be received as an exhibit unless offered by an adverse party."

Problem VIII-23
Burning Romeo

Action for libel. *P* testifies that on the day before his wedding his fiancee showed him the allegedly libelous letter written to her by *D* but that the letter is now unavailable because *P* burned it. *P*'s counsel asks him to testify to the contents of the letter. *D* objects.

What ruling and why?

This problem was inspired by the nineteenth century antics of "The Count Joannes," born "George Jones" in 1810. In the course of his career, Joannes instituted at least 16 libel suits, gained a conviction for barratry in Boston and admission to the Bar in New York, and played the role of Romeo a number of times, both on and off stage. The Count, who believed that his power of speech gained him in "one hour with a lady . . . [what took] three months with mere clods of humanity," brought his first libel suit pro se (Joannes v. Bennett, 87 Mass. (5 Allen) 169 (1862)):

[The Count] was apparently paying court to an eligible widow of the city. She was living with her parents, and both she and they were active in the church, she singing soprano in the church choir. Her name remains unknown, but her minister's name was Bennett. Apparently having no high opinion of the Count's qualifications as a son-in-law, her parents appealed to this minister for help and, concurring in their view, the latter undertook to write the lady in question attempting to dissuade her from the match. She promptly turned the letter over to her suitor, who just as promptly sued the Rev. Mr. Bennett for libel, the first gun in a salvo of litigation that was to continue for a dozen years or more.

The Count appeared as his own counsel, although there is no indication that he had ever been admitted to the Massachusetts Bar. His case was considerably weakened by the fact that he had destroyed the letter and was unable to produce it in court. His damages were also considerably mitigated due to the circumstance that despite the remonstrance of her parents and the Rev. Bennett, he subsequently married the lady. A more serious obstacle than even their disapproval, however, would appear to be the continued existence of Mrs. Melinda Jones, still legally his wife; but fortunately this was known neither to the lady, her parents, the court, nor the Rev. Bennett, but only to the Count, who chose not to reveal it, and Melinda, who was not present. In any event, the jury returned a verdict in his favor for $2,000.00.

On appeal the case was reversed and a new trial ordered, on the ground that the Count, having destroyed the letter under unexplained circumstances, should not have been permitted to introduce secondary evidence of its contents. The outcome of the second trial does not appear. . . .

Armstrong, The Count Joannes: A Vindication of a Much-Maligned Man," 36 A.B.A.J. 829 (1956).

Problem VIII-24
Close Enough for Government Work?

Action by the government against *D* for collection of unpaid taxes. *D* asserts the statute of limitations as a defense. The government contends that *D* is estopped from pleading the statute of limitations because she executed a written waiver of the limitations period, as specifically authorized by 26 U.S.C. §§6501(c)(4) and 6502(a)(2). *D* denies having executed the waiver.

At trial, the government cannot produce the written waiver. *W*, an IRS agent, is called to testify that the waiver was destroyed according to standard IRS procedure. The government also offers evidence of the normal practice of the IRS, which, it contends, establishes the likelihood that *D* did execute a waiver. *D* objects to *W*'s testimony and to the introduction of the government's other evidence.

What ruling and why?

UNITED STATES v. TAYLOR
648 F.2d 565 (9th Cir. 1981)

ELY, J. Taylor and Dennis B. Wittman were jointly indicted for their part in the assertedly fraudulent acquisition of a substantial loan from the Continental Bank of Texas ("Continental"), in Houston, Texas. During the period of time covered by the indictment, late 1974 to early 1975, Taylor was a vice-president of the real estate department of Home Federal Savings and Loan Association ("Home Federal"), located in San Diego, California. The fraudulent "scheme or artifice" alleged by the Government was that Taylor and Wittman, who was a principal in several San Diego real estate development entities, had induced Continental to make a $1.97 million loan to a corporation run by Wittman, on the basis of their false representations of several material facts. In a January 16, 1975 letter signed by Taylor and containing an initialed postscript, Taylor and Wittman blatantly misrepresented to Continental that Home Federal held a first lien on certain California real property. This letter was telecopied from San Diego to Houston, where Wittman received it, photocopied it, and delivered the photocopy to a loan officer of Continental. The photocopy tendered to Continental, which was the copy of the letter Continental relied on in approving the loan, was admitted into evidence at Taylor's trial as Government Exhibit "24." On January 23, 1975, Taylor signed a letter agreement with Continental purporting to confirm Home Federal's first lien commitment. After Taylor signed the letter agreement, without authorization, in his capacity as an officer of Home Federal, Continental funded the $1.97 million loan.

In July 1975, Wittman's corporation defaulted on the loan. Taylor and Wittman were indicted in June 1977. . . .

An issue at trial critical to the jurisdictional element of the crime charged[2] was whether Taylor had already signed the fraudulent letter dated January 16, 1975 (the predecessor of Exhibit "24") when it was telecopied from California to Texas, or whether Taylor had signed it after its transmission to Texas. Neither the "original" nor the telecopy was ever produced at trial. Instead, the Government introduced Exhibit "24," which was either a photocopy of the telecopy or a more remote reproduction.[3] While Exhibit "24" did reflect Taylor's signature, it was never conclusively established that the exhibit was a direct copy of the telecopy, leaving open the possibility that the signature was not affixed prior to interstate communication. Taylor's counsel at trial objected to the admission of this potentially spurious document on the basis of the "best evidence rule." The trial court ultimately admitted Exhibit "24" as secondary evidence, relying on the Government's claim that the original document had been unsuccessfully subpoenaed from the relevant parties, i.e., Continental, Home Federal, and Wittman's corporation.

In the course of the District Court's probe of the prosecuting attorney on the subpoena issue, Taylor's trial counsel made a qualified stipulation to the admission of the exhibit based on the truth of the Government's representations.[5]

---

2. 18 U.S.C. §1343 (1976) requires that the "scheme or artifice to defraud" involve the transmission "by means of wire, radio, or television communication in interstate or foreign commerce, any writings, signs, signals, pictures, or sounds for the purpose of executing such scheme or artifice."

3. An argument can be made that the "original" letter typed in San Diego is not the original, legally operative document for purposes of "best evidence" analysis because the officer of the defrauded Texas bank made the loan in reliance of either the telecopy or a photocopy of the telecopy. Under this view, the latter documents, rather than the "original" typed letter, must be treated as legally operative originals. See United States v. Gerhart, 538 F.2d 807, 810 n.4 (8th Cir. 1976); 5 J. Weinstein & M. Berger, Weinstein's Evidence ¶1001(3)[01] to [02] (1978 & Supp. 1979). Because we decide the admissibility issue on other grounds, we need not rule on this rationale.

5. At trial, the following colloquy between the district judge, defense counsel, and prosecutor took place:

The Court: Well, now, here's my ruling. I understand your point. I am going to overrule your objection to the admissibility, and the evidence in the case will have to be whatever it is concerning what [Exhibit "24"] purports to be — ultimately turns out to be.

Mr. Shenas [Defense Counsel]: Is that ruling based on a representation that the original of this letter has been subpoenaed from [Continental], from [Wittman's corporation], and from Home Federal by the Government?

The Court: Yes.

Mr. Shenas: Thank you.

The Court: Now, do you want something — and that's a representation you are willing to rely on?

Exhibit "24" proved to be a vital piece of evidence for the Government. It was used to rebut Taylor's contention that a fraudulent scheme did not exist at the time of the transmission of the January 16, 1975 letter; it was used to corroborate in important respects the testimony of the prosecution's key witness, Continental loan officer Michael Wells; and, most importantly, it provided evidence of an essential element of the charged offense — interstate communication to execute a fraud.

The jury rendered a guilty verdict on March 29, 1978. Taylor was sentenced to a term of one year and a day. On July 12, 1978, Taylor filed a direct appeal from his conviction (No. 78-2512), assigning a variety of trial errors. The most significant allegation of error was that the District

---

Mr. Shenas: Your Honor, I don't know if that's true or not. *If counsel will tell me that's true, I will believe it.* He hasn't said that — anything.

Mr. Kelton [Prosecuting Attorney]:   What?

Mr. Shenas: That the original of that document was subpoenaed by the Government from [Continental], [Wittman's corporation], and Home Federal.

Mr. Kelton: When the Grand Jury investigation was —

The Court: Now, can't you answer that question directly?

Mr. Kelton: When the Grand Jury investigation was initiated —

The Court: Can't you answer "yes" or "no"?

Mr. Kelton: Yes.

The Court: Is that the answer, "Yes"? All right. Now, this is important when you come down to make a representation of that kind.

Mr. Kelton: Judge, I must say for the record that there's no original that could be located. But I am making this statement after subpoenaes, after speaking to the attorneys, after speaking to everybody involved in this transaction, and I really object to Mr. Shenas' implication that somebody has tampered with this evidence.

The Court: Just a minute. I am the person who is asking the question, whether [Wittman's corporation] has been subpoenaed, Home Federal has been subpoenaed, and the bank in Texas has been subpoenaed for the production of the original letter of January 16, 1975 — which was Telexed to Texas.

Mr. Kelton: Yes, they have, and I would also say this, your Honor: There is no way that the original letter could have been in Texas because it was Telexed. That's the point.

The Court: Well, it would then show up with Home Federal, wouldn't it?

Mr. Kelton: Home Federal does not have it.

The Court: All right. It's been subpoenaed there. That's the only thing I am asking about, and you said it has been. So that's enough. That's what you have said and we needn't have any more explanation.

And on that basis, I will accept this in evidence.

Now, you know the responsibility you are assuming when you say it's been subpoenaed. Don't look so disheartened.

Mr. Kelton: I'm not disheartened, Judge. The only point I am trying to make is that I made a good faith offer of proof to the Court —

The Court: I am not suggesting you didn't make it in good faith. I am asking about a foundation for it, for my accepting in evidence secondary evidence.

Mr. Kelton: I would just like to put my position on the record, your Honor. It would take one second. That is this: That all I have to do to lay that foundation through this witness is establish a record that that was kept in the ordinary course of business at [Wittman's corporation], and that they do not have the original available. And that is my position under the Federal Rules. And I think I have made that clear.

The Court: All right. I will admit the document on the basis of secondary evidence because of your inability through subpoena power to produce the originals.

R.T., Vol. V, at 51-54 (emphasis added).

Court erred in the admission of Exhibit "24" because, inter alia, the copy was improper under the "best evidence rule" of the Federal Rules of Evidence. In his direct appeal Taylor did not impugn the veracity of the Government's statements concerning the inability of the subpoena power to uncover the original document, since resolution of that matter necessarily involved matters outside the trial record. Taylor made a personal request for proof of the subpoenas. Unfortunately, the Government did not respond with such proof. . . .

Taylor raises several claims of error in his direct appeal, the most serious of which is that the District Court erred in admitting Exhibit "24" into evidence. Having determined that these claims are without merit, we affirm Taylor's conviction.

Taylor argues that because Exhibit "24" is at best a photocopy of the telecopied January 16, 1975 letter, it was improperly admitted into evidence. Federal Rule of Evidence 1002, Taylor correctly asserts, requires the production of the "original" writing to prove the contents thereof, "except as otherwise provided." Taylor contends that since Exhibit "24" is neither an "original" under Rule 1002 nor a "duplicate" within the exception of Rule 1003, it should not have been admitted into evidence. Taylor's argument overlooks the state of the trial record and the clear application of the exception of Rule 1004(2), which allows the admission of secondary evidence when the "original" cannot be obtained by available judicial procedures. When Exhibit "24" was offered for introduction into evidence at trial, the Government represented to the District Court that subpoenas requesting the "original" letter — i.e., the one typed in San Diego — had been served on the parties and that the "original" was not produced. In reliance on this representation, the District Court admitted Exhibit "24" into evidence. Taylor's counsel did not object to the exhibit's admission. Because Taylor's counsel failed to object to the admission of Exhibit "24," and even stipulated to the unavailability of the "original" letter, the record on direct appeal compels that we reject Taylor's "best evidence" argument.

We have carefully considered Taylor's remaining claims and find that the District Court did not abuse its discretion, that the jury was properly instructed, and that the evidence was adequate to support the jury verdict. Therefore, Taylor's conviction of wire fraud in the District Court is affirmed. . . .

FRE 1005
Public Records

The contents of an official record, or of a document authorized to be recorded or filed and actually recorded or filed, including data compilations in any form, if otherwise admissible, may be proved by copy, certified as correct in accordance with rule 902 or testified to be correct by a witness who has compared it with the original. If a copy which complies with the foregoing cannot be obtained by the exercise of reasonable diligence, then other evidence of the contents may be given.

AMOCO PRODUCTION CO. v. UNITED STATES
619 F.2d 1383 (10th Cir. 1980)

McKay, J. In 1942, the Federal Farm Mortgage Corporation (FFMC) conveyed by special warranty deed a fee simple interest in certain land in Summit County, Utah, to Hyrum and Florence Newton. The original deed and all copies other than a recorded version kept in the Summit County Recorder's Office are apparently no longer in existence. The parties dispute the exact contents of the original 1942 deed. Appellants claim that the deed reserved to the FFMC a one-half mineral interest in the property. As recorded, however, the deed contains no such reservation.

In 1957, the FFMC conveyed by quitclaim deed to the United States all of its mineral interest in various tracts of property, including the Newtons' property. The United States subsequently leased its claimed one-half mineral interest to the other appellants in this case.

In 1960, the Newtons conveyed their entire interest in the property to a family corporation, the Hyrum J. Newton & Sons Sheep Company (Newton Company). Beginning in 1971, this family corporation leased the entire mineral interest in the property to the appellees.

Appellees brought suit on January 21, 1976, under 28 U.S.C. §2409a to quiet title to the disputed mineral rights. . . . [The appellees moved for summary judgment.]

[T]he district court was faced with two alternative approaches to resolve the merits of the dispute. The court could have determined whether the Newton Company or any of its successors in interest was a bona fide purchaser sufficient to cut off any interest in the appellants. The court selected, however, to decide first whether FFMC conveyed the disputed mineral interest to the Newtons in the 1942 deed, or whether it reserved the interest to itself. If the original 1942 deed contained no mineral reservation clause, the appellants obviously have no mineral interest in the property.

Because appellees brought this quiet title action, they have the burden of establishing their title to the disputed interest. By introducing the recorded version of the deed, which showed that they received the entire interest in the property, appellees established a prima facie right to relief. See Utah Code Ann. §78-25-3 (1953). The burden then shifted to the appellants to introduce evidence of the invalidity or inaccuracy of the recorded version of the deed. In granting summary judgment, the court excluded all of the evidence proffered by appellants.

ROUTINE PRACTICE

The appellants offered evidence in an attempt to show that the routine practice of the FFMC was to reserve a one-half mineral interest in all property transferred during the relevant period. The court excluded this evidence on the ground that under Rule 1005 of the Federal Rules of Evidence, the availability of a properly recorded version of the 1942 deed precluded admission of any other evidence of the contents of the deed. We believe the court misinterpreted the purpose and effect of Rule 1005. . . .

The notes of the Advisory Committee on the proposed rules of evidence help explain the purpose of this rule:

> Public records call for somewhat different treatment. Removing them from their usual place of keeping would be attended by serious inconvenience to the public and to the custodian. As a consequence judicial decisions and statutes commonly hold that no explanation need be given for failure to produce the original of a public record. . . . This blanket dispensation from producing or accounting for the original would open the door to the introduction of every kind of secondary evidence of contents of public records were it not for the preference given certified or compared copies. Recognition of degrees of secondary evidence in this situation is an appropriate quid pro quo for not applying the requirement of producing the original.

Rule 1005 authorizes the admission of certified copies of records and documents filed and stored in public offices. The purpose of the rule is to eliminate the necessity of the custodian of public records producing the originals in court. This purpose is not furthered by extending the rule to encompass documents not filed and stored in public offices.

Rule 1005, by its terms, extends to "a document authorized to be recorded or filed and actually recorded or filed." This language encompasses deeds, mortgages and other documents filed in a county recorder's office. However, it is the actual record maintained by the public office which is the object of Rule 1005, not the original deed from which the record is made. If the original deed is returned to the parties after it is recorded, it is not a public record as contemplated by Rule 1005.

Applying Rule 1005 to exclude all other evidence of the contents of a deed is especially troublesome in a case such as this one. We cannot embrace an interpretation of the Rule which would exclude all evidence of the original deed other than the recorded version when the very question in controversy is whether the original deed was correctly transcribed onto the recorded version. Rule 1004(1), which authorizes the admission of other evidence of the contents of a writing if all originals are lost or destroyed, rather than Rule 1005, is applicable to the 1942 deed.[6] Accordingly, assuming it is otherwise admissible, evidence of a routine practice of the FFMC is relevant to prove conduct under Rule 406, and is admissible in lieu of the original under Rule 1004(1). Even if the evidence is not extremely probative, as indicated by the court, it is sufficient to create a question of fact and render summary judgment improper. Accordingly, the case must be remanded for the district court to consider admissibility of the evidence under a proper interpretation of Rules 1004 and 1005.

BLM FILE COPY

The appellants offered into evidence a photocopy of what is purportedly a conformed copy of the 1942 deed. The copy was found in a case file of the Bureau of Land Management (BLM). In excluding the file copy, the court indicated that it was "apparently incapable of being properly authenticated," and, in any event, admission would be "unfair" under Rule 1003 of the Federal Rules of Evidence.

Documentary evidence introduced in federal courts must be authenticated under the provisions of Rules 901 or 902 of the Federal Rules of Evidence. Specifically, the proponent of such evidence must produce evidence "sufficient to support a finding that the matter in question is what its proponent claims." Fed. R. Evid. 901(a). The district court did not decide that the file copy could not be properly authenticated, but rather that it was "apparently incapable" of proper authentication. On remand, the appellants should be given the opportunity to properly authenticate the file copy under the provisions of Rule 901.[7]

The court also excluded the file copy on the ground that it would be "unfair to admit the duplicate in lieu of the original" under Rule 1003.[8] The trial court felt that admission of the file copy would be unfair

6. The court properly applied Rule 1005 in admitting a certified copy of the deed as recorded by the county recorder. Furthermore, because such a certified copy was available, the court should properly exclude any other proffered evidence of the contents of the recorded version of the deed. However, Rule 1005 does not preclude the admission of other evidence of the contents of the original 1942 deed. That deed is not a public record and Rule 1005 does not apply to it.

7. Appellants urge that the file copy can be authenticated as a public record under Rules 901(b)(7) or 902(4). However, the mere fact that a document is kept in a working file of a governmental agency does not automatically qualify it as a public record for purposes of authentication or hearsay. Although the recorded version of a deed is a public record, a copy of a deed deposited in a working file of the BLM is not, by that fact alone, a public record.

8. Although the BLM file copy is not a "duplicate" of the original 1942 deed, see Rule 1001(4), it is apparently a duplicate of the original conformed copy of the deed. As such, it is admissible to the same extent as the original conformed copy unless the trial court exercises its discretion under Rule 1003 to exclude it as "unfair."

because the most critical part of the original conformed copy (the reservation clause) is not completely reproduced in the "duplicate." We find no abuse of discretion in this holding.

In determining that admission of the file copy would be "unfair," the court was apparently considering admission for purposes of proving the contents of the original conformed copy (and ultimately, the original 1942 deed). However, the appellants also urge admissibility of the file copy for other purposes. They argue that the file copy supports their claim that the original 1942 deed was prepared on standard form 657, that it bears the same identification number as the county recorder's copy and the Federal Land Bank ledger, and that it demonstrates the physical length of the land description, supporting the theory that a flapped attachment was used on the 1942 deed. Even if admission of the file copy is unfair for the purpose of proving the contents of the original conformed copy, it may not be unfair for other purposes. Assuming the appellants can satisfactorily authenticate the file copy, on remand the district court should consider admissibility for these purposes.

BLM PLAT AND INDEX

The appellants urge that the district court improperly failed to consider an official BLM land office plat and a historical index which reflect the government's retained mineral interest. The court did not rule on this evidence, but said in a footnote: "[D]efendants allege that certain official land office plats or indexes reflect a mineral reservation in the federal government. The court, however, has seen no evidence supporting this allegation or the inference defendants wish to be drawn therefrom."

In fact, the evidence was before the court. The index and plat were submitted by some of the appellants as exhibits to a July 6, 1976, motion for summary judgment. Furthermore, they were specifically mentioned in the appellants' memorandum in opposition to the appellees' motion for summary judgment. Accordingly, on remand the district court should consider this evidence.[9]

OTHER EVIDENCE

The appellants also offered other evidence including a blank standard deed form 657, a copy of the 1957 quitclaim deed and certain working files of the BLM. On remand, the court should consider the

---

9. Unlike the file copy which is not a public record simply by virtue of its presence in a BLM working file, the BLM land office plat and historical index appear to be official records of a governmental agency and may qualify as "public records" under the federal rules.

admissibility of such evidence. The blank standard deed form would be relevant upon sufficient showing that the 1942 deed was prepared on a similar form. The 1957 quitclaim deed is not a "nullity" as suggested by the court. Rather, it represents a valid transfer of all interest retained by the FFMC, if any, to the United States. However, the appellants must show that it is relevant to issues in this case and otherwise admissible. The working files of the BLM, although not necessarily admissible as public records, may be admissible to show the practice of the agency and the manner in which deeds with lengthy descriptions were constructed. . . .

Reversed and remanded.

FRE 1006
Summaries

The contents of voluminous writings, recordings, or photographs which cannot conveniently be examined in court may be presented in the form of a chart, summary, or calculation. The originals, or duplicates, shall be made available for examination or copying, or both, by other parties at reasonable time and place. The court may order that they be produced in court.

Problem VIII-25
The Thunderbird Valley Scam

Charge: mail fraud. The government charged defendants with an elaborate land sale fraud involving Thunderbird Valley corporation, of which the defendants were stockholders, officers, and directors. The essence of the case against defendants was that they had double assigned mortgages to defraud investors and lenders. Defendants claimed they were unaware of any improprieties and that the defalcations shown by the government were inadvertent.

At trial the government offered the testimony of W, a postal inspector, that he had made a summary of records seized from the offices of Thunderbird Valley corporation that established 80 double assignments out of 260 files of transactions perused.

Is W's testimony admissible? What foundation must the government lay before this evidence is admitted? Must the government show it would be impossible, difficult, or simply inconvenient to produce the 260 files? Must the government show that the underlying, summarized documents are admissible? May W testify to what the summary shows, or must the summary itself be produced? Is the actual summary admissible as an exhibit? Does this make any difference to the jury? Does it make any difference if *W* is qualified as an expert? *Must W* be qualified as an expert? Is the government required to give advance notice to defendants that they intend to rely on a summary? Does notice obviate any of the necessary foundational requirements? Is there a sixth amendment problem in the use of summaries in criminal cases?

UNITED STATES v. SCALES
594 F.2d 558 (6th Cir. 1979), cert. denied, 441 U.S. 946 (1979)

TAYLOR, J. John E. Scales has appealed his conviction on nine counts of unlawfully converting to his own use assets of Local 423 of the Laborer's International Union in violation of 29 U.S.C. §501(c) and one count of conspiracy in violation of 18 U.S.C. §371. He was acquitted on the six remaining counts, which included three charges under Section 501(c), two charges for conversion of funds from an employee insurance fund in violation of 18 U.S.C. §664, and one charge of mail fraud in violation of 18 U.S.C. §1341. He was given an aggregate sentence of ten years.

From 1968 through 1977, appellant was the business manager of Local 423 of the Laborer's International Union, a labor organization as that term is used in 29 U.S.C. §§401-531. Count I of the indictment charged him with conspiracy to embezzle and misapply the funds of Local 423 and the Ohio Laborer's District Council — Ohio Contractor's Association Insurance Fund. A number of overt acts were alleged in furtherance of the conspiracy including receiving double payments for expenses, receiving payment for expenses not incurred, using Local 423 funds for personal expenses of no benefit to the members of the Union and receiving interest free loans made for fraudulent purposes from union funds. All but one of the substantive counts upon which appellant was convicted were also charged as overt acts. Count XV involved similar self dealing with union funds.

At trial, the Government introduced 161 exhibits, consisting of thousands of pages of documents, and the testimony of eight co-conspirators who had previously pleaded guilty to conspiring with appellant to embezzle union funds. Seventeen other witnesses also testified, including FBI Agent Charles A. Tosi, who prepared Government's summary exhibit, Exhibit 145. The trial lasted eight days.

Appellant question[s] on appeal . . . whether the trial judge erred prejudicially in admitting Government Exhibit 145 and in admitting the testimony of Special Agent Tosi of the FBI in connection with said exhibit. . . .

GOVERNMENT EXHIBIT 145 AND RELATED TESTIMONY

Appellant contends that the trial judge erred in allowing Government Exhibit 145 to be admitted into evidence as well as in permitting Special

Agent Charles Tosi to testify concerning the exhibit. Appellant argues that the exhibit was inadmissible and prejudicial because it summarized the indictment and part of the Government's proof, thereby constituting conclusion and argument, and that Agent Tosi's testimony contained improper conclusions and argument.

Exhibit 145 consisted of a series of large charts. The first chart summarized all the charges contained in the indictment. Each of the remaining charts summarized a count or an overt act, or both, by reproducing, or making reference to, some of the documentary proof already in evidence. The only references in Exhibit 145 that were not to documents admitted previously into evidence were several statements in the charts that union records did not contain certain information. The charts were authenticated by Agent Tosi.

There was no prejudicial error committed by the admission of Exhibit 145. In regard to the summary of the indictment, the rule is clear that the trial judge has discretion to submit the indictment to the jury in a criminal case as long as limiting instructions are given to the effect that the indictment is not to be considered as evidence of the guilt of the accused. Such a charge was given in this case. Indeed, the actual indictment was submitted to the jury in this case, and appellant raises no objection in that regard.

Nor can appellant claim that he was prejudiced by this chart because it was a summary rather than a copy of the full indictment. Not only was the Government's summary not inflammatory or prejudicially worded, the summary contained only enough description of the charges to remind the jury of the substance of each count. The trial judge carefully charged the jury as to all of the elements necessary for conviction on each count. The summary of the indictment clearly was intended to aid the jury in organizing the proof and no rights of appellant were prejudiced by its admission into evidence.

The remainder of Exhibit 145 consisted of a summary of some of the objective proof relating to a number of the counts and overt acts charged. The Government argues that the exhibit was admissible under Fed. R. Evid. 1006. . . .

Insofar as Exhibit 145 contained summaries of other exhibits in evidence, appellant contends that Rule 1006 does not apply because each document listed could have been, and was, examined at the time of its admission. There is no requirement in Rule 1006, however, that it be literally impossible to examine the underlying records before a summary or chart may be utilized. All that is required for the rule to apply is that the underlying "writings" be "voluminous" and that in-court examination not be convenient. With 161 exhibits, involving facts relevant to sixteen counts and twenty-one overt acts, comprehension of the exhibits would have been difficult, and certainly would have been inconvenient, without the charts utilized by the Government.

Exhibit 145 also contained written statements that union records did not contain certain information, primarily authorization for travel. Appellant argues that this information is not covered by Rule 1006 because this is information that records *do not* contain, and thus is not a summary of their contents as required by the rule.

Appellant admits that the underlying union records could have been introduced to prove the nonoccurrence of the relevant matters under Fed. R. Evid. 803(7). If the records themselves could have been admitted to show what their contents did not include, there appears to be no reason why Rule 1006 would not apply to a summary of their contents. It is true that in such an instance the content of the records is negative, but that does not render the fact of omission any less an accurate summary of the content of the records. The Court is strengthened in this conclusion by the similar view of 4 Wigmore, Evidence §1230 (Chadbourn rev. 1972):

> [T]estimony, by one who has examined records, that *no record* of a specific tenor is there contained is receivable instead of producing the entire mass for perusal in the courtroom.

(Emphasis in original). . . .

Of course even under Rule 1006, the summary or chart must be accurate, authentic and properly introduced before it may be admitted in evidence. In this regard appellant urges in general terms that Exhibit 145 is replete with characterizations and conclusions, and is deceptive. After a careful examination of Exhibit 145, the Court is unable to find any misleading or conclusory references. Exhibit 145 appears to present merely an organization of some of the undisputed objective evidence in terms of the relevant counts of the indictment.

Appellant also complains that the charts were too large and that the authenticating testimony was insufficient because Agent Tosi was not an expert. Size alone does not render inadmissible an exhibit containing otherwise unobjectionable objective evidence. Given the nature of Exhibit 145, it is difficult to see how Agent Tosi's lack of expertise could have prejudiced appellant. The chart did not contain complicated calculations that would require an expert for accuracy. In order to authenticate Exhibit 145 it was necessary only that Agent Tosi had properly catalogued the exhibits previously admitted and had knowledge of the analysis of the union records referred to in the exhibit. Neither of these requirements necessitated any special expertise. As the one who supervised the compilation of Exhibit 145, Agent Tosi was the proper person to attest to the authenticity and accuracy of the chart. See Weinstein's Evidence, ¶1006[06].

Entirely aside from Rule 1006, there would still be ample authority for the admission of Exhibit 145 into evidence. There is an established tradition, both within this circuit and in other circuits, that permits a summary of evidence to be put before the jury with proper limiting instructions. Some cases allow the summary of purely testimonial evidence, e.g., Epstein v. United States, 246 F.2d at 570; Barber v. United States, [271 F.2d 265 (6th Cir. 1959)], so strictly speaking, such summaries cannot be said to come within the requirements of Rule 1006. The purpose of the summaries in these cases is simply to aid the jury in its examination of the evidence already admitted. See United States v. Downen, [496 F.2d 314 (10th Cir. 1974), cert. denied, 419 U.S. 897]. Authority for such summaries is not usually cited, but would certainly exist under Fed. R. Evid. 611(a). See Weinstein's Evidence ¶1006[03].

The danger of permitting presentation of a summary of some of the evidence in a criminal case is plain. The jury might rely upon the alleged facts in the summary as if these facts had already been proved, or as a substitute for assessing the credibility of witnesses. This danger has led to the requirement of "guarding instructions" to the effect that the chart is not itself evidence but is only an aid in evaluating the evidence. See Holland v. United States, 348 U.S. 121, 128 (1954). Even with such instructions, a summary may still be considered as too conclusory or as emphasizing too much certain portions of the Government's case, or as presenting incompetent facts. Trial courts may take care that such unfair summaries are not presented to juries.

Despite the danger, however, most summaries are routinely admitted. In fact, not only are the summaries themselves admitted, but computations and evaluations are often permitted on the basis of such summaries.

In contrast to such extensive use, this appeal presents a very limited utilization of an evidence summary. The facts of the case were complex. Thus the summary was likely to have been very helpful to the jury. The facts summarized were entirely objective, and, for all that appears from this appeal, uncontested. No issue of credibility was presented. The exhibit was in no sense conclusory, but stated the facts shown in a neutral way. The facts summarized did not even directly undermine appellant's theory of the case. Finally, the trial judge did instruct the jury as to the limited purpose that such a summary could serve.[3]

---

3. Appellant has not specifically raised the issue of permitting such a summary to go to the jury during deliberations. As it appears that Exhibit 145 did accompany the jury, appellant's objection to this course may be viewed as implicit. It is certainly not unusual for such demonstrative evidence to go to the jury. In most cases, however, once the summary is considered properly admitted, the issue of its going to the jury is not separately raised. It appears generally that when such summaries are kept from the jury, it is either because they were not properly offered into evidence, or because the summary was considered unfair or unreliable for the reasons listed above. For essentially the same reasons we rule that this exhibit was properly admitted, we conclude that no right of appellant was prejudiced by its submission to the jury.

Appellant's final argument is that the trial court improperly permitted Agent Tosi to deliver a closing argument during his authentication of the summary. Ultimately the trial court accepted appellant's objection and limited Agent Tosi's testimony. Because Exhibit 145 was essentially a presentation of objective material which aided the jury in remembering portions of the evidence and sorting out the charges, there was really no need for Agent Tosi to restate the portions of the evidence contained in Exhibit 145. Under these circumstances, it would perhaps have been preferable had the trial judge ruled from the start of Agent Tosi's testimony that Exhibit 145 was essentially self-explanatory. The Court need not decide this issue, however, because the early portion of Agent Tosi's testimony consisted of an accurate recounting of certain objective evidence already before the jury. No rights of appellant could have been prejudiced by such a recital.

For the foregoing reasons, the judgment of the trial court is affirmed.

CHAPTER IX

Allocation, Inference, Burdens, and Presumptions

More than any other aspect of evidence, presumptions pose the deep epistemological question, What does it mean to prove something? As a result, evidence scholars over the years have been fascinated with presumptions. More than a few have set out to solve their mysteries, only to become lost in philosophical and operational details. In approaching this material we are well aware of Professor Morgan's warning, "Every writer of sufficient intelligence to appreciate the difficulty of the subject matter has approached the topic of presumptions with a sense of hopelessness and has left it with a feeling of despair." Morgan, Presumptions, 12 Wash. L. Rev. 255 (1937).

The problem may be that we have been asking the wrong questions about presumptions. As John Hart Ely has said in another context, "No answer is what the wrong question begets." Ely, Democracy and Distrust 72 (1980). We believe that the right question to ask about presumptions is, What is their *function*? Since presumptions are commonly justified as procedural tools, they can be truly understood only by understanding their function.

The functional theory of presumptions on which this chapter is based assumes that presumptions work to create the epistemological phenomenon of coming to a conclusion (a belief) about the happening of a disputed past event. This may be contrasted with the more common — and seemingly more rationalistic — approach of justifying presumptions on the grounds that they yield an acceptable probability statement assessing the odds that the disputed past event occurred. Choosing between these two approaches requires one to speculate about the role that these two quite different states of mind play in the process of judicial proof. In the realist world of twentieth-century American legal thought, the second approach has predominated, bolstered by the tendency on the part of many jurists and scholars to incorporate in law the quantification techniques of the scientific method. We believe, however, that overemphasis on the probabilistic-based approach obscures the ways in which presumptions work to bridge the gap between doubt and proof at individual trials and, on a broader scale, between doubt and faith in the justice system. Thinking about presumptions in terms of their contribution to belief-formation illuminates these functions. It also reveals the connections between presumptions and allocations of burdens of proof, inferential reasoning, and choices of substantive rules of law. Seeing these connections tends to lend some coherence to what otherwise appears to be a chaotic mixture of rules and doctrines.

Congress was not troubled by these larger concerns when adopting the Federal Rules. The Advisory Committee Notes reveal little in the way of deep structure in this area. Nor have the courts concerned themselves with epistemology in interpreting the presumption rules. Nonetheless, we commend the theoretical inquiry to you. It is interesting for its own sake and even if the theoretical approach suggested here does not fully convince you, it provides a practical framework for understanding not only the rules relating to presumptions but also how they fit within the broader subject of judicial proof.

We begin by addressing the problem of allocation of burdens of proof in civil and criminal cases. This subject is sometimes treated in courses in civil procedure, torts, contracts, and property but not always in connection with presumptions, inferences, judicial comment, and choices of substantive rules of law. As the following sections indicate, these subjects are all parts of the same machine and must fit together for the machine to work properly. Thinking about burdens of proof inevitably involves consideration of the use of probabilistic and mathematical proof, a subject already touched on in Chapter I. As mentioned there, the difference between our consideration of probabilistic evidence in Chapter I and in this chapter is that in Chapter I we were concerned with the *relevance* (and hence the *admissibility*) of such evidence, while in this chapter the focus is on the *sufficiency* of such evidence to *establish* an element of the case.

Our discussion of presumptions in civil cases is organized around three ways ("strategies") in which they and other devices can bridge the gap between speculation (which is unacceptable in court) and inference (acceptable). This approach is not explicit in the Federal Rules or in the cases. Indeed, the series of recent federal court cases dealing with presumptions, including the *Burdine* 1981 Supreme Court case, that we have included in this chapter reveal a tendency to confuse these three strategies in most instances. In addition to pointing out various problems courts have in applying Rule 301, these cases demonstrate the continuing validity of Professor Morgan's nearly half-century old warning. The *Sindell* case from the California Supreme Court, which concludes the section on presumptions in civil cases, is an interesting example of one of the three described strategies in disguise.

The section on presumptions in criminal cases again focuses on the

connection between the initial allocation of burdens of proof and presumptions. To what extent can the legislature constitutionally shift burdens of proof through reallocation of elements *or* by the use of
presumptions? Does it make any difference in which manner the burden
of proof is shifted? A series of problems and cases and a lengthy dialogue between Professor Nesson and Professor Allen raise these and a
host of other thorny constitutional and policy issues.

A. Allocation in Civil Cases

CLEARY, PRESUMING AND PLEADING: AN ESSAY ON JURISTIC IMMATURITY
12 Stan. L. Rev. 5-14 (1959)

THE SUBSTANTIVE LAW

Since all are agreed that procedure exists only for the purpose of
putting the substantive law effectively to work, a preliminary look at the
nature of substantive law, as viewed procedurally, is appropriate.

Every dog, said the common law, is entitled to one bite. This result
was reached from reasoning that man's best friend was not in general
dangerous, and hence the owner should not be liable when the dog
departed from his normally peaceable pursuits and inflicted injury. Liability should follow only when the owner had reason to know of the
dangerous proclivities of his dog, and the one bite afforded notice of
those proclivities. So the formula for holding a dog owner liable at
common law is: + *ownership* + *notice of dangerous character* + *biting.*

This rule of law becomes monotonous to postmen. Hence the postmen cause to be introduced in the legislature a bill making owners of
dogs absolutely liable, i.e., eliminating notice from the formula for liability. At the hearing on the bill, however, the dog lovers appear and, while
admitting the justness of the postmen's complaint, point out that a dog
ought at least to be entitled to defend himself against human aggression.
Then the home owners' lobby points out the usefulness of dogs in
guarding premises against prowlers. Balancing these factors, there
emerges a statute making dog owners liable for bites inflicted except
upon persons tormenting the dog or unlawfully on the owner's premises. The formula for liability now becomes: + *ownership* + *biting* − *being
tormented* − *unlawful presence on the premises.*

So in any given situation, the law recognizes certain elements as material to the case, and the presence or absence of each of them is properly
to be considered in deciding the case. Or, to rephrase in somewhat more

involved language, rules of substantive law are "statements of the specific factual conditions upon which specific legal consequences depend. . . . Rules of substantive law are conditional imperatives, having the form: *If* such and such *and* so and so, *etc.* is the case, *and unless* such and such *or unless* so and so, *etc.* is the case, *then* the defendant is liable. . . ." Now obviously the weighing and balancing required to determine what elements ought to be considered material cannot be accomplished by any of the methodologies of procedure. The result is purely a matter of substantive law, to be decided according to those imponderables which travel under the name of jurisprudence.

This view of the substantive law may seem unduly Euclidean, yet some system of analysis and classification is necessary if the law is to possess a measure of continuity and to be accessible and usable.

Prima Facie Case and Defense

Under our adversary method of litigation a trial is essentially not an inquest or investigation but rather a demonstration conducted by the parties.

Since plaintiff is the party seeking to disturb the existing situation by inducing the court to take some measure in his favor, it seems reasonable to require him to demonstrate his right to relief. How extensive must this demonstration be? Should it include every substantive element, which either by its existence or nonexistence may condition his right to relief? If the answer is "yes," then plaintiff under our dog statute would be required to demonstrate each of the elements in the formula: + *ownership* + *biting* − *tormenting* − *illegal presence on the premises.*

In the ordinary dog case this would not be unduly burdensome, but if the suit is on a contract and we require plaintiff to establish the existence or nonexistence, as may be appropriate, of every concept treated in Corbin and Williston, then the responsibility of plaintiff becomes burdensome indeed and the lawsuit itself may include a large amount of unnecessary territory. Actually, of course, the responsibility for dealing with every element is not placed on plaintiff. Instead we settle for a "prima facie case" or "cause of action," consisting of certain selected elements which are regarded as sufficient to entitle plaintiff to recover, *if* he proves them and *unless* defendant in turn establishes other elements which would offset them. Thus in a simple contract case, by establishing + *offer* + *acceptance* + *consideration* + *breach,* plaintiff is entitled to recover, unless defendant establishes + *accord and satisfaction* or + *failure of consideration* or + *illegality* or − *capacity to contract,* and so on.

Observe that the plus and minus signs change, in accord with proper mathematical rules, when we shift elements to the defendant's side of the equation as "defenses." For example, if plaintiff were required to deal with capacity to contract, it would become + *capacity to contract* as a part of his case, rather than the − *capacity to contract* of defendant's case.

Defenses, too, may be prima facie only and subject to being offset by further matters produced by plaintiff, as in the case of the defense of release, offset by the further fact of fraud in the inducement for the release. The entire process is the familiar confessing and avoiding of the common law.

Allocating the Elements

The next step to be taken is the determination whether a particular material element is a part of plaintiff's prima facie case or a defense. Or, referring back to the statement that rules of substantive law are "conditional imperatives, having the form: *If* such and such *and* so and so, *etc.,* is the case . . . *then* the defendant is liable," should the element in question be listed as an *if* or as an *unless?*

In some types of situations, the test has been purely mechanical, with the mechanics in turn likely to be accidental and casual. Thus, in causes of action based on statute, if an exception appears in the enacting clause, i.e., the clause creating the right of action, then the party relying on the statute must show that the case is not within the exception; otherwise the responsibility for bringing the case within an exception falls upon the opposite party. The principle is widely recognized, but the vagaries of statutory draftsmanship detract largely from its certainty of application. Returning to our dogs, two statutes will serve as illustrations.

> If any dog shall do any damage to either the body or property of any person, the owner . . . shall be liable for such damage, unless such damage shall have been occasioned to the body or property of a person who, at the time such damage was sustained, was committing a trespass or other tort, or was teasing, tormenting or abusing such dog. Mass. Ann. Laws ch. 140, §155 (1950).

> Every person owning or harboring a dog shall be liable to the party injured for all damages done by such dog; but no recovery shall be had for personal injuries to any person when they [sic] are upon the premises of the owner of the dog after night, or upon the owner's premises engaged in some unlawful act in the day time. Ky. Laws 1906, ch. 10, at 25, Ky. Stats. 1936, §68a-5.

The Massachusetts statute was construed as imposing on a two and one quarter year old plaintiff the burden of establishing that he was not teasing, tormenting or abusing the dog, while under the Kentucky statute a plaintiff was held to have stated a prima facie case by alleging only that he was bitten by a dog owned by defendant, leaving questions of presence on the premises at night or unlawful activities in the day time to be brought in as defenses. The difference in result can scarcely be regarded as calculated but is typical. Unfortunately, the statute which states in so many words the procedural effects of its terms is a rarity.

Exceptions in contracts receive similar treatment. If the words of promising are broad, followed by exceptions, the general disposition is to place on defendant the responsibility of invoking the exception. Of course, many of the cases involve insurance policies, with all that implies. In Munro, Brice & Co. v. War Risks Ass'n, during World War I one underwriter insured plaintiffs' ship against loss due to hostilities and another underwriter insured it against perils of the sea except consequences of hostilities. The ship was lost, and plaintiffs sued on both policies. The King's Bench Division held that as regards the first policy plaintiffs must show the loss to have been due to hostilities, but that under the second policy merely establishing the loss was sufficient, leaving it to the underwriter to bring in loss by hostilities as a defense. Since evidence of the cause of loss was wholly lacking, the loss fell on the second underwriter.

Julius Stone commented as follows: "Every qualification of a class can equally be stated without any change of meaning as an exception to a class not so qualified. Thus the proposition 'All animals have four legs except gorillas,' and the proposition 'all animals which are not gorillas have four legs,' are, so far as their meanings are concerned, identical. . . .

"If the distinction between an element of the rule and an exception to it does not represent any distinction in meaning, it may still remain a valid distinction for legal purposes. In that case, however, it must turn upon something other than the meaning of the propositions involved. It may turn, for instance, merely upon their relative form or order."

So in a few kinds of cases the answer to the question of allocation is found in the structure of a statute or contract, perhaps with some tenuous reference to intent, either of the legislature or of the contracting parties. But what of the great bulk of the cases, involving neither exception in a statute nor limitation upon words of promising? What general considerations should govern the allocation of responsibility for the elements of the case between the parties?

Precedent may settle the manner in a particular jurisdiction, but precedent as such does nothing for the inquiring mind. Thayer was of the view that questions of allocation were to be referred to the principles of pleading, or perhaps to analysis of the substantive law, and "one has no right to look to the law of evidence for a solution of such questions as these. . . ." Books about pleading, however, have not been numerous in recent years, except for the local practice works; and aside from a brief but provocative treatment by Judge Clark they offer slight assistance. The substantive law texts, when they deal with the matter at all, tend to describe results rather than reasons.

Despite Thayer's strictures, his descendants in the field of writing about evidence, by assuming to deal with problems of burden of proof as an aspect of the law of evidence, have found themselves inevitably enmeshed in the problems of allocation and have contributed most of the literature on the subject, although in an introductory and incidental fashion.

Before trying to establish some bench marks for allocation, let us note, though only for the purpose of rejecting them, two which are sometimes suggested. (a) That the burden is on the party having the affirmative; or, conversely stated, that a party is not required to prove a negative. This is no more than a play on words, since practically any proposition may be stated in either affirmative or negative form. Thus a plaintiff's exercise of ordinary care equals absence of contributory negligence, in the minority jurisdictions which place this element in plaintiff's case. In any event, the proposition seems simply not to be so. (b) That the burden is on the party to whose case the element is essential. This does no more than restate the question.

Actually the reported decisions involving problems of allocation rarely contain any satisfying disclosure of the ratio decidendi. Implicit, however, seem to be considerations of policy, fairness and probability. None affords a complete working rule. Much overlap is apparent, as sound policy implies not too great a departure from fairness, and probability may constitute an aspect of both policy and fairness. But despite the vagueness of their generality, it is possible to pour enough content into these concepts to give them some real meaning.

(1) POLICY

As Judge Clark remarks, "One who must bear the risk of getting the matter properly set before the court, if it is to be considered at all, has to that extent the dice loaded against him." While policy more obviously predominates at the stage of determining what elements are material, its influence may nevertheless extend into the stage of allocating those elements by way of favoring one or the other party to a particular kind of litigation. Thus a court which is willing to permit a recovery for negligence may still choose to exercise restraints by imposing on plaintiff the burden of freedom from contributory negligence, as a theoretical, though perhaps not a practical, handicap. Or the bringing of actions for defamation may in some measure be discouraged by allocating untruth to plaintiff as an element of his prima facie case, rather than by treating truth as an affirmative defense. And it must be apparent that a complete lack of proof as to a particular element moves allocation out of the class of a mere handicap and makes it decisive as to the element, and perhaps as to the case itself. In Summers v. Tice plaintiff was hunting with two defendants and was shot in the eye when both fired simultaneously at the same bird. The court placed on each defendant the burden of proving that his shot did not cause the injury. To discharge this burden was impossible, since each gun was loaded with identical shot. In Munro, Brice & Co. v. War Risks Ass'n the absence of proof of the cause of the ship's loss meant that the party on whom that burden was cast lost the case. In these cases the admonition of Julius Stone is particularly apt: "the Courts should not essay the impossible task of making the bricks of judge-made law without handling the straw of policy."

(2) FAIRNESS

The nature of a particular element may indicate that evidence relating to it lies more within the control of one party, which suggests the fairness of allocating that element to him. Examples are payment, discharge in bankruptcy, and license, all of which are commonly treated as affirmative defenses. However, caution in making any extensive generalization is indicated by the classification of contributory negligence, illegality, and failure of consideration also as affirmative defenses, despite the fact that knowledge more probably lies with plaintiff. Certainly in the usual tort cases, knowledge of his own wrongdoing rests more intimately in defendant, though the accepted general pattern imposes this burden on plaintiff.

(3) PROBABILITY

A further factor which seems to enter into many decisions as to allocation is a judicial, i.e., wholly nonstatistical, estimate of the probabilities of the situation, with the burden being put on the party who will be benefited by a departure from the supposed norm.

The probabilities may relate to the type of situation out of which the litigation arises or they may relate to the type of litigation itself. The standards are quite different and may produce differences in result. To illustrate: If it be assumed that most people pay their bills, the probabilities are that any bill selected at random has been paid; therefore, a plaintiff suing to collect a bill would be responsible for nonpayment as an element of his prima facie case. If, however, attention is limited to bills upon which suit is brought, a contrary conclusion is reached. Plaintiffs are not prone to sue for paid bills, and the probabilities are that the bill is unpaid. Hence payment would be an affirmative defense. Or again, "guest" statutes prohibit nonpaying passengers from recovering for the negligence of the driver. If most passengers are nonpaying, then the element of compensation for the ride would belong in the prima facie case of the passenger-plaintiff. If, however, most passengers in the litigated cases ride for compensation, then absence of compensation would be an affirmative defense. In the payment-of-a-bill situation the probabilities are estimated with regard to the litigated situation, payment being regarded generally as an affirmative defense, while in the guest situation they are estimated with regard to such situations generally and not limited to those which are litigated, status as a nonguest being a part of plaintiff's prima facie case. No reason for the shift is apparent, and it may be unconscious. The litigated cases would seem to furnish the more appropriate basis for estimating probabilities.

Matters occurring after the accrual of the plaintiff's right are almost always placed in the category of affirmative defenses. Examples are payment, release, accord and satisfaction, discharge in bankruptcy, and limitations. A plausible explanation is that a condition once established is likely to continue; hence the burden ought to fall on the party benefited by a change.

In the cases of complete absence of proof, a proper application of the probability factor is calculated to produce a minimum of unjust results, and the same is true, though less impressively, even if proof is available.

Problem IX-1
Civil Allocation in Idylia

In the past Idylia operated without an adversary system of justice. All civil disputes were brought to the Tribunal of Inquiry which thoroughly investigated and reached factual conclusions about each and every element that the Idylia legislature specified as essential to recovery. In some cases the Tribunal of Inquiry would remain uncertain even after exhaustive investigation. These cases would be decided by coin flip. The system was enormously expensive and the results unsatisfying, particularly in the coin-flip cases.

You are commissioned to allocate the proof of elements between plaintiff and defendant in contract suits and to provide a coherent theoretical justification for your allocation.

The elements for breach of contract in Idylia are as follows: agreement, consideration, breach, and lack of mistake. Records of the Tribunal of Inquiry show that in the last year (consider it representative) there were 3,000 disputed contracts. Estimates are that this is approximately 5 percent of all contracts. Damages were awarded in 1,000 cases.

	Number of cases in which the element was the major disputed issue	Number of cases in which Tribunal decided for recovery	Number of cases in which decision was for no recovery	Number of cases in which Tribunal wound up uncertain and flipped a coin
Agreement	850	325	275	250
Consideration	400	200	150	50
Breach	1,700	440	970	290
Absence of mistake	50	35	5	10
	3,000	1,000	1,400	600

What do you recommend, and why?

B. Inference and Speculation: What Is the Difference Between "Reasoning" and "Guessing"?

Problem IX-2
Big-Time Charlie

D, prosecuted for passing counterfeit money, admits that he bought drinks at a bar for himself and two friends and paid for the drinks with a counterfeit $20 bill but claims ignorance that the bill was counterfeit. The only evidence against him on the issue of knowledge is testimony that while in the company of his two friends, *D* lit a cigar with a $20 bill. *D* moves for a directed verdict. How should the judge rule?

Problem IX-3
Prison Yard

In an enclosed yard are 25 identically dressed prisoners and a prison guard. The sole witness is too far away to distinguish features. He sees the guard, recognizable by his uniform, trip and fall, apparently knocking himself out. The prisoners huddle and argue. One breaks away from the others and goes to a shed in the corner of the yard to hide. The other 24 set upon the fallen guard and kill him. After the killing, the hidden prisoner emerges from the shed and mixes with the other prisoners. When the authorities later enter the yard, they find the dead guard and the 25 prisoners.

The prosecutor indicts one of the prisoners — call him prisoner #1. If the only evidence at trial is the testimony of the distant witness, is prisoner #1 entitled to a directed verdict of acquittal?

Suppose, in addition, that the prosecutor calls prisoner #2 as a witness for the prosecution and prisoner #2 testifies that it was he who disassociated himself from the others and hid in the shed. Is prisoner #1 entitled to a directed verdict of acquittal?

If you conclude that a directed verdict of acquittal is appropriate in the first instance but not the second, then consider the following.

NESSON, REASONABLE DOUBT AND PERMISSIVE INFERENCE: THE VALUE OF COMPLEXITY, 92 Harv. L. Rev. 1187, 1194 (1979): Why should it be that the high likelihood but starkly numerical case is thrown out of court while the cases based on self-serving testimony or additional circumstantial evidence will be put to the jury? The question becomes truly puzzling when one considers that even a case in which the quantifiable likelihood of guilt was much lower — for example, where originally only two prisoners were in the yard — might be allowed to go to the jury as long as the prosecutor's case was bolstered by additional circumstantial evidence or by other evidence distinguishing the defendant.

Why should evidence which generates a clearcut mathematical statement of the likelihood of guilt be considered insufficient, even when the probability of guilt is high, while other evidence of a testimonial or circumstantial nature is much more readily considered by the courts to be sufficient to sustain a prosecutor's case? Do we actually consider the jury to be accurate in assessing the credibility of witnesses and the strength of circumstantial evidence? Or are some risks of inaccurate verdicts more acceptable than others?

———————

Is the problem of speculation limited to criminal cases? If the prison yard case were a civil action by the estate of the murdered guard against prisoner #1, would the analysis of issues be different?

Problem IX-4
Rapid Transit

While *P* was driving an automobile easterly on Main Street, Winthrop, at about 1:00 AM, she observed a bus coming toward her which she described as a "great big long wide affair." The bus, which was exceeding the speed limit and driving in the center of the road, forced *P* to turn right and hit a parked car. *P* could not specifically identify the bus that ran her off the road. She proved that *D* Rapid Transit Line was the only bus company to run a regular route on Main Street, with buses departing every half-hour on the Main Street route. Private and chartered buses could, however, use the route also.

P rests with this the only proof. Is *D* entitled to a directed verdict?

Problem IX-5
Blue Bus (A Reprise)[1]

P is negligently run off the road into a parked car (as in the preceding problem) by a blue bus. *P* is prepared to prove that *D* operates four-fifths of all the blue buses that use the route. What effect, if any, should such proof be given? If there is no other proof presented by either party, is a directed verdict in order? For which side? Would you bet that it was

1. See Problem I-16, p. 51, above.

D's bus that forced *P* off the road? Is it useful to think in terms of odds or wagers when considering admissibility or sufficiency of evidence? Consider the following.

L. COHEN, THE PROBABLE AND THE PROVABLE §30 (1977): *The inapplicability of betting odds.* Another commonly invoked criterion for the assignment of a mathematical probability is the acceptance or acceptability of appropriate betting odds within a coherent betting policy. So perhaps well-behaved jurors, who are fully self-conscious in their reasoning, should be supposed to measure the strength of their belief in the correctness of a particular verdict by reference to the odds they would accept if wagering on its correctness? This measure, the betting quotient, would be the ratio of the favourable figure to the sum of the two figures, and would have the structure of a mathematical probability. Odds of 4 to 1 on the plaintiff's case, say, would give a betting quotient or mathematical probability of .8. It would then apparently be possible for judges or legislators to stipulate a degree of mathematical probability that could be taken as putting the guilt of an accused person beyond reasonable doubt and a lower degree of mathematical probability that would suffice for the decision of civil cases.

But in fact such a procedure would be grossly fallacious. A reasonable man's betting practice is subject to two additional constraints, besides his knowledge of relevant data.

One constraint is that he only wagers on discoverable outcomes. Bets must be settlable. In each case the outcome must be knowable otherwise than from the data on which the odds themselves are based. When the horse-race is finally run, the winner is photographed as he passes the winning-post. When the football match is finally played, each goal is seen as it is kicked. Consequently wagers on past events or on the truth of scientific generalizations over an unbounded domain, or on any issue where the whole truth cannot be directly observed, are only intelligible in a context of total or partial ignorance about the relevant data. Knowing nothing, or only a little, about the local archaeological evidence I can wager you, on the basis of experience elsewhere, that there was no Roman settlement at Banbury; and to settle the bet we can excavate and see. But, if all the appropriate excavations have already been done, and we know their results, there is nothing to wager about. Similarly, to request a juryman to envisage a wager on a past event, when, ex hypothesi, he normally already knows all the relevant evidence that is likely to be readily obtainable, is to employ the concept of a wager in a context to which it is hardly appropriate. There is no time machine to take us back into the past. So there is no sure way of discovering whether the accused is guilty, or the plaintiff's statement of claim is true, except by looking at the relevant evidence. If one asks a juryman to envisage a wager in such a context, one is hardly entitled to expect a rational response.

Perhaps it will be objected that since people do sometimes wager sensibly about past events, as on the existence of a Roman settlement at Banbury, they can reasonably be assumed to have a general technique for assigning betting-quotient probabilities to past events on given evidence. Why then cannot a jury employ such a technique for the solution of its own special problems about probabilities? The answer to this objection is that it still does not succeed in attaching significance to the conception of judicial probabilities as betting quotients. The argument against a betting-quotient analysis of judicial probability is not that there is no sufficiently general technique for devising betting-quotients: the argument is rather that in certain situations the operational acceptance of a betting quotient is irrational. So talk about assigning probabilities, when probabilities are understood in the proposed way, involves the absurdity of talk about accepting reasonable bets on unsettlable issues.

Moreover, another constraint on rational betting practice has to be mentioned here. No one bothers about odds unless the amounts at stake are of some consequence. Only the very poor bet seriously in pennies. But when the amounts at stake begin to rise a prudent man tends to be more and more cautious about the odds he will accept for a given size of stake. Bookmakers shorten the odds on a horse not only when they hear of its latest wins elsewhere but also when they begin to be concerned about how much they would lose if it won the current race. So there is little sense in asking a man what odds he would accept on a certain outcome unless the value of the units wagered is also specified. Every juryman would have to be instructed separately by the judge, in accordance with the judge's estimate of what would be an appropriate sum of money for that juryman to envisage wagering. Consequently every accused would be at risk not only in relation to the evidence, but also in relation to the judge's estimates of how much importance each juryman attaches to the gain or loss of this or that sum of money. Such a system certainly does not yet exist anywhere, and its institution seems scarcely likely to promote the ends of justice.

NOTE: THE SUFFICIENCY OF MATHEMATICAL AND
PROBABILISTIC PROOF IN THE TRIAL PROCESS

The preceding four problems present the second subquestion posed, but deferred, in Chapter I, as to the sufficiency of probabilistic evidence to support a criminal or civil finding. At this point, you may want to review the material at pages 40-64, concerning the *admissibility* of such evidence. Not surprisingly, given his view as to the dangers of the use of mathematical models at trial, Professor Tribe is reluctant to concede that probabilistic data alone can support a judgment even in a civil case:

> In Smith v. Rapid Transit, Inc., 317 Mass. 469, 58 N.E.2d 754 (1945), the actual case on which this famous chestnut is based [the Rapid Transit and Blue Bus problems], no statistical data were in fact presented, but the plaintiff did introduce evidence sufficient to show that the defendant's bus line was the only one chartered to operate on the street where the accident occurred. Affirming the direction of a verdict for the defendant, the court observed: "The most that can be said of the evidence in the instant case is that perhaps the mathematical chances somewhat favor the proposition that a bus of the defendant caused the accident. This was not enough." 317 Mass. at 470. If understood as insisting on a numerically higher showing — an "extra margin" of probability above, say, .55 — then the decision in *Smith* would make no sense, at least if the court's objective were the minimization of the total number of judicial errors in situations of this kind, an objective essentially implicit in the adoption of a "preponderance of the evidence" standard. But cases like *Smith* are entirely sensible if understood instead as insisting on the presentation of some non-statistical and "individualized" proof of identity before compelling a party to pay damages, and even before compelling him to come forward with defensive evidence, absent an adequate explanation of the failure to present such individualized proof.

Tribe, Trial by Mathematics: Precision and Ritual in the Trial Process, 84 Harv. L. Rev. 1329, 1341 n.37 (1971). Later, Tribe modifies this point slightly, but only with regard to *admissibility,* in the following way:

> If the statistical evidence standing alone establishes a sufficiently high prior probability of X, and a satisfactory explanation is provided for the failure to adduce more individualized proof, there seems no defensible alternative (absent believable evidence contrary to X) to directing a verdict for the party claiming X, for no factual question remains about which the jury can reason, and directing a verdict the other way would be more likely to lead to an unjust result. If, however, more individualized proof is adduced, and if the party opposing X has discharged the burden (created by the statistical evidence) of producing believable evidence to the contrary, the question remains whether the risk of distortion created by informing the trier of fact of the potentially overbearing statistics so outweighs the probative value of such statistics as to compel their judicial exclusion. If this situation arises in the bus hypothetical, all that I am now prepared to say is that the question of admissibility seems to me a very close one.

Id. at 1361 n.102.

A fortiori, Tribe finds that the use of probabilistic data to support a criminal conviction, as in the prison yard problem, conflicts with fundamental, even constitutional, values. In a section of his article headed "The Quantification of Sacrifice," Tribe states:

Limiting myself here to the ordinary criminal proceeding, I suggest that the acceptance of [a specific mathematical method proposed by others], given the precision and explicitness its use demands, could dangerously undermine yet another complex of values — the values surrounding the notion that juries should convict only when guilt is beyond real doubt.

An inescapable corollary of the proposed method, and indeed of any method that aims to assimilate mathematical proof by quantifying the probative force of evidence generally, is that it leaves the trier of fact, when all is said and done, with a number that purports to represent his assessment of the probability that the defendant is guilty as charged. Needless to say, that number will never quite equal 1.0, so the result will be to produce a quantity — take .95 for the sake of illustration — which openly signifies a measurable (and potentially reducible) margin of doubt, here a margin of .05, or 1/20.

Now it may well be, as I have argued elsewhere, that there is something intrinsically immoral about condemning a man as a criminal while telling oneself, "I believe that there is a chance of one in twenty that this defendant is innocent, but a 1/20 risk of sacrificing him erroneously is one I am willing to run in the interest of the public's — and my own — safety." It may be that — quite apart from the particular number — there is something basically immoral in this posture, but I do not insist here on that position. All I suggest is that a useful purpose may be served by structuring a system of criminal justice so that it can avoid having to proclaim, as the suggested procedure would force us to proclaim, that it will impose its sanctions in the face of a recognized and quantitatively measured doubt in the particular case.

If the system in fact did exactly that, such compelled candor about its operation might have great value. It could generate pressure for useful procedural reform, and it should probably be considered worthwhile in itself. But to let the matter rest there would be wrong, for the system does *not* in fact authorize the imposition of criminal punishment when the trier recognizes a quantifiable doubt as to the defendant's guilt. Instead, the system dramatically — if imprecisely — insists upon as close an approximation to certainty as seems humanly attainable in the circumstances. The jury is charged that any "reasonable doubt," of whatever magnitude, must be resolved in favor of the accused. Such insistence on the greatest certainty that seems reasonably attainable can serve at the trial's end, like the presumption of innocence at the trial's start, to affirm the dignity of the accused and to display respect for his rights as a person — in this instance, by declining to put those rights in deliberate jeopardy and by refusing to sacrifice him to the interests of others.

In contrast, for the jury to announce that it is prepared to convict the defendant in the face of an acknowledged and numerically measurable doubt as to his guilt is to tell the accused that those who judge him find it preferable to accept the resulting risk of his unjust conviction than to reduce that risk by demanding any further or more convincing proof of his guilt. I am far from persuaded that this represents the sort of thought process through which jurors do, or should, arrive at verdicts of guilt. Many jurors would no doubt describe themselves as being "completely sure," or at least as being "as sure as possible," before they vote to convict. That some mistaken verdicts are inevitably returned even by jurors who regard themselves as "certain" is of course true but is irrelevant; such unavoidable errors are in no sense *intended*,[143] and the fact that they must occur if trials are to be conducted at all need not undermine the effort, through the symbols of trial procedure, to express society's fundamental commitment to the protection of the defendant's rights as a person, as an end in himself. On the other hand, formulating an "acceptable" risk of error to which the trier is willing deliberately to subject the defendant would interfere seriously with this expressive role of the demand for certitude — however unattainable real certitude may be, and however clearly all may ultimately recognize its unattainability.

In short, to say that society recognizes the necessity of tolerating the erroneous "conviction of some innocent suspects in order to assure the confinement of a vastly larger number of guilty criminals"[144] is not at all to say that society does, or should, embrace a policy that juries, *conscious of the magnitude of their doubts in a particular case,* ought to convict in the face of this acknowledged and quantified uncertainty. It is to the complex difference between these two propositions that the concept of "guilt beyond a reasonable doubt" inevitably speaks. The concept signifies not any mathematical measure of the precise degree of certitude we require of juries in criminal cases, but a subtle compromise between the knowledge, on the one hand, that we cannot realistically insist on acquittal whenever guilt is less than absolutely certain, and the realization, on the other hand, that the cost of spelling that out explicitly and with calculated precision in the trial itself would be too high.

Id. at 1372-1375.

Also not surprisingly, Saks and Kidd contend that there is really no difference between a judgment based on probabilistic data and one based on particularized, intuitive judgment except that the latter is naive:

> By disposing of the false distinction between probabilistic and particularistic evidence, we also obviate the interesting worry that probability evidence cannot support a finding of liability or guilt in the way that particularistic evidence can, by virtue of the latter's ability to pinpoint.

Saks and Kidd, Human Information Processing and Adjudication: Trial by Heuristics, 15 Law & Socy. Rev. 123, 154 (1980-1981).

Moreover, they contend, acknowledging the place of probabilistic methods in the process would further larger values served by the legal system:

> The harm that may be done a defendant is that behind this mask of certainty [created by the insistence on the use of nonquantifiable proof] can hide not only minute quantities of uncertainty, but massive quantities. Rele-

---

143. Tolerating a system in which perhaps one innocent man in a hundred is erroneously convicted despite each jury's attempt to make *as few mistakes as possible* is in this respect vastly different from instructing a jury to *aim* at a 1% rate (or even a .1% rate) of mistaken convictions.

144. Dershowitz, Preventive Detention: Social Threat, Trial, Dec.-Jan. 1969-70, at 22.

vant evidence might be weak indeed, but so long as it is kept fuzzy, a finding against a defendant could be rendered and claimed to be certain. Is this an affirmation of the accused's dignity?

Candid announcement of unavoidable margins of error may be a greater service to individual defendants and to the legal system. With such awareness we may be motivated to modify one of our most important social inventions to make it work better (err less); we may recognize that truth is not merely anything that a court asserts it to be; and both legal policy makers and case-by-case fact finders will not be able to hide from the implications and consequences of their own decisions nor from the context in which they must decide.

Id. at 156.

C.   Strategies for Bridging the Gap

Faced with a gap between speculation and inference courts have the obvious choice of directing the verdict against the plaintiff. This is what happened in Rapid Transit and probably would happen in the hypothetical Prisoners and Blue Bus cases. In some cases, however, the evidence may be circumstantial and thin, posing the same kind of uncertainty about what happened as the Rapid Transit, Blue Bus, and Prisoners cases did, and yet in these cases a directed verdict against the plaintiff might not be the best result. There will be *recurrent* types of cases where imposition of the burden of displacing uncertainty on the class of plaintiffs is deemed undesirable. For example, at the turn of the century people often were killed at railroad crossings. Their next of kin would bring suit but be unable to prove that the railroad was negligent (no witnesses — just a body by the crossing). One can well imagine concluding (1) that the defendant might be able to add to knowledge about what happened and that a procedure to elicit this knowledge should be adopted, or (2) that cases that result in uncertainty on the negligence issue should be resolved against the railroad, perhaps on a deep-pocket or easy-to-spread-the-loss theory, or (3) that the case should be decided on the basis of the kind of safety device at the crossing. Each of these approaches would allow us to reach a judgment for the plaintiff without having obviously to jump to a conclusion. These approaches are worth abstracting and naming.

1. *The Explanation Seeker.* Fill in the gap with more information. Specifically, impose a burden on the defendant to come forward with an explanation for the suggestive but not sufficient circumstantial evidence and authorize an inference to be drawn from his failure to do so. If he comes forward with more information the gap will have been bridged. If

he does not and it appears to the fact-finder that the defendant was in a position to come forward with an explanation favorable to himself, had there been one, then an inference can be drawn from his failure that will help bridge the gap. If it appears that the defendant is not in such a position, then this strategy will not help.

2. *The Allocation Shifter.* Bridge the gap by changing the starting assumption on the troublesome issue. Once the suggestive but insufficient circumstance is proved, a rule could be devised that changes the starting assumption on the issue in question, shifting the burden of displacing uncertainty to the defendant. As the rule stands today, if the case continues in an uncertain state the defendant will lose.

3. *The Issue Switcher.* The gap could be bridged by foresaking the initial troublesome issue altogether once it appears unresolvable and switching to another (not necessarily related) issue as a basis for resolving the controversy.

In the following problems, which strategy would you suggest to bridge the gap?

Problem IX-6
Family Car

A recurrent problem arises in auto accident cases in which the party at fault is a minor driving a car owned by a parent. The plaintiff sues the parent-owner, but to recover the plaintiff must prove that the minor was driving the car with the parent-owner's permission. Typically the plaintiff has no proof of this beyond proof of the relationship between the parent and the driver.

What procedural strategies would make sense for resolving these cases?

Problem IX-7
Post Office

P sues D for breach of contract. P proves that he mailed his acceptance of D's offer to D at D's proper address. D claims that he never received it. How should the issue be decided?

Problem IX-8
Last Carrier

P ships a crate of parts from Boston to Phoenix by rail. The crate is in good shape when sent but arrives damaged. Three different rail companies, $D1$, $D2$, $D3$, have handled the goods along the route of shipment. P has no way of knowing which one damaged the crate. P sues $D1$, $D2$, and $D3$. How should the case be resolved?

D. Civil Presumptions and Rule 301

The tremendous confusion that has characterized the law of civil presumptions stems primarily from a concept known as the "bursting bubble" theory of presumptions. The bursting bubble approach comes close to embodying the explanation-seeking strategy but misses. Under the bursting bubble theory, the only effect of a presumption is to shift a burden of producing evidence regarding the presumed fact. If evidence is produced by the adversary to meet that burden, the presumption disappears — the bubble bursts. Many problems have been associated with the bursting bubble approach:

(1) The burden of production imposed by this form of presumption has been thought to carry with it the risk of losing by directed verdict if the burden of production is not discharged.

(2) There has been much difference of opinion over the appropriate standard for determining whether the burden has been discharged: Can it be discharged by an offer of a scintilla of evidence or evidence sufficient to support a finding?

(3) Since the question of whether the burden has been discharged is for the judge to decide, it is possible that the presumption will be made to disappear on the basis of evidence that the jury will wholly discredit. This seems to give the presumption "too slight and evanescent" an effect (note the language of the FRE Advisory Committee Note). This criticism spurred the other major presumption theories (presumptions as evidence and burden-shifting presumptions). See Rule 301 as originally proposed and as amended by the House.

FRE 301
Presumptions in General in Civil Actions and Proceedings

In all civil actions and proceedings not otherwise provided for by Act of Congress or by these rules, a presumption imposes on the party against whom it is directed the burden of going forward with evidence to rebut or meet the presumption, but does not shift to such party the burden of

proof in the sense of the risk of nonpersuasion, which remains throughout the trial upon the party on whom it was originally cast.

Rule 301 as enacted appears to be an adaptation of the bursting
bubble approach and certainly is a rejection of the burden-shifting and
presumptions-as-evidence approaches. What it actually is, as we shall
see, remains somewhat unclear. Apparently the Senate Committee
thought that the burden of production described by Rule 301 would not
result in a directed verdict. The Senate report says that "it would be
inappropriate under this rule to instruct the jury that the inference they
are to draw is conclusive." But what did the draftmen think the jury
should be told? Here the legislative history offers up gibberish:

> If the adverse party offers no evidence contradicting the presumed fact,
> the court will instruct the jury that if it finds the basic facts, it *may presume* the
> existence of the presumed fact. If the adverse party does offer evidence
> contradicting the presumed fact, the court cannot instruct the jury that it may
> *presume* (emphasis in the original) the existence of the presumed fact from
> proof of the basic facts. The court may, however, instruct the jury that it *may
> infer* the existence of the presumed fact from proof of the basic facts.

Do the drafters presume that jurors know the difference between "presume" and "infer"?

Suppose a juror who is told that he "may presume" a fact says, "Well, I
understand that I *may* do so, but by what criteria do I decide whether I
should do so?"

Suppose a judge wanted to use Rule 301 as an explanation-seeker?
How would he instruct the jury? And would the instructions be consistent with the legislative history of 301?

TEXAS DEPARTMENT OF COMMUNITY AFFAIRS v. BURDINE
450 U.S. 248 (1981)

Justice POWELL delivered the opinion of the Court.
This case requires us to address again the nature of the evidentiary
burden placed upon the defendant in an employment discrimination
suit brought under Title VII of the Civil Rights Act of 1964, 42 U.S.C.
§2000e et seq. The narrow question presented is whether, after the
plaintiff has proved a prima facie case of discriminatory treatment, the
burden shifts to the defendant to persuade the court by a preponderance of the evidence that legitimate, nondiscriminatory reasons for the
challenged employment action existed.

I

Petitioner, the Texas Department of Community Affairs (TDCA), hired respondent, a female, in January 1972, for the position of accounting clerk in the Public Service Careers Division (PSC). PSC provided training and employment opportunities in the public sector for unskilled workers. When hired, respondent possessed several years' experience in employment training. She was promoted to Field Services Coordinator in July 1972. Her supervisor resigned in November of that year, and respondent was assigned additional duties. Although she applied for the supervisor's position of Project Director, the position remained vacant for six months.

PSC was funded completely by the United States Department of Labor. The Department was seriously concerned about inefficiencies at PSC. In February, 1973, the Department notified the Executive Director of TDCA, B. R. Fuller, that it would terminate PSC the following month. TDCA officials, assisted by respondent, persuaded the Department to continue funding the program, conditioned upon PSC reforming its operations. Among the agreed conditions were the appointment of a permanent Project Director and a complete reorganization of the PSC staff.

After consulting with personnel within TDCA, Fuller hired a male from another division of the agency as Project Director. In reducing the PSC staff, he fired respondent along with two other employees, and retained another male, Walz, as the only professional employee in the division. It is undisputed that respondent had maintained her application for the position of Project Director and had requested to remain with TDCA. Respondent soon was rehired by TDCA and assigned to another division of the agency. She received the exact salary paid to the Project Director at PSC, and the subsequent promotions she has received have kept her salary and responsibility commensurate with what she would have received had she been appointed Project Director.

Respondent filed this suit in the United States District Court for the Western District of Texas. She alleged that the failure to promote and the subsequent decision to terminate her had been predicated on gender discrimination in violation of Title VII. After a bench trial, the District Court held that neither decision was based on gender discrimination. The court relied on the testimony of Fuller that the employment decisions necessitated by the commands of the Department of Labor were based on consultation among trusted advisors and a nondiscriminatory evaluation of the relative qualifications of the individuals involved. He testified that the three individuals terminated did not work well together, and that TDCA thought that eliminating this problem would improve PSC's efficiency. The court accepted this explanation as rational and, in effect, found no evidence that the decisions not to promote and to terminate respondent were prompted by gender discrimination.

The Court of Appeals for the Fifth Circuit reversed in part. 608 F.2d 563 (1979). The court held that the District Court's "implicit evidentiary finding" that the male hired as Project Director was better qualified for that position than respondent was not clearly erroneous. Accordingly, the court affirmed the District Court's finding that respondent was not discriminated against when she was not promoted. The Court of Appeals, however, reversed the District Court's finding that Fuller's testimony sufficiently had rebutted respondent's prima facie case of gender discrimination in the decision to terminate her employment at PSC. The court reaffirmed its previously announced views that the defendant in a Title VII case bears the burden of proving by a preponderance of the evidence the existence of legitimate nondiscriminatory reasons for the employment action and that the defendant also must prove by objective evidence that those hired or promoted were better qualified than the plaintiff. The court found that Fuller's testimony did not carry either of these evidentiary burdens. It, therefore, reversed the judgment of the District Court and remanded the case for computation of backpay. Because the decision of the Court of Appeals as to the burden of proof borne by the defendant conflicts with interpretations of our precedents adopted by other courts of appeals, we granted certiorari, — U.S. — (1980). We now vacate the Fifth Circuit's decision and remand for application of the correct standard.

II

In McDonnell Douglas Corp. v. Green, 411 U.S. 792 (1973), we set forth the basic allocation of burdens and order of presentation of proof in a Title VII case alleging discriminatory treatment. First, the plaintiff has the burden of proving by the preponderance of the evidence a prima facie case of discrimination. Second, if the plaintiff succeeds in proving the prima facie case, the burden shifts to the defendant "to articulate some legitimate, nondiscriminatory reason for the employee's rejection." Id., at 802. Third, should the defendant carry this burden, the plaintiff must then have an opportunity to prove by a preponderance of the evidence that the legitimate reasons offered by the defendant were not its true reasons, but were a pretext for discrimination. Id., at 804.

The nature of the burden that shifts to the defendant should be understood in light of the plaintiff's ultimate and intermediate burdens. The ultimate burden of persuading the trier of fact that the defendant intentionally discriminated against the plaintiff remains at all time with the plaintiff. See Board of Trustees of Keene State College v. Sweeney, 439 U.S. 24, 25, n.2 (1979); id., at 29 (Stevens, J., dissenting). See generally 9 Wigmore, Evidence §2489 (3d ed. 1940) (the burden of persuasion "never shifts"). The McDonnell Douglas division of intermediate evidentiary burdens serves to bring the litigants and the court expeditiously and fairly to this ultimate question.

The burden of establishing a prima facie case of disparate treatment is not onerous. The plaintiff must prove by a preponderence of the evidence that she applied for an available position, for which she was qualified, but was rejected under circumstances which give rise to an inference of unlawful discrimination.[6] The prima facie case serves an important function in the litigation: it eliminates the most common non-discriminatory reasons for the plaintiff's rejection. As the Court explained in Furnco Construction Co. v. Waters, 438 U.S. 567, 577 (1978), the prima facie case "raises an inference of discrimination only because we presume these acts, if otherwise unexplained, are more likely than not based on the consideration of impermissible factors." Establishment of the prima facie case in effect creates a presumption that the employer unlawfully discriminated against the employee. If the trier of fact believes the plaintiff's evidence, and if the employer is silent in the face of the presumption, the court must enter judgment for the plaintiff because no issue of fact remains in the case.

The burden that shifts to the defendant, therefore, is to rebut the presumption of discrimination by producing evidence that the plaintiff was rejected, or someone else was preferred, for a legitimate, nondiscriminatory reason. The defendant need not persuade the court that it was actually motivated by the proffered reasons. It is sufficient if the defendant's evidence raises a genuine issue of fact as to whether it discriminated against the plaintiff.[8] To accomplish this, the defendant must

---

6. In *McDonnell Douglas*, supra, we described an appropriate model for a prima facie case of racial discrimination. The plaintiff must show: "(i) that he belongs to a racial minority; (ii) that he applied and was qualified for a job for which the employer was seeking applicants; (iii) that, despite his qualifications, he was rejected; and (iv) that, after his rejection, the position remained open and the employer continued to seek applicants from persons of complainant's qualifications." 411 U.S., at 802. We added, however, that this standard is not inflexible, as "[t]he facts necessarily will vary in Title VII cases, and the specification above of the prima facie proof required from respondent is not necessarily applicable in every respect in differing factual situations." Id., at 802, n.13.

In the instant case, it is not seriously contested that respondent has proved a prima facie case. She showed that she was a qualified woman who sought an available position, but the position was left open for several months before she finally was rejected in favor of a male who had been under her supervision.

8. This evidentiary relationship between the presumption created by a prima facie case and the consequential burden of production placed on the defendant is a traditional feature of the common law. "The word 'presumption' properly used refers only to a device for allocating the production burden." F. James & G. Hazard, Civil Procedure §7.9, at 255 (2d ed. 1977) (footnote omitted). See Fed. Rule Evid. 301. See generally 9 Wigmore, Evidence §2491 (3d ed. 1940). Cf. J. Maguire, Evidence, Common Sense and Common Law, 185-186 (1947). Usually, assessing the burden of production helps the judge determine whether the litigants have created an issue of fact to be decided by the jury. In a Title VII case, the allocation of burdens and the creation of a presumption by the establishment of a prima facie case is intended progressively to sharpen the inquiry into the elusive factual question of intentional discrimination.

clearly set forth, through the introduction of admissible evidence, the reasons for the plaintiff's rejection. The explanation provided must be legally sufficient to justify a judgment for the defendant. If the defendant carries this burden of production, the presumption raised by the prima facie case is rebutted,[10] and the factual inquiry proceeds to a new level of specificity. Placing this burden of production on the defendant thus serves simultaneously to meet the plaintiff's prima facie case by presenting a legitimate reason for the action and to frame the factual issue with sufficient clarity so that the plaintiff will have a full and fair opportunity to demonstrate pretext. The sufficiency of the defendant's evidence should be evaluated by the extent to which it fulfills these functions.

The plaintiff retains the burden of persuasion. She now must have the opportunity to demonstrate that the proffered reason was not the true reason for the employment decision. This burden now merges with the ultimate burden of persuading the court that she has been the victim of intentional discrimination. She may succeed in this either directly by persuading the court that a discriminatory reason more likely motivated the employer or indirectly by showing that the employer's proffered explanation is unworthy of credence. See *McDonnell Douglas,* supra, at 804-805.

III

In reversing the judgment of the District Court that the discharge of respondent from PSC was unrelated to her sex, the Court of Appeals adhered to two rules it had developed to elaborate the defendant's burden of proof. First, the defendant must prove by a preponderance of the evidence that legitimate, nondiscriminatory reasons for the discharge existed. 608 F.2d, at 567. See Turner v. Texas Instruments, Inc., 555 F.2d 1251, 1255 (C.A.5 1977). Second, to satisfy this burden, the defendant "must prove that those he hired . . . were somehow *better* qualified than was plaintiff; in other words, comparative evidence is needed." 608 F.2d, at 567 (emphasis in original). See East v. Romine, Inc., 518 F.2d 332, 339-340 (C.A.5 1975).

---

10. See generally J. Thayer, Preliminary Treatise on Evidence 346 (1898). In saying that the presumption drops from the case, we do not imply that the trier of fact no longer may consider evidence previously introduced by the plaintiff to establish a prima facie case. A satisfactory explanation by the defendant destroys the legally mandatory inference of discrimination arising from the plaintiff's initial evidence. Nonetheless, this evidence and inferences properly drawn therefrom may be considered by the trier of fact on the issue of whether the defendant's explanation is pretextual. Indeed, there may be some cases where the plaintiff's initial evidence, combined with effective cross-examination of the defendant, will suffice to discredit the defendant's explanation.

A

The Court of Appeals has misconstrued the nature of the burden that *McDonnell Douglas* and its progeny place on the defendant. See Part II, supra. We stated in *Sweeney* that "the employer's burden is satisfied if he simply 'explains what he has done' or 'produc[es] evidence of legitimate nondiscriminatory reasons.' " 439 U.S., at 25, n.2 (Stevens, J., dissenting). It is plain that the Court of Appeals required much more: it placed on the defendant the burden of persuading the court that it had convincing, objective reasons for preferring the chosen applicant above the plaintiff.

We have stated consistently that the employee's prima facie case of discrimination will be rebutted if the employer articulates lawful reasons for the action; that is, to satisfy this intermediate burden, the employer need only produce admissible evidence which would allow the trier of fact rationally to conclude that the employment decision had not been motivated by discriminatory animus. The Court of Appeals would require the defendant to introduce evidence which, in the absence of any evidence of pretext, would *persuade* the trier of fact that the employment action was lawful. This exceeds what properly can be demanded to satisfy a burden of production.

The court placed the burden of persuasion on the defendant apparently because it feared that "[i]f an employer need only *articulate* — not prove — a legitimate, nondiscriminatory reason for his action, he may compose fictitious, but legitimate, reasons for his actions." Turner v. Texas Instruments, Inc., supra, at 1255 (emphasis in original). We do not believe, however, that limiting the defendant's evidentiary obligation to a burden of production will unduly hinder the plaintiff. First, as noted above, the defendant's explanation of its legitimate reasons must be clear and reasonably specific. This obligation arises both from the necessity of rebutting the inference of discrimination arising from the prima facie case and from the requirement that the plaintiff be afforded "a full and fair opportunity" to demonstrate pretext. Second, although the defendant does not bear a formal burden of persuasion, the defendant nevertheless retains an incentive to persuade the trier of fact that the employment decision was lawful. Thus, the defendant normally will attempt to prove the factual basis for its explanation.

B

The Court of Appeals also erred in requiring the defendant to prove by objective evidence that the person hired or promoted was more qualified than the plaintiff. *McDonnell Douglas* teaches that it is the plaintiff's task to demonstrate that similarly situated employees were not treated equally. 411 U.S., at 804. The Court of Appeals' rule would require the employer to show that the plaintiff's objective qualifications were inferior to those of the person selected. If it cannot, a court would, in effect, conclude that it has discriminated.

The court's procedural rule harbors a substantive error. Title VII prohibits all discrimination in employment based upon race, sex and national origin. "The broad, overriding interest, shared by employer, employee, and consumer, is efficient and trustworthy workmanship assured through fair and . . . neutral employment and personnel decisions." *McDonnell Douglas,* supra, at 801. Title VII, however, does not demand that an employer give preferential treatment to minorities or women. 42 U.S.C. §2000e-2(j). See Steelworkers v. Weber, 443 U.S. 193, 205-206 (1979). The statute was not intended to "diminish traditional management prerogatives." Id., at 207. It does not require the employer to restructure his employment practices to maximize the number of minorities and women hired.

The views of the Court of Appeals can be read, we think, as requiring the employer to hire the minority or female applicant whenever that person's objective qualifications were equal to those of a white male applicant. But Title VII does not obligate an employer to accord this preference. Rather, the employer has discretion to choose among equally qualified candidates, provided the decision is not based upon unlawful criteria. The fact that a court may think that the employer misjudged the qualifications of the applicants does not in itself expose him to Title VII liability, although this may be probative of whether the employer's reasons are pretexts for discrimination.

IV

In summary, the Court of Appeals erred by requiring the defendant to prove by a preponderance of the evidence the existence of nondiscriminatory reasons for terminating the respondent and that the person retained in her stead had superior objective qualifications for the position. When the plaintiff has proved a prima facie case of discrimination, the defendant bears only the burden of explaining clearly the nondiscriminatory reasons for its actions. The judgment of the Court of Appeals is vacated and the case is remanded for further proceedings consistent with this opinion.

It is so ordered.

Was the Court in *Burdine* applying Rule 301? (The only citation to Rule 301 in the opinion is the "see" cite in footnote 8.) What is left of the apparent legislative objectives of Rule 301 after *Burdine*? Had the *Bur-*

dine Court wanted to use an "explanation seeker" approach, could the Court have done so?

In reading the following cases ask yourself what kind of presumption was involved, and focus carefully on the different ways in which the court treated the presumptions. Did the court in each case apply Rule 301? Did the court adequately reconcile Rule 301 with other rules, statutes, and common law doctrines in the cases?

AUTREY v. HARRIS
639 F.2d 1233 (5th Cir. 1981)

Before AINSWORTH, GARZA and JOHNSON, JJ.

PER CURIAM. This is an appeal from the denial of surviving child insurance benefits sought under the Social Security Act, 42 U.S.C. §402(d)(1). Appellant Leona Autrey was divorced from Herman George Fisher in 1967. Fisher was the natural father of appellant's son Ross, and the adoptive father of her daughters, Catherine and Debra Sue. She has testified that no hostility resulted, and that both she and the children had frequent contact with Fisher after the divorce.

That contact came to an abrupt end in June of 1969. Fisher, evidently piloting a small plane, departed a Kansas airport and radioed an airport for weather information for a flight to Las Vegas. He has not been heard from since, and the plane has never been found.

Mrs. Autrey applied for surviving child social security benefits in 1970, based on Fisher's employment records. The application was initially denied. In 1976, she requested that the prior application be reopened so that she could provide proof of death in accordance with applicable provisions of the Social Security Act and regulations pursuant. Specifically, she relied upon the presumption of death established by regulation. This application was denied initially and after reconsideration by the Bureau of Retirement and Survivors Insurance of the Social Security Administration.

Appellant then requested a hearing, which was held on December 15, 1978. The issue relevant to this appeal was whether Fisher's death could be presumed under 20 C.F.R. §404.705 (currently 20 C.F.R. §404.721), allowing such a presumption where a person is "unexplainedly absent from his residence and unheard of for a period of 7 years." The administrative law judge ruled against Mrs. Autrey, finding that she had not proved her husband's disappearance to be "unexplained." The finding became a final decision of the Secretary of Health, Education and Welfare through approval of the department of appeal council. Mrs. Autrey appealed by filing a complaint in the district court. In a one-page order, without stating reasons, the court affirmed the Secretary's decision.

The issue before us, both appellant and appellee agree, is whether the Secretary's decision is supported by substantial evidence. We conclude that it is not, and reverse.

The presumption of death under this regulation attaches when the claimant presents facts sufficient to establish that the wage earner has been absent from his residence and unheard of for seven years. Nothing in the regulation requires the claimant to refute every reasonable theory or explanation offered by the Secretary. Aubrey v. Richardson, 462 F.2d 782, 784 (3 Cir. 1972). Once the applicant creates the presumption, the burden shifts to the Secretary to rebut it. On this record, we find it perfectly apparent that Mrs. Autrey raised the presumption.[1]

In Mulder v. Weinberger, No. 74-3595 (5 Cir. April 29, 1975), an unpublished opinion, a panel of this court endorsed the standard for rebuttal proof articulated in Secretary of Health, Education and Welfare v. Meza, 368 F.2d 389 (9 Cir. 1966). We will adhere to that formulation. The Ninth Circuit stated in *Meza* that the presumption can be dissipated in two ways: "One would be by presenting evidence that the missing person is alive. . . . The other showing would be by proof of facts that rationally explain the anomaly of the disappearance in a manner consistent with continued life." 368 F.2d 389 at 392.

The administrative law judge relied on the second manner of rebuttal, holding that due to "personal, legal and familial difficulties, the wage earner had sufficient justification for disappearing and changing his identity." To support this conclusion, the following were cited: (1) Fisher's failure to file federal income tax returns in 1967, 1968 and 1969; (2) a suggestion that he was trying to avoid child support payments; and (3) several random comments by the appellant and her children that there may have been minor family difficulties.

Plainly, these are not sufficient to satisfy the Secretary's rebuttal burden, and are not enough to justify a conclusion that Fisher engineered a phony disappearance in order to change his identity. The burden of the Secretary requires more than mere conjecture as to possible explanations, *Aubrey*, supra at 785; *Meza* at 393. Here, the Secretary did no more than present facts which hardly support a somewhat bizarre and certainly speculative conclusion. The judgment of the district court must be reversed, and remanded with directions to enter a contrary judgment in favor of the appellant.

Reversed and remanded with instructions.

---

1. Mrs. Autrey testified that she made an exhaustive search for her former husband by checking with state and federal agencies, nursing homes and hospitals, the Wage Earner's Union and other sources. The search was detailed in a letter to a Texas Congressman which has been incorporated in the record as an exhibit.

There was no testimony from any party as to contact with Fisher after his disappearance. Appellant stated that if the plane crashed in the Rocky Mountains, wreckage might never be found.

SHARP v. COOPERS & LYBRAND
649 F.2d 175 (3rd Cir. 1981)

[Class action by investors under Section 10(b) of the Securities Exchange Act of 1934, 15 U.S.C. §78j(b), and SEC Rule 10(b)(5) against accountant-defendants for alleged omissions and misrepresentations by the accountants in a tax opinion letter on oil and gas limited partnership. Judgment for plaintiffs at trial.]

V . . .

Appellant next argues that the trial judge erred in his instruction to the jury on reliance and in formulating the special interrogatory to the jury on that issue. The trial judge instructed the jury that the appellees were entitled to a rebuttable presumption of reliance.[14] In the special interrogatories to the jury regarding reliance, the trial court asked with respect to each named plaintiff: "Would [the plaintiff] have purchased his investment in the 1971 WMC Ohio Program . . . even if the truth had been told in defendant's opinion letter?" The jury answered in the negative with regard to each class representative. Appellant argues first that the court erred in creating a presumption of reliance favoring the appellees, and second that the effect of the interrogatory was to create an irrebuttable presumption of reliance. We conclude that in the circumstances presented by this case, which involves both misrepresentations and omissions, the district court correctly allowed a presumption of reliance. In addition, we find no support for appellant's assertion that the trial court employed an irrebuttable presumption. We therefore reject both arguments.

14. In his instruction to the jury on reliance, the trial judge said:
"In a case of this type it must be found that the plaintiff . . . relied on the misrepresentations or was influenced to the point of purchasing by the omission. . . .
"In this respect the plaintiffs are entitled to a presumption of reliance. . . . By a presumption we mean that a given fact is established by the establishment of certain other facts, thus putting upon the other side the duty to persuade you to the contrary.
"In this case where there are material omissions and where there are material omissions mingled with misrepresentations, the plaintiffs are presumed to rely upon the contents of that letter. Of course, the bottom line was that there would be a double tax deduction, but the others, the omissions in particular are woven into that conclusion that there would be a double tax deduction, when in fact of course there was not.
"When there is a presumption as there is here in that respect the defendant has the burden of going forward and persuading you by a fair preponderance of the evidence that the plaintiffs would have purchased the securities at the same price even had they known there was no double tax deduction; even had they known there would not be a bona fide loan; even had they known the other omissions that were in the letter. This is the defendant's burden." App. at 2682a-83a.

A

Reliance is an element of a plaintiff's action for damages under rule 10b-5. . . . Normally, a plaintiff suing under rule 10b-5 bears the burden of proving all the elements of his case. See McLean v. Alexander, 599 F.2d 1190, 1196-97 (3d Cir. 1979). Nevertheless, the necessity of an element to a valid claim does not determine the allocation of the burdens of going forward and persuasion with respect to that element.

The Supreme Court authoritatively addressed the requirement of proving reliance in rule 10b-5 actions in Affiliated Ute Citizens of Utah v. United States, 406 U.S. 128 (1972), stating:

"Under the circumstances of this case, involving primarily a failure to disclose, positive proof of reliance is not a prerequisite to recovery. All that is necessary is that the facts withheld be material in the sense that a reasonable investor might have considered them important in the making of this decision. This obligation to disclose and this withholding of a material fact establish the requisite element of causation in fact." Id. at 153-54 (citations omitted).

The Court has subsequently defined a material omission in the context of proxy statements under rule 14a-9 as "a substantial likelihood that a reasonable [investor] would consider it important. . . . [T]here must be a substantial likelihood that the disclosure of the omitted fact would have been viewed by the reasonable investor as having significantly altered the 'total mix' of information made available." TSC Industries, Inc. v. Northway, Inc., 426 U.S. 438, 449 (1976). We have held this standard of materiality applicable to rule 10b-5 actions as well. See Healey v. Catalyst Recovery of Pennsylvania, Inc., 616 F.2d 641, 647 (3d Cir. 1980); id., at 653 (Aldisert, J., dissenting). Affiliated Ute makes clear that in at least some situations a presumption of reliance in favor of the rule 10b-5 plaintiff is proper. See Rochez I, 491 F.2d at 410. Our present task is to determine whether that presumption was properly applied in this case.

Both parties in this case cite decisions indicating that the presumption of reliance is proper in cases of alleged omissions, whereas no presumption arises in cases of alleged misrepresentations. This distinction has led Coopers & Lybrand to argue that its wrongful conduct in this case arose from misrepresentations in the opinion letter, whereas the class representatives argue that the violation resulted from the appellant's failure to disclose certain material facts.

We have concluded that both misrepresentations and omissions are present in this case. The jury heard evidence that Coopers & Lybrand had misrepresented certain crucial facts in the letter, such as its disclaimer of verification of the facts on which the opinion letter was based and its assertion that cash supplemental to the limited partner's contributions would be borrowed "from suitable banks or other lending agencies. . . ." The jury also heard evidence that Coopers & Lybrand had failed to disclose certain material facts, such as the affiliation between the putative lender, the Bahamian bank, and WMC. A strict application of the omissions-misrepresentations dichotomy would require the trial judge to instruct the jury to presume reliance with regard to the omitted facts, and not to presume reliance with regard to the misrepresented facts. Although this resolution would have great appeal to graduate logicians in a classroom, we are not persuaded to adopt it for use in a courtroom.

B

We begin by embracing the obvious proposition recently stated by the second circuit: "We therefore presume reliance only 'where it is logical' to do so." Lewis v. McGraw, 619 F.2d 192, 195 (2d Cir. 1980) (action under §14(e) of the Williams Act, 15 U.S.C. §78n(e)), cert. denied, — U.S. — (1980). A steadfast rule requiring the defendant to refute a presumption of reliance would be neither equitable nor logical. The plaintiff traditionally assumes the burden of demonstrating causation. Only in unusual circumstances is this burden shifted from the plaintiff to the defendant. The reason for shifting the burden on the reliance issue has been an assumption that the plaintiff is generally incapable of proving that he relied on a material omission. Lewis v. McGraw, 619 F.2d at 195; Thomas v. Duralite Co., 524 F.2d at 585. This incapacity arises from the difficulty of proving a speculative state of facts: Had the facts not been omitted, would plaintiff have acted on the information made available and thereby averted his loss? But this observation does not justify a clear distinction between the treatment of misrepresentations and omissions. First, the defendant confronts the same problem of speculation in trying to refute the presumption of reliance because he possesses no more information on the plaintiff's hypothetical behavior than does the plaintiff. Second, the problem of speculation is not unique to situations in which omissions have occurred. In misrepresentation actions as well, proof of reliance requires a degree of speculation on the action that the plaintiff would have taken had no misrepresentation occurred. Therefore, we are unpersuaded that the existence of misrepresentations *and* omissions, without more, necessitates any particular treatment of the reliance issue.

A further consideration guides our decision. If we were to follow blindly the omission-misrepresentation distinction in this case, we would be compelled to require a dual jury instruction. The jury would be instructed to search for proof of reliance by the plaintiff with regard to the misrepresentations, and to search for proof of nonreliance by the defendant with regard to the omissions. The problems with such a complicated approach before a lay jury are legion. We conclude that the proper approach to the problem of reliance is to analyze the plaintiff's allegations, in light of the likely proof at trial, and determine the most reasonable placement of the burden of proof of reliance. . . . Such a flexible approach avoids the potential problems of a broad judicial pronouncement of a precept governing reliance.

We agree with the district court that the burden in this case should fall on Coopers & Lybrand. The opinion letter issued by Coopers & Lybrand was intended to influence the investment decisions of persons interested in WMC partnerships. The appellant undoubtedly foresaw that it would have that effect. As in *Affiliated Ute,* Coopers & Lybrand by its action facilitated the transactions at issue but failed to disclose certain facts. Its misrepresentation of other facts should not alleviate its burden of proving nonreliance. Considering the likelihood that investors would rely on the opinion letter, we conclude that the trial judge properly placed the burden of refuting a presumption of reliance on the appellant.

C

Although we agree with appellant that the presumption of reliance, when appropriate, is rebuttable, see Thomas v. Duralite Co., 524 F.2d at 585, we reject its argument that the interrogatories made the presumption irrebuttable. The interrogatories on reliance did not, to be sure, emphasize this point, but if the trial judge had intended to make the presumption irrebuttable, no interrogatories on reliance would have been submitted. In addition, the jury instructions made crystal clear that the presumption was rebuttable. We therefore find no error in the trial court's treatment of reliance.

PLOUGH, INC. v. THE MASON AND DIXON LINES
630 F.2d 468 (6th Cir. 1980)

LIVELY, J. This case deals with the burden of proof in an action by a shipper for injury to goods transported by a motor carrier. Following a non-jury trial, the district court found that the carrier had met its burden of proving that the goods of the shipper had an "inherent vice" and that the carrier was free of negligence, but that the shipper had failed to prove that the carrier had transported the goods in a soiled or defective trailer. We conclude that the district court misallocated the burden of proof and, accordingly, we vacate the judgment and remand for further proceedings.

I

Many of the facts were stipulated. The shipper, Plough, delivered two trailer loads — a total of 198,568 cans of Solarcaine spray to the Mason and Dixon Lines, Inc. (M-D) at Melford, Connecticut for transportation to Memphis, Tennessee. The cans of Solarcaine spray and their plastic caps were in apparent good condition when delivered to M-D. When the trailers arrived at Memphis the contents were inspected by Plough's quality control personnel. The plastic caps on the cans in the top two layers of shipping containers inside each trailer were found to be discolored. The Plough inspectors rejected both shipments. One of the trailers (No. 7413) was moved immediately after it was unloaded and it was never examined by Plough's employees. Before the second trailer (No. 7488) was unloaded, Plough inspectors found dirt inside the trailer, on its floor, sides and roof, which was similar to that found on the top two layers of Solarcaine cartons. A small hole was also found in the upper front end of trailer No. 7488. Plough shipped five loads of Solarcaine from Melford to Memphis in its own trailers at about the same time the M-D shipment was made. All seven loads were from the same lot. There were no soiled plastic caps in any of the loads carried in Plough's own trailers.

It was stipulated that the plastic caps on the aerosol cans of Solarcaine are conductors which may become charged with static electricity. When this occurs, the caps attract particles of dust and other contaminants from the air. The caps become discolored and unfit for commercial use if the atmosphere is sufficiently contaminated. During manufacture of the plastic caps used on the Plough product an antistatic agent was added to dissipate any electrostatic charge and thus prevent discoloration or other contamination.

Plough's inspectors ascribed the discoloration of the caps to "diesel smoke." There was evidence that the contamination in trailer No. 7488 was not diesel smoke, but general dust and dirt. The district court concluded from the presence of the hole and of excessive dust and dirt particles in the interior of trailer No. 7488 that "defendant has failed to establish its affirmative defenses with regard to damage occasioned to plaintiff's products." Concerning trailer No. 7413, M-D argued that the sole cause of the discoloration was the "inherent vice of the caps in that the antistatic agent used in them was ineffective." The district court found that no defect was noted in trailer No. 7413 comparable to the hole in No. 7488, and that there was no excessive dirt or dust inside it. Since it was conceded by Plough that an inherent characteristic of the plastic caps was the buildup of static electricity, the district court concluded that M-D should prevail on its affirmative defense of inherent vice with respect to trailer No. 7413. . . . Plough has appealed from the district court's denial of damages for the same costs incurred to bring the products transported in trailer No. 7413 up to commercial standards.

II

The 1906 Carmack Amendment to the Interstate Commerce Act, 49 U.S.C. §20(11), makes common carriers liable "for any loss, damage or injury" caused by such carriers to property received by them for transportation. The Supreme Court has construed the Carmack Amendment as follows: "[T]he statute codifies the common-law rule that a carrier, though not an absolute insurer, is liable for damage to goods transported by it unless it can show that the damage was caused by '(a) the act of God; (b) the public enemy; (c) the act of the shipper himself; (d) public authority; (e) or the inherent vice or nature of the goods.' " Missouri Pacific R.R. v. Elmore & Stahl, 377 U.S. 134, 137 (1964) (citations omitted).

The Court dealt with the burden of proof in such cases as follows: "Accordingly, under federal law, in an action to recover from a carrier for damage to a shipment, the shipper establishes his prima facie case when he shows delivery in good condition, arrival in damaged condition, and the amount of damages. Thereupon, the burden of proof is upon the carrier to show both that it was free from negligence and that the damage to the cargo was due to one of the excepted causes relieving the carrier of liability." Id. at 138 (citations omitted).

The district court appeared to recognize these standards in colloquy with counsel during the course of the trial. However, early in its memorandum opinion the court wrote: "When a shipper makes out a prima facie case of damages, as here, an *inference* of negligence or fault on the part of the carrier may be drawn, thereby *shifting to the carrier the burden of going forward with the proof* that the shipment was not in good condition and properly packed when received by the carrier, and/or that it was not damaged by carrier's fault when delivered to the consignee." Railway Express Agency v. Smith, 212 F.2d 47 (6th Cir. 1954); United States v. Central of Georgia Railway, 411 F. Supp. 1023 (E.D. Tenn. 1976).

In fact, the carrier's delivery of damaged goods which were in good condition when it received them created a presumption of negligence, not a mere inference. The burden which shifts to the carrier once a shipper makes out a prima facie case is not the burden of going forward with the evidence. It is the burden of proof which "shifts to the carrier and remains there." Super Service Motor Freight Co. v. United States, 350 F.2d 541, 543 (6th Cir. 1965). In order to avoid liability the carrier must then prove two things: that it was not negligent and that the *sole* cause of the injury was one of the five exceptions listed in *Elmore & Stahl,* supra. American Hoist & Derrick Co. v. Chicago, Milwaukee, St. Paul & Pacific R.R., 414 F.2d 68, 72 (6th Cir. 1969).

Though the evidence of the hole in the front and the excessive dirt inside trailer No. 7488 was relevant, it was not required in order for Plough to make out a prima facie case of liability. That was accomplished when the merchandise, undamaged when received by the carrier, was delivered to Plough in a damaged condition. In its order on motion for clarification the district court wrote:

"The Memorandum Opinion of the Court clearly granted recovery to plaintiff with regard to the shipment contained in Trailer #7488, but found that as to Trailer #7413, the defendant had met its burden of proving inherent vice and freedom from negligence, the plaintiff having failed to show, as to trailer #7413, that defendant had negligently transported the goods in a soiled or defective trailer."

The district court erred in requiring Plough to produce similar evidence as to trailer No. 7413 as a prerequisite to recovery. Once Plough made its prima facie case, M-D could avoid liability only by proving both that it was free of negligence and that the inherent qualities of the goods were the sole cause of the damage.

The judgment of the district court must be vacated for two deficiencies in the court's findings. At no point did the court find that the "inherent vice" of the product was the sole cause of the damage. Though the district court found that M-D was free of negligence, the language in the order on motion for clarification clearly appears to have placed the burden on the shipper to prove specific acts of negligence by the carrier. As Plough pointed out, its stipulation that the plastic caps were prone to build up static electricity did not relieve M-D of its two-fold burden of proving that the inherent quality of the caps was the sole cause of their discoloration and that the carrier did not create or permit an atmosphere within the trailer in which the static electricity led or contributed to this discoloration.

III

At oral argument counsel for M-D contended that this court should re-examine its holding in Super Service Motor Freight Co. v. United States, supra. We were urged to adopt the dissenting opinion in *Super Service* as the better reasoned interpretation of the Carmack Amendment.

Counsel for M-D also argued that Rule 301 of the Federal Rules of Evidence requires such a re-examination. . . . It is immediately apparent that Rule 301 does not affect the burden of proof in Carmack Amendment cases. For well articulated reasons Congress chose to place the burden of proof on a carrier in whose hands goods are damaged rather than on the shipper. This is more than a burden of going forward with the evidence. It is a true burden of proof in the sense of the risk of nonpersuasion and it remains on the carrier once the prima facie showing has been made.

The judgment of the district court is vacated and the cause is remanded for further consideration and findings in the light of this opinion.

SINDELL v. ABBOTT LABORATORIES
26 Cal. 3d 588, 163 Cal. Rptr. 132, 607 P.2d 924 (1980)

Mosk, J. This case involves a complex problem both timely and significant; may a plaintiff, injured as the result of a drug administered to her mother during pregnancy, who knows the type of drug involved but cannot identify the manufacturer of the precise product, hold liable for her injuries a maker of a drug produced from an identical formula?

Plaintiff Judith Sindell brought an action against eleven drug companies and Does 1 through 100, on behalf of herself and other women similarly situated. The complaint alleges as follows:

Between 1941 and 1971, defendants were engaged in the business of manufacturing, promoting, and marketing diethylstilbesterol (DES), a drug which is a synthetic compound of the female hormone estrogen. The drug was administered to plaintiff's mother and the mothers of the class she represents,[1] for the purpose of preventing miscarriage. In 1947, the Food and Drug Administration authorized the marketing of DES as a miscarriage preventative, but only on an experimental basis, with a requirement that the drug contain a warning label to that effect.

DES may cause cancerous vaginal and cervical growths in the daughters exposed to it before birth, because their mothers took the drug during pregnancy. The form of cancer from which these daughters suffer is known as adenocarcinoma, and it manifests itself after a minimum latent period of 10 or 12 years. It is a fast-spreading and deadly disease, and radical surgery is required to prevent it from spreading. DES also causes adenosis, precancerous vaginal and cervical growths which may spread to other areas of the body. The treatment for adenosis is cauterization, surgery, or cryosurgery. Women who suffer from this condition must be monitored by biopsy or colposcopic examination twice a year, a painful and expensive procedure. Thousands of women whose mothers received DES during pregnancy are unaware of the effects of the drug. . . .

---

1. The plaintiff class alleged consists of "girls and women who are residents of California and who have been exposed to DES before birth and who may or may not know that fact or the dangers" to which they were exposed. Defendants are also sued as representatives of a class of drug manufacturers which sold DES after 1941.

Defendants demurred to the complaint. While the complaint did not expressly allege that plaintiff could not identify the manufacturer of the precise drug ingested by her mother, she stated in her points and authorities in opposition to the demurrers filed by some of the defendants that she was unable to make the identification, and the trial court sustained the demurrers of these defendants without leave to amend on the ground that plaintiff did not and stated she could not identify which defendant had manufactured the drug responsible for her injuries. Thereupon, the court dismissed the action. This appeal involves only five of ten defendants named in the complaint. . . .

This case is but one of a number filed throughout the country seeking to hold drug manufacturers liable for injuries allegedly resulting from DES prescribed to the plaintiffs' mothers since 1947. According to a note in the Fordham Law Review, estimates of the number of women who took the drug during pregnancy range from 1½ million to 3 million. Hundreds, perhaps thousands, of the daughters of these women suffer from adenocarcinoma, and the incidence of vaginal adenosis among them is 30 to 90 percent. (Comment, DES and a Proposed Theory of Enterprise Liability (1978) 46 Fordham L. Rev. 963, 964-967 [hereafter Fordham Comment].) Most of the cases are still pending. With two exceptions, those that have been decided resulted in judgments in favor of the drug company defendants because of the failure of the plaintiffs to identify the manufacturer of the DES prescribed to their mothers. The same result was reached in a recent California case. (McCreery v. Eli Lilly & Co. (1978) 87 Cal. App. 3d 77, 82-84, 150 Cal. Rptr. 730.) The present action is another attempt to overcome this obstacle to recovery.

We begin with the proposition that, as a general rule, the imposition of liability depends upon a showing by the plaintiff that his or her injuries were caused by the act of the defendant or by an instrumentality under the defendant's control. . . .

There are, however, exceptions to this rule. Plaintiff's complaint suggests several bases upon which defendants may be held liable for her injuries even though she cannot demonstrate the name of the manufacturer which produced the DES actually taken by her mother. The first of these theories, classically illustrated by Summers v. Tice (1948) 33 Cal. 2d 80, 199 P.2d 1, places the burden of proof of causation upon tortious defendants in certain circumstances. The second basis of liability emerging from the complaint is that defendants acted in concert to cause injury to plaintiff. There is a third and novel approach to the problem, sometimes called the theory of "enterprise liability," but which we prefer to designate by the more accurate term of "industry-wide" liability,[9]

---

9. The term "enterprise liability" is sometimes used broadly to mean that losses caused

which might obviate the necessity for identifying the manufacturer of the injury-causing drug. We shall conclude that these doctrines, as previously interpreted, may not be applied to hold defendants liable under the allegations of this complaint. However, we shall propose and adopt a fourth basis for permitting the action to be tried, grounded upon an extension of the *Summers* doctrine.

I

Plaintiff places primary reliance upon cases which hold that if a party cannot identify which of two or more defendants caused an injury, the burden of proof may shift to the defendants to show that they were not responsible for the harm. This principle is sometimes referred to as the "alternative liability" theory.

The celebrated case of Summers v. Tice, supra, 33 Cal. 2d 80, 199 P.2d 1, a unanimous opinion of this court, best exemplifies the rule. In *Summers,* the plaintiff was injured when two hunters negligently shot in his direction. It could not be determined which of them had fired the shot which actually caused the injury to the plaintiff's eye, but both defendants were nevertheless held jointly and severally liable for the whole of the damages. We reasoned that both were wrongdoers, both were negligent toward the plaintiff, and that it would be unfair to require plaintiff to isolate the defendant responsible, because if the one pointed out were to escape liability, the other might also, and the plaintiff-victim would be shorn of any remedy. In these circumstances, we held, the burden of proof shifted to the defendants, "each to absolve himself if he can." (Id., p. 86, 199 P.2d p.4.) . . .

In *Summers,* we relied upon Ybarra v. Spangard (1944) 25 Cal. 2d 486, 154 P.2d 687. There, the plaintiff was injured while he was unconscious during the course of surgery. He sought damages against several doctors and a nurse who attended him while he was unconscious. We held that it would be unreasonable to require him to identify the particular defendant who had performed the alleged negligent act because he was unconscious at the time of the injury and the defendants exercised control over the instrumentalities which caused the harm. Therefore, under the doctrine of res ipsa loquitur, an inference of negligence arose that defendants were required to meet by explaining their conduct. . . .

Defendants assert that these principles are inapplicable here. First, they insist that a predicate to shifting the burden of proof under *Summers-Ybarra* is that the defendants must have greater access to information regarding the cause of the injuries than the plaintiff, whereas in the present case the reverse appears.

---

by an enterprise should be borne by it. (Klemme Enterprise Liability (1976) 47 Colo. L. Rev. 153, 158.)

Plaintiff does not claim that defendants are in a better position than she to identify the manufacturer of the drug taken by her mother or, indeed, that they have the ability to do so at all, but argues, rather, that *Summers* does not impose such a requirement as a condition to the shifting of the burden of proof. In this respect we believe plaintiff is correct. . . .

Here, as in *Summers,* the circumstances of the injury appear to render identification of the manufacturer of the drug ingested by plaintiff's mother impossible by either plaintiff or defendants, and it cannot reasonably be said that one is in a better position than the other to make the identification. Because many years elapsed between the time the drug was taken and the manifestation of plaintiff's injuries she, and many other daughters of mothers who took DES, are unable to make such identification. Certainly there can be no implication that plaintiff is at fault in failing to do so — the event occurred while plaintiff was in utero, a generation ago.

On the other hand, it cannot be said with assurance that defendants have the means to make the identification. In this connection, they point out that drug manufacturers ordinarily have no direct contact with the patients who take a drug prescribed by their doctors. Defendants sell to wholesalers, who in turn supply the product to physicians and pharmacies. Manufacturers do not maintain records of the persons who take the drugs they produce, and the selection of the medication is made by the physician rather than the manufacturer. Nor do we conclude that the absence of evidence on this subject is due to the fault of defendants. While it is alleged that they produced a defective product with delayed effects and without adequate warnings, the difficulty or impossibility of identification results primarily from the passage of time rather than from their allegedly negligent acts of failing to provide adequate warnings. . . .

It is important to observe, however, that while defendants do not have means superior to plaintiff to identify the maker of the precise drug taken by her mother, they may in some instances be able to prove that they did not manufacture the injury-causing substance. In the present case, for example, one of the original defendants was dismissed from the action upon proof that it did not manufacture DES until after plaintiff was born. . . . Nevertheless, plaintiff may not prevail in her claim that the *Summers* rationale should be employed to fix the whole liability for her injuries upon defendants, at least as those principles have previously been applied. There is an important difference between the situation involved in *Summers* and the present case. There, all the parties who were or could have been responsible for the harm to the plaintiff were joined as defendants. Here, by contrast, there are approximately 200 drug companies which made DES, any of which might have manufactured the injury-producing drug.

Defendants maintain that, while in *Summers* there was a 50 percent chance that one of the two defendants was responsible for the plaintiff's injuries, here since any one of 200 companies which manufactured DES might have made the product which harmed plaintiff, there is no rational basis upon which to infer that any defendant in this action caused plaintiff's injuries, nor even a reasonable possibility that they were responsible.

These arguments are persuasive if we measure the chance that any one of the defendants supplied the injury-causing drug by the number of possible tortfeasors. In such a context, the possibility that any of the five defendants supplied the DES to plaintiff's mother is so remote that it would be unfair to require each defendant to exonerate itself. There may be a substantial likelihood that none of the five defendants joined in the action made the DES which caused the injury, and that the offending producer not named would escape liability altogether. While we propose, infra, an adaptation of the rule in *Summers* which will substantially overcome these difficulties, defendants appear to be correct that the rule, as previously applied, cannot relieve plaintiff of the burden of proving the identity of the manufacturer which made the drug causing her injuries. . . .

III

A [further] theory upon which plaintiff relies is the concept of industry-wide liability, or according to the terminology of the parties, "enterprise liability." This theory was suggested in Hall v. E. I. DuPont de Nemours & Co., Inc. (E.D.N.Y. 1972) 345 F. Supp. 353. In that case, plaintiffs were 13 children injured by the explosion of blasting caps in 12 separate incidents which occurred in 10 different states between 1955 and 1959. The defendants were six blasting cap manufacturers, comprising virtually the entire blasting cap industry in the United States, and their trade association. There were, however, a number of Canadian blasting cap manufacturers which could have supplied the caps. The gravamen of the complaint was that the practice of the industry of omitting a warning on individual blasting caps and of failing to take other safety measures created an unreasonable risk of harm, resulting in the plaintiffs' injuries. The complaint did not identify a particular manufacturer of a cap which caused a particular injury.

The court reasoned as follows: there was evidence that defendants, acting independently, had adhered to an industry-wide standard with regard to the safety features of blasting caps, that they had in effect delegated some functions of safety investigation and design, such as labelling, to their trade association, and that there was industry-wide cooperation in the manufacture and design of blasting caps. In these circumstances, the evidence supported a conclusion that all the defendants jointly controlled the risk. Thus, if plaintiffs could establish by a preponderance of the evidence that the caps were manufactured by one of the defendants, the burden of proof as to the causation would shift to all the defendants. The court noted that this theory of liability applied to industries composed of a small number of units, and that what would be fair and reasonable with regard to an industry of five or ten producers might be manifestly unreasonable if applied to a decentralized industry composed of countless small producers.

Plaintiff attempts to state a cause of action under the rationale of *Hall*. She alleges joint enterprise and collaboration among defendants in the production, marketing, promotion and testing of DES, and "concerted promulgation and adherence to industry-wide testing, safety, warning and efficacy standards" for the drug. We have concluded above that allegations that defendants relied upon one another's testing and promotion methods do not state a cause of action for concerted conduct to commit a tortious act. Under the theory of industry-wide liability, however, each manufacturer could be liable for all injuries caused by DES by virtue of adherence to an industry-wide standard of safety. . . .

We decline to apply this theory in the present case. At least 200 manufacturers produced DES; *Hall*, which involved 6 manufacturers representing the entire blasting cap industry in the United States, cautioned against application of the doctrine espoused therein to a large number of producers. (345 F. Supp. at p. 378). Moreover, in *Hall*, the conclusion that the defendants jointly controlled the risk was based upon allegations that they had delegated some functions relating to safety to a trade association. There are no such allegations here, and we have concluded above that plaintiff has failed to allege liability on a concert of action theory. . . .

IV

If we were confined to the theories of *Summers* and *Hall*, we would be constrained to hold that the judgment must be sustained. Should we require that plaintiff identify the manufacturer which supplied the DES used by her mother or that all DES manufacturers be joined in the action, she would effectively be precluded from any recovery. As defendants candidly admit, there is little likelihood that all the manufacturers who made DES at the time in question are still in business or that they are subject to the jurisdiction of the California courts. There are, however, forceful arguments in favor of holding that plaintiff has a cause of action. . . .

The most persuasive reason for finding plaintiff states a cause of action is that advanced in *Summers*: as between an innocent plaintiff and negligent defendants, the latter should bear the cost of the injury. Here, as in *Summers*, plaintiff is not at fault in failing to provide evidence of causation, and although the absence of such evidence is not attributable to the defendants either, their conduct in marketing a drug the effects of which are delayed for many years played a significant role in creating the unavailability of proof.

From a broader policy standpoint, defendants are better able to bear the cost of injury resulting from the manufacture of a defective product. As was said by Justice Traynor in *Escola,* "[t]he cost of an injury and the loss of time or health may be an overwhelming misfortune to the person injured, and a needless one, for the risk of injury can be insured by the manufacturer and distributed among the public as a cost of doing business." The manufacturer is in the best position to discover and guard against defects in its products and to warn of harmful effects; thus, holding it liable for defects and failure to warn of harmful effects will provide an incentive to product safety. (Cronin v. J. B. E. Olson Corp. (1972) 8 Cal. 3d 121, 129, 104 Cal. Rptr. 433, 501 P.2d 1153; Beech Aircraft Corp. v. Superior Court (1976) 61 Cal. App. 3d 501, 522-523, 132 Cal. Rptr. 541.) These considerations are particularly significant where medication is involved, for the consumer is virtually helpless to protect himself from serious, sometimes permanent, sometimes fatal, injuries caused by deleterious drugs.

Where, as here, all defendants produced a drug from an identical formula and the manufacturer of the DES which caused plaintiff's injuries cannot be identified through no fault of plaintiff, a modification of the rule of *Summers* is warranted. As we have seen, an undiluted *Summers* rationale is inappropriate to shift the burden of proof of causation to defendants because if we measure the chance that any particular manufacturer supplied the injury-causing product by the number of producers of DES, there is a possibility that none of the five defendants in this case produced the offending substance and that the responsible manufacturer, not named in the action, will escape liability.

But we approach the issue of causation from a different perspective: we hold it to be reasonable in the present context to measure the likelihood that any of the defendants supplied the product which allegedly injured plaintiff by the percentage which the DES sold by each of them for the purpose of preventing miscarriage bears to the entire production of the drug sold by all for that purpose. Plaintiff asserts in her briefs that Eli Lilly and Company and 5 or 6 other companies produced 90 percent of the DES marketed. If at trial this is established to be the fact, then there is a corresponding likelihood that this comparative handful of producers manufactured the DES which caused plaintiff's injuries, and only a 10 percent likelihood that the offending producer would escape liability.

If plaintiff joins in the action the manufacturers of a substantial share of the DES which her mother might have taken, the injustice of shifting the burden of proof to defendants to demonstrate that they could not have made the substance which injured plaintiff is significantly diminished. While 75 to 80 percent of the market is suggested as the requirement . . . , we hold only that a substantial percentage is required.

The presence in the action of a substantial share of the appropriate market also provides a ready means to apportion damages among the defendants. Each defendant will be held liable for the proportion of the judgment represented by its share of that market unless it demonstrates that it could not have made the product which caused plaintiff's injuries. In the present case, as we have seen, one DES manufacturer was dismissed from the action upon filing a declaration that it had not manufactured DES until after plaintiff was born. Once plaintiff has met her burden of joining the required defendants, they in turn may crosscomplaint against other DES manufacturers, not joined in the action, which they can allege might have supplied the injury-causing product.

Under this approach, each manufacturer's liability would approximate its responsibility for the injuries caused by its own products. Some minor discrepancy in the correlation between market share and liability is inevitable; therefore, a defendant may be held liable for a somewhat different percentage of the damage than its share of the appropriate market would justify. It is probably impossible, with the passage of time, to determine market share with mathematical exactitude. But just as a jury cannot be expected to determine the precise relationship between fault and liability in applying the doctrine of comparative fault (Li v. Yellow Cab Co. (1975) 13 Cal. 3d 804, 119 Cal. Rptr. 858, 532 P.2d 1226) or partial indemnity (American Motorcycle Ass'n v. Superior Court (1978) 20 Cal. 3d 578, 146 Cal. Rptr. 182, 578 P.2d 899), the difficulty of apportioning damages among the defendant producers in exact relation to their market share does not seriously militate against the rule we adopt. As we said in *Summers* with regard to the liability of independent tortfeasors, where a correct division of liability cannot be made "the trier of fact may make it the best it can." (33 Cal. 2d at p.88, 199 P.2d at p.5.)

We are not unmindful of the practical problems involved in defining the market and determining market share, but these are largely matters of proof which properly cannot be determined at the pleading stage of these proceedings. Defendants urge that it would be both unfair and contrary to public policy to hold them liable for plaintiff's injuries in the absence of proof that one of them supplied the drug responsible for the damage. Most of their arguments, however, are based upon the assumption that one manufacturer would be held responsible for the products of another or for those of all other manufacturers if plaintiff ultimately prevails. But under the rule we adopt, each manufacturer's liability for an injury would be approximately equivalent to the damages caused by the DES it manufactured.

The judgments are reversed.

Bird, C.J., and Newman and White, JJ., concur.

E.   Allocation and Presumptions in Criminal Cases

Problem IX-9
Criminal Allocation in Idylia

The Idylia constitution, like our own, is interpreted to require the prosecution in criminal cases to prove each and every element of a criminal offense beyond reasonable doubt. See In re Winship, 397 U.S. 358 (1970). But what is an "element" to which this mandate applies?

Idylia has adopted a criminal statute that defines the offense of first-degree touching. The elements of this offense, to be proved by the prosecution beyond reasonable doubt, are (1) a touching, (2) lack of consent of the touchee, and (3) intent. Conviction of first-degree touching carries a penalty of life imprisonment. The defendant may present various affirmative defenses, as follows:

(1) The touching was not premeditated (this reduces the offense to second degree, with a maximum penalty of 20 years);

(2) The touching did not result in the touchee's death (this reduces the offense to third degree, with a maximum penalty of 10 years); and

(3) The touching did not result in serious bodily harm (this reduces the offense to fourth degree, with a maximum penalty of one year).

Is this statute constitutional? Could Idylia have gone even further and made consent to the touching a defense? Consider these questions in light of the next two cases and the commentary that follows.

MULLANEY v. WILBUR
421 U.S. 684 (1975)

Mr. Justice POWELL delivered the opinion of the Court.

The State of Maine requires a defendant charged with murder to prove that he acted "in the heat of passion on sudden provocation" in order to reduce the homicide to manslaughter. We must decide whether this rule comports with the due process requirement, as defined in In re Winship, 397 U.S. 358, 364 (1970), that the prosecution prove beyond a reasonable doubt every fact necessary to constitute the crime charged. . . .

Petitioners, the warden of the Maine Prison and the State of Maine, argue that . . . Winship should not be extended to the present case. They note that as a formal matter the absence of the heat of passion on sudden provocation is not a "fact necessary to constitute the *crime*" of felonious homicide in Maine. In re Winship, 397 U.S., at 364 (emphasis supplied). This distinction is relevant, according to petitioners, because in *Winship* the facts at issue were essential to establish criminality in the first instance, whereas the fact in question here does not come into play until the jury already has determined that the defendant is guilty and may be punished at least for manslaughter. . . . In short, petitioners would limit *Winship* to those facts which, if not proved, would wholly exonerate the defendant.

This analysis fails to recognize that the criminal law of Maine, like that of other jurisdictions, is concerned not only with guilt or innocence in the abstract but also with the degree of criminal culpability. Maine has chosen to distinguish those who kill in the heat of passion from those who kill in the absence of this factor. Because the former are less "blameworth[y]," State v. Lafferty, 309 A.2d, at 671, 673 (concurring opinion), they are subject to substantially less severe penalties. By drawing this distinction, while refusing to require the prosecution to establish beyond a reasonable doubt the fact upon which it turns, Maine denigrates the interests found critical in *Winship*.

The safeguards of due process are not rendered unavailing simply because a determination may already have been reached that would stigmatize the defendant and that might lead to a significant impairment of personal liberty. The fact remains that the consequences resulting from a verdict of murder, as compared with a verdict of manslaughter, differ significantly. Indeed, when viewed in terms of the potential difference in restrictions of personal liberty attendant to each conviction, the distinction established by Maine between murder and manslaughter may be of greater importance than the difference between guilt or innocence for many lesser crimes.

Moreover, if *Winship* were limited to those facts that constitute a crime as defined by state law, a State could undermine many of the interests that decision sought to protect without effecting any substantive change in its law. It would only be necessary to redefine the elements that constitute different crimes, characterizing them as factors that bear solely on the extent of punishment. . . .

Winship is concerned with substance rather than this kind of formalism. . . .

PATTERSON v. NEW YORK
432 U.S. 197 (1977)

Mr. Justice WHITE delivered the opinion of the Court.

The question here is the constitutionality under the Fourteenth Amendment's Due Process Clause of burdening the defendant in a New York State murder trial with proving the affirmative defense of extreme emotional disturbance as defined by New York law. . . .

We decline to adopt as a constitutional imperative, operative countrywide, that a State must disprove beyond a reasonable doubt every fact

constituting any and all affirmative defenses related to the culpability of
an accused. Traditionally, due process has required that only the most
basic procedural safeguards be observed; more subtle balancing of society's interests against those of the accused have been left to the legislative
branch. We therefore will not disturb the balance struck in previous
cases holding that the Due Process Clause requires the prosecution to
prove beyond a reasonable doubt all of the elements included in the
definition of the offense of which the defendant is charged. Proof of the
non-existence of all affirmative defenses has never been constitutionally
required; and we perceive no reason to fashion such a rule in this case
and apply it to the statutory defense at issue here.

This view may seem to permit state legislatures to reallocate burdens
of proof by labeling as affirmative defenses at least some elements of the
crimes now defined in their statutes. But there are obviously constitutional limits beyond which the States may not go in this regard. "[I]t is
not within the province of a legislature to declare an individual guilty or
presumptively guilty of a crime." McFarland v. American Sugar Rfg.
Co., 241 U.S. 79, 86 (1916). The legislature cannot "validly command
that the finding of an indictment, or mere proof of the identity of the
accused, should create a presumption of the existence of all the facts
essential to guilt." Tot v. United States, 319 U.S. 463, 469 (1943). . . .

It is urged that Mullaney v. Wilbur necessarily invalidates Patterson's
conviction. In *Mullaney* the charge was murder, which the Maine statute
defined as the unlawful killing of a human being "with malice aforethought, either express or implied." The trial court instructed the jury
that the words "malice aforethought" were most important because
"malice aforethought is an essential and indispensable element of the
crime of murder." Malice, as the statute indicated and as the court instructed, could be implied and was to be implied from "any deliberate,
cruel act committed by one person against another suddenly . . . or
without a considerable provocation," in which event an intentional
killing was murder unless by a preponderance of the evidence it was
shown that the act was committed "in the heat of passion, on sudden
provocation." The instructions emphasized that " 'malice aforethought
and heat of passion on sudden provocation are two inconsistent things';
thus, by proving the latter the defendant would negate the former." 421
U.S., at 686-687. . . .

Mullaney's holding, it is argued, is that the State may not permit the
blameworthiness of an act or the severity of punishment authorized for
its commission to depend on the presence or absence of an identified
fact without assuming the burden of proving the presence or absence of
that fact, as the case may be, beyond a reasonable doubt. In our view, the
Mullaney holding should not be so broadly read. . . .

Mullaney surely held that a State must prove every ingredient of an
offense beyond a reasonable doubt, and that it may not shift the burden

of proof to the defendant by presuming that ingredient upon proof of the other elements of the offense. This is true even though the State's practice, as in Maine, had been traditionally to the contrary. Such shifting of the burden of persuasion with respect to a fact which the State deems so important that it must be either proved or presumed is impermissible under the Due Process Clause.

It was unnecessary to go further in *Mullaney*. The Maine Supreme Judicial Court made it clear that malice aforethought, which was mentioned in the statutory definition of the crime, was not equivalent to premeditation and that the presumption of malice traditionally arising in intentional homicide cases carried no factual meaning insofar as premeditation was concerned. Even so, a killing became murder in Maine when it resulted from a deliberate, cruel act committed by one person against another, "suddenly without any, or without a considerable provocation." State v. Lafferty, supra, at 665. Premeditation was not within the definition of murder; but malice, in the sense of the absence of provocation, was part of the definition of that crime. Yet malice, i.e., lack of provocation, was presumed and could be rebutted by the defendant only by proving by a preponderance of the evidence that he acted with heat of passion upon sudden provocation. In *Mullaney* we held that however traditional this mode of proceeding might have been, it is contrary to the Due Process Clause as construed in *Winship*.

As we have explained, nothing was presumed or implied against Patterson; and his conviction is not invalid under any of our prior cases. The judgment of the New York Court of Appeals is affirmed.

Mr. Justice REHNQUIST took no part in the consideration or decision of this case.

Mr. Justice POWELL, with whom Mr. Justice BRENNAN and Mr. Justice MARSHALL join, dissenting.

In the name of preserving legislative flexibility, the Court today drains In re Winship, 397 U.S. 358 (1970), of much of its vitality. Legislatures do require broad discretion in the drafting of criminal laws, but the Court surrenders to the legislative branch a significant part of its responsibility to protect the presumption of innocence. . . .

Mullaney held invalid Maine's requirement that the defendant prove heat of passion. The Court today, without disavowing the unanimous holding of *Mullaney*, approves New York's requirement that the defendant prove extreme emotional disturbance. The Court manages to run a constitutional boundary line through the barely visible space that separates Maine's law from New York's. It does so on the basis of distinctions in language that are formalistic rather than substantive.

This result is achieved by a narrowly literal parsing of the holding in *Winship*: "[T]he Due Process Clause protects the accused against conviction except upon proof beyond a reasonable doubt of every fact necessary to constitute the crime with which he is charged." 397 U.S., at 364. The only "facts" necessary to constitute a crime are said to be those that appear on the face of the statute as a part of the definition of the crime. Maine's statute was invalid, the Court reasons, because it "defined [murder] as the unlawful killing of a human being 'with malice aforethought, either express or implied.'" Ante, at 212. "[M]alice," the Court reiterates, "in the sense of the absence of provocation, was part of the definition of that crime." Ante, at 216. *Winship* was violated only because this "fact" — malice — was "presumed" unless the defendant persuaded the jury otherwise by showing that he acted in the heat of passion. New York, in form presuming no affirmative "fact" against Patterson, and blessed with a statute drafted in the leaner language of the 20th century, escapes constitutional scrutiny unscathed even though the effect on the defendant of New York's placement of the burden of persuasion is exactly the same as Maine's.

This explanation of the *Mullaney* holding bears little resemblance to the basic rationale of that decision. But this is not the cause of greatest concern. The test the Court today establishes allows a legislature to shift, virtually at will, the burden of persuasion with respect to any factor in a criminal case, so long as it is careful not to mention the nonexistence of that factor in the statutory language that defines the crime. The sole requirement is that any references to the factor be confined to those sections that provide for an affirmative defense. . . .

With all respect, this type of constitutional adjudication is indefensibly formalistic. A limited but significant check on possible abuses in the criminal law now becomes an exercise in arid formalities. What *Winship* and *Mullaney* had sought to teach about the limits a free society places on its procedures to safeguard the liberty of its citizens becomes a rather simplistic lesson in statutory draftsmanship. Nothing in the Court's opinion prevents a legislature from applying this new learning to many of the classical elements of the crimes it punishes. It would be preferable, if the Court has found reason to reject the rationale of *Winship* and *Mullaney*, simply and straightforwardly to overrule those precedents.

The Court understandably manifests some uneasiness that its formalistic approach will give legislatures too much latitude in shifting the burden of persuasion. And so it issues a warning that "there are obviously constitutional limits beyond which the States may not go in this regard." Ante, at 210. The Court thereby concedes that legislative abuses may occur and that they must be curbed by the judicial branch. But if the State is careful to conform to the drafting formulas articulated today, the constitutional limits are anything but "obvious." This decision simply leaves us without a conceptual framework for distinguishing abuses from legitimate legislative adjustments of the burden of persuasion in criminal cases. . . .

ALLEN, STRUCTURING JURY DECISIONMAKING IN CRIMINAL CASES: A UNIFIED CONSTITUTIONAL APPROACH TO EVIDENTIARY DEVICES
94 Harv. L. Rev. 321, 338-353 (1980)

[T]he superficially distinct evidentiary devices employed in criminal trials — affirmative defenses, placement of burdens of production and the concomitant possibility of a directed verdict on an issue, judicial comment on the evidence, and instructions on presumptions and inferences — are actually very similar. Their primary unifying trait is that they all modify the evidentiary relationship of the parties at trial by manipulating burdens of persuasion. Affirmative defenses and burdens of production manipulate the relative burden of persuasion explicitly, while the other devices do so implicitly.

Moreover, these devices cannot be distinguished on the basis of the magnitude of their effect on the burden of persuasion, for that effect unmistakably varies within each category. Comments on the evidence, or presumptive instructions, may be very influential with a jury, and thus have a great impact on the relative burden of persuasion, or may have little influence and little or no effect on the relative burden. Similarly, one affirmative defense may be much easier to establish than another, even though the formal burden of persuasion is the same in both cases. Moreover, instructions that comment on the evidence, either explicitly or implicitly, involve essentially the same problems of ensuring the accuracy of the comment. Both explicit judicial comment and presumptive instructions may enhance the likelihood of a correct outcome; but both may also do just the opposite, thereby unconstitutionally abridging the defendant's right to have the state prove its case against him beyond a reasonable doubt.

Finally, the detrimental impact on the defendant does not adequately distinguish any of these evidentiary devices. Compare, for example, shifts in burdens of "persuasion" and "production." As a rule, it may be more damaging to a defendant to have to prove something by a preponderance of the evidence instead of to some lower degree. If, however, the defendant has access to little or no convincing evidence on an issue, he will not be able to meet either standard. Similarly, the prevailing view that shifts in burdens of persuasion are more damaging than instructions on inferences seems erroneous. A shift in the explicit burden of persuasion conceivably may have no impact upon the outcome. If, for example, after all the evidence is in, the jury would conclude that there is a sixty-five percent chance that the defendant committed a homicide in the heat of passion, then the result will be the same — mitigation to manslaughter — regardless of whether the state has to prove the absence of provocation beyond reasonable doubt or the defendant has to establish it by a preponderance of the evidence. By contrast, judicial comment on that evidence conceivably could cause the same jury to find that provocation has been disproven beyond reasonable doubt.

The actual effect in a particular case of any of the evidentiary devices discussed above is an empirical question that probably is not subject to very satisfactory empirical investigation, but the devices all share the function of allocating burdens of persuasion to the state and to the defendant. Consequently, they all raise essentially the same two issues, despite the diversity of their manifestations in the current case law. The first issue is the compatibility of the devices with In re Winship's imposition of the reasonable doubt standard as a constitutional mandate. The second is the effect of the devices on our conception of the right to a jury trial.

Because of the functional similarity of these devices, a unified analysis of their constitutionality can be developed. . . .

Such a framework can be constructed by asking three fundamental questions. The first two questions respond specifically to *Winship*'s requirement of proof beyond a reasonable doubt, and the last relates to both *Winship* and the right to a jury trial. First, we must determine whether the evidentiary device has a favorable or unfavorable effect on the defendant's case, since there is no danger of the state's burden being lowered and therefore no question of constitutionality if the effect is favorable. Second, if the effect is unfavorable, we must establish whether the device affects a fact that the state is constitutionally required to demonstrate as an element of criminality. This step is a necessary part of the analysis because imposing a constitutional standard of proof makes sense *only* if it is linked to a theory that indicates what facts constitutionally must be proved under the standard; otherwise, the standard could be circumvented by a state choosing to redefine the factual elements constituting a crime. The third step of this analysis, which applies if the fact affected is one that the state cannot constitutionally remove from its definition of the crime in question, is to ask whether the device amounts to an accurate judicial comment on the evidence. Manipulations of the burden of persuasion are permitted *only* if the device moves the jury toward a more rational, accurate result. This last inquiry guards against undermining the jury's fact-finding role, and ensures that the jury does not reach its conclusion on the basis of inaccurate commentary that would lower the state's burden of proof.

A. A FAVORABLE EFFECT

The first standard applicable to the evidentiary devices is obvious and requires no extended discussion. If a state employs an evidentiary device that is favorable to a defendant, it should not be struck down on constitutional grounds. "Favorable" in this context means only that the explicit burden of persuasion on the issue involved remains with the government at least to the level of beyond reasonable doubt, and that the comment, whether accurate or not, tends to dispose the jury more in favor of the defendant on that issue than the jury would have been without the comment. Under such circumstances, a defendant has no basis for complaint. The constitutionally required burden of persuasion has been maintained, and the jury's evaluation of the factual issue will be at least as fair as he has a right to expect.

B. THE CONSTITUTIONAL NECESSITY OF PROVING THE FACT IN ISSUE

In the second step of the analysis, the nature of a particular fact in issue is examined to determine whether it is one that the state is required by the Constitution to prove beyond a reasonable doubt. Because forcing a defendant to bear the burden of persuasion in proving facts that establish a defense is functionally the same as requiring the state to prove the absence of those facts, constitutional analysis must not depend upon whether a state legislature chose to label a factual issue a defense or an "element of the offense." Without some substantive restriction on a legislature's discretion to define crime, *Winship* may be eviscerated. Therefore, step two inquires whether the state has increased the defendant's relative burden of persuasion with respect to an issue that is critical to culpability. . . .

Commentators who advocate the substantive due process test argue that "in evaluating the constitutionality of an affirmative defense, the ultimate question should be whether the issue is so critical to culpability that it would offend 'the deepest notions of what is fair and right and just' to obtain a conviction where a reasonable doubt remains as to that issue." To say that a fact "so critical to culpability" has not been proven beyond reasonable doubt, however, is simply another way of saying that the conditions for imposing punishment have not been satisfied. To subject a person to substantial punishment when such a critical fact has not been proven beyond reasonable doubt would distort the relationship between what the defendant has been proven to have done and what the state does to him. Unmistakably, this "due process" test is yet another manifestation of the concern that a proper relationship between crime and punishment be maintained, and thus is simply a variation on the theme of maintaining proportionate punishment. . . .

If the Constitution does not limit a state's ability simply to remove a particular element from the definition of criminality, there is no point in attempting to limit the state's power to shift the burden as to that element by creating an affirmative defense; nor, for that matter, is there any point in forbidding jury instructions that permit an element to be "presumed" on the basis of some other fact that lacks a rational relationship with that element. . . . [I]t seems to me that if a state limits its manipulation of burdens of persuasion to issues that need not be proved under the eighth amendment's proportionality standard or principles of substantive fairness imposed by due process, then whatever the state does should be acceptable. If, by contrast, the state manipulates a burden on an issue that constitutionally it must establish, then it must do so in a way that either favors the defendant or amounts to accurate judicial comment.

C.   Accurate Judicial Comment

Judicial comment on the evidence may be either accurate or inaccurate. Comment that is accurate enhances the jury's conception of reality, and permits the jury to deliberate in a more accurate and realistic factual matrix. Inaccurate comment also changes the factual matrix within which the jury operates, but it skews the decisionmaking process away from reality. . . . [I]naccurate judicial comment detrimental to the defendant, on an issue that constitutionally must be included in a state's definition of a crime, violates the mandate of In re Winship by effectively lowering the state's burden of proving guilt beyond a reasonable doubt. In fact, inaccurate comment on an issue is tantamount to creating an affirmative defense since the defendant is forced to show the existence of more than a reasonable doubt on the issue. Accurate comment, on the other hand, can prevent an erroneous verdict when the jury is unable to appreciate the implications of certain facts proven at trial. Certainly a state should be permitted to fill in gaps in the jury's knowledge. Since accurate judicial comment serves this important function without undercutting the reasonable doubt standard, it should be constitutionally permissible — as should its functional equivalents — so long as the comment does not violate the right to a jury trial. Accordingly, the impact of judicial comment on that right must be examined.

The effect of judicial comment on the right to a jury trial raises three questions that may generate constitutional problems: first, does the right to a jury trial limit the manner in which the jury may acquire information; second, how constrained may a jury be made to feel concerning the content of the comment; and third, what is the significance of ambiguity or incoherence in the comment?

1.   THE MANNER OF PRESENTING INFORMATION TO THE JURY

The first difficulty results from the very nature of judicial comment. Judicial comment is, in essence, a method of presenting evidence to the jury. Legislative investigation[105] or judicial experience[106] may result in

---

105. See, e.g., Turner v. United States, 396 U.S. 398, 410 & n.10 (1970); Comment, supra note 32, at 179-81.

106. See, e.g., Barnes v. United States, 412 U.S. 837 (1973).

the conclusion that certain facts usually present themselves in a certain relationship, a relationship that may not be known by the jury. One method of communicating the substance of that relationship is by judicial comment, which is precisely the dynamic the Supreme Court was referring to when it commented that "a valid presumption may . . . be created upon a view of relation broader than that a jury might take in a specific case."[107]

There are alternatives to comment, however. The facts that the comment is based upon could be presented to the jury. Prosecutorial argument on the basis of those data and the other evidence in the case may often be sufficient. Nonetheless, there does not seem to be any constitutional basis for preferring these procedures to judicial comment. Since the Constitution does not dictate a specific method of introducing evidence, accurate judicial comment does not contravene any constitutional command.

2. JURY INDEPENDENCE FROM JUDICIAL COMMENT

Though judicial comment is a permissible method of presenting evidence, it still raises problems with respect to the right to an independent evaluation of the evidence by a jury, which is implicit in the constitutional right to a jury trial. To be permissible, judicial comment must not convey to the jury a sense that it is bound by the content of the comment. The comment must be in permissive language and make very clear that the jury is simply being presented with another matter for its consideration. Obviously, the jury may be influenced by the comment, but if the comment is accurate, it ought to be influential. It ought to be influential, however, only to its degree of accuracy as determined by the jury, which raises the third problem with judicial comment.

3. AMBIGUITY IN JUDICIAL COMMENT

The judge is quite likely to be viewed with some respect by the jurors, and there will surely be a strong inclination to accept what he says as true. Accordingly, he must be careful to make sure that his comment is clear and coherent. Thus, instructions that say only that a jury "may but need not" infer or presume one fact from another should be struck down on the ground that they lead to irrational jury decisionmaking in contravention of the right to a trial by jury. The judge should be required to elaborate on what the word "may" means — what is the basis for concluding that one fact implies another, how close does the relationship seem to be, what are the levels of confidence that the data possess? These questions, of course, prompted the development of the "rational relationship" test in the first place. This test was created in order to

---

107. Tot v. United States, 319 U.S. 463, 468 (1943) (footnote omitted).

ensure that a reasonable connection exists between an "inferred fact" and one proved at trial so that an instruction on the inference would not skew the jury's deliberations away from reality. However, the rational relationship test is, at best, only a crude guarantor of jury rationality because the instructions on inferences and presumptions are usually so ambiguous that it is difficult to assess their impact on the jury's inferential process. The goal of the test would be accomplished better by requiring thorough, cautious comment in place of current instructions.

NESSON, RATIONALITY, PRESUMPTIONS, AND JUDICIAL COMMENT: A RESPONSE TO PROFESSOR ALLEN
94 Harv. L. Rev. 1574, 1576-1583 (1981)

. . . Allen's approach is flawed in that it only tests for the accuracy and rationality of judicial comment *after* finding that the issue affected is constitutionally essential to culpability.

Restricting his test in this way is problematic for two reasons. First, Allen fails to appreciate how limited and difficult the application of a substantive limitation theory will be, and therefore does not realize that his approach would virtually eliminate the requirement of rationality in instructing jurors. Second, rationality is a necessary, albeit not sufficient, condition for the constitutionality of every criminal presumption, whether or not the presumed fact is a constitutionally essential element of a crime.

A. The Impracticality of Substantive Limitation Theory

Allen's analysis begins with In re Winship and the puzzle that it posed. *Winship* announced the constitutional requirement that a state prove every "element" of a criminal offense beyond a reasonable doubt. That holding raised doubts about any use of affirmative defenses. If the statutory definition of a particular crime recognizes an affirmative defense, then it is possible to see the absence of that defense as an element that the state must prove beyond a reasonable doubt. Such a reading of *Winship* gained currency in Mullaney v. Wilbur. In *Mullaney,* the Court struck down a statute allowing the prosecution to rely on a presumption to prove malice, a statutorily prescribed element of homicide. The effect of the presumption was to impose on the defendant the burden of rebutting it (in order to mitigate the crime) by showing that the act was committed in the heat of passion.

Two years later, however, in Patterson v. New York, the Court adopted a narrow reading of *Mullaney*. The Court upheld a statute that shifted the burden to the defendant, not by a presumption as in *Mul-*

laney, but by a requirement that the defendant prove an affirmative defense. The Court took as its starting point the strict legislative definition of the offense: Only if the state expressly defined malice as an "element" of the crime would *Winship* require the prosecution to prove it beyond a reasonable doubt, unaided by any presumptions. Apparently, the state would be permitted to undercut the force of *Winship* merely by shifting elements from the prosecution to the defense.

Abhorrence of *Patterson's* arid formalism stimulated a wave of commentary, including a fine article by Professors Jeffries and Stephan. Jeffries and Stephan* rejected the purely formalistic approach that would have left the *Winship* issue up to state definition. However, they found equally untenable a reading of *Mullaney* that would require the state to prove beyond a reasonable doubt each and every issue affecting stigma or penalty. Such an approach would effectively eliminate all evidentiary devices, including affirmative defenses, by forcing the state to choose between two extremes. Either it must require the prosecution to prove an element beyond reasonable doubt, or it must eliminate it altogether from the definition of the crime. Jeffries and Stephan could find no substantive or procedural justification for this Hobson's choice. Indeed, putting states to such a choice might lead to harsher, less discriminating definitions of crimes. Further, it would be paradoxical to deny states the opportunity to use moderating measures (such as affirmative defenses and presumptions) to shift the burden on an element of an offense, but to allow them to eliminate the element altogether.

Attempting to cut between the two extreme solutions to the *Winship* puzzle, Jeffries and Stephan confronted the need for a constitutional jurisprudence defining the elements a state must prove to convict someone of a crime. Drawing on classic common law notions of actus reus and mens rea, as well as on the eighth amendment's prohibition of cruel and unusual punishment, they attempted to sketch out substantive constitutional limitations on the minimum definition of crime and on the maximum punishment that can be imposed for a particular offense.

Although Jeffries and Stephan presented their ideas of substantive limitation merely as directions for analysis, Allen seizes the theory, without developing it further, and makes it the keystone of his integrated test. . . . [S]ubstantive limitation embodies requirements of act, intent, and proportionality of punishment. It is difficult, however, to give content to these components. The "act" requirement is intended to guard against the possibility that the state would punish mere intention or status, an important but obviously limited protection given the minimal nature of the act necessary to meet the requirement.[31] The "intent"

---

*Jeffries and Stephan, Defenses, Presumptions, and Burden of Proof in the Criminal Law, 88 Yale L.J. 1325 (1979).

31. Consider, for example, the act requirement associated with the crime of conspiracy,

requirement is meant to ensure that a defendant's conduct is morally blameworthy, but its content too is both limited and obscure. Some crimes, for example, require no showing of intent at all.[32] As to proportionality, Jeffries and Stephan recognize that there is "no way to calculate exact relationships between wrong done and punishment earned, for the perception of good and bad and harm and blame flows from normative judgments that defy precise quantification."[33] The Constitution would at most require "some rough sense of proportion in the assignment of sanctions."[34] Because any finer honing of a proportionality standard would require articulation of a coherent theory of punishment, the authors in effect suggest that the test apply only when punishment is excessive in light of all possible justifications.

B. RATIONALITY: AN INDEPENDENT CONSTITUTIONAL REQUISITE

Allen's test demands accuracy and rationality of evidentiary devices only in cases running afoul of a substantive limitation theory. The problem that this poses is illustrated by Tot v. United States,[49] in which the defendant was convicted for violating a federal prohibition against possession of firearms by a felon. Tot's conviction was in part based on a statutory presumption authorizing the jury to infer from mere possession of a firearm that the firearm had been obtained in an interstate transaction. The Court invalidated the presumption, finding no "rational connection" between possession and interstate transport. Despite this irrationality, Professor Allen's theory leads to the conclusion that the case was wrongly decided, unless he were to argue that movement of the gun in interstate commerce was an issue constitutionally essential to culpability (as opposed to federal jurisdiction) under his proportionality analysis.

Allen . . . fails to recognize that rationality serves an independent constitutional value. The authority and integrity of courts rest to a significant degree on the extent to which society perceives them to be fair and rational arbiters of justice. It is one thing for the courts to tolerate a legislature's being ambiguous or arbitrary in defining a crime or establishing sentencing limits, and quite another to permit a legisla-

---

see, e.g., Yates v. United States, 354 U.S. 298 (1957), the act of an alcoholic in being publicly drunk, see, e.g., Powell v. Texas, 392 U.S. 514 (1968), and the "act" of nonfeasance, see Jones v. United States, 308 F.2d 307, 310 & nn. 8-11 (D.C. Cir. 1962).

32. See, e.g., United States v. Park, 421 U.S. 658 (1975) (interstate shipment of contaminated food); United States v. Dotterweich, 320 U.S. 277 (1943) (interstate shipment of adulterated food and mislabeled drugs).

33. Jeffries & Stephan, supra.

34. Id. at 1377.

49. 319 U.S. 463 (1943).

ture to insist on judicial arbitrariness in adjudicating criminal prosecutions. A legislatively established presumption that lacks a rational connection between predicate and conclusion makes the court administering it appear to be arbitrary. The very statement of the contrary proposition suggests Gilbert and Sullivan rules of procedure: "Jurors, you may presume *A* from proof of *B*, even though there is no rational connection between the two." One need not look further for the roots of the rational connection test. It does not depend on any theory of clear legislative statement or substantive due process, but rather on the notion that the legitimacy of judicial process requires that issues to be proved in court be proved rationally.

F. Criminal Presumptions: Are There Problems with the Fifth Amendment and the Presumption of Innocence?

Proposed FRE 303
Presumptions in Criminal Cases

(a) *Scope.* Except as otherwise provided by Act of Congress, in criminal cases, presumptions against an accused, recognized at common law or created by statute, including statutory provisions that certain facts are prima facie evidence of other facts or of guilt, are governed by this rule.

(b) *Submission to jury.* The judge is not authorized to direct the jury to find a presumed fact against the accused. When the presumed fact establishes guilt or is an element of the offense or negatives a defense, the judge may submit the question of guilt or of the existence of the presumed fact to the jury, if, but only if, a reasonable juror on the evidence as a whole, including the evidence of the basic facts, could find guilt or the presumed fact beyond a reasonable doubt. When the presumed fact has a lesser effect, its existence may be submitted to the jury if the basic facts are supported by substantial evidence, or are otherwise established, unless the evidence as a whole negatives the existence of the presumed fact.

(c) *Instructing the jury.* Whenever the existence of a presumed fact against the accused is submitted to the jury, the judge shall give an instruction that the law declares that the jury may regard the basic facts as sufficient evidence of the presumed fact but does not require it to do so. In addition, if the presumed fact establishes guilt or is an element of the offense or negatives a defense, the judge shall instruct the jury that its existence must, on all the evidence, be proved beyond a reasonable doubt.

The Advisory Committee deleted this rule because the subject of presumptions in criminal cases was to be addressed in revisions to the federal criminal code. What would a judge, using this presumption, say to a jury?

Problem IX-10
Moonshine

D is prosecuted for operating an illegal whiskey still. The prosecution's only proof is that *D* was found at the site of an illegal whiskey still. Is that a sufficient basis for inferring that *D* was operating the still? Can the jury take into account the fact that *D* offered no alternative explanation of what he was doing at the site of the still?

Does it help if based upon the state legislature's adoption of a presumption the trial judge gives the jury the following instruction?

> Under a statute enacted by the Legislature, when the defendant is shown to have been present at the site of the still such presence shall be deemed sufficient evidence to authorize conviction, unless the defendant explains such presence to the satisfaction of the jury.

How is the problem different if instead of the instruction above, the judge gives the following instruction?

> If you find that the defendant was present at the still, then that fact should be highly significant in your consideration whether the defendant was operating the still. You should consider that fact together with all the other facts of the case — the time of day, what the defendant was seen doing, what he was wearing, the equipment in his car — in deciding whether you are convinced beyond reasonable doubt that he was operating the still. This is a case based on circumstantial evidence. The fact that I leave it to you jurors to decide means that in my judgment it would be reasonable and legally supportable for you to reach a conclusion of guilt. It would also be reasonable and legally supportable for you to reach a conclusion of not guilty. It is up to you to decide whether, on considering all the facts and the defendant's explanation or lack of explanation, you are convinced beyond reasonable doubt that the defendant was operating the still.

Does it make any difference that the only way *D* can put forward an explanation is by testifying himself? How do the next two cases, Yee Hem v. United States and Griffin v. California, relate to these questions and to each other?

YEE HEM v. UNITED STATES
268 U.S. 178 (1925)

Mr. Justice SUTHERLAND delivered the opinion of the Court.

Plaintiff in error was convicted in the court below of the offense of concealing a quantity of smoking opium after importation, with knowledge that it had been imported in violation of the Act of February 9, 1909, c.100, 35 Stat. 614, as amended by the Act of January 17, 1914, c.9, 38 Stat. 275. Sections 2 and 3 of the act as amended are challenged as unconstitutional, on the ground that they contravene the due process of law and the compulsory self-incrimination clauses of the Fifth Amendment of the federal Constitution.

Section 1 of the act prohibits the importation into the United States of opium in any form after April 1, 1909, except that opium and preparations and derivatives thereof, other than smoking opium or opium prepared for smoking, may be imported for medicinal purposes only, under regulations prescribed by the Secretary of the Treasury. Section 2 provides, among other things, that if any person shall conceal or facilitate the concealment of such opium, etc., after importation, knowing the same to have been imported contrary to law, the offender shall be subject to fine or imprisonment or both. It further provides that whenever the defendant on trial is shown to have, or to have had, possession of such opium, etc., "such possession shall be deemed sufficient evidence to authorize conviction unless the defendant shall explain the possession to the satisfaction of the jury." Section 3 provides that on and after July 1, 1913, "all smoking opium or opium prepared for smoking found within the United States shall be presumed to have been imported after the first day of April, nineteen hundred and nine, and the burden of proof shall be on the claimant or the accused to rebut such presumption."

The plaintiff in error, at the time of his arrest in August, 1923, was found in possession of and concealing a quantity of smoking opium. The lower court overruled a motion for an instructed verdict of not guilty, and, after stating the foregoing statutory presumptions, charged the jury in substance that the burden of proof was on the accused to rebut such presumptions; and that it devolved upon him to explain that he was rightfully in possession of the smoking opium, — "at least explain it to the satisfaction of the jury." The court further charged that the defendant was presumed to be innocent until the government had satisfied the minds of the jurors of his guilt beyond a reasonable doubt; that the burden to adduce such proof of guilt beyond the existence of a reasonable doubt rested on the government at all times and throughout the trial; and that a conviction could not be had "while a rational doubt remains in the minds of the jury." . . .

We think it is not an illogical inference that opium, found in this country more than four years (in the present case, more than fourteen years) after its importation had been prohibited, was unlawfully imported. Nor do we think the further provision, that possession of such opium in the absence of a satisfactory explanation shall create a presumption of guilt, is "so unreasonable as to be a purely arbitrary mandate." By universal sentiment, and settled policy as evidenced by state and local legislation for more than half a century, opium is an illegitimate commodity, the use of which, except as a medicinal agent, is rigidly condemned. Legitimate possession, unless for medicinal use, is so highly improbable that to say to any person who obtains the outlawed commodity, "since you are bound to know that it cannot be brought into this country at all, except under regulation for medicinal use, you must at your peril ascertain and be prepared to show the facts and circumstances which rebut, or tend to rebut, the natural inference of unlawful importation, or your knowledge of it," is not such an unreasonable requirement as to cause it to fall outside the constitutional power of Congress.

Every accused person, of course, enters upon his trial clothed with the presumption of innocence. But that presumption may be overcome, not only by direct proof, but, in many cases, when the facts standing alone are not enough, by the additional weight of a countervailing legislative presumption. If the effect of the legislative act is to give to the facts from which the presumption is drawn an artificial value to some extent, it is no more than happens in respect of a great variety of presumptions not resting upon statute. See . . . Wilson v. United States, 162 U.S. 613, 619. In the *Wilson* case the accused, charged with murder, was found, soon after the homicide, in possession of property that had belonged to the dead man. This Court upheld a charge of the trial court to the effect that such possession required the accused to account for it, to show that as far as he was concerned the possession was innocent and honest, and that if not so accounted for it became "the foundation for a presumption of guilt against the defendant."

The point that the practical effect of the statute creating the presumption is to compel the accused person to be a witness against himself may be put aside with slight discussion. The statute compels nothing. It does no more than to make possession of the prohibited article prima facie evidence of guilt. It leaves the accused entirely free to testify or not as he chooses. If the accused happens to be the only repository of the facts necessary to negative the presumption arising from his possession, that is a misfortune which the statute under review does not create but which is inherent in the case. The same situation might present itself if there were no statutory presumption and a prima facie case of concealment with knowledge of unlawful importation were made by the evidence. The necessity of an explanation by the accused would be quite as compelling in that case as in this; but the constraint upon him to give testimony would arise there, as it arises here, simply from the force of circumstances and not from any form of compulsion forbidden by the Constitution.

Judgment affirmed.

GRIFFIN v. CALIFORNIA
380 U.S. 609 (1965)

Mr. Justice DOUGLAS delivered the opinion of the Court.

Petitioner was convicted of murder in the first degree after a jury trial in a California court. He did not testify at the trial on the issue of guilt. . . . The trial court instructed the jury on the issue of guilt, stating that a defendant has a constitutional right not to testify. But it told the jury:

> As to any evidence or facts against him which the defendant can reasonably be expected to deny or explain because of facts within his knowledge, if he does not testify or if, though he does testify, he fails to deny or explain such evidence, the jury may take that failure into consideration as tending to indicate the truth of such evidence and as indicating that among the inferences that may be reasonably drawn therefrom those unfavorable to the defendant are the more probable.

It added, however, that no such inference could be drawn as to evidence respecting which he had no knowledge. It stated that failure of a defendant to deny or explain the evidence of which he had knowledge does not create a presumption of guilt nor by itself warrant an inference of guilt nor relieve the prosecution of any of its burden of proof.

Petitioner had been seen with the deceased the evening of her death, the evidence placing him with her in the alley where her body was found. The prosecutor made much of the failure of petitioner to testify:

> The defendant certainly knows whether Essie Mae had this beat up appearance at the time he left her apartment and went down the alley with her.
>
> What kind of a man is it that would want to have sex with a woman that beat up if she was beat up at the time he left?
>
> He would know that. He would know how she got down the alley. He would know how the blood got on the bottom of the concrete steps. He would know how long he was with her in that box. He would know how her wig got off. He would know whether he beat her or mistreated her. He would know whether he walked away from that place cool as a cucumber when he saw Mr. Villasenor because he was conscious of his own guilt and wanted to get away from that damaged or injured woman.
>
> These things he has not seen fit to take the stand and deny or explain.
>
> And in the whole world, if anybody would know, this defendant would know.
>
> Essie Mae is dead, she can't tell you her side of the story. The defendant won't.

The death penalty was imposed and the California Supreme Court affirmed. 60 Cal. 2d 182, 383 P.2d 432. The case is here on a writ of certiorari which we granted, 377 U.S. 989, to consider whether comment on the failure to testify violated the Self-Incrimination Clause of the

Fifth Amendment which we made applicable to the States by the Fourteenth in Malloy v. Hogan, 378 U.S. 1, decided after the Supreme Court of California had affirmed the present conviction. . . .

If this were a federal trial, reversible error would have been committed. Wilson v. United States, 149 U.S. 60, so holds. It is said, however, that the *Wilson* decision rested not on the Fifth Amendment, but on an Act of Congress, now 18 U.S.C. §3481. That indeed is the fact, as the opinion of the Court in the *Wilson* case states. And see Adamson v. California, 332 U.S. 46, 50, n.6; Bruno v. United States, 308 U.S. 287, 294. But that is the beginning, not the end, of our inquiry. The question remains whether, statute or not, the comment rule, approved by California, violates the Fifth Amendment. . . .

We think it does. It is in substance a rule of evidence that allows the State the privilege of tendering to the jury for its consideration the failure of the accused to testify. No formal offer of proof is made as in other situations; but the prosecutor's comment and the court's acquiescence are the equivalent of an offer of evidence and its acceptance. The Court in the *Wilson* case stated: ". . . the act was framed with a due regard also to those who might prefer to rely upon the presumption of innocence which the law gives to every one, and not wish to be witnesses. It is not every one who can safely venture on the witness stand though entirely innocent of the charge against him. Excessive timidity, nervousness when facing others and attempting to explain transactions of a suspicious character, and offences charged against him, will often confuse and embarrass him to such a degree as to increase rather than remove prejudices against him. It is not every one, however honest, who would, therefore, willingly be placed on the witness stand. The statute, in tenderness to the weakness to those who from the causes mentioned might refuse to ask to be a witness, particularly when they may have been in some degree compromised by their association with others, declares that the failure of the defendant in a criminal action to request to be a witness shall not create any presumption against him." 149 U.S., p.66.

If the words "Fifth Amendment" are substituted for "act" and for "statute," the spirit of the Self-Incrimination Clause is reflected. For comment on the refusal to testify is a remnant of the "inquisitorial system of criminal justice," Murphy v. Waterfront Comm'n, 378 U.S. 52, 55, which the Fifth Amendment outlaws. It is a penalty imposed by courts for exercising a constitutional privilege. It cuts down on the privilege by making its assertion costly. It is said, however, that the inference of guilt for failure to testify as to facts peculiarly within the accused's knowledge is in any event natural and irresistible, and that comment on the failure does not magnify that inference into a penalty for asserting a constitutional privilege. People v. Modesto, 62 Cal. 2d 436, 452-453, 398 P.2d 753, 762-763. What the jury may infer, given no help from the court, is one thing. What it may infer when the court solemnizes the silence of the accused into evidence against him is quite another. That the inference of guilt is not always so natural or irresistible is brought out in the *Modesto* opinion itself:

"Defendant contends that the reason a defendant refuses to testify is that his prior convictions will be introduced in evidence to impeach him ([Cal.] Code Civ. Proc. §2051) and not that he is unable to deny the accusations. It is true that the defendant might fear that his prior convictions will prejudice the jury, and therefore another possible inference can be drawn from his refusal to take the stand." Id., p. 453, 398 P.2d, p.763.

We said in Malloy v. Hogan, supra, p.11, that "the same standards must determine whether an accused's silence in either a federal or state proceeding is justified." We take that in its literal sense and hold that the Fifth Amendment, in its direct application to the Federal Government, and in its bearing on the States by reason of the Fourteenth Amendment, forbids either comment by the prosecution on the accused's silence or instructions by the court that such silence is evidence of guilt.

Reversed.

THE CHIEF JUSTICE took no part in the decision of this case. Mr. Justice HARLAN concurred. Justices STEWART and WHITE dissented.

NESSON, REASONABLE DOUBT AND PERMISSIVE INFERENCES: THE VALUE OF COMPLEXITY
92 Harv. L. Rev. 1187, 1208-1213 (1979)

LACK OF SATISFACTORY EXPLANATION

It should be clear by this point that the concept of reasonable doubt is inconsistent with a procedure that permits an otherwise unassisted leap from aggregate likelihood to a conclusion of guilt in a specific case. There is, however, a frequent limitation on permissive inferences which, to some, has appeared to solve the problem: the factfinder typically is only allowed to infer the requisite conclusion from the predicate fact if there is a lack of satisfactory explanation. In *Gainey*, for example [the case from which the Moonshine problem was drawn, United States v. Gainey, 380 U.S. 63 (1965)], the jury was told that it was permitted to infer from the presence of the defendant at the still that he was operating the still, "unless the defendant . . . explains such presence to the satisfaction of the jury." The statute unsuccessfully challenged in *Turner* placed a similar qualification on the jury's authority to infer importation and knowledge from possession of heroin. If an inference can legitimately be drawn from a failure to explain a suggestive circumstance, that additional datum could bridge the gap between aggregate likelihood and a conclusion beyond reasonable doubt in the specific case. Moreover, if a defendant understands that an adverse inference will be drawn from the lack of a satisfactory explanation, the conclusion that there is no innocent explanation becomes more logical when he fails to offer one. Indeed, the statutory declaration of the permissive inference may be seen as notifying the defendant of the circumstances in which his passivity in defending will be counted against him. This, however, presents an obvious fifth amendment problem: is it constitutional to draw an inference against the defendant from his refusal to defend?

The fifth amendment is not a guarantee of acquittal. If the prosecution has offered proof which is sufficient to warrant a conclusion of guilt beyond reasonable doubt, a defendant may feel considerable pressure to take the stand and dispute the prosecution's case. Practically speaking, it may be his only chance for acquittal. The "compulsion" which the defendant feels in such a case is the natural consequence of the prosecution's presentation of a strong case, and clearly does not result in any violation of the fifth amendment.

But the situation created by permissive inferences is different. If proof of the predicate fact is sufficient to warrant a conclusion beyond reasonable doubt, then the case is no different from other cases in which the prosecution survives a motion for a directed verdict and puts to the defendant the strategic choice of testifying or not. If, on the other hand, proof of the predicate fact alone is not sufficient to warrant a conclusion of guilt beyond reasonable doubt, then the permissive inference instruction, by requiring the defendant to put forward a satisfactory explanation, significantly changes the situation. Now it is not simply the force of the prosecution's proof which warrants a verdict and puts pressure on the defendant to testify. The defendant's decision not to explain himself becomes an essential part of the prosecution's case, and the pressure to testify now comes from the statutory inference which the jury is invited to draw from the lack of any satisfactory explanation.

This fifth amendment problem implicit in permissive inferences was first raised before the Supreme Court in 1925, in Yee Hem v. United States. The case involved a prosecution for concealing imported opium. The trial judge had instructed the jury in the terms typical of the federal narcotics presumption: whenever the defendant is shown to have possessed opium, "such possession shall be deemed sufficient evidence to authorize conviction [i.e., for the jury to find knowledge and importation] unless the defendant shall explain the possession to the satisfaction of the jury." Yee Hem challenged this permissive inference on the grounds that the "satisfactory explanation" clause made the permissive inference an unconstitutional burden on his right to remain silent.

The Supreme Court, by its own admission, "put aside" the question "with slight discussion." The permissive inference, said the Court, "compels nothing":

It leaves the accused entirely free to testify or not as he chooses. If the accused happens to be the only repository of the facts necessary to negative the presumption arising from his possession, that is a misfortune which the statute under review does not create but which is inherent in the case. The same situation might present itself if there were no statutory presumption and a prima facie case of concealment with knowledge of unlawful importation were made by the evidence. . . . [T]he constraint upon him to give testimony would arise there, as it arises here, simply from the force of circumstances and not from any form of compulsion forbidden by the Constitution.

There are two basic flaws in this reasoning. First, it ignores the question which this Article poses: can the prosecution be considered to have offered a prima facie case of knowledge and importation merely by proving possession? The Court in *Yee Hem* merely assumed an affirmative answer. Second, even if proof of mere possession could constitute a prima facie case, and thus constitutionally impel the defendant to explain his possession, it does not follow that the jury may be told that it can supplement the prosecution's case with an inference based on the defendant's silence. In Griffin v. California, the Court examined the difference between a conviction based on the strength of the prosecution's case and one based on the prosecution's case supplemented by an inference drawn from the defendant's decision not to testify, and held that neither prosecutor nor judge may urge the jury to draw an adverse inference from a defendant's silence.

The Court's language in the latter case is particularly germane here. The remarks of the prosecutor and the judge in *Griffin* were held to violate the privilege against self-incrimination because the California rule permitting comment upon the defendant's silence by the prosecutor was "in substance a rule of evidence that allows the State the privilege of tendering to the jury for its consideration the failure of the accused to testify." *Griffin* held that "when the court solemnizes the silence of the accused into evidence against him," the state is in practical effect exercising that compulsion which the fifth amendment forbids.

If one accepts the proposition that the aggregate likelihood presupposed by the permissive inference is not itself enough to sustain a verdict beyond reasonable doubt, then any attempt to draw additional strength for the permissive inference from the defendant's lack of explanation means necessarily that the defendant's silence is functioning as an added piece of "evidence," "solemnized" by the statute and the jury instruction. *Griffin* thus suggests that permissive inferences must stand or fall on the strength of the inference to be drawn from the predicate fact, unaided by any inference from the lack of satisfactory explanation.

The best defense of the "lack of satisfactory explanation" language against fifth amendment challenge is not to deny that an inference is being drawn from the lack of a satisfactory explanation, but to argue that the explanation could have come from witnesses other than the defendant, and therefore that no inference is being drawn from the *defendant's* failure to testify. This argument, however, conveniently glosses over the fact that the defendant is the obvious person from whom the jury would expect explanation, particularly so in cases involving issues of intent and knowledge, issues which permissive inferences often address. The "unless satisfactorily explained" instruction, however phrased, is thus likely to be *understood by jurors* as an invitation to draw an inference from the *defendant's* silence. This in itself might be considered enough to invalidate it.

But there is a more fundamental weakness in the argument: it assumes that it is constitutional to require a defendant to put on a defense. A defendant cannot be constitutionally required to come forward with a defense unless the prosecution has first met its burden of proof. As Wigmore long ago explained, the presumption of innocence is merely a corollary of the rule that the prosecution must adduce evidence and produce persuasion beyond reasonable doubt; and by reason of this rule, the accused "may remain inactive and secure, until the prosecution has taken up its burden and produced evidence and effected persuasion."[84] The question, then, of whether any inference may be drawn from a defendant's failure to provide a satisfactory explanation, even if he might be able to do so by calling witnesses other than himself, depends upon whether the prosecution has first discharged its burden of production. But if the analysis so far presented in this Article is credited, the proof of the predicate fact of a permissive inference cannot by itself meet that burden, and therefore cannot provide a constitutional basis for authorizing an inference to be drawn against the defendant who fails to come forward with a defense. If the prosecution can only overcome the presumption of innocence by meeting its burden of persuasion, then allowing the prosecution to discharge this burden by means of any inference based on the defendant's failure to defend is inconsistent with the presumption of innocence.

G. Criminal Presumptions and Rationality

UNITED STATES v. DUBE
520 F.2d 250 (1st Cir. 1975)

Before COFFIN, C.J., McENTEE and CAMPBELL, JJ.
McENTEE, J. Defendant Dube was tried on an indictment charging him with robbery of a federally insured bank. He did not deny that he

84. 9 J. Wigmore, supra note 7, §2511, at 407.

committed the robbery, but introduced the testimony of a psychiatrist and a psychologist that he was insane when he committed the offense. The prosecution did not present expert opinion evidence but relied instead on cross-examination and the lay testimony of two bank tellers and Dube's accomplice to rebut his case. Dube moved for a judgment of acquittal on the ground that the prosecution had failed as a matter of law to sustain its burden of proving his sanity beyond a reasonable doubt, but the motion was denied. The jury returned a verdict of guilty and Dube appeals.

A criminal defendant is presumed sane, but the introduction of evidence of insanity dispels the presumption and subjects the prosecution to the burden of proving sanity beyond a reasonable doubt. Beltran v. United States, 302 F.2d 48, 52 (1st Cir. 1962). . . . There is no general principle that the prosecution must counter defendant's expert medical evidence with expert testimony of its own. The expert testimony is not conclusive even where uncontradicted; its weight and credibility are for the jury to determine, and it may be rebutted in various ways apart from the introduction of countervailing expert opinion.[1]

We do not think the evidence in this case was such that a reasonable man must necessarily have entertained doubts as to defendant's sanity. Both Dr. Voss, the psychiatrist, and Dr. Bishop, the psychologist, testified that in their opinion defendant was a schizophrenic and substantially incapable of conforming his conduct to the requirements of the law at the time of the crime. They arrived at those diagnoses nearly five months after the robbery and only a week before trial. Dr. Voss's opinion was based on two hours of interviews and Dr. Bishop's on a one-hour interview and three hours of intelligence and personality testing. . . .

Most importantly, Dr. Voss's diagnosis was based almost entirely on the subjective history narrated by defendant and his counsel, see United States v. Ingman, 426 F.2d 973 (9th Cir. 1970), and Dr. Bishop undoubtedly interpreted the test results in light of the history he received. Both

---

1. In Mims v. United States, 375 F.2d 135, 143-44 (5th Cir. 1967), the court stated that expert testimony may be rebutted "by showing the incorrectness or inadequacy of the factual assumptions upon which the opinion is based, 'the reasoning by which he progresses from his material to his conclusion,' the interest or bias of the expert, inconsistencies or contradiction in his testimony as to material matters, material variations between the experts themselves, and defendant's lack of co-operation with the expert. Also in cases involving opinions of medical experts, the probative force of that character of testimony is lessened where it is predicated on subjective symptoms, or where it is based on narrative statements to the expert as to past events not in evidence at the trial. In some cases, the cross-examination of the expert may be such as to justify the trier of facts in not being convinced by him. One or more of these factors may, depending on the particular facts of each case, make a jury issue as to the credibility and weight to be given to the expert testimony . . ." (footnotes omitted). See also United States v. McGraw, 515 F.2d 758 (9th Cir. 1975), holding that defendant's expert testimony may be rebutted by cross-examination or evidence from which the jury could infer that the defendant's expert testimony depended upon an incorrect view of the facts.

testified that they were able to detect malingering and that defendant could not fabricate a history suggesting schizophrenia, but of course a jury would not be bound to believe these assertions. Id. Indeed the factual assumptions they derived from Dube's narrative, on which they predicated their conclusions, did not comport with the testimony at trial. On the basis of defendant's statements, both regarded the robbery as compulsive and irrational, but the testimony of Mrs. Kyllonen, the accomplice, furnished abundant evidence of a carefully planned and executed crime. The experts' testimony also seemed to rest in part on the notion that bank robbery is an irrational activity in the first place, making the competence of a bank robber at least suspect. Both concluded that defendant was shy, a "loner," unable to form emotional attachments to others, but Mrs. Kyllonen testified that she was in love with defendant, that they had lived together for as long as three weeks before the robbery and that they had arranged to get back together after defendant disposed of some stolen checks in New York. She also testified that during the period immediately after the robbery she did not notice anything peculiar about defendant's activities. . . .

We agree with our concurring brother that the prosecution was remiss in not offering psychiatric testimony of its own. However, on all the evidence we think the court correctly allowed the case to go to the jury. See United States v. Coleman, supra.

Affirmed.

CAMPBELL, J. (concurring). I find this a difficult case to analyze though, on the facts, I concur in the result. The court dwells on the inadequacy of the psychiatrist's and psychologist's diagnoses. While in certain respects I think it is overly critical, I agree that the jury was entitled to be skeptical of opinions of insanity based upon relatively brief examinations made several months after the crime and at a time when Dube had everything to gain from a finding of insanity. . . .

Still it is not simple to identify the affirmative evidence from which the jury could find defendant sane *beyond a reasonable doubt.* Certain conclusions, could, it is true, be drawn from Dube's girl friend's description of his conduct before and after the crime. She had lived with Dube for several weeks and was in his company when he fled. While the defense argues that by selecting a bank to rob on the spur of the moment, Dube behaved in a bizarre manner, this behavior does not necessarily compel an inference of mental abnormality; and his conduct during and after the robbery, including precautions to avoid detection such as discarding the gun and driving to a city where he felt the police were less likely to be on the lookout, seems rational enough. The two tellers, who saw him briefly during the robbery, observed nothing bizarre, and the jury was able to add to this evidence its own observations of Dube while in the courtroom. Thus, there was evidence that Dube at certain times had behaved in a way which, to the average eyes, might seem normal. Still one wonders by what standard the fleeting glimpses of behavior transmitted by Dube's girl friend and the tellers allowed a finding of sanity beyond a reasonable doubt.* Dr. Voss, the psychiatrist, testified that the girl friend's version of Dube's behavior was consistent with a diagnosis of schizophrenia. Whether or not that is so, it is questionable whether her association with Dube was extensive enough, and her behavioral testimony detailed enough, to permit a positive diagnosis of sanity either by a layman or an expert.

Yet not without some hesitation I think the jury was entitled to receive help from another quarter. In Davis v. United States, 160 U.S. 469 (1895), the Supreme Court did not characterize the presumption of sanity as belonging to that category of presumption which vanishes once the defense shows evidence of insanity. Instead, it stated, "If the whole evidence, *including that supplied by the presumption of sanity,* does not exclude beyond a reasonable doubt the hypothesis of insanity, of which some proof is adduced, the accused is entitled to an acquittal. . . ." 160 U.S. at 488 [Emphasis supplied].

Except for the quoted reference in *Davis* (which was the case that established the federal rule requiring the prosecution to prove sanity beyond a reasonable doubt) there has been little attention paid in federal cases to whether the presumption of sanity, once questioned, continues to have evidentiary force. Some courts, like the court here, see it as a presumption that evaporates once evidence of insanity is introduced. Yet viewed as a common sense inference that a person without marked symptoms to the contrary is likely to be sane, I think the presumption is entitled to be given reasonable weight in determining whether on all the evidence the Government gets to a jury. . . .

In the present case, given the evidence of an ability to function normally, and an absence of evidence of abnormal behavior, I think the jury could summons assistance from the inference, or presumption, that Dube was sane. Evidence bearing upon insanity has never been restricted to expert evidence. Conduct, lay observations and even lay opinions have traditionally been given much weight. 2 J. Wigmore, Evidence, §§227 et seq. (3d ed. 1940). And the jury could add to factors such as the reasonableness of Dube's conduct before and after the crime and his apparent lack of any history of mental disturbance, an inference of

---

*Our approach is not easily reconciled with that taken in Beltran v. United States, 302 F.2d 48 (1st Cir. 1962), in which Judge Aldrich wrote, 302 F.2d at 52,

"The introduction of evidence of insanity places a burden on the government of proving sanity beyond a reasonable doubt. . . . This burden cannot be spirited away by the simple method proposed by the government of the court's saying it does not believe the evidence, therefore there is no evidence, therefore there is no burden. . . . [S]uch thinking would render the whole principle meaningless. Rather, the record must be looked at as a whole, with the burden on the government to overcome any reasonable doubt." . . .

sanity drawn from its common experience that most people (at least those without marked outward symptoms) are sane. With the aid of this inference it could reach the conclusion that he was sane beyond a reasonable doubt. I recognize that this rationale is not without its difficulties, but it seems more satisfying than to pretend that the Government's meager evidence of Dube's conduct established, or could establish, by itself, much of anything.

Had there been somewhat less evidence of ordinary behavior, or slightly stronger evidence of abnormality, reversal might be in order. But without condoning the Government's failure to call an expert or otherwise bolster its case I think the issue was properly submitted to the jury.

Does *Dube* present a problem of allocation or presumption? Suppose the court had recognized that a burden of persuasion could have been placed on the defendant *without* altering the degree of certainty to which the insanity issue had to be proved; i.e., suppose that the court had imposed on the defendant the burden of persuading the jury that there was at least a doubt about his sanity? Would that approach have solved the problem here? Would it have been constitutional?

Recall that the major historical debate with civil presumptions has been between the "bursting bubble" and the "shifting burden" approaches, with the first criticized for producing too slight an effect and the second for producing too great an effect. Would a workable middle ground be an approach that keeps the degree of certainty fixed but simply changes the direction from which the parties come at it? It seems to be so in the criminal context but not in the civil. The reciprocal of the plaintiff proving that an element is more probable than not would seem to be the defendant proving that the element is "as likely as not." But how does this differ from total ignorance?

COUNTY COURT OF ULSTER CITY v. ALLEN
442 U.S. 140 (1979)

Mr. Justice STEVENS delivered the opinion of the Court.

A New York statute provides that, with certain exceptions, the presence of a firearm in an automobile is presumptive evidence of its illegal possession by all persons then occupying the vehicle. The United States Court of Appeals for the Second Circuit held that respondents may challenge the constitutionality of this statute in a federal habeas corpus proceeding and that the statute is "unconstitutional on its face." 568 F.2d 998, 1009. We granted certiorari to review these holdings and also to consider whether the statute is constitutional in its application to respondents. 439 U.S. 815.

Four persons, three adult males (respondents) and a 16-year-old girl (Jane Doe, who is not a respondent here), were jointly tried on charges that they possessed two loaded handguns, a loaded machinegun, and over a pound of heroin found in a Chevrolet in which they were riding when it was stopped for speeding on the New York Thruway shortly after noon on March 28, 1973. The two large-caliber handguns, which together with their ammunition weighed approximately six pounds, were seen through the window of the car by the investigating police officer. They were positioned crosswise in an open handbag on either the front floor or the front seat of the car on the passenger side where Jane Doe was sitting. Jane Doe admitted that the handbag was hers. The machinegun and the heroin were discovered in the trunk after the police pried it open. The car had been borrowed from the driver's brother earlier that day; the key to the trunk could not be found in the car or on the person of any of its occupants, although there was testimony that two of the occupants had placed something in the trunk before embarking in the borrowed car. The jury convicted all four of possession of the handguns and acquitted them of possession of the contents of the trunk.

Counsel for all four defendants objected to the introduction into evidence of the two handguns, the machinegun, and the drugs, arguing that the State had not adequately demonstrated a connection between their clients and the contraband. The trial court overruled the objection, relying on the presumption of possession created by the New York statute. Tr. 474-483. Because that presumption does not apply if a weapon is found "upon the person" of one of the occupants of the car, . . . the three male defendants also moved to dismiss the charges relating to the handguns on the ground that the guns were found on the person of Jane Doe. Respondents made this motion both at the close of the prosecution's case and at the close of all evidence. The trial judge twice denied it, concluding that the applicability of the "upon the person" exception was a question of fact for the jury. . . .

At the close of the trial, the judge instructed the jurors that they were entitled to infer possession from the defendants' presence in the car. He did not make any reference to the "upon the person" exception in his explanation of the statutory presumption, nor did any of the defendants object to this omission or request alternative or additional instructions on the subject. . . .

In this case, the Court of Appeals undertook the task of deciding the constitutionality of the New York statute "on its face." Its conclusion that the statutory presumption was arbitrary rested entirely on its view of the fairness of applying the presumption in hypothetical situations — situations, indeed, in which it is improbable that a jury would return a conviction, or that a prosecution would ever be instituted. We must accordingly inquire whether these respondents had standing to advance the arguments that the Court of Appeals considered decisive. An analysis of our prior cases indicates that the answer to this inquiry depends on the type of presumption that is involved in the case.

Inferences and presumptions are a staple of our adversary system of factfinding. It is often necessary for the trier of fact to determine the existence of an element of the crime — that is, an "ultimate" or "elemental" fact — from the existence of one or more "evidentiary" or "basic" facts. E.g., Barnes v. United States, 412 U.S. 837, 843-844; Tot v. United States, 319 U.S. 463, 467; Mobile, J. & K.C.R. Co. v. Turnipseed, 219 U.S. 35, 42. The value of these evidentiary devices, and their validity under the Due Process Clause, vary from case to case, however, depending on the strength of the connection between the particular basic and elemental facts involved and on the degree to which the device curtails the factfinder's freedom to assess the evidence independently. Nonetheless, in criminal cases, the ultimate test of any device's constitutional validity in a given case remains constant: the device must not undermine the factfinder's responsibility at trial, based on evidence adduced by the State, to find the ultimate facts beyond a reasonable doubt. See In re Winship, 397 U.S. 358, 364; Mullaney v. Wilbur, 421 U.S., at 702-703, n.31.

The most common evidentiary device is the entirely permissive inference or presumption, which allows — but does not require — the trier of fact to infer the elemental fact from proof by the prosecutor of the basic one and which places no burden of any kind on the defendant. See, e.g., Barnes v. United States, supra, at 840 n.3. In that situation the basic fact may constitute prima facie evidence of the elemental fact. See, e.g., Turner v. United States, 396 U.S. 398, 402 n.2. When reviewing this type of device, the Court has required the party challenging it to demonstrate its invalidity as applied to him. Because this permissive presumption leaves the trier of fact free to credit or reject the inference and does not shift the burden of proof, it affects the application of the "beyond a reasonable doubt" standard only if, under the facts of the case, there is no rational way the trier could make the connection permitted by the inference. For only in that situation is there any risk that an explanation of the permissible inference to a jury, or its use by a jury, has caused the presumptively rational factfinder to make an erroneous factual determination.

A mandatory presumption is a far more troublesome evidentiary device. For it may affect not only the strength of the "no reasonable doubt" burden but also the placement of that burden; it tells the trier that he or they *must* find the elemental fact upon proof of the basic fact, at least unless the defendant has come forward with some evidence to rebut the presumed connection between the two facts. In this situation, the Court has generally examined the presumption on its face to determine the extent to which the basic and elemental facts coincide. To the extent that the trier of fact is forced to abide by the presumption, and may not reject it based on an independent evaluation of the particular facts presented by the State, the analysis of the presumption's constitutional validity is logically divorced from those facts and based on the presumption's accuracy in the run of cases. It is for this reason that the Court had held it irrelevant in analyzing a mandatory presumption, but not in analyzing a purely permissive one, that there is ample evidence in the record other than the presumption to support a conviction.

Without determining whether the presumption in this case was mandatory, the Court of Appeals analyzed it on its face as if it were. In fact, it was not, as the New York Court of Appeals had earlier pointed out. 40 N.Y.2d, at 510-511, 354 N.E.2d, at 840.

The trial judge's instructions make it clear that the presumption was merely a part of the prosecution's case, that it gave rise to a permissive inference available only in certain circumstances, rather than a mandatory conclusion of possession, and that it could be ignored by the jury even if there was no affirmative proof offered by defendants in rebuttal. The judge explained that possession could be actual or constructive, but that constructive possession could not exist without the intent and ability to exercise control or dominion over the weapons. He also carefully instructed the jury that there is a mandatory presumption of innocence in favor of the defendants that controls unless it, as the exclusive trier of fact, is satisfied beyond a reasonable doubt that the defendants possessed the handguns in the manner described by the judge. In short, the instructions plainly directed the jury to consider all the circumstances tending to support or contradict the inference that all four occupants of the car had possession of the two loaded handguns and to decide the matter for itself without regard to how much evidence the defendants introduced.

Our cases considering the validity of permissive statutory presumptions such as the one involved here have rested on an evaluation of the presumption as applied to the record before the Court. None suggests that a court should pass on the constitutionality of this kind of statute "on its face." It was error for the Court of Appeals to make such a determination in this case.

III

As applied to the facts of this case, the presumption of possession is entirely rational. Notwithstanding the Court of Appeals' analysis, respondents were not "hitchhikers or other casual passengers," and the guns were neither "a few inches in length" nor "out of [respondents'] sight." . . . The argument against possession by any of the respondents was predicated solely on the fact that the guns were in Jane Doe's pocketbook. But several circumstances — which, not surprisingly, her counsel repeatedly emphasized in his questions and his argument — made it highly improbable that she was the sole custodian of those weapons.

Even if it was reasonable to conclude that she had placed the guns in her purse before the car was stopped by police, the facts strongly suggest that Jane Doe was not the only person able to exercise dominion over them. The two guns were too large to be concealed in her handbag. The bag was consequently open, and part of one of the guns was in plain view, within easy access of the driver of the car and even, perhaps, of the other two respondents who were riding in the rear seat.

Moreover, it is highly improbable that the loaded guns belonged to Jane Doe or that she was solely responsible for their being in her purse. As a 16-year-old girl in the company of three adult men she was the least likely of the four to be carrying one, let alone two, heavy handguns. It is far more probable that she relied on the pocketknife found in her brassiere for any necessary self-protection. Under these circumstances, it was not unreasonable for her counsel to argue and for the jury to infer that when the car was halted for speeding, the other passengers in the car anticipated the risk of a search and attempted to conceal their weapons in a pocketbook in the front seat. The inference is surely more likely than the notion that these weapons were the sole property of the 16-year-old girl.

Under these circumstances, the jury would have been entirely reasonable in rejecting the suggestion — which, incidentally, defense counsel did not even advance in their closing arguments to the jury — that the handguns were in the sole possession of Jane Doe. Assuming that the jury did reject it, the case is tantamount to one in which the guns were lying on the floor or the seat of the car in the plain view of the three other occupants of the automobile. In such a case, it is surely rational to infer that each of the respondents was fully aware of the presence of the guns and had both the ability and the intent to exercise dominion and control over the weapons. The application of the statutory presumption in this case therefore comports with the standard laid down in Tot v. United States, 319 U.S., at 467, and restated in Leary v. United States, 395 U.S., at 36. For there is a "rational connection" between the basic facts that the prosecution proved and the ultimate fact presumed, and the latter is "more likely than not to flow from" the former.

Respondents argue, however, that the validity of the New York presumption must be judged by a "reasonable doubt" test rather than the "more likely than not" standard employed in *Leary*. Under the more stringent test, it is argued that a statutory presumption must be rejected unless the evidence necessary to invoke the inference is sufficient for a rational jury to find the inferred fact beyond a reasonable doubt. See Barnes v. United States, 412 U.S., at 842-843. Respondents' argument again overlooks the distinction between a permissive presumption on which the prosecution is entitled to rely as one not necessarily sufficient part of its proof and a mandatory presumption which the jury must accept even if it is the sole evidence of an element of the offense.

In the latter situation, since the prosecution bears the burden of establishing guilt, it may not rest its case entirely on a presumption unless the fact proved is sufficient to support the inference of guilt beyond a reasonable doubt. But in the former situation, the prosecution may rely on all of the evidence in the record to meet the reasonable-doubt standard. There is no more reason to require a permissive statutory presumption to meet a reasonable-doubt standard before it may be permitted to play any part in a trial than there is to require that degree of probative force for other relevant evidence before it may be admitted. As long as it is clear that the presumption is not the sole and sufficient basis for a finding of guilt, it need only satisfy the test described in *Leary*.

The permissive presumption, as used in this case, satisfied the *Leary* test. And, as already noted, the New York Court of Appeals has concluded that the record as a whole was sufficient to establish guilt beyond a reasonable doubt.

The judgment is reversed.

Mr. Justice Powell, with whom Mr. Justice Brennan, Mr. Justice Stewart, and Mr. Justice Marshall join, dissenting.

I agree with the Court that there is no procedural bar to our considering the underlying constitutional question presented by this case. I am not in agreement, however, with the Court's conclusion that the presumption as charged to the jury in this case meets the constitutional requirements of due process as set forth in our prior decisions. On the contrary, an individual's mere presence in an automobile where there is a handgun does not even make it "more likely than not" that the individual possesses the weapon.

I

In the criminal law, presumptions are used to encourage the jury to find certain facts, with respect to which no direct evidence is presented, solely because other facts have been proved.[1] See, e.g., Barnes v. United States, 412 U.S. 837, 840 n.3, United States v. Romano, 382 U.S. 136, 138 (1965). The purpose of such presumptions is plain: Like certain

---

1. Such encouragement can be provided either by statutory presumptions, see, e.g., 18 U.S.C. §1201(b), or by presumptions created in the common law. See, e.g., Barnes v. United States, 412 U.S. 837 (1973). Unless otherwise specified, "presumption" will be used herein to "permissible inferences," as well as to "true" presumptions. See F. James, Civil Procedure §7.9 (1965).

other jury instructions, they provide guidance for jurors' thinking in considering the evidence laid before them. Once in the juryroom, jurors necessarily draw inferences from the evidence — both direct and circumstantial. Through the use of presumptions, certain inferences are commended to the attention of jurors by legislatures or courts.

Legitimate guidance of a jury's deliberations is an indispensable part of our criminal justice system. Nonetheless, the use of presumptions in criminal cases poses at least two distinct perils for defendants' constitutional rights. The Court accurately identifies the first of these as being the danger of interference with "the factfinder's responsibility at trial, based on evidence adduced by the State, to find the ultimate facts beyond a reasonable doubt." If the jury is instructed that it must infer some ultimate fact (that is, some element of the offense) from proof of other facts unless the defendant disproves the ultimate fact by a preponderance of the evidence, then the presumption shifts the burden of proof to the defendant concerning the element thus inferred.[2]

But I do not agree with the Court's conclusion that the only constitutional difficulty with presumptions lies in the danger of lessening the burden of proof the prosecution must bear. As the Court notes, the presumptions thus far reviewed by the Court have not shifted the burden of persuasion; instead they either have required only that the defendant produce some evidence to rebut the inference suggested by the prosecution's evidence, see Tot v. United States, 319 U.S. 463 (1943), or merely have been suggestions to the jury that it would be sensible to draw certain conclusions on the basis of the evidence presented. See Barnes v. United States, supra, 412 U.S. at 840 n.3. Evolving from our decisions, therefore, is a second standard for judging the constitutionality of criminal presumptions which is based — not on the constitutional requirement that the State be put to its proof — but rather on the due process rule that when the jury is encouraged to make factual inferences, those inferences must reflect some valid general observation about the natural connection between events as they occur in our society.

This due process rule was first articulated by the Court in Tot v. United States, supra, in which the Court reviewed the constitutionality of §2(f) of the Federal Firearms Act. That statute provided in part that "possession of a firearm or ammunition by any . . . person [who has been convicted of a crime of violence] shall be presumptive evidence that such

---

2. The Court suggests that presumptions that shift the burden of persuasion to the defendant in this way can be upheld provided that "the fact proved is sufficient to support the inference of guilt beyond a reasonable doubt." As the present case involves no shifting of the burden of persuasion, the constitutional restrictions on such presumptions are not before us, and I express no views on them.

It may well be that even those presumptions that do not shift the burden of persuasion cannot be used to prove an element of the offense, if the facts proved would not permit a reasonable mind to find the presumed fact beyond a reasonable doubt. My conclusion in Part II, infra, makes it unnecessary for me to address this concern here.

firearm or ammunition was shipped or transported [in interstate or foreign commerce]." As the Court interpreted the presumption, it placed upon a defendant only the obligation of presenting some exculpatory evidence concerning the origins of a firearm or ammunition, once the Government proved that the defendant had possessed the weapon and had been convicted of a crime of violence. Noting that juries must be permitted to infer from one fact the existence of another essential to guilt, "if reason and experience support the inference," id., at 467, the Court concluded that under some circumstances juries may be guided in making these inferences by legislative or common-law presumptions, even though they may be based "upon a view of relation broader than that a jury might take in a specific case," 319 U.S., at 468. To provide due process, however, there must be at least "a rational connection between the facts proved and the fact presumed" — a connection grounded in "common experience." Id., at 467. In *Tot,* the Court found that connection to be lacking.

Subsequently, in Leary v. United States, 395 U.S. 6 (1969), the Court reaffirmed and refined the due process requirement of *Tot* that inferences specifically commended to the attention of jurors must reflect generally accepted connections between related events. At issue in *Leary* was the constitutionality of a federal statute making it a crime to receive, conceal, buy, or sell marihuana illegally brought into the United States, knowing it to have been illegally imported. The statute provided that mere possession of marihuana "shall be deemed sufficient evidence to authorize conviction unless the defendant explains his possession to the satisfaction of the jury." After reviewing the Court's decisions in Tot v. United States, supra, and other criminal presumption cases, Mr. Justice Harlan, writing for the Court, concluded "that a criminal statutory presumption must be regarded as 'irrational' or 'arbitrary,' and hence unconstitutional, unless it can be said with substantial assurance that the presumed fact is more likely than not to flow from the proved fact on which it is made to depend." 395 U.S., at 36 (footnote omitted). The Court invalidated the statute, finding there to be insufficient basis in fact for the conclusion that those who possess marihuana are more likely than not to know that it was imported illegally.[5]

Most recently, in Barnes v. United States, supra, we considered the constitutionality of a quite different sort of presumption — one that suggested to the jury that "[p]ossession of recently stolen property, if not satisfactorily explained, is ordinarily a circumstance from which you may

5. Because the statute in Leary v. United States, 395 U.S. 6 (1969), was found to be unconstitutional under the "more likely than not" standard, the Court explicitly declined to consider whether criminal presumptions also must follow "beyond a reasonable doubt" from their premises, if an essential element of the crime depends upon the presumption's use. Id., at 36 n.64. See supra n.2. The Court similarly avoided this question in Turner v. United States, 396 U.S. 398 (1970).

reasonably draw the inference . . . that the person in possession knew the property had been stolen." Id., 412 U.S. at 840 n.3. After reviewing the various formulations used by the Court to articulate the constitutionally required basis for a criminal presumption, we once again found it unnecessary to choose among them. As for the presumption suggested to the jury in *Barnes,* we found that it was well founded in history, common sense, and experience, and therefore upheld it as being "clearly sufficient to enable the jury to find beyond a reasonable doubt" that those in the unexplained possession of recently stolen property know it to have been stolen. Id., at 845.

In sum, our decisions uniformly have recognized that due process requires more than merely that the prosecution be put to its proof.[6] In addition, the Constitution restricts the court in its charge to the jury by requiring that, when particular factual inferences are recommended to the jury, those factual inferences be accurate reflections of what history, common sense, and experience tell us about the relations between events in our society. Generally this due process rule has been articulated as requiring that the truth of the inferred fact be more likely than not whenever the premise for the inference is true. Thus, to be constitutional a presumption must be at least more likely than not true.

II

In the present case, the jury was told that,

> Our Penal Law also provides that the presence in an automobile of any machine gun or of any handgun or firearm which is loaded is presumptive evidence of their unlawful possession. In other words, [under] these presumptions or this latter presumption upon proof of the presence of the machine gun and the hand weapons, you may infer and draw a conclusion that such prohibited weapon was possessed by each of the defendants who occupied the automobile at the time when such instruments were found. The presumption or presumptions is effective only so long as there is no substantial evidence contradicting the conclusion flowing from the presumption, and the presumption is said to disappear when such contradictory evidence is adduced.

Undeniably, the presumption charged in this case encouraged the jury to draw a particular factual inference regardless of any other evidence presented: to infer that respondents possessed the weapons found in the automobile "upon proof of the presence of the machine gun and the hand weapon" and proof that respondents "occupied the automobile

---

6. The Court apparently disagrees, contending that "the factfinder's responsibility . . . to find the ultimate facts beyond a reasonable doubt" is the only constitutional restraint upon the use of criminal presumptions at trial.

at the time such instruments were found." I believe that the presumption thus charged was unconstitutional because it did not fairly reflect what common sense and experience tell us about passengers in automobiles and the possession of handguns. People present in automobiles where there are weapons simply are not "more likely than not" the possessors of those weapons.

Under New York law, "to possess" is "to have physical possession or otherwise to exercise dominion or control over tangible property." N.Y. Penal Law §10.00(8). Plainly the mere presence of an individual in an automobile — without more — does not indicate that he exercises "dominion or control over" everything within it. As the Court of Appeals noted, there are countless situations in which individuals are invited as guests into vehicles the contents of which they know nothing about, much less have control over. Similarly, those who invite others into their automobile do not generally search them to determine what they may have on their person; nor do they insist that any handguns be identified and placed within reach of the occupants of the automobile. Indeed, handguns are particularly susceptible to concealment and therefore are less likely than are other objects to be observed by those in an automobile.

In another context, this Court has been particularly hesitant to infer possession from mere presence in a location, noting that "[p]resence is relevant and admissible evidence in a trial on a possession charge; but absent some showing of the defendant's function at [the illegal] still, its connection with possession is too tenuous to permit a reasonable inference of guilt — 'the inference of the one from proof of the other is arbitrary. . . .' Tot v. United States, 319 U.S. 463, 467." United States v. Romano, 382 U.S. 136, 141 (1965). We should be even more hesitant to uphold the inference of possession of a handgun from mere presence in an automobile, in light of common experience concerning automobiles and handguns. Because the specific factual inference recommended to the jury in this case is not one that is supported by the general experience of our society, I cannot say that the presumption charged is "more likely than not" to be true. Accordingly, respondents' due process rights were violated by the presumption's use.

As I understand it, the Court today does not contend that in general those who are present in automobiles are more likely than not to possess any gun contained within their vehicles. It argues, however, that the nature of the presumption here involved requires that we look, not only to the immediate facts upon which the jury was encouraged to base its inference, but to the other facts "proved" by the prosecution as well. The Court suggests that this is the proper approach when reviewing what it calls "permissive" presumptions because the jury was urged "to consider all the circumstances tending to support or contradict the inference."

It seems to me that the Court mischaracterizes the function of the presumption charged in this case. As it acknowledges was the case in *Romano,* supra, the "instruction authorized conviction even if the jury disbelieved all of the testimony except the proof of presence" in the automobile.[7] The Court nevertheless relies on all of the evidence introduced by the prosecution and argues that the "permissive" presumption could not have prejudiced defendants. The possibility that the jury disbelieved all of this evidence, and relied on the presumption, is simply ignored.

I agree that the circumstances relied upon by the Court in determining the plausibility of the presumption charged in this case would have made it reasonable for the jury to "infer that each of the respondents was fully aware of the presence of the guns and had both the ability and the intent to exercise dominion and control over the weapons." But the jury was told that it could conclude that respondents possessed the weapons found therein from proof of the mere fact of respondents' presence in the automobile. For all we know, the jury rejected all of the prosecution's evidence concerning the location and origin of the guns, and based its conclusion that respondents possessed the weapons solely upon its belief that respondents had been present in the automobile.[8] For purposes of reviewing the constitutionality of the presumption at issue here, we must assume that this was the case.

The Court's novel approach in this case appears to contradict prior decisions of this Court reviewing such presumptions. Under the Court's analysis, whenever it is determined that an inference is "permissive," the only question is whether, in light of all of the evidence adduced at trial, the inference recommended to the jury is a reasonable one. The Court

---

7. In commending the presumption to the jury, the court gave no instruction that would have required a finding of possession to be based on anything more than mere presence in the automobile. Thus, the jury was not instructed that it should infer that respondents possessed the handguns only if it found that the guns were too large to be concealed in Jane Doe's handbag; that the guns accordingly were in the plain view of respondents; that the weapons were within "easy access of the driver of the car and even, perhaps, of the other two respondents who were riding in the rear seat"; that it was unlikely that Jane Doe was solely responsible for the placement of the weapons in her purse, id.; or that the case was "tantamount to one in which the guns were lying on the floor or the seat of the car in the plain view of the three other occupants of the automobile."

8. The Court is therefore mistaken in its conclusion that, because "respondents were not 'hitch-hikers or other casual passengers,' and the guns were neither 'a few inches in length' nor 'out of [respondents'] sight,' " reference to these possibilities is inappropriate in considering the constitutionality of the presumption as charged in this case. To be sure, respondents' challenge is to the presumption as charged to the jury in this case. But in assessing its application here, we are not free, as the Court apparently believes, to disregard the possibility that the jury may have disbelieved all other evidence supporting an inference of possession. The jury may have concluded that respondents — like hitchhikers — had only an incidental relationship to the auto in which they were traveling, or that, contrary to some of the testimony at trial, the weapons were indeed out of respondents' sight.

has never suggested that the inquiry into the rational basis of a permissible inference may be circumvented in this manner. Quite the contrary, the Court has required that the "evidence *necessary to invoke the inference* [be] sufficient for a rational juror to find the inferred fact. . . ." Barnes v. United States, 412 U.S. 843 (1973) (emphasis supplied). See Turner v. United States, 396 U.S. 398, 407 (1970). Under the presumption charged in this case, the only evidence necessary to invoke the inference was the presence of the weapons in the automobile with respondents — an inference that is plainly irrational.

In sum, it seems to me that the Court today ignores the teaching of our prior decisions. By speculating about what the jury may have done with the factual inference thrust upon it, the Court in effect assumes away the inference altogether, constructing a rule that permits the use of any inference — no matter how irrational in itself — provided that otherwise there is sufficient evidence in the record to support a finding of guilt. Applying this novel analysis to the present case, the Court upholds the use of a presumption that it makes no effort to defend in isolation. In substance, the Court — applying an unarticulated harmless error standard — simply finds that the respondents were guilty as charged. They may well have been but rather than acknowledging this rationale, the Court seems to have made new law with respect to presumptions that could seriously jeopardize a defendant's right to a fair trial. Accordingly, I dissent.

Do you agree with the majority's characterization of the device involved in *Ulster County* as a "permissive inference"? If the factfinder's responsibility is to find the ultimate facts beyond a reasonable doubt based on evidence presented by the prosecution, how can the court apply *any* standard other than the "beyond-a-reasonable-doubt-rational-connection test" to this device, regardless of how it is characterized? Has the majority applied a standard even lower than the preponderance standard, i.e., "not-irrational"? Is the majority correct in considering all the evidence in the case in deciding whether the presumption passes constitutional muster? Is the dissent correct in insisting that the presumption be judged solely on the basis of the relationship between the basic fact and the presumed fact? Did the device in this case operate to shift the burden of production to the defendant? Is this constitutional? Is the decision in this case consistent with proposed Rule 303?

CHAPTER X

Judicial Notice

Judicial notice is a method of establishing a proposition without introducing evidence to prove it. Not surprisingly, there is considerable conceptual overlap between the devices discussed in the preceding chapter — presumptions, inferences, and allocations of burdens of proof — and judicial notice. The most commonly voiced justification for all such devices is efficiency — avoiding needless waste of time in proving something about which there ordinarily is no dispute. With greater effort, most matters that are judicially noticed could be made the subject of explicit proof, but in the majority of cases, the process of proof is not worth the time and cost. Noticing the fact places the burden of disproving it on the party contesting the fact. Thus, a disputable judicially noticed fact (Rule 201) and a rebuttable presumption (Rule 301) operate in the same way. A second function of judicial notice is to avoid embarrassment. As frequently happens, the point in question may be so obvious that the attorneys simply forget to prove it and the point is "saved" by judicial notice. In this way judicial notice is similar to presumptions in that judicial notice contributes to the process of belief-formation on a case-by-case as well as system-wide basis.

The framers of the federal rule, Rule 201, wrote a provision with five major restrictions:

(1) Rule 201 applies only to facts; the rule leaves questions of noticing law untouched;

(2) The facts must be adjudicative, as opposed to legislative; that is, the facts must pertain to the litigated event, not to the laws or policies behind the laws that relate to the event;

(3) For judicial notice to be taken, the adjudicative facts must be beyond "reasonable dispute";

(4) In a civil case there is no rebuttal of a judicially noticed fact; in a criminal case there may be, and the jury must be instructed that it is not requested to accept as conclusive any fact judicially noticed; and

(5) The opposing party has a right to be heard on any proposition to be noticed.

FRE 201
Judicial Notice of Adjudicative Facts

(a) *Scope of Rule.* This rule governs only judicial notice of adjudicative facts.

(b) *Kinds of Facts.* A judicially noticed fact must be one not subject to reasonable dispute in that it is either (1) generally known within the territorial jurisdiction of the trial court or (2) capable of accurate and ready determination by resort to sources whose accuracy cannot reasonably be questioned.

(c) *When Discretionary.* A court may take judicial notice, whether requested or not.

(d) *When Mandatory.* A court shall take judicial notice if requested by a party and supplied with the necessary information.

(e) *Opportunity to be Heard.* A party is entitled upon timely request to an opportunity to be heard as to the propriety of taking judicial notice and the tenor of the matter noticed. In the absence of prior notification, the request may be made after judicial notice has been taken.

(f) *Time of Taking Notice.* Judicial notice may be taken at any stage of the proceeding.

(g) *Instructing Jury.* In a civil action or proceeding, the court shall instruct the jury to accept as conclusive any fact judicially noticed. In a criminal case, the court shall instruct the jury that it may, but is not required to, accept as conclusive any fact judicially noticed.

NOTE: JUDICIAL NOTICE IN THEORY AND PRACTICE

With regard to the limitation of Rule 201 to adjudicative facts beyond reasonable dispute, the Advisory Committee's Note states:

> This is the only evidence rule on the subject of judicial notice. It deals only with judicial notice of "adjudicative" facts. No rule deals with judicial notice of "legislative" facts. . . .
>
> The omission of any treatment of legislative facts results from fundamental differences between adjudicative facts and legislative facts. Adjudicative facts are simply the facts of the particular case. Legislative facts, on the other hand, are those which have relevance to legal reasoning and the lawmaking process, whether in the formulation of a legal principle or ruling by a judge or court or in the enactment of a legislative body. The terminology was coined by Professor Kenneth Davis in his article An Approach to Problems of Evidence in the Administrative Process, 55 Harv. L. Rev. 364, 404-407 (1942). . . .
>
> The usual method of establishing adjudicative facts is through the introduction of evidence, ordinarily consisting of the testimony of witnesses. If particular facts are outside the area of reasonable controversy, this process is

dispensed with as unnecessary. A high degree of indisputability is the essential prerequisite.

Leglislative facts are quite different. As Professor Davis says:

> My opinion is that judge-made law would stop growing if judges, in thinking about questions of law and policy, were forbidden to take into account the facts they believe, as distinguished from facts which are "clearly . . . within the domain of the indisputable." Facts most needed in thinking about difficult problems of law and policy have a way of being outside the domain of the clearly indisputable. . . .

Similar considerations govern the judicial use of non-adjudicative facts in ways other than formulating laws and rules. Thayer described them as a part of the judicial reasoning process.

> In conducting a process of judicial reasoning, as of other reasoning, not a step can be taken without assuming something which has not been proved; and the capacity to do this with competent judgment and efficiency, is imputed to judges and juries as part of their necessary mental outfit.

Thayer, Preliminary Treatise on Evidence 279-280 (1898).

As Professor Davis points out, . . . every case involves the use of hundreds or thousands of non-evidence facts. When a witness in an automobile accident case says "car," everyone, judge and jury included, furnishes, from non-evidence sources within himself, the supplementing information that the "car" is an automobile, not a railroad car, that it is self-propelled, probably by an internal combustion engine, that it may be assumed to have four wheels with pneumatic rubber tires, and so on. The judicial process cannot construct every case from scratch, like Descartes creating a world based on the postulate *Cogito, ergo sum.* These items could not possibly be introduced into evidence, and no one suggests that they be. Nor are they appropriate subjects for any formalized treatment of judicial notice of facts. . . .

In view of these considerations, the regulation of judicial notice of facts by the present rule extends only to adjudicative facts.

What, then, are "adjudicative" facts? Davis refers to them as those "which relate to the parties," or more fully:

> When a court or an agency finds facts concerning the immediate parties — who did what, where, when, how, and with what motive or intent — the court or agency is performing an adjudicative function, and the facts are conveniently called adjudicative facts. . . .
>
> Stated in other terms, the adjudicative facts are those to which the law is applied in the process of adjudication. They are the facts that normally go to the jury in a jury case. They relate to the parties, their activities, their properties, their businesses.

2 Administrative Law Treatise 353.

As the federal rule states, a fact may be beyond reasonable dispute *either* because it is generally known within the territorial jurisdiction of the court or easily verifiable from sources whose accuracy "cannot reasonably be questioned." A typical example of judicial notice of an adjudicative fact of the latter sort is that the date on which a contract was executed was a Sunday. An example of the former type of fact is that Main Street in a certain city is a public way. Note that under the rule what a judge knows and what the judge may judicially notice are not the same. Thus, a judge could not properly take judicial notice that a certain street was under construction even though he had seen the construction, unless it were generally known within the jurisdiction or could be easily verified from reliable sources. The same restriction applies to jury members, except that anything all members of the jury know is likely to fall within Rule 201(b)(1).

As might be expected, it is sometimes difficult to say with certainty in a given case whether a fact is adjudicative or legislative. An example of a fact that most would agree is legislative is that forcing one unwilling spouse to testify against the other concerning confidential marital communications threatens the stability of marriages. Cf. Trammel v. United States, 445 U.S. 40 (1980), pp. 623-629, above.

The process of taking judicial notice appears to be carefully regulated by the federal rule, but certain questions are not explicitly answered. For example, Rule 201(e) provides that a party is entitled to be heard as to the propriety of taking judicial notice and that in the absence of prior notification, the request may be made after judicial notice has been taken. Rule 201(f) provides that notice may be taken "at any stage of the proceeding." Does this include after all parties have rested? After the trial has been concluded? On appeal? If so, how will an objecting party be heard? Must notification be given in all cases on all matters to be judicially noticed? If a party objects to the propriety of the court's taking judicial notice of a fact, what does the "not subject to reasonable dispute" standard mean? Certainty? Beyond a reasonable doubt? More probable than not? Should the standard shift depending on how central the fact is to the case? Once a fact has been judicially noticed, is contrary evidence admissible? On a related point, is judicial notice of a fact ever really mandatory? What does "supplied with the necessary information" in Rule 201(d) mean? How is such information supplied in practice? Must such "information" itself be admissible? Finally, in a criminal case, what exactly should the jury be told about a fact that the court has noticed over the objection of the defendant? What constitutional limitations are there on judicial notice of adjudicative and legislative facts? For example, could Rule 201(f) be applied to notice a fact in a criminal case on appeal?

Professor Warren Schwartz has criticized the present use of judicial notice and suggested that problems now handled by judicial notice could be better resolved by (1) greater use of summary judgment and directed verdict rulings to eliminate spurious issues, (2) relaxation of hearsay limitations on the use of scholarly works, and (3) greater flexibility in opening up the trial record to rectify inadequacies. Schwartz, A Suggestion for the Demise of Judicial Notice of "Judicial Facts," 45 Tex. L. Rev. 1212 (1967). According to Professor Schwartz, the doctrine of judicial notice of adjudicative facts is inadequate because "it fails as a means of identifying issues that need not be tried" and in "achieving a just result despite the failure of the parties to produce adequate proof." More fundamentally, Schwartz argues that contemporary judicial notice doctrine fails "to face squarely the questions of what should be the judge's responsibility in determining whether a factual record is inadequate and whether to take steps to cure it." In Schwartz's opinion, this failure is attributable to the doctrine's emphasis on facts that are of common notoriety or capable of ready verification, rather than on whether a particular factual issue is genuinely in dispute. Schwartz states,

> Whether the matter is commonly known or subject to immediate and accurate determination should be irrelevant if the truth of the particular fact in issue can be plainly demonstrated. This is precisely the approach of summary judgment and directed verdict, which foreclose the matter if the particular issue is not "genuine." These devices, moreover, should cover all cases where judicial notice can now be taken. If the matter is of "common notoriety," the affidavit or testimony of a knowledgeable person will be sufficient because presumably no denial will be possible. If the matter can be determined by reference to sources of "indisputable accuracy" the moving party will offer them; if indeed they are indisputable, they will not be disputed.

Id. at 1214-1215.

Schwartz proposes the following statute, together with summary judgment and directed verdict motions, as a "more inclusive and rational means for dealing with these problems":

> (1) If the trial court in a case in which both sides have rested and the case has not been decided shall determine that the evidence with respect to a material issue of fact is significantly less than may be available and that there is a substantial risk that decision based on the evidence of record measured by the applicable burdens of proof and persuasion may not comport with actual fact it may
> (a) in all cases where there is no jury and in jury cases where the additional evidence can be obtained without substantial delay stay all proceedings until the parties have an opportunity to obtain the additional evidence and then permit the evidence to be introduced and considered in the decision of the case, or
> (b) in jury cases where the additional evidence cannot be obtained without substantial delay discharge the jury and direct retrial of the case when the additional evidence is obtained.[2]

---

2. There are procedural devices that provide alternatives to directing complete retrial. Thus if the issue with respect to which the evidence is to be offered is severable the court can sever it and hear the remainder of the case. The jury verdict may then make the severed issue moot. A second possibility is that the party who will have to bear the expense of the extra proceedings (as provided in paragraph 3) may be agreeable to waiving jury trial. If the other party concurs, the case can simply be continued until the additional evidence is available. It is also possible that after the additional evidence is obtained summary judgment can be awarded and retrial thus avoided.

(2) If the trial court after the case has been decided or an appellate court shall determine that the evidence with respect to a material issue of fact is significantly less than may be available and that there is a substantial risk that decision based on the evidence of record measured by the applicable burdens of proof and persuasion may not comport with actual fact it may

(a) afford the parties the opportunity to demonstrate to the Court before whom the matter is pending their respective rights to summary judgment[3] with respect to the issue, or

(b) remand the case for the taking of further evidence and reconsideration by the judge before whom the case was originally heard (who may be the judge issuing the order) or a retrial of the issue before a jury as may be appropriate.[4]

(3) The party or parties against whom the issue would be resolved on the state of the record prior to the proceedings authorized by this Rule shall be responsible for all costs, including reasonable attorney's fees, incurred by the other parties in connection with proceedings authorized by this Rule.

Id. at 1213-1214.

Is Schwartz's proposal an improvement on the Federal Rules approach? Is it practical? Does it avoid or resolve questions left open by Rule 201? Does it raise new questions?

In the next three cases, Javins v. First National Realty Corp., Smith v. Pro-Football, Inc., and State v. Tavone, are the courts taking judicial notice of facts that should be the subject of proof? If so, are these facts legislative or adjudicative? Under the Federal Rules, how should such matters be handled by courts?

JAVINS v. FIRST NATIONAL REALTY CORP.
428 F.2d 1071 (D.C. Cir.), cert. denied, 400 U.S. 925 (1970)

WRIGHT, J. These cases present the question whether housing code violations which arise during the term of a lease have any effect upon the tenant's obligation to pay rent. The Landlord and Tenant Branch of the District of Columbia Court of General Sessions ruled proof of such violations inadmissible when proffered as a defense to an eviction action for nonpayment of rent. The District of Columbia Court of Appeals upheld this ruling. . . . We now reverse and hold that a warranty of habitability, measured by the standards set out in the Housing Regulations for the District of Columbia, is implied by operation of law into

---

3. A motion for summary judgment before the appellate court would be an unprecedented innovation. Since no oral testimony is required and the appellate court has gained familiarity with the case by hearing the appeal, there is no reason for a remand to the trial court.

4. Of course, waiver of jury trial will avoid the necessity of repeating the evidence previously admitted on the issue.

leases of urban dwelling units covered by those Regulations and that breach of this warranty gives rise to the usual remedies for breach of contract.

I

The facts revealed by the record are simple. By separate written leases, each of the appellants rented an apartment in a three-building apartment complex in Northwest Washington known as Clifton Terrace. The landlord, First National Realty Corporation, filed separate actions in the Landlord and Tenant Branch of the Court of General Sessions on April 8, 1966, seeking possession on the ground that each of the appellants had defaulted in the payment of rent due for the month of April. The tenants, appellants here, admitted that they had not paid the landlord any rent for April. However, they alleged numerous violations of the Housing Regulations as "an equitable defense or [a] claim by way of recoupment or set-off in an amount equal to the rent claim," as provided in the rules of the Court of General Sessions. They offered to prove

> [t]hat there are approximately 1500 violations of the Housing Regulations of the District of Columbia in the building at Clifton Terrace, where Defendant resides some affecting the premises of this Defendant directly, others indirectly, and all tending to establish a course of conduct of violation of the Housing Regulations to the damage of Defendants. . . .

Settled Statement of Proceedings and Evidence, p.2 (1966). Appellants conceded at trial, however, that this offer of proof reached only violations which had arisen since the term of the lease had commenced. The Court of General Sessions refused appellants' offer of proof[4] and entered judgment for the landlord. The District of Columbia Court of Appeals affirmed, rejecting the argument made by appellants that the landlord was under a contractual duty to maintain the premises in compliance with the Housing Regulations.

II

Since, in traditional analysis, a lease was the conveyance of an interest in land, courts have usually utilized the special rules governing real property transactions to resolve controversies involving leases. However,

4. According to established procedure, this case was submitted to both the District of Columbia Court of Appeals and this court on the basis of a sparse "Settled Statement of Proceedings and Evidence," as approved by both parties and the trial judge. Unfortunately, the court's ruling on the offer of proof was made from the bench, and the basis of the ruling is not reflected in the "Settled Statement." We have recently noted the inadequacy of such records for review by an appellate court.

as the Supreme Court has noted in another context, "the body of private property law . . . , more than almost any other branch of law, has been shaped by distinctions whose validity is largely historical." Courts have a duty to reappraise old doctrines in the light of the facts and values of contemporary life — particularly old common law doctrines which the courts themselves created and developed. As we have said before, "[T]he continued vitality of the common law . . . depends upon its ability to reflect contemporary community values and ethics."

The assumption of landlord-tenant law, derived from feudal property law, that a lease primarily conveyed to the tenant an interest in land may have been reasonable in a rural, agrarian society; it may continue to be reasonable in some leases involving farming or commercial land. In these cases, the value of the lease to the tenant is the land itself. But in the case of the modern apartment dweller, the value of the lease is that it gives him a place to live. The city dweller who seeks to lease an apartment on the third floor of a tenement has little interest in the land 30 or 40 feet below, or even in the bare right to possession within the four walls of his apartment. When American city dwellers, both rich and poor, seek "shelter" today, they seek a well known package of goods and services[9] — a package which includes not merely walls and ceilings, but also adequate heat, light and ventilation, serviceable plumbing facilities, secure windows and doors, proper sanitation, and proper maintenance.

Professor Powell summarizes the present state of the law:

> The complexities of city life, and the proliferated problems of modern society in general, have created new problems for lessors and lessees and these have been commonly handled by specific clauses inserted in leases. This growth in the number and detail of specific lease covenants has reintroduced into the law of estates for years a predominantly contractual ingredient. In practice, the law today concerning estates for years consists chiefly of rules determining the construction and effect of lease covenants. . . .[10]

Ironically, however, the rules governing the construction and interpretation of "predominantly contractual" obligations in leases have too often remained rooted in old property law.

Some courts have realized that certain of the old rules of property law governing leases are inappropriate for today's transactions. In order to reach results more in accord with the legitimate expectations of the parties and the standards of the community, courts have been gradually introducing more modern precepts of contract law in interpreting leases. Proceeding piecemeal has, however, led to confusion where "de-

9. See, e.g., National Commission on Urban Problems, Building the American City 9 (1968). The extensive standards set out in the Housing Regulations provide a good guide to community expectations.
10. 2 R. Powell, Real Property ¶221[1] at 179 (1967).

cisions are frequently conflicting, not because of a healthy disagreement on social policy, but because of the lingering impact of rules whose policies are long since dead."

In our judgment the trend toward treating leases as contracts is wise and well considered. Our holding in this case reflects a belief that leases of urban dwelling units should be interpreted and construed like any other contract. . . .

IV

In our judgment the common law itself must recognize the landlord's obligation to keep his premises in a habitable condition. This conclusion is compelled by three separate considerations. First, we believe that the old rule was based on certain factual assumptions which are no longer true; on its own terms, it can no longer be justified. Second, we believe that the consumer protection cases . . . require that the old rule be abandoned in order to bring residential landlord-tenant law into harmony with the principles on which those cases rest. Third, we think that the nature of today's urban housing market also dictates abandonment of the old rule. . . .

[S]ome courts began some time ago to question the common law's assumptions that the land was the most important feature of a leasehold and that the tenant could feasibly make any necessary repairs himself. Where those assumptions no longer reflect contemporary housing patterns, the courts have created exceptions to the general rule that landlords have no duty to keep their premises in repair.

It is overdue for courts to admit that these assumptions are no longer true with regard to all urban housing. Today's urban[39] tenants, the vast majority of whom live in multiple dwelling houses, are interested, not in the land, but solely in "a house suitable for occupation." Furthermore, today's city dweller usually has a single, specialized skill unrelated to maintenance work; he is unable to make repairs like the "jack-of-all-trades" farmer who was the common law's model of the lessee. Further, unlike his agrarian predecessor who often remained on one piece of land for his entire life, urban tenants today are more mobile than ever before. A tenant's tenure in a specific apartment will often not be sufficient to justify efforts at repairs. In addition, the increasing complexity of today's dwellings renders them much more difficult to repair than the structures of earlier times. In a multiple dwelling repair may require access to equipment and areas in the control of the landlord. Low and middle income tenants, even if they were interested in making

---

39. In 1968 more than two thirds of America's people lived in the 228 largest metropolitan areas. Only 5.2% lived on farms. The World Almanac 1970 at 251 (L. Long ed.). More than 98% of all housing starts in 1968 were non-farm. Id. at 313.

repairs, would be unable to obtain any financing for major repairs since they have no long-term interest in the property.

Our approach to the common law of landlord and tenant ought to be aided by principles derived from consumer protection cases. . . . In a lease contract, a tenant seeks to purchase from his landlord shelter for a specified period of time. The landlord sells housing as a commercial businessman and has much greater opportunity, incentive and capacity to inspect and maintain the condition of his building. Moreover, the tenant must rely upon the skill and bona fides of his landlord at least as much as a car buyer must rely upon the car manufacturer. In dealing with major problems, such as heating, plumbing, electrical or structural defects, the tenant's position corresponds precisely with "the ordinary consumer who cannot be expected to have the knowledge or capacity or even the opportunity to make adequate inspection of mechanical instrumentalities, like automobiles, and to decide for himself whether they are reasonably fit for the designed purpose." Henningsen v. Bloomfield Motors, Inc., 32 N.J. 358, 375, 161 A.2d 69, 78 (1960).[42]

Since a lease contract specifies a particular period of time during which the tenant has a right to use his apartment for shelter, he may legitimately expect that the apartment will be fit for habitation for the time period for which it is rented. . . .

Even beyond the rationale of traditional products liability law, the relationship of landlord and tenant suggests further compelling reasons for the law's protection of the tenants' legitimate expectations of quality. The inequality in bargaining power between landlord and tenant has been well documented.[44] Tenants have very little leverage to enforce demands for better housing. Various impediments to competition in the rental housing market, such as racial and class discrimination[45] and standardized form leases,[46] mean that landlords place tenants in a take it or leave it situation. The increasingly severe shortage[47] of adequate housing further increases the landlord's bargaining power and escalates the need for maintaining and improving the existing stock. Finally, the findings by various studies of the social impact of bad housing has led to the realization that poor housing is detrimental to the whole society, not

42. Nor should the average tenant be thought capable of "inspecting" plaster, floorboards, roofing, kitchen appliances, etc. To the extent, however, that some defects *are* obvious, the law must take note of the present housing shortage. Tenants may have no real alternative but to accept such housing with the expectation that the landlord will make necessary repairs. Where this is so, caveat emptor must of necessity be rejected.

44. See Edwards v. Habib, 130 U.S. App. D.C. 126, 140, 397 F.2d 687, 701 (1968); 2 R. Powell, supra Note 10, ¶221[1] at 183; President's Committee on Urban Housing, A Decent Home 96 (1968).

45. President's Committee, supra Note 44, at 96; National Commission, supra Note 9, at 18-19; G. Sternlieb, The Tenement Landlord 71 (1966).

46. R. Powell, supra Note 10, ¶221[1] at 183 n.13.

47. See generally President's Committee, supra Note 44.

merely to the unlucky ones who must suffer the daily indignity of living in a slum.[48]

Thus we are led by our inspection of the relevant legal principles and precedents to the conclusion that the old common law rule imposing an obligation upon the lessee to repair during the lease term was really never intended to apply to residential urban leaseholds. Contract principles established in other areas of the law provide a more rational framework for the apportionment of landlord-tenant responsibilities; they strongly suggest that a warranty of habitability be implied into all contracts for urban dwellings. . . .

We follow the Illinois court in holding that the housing code must be read into housing contracts — a holding also required by the purposes and the structure of the code itself.[57] The duties imposed by the Housing Regulations may not be waived or shifted by agreement if the Regulations specifically place the duty upon the lessor. Criminal penalties are provided if these duties are ignored. This regulatory structure was established by the Commissioners because, in their judgment, the grave conditions in the housing market required serious action. Yet official enforcement of the housing code has been far from uniformly effective.[59] Innumerable studies have documented the desperate condition of rental housing in the District of Columbia and in the nation. . . .

We therefore hold that the Housing Regulations imply a warranty of habitability, measured by the standards which they set out, into leases of all housing that they cover. . . .

SMITH v. PRO-FOOTBALL, INC.
593 F.2d 1173 (D.C. Cir. 1978)

WILKEY, J. This private antitrust action challenges the legality of the National Football League (NFL) player selection system, commonly called the "draft." The plaintiff is James McCoy (Yazoo) Smith, a former professional football player who played one season for the Washington Redskins after being drafted by them in 1968. The defendants are Pro-Football, Inc., which operates the Redskins, and the NFL. Smith contends that the draft as it existed in 1968 was an unreasonable restraint of trade in violation of §§1 and 3 of the Sherman Act, and that, but for the

48. A. Schorr, Slums and Insecurity (1963). . . .

57. "The housing and sanitary codes, especially in light of Congress' explicit direction for their enactment, indicate a strong and pervasive congressional concern to secure for the city's slum dwellers decent, or at least safe and sanitary, places to live." Edwards v. Habib, supra Note 44, 130 U.S. App. D.C. at 139, 397 F.2d at 700.

59. See Gribetz & Grad, Housing Code Enforcement: Sanctions and Remedies, 66 Colum. L. Rev. 1254 (1966); Note, Enforcement of Municipal Housing Codes, 78 Harv. L. Rev. 801 (1965).

draft, he would have negotiated a far more lucrative contract when he signed as a player in that year. Smith alleges that he has been injured in his business or property in the amount of the difference between the compensation he actually received and the compensation he would have received had there existed a "free market" for his services.

After a trial to the court, District Judge Bryant held that the NFL draft as it existed in 1968 constituted a "group boycott" and was thus a per se violation of the Sherman Act. Alternatively, he held that the draft, tested under the rule of reason, was an unreasonable restraint because it was "significantly more restrictive than necessary" to accomplish whatever legitimate goals the NFL had. Judge Bryant awarded Smith treble damages totaling $276,000. The Redskins and the NFL have appealed the finding of antitrust liability; both sides have appealed the damage award. Relying on the rule of reason, we affirm the finding of antitrust liability and remand for recomputation of damages.

I. BACKGROUND

The NFL draft, which has been in effect since 1935, is a procedure under which negotiating rights to graduating college football players are allocated each year among the NFL clubs in inverse order of the clubs' standing. Under the draft procedures generally followed, the team with the poorest playing-field record during the preceding season has the first opportunity, as among the NFL teams, to select a college player of its choice; the team with the next poorest record has the next choice, and so on until the team with the best record (the winner of the previous year's "Super Bowl") has picked last. At this point, the first "round" of the draft is completed. In 1968 there were 16 succeeding rounds in the yearly draft, the same order of selection being followed in each round. Teams had one choice per round unless they had traded their choice in that round to another team (a fairly common practice). When Smith was selected by the Redskins there were 26 teams choosing in the draft.

The NFL draft, like similar procedures in other professional sports, is designed to promote "competitive balance." By dispersing newly arriving player talent equally among all NFL teams, with preferences to the weaker clubs, the draft aims to produce teams that are as evenly-matched on the playing field as possible. Evenly-matched teams make for closer games, tighter pennant races, and better player morale, thus maximizing fan interest, broadcast revenues, and overall health of the sport.

The draft is effectuated through the NFL's "no-tampering" rule. Under this rule as it existed in 1968, no team was permitted to negotiate prior to the draft with any player eligible to be drafted, and no team could negotiate with (or sign) any player selected by another team in the draft. The net result of these restrictions was that the right to negotiate with any given player was exclusively held by one team at any given time. If a college player could not reach a satisfactory agreement with the team holding the rights to his services he could not play in the NFL.

Plaintiff Smith became subject to the draft when he graduated as an All-American football player from the University of Oregon in 1968. The Redskins, choosing twelfth, picked Smith as their first-round draft choice. After several months of negotiations, in which he was represented by an agent, Smith and the Redskins signed a one-year contract — a version of the Standard Player Contract that the NFL requires all players to sign. The contract awarded Smith a $23,000 "bonus" for signing, an additional $5,000 if he made the team, and a salary of $22,000, for a total first-year compensation of $50,000.

Smith made the team and performed at a high level of play as a defensive back until he suffered a serious neck injury in the final game of the 1968 season. His doctors advised him not to continue his football career. After his injury the Redskins paid Smith an additional $19,800, representing the amount he would ordinarily have received had he played out the second ("option") year of his contract.

Two years after his injury Smith filed suit in the District Court. After finding that the draft violated the antitrust laws, Judge Bryant awarded Smith damages equal to the difference between his actual compensation and the compensation he could have received in a free market. To compute the latter amount, Judge Bryant assumed that plaintiff in a free market would have been able to negotiate a three-year contract with an "injury protection clause," i.e., a clause guaranteeing payment for the full term of a player's contract even if he should be incapacitated. Judge Bryant estimated Smith's annual "free market salary" by taking the annual salary ($54,000) of another defensive back (Pat Fischer) who signed as a "free agent" with the Redskins in 1968. The resulting calculation yielded $162,000 as the contractual value of Smith's services in a free market. From this sum Judge Bryant subtracted the $69,800 that Smith in fact received, netting actual damages in the amount of $92,200. This figure was trebled to $276,600 in accordance with the antitrust laws.

II. ANALYSIS

The legality of the NFL player draft under the antitrust laws is essentially a question of first impression. This case requires us to consider (1) whether the legality of the draft is governed by a per se rule or by the rule of reason; (2) whether the draft, if tested by the rule of reason, is a reasonable restraint; and (3) whether, if the draft violates the antitrust laws, the measure of damages adopted by the District Judge was proper. We discuss these issues in turn. . . .

[In this part of the opinion, the Court found no per se violation.]

B. RULE OF REASON

Under the rule of reason, a restraint must be evaluated to determine whether it is significantly anticompetitive in purpose or effect. In making this evaluation, a court generally will be required to analyze "the facts peculiar to the business, the history of the restraint, and the reasons why it was imposed." If, on analysis, the restraint is found to have legitimate business purposes whose realization serves to promote competition, the "anticompetitive evils" of the challenged practice must be carefully balanced against its "procompetitive virtues" to ascertain whether the former outweigh the latter. A restraint is unreasonable if it has the "net effect" of substantially impeding competition.

After undertaking the analysis mandated by the rule of reason, the District Court concluded that the NFL draft as it existed in 1968 had a severely anticompetitive impact on the market for players' services, and that it went beyond the level of restraint reasonably necessary to accomplish whatever legitimate business purposes might be asserted for it. We have no basis for disturbing the District Court's findings of fact; and while our legal analysis differs slightly from that of the trial judge, having benefited from intervening guidance from the Supreme Court, we agree with the District Court's conclusion that the NFL draft as it existed in 1968 constituted an unreasonable restraint of trade.

The draft that has been challenged here is undeniably anticompetitive both in its purpose and in its effect. The defendants have conceded that the draft "restricts competition among the NFL clubs for the services of graduating college players" and, indeed, that the draft "is designed to limit competition" and "to be a 'purposive' restraint" on the player-service market. The fact that the draft assertedly was designed to promote the teams' playing-field equality rather than to inflate their profit margins may prevent the draft's purpose from being described, in subjective terms, as nefarious. But this fact does not prevent its purpose from being described, in objective terms, as anticompetitive, for suppressing competition, is the *telos*, the very essence of the restraint.

The trial judge was likewise correct in finding that the draft was significantly anticompetitive in its *effect*. The draft inescapably forces each seller of football services to deal with one, and only one buyer, robbing the seller, as in any monopsonistic market, of any real bargaining power. The draft, as the District Court found, "leaves no room whatever for competition among the teams for the services of college players, and utterly strips them of any measure of control over the marketing of their talents." The predictable effect of the draft, as the evidence established and as the District Court found, was to lower the salary levels of the best college players. There can be no doubt that the effect of the draft as it existed in 1968 was to "suppress or even destroy competition" in the market for players' services.

The justification asserted for the draft is that it has the legitimate business purpose of promoting "competitive balance" and playing-field equality among the teams, producing better entertainment for the public, higher salaries for the players, and increased financial security for the clubs. The NFL has endeavored to summarize this justification by saying that the draft ultimately has a "procompetitive" effect, yet this shorthand entails no small risk of confusion. The draft is "procompetitive," if at all, in a very different sense from that in which it is anticompetitive. The draft is anticompetitive in its effect on the market for players' services, because it virtually eliminates economic competition among buyers for the services of sellers. The draft is allegedly "procompetitive" in its effect on the playing field; but the NFL teams are not economic competitors on the playing field, and the draft, while it may heighten athletic competition and thus improve the entertainment product offered to the public, does not increase competition in the economic sense of encouraging others to enter the market and to offer the product at lower cost. Because the draft's "anticompetitive" and "procompetitive" effects are not comparable, it is impossible to "net them out" in the usual rule-of-reason balancing. The draft's "anticompetitive evils," in other words, cannot be balanced against its "procompetitive virtues," and the draft be upheld if the latter outweigh the former. In strict economic terms, the draft's demonstrated procompetitive effects are nil.

The defendants' justification for the draft reduces in fine to an assertion that competition in the market for entering players' services would not serve the best interests of the public, the clubs, or the players themselves. This is precisely the type of argument that the Supreme Court only recently has declared to be unavailing. In National Society of Professional Engineers v. United States [435 U.S. 679 (1978)], the Court held that a professional society's ban on competitive bidding violated §1 of the Sherman Act. In so holding the Court rejected a defense that unbridled competitive bidding would lead to deceptively low bids and inferior work "with consequent risk to public safety and health," terming this justification "nothing less than a frontal assault on the basic policy of the Sherman Act." Ending decades of uncertainty as to the proper scope of inquiry under the rule of reason, the Court stated categorically that the rule, contrary to its name, "does not open the field of antitrust inquiry to any argument in favor of a challenged restraint that may fall within the realm of reason," and that the inquiry instead must be "confined to a consideration of [the restraint's] impact on competitive conditions." The purpose of antitrust analysis, the Court concluded, "is to form a judgment about the competitive significance of the restraint; it is not to decide whether a policy favoring competition is in the public interest, or in the interest of the members of an industry. Subject to exceptions defined by statute, that policy decision has been made by Congress."

Confining our inquiry, as we must, to the draft's impact on competitive conditions, we conclude that the draft as it existed in 1968 was an unreasonable restraint of trade. The draft was concededly anticompetitive in purpose. It was severely anticompetitive in effect. It was not shown to have any significant offsetting procompetitive impact in the economic sense. Balancing the draft's anticompetitive evils against its procompetitive virtues, the outcome is plain. The NFL's defenses, premised on the assertion that competition for players' services would harm both the football industry and society, are unavailing; there is nothing of procompetitive virtue to balance, because "the Rule of Reason does not support a defense based on the assumption that competition itself is unreasonable." . . .

Affirmed in part, reversed in part, and remanded for proceedings consistent with this opinion.

MacKinnon, J., concurring in part and dissenting in part. . . . I disagree with the majority's holding that the draft is a violation of the Rule of Reason and with its reasoning that the Supreme Court's decision in *Engineers* requires that conclusion.

B.   THE BUSINESS OF FOOTBALL, AND THE HISTORY AND PURPOSE OF THE DRAFT

(1) The Need for this Analysis. Since the draft is not illegal "per se," it must be analyzed under the Rule of Reason, the "second category" referred to by *Engineers*, 435 U.S. at 693. Under this standard, the "competitive effect" of the agreement of the teams to maintain a college player draft must "be evaluated by analyzing the facts peculiar to the business, the history of the restraint, and the reasons why it was imposed. . . . [T]he purpose of [this] analysis is to form a judgment about the competitive significance of the restraint. . . ." Id. After analysis of the opinions of the trial court and of the majority and their discussion of the business of professional football as operated in 1968 by the National Football League, I find that the majority and the trial court have overlooked and not given adequate consideration to many significant facts concerning the history of the draft, the reasons which brought it into being and compel its continuance, and the peculiar nature of the business of professional football in the United States.

(2) The Nature of the Business. A critical fact "peculiar to the business" as presently constituted is that the component members of the NFL are not *economically* competitive with each other. In 1968, the NFL operated through 26 separate corporations in an economic joint venture which fielded teams and thereby furnished entertainment — and continue to do so today — to paid spectators and a large television audience. Each

team has a substantial economic stake in the financial success of all the other teams. . . .

Application of the policy of competition to professional sports, just as with the application of the policy to other unique, exceptional industries, presents special problems that the Court recognized in *Engineers* do occasionally arise. Professional sports teams are in some respects traditional economic units seeking to sell a product to the public. But economic competition between teams is not and cannot be the sole determinant of their behavior. Professional sports leagues are uniquely organized economic entities; the ultimate success of the league depends on the economic *cooperation* rather than the economic competition of its members. United States v. National Football League, 116 F. Supp. 319, 323-24 (E.D. Pa. 1953); Note, The Super Bowl and the Sherman Act: Professional Sports and the Antitrust Laws, 81 Harv. L. Rev. 418, 418 (1967). The product being offered to the public is more than an isolated exhibition — it is a series of connected exhibitions that culminate in the annual grand finale contest between the two teams with the best records in the League, which have demonstrated their prowess in organized, rigidly scheduled League competition. The product being offered the public is the "league sport," and the value of this product at the stadium gate and to the television networks depends on the competitive balance of the teams in the league. Spectators and television viewers are not interested in lopsided games or contests between weak teams.

In many respects, the business of professional football as carried on by the NFL resembles a "natural monopoly." . . . Anyone who wishes to watch a major professional football game must watch an NFL game, played under NFL rules with NFL teams and players. History suggests that it is easier for the NFL to expand the number of teams than it is for another league to form and operate successfully. Competition may exist for a time, as the experiences of the American Football League and the World Football League demonstrate, but in the long run such competition is destructive and many teams fail, even as they did within the NFL in its free market formative years.

(3) The History and Effect of the Draft. The draft was adopted in 1935 at a time when baseball was recognized as the national sport. In order to consider and evaluate properly the role and effect of the draft, it is necessary to view the conditions that existed in professional football at that time. Books could be written on the changes in professional football between 1935 and 1968; we have room only for a few of the most significant details.

In 1935, there were only nine teams in the NFL; four in the Western Division and five in the Eastern Division. The League was confined to a few cities in the east, and extended no further west than Chicago. Squads were much smaller (around 22 players, instead of 43 to 47), a free market existed for players' services, and salaries were much lower. Even the game itself was substantially different. The rules were designed to create a game for the players rather than to attract spectators by what today in many contests results in what may accurately be described as basketball on grass. Players formerly had to be able to play both on offense and defense and to be in condition to play 60 minutes if necessary rather than only one way for less than 30 minutes; substitution was greatly limited; platooning of offensive, defensive, kicking, and special teams was *not* permitted; and winning teams stressed the running game from various formations, instead of forward passing from the "T formation" where 9 men are called upon to try to block 11 on running plays with little or no deception that characterized the T formation when it was revived in the 30's. There were fewer crippling injuries because players were younger and they did not play at the excessive weights that are prevalent today. Four teams generally dominated the League — the Chicago Bears, the New York Giants, the Green Bay Packers, and the Boston (later Washington) Redskins. The 1935 regular season consisted of 12 games, which included home and away games with teams in the same division; the season was followed by one championship game between the winners of each division.

During this era of the sport, the League was in substantial competition with business in general and coaching positions for college graduates. For many good football players coming out of college the professional football teams could not compete with the salaries, security and future prospects that were offered by business, the professions, and coaching jobs in colleges, universities and other educational institutions and so they elected not to sign pro contracts. Also, the best coaches chose to remain with colleges and universities. Many players recognized that professional football, at best, was only a seasonal occupation of limited duration at best, that the pay was modest, that it offered only temporary income with some risk of injury, and that once their playing days were over (even today, the average playing life of a player is only about four and one-half years), they would have to start belatedly in their life's work. Many players recognized that the delay in starting their permanent career, or in interrupting it for a few professional seasons, could impair their permanent careers. For that reason, many college players passed up professional football and went directly into business. Lucrative jobs coaching college football, with the opportunity for embarking on a well-paying lifetime career with considerable stability, presented substantial competition for the outstanding players, and these job opportunities in the teaching profession also carried the opportunity for eventual tenure and retirement. As Paul Brown, a former coach at Ohio State University and later coach of the Cleveland Browns and the Cincinnati Bengals, testified, graduating players at Ohio State never thought about playing professional football. A great many of those who played did so because "they liked to play football";[23] and it is fair to say that the "mercenary" element had not affected the sport to the extent it has today (and that has produced a host of complications). Some college players also went to graduate school to prepare for a profession; some went into other professional sports. In 1935, professional football was thus in substantial competition with a host of other vocations and occupations for graduating college players. Even among those who played, many only devoted a half-day to the team, and thus did not give the game the effort that it would come to demand in 1968.

Prior to the first draft, there was a "free market" for players' services. Even so, players' salaries were very modest, and limited club incomes made many franchises precarious. The League would go through 40 franchises before it reached its present stability, with 28 teams. The testimony shows that the Chicago Bears, even though they won the League Championship in 1932, lost $18,000; George Halas, their coach and owner, at the end of the season had to give promissory notes for $1,000 each to Bronko Nagurski and Red Grange for the balance due on their salaries.

The college player draft was adopted in 1935 at the suggestion of Bert Bell, after Cincinnati (which finished the season as the St. Louis Gunners), the bottom team in the Western Division in 1934, had been forced to drop out of the then 10 team league.[27] The 1935 draft as adopted was a pure draft — simple, uncomplicated, and complete. The team with the poorest winning record drafted first; the others followed in inverse order to their won-lost record; the team with the best record in the prior season drafted last. In its early years, the draft covered 30 rounds, but was later reduced to 17 rounds.

The draft was first conducted in 1936 and has continued annually for

23. On December 14, 1941, I was having breakfast in Chicago with Red Smith, a former playing opponent of mine of Notre Dame ('25, '26), then line coach of the Green Bay Packers, who were scheduled that afternoon to play the Chicago Bears for the Western Division Championship. One by one, as the Green Bay players came in for breakfast, I noticed an unusual number of former players from the University of Minnesota. Most of them had been average football players on fine teams at Minnesota, but all were not the outstanding "stars" the public expect to be on the roster of one of the top professional teams that was playing for the championship. When the number of former Minnesota players on the small squad that Green Bay carried in those days got to eight (Hal Van Every, Andy Uram, Bill Johnson, Bill Kuusisto, Larry Buhler, Charlie Schultz, George Svendson, Lou Midler — the NFL Encyclopedia erroneously lists Midler as being from Northwestern, see Encyc. at 144), all of whom I had known initially since they were freshmen and some from their high school days, I said to Red, "You have a great many Minnesota boys?" He replied, "Yes, we like them." I then asked, "What do you like about them?" He thought a minute, and replied, "I guess they just like to play football."

27. [The NFL's Official Encyclopedia History of Professional Football] 28-29 (1977). The Cincinnati Reds lost eight straight games, after which the franchise and some of the players moved to St. Louis. The St. Louis Gunners played three games during the remainder of the season, losing two of them. Id. The Reds-Gunners franchise did not return for the 1935 season. Id., at 29.

the last 42 years. If we assume that roughly 400 players have been drafted each year, approximately 17,000 players have been drafted by professional football teams. What is significant about this large number is that, although a great many players have been affected by the draft, there have been a relatively insignificant number of lawsuits challenging the validity of the draft as conducted by the NFL. This case is stated to be one of first impression attacking the legality of the draft under the antitrust laws. It is also a material fact, of considerable significance, that no case has been pointed to where the Antitrust Division of the Department of Justice has ever attacked the validity of a player draft in any professional sport.

In my view, there are compelling reasons why the draft has continued so long without serious challenge. In effect a player draft is *natural* for league sports. Competitive equality among the component teams is an inherent requirement for meaningful sports competition and the survival of a conference or league — high school, college, or professional — and all of its members. Close rivalries are the backbone of any successful sport. When the NFL established the draft, its objective was to give each team the same fair *opportunity* to be competitive; it sought to achieve a competitive balance among all the League's teams, that is, to "try to equalize the teams." The intended result was to create a situation where each League game would become a closer contest, where spectator interest in the game and the players themselves would be increased, where the interesting individual contests would create an interesting League championship race, and where ultimately the teams and their players would benefit from the greater income resulting from the increased fan interest.

A player draft to achieve competing balance is not new. Early explorers in the American west found the Indians employing a-form of the draft in their game of shinny, played with curved sticks and a wooden ball. The Aborigines of Minnesota, Minnesota Historical Society (1911), quotes the following description from George P. Belden, "The White Chief" (p.37):

> [T]he young men . . . go out on the prairie near the camp . . . [and] having found a smooth spot, they halt, and two of the youths, by common consent, take opposite sides and pick out the players, first one and then another, until enough are had.

The need for and the benefits derived from competitive equality are apparent even on sand lots, where two captains "choose up sides"; the flip of a coin determines who chooses ("drafts") first, and subsequent choices are exercised in alternating fashion. If one side was certain to lose the game, the number of people who would be interested in playing or watching would be seriously diminished. Spectators and players are not attached to athletic slaughters or to contests where the result is foreordained.

What lack of competitive balance in a football league can do to spectator attendance was demonstrated during the existence of the All-America Football Conference and is spelled out in the record here. In that League the Cleveland Browns coached by Paul Brown started out drawing 60,000 to 70,000 people for its home games. They won the championship every year, and their "attendance fell down to under 20,000" because the fans said, "Oh, they are going to win anyway. What is the use of going out there?" This is an absolute answer to the contention that the league can survive if competitive equality of the teams is destroyed. There will always be a league but constant losses by their teams would cause many areas to lose their franchises.

All major sports, in recognition of the need for competitive balance, have drafts. Hockey and basketball have drafts, and baseball instituted a draft when it became clear from the long domination of the New York Yankees that the farm system was not producing competitive balance. . . .

Since 1935, the number of teams has increased from 9 to today's League of 28 teams, and the number of players per team has also been increased substantially. Instead of the small squads of around 26 players in the early days of the sport, the modern team's roster once swelled to 47 and was later reduced to 43 players. This has increased the total number of active players in the League as a whole to slightly over 1,200. Gate receipts have increased tremendously due to the increased popular interest in the game. Also important are the television revenues, which constitute a large part of each team's annual income. The NFL television contracts between the League and the television networks have distributed hundreds of millions of dollars to all teams in the League; and current news reports indicate that the payments are to be substantially increased. The lucrative television contract, made possible by an *exemption* from the antitrust laws enacted by Congress, is negotiated for all teams by the League Commissioner. These moneys are distributed *equally* to each team in the League without regard to the size of the team's local television market. In 1968 the revenues from television accounted for approximately 30 percent of the total revenue of the Redskins and this was approximately the same percentage as the average for all NFL teams in that year. Team revenue from gate receipts, television contracts, and other sources has increased tremendously since 1935, and the NFL teams and their players are the direct recipients of the benefits of the increased national interest in NFL games. College players, 22 years old, coming out of college in 1976 and playing in the NFL were making $20,000 to $150,000 their first year. . . .

Football, it is claimed, has now become the national game, supplanting baseball. Fan interest in the nearest local team has become so intense that city after city has secured a franchise for a local team and has substantially *subsidized* the entire professional football industry (a fact not generally recognized) by erecting huge stadiums with hundreds of millions of dollars of taxpayers' money or pledges of public credit and with exemptions from the payment of real estate taxes on account of their municipal ownership. There is also an additional subsidy in raising construction'funds through tax exempt municipal bonds which because of the tax exemption carry lower interest rates on the borrowed funds. Twenty cities have erected these huge new stadiums with "amortized tax dollars" and of the 29 stadiums in use only four were privately financed. These stadiums facilitate the large crowds that are necessary to enable the "local" team to compete in gate receipts with the teams of other localities that are considered rivals. The local fans in most areas where the teams have established reasonably respectable winning records acquire a strong interest in their local team and a powerful attachment to certain players whose performance they admire. Such interest lags if the team becomes a "loser." . . .

The argument that the draft could successfully be limited to a very few rounds is based on the false premise that only the "blue-chip" players or super-stars in college contribute to the success of the professional team. No creditable testimony supports the conclusion that the necessary competitive balance could be assured if the draft were limited to those 56 graduating college players that the scouts deemed the best prospects at the time, much less if it were limited to the 5 to 8 superstars that generally develop annually. Football is a *team* game and a team is generally not made by drafting one or two graduating college "stars." Notwithstanding the fact that the "stars" get the billing, a passing quarterback, for instance, cannot succeed unless the rest of the team are of sufficient ability to do their jobs. If his blockers cannot stop the defensive rush, or his receivers cannot get free, the quarterback's ability will never show. Thus, it is pure illusion to suggest that if a few so-called stars or "blue-chip" players were distributed equally by a draft confined to two rounds that a continuation of competitive equality could be assured. So-called "stars" soon become "black-and-blue" chip players if their teammates who are necessary to their success are overshadowed by players on other teams. The pitiful showing of the "great" O. J. Simpson for this year with the San Francisco 49ers, after moving from his successful years with the Buffalo Bills, is current proof. Winning teams need strong players at all positions,[53] and good players to substitute for those who inevitably be-

53. A good example of the need for a strong supporting cast for a star is provided by the drafting of O. J. Simpson by the Buffalo Bills. The circumstances are well known. Simpson won the Heisman Trophy and was drafted by the Bills in the first round in 1969. In 1969 and 1970, Simpson was something of a disappointment because of weaknesses in the Bills' offensive line (J.A. 1831-32). Then as the statistics and personnel roster prove, Encyc. at 103-05, Simpson's performance and the team's success began to improve when the Bills in 1972 began drafting linemen capable of blocking for Simpson. In 1970, the

come injured. These are not produced solely from first and second round draft choices.

The majority frame the issue as a balancing of the procompetitive effects and the anticompetitive effects of the draft with respect to the market for players' services. It is important to understand the nature of this market. The teams' owners, the purchasers of players' services, are "adverse" to each other in the sense that each owner desires to obtain the most talented available players. The players are to some extent "adverse" to each other, as the players desire to play for the best teams, though what is "best" may vary in the perceptions of different players, just as some people like different foods or colors. It is fair to say that a large percentage of the players are attracted toward the teams that pay the most, have winning records, are located in large cities, and play in a warm climate. Some want to play close to home or where they made their college reputations; or some prefer an invigorating climate with knowledgeable sportswriters and fans who understand the basics of the game. The weight of any particular factor varies according to individual taste and preference, thus rendering the notion of the "best" team from the players' perspective somewhat variable.

Given this market, the majority opinion assesses the competitive impact of the draft on the competition among the teams' owners for players' services. The majority see the draft as an absolute ban on competition between teams for the services of players just out of college. Finding an absolute anticompetitive effect, the majority conclude there can be no procompetitive benefit. After stating that it is impossible to balance, the majority proceed to balance and find what essentially amounts to a predicted outcome to be plain — the anticompetitive effects outweigh the procompetitive benefits, and the draft is invalid.

In my opinion this result is not required by *Engineers* or the Rule of Reason. . . . [T]he restraint that actually results on the player from being restricted to bargaining with one team can be overestimated if one just reads the majority opinion and looks no further than the written word. Actually there are a number of league practices that alleviate what might

---

team's record was 1-13; . . . with the addition of linemen chosen early in the draft, the record improved to 9-5 in 1972, which record was duplicated in 1973. Simpson gained over 1000 yards in 1972, 1974, and 1975; in 1973, he gained a record 2003 yards and interest in the team skyrocketed. In 1976, he gained 1503 yards. A new stadium was built in 1973 and a sell-out crowd of 80,000 watched the first game in it. None of this success occurred until Buffalo used its early draft choices to select outstanding linemen. Simpson was eventually to sign a three-year contract for over two million dollars (Encyc., at 103). It is hard to find a better example to disprove the theory that a few so-called "stars" can make a team a winner. Other similar examples can be pointed to by any sports follower.

The majority object to the use of the Encyclopedia published in 1976 because this case was tried before that date. However, the *facts* occurred before the trial, were well known, and were referred to in the testimony.

appear to be the strict requirements of the draft. It is a "common practice" for a player to be drafted by one team, and then to deal with another team, followed by a trade between the club having the negotiating rights and the club wanting the player. At oral argument, it was brought out that Jack Snow of Notre Dame was drafted as a wide receiver by the Minnesota Vikings in the first round.[71] However, Snow expressed a dislike for playing in the Minnesota climate, refused to negotiate with the Vikings, and was traded to the Los Angeles Rams where he played eleven seasons, 1965 to 1975. Joe Namath was also selected on a first round draft choice obtained in a player trade. Encyc., 184. It is common knowledge that teams frequently trade players to satisfy compelling personal preferences of the players. So in practical reality the draft is not as restrictive as it may seem to those who are unfamiliar with it or who blind themselves to how it works in practice. . . . The majority admit that the draft is not pernicious and that it does contribute to the accomplishment of a legitimate business purpose — the improvement of the league product so all players and teams may benefit. All that remains is to find that the net anticompetitive effect is "insubstantial." If we find with the majority that there is no procompetitive effect then it is purely a question of evaluating the anticompetitive effect of the draft. This brings us in this case to the effect of the draft on Smith's salary. Smith's salary was in line with those of other Redskins. J.A. 423-575. Since the financial records for 1968 indicate that the Redskins and the other league teams were paying out practically all their income in players' salaries and other operating costs it is obvious that, draft or no draft, Smith's chance of getting a higher salary was practically non-existent. Thus, the effect of the draft on him was *insubstantial* and under the majority's formulation the draft would survive. I would concur in that conclusion. It is merely another way of saying that Smith has no cause of action because he obtained as favorable a contract as he could even if there were no draft.

Judge WILKEY, in a footnote rejoinder to the dissent: Our colleague has reinforced his own encyclopedic knowledge of football with repeated references to The NFL's Official Encyclopedia History of Professional Football (1977), beginning with note 3. Whatever may be the propriety of a trial court taking judicial notice of an "encyclopedia" to establish facts (and an encyclopedia whose occasional inaccuracy our colleague himself corrects, note 23), see McCormick's Handbook of the Law of Evidence §§329-31 (1972) (2d ed.), we think it improper and a bit unfair to ground an opinion urging reversal of the trial court's principal factual conclusions (that the evidence was equivocal whether the draft was essential to preserve competitive balance, and that the draft had a

71. Encyc., at 165.

severely anticompetitive impact) on "facts" culled from a book appearing a year after the trial court's decision. We suggest the factual bases, and therefore legal validity, of the dissent is similarly flawed by reliance on personal observation (note 23) and common knowledge in the community (notes 51 and 69).

Indeed, there are frequent references to events occurring after the oral argument in this case, e.g., O. J. Simpson's 1978 record (p.29), Terry Metcalf's 1978 Canadian contract (note 69), the New York Yankees' recent success (p.53). One man's reminiscences of a popular sport should not be confused with a judicial decision.

If Judge Bryant's principal factual conclusion is to be set aside, as our colleague urges, it must be on the ground that it was clearly erroneous, see Daniels v. Hadley Memorial Hospital, 185 U.S. App. D.C. 84, 91, 566 F.2d 749, 756 (1977), and, surely, clearly erroneous on the record before him, . . . without the wholesale importation of "facts" judicially noticed for the first time on appeal.

The bulk of our colleague's dissent is devoted to a recitation and analysis of detailed facts relating to the history of professional football, some in the record before the district court and some supplemental thereto. . . . Our colleague then makes his own findings of fact as to the benefits derived in 1968 and currently from the professional football draft, and its effect on competition, these findings of fact differing from those of the trial court. For example, "[s]ome argue that this [competitive balance] has been caused by other factors, but the preponderance of the *factual* testimony and record evidence supports a conclusion that the college player draft was the key factor which produced the competitive balance of the teams. . . . There was no showing to the contrary in the 2,000 page record."

First, we believe that the NFL's theory of competitive balance, even were it empirically valid, is legally wide of the mark in a rule of reason inquiry. Moreover, there *was* a showing in the record which contradicts the findings of the dissent as our colleague himself realizes: "The court concluded that the evidence on whether the draft was essential to competitive balance was 'at best equivocal,' and that no correlation was demonstrated between the draft and survival of the League."

We suggest this finding of fact by the trial court, as recited by our colleague, must be affirmed if there is evidence in the record to support it, and that an appellate court cannot make a different finding of fact, particularly when the record evidence obviously lends itself to the conclusion reached by the trial court. See Daniels v. Hadley Memorial Hospital, 185 U.S. App. D.C. 84, 91, 566 F.2d 749, 756 (1977).

First, to the extent the defendant's theory relies on the draft as a device to allocate player talent evenly, without which wealthy owners would be free to corner the market, Judge Bryant found "abundant convincing testimony" that factors other than money are often decisive in players' choice of teams. 420 F. Supp. at 746. See J.A. at 945 (unrelated business opportunities); id. at 1049-52 (same); id. 1073-74 (racial discrimination and general community atmosphere); id. at 1080-84 (preference for NFL over AFL); id. at 1086, 1091-92 (dispute with owner); id. at 1112 (climate); id. at 1212 (educational opportunities); id. at 1214-15 (disagreement with coaching staff and management). Further, the evidence with regard to the movement of free agents and former World Football League players who were ungoverned by the draft did not reveal any trend for the best players to become concentrated with teams "offering money, glamour and success." 420 F. Supp. at 746, citing Free Agents' First Wave On the Move, Washington Post, 7 July 1976, at D1.

Second, it is doubtful whether the draft was effective in maintaining whatever competitive balance did exist in the League. Although from year to year the worst teams usually got somewhat better and the best teams somewhat worse, it is uncertain how much, if any, of this is explained by the draft. See J.A. at 939-40, 990, 1975 (testimony of Dr. George Burman); id. at 1968-69 (testimony of Bruce Caputo).

Without by any means going into the minute detail furnished with such relish by our colleague, we think that two other factors contribute at least as much as the player draft to producing and maintaining a competitive balance in the league — *television* revenues and *coaching* changes.

The player draft originated in 1935 and was in full effect from then on, but none of the wonderful development of the professional football game pointed to by the appellant, and encored by our colleague, occurred until the mid-1950's. The advent of professional football on television created a synergistic effect between television and the sport. Television exposure brought more fans, produced more revenues, which in turn produced better paid players, more profitable franchises, and generally a better entertainment feature for television. This sort of ratchet effect started working in the mid-1950's with the advent of television and has continued over the years. See Proceedings, Conference on the Economics of Professional Sports, Washington, D.C., 7 May 1974, at 30, J.A. at 290.

It is possible to say that in the 1935-1955 period the player draft had some importance in preserving a kind of competitive balance, preventing rich owners from running away with the league (if there were any independently rich owners of the then only nine professional football teams). But by 1968, as now, the impact of the player draft is clearly different from what arguably it had been in 1935-1955.

The great equalizing feature now is not the player draft, but the league's arrangement to place the teams financially on nearly equal footing — equal sharing of television revenues. In 1968 each team in the NFL received nearly one third of its revenues from television and radio, averaging $1.13 million. See J.A. at 618. (In 1974, the most recent year for which figures appear in the record, such revenues averaged $2.28 million and were 34.5 percent of total revenues. Id. at 655.) We were told at oral argument by counsel for the NFL that such revenues now represent over half of average team income. If one realizes that at the present time all teams in the league will receive more than one half of their revenues in exactly equal shares from television, and nearly every team in the league is able to sell out its stadium for all the league games, then it appears that the financial sinews for a competitive player balance have been equalized. See J.A. at 1978 (testimony of Dr. George Burman).

The second factor producing competitive balance (or lack of it) is the impact of the *coach* on the success or failure of the team. Despite the claims to "competitive balance" from whatever factors, it is clear that a small number of the teams have dominated the play-offs year after year. The record shows nine teams as occupying twenty-two out of the available twenty-four places in the play-offs in the 1973-1975 seasons. See 420 F. Supp. at 746, citing N.Y. Times, 6 June 1976, at 56. These nine teams include teams with long records of success year after year with the same coach: (1) Dallas Cowboys with Landry; (2) Washington Redskins with Lombardi and Allen; (3) Minnesota Vikings with Grant; (4) Oakland Raiders with Madden; (5) Miami Dolphins with Shula; (6) Pittsburgh Steelers with Noll. These teams have consistently been in the play-offs and won titles, despite the fact that under the draft they have been getting the worst picks year after year. It would appear that the effects of fine coaching swamp whatever effect the draft may have on team performance.

Analysis of the record of coaching changes, or lack of changes, illustrates at least two things. First, that the player draft does not have an equalizing effect to the extent of knocking out the top teams, if the top teams have good coaches. Second, it is certainly arguable that what happens to change the position of teams in the league is not a draft choice advantage, but that the losing teams fire the losing coaches.

Our colleague argues "[i]n only one of twelve seasons from 1964-1975 did those teams in the bottom half of the NFL's standings fail to win a greater number of games in the next following priority selections in the draft. Statistical analysis shows that this could not have been the product of chance occurring without regard to the draft." Our dissenting colleague did not tell us how many of the teams in the bottom half of the standings not only received the usual priority in draft selection, but also fired their losing coaches. Whatever statistical analysis our colleague is talking about, it is obviously worthless unless it takes account of the changes in the head coaches and the coaching staffs as well.

The changes in position in the league effected by changes in head coaches is easily seen from the record by what happened after the arrival of Lombardi in Green Bay, the arrival of Lombardi and thereafter Allen at Washington, the move of Shula to the Miami Dolphins, and the move of Noll to the Pittsburgh Steelers. See J.A. at 658-76; id. at 950-52, 1978-79 (testimony of Dr. George Burman); id. at 904-05 (testimony of Edward Garvey); id. at 1116-18 (testimony of Bart Starr). In each of these four instances teams with a long series of losing seasons, during which they had had the benefit of priority in the player draft, were very shortly upgraded into title contenders after the arrival of these coaches of recognized high ability.

We think the trial court was eminently correct when he "concluded that the evidence on whether the draft was essential to competitive balance was 'at best equivocal,' and that no correlation was demonstrated between the draft and survival in the league."

Judge MACKINNON, in a footnote response to Judge Wilkey: The majority complains of reference to facts disclosed in the Encyclopedia of Pro Football and to matters of common knowledge that can be readily verified by reference to encyclopedias, books and other publications of established authenticity. This however is clearly permissible and may be done for the first time on appeal as is recognized by the Federal Rules of Evidence, Rule 201(f) which states: "Judicial notice may be taken at any stage of the proceedings." Judicial notice also may be taken of facts "though they are neither actually notorious nor bound to be judicially known, yet they would be capable of such instant and unquestionable demonstration, if desired, that no party would think of imposing a falsity on the tribunal in the face of an intelligent adversary." [Citing Wigmore on Evidence, Third Edition (1940), Vol. IX, Section 2571(3)].

It is a complete answer to the majority's complaint of the few references by this opinion to recent events that the majority does not question the *validity* of any of the facts so referred to. Actually, such recent facts are merely duplicative of facts already in the trial record. The invalidity of a court's prior factual assumptions that are predictive of future consequences may be demonstrated by pointing out that the results were different than was predicted; and the fact that some of these results occurred after the court's decision does not prevent their use. In fact, since the court indulged in predictive assumptions it invited testing by the subsequent outcome. . . .

The majority . . . assert that competitive balance is produced today by equal sharing of television revenues and by the impact of the *coach*. This of course ignores the historical fact, which we are to consider in applying the rule of reason, that the achievement of competitive balance was the purpose of the draft, and that this produced the exciting games throughout the league, that led to the original television contracts and to the increased revenues therefrom. Moreover, the equal sharing of television revenues would not overcome the unlimited financial resources that a few owners are able and willing to make available to produce a winning team.

As to coaches, the majority seek to attack the *fact* that losing teams almost invariably improved their record with players from the succeeding draft, by arguing that firing of "losing coaches" may have been the cause. Naturally some coaches are better than others but the record does not indicate that coaching changes exceed draft results as a factor in producing the improvement in the record of losing teams. Of the Twenty-Three "Winningest coaches" in Pro-football history 15 moved to other teams and only two, Shula and Allen, had winning records with the new team. This excludes Lombardi who was only one year at Washington and had a record of 7 wins, 5 losses and 2 ties. Encyc. p.452. Thus, a new coach is no panacea. Also coaching in the NFL today is not a one man job — staffs are enormous — and the movement of a head coach may not be the critical element. Coaches can make their contribution but in the last analysis the game is played by the players and not even a court should try to deny that fact. When it does, its position is obviously untenable.

As for the majority's statement that the draft did not produce until the 50's and then television did the job, this again is a near-sighted approach and evaluation that blinds itself to the fact that it is the game on the field that is being sold. The statistics indicate that paid attendance at professional games has *regularly increased* steadily to 11,044,018 in 1976, Encyc., p.437, as the number of league teams has increased from 9 to 28 and their competitive balance has spread throughout the United States. Also 17 of the stadiums presently in use were built, occupied by new teams, or substantially enlarged to their present capacity in the last 10 years. Encyc., pp. 454-463. The organization of new teams and the building of huge stadiums have *combined* with the improved quality of the product and the advertising it receives from the media to produce its present popularity. This is part of the growth in general sports' interest in the nation which has seen 42 major league teams in all sports in 1959 grow to 117 teams at the last counting.

STATE v. TAVONE
446 A.2d 741 (R.I. 1982)

KELLEHER, J. The defendant, John Tavone (Tavone), stands convicted by a Superior Court jury of having knowingly presented for commercial gain an obscene motion picture. Subsequent to the conviction the trial justice imposed a two-year prison sentence. Thereafter, the trial justice released Tavone on bail pending our determination of his appeal. One of the conditions involved in the grant of bail was that while Tavone's appeal was pending, he would not exhibit at the theater he owns and operates any X rated motion pictures. Tavone is before us pursuant to our Rule 9, seeking a nullification of the "X rated" stipulation.

Tavone's theater is located in West Warwick, and its operation is licensed by the town council of that municipality. The indictment that led to Tavone's conviction consisted of three counts, two of which related to one movie and the third of which concerned a second movie. The jury acquitted Tavone on the charges included within the two-count movie but convicted him so far as the one-count motion picture was concerned.

In setting the "X rated" prohibition, the trial justice acknowledged that "X rated movies are not automatically to be equated with obscene movies. . . . And if an X rated movie cannot be equated with an obscene movie, Lord knows what distinguishes it from an R rated movie."[1] However, in opting for a blanket exclusion of X rated movies, the trial justice expressed a concern that the public's "confidence in its court system is going to be eroded" if he released Tavone on bail and "then he goes right back into business doing what he has been doing day in and day out." The trial justice warned Tavone that a showing of any X rated movie might be considered ground for revocation of bail.

In State v. Abbott and Freeman, 113 R.I. 430, 432, 322 A.2d 33, 35 (1974), this court emphasized that the primary purpose of bail, "be it of the pretrial or the post conviction variety, is to assure a defendant's appearance in court at the appointed time." The trial justice's concern for the judiciary's image is laudable; however, we fail to see the relationship between Tavone's abstention from the showing of a movie bearing an X classification and assurance of his subsequent appearances as well as his submission to the court's judgment. See also Carter v. Carson, 370 So. 2d 1241 (Fla. 1st D.C.A. 1979).

Accordingly, that portion of the order granting bail which refers to the showing of X rated movies is hereby vacated.

---

1. A most interesting and enlightening discussion of the movie-rating system can be found in the February 21, 1982 edition of the Providence Sunday Journal at pages H-7 and -8 of the "Arts/Travel/Leisure" section. Michael Janusonis, a Journal arts writer, reports that the rating system was intended by its originator, the Motion Picture Association of America, to serve as a guide for parents. The association obtains its financial support from three groups: movie producers, distributors, and theater owners.

At present a seven-member rating board can place a movie submitted to the board for its review in any one of four categories. A movie rated "G" assures the parents that the film is suitable for the viewing of all. A parent who learns that a movie has been rated "PG" is being told that he or she must make an independent determination as to whether the film in question should be seen by his or her children. Films rated "R" or "X" are considered to be adult material which is not intended for minors. Attendance at an R rated movie is possible for any child who is accompanied to the movie by an adult. Vulgarity will usually earn for a movie an automatic R. Although an X rated movie is presumed to be pornography, some movies have been rated X because of the violence they portray.

According to Mr. Janusonis, there is a belief by some members of the moving-picture industry that the rating system is not in tune with contemporary mores, but as the chairman of the National Association of Theater Owners observed when asked about the rating system: "It's imperfect, but it's the best thing we've got."

Problem X-1
Bad Trip

Defendants were indicted for a violation of 21 U.S.C. §841(a)(1), possession with intent to distribute a controlled substance, namely lysergic acid diethylamide (LSD). At trial the court was asked by the government to instruct the jury as a matter of law that LSD was a controlled substance as of the date of the offense. Defendants argued that this was a fact for the jury to determine. Can the court judicially notice that LSD is a Schedule I controlled substance in the Federal Register? Is this an adjudicative or a legislative fact? What should the court instruct the jury on this issue?

Problem X-2
Head Shop

P, a retailer of popular records and novelty items, sues to enjoin the enforcement of a town ordinance that forbids the display of "narcotics paraphernalia" and asks the court to take judicial notice of "the phenomenon known as the Counterculture of the Seventies wherein untraditional attire such as spoons and hand-crafted pipes adorn both home and person." May the judge do so? Is this a legislative or an adjudicative fact, or a fact at all?

Problem X-3
Hoist on One's Own Petard

The Ku Klux Klan sues the FBI alleging that from 1966 through 1972, as part of its covert operation known as COINTELPRO, the FBI attempted to destroy the Klan in violation of its first and fourteenth amendment rights. The FBI pleads the statute of limitations, claiming that in November 1974 the FBI disclosed that it was targeting white hate groups for COINTELPRO covert operations and that the statute of limitations began to run at that time. The Klan claims that it is not a "white hate group," and the Klan leader states in affidavit that the Klan has never advocated hatred against blacks and jews. May the trial judge judicially notice that the Klan is in fact a white hate group that advocates hatred of blacks and jews? If the judge notices this fact, would she do so under Rule 201(b)(1) or (2)? If under Rule 201(b)(2) what sources could be used consistent with the rule? What information could be supplied to bring notice of the fact with Rule 201(d)? If under Rule 201(b)(1), does it matter where the court is sitting and what the background of the judge happens to be?

Problem X-4
Boycott or Business?

P seeks to void his oil shipping contract on the ground that it is illegal under U.S. law and against public policy because under the contract loading must be "at one or two safe ports Mediterranean Sea, excluding Israel." *D* contends that the Israeli limitation is based on a "safe ports" policy rather than a political or economic boycott. At *P*'s request could the court take judicial notice that the loading provision furthers an Arab boycott of Israel which is against U.S. law and policy?

Problem X-5
Canal Zone Confusion

Territorial criminal jurisdiction depends on two distinct elements: (1) the location of commission of the crime and (2) the location of the territorial boundary. *D* was convicted of larceny within the Canal Zone. The place of the larceny was proved but not the location of the boundary. On appeal from the conviction, may the appellate court consult maps of the Zone and take judicial notice that the location of the crime was within the Zone? Is this consistent with Rule 201(g)? Is it constitutional?

Problem X-6
Joyride Junker

Charge: grand larceny arising out of the theft of an automobile. At trial there was no direct evidence on the value of the automobile, and the only testimony in the record upon which finding of value could be based was testimony by the owner that the automobile was a four-year-old Ford sedan that was in excellent condition. At the close of the prosecution's case-in-chief defense counsel moved for a directed verdict on the ground that there had been no evidence that the value of the car exceeded $50, the statutory requirement for grand larceny. The court denied defendant's motion and instructed the jury, "You will take the value of this property as being in excess of $50 and therefore the defendant, if he is guilty at all, is guilty of grand larceny." Defendant was convicted. Did the trial court commit reversible error?

Table of Cases

907

Table of Secondary Authorities

Books and Treatises

Ayer, A. J., Probability and Evidence (1972), 16
Bentham, Jeremy, Rationale of Judicial Evidence (Wigmore 1961 ed.), 537
Cleary, Edward, McCormick on Evidence (1972), 81, 645, 662
Cohen, L., The Probable and the Provable (1977), 804
Copi, Irving, Introduction to Logic (1972), 20
Durand, P., Evidence for Magistrates (1969), 214
Hart, H., & J. McNaughton, Evidence and Inference (1959), 14
King, W., & D. Pillinger, Opinion Evidence in Illinois (1942), 634
Maguire, J., Evidence: Common Sense and Common Law (1947), 247
Maguire, J., J. Weinstein, J. H. Chadbourn, & J. H. Mansfield, Evidence
    (1973), 214
Morgan, Edmund, Basic Problems of Evidence (1954), 5
Thayer, James, Preliminary Treatise on Evidence (1898), 1, 27
Weinstein, J., & M. Berger, Weinstein's Evidence (1981), 700
Westin, Alan, Privacy and Freedom (1967), 522
Wigmore, John, A Student's Textbook on the Law of Evidence (1935), 2
Wigmore, John, Wigmore on Evidence, 234, 240, 439, 520, 642, 645, 671,
    732, 789

Articles

Allen, Ronald, "Structuring Jury Decisionmaking in Criminal Cases: A
    Unified Constitutional Approach to Evidentiary Devices" (1980), 841
Armstrong, Walter P., Jr., "The Count Joannes: A Vindication of a
    Much-Maligned Man" (1956), 778
Cleary, Edward W., "Presuming and Pleading: An Essay on Juristic
    Immaturity" (1959), 795
Falknor, Judson F., "The 'Hear-Say' Rule as a 'See-Do' Rule: Evidence of
    Conduct" (1960), 284
Gardner, Dillard S., "The Camera Goes to Court" (1946), 240
Giannelli, Paul C., "The Admissibility of Novel Scientific Evidence: *Frye v.
    United States*, A Half-Century Later" (1980), 651
Green, Eric, "Expanded Use of the Mini-Trial, Private Judging,
    Neutral-Expert Fact-Finding, Patent Arbitration and Industry
    Self-Regulation" (1981), 700
James, George, "Relevancy, Probability and the Law" (1941), 21
Krattenmaker, Thomas "Testimonial Privileges in Federal Courts: An
    Alternative to the Proposed Federal Rules of Evidence" (1973), 522
Ladd, Mason, "Expert and Other Opinion Testimony" (1956), 635

Rules

Miscellaneous

Index